JOAN ROBINSON AND MODERN ECONOMIC THEORY

JOAN ROBINSON

From the Ramsey and Muspratt Collection. © Peter Lofts: Anglia Supercolor Studios.

Joan Robinson and Modern Economic Theory

Edited by
George R. Feiwel

 NEW YORK UNIVERSITY PRESS
Washington Square, New York

First published in 1989 in the U.S.A. by
NEW YORK UNIVERSITY PRESS
Washington Square
New York, N.Y. 10003

Printed in Hong Kong

Library of Congress Cataloging-in-Publication Data
Joan Robinson and modern economic theory.
   Bibliography: p.
   Includes index.
   1. Robinson, Joan, 1903– . 2. Economics.
I. Feiwel, George R.
HB103.R63J63   1989   330.1   88–15135
ISBN 0–8147–2591–0

Contents

Notes on the Contributors

Irma Adelman is Professor of Agricultural and Resource Economics and Professor of Economics, University of California (Berkeley). She has taught at the University of Maryland, Northwestern University, Johns Hopkins University, and Stanford University. A Fellow of the Econometric Society, the American Academy of Arts and Science, the Netherlands Institute of Advanced Study, and the Center for Advanced Study in the Behavioral Sciences, she has held the Cleveringa Chair at Leiden University, and has been Senior Economist, Development Research Center, International Bank for Reconstruction and Development. She has served as Vice-President of the American Economic Association and has been awarded the Order of the Bronze Tower by the government of South Korea. Formerly on the editorial boards of *Behavioral Science*, *Journal of Economic Literature*, and *American Economic Review*, she is now on the editorial boards of *Quarterly Journal of Economics*, *World Development*, *Journal of Policy Modeling*, and *Journal of Comparative Economics* and is associate editor of *Journal of Development Economics*. She has written nearly one hundred articles in the broad areas of development, income distribution, and planning, combining empirical analysis with a broad range of statistical and operations research techniques to analyze interactions among economic, social and political forces. She is the author of nearly ten books, including *Society, Politics, and Economic Development* (with C. T. Morris, 1967); *Economic Growth and Social Equity in Developing Countries* (with C. T. Morris, 1973); and *Income Distribution in Developing Countries* (with S. Robinson, 1978).

Kenneth J. Arrow, whose name is largely synonymous with modern economic theory, our protagonist in *Arrow and the Ascent of Modern Economic Theory* and *Arrow and the Foundations of the Theory of Economic Policy*, is Joan Kenney Professor of Economics, Professor of Operations Research and member of the IMSSS, Stanford University. He was formerly James Bryant Conant University Professor of Economics, Harvard University. He has been President of the Econometric Society, the American Economic Association, the Institute of Management Sciences, the Western Economic Association, the International Society for Inventory Research, and the International Economic Association. He has received the John Bates Clark medal of the American Economic Association and in 1972 the Nobel Memorial Prize in Economic Science. A recipient of numerous honorary degrees, most recently from the University of Cambridge, he is a Fellow and past Vice-President of the American Academy of Arts and Sciences, a Member of the National Academy of Sciences, and a Corresponding Fellow of the British Academy. His many contributions include *Social Choice and Individual Values* (1951,

1963); *Essays in the Theory of Risk Bearing* (1971); *The Limits of Organization* (1974); *General Competitive Analysis* (with F. H. Hahn, 1971); *Social Choice and Multicriterion Decision Making* (with H. Raynaud, 1986); and six volumes of *Collected Papers of Kenneth J. Arrow* (1983, 1984, 1985). He has also contributed to *Issues in Contemporary Microeconomics and Welfare* (1985) and *Issues in Contemporary Macroeconomics and Distribution* (1985).

William J. Baumol is Joseph Douglas Green Professor of Economics, Princeton University and Professor of Economics, New York University. He is a Guggenheim and Ford Faculty Fellow, an Honorary Fellow of the London School of Economics and Political Science, a Fellow of the American Academy of Arts and Sciences and of the Econometric Society, and a Distinguished Fellow of the American Economic Association. Past President of the American Economic Association, Eastern Economic Association, the Association of Environmental and Resource Economists, and the Atlantic Economic Society, and recipient of several honorary degrees, he is a Founding Member of the World Resources Institute. He has contributed extensively to a wide range of topics, including microeconomic theory, industrial organization theory, and environmental economics. He is the author of sixteen books, including *Welfare Economics and the Theory of the State* (1952, 1965); *Business Behavior, Value and Growth* (1959, 1966); *Economic Theory and Operations Analysis* (1961, 1976); *Performing Arts: the Economic Dilemma* (with G. Bowen, 1966); *The Theory of Environmental Policy* (with W. E. Oates, 1975); *Contestable Markets and the Theory of Industry Structure* (with J. C. Panzar and R. D. Willig, 1982); *Superfairness* (1986), and the successful textbook *Economics: Principles and Policy* (with A. Blinder 1979, 1984). He is also a contributor to *Issues in Contemporary Microeconomics and Welfare* (1985), and *Arrow and the Foundations of the Theory of Economic Policy* (1987).

Robert A Becker is Associate Professor of Economics, Indiana University. He has made numerous invited presentations at faculty and government agency seminars and conferences of the Econometric Society and the Midwestern Mathematical Economics Assocation. He is among the newer crop of mathematical economic theorists and has published more than fifteen articles in capital theory, general equilibrium theory, and microeconomic theory.

Kenneth E. Boulding is Distinguished Professor of Economics, Emeritus, University of Colorado. He has taught at a number of universities, including Edinburgh, Colgate, McGill, Iowa State College, and University of Michigan and has held various distinguished visiting professorships in different institutions, including Cornell University, Wellesley College, Dartmouth College, Swarthmore College, University of Pennsylvania, and University of

Texas (Austin). He has been awarded the John Bates Clark Medal and is a Distinguished Fellow of the American Economic Association. He is past President of the American Economic Association, American Association for the Advancement of Science, Peace Research Society, British Association for the Advancement of Science (Section F, Economics), Co-president of the Academy of Independent Scholars, and since 1970 has been the President of the Association for the Study of the Grants Economy. A holder of more than thirty honorary degrees, he is a Fellow of the American Academy of Arts and Sciences and the American Philosophical Society. He is a Member of the National Academy of Sciences and a Corresponding Fellow of the British Academy. In economics he is a maverick, at home both inside and outside the mainstream. Among his more innovative approaches is the attempt to integrate economics with biological concepts of ecological equilibrium and dynamics and genetic production. He is a prolific writer whose nearly forty books include six volumes of *The Collected Papers of Kenneth E. Boulding* (1971, 1973, 1974, 1975, and 1985); a standard textbook *Economic Analysis* (1941, 4th ed. 1966); *A Reconstruction of Economics* (1950, 1962); *Beyond Economics* (1968); *Sonnets from the Interior Life and other Autobiographical Verse* (1975); *Evolutionary Economics* (1981); and *The World as a Total System* (1985).

William A. Brock, formerly Professor of Economics, University of Chicago, Cornell University, and the University of Rochester, is F.P. Ramsey Professor of Economics, University of Wisconsin (Madison). A Fellow of the Econometric Society and a Romnes Faculty Fellow, he has been Sherman Fairchild Distinguished Scholar, California Institute of Technology and on two occasions Visiting Professor, University of California (San Diego) and participant of the summer seminars IMSSS (Stanford University). He is Associate Editor, *Journal of Economic Theory* and *International Economic Review*. He has published more than fifty articles in general equilibrium theory, uncertainty, rational expectations, business cycles, asset prices, and natural monopoly. He is also the co-author of *The Impact of Federal Regulations and Taxes on Business Formation, Dissolution, and Growth* (with D. S. Evans, 1985) and *Stability Analysis in Economic Theory* (with A. G. Malliaris, 1985). He is at work (together with S. P. Magee and L. Young) on *Endogenous Tariff Theory*.

Martin Bronfenbrenner, Kenan Professor of Economics Emeritus (and Lecturer on Japanese History), Duke University, is Professor of International Economics, School of International Politics, Economics, and Business, Aoyama Gakuin University, Tokyo, Japan. A knowledgeable observer of the Japanese economy since the Second World War, he has written extensively in many areas of economics. He has taught at a number of US universities, including the University of Wisconsin, University of Minnesota, and Carnegie-Mellon University. He has acted as President, Southern Economic

Association, History of Economics Society, Atlantic Economic Association, and Vice-President, American Economic Association. He has served on the editorial boards of *American Economic Review*, *Journal of Economic Literature*, and *Southern Economic Journal*. His numerous publications include *Is the Business Cycle Obsolete?* (1969); *Academic Encounter* (1969); *Income Distribution Theory* (1971); *Macroeconomic Alternatives* (1979); and the successful textbook *Economics* (with W. Gardner and W. Sichel, 1983). His literary skills are also reflected in his recollections of Japan under the American occupation *Tomioka Stories* (1976). He is also a contributor to *Issues in Contemporary Macroeconomics and Distribution* (1985).

John S. Chipman, formerly at the Cowles Commission and Harvard University, is Regents' Professor of Economics, University of Minnesota and Standiger Gastprofessor, University of Konstanz. He was visiting Professor at the following universities: Harvard, Vanderbilt, Chicago, and Rochester and the Stockholm School of Economics; a Fellow of the Center for Advanced Study in the Behavioral Sciences; Associate Editor of *Econometrica* and the *Canadian Journal of Statistics*; and editor of the *Journal of International Economics*. A fellow of the Econometric Society, the American Statistical Association, and the American Academy of Arts and Sciences, he has received the James Murray Luck Award of the National Academy of Sciences. He has contributed significantly to welfare economics, international trade theory, and statistics and is a keen student of the history of economic thought. In addition to numerous articles, he has written *The Theory of Inter-Sectoral Money Flows and Income Formation*. He is also a contributor to *Arrow and the Foundations of the Theory of Economic Policy* (1987).

Gregory Clark, educated at the University of Cambridge and Harvard University, is Assistant Professor of Economics. Stanford University. A holder of the Wrenbury Scholarship, University of Cambridge and an Honorary Senior Scholar, King's College, Cambridge, he was awarded the Certificate of Distinction in Teaching, Harvard University. He is among the youngest crop of economic historians and his several articles have dealt primarily with certain aspects of the industrial revolution in the UK, labor and management in the late nineteenth century, and agricultural development.

Gerard Debreu, a mathematical economist par excellence, is University Professor and Professor of Economics and Mathematics, University of California (Berkeley). He was a Research Associate at the Cowles Commission and later Associate Professor of Economics, Cowles Foundation for Research in Economics, Yale University. A recipient of several honorary degrees, he was a Visiting Professor at the Center for Operations Research and Econometrics, Université Catholique de Louvain, Erskine Fellow and Visiting Professor, University of Canterbury (New Zealand), and Overseas Fellow, Churchill College, Cambridge. A former Fellow of the Center for Advanced Study in the Behavioral Sciences and Guggenheim Fellow, he is a Fellow of the American Academy of Arts and Sciences and a Member of the National Academy of Sciences, a Distinguished Fellow of the American Economic Association, a Chevalier de la Légion d'Honneur and past President of the Econometric Society. In 1983 he was awarded the Nobel Memorial Prize in Economic Science. His many landmark contributions to general equilibrium theory include the classic *Theory of Value* (1959) and *Mathematical Economics: Twenty Papers of Gerard Debreu* (1983). He is also a contributor to *Arrow and the Ascent of Modern Economic Theory* (1987).

Robert Dixon is Senior Lecturer, University of Melbourne (Australia). An associate editor of the *Cambridge Journal of Economics*, he is a member of the advisory board of the National Institute of Economic and Industry Research (Australia). He has written nearly thirty articles on income distribution, agricultural economics, regional growth, and industry structure. He is the co-author of *Regional Growth and Unemployment in the United Kingdom* (with A. P. Thirlwall, 1975). He is at work on a monograph on Cambridge-style economic theory.

George R. Feiwel is Alumni Distinguished Service Professor and Professor of Economics, University of Tennessee. He has been on several occasions Visiting Professor, Harvard University and University of California (Berkeley), Visiting Professor, University of Stockholm, and has more than once been Senior Faculty Visitor, University of Cambridge. He has served on the editorial board of the *Journal of Economic Literature* and has participated in the summer IMSSS Seminars (Stanford University). A Guggenheim Fellow, he is the author of more than fifteen books, including *The Economics of a Socialist Enterprise* (1965); *The Soviet Quest for Economic Efficiency* (1967, 1972); *Industrialization Policy and Planning Under Polish Socialism*, 2 vols (1971); *The Intellectual Capital of Michał Kalecki* (1975); and *Growth and Reforms in Centrally Planned Economies* (1977). He is also a contributor to and editor of *Samuelson and Neoclassical Economics* (1982); *Issues in Contemporary Microeconomics and Welfare* (1985); *Issues in Contemporary Macroeconomics and Distribution* (1985); *Arrow and the Ascent of Modern Economic Theory* (1987), and *Arrow and the Foundations of the Theory of Economic Policy* (1987).

Franklin M. Fisher is Professor of Economics, Massachusetts Institute of Technology. He has taught at the University of Chicago and Harvard University, and has been on various occasions Visiting Professor, Hebrew University of Jerusalem and Tel-Aviv University (of which he is also a member of the Board of Governors and a participant of the summer IMSSS seminars (Stanford University). A Fellow of the Econometric Society and of the American Academy of Arts and Sciences, he is also a Guggenheim Fellow and Erskine Fellow (University of Canterbury), and has been a Ford Foundation Faculty Research Fellow, London School of Economics. He was awarded the John Bates Clark medal of the American Economic Association and has served as President of the Econometric Society of which he is also a Council member. He has acted as associate editor of the *Journal of the American Statistical Association*, American editor of the *Review of Economic Studies*, and editor of *Econometrica*, and is a research associate of the National Bureau of Economic Research. He is the author of more than one hundred articles ranging over the fields of econometrics, aggregate production functions, price indices, industrial organization, and most notably in the underrated field of mathematical stability theory. He has published more than ten books, including *A Priori Information and Time Series Analysis* (1962); *Essays on the Structure of Social Science Models* (with A. Ando and H. A. Simon, 1963); The *Economic Theory of Price Indices* (with K. Shell, 1972); *Folded, Spindled, and Mutilated: Economic Analysis and U.S. v IBM* (with J. J. McGowan and J. E. Greenwood, 1983); and *Disequilibrium Foundations of Equilibrium Economics* (1983).

Duncan K. Foley, formerly at MIT and Stanford University, is Professor of Economics, Barnard College and Columbia University Graduate Faculty of Arts and Sciences. A former associate editor of the *Journal of Economic Theory*, he is a member of the editorial board of the *Journal of Economic Literature*. He has written a number of articles exhibiting the progression of his interests from an extension of the general equilibrium model to economies with public goods (using game theoretic solutions), through the role of money in the business cycle in neoclassical formulation, to a search for alternatives to the neoclassical paradigm (using modern mathematical techniques). He is the author of *Monetary and Fiscal Policy in a Growing Economy* (with M. Sidrauski, 1971); *Understanding Capital: Marx's Economic Theory* (1986); and *Money, Accumulation and Crisis* (1986).

Pierangelo Garegnani is Professor of Economics, University of Rome. He has been Professor of Economics, University of Pavia and University of Florence and Visiting Professor, University of Cambridge (Fellow, Trinity College), and Visiting Professor, Stanford University. A foremost disciple of Sraffa, he has been involved in the capital controversies on the side of Anglo-Italians and in a 'family quarrel' with Joan Robinson. His many publications include *Il Capitale nele Teorie della Distribuzione* (1960); *Il Problema della Domanda Effetiva nello Sviluppo Economico Italiano* (1962); *Valore e Domanda Effetiva* (1979); and *Marx e gli Economisti Classici* (1981).

Richard M. Goodwin is Professor of Economics, University of Siena. Early in his career he taught at Harvard University where he achieved the distinction of being both a student and teacher (in mathematics) of Schumpeter, and where he taught not only economics but also physics. A pre-war Rhodes Scholar, in 1950 he travelled on a Fulbright Fellowship to the University of Cambridge where he remained for thirty years, first as Instructor then as Reader. Throughout this period he was closely associated with Joan Robinson and Richard Kahn and was a member of the 'secret seminar' during the period when Cambridge growth theory was being thrashed out. Emeritus Fellow, Peterhouse College, Cambridge, he has spent a year at the Institute of Statistics, Calcutta, cooperating in the preparation of the Indian Second Five-Year Plan and has been Visiting Professor, University of Vienna. He has made significant contributions to economic dynamics, in particular to integration of cycle and trend and recently he has returned to his original interests in Schumpeter's contributions, sparked by the development of catastrophy theory and the concept of bifurcation. His many articles have been collected in *Essays in Economic Dynamics* (1982) and *Essays in Linear Economic Structures* (1983). He is also the author of *Elementary Economics from the Higher Standpoint* (1970) and is at work on *The Dynamics of a Capitalist Economy* (with L. Punzo).

Harvey Gram is Professor of Economics, Queens College, City University of New York. He has taught at the University of Waterloo, New York University, and the New School for Social Research. He has written on general equilibrium theory and capital and growth theory. He is the co-author (with V. C. Walsh) of a review article of Joan Robinson's contributions and of *Classical and Neoclassical Theories of General Equilibrium* (with V. C. Walsh, 1980).

Frank Hahn, a younger colleague, sometime protégé and antagonist of Joan Robinson, and from within the citadel a leading defender and critic of neoclassical economics, is Professor of Economics, University of Cambridge and Fellow, Churchill College (Cambridge). He was formerly Professor of Economics, London School of Economics; Visiting Professor, University of California (Berkeley); Taussig Research Professor, Harvard University; Schumpeter Professor, University of Vienna; and on several occasions Visiting Professor, MIT. He is the *enfant terrible* in residence of the summer seminars, IMSSS (Stanford University). A Fellow of the British Academy, he is a Corresponding Fellow and Foreign Honorary Member of the American Academy of Arts and Science; an honorary member of the American Economic Association; and a Fellow of the Center of Advanced Study in the Behavioral Sciences (Stanford). A recipient of honorary degrees from the University(ies) of Birmingham, Strasbourg, East Anglia, and London, he has served as President of the Econometric Society and the Royal Economic Society and as managing editor of the *Review of Economic Studies* and assistant editor of the *Journal of Economic Theory*. A significant contributor to modern general equilibrium analysis, he has published numerous articles analyzing sequential markets, money in a general equilibrium system, stability theory, economics with heterogeneous capital goods, and overlapping generations. His most recent work (with R. M. Solow) concentrates on employment theory and contracts and conjectural equilibria. He is the author and editor of several books, including *The Share of Wages in National Income* (1972); *Money and Inflation* (1982); *Equilibrium and Macroeconomics* (1984); *Money, Growth and Stability* (1985); and *General Competitive Analysis* (with K. J. Arrow, 1971).

Peter J. Hammond, formerly Professor of Economics, University of Essex, is Professor of Economics, and member of the IMSSS (Stanford University). A Fellow of the Econometric Society, he was a Fellow of the Institute of Advanced Studies, the Hebrew University of Jerusalem, Joseph A. Schumpeter Visiting Professor, University of Graz, Visiting Professor, Center for Operations Research and Econometrics, Université Catholique de Louvain, and Princeton University. A major contributor to welfare economics and social choice theory, he has written over fifty papers also ranging over the fields of optimal growth and exhausible resources, rational individual choice, distributional objectives in welfare economics, uncertainty, information, incentives, general equilibrium theory, incomplete markets, and extensive games. He is the author of four lectures on Schumpeterian themes in the modern welfare economics of production published in *Lectures on Schumpeterian Economics* (ed. C. Seidl, 1984) and a contributor to *Issues in Contemporary Microeconomics and Welfare* (1985) and *Arrow and the Foundations of the Theory of Economic Policy* (1987). He is currently at work on a book, *Welfare Economic Theory*.

Daniel M. Hausman is Professor of Philosophy, Carnegie-Mellon University. After undergraduate training at Harvard and New York Universities, he studied at the University of Cambridge in the early 1970s. He has taught at the University of Maryland and was a Visitor, Institute for Advanced Study, Princeton. Starting with his PhD thesis on capital theory his research interests have centered on economic philosophy. He is the author of *Capital, Profits and Prices: An Essay in The Philosophy of Economics* (1981) and the editor of *The Philosophy of Economics* (1984).

Timothy J. Kehoe is Professor of Economics, University of Minnesota. He has taught at Wesleyan University, MIT, and the University of Cambridge where he was Fellow at Clare College and Churchill College. A former consultant to the World Bank and the Bank of Mexico, he has held fellowships of the Sloan Foundation and the Mathematical Sciences Research Institute (Berkeley). He is co-director of the Model of Applied General Equilibrium, Universidad Autonoma de Barcelona and Associate editor of the *Journal of Mathematical Economics*. He has written nearly thirty papers in pure and applied general equilibrium theory, comparative statistics, and intertemporal economics. He is also the author of *Regularity and Index Theory for Economic Equilibrium Models* (forthcoming) and is at present revising *General Competitive Analysis* (with K. J. Arrow and F. H. Hahn).

Murray C. Kemp is Research Professor of Economics, University of New South Wales. He has been Visiting Professor at the Universities of Paris, Mannheim, Essex, and Minnesota, and at Columbia University and MIT. A Fellow of the Econometric Society, he has contributed significantly to the theory of international trade, resource economics and welfare economics. His many publications include *The Pure Theory of International Trade and Investment* (1964, 1969); *Three Topics in the Theory of International Trade: Distribution, Welfare, and Uncertainty* (1976); *Variational Methods in Economics* (with G. Hadley, 1971) and *Essays in the Economics of Exhausible Resources* (ed. with N. V. Long, 1984). He is also a contributor to *Issues in Contemporary Microeconomics and Welfare* (1985) and *Arrow and the Foundations of the Theory of Economic Policy* (1987).

Lawrence R. Klein, one of the principal architects of modern macroeconometrics, is Benjamin Franklin Professor of Economics, University of Pennsylvania. He was formerly at the University of Chicago, University of Michigan, and the Oxford Institute of Statistics. He is Chairman of the Professional Board, Wharton Econometric Forecasting Associates, Inc.; principal investigator, Project LINK; and a Member of the National Academy of Sciences. A recipient of several honorary degrees, including the University(ies) of Vienna, Paris, Brussels, and Oxford he is past President of the American Economic Association, the Econometric Society, and the Eastern Economic Association. In 1976 he served as coordinator of Jimmy Carter's Economic Task Force and as Consultant to President Carter's Council of Economic Advisers and to the Federal Reserve Board. He was awarded the John Bates Clark medal of the American Economic Association and in 1980 the Nobel Memorial Prize in Economic Science. His numerous contributions include *The Keynesian Revolution* (1947, 1966); *An Econometric Model of the United States, 1929–1952* (with A. S. Goldberger, 1955); *Essay on the Theory of Economic Prediction* (1968); and *An Introduction to Econometric Forecasting and Forecasting Models* (1980). He has also contributed to *Issues in Contemporary Macroeconomics and Distribution* (1985) and *Arrow and the Ascent of Modern Economic Theory* (1987).

David K. Levine is Associate Professor of Economics, University of California (Los Angeles). A Visitor, Mathematical Sciences Research Institute (Berkeley) and a participant in the summer seminars, IMSSS (Stanford University), he was Visiting Scholar, Department of Applied Economics, University of Cambridge. He has written more than thirty papers on general equilibrium theory and game theory, incomplete information, and intertemporal economics. He is also the author of *Theory of Microeconomics* (1986) and is at present working on two books *Microeconomics: A Computer Text* (with D. Barkley, L. Glover, and B. Ellickson) and *Overlapping Generations with Perfect Capital Markets* (with T. Kehoe, W. Muller, and M. Woodford).

Mukul Majumdar is Warshow Professor of Economics, Cornell University. He has taught at Stanford University, and has been Visiting Lecturer, London School of Economics and University of Canterbury; Visiting Research Professor, University of Bonn; Visiting Ford Rotating Professor, University of California (Berkeley); Visiting Professor University of Wisconsin (Madison); and participant of the summer seminars, IMSSS (Stanford University). A Fellow of the Econometric Society and a Guggenheim Fellow, he has been a coordinating foreign editor of the *Review of Economic Studies*. He serves on the editorial board of the *Journal of Mathematical Economics* and is an associate editor of the *Journal of Economic Theory*. He has written nearly forty articles on general equilibrium theory, welfare economics, capital theory, and stochastic methods. He is at present at work (with T. Mitra) on a monograph *Intertemporal Economics*.

Andreu Mas-Colell is Professor of Economics, Harvard University. Formerly Professor of Economics and Mathematics, University of California (Berkeley); he was a Sloan Fellow; a Visiting Scholar, University of Bonn; Visiting Professor, Universitat Autonoma de Barcelona and Mathematical Sciences Research Institute (Berkeley); and associate editor of the *Journal of Economic Theory* and of the *SIAM Journal of Applied Mathematics*. He is a Fellow of the Econometric Society and a Member of its Council, an associate editor of *Econometrica*, and the editor of the *Journal of Mathematical Economics*. He has written some fifty research papers on subjects ranging from abstract social choice problems to pricing policy for public firms. But in the main he has focused on general equilibrium theory where he has concentrated on extensions of the model to new areas and on treatment via calculus techniques. His publications include *The Theory of General Economic Equilibrium: A Differentiable Approach* (1985). He is also a contributor to *Arrow and the Ascent of Modern Economic Theory* (1987).

Gautam Mathur, a student of Joan Robinson (who supervised his PhD dissertation), is Director, Institute of Applied Manpower Research (India). He has had a distinguished academic and civil service career in India.

Formerly at Punjab University, he became Dean, Faculty of Social Sciences, Osmania University and later Vice-Chancellor, Utkal University. He has served in a number of consultative posts to the United Nations and the government of India. He has held a number of academic visiting appointments, among them at Nuffield College (Oxford); Faculty of Economics and Politics, University of Cambridge; Ruhr University; University of Manchester; University of Rome; and University of Portland. A past President of the Indian Economic Association, Indian Academy of Social Sciences, and Indian Society of Labour Economics, he serves on the advisory board of editors of *World Development*. He has written about eighty articles ranging over many fields, including capital theory, development policy and planning, public finance, science and education policy and manpower planning, and law and economics. He is also the author of *Planning for Steady Growth* (1965); *Disparity Tax in a Composite Economy* (1975); and *Economic Justice in a Free Society* (forthcoming).

R. C. O. (Robin) Matthews is Master of Clare College, Cambridge and Professor of Political Economy, University of Cambridge. Formerly Drummond Professor of Political Economy, Oxford University; Fellow of All Souls College; Lecturer, University of Cambridge, Fellow St. John's College; and Chairman of the Social Science Research Council; he was President of the Royal Economic Society, Chairman of the Panel of Academic Consultants, Bank of England, and a Member of the Economic Policy Committee, Social Democratic Party. A fellow of the British Academy, he has been Visiting Professor, University of California (Berkeley) and Stanford University; and for many years has served in various editorial capacities, most recently as editor, *The Economic Journal*. His many publications in economic history, growth theory, and business cycle theory include *A Study in Trade Cycle Theory* (1954), *The Business Cycle* (1958), and *British Economic Growth 1856–1973* (with C. H. Feinstein and J. C. Odling-Smee, 1982). More recently his interests have shifted towards a greater stress of the interdisciplinary approach. He is also a contributor to *Arrow and the Foundations of the Theory of Economic Policy* (1987).

Tapan Mitra is Professor of Economics, Cornell University. He has taught at the University(ies) of Rochester and Illinois and the State University of New York (Stony Brook). A Sloan Research Fellow, he has been academic visitor, International Centre for Economics and Related Disciplines, London School of Economics. A close collaborator of M. Majumdar, he has published about thirty articles ranging over the fields of capital and growth theory, welfare economics, exhaustible resources, international trade, population growth, and the economics of forestry.

Edward Nell is Professor and Chairman, Department of Economics, New

School of Social Research. He has taught at Wesleyan University and the University of East Anglia and has been visiting Professor at Bennington College, McGill University, University of Brenen, and Université d'Orléans. A Fellow of the Lehrman Institute, a Bard Center Fellow, and Fellow and teaching member of the Centro di Studi Economici Avanzati, he is on the editorial board of the *Journal of Post-Keynesian Economics*. A former Rhodes scholar, he studied for several years at Oxford, made contact with Cambridge and, in particular, with Joan Robinson. He has written more than fifty articles dealing with capital theory, the Cambridge controversies, critique of neoclassical economics, and the economics of Marx, Keynes, and Sraffa. He is the author of nearly ten books including *Rational Economic Man* (with M. Hollis, 1974); *Growth, Profits and Property* (ed., 1980); *Free Market Conservatism* (1984); *Prosperity and Public Spending* (1986); and *Keynes After Sraffa* (1986).

Yaw Nyarko, a graduate student of M. Majumdar and among the newest crop of mathematical theorists, is Assistant Professor of Economics, Brown University. He has held the A. D. White Presidential Fellowship and the Floyd Mundy Fellowship. Aside from his chapter in this volume, he has written five other research papers in the general area of growth theory, stressing uncertainty, incomplete information, and optimal strategies, and using a game-theoretic approach.

I. G. Patel, Director of the London School of Economics and Political Science, a student of Joan Robinson's, has had a distinguished career as an economist in public service. He was Division Chief, Research Department, International Monetary Fund (IMF); Alternate Executive Director for India on the Board of the IMF; Chief Economic Adviser (later Special Secretary), Ministry of Finance and Economic Adviser, Planning Commission (India); Deputy Administrator, United Nations Development Programme; Governor, Reserve Bank of India; and Director, Indian Institute of Management. He is a Member of the United Nations Committee on Development Planning and of the Advisory Group, General Agreement on Trade and Tariffs, and an Honorary Fellow, King's College, Cambridge. He is the author of *Essays in Economic Policy and Economic Growth* (1986).

John E. Roemer is Professor of Economics, University of California (Davis). A Guggenheim Fellow, he has been a Visiting Professor, Yale University and has held the National Science Foundation Needs Fellowship. He was a member of the editorial board of the *Review of Radical Political Economics* and serves in such capacity on the board of *Economics and Philosophy*. He has published nearly fifty articles in economics and philosophy. After writing extensively on how the Marxian theory of exploitation and class could be given rigorous foundations, using tools of equilibrium theory and game theory, he is now studying theories of distributive justice, using an axiomatic approach. He also attempts to apply methods of contemporary economic modelling to the study of political philosophy problems. He is the author of *Analytical Foundations of Marxian Economic Theory* (1981), *A General Theory of Exploitation and Class* (1982), and *Free to Lose* (forthcoming).

Paul M. Romer is Assistant Professor of Economics, University of Rochester. A student of Robert E. Lucas, Jr and Jose A. Scheinkman at the University of Chicago where he has held the Starr and Earheart Fellowships, he has published several papers in mathematical economics on such topics as increasing returns, growth and scarcity, information and optimal contracts, and productivity.

Michael Rothschild, formerly Professor of Economics University of California (San Diego), University of Wisconsin (Madison), Princeton University, and Harvard University, is Dean, Division of Social Sciences, University of California (San Diego). A Fellow of the Econometric Society, Guggenheim Fellow, Romnes Faculty Fellow, and Oskar Morgenstern Distinguished Fellow, he is a Research Associate, National Bureau of Economic Research and a member, Council of the Econometric Society. He has served on the board of editors of the *Journal of Economic Literature* and is associate editor of *Econometrica* and the *Journal of Economic Theory*. His more than thirty articles range over the fields of risk and uncertainty, income distribution, information, and capital theory. He is the editor of *Uncertainty in Economics* (with P. A. Diamond, 1978).

Thomas K. Rymes is Professor of Economics, Carleton University (Canada), A Visiting Fellow, Wolfson College, Cambridge, he was on several occasions Visiting Professor, McGill University. A Canada Council Fellow, he has served on the executive council of the Canadian Economic Association, and as member of the editorial board of the *Canadian Journal of Economics* (of which he has also been associate editor) and *Review of Income and Wealth*. He has published more than twenty articles on capital theory and growth, money and banking, and productivity. He is also the author of *Fixed Capital Flows and Stocks, Manufacturing, Canada, 1926–1960* (2 vols., 1967) and the editor of *Papers on Regional Statistical Studies* (with S. Ostry, 1966).

Paul A. Samuelson, a master economist *par excellence*, is the first American Nobel Laureate in economic science, Institute Professor at MIT (and an 'institution' in his own right), and our protagonist in *Samuelson and Neoclassical Economics*. He has been President of the Econometric Society, the American Economic Association, and the International Economic Association. A recipient of the John Bates Clark medal, the Albert Einstein Commemorative award, and more than twenty-five honorary degrees (including from the University of Chicago and Harvard University – his alma mater), he is a Corresponding Fellow of the British Academy, a Fellow of the American Academy of Arts and Sciences, and a Member of the National Academy. An active consultant to many government agencies, Economic Adviser to President Kennedy, and in 1964 Chairman of the President's Task Force for Maintaining American Prosperity, he was for nearly twenty years bi-weekly columnist for *Newsweek* magazine. His rich output of papers is now available in five volumes of *The Collected Scientific Papers of Paul A. Samuelson*. He is also the author of *Foundations of Economic Analysis, Linear Programming and Economic Analysis* (with R. Dorfman and R. M. Solow), and of the most influential modern economics textbook, *Economics*, now in its twelfth 'incarnation'. He is also a contributor to *Arrow and the Foundations of the Theory of Economic Policy* (1987).

Tibor Scitovsky is Eberle Professor of Development Economics, Emeritus, Stanford University. He has been Professor of Economics, University of California (Berkeley and Santa Cruz) and London School of Economics; Heinz Professor of Economics, Yale University; and Visiting Fellow, All Souls College, Oxford. A Fellow, Development Centre, OECD (Paris) and a Guggenheim Fellow, he is a Distinguished Fellow of the American Economic Association, a Corresponding Fellow of the British Academy, an Honorary Fellow of the London School of Economics, and a Fellow of the American Academy of Arts and Sciences. In his numerous papers he has contributed to many fields including welfare economics, international trade, and a new approach to rational consumer behavior. He has written nearly ten books, including *Welfare and Competition* (1951, 1971); *Economic Theory and Western European Integration* (1958); *Industry and Trade in Some Developing Countries* (with I. M. D. Little and M. F. Scott, 1970); and *The Joyless Economy* (1976).

Koji Shimomura is Associate Professor of Economics, Research Institute for Economics and Business Administration, Kobe University (Japan). His professional association with Murray Kemp began at the University of New South Wales where he got a PhD in economics in 1983. He has written papers on renewable resources and on labor unions and is also the author of *Essays in Some Topics of Modern Economic Theory* (1984), and the co-author (with Murray Kemp) of *Labour Unions and the Theory of International Trade* (forthcoming).

T. N. Srinivasan, Samuel C. Park, Jr Professor of Economics, Yale University, was formerly Research Professor, Indian Statistical Institute. A Visiting Professor at MIT, University of Minnesota, and Stanford University (where he was also Ford Faculty Research Fellow), he has been a Special Adviser, Development Research Center, The World Bank, to which he is also a consultant. He is a Fellow of the Econometric Society and the American Academy of Arts and Sciences, an honorary member of the American Economic Association, and a recipient (with Marc Nerlove) of the Mahalanobis Memorial medal of the Indian Econometric Society. A former coeditor of *Econometrica* and the *Journal of Development Economics* and associate editor of the *Journal of International Economics*, he is associate editor of the *International Economic Review* and member of the editorial board of the *World Bank Economic Review*. He is the author of more than one hundred articles concentrating on dynamic models of growth and development, empirical planning models for India, the pure theory of international trade, uncertainty (especially as applied to agriculture), agricultural development and institutions, and poverty and malnutrition. He has co-authored and co-edited nearly ten books, including *Foreign Trade Regimes and Economic Development* (with J. N. Bhagwati, 1975); *Lectures on International Trade* (with J. N. Bhagwati, 1983); and *Handbook of Development Economics* (ed. with H. B. Chenery, forthcoming).

Joseph E. Stiglitz is Professor of Economics, Princeton University. Formerly Drummond Professor of Political Economy, Oxford University and Professor of Economics, Stanford University and Yale University, he was Oskar Morgenstern Distinguished Fellow and Visiting Professor, Institute for Advanced Studies and Mathematics; Visiting Fellow, St Catherine's College, Oxford; Visiting Professor, University of Canterbury (New Zealand), and Tapp Research Fellow, Gonville and Caius College, Cambridge. A Guggenheim and Fulbright Fellow, he is a Fellow of the Econometric Society and of the American Academy of Arts and Sciences and recipient of the John Bates Clark medal of the American Economic Association. A former associate editor of the *Journal of Economic Theory* and *American Economic Review* and American editor of the *Review of Economic Studies*, he is associate editor of *Energy Economics* and *Managerial and Decision Economics* and co-editor of the *Journal of Public Economics*. He is the author of nearly two hundred papers in a very broad range of fields covering the economics of information, uncertainty (basic concepts, market equilibrium, risk and agriculture, portfolio analysis, and theory of corporate finance), theory of taxation, public economics, distribution of income and wealth, growth and capital theory, natural resources, development and trade, macroeconomics, and the theory of imperfect competition. He is also the co-author of *The Theory of Commodity Price Stabilization* (with D. Newberry, 1981); *Lectures in Public Economics* (with A. B. Atkinson, 1980); co-editor of *New Developments in the Theory of Market Structure* (with E. Mathewson, 1985) and has recently published a textbook, *Economics of the Public Sector* (1986). He is also a contributor to *Arrow and the Foundations of the Theory of Economic Policy* (1987).

Paul Streeten is Professor of Economics and Director, World Development Institute, Boston University. A former Warden, Queen Elizabeth House; Director, Institute of Commonwealth Studies; and Fellow, Balliol College, Oxford, he was also Professor of Economics and Fellow (Deputy and Acting Director), Institute of Development Studies, University of Sussex. He has also served as Deputy Director-General of Economic Planning, UK Ministry of Overseas Development. He was a Special Adviser, Policy Planning and Program Review Department, World Bank and Director of Studies, Overseas Development Council. A former editor of the *Bulletin of the Oxford Institute of Statistics*, he was also on the board of editors of the *Journal of Development Studies*. He was a member of the Board of Commonwealth Development Corporation and of the Royal Commission on Environmental Pollution. He has written numerous articles in such diverse fields as methodology, welfare economics, public finance, international trade, and economic planning and development. He has published more than ten books, including *Economic Integration* (1961, 1964); *Unfashionable Economics* (1970); *The Frontiers of Development Studies* (1972); *Development Perspectives* (1981); and *What Price Food?* (1987).

David Sunding is a graduate student in the Department of Agricultural and Resource Economics at the University of California, (Berkeley). He specializes in economic development, economic theory, and the study of institutions and their effect on economic growth.

Paolo Sylos Labini, formerly at the Universities of Catania and Bologna, is Professor of Economics, University of Rome. He has been Visiting Professor at the University(ies) of Cambridge, Yamaguchi, Rio de Janeiro, Sidney, and Roskilde, and Oxford University, Harvard University, MIT, and Universidad Autonoma Nacional, Mexico. On several occasions he has served as economic adviser to the Italian government. A member of the Academia Nazionale dei Lincei, he is on the board of editors of the *International Journal of Industrial Organization, Moneta e credito*, and *Banca Nazionale del Lavoro Quarterly Review*. His writings are a blend of the theoretical, empirical, and policy-oriented aproach. He has made important contributions to industrial organization and his early interest in the economics of technical change led him to study growth theory and development and planning. Among his many publications are *Oligopoly and Technical Progress* (1962, 1964); *Trade Unions, Inflation and Productivity* (1974); *The Forces of Economic Growth and Decline* (1984); and *Le classi sociali negli anni ottanta* (1986).

Lorie Tarshis is chairman, Department of Economics, Glendon College, York University (Canada). He has taught at Tufts University; Stanford University; and Scarborough College, University of Toronto, and served as

Research Director, Ontario Economic Council. A Guggenheim Fellow and Fulbright Fellow, he has been Visiting Professor, University of Washington, University of British Columbia, and Tokyo University. A member of Keynes's Political Economy Club, a student of Keynes, and in touch with the members of the 'Circus' he was a research scholar at Trinity College during the fateful years when the *General Theory* was being written and immediately after its publication. He was one of the first to bring 'Keynes to America' and cooperated (with Emile Despres, Walter Salant, Paul Sweezy, and others) on a tract on fiscal policy, *An Economic Program for American Democracy* (1938), which influenced Roosevelt's advisers. Soon after the war he published the widely acclaimed Keynesian textbook *Elements of Economics*, a book that came under strong right-wing attack in the McCarthy era and that had a second incarnation as *Modern Economics* in 1966. His many accomplishments include work in international economics and finance. He is also the author of *Mobilizing Resources for War* (with T. Scitovsky and E. S. Shaw, 1951); *International Economics* (1955); and *The U.S. Balance of Payments in 1964* (with W. Salant *et al.*, 1962).

Lance Taylor, formerly at Harvard University, is Professor of Economics, Massachusetts Institute of Technology. A Visiting Professor at the Universidade de Brasilia and the University of Minnesota, he has given the Marshall Lectures, University of Cambridge and the W. Arthur Lewis Lecture, American Social Science Association. He has published more than fifty papers in economic development and planning, growth modelling, income distribution, and applied general equilibrium. He is also the author of *Notes and Problems in Microeconomic Theory* (with S. Bowles, D. Kendrick, and M. Roberts, 1970); *Macro Models for Developing Countries* (1979); *Models of Growth and Distribution for Brazil* (with E. L. Bacha, E. A. Cardoso, and F. J. Lysy, 1980); *Egypt: Economic Management in a Period of Transition* (with K. Ikram, and others, 1980); and *Structuralist Macroeconomics: Applicable Models for the Third World* (1983).

Vivian Walsh, educated at Trinity College (Dublin), is Professor of Economics, Guilford College. He was on the faculty of the London School of Economics for several years before coming to the USA where he has taught at a number of institutions, most recently as Distinguished Visiting Professor of Economics and Philosophy, University of Tulsa. Throughout his career, his teaching and research interests have centered on economic theory, history of economic thought, and analytic philosophy. His approach to economics, hitherto strictly neoclassical, suffered an exogenous shock on being exposed to Joan Robinson's teaching in the early 1970s. He has written an article reviewing Joan Robinson's contributions (with H. Gram). He is also the author of *Scarcity and Evil* (1961); *Introduction to Contemporary Microeco-*

nomics (1970); and *Classical and Neoclassical Theories of General Equilibrium* (with H. Gram, 1980).

Edward N. Wolff Is Professor of Economics, New York University. Formerly a Research Associate of the National Bureau of Economic Research, he has been affiliated, *inter alia*, with the Department of Urban Studies and Planning, MIT; the World Bank, Equal Employment Opportunity Research; the Committee for Economic Development; and the Institute for Research on Poverty. He is on the editorial board of the *Review of Income and Wealth*. Since 1975 he has published nearly forty papers on development and trade, income distribution, and productivity. He is also the author of *Growth, Accumulation, and Unproductive Activity* (1986) and the editor of *International Comparisons of Household Wealth Distribution* (forthcoming). He is at present writing *Economics of the Labor Force*.

Preface

With the passing of Joan Robinson a vital flame has gone out of economics. We are all the poorer for it. We all recognize that there was more than one Joan Robinson. She means different things to different people. There were different Joans at any one time and different Joans in time. The dynamics of change in Joan can be considered an ascending or descending trend or even a growth cycle, given the beholders' preconceptions and predispositions.

There was Joan Robinson who initially was fascinated by economic theory as an essentially tool-making process (the subject matter of economics 'is neither more nor less than its own technique' (Joan Robinson, 1932, p.3)), and who later in life revolted against developing a fully-fledged alternative theory to neoclassical economics on the grounds that it would only be another box of tricks. She stressed that what economic theory needs now is a different way of thinking: 'to eschew fudging, to respect facts and to admit ignorance of what we do not know' (1979, p.119). There was Joan, the challenging critic, asking profound questions, but often providing no more than hints to answers. She said of Myrdal (whom she admired) that he saw problems more clearly than solutions and of Sraffa that he was far more negative than positive. *Mutatis mutandis*, the same could be said of her.

There was Joan Robinson, the great Marshallian, trying to escape Marshall's moralizing and fudging, who broke out of the 'Marshallian incubus' and wrote the neoclassical, tool-making *Economics of Imperfect Competition* in Pigovian tradition, inspired by Sraffa's pregnant suggestions and sacrilegious questioning of Marshall.

There was Joan Robinson who at times showed a remarkable grasp of the grand conception of general economic interdependence and asked searching questions about the limitations of Walrasian general equilibrium theory, while she sometimes downgraded its usefulness and its historical achievement.

There was Joan Robinson, political economist *par excellence* in the best Cambridge tradition, who was inspired and enthused by the unique experience and opportunity of participating in Keynes's Circus and who became a formative figure in the Keynesian revolution. There was Joan who increasingly perceived the Keynesian revolution through Kaleckian eyes. Loyal to Keynes her mentor, she increasingly reinterpreted his great teaching in the Kaleckian mode.

There was Joan Robinson, the contributor and interpreter of the Keynesian revolution on the theoretical plane, who incessantly sought to go beyond the *General Theory*; to generalize it into a long-term theory of employment and to 'open' it to an open economy.

There was the Joan Robinson of *The Accumulation of Capital*, a great model builder, who fully understood the need to simplify drastically and was accused of unnecessary abstraction. There was the Joan of the very formalistic book with at least one foot in the mainstream, who seethed with new ideas and concentrated on large themes, but whose execution fell short of the mark in articulating her conception of the vicissitudes of the capitalist economy. To paraphrase Pigou, when a person has devised a new way of climbing a mountain, we may indeed regret that her way has not led to the top, but for the effort that has advanced her towards the top nothing is due but praise.

There was Joan Robinson who perceived economic processes as a Keynesian (Kaleckian) and was critical of Sraffa's prelude to a critique of economic theory. Yet, she was attracted to and influenced by the Sraffian approach and vacillated between Keynesian and Sraffian themes. There was Joan who reinstated Marx as an economist and made his reproduction schemes respectable, while committing the 'sacrilege' of debunking his labor theory of value.

There was Joan Robinson, the astute theoretician in the Cambridge tradition, innocent of sophisticated mathematics in the age of mathematization of economic theory. As she (1979, p.115) said of herself. 'I had a very literary education and to this day I know only the mathematics that I was able to pick up in the course of trying to formalize economic arguments'. She knew some calculus, was brilliant at geometry, knew elementary differential equations, was at home in ordinary algebra and knew the basics of matrix algebra. She understood elementary statistics and the rudiments of econometrics. (She understood the mathematics of reswitching and she saw it intuitively long before anyone except Sraffa had worked it out. She worked out the Golden Rule geometrically without recourse to differential equations, as she did in her critique of the Solow-Swan approach.)

She was gifted with remarkable intuitive and analytical powers and an exceptionally logical mind. She had the enthusiasm of the creatively destructive innovator and pursued a relentless quest to get the logical arguments right. She emerged as a respected, technically competent analytical economist in an age when progress in economics is frequently measured by the sophistication of the contributions to techniques of economic analysis.

There was Joan Robinson who argued that mathematics is a powerful tool of thought, but that its application to economic theory often consists of putting circular arguments into sophisticated mathematical forms. There was Joan who knew her comparative advantage. When asked by Ragnar Frisch to be vice-president of the Econometric Society, she declined the honor on the grounds that it would do no good for her name to appear on the cover of a journal when she could not understand anything inside it. She was annoyed by the modern neoclassical practitioners who take refuge in building increasingly elaborate mathematical manipulations and who resent anyone asking them what it is they are supposed to be manipulating. In her hostility to sophisticated mathematical economics, she unfortunately did not trouble to differentiate between the trivial niceties and the substantive advances in economic content. She wanted to think about the economic issues and did not want to be distracted by what she considered to be purely mathematical questions which, as a matter of division of labor, she preferred to leave to others. There was Joan who believed that the success of economics depends more on insight than precision and that its affinity must be with history as much as with mathematics.

There was Joan Robinson who criticized economic theory for being far removed from reality, abstract, formalistic, esoteric, and all that, while Joan, the theorist, committed similar sins. She was hypercritical of the pervasive concept of equilibrium in economic theory, while she herself used it to advantage in *The Accumulation of Capital*. She was particularly critical of the drawing of practical conclusions from equilibrium analysis, which she did not do.

There was the unfashionable and fierce Joan Robinson who did not appeal to some fledgeling economists because she did not communicate in their language, while telling them that anyway their language is unsuitable for economics, and/or who irritated them by telling them what they had no wish to hear. But there was also Joan the great teacher who influenced her students in subtle ways. She taught them to think for themselves; she injected them with a healthy dose of scepticism; she showed them how to discuss economic theory without resorting to mathematical symbols; and, above all, she fired them with earnestness for their subject.

There was Joan who, in an age when many of her peers tended to concentrate their energies on narrow subjects amenable to mathematically-complicated 'easy' answers, embarked on difficult broad questions to which she did not always have answers. There was Joan in whose work history, institutions, anthropology, politics, and philosophy all played an important role. She (1979, p.118) admitted that 'history can never give a final knockdown answer to any question. Each generation rewrites its own past in accord with its current ideology'. However, she believed 'that there is a lot of difference between good analysis and bad, apart from ideological tendencies'.

There was Joan who came to economics because she hoped to find in it answers to the plight of the poor and who remained in economics fired by social enthusiasm. She tried to show how orthodox theory fails to understand how the capitalist economy works. She sought to establish that government policy had the capacity to improve economic performance and to make society more humane and just. But in her work there is little directly about policy. The argument is implied. While she had an exaggerated view of the potency of intelligent argument, she increasingly came to realize that economic answers are but political questions.

There was Joan the social critic who, in her search for a better world, aligned herself with alternative social designs that appeared to promulgate a better society. Her critics have made much of this, and it may have lost her the Nobel Prize. But we should respect the fact that even in old age she retained a youthful ability to respond with enthusiasm to the promise of a dream. She did not always see the grim realities at first, but when she came to see them – as she always did, for she was as severe a critic of political ideology as of economic ideology – she was merciless in denouncing them. Like many Europeans, she was revolted by certain aspects of the US establishment (social, political, and intellectual) – a feeling that spilled over into economics. She strongly denounced the creation of prosperity by building up the arsenal of military hardware. And she was critical, even contemptuous of 'Hollywood culture'; unlike the French she could not see any value in its creations.

There was Joan Robinson, the great expositor, truly guilty of 'Koopmans's sin' of lucid and persuasive use of language, who, in a few well-chosen words, could rout her opponents. She was a master of controversy. An apt pupil of Keynes, she was blunt spoken and disregarded the niceties of social intercourse. She was a campaigner and preacher in Cambridge-style earnestness, seeker after truth, incorruptible, fiercely courageous, and honest.

There was Joan Robinson of the mordant sense of humor, the antagonist who did not always play cricket, and the forbidding and austere personality. But there was also Joan, the warm and devoted friend whose limpid and sparkling blue eyes and wicked smile conveyed warmth and often said more than mere words could express.

Yes, she was irritating, irascible, intolerant, impractical, angry, difficult, dictatorial, and domineering. But she was also inspiring, incisive, insightful, ingenious, independent, indomitable, and pertinacious; a shrewd and subtle thinker, dedicated to her cause. She had a special blend of vigor, fervor, tenacity, persuasiveness and polemical brilliance in arguing her position. She represented economics at its best, urged us to think for ourselves, and showed us the strengths and limits of economic theorizing. She also showed us what great satisfaction could be derived when economics is put to higher uses for the betterment of mankind. For this and much more she could serve as an admirable figure for future economists to emulate.

Samuelson (1966, p.1593) aptly noted: 'Cambridge economists, God bless them, also deserve justice; and since they cannot always be counted on to pour it on each other in buckets, it is up to us barbarians to join in the rituals'. It is in this spirit that he (1970, p.397) went on to extol his most faithful and severe critic:

> If an ignoramus in economics says that the current economic system cannot be interpreted as a rational scheme, that is nothing. But if one of the greatest analytical economists of our era says this, she is worth listening to. Joan Robinson . . . won fame young as one of the inventors of the theory of imperfect competition. She consolidated her worldwide reputation by becoming one of the leading contributors to the Keynesian macroeconomic literature . . . In recent decades Mrs. Robinson has been

an important pioneer and critic of growth models. For any of these accomplishments she might well be awarded the Nobel Prize in Economics.

And in his masterly introduction (Chapter 2) to *Joan Robinson and Modern Economic Theory*, Paul shows why Joan was a scholar who will enjoy a permanent niche in the Pantheon of economic science.

Reluctant 'admirer', Bronfenbrenner (1979, p.446), comments:

> Voltaire is supposed to have said "I do not agree with a word you say, but shall defend to the death your right to say it." May I paraphrase him, speaking as a "bastard Keynesian" purveyor of "rubbish" and "stinking fish"? I do not agree with most of what Joan Robinson has been saying these past forty years, but hope she wins a Nobel Prize for saying it." Mrs. Robinson has done more than any other contemporary economist (Milton Friedman being her only rival) to save our discipline from ossified cut-and-driedness; also it occasionally occurs to me that she may be right about some matters in dispute, or that some of my favourite fish may be getting a trifle over-ripe with age.

A far more reluctant 'admirer' – one whose views were the butt of Joan's virulent attacks – Milton Friedman (1986, p.77) mused that for economists 'the most important thing to do if you want to be a Nobel laureate is to be a male'. But, he adds

> the absence of females is not, I believe, attributable to male chauvinist bias on the part of the Swedish Nobel Committee. I believe that the economics profession as a whole would have been nearly unanimous that, during the period in question, only one female candidate met the relevant standards – the English economist Joan Robinson, who has since died. The failure of the Nobel Committee to award her a prize may well have reflected bias but not sex bias.

That Joan Robinson's influence on the development of modern economics is much greater than is commonly recognized, the contributions to these two volumes, coming as they do from different streams of thought, eloquently attest. This is not a forum for only those who agree with Joan to pay her tribute. Indeed, she dedicated one of her books (*What are the Questions?*) to her critics and here is an opportunity for both her admirers and critics to reciprocate. As she was the first to admit, a real compliment to a scholar is paid when his/her work is taken seriously and critically. She would have hated hagiography and would have considered it condescending. While Joan cared not at all for self-promotion and embarked on no ego trips, she cared much for how her ideas were received by those who disagreed with her. In these two volumes we try to pay tribute to her memory by taking her ideas, themes and concerns seriously as they deserve to be taken and to convey the advances, lacunae, and vicissitudes of the subject she made most particularly her own. Joan would have especially appreciated the essays by her critics and we are all saddened that the voice that would have answered them so well is stilled.

INTRODUCTION TO THE TWO VOLUMES

Joan Robinson and Modern Economic Theory

There are many paradoxes in the economics of Joan Robinson. In Chapter 1 we provide some clues to help us solve the riddles. She was one of the original architects of the imperfect competition revolution and a creative participant of the Keynesian revolution whose ideas she later attempted to generalize and reconstruct. In this chapter we make a selective attempt at conveying Joan Robinson's perspective on economic theory and policy and to touch only on the opposing positions. We first look at her formative years as an economist and her first steps in her 'long struggle' to escape from Marshall and Pigou which culminated in her first *magnum opus* and discuss the grounds on which she later repudiated it. We then proceed to some aspects of the Keynesian revolution and her later attempts at extending it to the long run. In the next section we present the gist of the capital controversies. Thereafter we pause only selectively on her views on the state of economic theory, the questions asked by modern economists, and her attitude towards alternative approaches.

It is a distinct privilege to present the reader with a complementary introduction – the masterful and reflective Chapter 2 by Paul Samuelson – one of the main contestants of the capital controversies and the target of much of Joan's ascerbic criticism. This insightful and sympathetic essay, intended by Paul as a scholarly assessment and a tribute to Joan, is quite revealing about the author himself. Samuelson recalls that in his lifetime as an economist 'Joan Robinson was always there at the frontier of science'. He considers Joan's work on Marxian economics as the dividing line between her early work on imperfect competition and the theory of employment and her post-war work in growth, distribution and capital theory. It is 'particularly her work in the foundations of capital theory' that Samuelson regards 'as valuable and constructive'. He also emphasizes Joan's analysis of the rising supply price as a 'first case of a scholar in the Marshallian tradition breaking through to sight the Pacific of general equilibrium analysis'. He discusses Sraffa's 1926 bombshell about increasing returns and his inspiration for the imperfect competition and adds: 'Joan and Piero may not have much liked the Egypt of constant returns to scale, but it was not vouchsafed for them to pass in their lifetimes to the Canaan of increasing returns to scale.' Samuelson touches with first-hand knowledge on the personalities of Chamberlin, Schumpeter, Kahn, Sraffa, Pigou, and, of course, Joan Robinson and his interaction with them. He deplores the fact that Joan Robinson actually did not have a clear-cut income distribution theory. He then undertakes a simplified thought experiment involving the 'ultra surrogate' capital model. Samuelson emphasizes how much he learned from Joan in the capital controversies. 'Beyond the effect of rallying the spirits of economists disliking the market order, these Robinson–Sraffa–Pasinetti–Garegnani contributions deepen our understanding of how a time-phased competitive micro-system works.' He also mentions Joan's political leanings, loyalties, and independence of spirit and reminds us that she 'will be long remembered for her originality and breadth – and for the person she was'.

Part I provides a background for analyzing Joan Robinson's work and an insight into how her critique and work affected that of others. It is gratifying to open it with Arrow – who shares with her 'a critical attitude to the existing structure', though they did not agree in their perspectives on economic analysis. In Chapter 3, Arrow shares with us his profound thoughts on a broad range of subjects. He discusses authoritatively developments in modern economic theory, particularly as they relate to Joan Robinson's work. He speaks of Walrasian intertemporal equilibrium and the steady state and the problems of getting into equilibrium (stability analysis). He clarifies the term equilibrium in the Walrasian, Marshallian, Ricardian, and Keynesian sense. He praises Joan for having forced the question of heterogeneity of capital. He then proceeds to questions of income distribution: he denies a connection between the capital controversies and views on income distribution, he contends that the distributional implications of marginal productivity theory are much weaker than they appear, and he speaks of income inequalities within the labor force – a topic he considers more serious in our times than questions of functional distribution. Arrow is critical of Sraffian economics as a new paradigm. He speaks of the rift between micro and macro economics and of the difficulty of theoretical integration when one is convinced, as he is, 'that there *really* is disequilibrium in the sense of non-market clearing', and criticizes the new classical macroeconomics. Arrow then discusses the difficulties of integrating imperfect competition into the general equilibrium system and the relationship of imperfect competition and imperfect information. He suggests how much economists can learn from the problems of computation and measures of differential complexity of different kinds of computation being debated currently by mathematicians and computer scientists. He then turns to growth theory and casts doubts on the validity of a problem of long-run effective demand. He disputes (Joan Robinson's and others') identification of neoclassical economics with capitalist apologetics. 'As one who has had, and still has, a socialist bias of some not very clear kind ... I do not feel that I adopted neoclassical economics *because* it defended capitalism.' Arrow then speaks of Joan's criticism of mainstream economics and of the insuperable difficulties in tackling some important problems. Finally, he concentrates on evaluating Joan's approach to economic theory, her attitude as social and economic critic, and offers glimpses of her personality that impressed him.

In Chapter 4, Hammond – a former student of Joan who, though she did not prevent him from becoming a leading neoclassical and welfare economist, at least taught him to doubt and to discuss theory without necessarily using mathematics (though he is adept at both) – casts a critical look at the assumptions underlying his own chosen field. Inspired by the writings of Joan Robinson, especially her books *Economic Philosophy* and *Economic Heresies*, and liberally spiced with relevant quotations from many of her works, Hammond discusses the following assumptions, all of which – except the last – are all too commonly found within neoclassical economics: (1) assumptions are not to be compared with reality; (2) consumer sovereignty; (3) unbounded rationality; (4) unbounded foresight; (5) unbounded cooperation; (6) Pareto efficiency is sufficient for ethical acceptability; (7) the distribution of wealth is ethically acceptable; (8) consumers can survive without trade; (9) income effects are negligible; (10) Pareto efficiency is necessary for ethical acceptability; (11) there is a representative consumer; (12) distortionary taxes create deadweight losses; (13) domestic public expenditure programs are wasteful; (14) transfer programs confer no benefits; (15) capital markets are perfect; (16) anticipated monetary and fiscal policies are ineffective; (17) inflation is caused by an expanding money supply; (18) there is a representative worker; (19) the current level of unemployment is ethically acceptable (20) there is a representative capital good; (21) product markets are perfectly competitive or at least contestable (22) neoclassical economics need not be theological.

In the next chapter (5), Klein acknowledges that Joan Robinson's claim to fame is for her ingenious handling of intricate and subtle problems of capital theory, employment theory, imperfect competition, Marxian theory, and many other subjects quite beyond the uninitiated. But, Klein contends, Book I of her *Accumulation of Capital* 'is truly a masterful statement of economic principles, especially principles of macroeconomics, that could serve better than almost any other "Principles" textbook in laying bare the fundamental aspects of our subject to the beginner'. Klein stresses that from Joan Robinson the student will learn a great deal about the structure of the capitalist economy, its differences from the socialist one, and how the various macroeconomic departments of the total system fit together. The student could also learn not to be overly pedantic and to settle for some common-sense distinctions. She provides the maximum framework that is still institution-free. She distills the essence of the working of the credit market and castigates unproductive financial speculation. She points to the various sources of personal income and makes the clear distinction between income and wealth. She points to the intrinsic difficulties of measuring wealth and of providing an index number for measuring purchasing power. In discussing financial market strategies, she demonstrates a clear grasp of the fundamentals of portfolio management. She fully recognizes and appreciates the role of profit as a driving force in the capitalist economy. In her consumption and investment schema she clearly perceives the double-edged role of savings and points to the paradoxical nature of the capitalist system and the role of thrift in it. There is also an excellent early appreciation of the role of expectations and their relation to decision making in a dynamic system. She develops the highly abstract and unrealistic conditions of tranquillity, lucidity, and harmony. If such conditions were to prevail, she reasons, there would have been no incentives for entrepreneurs to break out in new directions. But if the disturbances were too severe, the economy would have collapsed. She acknowledges that some coherence is embedded in all the confusion.

In view of Joan Robinson's critical attitude towards the mathematization of economic theory, the explanation of the historical development of mathematical economics by no less an authority than Gerard Debreu is particularly relevant. In Chapter 6, Debreu considers the changes in the mathematical form of theoretic models of an economy during the past four decades, and the growth of mathematical economics in that period in relation to each other and to the development of the profession. He then examines the fit of the mathematical form to the economic content of theoretic models, their separation in a completed axiomatic theory and their interplay in its elaboration. He also analyzes the consequence of the axiomatization of economic theory.

In Chapter 7, Goodwin – a close associate of Joan's during 'the age of capital theory' – aims to put forth in simple, plausible form the dynamics of a capitalist economy. This is what Joan devoted most of the latter half of her life to developing in a new and stimulating way. Chapter 7 is phrased in simple mathematical form – a form Joan neither approved of nor was at ease with. Nevertheless, Goodwin attempts to follow along the path on which Joan strove unceasingly to amplify Keynes's central message. Whilst avoiding the manifold complexities of reality, Goodwin attempts to make precise the basic conception (with some complications) of the notion that investment determines demand which, in turn, determines investment, keeping in mind that this is not always so.

Part II deals with one of Joan Robinson's major critiques of modern economics – the problem of stability or as she called it 'getting into equilibrium'. It opens with Chapter 8 where Gram points to Joan Robinson's arguments that 'the lack of comprehensible treatment of historical time, and the failure to specify the rules of the game in the type of economy under discussion' renders useless the bulk of traditional economic theory. Gram suggests that a perfectly coherent basis for this indictment is to be found within the structure of general equilibrium theory itself, a theory that adroitly finesses the problems raised by Robinson either by treating them as formal difficulties (to be solved by an appropriate choice of assumptions), or by reformulating them in ways that appear to leave them permanently on the agenda for further research. Robinson saw in the fascination with equilibrium analysis a misguided refusal to recognize the unavoidable ideological component in economic analysis and an unwillingness to come to terms with the fact that the present is a break in time between the unpredicted consequences of an irrevocable past and the unpredictable developments of an unknowable future. For these reasons she saw economic theory as cutting itself off from making any useful contribution to the discussion of contemporary problems.

In Chapter 9, Walsh offers a note on Joan Robinson's specific objections to the notion of 'getting into equilibrium', in both short- and long-period contexts. He argues that recent work, of which Robinson might not have approved, nevertheless lends support to some of her contentions. In the short period, what she objected to was a perfectly competitive equilibrium, with all markets clearing, of the sort found in an elementary time interval of a standard neo-Walrasian model. Certain recent models of temporary or quasi-equilibrium, where firms set prices and quantity rationing may arise, may represent the beginnings of a theoretical development ultimately capable of meeting some of her objections. In the context of the long period, Walsh argues that Robinson did not in fact change her views concerning Sraffa at the end of her life. Rather, he suggests, she had *always* accepted the Sraffa system as a snapshot of a model *in* long-period equilibrium, and had *always* rejected the view of it as the culmination of a real world process of gravitation. He argues that certain recent studies of gravitation (or more properly convergence) to equilibrium in the context of formal models show that even in this highly simplified context 'getting into equilibrium,' in the sense of a long-period position with reproduction prices, is highly problematical. He qualifies this argument by noting that work on gravitation has shown that, in the case of certain very simple modern classical models, a formal process of convergence to equilibrium *can* be specified, so that Robinson's claim needs some qualification.

Chapter 10 elucidates the problems of 'getting into equilibrium' by one of the leading modern specialists in stability analysis. Frank Fisher discusses the similarities and differences of stability analysis in microeconomic and macroeconomic settings. He then elaborates on the notion of equilibrium and on the serious difficulties of incorporating *real* dynamics into economic theory. He disputes the notion that the concept of equilibrium is inapplicable to study an economy primarily characterized by change. He stresses the 'big gaping hole in the center of what economists know, namely, the question of what happens out of equilibrium and whether we ever get close to equilibrium'. He considers it an 'important gaping hole because most of what we do depends on assuming that it is not a problem. And we really have very little basis for that'.

In Chapter 11, Nell argues that the concepts of 'temporary equilibrium' is defective because it does not allow for the formation of a rate of profit on capital; long-run equilibrium, on the other hand, does. But the same forces that tend to form a rate of profit also require balanced growth; moreover, the rate of growth and the rate of profit are connected through income distribution. Different social classes have different propensities to save, and so will tend to accumulate wealth at different rates. However, long-run equilibrium requires that the relative wealth of the different social classes remain constant; the different components of wealth cannot grow at different rates. If they did, then under plausible assumptions, the rich would become richer, and the poor, relatively poorer. Long-run equilibrium is therefore, according to Nell, not the appropriate concept for the analysis of capitalism, which would be better based on a classical–Marxian examination of the economic structure and its laws of motion.

Perforce in this book Sraffa enters in different guises. In the preface to his *magnum opus*, Sraffa wrote that his book is only a prelude to a critique of economic theory (as the subtitle indicates) and that he leaves it up to others, somewhat younger and better equipped to the task, to attempt a full-scale critique. Though I do not mean to imply that Sraffa had Garegnani in mind, we could not have called on anyone better qualified than Piero Garegnani who in Chapter 12 not only offers us the Sraffian perspective, but differentiates his position from Joan Robinson. Garegnani's dispute with Joan was sparked off in 1976 by his remark about a convergence between her and Samuelson's positions on the impossibility of analyzing changes in the economy by means of the traditional comparison between 'normal positions' of the system. Joan Robinson reacted to this by writing a short comment, reproduced as Appendix I of Chapter 12. Garegnani's reply constitutes the major part of the chapter and her rejoinder is printed as Appendix II. In particular, in the major part of Chapter 12, Garegnani focuses on three issues. The first pertains to the implications of the criticism of the traditional concept of capital. The second deals with Joan Robinson's critique of traditional theory, based on the impossibility of analyzing changes by comparing equilibria and with the methodological status of this critique. The third concerns the legitimacy of Joan Robinson's extension of her critique from the comparison of neoclassical equilibria to the more general method of comparing 'normal positions' of the economic system. The appendices show Joan Robinson's objections to Garegnani's criticism of neoclassical theory. She felt that his argument had conceded to neoclassical theory what it should never have granted; that is, the possibility of analyzing changes in the economy by means of a comparison between equilibria.

I have also prevailed on Garegnani to provide us in Chapter 13 with a non-technical introduction to Sraffa. In many ways this provides a backdrop for his discussion in Chapter 12 and was initially designed as an appendix to that chapter. However, it is included here as a separate entry to call attention to it for the reader who may wish for a more general discussion of Sraffa's contributions and Garegnani's conception of them.

From this 'family quarrel' we pass to Part III which deals with the serious questions of capital, growth, and distribution that preoccupied Joan Robinson in the post-war years. It opens with Chapter 14 where Nell points out that Joan Robinson's views on accumulation developed along with growth theory itself. She rejected the Harrod–Domar picture of instability as too extreme, but she found the neoclassical vision of substitution objectionable on two grounds. First, capital is not a factor of production, but consists of produced means of production, aggregated in value terms, on which profit is earned. There is no reason to expect that the value of produced means of production will vary in any regular way with the rate of return; nor can any useful notion of the marginal product of such a conglomeration of goods be defined. Second, factories and equipment will be established on the basis of beliefs and expectations that will often be mistaken or become quickly outdated. The economy's stock of equipment at any moment of historical time will not be in equilibrium; steady growth must be considered at best a useful fiction – and Joan Robinson had increasing doubts about its usefulness, although she continued to adhere to the view that growth and distribution were connected through the classical savings function. Nell notes, however, that this connection is open to two forms of criticism: one in capital theory – that *relative* price changes may generate pressures in the wrong direction, the other in investment theory – the capacity/acceleration relationship may lead to real wage movements in the wrong direction. He concludes that Joan's instincts in criticizing steady growth may have been sound, but the idea needed to take its place – transformational growth – has hardly been sketched.

Mathur, a student of Joan Robinson, derived the concept of platinum age from her work. In his earlier work he considered various states of steady growth in the long-run path of development and derived in this connection the properties of a turnpike. He imposed the minimum time for reaching the golden age as an optimality condition and determined the choice of turnpike therefrom. In Chapter 15 he conceives of development in a broader context of restructuring the capital stock in response to long-term growth of technical knowledge. According to this concept of development, the relatively more advanced countries are all considered to be underdeveloped (though less so than the ones in the take-off stage). A 'second industrial revolution' would require an efficient long-term path of capital accumulation as pointed out by Dorfman, Samuelson and Solow as far back as 1957. Mathur takes three sectors of heterogeneous capital into consideration and derives the guideposts of an alternative methodology to that pioneered by

Dorfman, Samuelson and Solow. He obtains this in the Robinsonian framework, using a structure developed for extending von Neumann and Sraffa models to the field of development problems. Thus he derives an optimal strategy for the so-called advanced countries that can be adopted either in the context of socialist, capitalist or mixed economies as guideline for encouraging investment into an optimal pattern. Mathur perceives the social advantage of the proposed strategy in combining rapid diffusion of high technology while securing social justice in the sense of a high degree of employment and favorable income distribution.

The next five chapters deal with capital theory in a more 'neoclassical vein'. In Chapter 16, Becker and Majumdar present their view of the major issues and results on optimality and decentralization in the class of deterministic, infinite horizon, discrete time, one sector models of capital accumulation. They focus on the qualitative properties of the solution obtained under alternative optimality criteria, the sensitivity of that solution with respect to variations in the initial data and the underlying parameters of the economy. They discuss decentralization of the optimum by means of competitive prices in terms of both the perfect foresight equivalence principle and an informationally decentralized viewpoint. They also study capital accumulation with heterogeneous households.

In Chapter 17, Mas-Colell points out that the line of research initiated by Joan Robinson culminated in the 1960s with the realization that many of the comparative statics theorems, valid for one capital good, do not generalize for the heterogeneous capital goods case. 'To a sensibility educated on the former, the heterogeneous capital goods case admitted models with behavior that appeared "bizarre", "exotic", "paradoxical".' However, Mas-Colell adds, 'this was no disappointment to Joan Robinson and her followers. It was rather their point and in this they were perceptive.' The central example with which Mas-Colell concerns himself in Chapter 17 is the dependence of steady-state consumption on the interest rate. He restricts himself to a world without population growth and without technological change. A basic and quite general theorem, the golden rule, asserts that the maximum consumption level is associated with a rate of interest equal to the rate of population growth, that is, zero. In addition, the standard one capital good case displays a monotonically decreasing relationship between consumption levels and the rate of interest. This does not generalize and it is now well understood that even with only two capital goods a non-monotone association is possible. The purpose of Chapter 17 is to bring this point to its logical conclusion, or, as Mas-Colell puts it, 'to out-Cambridge Cambridge', by showing that in general there is no other theorem on the association across steady states of consumption levels and rates of interest than a slightly strengthened version of the golden rule. Roughly, the result is that, given any set of consumption and rates of interest pairs, a well-behaved technology can be found having precisely this set as the steady-state comparative static locus. A minor positive pay-off of this reasearch strategy is the uncovering of a slight strengthening of the golden rule.

Joan Robinson argued that neoclassical general equilibrium theory could not determine the rates of interest in an intertemporal model. In Chapter 18, Kehoe, Levine, and Romer consider a production economy with a finite number of heterogeneous, infinitely lived consumers. They show that, for almost all endowments, equilibria that converge to a non-degenerate steady state or cycle are locally unique. They do so by stating the equilibrium conditions that equate spending and income for each consumer entirely in terms of first period factor endowments and derivatives of a social value function.

In Chapter 19, Majumdar, Mitra and Nyarko use the techniques of dynamic programming to analyze a problem of optimal intertemporal allocation under uncertainty. The technology constraining the set of feasible policies is non-convex and also assumed to be subjected to random shocks. The criterion for evaluation of alternative policies is maximization of a discounted sum of expected one period utilities derived from consumption. They show the optimal investment policy function to be monotonically non-decreasing; in fact, it is strictly increasing when the optimal program is characterized by a stochastic Ramsey–Euler condition. They show that non-uniqueness of optimal actions is restricted to the initial period only, and further, that the set of all initial stocks, from which there is a unique optimal action, coincides with the set on which the value function is differentiable. The dynamic process of optimal inputs converges to some steady state that depends on the initial stock. Their exercise provides a convenient overview of the recent literature dealing with non-convexities and uncertainty in the context of capital theory and the theory of renewable resources.

In Chapter 20, Brock, Rothschild, and Stiglitz argue that many problems involving the valuation of assets that evolve stochastically can be formulated as optimal stopping problems. Some of the examples they analyze include the problem of finding the optimum time to erect a plant with a given construction cost and whose profits are generated by a stochastic process. In this case, they seek the market value of the rights to construct such a plant as a function of the current state of profit potential. The optimal stopping time is just the time at which the plant is built. Formally identical is the problem of deciding when to stop accumulating human capital and start working. Here human capital is measured by the discounted value of expected future earnings. What distinguishes Chapter 20 from the existing literature on this problem is that its authors show how to derive comparative statics propositions for optimal stopping problems where the instantaneous mean and variance functions are arbitrary functions of the state variables. Brock, Rothschild, and Stiglitz analyze an asset whose growth follows a discrete time-stochastic process. They pose and solve the optimal stopping problem for assets whose intrinsic value follows a diffusion process with instantaneous mean and instantaneous variance. They show also how the same techniques can be applied to optimal stopping problems where the asset is described by a dimensional diffusion process.

With Chapter 21 we pass into other aspects of growth and distribution. Here Lance Taylor sets up a demand-driven two-sector model to analyze the effects on income distribution and steady-state growth of shifts in demand composition – from Engel effects, changes in social preference, or attempts at income redistribution through tax/transfer policies. He shows that distributional movements depend on labor intensity of the sectors, while growth effects depend on the sectoral sensitivity of investment demand functions to profit rates and technical change. With plausible parameter values, outcomes of either sign can result – a finding that sheds light on asserted causes for stagnation and income concentration that have appeared in the literature for at least 150 years.

In Chapter 22, Baumol and Wolff discuss three basic concepts of productivity growth: growth in welfare productivity, productive capacity and crude productivity. They show that these three concepts have very different meanings and uses. They demonstrate that all three of them are significant, even the crude productivity growth measure that makes no adjustment for quality changes and may seem basically indefensible. They show why any robust scalar representation of growth in productive capacity may be impossible and why explicit adjustments for changes in product quality may be unnecessary. That is, at least in principle, one can hope to deal with the quality change problem through reasonably accurate measurement of growth in welfare productivity, which may be, ultimately, the best measure of productivity growth. They use empirical evidence to show that estimates of both annual and annual average productivity growth over fairly long periods are very sensitive to the choice among productivity concepts. Moreover, estimates of capacity productivity growth are very sensitive to the assumptions used to impose an equiproportionate shift on the production function over time.

Joan Robinson's growth theory was essentially concerned with the relationship between the rate of technical progress and capital accumulation. In Chapter 23 Rymes extends her theory to the case of induced technical progress put in place by 'research and development' capital expenditures. He shows that traditional measures of total factor productivity or technical progress, both by industry and at the aggregate level, will generate measures of productivity change misleading when related to measures of R&D capital expenditure. Joan supported Harrod's conception of technical progress. Rymes also shows that new measures of Harrod–Robinson total factor productivity, when related to the R&D measures, will provide a better empirical foundation for the study of the relationship between induced technical progress and R&D expenditures. Joan's growth theory and conceptions of technical progress, adapted from Harrod, are thus seen to have immediate relevance to some very important contemporary empirical and policy questions in the economics of capital accumulation and technical progress.

Joan Robinson often wrote critically about the labor theory of value. She also subscribed to an elegant model of the real wage in which the wage is related to the average product of labor in the wage-goods sector and to the proportion of the total workforce which is engaged in the production of wage-goods. In the final chapter (24) of Part III, Dixon shows that her model of the real-wage can yield an expression for economy-wide wage-share in terms of the sectoral composition of employment and the (implicit) rate of exchange of labor time. The model is rich in classical and Marxian insights.

Part IV deals with development and international trade, both as they relate more specifically to Joan Robinson's thinking and to the development of modern economics as a whole. Joan Robinson was adamant that models of steady growth are futile and, unless the microeconomics of behavior of producers and consumers are plausible, the macroeconomics of the steady state is meaningless. In the opening chapter (25), Srinivasan shows that some of the radical critiques of neoclassical theory of international trade and its presumption of the optimality of free trade are based on wrong use of steady-state analysis. He shows that a class of models purporting to analyze the commodity trade and capital flow relations between developed and developing countries and arriving at conclusions contrary to neoclassical analysis have made implausible microbehavior assumptions. He discusses recent models of international trade based on increasing returns to scale and product differentiation in production and non-competitive market structure from the point of view of economic development. These models and their rehabilitation of interventionist international trade policy are unlikely to be appropriate for developing countries.

In Chapter 26, Adelman and Sunding examine Joan Robinson's writings on economic development and developing economies from the perspective of mainstream development economics. They argue that Joan's thinking about development may be divided into three periods: during the 1950s and 1960s she focused almost exclusively on growth and capital accumulation. She shared with early development economists a preoccupation with investment in physical capital as the major determinant of economic development, but she was more extreme than the mainstream development economists in her stress on the rate of capital accumulation. The second period was characterized by Joan's reaction against post-war changes in capitalist economies, her awareness of failures in East European countries, and her fascination with Maoist China. She was thus led to recognize agriculture's role in economic development. Finally, in the last years of her life, Joan Robinson expressed some disenchantment with China as a model for developing countries. Adelman and Sunding conclude with an assessment of Joan's writings on economic development in the light of the stylized facts of development reported by Chenery and others and in the light of China's performance since 1952.

Joan Robinson's essay on disguised unemployment analyzes the situation in an advanced industrialized country where, in a depression, people are thrown out of work and crowd into substantially lower productivity occupations. In Chapter 27, Streeten argues that this can be modelled in terms of a two-sector model. In one sector wages are rigid downwards and productivity is high. In the other sector incomes (from self-employment) are flexible downwards and productivity is low, in some cases approaching zero. To restore full employment, all that is needed is an increase in effective demand. When the concept has been applied to low-income countries, it is clear that additional assumptions have to be made. Streeten analyzes these in the context of a low-income rural sector with family farms and a high-income industrial sector with wage employment. He distinguishes a static from a dynamic concept. He spells out differently assumptions about what conditions have to change in the agricultural sector as workers are transferred to the industrial sector, if agricultural output is not to fall.

In Chapter 28, Bronfenbrenner offers us the confessions of a 'sinner' in international economics. He recalls the essence of the macroeconomics of international trade theory forty years ago. He speaks of his first-hand experience of post-war Japan, of the 'structural dollar-shortage' thesis as applied to the reconstruction of Japan, and of the thinking at the same time about exchange rates. He then lists six factors responsible for his misunderstandings and is able to provide a clearer conception of international trade theory: (1) lack of belief in the post-war Japanese policy to raise real-wages, to intensify investment in human capital, and to move 'up-market' in the world economy; (2) an underestimate of the difficulties of shifts or transitions between equilibrium positions, (3) an overestimate of the advantages of exchange-rate stability, even at 'wrong' rates; (4) an underestimate of the rising importance of 'processing economies' in international trade; (5) an underestimate of the international economic consequences for the US of its political commitment to high employment 'at whatever cost'; and possibly (6) some element of racism in his underestimate of the economic potential of Japanese labor.

In Chapter 29, Chipman develops a model where two countries each produce an export good and a non-tradable at constant costs (with a single factor of production); the countries do not produce import-competing goods. Thus, the 'elasticity of supply' of exports is infinite in each country. He shows that if the two countries have identical marginal propensities to consume the two tradables, and if the 'Marshall–Lerner' stability condition holds, then a transfer will improve the receiving country's terms of trade if the non-tradable is a superior good, and worsen it if the non-tradable is an inferior good. If the exchange rate is endogenous and each country pursues a monetary policy so as to stabilize the price of its non-tradable, the real and nominal exchange rates and the terms of trade are all proportional. Hence a transfer will strengthen the receiving country's exchange rate if the non-tradable is superior and stability holds. Chipman analyzes a model of pegged, adjustable exchange rates where the demand for money in each country is proportional to expenditure and the exchange rate is exogenously controlled by country 2. He shows that if the capital flow between the countries is exogenously determined in terms of country 1's currency, and if both the 'orthodox presumption' and stability hold, then a devaluation by country 2 will have no real effect; whereas if the capital flow is exogenously determined in terms of country 2's currency, and if both the 'orthodox presumption' and stability hold, then a devaluation by country 2 will improve or worsen its balance of payments (in country-1 currency) according to whether the initial balance is in deficit or surplus. He thus obtains a sharp contrast between regimes according as the exchange rate is endogenous or exogenous.

It is a striking fact (and, in view of her strong social sympathies, a puzzling one) that during no phase of her long professional career did Joan Robinson seriously interest herself in the economics of labor unions. Although she has made noteworthy, important contributions to the theory of international trade in Chapter 30, Kemp and Shimomura pay tribute to Joan Robinson not by elaborating one of her favorite themes but by plunging into territory she has conspicuously neglected. Their purpose is to outline a theory of international trade that incorporates a powerful labor union. As a more specific but subsidiary objective, they seek to discover whether there are circumstances where a maximizing union, by imposing a minimum wage, may so change the effective factor-endowment ratio of a country as to reverse the direction of its trade.

Joan Robinson and many other economists have considered technical progress and the accumulation of more capital per worker to be the only way to raise *per capita* output and income in the long run. Yet, in a study of British agriculture before its mechanization in the mid-nineteenth century, Clark, in Chapter 31, shows that while output *per capita* more than doubled between 1300 and 1841 the source was mainly an increase in work intensity. Simple hand tasks such as reaping and threshing were being done much more quickly in 1841. This increase of the work pace was not a consequence of economizing on more expensive labor in the latter period. For the price of grain relative to labor changed dramatically from year to year, and after the Black Death in 1349, yet such price fluctuations never caused the work pace to change. An increase in the intensity of labor thus has to be ranked above technical progress and capital accumulation as a source of increased incomes in pre-industrial Britain. Clark has every reason to expect similar results for the rest of Europe.

Part V follows up on topics Joan Robinson has touched upon deftly and with much grace and insight. In Chapter 32, Hausman focuses on Joan Robinson's view of the perennial concern of economists to demonstrate that selfish market behavior is morally acceptable, but that, in fact, there is an irreconcilable conflict between morality and economics. Along the way, he considers the extent to which this moral or ideological burden borne by economics affected the Cambridge controversy in the theory of capital, growth and distribution. Although he finds the moral conflict Joan emphasizes to be real and disturbing, he argues that she overstated her claims for the importance of ideology.

In 1942, Joan Robinson wrote that although she was sympathetic with the egalitarianism Marxism champions, the route to those ends through the labor theory of value was misdirected. In Chapter 33 Roemer goes further and argues that the theory of Marxian exploitation, even purged of the labor theory of value does not properly represent Marxian concerns with capitalist property relations. Marxism has championed exploitation as the statistic to measure the distributional injustice of capitalism; the inequality of income due to private ownership of the means of production should be remedied by public ownership. Roemer shows that exploitation, as classically defined, is an imperfect statistic for the distributional and ethical concerns which animate Marxism. He proposes an axiomatic approach to reflect more accurately the debate concerning what kinds of property rights are ethically defensible. He asks: What distributions of final output will respect both the self-ownership of persons (their rights to returns from their differential skills) and public ownership of productive resources in the external world? He presents a model showing that public ownership of the external world nullifies the possible returns to self-ownership. Methodologically, he shows how debates within political philosophy can be studied using tools of mechanism theory on spaces of economies. He intends the theorem in Chapter 33 as a challenge to neo-Lockeanism, an illustration of how Marxian ethical concerns can be represented using modern tools of analysis.

Part VI attempts to provide a composite sketch of Joan Robinson's personality and accomplishments as seen through the eyes of various beholders. No matter how perceptive and written with critical flair, yet with admiration and even affection, as their authors would be the first to admit, these images are but shadowy reflections of the vital flame that was Joan. In the opening chapter (34), Boulding recalls the sense of a 'new dawn' in economics in the 1930s in two aspects: Keynes with a great deal of help from Joan Robinson was throwing light on the dark problem of unemployment, and Joan Robinson herself, with *The Economics of Imperfect Competition*, was releasing us from the absurdities of the pure competition model of pricing. These were not false dawns, Boulding stresses, but they did turn out to be cloudy. Joan Robinson never repudiated Keynesianism, though she did abandon imperfect competition in a lifelong search for an adequate theory of capital and profit, that somehow always eluded her. She was a lonely voice, asking the right questions, in an era contented with easy mathematical answers to the wrong questions. Her sense of the great complexity of capital structures and economic relationships denied her access to simple solutions, but the questions she raised will be with us for a long time.

The next seven chapters constitute a series of vignettes of Joan where (in Chapter 35) Streeten stresses her incomparable quality of *Zivilcourage*; Patel (in Chapter 36) emphasizes her innate kindness and warm heart; Scitovsky (in Chapter 37) recalls the young Joan, her loveliness and her stern insistence that he learn to think for himself; Chipman (in Chapter 38) recalls the two sides of Joan – her kindness and her argumentativeness; Sylos Labini (in Chapter 39) shares with us more than thirty years of frequent contacts, her somewhat overbearing qualities and the essence of her friendliness; Foley (in Chapter 40) highlights the capital controversy he observed as an onlooker and junior member of the MIT economics department (he recalls her aggressive, non-discriminating, and impressive intellectual stance) and his personal exchange with her over the labor theory of value she continued to regard as a 'piece of mystical rubbish'; and Gram (in Chapter 41) remembers the Joan of the 1970s, the increasing terseness of her arguments and her growing disenchantment towards the end of her life.

In the following chapter (42) Walsh shares with us his perceptions of Joan in the last years of her life. He stresses her moral seriousness, her interest in and kindness to young people, her innate natural dignity, her stern purpose, and her mystery, her uncompromising stance, her wicked sense of humor, and the ravages of failing health in her last years. He recalls the perseverance with which she guided and advised him and Gram through the years they worked on their joint book and their points of disagreement with her.

In Chapter 43, Nell recalls Joan's commanding presence, her single-mindedness and partisanship. He stresses that it is as a critic that she will be best remembered. He emphasizes that only a theory can beat another theory. 'Only those protected by the amulet of another theory will be safe . . . that is the protection that many of Joan's students and followers sought, but which she never provided.' Yet, she had all the ingredients for such a theory, but the construction was lacking.

In the next three chapters we are offered views of Joan from three colleagues in Cambridge. In Chapter 44, Hahn speaks of certain misconceptions in Joan's critique of neoclassical economics, of her attitude towards equilibrium, of the potentially useful role her criticism could play for modern mathematical theorists, and of the acuteness of her criticism of 'bastard' Keynesians. According to Hahn, 'Joan had a number of very important things to say. If she had been trained in mathematics and had been technically more competent she could really have done more to clinch them.' He considers her work on interest rates and money her 'lasting achievement' and is quite irritated by her work in capital theory. He emphasizes that Joan was 'totally a heterodox upper-class Englishwoman' and 'a part of her personality was simply upper-class refusal to go with the herd'.

In the next chapter (45), Matthews speaks of Joan as a crusader whose work cannot be divorced from her overriding desire to establish the truth and to refute self-interested or lazy fallacies. He mentions that her essential originality lay perhaps in her ability to synthesize those who so profoundly influenced her. He stresses the quality of her criticism: 'she was better at pointing out that the Emperor had no clothes than in supplying him with clothing'. He recalls the exciting days when the 'secret seminar' was discussing capital and growth and muses about the Cambridge atmosphere at the time.

In Chapter 46, Goodwin – who strongly supported Joan and Kahn in Cambridge since the early 1950s – offers us an affectionate glimpse of Joan, the passionate seeker after truth. He recalls his first exposure to her as a student at Oxford: 'I understood little but sat spellbound, and, in a sense have remained so ever since.' He speaks of her 'totally self-abnegating dedication' in pursuit of truth, 'her clarity, her unswerving devotion to unpopular, progressive causes, her total sincerity and integrity, her high seriousness, and her unwillingness to suffer fools gladly'.

The last chapter (47) presents the recollections of Lorie Tarshis who first encountered Joan in the classroom in 1933. 'Her lectures were not only clear and crisp; they were delivered by a very attractive young lady ... A strong, handsome face, a lovely smile, white teeth and bright blue eyes and a liveliness that sparkled.' Not only as a student himself, but whenever he met her later, Tarshis was impressed by her sincere interest in and encouragement of students who demonstrated an ability for independent thought. He also stresses her commitment to truth, her willingness to fight for it no matter how powerful the opposition and the enmity she aroused on her way. There is no more fitting way of concluding than by citing the last paragraph of Chapter 47:

> Like my fellow contributors in these volumes, I dedicate my essay to her memory, and ... the hope that her example will be followed by many: her determination to discover how things work, her insistence on writing out her findings directly and clearly, her fierce will to hold her ground, once she was persuaded of its rightness, even if she had to stand alone; and all this combined with an unclouded conscience that recognized the claims of others, the worth of friendship and the beauties that man, women and children can create.

The Economics of Imperfect Competition and Employment: Joan Robinson and Beyond

This volume opens with a two chapter introductory part: the first chapter provides a background on the integration of imperfect competition and the theory of employment that inspired Joan Robinson's post-General Theory work; the second is a notable example of a current attempt at building a model of imperfect competition and unemployment in a game theoretic framework, and as such also fits into Part III.

The imperfect competition revolution had no bearing on the Keynesian revolution, though both of them took place at about the same time and in the same place and both involved at least some of the same *dramatis personae*. This is more than a doctrinal history puzzlement. Had it been otherwise, it would have fundamentally affected the course of the age after Keynes. Whatever the merits of Joan Robinson's *Economics of Imperfect Competition*, one of the reasons she came to reject it is because she was strongly influenced by Kalecki's pioneering integration of imperfect competition and macrodynamics. Throughout Chapter 1 we trace Kalecki's pervasive influence on Joan Robinson and her creative adaptation of his approach to pricing, distribution, and, with some reservation (particularly about the investment function), to growth, thus throwing a light on the key ingredients of the Robinsonian construct. In particular, we trace how Kalecki brought his version of the theory of employment to Cambridge and the reception it received; the differences between Kalecki and Keynes in non-economic dimensions, and their diverse intellectual roots. The major part of Chapter 1 examines the essential differences between the Kaleckian and Keynesian models and how these differences can be traced in Joan Robinson's work. To build a realistic theory, Kalecki explained how industrial prices are formed by mark-ups on costs and distinguished between 'cost-determined' and 'demand-determined' prices. The mark-ups depend on the relative strength of market imperfection he called the 'degree of monopoly'. Together with other distributional factors this is the key for the determination of macrodistribution. Kalecki's theory of profits was based on the principle that wage earners do not save, but spend what they get and that entrepreneurs get what they spend. Entrepreneurs' profits are governed by their propensity to invest and consume and not the other way round. Kalecki's model presented the economic process in motion; that is, how one sequence develops from the preceding ones. The model encompasses long-run dynamics and the capacity effects of investments and some other supply considerations. Kalecki approached the theory of effective demand through the theory of the business cycle which established two basic relations: (1) the impact of effective demand generated by investment on profits and national income; and (2) the investment decision function, where the rate of investment decisions at a given time is roughly determined by the level and the rate of change in economic activity at some earlier time. To Kalecki, the key prerequisite for becoming an entrepreneur is the ownership of capital. Investment decisions are related to the firm's 'internal' accumulation of gross savings. These savings allow the firm to make new investments without facing the problems of the limited capital market or 'increasing risk'. Kalecki dealt with an open system and treated the rate of export surplus as a promoter of prosperity and balance-of-payments difficulties as a factor limiting expansion. Kalecki realized that whatever the rationale of the *economics* of full employmet, the *political* problems are formidable. During World War II, while he wrote his masterful policy guidelines of the three ways to full employment, he realized the potential objections to such policies and predicted the emergence of the political business cycle.

The second chapter is an illustration of the most recent revival of interest in imperfect competition within a general equilibrium framework. While in the past this work has not borne the expected fruits, Roberts in Chapter 2 goes far beyond towards an integration of imperfect competition and macroeconomics, using the increasingly more fruitful (and one might add, fashionable) game-theoretic approach – an approach also applied by the contributors to Part III of this volume. Roberts considers a game-theoretic, non-Walrasian, general equilibrium model of price determination, production, and exchange. In this game, firms first select prices and wages, consumers/workers then make input supply and output demand offers, and finally firms select the fractions of these to accept. Equilibrium (pure strategy, subgame perfect, Nash equilibrium) involves each agent acting optimally from each point forward while correctly recognizing the results of taking any given course of action. In particular, firms correctly forecast the quantity responses to different prices and wages. Roberts shows that, with a particular structure of preferences, endowments and technology, for any equilibrium with positive levels of economic activity, there exists another equilibrium at the same prices and wages with lower levels of activity. The latter equilibrium corresponds to involuntary unemployment. This unemployment arises because of a failure of excess demand: expectations of low demand are self-confirming. Further, expectations are such that price and wage changes do not appear profitable, and, by the nature of equilibrium, these expectations are correct. He also considers existence issues.

Part II deals with imperfect competition in historical perspective and throws some light on future developments. In the opening chapter (3), Whitaker explores the intellectual background of Cambridge economics against which Joan Robinson's *The Economics of Imperfect Competition* was written. An extensive analysis of the ideas on monopoly and competition of Marshall, Pigou, and Sraffa paves the way for a reconsideration of the main themes of Joan Robinson's book in relation to the web of ideas from which they arose. Whitaker places Joan Robinson's later strictures on her own early work in historical perspective, and reaches somewhat revisionist conclusions on Pigou's deviation from Marshall, Sraffa's criticisms of the Cambridge school, and the way in which *The Economics of Imperfect Competition* related to Cambridge tradition and Sraffa's critique of it. He assigns a key influence to Gerald Shove as a source through which the Cambridge tradition was transmitted to Joan Robinson.

In Chapter 4, Bishop pays tribute to the scientific importance and specific analytical strengths of Joan Robinson's famous first book and attempts to identify and evaluate some of its principal shortcomings. The central strength is, of course, its presentation of the static equilibrium conditions of several leading types of imperfect competition, both monopolistic and monopsonistic – as a necessary step towards freeing economic analysis from its dependence on the perfectly competitive model. The weaknesses he stresses include the ambiguities of exploitation as an offence against justice or efficiency, the preoccupation with labor as persistently exploited and never exploiting, and some deficiencies in the analysis and evaluation of the removal of market imperfections.

In Chapter 5, Negishi takes us back to Edgeworth and then propels us much beyond. Edgeworth demonstrated the so-called equivalence theorem in which the outcome of an exchange economy where traders act cooperatively is identical to the Walrasian equilibrium of the perfect competition where traders act non-cooperatively as price takers, when the number of traders of the same type is infinitely large. Since the infinity of identical traders is a sufficient condition, however, a natural question Negishi asks is whether it is also a necessary one. According to Farell and Schitovitz, the equivalence theorem holds even in the case of duopoly where there are only two suppliers of a good though the number of demands is infinite. Negishi suggests that the theorem holds in a four-person case of an Edgeworth game of exchange, if indivisible lump-sum transactions are ruled out and competition is assured so as to satisfy Jevon's law of indifference. Finally, the theorem still holds in the case of bilateral monopoly or isolated exchange between two traders, if exchanges are repeated indefinitely through time. All this suggests to Negishi that what is essential for perfect competition is not so much the number of traders or the scale of traders relative to that of the economy as perfect information and no friction, also explicitly assumed by Edgeworth. Walrasian assumptions are vindicated by Edgeworth's theorem. Even though traders are actually not price takers and there are no auctioneers, we could assume that traders act as if they were taking prices set by auctioneers, if the information is perfect and there are no frictions. But, Negishi points out, for the development of non-Walrasian economics to provide microeconomic foundations for Keynesian fixprice economics, on the other hand, one has to assume that information is not perfect and there do exist such frictions as cost of organizing coalitions and cost of trade.

The Economics of Imperfect Competition evoked an initial response which was favorable in the extreme. Within a generation, however, considerable disillusion had set in. In Chapter 6, Sutton argues that the low point of the book's fortunes was reached in the 'Archibald versus Chicago' debate, that appeared in the *Review of Economic Studies* of 1961, in which all protagonists appeared to agree only on one thing: that the theory as it stood was empirically empty. The enormous resurgence of interest in imperfect competition that we have witnessed over the past decade has been built around the notion of putting more structure into the basic theory by specifying some explicit representation of consumer preferences over differentiated products. This has been an impressively fruitful line of development. It has led to important new departures in areas as widely separated as the theory of intra-industry trade, and the analysis of vertical restraints on trade. Yet, for all this progress, Sutton retains a nagging worry: is this theory 'consistent with anything'? In Chapter 6 he addresses himself to these continuing concerns.

Part III, consisting of studies of imperfect competition within the game-theoretic framework, opens with Chapter 7 by one of the ablest practitioners of the science and art of game theory. In it Rubinstein argues that it is a matter of judgment to decide when a market outcome is well described by the competitive price model and to decide what the units appearing on the quantity axis of the demand–supply diagram are. The literature he introduces in this chapter aims to assist us in this judgment. The method Rubinstein uses starts by specifying in detail the process by which the terms of transactions are determined. He describes the process of trade as a game and studies non-cooperative solution concepts. Finally, he checks under what circumstances the solution is close to the competitive outcome.

In Chapter 8, Wilson surveys a part of the recent literature on imperfect competition among firms. The topics he has selected emphasize incumbent firms' strategies of entry deterrence and battles for market share or survival. He describes the roles of pricing, supply, and investment in implementing these strategies. He presents the survey in expository form to convey how game-theoretic methods are used to formulate models of dynamic interactions among firms. Dynamic features reveal that firms' strategies are affected by powers of commitment, such as irreversible investment; and, there can be multiple equilibria depending on the firms' mutual expectations. Also, several models reveal the strong effects of informational asymmetries among the competitors: predation can deter entry, and among incumbents profits can be dissipated in wars of attrition; conversely, informational effects can sustain cooperative endeavors. The gist of the results is a verification of the rich complexity of the strategic aspects of imperfect competition, emphasized by Joan Robinson, and an illustration of the game-theoretic methods that have been developed recently to capture the roles of dynamics and informational asymmetries.

In Chapter 9, Hurwicz examines the effects of entry of new firms in a symmetric differentiated products industry; in particular, the effects on the profits of firms already in the industry. The industry is in equilibrium if additional entry would result in negative profits for everyone, but profits can be at equilibrium. He obtains an upper bound on the number of firms that could coexist in an industry under fairly general assumptions, without presupposing symmetry. Under more specialized assumptions, he shows that the profits of individual firms go down as the number of firms increases. This is the case both in the Cournot and Bertrand models. He confines himself to the study of symmetric equilibrium solutions. He shows that under Cournot duopoly *asymmetric* solutions do not exist, but he does not study the more general aspects of existence of asymmetric oligopoly solutions. Some of the results are also valid for *undifferentiated* commodities that is, where all firms sell identical products.

In Chapter 10, Milgrom makes two contributions to the theory of price discrimination. First, considering a monopolist that produces at constant unit costs, he observes that without some connection such as resale possibilities, laws prohibiting price discrimination, or reputational phenomena, the problem naturally decomposes into a set of bilateral monopoly problems with individual prices determined by bargaining. This view is inconsistent with the usual presumption that price discrimination is profitable for the seller. Indeed, when consortiums of buyers may form to negotiate prices, laws that prohibit price discrimination create a free rider problem that may result in higher prices for all. His second contribution is a new graphical analysis of the problem of third-degree price discrimination. Gabszewicz and Thisse (in Chapter 11) investigate the impact of price discrimination in a vertically differentiated market. They show that: (1) a discriminatory pricing equilibrium exists under rather general conditions; (2) the equilibrium qualities coincide with the Pareto-optimal qualities; and (3) all consumers are better off under discriminatory pricing than under uniform pricing.

Part IV on different approaches to imperfect competition opens with Chapter 12 where Archibald and Eaton remind us that spatial models *are* characteristics models, but not vice versa. In quite standard and general characteristics and spatial models, they deal with the resolution of two main problems: the 'combinability' of goods (or stores) to obtain preferred characteristics mixes; and the measurement of distance between goods (or stores). The resolution of these problems is the same in both models: although the models are not identical, they are easily seen to be particular applications of the general characteristics model. The main analytical tool they use is an indirect characterization of preferences in the appropriate space. For both models they identify the case in which characteristics are not satisfactory primitives. The nature, extent, and role of product differentiation in Joan Robinson's theory of imperfect competition were the major topics of dispute in Chamberlin's unrequited challenge to its realism. In the next chapter (13) Kuenne strives to clarify such questions as a prelude towards a formal incorporation of price and product quality in oligopolistic decision making. He suggests a means of measuring product qualities cardinally and explores the interrelations of price and quality choices in the firm's decisions. He shows the crucial dependence of the response of the firm to rivals' changes in product quality upon the convexity or concavity of its sales function and studies the nature of oligopolistic competition in these dimensions under rivalrous consonance. He develops a framework of analysis to seek the difficult-to-obtain general propositions independent of firm and industry specifics.

Chapter 14 is an investigation of the welfare of the different groups of individuals in unemployment situations. The framework is the familiar three-good model studied among others by Barro and Grossman, Benassy, and Malinvaud. Silvestre assumes that, in situations of less than full employment, some workers are fully employed and some others are totally unemployed. This makes the analysis more complex than in the usual models with representative workers since one must consider separately three welfare magnitudes: the number of workers employed, the welfare of the employed workers, and that of the unemployed. Both the framework and the question fit well in Joan Robinson's view of the economic world. The framework is one where economic activity is carried out at prices not necessarily Walrasian, and where unemployment situations are typical. It can be interpreted as a short-run model, but also as a model where agents have monopoly or monopsony power. This second interpretation actually agrees better with Joan Robinson and Kalecki than with Keynes. The question, on the other hand, is in the spirit of Joan Robinson's study of the monopolistic and monopsonistic exploitation of workers, though it is placed in a set-up where the interaction between the labor market and the output market is explicit and where unemployment plays a central role. Silvestre's results characterize the price–wage pairs with the property that any movement away from them makes someone (an owner of a firm or a worker who is employed or unemployed or marginally employed) worse off. One cannot move away from such a point with unanimous approval. Thus price–wage pairs satisfying this property are states of conflict interests. He shows that price–wage pairs close to what he calls the Keynesian–classical boundary (defined by the presence of unemployment and the equality between price and marginal cost) have this property and that those away from it do not.

Part V deals with imperfect competition in specific markets. In the opening chapter (15) Stiglitz, a student of Joan Robinson, relates his work not only to her *Economics of Imperfect Competition*, but also to her 1951 development of a general portfolio theory, 'A clear predecessor of the later work of Tobin' for which Stiglitz believes 'she may have received insufficient credit'. Stiglitz examines imperfect competition in the capital market, using a simple general-equilibrium portfolio model. He shows that the market economy is not, in general, Pareto efficient. In particular, he investigates whether there are too few or too many risky firms, whether they will be too small or too large, whether there will be 'errors' in the choice of techniques, and the like. He investigates in detail the interpretation that, in the absence of a complete set of securities, the market ought to be viewed as monopolistically competitive. He shows that when the number of firms is not fixed, the market solution will err both with respect to the number and choice of firms, even when all firms take as given their value per unit scale of output. More generally, Stiglitz's second motivation is provided by the analysis of equilibrium in the capital market with entry under competitive conditions. And the third motivation is to understand more fully monopolistic competitive equilibrium. Thus, in

Chapter 15, Stiglitz considers a simplified version of the capital market model. He assumes all risky firms to be identical, but perfectly correlated and all safe firms (those whose returns are perfectly certain) to be identical. As one safe security is a perfect substitute for another, the safe firms in this model constitute a perfectly competitive industry and the risky firms a monopolistically competitive industry. He then proceeds to assume the returns to the risky firms to be independently (but identically) distributed and then correlated with a general market factor. He assumes all individuals to be identical and risk averse. This formulation allows him to avoid the pitfalls of previous studies of monopolistic competition: individuals purchase not one but all produced commodities; there is a perfectly competitive sector, so he can enquire into the diversion of resources from the perfectly competitive to the monopolistically competitive sector; and since all individuals are identical and purchase the same portfolio, they are all worse off in the competitive situation than in the optimal. Hence, Stiglitz argues, his results are of interest not only for what they suggest about the workings of the capital market, but for the light they shed on the more general question of resource allocation in economies with a monopolistically competitive sector.

In Chapter 16, Kurz examines the properties of competition in the market for credit when the lender must bear the risk of default by the borrower. In the formal model there are many borrowers and many depositors with an intermediary who lends the depositors' funds to the borrowers but must bear the risk of default. Each borrower provides some of his own equity (i.e. collateral) and, to protect the depositors, the intermediary must also have some equity capital. He shows that when taking into account the possibility of default by the intermediary, a competitive equilibrium will often require rationing. He states the characteristics of rationing equilibria and shows that the intermediary will resist, in equilibrium, offers of a higher interest rate by the rationed out borrowers, since higher interest rates will induce a reduction in the collateral offered by all the borrowers. This will reduce the expected profits of the intermediary. These results supplement earlier papers where equilibrium in credit markets resulted in non-linear pricing but without an explicit rationing constraint.

Joan Robinson insisted that the existence of considerable unemployed resources should not be viewed as a troublesome problem, but rather as a splendid exploitable opportunity of doing something really useful. As other 'Keynesians', she maintained that capitalism, managed with intelligence and goodwill, can continue to flourish in already developed economies. She had her own predilections about the ways and means to and content of full employment and about the message of the Keynesian revolution on planes of theory and policy. According to the proverbial view of the cup as either half full or half empty, there are considerable similarities and differences between her and the mainstream synthesis of neoclassical and Keynesian theory (and policy) represented in Part VI by some of its most distinguished proponents.

At a time when the resurgence of classical macroeconomics attempts to bury Keynes, the differences between the various Keynesian factions seem to be somewhat less important.

In Chapter 17, Solow stresses that he is first and foremost a Keynesian and disparages in some degree the academic discussions of 'what Keynes really meant'. He speaks of the work he is doing (with Frank Hahn) to provide a modern theoretical foundation for Keynes's notion of unemployment equilibrium through the modern developments of multiple equilibria. He suggests that Joan Robinson was a superb critic of neoclassical analysis, but also an apt user of its tools in her own work. He then discusses the meaning of 'neoclassical' and suggests that, according to his understanding of the term, Sraffa was also neoclassical. Solow points out that his vision is not so very different from Joan's. He speaks of his slight differences with Tobin, his major differences with the new classical economists, his attitude to post-Keynesian economics, his view of microfoundations for macroeconomics, his position on the neoclassical synthesis, and finally his perspective on growth theory.

In the second testimony (Chapter 18), Tobin shares with us his interpretation of the Keynesian message on the planes of theory and policy and his view of Keynes and the canons of neoclassical economics, imperfect competition, and microfoundations for macroeconomics. He describes the essence of the neoclassical synthesis and negates the view that it inserted 'a few Keynesian contributions into an existing mainstream; it changed the mainstream altogether'. He emphasizes Joan Robinson's historical approach and agrees with her critique of American Keynesians' distortion of Keynes's investment function and entrepreneurial activity. Tobin elaborates on his views about incomes policy and income redistribution and comments on the relationship between Keynesian economics, monetarism, and the welfare state. He speaks of the ultimate emergence of a new synthesis that will borrow the best from all macro thinking: 'Rather than looking at Keynesian static analysis as something good for now, good for next year, and good for the year after that, one looks at it as a panel in a moving picture. In the dynamic system there are relations between periods, based on intertemporal behavior as well as expectations. There are both stock-flow relations, from past to present, and expectations of future variables, from future to present'. The vision behind the future synthesis 'will deviate from the Keynesian vision by taking more explicitly into account anticipations of government policies and by promoting monopolistic-competition features of markets from the vague background into explicitly modeled relationships'.

In the third testimony (Chapter 19), Modigliani stresses that the main difference between Kahn and himself is the former's belief in absolute wage rigidity and his belief in slow wage adjustment. Modigliani speaks about inflation, the Phillips curve, the deficit, and monetary economics. For him, Hicksian IS-LM distills 'the basic message of the *General Theory* in one easy lesson'. He speaks of the need to stabilize the economy and points to the post-war successes. He returns to the causes and consequences of inflation. He contrasts his vision and approach to economics with Milton Friedman and against this background speaks of his formulation of the life-cycle model. Modigliani also sheds light on the analysis of unemployment through search theory, some aspects of the capital controversy in which he participated, and some personal views of Joan Robinson.

In Chapter 20, Weitzman shares with us the essence of his significant work on profit sharing. He focuses on money labor costs which are too high relative to aggregate demand, in particular in the UK and continental Europe. He contends that if the wage would become more flexible in relation to the firm's performance, this would induce firms to hire more workers, thus alleviating the unemployment problem, particularly among the new entrants into the labor force. Although this would involve some uncertainty about take home pay, it would be a far less harmful uncertainty than the one we face in the wage system which involves inflation and large-scale unemployment. Weitzman also speaks about the acceptance and opposition to profit sharing from employers and workers. He mentions the statistically difficult-to-capture microeconomic benefits of profit sharing, but stresses that his development of the scheme was primarily motivated for macroeconomic reasons. He is somewhat reluctant to admit that his scheme has income distribution effects and perceives some opposition to it on the grounds of misperceptions as to who is going to gain. He perceives the scheme as a *supplement* to Keynesian policies. The model of price formation that underlies his scheme is in a sense Kaleckian. It is a model of 'monopolistic competition where basically the anchor is a payment system that is quasi-fixed in the short run'. In general, he views the present state in macroeconomics as being somewhat 'decadent' in that it does not address itself to real-world problems. In this connection he also muses on methodological problems, on the need to cut into a subject even if all foundations are lacking. He mentions the problem of increasing returns as 'fundamental' to our understanding of involuntary unemployment. Weitzman also shares with us his views of Joan Robinson, Cambridge economics, and critiques of general equilibrium theory.

Part VII deals with the place of money and finance in Joan Robinson's economics and with a comparison of Joan Robinson's and the new classical macroeconomists' critiques of the neoclassical synthesis. In the opening Chapter (21), Dillard considers it paradoxical that Joan Robinson dealt only perfunctorily with money in view of her deep involvement in the preparation of Keynes's *General Theory*. As the title suggests, Keynes explains unemployment in terms of money and a monetary theory of interest. Apart from Richard Kahn, Joan Robinson worked more closely than anyone else in developing and refining the ideas and concepts in the *General Theory*. Prior to and following publication of the *General Theory*, she wrote several books and numerous articles, usually with Keynes's explicit sanction, explaining and defending its ideas. Yet in the post-Keynesian years when Joan Robinson extended Keynesian theory to the long period, money occupied no significant place in her theory. This appears paradoxical in view of her earlier immersion in Keynes's monetary economics. Dillard explores this apparent paradox.

The term finance is often referred to in two totally different meanings, the one being the liquidity needed by firms in order to make current production possible, the second being the yield from the placement of long-term securities on the financial market. In most macroeconomic models the first problem is ignored, while the second is identified with the financing of investment. In Chapter 22, Graziani shows this procedure to be fully legitimate in the framework of a fully neoclassical model. But Joan Robinson's model of income distribution requires a different treatment of finance, where, on the one hand, means of payment supplied by banks to firms are explicitly dealt with, and on the other hand, investment is financed not only by saving out of wage income but also firms' profits. Graziani attempts a reconstruction of the financing of the economy according to Joan Robinson's indications. He provides an analytical support to Joan Robinson's view that investment does not seem to react to changes in the rate of interest.

A very unusual and striking parallel is drawn between Joan Robinson's and the new classical macroeconomists' critiques of the neoclassical synthesis in Chapter 23 by Sheffrin, the well-known specialist on the new classical approach. He argues that the criticisms that Joan Robinson raised against American neoclassical Keynesian macroeconomics are in many ways similar to those of the new classical macroeconomists. Although her substantive ideas differ sharply from the new classicals, their preoccupations are surprisingly similar. Sheffrin contends that Joan Robinson's views on time, history, dynamics and even econometrics echo in the writings of the new classicals.

Part VIII concentrates on the most striking market failure (unemployment), but also deals with some others (financial markets) and the need for public policy to step into the gap. In the opening chapter (24), Laroque presents a model in which rational inventory-holders with perfect foresight are responsible for the business cycle. At the same time, the model provides an explanation of why arbitrage may not force the price system to its competitive value in the long run. Inventories prevent the *tâtonnement* process to converge to the competitive equilibrium. Finally the model gives a rationale for the use of Keynesian fiscal and monetary policies.

In Chapter 25, building on the Cass–Shell notion of 'sunspot' phenomena, Cass explores the implications for competitive market allocation when there are too few financial instruments to guarantee Arrow–Debreu equilibrium. He conducts the analysis in terms of the leading example, where two households only have available a single bond for hedging between two possible future states of the world. The most striking result is that, with such market 'failure', there will generally be a continuum of distinct equilibrium allocations in which sunspots matter – and thus ample justification for government intervention in the financial market.

In the next chapter (26), Tarshis deplores the macroeconomists' inability to forge satisfactory explanations for the sharp movements in interest rates in the last fifty years. He examines three such attempts: an explanation of high interest rates as a consequence of a low saving rate; the doctrine that attributes high interest rates to inflation or expectations of inflation; and an explanation of the level of interest rates by reference to the size of the federal budget. He then proceeds to construct a theory to replace those implicit in the aforementioned three attempts – a theory general enough to deal with day-to-day problems, that takes account of the unique features of money and credit markets, and one that must be consistent with acceptable macroeconomic insights.

In a related chapter (27), Eisner suggests that Keynesian unemployment does not require rigid wages. Where wealth effects of government debt to the private sector cannot maintain or restore full employment equilibrium, a fixed wage serves to define the price level. Money is not neutral where it coexists with interest-bearing government debt. A government budget deficit involving proportionate increase of non-interest-bearing debt (money) and interest-bearing debt will raise current and planned future consumption demand and thus raise investment demand of rational entrepreneurs as well. Under conditions of less-than-full employment this should increase consumption *and* investment. With market-clearing full employment, a nominal deficit financed by proportionate increases of money and interest-bearing debt will cause inflation but no increase in the real value of money and debt.

Economists often assume that politicians have decided what the goals of economic policy are, while the political habit is merely to list goals without choosing among them. In Chapter 28, Jamie Galbraith reviews the goals of the Employment Act, as amended. He argues that the objective of full employment has lost relevance in a time when people are abandoning high-valued leisure for lower-valued jobs. If so, policy should strive instead to achieve sustainable increases in real household income, a process requiring emphasis on the exploitation of comparative advantage in world trade, and the substitution of fewer good jobs for a larger number of poor ones. Price stabilization, finally, is primarily a political imperative, necessary to reduce distributive conflicts that otherwise tend to overwhelm the limited decision-making resources of the political system.

Part IX picks up a theme closely related to Joan Robinson's critique of the American genus of Keynesian economics – namely, the content of full employment with which she challenged American economists in her Ely Lecture in 1971 as the second crisis in economic theory. It concentrates on Joan Robinson's denunciation of the creation of full employment by means of an armaments build-up and on her concern for ways of avoiding a costly arms race and preserving peace. In Chapter 29, Fischer outlines how economists can contribute to that goal by studying the economic consequences of war, analyzing the decision-making processes by which national governments choose between war and peace, and exploring how increased international trade and other forms of economic cooperation can help reduce tensions and increase each side's stakes in maintaining peace. Fischer argues that economists should begin to address also the crucial issues of war and peace – issues that have affected human welfare more seriously than business cycles, inflation, or trade statistics. He emphasizes that unless we can avoid a nuclear holocaust, all our other concerns would be futile.

In the closing chapter (30), the first Nobel laureate in economic science, Tinbergen enjoins the economic profession to follow in the footsteps of the legal and medical professions in accepting the responsibility of pointing out to the general public the dangers involved in nuclear war. His position is that 'the traditional attitude that warfare decisions are exogenous to the economist's realm can no longer be accepted'. In this 'sketch' of what the economics of warfare might consist of, Tinbergen begins with some spiritual and ideological aspects of warfare and a general historical survey of the subject. He then proceeds to a discussion of the economic and industrial aspects of warfare, followed by a retrospect on economists' contributions to the subject. He proposes the new elements to be added to the economics of warfare and suggests world-wide integration and changes in institutions as alternatives to warfare. 'Modern war is such an irrational activity, requiring such enormous sacrifices from humanity, that its elimination can make an unparalleled contribution to human happiness. Efforts made to further that elimination promise to be highly productive in comparison to many alternative efforts.'

References

Bronfenbrenner, M. (1979) 'Review of Joan Robinson's *Contributions to Modern Economics*', *Economic Journal*, 89 (June): 446–7.
Friedman, M. (1986) in W. Breit and R. W. Spencer (eds), *Lives of the Laureates* (Cambridge, Mass.: MIT Press) pp. 77–92.
Robinson, Joan (1932) *Economics is a Serious Subject* (Cambridge: Heffer).
Robinson, Joan (1979) *Collected Economic Papers*, vol. 5 (Oxford: Blackwell).
Samuelson, P. A. (1966) *The Collected Scientific Papers of Paul A. Samuelson*, ed. by J. E. Stiglitz, 2 vols (Cambridge, Mass.: MIT Press).
Samuelson, P. A. (ed) (1970) *Readings in Economics* (New York: McGraw-Hill).

Acknowledgments

Leo Hurwicz is to be 'blamed' for suggesting this undertaking commemorating Joan Robinson's contributions to economics; Ida and I for its execution. But there are many 'partners in crime' (aside from the obvious ones listed in the table of contents) and I am a bankrupt when it comes to distributing the 'blame' fairly.

It all started with a telephone call from Leo shortly after Joan died. I deeply appreciate his initiative, his 'utopian' system designer's confidence, and his wise counsel. The contributors' product is only partly identified in the table of contents. I am beholden to all of them and at a loss for words to express my gratitude for the spirit of cooperation, good workmanship, and the remarkable intellectual experience it has been.

At the formative stages and throughout the gestation of this project, I have had the good fortune to benefit from the support and advice of Kenneth Arrow, Dick Goodwin, Peter Hammond, Lawrie Klein, Mordecai Kurz, Robin Matthews, Ed Nell, Paul Samuelson, Joe Stiglitz, Lorie Tarshis, Jan Tinbergen, and John Whitaker. A very special thanks is due to Franco Modigliani, Bob Solow, and Jim Tobin who went out of their way to make time in their busy schedules, often at times inconvenient for them, to record their thoughts and for the extraordinary experience and the fun it has been.

It is my pleasant duty to record here my indebtedness to Richard (Lord) Kahn, Sir Austin Robinson, John Kenneth Galbraith, and (the late) Gunnar Myrdal for their encouragement and kind cooperation. Special thanks are also due to George Akerlof, John Hobakkuk, Rolf Henriksson, Sir Brian Hopkins, Ada Kalecki, (the late) Leonid Kantorovitch, Tadeusz Kowalik, Sir Arthur Lewis, Bill Nordhaus, K. N. Raj, Dick Stone, and Paul Sweezy.

I am glad to acknowledge all those who graciously commented on my two introductory chapters and preface. Thanks are due to Irma Adelman, Chris Archibald, Kenneth Arrow, Will Baumol, Bobby Becker, Buz Brock, David Cass, John Chipman, Gerard Debreu, Robert Dixon, Jamie Galbraith, Jean Gabszewicz, Harvey Gram, Augusto Graziani, Peter Hammond, Murray Kemp, Lawrie Klein, Andreu Mas-Colell, Robin Matthews, Ed Nell, Takashi Negishi, John Roberts, Paul Samuelson, Steve Sheffrin, T. S. Srinivasan, Lance Taylor, Vivien Walsh, and John Whitaker. Of course none of the above is responsible for any errors of omission or commission.

I am pleased to acknowledge the superb cooperation of the Head of the Reference Library at the University of Tennessee, Bob Bassett, and of the staff of the Stanford Libraries. Thanks are also due to René Olivieri of Blackwell for his kind cooperation. It was good to have again Keith Povey's editorial help. As always I appreciate the assistance, advice, and encouragement of Tim Farmiloe of Macmillan. He makes the task easier and enjoyable. What more could one ask of a publisher?

In the process of completing these two volumes, I benefited from a fellowship from the Jerome Levy Economics Institute of Bart College. Their financial assistance is appreciated as is David Levy's and Dimitry Papadimitriou's interest and elegance.

It was my good fortune to have known Joan and some of the 'old guard' in Cambridge reasonably well. I am grateful for the opportunity and privilege. Perhaps I should add that the very special relation I had with Joan emanated from my work on Michał Kalecki during the gestation of which Joan demonstrated her best qualities of supporter, scholar, critic, and friend. Ida and I cherish the memories. Joan set and demanded very high standards of personal and scholarly integrity for herself and her friends. As I am writing these words I cannot help but remember the last time we saw her in 1980. Ida and I entered a room full of people, her eyes lit with a unique spark (probably she was remembering Kalecki). She sat with Ida, was silent for a while, and then said how much she appreciated the 'outstanding' work we had done on Kalecki. These words of Joan and the support of the contributors were a sustaining force in the execution of this fascinating endeavor, not always conducted under the most auspicious circumstances. We can only hope the result would not have disappointed Joan and are deeply grateful to those who have shown us so much kindness, understanding, and encouragement.

There is also another lady near to my heart whose moral fortitude, high standards, and exemplary (unremunerated) labors served as an incessant inspiration, guide, and critic during the long and difficult process of gestation and fruition of this enterprise. My wife, Ida, brought to it her usual dedication, enthusiasm, and desire to do the right thing. Lucky is the person who can 'survive' such an environment.

Our thoughts could not be better expressed than in the words of Richard Goodwin (the note in Chapter 7 of *Joan Robinson and Modern Economic Theory*): We offer these two volumes 'as a tribute to the memory of one of the more remarkable persons' we have ever known.

Joan Robinson was an embodiment of 'the desire and pursuit of the whole' and her passing is a great loss to her friends, and, though often unacknowledged, to the profession as a whole. She had an uncanny and rare ability to unravel the daunting complexities of economic life by the exercise of logic alone. To this austere activity she dedicated unselfishly the bulk of her adult life. For the many of us who stood in awe and admiration of the purity and power of her devotion to the understanding of our world, a light has been extinguished.

1 Joan Robinson Inside and Outside the Stream

George R. Feiwel

I have always aimed to make my own prejudices sufficiently obvious to allow a reader, while studying the arguments, to discount them as he thinks fit, though, of course, this generally leads a reader of opposite prejudices to reject the argument in advance. (Joan Robinson, 1960, 1975, p.iv)

How can what an Englishman believes be heresy? It is a contradiction in terms. (G. B. Shaw, *St Joan*, Scene iv)

1 INTRODUCTION

In the 1930s there were three great waves in economics: the Keynesian revolution, the imperfect (monopolistic) competition revolution, and the 'fruitful clarification of the analysis of economic reality resulting from the mathematical and econometric handling of the subject' (Samuelson, 1977, p. 890). Joan Robinson was a creative participant (as a member of Keynes's Circus) and a generalizer of the first wave and one of the two independent (and complementary) architects of the second. Her position in the third is ambivalent. While she was innocent of modern mathematical techniques and showed some hostility towards their use in economics, her own theoretical writings (especially her major pre-war (1933) and post-war (1956, 1966) books) are very formalistic and abstract. She casts her argument in what may be called the axiomatic method, even though she is tinged with the 'Marshallian incubus' in execution.

There are many paradoxes in the economics of Joan Robinson and some clues to help us solve the riddle. Above all, she was a Cambridge economist and began her career when Cambridge ruled the seas of economics, at least in the English speaking world. At that time there still was such a thing as Cambridge imperialism.[1] England was still a great power, but it was perched on the brink of stagnation, and depression.

Joan Violet Maurice (as she was then known) was a product of the upper middle class. Her great grandfather was a well-known Christian Socialist. Her father, Major-General Sir Frederick Maurice, was the victim of the (in)famous Maurice debate in 1918. Some clues to the indomitable, pertinacious Joan, seeker after truth, campaigner and preacher can be found in her family background. In many ways she was the élitist upper-class English-woman, but she had a genuine concern for the plight of the poor and a strong belief in egalitarianism. She was intellectually seduced by left-wing politics but she did not get involved in direct action.

Another clue to her personality – a facet of it to which many of her American antagonists fell prey and strongly deplored – was that she was a product of and operated within the milieu of English academia. It was a world where controversies are cherished and nurtured, where personal clashes and assaults thrive, where combatants often do not speak to each other for years, and where even friends, with offices next to each other, write notes rather than speak. It was a world where the oral tradition was strong; ideas were thrashed out in select groups (like Keynes's Circus and later the 'secret seminar'). It was a world before the explosion of scholarly research in general, and of the economic profession in particular, where one knew and discussed at length what one's colleagues were doing and those that were far away did not matter anyway. It was a world where one formed one's opinion about the content and fundamental message of one's colleagues work on the basis of discussion and interpretation.[2] It was also a man's world where the barriers against women were only slowly crumbling. Whilst this undoubtedly created some problems she did not perceive this as a major difficulty, neither did she feel discriminated against. One of the puzzles of Joan's position in the economic profession in the post-war years was that she carried over the habits and traditions of the 1930s to an era when, for better or worse, economics became more cosmopolitan and was governed by different rules.

She had the extraordinary ability to zero in on the heart of the matter and in a few well-chosen words to convey its essence. She had an irritating penchant to dismiss as nonsense ideas with which she did not agree.[3] She had a great affinity for language. She wrote clearly, concisely and with elegance. Interspersed throughout her writings are jewels of perception, written with wit and sharply to the point. Such a flair for language is altogether rare among economists. Among her outstanding contemporaries perhaps Gal-braith and Samuelson also share this felicity.

A further clue to the paradox of Joan is that she matured as an economist at a time when literary economics was just about to be displaced by the third wave, the mathematization of economics and increasing fascination with sophisticated mathematical techniques. At the same time, the Marshallian mode of thinking (in which she was steeped, but which she struggled to escape, as we shall see later) was being displaced by the increasing dominance of modern Walrasian general equilibrium and the increasing role of the game-theoretic approach. In the latter part of her life, performance criteria shifted in her disfavor. In such an environment and with her prickly character and penchant for disputes, it is not surprising that, despite its relevance and intrinsic appeal to idealistic or questioning youth, her work did not always attract the best and brightest. But this tale has many other facets. Her conception of economic processes is not very conducive to adaptation in mathematical models. Indeed, when Findlay attempted to set out the formal relations of the model in *The Accumulation of Capital* (1956, 1966), she was dissatisfied with it on the grounds that the formalization deprived it of significance. Her potential influence should not be underestimated, however, as the contributions to these two volumes so eloquently attest.

Perhaps the most important clues to the economics of Joan Robinson can be found in the influences exerted on her by her antecedents and contemporaries. In her formative years Marshall and Pigou stand out as the most conspicuous influences. They are the strongholds of orthodoxy that she battled with all her life. Sraffa (1926), and particularly his teaching and discussions, provided the ferment for her questioning of the inherited theory of value and her work on imperfect competition. Throughout her life, discussions with Sraffa continued to be a dominant influence, though she complained that his attitude was negative rather than positive. At the same time, she also formed a close and lasting partnership with Richard Kahn who helped her in conceptualization and in constructing the technical apparatus of her major books. The pre-eminent influence of Keynes's personality and economics, her membership in the Circus, the disputes with Pigou and Robertson in Cambridge and Robbins and Hayek at LSE are all a part of this story. Another story is the pervasive influence of Kalecki (as told in Chapter 1 of the companion volume) – a fountainhead of many of her ideas. In later years she tended to see much of the Keynesian revolution through Kaleckian eyes. During the war she read Marx and Rosa Luxemburg (at the instigation of Kalecki and influenced by Sraffa) and was greatly impressed by the schemes of expanded reproduction as analytical tools and Marx's vision of capitalism in motion. But, like Kalecki, she was very critical of the labor theory of value which she considered to be metaphysical. Among her other influences, her critical attitude towards Wicksell, and her admiration for the man stand out. Further influences of contemporaries included Harrod's work in growth and her ambivalent relationship with Kaldor. Her continuous disputes with Hicks, Samuelson, Solow, Meade, Hahn, and others, as well as interaction with her 'favorites' among Cambridge colleagues, visitors and students, have all left a mark.

It is difficult in this introductory chapter to do justice to the richness and variety of Joan Robinson's contributions and the scholar and person she was. This is but a fragmentary attempt to convey *her* perspective on economic theory and economic philosophy. To understand her position, it might be helpful to glance at her formative years as an economist and the first step in her long struggle to escape from Marshall and Pigou which culminated in one of the neoclassical masterpieces of what Shackle called 'the years of high theory' – her *Economics of Imperfect Competition* and the grounds on which she rejected it (Sections 2–4). At the same time, a much greater storm was brewing: the Keynesian revolution and its almost unique impact not only on our heroine, but on a whole generation of economists the world over – a fascinating tale whose general outlines can be found in Section 5 (treated in greater detail in Chapter 1 of the companion volume). In the next section (6) we shall look at what Joan called the 'generalization of the General Theory', one of her main post-war preoccupations, and in Section 7 at the capital controversy in which she was enmeshed for so many years. Thereafter we shall pause (in Section 8) on her views on the state of economic theory, the questions asked by modern economists, her attitude towards alternative approaches, and her forays into economic philosophy and politics. The concluding section (9) shows that she has not (in Horace's words) died altogether.

2 IMPERFECT COMPETITION: MARSHALL, PIGOU, AND SRAFFA

When in 1921, Joan Robinson arrived in Cambridge, as a student 'Marshall *was* economics' and his '*Principles* was the Bible' (Joan Robinson 1973b, p.ix) (see Chapter 3 of the companion volume). In one of her last lectures (the so-called 'Spring Cleaning' lecture to the Eastern Economic Association in May 1980, that I had the privilege of including in a volume I edited), she (1985, p.157) recalled:

> I am one of the few survivors of the generation that learned economic theory before the Keynesian revolution. Alfred Marshall was the overmastering influence on teaching in the English-speaking world. There were many disputed points within the Marshallian canon, such as the meaning of the 'representative firm', but other schools – Walras, Pareto, the Austrians – were dismissed in footnotes. We used to say in Cambridge: 'Everything is in Marshall.' I added later: 'The trouble is that everything else is as well.'[4]

She came to study economics as many others without a clear idea of what it was about. She had some hazy notion that economics would help her understand the reasons for poverty and the means of alleviating it. She also hoped to find in economics greater scope for rational argument than in history – her school specialization. 'I was somewhat disappointed on both counts.' She reacted badly towards Marshall: 'I felt smothered by the moralizing and mystified by the theory' (Joan Robinson, 1978, p.ix). As her education passed from Marshall–Pigou to Keynes, she was not exposed to Walrasian general equilibrium. She (1978, p.xix) recalls that in the 1930s Walrasian doctrines were in vogue at the London School of Economics (see Hicks, 1983, pp.358–9). There they mocked 'the logical inconsistency in

Marshall's method of treating markets for commodities "one at a time", but the logical flaw in their own system was still more crippling'.

She graduated in 1925 and in 1926 married Austin Robinson – by then an already established Cambridge economist. They spent some time in India and returned to Cambridge in 1929 when Joan began teaching. By then,

> Mr. Sraffa's lectures were penetrating our insularity. He was calmly committing the sacrilege of pointing out inconsistencies in Marshall (his article of 1926, ... also, was still reverberating) and at the same time revealing that other schools existed (though they were no better). The elders reacted by defending Marshall as best they could, ... but the younger generation were not convinced by them. The profound inconsistency between the static base and the dynamic superstructure had become too obvious (Joan Robinson, 1951, 1978, p.vii).[5]

One clue to the economics of Joan Robinson is that she was a great Marshallian while she fought tooth and nail to escape from Marshall, particularly in his Pigovian incarnation. To her Marshall was a subtle thinker, with many valuable ideas, but in a terrible muddle.[6] She (1979a, pp.53–4) saw Marshall as, in a way, an heir of the classical tradition.[7] He concentrated on a recognizable economy in a specific phase of its development, where recognizable classes of the society interact within a specific legal and conventional framework.

> Marshall inherited from Ricardo two qualities which are lacking in the branch of the neo-classical school that derives from Walras. He had (though confusedly) a sense of time. The short period is here and now, with concrete stocks of means of production in existence. Incompatibilities in the situation – in particular between the capacity of equipment and expected demand for output – will determine what happens next. Long-period equilibrium is not at some date in the future; it is an imaginary state of affairs in which there are no incompatibilities in the existing situation, here and now. Secondly, Marshall had a sense of the structure of society. His world is peopled with types (though idealized in a way which nowadays sometimes seems comical) who have different parts to play – the businessman, the worker, the householder – each has his own characteristic motives and problems. (Joan Robinson, 1965, 1975, p. 101)

But she (1979a, p.12) adds that the trouble with Marshall's analysis is that it 'was half in historical time and half in equilibrium analysis'. In her (1973b, p.ix) opinion there was a deep-rooted conflict in Marshall's *Principles*.[8] It was a conflict of which Marshall was 'uneasily' aware, especially in connection with increasing returns. The conflict lay between the analysis, couched in purely static terms, and the conclusions drawn therefrom – conclusions that apply to a dynamic economy, developing through time. But 'somehow we managed to swallow it'.

In Samuelson's (1972, p.25) 'analysis' Marshall was a victim of self-hate. A good chess player, he was ashamed of playing chess. A good analytical economist, he was ashamed of analysis. He grasped Cournot's insistence that the marginal cost curve must not be declining for any maximizing pure competitor, but he resisted acceptance of that fact. Nothing, according to Samuelson, can 'change this fact: any price taker who can sell more at the going price than he is now selling and who has falling marginal cost will not be in equilibrium. Talk of birds and bees, giant trees in the forest, and declining entrepreneurial dynasties is all very well, but why blink at such an elementary point?'

Samuelson (1972, p.24) considers that Marshall confused two generations of scholars by 'his insistence on having his cake and eating it too'. He tried to deal with imperfect and perfect competition at the same time. 'He would try to achieve a spurious verisimilitude by talking about vague biological dynamics, and by failing to distinguish between reversible and irreversible developments'. He confused the question of external economies and diseconomies with the completely separate questions of varying laws of returns. 'Marshall was so afraid of being unrealistic that he merely ends up being fuzzy and confusing – and confused.' Samuelson correctly views much of the work done between 1920 and 1933 as 'merely the negative task of getting Marshall out of the way'.[9]

In the preface to the second edition of *The Economics of Imperfect Competition*, Joan Robinson (1933, 1969, pp.v–vi) spoke of the state of the Marshallian–Pigovian 'orthodoxy' when she originally wrote. 'Here we were, in 1930, in a deep slump, and this is what we were asked to believe':

1. The reaction of output and prices to unforeseen changes in demand for a particular commodity depends on the competitive conditions. Marshall's concept of competition was imprecise.[10] He assumed that a rise in demand would lead to an increase in output and a higher rate of utilization of capacity, with higher marginal cost accompanied by a higher price. In a slump firms do not reduce prices for 'fear of spoiling the market'.[11] In time as firms expand, invest in new techniques, and learn by doing, they reap internal economies of scale. The average cost per unit of output falls and is passed on to the public in the form of lower prices. Where are then the bounds to the size of the individual firm? Why does not a single firm undersell all others, expand and lower costs further, and finally conquer the market? Marshall's answer was to identify the lifecycle of the firm with that of the family. He suggested that the expansion of a firm would slacken as the coddled sons of the owner take over. In his view joint-stock companies stagnate. (See also Joan Robinson 1979a, pp.10–11 and 54; 1971, pp.58 and 97; and 1952, p.69.)

2. In Pigou's hands all this became an uncluttered, logical scheme.

> Perfect competition means that the individual producer can sell as much
> or as little as he likes at the ruling price. Each firm continuously produces
> the amount of output of which the marginal costs is equal to price. There
> are internal economies of scale only up to a certain size, at which average
> cost (including a normal profit) is at a minimum. When demand is such as
> to call forth output beyond this size from a particular firm, marginal cost,
> and therefore price, exceeds average costs. Super-normal profits call in
> fresh competition which brings down the market price and pushes back
> the output of the firm. When price is below average cost, some firms are
> driven out of business, and those that remain expand. Thus the optimum
> size of firm, with minimum average costs, is always tending to be
> established. (Joan Robinson, 1933, 1969, pp. v–vi)

Actually Joan Robinson was a 'second-hand' Marshallian. It was Pigou
and Shove who explained Marshall to her. It is the 'Pigovian orthodoxy' she
fought.[12] In her (1978, p.132) view 'Pigou emptied history out of Marshall
and reduced the analysis to a two-dimensional scheme'. Pigou attempted to
solve Marshall's above-mentioned quandary by introducing the equilibrium
size of the firm.

> Every week, a firm is maximizing profits by selling such an output as to
> make the marginal costs of its product equal to the ruling price; over the
> long run, competition forces it to operate at the minimum point of a U-
> shaped curve, where marginal and average cost are both equal to price.
> There is a rate of interest (somehow connected with the discount of the
> future of owners of wealth) at which every firm can borrow as much or as
> little as it likes; when it is in equilibrium, its net profit per annum is just
> sufficient to cover interest, at the ruling rate on the value of its capital.
> (Joan Robinson, 1978, p. 132)[13]

Joan Robinson (p.131) compares the economics of the classics and
neoclassics, in a way drawing a parallel between Marshall and Pigou. In her
perception, the classics (and to some extent even Marshall)

> were concerned with actual contemporary problems and put their argu-
> ments in terms of the structure and behaviour of the economy in which
> they were living, while the neoclassics enunciated what purported to be
> universal laws, based on human nature – greed, impatience and so forth.
> The latter rarely say anything at all about the kind of economy to which an
> argument is to be applied. The suggestion is that the same laws which
> govern the supposed behaviour of Robinson Crusoe are equally valid for
> the conduct of Gosplan, or rather what its conduct *ought* to be, and for
> analysing the vagaries of Wall Street.

From the vantage point of a quarter of a century later, in 1958 Joan Robinson (1960, 1975, pp.240–1) perceived the background of imperfect competition in Marshall's vague and unelaborated concept of 'fear of spoiling the market'.[14] Marshall also spoke of the specific demand curve for the output of a specific firm – which means that marginal cost is not equated with price, but with marginal revenue and that the wages of the employed workers are smaller than the value of their marginal product.

It was alien to Marshall's outlook to stress these implications and he passed lightly over them, but in the thirties it had become obvious that the exception swallowed up the rule, and Marshall's evasive references were no longer satisfactory.

The new analysis, stressing market imperfection, oligopoly, deliberate product differentiation and selling costs, appeared to give precision to Marshall's vague concept of 'fear of spoiling the market' and provided the means for elaborating problems which could no longer be dismissed in a footnote.

Unlike Marshall, who was generous in acknowledging his indebtedness to distant predecessors and ungenerous in acknowledging the contributions of contemporaries, in her (1933, 1969) book, Joan Robinson bends over backwards to acknowledge her contemporaries and appears to treat her elders (especially Marshall and Pigou) rather slightingly, but this is not entirely just. In her words (1933, 1969, p.xiii):

In general I have endeavoured to build on the foundations laid by Marshall and by Professor Pigou. This is a debt which all economists owe, and which may be taken for granted. I have for the most part referred to their works only where I believe that I have detected them in errors of detail.

Here she (p.xiii) also acknowledges Sraffa 'as the fount from which my work flows, for the chief aim of this book is to attempt to carry out his pregnant suggestion that the whole theory of value should be treated in terms of monopoly analysis'.[15]

In 1958, recollecting the birth of imperfect competition, Joan Robinson (1960, 1975, pp.239–40) points to Sraffa (1926) as shaking the foundations of orthodoxy. In particular she cites the following passage from Sraffa (1926, p.543):

Everyday experience shows that a very large number of undertakings – and the majority of those which produce manufactured consumers' goods – work under conditions of individual diminishing costs. Almost any producer of such goods, if he could rely upon the market in which he sells his products being prepared to take any quantity of them from him at the current price, without any trouble on his part except that of producing them, would extend his business enormously. It is not easy, in times of normal activity, to find an undertaking which systematically restricts its own production to an amount less than that which it could sell at the current price, and which is at the same time prevented by competition from exceeding that price. Business men, who regard themselves as being subject to competitive conditions, would consider absurd the assertion that the limit to their production is to be found in the internal conditions of production in their firm, which do not permit the production of a greater quantity without an increase in cost. The chief obstacle against which they have to contend when they want gradually to increase their production does not lie in the cost of production – which, indeed, generally favours them in that direction – but in the difficulty of selling the larger quantity of goods without reducing the price, or without having to face increased marketing expenses.

Speaking of Sraffa's (1926) influence on her, she (1960, 1975 p.240) muses that 'its wider significance was not generally recognized until the seeds of doubt about orthodox theory germinated in the atmosphere of discontent with *laisser-faire* policy which prevailed in the great depression'.

In *The Economics of Imperfect Competition*, Joan Robinson (1933, 1969, pp.118–19) perceives Sraffa's (1926) intentions and his relationship to monopoly analysis as follows:

He was concerned to show that economists who make use of the competitive analysis of value have a strong unconscious bias in favour of rising and falling supply price, simply because, if supply price is always constant, their analysis has nothing interesting to say. The monopoly analysis of value, inaugurated by Mr Sraffa himself, has no axe to grind in the matter. If the statisticians assure Mr Sraffa that he is right, and that almost every industry works under conditions of constant costs, the task of the monopoly analysis will be much simplified. But it will lose none of its validity, and will gain considerably in charm.

In 1934, writing for the first time in an American journal, Joan Robinson (1951, 1978 pp.20–1) stressed Sraffa's (1926) role in the imperfect competition revolution. She perceived him as 'emancipating economic analysis from the tyranny of the assumption of perfect competition' but 'he was not himself aware of the freedom he was winning for us'.

Sraffa (1926) was satisfied with the notion that when imperfect competition prevails, the problems of normal profits and free entry need not be considered, for in any case entry into an imperfect market is difficult. But, Joan Robinson contends, Sraffa's argument can be easily pushed to its logical conclusion. He showed that in the real world almost every market is imperfect 'and it would be impossible to contend that in the real world new firms hardly ever enter any industry'. The notion of free entry is closely entangled with that of normal profit (Joan Robinson, 1951, 1978, pp.20–2).

According to Joan Robinson (p.27), Sraffa conceived of market imperfection introduced through customers' specific preferences for the output of one firm over another and the existence of differential transport costs. Moreover, the same price throughout the market is not sufficient to call a market perfect, for if all firms are the same with respect to costs and demand conditions, the same price will prevail, no matter how imperfect the market is.

While she acknowledged Sraffa's inspiration, Joan Robinson (1933, 1969, p.xiii) attributed to Richard Kahn a degree of cooperation close to co-authorship: 'The whole technical apparatus was built up with his aid, and many of the major problems – notably the problems of Price Discrimination and of Exploitation – were solved as much by him as by me. He has also contributed a number of mathematical proofs which I should have been incapable of finding myself.' In later years (for example, 1979, p.112), she referred to *The Economics of Imperfect Competition* on which she said, she was 'working with R. F. Kahn'. In recommending the publication of the book to Harold Macmillan, Keynes observed that his confidence in Joan's work was boosted by the fact that she had worked so closely with Kahn, who, as the most careful and accurate of all younger economists, could be relied upon to ensure that the work would be relatively free of technical slips and errors.

One of the other contemporaries whom she acknowledged was E. G. Shove, not only for some specific contributions but for his teaching in Cambridge for many years which 'has influenced directly and indirectly the whole approach to many problems of economic analysis' (Joan Robinson, 1933, 1969, p.xiv). She (p.xiv) also thanked Austin Robinson whose 'work on the optimum size of firms is the foundation of my treatment of competitive equilibrium, and plays an important part in the Appendix on Increasing and Diminishing Returns'. Joan Robinson (pp.xiv–xv) makes much of the marginal revenue curve which 'plays a great part in my work, and my book arose out of the attempt to apply it to various problems'. (She mentions a number of 'explorers' of the concept, including R. F. Harrod, T. O. Yntema, and J. Viner. She even breaks through the Anglo-Saxon originality barrier by including E. Schneider, H. von Stackelberg and F. Zeuthen.)[16] But her book is much more than an application of the marginal revenue curve to various problems.

3 THE ECONOMICS OF IMPERFECT COMPETITION

It is not our purpose here either to evaluate the adequacy of Joan Robinson's

1933 book or to compare it with Chamberlin's (1933) or even to present the reception they received at the time and the evaluation to which they were subjected later,[17] but to sketch its main thrust and in the next section (4) to provide Joan Robinson's reconsideration of imperfect competition. However, we would be seriously remiss if we did not point out that when Joan Robinson's 1933 book appeared it was reviewed by Schumpeter, a colleague of Chamberlin. Schumpeter (1934, p.251) acknowledged 'that we owe substantial progress to the works of all the theorists of imperfect competition, among whom Mrs. Robinson in this book establishes a claim, certainly to a leading, and perhaps to the first, place'. Schumpeter praised the book for its great range and power. He (p.251) 'graded' it in his favorite expression as

> an admirable performance, both by virtue of its pioneer achievement and by the energy and straightforwardness of its exposition which eminently qualify it for classroom use, at least for such teachers as do not think it their duty to deal with their students as if they were feeble-minded. It is remarkably free from the blemishes (and flourishes) which so often disfigure and impair exposition of theoretical work. Its results, never irrelevant, mostly interesting, often novel, are presented in a thoroughly workmanlike way. It is an excellent example of what serious theory should be and well lives up to the standard of rigor set by the author in a pamphlet entitled *Economics Is a Serious Subject* (1932).

With a more than thirty-year perspective, Shackle (1967, p.53) placed the book as one of the important accomplishments of 'the years of high theory'.

> The care and thoroughness of her statement of definitions and assumptions, the candour of her declaration about the abstract character of her analysis, the systematic organization which lets us know these things at the beginning and offers a formal explanation and training in the pure technique of average and marginal curves without, at that stage, giving these curves any specific content or interpretation, were at that date something new in economic reasoning. Joan Robinson was a navigator, not a mere groping breaker of the jungle.

> In the Pigovian scheme that dominated Cambridge economics in 1930, 'under perfect competition, any plant that was working at all must be working up to capacity . . . Imperfect competition came in to explain the fact, in the world around us, that more or less all plants were working part time' (Joan Robinson, 1933, 1939, p.vi).

The theory of imperfect competition was propelled into existence by a notion that was in the air in Cambridge, but was yet in a nebulous state. The notion that every firm is facing a falling demand curve for its own product and that profits are maximized at the output for which marginal revenue is equal to marginal cost, provided an explanation for a situation in which firms could work their plants at less than full capacity and still earn a profit. (Joan Robinson, 1933, 1969, p.vi).

> I remember the moment when it was an exciting discovery (made by R. F. Kahn) that where two average curves are tangential, the corresponding marginal curves cut at the same abscissa. The apparatus which we worked out took on a kind of fascination for its own sake (though by modern standards it is childishly simple) and I set about to apply it to the rest of Pigou's system. This reached its culmination in the analysis of price discrimination. I think that this is still useful and that it is worthwhile to master the apparatus for its sake. But to apply the analysis to the so-called theory of the firm, I had to make a number of limitations and simplifications which led the argument astray. (Joan Robinson, 1933, 1969, p.vi)

In the pre-1930s setting, price theory concentrated on the analysis of perfect competition and treated monopoly as a special case. What Joan Robinson (1933–69) attempted to do was to invert the procedure. In the concluding chapter she (p.307) states: 'It has been the purpose of the foregoing argument to show that this process can with advantage be reversed and that it is more proper to set out the analysis of monopoly, treating perfect competition as a special case.'

Although the content of the book was revolutionary at the time, its general tenor is conciliatory: 'It has been the intention of this book to avoid wanton controversy' (Joan Robinson, 1933, 1969, p.116).

Before proceeding any further we should note that Joan Robinson's first publication (1932), which she later repudiated, dealt with what Sir Dennis Robertson called the distasteful subject of methodology. She dedicated it to 'the fundamental pessimist'. She (p.3) began by stating:

> The student's heart sinks when his is presented with a book on the Scope and Method of his subject. Let me make a start, he begs, and I will find out the scope and method as I go along. And the student is perfectly right. For a serious subject, in the academic sense, is neither more nor less than its own technique.

In a way this pamphlet could be read as a Manifesto of how she set to work in *The Economics of Imperfect Competition*. Referring to the discussions surrounding the germination of the latter, Shackle (1967, p.47) differentiated Joan's approach from that of the other 'good' Marshallians who 'examined the existing world in a spirit of respect, they brought as much of it intact into their discourse as they could, they valued the contours and features of the landscape they beheld and tried to mould their argument upon them rather than cut a path direct to rigorous conclusions'. On the other hand, Joan Robinson – 'a new participant of ruthless and incisive temper, determined to formulate everything in the new language and to follow the Sraffian path without distraction' –

> did the opposite. Clear and definite questions cannot be asked about a vague, richly detailed, fluid and living world. This world must therefore be exchanged for a *model*, a set of precise assumptions collectively simple enough to allow the play of logic and mathematics. The designer of a model works backwards and forwards, considering when he has made some inferences from a given set of assumptions, whether a different set would yield a total scheme, of premises, reasoning and results, more interesting and generally illuminating as a whole than the former set. The model is a work of art, freely composed within the constraints of a particular art-form, namely the logical binding together of propositions. In this bounded freedom it resembles any other art form, the sonnet, the symphony, the cabinet-maker's or architect's conception.

Thus *The Economics of Imperfect Competition* is an exercise in tool making and at the time Joan Robinson (1933, 1969, p.1) was proud of it: 'This book is presented to the analytical economist as a box of tools. It is an essay in the technique of economic analysis, and can make only an indirect contribution to our knowledge of the actual world.' She (p.1) went on to distinguish between tool makers and tool users:

> It is only by using their tools upon observed facts that economists can build up that working model of the actual world which it is their aim to construct. To tinker with the tool-box is merely a preliminary to the main attack, and, to those who are in haste for results, it may appear an idle occupation far inferior to the fruitful work of the tool-users. The gap between the tool-makers and the tool-users is a distressingly wide one, and no economist can fail to have sympathy with the impatience of the politician, the businessman, and the statistical investigator, who complain of the extremely poor, arid, or even misleading information with which the analytical economists provide him.

> In most cases the analytical economists and the practical men do not speak the same language. The former cannot answer the latter's questions without hedging them with a number of conditions that makes the answers rather useless for practical purposes.

> It is natural enough for the practical man to complain that he asks for bread and the economist gives him a stone. But the answer of the analytical economist to such complaints should not be to fling away his tools and plunge into the tangled problems of the real world, armed only with his naked hands. It should be rather to set about to elaborate his analysis so much that it can begin to be useful. (Joan Robinson, 1933, 1969, pp.1–2)

Joan Robinson (1933, 1969, p.2) sees a solution to this dilemma in the refining of analysis by relaxation of assumptions bringing them in closer to the complex conditions of the real world – along lines later advocated, *inter alia*, by such mathematical economists as Wald (1938, 1951) and Koopmans (1957); 'The practical man must be asked to have patience, and meanwhile the economist must perfect his tools in the hope of being able sooner or later to meet the practical man's requirements.'

Joan Robinson (1933, 1969, pp.2–3) is emphatic about the analytical economist's obligation to unequivocally set forth the assumptions on which his analysis is based. Here, but for her innocence of mathematics, she could be classed as a devotee of the axiomatic method (see Chapter 6 of this volume).

The best that the economist can do is use what implements he has with the greatest care and precision, and when he does give an answer to some general question to take the utmost pains to make clear what assumptions about the nature of the problem are implicit in his answer. If ... the assumptions are very abstract the economist will only bring the practical man into confusion and himself into disrepute by allowing him to suppose that the question which is being answered is the same as the question which is being asked.

She (1932, p.8) castigated her fellow English economists for

never giving a proper account of their assumptions. The search for Marshall's hidden assumptions has occupied a whole generation, and almost threatened at one time to turn the English economists into a school of higher-critical theologians. The economist who does not state his assumptions correctly, or does not state them at all, is a cause of great trouble to his colleagues.

She (p.8) attributes 'the prevalence of this vice' partly to optimism 'which leads them to concentrate on the technique and leave the assumptions to look after themselves' and partly to 'duplicity, which leads them to hope that no one will notice quite how unreal their assumptions are'. But there is also some humility involved here. The economist suffers an 'agonising sense of shame' when confronted with practical questions that he can either tackle by making assumptions closer to real conditions, but cannot answer with the tools at hand, or that he can answer by making quite unrealistic assumptions that he buries in footnotes and would be ashamed to expose to the critical eye of the practical man. This, however, is a 'scandalous breach of faith with the practical man' (Joan Robinson, 1933, 1969, pp.2–3).

The precept that Joan Robinson (1933, 1969, p.3) follows is to 'take a sardonic pleasure in shocking the practical man by the brutal frankness with which' she set out her assumptions. She finds solace in her conviction that she is following the only route by which there is some hope of finding the answer in the end.

My book attempts to live up to this standard, and if anywhere a necessary assumption is missing from the list, it must be taken to show that I have fallen into the third trap which besets the path of the economist: the danger that he does not himself quite know what his own assumptions are.

The concluding paragraph of *The Economics of Imperfect Competition* (p.327) sums up the spirit in which it was written:

The level of abstraction maintained in this book is distressingly high. The technique can only survive in an atmosphere rarefied by the adoption of very severe simplifying assumptions. The reader who is interested in results immediately applicable to the real world has every right to complain that these tools are of little use to him. The knives are of bone and the hammers of wood, only capable of cutting paper and driving pins into cardboard. But the analytical economist who is prepared to work stage by stage towards the still far-distant ideal of constructing an analysis which will be capable of solving the problems presented by the real world may perhaps find in this tool-box some implements which will serve his turn.

In very broad contours one can summarize *The Economics of Imperfect Competition* as follows: the main theme, as Joan Robinson (p.6) stresses is the theory of value. Her treatment radically departs from the tradional pre-1930s views.[18] It begins with the monopolist and then proceeds to groups of firms competing against each other in imperfect markets. The book consists of two main parts: monopoly and monopsony. The latter pertains primarily to prices of particular factors of production. Joan Robinson (1933, 1969, p.8) opens her exposition by 'brutally' setting out the assumptions 'in all their naked unreality', by providing some definitions, and by displaying the elements of techniques. Throughout the text she applies a geometric exposition with a high degree of virtuosity (aided by Kahn). The analysis is partial equilibrium and purely static in nature.

The technique set out in this book is a technique for studying equilibrium positions. No reference is made to the effects of the passage of time. Short-period and long-period equilibria are introduced into the argument to illustrate various technical devices, but no study is made of the process of moving from one position of equilibrium to another, and it is with long-period equilibrium that we shall be mainly concerned. (Joan Robinson, 1933, 1969, p.16)

Interestingly Joan (pp.20–1) is troubled by partial analysis and yearns for something more general, though she does not carry this out. Similarly, she is troubled by complications introduced into the individual demand curve by the problem of advertising, but, again unfortunately, does not pursue this topic. She recognizes the perplexing problem of oligopoly, but as she later admitted (see Section 4) she did not know how to tackle it.[19]

The analysis first centers on the determinants of the price charged by a single producer, taking into account the conditions of the producer and those of demand and cost. In this light the supply curve of a commodity is considered. Consideration is given to the reaction of monopoly profit on the number of firms producing a given commodity. She considers that the two aspects of the question how an alteration in the industry's output affects the price of a commodity – i.e. how demand for the individual seller is affected by an alteration in the output of the industry (assuming that his costs remain unaffected) and how the individual seller's costs are affected when the simplest kind of change in his demand is assumed to occur – though treated separately, can be combined to analyze the supply curve of a commodity.

Joan Robinson then proceeds to an analysis of how the output of a perfectly competitive industry is affected by the reduction of a number of independent producers to one, all else remaining unchanged. She shows that such comparisons and their corollaries are not only unrealistic but also logically inconsistent. The comparisons are not, however, entirely idle as they pave the way for analyzing a most important practical question – namely, what is the effect of combining imperfectly competitive firms into a single unit of control? The first part concludes with a discussion on price discrimination that includes a lapse from the strict line of analysis into what she calls the drawing of morals – some reflections on the desirability of price discrimination.

The opening chapters on monopsony contain some additional definitions and a review of the two building blocks thus far: the individual buyer and seller. For the sake of convenience, Joan Robinson adopts labor as the factor of production and analyzes the demand curve for a factor in a manner symmetrical to the analysis of the supply curve of a commodity, but not in as fully developed a manner. She then draws the comparison of monopoly and competitive demand for labor – comparisons symmetrical to those drawn previously and subject to the same objections and justifications.

Perhaps the last part of *The Economics of Imperfect Competition* is the most original, in the sense of being quite different from Chamberlin (1933), and the most important, in the sense of vision and continuity of Joan Robinson's life work. In later years, she (for example, 1979a, p.114) was fond of stressing how delighted she was to have shown that wages do not equal the marginal productivity of labor. Whether or not this was one of her chief objectives at the time is not now easily disentangled from time-distorted perspectives. This part consists of two sections – one on exploitation and the other on welfare implications of a 'world of monopolies'. In the first, labor no longer stands for any factor of production, but only for its own category, and the prices of this factor are not looked at from the employer's perspective but from that of the worker. Here perfect competition is used as a yardstick against which the imperfectly competitive situation is measured. Joan Robinson (1933, 1969, p.11) finds 'the temptation to stray from the path of analysis and to offer reflections of a moral character . . . too strong to be resisted'. The concluding chapter is a more general foray into welfare economics.

It behoves us to digress here, however briefly, to Joan Robinson's imaginative and controversial discussion of exploitation. She (1933, 1969, pp.310–11) defines exploitation

> as a state of affairs in which the wage of a factor is less than the value of its marginal physical production . . . and we have distinguished two types of exploitation, monopolistic exploitation which arises when the demand curve for the commodity is not perfectly elastic, and monopsonistic exploitation which arises when the supply curve of the factor is not perfectly elastic to the individual employer.

She (pp.289–90) speaks of quasi-exploitation in industries where the markets for commodities and labor are perfect, but there is no free entry. Here, though there will be no exploitation as she defines it, above normal profits may be earned. the wage will be below the average net productivity of labor, and a situation akin to exploitation may arise. Though monopolistic exploitation cannot be eliminated by raising wages, quasi-exploitation in a specific industry could be eliminated by raising wages until above normal profits are absorbed and full equilibrium conditions are restored.

Joan Robinson (p.291) does not shy away even from unpalatable conclusions: This may not be a desirable maneuvre. If normal profits are restored by an increase in wages, the result is a higher price for the commodity and less employment in the industry than if the adjustment had occurred via the industry's expansion. Other industries may also suffer unemployment or wage cuts. Also the cause of the above normal profits – the high demand for the commodity – will not result in an increase in supply. Here she (p.291) makes an argument that has not lost its relevance in the more than fifty years since it was written – an argument often repeated today.

> Under the perfectly *laissez-faire* conditions of the economic text-books the direction of resources into different types of manufacture is brought about by the fluctuation of profits above and below normal. When profits are more than normal the industry is supposed to expand, and when they fall below normal, to contract. By this means the changing demands of the consumer are implemented. If profits are kept at the normal level by

changes in wages (an assumption probably far more realistic than the assumption of the text-books), the mechanism by which resources are directed from one use to another breaks down. There is a moral here, both for those who seek to patch up our present economic system by introducing profit-sharing schemes in particular industries and for those who complain, when losses are being made, that wages in a particular trade are too high. The system of the text-books perhaps never existed, and perhaps if it did it would not have been a very admirable one. But it has some merits. A system of uncontrolled private enterprise in which wages are more plastic than profits must entail the misdirection of resources and the waste of potential wealth on an extensive scale.

With all her reservations and her critical attitude towards Pigou, Joan Robinson (1933, 1969) was not only influenced by him in her (over)emphasis of techniques, but also by his development of welfare economics. Many years later she (1962a, p.74) claimed that

> in Cambridge we had never been taught that economics should be *wertfrei* or that the positive and the normative can be sharply divided. We knew that the search was for fruit as well as light. But the anodyne of *laisser faire* had worked pretty thoroughly even in Cambridge ... Pigou set out the argument of his *Economics of Welfare* in terms of exceptions to the rule that *laisser faire* ensures maximum satisfaction; he did not question the rule.

Indeed, a good part of *The Economics of Imperfect Competition* is an excursion in the tradition of, and in reaction against, Cambridge-style welfare economics. It is not merely a variation on the themes of Pigou (1920) – the book that is often considered the cornerstone of welfare economics; it goes beyond it. Whatever else needs to be said about *The Economics of Imperfect Competition*, it is also not merely a book in tool-making. It is an attempt to provide a theoretical construct for a new vision of how markets function under more realistic conditions, whatever its imperfections in execution may be.

One should also remember that *The Economics of Imperfect Competition* is in the best Cambridge tradition not only a treatise but a teaching tool. Indeed, the point was brought up by Schumpeter (1934, p.252–3): 'In justice to the book we must always bear in mind, first, that besides being very much more it is also a textbook, the work of a mind eminently gifted for, and almost passionately fond of, teaching'.

It is with regard to this, her first *magnum opus*, written in her late twenties, that Joan Robinson has demonstrated two facets of the probity of her nature, all too rare among scholars in general, and social scientists in particular. First, when Chamberlin's book appeared almost simultaneously she did not get engaged in attempting to prove her essential originality or to show the superiority of her analysis. Nay, she leaned over backwards to point out in what respects Chamberlin was superior. Second, when in time she became disillusioned with the type of analysis she had attempted in this book, she did not hesitate openly to repudiate it. Nay, she took pleasure in self-criticism.

Whether or not the almost simultaneous publication of Chamberlin (1933) with her own book (1933, 1969) was a dismaying shock to her, Joan Robinson made little attempt immediately afterwards or at any other time to differentiate her product from Chamberlin. (For example, in 1953, she (1960, 1975, p.237) referred to the 'Chamberlin–Robinson duopoly' that 'set up in imperfectly monopolistic competition'.) Whether this was from the lofty ideals of scholarly integrity or because she was by then much preoccupied by the ferment of ideas surrounding the birth of the *General Theory* is another question. 'I soon abandoned the field; when I came under the influence of the incipient Keynesian revolution, I realized that my Pigovian book was leading up a blind alley' (Joan Robinson, 1978, p.x). Be that as it may, her writings, when they touch on this 'simultaneous discovery' display the highest scholarly integrity and personal disinterest.

For example, in 1934 in a paper published in the *Quarterly Journal of Economics* – Chamberlin's home ground – Joan Robinson (1951, 1978, p.21) praised Chamberlin for categorically separating the notions of perfect competition and free entry. She viewed, however, his distinction of 'pure' and 'perfect' competition (the former meaning a state of affairs where the demand for the output of each firm is perfectly elastic and the latter requiring the additional conditions of perfect mobility of factors, perfect certainty, and the like) as 'something misleading' and paying 'a verbal tribute to the old confusion'.

In the same paper, she (p.27) observed that Chamberlin seems to associate market imperfection simply with product differentiation. But there is a complex relationship between product differentiation and market imperfection. Physical differentiation is not a *necessary* condition for market imperfection. Two products may be essentially identical but produced by two different firms. The market for them will be imperfect if various customers have different preferences as to the two firms. Differentiation is also not a sufficient condition for market imperfection, for two firms may well produce two different products that may compete with each other in a perfect market.

In later years, Joan Robinson usually referred to the works jointly. In 1958, in a retrospect on imperfect competition, she (1960, 1975, p.239) noted the coincidence of Chamberlin's and her publication 'for he had been working on the subject much longer than I'. The enthusiastic reception they got she (p.239) attributed to the fact that 'the problems that we (along with a number of other writers who contributed to the new theory) were concerned with had become painfully obvious and were crying out for discussion'. She (p.24) also spoke of the new analysis as 'stressing market imperfection, oligopoly, deliberate product differentiation and selling costs'. And in 1953, in her counterpart to Chamberlin (1951), she stressed in a footnote that she could not understand the distinction Chamberlin made and she (1960, 1975, p.222) leaned over backwards to give credit to him:

> I should like to take this opportunity of saying that I have never been able to grasp the nature of the distinction between *imperfect* and *monopolistic* competition to which Professor Chamberlin attaches so much importance. (Cf. 'Monopolistic Competition Revisited', *Economica*, November 1951.) It appears to me that where we dealt with the same question, in our respective books, and made the same assumptions we reached the same results (errors and omissions excepted). When we dealt with different questions we naturally made different assumptions. In many respects Professor Chamberlin's assumptions were more interesting than mine, in particular in connection with oligopoly and with product differentiation as a dynamic process.

Fifteen years later in the preface to the second edition, Joan Robinson (1933, 1969, p.ix) again demonstrated exemplary self-criticism of the serious limitations of her argument:

> I did not attempt to tackle duopoly and oligopoly and, concentrating on price as the vehicle for competition, I said very little about non-price competition, such as artificial product-differentiation, advertising and sales promotion, which in fact accounts for the greatest part of the wastefulness of imperfect markets. The twin to my book, Chamberlin's *Monopolistic Competition*, opened up these subjects,

But she (pp.ix–x) was disappointed by his stand in subsequent controversies where he 'appeared to be more concerned to defend the market system than to expose its drawbacks'.[20] In her (1979a, p.156) view Chamberlin was reluctant 'to draw the conclusions that the market system cannot perform the function of an ideal allocation of resources when it is being manipulated by salesmanship'. It is an interesting twist of fate that Chamberlin, whose work was in the positive mould, introduced the problem of advertising as an element of imperfect markets, whereas Joan Robinson, whose work was couched in normative terms, and whose predisposition would have afforded her an opportunity to push the analysis much further, lacked the concept entirely (on Chamberlin see Kuenne, 1967, pp.251ff.)

More recently Joan Robinson (1979a, p.114) reflected on Chamberlin's one-sided controversy and on their twain purposes:

> My twin, Professor Chamberlin, spent many years protesting that his

'monopolistic competition' was quite different from my 'Imperfect Competition' (It used to be said at Harvard at one time that any student would be sure of getting a good degree by abusing Mrs. Robinson). This was partly, I think, due to human weakness. We had to share reviews and footnotes that Chamberlin would rather have had to himself. (The fact that I was quite bored with the subject annoyed him all the more.) But there was a deeper reason. I was delighted to find that I had proved (within the accepted assumptions) that it is not true to say that wages equal the marginal productivity of labour, while Chamberlin wanted to maintain that advertisement, salesmanship and monopolistic product differentiation in no way impaired the principle of consumer's sovereignty and the beneficial effect of the free play of market forces.

(In Chapter 2 of this volume, Samuelson – a student of Chamberlin – corroborates the first parenthetical statement in this quotation.)

The 'unnecessary controversy' was actually an ideological one – or, at least, this is how Joan Robinson (1978, p.x) saw it with a near-half-century perspective:

I had been very well pleased to refute the orthodox theory of wages, which had stuck in my gizzard as a student, while Chamberlin refused to admit that his argument damaged the image of the market producing the optimum allocation of given resources between alternative uses. This ideological difference underlay an otherwise unnecessary controversy.

4 IMPERFECT COMPETITION RECONSIDERED

In 1953,[21] after serving a short time on the Monopolies Commission, Joan Robinson (1960, 1975, p.xii) 'felt impelled to revisit imperfect competition'. She not only offered a searching criticism of her first *magnum opus*, but also an insightful perspective of the development in two decades. At the outset, she (1960, 1975, p.222) pointed an accusing finger at the formalism:

The Economics of Imperfect Competition was a scholastic book. It was directed to analysing the slogans of the text-books of twenty years ago: 'price tends to equal marginal cost' and 'wages equal the marginal product of labour'; and it treated of text-book questions, such as a comparison of the price and output of a commodity under conditions of monopoly and of competition, demand and costs being given. The assumptions which were adequate (or which I hope were adequate) for dealing with such questions are by no means a suitable basis for an analysis of the problems of prices, production and distribution which present themselves in reality.

She increasingly felt that the method she had used was flawed. In 1969, in a somewhat autobiographical mood, she (1973a, p.123) spoke of the neoclassical school as 'the dominant orthodoxy when I began to study economics in the twenties; I understand it very well – I even wrote a book in that style. It was a system of *a priori* argument. Choose assumptions and deduce conclusions from them. There was no attempt to check up with observations of what actually happens.' And in a later paper, she (1979a, p.114) faults the method in even stronger terms for starting 'the argument from a purely *a priori* set of assumptions' and then introducing 'a minor improvement in them instead of making a radical critique of the relationship between the traditional assumptions and the actual economy that they pretended to describe'. But she (p.114) does not consider the work altogether wasted, 'because, over the bridge of Kalecki's "degree of monopoly" it led on to the modern theory of the determination of profit margins and so was linked up with the theory of employment'.

Joan Robinson (1960, 1975, p.233–4) recalled that 'it was in connection with slump conditions that the imperfect-market analysis was evolved'. However, 'it now appears much too simple, and oligopoly, price leadership and a feeling for "playing the rules of the game" have to be brought in to supplement it'. As she saw it in 1974 (1979a, p.155), imperfect competition was an attempt 'to reconcile the principle of profit-maximization with under-capacity working' – an attempt criticized as unrealistic.

> The upshot of the debate was that strict profit maximizing is impossible in conditions of uncertainty, that prices of manufactures are generally formed by adding a margin to prime cost, which is calculated to cover overheads and yields a profit at less than capacity sales, and that an increase in capacity generally has to be accompanied by some kind of selling costs to ensure that it will be used at a remunerative level.

Although it was a product of the general dissatisfaction with *laissez-faire* policy during the slump, and was particularly meaningful in the context of the economic situation when the book appeared, the analysis was presented in terms that purported to be perfectly general.

More specifically Joan Robinson (1960, 1975, pp.222–38 and 240–4; 1933, 1969, pp.vi–xi; 1979, pp.112–14, 149–50, 156, 188) provided an intriguing retrospect on imperfect competition touching on the following topics: (1) industries and markets; (2) the entrepreneurs; (3) oligopoly and forms of competition; (4) price policy; (5) equilibrium and time; (6) the causes of monopoly; (7) the relationship between imperfect competition and the Keynesian revolution; and (8) the relevance of imperfect competition to contemporary capitalism.

(1) In her discussion of industries and markets, Joan Robinson (1960, 1975, pp.222–4) stressed how the assumption of the firm producing one commodity

slurs the distinction between the output of an industry and the market demand for commodities that are close substitutes for each other but are produced by different industries. An industry's degree of concentration is not necessarily related to market power. A number of small powerful monopolies over certain goods may exist in relatively unconcentrated industries, whereas highly concentrated ones may encounter competition in some or all of their products from substitutes produced by other industries. She felt that the scope of imperfect competition can be enlarged by relaxing the assumption of one-commodity firms (of course, at the cost of simplicity) and combining the treatment of polypoly in an imperfect market with that of price discrimination by a firm selling in various markets. For her (1960, 1975, pp.224–5):

The general moral of the *Economic of Imperfect Competition* which points to the rationalizing monopsonist as the best pilot to find a channel between the Scylla of competitive inefficiency and the Charybdis of monopolistic exploitation seems to remain valid when the assumption of one-commodity firms is dropped, though this is not the kind of proposition that can be established by geometry alone.

In her thirty-five year perspective, Joan Robinson (1933, 1969, p.xi) still criticises imperfect competition for the 'simplistic' conception of a one-commodity firm, but she also points to the changing situation with regard to multinational conglomerates:

Nowadays the definition of an industry is breaking down in another way. More and more, the great firms have a foot not only in many markets but in many industries, in several continents, the connections between their various activities being neither in know-how nor in marketing but merely in financial power.

In a longer version of an article written for the 1974 edition of the *Encyclopedia Britannica*, Joan Robinson (1979a, pp.149–50) describes the present-day imperfect market:

The market for manufactures is what economists call 'imperfect', because each company has its own style, its own reputation, and its own locations; and all of the arts of advertisement and salesmanship are devoted to making it even more perfect by attracting buyers to particular brand names. Even small businesses that depend upon the services of dealers have the final say in what prices they will charge, and great corporations can differentiate their goods in order to create demand for them.

In this type of market, supply normally is very elastic – that is, responsive to demand – in the short run. Stocks of inventories are held at some point in the chain of distribution; while stocks are running down or building up, there is time to change the level of production, and once a price has been set, it is rarely altered in response to moderate changes in demand. Even in a deep slump, defensive rings may often be formed to prevent price cutting.

(2) Joan Robinson (1960, 1975, p.225) criticized her (1933, 1969) treatment of the entrepreneur as 'extremely primitive'. Despite the bewildering array of modern forms of ownership and organization of firms, she sketched certain common characteristics such as the need for much cooperation and continuity. 'Industry, as opposed to commerce, could not have developed in an economy where the capitalists were all ruthlessly individualistic childless orphans.' A flourishing business is endowed with a certain personality like a college. Successive individuals identify with it and are loyal to it. Moreover, the interests of the casual shareholder (in search of short-run profit) are subordinated to those of management that succeeds as the business succeeds. Thus effectively (as distinct from legally) a public company much resembles a family business. Joan Robinson (1960, 1975, p.225) felt that 'for a first shot at a simple stylized analysis the most useful starting-point is still "the entrepreneur", regarded as the personification of a "firm" rather than as a particular individual in a pair of trousers'.

The entrepreneur's goal is the survival and growth of the firm. To achieve this, he pursues profit, but only to the extent that present action does not damage the firm's future position. She (p.226) is thus 'inclined to retort to those who grouse about the assumption that the entrepreneur's aim is to maximize profits in the immortal words of Old Bill: If you know a better 'ole, go to it'.

Joan Robinson (pp.226–7) was very skeptical about the notion of normal level of profit (though she searched for a theory of the profit rate) and was much more critical of the equilibrium size of the firm. She considered that they have very little application to reality. Imperfections of the capital market aside, and given time to accumulate capital out of profits and to acquire the necessary know-how and connections, 'there seems to be no limit to the ultimate size of the firm, until a condition of oligopoly is reached in each of the markets for the commodities supplied by the industry so that the last stages of the competitive struggle are too costly to be fought out'. And firms may well grow beyond that stage by crossing over into other or new industries (product lines) where they would not challenge too strong an opposition.

(3) Joan Robinson (1960, 1975, p.228; see also 1933, 1969, p.ix) confessed that she neglected oligopoly not because she thought it unimportant, but because she could not solve it: 'I tried to fence it off by means of what unfortunately was a fudge in the definition of the individual demand curve.'

She (p.228) enumerates many forms of competition such as product imitation, product differentiation (as regards quality that affects usefulness or pleasure but also as regards snob appeal and the like, and simply packaging), all kinds of services, advertising, pure salesmanship, higher price (to project the image of higher quality) and lower price. Joan Robinson (p.229) reveals a typical professional deformation (a hankering for the perfect market) in these words:

> The wastes of imperfect competition take many more forms besides sub-optimum scales of production, and the benefit of price competition, imposed by perfect markets (provided that it is not at the expense of wage rates), is in putting a premium on technical efficiency, as opposed to cunning salesmanship and strategic power, even more than in defending the consumer from exploitation.

(4) As soon as one recognizes that in the real world competition is never pure and perfect, one realizes that individual firms have great scope for varying their price policy and precise generalizations are not possible (Joan Robinson, 1979a, p.156). Joan Robinson (1960, 1975, pp.229–30) derides the lack of realism in the sketch of an entrepreneur attempting to find *à tâtonnement* the most profitable price for a commodity while cost and market conditions remain unaltered for the duration of the experiment. The entrepreneur is highly unlikely to change a price for the experiment's sake. He is even unlikely to increase the price when demand rises and usually waits for some 'justifiable' reason, such as an increase in costs. Moreover, he avoids overt price changes as much as possible, resorting to rebates and the like.

But, asks Joan Robinson, when price decisions have to be made, is the analysis of imperfect competition helpful? When a new product line is brought out the entrepreneur has some idea of the elasticity of demand; of what quantities he can sell at what prices. Sometimes he has an idea of what the 'right price' would be in view of the commodities already on the market. When asked how he sets prices, he retorts that he sets them according to costs, but obviously he does so taking into consideration demand conditions. Thus to think of the entrepreneur's decision as made on the basis of how he conceives the individual demand curve 'seems to be an over-formalization, rather than a totally misleading approach' (Joan Robinson 1960, 1975, p.231). Moreover, the span of time over which specific investment expenditures have to be recovered and the (uncertain) period of time during which the commodity will be marketable are crucial issues in pricing decisions.

Some firms produce fairly standard goods for which markets are more 'perfect' and specialties for which demand is more inelastic. In such cases, the profit margins on the latter are much higher than those on the former. This is often explained as an attempt to 'recover overheads', but it only means that the entrepreneur charges what the traffic will bear (p.231).

Imperfect competition has little to say about how an industry will respond when its labour and/or material costs arise. Here the oligopolistic element predominates. In such situations it is dangerous to take unconcerted action. Usually firms wait for the 'price leader' to take action. 'A price leader who is confident of the "good discipline" of his followers will be inclined to raise prices when costs go up and hold them up when costs go down' (p.232).

But there are many exceptions to this rule. For example, a strong leader who wishes to expand may not increase prices hoping to drive away weaker firms and take over their market share. Or when several strong firms are warring for supremacy, a decline in costs may precipitate a price war that may reduce prices even beyond the decline in costs.

When a firm's costs decline due to technical improvements, say, in the production of a low-cost substitute for an old commodity, it can either pass on the savings to the consumer (by adding to costs only the same profit margin that the firm earns on other lines) or price the new product in line with the old and earn a much higher profit margin. The latter action is particularly undetectable if the new commodity is protected by a patent, some secret know-how, or special scale economies.

In a seller's market (where even at high prices demand exceeds capacity), strong firms may choose to delay delivery rather than raise prices, promoting future goodwill. On the other hand, in more competitive situations (easy entry and large number of sellers) present moderation is no insurance of future gain. 'Thus, we find the apparently paradoxical phenomenon of the imperfection of competition keeping prices below the competitive level' (p.233).

In a buyer's market (where demand is declining) an oligopoly maintains prices. A firm that has a large share of the market is prevented from cutting prices by the knowledge that other firms will follow suit. In highly imperfect markets, prices will be maintained by the low elasticity of demand for specialties. In more competitive markets, prices will be maintained for no one wants to be the first to cut prices. Moreover, entrepreneurs will defend themselves from cutting prices in these situations by pointing to the increased average costs due to smaller production batches. They may even wish to raise prices, but usually they do not do so in view of the unfavorable demand conditions. 'In a prolonged slump, margins are cut sooner or later, unless there is a price agreement and it is usually said to be the high-cost producers who cut first, because they are threatened with bankruptcy unless they can increase sales somehow or other' (p.233).

Thirty-five years later, Joan Robinson's (1933, 1969, p.vii) realistic view of price setting centers on the gross margin (as a percentage of prime costs) to cover overheads, depreciation, and net profit. This can be calculated by estimating the sales from given capacity and evaluating what net profits may be expected, that is, what the traffic will bear. Realistically, she does not expect businessmen to draw her curves, 'but it is perfectly sensible to say that the "degree of monopoly" is higher, or price policy less competitive, when the producer, in setting his margin, calculates upon a lower level of utilisation of plant and upon a higher rate of profit on capital'.

In her view (1933, 1969, pp.vii–viii) nowadays the concept of perfect competition is not only completely inappropriate to manufacturing; she doubts that it is even appropriate to fish (to use Marshall's example). 'The prices of manufactures in the nature of the case are administered prices.' (see also 1956, 1966, pp.181–88). As long as costs do not change, prices usually do not vary with short-run alterations in demand. Output does, and so does the per unit overhead, and hence the share of net profit. Even in a seller's market, firms refrain from raising prices, preferring to ration or delay sales, in order not to choke off demand. Thus, prices remain virtually unaffected while profits are very much influenced by movements in demand.

One of the post-war 'rebellions' against the 'old orthodoxy' was the development of the full-cost principle (see, e.g., Andrews 1949). It negated the existence of the individual demand curve as a figment of the economist's imagination, unknown to the seller. Rather than maximizing profit, the businessman sets prices to cover costs plus a 'reasonable' rate of return on the investment. In Joan Robinson's (1960, 1975, p.242) view, 'as a protest against the extreme formalism of the imperfect competition analysis (especially my version of it) this is certainly salutary'. She found the full-cost principle appealing in its subversion of the 'old orthodoxy', as it strikes at the very heart of that system by denying the profit-maximization assumption. However, the theorist in her (p.243) was dissatisfied.

It leaves us in a state of perfect nescientness – anything may happen. The moral seems to be that the approach to price theory through individual decisions will never lead to fruitful generalizations, and that it would be better to tackle the problem of the behaviour of proft margins in the economy as a whole through over-all statistics of costs, prices and the share of wages in the value of output.

(5) 'In my opinion, the greatest weakness of the *Economics of Imperfect Competition* is one which it shares with the class of economic theory to which it belongs – the failure to deal with time' (Joan Robinson, 1960, 1975, p.234). The static analysis in that book is 'a shameless fudge – one that confuses comparisons of possible alternative equilibrium positions with the analysis of a process going on through time. Nowhere in the book is there a clear distinction between the relationships of long and short periods or between the future and the past. However, she (1978, p.x) noted that she 'avoided the horrible neoclassical methodology of drawing a plane diagram showing a timeless relation between two variables and then moving about on it'.

I postulated that a firm could find out the conditions of demand for its product by trial and error – that is, I treated the conditions of demand as being unchanged for an indefinitely long period and I assumed that experiments with prices would leave no traces in market conditions. The whole analysis, which in reality consists of comparisons of static equilibrium positions, is dressed up to appear to represent a process going on through time. (Joan Robinson, 1933, 1969, p.vi see also 1979a, p.112)

A movement of price, rate of output, wage, and the like takes place through time; the positions at any point of time depend on what they were in the past.

The point is not merely that any adjustment takes a certain time to complete and that (as has always been admitted) events may occur meanwhile which alter the position, so that the equilibrium towards which the system is said to be *tending* itself moves before it can be reached. The point is that the very process of moving has an effect upon the destination of the movement, so that there is no such thing as a position of long-run equilibrium which exists independently of the course which the economy is following at a particular date. (Joan Robinson, 1960, 1975, p.234)

Unlike the textbook examples of continuous small-step investment, in real life when there is a rise in demand for certain commodities, a number of firms producing them make investment plans and carry them out at the same time; that is, while profits are high. There is then an abrupt expansion of capacity followed by a sharp decline in profitability. Several years down the road the rate of profit in that industry will be lower than it would have been had the demand expansion not taken place. The situation is similar in regard to the wage and the age composition of the labor force. Thus all kinds of long-run supply curves have to be considered as irreversible and the concept of the two-dimensional, long-run supply curve goes overboard. 'This kind of difficulty underlies all problems connected with prices, profits and wages, and there seems to be little point in adding more and more subtleties to the superstructure of a theory which is based upon such shaky foundations' (Joan Robinson, 1960, 1975, p.235).

In the preface to the second edition, Joan Robinson (1933, 1969, pp.vi–vii) suggests that the argument can be recast in dynamic analysis by distinguishing between the short-run (price policy and capacity utilization) and the long-run (investment) aspects of competition.

(6) Though the causes of monopoly have been empirically documented, their analytical treatment is weak. One of the primary causes is competition which drives firms to expand and drives the stronger to swallow up the weaker.

An industry which is strongly competitive must be in the course of tending towards a condition of oligopoly; competition can be permanent only when it is hampered by highly imperfect markets or softened by a spirit of live and let live among the entrepreneurs concerned. (Joan Robinson, 1960, 1975, p.236)

(Also monopoly (or strong oligopoly) at one stage of the industrial structure promotes competition at the other.) Monopolization is also fostered when the abrupt expansion of capacity overshoots demand.

In a buyer's market profit margins may not be kept sufficiently high by imperfect competition discipline of price followers, or loyalty to the average cost principle. Driven by the fear of extinction, firms enter into price agreements–agreements that may be eroded by outside competition when prosperity returns, but may well persist for a very long time. Monopolies are particularly easy to form where the boundaries of the industry coincide with those of the market, such as minerals, specialized machinery and other specialized commodities where the scope for product differentiation is minimal and demand fairly inelastic. Once a monopoly is formed, in cases where either supply is circumscribed by natural resources, or scale economies are important, or know-how is very specialized, it is likely to persist.

A monopolistic price policy cannot be generally associated with a cautious investment policy that limits growth of capacity in relation to demand. For example, the firms that make the highest monopolistic profits are often those that grow most rapidly. In the US the showplaces of industry are among the least competitive industrial giants.

Competition is always in course of bringing itself to an end. At any moment, in prosperous modern industries, the number of firms is tending to fall and competition is becoming more oligopolistic. My old-fashioned comparison between monopoly and competition may still have some application to old-fashioned restrictive rings but it cannot comprehend the great octopuses of modern industry. (Joan Robinson, 1933, 1969, p.ix)

In Joan Robinson's view (1960, 1975, p.242), Galbraith (1952, 1956) finds perfect competition non-existent in reality for competition results in oligopoly as the winners expand and the losers disappear. Price cutting becomes rare where there are few firms aware of each other's reactions. The competitive effort is then geared towards cost cutting – a further incentive to technical progress. Competition also takes the form of advertising and other selling expenditures. Each oligopolist's advertising and selling expenditures escalate because those of others do, 'like military expenditure by rival nations in an arms race' (p.244). One of the reasons why national income is an inadequate measure of national welfare under modern conditions is that 'an appreciable proportion of it is made up of the "service" of persuading consumers to buy' (p.244).

Galbraith (p.102) admits that advertising and salesmanship may be a waste, 'but it is waste that exists because the community is too well-off to care'. Joan Robinson (p.244) objects that this 'inescapable concomitant of the productive efficiency of the oligopolistic economy' must not be the pattern followed by less wealthy economies than the US.

(7) Experience has borne out the Keynesian idea that the general price level moves more or less proportionately to the level of wage rates. There is a tendency to link this with imperfect competition for if producers were competitive they could not pass on a cost increase to consumers. But, Joan Robinson (1933, 1969, p.viii) retorts, if perfect competition (with prices equal to marginal costs) did exist, the movement would be automatic; increasing money wages would push the marginal cost curves proportionately upwards. Imperfect competition, on the other hand, injects an element of judgment into price policy; sometimes prices move more and sometimes less than proportionately to costs depending on the economic situation.

What Joan Robinson calls orthodox economic theory (pre-1930s) stated that any factory that is working at all is working at full capacity. In the slump, however, most plants were underutilized while prices did not decline. Profit margins were maintained even though marginal cost was no larger than average prime costs. She and others used the marginal revenue concept to explain this phenomenon but Keynes did not. (Instead he used the rather infelicitous concept of user cost to reconcile competition with the fact that a profit margin was part of the supply price even in a depression.) (See Joan Robinson, 1979a, p.158.)

In the 1930s the main thrust against the citadel of orthodoxy came from Keynes's *General Theory*. Joan Robinson (1960, 1975, p. 241) stresses that 'the theory of employment was, of course, far more important, both for analysis and for policy, than anything concerned with the theory of individual prices'.

As we show in Chapter 1 of the companion volume, Keynes was rather uninterested in price theory, but the two streams of thought were merged by Kalecki who showed how effective demand and the employment level are affected by the determination of the gross profit margin – the key to distribution of the product between wages and profits. Twenty-five years later Joan Robinson (1960, 1975, p.241) perceived that the Kaleckian analysis very much enhanced the analysis of imperfect competition: 'what began with Sraffa's objection to the lack of logic in orthodox economic theory and Professor Chamberlin's objection to its lack of realism opened up into a general indictment of the operations of the economic system itself'.

Though, as we know, her analysis of imperfect competition was stimulated by the British slump of the 1920s and she was a fully fledged member of Keynes's Circus, Joan Robinson (1933, 1969, p.viii) acknowledges that

it was Michal Kalecki rather than I who brought imperfect competition into touch with the theory of employment. He showed that a rise in profit margins, such as may come about by defensive monopolistic agreements in a slump, reduces real wages and so tends to increase unemployment. He also established the very striking proposition that a rise in margins increases the share of profit in the value of output only by reducing the share of wages. The total of profit over a period of time is not likely to be increased by it. Overall expenditure is not raised immediately, so that the main effect of raising prices is to sell less goods for more or less the same total receipts.

Applying this type of analysis she (1960, 1975, p.243) perceives under imperfect competition wages to be below marginal productivity and trade unions as 'necessary to reduce the imperfection of the labour market and bring it somewhat nearer to the competitive ideal'. Accordingly, in view of growing productivity with technical progress, 'the workers do better by accepting a given share in a growing total than they could do by securing a larger share in a total which, for that very reason, would be growing less fast'. The worker's pressure to raise money-wage rates is salutary to the system. As price competition is avoided in oligopolistic situations, with constant money-wage rates, given technical progress, costs would decline continually. The share of profits in national income would increase and that of wages decline. Aggregate demand would then not grow sufficiently quickly to absorb the increased output due to increased productivity. Thus, 'the upward pressure of money-wage rates checking this growth of margins is necessary in order to keep the share of wages more or less constant, and to prevent the oligopolists from frustrating themselves' (pp. 243–4).

(8) Twenty-five years after the publication of *The Economics of Imperfect Competition*, Joan Robinson (1960, 1975, pp.237–8) felt that

> a great deal of mental energy has been devoted to a theological discussion whether an existing state of imperfect (or impure) competition is (a) beneficial, (b) harmless, (c) a necessary evil or (d) an unnecessary evil, while an analysis (as opposed to historical studies) of the causes and consequences of the process of survival or decline of competition has hardly begun.

And with an additional fifteen-year perspective she (1933, 1969, p.xi) was appalled that some of the weaknesses of imperfect competition have been frozen into orthodox teaching; while its negative strong points (of which she particularly stresses three) were relatively neglected. To wit, firstly, by demonstrating the pervasiveness of imperfect competition in manufacturing, the analysis debunks the complex of ideas surrounding the concept of small variations of demand eliciting price changes in the short run (as it does in raw materials markets). Secondly, 'it draws the moral' that 'consumer's sovereignty can never be established as long as the initiative lies with the producer' (pp.xi–xii). 'Finally, what for me was the main point, I succeeded in proving within the framework of the orthodox theory, that it is not true that wages are normally equal to the value of the marginal product of labour' (p.xii).

To Joan Robinson (1960, 1975, p.xii) the theory of imperfect competition did not seem to have grown much during the twenty years she had been away: 'Micro-theory was rather left out of the Keynesian revolution and it was in need of a revolution of its own.' And forty years after, she (p.xii) saw great strides made in the study of business behavior, of the effects of uncertainty of expectations, of price setting, and of financial organization, 'while theory appears to have relapsed right back into perfect competition and correct foresight'. 'Perfect competition, supply and demand, consumer's sovereignty and marginal products still reign supreme in orthodox teaching' (Joan Robinson, 1933, 1969, p.xii). She (1979a, p.156) emphasized again and again that modern 'textbook teaching often seeks refuge in the illusory simplicity of conditions of perfect competition, correct foresight and general equilibrium in the markets for commodities and factors of production'.

But all is not so glum as Joan Robinson sees it. Samuelson (1972, p.51) observes that 'Chamberlin, Sraffa, Robinson, and their contemporaries have led economists into a new land from which their critics will never evict us'. He (p.21) is convinced that 'perfect competition provides an empirically inadequate model of the real world. This forces us to work with some versions of monopolistic or imperfect competition. Chicago economists can continue to shout until they are blue in the face that there is no elegant alternative to the theory of perfect competition'. If that is so, 'so much the worse for elegance', says Samuelson. And practicing the art of self-criticism, he (p.22) goes on to admit that 'we theorists, quite removed from Cook County, have retrogressed in the last quarter century, taking the coward's way of avoiding the important questions thrown up by the real economic world and fobbing off in their place nice answers to less interesting easy questions'.

Of course, Samuelson's quip about Cook county refers to his alma mater, the University of Chicago. There monopolistic (imperfect) competition came under strong attack. Alas, this is not the place to elaborate on and refute the criticism. Suffice to say that it was directed at the fact that imperfect competition is empirically empty in the Popperian sense; that the set of falsifiable predictions it gives us is meager. This is reflected in the paucity of formal empirical tests of imperfect competition theory. In contrast, they claim, perfect competition theory, when amended for contracts, rational expectations, and the like, generates a rich set of falsifiable predictions.[22]

Marshall's teaching was not only retrogressive for the theory of imperfect competition, it also inadvertently delayed the understanding of general equilibrium. It was only after World War II that economists – at least in the Anglo-Saxon world – began to think in terms of general equilibrium. Samuelson (p.26) believes that 'this represents an advance in logical clarity but something of a retreat in terms of realistic appraisal of actual imperfectly competitive markets'.

Triffin (1940) was one of the first to propel imperfect competition on to the path of general equilibrium theory.[23] For a long time this direction did not seem to lead very far. Despite a number of notable contributions beginning in the 1960s, progress has been disappointing (see Hart, 1985). One of the foremost makers of modern general equilibrium theory, Kenneth Arrow, feels strongly about the need to incorporate imperfect competition into the framework of general equilibrium theory. Not only does he remind us constantly of this lacuna, but he is at the forefront in attempting to go some way towards rectifying this unpalatable situation (see Feiwel 1987, pp.53–5). Certain most recent accomplishments in this direction are some of the contributions in Parts I–V of the companion volume.

5 THE KEYNESIAN REVOLUTION

Joan Robinson (1960, 1975, p.1) contrasted the attitudes of Marx, Marshall, and Keynes towards capitalism. Oversimplifying, Marx was the revolutionary socialist who tried to explain the system in order to destroy it. Marshall was the complacent defender of capitalism who tried to make it palatable by presenting the system in an agreeable light. Keynes was the disillusioned defender of capitalism who analyzed the system's failure in order to find the means to save it from self-destruction.

Further, she (p.12) warned that it is foolish to refuse to learn from an economist whose ideology one disapproves. It is equally imprudent to adopt the theories of another whose ideologies one favors. For economic theory is at best only a hypothesis. It merely suggests plausible explanations of some economic happening. It cannot be considered correct until confronted with facts. The task of the disciple of a great economist is not to propagandize his doctrine, but to test his hypothesis. If the hypothesis is disproved it must be rejected. It is of no use to choose a hypothesis by the color of the economist who puts it forward and then to reject the facts that do not agree with it.

As we know, when Joan began to study economics, Alfred Marshall was the dominant figure. He was a subtle analyst who dwelt on exceptions to every rule, but his docrines were usually interpreted as supporting *laissez-faire* and rejecting government intervention as being more of a bane than a benefit.

Economic theory drew a very flattering picture of the private-enterprise system. It was depicted as a beautiful machine with delicately-balanced interacting parts and with a self-righting mechanism that ensured that it kept itself in balance. Full employment of labour was regarded as a normal state of affairs and stability in the value of money taken for granted. Equilibrium in international trade only required the abolition of tariffs and the maintenance of the gold standard. Any departure of actual developments from the ideal equilibrium was regarded as due to frictions which the operation of the machine would overcome for itself, or were attributed to the stupid interference of governments which were often foolish enough to depart from the strict rule of *laissez-faire*. (Joan Robinson, 1960, 1975, p.271)

For Joan Robinson all that is the old orthodoxy, represented in the (in)famous White Paper of 1929 – the view of the Treasury held by Marshall's pupils who were then making policy. The old orthodoxy is also rooted in the (in)famous Say's Law of the Market – so blatantly disproved by the traumatic Great Depression. The old orthodoxy is the 'natural tendency to the establishment of equilibrium with full employment' (1979a, p.57). But in England there was massive unemployment even before the world depression set in. Academic teaching, however, was by and large oblivious of the problems of shocking reality. 'The Marxists abused the academics, but they shared their belief in the principles of sound finance. In this fog Keynes was groping for a theory of employment' (Joan Robinson, 1965, 1975, p.92).

Though theoretically unarmed Keynes's basic vision of the capitalist economy could already be discerned in the *Consequences*.[24] This vision was crystallized in an informal 1934 BBC discussion that appeared in *The Listener* (Keynes 1973a, pp.485–92) of which some excerpts are very enlightening:[25]

On the one side are those who believe that the existing economic system is, in the long run, a self-adjusting system, though with creaks and groans and jerks, and interrupted by time lags, outside interference and mistakes . . . These authorities do not, of course, believe that the system is automatically or immediately self-adjusting. But they do believe that it has an inherent tendency towards self-adjustment, if it is not interfered with and if the action of change and chance is not too rapid.

On the other side of the gulf are those who reject the idea that the existing economic system is, in any significant sense, self-adjusting. They believe that the failure of effective demand to reach the full potentialities of supply . . . is due to much more fundamental causes (p.486–7).

The strength of the self-adjusting school depends on its having behind it almost the whole body of organized economic thinking and doctrine of the last hundred years. This is a formidable power (p.488).

Now *I* range myself with the heretics. I believe their flair and their instinct move them towards the right conclusion. But I was brought up in the citadel and I recognise its power and might. A large part of the established body of economic doctrine I cannot but accept as broadly correct. I do not doubt it. For me, therefore, it is impossible to rest satisfied until I can put my finger on the flaw in that part of the orthodox reasoning which leads to the conclusions which for various reasons seem to me to be inacceptable. I believe that I am on my way to do so. There is, I am convinced, a fatal flaw in that part of the orthodox reasoning which deals with the theory of what determines the level of effective demand and the volume of aggregate employment; the flaw being largely due to the failure of the classical doctrine to develop a satisfactory theory of the rate of interest (p.489).

Now the school which believes in self-adjustment is, in fact, assuming that the rate of interest adjusts itself more or less automatically, so as to encourage just the right amount of production of capital goods to keep our incomes at the maximum level which our energies and our organization and our knowledge of how to produce efficiently are capable of providing. This is, however, pure assumption. There is no theoretical reason for believing it to be true (p.490).

Even as things are, there is a strong presumption that a greater equality of incomes would lead to increased employment and greater aggregate income ... At present, it is important to maintain a careful balance between stimulating consumption and stimulating investment ... The right course is to get rid of the scarcity of capital goods – which will rid us at the same time of most of the evils of capitalism – whilst also moving in the direction of increasing the share of income falling to those whose economic welfare will gain most by their having the chance to consume more.
    None of this, however, will happen by itself or of its own accord. The system is not self-adjusting, and, without purposive direction, it is incapable of translating our actual poverty into our potential plenty (p.491).

In the book that was the Magna Carta of the Keynesian revolution, Keynes (1936, p.249) depicted his contemporary capitalist economy:

In particular, it is an outstanding characteristic of the economic system in which we live that, whilst it is subject to severe fluctuations in respect of output and employment, it is not violently unstable. Indeed it seems capable of remaining in a chronic condition of sub-normal activity for a considerable period without any marked tendency either towards recovery or towards complete collapse.

Whatever else needs to be said about the Keynesian revolution in macroeconomics and monetary theory and its various interpretations,[26] it undermined the myth that full employment is the normal state of the economy. It focused on the seriousness of the macroeconomic failure of the system, on the sources of real disturbances, and on the opportunities for improvement. It stressed effective demand as a central problem, variously interpreted as the possibility of underemployment equilibrium with involuntary unemployment in which the economy can get stuck for a long time or persisting disequilibrium which conventional economic analysis found so awkward to accommodate. It pointed to the fallacies of the classical saving–investment–interest rate mechanism and the doctrine of full employment via flexible wages and prices and to the classical policy prescriptions in general.

The Keynesian revolution means different things to different people (see Chapter 1 of the companion volume). In the standard mainstream interpretation it refers to the impact of the theory of the determination of the level of aggregate output and employment. It underscores the dependence and impact of the level of effective demand on the degree of utilization of labor and capacity. It provides the analytical innovation of the consumption function. It focuses on expectations in an uncertain world in general and on marginal efficiency of investment and speculative liquidity preference in particular. It cogently distinguishes between the acts of saving and investment and the problems of finding offsets to saving. It emphasizes, *inter alia*, the fluctuations in total investment demand (and its dependence on shifts in expected profitability, which in turn depends on fairly unpredictable and subjective psychology, and is beneficially influenced by a reduction of uncertainty about the future when the economy is steadily working in high gear) as a source of macroeconomic instability.

As Keynes (1936, p.viii) stressed in the preface, the writing of the *General Theory* had been for him 'a long struggle to escape from habitual modes of thought and expression'. The difficulty in comprehending the argument lies not in the novelty of the ideas, which in themselves are quite simple, but in escaping from the traditional ones 'which ramify for those brought up as most of us have been, into every corner of our minds'.

In the opening page, Keynes (1936, p.3) argued that the postulates of (neo)classical (Pigovian) theory are applicable merely to a special case only and not to the general case as the postulates this theory assumes are a limiting point of the possible positions of equilibrium. In the preface to the 1939 French edition, Keynes noted that he called his book a general theory because he was mainly concerned with the aggregate behavior of the economic system. He argued that fundamental errors have been committed by extending to the aggregate conclusions correctly arrived at with reference to only an isolated part of the whole (see Kahn 1984, p.121).

As we know, Joan Robinson played a major role in the Circus where the ideas of the *General Theory* were thrashed out before they were written. She was also a major participant in its explication, reinterpretation, extension, and generalization. Her roles as contributor, interpreter, critic, and innovator of this historical achievement are inextricably intertwined. They are reflected in all of her post-General Theory work and only partly in the often fascinating correspondence of Keynes that has survived and been preserved in Keynes's Collected Works. In final analysis, it is not important what particular idea originated with her or what her specific contribution was, even if it could be detected. It was the unique opportunity of participating in this great creative effort and the circumstances of the time that affected her life. Whether what in later years she saw in Keynes was always there, and whatever the other influences at work (as pointed in Chapter 1 of the companion volume), she remained a great Keynesian for the rest of her life, not necessarily in any narrow, specific sense of the term, but in the spirit Shackle (1966, p.14) captured with such felicity.

There is a time, perhaps more than one, in the history of every science when it has its *mystique*: an idea, surprising, vaguely hinting at enormous powers of explanation, and far from being fully understood, takes command of some men's thought and imagination, and is followed to the stars. It is for these men a time of great happiness, a time filled with a sense of purpose, of conquest, of being members of a small *élite*, a time of achievement past and promised, of great prestige and a feeling of being borne upon irresistible waters of success. Such a time in England was the 1930s for those who had any share, however humble, in the Keynesian liberation. Whether a man was himself a liberator or a young convert whose feet were scarcely yet entangled in the classical net and was unknowingly eager for release, the time was magical.

Keynes's *Treatise* (1930) was barely published when he began rethinking his ideas and moving in a new direction.[27] A group of young economists (Richard Kahn, James Meade, Joan and Austin Robinson, and Piero Sraffa), known as the Circus, began to meet to discuss the basic issues. So little of their discussions has survived in written form that some economists disparage the importance of these discussions in clarifying Keynes's ideas and helping him write the *General Theory*. Kahn (the chief spokesman, or as Meade called him the 'Messenger Angel', for the Circus in its relations with Keynes) feels he should not enter into personal controversy because 'it would be unseemly to appear to be making a case for my friends and myself'. And he (1984, p.105) adds: 'Don Patinkin disputes the importance commonly attributed to us in assisting Keynes to write the *General Theory*. In so far as he relies on documents, he is fully entitled to make his case.' (Fortunately, in the last decade or so the members of the Circus have got together and written up their reminiscences of that glorious time (see Keynes, 1973, pp.337–43) and separate accounts have also appeared (see Kahn, 1984, pp.105–11; Joan Robinson, 1978, pp.xi–xvi; Joan Robinson (n.d.); A. Robinson, 1977; Kahn, 1985; A. Robinson, 1985).) In this connection, Austin Robinson's (1985, pp.53–4) comments are very much to the point:

There is no record, unfortunately, of what we talked about. Don Patinkin likes to think that if there is not a record on paper of something it cannot have happened. I do not happen to agree with that view myself. I think that Richard Kahn's memories, my own memories and the collective memories of all of us are worth something in the way of evidence. We did not *then* feel any need for there to be the establishment of evidence. For I think one thing that the present generation forgets is that private property in ideas was only invented with the Ph.D. In 1931 we were considerably more interested in truth than we were in establishing property rights in ideas. I think Richard Kahn will agree with me that some of the ideas that were fed to Maynard by Joan or by him may have come from Kahn himself or from Joan herself. They may have come from Piero. They may have come from James Meade. They may have come from any of the five of us individually or collectively. The amanuensis of our collective thinking was not necessarily the author of the particular idea.

To the question of who provided the ingredients of the *General Theory*, Sir Austin (p.57) answers:

I think the Circus put together *some* of the ingredients. But many of the ingredients were there already and Keynes was aware of them. He only had to be reminded of them. It was not we who created the ingredients. We reminded him that he could not build a satisfactory theory *unless* these ingredients were included. That is where I believe we made our contribution.

Kahn (1985, pp.43–4) recalls that in writing the *General Theory* Keynes was in a hurry and relied on the Circus for theoretical scrutiny and substantiation:

To secure conviction, he relied on sincerity and commonsense. He could display his skill at advocacy without arousing the resentment displayed by many of his academic colleagues. When it came to the more precise logic of the *General Theory* he had to demand from his readers the abandonment of firmly ingrained theoretical ideas. Keynes, the propagandist, was always forging ahead of the author of theoretical works. Indeed it was his zest as a reformer that set the pace for the writing of the *General Theory*.

Keynes's attitude towards the Circus is well described by Kahn (1985, p.49) who wonders at the magnanimity with which Keynes received his regular weekly reports of Circus debates, doubts, and tentative conclusions:

Keynes might well, had he been a lesser man, have been unreceptive. He was in fact the very opposite. He picked up our ideas, incorporated them in his own thinking and went ahead. And he asked me to take suggestions for further discussion back to the Circus. But it did not occur to any of us that we were doing more than adding glosses and embroideries to Keynes's work. Any further advance was made by Keynes.

Joan Robinson (1978, p.xi) recalled that from early 1931 until the completion of the *General Theory* 'I was involved, along with Kahn, in a continuous series of discussions, writings, lectures and correspondence around the development of Keynes' ideas'. She also admitted that Sraffa was secretly skeptical about the new ideas. She (pp.xi–xvi and n.d.) recorded that among the main topics discussed by the Circus was the elasticity of output in response to changes in demand. They were trying to convince Keynes that his theory was concerned with the analysis of 'output as a whole' She recalled (n.d., p.4) that an important step was 'the recognition that there could be a self-sustaining short-period equilibrium at *any* level of employment and Kahn's suggestion of drawing cordons round the investment and the consumption goods industries and studying the interchange between them (of course, none of us had heard of Marx's schema of expanded reproduction. Certainly, the English Marxists were no help; they were the stoutest defenders of "sound finance" that we had to contend with.)'

She (1978, pp.xii–xiii) recorded that among the topics discussed by the Circus was Austin Robinson's point about the fallacy of the widow's cruse under unemployment. (See Chapter 1 of the companion volume.) 'This was the first step from the theory of money to the analysis of output' described in her 1933 article on money and output (see 1978, pp.14–19). Another topic was modification of the definitions in the *Treatise* and clarifications of some confusions between accounting identities and causal relationships. Other topics included normal profits and the 'buckets-in-a-well' fallacy and confusion between a flow of income and stock of wealth. In her reading of *Collected Writings of John Maynard Keynes* she (1979a, p.170) commented on the upheavals and reformulations that led away from the *Treatise* to the *General Theory* and noted that there were 'moments when we had some trouble in getting Maynard to see what the point of his revolution really was'. In the end, however, when he summarized his views in 1937 in his reply to Taussig, Leontief, Robertson and Viner (Keynes, 1973b, pp.109–23) he got the point into focus.

On the question of Keynes's acknowledgment of the Circus' (and particularly Kahn's) inputs into the making of the *General Theory*, Joan Robinson (n.d., p.5) mused that at the time the members of the Circus did not think in terms of attributions. 'Keynes, and all of us, thought that it was of great and serious importance to get the argument right; taking credit for it was quite a secondary matter'. And she added: 'working with Keynes, though he could be exasperating at times, was an exhilarating experience. The profession nowadays is flat and tedious by comparison'.

Joan Robinson (1978, p.xiv) described the atmosphere in Cambridge at the time:

In the days following the meetings of the circus, there was a clear distinction between those who had seen the point and those who had not. Austin Robinson said that we went about asking: Brother are you saved?

And there were those who were not 'saved'.

Dennis Robertson was sarcastic about the circus, and came to only one meeting. He had an ambivalent attitude to Keynes, who had been a close friend. He admired Maynard's intellectual daring and yet was frightened by it. He clung to old doctrines, such as that a cut in wages must necessarily increase employment, and he kept up a running fire of criticisms, some of which were useful, though on peripheral points.
        As the argument went on, he became embittered. He tried to prevent me from expounding the new theory in my lectures (but Pigou ruled in favour of free speech). Lord Robbins . . . and others have drawn a pathetic picture of Dennis, but it was Keynes who was grieved by his hostility. After Keynes' death when Robertson had returned to Cambridge as Pigou's successor, he created a lasting schism in the faculty by trying to re-schedule the syllabus so that Keynes' theory could not be taught (if at all) before the final year.[28]

Joan Robinson's interpretation of the *General Theory* has shifted in time. Increasingly in the post-war period it has become more Kaleckian than Keynesian (as we show in Chapter 1 of the companion volume), consciously or unconsciously. In final analysis it matters little, for her interpretation and extensions have the Robinsonian flavor. Here we shall briefly and selectively illustrate her perception of the Keynesian revolution (staying away as much as possible from Kaleckian overtones).

Keynes had cleared the way for a new approach. He broke down the old dichotomy between *Principles* and *Money*, treating the financial system as part of the general functioning of the economy. He observed that, because prediction of the future is necessarily uncertain, behaviour affecting economic life (or private life, for that matter) cannot be governed by strictly rational calculations of the outcome. He pointed out that accumulation depends upon decisions about investment taken by business firms and governments, not by decisions about savings taken by households, and he drew a clear distinction (which was confused in the old orthodoxy) between interest, as the price that a businessman pays for the use of finance to be committed to an investment, and profit, which is the return that he hopes to get on it. He pointed out that wage rates are settled in terms of money and the level of real wages depends upon the operation of the economy as a whole. All this cleared the ground for a model appropriate to modern capitalism, but Keynes' own construction was confined to dealing with short-period analysis. (Joan Robinson, 1979a, p.59)

Keynes's model was constructed to tackle the causes and consequences of the variations in the rate of employment and utilization of existing capacity taking place with fluctuation of effective demand. Keynes recognized that in a capitalist economy the price level is primarily governed by the level of money wages, with far-reaching implications for the post-war economies. Keynes took it for granted that in a modern capitalist economy wages are set in terms of money. He 'brought the argument down from the cloudy realms of timeless equilibrium to here and now, with an irrevocable past, facing an uncertain future'. In a monetary economy, money enters the argument as the proverbial link between the present and the future. The *General Theory* is a monetary theory 'only in the sense that relationships and institutions concerned with money, credit, and finance are necessary elements in the "real" economy with which it is concerned' (Joan Robinson, 1971, pp.89–90).

Joan Robinson (1979a, p.170) emphasized that on the plane of economic theory 'the revolution lay in the change from the conception of equilibrium to the conception of history; from the principles of rational choice to the problems of decisions based on guess-work or on convention'. She reinterpreted Keynes with her own views of time, history, and uncertainty. To a student of modern mathematical economics this has the flavor of the imperfect information revolution and bounded rationality.

For Joan Robinson (1979a, p.210) the expression 'post-Keynesian' applies to a mode of analysis that takes into account the difference between the future and the past. She (1978, p.x) perceived Keynes as instinctively recognizing 'the nature of historical time in which today is an ever-moving break between the irrevocable past and the unknown future', but he did not articulate this point until after the publication of the *General Theory*. 'Once we admit that an economy exists in time, that history goes one way, from the irrevocable past into the unknown future, the conception of equilibrium based on the mechanical analogy of a pendulum swinging to and fro in space becomes untenable. The whole of traditional economics needs to be thought out afresh' (Joan Robinson, 1979a, p.172).

But what has become of Keynes? Joan Robinson (pp.172–3), the critic of modern economics, strongly disagreed with the mainstream merger of Keynesian and neoclassical economics (see Part VI of the companion volume):

After the war, Keynes' theory was accepted as a new orthodoxy without the old one being rethought. In modern text-books, the pendulum still swings, *tending* towards its equilibrium point. Market forces allocate given factors of production between alternative uses, investment is a sacrifice of present consumption, and the rate of interest measures society's discount of the future. All the slogans are repeated unchanged.

How has this trick been worked? First of all, simplifications in Keynes' own exposition, which were necessary at the first stage of the argument, have been used to smooth the meaning out of it. Keynes sometimes talked of total output at full employment as though it was a simple quantity. Obviously, the maximum output that can be produced in a given situation depends on the productive capacity in existence of plant and equipment for labour to be employed with, and productive capacity exists in concrete forms available for producing particular kinds of output. The notion of 'the level of investment that will ensure full employment' presupposes the existence of productive capacity for investment and consumption goods in the right proportions.

Moreover, it presupposes a particular ratio of consumption to investment. But the level of consumption from a given total income depends upon its distribution between consumers, and this depends on the distribution of wealth among households, the ratio of profits to wages, relative prices of commodities and the system of taxation.

All this is ignored in the vulgarized version of Keynes' theory. At any moment, the text-book argument runs, there is a certain amount of saving per annum that would occur at full employment. Let the government see to it that there is enough investment to absorb that amount and then all will be well.

So we return to the classical world where accumulation is determined by saving and the old theory slips back into place. But here there is a difficulty. Investment every year is to be just enough to absorb the year's savings. What about the new equipment that it creates? Will that be just enough to employ the labour then available, when investment is absorbing saving next year? The long period aspect of investment, that it creates capital goods, must be considered as well as the short-period aspect that it keeps up effective demand.

And, with a hint to the capital controversies (discussed in Section 7), she (p.173) continues:

Never mind! Never mind! cry the bastard Keynesians. We can pretend that capital goods are all made of putty. They can be squeezed up or spread out, without trouble or cost, to give whatever amount of employment is required. Moreover, there is no need to worry about mistaken investments or about technical change. Not only the putty added this year, but the whole lot, can be squeezed into any form that is needed so as to re-establish equilibrium instantaneously after any change.

There has been a lot of tiresome controversy over this putty. The bastard Keynesians try to make out that it is all about the problem of 'measuring capital'. But it has nothing to do either with measurement or with capital; it has to do with abolishing time. For a world that is always in equilibrium there is no difference between the future and the past, there is no history and there is no need for Keynes.

Joan Robinson's initial criticism was aimed at Hicks's (in)famous IS-LM. In her more recent restatement of the controversy, she (1979a, p.211) provided not only the flavor of her past anger, but also an ironic glimpse at Hicks's recantation, and her negation of Keynes's being half in historical time and half in equilibrium.

Whenever equilibrium theory is breached, economists rush like bees whose comb has been broken to patch up the damage. J. R. Hicks was one of the first, with his IS/LM, to try to reduce the *General Theory* to a system of equilibrium. This had a wide success and has distorted teaching for many generations of students. J. R. Hicks used to be fond of quoting a letter from Keynes which, because of its friendly tone, seemed to approve of IS/LM, but it contained a clear objection to a system that leaves out expectations of the future from the inducement to invest.

Forty years later, John Hicks noticed the difference between the future and the past and became dissatisfied with IS/LM but (presumably to save face for his predecessor, J. R.) he argued that Keynes' analysis was only half *in time* and half in equilibrium.

Regretfully, we can only hint here at the other side of the story. For example, Solow, in Chapter 17 of the companion volume, goes on record that he prefers J. R. to John (Hicks). Some economists would say that they prefer the young Joan to the mature one, say, her repudiated *Economics of Imperfect Competition* to her *Accumulation of Capital* and the earlier pre-war Keynesian Joan to the post-war Kaleckian Joan.

Joan Robinson's (1979a, p.91) recurring criticism of developments in modern economics targets the split into micro and macro economics: 'Keynes was safely corralled into the section called "macro economics" while the main stream of teaching returned to celebrating the establishment of equilibrium in a free market.' Her writings are permeated with continuous gibes at the neoclassical synthesis of 'illegitimate' Keynesians whom she calls by a less polite name – a name Solow in Chapter 17 of the companion volume considers a compliment for it suggests hybrid vigor (see Feiwel, 1982).

In a sense the germ of the synthesis can be found in a controversial passage by Keynes (1936, pp.378–9):[29]

If our central controls succeed in establishing an aggregate volume of output corresponding to full employment as nearly as is practicable, the classical theory comes into its own again from this point onwards. If we suppose the volume of output to be given, *i.e.* to be determined by forces outside the classical scheme of thought, then there is no objection to be raised against the classical analysis of the manner in which private self-interest will determine what in particular is produced, in what proportions the factors of production will be combined to produce it, and how the value of the final product will be distributed between them ... To put the point concretely, I see no reason to suppose that the existing system seriously misemploys the factors of production which are in use ... It is in determining the volume, not the direction, of actual employment that the existing system has broken down.

Keynes (p.379) went on to say that in order to fill the gaps in the 'classical theory' one should not dispose of the market economy, 'but to indicate the nature of the environment which the free play of economic forces requires if it is to realize the full potentialities of production'. Joan Robinson (1979a, pp.127–8) considers this as unfortunately an 'ill-considered remark', quite contrary to Keynes's main argument. And she adds: 'Here is the bastard Keynesian theory in its purest form.'

With the benefit of hindsight and foresight and a tinge of her own strong views about the message of the Keynesian revolution, Joan Robinson (1962a, pp.138–9) wrote:

It is possible to defend our economic system on the grounds that patched up with Keynesian correctives, it is, as he put it, the 'best in sight'. Or at any rate that it is not too bad, and change is painful. In short, that our system is the best system that we have got.

Or it is possible to take the tough-minded line that Schumpeter derived from Marx. The system is cruel, unjust, turbulent, but it does deliver the goods, and, damn it all, it's the goods that you want.

Or, conceding its defects, to defend it on political grounds – that democracy as we know it could not have grown up under any other system and cannot survive without it.

What is not possible, at this time of day, is to defend it, in the neoclassical style, as a delicate self-regulating mechanism, that has only to be left to itself to produce the greatest satisfaction for all.

6   *THE ACCUMULATION OF CAPITAL* AND VICISSITUDES OF CAPITALISM

After the war, when the problem of deficient effective demand seemed to have faded into the background, a fresh question came to the fore – long-run development.

The change arose partly from the internal evolution of economics as an academic subject. The solution of one problem opens up the next; once Keynes' short-period theory had been established, in which investment plays the key role, it was evidently necessary to discuss the consequences of the accumulation of capital that investment bring about.

Still more, the change in the centre of interest was due to urgent problems thrown up by the actual situation . . .

In this situation both static neo-classical analysis of the allocation of given resources between various uses, and Keynesian short-period analysis of how given resources are employed, appear quite inadequate. A dynamic long-run analysis of how resources can be increased is now what we require. (Joan Robinson 1962a, p.99–100).

In pursuing that goal, would Joan Robinson (1978, p.135) find her neoclassical heritage useful?

Before we can discuss accumulation, we must go back to the beginning and deal with the questions which Walras and Pigou left unanswered. In what kind of economy is accumulation taking place? Is it Frank Ramsey's classless co-operative, a collection of peasants and artisans, or a modern capitalist nation? Is it a property-owning democracy in which the rate of saving depends on the decisions of households? If so, by what means is saving converted into additions to the stock of inputs? Or if investment depends on the decisions of industrial firms, how do they get command of finance, and what expectations of profits are guiding their plans? Is there a mechanism in the system to ensure growth with continuous full employment? And if increasing value of capital per man leads to a prospective fall in the rate of profit, do the firms go meekly crawling down a pre-existing production function, or do they introduce new techniques that raise output per unit of investment as well as output per man?

How then does she (1962b, p.34) plan to concretize her model?

To build up a causal model, we must start not from equilibrium relations but from rules and motives governing human behaviour. We therefore have to specify to what kind of economy the model applies, for various kinds of economies have different sets of rules. (The *General Theory* was rooted in the situation of Great Britain in the 1930s; Keynes was rash in applying its conclusions equally to medieval England and ancient Egypt.) Our present purpose is to find the simplest kind of model that will reflect conditions in the modern capitalist world.[30]

Joan Robinson (1979b, p.ix) noted that when she wrote her (1952) book she took it for granted that Keynes' 'long struggle to escape' from 'habitual modes of thought and expression' had been made not only by her but by economists at large. Her goal then was to 'carry the modes of thought and expression of the *General Theory* into new fields, in particular, following Harrod, into the analysis of accumulation and growth'. Her program was to go beyond Keynes and to develop a long-run analysis, free from the need to assume conditions of static equilibrium (see Joan Robinson, 1980, p.105). As she (1979b, pp.xvii–xviii) perceived it, her

> generalization of the *General Theory* was an attempt to treat the analysis of accumulation according to Keynes' prescription. I worked out the internal relationships of a capitalist economy in steady growth – a golden age – omitting the large fields of foreign trade and government action which, however, are susceptible to be treated in the same manner. I used it as the background to analyse departures from it – that is to study the effect upon a growing economy of various types of vicissitudes that it may meet with. This propounds no doctrines but maps out a large area of the problems that should be investigated in the light of contemporary history. I still believe that something on these lines is a necessary preparation for 'applying our formal principles of thought' to economic reality.[31]

The road to *The Accumulation of Capital* was paved with the difficulties of translating the conception into an analytical structure and with replacing the tool-box she initially used (for example, she ultimately abandoned her ingenious use of the concept of elasticity of substitution that she (1933, 1969) introduced (see also Kahn, 1933; Hicks, 1983, pp.313–26)). While her presentation of the argument might be clearer in her 1952 essay (pp.67–164), her treatise (1956, 1966) is a much more satisfactory exposition. Though masterful in many ways, in others this book (1956, 1966) falls short of the mark.

Although it did not make the great splash that her first book did *The Accumulation of Capital* was generally well received, though some reviewers complained about the difficulties of presentation and the 'unnecessary' degree of abstraction. For instance, Lancaster (1960) found the chief fault of the book to have been a failure of communication, for he was certain that in her own mind, Joan clearly perceived what she was doing. Though he praised her for having rigorously avoided unnecessary sophistication and for calling a spade a spade, Worswick (1959) felt driven to translate the model into algebra for he found himself frequently at a loss in following the argument. Klein (1958) found Joan Robinson's book (1956, 1966) to be well written and well reasoned and a 'truly brilliant piece of theoretical work'. He also praised the 'many brilliant flashes of insight', but found it disappointing for, in his view it 'unfortunately does not seem to lead anywhere in particular'. Abba Lerner (1957) found the book irritating because it abounds in aphorisms, wisecracks, contradictions, and the like that smack of Marxist literature and because of the excessive abstraction. But he had a nagging doubt about his own strictures. He well remembered feeling 'somewhat similarly supercilious about queer things going on in Cambridge' at the time of the Keynesian revolution and that it was Joan Robinson and her friends who set him straight.

Joan Robinson was herself troubled by the lack of comprehension with which the book (1956, 1966) was received and produced a clarification thereafter (1962b). She (1962b, p.v) considered this clarification in the guise of an introduction rather than a supplement to her treatise (1956, 1966).[32] Probably an even better introduction to this subject is her (1960) book.

However remarkable its novelty, analytical pointers and the pearls of wisdom with which it abounds, in *The Accumulation of Capital* Joan Robinson did not succeed in meeting several demanding objectives in her grand design. She did not succeed in integrating the various streams of analysis and in truly generalizing Keynes's short-period analysis into long-run development. Neither did she succeed in integrating growth and fluctuations, nor did she provide a complete alternative theoretical structure to the neoclassical construct she tried to dislodge. *The Accumulation of Capital* enriches our knowledge about the nature and working of the capitalist economy and articulates an alternative conception, but it does not provide a fully fledged theory. What it does provide is a wealth of pointers and ingredients for constructing such an alternative theory, while shedding a light on the difficulties that can be expected in meeting this demanding objective.

To be fair, however, one should point out that Joan Robinson did not attempt a full-scale theory. Indeed, as she (1979a, p.119) put it:

It is often said that one theory can be driven out only by another; the neoclassicals have a complete theory (though I maintain that it is nothing but a circular argument) and we need a better theory to supplant them. I do not agree. I think any other 'complete theory' would be only another box of tricks. What we need is a different habit of mind – to eschew fudging, to respect facts and to admit ignorance of what we do not know.

The Accumulation of Capital is a very abstract and formalistic book with at least one foot (if not more) in the mainstream and in that respect it is not entirely unlike *The Economics of Imperfect Competition*. The criticism levelled against the formalism of this book (1956, 1966) is partly due to misunderstanding. She starts with the mythical world of the golden age,[33] but her very purpose is to descend to the vicissitudes of the capitalist economy as she so clearly articulates in her 1952 essay (see also 1962b, pp.16–17, 63–69; 1960, 101–19). The road by which she descends into the real world is not smooth, nor is it entirely analytically satisfactory. There are many virtues in models that articulate the requisite conditions for states that never have occurred and never will occur as long as they elucidate (as Joan Robinson does) the conditions needed to achieve such a state and the absence of these conditions in the real world. (This is one of the great advantages of the literature on competitive general equilibrium theory – an advantage that Joan Robinson does not seem to have perceived.)

Joan Robinson clearly states her assumptions at the very beginning of the book. Indeed, she stresses the unrealism of the heroic assumptions she makes. It is not cricket to take her to task for mistaking her mythical golden age, with full employment, for the real world. Her research strategy, as that of others, is to formulate first the stringent conditions required for steady growth which she identifies as a mythical state of affairs not likely to obtain in any actual economy.[34] She (1956, 1966, pp.59–60) describes the three important conditions: *tranquility* – a state where an economy 'develops in a smooth regular manner without internal contradictions or external shocks, so that expectations based upon past experience are . . . constantly fulfilled'; *lucidity* – a state where 'everyone is fully aware of the situation in all markets and understands the technical properties of all commodities' and where, therefore, 'there would be no scope for salesmanship, and profits could be made only by meeting the needs of consumers'; and *harmony* – a state where 'the rules of the game are fully understood and accepted by everyone' and where 'no one tries to alter his share . . . and all combine to increase the total to be shared'. Therefore, 'an economy which existed in a state of tranquility, lucidity and harmony would be devoted to the production and consumption of wealth in a rational manner'. That she presents this to show how much it differs from the real world is obvious from her words (p.60):

> It is only necessary to describe these conditions to see how remote they are from the states in which actual economies dwell. Capitalism, in particular, could never have come into existence in such conditions, for the divorce between work and property, which makes large-scale enterprise possible, entails conflict; and the rules of the game have been developed precisely to make accumulation and technical progress possible in conditions of uncertainty and imperfect knowledge. Yet too much disturbance, deception and conflict would break an economy to pieces. The persistence of capitalism till to-day is evidence that certain principles of coherence are imbedded in its confusion.

The last sentence of the above quotation may well be one of the most interesting in the whole book. Perhaps it is this idea that she failed to explain in her *magnum opus*.

Joan Robinson was a great model builder who fully understood the need to simplify drastically. ('In order to know anything it is necessary to know everything, but in order to talk about anything it is necessary to neglect a great deal' (Joan Robinson, 1951, 1978, p.42).) Like many other model builders she suffered from the gulf between her perception of the realities and her ability to articulate this in simplified terms, with imperfect techniques. It is ironic, however, that she showed considerable intolerance of others following the model-builder's path.[35] To be fair, one must point out that, unlike some other model builders, she had an uncanny flair for distilling the essence of the problems she tackled, and it is to her credit that she engaged in some of the most difficult and unsettled economic issues of all times and revived some of the large issues of classical political economy. That she was a leading question framer of our times is not in dispute. She asked questions that few others did. The answers she provided, however, are sometimes only clues, and there are many questions she did not pursue.

The Accumulation of Capital is a great work in the classical tradition. Probably a more descriptive title would have been 'Accumulation, Distribution, Effective Demand, and Employment'. It concentrated on the large classical, Keynesian and Kaleckian themes. In the preface Joan Robinson (1956, 1966, p.v) writes:

> Economic analysis, serving for two centuries to win an understanding of the Nature of Causes of the Wealth of Nations, has been fobbed off with another bride – a Theory of Value. There were no doubt deep-seated political reasons for the substitution but there was also a purely technical, intellectual reason. It is excessively difficult to conduct analysis of over-all movements of an economy through time, involving changes in population, capital accumulation and technical change, at the same time as an analysis of the detailed relations between input and price of particular commodities. Both sets of problems require to be solved, but each has to be tackled separately, ruling the other out by simplifying assumptions. Faced with the choice of which to sacrifice first, economists for the last hundred years have sacrificed dynamic theory in order to discuss relative prices. This has been unfortunate, first because an assumption of static over-all conditions is such a drastic departure from reality as to make it impossible to submit anything evolved within it to the test of verification and, secondly, because it ruled out the discussion of most of the problems that are actually interesting and condemned economics to the arid formalism.
>
> Keynes's *General Theory* ... left a huge area of long-run problems covered with fragments of broken glass from the static theory and gave only vague hints as to how the shattered structure could be rebuilt.

The book presents the economy in a two-sector (capital goods and consumer goods) growth and distribution aggregative model in the classical mould. While elsewhere (for example in 1962b) she criticizes the pervasive concept of equilibrium in economic theory, she employs it herself in elucidating her argument in this book (1956, 1966).[36] Indeed, one can make good use of an analytical tool without being committed to it. By concentrating on long-run growth equilibrium only, Joan Robinson rules out 'the more fundamental question what process of causation might be held conceptually responsible for the establishment and persistence of any particular Golden Age' (Kahn,

1959, p.149). Thus the problem of getting into equilibrium is not encountered in this context. The treatment rules out the problem (see Chapter 9 of this volume).

Joan Robinson has intuitively developed what is essentially a linear programming approach and does remarkably well with her own tool-box. However, there is a grain of truth in Klein's (1958, pp.623–4) observation that she was 'insular in her intellectual outlook and horizon'. He muses that had she gone into the modern development in linear programing, input–output analysis, mathematical general equilibrium system, and theory of balanced growth she would have achieved her results more generally and more directly. She would then not have been restricted to two sectors, but could have achieved full generality in a *n*-sector system by using input–output models and more general systems. She could also have avoided with greater ease much of the index number problem by forging on from the simple aggregative to more general systems. Fairness, however, requires us to observe that had she been familiar with all those modern developments and had she been a practitioner of mathematical techniques, she might have been inhibited in the development of the essentially original aspects of her model (especially her handling of historical time). Also, one cannot overstress that for her a model that is neatly expressed and rigorously formalized might lose its economic significance (for example, her objections to Findlay's mathematization of her model (1965, 1975, p.48) and to Kalecki's formalization of the investment function and her preference for 'animal spirits' and the major role it plays in her conception (see Chapter 1 of the companion volume)).

The Accumulation of Capital consists of eights parts called 'books'. The first book (as Klein suggests in Chapter 5) could be considered a major introduction to aggregative economics. Joan Robinson conceived the bulky second book, treating accumulation in the long run, as containing the central part of the work, although in later years she has emphasized the third book – the descent to the short period. Over and over again Joan Robinson insists that it is not possible to go back to the pre-Keynesian view that saving governs investment. She insists that it is investment decisions *not* saving decisions that govern the accumulation of wealth. Her (1962b, pp.82.3) model is 'designed to project into the long period the central thesis of the *General Theory*, that firms are free, within wide limits, to accumulate as they please, and that the rate of saving of the economy as a whole accommodates itself to the rate of investment that they decree'.

Indeed, she makes much of the distinction between the long and short period. Joan Robinson (1956, 1966, pp.179–80 and 198) describes the short period as not any definite period of time in the analytical sense, 'but a convenient theoretical abstraction meaning a period within which changes in the stock of capital equipment can be neglected'. During this period the stock of capital can be utilized at various rates by employing more or less labor. Within the technical limits, 'the short-period swings of output and consumption are governed by the movements of effective demand'. Moreover, 'everything that happens in an economy happens in a short-period situation, and every decision that is taken is taken in a short-period situation'. But whatever happens and whatever decision is made repercusses both in the short and long periods. 'Changes in output, employment and prices, taking place with a given stock of capital, are short-period changes; while changes in the stock of capital, the labour force and the techniques of production are long-period changes'. Thus 'a given short-period situation contains within itself a tendency to long-period change'. Furthermore, in the long run capital accumulates 'as the result of decisions to invest made in a succession of short-period situations'. If a seller's market prevails in the short period, on the basis of current experience, entrepreneurs will decide to invest. A high employment level in the capital goods sector portends high profits in the consumer goods sector. And if a buyer's market prevails, the excess capacity discourages investment and this, in turn, lowers profits. 'This double interaction between investment and profits is the most troublesome feature of the capitalist rules of the game, both from the point of view of entrepreneurs who have to play it and of economists who have to describe it'. In her later work, Joan Robinson has tended to lay greater stress on the short period and on the Kaleckian conception of the long period as a succession of short periods. She (1971, p.18) described the notion of 'being in the long period' as if it were a date in history. For her the short period is not a length of time but a state of affairs. 'Every event that occurs, occurs in a short-period situation; it has short-period and long-period consequences. The short-period consequences consist of reactions on output, employment, and, perhaps, prices; the long-period consequences concern changes in productive capacity.' All this is a question that became controversial between her and Garegnani (see Chapter 12) and that continues to be a sensitive issue (see also Eatwell and Milgate 1983).

The analytical strategy Joan Robinson uses is to proceed gradually from the most austere model through relaxation of assumptions to the more complex ones. Interestingly, her simple model of accumulation with a single technique contains the key propositions and the remainder of the book, in her view, involves complications and qualifications surrounding the main findings, but does not essentially alter them. 'A discussion of growth immediately raises the question of technical change' (Joan Robinson, 1979a, p.20). She discusses accumulation with constant techniques before introducing technical progress into the picture, though she views accumulation and technical progress as largely inseparable.[37] The fourth part of the book introduces finance and the monetary system. The fifth part brings in the rentier and consumption out of profit. The sixth part introduces scarcity of land and rent from which she previously abstracted, and concludes with a chapter on increasing and diminishing returns, also previously assumed away. The following two parts are devoted to the theories of relative prices and international trade respectively. The book concludes with notes on a broad range of topics with the purpose of assisting 'the reader to see in what respects the argument of this work conflicts with certain lines of thought with which he is likely to be familiar' (Joan Robinson, 1956, 1966, p.x). It is worth noting that 'the whole argument is set out, as far as possible, as an analytical construction with a minimum of controversy' (p.x).

The Accumulation of Capital abounds with innovative ideas (see Chapters 5 and 14 in this volume). Among them are her treatment of history and time (an attempt to present a historical model) and in this treatment her important distinction between difference and change.[38] As she (1956, 1966, p.71) pointed out:

> Throughout the argument it is necessary to distinguish *differences* from *changes*. The effect of having had in the past, and continuing to have, say, a higher rate of accumulation or a higher degree of monopoly, is not the same as the effect of a rise in the rate of accumulation or of an increase in monopoly. The analysis is therefore conducted in terms both of a comparison between economies with permanently different characteristics and of a single economy in which a change takes place at a moment of time.

In other words, 'the concept of equilibrium cannot be used to discuss the *effects* of *change*. It can only deal with *comparisons* of imagined *differences*' (Joan Robinson, 1978, p.xix). 'To account for the difference we have to delve into past history' (Joan Robinson, 1960, 1975, p.153). So, for Joan Robinson (1979a, p.15), 'the post-Keynesian system dwells in historical time; it is designed to analyse the consequences that may be expected to follow a change taking place at a particular date in particular circumstances. The system is set up like an artist's mobile. A flick on any point sets everything in motion, but it is possible to see which are the principle interactions and which way causation runs from one to another'. In other words, 'to make a comparison between two situations, each with its own future and its own past, is not the same thing as to trace a movement from one to the other' (Joan Robinson, 1960, p.v).

As early as 1953, Joan Robinson (1960, 1975, pp.120–1) made the clear distinction between logical and historical time.

> Time is unlike space in two very striking respects. In space, bodies moving from A to B may pass bodies moving from B to A, but in time the strictest possible rule of one-way traffic is always in force. And in space the distance from A to B is of the same order of magnitude (whatever allowance you like to make for the Trade Winds) as the distance from B to A; but in time the distance from to-day to to-morrow is twenty-four hours, while the distance from to-day to yesterday is infinite, as the poets have often

remarked. Therefore a space metaphor applied to time is a very tricky knife to handle, and the concept of equilibrium often cuts the arm that wields it.

Her most cogent explanation of the differences between logical and historical time was in a witty, whimsical and 'disobliging' lecture at Oxford University in the early 1950s (1973a, pp.254–63). In explaining these differences she used the famous Marshallian cross of supply and demand. Mainstream teaching tells us that if price is above the intersection point (equilibrium), supply exceeds demand and the price is decreasing. When price is below equilibrium, demand exceeds supply and the price is increasing. The price may well not settle at the equilibrium point but it *tends* to move towards it. Her initial quarrel is with the verb *tend*. It implies movement and movement implies a temporal sequence. But the cross diagram is devoid of time. 'To fill the story of a movement towards equilibrium, a complicated dynamic process must be specified and to specify a process that will actually reach equilibrium is by no means a simple matter' (Joan Robinson, 1980, p.87; see also Chapter 10 in this volume).

The movement described by the verb *tend* in mainstream teaching is, according to Joan Robinson, borrowed from space to explain a temporal process. Consider the bodies moving in space between points A and B as in the above 1953 quotation (or, for that matter, a swinging pendulum or the pairs of an old-fashioned scale). If they are in disequilibrium they move freely from A to B and from B to A (the pendulum swings and the pans of the scale wobble from side to side). And in space there is not the indefiniteness implied by the verb *tend*: given time the bodies *will get into equilibrium* (both the pendulum and the scales will settle). Finally, the distance between A and B is of about the same order of magnitude as between B and A. Not so in time, however.

'Today' is at the front edge of time. It moves continuously forward with an ever lengthening past behind it. Any event that occurred at any date in history occurred when that date was 'today'. We attempt to understand its causes, which lay in its own past and to trace its consequences which followed in its own future. The future up to today of any event in the past has already happened. As would-be social scientists – historians and economists – our relations to an event in the past and an event taking place 'today' are radically different. The consequences of past events can, in principle, be known, or at least discussed, while the consequences of a present event can, at best, be predicted with a range of possibilities which may turn out not to have been correctly anticipated. . . .

'Today' is influenced, but not completely bound, by the past. Any action or decision taken today is either the result of blind habit and convention or it is directed towards its future consequences, which cannot yet be fully known. (Joan Robinson, 1980, p.86)

Thus the analogy between space and time is misleading. Whereas on a scale, for instance, the weights can be moved from pan to pan and the former position can be restored, a temporal movement is unidirectional from the past to the future; when something happens today it repercusses tomorrow and yesterday cannot be restored.[39]

Introducing the inexorable arrows of time into the cross diagram is of no help: in one instance one gets something resembling a pig cycle, in another a damped cycle, and in a third a cycle tending towards infinity. Joan Robinson (1973a, pp.256–9) uses these diagrams to make the point that Marshall had a thorough understanding of time.

> Marshall had a remarkable intuitive genius and he knew by instinct how to find out the one case where you can say something without the arrow getting you all mixed up. The short period supply curve, under strictly perfect competition, when demand always rises, never falls. . . One hop up in time, and you have a position where the arrow will not worry you laterally, so long as you are in the short period.
>
> What did he do? The more I learn about economics the more I admire Marshall's intellect and the less I like his character.
>
> He worked out his short period for forward movements with great lucidity and then he filled the book with tear gas, so that no one would notice that he had fudged the whole of the rest of the argument. Just read Marshall's *Principles* through again with a gas mask on and you will see how right I am. (Joan Robinson, 1973a, pp.258–9)

And what about Marx? According to Joan Robinson (1973a, p.262) he not only understood time but played fair. He first discussed accumulation in terms of a model of simple reproduction – the equilibrium point in Marxian terms. Then he sent his model 'moving forward through history' and showed that it can never get back to equilibrium 'this side of doomsday'. Similarly, Harrod's point—the 'warranted rate of growth' – 'is not to show that the model tends towards an equilibrium line of development but that (just as Marx said) once it slips off the line it will never get back between now and doomsday' (p.263, see also 1971, pp.116 and passim).

Joan Robinson (1962b, pp. 23–4) perceived mainstream growth models – what she called the pseudo-causal model couched in logical time – as proceeding by designating 'a sufficient number of equations to determine its unknowns, and so finding values for them that are compatible with each other' (p.23). Such a model is not restricted only to stationary equilibrium relations; its equations may specify a time path (such as accumulation of capital or a specific pattern of fluctations). 'But the time through which such a model moves is, so to speak, logical time, not historical time'.

She illustrated this with the well-known example of a growth model of a perfectly competitive capitalist economy where the equations depict constant employment; a relationship between value of capital per worker and value of output per worker, implying a decelerating rate of profit on capital as total value of capital grows; and a savings–profits ratio, implying a decelerating rate of accumulation as total value of capital grows. This model depicts a process of continuously growing capital at a decreasing rate. 'The model is following a path in logical time approaching in one direction a "future" state with some limiting value of the rate of profit and in the other a "past" state of indefinitely rapid growth' (p.24).

Joan Robinson (1962b, pp.24–5) considered the question of stability of such a path a 'nonsense question' – to use one of her favorite terms – because of implied 'sufficient' foresight and equality between expected and actual levels of profit. 'A world in which expectations are liable to be falsified cannot be described by the simple equations of the equilibrium path.'

She perceived most of mainstream economics as pertaining to the analysis of relations among variables (such as prices, outputs, profit rate, and so on) in a stationary state. She (p.25) admitted:

There is much to be learned from *a priori* comparisons of equilibrium positions, but they must be kept in their logical place. They cannot be applied to actual situations; it is a mortal certainty that any particular actual situation which we want to discuss is not in equilibrium. Observed history cannot be interpreted in terms of a movement along an equilibrium path nor adduced as evidence to support any proposition drawn from it.

In this vein, she (1979a, pp.49–50) strongly objected to the praise of elegance showered on the general equilibrium model even by those who are critical of its usefulness:

A system of simultaneous equations need not specify any date nor does its solution involve history. But if any proposition drawn from it is applied to an economy inhabited by human beings, it immediately becomes self contradictory. Human life does not exist outside history and no one has correct foresight of his own future behaviour, let alone of the behaviour of all the other individuals which will impinge upon his. I do not think that it is right to praise the logical elegance of a system which becomes self-contradictory when it is applied to the question that it was designed to answer.

In such a model there is no causation. In the closed circle of simultaneous equations, 'the value of each element is entailed by the values of the rest. At any moment in logical time, the past is determined just as much as the future' (Joan Robinson, 1962b, p. 26).

Joan Robinson (1962b, pp.27–8) conceived of the emergence of what she called the pseudo-causal model as a response to Keynes's criticism.

> A bastard generation of theorems emerged – such as that, with unemployment, money-wage rates fall so that, provided the quantity of money is not reduced, the rate of interest is lowered, and (an unstated proviso, which has only to be stated to appear ridiculous) if expectations of profit in money terms are unaffected by the fall in prices, investment will increase. In these theorems (which continue to proliferate) Keynesian causal relations are fitted into an arbitrary set of assumptions fixed up so as to lead to the results once believed to be established by equilibrium analysis.

The pseudo-causal models, as she (1985, p.159 and 1979a, p.49) saw them, frequently feature a quest for equilibrium:

> *When* is the date when equilibrium is going to rule? It is usually said that, at any moment, markets are tending towards equilibrium, or that demand governs supply *in the long run*. Equilibrium, it seems, lies in the future. Why has it not been established already? Jam tomorrow but never jam today.

> Equilibrium is described as 'the end of an economic process ... If we interpret this as an historical process, it implies that, in the period of past time leading to 'today', equilibrium was not established. Why are the conditions that led to a non-equilibrium position 'today' not going to be present in the future?

To these mainstream models, Joan Robinson (1962b, pp.25–6) counterposed the historical model she utilized in her treatise (1956, 1966). Such a model is supposed to depict a specific set of values existing at a moment of time, generally not in mutual equilibrium, and to indicate how these values are expected to interact. Thus, using the historical model, one should be able to start anywhere either in or out of equilibrium and discuss what will happen next.

> A model applicable to actual history has to be capable of getting out of equilibrium; indeed, it must normally not be in it. To construct such a model we specify the technical conditions obtaining in an economy and the behaviour reactions of its inhabitants, and then, so to say, dump it down in a particular situation at a particular date in historic time and work out what will happen next. The initial position contains, as well as physical

data, the state of expectations of the characters concerned (whether based on past experience or on traditional beliefs). The system may be going to work itself out so as to fulfil them or so as to disappoint them.

The historical model requires specification of causal relations. 'Today is a break in time between an unknown future and an irrevocable past. What happens next will result from the interactions of the behaviour of human beings within the economy. Movement can only be forward' (p.26).

The economy may be in equilibrium in the short run, yet contain the seeds of inconsistencies that will soon disequilibrate it. Consider an economy that has lived through history on a path passing through an equilibrium point. At a certain date a change of tastes takes place. A change in the production pattern is likely to involve some investment, disinvestment, windfall losses or gains on (in)appropriate inventories, and the like. The story of the path and length of time for finding a new equilibrium involves the behavior of the economy out of equilibrium and how decisions are affected by disappointed expectations (Joan Robinson, 1979a, p.52).

The economy may also be in equilibrium in the long run, reproducing itself or expanding or contracting smoothly as long as there are no exogenous shocks. The model then follows a path similar to the equilibrium one. 'But it is still an historical, causal story that has to be told – the economy follows the path because the expectations and behaviour reactions of its inhabitants are causing it to do so' (Joan Robinson, 1962b, p.26).

When the economy is not in equilibrium to begin with, the historical model is supposed to trace the interactions of initial conditions in the future. When the equilibrium path is disturbed, the model is supposed to depict the economy's responses to shock.

In reality, disturbing events occur on disequilibrium paths. The resulting turbulence is beyond the skill of model builders to analyse. Historical analysis can be made only in very general terms. When the analysis leads to results that are contradicted by experience the model must be re-examined to see whether there was some error in its construction or only some ill-considered application of it in the analysis. (p.27)

As always, there is a conflict between reality and the causal historical model. In the real world, variables such as employment, labor force, price level, quantity of money, and the like are not sharply delineated and their internal structure is very complicated. In the causal model these variables are expressed in conventional homogeneous units. The conventional basis is made obvious and it is a matter of debate which convention makes more sense.

In the real world, changes in prices, employment, interest rates, and so on are followed by relative changes in specific markets and regions so that the pattern changes with the level. The causal model attempts to incorporate these complications.

The current rate of profit is distinguished from the expected one and the assumed connection between them is specified. A historical model that follows a smooth path, where the expected rate of profit has been constant for some time and has been realized, suggests that its population holds firm expectations that the current rate of profit will equal the past rate. The path will remain stable as long as discrepancies between expected and realized profits do not alter expectations. However, firm expectations cannot be held when past experience has varied considerably. There is then a tendency to attach much weight to current conditions in forming expectations; a slight change in current receipts influences investment decisions. Expectations might take different courses (that is, that the current situation will continue indefinitely, that change will continue in the same direction, or that after a time a departure from the past experience will either partly or fully reverse itself) and so does the model (Joan Robinson, 1962b, pp.28–30).

For Joan Robinson (1979a, p.48), when one admits the uncertainty of expectations – the pilot of economic behavior – 'equilibrium drops out of the argument and history takes its place'. Expectations of the outcome of an investment plan, of technical developments, of future prices, not to speak of exogenous (political and natural) shocks, are enshrouded in an uncertainty that cannot be reduced to 'calculated risk' by means of mathematical probability theory.

The historical causal model 'solves' the vexed question of measuring capital by drawing up schedules that depict for each economy the value of capital in terms of labor-time and commodities. But no conclusions can be drawn from this analysis. Economies with different profit rates obtain either at different times or in different spheres. In the first, technical knowledge alters, in the second, human and natural resources differ. 'The comparison of different economies with the same technical possibilities and different rates of profit is an exercise in pure economic logic without application to reality' (Joan Robinson, 1962b, p.33).

In the historical model the stock of capital goods at some base date is valued either at historical cost, at current reproduction cost, or in terms of its future earning power, discounted at an 'appropriate' rate of interest. 'Each measure . . . is vague and complex, and each gives a different result. This is certainly a very tiresome state of affairs for both private and social accountants, but it cannot be amended by pretending that it is not so' (p.33).

Building a historical model requires one to specify the roles and motives governing human behavior and the minimum of institutional arrangements. Joan Robinson (1956, 1966) first depicts an unfettered capitalist economy where production is organized by individual firms motivated by the competitive urge to grow and consumption is organized by individual households; all interacting without governmental shackles. Only by understanding how such an economy works can one hope to understand the objectives and effectiveness of national policies. In her model the firm is actuated by a competitive urge to grow. It is not a profit maximization model in the sense that the firm seeks profit for the sake of growth. Joan Robinson (1962b, pp.37–8) considers motivation of the firm not only a question of intrinsic traits of human nature but also a matter of conformist behavior – one that is stamped by society's approval.

Capitalism develops the spirit of emulation; without a competitive urge to grow, modern managerial capitalism could not flourish. At the same time there are costs and risks attached to growth that keep it within certain bounds. To attempt to account for what makes the propensity to accumulate high or low we must look into historical, political and psychological characteristics of an economy; with that sort of inquiry a model of this kind cannot help us. It seems reasonably plausible, however, to say that, given the general characteristics of an economy, to sustain a higher rate of accumulation requires a higher level of profits, both because it offers more favourable odds in the gamble and because it makes finance more readily available. For purposes of our model, therefore, the 'animal spirits' of the firms can be expressed in terms of a function relating the desired rate of growth of the stock of productive capital to the expected level of profits.

This passage is somewhat puzzling. She starts out with broad generalizations supposedly indicating a superior insight into capitalist motives for investment. Her emphasis on 'animal spirits' is supposed to be a rejection of neoclassical rationality. It all winds up with a great anticlimax; a function (in the model, a very rigid function) relating the desired rate of capital growth to the expected rate of profit. This is hardly an outcome that a narrow-minded neoclassicist (or for that matter, any kind of narrow-minded model builder) would regard as particularly shocking.

7   THE CAPITAL CONTROVERSY

Like Keynes and other Cantabrigians, Joan Robinson thrived on controversy, the ultimate benefits of which are themselves controversial.[40] In her last years Joan felt that she wasted much energy on controversy. It may even be argued that the negative effects offset any positive gains. If for no other reason, controversy diverted her from more constructive endeavors and tainted her with negativism so that her positive contributions tended to be underrated. True, she had tremendous comparative advantage in Cambridge-style controversy which most of her peers on the other side of the Atlantic (but also some on her shores and even on her home ground) considered excessively rude. She (1979a, p.111) pointed out, however, that the style does not aim to offend but to get points clear, even if shockingly so. She also complained that she had suffered a great deal in the US where she was often 'fobbed off with compliments' just as she was 'hoping to clinch an argument'. (Robin Matthews (1986, p.903) jests that one might consider 'the spiritual father of the Cambridge School' to have been William Cunningham, Archdeacon of Ely – famous as both an anti-theoretical institutionalist and polemicist – 'who once told his congregation that for him the bliss of Heaven would be incomplete if it lacked the pleasures of controversy'.)

Even her critics admit that she was a master of controversy. Harry Johnson (1978, p.130) provided a striking image of Joan's visit to the University of Chicago – that excellent US training ground in debate. His students 'looked at her and decided, "Well, we'll certainly show this old grandmother where she gets off." After they picked their heads up off the floor, having been ticked off with a few well chosen blunt squelches, they took a much more respectful attitude'.

Early on in her career Joan Robinson (1932, pp.5–6) was already fully aware of how controversies among economists arise and how they should be conducted:

> Economic controversies sometimes occur in which one of the contestants is right and the other is wrong. One has made a logical error, and the other has seen it. But this is the rarest kind of controversy. More often, like the two knights in the story, they are fighting about whether a shield is black or white only to find, after it is all over, that one side was black and the other side white. Now conducting an economic controversy is a delicate business. It is fatal to be too rude – an interchange of: It's black. No it's not, it's white – never leads to any results. On the other hand it is fatal to be too polite. When you are looking at a black shield, and the other man says it is white, it is of no use to say: Perhaps so, but I think on balance the evidence in favour of its being black is stronger; and then, he politely replies: But I think it is white, to part from him saying: Of course there is a lot of difference of opinion nowadays, and we each have a right to our own. The proper technique of controversy is to say: That's interesting – what makes you say it is white?
>
> Now when the argument is approached in this spirit the differences, other than logical, boil down to a difference of assumptions. One side of the shield is white, and the other is black, and there is no need to quarrel.

A few years later, she (1937, 1949, pp.99–100) provided a more exhaustive list of the causes of controversy:

> Controversies arise for five main reasons. First, they occur when the two parties fail to understand each other. Here patience and toleration should provide a cure. Second, controversies occur in which one (or both) of the

parties has made an error of logic. Here the spectators at least should be able to decide on which side reason lies. Third, the two parties may be making, unwittingly, different assumptions, and each maintaining something which is correct on the appropriate assumptions ... Fourth, there may not be sufficient evidence to settle a question of fact conclusively one way or the other. Here the remedy is for each party to preserve an open mind and to assist in the search of further evidence. Fifth, there may be differences of opinion as to what is a desirable state of affairs. Here no resolution is possible, since judgments of ultimate values cannot be settled by any purely intellectual process.

And she (p.100) correctly zeroed in on the fifth source of controversy as the most onerous one:

It is the fifth source of controversy which keeps all the rest alive. When some important issue of public policy is at stake each disputant clings desperately to his own opinion. Each refuses to understand the other, for fear that if he understood he might be compelled to make some concession. Each persists in his errors, for he who is convinced against his will is of the same opinion still. Each refuses to consider his assumptions for fear of being obliged to admit that his assumptions do not conform to reality. Each reads the incomplete evidence in his own favour.

Controversies in economics persist, not because economists are necessarily less intelligent or more bad-tempered than the rest of mankind, but because the issues involved arouse strong feelings. A bad argument which appears to favour a desired policy is obstinately and passionately upheld in the face of a better argument that appears to tell against it. But argument in the nature of the case can make no difference to ultimate judgments based on interest or moral feeling. The ideal is to set out all the arguments fairly on their merits, and agree to differ about ultimate values.

Later in her life, Joan Robinson (1960, 1975, p.275) became increasingly aware that 'with most problems nowadays the economic answers are only political questions'.

The map of modern economics is marked by many battlegrounds – none more 'bloody' than the theory of growth and capital (see Part III of this volume). But the amount of blood spilled is hardly a measure of the intrinsic importance of the issues discussed (see Bliss, 1975, pp.345–52; Sen 1970, pp.9–33). Joan Robinson's contributions to the theory of growth and distribution were heavily enmeshed in time-consuming and sometimes frustrating controversies.[41] What follows is only one example – perhaps one of the best known.

The notorious and often recondite Cambridge–Cambridge controversy transgresses the theory of capital and involves the whole corpus of economic theory and underlying ideologies. 'It is understandable that strong convictions should lead to strong language, as any reader of the "capital controversies" can document in quantitative detail, author by author' (Samuelson, 1977, p.141). The last word has not been said on what the shouting is all about, what the principal issues of controversy and central questions of theory are, and what is the appropriate methodology.

Clearly the personalities of the chief combatants – (i) the so-called Anglo-Italian offense (led by Joan Robinson, Kaldor, and Pasinetti, and inspired by Sraffa), and (ii) the MIT Institute Professors (Samuelson, Solow, and Modigliani, but also including 'residents' of Cambridge-on-the-Cam, Hahn and Meade) – matter, but much more is at stake. As Samuelson (1977, p.113) acknowledged: 'Behind an esoteric dispute over "reswitching" or heterogeneity of capital there often lurk contrasting views about fruitful ways of understanding distributional analysis and affecting its content by alternative policy measures.' For Joan Robinson (1979a, p.57) 'the long wrangle about "measuring capital" has been a great deal of fuss over a secondary question. The real source of trouble is the confusion between comparisons of equilibrium positions and the history of a process of accumulation.' And she (p.58) went on with her major tenet:

> The problem of the 'measurement of capital' is a minor element in the criticism of the neo-classical doctrines. The major point is that what they pretend to offer as an alternative or rival to the post-Keynesian theory of accumulation is nothing but an error in methodology – a confusion between comparisons of imagined equilibrium positions and a process of accumulation going on through history ...
>
> The lack of a comprehensible treatment of historical time, and failure to specify the rules of the game in the type of economy under discussion, make the theoretical apparatus in neo-classical text-books useless for the analysis of contemporary problems, both in the micro and macro sphere.

She (1973a, p.114) admitted that the drawn-out controversy may seem 'mere scholasticism, yet it has important implications both for the formation of ideology and for understanding the world we are living in'. Bliss (1975, p.351) rejects this view. He does not agree that 'the disputants who do battle in the theory of capital are really engaged in disputes about whether capitalism is an admirable form of social organization, and whether the distribution of income that it throws up is a good one. More plausibly they are engaged, for the most part, just as they seem to be engaged, in rather dry technical arguments'. Hahn (1975, p.364) considers the relation of ideology and theory as a non-issue for economists who discuss theory as theorists 'since it cannot be the case that a theory should be rejected or accepted by an appeal to the motives, conscious or otherwise, of proponents' (see Section 8 of this chapter and Chapter 4 of this volume).

What all the shouting was about continues to mystify not only the onlookers, but also some of the participants. Solow (1983, p.181), for instance, professes a 'continuing doubt as to what the controversy was about'. Joan described it as the Great Capital Debate, while the 'disagreeable' Frank Hahn characterizes it as the Great Charade. Burmeister (1980, p.154) asks why the controversy generated so much heat when there was so little fire.

In a standard survey of the controversies, Harcourt (1972) (with strong affinities for Cambridge-on-the-Cam) sees the main issues under discussion as those grand themes that preoccupied Ricardo and Marx; the relations between accumulation and income distribution and the origins of profits, their absolute and relative size at any point of time and intertemporally, and similar questions about wages. The debate revolves around value, capital, growth, and distribution theory. The Anglo-Italian criticism is directed against the neoclassical 'apologetic' conception loosely identified under the heading of marginal productivity theory and the neoclassical approach to growth theory, including the neglect of effective demand. Solow (1975, p.277) considers that the main battle is over the theory of profits and capital. He argues that the Anglo-Italians have 'gone after peripheral aspects of the profit-cum-interest story, and left its center untouched'. In a review article of Harcourt, Stiglitz (1974, pp.901–2) (another partisan of MIT) focused on what he considered to be the three major issues – the determination of savings and the interest rate, reswitching of techniques, and aggregate capital – where the Anglo-Italians have 'gone astray'. He argued, *inter alia*, that ideology plays a far less important role than Harcourt suggests. He claimed that 'there is a well-known propensity of individuals to dislike what they don't or can't understand', implying that his opponents 'do not understand neoclassical capital theory'. To him it appears that 'it is the confused attempt to discredit the marginal-productivity interpretation of the interest rate which imbues the topics of capital theory with their ideological interest to the devotees of Cambridge (UK) doctrine'. In the final analysis, Solow (1975, p.277) notes that this tempest has little to do with what economists do. If the contested features of neoclassical or mainstream economics 'were officially declared overthrown tomorrow, hardly anyone, perhaps no one, who is actually doing economics would do anything differently'.

The voluminous literature, including the growing industry of commentators, defies brief synopsis. As so much misunderstanding enshrouds the controversy, and since it might be illusory that the participants were actually communicating with each other, it might be wise to call attention here to some of the statements by the chief contestants themselves to convey an impression of their own perceptions of their positions and those of their opponents.

The controversies over so-called capital theory arose out of the search for a model appropriate to a modern western economy, which would allow for an analysis of accumulation and of the distribution of the net product of industry between wages and profits. (Robinson, 1978, p.114)

To recall, Keynes's *General Theory* is concerned only with a short period situation; the existing stock of capital can be represented by a 'who is who' of specific means of production. The book value depends on the accounting convention followed. The stock-exchange value of the business depends on the market's expectations of future profits and on the level of interest rates. Expectations are subject to marked shifts and interest rates are conditioned by monetary policy and by interdependencies of financial markets. As the value of capital is an imprecise concept, so is the rate of profit. Keynes was not concerned with all that; he did not need a theory of the rate of profit. But as soon as accumulation and growth come to the forefront, it becomes necessary to tackle the formidable question of the concepts of aggregate quantity of capital and rate of profit (see Joan Robinson, 1980, p.100; 1979a, pp.59–60). In her famous 'sermon' at Oxford in the early 1950s, Joan Robinson (1973a, p.261) contrasted the short and long periods:

> The short period means that capital equipment is fixed in kind. You do not have to ask: When is capital not capital? because there is a specific list of blast furnaces and rolling stock and other hard objects, and for Marshall a given number of trawlers.
>   In the long period capital equipment changes in quantity and in design. So you come slap up to the question: What is the quantity of capital?

Joan Robinson reminisced about the early stages of the discussion on long-run growth in the Keynesian tradition which was spurred by the publication in 1949 of Harrod's *Towards a Dynamic Economics*.[42] Whatever the shortcomings of the latter, 'he also lacked a rate of profit'. She acknowledged that it was not till she found the 'corn economy in Sraffa's *Introduction* to Ricardo's *Principles* that I saw a gleam of light on the question of the rate of profit on capital' (1978, pp.xvi–xvii). (See also 1973a, pp.125, 253; 1982, pp.90–1; 1980, pp.144–50; 1979b, pp.xx–xxiii; Kregel, 1971; Harcourt, 1986; Walsh and Gram, 1980; and Chapter 13 in this volume.)[43] She (1960, 1975, pp.114 and 130) fired the first round of the capital controversy in 1953 by stating:

> The dominance in neo-classical economic teaching of the concept of a production function ... has had an enervating effect upon the development of the subject, for by concentrating upon the question of the proportions of factors it has distracted attention from the more difficult

but more rewarding questions of the influences governing the supplies of the factors and of the causes and consequences of changes in technical knowledge.

And further:

When presented with the task of determining the distribution of the product of industry between labour and capital, the neo-classical production function comes to grief (even in the most perfect tranquility) on the failure to distinguish between 'capital' in the sense of means of production with particular technical characteristics and 'capital' in the sense of a command over finance.

When presented with the task of analysing a process of accumulation the production function comes to grief on the failure to distinguish between comparisons of equilibrium positions and movements from one to another.

Twenty years later she (1978, p.xvii) quipped that in this first round she was 'innocently remarking that the Emperor had no clothes'.

Solow (1955–6, p.101) responded by praising Joan Robinson for being annoyed by some of the practices of academic economists. 'We have reason to be grateful for her annoyance, for she seems to have written her article the way an oyster makes pearls – out of sheer irritation.' He went on to show that only in a very narrow class of cases can one sum up the various capital inputs in a single index-figure, so that the production function can be 'collapsed' to give output as a function of inputs of labour and capital-in-general.

Joan Robinson (1979a, p.116) recalled that when she fired her 1953 salvo, she was still naive. She believed that if she asked a reasonable question, she ought to get a serious answer. She was quite surprised at the indignation that her question aroused. She became the butt of such jokes and Solow's 'everybody in the profession, except Joan Robinson, knows perfectly well what capital means'.

Reflecting on her role in the development of the controversy, Joan Robinson (1982a, p.91) recalls that she

set about to dismantle the neoclassical production function by introducing what I called a book of blueprints showing the concrete stock of means of production required for each level of output with a given labor force. From this developed what Professor Solow called a pseudo-production function ... I do not think I ever misused it as Professor Samuelson does nowadays, but it certainly took me a long time to understand its meaning and its limitations.

And elsewhere:

The pseudo-production function consists of the specification of a set of mutually non-inferior techniques, each requiring a particular stock of means of production per man employed. Each is eligible for at least one rate of profit, and none is superior to the rest at every rate of profit. When the techniques are listed in order of the flow per man employed of a homogeneous net output, it can be seen that a higher output is not necessarily associated with 'more capital', that a technique that is eligible at a higher rate of profit may require a larger value of capital at the corresponding prices, and that the same technique may be eligible at widely different rates of profit. This killed off the doctrine of 'marginal productivity of capital' associated with the production function (though it has refused to get buried), but it does not, by itself, provide the basis for an alternative analysis of accumulation. If techniques are invented, one after the other in historical time, there is no reason to expect them to be mutually non-superior. A new technique is normally adopted because, at existing prices and wage rates, it promises a higher return than the one in use, per unit of financial investment. It does not have to wait for a change in prices to make it eligible. But it will not remain exceptionally profitable for long. Copiers wipe out the initial competitive advantage of new commodities and rising real wage rates, of higher productivity. Meanwhile, new, more eligible techniques are being introduced. At each moment, the prospect of higher profits is inducing change, while, over a run of years, the *ex post* average realized rate of profit may be constant or falling. (Joan Robinson, 1979a, pp. 20–21)

After much water had passed under the bridge and some sensibilities had been exacerbated, Joan Robinson (1978, pp.122–3) pointed out that Samuelson accepted, 'after some hesitation', the logic of the pseudo-production function and

he even referred to a 'general blueprint technology model of Joan Robinson and MIT type' but his interpretation of it was (and still is) very different from mine. He recognized that each point on a pseudo function is supposed to represent an economy in a steady state, in which inputs are being reproduced in unchanged physical form, and yet he supposed that saving could rise an economy from one point to the position at another. He envisages a process of accumulation creeping up the pseudo-production function from lower to higher shares of wages, and higher to lower rates of profit. But an increase in gross investment above the rate required to maintain a steady state would entail an enlargement of investment (which would have to shrink again when a new steady state was reached). The former pattern of prices would be upset. Inputs appropriate to one technique would have to be scrapped and replaced by those appropriate to another. And how are we to imagine that the prospect of a lower rate of profit in the future induces these changes to be made?

In 1975, Joan Robinson (1982a, p.91) stressed that the pseudo-production function 'permits only of comparisons of imaginary equilibrium positions already in existence, not a process of accumulation going on through time'.

> There is no such phenomenon in real life as accumulation taking place in a given state of technical knowledge. The idea was introduced into economic theory only to give a meaning to the concept of the marginal productivity of capital, just as the pseudo production function was constructed in order to show that it has no meaning. (Joan Robinson 1979a, pp.82–3)

From Samuelson's rebuttal (1977, pp.134–41) it appeared to Joan Robinson (1982a, p.91) that with respect to accumulation 'he is still a completely unreconstructed pre-Keynesian neoclassic. He expects to find the rate of interest (which is what he calls what Sraffa calls the rate of profits) lowered by successful saving-investment abstaining from consumption.'

'The furore about "reswitching" raged around the conception of a pseudo-production function' (Robinson, 1978, p.121). As Joan Robinson (1982a, p.92) sees Samuelson's interpretation:

> Evidently, we are in an era when a slow secular fall in the rate of profits is going on. Each time it passes a switch point (whether towards a technique which requires a higher or lower value of capital than the last) there must be a certain period of investment and disinvestment installing the stock required for the latest technique and clearing away the debris of the former one. We are not told anything about what goes on in these interludes, which seem to pass as though in a dream.
>
> The whole process may take centuries but all the while there is no technical progress or learning by doing. The specifications of all the techniques were available in the original book of blueprints.

And she (1982a, p.93) claims to have shattered the pseudo-production function again in 1974:

> Obviously, stocks of equipment appropriate to different techniques cannot coexist both in time and space. It should never have been drawn in a plane diagram in the first place. Different techniques are not isolated from each other on 'islands'. They succeed each other through time as new discoveries and inventions become operational. Normally, a new technique is *superior* to the one in use and does not have to wait for a change in the rate of profit to be installed.

Pseudo-production functions flourished again independently after the appearance in 1960 of Sraffa's classic *Production of Commodities by Means of Commodities*. In this model one of the ingredients among the inputs exists in two versions or brands. The difference between them is in the time pattern of reproduction, not any physical characteristic. Sraffa did not intend this for a pseudo-production function. His purpose was to refute marginalism by showing that the least conceivable difference alters the whole system. (Robinson, 1982a, p.93)

According to Joan Robinson (1982a, p.94) Samuelson's initial reaction to Sraffa was 'to produce a form of pseudo-production function in which, beyond each switch point, a higher rate of interest is associated with a lower ratio of value of capital to output so that backward switching cannot occur'. The Sraffians countered this by constructing an array of pseudo-production functions with all kinds of switching points. She (p.94) considered it a futile exercise. These production functions 'are now so elaborate, elegant and beautiful and their designers have become so fond of them, that it seems cruel to point out that they are unable to say anything without falling into Samuelson's fallacy'.

Looking over the controversy, Joan Robinson (1979a, p.xv) mused:

The participants in the controversy, on both sides, failed to observe that it had nothing whatever to do with the analysis of the choice of technique or the determination of the rate of profit in a process of accumulation going on through historical time.

Perhaps I am partly to blame for introducing the expression 'a book of blueprints' for an imaginary list of mutually non-superior techniques all available at once, but at least I did insist that my pseudo-production function could be used only for comparing stocks of capital each already in existence.

For Joan Robinson (1979a, pp.69–70) the pseudo-production function was a useful construct but it should not be incorporated in the construction of dynamic theory. The stocks of inputs pertaining to two different techniques cannot exist side by side in time and space. No such thing as a book of blueprints pertaining to various interest rates exists. When accumulation proceeds, techniques develop and future techniques are unknown today. In reality, no stock of capital is ever perfectly congruent with expectations of profit. 'The pseudo-production function is not a model for the analysis of capitalism but a device to smoke out the contradictions in mainstream teaching.'

In his numerous writings on the subject, Samuelson has reformulated his conceptions, admitted to some failings, but upheld the essence of his position:

Recently . . . I have insisted that capital theory can be rigorously developed without using any Clark-like concept of aggregate 'capital', instead relying upon a complete analysis of a great variety of heterogeneous physical capital goods and processes through time. Such an analysis leans heavily on the tools of modern linear and more general programming and might therefore be called neo-neo-classical. It takes the view that if we are to understand the trends in how incomes are distributed among different kinds of labor and different kinds of property owners, both in the aggregate and in the detailed composition, then studies of changing technologies, human and natural resources availabilities, taste patterns, and all the other matters of *micro*economics are likely to be very important.

... But must there always be a need for mutually exclusive choice? Cannot each in its place be useful? What I propose to do there is to show that a new concept, the 'Surrogate Production Function', can provide *some* rationalization for the validity of the simple J. B. Clark parables which pretend there is a single thing called 'capital' that can be put into a single production function and along with labor will produce total output (of a homogeneous good or of some desired market-basket of goods). (Samuelson, 1966, pp.325–6)

Until the laws of thermodynamics are repealed, I shall continue to relate outputs to inputs – i.e. to believe in production functions. Until factors cease to have their rewards determined by bidding in quasi-competitive markets, I shall adhere to (generalized) neoclassical approximations in which relative factor supplies are important in explaining their market remunerations. (Samuelson, 1972, p.174)

And, referring to his 1966 summary of the debate, where he clearly differentiates his position from that of his opponents (1972, pp.230–5) and the shots fired for another decade, Samuelson reports that his '1966 discussion seems to stand up very well, and it would be hypocritical of me to give it other than a clean bill of health as a representation of my 1975 views' (Samuelson, 1977, pp.134–5). It may be noted that for Solow (1967, pp.1259–60), who pokes fun at himself as a 'rank methodological opportunist', macroeconomic production functions are not a rigorously justifiable concept. 'In my mind it is either an illuminating parable, or else a mere device for handling data, to be used so long as it gives good empirical results, and to be abandoned as soon as it doesn't, or as soon as something better comes along.' (See also Joan Robinson, 1973a, pp.114, 117; 1979a, pp.72, 94, 95.)

An upshot of the capital controversy, was the disagreement between Joan Robinson and Garegnani (see Chapter 12 in this volume). The disagreement revolved around two issues: the essence and status of a pseudo-production function and the use of the concept of long-period equilibrium in historical analysis (see Joan Robinson, 1980, pp.121–34; Eatwell and Milgate, 1983). Joan Robinson's interpretation of and attitude to Sraffa (1960) is a contro-

versial subject (for her initial reaction, see 1965, 1975, pp.7–14). Whatever
else may be said she has found in it an inspiration for solving the vexed
problem of what is meant by 'quantity of capital'. In her last published paper
(1985, pp.163–5) she expressed misgivings about the standard commodity
and called attention to other puzzles of this 'enigmatic book' which,
however, could be put to good use 'in reconstructing analysis after the spring
cleaning has been completed'. In conclusion she (pp.164–5) wrote:

> To reconcile the two parts of Sraffa's analysis we may treat it as follows.
> The 'system' of production in use in an economy at a moment of time, and
> the stocks of inputs required to implement it, are set out in terms of a
> physical input–output table. It does not represent a stationary state or an
> equilibrium position. It is simply the position that has been reached,
> 'today', as a result of accumulation of stocks and of technical knowledge
> over the past history.
>
> At a moment of time there can be no change but if accumulation or
> decumulation is going on, say from week to week or from year to year,
> there must be technical change to accommodate changes in the relations of
> inputs to employment of labour and even when the total stock is in some
> sense constant choices are required about the form in which replacements
> are being made of items used up. Thus, as history marches on, there is slow
> gradual change. There may also be bouts of important changes from time
> to time, following major discoveries, and 'Keynesian' swings of effective
> demand run to and fro over the long-term evolution.
>
> The control of production may in principle be appropriate to any social
> and political system – socialist, co-operative or capitalist. Where the land
> and stocks are owned by a class of capitalists they are paying a certain
> wage bill per annum in terms of dollars. Dollar prices then determine the
> real wage rate per man-year of employment and the share of gross and net
> profits in proceeds. The ratio of net profit in dollars to the wage bill is the
> ratio of exploitation. According to Sraffa, the prices of commodities are
> such as to make the rate of profits on the dollar value of capital uniform
> and constant through time, but in real life this condition is not exactly
> fulfilled.
>
> The rate of exploitation (with the corresponding level of the rate of
> profits) may, in principle, be anything between zero (which permits only
> enough gross profit to keep stocks intact) and the maximum that permits
> the labour force just to exist and reproduce itself.
>
> There does not seem to be much point in making further systematic
> generalizations. We have here a broad frame within which detailed studies
> of actual history can be carried out.
>
> This is where Sraffa leaves us and hands us over to Keynes.

8 ECONOMIC PHILOSOPHY

I hold very strongly that the purpose of economic theory should be to try to throw some light on the world that we are living in . . . It should proceed by advancing hypotheses which are in principle refutable. But to sort out the questions to be discussed it is often necessary to pass through a phase of purely logical, *a priori* argument – intellectual experiment – before hypotheses can be formulated. (Joan Robinson, 1980, p.ix)

Speaking about her own work, Joan Robinson (1978, p.xxii) mused that during her fifty years or so of scholarly writing, she has 'aimed to bring theoretical analysis nearer the actual problems of economic life instead of further away from them'. She (1979a, p.1) considered that the reason much economic theory ends up in a blind alley is because it does not originate from actual economic problems. In the 1930s economic theorizing was not a purely intellectual movement.

In fact it arose out of the actual situation of the thirties – the breakdown of the world market economy in the great slump. Kalecki, Keynes, and Myrdal were trying to find an explanation for unemployment; the exploration of imperfect and monopolistic competition set afoot by the challenge from opposite directions, of Piero Straffa . . . and Allyn Young . . . to the orthodox theory of value, though it proved to be a blind alley, arose from the observation that, in a general buyers' market, it could not be true that prices are equal to marginal costs. The movement of the thirties was an attempt to bring analysis to bear on actual problems. Discussion of an actual problem cannot avoid the question of what should be done about it; questions of policy involve politics (laisser-faire is just as much a policy as any other). Politics involve ideology; there is no such thing as a 'purely economic' problem that can be settled by purely economic logic; political interests and political prejudice are involved in every discussion of actual questions.

Furthermore, she (1978, pp.63–4) considered that

the element of propaganda is inherent in the subject because it is concerned with policy. It would be of no interest if it were not. If you want a subject that is worth pursuing for its intrinsic appeal without any view to consequences you would not be attending a lecture on economics. You would be, say, doing pure mathematics or studying the behaviour of birds. . . . Economic theory, in its scientific aspect, is concerned with showing how a particular set of rules of the game operates, but in doing so it cannot help but make them appear in a favourable or an unfavourable light to the people who are playing the game. Even if a writer can school himself to perfect detachment he is still making propaganda, for his readers have interested views. Take, for example, a piece of pure analytical argument such as that the operation of the gold standard secures stability of the exchanges provided that money-wage rates are flexible. This means that it will not function well where Trade Unions are strong and prevent wages from falling when the preservation of the exchange rate requires that they should. This is a purely scientific statement and there is not much room for disagreement about it regarded as a description of the way the system works. But to some readers it will appear as strong propaganda against the trade unions, to others as strong propaganda against the gold standard.

This element of propaganda enters into even the most severally technical details of the subject. It cannot fail to be present when the broad issue of the operation of the system as a whole is under discussion.

Joan Robinson, the teacher by predisposition and temperament, was much concerned with what is being taught to future generations of economists. We know how harsh she was on orthodoxy. She (1980, p.112) admitted bitterly that her critical pieces are understood only by those who agree with her and do not need to read them.[44] In reforming teaching, she (1965, 1975, p.4) would first disregard the exam-passers who would anyway reduce what they were taught to slogans. 'and new slogans cannot be more mis-educating than the old ones'.

For the serious students, I would take the bull by the horns and start from the beginning to discuss various types of economic system. Every society (except Robinson Crusoe) has to have some rules of the game for organizing production and the distribution of the product. *Laissez-faire* capitalism is only one of the possible sets of rules, and one in fact which is unplayable in a pure form. It always has to be mixed with some measures of collective control. The Indian scene provides examples of pre-capitalist, capitalist and socialist games being played side by side. Students acquainted with the old fast-vanishing world can help in trying to puzzle out the economic analysis of its functioning and to test out the meaning of concepts such as wages and capital in non-capitalist contexts.

Adam Smith, Ricardo, Marx, Marshall and Keynes would be treated in terms of the model of an economic system that they each had in mind and of the actual problems that each sought to solve.

I should displace the theory of the relative prices of commodities from the centre of the picture and make the main topic production, accumulation and distribution, looked at from the point of view of an economy taken as a whole. Keynes' General Theory then falls into place as the short-period section of a truly general theory. Here price theory comes in as an element in the theory of distribution, for the relation of prices to money-wage rates in the industrial sector of an economy is one of the determinants of the distribution of proceeds between workers and capitalists or the state, and the relation of agricultural to manufacturing prices is a main determinant of distribution between sectors of the economy.

Markets and the laws of supply and demand I should treat not only in terms of an ideal equilibrium already achieved but also in terms of actual dealings in commodities, with their tendency to develop cobweb cycles, and the violent shocks that are given from time to time to the communities dependent on them.

Welfare I should treat in human terms and teach the students to look, not for 'preference surfaces', but for objective tests of standards of nutrition and health.

In all this I should emphasize that economic theory, in itself preaches no doctrines and cannot establish any universally valid laws. It is a method of ordering ideas and formulating questions. For this reason, I should pay a good deal of attention to method. I should insist upon the distinction between an accounting identity, a statement of equilibrium conditions and a summary of econometric facts . . . None of these tells us anything about causation; models built with these bricks will never stand up. To find causal relations we want to know how individuals behave and how the behaviour of various groups reacts on each other. I should try to break down the awe that students feel for formulae, not so as to induce a sceptical drift into intellectual nihilism, but so as to form the habit of picking them to pieces and putting them together again with the ambiguities cleaned off, and keeping them firmly in their place as useful adjuncts to common sense, not as substitutes for it . . .

Returning from this happy day-dream, my gloom is all the deeper. To write down what I want to see emphasizes how unlikely it is that I ever shall. But courage! We must try as best we may to do a little good here and there to set in the scales against all harm. (pp.4–6)

Reflecting on her life's work and on that of others during that time, in a soul-searching essay, provocatively entitled 'Thinking about Thinking', she (1979a, p.110) observed that she never had her early pamphlet *Economics is a Serious Subject* (1932) reprinted

because I soon ceased to believe in its main argument – that if economists could avoid certain bad habits and arrive at a consistent set of assumptions, however abstract, they could approach reality step by step merely by making more complicated models.

I soon realized that to avoid unacceptable methods of argument is a necessary but not a sufficient condition for establishing a genuine discipline. But some of the negative points in the essay still seem to be valid forty years after it was written. One of those points concerns controversy among economists. (See Section 7 of this chapter.)

She (1979a, p.111) provided a method for resolving controversies:

> When controversies arise through confronting contradictory conclusions, they can easily be resolved by examining the arguments that led to them. Each party should set out clearly the assumptions on which his argument is based; by mutual criticism they can arrive at agreement about what consequences follow from what assumptions and then they can join in an amicable discussion about what evidence must be found to show which set of assumptions (if either) is relevant to the problem in hand.
>
> For this method to be successful, both parties must follow it. An attempt by one party to proceed in this way is frustrated if the other continues to reiterate his conclusions or insists that his own set of assumptions is the only one that can legitimately be made. Unfortunately, the greater part of economic controversies arise from confronting dogmas. The style of argument is that of theology, not of science. This has grown with the growth of a large and flourishing profession, in which jobs depend on supporting opinions acceptable to those in authority.

Joan Robinson (1979a, p.112) believed that the Keynesian revolution featured many of the attributes of scientific revolutions:

> but the subsequent development of the subject was not at all like that of any natural science when a shift of paradigm has occurred. In economics, new ideas are treated, in theological style, as heresies and as far as possible kept out of the schools by drilling students in the habit of repeating the old dogmas, so as to prevent established orthodoxy from being undermined.

She admitted that disputes would continue to occur where political issues are involved, for they hinge on differences in judgement and moral values. But she (1973a, p.122) was distressed that lengthy controversies continue to surround purely logical points: 'In economics, unfortunately, logic is corrupted by opinions. Arguments are judged by their conclusions, not by their consistency. Terms are used without definitions, so that propositions containing them are merely incantations. Economics is a branch of theology.'

8.1 Ideology and Theory

In a highly provocative and most lucid book – one that Paul Baran (1964, p.455) has called 'A Brilliant Woman's Guide Away From Economics' –

Joan Robinson (1962a) set out to clear the impenetrable fog about why economists believe what they believe and what it is that makes them believe it. She (p.1) began by asserting that economics 'has always been partly a vehicle for the ruling ideology of each period as well as partly a method of scientific investigation'.

She (pp.2–3) attempted to distinguish ideology from science by pointing out that when 'an ideological proposition is treated in a logical manner, it either dissolves into a completely meaningless noise or turns out to be a circular argument'. And, as distinct from a scientific proposition, 'the hallmark of a metaphysical proposition is that it is not capable of being tested'. But the metaphysical propositions do have meanings. 'They express a point of view and formulate feelings which are a guide to conduct.' Moreover, 'metaphysical propositions also provide a quarry from which hypotheses can be drawn. They do not belong to the realm of science and yet they are necessary to it'. As an example of such a metaphysical proposition she pointed to the slogan 'all men are equal' as a research program.

> Let us find out whether class or colour is correlated with the statistical distribution of innate ability. It is not an easy task, for ideology has soaked right into material we are to deal with. What is ability? How can we devise measurements that separate what is innate from what is due to environment? We shall have a hard struggle to eliminate ideology from the answer, but the point is that without ideology we would never have thought of the question.

Unfortunately in economics, as in other fields, 'no one . . . is conscious of his own ideology, any more than he can smell his own breath' (p.41). Be that as it may,

> whether or not ideology can be eliminated from the world of thought in the social sciences, it is certainly indispensable in the world of action in social life. A society cannot exist unless its members have common feelings about what is the proper way of conducting its affairs, and these common feelings are expressed in ideology. (p.4)

She (pp.4–6) considered ideology as something of a substitute for instinct – a standard of morality inculcated at an early age. In order for the species to survive any animal must have some egoism, extended from the individual to the family. However, 'social life is impossible unless the pursuit of self-interest is mitigated by respect and compassion for others. A society of unmitigated egoists would knock itself to pieces; a perfectly altruistic individual would soon starve'. In most cases altruistic emotion is very unreliable; it is only 'strong enough to evoke self-sacrifice from a mother defending her young'. Therefore, 'since the egoistic impulses are stronger than the altruistic, the claims of others have to be imposed upon us. The mechanism by which they are imposed is the moral sense or conscience of the individual.' For example, though stealing is not morally as repugnant as cruelty and meanness, 'a lack of honesty is a very great nuisance in society. It is a source of expense and it is thoroughly tiresome – just as tiresome for thieves as for everyone else; without honour among thieves even thieving would be impracticable'. (See also Arrow, 1974, pp.15–29.)

Joan Robinson rejected the notion that morality derives either from religion or reason. For her (1962a, pp.11 and 12), 'the upshot of the argument is that moral feelings are not derived from theology or from reason. They are a separate part of our equipment, like our ability to learn to talk'. In other words,

> the ethical system implanted in each of us by our upbringing (even a rebel is influenced by what he rebels against) was not derived from any reasonable principles; those who conveyed it to us were rarely able to give any rational account of it, or indeed to formulate it explicitly at all. They handed on to us what society had taught to them, in the same way as they handed on to us the language that they had learned to speak.

There is a large variety of ethical systems, but we all believe in some absolutes:

> There are certain basic ethical feelings that we all share. We prefer kindness to cruelty and harmony to strife; we admire courage and respect justice. Those born without these feelings we treat as psychopaths; a society which trains its members to crush them we regard as a morbid growth. It is no good trying to pretend that we can think or speak about human questions without ethical values coming in. (p.14)

In a commencement address at the University of Maine in 1977, Joan Robinson (1979a, p.43) registered a strong protest against the unequal balance between morality and the market (see also Arrow, 1974):

> I want to speak about the philosophy of economics. It is an extremely important element in the view of life and the conceptions which prevail in this country. Freedom is the great ideal. Along with the concept of freedom goes freedom of the market, and the philosophy of orthodox economics is that the pursuit of self-interest will lead to the benefit of society. By this means the moral problem is abolished. The moral problem is concerned with the conflict between individual interest and the interest of society. And since doctrine tells us that there is no conflict, we can all pursue our self-interest with a good conscience.

'Any economic system requires a set of rules, an ideology to justify them, and conscience in the individual which makes him strive to carry them out' (Joan Robinson, 1962a, p.13). However, even economic terminology is value-loaded: 'Bigger is close to better; equal to equitable; goods sound good; disequilibrium sounds uncomfortable; exploitation, wicked; and sub-normal profits, rather sad' (p.14). Nevertheless, the technical features of a given economic system can be described objectively.

> But it is not possible to describe a *system* without moral judgments creeping in. For to look at a system from the outside implies that it is not the only possible system; in describing it we compare it (openly or tacitly) with other actual or imagined systems. Differences imply choices, and choices imply judgment. We cannot escape from making judgments and the judgments that we make arise from the ethical preconceptions that have soaked into our view of life and are somehow printed in our brains. (p.14)

This need to rely on judgment has a side effect. It makes economists more uncomfortable and contentious. 'The reason is that, when a writer's personal judgment is involved in an argument, disagreement is insulting' (p.24). Perhaps the acceptance of economics as value-loaded and infiltrated by judgment came easier to Joan Robinson than to most of her American colleagues because, as she (p.74) admitted, she was not taught in Cambridge that economics should be value-free or that a sharp line of demarcation could be drawn between positive and normative economics.

The question of value judgment in economics seethes with controversy (see Feiwel, 1985a, pp.62–86 and references therein; Dobb, 1973; Hutchison, 1981). In Joan Robinson's (1970, p.122) view (and here she spoke of herself, but left that conclusion to the reader),

> every human being has ideological, moral and political views. To pretend to have none and to be *purely objective* must necessarily be either self-deception or a device to deceive others. A candid writer will make his preconceptions clear and allow the reader to discount them if he does not accept them. This concerns the professional honour of the scientist. But to eliminate value judgments from the subject-matter of social science is to eliminate the subject itself, for since it concerns human behaviour it must be concerned with the value judgments that people make. The social scientist (whatever he may privately believe) has no right to pretend to know any better than his neighbours what ends society should serve. His business is to show them why they believe what they purport to believe (as far as he can make it out) and what influence beliefs have on behaviour.

When all is said and done, however, 'economics is only a branch of theology. All along it has been striving to escape from sentiment and to win for itself the status of science' (Joan Robinson, 1962a, p.21). Economists eagerly look to the natural sciences as pointing a way for them to emerge from the morass of ideology.

> The great prestige of the natural sciences and the spectacular technology founded upon them leads to the hope that if only scientific method could be applied to the study of society we might hope to find a solution for the dreadful problems hanging over our life today.
>
> There is not yet much reason to expect that such a grand programme can be fulfilled. The methods to which the natural sciences owe their success – controlled experiment and exact observation of continually recurring phenomana – cannot be applied to the study of human beings by human beings. So far, no equally successful method of establishing reliable natural laws has been suggested. (Joan Robinson, 1970, p.119)

> In the natural sciences, controversies are settled in a few months, or at a time of crisis, in a year or two, but in the social so-called sciences, absurd misunderstanding can continue for sixty or a hundred years without being cleared up.
>
> The cause of this difference, of course, lies in the difference of methods. My saying: 'A serious subject is neither more nor less than its own technique' was a half truth, but it is the important half. In the natural sciences, experiments can be repeated and observations checked so that a false hypothesis is quickly knocked out. I agree with Kuhn's view of science as a particular kind of social activity which is carried on for its own sake, with a particular set of accepted rules. That it enables us to understand an aspect of the universe is, so to speak, an accidental by-product of this activity. Economics is also a social activity but its rules are such that its by-products are much less impressive. (Joan Robinson, 1979a, p.116)[45]

All this does not mean that the social scientists (and particularly economists) should jump to conclusions, propound circular arguments, or resolve disputes by abuse. Neither does it mean

> that economic theory is useless. We cannot help trying to understand the world we are living in, and we need to construct some kind of picture of an economy from which to draw hypotheses about its mode of operation. We cannot hope ever to get neat and precise answers to the questions that hypotheses raise, but we can discriminate among the pictures of reality that are offered and choose the least implausible ones to elaborate and to confront with whatever evidence we can find. (p.10)

Joan Robinson (1951, 1978, p.171) sounded a note of warning:

> It is a common vice of present-day economic argument to jump from a highly abstract piece of analysis straight to prescriptions for policy, without going through the intermediate stage of examining how far the assumptions in the analysis fit the facts of the actual situation.

Economists should investigate the nature of their differences and embark on a research program in an attempt to resolve them (Joan Robinson, 1970, p.119). It is difficult, however, to apply the scientific method in the social sciences, mainly because 'we have not yet established an agreed standard for the disproof of an hypothesis. Without the possibility of controlled experiment, we have to rely on interpretation of evidence, and interpretation involves judgment; we can never get a knock-down answer. But because the subject is necessarily soaked in moral feelings, judgment is coloured by prejudice' (Joan Robinson, 1962a, pp.22–3). But the problem cannot be resolved by shedding prejudice and approaching the issue under discussion with full objectivity. She (1960, 1975, p.113) does not think that a 'purely economic argument can ever finally settle any question, for political and human considerations are always involved in every question and are usually decisive'. However, 'analysis that is put at the service of ideology is not interesting, because we know in advance what the answer is going to be. When we consider the world evolving around us, we see a great number of questions that need to be explored because the answers are not obvious at all' (Joan Robinson, 1979a, p.261). She (1962a, p.23) warns us that 'anyone who says to you: "Believe me, I have no prejudices," is either succeeding in deceiving himself or trying to deceive you'. In final analysis, 'economists are not strictly enough compelled to reduce metaphysical concepts to falsifiable terms and cannot compel each other to agree as to what has been falsified. So economics limps along with one foot in untested hypotheses and the other in untestable slogans' (p.25).

> Then, the question may be raised: if the choice between one theory and another is always made by their ideological colour, not their logic, why is a reasonable theory any more use than a spurious one? Is there any point, after all, in trying to make economics into a serious subject? . . . Logic is the same for everyone . . . and the reading of evidence, though always biassed to some extent, can be more or less fair . . . My old saying about technique was a half truth. The other half concerns the subject to which technique is to be applied. I believe that the proper subject matter of economics is an examination of the manner of operation of various economic systems, particularly our own, and as long as our economic system continues to survive, a clear-sighted examination of it is more likely to favour radical views than to support the defenders of the status quo. (Joan Robinson, 1979a, pp.118–9)

Joan Robinson (and Wilkinson, 1985, p.73) drew a telling parallel between religion and economics:

I have always felt that it was a serious misfortune that religion came to the West in the form of an implausible piece of history for this created a clash between the requirements for the development of spiritual life and the requirements of intellectual honesty. At a lower level – the sphere of economic theory – there is a similar conflict between ideology and logic.

And the same is true of the human race as a whole.

For the most part the human race, even today, does not attach importance to the distinction between a thing being the case and not being the case. Myths, superstitions and slogans satisfy them. Logic, inquiry by experiment and a rationalist view of history were highly developed in Athens, but since they were the occupation of gentlemen, methods of production were not much affected by them. (Joan Robinson, 1970, p.60)

Joan Robinson (1962a, pp.20–21) pointed out that the pursuit of profit harms the prestige of the businessman. 'While wealth can buy all forms of respect, it never finds them freely given'. Therefore, 'it was the task of the economist to overcome these sentiments and justify the ways of Mammon to man. No one likes to have a bad conscience. Pure cynicism is rather rare . . . It is the business of the economists, not to tell us what to do, but show why what we are doing anyway is in accord with proper principles'.

She singled out *at least* five areas in economics where this justification has resulted not in clarifying the issues, but rather in obscuring them; in throwing a veil over the actual motives and outcomes. Her targets were: (1) income distribution, (2) utility theory, (3) equilibrium analysis, (4) free trade, and (5) monetarism (see also Chapter 4 in this volume):

(1) 'The doctrine that unequal distribution of income is helpful to growth because the rich save, is the reverse of the truth for there would be less unnecessary expenditure if they were less rich' (Joan Robinson, 1979c, p.13; see also 1967, pp.3–6 and *passim*). She (1979c, p.17) considered that on the whole 'the calculation of GNP *per capita* is a smoke screen to keep the problems of distribution out of view'. She (p.5) stressed how misleading are the per capita GNP statistics because 'from the point of view of welfare, information about *average* income is meaningless unless we know how consuming power is distributed'. As an example, she (p.5) pointed to the oil-rich Arab states where after 1973 'GNP *per capita* suddenly jumped to levels which exceed that of the richest Western states, yet in these countries are found some of the poorest and least "developed" communities in the world'. Using these conventional measures of GNP per capita, the world is divided into rich and poor countries, while the division between rich and poor people

within each country is disregarded. 'In fact, the highest level of luxurious living is often found in the poorest countries and, with it, the greatest concentration of power in the hands of a few' (p.34).

> Accepted orthodoxy is very heavily impregnated by the teaching of the economists which, combined with patriotism, makes the 'growth of national income' the aim of policy and the criterion of success. Statistics of the overall total of national income pay no attention to the distribution of consumption between families or to the composition of the flow of goods and services which it measures. The composition of output is very largely determined by what is profitable for business to sell. In the heyday of economic orthodoxy this was presented as the greatest merit of the system – profit depends upon meeting demand, and demand expresses the free choice of the consumer as to how to dispose of his purchasing power. (Purchasing power is admittedly not distributed according to needs but somehow that was not allowed to spoil the argument.) (Joan Robinson, 1970, p.113)
>
> The whole subject is so embarrassing that in fact it is scarcely mentioned. There is no treatment at all of the determination of the distribution of income in orthodox teaching, and precious little about its consequences. What to the general public appears one of the most interesting of all questions in economics is simply left out of the syllabus. (Joan Robinson, 1985, p.160)

(2) '*Utility* is a metaphysical concept of impregnable circularity; *utility* is the quality in commodities that makes individuals want them, and the fact that individuals want to buy commodities shows that they have *utility*' (Joan Robinson, 1962a, p.47). Joan Robinson (pp.47–9) traced the concept of utility through Jevons, Marshall, and Edgeworth and noted that

> we are told nowadays that since *utility* cannot be measured it is not an operational concept, and that 'revealed preference' should be put in its place. Observable market behaviour will show what an individual chooses. Preference is just what the individual under discussion prefers; there is no value judgment involved. Yet, as the argument goes on, it is clear that it is a Good Thing for the individual to have what he prefers. This, it may be held, is not a question of satisfaction, but freedom – we want him to have what he prefers so as to avoid having to restrain his behaviour. (p.49)

But value judgment creeps in nonetheless: 'drug-fiends should be cured; children should go to school. How do we decide what preferences should be respected and what restrained unless we judge the preferences themselves?' (p.49) Furthermore, she (p.49) negates that market behavior can reveal preferences. One objection is that 'the experiment of offering an individual alternative bundles of goods, or changing his income just to see what he will buy, could never be carried out in practice'. The other objection is logical.

> We can observe the reaction of an individual to two different sets of prices only at two different times. How can we tell what part of the difference in his purchases is due to the difference in prices and what part to the change in preferences that has taken place meanwhile? There is certainly no presumption that his character has *not* changed, for soap and whisky are not the only goods whose use affects tastes. Practically everything develops either an inertia of habit or a desire for change. (p.50)

There is an egalitarian moral to utility (see Arrow, 1983a and 1983b). Joan Robinson (1962a, p.52) saw this moral in the writings of Marshall. It all 'points to egalitarian principles, justifies Trade Unions, progressive taxation and the Welfare State, if not more radical means to interfere with an economic system that allows so much of the good juice of *utility* to evaporate out of commodities by distributing them unequally'. All the same, Marshall used an 'elegant conjuring trick by which the egalitarian moral of the *utility* theory was made to vanish before our eyes' (p.57; see also 1979a, pp.43–7).

(3) In Joan Robinson's perception, one of the reasons the neoclassicists are so isolated from the real world is the dominance of the concept of equilibrium in theory.

> The dominance of equilibrium was excused by the fact that it is excessively complicated to bring into a single model both movements of the whole through time and the detailed interaction of the parts. It was necessary for purely intellectual reasons to choose between a simple dynamic model and an elaborate static one. But it was no accident that the static one was chosen; the soothing harmonies of equilibrium supported *laisser-faire* ideology and the elaboration of the argument kept us all too busy to have any time for dangerous thoughts. (Joan Robinson, 1962a, pp.71–2)

She (pp.80–1) attributed the survival of equilibrium theory to a psychological element.

> There is an irresistible attraction about the concept of equilibrium – the almost silent hum of a perfectly running machine; the apparent stillness of the exact balance of counteracting pressures; the automatic smooth recovery from a chance disturbance. Is there perhaps something Freudian about it? Does it connect with a longing to return to the womb? We have to look for a psychological explanation to account for the powerful influence of an idea that is intellectually unsatisfactory.

Moreover,

> long-run equilibrium is a slippery eel . . . No one would deny that to speak of a tendency towards equilibrium that itself shifts the position towards which it is tending is a contradiction in terms. And yet it still persists. It is for this reason that we must attribute its survival to some kind of psychological appeal that transcends reason. (p.82; see also 1979a, 48–58)

(4) One of Joan Robinson's *bêtes noires* was free trade.

> The most pervasive and strongly held of all neoclassical doctrines is that of the universal benefits of free trade, but unfortunately the theory in terms of which it is expounded has no relevance to the question that it purports to discuss. The argument is conducted in terms of comparisons of static equilibrium positions in which each trading nation is enjoying full employment of all resources and balanced payments, the flow of exports, valued at world prices, being equal to the flow of imports. In such conditions, there is no motive for resorting to protection of home industry. Since full employment of given resources is assumed, there is no need for protection to increase home industry, and since timeless equilibrium is assumed there can never be a deficit in the balance of payments. Moreover, since all countries are treated as having the same level of development, there can be no question of 'unequal exchange'. (1979c, p.102)[46]

She (p.103) considered that 'the most misleading feature of the classical case for free trade (and the arguments based upon it in modern textbooks) is that it is purely static. It is set out in terms of a comparison of the productivity of *given* resources (fully employed) with or without trade'. Moreover, the free-trade doctrine is highly inequitable. It 'was part of the general defence of *laisser faire*. Protection is an interference with the free play of market forces. For this reason, the doctrine suits the interests of whichever nation is in the strongest competitive position in world markets' (p.104).

(5) 'The enormous ideological attraction of the Quantity Theory of Money, that kept it going for nearly forty years after its logical content was exploded, . . . is due to the fact that it conceals the problem of political choice under an apparently impersonal mechanism' (Joan Robinson, 1962a, p.98). Joan Robinson (1982b, p.280) criticized the circularity in the monetarist argument.

> It requires years of eduction in economics to grasp this idea, for any sensible person can see that it is merely mistaking a symptom for a cause – when demand is slack, unemployment prevalent, and over-all earnings relatively low, there is less money in circulation at a given level of prices. It

is the lack of expenditure which keeps down the quantity of money in circulation, not a limited stock of money that keeps down expenditure.

And, in one of her last published essays (with Wilkenson, 1985, pp.97–8), without precisely naming them, she targeted monetarists old and new and supply-side economists. She pointed out that within orthodox thought

> Keynes's system has been relegated to a special case of wage and price inflexibility and Keynesian policies have been increasingly regarded as additional interferences with the 'invisible hand'. By advocating the adjustment of the money supply as the answer to inflation and by offering 'market' solutions to unemployment, the economics profession has progressively abandoned logic for ideology and set us back precisely where we started.

She concluded her *Economic Philosophy* (1962a, pp.146–7) on a pessimistic/optimistic note:

> Perhaps all this seems negative and destructive. To some, perhaps, it even recommends the old doctrines, since it offers no "better 'ole" to go to. The contention of this essay is precisely that there is no "better 'ole."
>
> The moral problem is a conflict that can never be settled. Social life will always present mankind with a choice of evils. No metaphysical solution that can ever be formulated will seem satisfactory for long. The solutions offered by economists were no less delusory than those of the theologians that they displaced.
>
> All the same we must not abandon the hope that economics can make an advance towards science, or the faith that enlightenment is not useless. It is necessary to clear the decaying remnants of obsolete metaphysics out of the way before we can go forward.
>
> The first essential for economists, arguing amongst themselves, is to "try very seriously," as Professor Popper says that natural scientists do, "to avoid talking at cross purposes" and, addressing the world, reading their own doctrines aright, to combat, not foster, the ideology which pretends that values which can be measured in terms of money are the only ones that ought to count.

But in the last years of her life, she became increasingly despondent and pessimistic, as indicated in the last part of this section (see also Chapters 41 and 42 of this volume).

8.2   On Marx and Marxism

At the beginning of the war, as a distraction from the news, Joan Robinson began a serious study of Marx and Rosa Luxemburg. For her, the principal message of Marx was the injunction to think in terms of history, not of equilibrium. Her own 'Marxian heresy' (1942, 1966) has done much to reinstate Marx as a serious, though sometimes misguided, economist.[47] With the passion that Marx arouses among both his critics and disciples and the intolerance of some disciples towards criticism of the prophet, it is natural that her venture met with a mixed reception. Whatever the inherent merit of her treatment of Marx and her contribution to the comparisons of the economic analysis of *Capital* with mainstream academic teaching, her (1942, 1966) book had an indelible impact on her. It is one of the inspirations for *The Accumulation of Capital*. It provides, *inter alia*, a clue to her view of history and time; of the capitalist rules of the game pertaining to how property and work are combined in production and with the rights they bestow to share in proceeds; of the evolving system beset by conflict; of the inflationary barrier; and of animal spirits (initially influenced by Keynes).

I began to read *Capital*, just as one reads any book, to see what was in it; I found a great deal that neither its followers nor its opponents had prepared me to expect. Piero Sraffa teased me, saying that I treated Marx as a little-known forerunner of Kalecki. There is a certain sense in which this is not a joke. There are many pointers in *Capital* to a theory of effective demand. Marx's disciples could have worked it out before Keynes and Kalecki learned it from the brutal teaching of the great slump; but they did not do so. The professional Marxists in England greeted the *General Theory* with the slogans of sound finance. The 'Keynesian' element in Marx *was* little-known.

The academics did not even pretend to understand Marx. It seemed to me that, apart from prejudice, a barrier was created for them by his nineteenth-century metaphysical habits of thought, which are alien to a generation brought up to inquire into the meaning of meaning. I therefore tried to translate Marx's concepts into language that an academic could understand. This puzzled and angered the professed Marxists, to whom the metaphysics is precious for its own sake. (Joan Robinson, 1942, 1966, pp.vi–vii)

Keynes was, of course, right when he warned Joan Robinson, that her fierceness might get her into trouble in some quarters. At the time, Keynes was not to know in how many diverse quarters she would arouse tempers. We have seen the running controversies she had with the mainstream. We also hinted at some disputes with her 'fellow travellers'. Her passionate outbursts against monetarism in all its guises can even be left to the imagination of the reader (but to set the record straight, see Joan Robinson, 1971). Her disputes with orthodox Marxists are summarized in her hilarious 'Open Letter from a Keynesian to a Marxist' (Ronald Meek), first published in 1953 (Joan Robinson, 1973a, pp.264–8). This is very revealing of what Joan stood for and what she opposed and warrants lengthy extracts.

I must warn you that you are going to find this letter very hard to follow. Not, I hope, because it is difficult (I am not going to bother you with algebra, or indifference curves) but because you will find it so extremely shocking that you will be too numb to take it in.

First I would like to make a personal statement. You are very polite, and try not to let me see it, but, as I am a bourgeois economist, your only possible interest in listening to me is to hear which particular kind of nonsense I am going to talk. Still worse – I am a left-wing Keynesian. Please do not bother to be polite about that, because I know what you think about left-wing Keynesians.

You might also say I am the archetypal left-wing Keynesian. I was drawing pinkish rather than bluish conclusions from the *General Theory* long before it was published. (I was in the privileged position of being one of a group of friends who worked with Keynes while it was being written.) Thus I was the very first drop that ever got into the jar labelled 'Left-wing Keynesian'. Moreover, I am quite a large percentage of the contents of the jar today, because so much of the rest has seeped out of it meanwhile. Now you know the worst.

But I want you to think about me dialectically. The first principle of the dialectic is that the meaning of a proposition depends on what it denies. Thus the very same proposition has two opposite meanings according to whether you come to it from above or from below. I know roughly from what angle you come to Keynes, and I quite see your point of view. Just use a little dialectic, and try to see mine.

I was a student at a time when vulgar economics was in a particularly vulgar state. There was Great Britain with never less than a million workers unemployed, and there was I with my supervisor teaching me that it is logically impossible to have unemployment because of Say's Law.

Now comes Keynes and proves that Say's Law is nonsense (so did Marx, of course, but my supervisor never drew my attention to Marx's views on the subject). Moreover (and that is where I am a left-wing Keynesian instead of the other kind), I see at a glance that Keynes is showing that unemployment is going to be a very tough nut to crack, because it is not just an accident – it has a function. In short, Keynes put into my head the very idea of the reserve army of labour that my supervisor had been so careful to keep out of it . . .

The thing I am going to say that will make you too numb or too hot (according to temperature) to understand the rest of my letter is this: I understand Marx far and away better than you do. (I shall give you an interesting historical explanation of why this is so in a minute, if you are not completely frozen stiff or boiling over before you get to that bit.)

When I say I understand Marx better than you, I don't mean to say that I know the text better than you do. If you start throwing quotations at me you will have me baffled in no time. In fact, I refuse to play before you begin.

What I mean is that I have Marx in my bones and you have him in your mouth ...

Suppose we each want to recall some tricky point in *Capital*, for instance the schema at the end of Volume II. What do you do? You take down the volume and look it up. What do I do? I take the back of an old envelope and work it out.

Now I am going to say something still worse. Suppose that, just as a matter of interest, I do look it up, and I find that the answer on my old envelope is not the one that is actually in the book. What do I do? I check my working, and if I cannot find any error in it, I look for an error in the book. Now I suppose I might as well stop writing, because you think I am stark staring mad. But if you can read on a moment longer I will try to explain.

I was brought up at Cambridge, as I told you, in a period when vulgar economics had reached the very depth of vulgarity. But all the same, inside the twaddle had been preserved a precious heritage – Ricardo's habit of thought.

It isn't a thing you can learn from books. If you wanted to learn to ride a bicycle, would you take a correspondence course on bicycle riding? No. You would borrow an old bicycle, and hop on and fall off and bark your shins and wobble about, and then all of a sudden, Hey presto! You can ride a bicycle. It is just like that being put through the economics course at Cambridge. Also like riding a bicycle, once you can do it, it is second nature.

When I am reading a passage in *Capital* I first have to make out which meaning of c Marx has in mind at that point, whether it is the total stock of embodied labour, or the annual flow of value given up by embodied labour (he does not often help by mentioning which it is – it has to be worked out from the context) and then I am off riding my bicycle, feeling perfectly at home.

A Marxist is quite different. He knows that what Marx says is bound to be right in either case, so why waste his own mental powers on working out whether c is a stock or a flow?

Then I come to a place where Marx says that he means the flow, although it is pretty clear from the context that he ought to mean the stock. Would you credit what I do? I get off my bicycle and put the error right, and then I jump on again and off I go.

Now, suppose I say to a Marxist: 'Look at this bit – does he mean the stock or the flow?' The Marxist says: 'C means constant capital,' and he gives me a little lecture about the philosophical meaning of constant capital. I say: 'Never mind about constant capital, hasn't he mistaken the stock for the flow?' Then the Marxist says: 'How could he make a mistake? Don't you know that he was a genius?' And he gives me a little lecture on Marx's genius. I think to myself: This man may be a Marxist, but he doesn't know much about geniuses. Your plodding mind goes step by step, and has time to be careful and avoids slips. Your genius wears seven-league boots, and goes striding along, leaving a paper-chase of little mistakes behind him (and who cares?). I say: 'Never mind about Marx's genius. *Is* this the stock or is it the flow?' Then the Marxist gets rather huffy and changes the subject. And I think to myself; This man may be a Marxist, but he doesn't know much about riding a bicycle.

The thing that is interesting and curious in all this is that the ideology which hung as a fog round my bicycle when I first got on to it should have been so different from Marx's ideology, and yet my bicycle should be just the same as his, with a few modern improvements and a few modern disimprovements. Here what I am going to say is more in your line, so you can relax for a minute.

Ricardo existed at a particular point when English history was going round a corner so sharply that the progressive and the reactionary positions changed places in a generation ...

Ricardo was followed by two able and well-trained pupils – Marx and Marshall. Meanwhile English history had gone right round the corner, and landlords were not any longer the question. Now it was capitalists. Marx turned Ricardo's argument round this way: Capitalists are very much like landlords. And Marshall turned it round the other way: Landlords are very much like capitalists. Just round the corner in English history you see two bicycles of the very same make – one being ridden off to the left and the other to the right.

Marshall did something much more effective than changing the answer. He changed the question. For Ricardo the Theory of Value was a means of studying the distribution of total output between wages, rent and profit, each considered as a whole. This is a big question. Marshall turned the meaning of Value into a little question: Why does an egg cost more than a cup of tea? It may be a small question but it is a very difficult and complicated one. It takes a lot of time and a lot of algebra to work out the theory of it. So it kept all Marshall's pupils preoccupied for fifty years. They had no time to think about the big question, or even to remember that there was a big question, because they had to keep their noses right down to the grindstone, working out the theory of the price of a cup of tea.

Keynes changed the question back again. He started thinking in Ricardo's terms: output as a whole and why worry about a cup of tea? When you are thinking about output as a whole, relative prices come out in the wash – including the relative price of money and labour. The price level comes into the argument, but it comes in as a complication, not as the main point. If you have had some practice on Ricardo's bicycle you do not need to stop and ask yourself what to do in a case like that, you just do it. You assume away the complication till you have got the main problem worked out. So Keynes began by getting money prices out of the way. Marshall's cup of tea dissolved into thin air. But if you cannot use money, what unit of value do you take? A man hour of labour time. It is the most handy and sensible measure of value, so naturally you take it. You do not have to prove anything, you just do it.

Well there you are – we are back on Ricardo's large questions, and we are using Marx's unit of value. What is it that you are complaining about?

Do not for heaven's sake bring Hegel into it. What business has Hegel putting his nose in between me and Ricardo?

8.3 Social and Policy Questions

Joan Robinson was a special champion of the Third World. Her sympathy for the misery of the poor in these regions was probably aroused very early in life when, as a new bride, she accompanied Austin Robinson to India where they lived in the late 1920s. In the 1930s, as we know, she participated actively in the Keynesian revolution, but it was primarily on a theoretical not a policy level. Thereafter the main thrust of her writings on social and policy implications was aimed at improving conditions in the Third World. She provided the examples of (1) the US and the modern welfare state, (2) the Soviet system, and (3) the Chinese way, to illustrate how (4) the underdeveloped countries, with their special problems, could approach a satisfactory development strategy (see also Chapter 26 in this volume). And throughout she continued to warn mankind of (5) the tragedy of nuclear war hanging over it.

(1) Joan Robinson (1970, p.60) saw all of human history from the beginning to the eighteenth century as one period and from the industrial revolution until today as another. The same patterns recur.

> The British Empire had something in common with the Roman; the destruction of Greece through internecine war leading to the dominance of Macedon are repeated in this century in European wars leading to the dominance of the United States. But there are three characteristics of the modern age which distinguish it from the past – the hypertrophy of the nation state (which some modern attempts at internationalism have done little to check), the application of science to production and the penetration of money values into every aspect of life.
>
> The exaltation of making money for its own sake to respectability, indeed to dominance, in society was the new feature of the capitalist system which distinguished it from all former civilizations. A temperamen-

tal inclination to avarice or generosity is no doubt distributed statistically in much the same way in all human populations. There is no reason to suppose that the natural passions were changed in the nineteenth century. Rather a society developed in which ambition and love of power could be satisfied by accumulating wealth, and this met with technical and historical conditions which enabled it to grow and flourish and stretch its tentacles over the world. (p.67)

She (pp.82–7) perceived the predominant element of the capitalist world to be in the US. It is there that she looked for the mechanism of the new system.

The era of personal capitalism, when the 'robber barons' built up large fortunes, had come to an end (though some areas for wheeling and dealing still remain). They were succeeded by great bureaucratized concerns adapted to the application of scientific methods to technology, management and salesmanship. Second, the greatly enlarged concern of the State in economic affairs, which had begun in the slump and grown in the war, continued into quasi-peacetime.

The great corporations inherited the aims and attitudes individual capitalists but there are important differences in their mode of operation. Once launched they do not depend for finance upon individual saving. Each consists in a self-perpetuating and self-expanding fund controlled and serviced by a self-perpetuating cadre of managers and technicians ...

There is a strong propensity in human nature – perhaps rooted in the instincts which give social cohesion to a company of apes – to develop loyalty to whatever institution an individual finds himself in. Managerial capitalism requires a high degree of attachment of the staff to a corporation. Self-interest, of course, is involved but pure self-interest would lead to great mobility between businesses and the disclosure of the secrets of one to another. Loyalty which invests the ego of the individuals in his corporation is an essential feature of the system...

The managers are continually striving to increase profits by investments which reduce costs so as to improve their selling power. This makes it possible for real wages to rise without reducing the rate of profit. The major part of this investment is financed out of profits and the earning power of the capital so created is the property of whoever happens to be holding the shares. Thus the position of the stockholder is anomalous ...

This system ensures for the managements a high degree of independence from bankers and governments and for that reason they tolerate the drain on the firm's resources represented by the necessity to pay out enough dividends to secure its good standing on the Stock Exchange ...

There is an ever-rising consumption of industrial products by the middle class of farmers, small businesses, professionals including the personnel of the technostructure itself, and that part of the working class which had become absorbed into the system; the system has come to be known as the 'consumer society'. But this is not a sufficient base to provide an outlet for the sheer mass of investible funds which the system generates. Moreover the inherent instability of investment which the private enterprise economy had manifested before the war is now coupled with a potential instability in consumption . . .

The system *has* however kept running with only moderate fluctuations. State expenditure has provided a balancing element in demand to preserve near-stability and continuous growth in the market for goods. The easiest line of expenditure for the state to undertake is for so-called defence . . .

There may have been some far-sighted government advisors who saw the arms race as a solution of the problem of maintaining economic stability, but it seems plausible to suppose that this formula came from a convergence of a variety of forces. The military and all the authorities who had risen to positions of power and honour in the war were reluctant to step down. A number of important industries would have suffered a sharp decline if armaments production had fallen off; the scientists who had committed themselves to the atom bomb did not want to believe that it was unnecessary; politicians, financiers and industrialists feared that sympathy with the Russian people might encourage communism at home; broad masses of white workers, small businessmen, members of the technostructure and intellectuals still held the faith [in the opportunities the system offers] . . .

Whatever its causes, the consequence of the Cold War was to provide an outlet for government expenditure which did not compete with private enterprise and which did not saturate demand by producing anything that the public could consume . . .

The vested interest of all who depend for profits or employment on the arms industry (including a large proportion of the universities and research institutes) gave it a solid backing, and the crusade for 'freedom' gave it a noble aim.

This system has proved itself remarkably successful, not for fighting wars, but for maintaining continuous profitability and so permitting a continuous growth of industry, which, so to speak as a by-product, could continuously expand the output and consumption of marketable goods. The relations of production were better adapted to the forces of scientific technology than ever before . . . Rationality requires that the prime aim of policy should be to make war obsolete and to find alternative ways of dealing with the problems that give rise to it; but it is precisely the economic success of the military-industrial complex (though it has over-reached itself in Vietnam) that puts the greatest obstacle in the way of any such attempt.

To maintain near-full employment, it is not enough merely to preserve stability. It is necessary also to ensure that the number of jobs that the economy offers grows at the same pace as the working population. Technical progress is continually reducing the number of man-hours of work required, this year, to produce last year's output. At the same time, when the population is growing, greater numbers are seeking employment this year than last. To prevent unemployment requires the demand for labour to rise along with the supply.

An adequate rate of increase of total output together with a reduction in man-hours of work per man-year and a lengthening of the period of education enables the system to digest technical change which is gradual and widely diffused throughout industry, though there does not seem much logic in allowing the 'passive and functionless' shareholder to enjoy a large part of the benefit. But the profit motive contains no mechanism to ensure that technical progress will take digestible forms . . .

Modern capitalism is well adapted to produce fabulous technical successes, but not to provide the basis for the noble life accessible to all that Marshall dreamed of.

Joan Robinson (pp.89–93) saw the development of the welfare state as an outgrowth of

the demands of democracy and humanitarian sentiment combined with the enlightened self-interest of the business community. A destitute citizen is a reproach to the economy and of no use to it as a worker to produce, or a market to absorb, saleable goods; ill-health is wasteful and public education is necessary to produce skilled workers and the lower echelons of the technostructure. Thus modern capitalism takes a turn towards the welfare state . . .

It is possible to argue that in Sweden democratic public opinion has mastered the industrialists and made them its servants, while in USA the state has become the servant of the industrialists. Other Western countries lie somewhere in between . . .

Boring or not, the welfare state has very much softened the harshness of raw capitalism and has played a large part in saving it, till now, from the doom that Marx foresaw a hundred years ago.

As well as industrial technology, the second ingredient in the high standard of life of the developed nations is birth control . . . A cessation of growth of numbers in a near-full employment welfare economy would make possible a more rapid rise in the average standard of consumption with less destruction of amenities in space, water and air. All the capitalist industrial nations are still suffering from growing numbers; and the humanitarians are in a cruel dilemma between wanting to rescue all the children who do get born from poverty and fear of encouraging their parents to bear more.

The welfare state, just as much as the needs of 'defence', promotes nationalism. Each government is concerned for its own people and policy cannot distinguish between benefits to them which are absolute and those which are at the expense of other peoples ...

An ideal solution (from the point of view of the native capitalists) has been found in Western Germany where workers from poorer countries are brought in, ready-made with no cost for their rearing, when industry is booming, and expelled when unemployment threatens. In such situations, it is taken for granted that the welfare only of the natives is the concern of the home government, whether the system offers any advantages to foreigners or not ...

The requirements of the warfare state and the welfare state meet in the export of armaments, which keep industry in ex-imperialist countries prosperous and permit enmities in the ex-colonial countries, which were frozen at the level of bows and arrows or flintlocks, to break out with bombs and tanks.

(2) In her later writings, Joan Robinson was also harshly critical of the Soviet system. Of Marxism she (1962a, p.41) said that 'in its original form (like Christianity)' it 'had the appeal of the cause of the under-dog. As with Christianity, the wheel of time has brought it to be a creed for top dogs and its moral appeal has been much weakened thereby'. She (1970, pp.94–74) spoke of the Soviet system after World War II when the Soviet sphere of influence extended to a number of East European countries.

The Russian system was transplanted into all these countries, including its tyranny and injustice. In spite of all, the powerful effect of planned development has raised production (including armaments) over the whole area to such a level that a policy of relaxation becomes possible and the demands of the public for some benefit from their toil and abstinence become insistent.

The era of potential affluence took the Soviet planners by surprise. During the period of heavy accumulation it was considered to be a 'law of socialism' that the proportion of annual investment devoted to expanding the investment industries should be greater than the proportion devoted to building up capacity in consumer good industries ...

During the period of accelerating accumulation, a kind of anti-consumer ideology was developed by the planners. Only heavy industry was taken seriously. The Soviet system proved to be very efficient for producing sputniks but very inefficient at meeting the housewife's daily needs. Unnecessary hardships were imposed upon the consumer, for instance by failure to provide for services such as repairs for shoes and watches, over and above the hardships necessarily entailed by high accumulation and an economy dominated by defence. The method of controlling industry by

commands from above which were often incompatible with each other, the statement of plans in terms of gross output which encouraged a wasteful use of materials, and an arbitrary system of prices, led to inefficiency in production. The economic system which proved successful in applying a forced draft to accumulation was proving to be an impediment to enjoying its fruits. The relations of production had to be adapted to a new situation.
... Perhaps the most important achievement of the Soviet system was the development of public education, far ahead of anything seen in welfare capitalism, and the opening of opportunity to talent for all the peoples of the Union. This was accompanied by a stratification of income and status according to the educational level required for various kinds of work. For a long time the requirements for trained personnel of the administration, industry (including armaments and space travel) and the social services, including education itself, was running ahead of what the system could provide; recently it was found that supply had caught up upon requirements so that there begin to be more qualified candidates than places carrying the privileges which they expected to enjoy. In the severely utilitarian drive for production, the concept of education as an end in itself had been lost. The idea was even suggested of limiting entry to higher education so that there would be a sufficient number of workers obliged to remain in the lower ranks.

(3) Someone once said that there are things about which one ought to write a great deal or nothing at all. Joan's writings on Mao's China are a case in point. Why she was attracted to and fascinated by the possibilities of an alternate social and economic design is fairly clear, but why she wore blinkers when she looked at China is something of an enigma. The puritan in Joan was attracted to the aims of the Cultural Revolution: combat egoism and eschew privilege. One wonders how it is possible that Joan Robinson, the realist, did not perceive the human and material costs of the undertaking in practice.

(4) In many ways, Joan Robinson (1976, pp.9–10) saw the principal problems of underdeveloped economies in the same light as Kalecki (see Feiwel, 1975, ch. 16).

Non employment in the underdeveloped economies is of a totally different nature from unemployment in the developed economies; it cannot be overcome merely by increasing effective demand. The objective of development is to increase productive capacity. To embark upon large schemes of investment without a coherent plan will mean a great deal of wasted effort. Moreover, even well directed investment sets up inflationary pressure. To avoid inflation requires a massive increase in the supply of necessities for consumption – in particular food – but at the same time investment itself enriches the old feudal and the new business families, deflecting resources into the production of luxuries. A successful programme of development, therefore, requires strong measures to prevent growing inequality in incomes.

She asked the most pertinent question: what is development for and who is to benefit from its fruits? (see 1979a, p.29).

Like many others, she was troubled by the excessive growth of population in Third World countries. In most of these countries throughout the postwar period employment has been increasing at a slower rate than population. Agriculture cannot provide even a subsistence level for the new generation of peasants. And the new jobs in industry and services are insufficient to absorb the influx from the countryside. 'A flow of dispossessed families has drifted into shanty towns and slums or on to the streets of cities, living on a physical and social standard of existence at the limit of human endurance' (Joan Robinson, 1979c, p.6).

> Marx, in his desire to combat the reactionary doctrines of Malthus, did not stress the point that growth of population, under capitalism, is inimical to the interests of the working class, though his own theory clearly indicates that this is the case. When capital accumulation goes on faster than the labour force is growing, the reserve army of the unemployed is absorbed and competition between capitalists for hands causes real wage rates to rise. The consequent reduction in the share of profit in the proceeds of industry slows down accumulation, and when numbers continue to grow, the reserve army is replenished and wages fall again. When the labour force is not growing, accumulation takes the form of technical change which raises output per man employed. Then organised labour can catch a share in the growth of productivity by raising real-wage rates. This, indeed, has happened in the Western economies. The moral seems clear, but some fanatically dogmatic Marxists have joined with the Pope in refusing to admit that the growth of population, in modern conditions, is an impediment to the growth of human welfare. (p.8)

And, in typical Robinsonian fashion, she (1962a, p.115) replied to the religious aphorism, ' "with every mouth God sends a pair of hands." True enough, but he does not send a combine-harvester'.

Joan Robinson was not much impressed by the attempts at industrializing Third World countries under the banner of capitalism. She (1962a, pp.124–8) admitted that 'the aspirations of the developing countries are more for national independence and national self-respect than just for bread to eat' (p.124). Genuine universalism is very rare. 'The prosperity of others is not desirable for *their* sake, but as a contribution to *our* comfort; when their prosperity seems likely to threaten ours, it is not desirable at all' (p.126).

Foreign aid is self-interested. 'We help India (as much as we do) not because we want to multiply "units of happiness" by giving starving people a square meal, but because we hope it will keep up the prestige of the West against the Soviet Union' (p.128).

She was scornful of the 'Far Eastern miracles' (South Korea, Hong Kong, Taiwan, Singapore) achieved through free trade. 'Low wages do not necessarily mean cheap labour, but it seems that in these countries workers are exceptionally patient, dextrous and well disciplined, so that low wages give their employers a powerful competitive advantage in export markets. Since they are in competition with each other in keeping down costs, the authorities try to avoid the expenses involved in social services' (Joan Robinson, 1979c, pp.107–8). However, 'if development means overcoming poverty and building up national self-reliance, these miracles can hardly be regarded as examples of success' (pp.109–10). And not least important, in these countries 'there are strong dictatorships which do not tolerate unrest' (p.119). She (1979c, pp.123–4) drew a sharp contrast between the development of capitalism in the West and in the Third World:

> Capitalism grew up in the traditions of democratic liberalism and however much hypocrisy and ideological manipulation there may be in that tradition, it has meant that, with growing wealth, there has been a great diffusion of consumption and of education throughout the populations of the Western countries. There have been Factory Acts, limitations of hours of work, prohibition of child labour. Housing is not much to boast about, but cities at least provide sewage and clean water for almost every family, while the families of industrial workers have come to expect many formerly middle-class luxuries. Parliament and the press are free to criticise the authorities and the imposition of orthodoxy on intellectual life operates more through self-censorship than overt oppression.
>
> When capitalism is transplanted into backward regions, it does not develop on these lines but (combined with growth of numbers) generates a trend towards inequality and misery. Tyrannous governments are therefore necessary to hold society together. Any attempt to organise a labour movement is soon crushed and it is a commonplace for priests and intellectuals to be tortured to cure them of uttering dangerous thoughts.

In Joan Robinson's opinion some form of 'benign' socialism and economic planning would be most beneficial for an underdeveloped country seriously and successfully embarking on industrialization. 'It is not easy to see how the Third World can mount the attack while preserving private property in the means of production and respecting the rules of the free-market economy' (p.10) True enough, 'it is far easier to build machines than to reorganise society' (1962a, p.114). At the present juncture in many Third World countries 'national planning is still in fashion among economists and many models are produced showing how growth can be achieved by investment, but this concept of planning is a day-dream, for the governments concerned do not in fact have sufficient control over resources to carry plans into effect ... This kind of "planning" is merely an amusement for theoretical economists' (1979c, p.12). But when the planner has command over resources he could benefit from 'the statistical and mathematical methods evolved by modern economics ... provided that they are thoroughly well scrubbed to get the metaphysical concepts cleaned off them' (1962a, p.123).

When national authorities take it upon themselves to direct economic development, investment has to be controlled by a conscious plan instead of following the fluctuating animal spirits of private enterprise. Proportions derived from the formula for growth ($g = s/v$) then have something to say. For instance the formula shows that, if a particular rate of growth is to be achieved, the more capital-saving the type of investments to be made, the higher is the ratio of consumption to income that can be permitted (given g, a lower value of v entails a lower value of s) or that, given the type of investment that is to be undertaken, the rate of growth achieved depends upon the ratio of investment consumption (given v, a higher value of g requires a higher value of s).

All the same, the emphasis on saving is more misleading than helpful. The characteristic problem of an under-developed economy is that its present rate of accumulation is too low (in some cases too low even to keep up with the growth of population, let alone to start reducing under-employment and raising the standard of life). Such economies have before them the heavy task of raising their growth rates, and, however much ingenuity they use in keeping the capital/output ratio down, this must entail (in terms of the formula) an overall rise in the ratio of saving to income. But for the most part, the mass of their people are living below the minimum of subsistence necessary for working efficiency. The problem can be stated in a straightforward manner in terms of the need to provide for an increase in necessary consumption while restraining unnecessary consumption. The overall saving ratio (s in the formula) distracts attention from the distribution of income between individual families. It helps to disguise the awkward problem of what the Indians have begun to call the 'growth of the U-sector,' which takes place when private wealth is swollen by the overflow from public investment.

The need to restrain consumption in order to permit the rate of accumulation to increase gives an advantage to the economies carrying out development under socialist institutions. A revolution which nationalizes property without compensation makes resources that formerly fed U-consumption available for investment. The pre-existing surplus of unnecessary consumption is small, however, in relation to the accumulation required. The main advantage of wiping out unearned income is that it makes it easier, morally and politically, to prevent real wages from rising too fast. Moreover collective consumption in the form of medical services, entertainments, and so forth (which are easier to provide in a collectivized economy) contribute more, per unit of national expenditure, to the general welfare (on any reasonable basis of judgment) than a rise of wages spread thinly over individual families.

(5) In many places throughout this chapter we have alluded to Joan Robinson's condemnation of the creation of prosperity in the West through military build-up. At no time was this stronger than in her last years when she became increasingly dejected. It took overtones of warnings against nuclear self-destruction. In 1980 in a talk in Montreal, she (1983, pp.15 and 17) is reported to have said:

> We are sitting around discussing ideas totally beside the point. The important question is not whether the rate of inflation is high or low or can be brought under control but whether our generation will succeed in destroying the world. We are seeing the supply of arms pile up as the Americans and Soviets advance from one missile system to the next. This same threat lies before the next generation. We should realize that the stock-piling of destruction precedes discussion of inflation and unemployment. The arms race is too serious a matter for us to be content to dispute economic theories that float off into the stratosphere.
>
> Economics should begin to address the important issue of our impending doom.

In *The Tanner Lectures on Human Values*,[48] she (1982b) took up the theme (eloquently advanced in Chapters 29 and 30 of the companion volume) of the nuclear peril facing us today.

> Fanciful scientists have discussed the possibility of colonising the solar system, but meanwhile we have only one world and we have created a situation which threatens to make it uninhabitable. When I say *we* I am referring to the generation of the human race now extant, led and manipulated by the ruling powers of the great industrial nations. The peril threatening the world arises from a technological development in warfare. Over the centuries wars have been growing more and more destructive, but up till now it was always possible to restore the economic base of the countries concerned after the war was over. From nuclear destruction there is no recovery. (p.257)
>
> How has this situation been allowed to arise? Mainly, I suppose, because the whole subject is so horrifying that we prefer not to think about it and, in each country, leave the notions of various so-called experts and the

interplay of various vested interests to shape our history for us. But just not to think about it makes it all the more dangerous. (p.258)

The nuclear weapons that are now being developed cannot provide defense. If they are not to be used for aggression they could only be used for revenge. This was forcibly illustrated for us in Cambridgeshire when there was a false alarm last summer. In eastern England automatic gadgets are set up which are intended to give a warning signal when a rocket is detected on its way. This was set off by (I think) a flight of geese. Immediately, from the surrounding aerodromes, loaded planes shot into the air, ready to fly east and drop bombs over there. Their function was evidently not defense but retaliation. What satisfaction would it be, when our homeland was destroyed, to go and destroy the homeland of a supposed enemy? It is certainly a misnomer to describe this as defense. (p.261)

Far from contributing to defense, the production of weapons increases peril. A quaint system has developed of announcing that some new horror will be available in three or five years' time, so that if the other side is as hostile and aggressive as our propaganda pretends, they would be well advised to "take it out," as the phrase is, before it can be installed.

Perhaps in the deepest sense we can never understand our own history, but it seems to me to be worthwhile to try to discuss how this dangerous situation has arisen. I suggest three aspects – the Cold War, the momentum of research and development, and the connection of armaments with the problem of employment ...

First, the Cold War. The kaleidoscope of history has brought into existence two great national powers each with its troop of allies and satellites. This would in any case have been a cause of tension and rivalry, but it so happens that they support two different ideologies – so called communism in the Eastern camp and so-called freedom in the West – which gives the conflict between them something of the character of the wars of religion ...

The conflicts of ideologies smothers self-criticism ... This is most damaging to the side that professes freedom as its ideology, for obscurantism and self-righteousness are liable to tarnish that very openness and objectivity which is supposed to be the glory of the Western side ...

The second, and perhaps the main cause of the situation we have got ourselves into is the momentum of research and development. When an idea has once been started it must be pursued without regard to consequences, and once a new weapon or means of attack has been perfected it is extremely difficult to prevent it being added to the stock of means of destruction. (pp.262–3)

Robert Oppenheimer agonised over his responsibility for Hiroshima. In 1951 his rival, Edward Teller, was working on the next generation of means of devastation, the hydrogen bomb. Oppenheimer opposed it and, presumably for that reason, a case was fabricated for questioning his loyalty. He gave way, however, to the momentum of research. The new conception was "technically so sweet you could not argue about that." "You go ahead and do it and you argue about what to do about it only after you have had your technical success." ... Here is the clearest statement of the process which has brought us to where we are. (p.267)

During the 1970's research and development continued. Technological advance went into improving the accuracy of aim of rockets and the secrecy with which a sudden attack could be launched. These new devices are designed for aggression. The notion of defense has faded from the scene. In particular, the neutron bomb, which is designed to wipe out the defenders of a city with a minimum of damage to buildings, seems to be designed for the requirements of a conqueror ...

Official pronouncements made in the West and discussed in the media seem to be mainly aimed at providing soothing syrup to discourage the general public from forming any opinion in this situation; when some warnings are emitted, they are mainly confined (apart from Mountbatten's) to the loss of life that could be caused by nuclear war. This seems to be a kind of collective egoism. What is at risk is not just the lives of the present generation of the inhabitants of the northern hemisphere or of the whole globe, it is, as Mountbatten recognised, the continuance of our civilization. No doubt that civilization, East and West together, is imperfect, bloodstained, full of injustice, but all the same it is a great achievement and full of new possibilities. We surely should be concerned not to throw it away? Supposing that we squeak through the present era of crisis and manage to survive for twenty or fifty years, we should still leave the world in peril of a future disaster. Unless mankind can give up the habit of making national wars, it seems that sooner or later it will destroy itself. (pp.272–3)

The Keynesian revolution in economic theory which emerged from the great slump of the 1930's is often identified merely with a policy of running a budget deficit to reduce unemployment; but it was more than that. It was a great gain in insight into the manner of operation of a capitalist industrial economy. The *principle of effective demand* means that the accumulation of capital in the sense of productive capacity is not directly due to saving in terms of money – finance – but to investment in creating physical means of production ...

In the slump of the thirties, the advocates of public loan expenditure were mocked by the argument that they were advocating the policy of paying workers to dig holes in the ground and fill them up again. They replied that wages are spent on goods and services. The excess of what a family can buy when the breadwinner is earning over what they spend when he is on the dole calls into being a genuine increase in real national income ...

In the 1930's, unbeknownst to Keynes, the principle of effective demand had been discovered independently in defeated Germany; not only discovered but actually put into practice. (pp.274–7)

We may ask, is the employment motive playing a part on the Western side in maintaining the arms race? Are we back at the policy of digging holes in the ground to maintain jobs?

Of course the danger of confrontation between the armed giants and the international tensions that it breeds are far and away more important than the problem of unemployment, however grave that may be, but perhaps the problem of employment is playing a minor part in keeping tension alive? To call off the arms race does not require any prior agreement between the two sides. It is open to either great power to state that enough is enough. The initiator has sufficient power to destroy the other side several times over and does not propose to add any more to its stockpile of redundant weapons.

Such an outbreak of common sense in international relations is not to be expected in this mad world, but just for the sake of argument we might enquire whether such a move would have a tendency to precipitate a slump. Some care would have to be taken to prevent a sudden drop in profits and jump in unemployment. Where contracts were broken or legitimate expectations disappointed, the firms concerned should be offered credits on favourable terms and encouraged to switch *r* and *d* to constructive forms, in particular the search for new sources of energy. After perhaps a short period of confusion, the effect on employment should be highly favourable. Present policy which combines cutting public expenditure with increasing military investments has introduced a serious distortion into development. From a short-period point of view, man-power, including the most expensively trained scientific man-power, is shifting from services such as health and education and the production of civilian goods in general into production of war-like stores.

Research conducted by one of the big trade unions involved appears to show what when a certain flow of finance is deflected from civilian to military production there is a reduction of employment. The cost of materials handled and allowance for profits is higher per man employed on the average than in civilian branches of industry, so that cost per unit of employment is greater... Moreover, part of the cost is for mining the earth's crust for rare minerals and embodying them in forms that can be used only for destruction ...

From a long-period point of view the loss due to the arms race is literally incalculable, for we cannot know what benefits would have been derived from applying the mental and material resources involved to constructive ends.

What form would increased civilian employment take? Emma Rothschild has made a very interesting analysis of the tendency of the structure of employment in the USA to shift from manufacture towards services ...

Emma Rothschild sees in this a symptom of decay. These are low-wage activities giving little scope for technically progressive investments.

I do not see the force of this argument. If what the consumer most wants is to be freed from the chores of cooking and cleaning at home why is it less progressive to meet this demand than demand for objects made out of metals or chemicals? If they are low-wage occupations, the remedy is to unionise the workers and push up wages so that it would be profitable to mechanise the services, making fast food all the faster. This is certainly not a recipe for gracious living, but if it is what is wanted, why should it not be provided? (pp.283–5)

9   *NON OMNIS MORIAR*

Shortly before her eightieth birthday (31 October, 1983) after a prolonged illness, Joan Robinson died on 5 August, 1983. She left an imperishable and incalculable scholarly legacy and fond memories of the person and scholar she was.

Within the broad context of accretion of economic knowledge, perceptions of her achievements (and of the relative merits of specific contributions) do and will differ, but the overall picture that emerges is one of an economist who will live forever.

I believe future generations of economists will be inspired to emulate her and explore the profound questions she raised with such perspicacity, perspicuity, and persistence. Economics lives by its unresolved problems. What matters is whom it attracts, for what reasons, what do the 'young' do, and how do they go about it.

Those who complain that economics is dull should read Joan Robinson. As Al Jolson used to say, 'you ain't seen nothing yet'. She not only challenged orthodoxy, fallacies, complacency, fudging, sloppy thinking, and circular reasoning as she saw them, but showed us that economics is a serious subject. She once said that the genius of Ricardo was in his analysis and not in his ideology. *Mutatis mutandis* the same can be said of her. By and large, she had a remarkable grasp of the potentials and limits of economic theorizing and was a gifted practitioner of the art of economic model building. Some of her critics feel that she suffered from (what Schumpeter called) Ricardo's Vice, but this is not a view to which I subscribe. Those who find comfort in anti-theory or, for that matter, those who build models for the sake of models further and further removed from reality, will hardly find an ally and champion in Joan. She practiced and preached economics as a serious subject in the service of human betterment. Marshall once said that Cambridge sends into the world the best of men with cool heads and warm hearts. Joan Robinson was a living example of this aphorism with the set expanded to women.[49]

Yes there are and will be different Joans for different people. The diversity is rather reassuring.

In this chapter, I have tried to show that economics, as a living and serious subject, is the richer in an essential sense for Joan Robinson's overall and specific contributions. I have not shied away from mentioning (sometimes sharp) criticism of her work, for in a serious subject, serious criticism is a higher form of praise than mere following. In the chapters that follow different perceptions of Joan Robinson's contributions and of various facets of subjects she touched upon are presented. What has made this enterprise really worth while is the richness and variety of approaches and emphases.

For those of us who had the privilege of knowing Joan, she was much more than a great economist. Memories of her are vivid and cherished by those of us who were so deeply touched by her. *The Times* (10 August, 1983), after recording her great contributions to economics, described her in these words:

Her work drew to her an army of admirers of all ages and in all parts of the world. Throughout her life her fierce independence of spirit led her to espouse humanitarian causes without regard to prevailing prejudices or fashions. It was part of her humanitarianism that she spent a good deal of time in making economics understandable to ordinary men and women, prompted by the realization that an understanding of how capitalist economies work is essential to the understanding of the world in which we live. She displayed remarkable intellectual vitality which made her interested in every promising new initiative in the subject and eager to explore its validity and significance.

As a teacher she was brilliant, clear, stimulating and original. As a conversationalist she was alarming. She was determined to thrash out differences in logic and assumptions and would pertinaciously continue when her antagonist wished to stop. She held views with great conviction and wished others to share her logical approach. But behind her somewhat alarming facade she possessed great warmth and sympathy.[50]

At a memorial service for Joan at King's College Chapel (29 October, 1983), Ruth Cohen (a life long friend and Principal of Newnham College) spoke of 'Joan as a person and a friend', 'a great economist and one of the most remarkable personalities of her generation' (Cohen, 1983, p.3). More specifically, she (pp.1–2) said:

Her work was original over many fields and her reputation as an economist of the first rank has been world-wide for many decades. Most of

us, I think, regard it as outrageous that she never received the Nobel Prize.
... As an economist she would accept no theory as granted, and would
reconsider accepted assumptions, of the right certainly, but of the left too.
... In the last few years of her life she became very depressed at the state of
economic doctrine, struggling towards a theory that could create models
that could grapple with history, with ecological balances in individual
communities, and particularly with technological change. She was trying
to evolve a different technique of thought.

And Ruth Cohen (p.3) also spoke of the human side of Joan:

She was one of the warmest, most loyal and delicate of friends ... She had
a great gift for life – warmth and humanity, ready joys and angers, and a
fulness of response, to people who touched her, to civilisation and to
nature.

She loved her family. To quote Joan ... 'It's much easier being a
woman. You can be so creative having a child'. She actively enjoyed pram-
pushing, for her grandchildren as well as for her daughters. To my great
surprise she knitted for them! ...

Indeed, she loved the young generally, undergraduates as well as
children. And she had faith in them.

Notes

1. For a background on the Cambridge tradition and the Cambridge school of
   economics from different perspectives see, *inter alia*, Chapter 3 of the companion volume; A. Robinson, 1977 and 1985; Kahn, 1984 and 1985; Skidelsky,
   1983; Keynes, 1963; Hutchison, 1981; Johnson, 1978; and O'Brien and Presley,
   1981.
2. For example, Keynes (1973b, p.35) wrote in a letter to Hawtrey (dated 28 May,
   1936: 'You must remember that I was brought up by these teachers and
   lectured their stuff for many years and my impression is just as much derived
   from what I was taught in my turn as from chapter and verse'.
3. She defined 'nonsense' (1973a, p.261) in the strict sense given to that word by
   Wittgenstein: 'What can be thought can be thought clearly. What can be said
   can be said clearly. What can be shown cannot be said'.
4. With similar scorn, Samuelson (1972, p.25) points out:

   'It is all in Marshall,' they say, failing to add, 'All the words of economics are
   in Webster's dictionary or in the fingertips of monkeys in the British
   Museum.' But just as it takes more than monkeys to find the Michelangelo
   statues that lurk in an old cube of marble, so it takes more than can be
   learned in Marshall to isolate the good sense that is embalmed therein.

5. The strong impact of the young Piero Sraffa on the Cambridge of the 1920s was
   acknowledged and described by Kahn, 1984, pp.23–6. Shackle (1967, p.12)
   noted that the years of high theory opened with the Sraffian Manifesto (Sraffa,
   1926). (See also Shackle, 1967, ch. 3.)

6. Joan Robinson (1979a, p.169) noted a very striking example of Marshall's confusion:

> Marshall had a foxy way of salving his conscience by mentioning exceptions, but doing so in such a way that his pupils would continue to believe in the rule. He pointed out that Say's Law – supply creates its own demand – breaks down when there is a failure of confidence, which causes investment to fall off and contraction to spread from one market to another. This was mentioned by the way. It was not meant to disturb the general faith in equilibrium under laisser-faire.

7. In 1978 (p.xi) Joan Robinson wrote: 'After passing through another intellectual revolution, I took a more kindly view of Marshall. Though he fudged the problem of time, he was aware of it, and he took pains to avoid the spurious neoclassical methodology'. But in 1973b (p.ix) she wrote: 'Recently I have used Pigou's name as a convenient label for the static element in Marshall and credited Marshall himself with the dynamic element ... Perhaps this is too flattering to Marshall. Both elements were present in his thinking and he showed great agility in appealing, in each context, to whichever would best suit his purpose of presenting a mollifying picture of the private-enterprise economy'.

8. This conflict was not confined to *Principles*. 'The most powerful and all-pervasive doctrine in pre-Keynesian orthodoxy was the case in favour of free trade. This was not invented by the neoclassicists, but derived via Marshall from David Richardo' (Joan Robinson, 1979a, p.25).

> Whether convincing or not, Ricardo's analysis is perfectly clear. The model in Marshall's *Pure Theory of Foreign Trade*, expressed in terms of 'offer curves', is not so easy to grasp. He refers to the *Pure Theory of Domestic Values* for the analysis of costs and prices in each country, but this theory is an inextricable mixture of static and dynamic elements. 'Increasing returns' is the result of investment and technical progress going on through time as the output of a particular commodity is growing. How can this be fitted in to the comparisons of static equilibrium. He was aware of the contradiction but did not feel able to deal with it. (Joan Robinson, 1973a, p.17, see also Joan Robinson, 1951, 1978, pp.182–205; 1973a, pp.14–24.)

9. But again one should not forget alternative views of Marshall. For example, Gram and Walsh (1983, p.521) write (see also O'Brien and Presley, 1981, ch.2; Feiwel, 1987, pp.145–59; and Chapter 3 of the companion volume):

> The strength of Marshall's method, mirrored in much of Robinson's work, is that it highlights those partial and ultimately inconsistent equilibria which may be the nearest we can come to depicting certain aspects of real life – the *formation* of short-run relative prices, for example. The analytical perfection of a general equilibrium model evades this problem, concerning itself instead with the *existence* of prices compatible with given conditions of static or intertemporal supply and demand. Even if Marshall's method is bound to be wrong to some extent, it gives an invaluable picture of an aspect of economic reality which general equilibrium models cannot offer. Were this not so, it would be impossible to explain the eternal youthfulness and survival of essentially Marshallian treatments of microtheory now that we have systems of general equilibrium which exhibit rigorously those properties of an economy with which they can properly be expected to deal. There would appear to be a terrain from which Marshall is extremely difficult to dislodge.

10.   On the distinctions between 'pure', 'perfect', and other types of competition see Joan Robinson, 1951, 1978, pp.20–34; see also 1979a, pp.6, 8–9, 146–67; 1962b, pp.1–2 and *passim*.

11.   Which of us has not been brought up short in his reading of Marshall when suddenly, in the midst of what was thought to be a discussion of 'competition', it turns out that some entrepreneur fails to do something because of his 'fear of spoiling the market,' a sure sign of some kind of imperfection of competition? Such aberrations as these, to which I point in horror, are taken by some modern writers as signs of Marshall's genius and erudite wisdom about the facts of life. (Samuelson, 1972, p.25)

12.   Joan Robinson (1979a, pp.11–12) saw the roots of what she later perceived as her wrong turn in Pigou's own wrong turn (see 1951, 1978, pp.vii–viii):

> A. C. Pigou ... was a loyal disciple of Marshall and quite innocent of any knowledge of industry. He therefore constructed a U-shaped average cost curve for a firm, showing economies of scale up to a certain size and rising costs beyond it. Pigou's firm, in a perfectly competitive market, is always selling the output that maximizes profits, that is, at which a small increase in production would cause marginal cost to exceed the price; when price exceeds average cost, the firm is making a super-normal profit, which will attract new competition; when price is below average costs, some firms are dropping out. Equilibrium requires that both marginal and average costs are equal to price, that is, that the size of the firm is such that it is producing at minimum cost. In the ultimate equilibrium of a stationary state, the flow of profits obtained by each firm is just sufficient to cover interest at the ruling rate on the value of the capital that it operates, leaving nothing over as the 'reward of enterprise'.
>
> In Marshall's world, however, profits accrue to 'business ability in command of capital'; successful firms retain part of their profits to invest in expanding their activities, and the more capital they own the easier it is to borrow outside finance. The conception is absurd that a firm when it is making more than normal profits sits around waiting for competition to invade its markets and drive it back towards its optimum size. It would be the height of imprudence for a business to distribute the whole of its net profit to the family or to shareholders, and no business could borrow if prospective profits did not exceed its interest bill.
>
> If Marshall's theory had been taken on its merits as a hypothesis, it would have soon appeared that the way out of his dilemma was the opposite of that proposed by Pigou. Successful firms accumulate finance and devour the unsuccessful ones. Most joint-stock companies continue to grow, and many competitive industries tend towards a condition of dominance by one or a few firms. But the great corporations do not behave monopolistically in the sense of restricting output in order to raise prices. They continue to compete with each other, invading new markets, introducing new products, and evolving new techniques, while at the same time throwing up opportunities for new small businesses to make a start.

13.   Joan (1978, p.132) complains that 'this rigmarole was the only legacy from Marshall that has been incorporated into modern orthodoxy'.

14.   The experience of an all-round buyer's market in the 1930s shocked us into realizing (what Marshall always knew) ... that prices may be held above prime costs and plants worked at less than full capacity; and the experience

of seller's markets in recent times has shown that long delivery dates and rationing of customers accompany prices held below the level that chokes off excess demand. In short, imperfect competition is the general rule in manufacturing industry. (Joan Robinson, 1971, pp.19–20)

15. There are various interpretations of the content and message of Sraffa's pathbreaking 1926 contribution and of its relation to its previous longer version in Italian. Moreover, Sraffa (1926) and its earlier Italian version are helpful in understanding many of the controversies that surround Sraffa (1960). The negative and positive implications of Sraffa (1926) and the relative merits of the alternative routes that could be followed after discarding Marshall's partial equilibrium analysis, indicated or implied by Sraffa (1926) and those that he eventually followed in the 'classical revival', and those followed by modern general equilibrium theorists and other streams – all those are sensitive issues that would require a book to explore. Only some aspects will be touched upon in the pages that follow. For the many facets of these questions, see *inter alia*, Chapter 13 of this volume; Roncaglia, 1978; Harcourt, 1986; Walsh and Gram, 1980; Hahn, 1975, 1982; Dobb, 1973; Sylos Labini 1985; Shackle, 1967; Samuelson, 1972, pp.28–30; Maneschi, 1986; Kregel, 1971, 1983; and Harris, 1978.

16. Writing in 1967 in a *Festschrift* for Chamberlin, Samuelson (1972, p.23) wrote:

That grown men argued seriously in 1930 about who had first used or named the curve that we now call "marginal revenue" is a joke. Cournot had settled all that a century earlier and in a completely modern manner, so that the reader who picks up the English translations of his book and has to guess at the date of its authorship merely on the basis of an understanding of the cost-controversy literature ought to guess 1927 or 1933.

(For an opposite point of view see Shackle, 1967, p.22). In a similar vein, Shubik (1970, p.416) noted that Joan Robinson

managed to write a book on imperfect competition in which the work of Cournot was not even mentioned. The mathematical apparatus she assembled to do this job was such that von Neumann once remarked that if the archeologists of some future civilization were to dig up the remains of ours and find a cache of books, *The Economics of Imperfect Competition* would probably be dated as an early precursor of Newton.

17. Schumpeter (1934, pp.251–2) was of the opinion that Joan's book gained by coming out almost at the same time as Chamberlin's.

For we have now before us in addition to the individual gifts we owe to Chamberlin, Harrod, Robinson, Schneider, Shove, Sraffa, Stackelberg, Zeuthen and others, also what they contributed jointly in the settings peculiar to their different mentalities, and this is much more useful and stimulating than the results of a "planned economy" would have been in this case. Mrs. Robinson's genuine originality stands out from the whole perhaps better than it would if her book stood alone.

Interestingly, even in the *Festschrift* for Chamberlin (Kuenne, 1967), Joan Robinson is treated as a co-heroine.

By now *The Economics of Imperfect Competition* has permeated economics textbooks both in price theory and in history of thought. Even authors of different orientations side in praising Joan Robinson's achievement. For example, Seligman (1962, p.721) considered it as 'one of the great landmarks of the history of economic analysis'. And Ekelund and Hébert (1983, p.483) wrote that the book 'is an analytical tour de force', and Joan Robinson, 'within the confines of her method of analysis', 'was able to make contributions of the first rank to the theory of the firm under all competitive market structures'. However, O'Brien (1984) downgraded and was altogether hostile to Joan Robinson's contributions.

18. Shackle (1967, p.11) noted that Joan Robinson 'abandoned value theory itself in favour of her new invention, the theory of the firm'.

19. In his comments on *The Economics of Imperfect Competition*, Schumpeter (1934, pp.253–4) remarked that

> justice requires us to bear in mind that the book is Marshallian to the core. Everything about it is Marshallian: the approach, the fundamental "conceptual scheme," the manner of reasoning, the starting-points . . . as well as the goals, even the general social vision (although somewhat "modernized") which floats about it. The author steps out of the Cambridge circle only as far as the marginal revenue curve makes it necessary to do so by virtue of the fact that it was simultaneously discovered by a number of economists outside of Cambridge. But on no other occasion. She even fails to pay her respects to Cournot. Excepting her recognition of Mr. Harrod's work in her special field, she found even Oxford too far off – for she does not mention or use the indifference curve. And Walras and Pareto have not written for her. Hence her analysis is strictly an analysis of partial equilibria of single firms or industries . . .
>
> This is not meant to imply adverse criticism. I am too strong an admirer of Marshall's teaching to mean that. I also admire too much the vigorous contour lines of the analytic system which I conceive to be Mrs. Robinson's. For part of our way her machine works more efficiently than any other would, but it is none the less true that it stops of itself after a certain point and that it does so not only, as Mrs. Robinson herself emphasizes, because its parts are as yet imperfect, but because of imperfections inherent to its fundamental design.

It should be noted that Joan Robinson (1933, 1969, pp.37–8, 48, 72–3, and 81) invented and explained the implications of the kinky demand curve (usually identified with Sweezy).

20. As early as 1935, Joan Robinson (1951, 1978, pp.49–51) published a fundamental objection to *laissez-faire* where she pointed to its inherent defects as she then saw them.

21. Already in 1934, writing in the *Quarterly Journal of Economics*, on what is and is not (im)perfect competition, Joan Robinson (1951, 1978, pp.20–34) observed that when she wrote *The Economics of Imperfect Competition* she was 'too much under the influence of tradition to imagine that there was anything more to be said about the matter, but I now feel that the argument must be pushed a stage further'. (p.3)

22. Even the references to this whole debate have to be treated in summary fashion. For the Chicago and refuting arguments see Samuelson, 1972, p.21. For the development of the Chicago school see Reder, 1982 and for a discussion of the more up-to-date developments at Chicago see Feiwel 1985b, pp.24–56 and 116–25 and references therein.

23. 'In the general pure theory of value, the group and the industry are useless concepts. The new wine of monopolistic competition should not be poured into the old goatskins of particular equilibrium methodology' (Triffin, 1940, p.89).

24. Every comprehensive 'theory' of an economic state of society consists of two

complementary but essentially distinct elements. There is, first, the theorist's view about the basic features of that state of society, about what is and what is not important in order to understand its life at a given time. Let us call this his vision. And there is, second, the theorist's technique, an apparatus by which he conceptualizes his vision and which turns the latter into concrete propositions or 'theories'. In those pages of the *Economic Consequences of the Peace* we find nothing of the theoretical apparatus of the *General Theory*. But we find the whole of the vision of things social and economic of which that apparatus is the technical complement. The *General Theory* is the final result of a long struggle *to make that vision of our age analytically operative*. (Schumpeter, 1951, p.268)

25.   In a letter to Hawtrey (dated 15 April, 1936) Keynes (1973b, p.26) wrote:

They consider that the economic system is a self-adjusting one; and that, apart from difficulties due to resources being specialised in mistaken directions, there is no obstacle to the full employment of everyone who is willing to work at a real wage not greater than his marginal productivity. They assume, that is to say, that, if resources were fluid and could be applied equally well in any direction, there would never be any obstacle to full employment, and there would be no unemployment except that which I describe as voluntary. This is the thesis of theirs which I am denying and which I consider it important to deny.

26.   Joan Robinson (1962a, p.73) noted that 'some of Keynes' contemporaries and seniors dislike the expression "the Keynesian Revolution." there was nothing, they say, so very new in the *General Theory*'. And she added, 'they are in a very weak position to say that to the present writer, who learned the pre-Keynesian orthodoxy at their feet'.

27.   Keynes started life as a monetary economist. When he was working on his *Treatise on Money*, he thought that he had to be concerned strictly with the general price level. He rejected the suggestion that his subject was connected with the problem of unemployment ... The ink was not dry on the first copies of the *Treatise* before Keynes began to acknowledge that employment was after all the central point. (Joan Robinson, 1379a, p.169; see also, p.185)

28.   On the unpleasant relations between Keynes and the Circus on the one hand and Robertson and Pigou on the other, see, *inter alia*, Kahn, 1984, pp.185–99; Johnson, 1978, ch. 7 and *passim*; and O'Brien and Presley, 1981, chs. 4 and 6.

29.   Had Keynes actually worked out such a synthesis it naturally would have been one of Marshall-Pigou-Keynes rather than the Walras-Hicks-Samuelson-Keynes variety that eventually emerged.

30.   Joan Robinson (1962b, pp.78–84) classifies models of private-enterprise economy according to the mechanism that determines distribution of national income between wages and profit. She speaks of classical models where the real wage is fixed (by the 'subsistence level' of the worker) and profit is the residual surplus. The neoclassical model is most at ease in a stationary state. The rate of interest is the supply price of capital and wages constitute the residual. Models in the Keynesian tradition involve distribution governed by investment and thrift. Those models can be classified according to assumptions made about the inducement to invest. The models could also be classified according to their assumptions about the propensities to consume – whether they postulate an aggregate propensity to consume or whether the latter depends on the distribution of income between classes. (See also Joan Robinson 1960, 1975, pp.89–99.)

31. On a self-critical note, Joan Robinson (1960, 1975, p.vi) noted that the defect in the last chapter in her (1952) book (whose title became the new title of the reprinted version of her book (1979b)) 'was the lack of an adequate conception of the rate of profit and of its relation to the choice of technique'. In paving the way for a second attempt in her (1956, 1966) book she 'raised the question of the meaning of a quantity of capital as a fund of finance or as a stock of equipment'. For her view of some other blemishes and her attempts to straighten them out see 1979b, pp.ix–xxviii.

32. The essays in this volume might be regarded as an introduction rather than as a supplement to my *Accumulation of Capital*. That book was found excessively difficult. The main fault, I think, lay in too terse an exposition of the main ideas, particularly in Chapter 8 [Accumulation with Constant Technique], and a failure to mark sufficiently sharply the departure from the confused but weighty corpus of traditional teaching that we are required to make when we adopt a Keynesian approach to long-period problems. I offer the present volume with apologies to readers whose heads ached over the earlier one. (Joan Robinson, 1962b, p.v)

33. 'The conditions which steady accumulation requires are such as never to be found in reality . . . All the same, it is useful to set them out, in order to see what their absence entails' (Joan Robinson, 1952, p.92). The explicit statement of conditions for steady growth 'suggests that there is no necessary and inevitable collapse of capitalism in prospect' but it simultaneously shows how hard it is to satisfy the conditions in reality and 'how many weak points there are in the mechanism that keeps the system running' (Joan Robinson, 1960, 1975, p.103).

34. Discussing the characteristics of steady states, Solow (1970, p.2) observed that 'there are always aspects of economic life that are left out of any simplified model. There will therefore be problems on which it throws no light at all; worse yet, there may be problems on which it appears to throw light, but on which it actually propagates error'. And, he (p.7) added 'that the steady state is not a bad place for the theory of growth to start, but may be a dangerous place for it to end'.

Solow (1956, p.65) began by stating that 'the art of successful theorizing is to make the inevitable simplifying assumptions in such a way that the final results are not very sensitive'. Furthermore, he (p.91) qualified his contribution in the following manner:

> Everything above is the neoclassical side of the coin. Most especially it is full employment economics – in the dual aspect of equilibrium condition and frictionless, competitive, causal system. All the difficulties and rigidities which go into modern Keynesian income analysis have been shunted aside. It is not my contention that these problems don't exist, nor that they are of no significance in the long run. My purpose was to examine what might be called the tightrope view of economic growth and to see where more flexible assumptions about production would lead a simple model.

35. It is interesting to note that in describing the reasons why she used the mythical golden age, Joan Robinson (1979a, pp.19–20) drew a parallel between her thinking and that of Hicks. She mentions Hicks's 'long struggle to escape' from *Value and Capital* and his conclusion that models of steady growth are futile and his attempt to analyze disequilibrium growth in *Capital and Time*. Hicks defends his initial position by explaining that he had got hold of a model that was firm and that he thought he understood, but the point of this steady-state model was that it had to be disturbed. And, says Joan: 'I intended my golden age . . . to be used in this way.' (See also Joan Robinson, 1960, p.145.)

36. The concept of equilibrium has many meanings and may be a treacherous one. See Joan Robinson, 1956, 1966, chapter 6 and 1979a, pp.48–58. This is not the place to go into the many meanings of equilibrium, see, *inter alia*, Feiwel, 1987. What equilibrium means for the purposes at hand has been felicitously stated by Bliss (1975, pp.27–8):

> Broadly, there are two approaches that have been adopted with regard to economic equilibrium. On the one hand, equilibrium may be regarded as something which would be expected to be realized, because the dynamic forces which operate upon the economy operate in such a way, and sufficiently rapidly, to bring the economy to an equilibrium. In this case, equilibrium being something which is expected to occur, anything which can be shown to be a feature of equilibrium will itself be expected to occur. It should then be possible in principle to give to the relations of the economy a dynamic formulation of which the equilibrium solution would be one particular solution state, but a particular state which could be shown to be attained rather rapidly. The study of the behaviour of the economy out of equilibrium will be called *disequilibrium dynamics*. Alternatively, we may regard the assumption that equilibrium obtains as no more than an analytical stepping stone, as a necessary simplification to render possible some progress in an otherwise hopelessly difficult analytical endeavour. Either approach is possible; both have been adopted fairly explicity by those writers who have taken the trouble to make clear how they regard equilibrium; and both suffer from serious shortcomings between which, inescapably, the theorist must make his choice.
>
> The disadvantage of regarding the equilibrium state as the culmination of disequilibrium dynamic adjustment is simply that the formulation of models of disequilibrium dynamics is hard and uncertain work ...
>
> In the face of all the foregoing problems it may seem more sensible to simply assume that equilibrium will prevail and to thus confine our investigations to the equilibrium state. We could regard the object of our investigations not as 'the economy' but as 'economic equilibrium' and we could attempt to justify this procedure as a useful starting point to what one might eventually hope to see realized in a complete account of the behaviour of the economy, including a full specification of its disequilibrium dynamics. This approach, while less ambitious than a full dynamic approach, may seem to be more attractive, if only because more tractable, than the Herculean programme of constructing a complete theory of the behaviour of the economy out of equilibrium.

In this connection see also Chapters 3, 4, 8, 9, and 10 of this volume.

37. In a Schumpeterian vein, commenting on the assumptions of her simple model, Joan Robinson (1956, 1966, p.65) states: 'In reality, in capitalist economies, technical change is always taking place; indeed we might say that the *raison d'être* of the capitalist rules of the game is that their development was favourable to technical progress. It would therefore be absurd to rule technical progress out of our model.' According to Joan Robinson (1980, p.90), 'the construction of a long-run model does not lead up to any plausible hypotheses about reality. It is useful for eliminating contradictions and pointing towards causal relations that will have to be taken into account in interpreting history. Nor should we expect to find a period in which technology can be represented in a single system of equations or in an orderly series of vintages'. Moreover, as she (1962b, p.88) pointed out the model of an economy characterized by technical dynamism cannot be 'both neat and lifelike'.

There is nothing in reality which remains constant through time to provide us with neat units in which to calculate. Workers are acquiring new skills and losing old ones. Products are changing in physical character, in saleability and in capacity to satisfy wants. The wants themselves are changing with the products. The purchasing power of money over commodities, or over labour-time, or even both, is changing not only in general level but also in pattern. Above all, capital goods are changing, so that the means of production required for a later technique have little or nothing in common with those of earlier design. On the other hand, analysis which does not take account of technical change can be very neat but it is of no interest.

38.   In the preface to her *Exercises in Economic Analysis*, Joan Robinson (1960, p.v) gave a sermon on methodology. She stressed three methodological rules that she attempts to follow: (1) we must take time seriously: (2) a quantity has no meaning unless the units in which it is measured can be specified; and (3) technical and physical relations between man and nature have to be distinguished from social relations between man and man (with an intermediate class – incentives of behavior – where the technical situation involves human nature itself). Of course, it involves distinction between difference and change stressed in the relevant exercises.

Among Joan Robinson's unpublished papers there is an unpublished preface to *The Accumulation of Capital* (apparently intended as a draft for a future revision). In it she (quoted after Harcourt, 1986, p.101) stressed 'four distinct groups of questions':

1. We make comparisons of situations, each with its own past, developing into its own future, which are different in some respect (for instance the rate of accumulation going on in each) in order to see what the postulated difference entails.
2. We trace the path which a single economy follows when the technical conditions (including their rate of change) and the propensities to consume and to invest are constant through time.
3. We trace the consequences of a change in any of these conditions for the future development of the economy.
4. We examine the short period reaction of the economy to unexpected events.

39.   Some modern general equilibrium theorists feel that the distinction between space and time is true but trivial. It is a question on which no one would disagree. Good theorists usually do not fall into the error of supposing that causation runs from the future to the present (see Feiwel, 1987, chs. 2 and 4).

40.   Indeed, controversies, while they are sometimes fun and exhilarating, are a considerable waste of time. To some extent they discredit the social scientists in the eyes of their colleagues in the natural sciences. One advantage of serious mathematical economics is to knock out a lot of nonsense. Unfortunately, mathematical economics is limited as to what it can cover.

41.   In a witty and perceptive piece, Sen (1974) casts the issues in a discourse between the Venerable Subhuti and Buddha. Subhuti, who on the whole led a virtuous life had some lapses, and was born again in this century as an economist destined to specialize in capital theory since he was a 'hair-splitting Brahmin'. The piece needs to be read in its entirety to appreciate its finer points and the hilarious way they are articulated.

42.   For Joan Robinson's short statement of the influence of Harrod and Kalecki on her when she set out to generalize *General Theory*, see 1979a, pp.77–8; see also 1952, pp.159–6; and 1979b, pp.ix–xxviii.

43. 'For me, the Sraffa revolution dates from 1951, the *Introduction* to Ricardo's
    Principles ..., not from 1960' (Joan Robinson, 1982a, p.91). 'Piero Sraffa's
    formal analysis re-established (though in a somewhat cryptic manner) the
    classical doctrine that the rate of profit on capital depends upon the technical
    structure of production and the share of wages in net output' (Joan Robinson,
    1979a, p.95; see also Robinson and Eatwell, 1973). On Ricardo via Sraffa and
    on Sraffa's illumination or critique of Marx, see 1979a, pp.212–6, 275–9. See
    also Dobb, 1973 ('in general a most admirable book' (Joan Robinson, 1980,
    p.122)).

44.   I have been trying for the last twenty years to trace the confusions and
        sophistries of current neo-classical doctrines to their origin in the neglect of
        historic time in the static equilibrium theory of the neoclassics and at the
        same time to find a more hopeful alternative in the classical tradition,
        revived by Sraffa, which flows from Ricardo through Marx, diluted by
        Marshall and enriched by the analysis of effective demand of Keynes and
        Kalecki. (Joan Robinson, 1973b, p.xii)

Joan Robinson (1980, pp.94–5) sees the challenge to the new generation of
economists in these terms:

> We must throw out concepts and theorems that are logically self-contradic-
> tory, such as the general equilibrium of supply and demand, the long-run
> production function, the marginal productivity of capital and the equili-
> brium size of firms ...
>
> Swings of activity must be seen, not as starting up from cold, but as
> overlaying slow long-run changes in productive capacity produced by
> accumulation, technical change (including changes in methods of operation
> of the labour force) and alterations in the composition of output. The
> interaction between the long-run and the short-run consequences of techni-
> cal innovations is a complicated subject which requires more study.
>
> The evolution of business activity and trade-union policy should be
> approached in the spirit of natural-history observation of the behaviour of
> classes and groups.
>
> The analysis of international trade should be preceded by an inquiry into
> the meaning of a 'nation' in the relevant respects – a question which
> nowadays is not so simple as used to be supposed.
>
> All this, and much more, indicates work to be done, provided that we give
> up the search for grand general laws and are content to try to enquire how
> things happen.

Her (1978, p.75) typical advice to students of economics is: Any theory that
we follow blindly will lead us astray. To make good use of an economic theory
we must first sort out the relations of the propagandist and the scientific
elements in it, then by checking with experience, see how far the scientific
element appears convincing, and finally recombine it with our own political
views. The purpose of studying economics is not to acquire a set of ready-made
answers to economic questions, but to learn how to avoid being deceived by
economists.

45. Joan Robinson (1979a, pp.116–7) continued as follows:

> The modern style of so-called mathematical economists came into fashion
> after the period when my pamphlet was written. Mathematical logic is a
> powerful tool of thought, but its application in economic theory generally
> seems to consist merely of putting circular arguments into algebra. Mathe-
> matical theory of statistics, also, was developing fast. At first there were high

hopes that observations of reality by the method of econometrics would produce truly scientific results.

Since I have confessed that I am no mathematician, my views on this subject might be thought to be those of the fox who had lost his tail, but that reproach could not be made to Norbert Wiener. . . [*God and Golem*]:

> An econometrician will develop an elaborate and ingenious theory of demand and supply, inventories and unemployment, and the like, with a relative or total indifference to the methods by which these elusive quantities are observed or measured. Their quantitative theories are treated with the unquestioning respect with which the physicists of a less sophisticated age treated the concepts of the Newtonian physics. Very few econometricians are aware that if they are to imitate the procedure of modern physics and not its mere appearances, a mathematical economics must begin with a critical account of these quantitative notions and the means adopted for collecting and measuring them.

He continues: 'Difficult as it is to collect good physical data, it is far more difficult to collect long runs of economic or social data so that the whole of the run shall have a uniform significance? This means that an attempt to test hypotheses by data in the form of time series is posing two questions at once – whether the forces at work were correctly diagnosed for one period and whether they have remained the same over subsequent periods. When there are elements in the forces involved such as the militancy of trade unions or the effect of advertising on household expenditure, this difficulty appears to be insuperable.

46.   In modern teaching, Keynes is kept in a separate compartment. In that compartment it is permissible to discuss the relation of the balance of trade to the level of employment, but the so-called theory of international trade is still conducted in terms of comparisons of equilibrium conditions, with 'given resources' always fully utilized. Instead of following the path that Ricardo opened out and linking it up with Keynes, the modern theory never escapes from the blind alley of comparisons of stationary states. It is therefore worse than useless for a discussion of the problems of management of a national economy or the role of export-led growth and import-led stagnation in international competition. (Joan Robinson, 1979a, p.142; see also pp.25–9, 130–45; 1973a, pp.1–24, 212–40)

47.   I did not intend my *Essay on Marxian Economics* . . . as a criticism of Marx. I wrote it to alert my bourgeois colleagues to the existence of penetrating and important ideas in *Capital* that they ought not to continue to neglect. In this the book had some success, which it certainly would not have done if it had been written in Marxist terminology, but since I was a bourgeois myself I must have been trying to reconstruct orthodox equilibrium theory. (Joan Robinson, 1979a, p.280)

And elsewhere she (1973a, p.250) wrote:

> My academic colleagues thought it queer (if not something much worse) that I should be interested in Marx's logic, because they had been taught as undergraduates that he has none. The Marxists just did not make head or tail of what I was trying to say. You cannot talk to a Marxist in English because he only understands Hegelese, a language I have never mastered and which seems to me, in any case, a very poor medium of communication for ideas about pure logic.

Those interested in the evolution (if not dialectics) of the Cambridge school of economics would find of particular interest the review article by Shove (1944). He generally praised Joan for her admirably clear, concise, and thoroughly well-documented exposition and critique of Marx, but found her onslaught on the orthodox economists difficult to digest and not nearly as well-documented (see also Hutchison, 1981, pp.87–95). (Shove's attitude towards Joan and Marx becomes somewhat clearer in the light of Austin Robinson's (1977, p.28) characterization of Shove. He described Shove as having a tinge of the Bloomsbury group. He was an economist with central interests in Marshallian value theory whose gifts were critical rather than creative. He resembled Dennis Robertson in insisting that the world is not as simple as economic models make it look – 'nothing is wholly black or wholly white, but everything grey'. He regarded economic models as dangerous oversimplifications.)

On the other hand, Cuyvers (1979) confirms that Marxists have often been irritated by Joan Robinson's provocative criticism of Marx's theory of value and have generally considered her work as esoteric and highy academic. His neo-Marxist, sympathetic, critical, and learned perspective on Joan's work is enlightening.

For Joan Robinson's evolving views on Marx and Marxism see, *inter alia*, 1942, 1966, pp.xi–xxi; 1965, 1977, part 3; 1979c, ch. 2; 1980, pp.155–202; and Robinson and Eatwell, 1973.

Whatever also needs to be said about Marx (and so much was and is still being said that even references would constitute a book), there is much to Schumpeter's (1951, p.54) perceptive, revealing and instructive passage. He argues that in the court that sits on theoretical techniques, the verdict on Marx would be rather adverse:

> But a court of appeal – even though still confined to theoretical matters – might feel inclined to reverse this verdict altogether. For there is one truly great achievement to be set against Marx's theoretical misdemeanors. Through all that is faulty or even unscientific in his analysis runs a fundamental idea that is neither – the idea of a theory, not merely of an indefinite number of disjointed individual patterns or of the logic of economic quantities in general, but of the actual sequence of those patterns or of the economic process as it goes on, under its own steam, in historic time, producing at every instant that state which will of itself determine the next one. Thus, the author of so many misconceptions was also the first to visualize what even at the present time is still the economic theory of the future for which we are slowly and laboriously accumulating stone and mortar, statistical facts and functional equations.

On Marx see also, *inter alia*, Dobb, 1973; Harris, 1978; Walsh and Gram, 1980; Morishima, 1973; Samuelson, 1972, part 3; and Chapters 11 and 33 in this volume.

48. She was exceedingly ill and frail when she travelled to deliver her lectures at the University of Utah. Her health was so poor that she had serious problems reading her notes (apparently she stumbled several times and at one time read the same page twice). But her indomitable spirit shone bright to the very end.

49. Ruth Cohen (1983, p.2) recalled the following story: 'A distinguished visiting economist at a party had made no effort to talk to her. A theoretical discussion started and Joan chipped in. "But that is very important" said the visitor in tones of great surprise. "I'm Joan Robinson" she replied. "Oh, I thought you were a mere woman" '.

50.   In a letter to the editor (*Times*, 30 August, 1983), Dr. Carmen Blacker provided this charming and rare glimpse of Joan:

> May I, who lived for more than 10 years in a large room of her house, add to your obituary notice of Professor Joan Robinson . . . with some recollections of her personal kindness as a Cambridge landlady and of her spartan way of life.
>
> A strict vegetarian, she slept all the year round in a small creeper-covered hut at the bottom of the garden. It was entirely unheated, and open on one side to all weathers, but no storm, deluge or frost could persuade her to sleep in the house.
>
> Every morning at five minutes to eight I would see her walking over the lawn to her breakfast of yoghurt, in a maroon dressing gown and with her long grey hair hanging down her back. In the early spring she was often woken by tits pecking at her hair for material for their nests.
>
> Once she awoke to find a new pair of Marks and Spencer bedroom slippers entirely filled with nuts. 'The squirrel came from Trinity', she declared, promptly and considerately reverting to her old pair.

References

Andrews, P. W. S. (1949) *Manufacturing Business* (London: Macmillan).

Arrow, K. J. (1974) *The Limits of Organization* (New York: Norton).

Arrow, K. J. (1983a) *Collected Papers of Kenneth J. Arrow*: v. 1: *Social Choice and Justice* (Cambridge, Mass.: Harvard University Press).

Arrow, K. J. (1983b) *Collected Papers of Kenneth J. Arrow*: v. 2: *General Equilibrium* (Cambridge, Mass.: Harvard University Press).

Baran, P. A. (1964) 'Review of Joan Robinson's *Economic Philosophy*' *American Economic Review* 54: 455–8.

Bliss, C. J. (1975) *Capital Theory and the Distribution of Income* (Amsterdam: North Holland).

Burmeister, E. (1980) *Capital Theory and Dynamics* (Cambridge: Cambridge University Press).

Cambridge Journal of Economics (1983) Special Issue Prepared in Honor of Joan Robinson's Eightieth Birthday 7 (October).

Chamberlin, E. H. (1933) *The Theory of Monopolistic Competition* (Cambridge, Mass.: Harvard University Press).

Chamberlin, E. H. (1951) 'Monopolistic Competition Revisited', *Economica*, NS 18 (November): 343–62.

Cohen, R. (1983) 'Address at the Memorial Service in King's College Chapel for Joan Robinson' (29 October), mimeo.

Cuyvers, L. (1979) 'Joan Robinson's Theory of Economic Growth', *Science and Society* 43 (Fall): 326–48.

Dobb, M. H. (1973) *Theories of Value and Distribution* (Cambridge: Cambridge University Press).

Eatwell, J. and M. Milgate (eds) (1983) *Keynes' Economics and the Theory of Value and Distribution* (New York: Oxford University Press).

Ekelund, R. B. Jr and R. F. Hébert (1983) *A History of Economic Theory and Method* (New York: McGraw-Hill).

Feiwel, G. R. (1975) *The Intellectual Capital of Michal Kalecki* (Knoxville: The University of Tennessee Press).

Feiwel, G. R. (1982) 'Samuelson and the Age After Keynes' in Feiwel (ed) *Samuelson and Neoclassical Economics* (Boston: Kluwer-Nijhoff), pp.202–43.

Feiwel, G. R. (1985a) (ed) *Issues in Contemporary Microeconomics and Welfare* (London: Macmillan).

Feiwel, G. R. (1985b) (ed) *Issues in Contemporary Macroeconomics and Distribution* (London: Macmillan).

Feiwel, G. R. (1987) (ed) *Arrow and the Ascent of Modern Economic Theory* (London: Macmillan).

Galbraith, J. K. (1952, 1956) *American Capitalism* (Boston: Houghton Mifflin).

Galbraith, J. K. (1967) *The New Industrial State* (Boston: Houghton Mifflin).

Gram, H. and V. Walsh (1983) 'Joan Robinson's Economics in Retrospect', *Journal of Economic Literature* 21 (June): 518–50.

Hahn, F. H. (1975) 'Revival of Political Economy: The Wrong Issues and the Wrong Argument', *Economic Record* (September): 360–64.

Hahn, F. H. (1982) 'The Neo-Ricardians', *Cambridge Journal of Economics* 6 (December): 353–74.

Harcourt, G. C. (1972) *Some Cambridge Controversies in the Theory of Capital* (Cambridge: Cambridge University Press).

Harcourt, G. C. (1986) *Controversies in Political Economy* (New York: New York University Press).

Harris, D. J. (1978) *Capital Accumulation and Income Distribution* (Stanford: Stanford University Press).

Hart, O. D. (1985) 'Imperfect Competition in General Equilibrium' in K. J. Arrow and S. Honkapohja (eds) *Frontiers of Economics* (Oxford: Blackwell), pp.100–49.

Hicks, J. R. (1982) *Money, Interest and Wages* (Oxford: Blackwell).

Hicks, J. R. (1983) *Classics and Moderns* (Oxford: Blackwell).

Hutchison, T. W. (1981) *The Politics and Philosophy of Economics* (New York: New York University Press).

Johnson, E. S. and Johnson, H. G. (1978) *The Shadow of Keynes* (Oxford: Blackwell).

Kahn, R. F. (1933) 'The Elasticity of Substitution and the Relative Share of a Factor', *Review of Economic Studies*, 1 (October): 72–8.

Kahn, R. F. (1959) 'Exercises in the Analysis of Growth', *Oxford Economic Papers* NS 11 (June): 143–56.

Kahn, R. F. (1984) *The Making of the General Theory* (Cambridge: Cambridge University Press).

Kahn, R. F. (1985) 'The Cambridge Circus "1" ', in G. C. Harcourt (ed.) *Keynes and his Contemporaries* (London: Macmillan), pp. 42–51.

Kalecki, M. (1971) *Selected Essays on the Dynamics of the Capitalist Economy* (Cambridge: Cambridge University Press).

Keynes, J. M. (1930) *A Treatise on Money* (London: Macmillan).

Keynes, J. M. (1936) *The General Theory of Employment, Interest and Money* (London: Macmillan).

Keynes, J. M. (1963) *Essays in Biography* (New York: Norton).

Keynes, J. M. (1973a) *The Collected Writings of John Maynard Keynes*, vol. 13 (London: Macmillan).

Keynes, J. M. (1973b) *The Collected Writings of John Maynard Keynes*, vol. 14 (London: Macmillan).

Klein, L. R. (1958) 'Review of Joan Robinson's *The Accumulation of Capital*', *Econometrica* 26: 622–24.

Koopmans, T. C. (1957) *Three Essays on the State of Economic Science* (New York: McGraw-Hill).

Kregel, J. (1971), *Rate of Profit, Distribution and Growth* (London: Macmillan).

Kregel, J. (1983) (ed) *Distribution, Effective Demand and International Economic Relations* (London: Macmillan).

Kuenne, R. E. (1967) (ed) *Monopolistic Competition Theory* (New York: Wiley).

Lancaster, K. (1960) 'Mrs. Robinson's Dynamics', *Economica* NS 27 (February): 63–70.

Lerner, A. P. (1957) 'Review of Joan Robinson's *The Accumulation of Capital*', *American Economic Review* 47: 693–99.

Maneschi, A. (1986) 'A Comparative Evaluation of Sraffa's "The Laws of Returns Under Competitive Conditions" and its Italian Precursor', *Cambridge Journal of Economics* 10: 1–12.

Matthews, R. C. O. (1986) 'The Economics of Institutions and the Sources of Growth', *Economic Journal* 96 (December): 903–18.

Morishima, M. (1973) *Marx's Economics* (Cambridge: Cambridge University Press).

O'Brien, D. P. (1984) 'Research Programmes in Competitive Structure', *Journal of Economic Studies* 10 (4): 29–51.

O'Brien, D. P. and Presley, J. R. (eds) (1981) *Pioneers of Modern Economics in Britain* (London: Macmillan).

Pigou, A. C. (1920) *Economics of Welfare* (London: Macmillan).

Reder, M. W. (1982) 'Chicago Economics: Permanence and Change', *Journal of Economic Literature* 20 (March): 1–38.

Robinson, A. (1977) 'Keynes and his Cambridge Colleagues', in D. Patinkin and J. C. Leith (eds), *Keynes, Cambridge and 'The General Theory'* (London: Macmillan).

Robinson, A. (1985) 'The Cambridge Circus "2" ', in G. C. Harcourt (ed.) *Keynes and His Contemporaries* (London: Macmillan), pp. 52–7.

Robinson, Joan (1932) *Economics is a Serious Subject* (Cambridge: Heffer).

Robinson, Joan (1933, 1969) *The Economics of Imperfect Competition* (London: Macmillan).

Robinson, Joan (1937, 1949) *Introduction to the Theory of Employment* (London: Macmillan).

Robinson, Joan (1942, 1966) *An Essay on Marxian Economics* (London: Macmillan).

Robinson, Joan (1951, 1978) *Collected Economic Papers*, Vol. 1 (Oxford: Blackwell).

Robinson, Joan (1952) *The Rate of Interest and Other Essays* (London: Macmillan).

Robinson, Joan (1956, 1966) *The Accumulation of Capital* (London: Macmillan).

Robinson, Joan (1960) *Exercises in Economic Analysis* (London: Macmillan).

Robinson, Joan (1960, 1975) *Collected Economic Papers*, Vol. 2 (Oxford: Blackwell).

Robinson, Joan (1962a) *Economic Philosophy* (Chicago: Aldine).

Robinson, Joan (1962b) *Essays in the Theory of Economic Growth* (London: Macmillan).

Robinson, Joan (1965, 1975) *Collected Economic Papers*, Vol. 3 (Oxford: Blackwell).

Robinson, Joan (1967) *Economics: An Awkward Corner* (New York: Random House).

Robinson, Joan (1970) *Freedom and Necessity* (New York: Pantheon Books).

Robinson, Joan (1971) *Economic Heresies* (New York: Basic Books).

Robinson, Joan (1973a) *Collected Economic Papers*, Vol. 4 (Oxford: Blackwell).

Robinson, Joan (1973b) 'Foreword' to J. Kregel, *The Reconstruction of Political Economy* (New York: Wiley).

Robinson, Joan (1976) 'Introduction' to M. Kalecki, *Essays in Developing Economies* (Hassocks: Harvester Press).

Robinson, Joan (1978) *Contributions to Modern Economics* (New York: Academic Press).

Robinson, Joan (1979a) *Collected Economic Papers*, Vol. 5, (Oxford: Blackwell).

Robinson, Joan (1979b) *The Generalization of the General Theory* (London: Macmillan).

Robinson, Joan (1979c) *Aspects of Development and Underdevelopment* (Cambridge: Cambridge University Press).

Robinson, Joan (1980) *What are the Questions?* (Armonk, NY: Sharpe).

Robinson, Joan (1982a) 'Misunderstandings in the Theory of Production', in G. R. Feiwel (ed), *Samuelson and Neoclassical Economics* (Boston: Kluwer-Nijhoff), pp.90–6.

Robinson, Joan (1982b) 'The Arms Race' in S. M. McMurrin (ed) *The Tanner Lectures on Human Values* III (Cambridge: Cambridge University Press), pp. 257–89.

Robinson, Joan (1983) 'The Economics of Destruction' (transcribed from notes taken by Hal Kursk), *Monthly Review* 35 (October): 15–7.

Robinson, Joan (1985) 'The Theory of Normal Prices and Reconstruction of Economic Theory' in G. R. Feiwel (ed) *Issues in Contemporary Macroeconomics and Distribution* (London: Macmillan), pp.157–65.

Robinson, Joan (n.d.) 'Introduction' (written for a collection of R. F. Kahn's early essays; forthcoming) mimeo.

Robinson, Joan and J. Eatwell (1973) *An Introduction to Modern Economics* (London: McGraw-Hill).

Robinson, Joan and F. Wilkinson (1985) 'Ideology and Logic' in F. Vicarelli (ed) *Keynes's Relevance Today* (Philadelphia: University of Pennsylvania Press).

Roncaglia, A. (1978) *Sraffa and the Theory of Prices* (New York: Wiley).

Samuelson, P. A. (1966) *The Collected Scientific Papers of Paul A. Samuelson*, 2 vols, ed. by J. E. Stiglitz (Cambridge, Mass.: MIT Press).

Samuelson, P. A. (1972) *The Collected Scientific Papers of Paul A. Samuelson*, Vol. 3, ed. by R. C. Merton (Cambridge, Mass.: MIT Press).

Samuelson, P. A. (1977) *The Collected Scientific Papers of Paul A. Samuelson*, vol. 4 ed. by H. Nagatani and K. Crawley, (Cambridge, Mass.: MIT Press).

Schumpeter, J. A. (1934) 'Robinson's Economics of Imperfect Competition', *Journal of Political Economy* 42: 249–57.

Schumpeter, J. A. (1951) *Ten Great Economists* (New York: Oxford University Press).

Seligman, B. B. (1962) *Main Currents in Modern Economics* (New York: Free Press).

Sen, A. K. (1974) 'On Some Debates in Capital Theory', *Economica* 41 (August): 328–35.

Sen, A. K. (ed) (1970) *Growth Economics* (Harmondsworth: Penguin).

Shackle, G. L. S. (1966) *The Nature of Economic Thought* (Cambridge: Cambridge University Press.

Shackle, G. L. S. (1967) *The Years of High Theory* (Cambridge: Cambridge University Press).

Shove, G. F. (1944) 'Mrs. Robinson on Marxian Economics', *Economic Journal* 54 (April): 47–61.

Shubik, M. (1970) 'A Curmudgeon's Guide to Microeconomics', *Journal of Economic Literature* 8 (June): 405–34.

Skidelsky, R. (1983) *John Maynard Keynes* vol. 1 (London: Macmillan).

Solow, R. M. (1955–6) 'The Production Function and the Theory of Capital', *Review of Economic Studies* 23: 101–8.

Solow, R. M. (1956) 'Contribution to the Theory of Economic Growth', *Quarterly Journal of Economics* 70 (February): 65–94.

Solow, R. M. (1967) 'Review of Hicks's *Capital and Growth*', *American Economic Review* 57 (December): 1257–60.

Solow, R. M. (1970) *Growth Theory* (New York: Oxford University Press).

Solow, R. M. (1975) 'Cambridge and the Real World', *Times Literary Supplement*, 14 March, pp.277–8.

Sraffa, P. (1926) 'The Laws of Returns Under Competitive Conditions', *Economic Journal*, 36 (December): 535–50.

Sraffa, P. (1960) *Production of Commodities by Means of Commodities* (Cambridge: Cambridge University Press).

Stiglitz, J. E. (1974) 'The Cambridge-Cambridge Controversy in the Theory of Capital: A View from New Haven', *Journal of Political Economy* 82 (4): 893–903.

Sylos Labini, P. (1985) 'Sraffa's Critique of the Marshallian Theory of Prices', *Political Economy – Studies in the Surplus Approach* 1 (2): 51–71.

Tobin, J. (1973) 'Cambridge (UK) v. Cambridge (Mass.)', *Public Interest* 31 (Spring): 102–9.

Triffin, R. (1940) *Monopolistic Competition and General Equilibrium Theory* (Cambridge, Mass.: Harvard University Press).

Wald, A. (1938, 1951) 'On Systems of Equations of Mathematical Economics', (Translated from German), *Econometrica* 19 (October): 368–403.

Walsh, V. C. and Gram, H. (1980) *Classical and Neoclassical Theories of General Equilibrium* (New York: Oxford University Press).

Waintraub, E. R. (1985) 'Joan Robinson's Critique of Equilibrium: An Appraisal', *American Economic Review* (May): 146–9.

Worswick, G. D. N. (1959) 'Mrs. Robinson on Simple Accumulation', *Oxford Economic Papers* NS 11: 125–41.

2 Remembering Joan

Paul A. Samuelson

1 INTRODUCTION

Throughout my lifetime as an economist Joan Robinson was always there at the frontier of science. We began together in 1932: I as a student at Chicago; she in her first publishing phase. Many times, in print and elsewhere, I expressed the considered opinion that the corpus of her work richly deserved a Nobel Prize.

For half a century after 1932, Joan Robinson contributed to every major field of political economy. The 1933 Robinson and Chamberlin classics in imperfect competition nicely complemented each other. The first intimation we outsiders had that Keynes (with the help of the 'Circus' which included Richard Kahn, Joan, Austin Robinson, Roy Harrod, James Meade, Piero Sraffa, and others) was forging a theory of output as a whole, came from Robinson (1933b). As an escape from the war and a digression from her nascent Marxian studies, Joan wrote her famous analysis of rising supply price, (Robinson, 1941), which was the first case of a scholar in the Marshallian tradition breaking through to sight the great Pacific of general–equilibrium analysis. I know how original this work was since Wolfgang Stolper and I were at the same time pursuing similar paths in connection with Stolper and Samuelson (1941). Joan's work on foreign exchange rates and the terms of trade, Robinson (1937), was the first quantum jump in that subject since C. F. Bickerdike (1920): before 1937 we all believed that depreciating a currency would, in stable equilibrium *necessarily* depreciate its terms of trade – a logical misapprehension.

Joan's education was as innocent of Marxian instruction as of mathematics. It was only the former that she considered a deprivation. She wore her lack of mathematical knowledge proudly: 'If you don't have it, flaunt it,' that was her motto. 'You think the Emperor has clothes? You think that Euler's Theorem is heap big stuff? Well, let this honest child tell you that ordinary glands are showing through, and all that is needed for competitive factor prices to exhaust market revenues is that total market demand be large enough to be served by numerous replicated firms.'

James Mill and the late Tjalling Koopmans considered it a sin if scholars wrote too well. That brought unearned importance to their offerings. If this be a sin, it is not a sin run rampant in economics. But Joan Robinson, before the seat of judgment of St Peter, would have to plead guilty to flagrant abuse of the art. Eschewing jokes and elegant rhetoric, in plain forceful prose she explicated complex relationships and seduced readers' belief. She could even make 'reswitching' in capital theory exciting, offering it as a lifeline to generous-minded Indians, Italians, and East Anglians feeling buried under the Leviathan of topological proofs that market capitalism delivered the goods of Pareto optimality.

Joan's *An Essay on Marxian Analysis* (1942) marks the division between (1) her early work in the mainstream tradition of post-Marshallian orthodoxy and of Keynesian macroeconomics and (2) her later work in post-Keynesian distribution theory and in Sraffian capital theory. Particularly her work in the foundations of capital theory I regard as valuable and constructive. A Nobel Prize to Joan Robinson alone, or to the pair Robinson–Sraffa, or Robinson–Harrod, or Robinson–Kalecki, or Robinson-Kaldor, I would judge to have been well deserved. And in making this evaluation, I give zero weight to the desirability that a female scholar should receive such an award.

The Marx essay deserves comment in its own right. And also for the light it casts on Joan's developing viewpoints.

2   MARXIAN STUDIES

St Paul's School and Girton College were silent on Marx. Maynard Keynes, whom Joan admired and only later was to patronize, regarded Karl Marx as a waste of time. Before World War II Robinson seems to have been ignorant of Marx's economic works. Robinson (1937, final essay) is a patronizing criticism of John Strachey's superficial use of Marxian patter to predict capitalist depression and to reject Hayekian orthodoxy: Marxians, it appeared, were guilty in Joan's eyes of not knowing elementary Model T Keynesianism.

By 1941 Robinson had mastered the three volumes of *Capital* and some of the Marx–Engels correspondence. (At that date no one knew the 1958 *Grundrisse*, and few had studied the early 1840s writings of the Marx who had not yet become a Marxian.) Joan's admiration for Michal Kalecki, whose originality in independently discovering Keynesian effective demand she if anything exaggerated, I suspect played a role in her investigating Marx.

Robinson pays Marx the compliment of taking him seriously as a scholar. This means no condemnation or praise for subversiveness. It means no patronizing or condescension. It means no reverence as to a sage or a God. She has somewhere expressed her impatience with mindless idolators of the Master who, if asked whether Marx's constant capital is a stock or a flow, reply that Karl Marx was a genius. By her code one must never encounter error or obscurity in *Capital* without calling it by its name; and never fail to hail greatness.

The Robinson *Essay* is an unsparing critique of Marx's paradigm, redeemed by the author's evident approval of Karl Marx and wholehearted rejection of capitalistic apologetics. In commemorating the centennial of *Capital*, Volume I, I said in effect, 'with Joan Robinson as a friend, Karl Marx had no need for an enemy'. (Samuelson 1967, p.622). Robinson then, and ever, rejected Marx's labor theory of value and his *uniform rate-of-surplus-value* (or of rate-of-*exploitation*) paradigm: even in socialism, making labor values determine the price ratio of land-intensive wheat to labor-intensive sugar beets was shown by her to be foolishly inefficient; not yet, apparently, could she show that a Sraffian system with price ratios made to be proportional to embodied (undated!) labor would lead to a similar gratuitous intertemporal inefficiency at profit rates conducive to switch points. What Joan Robinson began in 1942, the purification of Marxism *from within* the camp, has been continued by Ian Steedman's *Marx After Sraffa* (1977), by the many writings of John Roemer, and by a number of other modern Marxians.[1]

Robinson believes it is absurd for Marx to aver that labor is alone productive and that capital goods are not. Marx should recognize that such goods are productive: all Marx needs for his ethical message is that *ownership* of capital by capitalists is not productive. She is scathing – too scathing – on the Marshall–Senior apologetics which try to justify interest as the return to compensate for *waiting* in the part of savers. (It is interesting that, for a socialist state, Robinson then and ever afterwards did perceive the need for current generations to abstain from consuming in the interests of higher consuming by later generations. In reply at MIT to a questioner from an LDC, Joan in 1962 suggested that planners in a poor country ought first to use their limited resources for high-yield projects; after those had been exploited, and as resource availability improved, planners would naturally move down to lower-yield projects. God in heaven will forgive Joan for this neoclassical heresy, for at the moment she did not quite realize what she was saying. But on the issue of Wall Street's usefulness, Robinson never deviated into heresy.)[2]

The *Essay* devotes a short chapter to demolishing Marx's demonstration of a law of the declining rate or profit. Gross output (of an industry or a society) is broken down into Wages + Capital costs + Surplus = $v + c + s$. She then exposes as an empty tautology the syllogism:

> If the *rate of exploitation* is somehow constant (s/v is unchanged); and if the *organic composition of capital* rises ($v/[c + v]$ is down); then the *rate of profit* must fall ($s/[c + v] = [s/v] [v/(c + v)]$ has to be down).

This tautology she differentiates from the neoclassical 'deepening of capital', in which a rise in Clarkian K/L must reduce the marginal-product-of-capital rate of return or of profit $- s/[c + v] = \delta Q/\delta K$ to be a declining function of K/L. Not yet does she express her post-1952 condemnation of platonic aggregate capital; not yet does she articulate Sraffa's demonstration that lower profit rates can accompany *lower* ratios of aggregate capital to aggregate labor, but we see already in 1942 a mind ready to be skeptical on this subject.

For an instant, I thought I glimpsed in Robinson's exposition, (Robinson, 1942, pp.42–6) an early recognition[3] of the 1950's *factor price*, or (real-wage, profit rate), *tradeoff frontier*. How can the profit rate fall if (as Marxians believe) the real-wage rate does not rise? Unfortunately, as our hopes are raised that she understands, Robinson wrongly concedes (p.44) that the competitive profit rate could fall provided $\delta Q/\delta$ capital falls fast enough. (I once suggested she correct this blemish in any new edition; but she had apparently forgotten the point and the slip remains in the *Essay*'s 1967 second edition.)

Conceding defects in Marx's analysis, we should not deny too much. Even in the most complicated Sraffa–Neumann model, when a stationary work-force goes from a non-golden-rule technology to a golden-rule equilibrium configuration, the rate of profit does have to fall (while, to be sure, the real-wage rate does rise). Reswitching does not vitiate this germ of truth concerning 'capital deepening'.

We can provide an out for Robinson if we suppose her not to be dealing with competition. Most of the Marx-Morishima relationships of M. Morishima (1973), like those of Piero Sraffa (1960), lose relevance and content if *constant returns to scale* is specifically denied. Early on (Robinson, 1942, p.4) she attributes to Marx the view that concentration of capital in ever larger concerns, forced on by the development of technique, turns the capitalists towards the anti-social practises of monopoly'. The $c + v + s$ paradigms of Marx, Ricardo, and Sraffa never grapple with these increasing-returns analytical issues. Robinson (1942, pp.3–4) never explains why workers should be forced below their pre-capitalism real income levels by the following developments, which make no mention of land enclosures, of expropriations of peasants' capital, of profit rates elevated by capitalistic encroachments or by capital-favoring inventions. She writes:

> But the workers, who under the compulsion of capitalism, produce the wealth, obtain no benefit from the increase in their productivity power. All the benefit accrues to the class of capitalists, for the efficiency of large-scale enterprise breaks down the competition of the peasant and craftsman, and reduces all who have not property enough to join the ranks of the capitalists to selling their labour for the mere means of existence.

Aside from the problem of reconciling this with history, as game theory it is primitive. It reminds me of a time when MIT graduate students listened with disdain to the claim of Professor Stephen Marglin of Harvard that the factories of the industrial revolution neither increased workers' productivity nor their real wages but served merely to render them more docile. Our von-Neumann sophisticates found this hard to reconcile with the existence of a blocking collusion by workers who merely stay at home and buy raw materials at their unchanged competitive scarcity.

3 CONSTANT RETURNS?

Among Robinson's patron saints are Keynes, Kahn, Kalecki, and Sraffa. To Americans, Sraffa (1926) is one of several important articles of the mid-1920s that initiated the monopolistic competition revolution. To Joan it is the grand progenitor of that revolution. Two different themes are argued by Sraffa.

The first theme is substantive. Real-life firms do face sloped demand curves. They definitely cannot sell all the *q* they wish at some *p* that is named by the perfect-competition market. By incurring promotion and advertising costs, they can entice new customers and widen *their* market. By lowering their *p*, they may coax out some new *q* sales from consumers and divert some *q* sales from rival firms. All this is realistic – nearly trite. Marshall was, of course, aware of it; but he muddied the waters for his disciples by pretending that all this was still *competition* theory. Since these firms we are talking about can well enjoy declining marginal cost curves, Marshall persisted in the nonsense that decreasing MC phenomena – increasing returns to scale – were compatible with perfect competition. Sraffa (1926) in a common-sense way emphasizes that all this is imperfect and not perfect competition. Sraffa's task is well done. His Marshallian audience needed for him to do it. But there is nothing earthshaking or, by 1926, even original in this Sraffian message. All the treatises on industrial organization from the 1890s to 1930 took for granted what Sraffa was neatly expressing. J. M. Clark (1923) had tried to provide analytical insight concerning the breakdown of perfect competition, by invoking the economics of increasing-return-to-scale ('of overhead costs', Clark called it). Edward Chamberlin (1933), a pupil of the author Allyn Young (1928), never ceased to emphasize this technical returns background of product differentiation and oligopoly.

A youngster in his twenties does not gain Byronic fame and a life fellowship at a Cambridge college by polishing up a neat description of realistic markets. The second theme in Sraffa (1926) was the one that commanded the admiration of Keynes and readers of the *Economic Journal*. It is purely definitional and analytic, a first exercise in the history of economic thought – that area in which Sraffa's Ricardian studies were to win him imperishable fame.

This second Sraffian theme deals with what Marshall's partial equilibrium should 'really' have called for. Alfred Marshall, it will be recalled, was at the peak of his fame when he died in 1924. Two-thirds of a century later, after the Anglo-Saxon world had come to digest the contributions of Leon Walras, Knut Wicksell, and Irving Fisher, it is realized that Alfred Marshall's reputation – deservedly great – was overrated in the 1900–30 period. If the world excessively overvalued Marshall, Oxbridge outrageously treasured his writings. A. C. Pigou, as successor to Marshall's Cambridge chair, protected his memory like a watchdog (and, in consequence, Pigou's own great originality was never properly recognized).

J. H. Clapham, another Marshall pupil and an eminent economic historian, was the one who initiated the so-called 'cost controversy' that brought the Anglo-Saxon literary tradition almost up to where A. A. Cournot (1838) had arrived a century earlier. Clapham (1922) spoke of those 'Empty Economic Boxes': it was a scandal, he suggested, that economists could not empirically allocate industries to one or another of Marshall's box of (1) increasing-cost industries, (2) decreasing-cost industries, and (3) constant-cost industries.

Sraffa's second theme was the bombshell that the only category compatible with Marshallian partial-equilibrium analysis of competition was, after all, the constant-cost case. This Sraffian theme is simply wrong. But, as far as I can recall, no one has explicated the error of his reasoning and conclusion. Actually, Robinson (1941), an article that I mentioned earlier with admiration and which elicited praise from the hypercritical Jacob Viner,[4] lays out clearly how misled a reader of Sraffa (1926) would be to deny the existence of important competitive industries that produce under rising marginal costs.

Robinson (1941) demonstrates, without apparently ever connecting up its analysis with Sraffa (1926), that the box of increasing-cost competitive industry is indeed not an empty one.[5]

The writers that Sraffa knew well, Smith and Ricardo understood from the beginning that a shift of demand towards hill-grown wine and away from plain-grown rye would raise the price of wine (relative to the wage and the price of rye), a deviation from the 1926 presumption of horizontal *SS* supply curve. Ricardo was able to forget this two-factor-costs-in-price truth in favor of the erroneous doctrine that unit labor costs alone determine price ratios in a time-free system by the bogus device of supposing that he could get rid of the complication of rent by concentrating on production at the external margin of rent-free land. When Piero Sraffa came at last to write the introduction to his edition of Ricardo's *Principles*, Sraffa (1951, p.xxiii), I was incredulous to read that so sophisticated a mind blandly accepted this fatally flawed error of Ricardo: if Sraffa did not himself realize that *where the external margin falls is itself an endogenous variable dependent on consumers tastes for corn and services*, the scandal is all the greater. That the many solemn reviewers of Sraffa's great Ricardo edition pass over the matter in silence is further occasion for surprise.

An essay remembering Joan must inevitably involve remembering Piero, Nicky, Luigi, and many others. It is rewarding to discern in Sraffa's 1926 preoccupation with the constant-cost case (1) his nostalgia for the classical writers before and after Ricardo; (2) his lifelong interest in Marxian analysis;

and (3) a foreshadowing of his 1960 classic input–output model, which we know he began shortly after 1925 and resumed only in the 1950s after his long confinement with Ricardo's works had been relieved by the parturition of publication. Robinson held Sraffa uniquely in respect.

Where Joan's own work of the 1950s and 1960s is concerned her blueprint technologies of the *Accumulation of Capital* eschew the special complications involved in increasing-returns-to-scale technologies. Joan and Piero may not have much liked the Egypt of constant-returns-to-scale, but it was not vouchsafed for them to pass in their lifetimes into the Canaan of inceasing returns to scale.[6]

4 PERSONALITIES

Until the end of World War II Joan Robinson was still a name in print to me. She was an admired authority but a little distrusted for her enthusiasms. My Harvard friend, Sidney Alexander, who was just about Keynes's last tutee in Cambridge, passed on to me the aphorism he distilled from his King's College experience 'To Joan everything is either absurdly simple or simply absurd.'

One reason I chose to go to Harvard for graduate work in 1935 was my admiration for Edward Chamberlin's *Theory of Monopolistic Competition* (1933). Taking his so-called advanced course in the fall of 1935 deflated my esteem for him. What completed the operation was his comment on the margin of the term paper I wrote for his course. It was a very good paper for the time – my fellow student Robert Triffin assured me of that. But what really browned me off was the fact that Chamberlin's only remark on my paper was a pencilled in 'Good' next to a paragraph in which, while criticizing some implicit theorizing in passages from Joan's *Economics of Imperfect Competition* (1933a), I referred to her cheaply as Madame Robinson.

For Americans of my time Joan Robinson was a fascinating figure. Women economists were rare enough. Great ones could be counted on one thumb. Once at the old Merle, the coffee shop across from Widener library where Schumpeter and the in-crowd of Harvard economics gathered for gossip, I asked Joseph Schumpeter: 'How old is Joan Robinson?' That wicked raconteur replied ungallantly: 'I am over 30. She is over 30.' (Actually he was then about 53, she 33.)

I went on rashly and in evident bad taste: 'Is Joan Violet pretty?' Schumpeter in his best mock-Viennese caddishness replied: 'Let me put it this way, my dear Samuelson. Joan Robinson is the kind of person one would kiss in an English garden.' I recount this childish tale of not-kiss-and-tell only because it involves scholars with a permanent niche in the pantheon of economic science. Underneath the veil of his Viennese gaiety, Schumpeter gave, I thought, an impression of sadness in those days of his widowerhood prior to his final marriage with Elizabeth Schumpeter, the American economic historian.

5 FACTOR–PRICE FLAP

When I wrote my obituary of Keynes, Samuelson (1946), Joan Robinson wrote to me to express her wonder that an outsider could have discerned so accurate a picture of the *General Theory*'s genesis. Our intense correspondence began, however, after my 1948 article on factor–price equalization appeared. Parallel with her epistolary dialogue, I carried on a separate discussion with Richard Kahn. (All British economists seemed to take time out in 1948 to object to factor–price equalization. Both A. C. Pigou and (Sir) Donald McDougall wrote refutations for the *Economic Journal*, which had reached the stage of galley proofs before being withdrawn by their authors.[7] Jan Tinbergen (1949), James Meade (1950), S. F. James and I. Pearce (1952), Roy Harrod (1958), and D. Gale and H. Nikaido (1965) were only some of the reactors to the 1948–9 factor-price papers.

One of the valid points I remember Robinson's letters dealing with went like this: for the case where both goods always involve the same factor proportions, free trade in goods can't prevent the region with higher labor/land endowments from enjoying higher real rents and lower real wage rates. Samuelson (1948) had only belatedly stressed the important axiom that food was to be *uniformly* more land-intensive than clothing; not until Samuelson (1949, pp.188, 192) was this key aspect of the syllogism sufficiently stressed.

The factor–prices incident gained in international interest because, during my autumn 1948 sojourn in London, Cambridge, and Oxford, Lionel Robbins as my dinner host at the Reform Club said: 'I think that Abba Lerner, when he was my LSE student around 1933, wrote a paper on factor–price equalization much like your 1948 *EJ* paper. And I think I can locate a copy in my files.'

Robbins' memory was accurate. And, since A. P. Lerner had forgotten completely that he had ever written such a paper, it was the happy chance that Robbins did have a file copy that made possible publication of the classic Lerner (1952), which beautifully paralleled my independent effort.

Lerner was not the only forgetful scholar. There appeared in his 1933 manuscript a footnote thanking Mrs J. Robinson for pointing out the failure of factor-price equalization in the singular case of identical factor intensities. Joan had quite forgotten all this and her mind generated fifteen years later in our correspondence the same logical objection that had occurred to her earlier. With the voracious memory that I had in those days, I found such Lerner and Robinson absentmindednesses astonishing.

When my Guggenheim fellowship finally brought me to King's College, I enjoyed the delicious privileges of the don in the *ancien régime*, living in the comfortable rooms of old Professor Reddaway (Brian's father, the expert in Polish history) and walking through the Backs conversing with Piero Sraffa. Richard Kahn was the gracious host who arranged all things. As Bursar of King's and Executor to Keynes' estate, Kahn kept me from starving in post-war Britain by his hospitality at the Cambridge Arts Theatre Restaurant. (A woman at a neighboring table, past the first bloom of youth, rather annoyed me by her loud chatter. Imagine my surprise when she rose to grasp Richard by his lapels and asked: 'Darling can I afford a new fur coat?' He nodded gravely and proceded to puncture the bubble of scandal by introducing me to Lydia, Keynes's ballerina widow.)

The big evening came when I was invited to Kahn's rooms, as I thought to discuss factor–price equalization. It was to be a seminar *pour trois*, it seemed, when Joan Robinson appeared in what looked at first to be red-orange pyjamas, but which I worked out to be some kind of Indian jodhpurs that would have graced a Harvard academic processional.

After providing whisky and the only ice cubes then obtainable in the other Cambridge, Richard was not to be seen. When Joan began speaking of factor intensities, I dragged my heels, suggesting that we delay until Kahn's return. Finally, it dawned on me that this was to be a dialogue and not a threesome. Since Kahn's letters had been no less creative than Robinson's, I found such self-effacement remarkable. For a long time I was overly gullible to gratuitous gossipings that gave Richard Kahn enormous credit for good things that appeared under the signature of John Maynard Keynes and J. V. Robinson. The number of those who can testify cogently on this matter are, alas, shrinking.

In any case, we had a good talk. Since I was sitting with a poker hand containing four aces, the whisky tasted exceptionally good. Sure enough, at about 11 p.m., Richard Kahn returned with a fresh supply of ice cubes and the memorable evening came to an end.

A second time I missed my cue with Richard. He mentioned to me: 'I think if you were to go to Pigou's rooms around four tomorrow he'd be in.' Two days later, Kahn asked me why I hadn't kept my appointment with Pigou. Knowing how reclusive Pigou was reputed to be, I had not understood that a command was being given. The next day I did get admitted to the old rooms of Clapham where Pigou chose to live after his heart began to act up.

I recall Pigou as sitting in an old robe, and complaining that he was going gaga with age. Actually, he was a deal younger than I am now and I thought that the articles he couldn't stop writing were worthwhile in their own right. One foolish conversational gambit by me I have to report. Looking at the picture of a handsome young oarsman on Pigou's mantle, I asked fatuously, 'Is that Frank Ramsey?' 'Good God, no,' Pigou replied.

I am glad I got to Cambridge in its 1930–55 prime. That was something of a highwater mark, nipped if not in its bud then in its blossom, by the internecine warfare between the Kahn–Robinson–Sraffa–Kaldor and the Dennis Robertson factions. Richard Stone stayed aloof. Harry Johnson managed still to be on polite terms with both parties but it was a tightrope that impatient soul could not continue to walk. Observing life in Cambridge made me happy I had refused an earlier call to a chair in Chicago. I realized that the adversary procedure may possibly work for the law, but is an ineffecient and unpleasant way of doing science. I've never changed my mind on this.

One last anecdote.[8] To josh Joan, I said we Americans took an unfair advantage over the English: we were able to read both English and American. She replied that one would want to benefit from the American literature but where in that vast terrain would one know where to begin? My mentioning of the *AER* exhausted this unprofitable topic.

6   AGNOSTICISM

Joan Robinson to the end of her life lacked a theory of the distribution of income. I do not say this lightly. It was a conclusion I resisted for many years. Yet, when I wanted to reproduce her verbatim views on the subject in a book of *Readings*, a search through all her writings – no mean task in itself – turned up no quotable passages, nor even brief ones.

I was therefore not surprised when I read Maurice Dobb's last book (Dobb, 1973), on theories of value and distribution, to see that he went to his grave regretfully conscious that it was impossible to specify how the shares of rent, profit, and wages were determined under capitalism; and *a fortiori* impossible to explain the Gini and Pareto statistics or the distribution of incomes among the poor and the rich.

Nicholas Kaldor, of course, differed in this respect from Joan. As his readers used to quip, in any month Kaldor had at least one theory of distribution. Similarly, readers were never in doubt about Luigi Pasinetti's neo-Keynesian model of distribution. Robinson did share with these authors Harrodian and Kaleckian macroidentities such as

natural growth rate = saving rate ÷ capital/output ratio
= saving rate of capitalists × profit rate

But Robinson repeatedly insisted that golden-age exponential paths were only classroom idealizations with no possible real-life applications. And I can recall no writing in which she expressed agreement with Kaldor's mid-1950s infatuation with full-employment equilibrium and with the relevant view in Kaldor (1956) that Keynes's *Treatise* and not his *General Theory* was the great breakthrough.

For more than a century of history, each 1 per cent variation in nominal

GNP (or PQ) has involved about $\frac{1}{3}$ of 1 per cent change in P and a $\frac{2}{3}$ of 1 per cent change in Q: suppose Kaldor's model were realistic, in which autonomous change in investment alters the wage–profit shares of income just enough to evoke full-employment saving (from unthrifty workers and thrifty capitalists) of exactly enough to match whatever the autonomous investment is; then Q's percentage change should be virtually zero and P's change virtually 1 per cent. Curiously, just when President Eisenhower was enjoying three recessions within his two four-year terms, Dr Kaldor was proclaiming the demise of the business cycle and of underemployment equilibrium. Robinson sensibly refrained from joining in that waltz.

During the short segment that I could stand of Solow's debate with Joan Robinson at the 1970 World Econometric Congress in Cambridge, I did hear her commit herself to a definite theory of what determines a society's wage-share: it is the militancy of bargaining by the laboring class, through formal unions or otherwise, that can elevate real-wage rates and depress the aggregate of profits, she seemed to be saying on that occasion. I almost doubted the correctness of my hearing, because of my reluctance to attribute to so sophisticated a scholar so simple a view. But actually, in preparing this memoir, I note in Robinson (1965, pp.179–80), an earlier echo of this same bargaining-power theory, namely

> we find (1953) a low share of wages (corresponding to a high rate of exploitation) in manufacturing industry in countries like Cost Rica (less than 20%), Turkey (30%), Japan (40%) and a relatively higher share in Australia, Finland and UK (58%) and only slightly less in the USA (55%) ... [These] figures ... certainly suggest that the rate of exploitation depends far more upon the bargaining power of the workers than upon the rate of profit and the capital/labour ratio ...
>
> ... All this seems to justify Marx's conception that the rate of exploitation is a more fundamental relationship than the rate of profit.

If Joan believed that society obeys a Sraffa input – output model with but one possible set of techniques – fixed (a_{ij}) coefficients and fixed direct-labor coefficients ($a_{01} \ldots a_{0n}$) – then the interest rate could be anything from its maximum to zero, with the wage-share going from a zero share to a share of unity. This bargaining notion, however, does not so much answer a puzzle as create one. What was the purpose of her sheaf of blueprints in the *Accumulation of Capital* if not to deny the adequacy of a one-technique view of the world?

Momentary lapses into so narrow and special a view of fixed-coefficients would rationalize her simple view that, since existing capital is already here, its owners can safely be expropriated of any profit income the market accords it. However, if socialist societies can benefit from having more of a great variety of capital goods, that basic technological property ought to characterize capitalist and mixed economies. Not only is there the problem of motivating the expropriated capitalists to maintain existing capital goods intact, there is also a tremendous *informational* problem in every society. In the absence of markets, thousands of heterogeneous capital items will not get themselves, and keep getting themselves, rationed properly in an automatic way: effective technology can erode and disappear as well as be born.

If Robinson were to specify for a many-sector economy the many alternative blueprint activities that she herself envisages, most societies observed in history or nowadays are far from the golden-rule endowments of heterogeneous inputs that gives a stationary population maximal *per capita* consumption. A zero rate of profit could not sustain the currently observed non-golden-rule vectors of inputs and outputs.

The positivity of competitive interest rates, with all that this implies for a wage-share of less than 100 per cent of national income, thus seems genuinely to be a result of scarcity of capital(s). Very poor regions are especially poorly endowed with the elements in their vectors of heterogeneous capital goods and of natural resources. That ought, one would think, to be cogently related to the gross inequalities of wage and property incomes that so often are reported in poor regions. In stressing this role of economic law, as against the role of economic power, I am, of course, cognizant of all the Sraffian complications. Reswitching can occur, so that a simple identification of more-roundabout, more-mechanized, more-time-intensive configurations with lower market interest rates is in general not valid.

To me, the facts of twentieth-century history, to say nothing of experience in earlier times, suggest how stubborn rather than loose are the market forces constraining what real wage gains can be secured by militant collusions to limit labor supplies. Thus, when the populist dictator Juan Perron tried many decades ago to raise wage rates quickly by 40 per cent, he did not succeed in materially raising the mean Argentine *real*-wage on a sustained basis. Inflation, unemployment, and other reactions to higher nominal wage rates characterized this and innumerable other similar incidents in history. No 1-technique Sraffa hypothesis could convincingly cover those facts of real life.

7 A SIMPLIFIED THOUGHT EXPERIMENT

At this point I am not arguing that Joan should take up with marginal-product notions of the simplest Clarkian type. My point can be made within the framework of a von Neumann–Sraffa technology where $\delta Q/\delta K$ coefficients are not everywhere definable for the system.

Let me begin with what may be called the case of *ultra-surrogate* capital. There are *n* sectors (perhaps *n* equals 100). Each produces a heterogeneous good to be consumed or used as an input in the many industries. To conserve space, I'll ignore the durability of the diverse inputs. Each industry may well have dozens of different techniques that convert direct-homogeneous-labor and the heterogeneous inputs into the respective goods: Robinson's book has many pages of blueprints, adjacent technologies being close to each other and spanning diverse input ratios for $(Q_{ij}/L_j, Q_{1j}/Q_{2j})$.

What makes my scenario a Santa Claus case of *ultra*-surrogate capital is the very special assumption that *all* industries are posited to happen to have *exactly the same choices of blueprints*. This is a much stronger and more special axiom than what is involved in Marx's case of 'equal organic compositions of capital(s)'. What makes the ultra simplification worth examining is that, despite the heterogeneity of the capital items themselves, and despite the lack of smooth differentiabilities of the production functions with the implied illegitimacy of marginal products and $\delta Q_i/\delta Q_{ij}$ terms, a Joan Robinson could find in the ultra-surrogate capital model a manageable suppy and demand model of income distribution. Her bogey of a razor's edge for Harrod's model evaporates into something close to the Solow–Meade non-exponential growth paths. No neoclassical faking or cheating, of the kind that Robinson abhorred, is involved within the ultra rules of the game. Also, the complications of the Hahn Problem (Hahn, 1966) which Joan perceived as the problem of consistent expectations in a world not growing in balanced exponentials, are made manageable in this special Santa Claus case.

If Joan were given this ultra model as a Tripos problem, she could discern how it would develop under the Marx–Kalecki hypothesis that all profits are saved and all wages are consumed; or under the Harrod hypothesis of a constant fraction of all net income saved; or under a Kalecki–Harrod–Kaldor blend in which the constant fraction s_w of wages are saved and the constant fraction s_r of profits are saved; or under the oft-observed life-cycle saving patterns of Modigliani (1986).

The advantage of this model is that it can be regarded as neo-Keynesian rather than neoclassical. It will accommodate to post-Keynesian macroidentities while exhibiting a macrodistribution of income that is truly the resultant of all the micro-supply-and-demand relations of the separate markets. At the same time that Kalecki could apply his saving insights to the model, a Walras or Wicksell could do the same.

I shall describe only two scenarios of the model. In the Pasinetti (1962) 2-caste version, let caste 1 be non-workers who always save the positive fraction s_1 of their profit incomes. The rest belong to caste 2, people who both work and earn profit on their past saving: these people save the positive fraction s_2 of their net income from whatever source it may come.

Begin the *ultra* technology with society having sparse elements of every heterogeneous good, sparse relative to the existing labor force which we can take to be growing very slowly at the exponential rate $(1+g)^t$. Early on there could be labor redundancy and low imputed market real-wages; or, if low-productivity direct-labor methods always exist, early on real-wages could be very low and the profit very high. Given early initial *per capita* capitals very sparse and several alternative techniques feasible, with the s_1 saving coefficient large, the ultra model will begin with the heterogeneous capitals growing faster than labor. In the ultra case, the profit rate falls and the real wage rises as capital(s) meaningfully 'deepen'. The process is slow and people understand it to be going on. In this stage the observed profit rate at the successive switch points reached can be considerably higher than g/s_1. If the profit rate, $r(t)$, should drop down to g/s_1 and if s_2 is less than s_1 times the wage-share of income at that profit level, the system could stay forever in a primal Pasinetti equilibrium with only widening of capital going on and both castes having wealth growing at the same $(1+g)^t$ rate.

If the profit rate g/s_1 brings for low g a wage-share such that $s_2 >$ (wage-share) times s_1, capital will continue to deepen because of caste 2 saving. Indeed, this could result in a profit rate that goes foolishly below the golden-rule of g and becomes even virtually zero.

What is the moral of the simple ultra scenario? It provides a case that can lack all neoclassical marginal products (or partial derivatives) and yet give for Robinson and Dobb a determinate supply-and-demand micro handle on distributive factor shares at *all* times – including the special long-run macro asymptotes that would hold if certain simple macro saving propensities could be validly hypothesized. In the ultra model, when effective labor supplies depart systematically from simple exponentials, the micro foundations of distribution still hold firm even when macro theories cease to apply.

Consider the gross facts of present-time experience. In the 1980s, there are no Harrodian natural rates of labor-supply growth that display constancies. But if we calculate approximate constants estimated for OECD nations, we find them to be little above zero. Demography is stagnant and post-OPEC productivity sluggish. At the same time, real interest rates are unprecedentedly high in the 1980s. I cannot glean much help from macrodistribution models to rationalize these trends. Robinson, while spurning micro models, seems to have done well to remain agnostic concerning post-Keynesian theories of distribution.

The second scenario for the ultra technology could be one that Cassel or Ramsey might have more interest in. Suppose we are all born into a clan that lives forever in unchanged population size. Suppose clan saving behavior acts to maximize the integral of all future utilities from final consumption, but with all future utilities systematically discounted at the subjective rate $(1+R)^{-t}$. Then even though there are no partial derivatives of the marginal-productivity type, the ultra system will have the following properties:

If it begins with sparse *per capita* stocks of heterogeneous capital goods, people will save: the deepening of capital thus induced lowers the objective own-rate-of-interest of the heterogeneous capital stock(s), $r(t)$, until as $t \to \infty$ we observe $r(t) \to R$ from above. Etc.

A similar but more complicated story holds when we drop the ultra-surrogate singularities and still deal with a von Neumann system whose alternative techniques are many but are still only finite in number. When Robinson decided no one could analyze non-steady states of capitalistic development, she abdicated from the only game in town – the one spelled out by economic history.

8   JOAN ROBINSON, LEFTIST

Superficially, but only superficially, Robinson was easy to classify. She rejected perfect-competition Hayekianism. She rebelled against Marshallian Say's-Lawism in favor of *General Theory* Keynesianism. She successively waxed enthusiastic about Stalin's Soviet Union; Mao's China; North Korea; Castro's Cuba; American students' new leftism.

The above paragraph fails to convey her independence of mind. Joan wore no man's collar (or woman's either). I once remarked to an old Cambridge hand that she must think well of another leftist scholar there. He corrected me: 'Oh no, she is contemptuous of him as a lackey of the Party Line.' I stood corrected.

A Polish scholar once volunteered to me: 'I love that woman. When she visited Poland all the brass turned out to give her the royal treatment. Replying to the toasts and fine words, she proceeded at once to the forbidden topic that all of us were thinking about, saying, "Why are we wasting our time on these matters when the workers in Posen are rebelling? What is the reason for that?" We young people revered her for that.'

By temperament Joan was, apparently, mercurial. I happened to be in Cambridge in the spring of 1952, on my way home from the famous Paris colloquium on risk. She had just returned from the Moscow conference orchestrated for scholars by Oskar Lange, by then a stalwart of the Polish apparatus.[9] Robinson was on a high. The return of a lost wallet with its currency gone but its papers intact was deemed by her evidence of a new spirit of mankind under (Stalin's) socialism. After Joan's enthusiastic lecture to a Cambridge audience on her Sydney-and-Beatrice-Webb visit to utopia, an undergraduate asked: 'But, what about the alleged plot of Jewish doctors to kill Joseph Stalin?' Robinson, no bigot, could only rebut with a *tu quoque*: 'And how about your lynchings in the South?'

Although she was no member of the Bloomsbury set, her reply to a *Commentary* survey on whether Britain should join the Common Market had echoes in it of E. M. Forster. Having more friends in the Third World than in Europe, she asked why then should she favor the move.

As far as I can recall, she never lost her heart to Albania. But it says something for her kindliness that she could, even momentarily, admire North Korean totalitarianism and take seriously allegations of 18 per cent per annum trends of real growth there. In her 1964 view, but for the black-out in South Korea of news of progress in the North, spontaneous immigration would explode from South to North!

At those times in the late 1950s when we now know the Great Leap Forward was being followed by the greatest economic distress – including famine that may have killed tens of millions of people – the testimony of her eyes told of bonny people in the streets. While criticisms of the cultural revolution were growing in the West, she told me pointedly that it would be good for sedentary professors to lead a more active life in the countryside.

Like my old teacher in Schumpeter's classroom, Paul Sweezy, Joan Robinson became successivly disillusioned with the perversions of socialism perpetrated by the bureaucracies of Eastern Europe and elsewhere. 'True socialism' was her first and ever love, not the pretenders who took its name in vain.

Who is to say her value judgments were wrong, or other than noble? What I regret is the loss of her keen mind in helping understand and improve the trend of mixed capitalism. Reswitching captured and emasculated a whole generation of economists in East Anglia, Italy, and India. If only they could have spent six days of the week on researching the causes of stagflation, productivity slowdowns, and of waxing natural-resources fortunes, and only Mondays on input–output matrices!

I had Joan Robinson in mind when one edition of my *Economics* improved on John Morley's aphorism, 'Where it is a duty to worship the sun, the laws of heat will be ill understood.' The laws of heat will also be poorly understood where it is a duty to hate the sun.

Joan Robinson came to have a profound distaste for American society. She would have smiled grimly at Laski's quip: 'America is the only society that has managed to go from savagery to decadence without passing through civilization.'

Because it reflects an important strand in her thinking, I reproduce in its entirety the letter she wrote to my dear colleague, Harold A. Freeman, an eminent statistician who wrote in his retirement a 1979 book documenting the evils of American capitalism, *Towards Socialism*.

29 October 1979

Dear Professor Freeman

I was absolutely amazed that such a sensible book could be written in the Economics Department at MIT. How did you hit it off with Samuelson and company?

Your statement of the case is very clear, but the 'towards' seems rather Utopian! The obstacles now are formidable.

I thought perhaps that section 14 is too optimistic. It implies that once Socialism is installed people will become enlightened and cooperative, but Socialism, particularly in United States, will have to cope with a profoundly corrupted society and a great deal of neurosis and sheer wickedness.

Wishing you the best success,

Yours

JOAN ROBINSON

9   WHAT THE CAPITAL CONTROVERSY TAUGHT ME

Onlookers like high drama. Controversy between the two Cambridges – with Joan Robinson against Robert Solow, or against Robert Solow and Paul Samuelson – captures economists' attention.

But then, after a time, the crowd's enthusiasm ebbs. The action moves elsewhere: to Friedman's monetarism versus Tobin's eclectic post-Keynesianism; or, to descend from the sublime to the ridiculous, radical-right supplyside economics grabs the limelight.

On one of Joan Robinson's return visits to Cambridge, Massachusetts, as she explicated the intricacies of Wicksell effects, one of the radical students stomped out of the room muttering loudly 'A plague on both your houses.' More serious researchers resolved their perplexities one way or another concerning the intricacies of time-phased systems and wanted to move on to new frontiers.

Joan Robinson complained of deaf adders who would not hear. I don't know whether she determined that I just could not understand her message, or whether she decided that perversely I chose to disregard it. For my part, I read all her writings and did not find the calculus of time-phased systems a transcendental mystery. That part of my work dealing with equilibrium paths of heterogeneous capital vectors I never expected her to read, any more than I expected my good friend and mentor, Alvin Hanson, to spend his sixth and seventh decades swotting the intermediate mathematics involved in my accelerator–multiplier models or in Richard Goodwin's autorelaxation limit cycles.

Something precious I gained from Robinson's work and that of her colleagues working in the Sraffian tradition. As I have described elsewhere, prior to 1952 when Joan began her last phase of capital research, I operated under an important misapprehension concerning the curvature properties of a general Fisher—von Neumann technology.

What I learned from Joan Robinson was more than she taught. I learned, not that the general differentiable neoclassical model was special and wrong but that a general neoclassical technology does not necessarily involve a higher steady-state output when the interest rate is lower. I had thought that such a property generalized from the simplest one-sector Ramsey–Solow parable to the most general Fisher case. That was a subtle error and, even before the 1960 Sraffa book on input-input, Joan Robinson's 1956 explorations in *Accumulation of Capital* alerted me to the subtle complexities of general neoclassicism.

These complexities have naught to do with *finiteness* of the number of alternative activities, and naught to do with the phenomenon in which, to produce a good like steel you need directly or indirectly to use steel itself as an input. In other words, what is wrong and special in the simplest neoclassical or Austrian parables can be completely divorced from the basic critique of marginalism that Sraffa was ultimately aiming at when he began in the 1920s to compose his classic: Sraffa (1960). To drive home this fundamental truth, I shall illustrate with the most general Wicksell–Austrian case that involves time-phasing of labor with no production of any good by means of itself as a raw material.

As in the 1893–1906 works of Knut Wicksell, translated in Wicksell (1934, Volume I), let corn now be producible by combining (labor yesterday, labor day-before-yesterday, etc.):

$$Q_t = f(L_{t-1}, L_{t-2}, \ldots, L_{t-T}) = f(L) \tag{1}$$

$$Q = f(L_1, L_2, \ldots, L_T) \quad \text{in steady states} \tag{2}$$

$$= L_1 f(1, L_2/L_1, \ldots, L_T/L_1), \quad \text{1st°-homogeneous and concave} \tag{3}$$

$$= \sum_1^T L_j(\delta f(L)/\delta L_j), \quad \text{Euler's theorem} \tag{4}$$

$$\delta f/\delta L_j = f_j(L), \ \delta^2 f/\delta L_i \delta L_j = f_{ij}(L) \quad \text{exist for } L \geqq 0 \tag{5}$$

$$f_j > 0, \ (z_1 \ldots z_T)[f_{ij}(L)](z_1, \ldots, z_T)' < 0 \text{ for } z_j \neq bL_j > 0 \tag{6}$$

Nothing could be more neoclassical than (1)–(6). *If* it obtained in the real world, a Sraffian critique could not get off the ground.

Yet it can involve (a) the qualitative phenomena much like 'reswitching', (b) so-called perverse 'Wicksell effects', (c) a locus between steady-state *per capita* consumption and the interest rate, a (*i,c*) locus, which is *not* necessarily monotonically negative once we get away from very low *i* rates. This cannot happen for the 2-period case where $T = 2$. But for $T \geqq 3$, all these 'pathologies' can occur, and there is really nothing pathological about them. No matter how much they occur, the marginal productivity doctrine does directly apply here to the general equilibrium solution of the problem of the distribution of income.

Remarks. What eternal verities do always obtain, even when corners in the technology make derivatives $[\delta Q_j/\delta L_j, \delta Q_j/\delta Q_{ij}]$ be somewhere undefined? Always, it remains true:

(a) To go from an initial sub-golden-rule steady state to a maintainable golden-rule steady state of maximal *per capita* consumption, must involve for society *a transient sacrifice of current consumptions* ('waiting' or 'abstinence' à la Senior, Böhm, and Fisher!).

(b) For non-joint-product systems, there is a steady-state trade-off frontier between the interest rate and the real-wage (expressed in terms of any good).

This monotone relation between $(W/P_j,i)$ was obscurely glimpsed by Thünen and other classicists and by Wicksell and other neoclassicists. But the *factor–price trade-off frontier* did not explicitly surface in the modern literature until 1953, as in R. Sheppard (1953), P. Samuelson (1953), and D. Champernowne (1954). One can prove it to be well behaved for (1)–(3), or any convex-technology case, by modern duality theory. Before Robinson (1956), I wrongly took for granted that a similar monotone-decreasing relation between $(i,Q/\Sigma_1^T L_j)$ must also follow from mere concavity – just as does the relation $-\delta^2 C_{t+1}/(\delta C_t)^2 = \delta i_t/\delta C_t > 0$. But this blythe expectation is simply wrong! I refer readers to my summing up on reswitching: Samuelson (1966).

I realize that there are many economists who tired of Robinson's repeated critiques of capital theory as tedious and sterile naggings. I cannot agree. Beyond the effect of rallying the spirits of economists disliking the market order, these Robinson–Sraffa–Pasinetti–Garegnani contributions deepen our understanding of how a time-phased competitive microsystem works.

10   FINALE

The life of science is performed on a stage. The same actors come and go for a while. New scholars emerge. Each scholar someday drops out permanently.

Great scholars leave their mark on the drama of accumulated scholarship. Joan Robinson will be long remembered for her originality and breadth – and for the person she was.

Notes

1. During the bad McCarthy years of the 1950s, Joan Robinson once said to me: 'I understand it is a dangerous and reportable act to buy my *Essay* in a Washington, DC bookstore – even though the book is, after all, a critique of Marx!' My 1967 remark about Robinson as a friend had reference to Robinson (1965, pp.154–5): 'The prediction of "growing misery" for the workers under capitalism . . . today has been obviously falsified. . . . This error, like Jesus' belief that the world was shortly coming to an end, is so central to the whole doctrine, that it is hard to see how it could have been put afloat without it . . . "You [workers] have nothing to lose but the prospect of a suburban home and a motor car" would not have been much of a slogan.'

2. See Robinson (1965, p.410) for '. . . there is one point on which I agree with him [Solow] – that the notion of factor allocation in conditions of perfect competi-

tion makes sense in a normative theory for a planned economy rather than in a descriptive theory for a capitalistic economy, and that the notion of the marginal productivity of investment makes sense in the context of socialist planning.'

3. Often one found in Robinson's writings prescient insights. Browsing through an early collection of her papers, I spotted what was essentially a statement of the Nonsubstitution Theorem.

4. J. Viner (1931) is the famous article in which the mathematical draftsman Y. K. Wong corrected Viner's boo-boo concerning the envelope to the U-shaped cost curves, insisting that Viner should make the envelope's slope negative where it touches tangentially the short-run Us that are still falling. In Viner (1931) there is the 'pure Ricardian case' – today often called the Jones–Samuelson or Ricardo–Viner–Samuelson–Jones case: in this case, each good requires transferable labor and a land specific to itself; here an expansion of demand for such a good (burgundy wine, for example) *must* raise its relative price – a clear negation of any Sraffian contention that only constant costs are truly compatible with perfect competition. Cf. Ronald Jones (1971) and Samuelson (1971a).

5. A close reading of Sraffa (1926) suggests a technical defence for Sraffa. The increasing-cost box, if not empty, is 'almost empty' in that the cases where it occurs are alleged to be unimportant. Will this wash? From the standpoint of the mathematical theory of what is generic and what is singular – of what is 'almost always' the case in the space of all possible (labor/output, land/output) coefficients, constant costs is the singular case that is as rare as Marx's configuration of 'equal organic compositions of capital'. Counsel for Sraffa can retreat to a different defensive tack: Sraffa is not so much denying the empirical relevance of competitive increasing costs, as he is pointing out the limitations of Marshall's *partial* equilibrium methodology. You might object: 'Outside East Anglia in the flapper age who cares all that much about Marshall's idiosyncratic constructs?' The answer is that we economists everywhere did take Marshall seriously in every respect; and so any cogent comment by Sraffa on the matter would indeed be important for the time. But, substantively, would a Sraffian claim be correct, that constant costs are appropriately handled by partial equilibrium paradigms while increasing costs are not? In its own right, the claim cannot be sustained. Increasing costs can be rigorously handled in certain special models by Marshallian-cross diagrams – as can be seen in Samuelson (1971b); and, conversely, it is not correct that the general constant-cost case can dispense with Walras–Pareto general–equilibrium methodology and be adequately handled by partial–equilibrium techniques. *Remark*: I have ignored completely the topic of 'externalities'. These can be important in their own right but they were red herrings that befuddled the post-Clapham polemics of the Marshallians.

6. Scholars more learned in the genesis of Marx's thought than I am will know that, when the young Marx was fumbling towards an understanding of economics, he entertained the notion of a normal price for a good around which its supply-and-demand oscillations would take place. At first he resisted, I am given to understand, the hypothesis that labor costs alone determined this normal level of price. Had he stayed in such a viewpoint, Marx would not only have been near to the Marshall to come (and the Walras!) but also would have been in general agreement with Smith's eclectic wage + rent + interest resolution of competitive price. Anti-Marxians and Marxians do not sufficiently realize how many tens of thousands of words Marx devoted to criticizing this Smithian 3-component resolution of price. Robinson (1965, p.12) reads Sraffa (1960) 180° backward: Sraffa's dated-labor resolution, which in matrix terms says

$P = Wa_0[I + a(1 + i) + a^2(1 + i)^2 + \ldots)$, is a vindication of Smith's value-added approach and not a 'rejection' of it. Paradoxically, Marx's Volume II tableau of reproduction, without his realizing it, gives the simultaneous-equation vindications for Smith's resolution: ignoring fine points connected with differences in sectors' organic composition of capital, in matrix terms it says $P(Q - aQ) = WL + i(PaQ) = Wa_0Q + i(PaQ)$, where by convention the wage is defined to be paid *post-factum*. It is trivial to add land and rent to this Smith–Sraffa system. V. Dmitriev (1898) was the first to dot the i and cross the t of this vindication of Smith.

7.   Pigou amused Kahn by saying, 'Samuelson's argument, which seems to have more merit than I at first believed, should be vetted by a mathematician.' 'But', responded Kahn (somewhat generously), 'Samuelson is a mathematican.' To which, the sexagenarian Pigou replied, 'I mean a good British mathematician.'

The joke evolved into romance. The great A. W. Turing, of Turing-machine Godel-like fame, was a chess partner of Pigou and looked into the matter. He pointed out for me, correctly and usefully, that a vector transformation, $y = f(x)$, with everywhere one signed, $\det[f'(x)] \neq 0$, could have a multivalued inverse $f^{-1}(y)$ – as in the case of the complex-number equation(s) $e^x = 1$. All this led in the end to the Gale–Nikaido breakthrough on univalent functions – as in Gale–Nikaido (1965), L. W. McKenzie (1955, 1967), I. Pearce (1959, 1967), Samuelson (1949, 1953, 1967).

8.   When I was introduced to Provost Sheppard of Kings, he inquired where I had come from. On learning that I had just been in Oxford, Sheppard replied: 'Quite proper. As the old Baedekker says: "Oxford and Cambridge – if time is short, skip Cambridge." '

At Oxford I lived in what was then called Halifax House, but which for a century had been an Anglican nunnery. Its walls had collected the frigidities of a full century and I was the coldest Yank in Britain. During my sojourn there double tragedies struck Oxford: Magdalen budgetary pinch cost it the waiting staff, and All Souls for the first time since the Middle Ages stopped brewing its own beer.

9.   I believe no American accepted Lange's invitation, and seem to recall being told by Harvard's Edward Mason that he had refused at the suggestion of the State Department. The apolitical Herman Wold of Uppsala attended, grateful for the rare opportunity to meet again with the great mathematician Kolmogorov.

References

Bickerdike, C. F. (1920) 'The Instability of Foreign Exchange', *Economic Journal*, 30 (March): 118–22.

Chamberlin, E. H. (1933) *Theory of Monopolistic Competition* (Cambridge, Mass.: Harvard University Press).

Champernowne, D. G. (1954) 'The Production Function and the Theory of Capital: A Comment', *Review of Economic Studies*, 21(2): 112–35.

Clapham, J. H. (1922) 'Of Empty Boxes', *Economic Journal* 32 (September): 305–14.

Clark, J. M. (1923) *Studies in the Economics of Overhead Costs* (Chicago: University of Chicago Press).

Cournot, A. A. (1838) *Researches into the Mathematical Theory of Wealth*. English translation (1897).

Dmitriev, V. (1898, 1902, 1974) *Economic Essays on Value, Competition, and Utility* (London: Cambridge University Press).

Dobb, M. H. (1973) *Theories of Value and Distribution Since Adam Smith* (Cambridge: Cambridge University Press).

Freeman, H. A. (1979) *Toward Socialism in America* (Cambridge, Mass.: Schenkman).

Gale, D. and H. Nikaido (1965) 'The Jacobian Matrix and Global Univalence of Mappings', *Mathematische Annalen*, Bd. 159 (Heft 2): 81–93.

Hahn, F. H. (1966) 'Equilibrium Dynamics with Heterogeneous Capital Goods', *Quarterly Journal of Economics*, 80 (November): 633–46.

Harrod, R. F. (1958) 'Factor–Price Relations under Free Trade', *Economic Journal*, 68 (June): 245–55.

James, S. F. and I. F. Pearce (1952) 'The Factor–Price Equalisation Myth', *Review of Economic Studies*, 19(2): 111–20.

Jones, R. W. (1971) 'A Three-Factor Model in Theory, Trade and History', in *Trade, Balance of Payments and Growth*, J. N. Bhagwati *et al.* (eds) (Amsterdam: North-Holland), pp.3–21.

Kaldor, N. (1956) 'Alternative Theories of Distribution', *Review of Economic Studies*, 23(2): 83–100.

Lerner, A. P. (1952) 'Factor Prices and International Trade', *Economica*, 19 (February): 1–15.

Marx, K. (1867, 1885, 1894) *Capital.*

McKenzie, L. W. (1955) 'Equality of Factor Prices in World Trade', *Econometrica*, 23 (July): 239–57.

McKenzie, L. W. (1967) 'The Inversion of Cost Functions: A Counterexample', *International Economic Review* 8 (October): 271–85.

Meade, J. E. (1950) 'The Equalisation of Factor Prices: The Two-Country Two-Factor Three-Product Case', *Metroeconomica*, 2 (December): 129–33.

Modigliani, F. (1986) 'Life Cycle, Individual Thrift, and the Wealth of Nations', *American Economic Review*, 76(3) (June): 297–313.

Morishima, M. (1973) *Marx's Economics: A Dual Theory of Value and Growth* (Cambridge: Cambridge University Press).

Pasinetti, L. (1962) 'Rate of Profit and Income Distribution in Relation to the Rate of Economic Growth', *Review of Economic Studies*, 29 (October): 267–79.

Pearce, I. (1959) 'A Further Note on Factor-Commodity Price Relationships', *Economic Journal*, 69 (December): 725–32.

Pearce, I. (1967) 'More About Factor Price Equalization', *International Economic Review*, 8 (October): 255–70.

Robinson, J. (1933a) *Economics of Imperfect Competition* (London: Macmillan).

Robinson, J. (1933b) 'The Theory of Money and the Analysis of Output', *Review of Economic Studies*, 1 (October): 22–6.

Robinson, J. (1937) *Essays in the Theory of Employment* (London: Macmillan).

Robinson, J. (1941) 'Rising Supply Price', *Economica*, NS 8 (February): 1–8. Also *Collected Economic Papers*, Vol. II (Oxford: Blackwell).

Robinson, J. (1942) *An Essay on Marxian Analysis* (London: Macmillan).

Robinson, J. (1952) *The Rate of Interest and Other Essays* (London: Macmillan).

Robinson, J. (1956) *The Accumulation of Capital* (London: Macmillan).

Robinson, J. (1965) *Collected Economic Papers*, Vol. III (Oxford: Blackwell).

Samuelson, P. A. (1946) 'Lord Keynes and the General Theory', *Econometrica*, 14 (July): 187–200. Also(1966) chapter 114 in Vol. 2 of *Collected Scientific Papers of Paul A. Samuelson* (Cambridge, Mass.: MIT Press).

Samuelson, P. A. (1948) 'International Trade and the Equalisation of Factor Prices', *Economic Journal*, 58 (June): 163–84. Also (1966) chapter 67 in Vol. 2 of *Collected Scientific Papers of Paul A. Samuelson* (Cambridge, Mass.: MIT Press).

Samuelson, P. A. (1949) 'International Factor–Price Equalisation Once Again', *Economic Journal*, 59 (June): 181–97. Also (1966) chapter 68 in Vol. 2 of *Collected Scientific Papers of Paul A. Samuelson* (Cambridge, Mass.: MIT Press).

Samuelson, P. A. (1953) 'Prices of Factors and Goods in General Equilibrium', *Review of Economic Studies*, 21(1): 1–20. Also (1966) chapter 70 in Vol. 2 of *Collected Scientific Papers of Paul A. Samuelson* (Cambridge, Mass.: MIT Press).

Samuelson, P. A. (1967) 'Marxian Economics as Economics', *American Economic Review*, 57 (May): 616–23. Also (1972) chapter 152 in Vol. 3 of *Collected Scientific Papers of Paul A. Samuelson* (Cambridge, Mass.: MIT Press).

Samuelson, P. A. (1971a) 'Ohlin Was Right', *Swedish Journal of Economics*, 73(4) (December): 365–84. Also (1977) chapter 254 in Vol. 4 of *Collected Scientific Papers of Paul A. Samuelson* (Cambridge, Mass.: MIT Press).

Samuelson, P. A. (1971b) 'An Exact Hume–Ricardo–Marshall Model of International Trade', *Journal of International Economics*, 1 (February): 1–17. Also (1972) chapter 162 in Vol. 3 of *Collected Scientific Papers of Paul A. Samuelson* (Cambridge, Mass.: MIT Press).

Sheppard, R. W. (1953) *Cost and Production Functions* (Princeton NJ: Princeton University Press).

Sraffa, P. (1926) 'The Laws of Returns under Competitive Conditions', *Economic Journal*, 36 (December): 535–50.

Sraffa, P. (1951) (ed.), *The Works and Correspondence of David Ricardo*. Vol. I, *On the Principles of Political Economy and Taxation* (Cambridge: Cambridge University Press).

Sraffa, P. (1960) *Production of Commodities by Means of Commodities* (Cambridge: Cambridge University Press).

Steedman, I. (1977) *Marx after Sraffa* (London: NLB; also (1981) London: Verso).

Stolper, W. F. and P. A. Samuelson (1941) 'Protection and Real Wages', *Review of Economic Studies*, 9 (November): 58–73.

Tinbergen, J. (1949) 'The Equalisation of Factor Prices Between Free-Trade Areas', *Metroeconomica*, 1 (April): 39–47.

Viner, J. (1931) 'Cost Curves and Supply Curves', *Zeitschrift fur Nationalokonomie*, 3, 23–46, reprinted (1959) in *The Long View and the Short*, J. Viner (Glencoe, Il.: The Free Press).

Wicksell, K. (1893–1906) *Lectures on Political Economy*, Vol. 1 *General Theory*. English translation (1934) (New York: Macmillan).

Young, Allyn (1928) 'Increasing Returns and Economic Progress', *Economic Journal*, 38 (December): 527–42.

Part I

Content and Method of Economic Theory

3 Joan Robinson and Modern Economic Theory: An Interview

Kenneth J. Arrow

Feiwel: Would you be good enough to reflect on the nature of equilibrium in accumulation of capital? What sensible long run is there in the Walrasian system? What kind of equilibria are possible?

Arrow: The Walrasian system in its modern form is not actually very interested in the idea of the steady state or long-run equilibria. Perhaps I should define my terms somewhat. Almost exactly fifty years ago Ragnar Frisch drew a distinction between equilibrium and the steady state (or the stationary state, as I think he called it). In the neoclassical framework equilibrium really means market clearing. It has nothing to do with stationarity over time in and of itself. The full modernized Walrasian general equilibrium system, as set forth, for example, in Debreu's *Theory of Value* (or in our joint paper five years before that), involves equilibrium *over time*. That does not mean stationary state. It means that at any moment of time we have a set of prices for the present and for the future and that there are demands and supplies of products for the present and for the future. So, at time 0, say today, we have planned demand for and supply of each product for each future period. If you find a set of prices such that all markets clear, that is an equilibrium. That equilibrium may, and in general will, involve changes over time. I should add, of course, parenthetically for it is not directly relevant here, the fact that we also provide for uncertainty. But let me avoid that question for the time being. Let us imagine a world of certainty where the basic factors about the future are known – the production possibilities, utility functions, and resources.

The question may arise: Nevertheless, would not we expect that in this story we have where everybody is optimizing, making plans today for the indefinite future, that the process will tend towards a steady state? The answer is that it is not a valid theorem of Walrasian economics. We can have perfectly good examples, known today, where you set forth an economy that is quite simple – for example, two sectors – where everybody perfectly foresees the future and seeks to equilibrate supply and demand on all markets present and future simultaneously, and where the economy simply whirls around; it does not converge to any steady state. We have fully understood this only recently because of the use of modern dynamic theory, but we did know that we were never able to prove convergence in complicated models. I say 'complicated', but they do not have to be very complicated either. It is true, of course, if you take the one-good world, where you have one good used either for capital or for consumption, then, indeed, you tend to have a convergence to a steady state. However, with different kinds of goods (say, both capital and consumption goods, to go no further), it is possible to produce examples where the economy will exhibit almost any kind of behavior you would like. It can cycle indefinitely – that has been the subject of recent research. You can also have what is currently called 'chaotic' behavior – and that is a very recent result by Boldrin and Montrucchio.

In general, the Walrasian intertemporal equilibrium (which is an equilibrium) may not necessarily converge to a steady state. It is true that there are steady-state solutions, in general. That is to say, if you happen to start with a certain configuration of capital goods, then at least under some assumptions (if you assume no technological progress, no growth in population, and a lot of other things), you generally reproduce those goods; at the end of each period people save just enough to maintain the capital intact. However, if the initial situation is not such that the capital goods are at those steady-state values but at different values, then, in general, there is no particular reason to assume it converges, as far as we know now. Now, this is at the broad theoretical level where all production functions are possible, all utility functions are possible. It may well be that if you take empirically valid production and utility functions, it will not happen. That is very difficult to tell without a lot of detailed investigations.

I would like now to make one further remark: Typically, these problems of possibly cyclical or other behavior do depend on the extent to which people discount the future. They tend not to occur if the discount rates are relatively high; that is, if the future is not discounted very much – if you tend to value tomorrow at a very high fraction (close to 1) of today. In that case you tend to have a monotone convergence to a steady state. That seems to have been our experience.

So, for current Walrasian thinking, the really interesting thing is intertemporal equilibrium. The steady state is nice to have happen analytically because it makes talk a lot easier if you have a steady state. But it is not necessary to have it from the point of view of welfare, nor from other points of view.

I may add that as soon as one enlarges one's horizon a little and admits some kind of technological progress, then steady states are sheer nonsense under any system of economics, be it neo-Ricardian, neoclassical, or anything else. The reason is this: If you assume that individuals are growing wealthier *per capita* and are capable of such indefinite growth, then we expect the proportions in which different goods are consumed to change over time – the well-known Engel's laws. Therefore, steady states are essentially an impossibility, and that is true under any system one could think of.

So, the search for the steady state is something of a chimera, although I can understand that it makes analysis much easier if one can think in terms of steady states. I suppose that is why Joan Robinson has spent so much of her efforts on finding steady states, even though her view of the capitalist world is that it tends to be extremely chaotic and uncertain.

Feiwel: Joan Robinson criticized equilibrium theorists for being too concerned with being in equilibrium rather than with the fundamental problem of getting into equilibrium. To what extent was she right and/or wrong?

Arrow: That is a very striking question. In fairness it must be said to have been the object of a great deal of research, both neoclassical and otherwise. It is what is usually called stability analysis; the idea being, supposing you are out of equilibrium, will you tend to converge towards equilibrium? I am using 'equilibrium' now in the market clearing sense, rather than in the stationary state sense, for, as I said before, that may not be achievable, in any case.

Stability analysis is a subject that has been broached by many economists. I believe the originator of this analysis was Walras. In reading him, one is struck with the enormous amount of time he devoted to what he called *tâtonnements*: suppose you have a system of prices, 'called out by chance' – to use his phrase – what happens then? At every stage of his analysis, from pure exchange through production to capital, he repeats (not necessarily with much gain in clarity) the discussion.

Everybody who talks about equilibrium (in the sense of market clearing) always gives some sense of an argument about what would happen out of equilibrium. For example, Ricardo, or even Smith, say 'well, supposing the price was such that more than normal rate of profit was earned'. Then they tell a story: capital will flow into this activity, etc. Always there is a story to justify the equilibrium concept by some rudimentary dynamics discussion; the idea of what would happen were it not in equilibrium. A price above or below the natural price could not survive.

Most of these discussions were extremely rudimentary even for a single market. But Walras not only stated it quite explicitly for a single market, but he was concerned with the interrelation among markets. That was the big and damaging new development. You could tell some kind of story easily enough with supply and demand curves crossing on a single market, as to why they should come into equilibrium. But the story became more complicated when a change of price on one market affected supply and demand on other markets. I will not go into the full intellectual history of all that. Unfortunately, today we know that if we take the out-of-equilibrium system that is most common, namely, the Samuelsonian dynamics in which price responds roughly proportionally to a difference in supply and demand, then we have lots of examples of perfectly well behaved systems that nevertheless are unstable. The definitive paper on this was Herbert Scarf's; in 1960 he first gave a clear-cut, fully defined general equilibrium system satisfying all the requirements that nevertheless had no stable equilibrium; it had only one equilibrium point and that was unstable.

This can be regarded as a damaging result. But it is equally true of any other system I know of. I do not see that neo-Ricardian economics has spelled out its dynamics. It has the same kind of verbal dynamics that we all use: say demand exceeds supply, price rises, this attracts more resources; something shifts, this shifts, that shifts, etc. ... we tell a story. That kind of verbal story is the same kind of story that is told in a neo-Ricardian setting with different topics. So all systems have the same difficulty of showing stability in a multi-market context. There is nothing peculiar to the difficulties encountered in the neoclassical setting.

The question of the necessity of a stability story is an interesting one. You might say, 'well, every hypothesis is entitled to be taken on its own merits'. One might say that the world is such that markets always clear at every moment (a proposition now being pushed very hard by our so-called new classical friends); never mind how they come to clear, they clear. We can then say 'that is a hypothesis about the world'. We can spell out its implications. We can see whether they check with our experience and our empirical evidence or whether they do not. If they check, well, there may be another interesting question as to how we get into that equilibrium. On the other hand, by the same token, the statement that the world is out of equilibrium, that markets do not clear most of the time, at least not completely, is also a perfectly good hypothesis whose implications should also be studied. So, unlike say Lucas, I do not think there is any reason why theory *has* to be market clearing theory. There is no end to the extent to which one can push back the chain of causation about everything. Any theory, if accepted, raises the question: why is it true and not something else? And we always appeal to a deeper theory. I would not go so far as to say that stability theory is necessary; I admit it would be desirable.

My own present view is that we actually do not observe very often, except in the labor market, violent disequilibria and we have to ask: why is that so? There are several possible conjectures. One is, of course, that the Samuelsonian stability theory (or indeed that of Marshall or Walras), when you look at it closely, is lacking in certain rather obvious dimensions which suggests necessary modifications. In particular, there is no memory;

a price responds to current supply and demand. The point of it is that the history of what has happened in the course of price adjustment is information that could be exploited at any current moment and, therefore, it may be that the price adjustment process is one that itself is modified over time in response to learning. It *may* be (though I do not know whether it is true or not) that one could thus derive adjustment processes. It is certainly true that we can find adjustment processes requiring more information than just supply and demand that will almost always converge. This has been shown by people like Smale – essentially a first cousin of the algorithms, developed first by Scarf and later by others, that actually show you how you can solve for an equilibrium economy. It is an iterative process and you can conceive of the market as doing it. Actually the process demands much information; that is, the adjustment on one market demands information about other markets. That may or may not be regarded as desirable.

I can only repeat that there are open ends in the stability theory, and all multimarket models of any kind have very similar problems.

Feiwel: One clarifying question: is there a difference in the understanding of the 'short run' in the modern Walrasian sense and the usual Marshallian textbook-type concept?

Arrow: Of course, we do not use phrases like that. It is true that we have a succession of periods: We have markets clearing at time 1, markets clearing at time 2, markets clearing at time 3. Now, if you look at the market clearing at time 1, we think of everything that relates to the future as given. In particular it is going to be true that if you have durable goods, the demand for these goods is going to depend on the present and the future and, therefore, the stock of existing durable goods is going to change relatively slowly. The point about durable producers' goods is that you have a stock of them. To put it differently, in the von Neumann terminology, durable goods today produce durable goods tomorrow (a little older durable goods tomorrow). Therefore the stock of durable goods is going to change relatively slowly. And it has to. You cannot have a discontinuous jump in that for it would mean an infinite rate of output, and you cannot have that. Therefore, in that sense I would say not that there is a contradiction between the Marshallian and Walrasian point of view, but that the Walrasian is essentially a little clearer and a more carefully worked out statement of the Marshallian position that the durable goods are going to adjust in a different way than the flow variables like labor, and, therefore, there are going to be cost curves relevant to the short run. Of course, in equilibrium the short-run and long-run conditions have to be satisfied. They are made consistent, as Marshall said, by varying the quasi-rents on the durable goods. I believe it is correct to say that looking at the Walrasian equilibrium as of a moment of time, then it is in effect like a short-run equilibrium in the Marshallian sense.

Feiwel: Could you elaborate on the differences in the use of the term 'equilibrium' by the modern Walrasians and, say, the classical economists, Marshall, and Joan Robinson (who, for instance, tends to speak about the tendency of getting to long-term equilibrium or the stationary state)?

Arrow: You are right, there is a lot of murkiness about this. I think the classicists had both the statesman, state and what amounts to supply equalling demand, but it is not very explicit. Certainly, in Ricardo there is the idea of an equilibrium at a moment of time. He does not have a great deal to say about the determination of quantities. It does not occupy nearly as much bulk as does the concept of natural prices. One of the reasons for this emphasis is that the prices are supposed to be determined in some way independent of demand. Therefore, one can talk about prices and concern oneself with demand only at those prices. The allocation of resources among industries does depend upon demand. Given the natural prices and at those prices a certain demand, the silk industry, for example, had better produce the amount to meet the demand, not more and not less. Ricardo explains this tendency by the idea that the market price might deviate from the natural price and attract capital and so forth.

He has roughly the idea (although I find it hard to make a thoroughly consistent statement of Ricardo) that the price of labor is given by the subsistence level. It is true the subsistence level is not a physiological subsistence level; that is absolutely clear. But what determines it is left totally unclear, so let us take it as exogenous to some extent. If the price of labor is given, the price of goods is then determined by the statement that the return to capital is to be equated among all industries and, if you make the very simple assumption that in effect the period of production is the same in all industries, that is, all industries are equally capital intensive, then you can say that the relative prices of goods equal their labor content. Actually by the time you get through the first five chapters, there are all kinds of exceptions in little notes. There are enough exceptions to drive the whole of neoclassical economics through it. Nevertheless, that is the lesson that has been drawn by others.

In the Ricardian system, at a given moment the rate of return is determined by the profit rate in the agricultural sector. Actually there is a simultaneous element there which I think has been neglected, because the size of the population affects the rents. The feedback of rents on the whole system is entirely neglected. At any rate, the rate of return on capital is essentially determined by the returns on capital in the agricultural sector. In some sense that is a short-run equilibrium, because Ricardo does talk towards the end about the accumulation of capital and the decline in the rate of return. The discussion of that is quite explicit, so presumably the central model is not a long-term steady state.

The economy can depart from normal prices for periods of time, because, for example, the wages might be above the subsistence level and that would be followed by an increase of population. In effect, the supply of labor is infinitely elastic, but with a lag. It is not elastic immediately. In fact it is inelastic in a very short run and gets more and more elastic as time goes on. So there is a long and short run even with a given stock of capital. Then, in addition, there is capital accumulation. The labor force has a kind of capital aspect in all this. Then there is a very, very long run where the rates of return are driven down to their minimal level; the country is very heavily populated and the landlords are presumably getting very, very rich because of the high rent situation.

If you try to tease a consistent story out of Ricardo, the story would be fairly complex. The same is true of the neoclassicists.

Keynes has an interpretation of equilibrium that is not market clearing. That, by the way, is subject to some argument. Some say that actually the supply of labor is somehow given and demand can be raised by raising prices, but cannot be decreased by lowering wages. I spoke about market clearing. Now, one could have a more general concept of equilibrium at a moment of time, not based on market clearing but based on some other concept. But it is essential to have a definition of market equilibrium. One possibility (implicit in Keynes and articulated by some of the economists of the European school, particularly, Malinvaud, Drèze, Hahn, and Benassy – and in this country by Barro and Grossman, though they have both repudiated it since) is to argue that sticky prices define an equilibrium without market clearing. But then there must be some method of allocating either the excess demand or the excess supply (usually the latter), that is, a rationing scheme. In other words, the substitute for the price-taking behavior of the Walrasian scheme is one where prices are rigid or sticky and there are non-price ways of allocating goods. This viewpoint has given rise to a considerable literature that people are taking seriously, and not only theoretically. There is a fair amount of empirical work, especially in Europe where it is a popular and important subject.

That is a kind of equilibrium. It is still not the long-run Keynesian equilibrium of which Joan spoke. In Keynes after all it is quite clear that investment goes up and down a lot. As far as I know, he does not talk at all about long-run investment policy. There are some elements of an idea that long-run investment is not going to be sufficient to sustain full employment, but he does not have, as far, as I can see, any idea of a long-run steady state. He does not contradict the idea; he just does not discuss it. The stagnationists, like Alvin Hansen and certainly Joan, have held that underemployment can be steady state. That is partly derived from Harrod.

He is actually the first to discuss this in terms of the theory that investment is justified in part by growth. At the same time, because of the Keynesian story, investment determines growth. There are some simultaneous equations there that can be exploited in various forms with the lack of market clearing to give rise to these various accumulation paths – golden ages and all that – that Joan plays with in *The Accumulation of Capital*. So there can be a steady state of Keynesian equilibrium. It is not clear in Keynes that there is one or that there can be one. Certainly, his emphasis was in a way like that in Walras; it was a little more short run.

Feiwel: How important is the discussion about the heterogeneity of capital?

Arrow: In some ways it is very important; I have to give Joan a lot of credit for having pushed the subject. I do not think that any *true* Walrasian can learn much from it, because he or she never assumed that there is only one kind of capital good; it is only important for the applied Walrasians – if I may put it that way. From the pure Walrasian viewpoint everything is fully heterogeneous – no questions about that – there are lots of goods of all kinds; capital goods, consumer goods, and the like. The trouble is to have that system tell you anything. Of course, there is a certain impatience on the part of every economist, certainly anyone concerned with practical affairs to say, 'look, I have this complicated system, that is very nice, but what does it tell me in understandable terms?' Then, the propensity is to take the system and boil it down. Thus it is boiled by many (including Harrod, by the way, not just the neoclassicists) to a one-dimensional system.

Now, it turns out that one-dimensional systems have a lot of very special properties. The one-good system simply is not general. I already referred to that before when I pointed out that in such a case you have to have monotone convergence to a steady state. That is more or less what Bob Solow did in his famous papers. I say more or less because his savings function is not neoclassical. Despite the usual reference to it as a neoclassical growth model, it is no such thing. It is a mixture. In a true neoclassical model savings is determined at the same time as consumption is by optimization over an infinite horizon, whereas Solow just assumed that the savings rate is a constant. His model is a mixture of Keynesian and neoclassical. It is neoclassical in the sense that markets always clear, but the savings behavior is not neoclassical. That is important because actually the asymptotic behavior is quite different. For example, he had trouble getting a steady state, unless he brought in depreciation of capital, or growth in population, or technology. These obviously exist in the real world, but it is peculiar that the existence of a steady state should depend on them. The answer is: if properly done, it does not. The point is that people eventually stop saving. In fact, at that time the true infinite-horizon

Walrasian is just like a neo-Ricardian. *By definition*, in steady states, with constant population, there is zero capital accumulation. Therefore, the economy has to somehow come to the point where savings gets to zero. In the Solow model that is not possible. I simply wanted to differentiate those growth models from the true neoclassical growth models of the optimal kind, the McKenzie (and going back to Ramsey) and all the modern variations of the Ramsey models.

It is also true that neoclassists emphasize the role of the heterogeneity of capital and not only in the broad theoretical sense, but in the practical sense as well. Hahn wrote a very famous paper where he pointed out that with heterogeneous capital goods the concept of perfect foresight gives rise to all sorts of problems because of saddle point properties. Except on the unique right path, it is impossible to be on a competitive path forever. Therefore the analysis is very much constrained. Certainly, it is true that the heterogeneity of capital does make a difference. The more we go into it, the more we appreciate, I think, the possibility that it makes a difference.

The idea of reswitching – the idea that the capital intensity does not rise as the interest rate falls – it based on heterogeneous capital goods. Of course, there is a problem of measurement of what one means by capital. If there are several capital goods, what is meant by the stock of capital? Consumption was taken as a numeraire, but that does not have any special validity. There is probably no sense in which an aggregate measure of capital will automatically follow the rate of interest, once there is a multiplicity of capital goods. Pasinetti was quite correct. The trouble is that with heterogeneous capital goods almost anything is possible.

Now, I do not think this in any way interferes with the consistency of the general equilibrium theory of capital formation based on perfect foresight. You may not like the assumption of perfect foresight; that I can understand. But what I am saying is that there is no logical inconsistency in the perfect foresight model. One restricted way of looking at it is that in a way the rate of interest is a funny thing to look at. What we are actually interested in is prices. We have the price of a capital good today and the price of a future capital good which we can interpret as a discounted price, but in itself it is a price. It is only because we want to have some kind of geometric average, called the rate of interest, that we get some of these paradoxes. They are not really contradictions. Now, it is true that intertemporal allocation can be discussed without ever mentioning the rate of interest. The variables are today's prices for future goods. There is then a perfectly consistent story that does not look any different from the story about choosing commodities today – one that the neo-Ricardians do not seem to object to particularly. There are, of course, others objecting to that story on the grounds that people choose things by habit or something else, by endogenous tastes or what not. It is true that the Robinson–Sraffa school tends not to discuss utility concepts at all. The question, however, is: what do they replace them with? One of the reasons they do not worry about it is that they are not really interested in consumer demand. They do not actually address the question. All that I am saying, however, is that choice over time is a form of consumer demand and the question is whether that concept can be easily discarded.

A point that I mentioned previously is that of discounting for the future. One of the questions involved in the choice of the present for the future is that you have discounts for the future. I think that in most of the Robinson–Sraffa type work the idea of discounting the future does not play any role. They do not seem to think in terms of what determines savings, for example. This fits into our discussion at this point in the sense that it deals with the theory of distribution. That is why Joan Robinson can be so interested in the golden rule which essentially is the maximum sustainable consumption. That was a very interesting piece of analysis, by the way. But, I do not regard the golden rule of consumption as having any particular normative significance because to me future consumption is discounted. It means that the marginal product of capital is being driven not to zero but to the subjective rate of discount. That is a different story. This is all very suggestive. It is a question of what governs capital accumulation. We shall come back to its ideological significance. But obviously it can be argued that the discounting of the future can be used as a justification for the rate of interest: 'I do not want to give up my goods without some positive return because, obviously, I would rather have them today than tomorrow'. That is the old argument of abstinence or waiting used by Marshall, Senior, and others.

What I am saying is this: the heterogeneity of capital is indeed an important question, but I cannot see it in any way as destructive of the neoclassical paradigm. I cannot see how it could be because it is stated within that paradigm. All it says is: the stories told with a single capital good are not valid, and maybe (although we still do not have a very clear idea) they are very misleading. There is evidence that as soon as stories with heterogeneous capital goods are told cycles and similar dynamic phenomena occur. And since we do have cycles, maybe this story should not be thrown out too quickly.

Feiwel: What in your opinion are the real issues of the capital controversy? Has it contributed to our understanding of income distribution and of ways to affect its content by policy measures?

Arrow: Obviously, in the way it has been used (say by Garegniani, for example, whom I take to be an authoritative representative) has been to show that the neoclassical theory cannot be right; that it shows instability. I think that all it shows is that you can never talk about a single capital good; that is all there is to it. I do not see that it proves anything whatever, particularly when the alternative theories seem to be arbitrary.

To answer the second part of your question, I do not see any particular connection between the capital controversy and a really interesting story about income distribution. The neo-Ricardians, of course, have a theory of distribution which was actually first articulated, as far as I know, in Frank Hahn's doctoral dissertation, but was not published at the time. It was later published by Kaldor. Essentially it means that the propensities to save determine the distribution of income. If you look at this perfectly innocuous equation (savings equal investment and investment is whatever it is; savings is determined by the propensity to save, for the moment taking that as a meaningful concept), the only way you get the distribution of income into this is to say, 'if you have different income classes and only one group saves and the other does not, then the savings times the income of that class must equal investment'. If you assume that the investment has some rate of growth and you have a fixed capital–output ratio, then you have an identity that tells you the income of that class has to be big enough that at the savings propensity it provides the needed investment. That equation must be true; it must be true in any system whatever, neoclassical, neo-Ricardian ... there cannot be any system where it is not true that savings equals investment in that sense. There is a question whether it is intended or unintended investment, but actually at this point that is not a difference; these are intended magnitudes even in the neo-Ricardian formulation.

Then how can I deny the neo-Ricardian theory? The answer to this is: there are many things held constant there. It is an equation, but it only tells you anything if you assume the growth rate is given, if you assume the savings rate is given, etc. If, for example, the savings rate is affected by the rate of interest, the equation is still valid, but the implications drawn are not. The rate of growth of the capital stock is not given; it is the result of various economic forces. So the prices and other things that determine that may change so as to make it true. It is also true that one of the reasons they get by with this is that they assume a fixed capital–output ratio, so that the usual marginal productivity story does not tell you anything. There are a lot of supporting hyperplanes at the point where capital is fully employed. Therefore, there is nothing that ties this down. On the contrary, if you had a smooth production function then the rate of interest would be completely determined and there would be other things that would have to give. So the equation is close to a tautology, depending on how you interpret it. It is a tautology if you say that what is actually saved is actually invested. It is a real equation if you say that it is intended. But that is not really the distinction. In any case, it is either a tautology or it is an equation so elementary that no system could deny it. Therefore, it cannot be a way of distinguishing one system from another. In my opinion, you get a distribution theory that is only sharp if you assume a lot of things to be constant that you have no reason to think of as constant. For example, the rate of savings ought to depend on the pre-existing level of capital. If people are very capital-rich they may save less. That is what Ricardo said. This may be neo-Ricardian theory, but when you go to paleo-Ricardian theory it looks more like neoclassical. I really do not think it is a genuine theory of distribution.

Feiwel: May we have your view on the distributional implications of marginal productivity theory?

Arrow: To some extent they are not as strong as they appear. The rate of return on capital has to include capital gains. Therefore, in some sense, you have the same sort of problems to which I just objected in the neo-Ricardian story. It only becomes a completely deterministic, a completely tied-down theory if you assume away something like capital gains. (I am speaking of real capital gains, that is, changes in the relative prices of consumer goods and capital goods, for the moment forgetting about the aggregation problem.) So it is not a complete theory without putting it through the full dynamic model. It is in some sense a short-run theory of wages. I think that is correct. I do not see what is wrong with the proposition that the wages at any moment of time are governed by the marginal productivity of labor, given of course all the other factors like capital and so on, which can, however, be reasonably thought of as constant in the short run. It is not a long-run theory of distribution because the wages, the rates of return, and everything else are evolving over time. It will hold in the long run, but it is not a complete system. Like the savings–investment identity we spoke of before, it is only one equation of a complete theory. For certain purposes it may be ruling, but it is not ruling in the long run. It is true that in modern theories the labor force is thought of as exogenous – it is whatever it is. But the capital stock that goes with it is not exogenous. Therefore, one cannot rely on simple rules like that.

The simplest idea of a steady state in a Walrasian system assumes that in fact the utility function for an individual over time is the sum of discounted utilities. That is only one possible utility function, but it is a convenient one – the constant discount rate of utilities. Then the long-run steady state would have to be one where the rate of return on capital is that subjective rate of discount – that is, in the steady state if there were one. Therefore, the return on capital is given by wealth. The point is not so much whether this is true or not, but it determines what the steady-state capital–output ratio is and that, in turn, determines the wage rate again through marginal productivity. So marginal productivity theory is there as part of the story, but it simply is not the full story. I am afraid that one of the unpleasant lessons of general equilibrium theory is that you always have to work with complete systems. Some things may be more important than others, you may not have to think of everything, but you rarely can get by with one equation. For example, the monetarists with their stable demand for money have their fallacies, the Keynesians or neo-Keynesians have theirs, but the Walrasians are always cautious, or should be.

Feiwel: This raises another question: can you share with us what specifically you mean by income distribution?

Arrow: As is well known, there are two (at least, and one could think probably of more) quite distinct meanings. One is what is called the functional distribution of income; what is given to capital, to labor, and so forth. As soon as you have that question, you can say, 'after all there are all kinds of capital . . .' Then, of course, the first thing a Walrasian would say would be 'yes, but this is not really a well-posed question, after all there are many various kinds of labor'. Now, that is a fact one can hardly dispute. It is interesting, however, that whole systems are created on the assumption of homogenous labor, when labor is not merely heterogenous, but strikingly so. Although Ricardo is embarrassed about that, he has a passage where he discusses it, but he passes on and buries it. Marx does too; he also recognizes it. It is hard to deny this fact. Smith and Mill do talk about 'compensating advantages' – that is, net advantages, when the people doing very dirty work get paid more. In some sense all that means is that real wages are equated. But the definition of real wages is a little more complex and includes the disutility of labor. But the point is that it is quite clear that this is not true either – people doing pleasanter jobs are paid more than those doing unpleasant jobs, not less on the average (with exceptions, of course). Mill conceded that without having any particular substitute for it. It was true then; it is true now. Therefore, the only real answer consistent with neoclassical theory is that people are different. There may well be other answers to this story. We are talking here about labor income, not about the usual picture in Marx or Ricardo where there are rich capitalists who have enough capital on which the return yields them a high income, and then there are others – the laborers. Therefore, the impression is that the inequality of incomes is due to the fact that some people have capital and some do not.

In fact, we know that in our modern society (whatever the problems of definition) most inequality of incomes is within the labor force. The question whether to classify executives within the labor force is a difficult one; it seems metaphysical to deny that they are for one would have to explain why they are not laborers. At what point of the hierarchy do you draw the line? They are certainly not capitalists. There are many executives who, whatever wealth they have, have accumulated it as a result of their own savings. Their wealth is a result of their high incomes, not the cause of it. So you have to ask the question: how does it come about that there is a significant class of people who are well off, yet not because they are capitalists? One might say that this group is relatively small and should not count. But there are a lot of people below this category in the US who are getting annual incomes of, say $50,000 or $60,000. These are not really astronomical figures, but at least two or three times what a semi-skilled worker (say, a steel worker) would get. You then have to ask yourself, 'what is it about these people that makes it so?' One answer, of course, is that they are different; genetically, culturally, family, whatever. They are different; they have different productivities. This strongly overlaps the distribution of income to wealth. It is true that the highest possible incomes, for the most part, go to people who are wealthy. And the very wealthiest people inherit the bulk of wealth. This is a very small number of people, a large percentage of the wealth, but not a large percentage of total incomes.

The Ricardian question was, of course, how is income distributed – 'the annual produce' was, I believe, the phrase he used. The question then is: why does the functional distribution of income not provide a full answer? First, there is an ambiguity in the concept of functional distribution. But even that ambiguity aside, there is a tremendous amount of inequality among people who have no capital. You certainly are not getting at all (and in some sense not even at half) of the inequality by considering the functional distribution of income. We then come to the interesting question of what governs the distribution of income within the labor force and also among capitalists. That is an interesting and open question. Some people think that people get different rates of return. Some people are better capitalists than others. It is not as if there was a market on which one simply puts out one's capital. And rates of return are, in fact, very far from equalized over industries, by the way. We say, 'yes, but that is because of different riskiness' and stories like that. This is to a considerable extent true, but not entirely.

The question then is: by distribution of income do you mean the Ricardian distribution, as you put it, or the question of inequality? Although there is some overlap to them, these are very, very far from being the same question. If you would ask: what is a good theory of the inequality of income? Neoclassical economics provides a kind of answer. It does not provide a terribly good answer because it says 'everybody is different'. Therefore, in some sense, the answer is rather vague. It does not explain the inequalities. It ultimately says that income among laborers is different because they are different people. Essentially you then have to go to the non-competing groups. That is the basic explanation: there are a lot of classes of people capable of supplying different kinds of labor and when a certain kind of labor commands a high price on the market, those people get high wages. That is an explanation of sorts. It is a logical explanation but it is not one on which you can operate very effectively. It explains why people might have different amounts of capital, partly because they have different human assets (analogous to different amounts of land) that they then use to accumulate savings, partly because they may have different discount rates and are more or less willing to accumulate. The Walrasian story, being a rather weak story, can certainly be made compatible with almost any set of facts about distribution by putting in assumptions about demand and supply of different kinds of goods and different rates of discount.

People have, of course, made various efforts to try to build in theories that are sometimes rather of an *ad hoc* character. For example, that individual income varies randomly over time and then people make efforts to smooth their income, and you work through the optimal reactions. You get a kind of theory ... There is not much of economics to that kind of theory. Another kind of approach is that followed by Tinbergen (and not much picked up by others). It is based on a kind of sorting process. People are capable of earning different amounts of money at different jobs. They go to the one with the highest rate of return. That creates a supply and demand situation. Wages have to alter to adjust to that. If you make some simple assumptions, you probably have a manageable theory. My feeling is that a general theory of distribution – and here I mean a manageable theory, not a formal theory (I do not think there is anything wrong with the formal theory, it just does not tell you much) – is going to be hard to develop.

In fact, I am somewhat depressed with the way people who use the neoclassical paradigm in empirical work essentially tend to make assumptions from which distribution disappears completely. I am not talking about people who analyze distribution, but about those who have some other concerns, such as, for example, the course of securities prices as a research topic. The theories of the securities market typically tend to assume that everybody is exactly like everybody else. There are then various random things happening and anticipated. One peculiar implication of this theory is that no trade will ever take place. What is true is that prices will change, but just in such a way that everybody will hold on to what they initially had. This is an interesting question. Some people say 'well, trading is really a very small amount of the stock of securities trades; therefore this is a first approximation and as such not so bad'. Others say, however, 'no, the characteristic features of the market are lost when this is allowed to happen; for example, things like the relationship between long- and short-term rates of interest that are really inexplicable unless in terms that some people prefer long-term and others short-term bonds and that is because they must be different, otherwise they would all want the same thing'. It is easy to imagine, when you bring in life-cycle considerations, that people are different. Some people have different tastes and whatnot; in fact, just differences in wealth would play a role. If you assume that everything is not homogenous (and Engel's laws alone show that this is true) then income distribution means that even if people have the same utility function, they are at quite different points on it. Their marginal rates of substitution, as you go along the rays, will be different, so there will be different points; there will be different rays from the origin in their securities space. And if their wealth changes, they will want to move, they will want to trade. If they have an unexpected loss, they will want to trade off, to shift the composition of the stocks. The current theories – those that are made practical for empirical investigation – do not actually allow for this. One might give many examples of that sort of thing. This is a case where we are not worried as much about the causes of the distribution of income as about the implications of distributions of all kinds (including the distribution of characteristics, but particularly the distribution of income).

One particular aspect that I find very interesting and neglected is the fact that on the surface there seems to be overwhelming evidence that the savings ratio or propensity depends on wealth. The sophisticated concepts of permanent and transient income and the like were attempts at undermining this, that the evidence was not quite what it was cracked up to be. Nevertheless, it seems that on the face it is quite clear that savings is probably a non-linear function of income. That was, of course, the orthodox doctrine before. When Keynes wrote, for example, he talked about redistribution of income as having an effect on the propensity to save. Was it not one of his ideas to raise the propensity to consume by redistributing income? After the war people began to fit savings relations, but the evidence was not quite clear; some said that it was approximately linear at least, though not homogenous, others that it was homogenous. But you can find even very careful evidence for non-linearity. That would imply that income distribution has something to do with changing the balance of saving and consumption. The fact is that there is no very good empirical integration of this point of view with the facts.

Take, for example, the controversy over the effect of social security wealth on savings. There are a number of factors involved. The one that strikes me is that the people who do the saving are those to whom social security makes very little difference. Therefore, it is hard to see why it should have any significant effect. The large majority of recipients of social security are essentially saving very little anyway. Thus it cannot possibly have an adverse effect on saving. The models used to test this were all based on the 'representative saver'. That was true of Feldstein's model and it was true of the models of those who attacked him. What I am saying is that the neglect of distribution works both ways. The difficulties are real.

There are problems in grasping even a simplified story about income distribution compatible with any model. And the neo-Ricardian model seems to be doing nothing in this respect.

Feiwel: Is Sraffian economics a new paradigm?

Arrow: I must admit that I do not really have a high respect for what is regarded as Sraffa's great contributions. Sraffa's did discover a very nice and interesting theorem – a perfectly good neoclassical theorem. He said that 'in the absence of joint production, if some other assumptions hold, and if a particular index number among all other possible ways of measuring price levels is used, then, even though there are many commodities, the wage–profit rate frontier is a straight line'. That is surprising, unusual, a nice theory, but I fail to see it as a great conceptual breakthrough.

What he uses it for is to say, 'well, you have this frontier, and therefore the point on it is undetermined'. Of course, all he has done is to drop an equation. And this story comes back to the discount rate again. The question is: why do we hold the capital we do? Why don't we simply spend it on consumption? There has to be some reason, one of which is a regard for the future. This adds another equation. Then the point on the wage-profit rate frontier is determined.

If you go into more detail you see that Sraffa makes a lot of methodological statements that are just hogwash – and I cannot put it much stronger. He makes a statement that he does not have any marginal productivity in his theory at all. I do not think that is true. Let us take an elementary point. He assumes that the profit rates in all industries are the same. Why should they be the same? Of course, you can axiomatize or assume anything. But the classicists gave a reason: namely, capital would flow. Now, that implies constant returns to scale because if capital flows from one industry to another it means that the new capitalists can invest on the same terms as the old ones did. The same applies if one expands one's operations. Otherwise you are equating only at the margin. I presume that if you have diminishing returns to scale, for example, you would not be equating profit rates, you would only be equating *marginal* profit rates. Marginal profit rates equal average profit rates only on the assumption of constant returns to scale. Further, he speaks of an expanding economy and he has the same coefficients as the economy expands. He wants to get the steady growth model, at least as a measuring rod. But to assume that the same coefficients hold as the economy expands is to assume constant returns.

Another interesting question is: why should the price in period $t+1$ be proportional to the cost measured in period t? How does he get that equation? The idea is that this is some time theory of profit, with presumably mobility of labor. But there is no reason for the price at time

$t+1$ to be the same as at time t. The steady-state assumption is an additional assumption.

There are technical and conceptual problems with the Sraffian theory. And its results, just like the golden rule, are no particular blow to neoclassical economics. The idea that commodities are produced by means of commodities is something that Walrasians have no particular difficulties with. There is nothing startling in that story from a Walrasian point of view. I do not really understand why it is considered revolutionary.

Feiwel: Why is it so difficult to integrate micro and macro theory? What are the most hopeful avenues for achieving such an integration?

Arrow: That is a very good question! The fundamental problem is that micro theory (or at least the general equilibrium theory) is a perfectly complete theory. It should explain everything; there is nothing left out. So how can it it be a problem? The answer is, of course, something to which I referred earlier: the difference between the formal general theory and the realization in actuality. One problem with micro theory is empirical; the only reason why we have a macro theory is empirical evidence. It has been noted since 1821, I believe, that the capitalist economies seem to be subject to rhythmic fluctuations. These fluctuations are not thoroughly regular; some people even argue whether they occur at all. Some econometricians have claimed that it is not so clear that you can find this periodicity. Most people have, however, no difficulty in seeing the economy as sometimes better off, sometimes worse off. The different parts of the economy do not co-move perfectly, but there is some correlation among the movements of the different parts. Typically we find something that traditionally we have been brought up to call 'unemployment' and that nowadays my new classical friends call 'countercyclical movements of the demand for leisure'. In their view the 'demand for leisure' is high at the bottom of the cycle! (I did not make up that phrase; that was actually said by Edward Prescott, believe it or not!)

The reason why we have a macro story is not so much a contradiction between micro and macro as that some of our micro seems to have failed. The reason I say 'seems to' is because our new classical friends say, 'no, it has not failed; one has to be a little more sophisticated about it, there are lags, there are random shocks, and the economy is always in equilibrium in a market-clearing sense, but sometimes it is better off and sometimes worse'. It is quite clear if you have uncertainty, you are going to have shocks. The neoclassical system (or any other) has lags if only because capital takes time to build. It is well known that a system involving lags and shocks will generate fluctuations (as shown by Slutsky and Frisch who cites Wicksell). The different parts of the system are linked – general equilibrium theory says that. Therefore, something happening in one part is likely to repercuss in others. It is not always clear how this works; it may be offsetting as well as reinforcing. For instance, if one commodity becomes suddenly dear, if there is a frost killing oranges, you might expect the demand for grapefruit to go up not down. Then the orange growers get poorer, they spend less – you can tell some story like that. In some sense it may be possible to argue that these fluctuations are a passing thing. Others point out, 'yes, but these fluctuations are sometimes awfully big'. The question is one of interpretation: are these people ready to work at some kind of a going wage and cannot, or do they prefer to wait until wages get higher? The new classical economists tell various stories that I do not find very convincing. I am perfectly prepared to say that the general equilibrium story (or any similar version) does not really explain the facts. I might add that a steady state of Keynesian unemployment is not particularly responsive to the facts either.

Keynes did have the effect of shifting attention from movements in the economy to unemployment equilibria. It is true that he had an investment that was fluctuating so much that presumably he could write these equilibria up and down. So in some sense he left room for fluctuations. He did have a discussion of the trade cycle in his notes and in one chapter.

As I said, in a sense, the proper way of looking at macro is as a set of phenomena, not so much as theory, that does not really fit into general equilibrium theory. Admittedly, one can try to reconcile them – that is the new classical viewpoint – or one can introduce new concepts of equilibrium – such as the fixed-price equilibria. The latter might provide a partial answer, but unfortunately it does not provide a complete system to answer the question why prices are whatever they are. This was certainly clear when prices were moving rapidly under general inflation. It was then a little hard to think in terms of prices being fixed. They may be rigid in some other sense, but they are not fixed in a nominal one.

One dilemma this gives rise to is the use of microeconomics for policy to answer such questions as: should you build a dam, the whole spectrum of planning public works and the like, regulation, etc. All these questions involve microeconomic tools that imply full employment. How does one reconcile this? Well, one argument that I think is not a bad one is that it is actually proper to think in terms of full employment in the long run. If unemployment varies between 10 and 4 per cent that may be quite good enough for the purpose of this calculation. Remember that our estimates of marginal productivity are drawn from data that already reflect the level of unemployment. Therefore, the numbers we derive from theory to use this can, in a sense, be consistent with this viewpoint to a reasonable degree.

For example, I have recently participated in a statement attacking protectionist measures. I know that under present conditions of consumer spending and unemployment, protectionist measures that reduce our balance-of-payments deficit would have a positive effect on employment. I think that the numbers would definitely justify this Keynesian position. You could even justify it by bringing in sort of quasi-neoclassical stories of search and efficiency wage kind. But somehow or other, for me, it is the wrong way of looking at it, because a couple of years from now there will not be this unemployment – at least we hope not! There are a lot of other problems here as well. One is that the other country can do the same thing, so it is not a real solution. If we go to protectionism, others will as well, and we are back where we started from. That is an argument against protectionism even in a Keynesian world. Aside from that there are still other arguments such as: why should we pay more for things that we could have got cheaper? One really has to think in terms of full employment averaging out over a period of a few years, even though it may be a constant level below.

Another example is one of the best pieces of applied economics I have ever seen. It is a study made by the Brookings Institution (by Ed Fried, Charlie Schultze, and others) at the time of the 1973 oil price increase. In effect they argued that the impact today is Keynesian and the impact in three years is neoclassical. These large OPEC surpluses will somehow come back. They will generate credit market changes, demands, and the like. As far as tracking the real effects of the oil crisis, it was a very good piece of forecasting. The immediate effect was a lot of unemployment due to the trade deficit and the ultimate effect was neutral. That is, given all this, the system is going to adjust by mechanisms that you can call not precisely neoclassical, but having much the same effect. Now, this is not a theoretical foundation, it is a good working rule.

Now, you could object – and I have made this objection myself at times – that if the system can give rise to the general disequilibria in the market place, then we do not have the laws right. Therefore, what reason have we to use it at all? At the ultimate level that is, I think, a good objection. At the practical level I am willing to take this kind of *ad hoc* compromise. That is in a sense an explanation of the practical way of integrating micro and macro.

On a theoretical plane, if you accept the view – which I do – that there *really* is disequilibrium in the sense of non-market clearing, then the question is how do you explain this. There is, of course, one in terms of wage and price stickiness, but that is one almost by definition because by sticky wages and prices you mean those that do not clear the market.

Feiwel: Can we provide convincing explanations of short-run price and wage stickiness and adjustment over time?

Arrow: I must say I am having trouble with that. There is no difficulty in making up stories that show stickiness. Take, for example, the cost of changing prices that Sheshinski has been stressing lately. Alternatively, there is the explanation that customers want to have firm expectations and cannot take highly variable prices. By the way, they do in the securities market. That is interesting: there are markets where prices change immediately – of course, these are organized markets. I find it all somewhat unclear. You have some startling cases of industries (not wages) where prices of some goods remain constant over long periods of time. What happens is that occasionally there is excess demand and a queue develops. These are typically producers' goods, by the way; both sides of the market are highly rational; you are not dealing with irrational consumers or workers. In wages you know that there is a human element so you expect the wage recipients to take a rather possessive attitude, exerting power in various ways, and so on. But when you ask: why does a particular grade of steel have a rigid price? – the non-economic reasons should not apply.

Take for instance, Stigler and Kindahl's *The Behavior of Industrial Prices*, that supposedly demonstrates the flexibility of prices. Looked at closely, their evidence shows some but far from total flexibility. Prices do not adjust rapidly. The same result can be found in other studies, by Dennis Carlton and others. There is much evidence of rigidities.

I myself have a little experience of this. For example, in the market for durable producer goods, when demand conditions get high, the delivery time grows. Pure theory would say, 'these are at least two kinds of goods: goods for immediate delivery and goods for, say, six months delivery. If you want immediate delivery, there is one price (higher) and if you want to wait, there is a lower price.' But in fact that is not what happens. The producers charge one price! It is a well-known phenomenon. Obviously when conditions are slack, you can make deliveries out of inventory – if it is the kind of good that can be delivered out of inventory. Theoretically, one can understand that in the short run it may not be possible to deliver these goods to meet all orders. Well, it should be expected either that the price will go up to keep the delivery date constant, or, more sophisticatedly, there should be a variety of prices. Whatever is contracted for should be done. But in fact it is not. What is being bought is a variable commodity not a definite commodity, if the delivery date is taken as one of the characteristics of the commodity.

There is another interesting story about justice that refers to wages in particular. The employers have certain inhibitions about some wage changes that are considered unjust. Somehow it is just to fire the workers, but not just to cut their salaries! This seems to be clearly the case. If you ask people, they will say it. There is an idea that certain changes are thought of as unjust. When you take surveys, people will say that it is unjust to cut wages under these conditions. These feelings of justice may or may not – we do not really know – have a direct influence on the market. A factory does have a social structure to it and it may not be so easy to change it.

All this, however, does not add up to a clear-cut theory, to the extent that as a theory it undercuts the neoclassical general equilibrium because these are the terms that are left out of these equations.

Feiwel: Can we return to the question of 'new classical macroeconomics'? How do you feel about it?

Arrow: I think it is wrong. But I think it has been illuminating, in the sense that afterwards we have never been the same. There is one point on which everybody agrees: expectations may be altered by policy changes. Without accepting a complete impotence theorem (that is, that government policy has no power), it is a fact that if the government changes policy people's expectations will alter. The government cannot just play on existing expectations. Even before I heard about new classical macroeconomics, I always thought it is very hard to talk about expectations without being more specific about it. To build a theory that people are systematically wrong is a little disturbing. For one, it implies that you could make a lot of money. Since I know I cannot make a lot of money, then people must be somehow right. That is why it is hard to deny something like this ...

Now, I think what is wrong is not rational expectations exactly (although that has some cognitive problems of its own), but just the assumption that in the future markets will clear. In other words, if I have an opportunity of selling my labor now, I will do so, even though I would rather take a rest now and work later, because I am not sure that there will be employment for me next year. So, I may be rationed as to my sales and I may act in anticipation of quantity constraints. Rationing may be rational. I may correctly anticipate unemployment next year, or at least the probability of unemployment. From an individual point of view that is an important variable; the fact that we might be unemployed even if we were willing to work at the going wage rate.

So, I think the idea of rational expectations has some validity. The new classical macroeconomics is, of course, built on market clearing. And I do not believe that markets clear. I do not think that there is any demonstrated effect that they do. But I would not dispute that what we call unemployment could be given some other, more useful, name. Of course, every now and then one reads newspaper stories about job openings and 200 or 300 people lined up for three jobs. That sort of thing suggests to me that it can be probably attributed to unemployment. The fundamental question is one of market clearing. I believe there is no market clearing and for the short-run fluctuations of the economy it is a very important fact.

Feiwel: What are the obstacles to integrating imperfect competition into general equilibrium analysis? Where are we now?

Arrow: They are very severe. The biggest problem is this: take the simplest case, one monopoly in an otherwise perfectly competitive world. Then the monopolist says, 'what happens if I change my price or vary the quantity'? – it does not matter which. The demand curve that is relevant is the one sometimes called the *mutatis mutandis* demand curve not a *ceteris paribus* one, because when he changes the price this changes all the rest of the economy. The buyers will then have less income so that they will buy less of something else; this may release some factors, reduce the price of factors to our monopolist or even increase them ... the chain is endless. So, what does that mean? It means that the monopolist must have in his head a general equilibrium model of the entire economy. Well ... we can assume that; that is what game theorists assume. You can work through all the implications. But it does give one pause ...

Things are further complicated when one has more than one power center. Even if it is only two monopolies in different industries, theoretically they have to take account of each other. They would be essentially equivalent to a duopoly, with all that that implies. Theoretically, one could have, I imagine, a game story where there are a number of isolated power centers and a mass of powerless producers and consumers. You can model this as a game. You have all the ambiguities that game theory has even in the simplest duopoly problem such as, for example, the question: what are the strategic variables? The fact is that for 114 years we have had two competing theories of duopoly – the Bertrand and Cournot. They are totally different. They lead to very different implications. In all this time nobody has been able to choose between them. Neither one is more natural than the other. So, the question would be: if you have isolated firms in different industries, what do they do, do they set quantities or do they set prices? If there is only one, it does not make any difference. But as soon as you have two, it does. So, the questions are: what are the tactics? What is the game? You might model the mass as mechanically responsive. That may be all right in a general equilibrium model. But the power centers are another story. I think we can formulate this as a general existence theorem, ask whether equilibria exist, about mixed strategies, and all the rest of it ...

Of course, the basic problem in all this is that you may well ask: how can a monopoly even originate? Well, you can tell some stories that revolve around patents and so on. But aside from those so-called artificial monopolies, the only interesting cases are non-concavities. As soon as you have non-concave situations, you have troubles! Questions whether equilibria exist or not are hard to answer. In the book that Hahn and I wrote we attempted to set forth a general equilibrium model of that sort. I must confess it has not made a big impact on the profession. Even to show the existence of equilibrium, we had to make all sorts of assumptions.

I think the natural story has got to be one where there is free entry and the only reason why there are not many firms is because of a non-concavity. No one finds a problem in entering, but every firm must work at an appreciable scale. But the market is of such a size that only a few firms can exist. That means that there are a lot of firms out there that could enter. It does not quite mean, however, that there will be zero profits; there is a kind of discontinuity if a firm enters or not.

It is very hard to discuss this question in great detail. The nearest thing to it, along a Cournot line, is the work of Novshek and Sonnenschein. What they do is prove existence if the oligopolists together are rather small (not zero) compared to the market. That is an essential; the market has got to be large relative to any one firm. They do have one of the few good general equilibrium treatments of this question.

There are some other technical problems, but those can probably be finessed with a little cleverness. One is that the owners of the monopoly have utility functions. Therefore, their utilities are going to be affected by the prices charged by the monopolist and their own consumption may suffer. But I think that can be avoided by assuming that there are many owners and their interests are basically in making higher profits for the monopoly, ignoring the fact that they themselves have to pay a higher price for that commodity. Probably only a true game-theoretic formulation would work. I plan to spend some time on this next year . . .

Feiwel: In *Value and Capital*, Hicks wrote that the theory of imperfect competition is destructive of neoclassical theory. Is this so?

Arrow: I do not know whether it is a necessary statement, but as an empirical statement it is certainly true that it is very, very hard to arrive at a coherent theory of imperfect competition in the neoclassical general equilibrium framework. It seems as though one ought to be able to modify the story to take account of it, but so far it has proven to be quite an intractable problem. And the other thing is: if you get a formal model and you show existence, do you have any real interesting properties?

Feiwel: Would you be good enough to relate imperfect competition to imperfect information?

Arrow: I think there is a problem of terminology here. Chamberlin made the distinction between 'pure' and 'perfect' competition – a distinction that has not caught on. But it is a distinction that would be relevant here, because 'perfect competition' included perfect knowledge. Now, the term perfect knowledge has to be understood carefully; it does not mean that you actually know everything. What it means is that you do not have private information, but there may be uncertainty. 'Pure competition' is just the absence of market power. We now have a great many theories of 'pure competition' (or more appropriately perfect competition – as the term is now ordinarily used), with various forms of imperfection in the information. There are all these questions of the rational expectations equilibrium: if I see what the price is I realize that other people must know something that I do not know, therefore, I make an inference, I add that to my private information, and so forth and so on. There is a whole set of interesting theories, but they are all within the realms of perfect (or 'pure') competition. They deal, however, with results quite different from perfect competition.

There is another sense in which there seems to be, at least in some cases (particularly in the so-called signalling equilibria of Michael Spence and others), where it does look as though the existence of private information creates the possibility of something like imperfect competition, even though the objective conditions are not there – by which I mean that the market is filled with people all of whom are very small, whatever way one wants to formalize that concept. Take the typical model where workers get educated and use their education as a signal, and let us say that a competitive equilibrium is established and there is a wage–education relationship. That is, there is a wage for every education level, such that the workers with given abilities choose more or less education and then sort themselves out so that those with a given education level in fact have an ability equal to the wage. Behind that there is the assumption of perfect competition on the employer's (buyer's) side, because that is why wage equals ability (productivity). If you had a competitive equilibrium, so that everyone takes that curve as given and responds to it passively, then there is an equilibrium. However, it turns out that it pays a firm in general to offer a different wage–education relationship and it will make a positive profit. Of course, that is presumably unsustainable because then other people would do it. But the point is that the competitive equilibrium is not sustainable. Usually, under perfect competition, it would not pay a firm to offer either a higher or lower wage than the market one; it would make no difference whatever. If there were no private information, if wages were paid for education because education really is ability, then it would not pay a firm to ever offer a different curve. Either it would be paying too much for workers at a given level or it would be paying below the market level in which case it could not attract any. But in this case if you offer a certain curve, you can attract certain people whose average level of ability is higher than the wage you are paying them, yet they are better off because they can economize on their education.

I have a suspicion this may be the beginning of a broader concept. It turns out that small firms can possess market power; that is, a trivial firm does not have to accept the wage structure and finds it profitable to do so. That is a striking fact that may have far more generality. I have a feeling whenever there is private information, there may be some room for people without private information to exploit this by looking at the behavior of others. What equilibrium is in this context is a little hard to discuss. People still argue about it (Charles Wilson and Riley first made this observation). So there is a sense in which highly imperfect information or asymmetry of information can give rise to such behavior that even a very tiny individual can depart from market prices; that is, he does not find it necessary to be a price taker.

Feiwel: Lately much has been made of the usefulness for economists of the current research among mathematicians and computer scientists on the question of computation and measures of differential complexity of different kinds of computation. Would you be good enough to elaborate on what we can learn from them?

Arrow: Obviously, as we all know, the hypothesis on which modern economics by the 1870s rested is the idea of rationality of economic agents. In a way this was true of economics before then, but the economists did not quite realize the interesting nature of what was involved in optimization. Indeed, it is true of each generation which finds newer and newer problems. What seemed quite simple: 'maximize profits, and, therefore, price equals marginal cost, etc.', we now learn is infinitely ramified.

Clearly, there are two aspects in which computation impinges on economics. Conceptually they are of rather different importance. The fundamental question is: since human beings are supposed to be the agents taking action, are they capable of highly rational computations of the kind that we envisage in our theory? When you actually try to solve a problem, you realize that the resources required for the solution of the problem are enormous. Take, for instance, the calculation of whether to increase anti-pollution measures done on the basis of a benefit–cost analysis. It is well known that this analysis is a time-consuming operation. Part of it is for reasons not really the subject of this discussion – and that is information gathering. The other part is just the cost of analyzing the information gathered and using it to arrive at the best decision. These calculations, even making assumptions that are unrealistically simple, turn out to be fairly complex. Complexity, from the point of view of the practitioner here, means resources in a real sense, perfectly comparable to resources we usually talk about – resources actually used for a new sewage plant or those used when you substitute lead-free gasoline for leaded gasoline (i.e., a higher cost of resources in the manfuacturing process, lower efficiency of automobiles, and whatnot). Resources used in computation are the same kind of resources. One needs labor, engineering skills, capital, and time to produce all these results. So, obviously, the natural question from an ultrarationalist point of view is: at what point do you stop being rational? Or, to be exact, how do you trade-off accuracy in the computation against the cost of computation?

As a preliminary to that, one obviously needs to know what are the costs of computation. How hard is it to solve these problems? And some problems turn out to be much simpler than others. What we really want is a cost function of computation. Even then there are some deep conceptual questions as to what you do with the information once you have it. But let us not even worry about those at this time. Let us just worry about the question of costs.

This theme is not exactly new. Thorstein Veblen, in reviewing John Bates Clark's work,* said that among his other complaints of Clark's model of economic man was that he was a lightning calculator. Any psychophysics that had emerged from the middle of the nineteenth century always had lags between stimulus and response. Something was going on internally. This research was indeed an important part of the research projects of the early psychophysicists in Germany and later in the US and elsewhere.

Now I jump ahead to the time when internal to mathematics this problem began to exist in a different form. Intuitively we had a good idea of what a proof was; people like Russell and Whitehead formalized this rather considerably in the early twentieth century. But a proof is a kind of algorithm. It is a calculated thing where each step follows from preceding steps by certain permitted operations – and there is a rather short list of permitted operations. So a proof was a finite object. Then people began to worry: can you prove everything? And this is what led to Gödel's famous results.

Here was, so to speak, a problem of the infinite cost of certain kinds of thought process that arose internal to the most internalist form – the most removed from the material world. Physiologists, who were well acquainted with the work on the nervous system, began to ask how one could combine the elementary knowledge one could get from anatomy and from simulated experiments on frogs and whatnot to get an idea of how the brain might work. Various models were proposed. Some mathematicians, particularly Norbert Weiner and John von Neumann, had contact with this group. As the ideas of the systematic theory of computing (associated with names like Turing in the late 1930s) developed, these people thought – certainly von Neumann did – along these lines as a model for the brain. Von Neumann's last lectures were reproduced in a book, published posthumously, under the title *The Computer and the Brain*. The analogy between the then brand new, very clumsy, electronic computer and the brain went in both directions. One of the directions was to get some ideas of how to compute from the way one thought the brain worked. That has

---

*Veblen's review of J. B. Clark, *The Essentials of Economic Theory as Applied to Modern Problems of Industry and Public Policy* (London: Macmillan, 1907), appeared as 'Professor Clark's Economics' *Quarterly Journal of Economics* 22 (1908): 147–95.

turned out to be very treacherous because the brain may not work the way one thought it does. The other direction was, of course, of the computer as a model for the brain.

It was out of this context, out of both the feedback ideas of Wiener and the use of the computer as a problem solver (and as an optimizer) of von Neumann, that Herbert Simon revived these old problems about the limitation of the intellect and introduced the now familiar concept of bounded rationality. The relationship between the two has been tenuously put together and has drifted apart. Simon enunciated these ideas to a very considerable attention, but they turned out to have essentially no impact on the development of economic theory. There was a school that immediately followed Simon; his disciples concentrated on very detailed case studies. They concluded logically that from the fact of bounded rationality follows that you have to use simple rules. Which simple rules was a question they finessed. They went around and asked people what rules they used, and they used these rules to figure out behavior. Actually, they had some astounding successes, by the way. They arrived at prediction of the kind we never see in economics. But it had absolutely no impact! Take the Cyert–March study of a canning company; it turned out when they went to another canning company their operating rules were entirely different, at least as announced on a conscious level.

So, a fundamental question for us is: people are rational, they are cost accommodating. To be sure, there are second order costs that are not negligible compared to other problems. What is getting to be frightening is that the more you do the economics of information, the more extended is the computational complexity of the rules. As a result people, I think, are getting a little frightened about what is implicit when everybody has to have his or her own model of the total economy and have to be able to solve it for equilibrium conditions and everything else. You can get a little nervous about this as a demand for human action. One used to have a confident view – about all one had to have was prices; that was all one need know. And even that turns out to be non-trivial. It is a relatively simple computation, but when one brings in incomplete markets, one has to be able to project all sorts of other things. People who up to this point were perfectly willing to go ahead are beginning to get frightened as to what assumptions are being made about the agents involved.

I mentioned a second, less important, aspect of computational complexity: the question of how the outside analyst solves the economic system. Supposing somehow or other demand and supply functions, however generalized, are known, how do you solve it? Pareto refers to this question. He gives the example of a very tiny economy (something like 100 people, 10 commodities) and quickly gets up to 71 000 equations. And he says: this is well beyond the capacity of the biggest computer (in the French translation the word used is 'ordinateur', currently the word used for computer). And yet the market solves such problems. Thus, somehow the market becomes an efficient computer. This is not at the individual behavior level, but rather at the market clearing level. Thus the question of the complexity of the market is in some sense more of a problem for the analyst and a statement about the usefulness of the models than it is a statement about the behavior of the people in the model. Except to the extent that we have incomplete markets, then each individual has to solve his or her own equilibrium problem.

Feiwel: Is the problem of long-run effective demand disregarded by the neoclassical growth literature? Why is growth theory no longer a fashionable subject?

Arrow: Part of the reason it is no longer fashionable is that what was done was done. Most of the simple lessons were already drawn; there was not much further to go. There were two sector growth models, and they turned out to be just a mess of complications not telling us much in the way of stories. I know there is a question as to whether we learn anything from stories that are not simple.

Now, the problem of long-run effective demand is neglected in the neoclassical growth models (built on Solow's work) that typically assume full employment. On the other hand, as I have said before, I think that the idea of *long-run* effective demand may be a chimera. I am not sure that I am prepared to believe in long-run effective demand. I do believe in short-run effective demand. I believe in fluctuations, in markets not clearing and in all that. It would be very useful to overcome that. If we could have a feasible government intervention to overcome that it would increase output very considerably, even aside from other considerations – for example, the effects on the people involved – even if one looks at it only from an output point of view, it would be beneficial. I do not know that there can be a long-run effective demand policy.

As I suggested before, a model that says that in the long run you have full employment is the right one. If you do not accept that, you get into these leaden ages and so forth where the rate of growth of the labor force plays no role. In other words, you have a model where expectations determine employment. But unemployment is whatever it is. As long as the labor force is larger than what is demanded, you are going to have unemployment rates secularly approaching 1. Well, that is nonsense. I firmly believe that the size of the labor force has repercussions on the economy. For example, the US is pointed to as having created a great many more jobs in the last ten or fifteen years than Europe has. Some people attribute this to the superior dynamism of the US economy. On the other hand, the US labor force has during these years grown a lot more than the European has. And that is not a coincidence! If the Europeans had a lot more people looking for jobs, there would *be* more jobs. Now, the neoclassicists will tell you that this would happen by lowering real wages. But you can also tell another story. Perhaps the demand from a lot more people creates the jobs . . . perhaps you can tell a more Keynesian story. But one way or another, the labor force is going to have a repercussion on economic activity; someday as unemployment gets to be too big it will be contracted. This process may work slowly, imperfectly, and everything else, but I really do not believe that you can expect that over the long run we will have secularly growing unemployment. Now, it is true that statistically it is probably wrong to say that we have full employment in the long run. What I mean is that the average level of employment is fairly steady. Why it is not zero is another question.

Of course, there is the old Marxian story – one that has recently been given a great neoclassical formulation – namely, that the capitalist system needs a reserve army of unemployed. If the capitalist system actually needs such a reserve army, it should be thought of as part of the cost of the system. It would then be a necessary fact and not count as unemployment. Let us take an analogy: think of a firm and the control of inventories. You can well say, 'inventories are wasteful, they tie up capital, and so on'. But you need them and for reasons that are sometimes hard to explain in ordinary economic terms. There are, of course, reasons that are perfectly ordinary in economics. But others are due to the fact that we are not really modelling the economy in quite such micro detail so that, for example, there are very, very short-term fluctuations in demand. Your customer is planning to buy from you, but he does so tomorrow rather than today – that sort of thing. Then you have the inventories on hand and you maintain a stock of them. And they are productive! If you did not have them, every now and then you would miss a sale. In the same way, a certain body of unemployment may be necessary for the smooth working of the economy.

In the modern version this is called the efficiency–wage theory. It pays the firm to pay above market clearing wages to acquire loyalty. Obviously, you cannot check on workers in detail (you cannot tell what they do every minute), but over a period of time you can tell whether they are shirking or doing what you want them to. If you are not satisfied you can fire them. If you are only paying the market wage, firing is not much of a threat; the worker can find another job. If you are paying, however, above the market wage, the worker is losing something when he is fired. So, it is in the firm's private interest to raise the wage above the market wage. One can then tell a neoclassical story in the sense that it is in the *individual* (not class) interest of the individual employer to raise wages above the market level. Of course, if everybody raises wages above the market wage, there is going to be some unemployment. And that will reinforce the penalty of getting fired. You can work this out . . . Stiglitz, Shapiro, Calvo and many others have done it. In fact, a Marxist, Sam Bowles, has written a paper which, if not basically neoclassical, is at least neo-neoclassical, if you will; limited information neoclassical. It shows that you can have a story that explains why on the average there is going to be unemployment (though it does not explain why there are fluctuations). What I am saying is that something that may look like a failure in the long run may well have a different interpretation.

Feiwel: There is a view (strongly held by Joan Robinson, but also by Hicks and others) that neoclassical economics, particularly in its modern American 'incarnation', has a strong ideological, defense-of-capitalism, underpinning. May we have your reaction to this?

Arrow: Of course, there is always a problem as to which is underpinning and which is derived. One can argue that we teach neoclassical economics because it defends capitalism. One can also argue that we defend capitalism because neoclassical economics has taught us how good it is; because neoclassical economics is sound. If I have a theory that says that the price system achieves a high degree of efficiency in a decentralized world, then I may say, 'well, that might be an argument for capitalism against socialism – or, at least for market socialism against non-market socialism'. As one who has had, and still has, a socialist bias of some not very clear kind (and I had a stronger one in the past), I do not feel that I adopted neoclassical economics *because* it defended capitalism.

I would dispute the word 'underpinning'. The idea that there is some *association* between neoclassical economics and the defense of capitalism is certainly real. Of course, a lot of people who defend capitalism regard the neoclassical defense as a kind of sell-out. For instance, the whole Schumpeterian school, now enjoying a big revival, claims that the virtue of capitalism is not perfect competition, but rather imperfect competition. I am, of course, oversimplifying ... it is more complicated than that. Essentially, the virtue is in the new formation of monopolies so that existing monopolies cannot thrive. Certainly, it is not some delicate observance of prices at marginal costs, it is freedom to innovate – an ability that presumably would be lessened in a bureaucratic system of any kind, socialist or capitalist. Indeed, Schumpeter was worried about large corporations and their reduced ability to innovate. So, one argument is that the decentralized free enterprise system has a power not really explained by the price system.

Also Friedman's defense of capitalism does not usually run in terms of its Pareto efficiency. In the first place, he equates it with political liberty and, in the second place, people's self-interest is the most important powerful motive and in pushing their self-interest, people are likely to improve efficiency and all that. This is then going to leak out and be good

for the world as a whole. His position is somewhere between the Schumpeterian and the strict neoclassical welfare economics exercise. So, I am not
really prepared to say that neoclassical economics serves as a justification.

It is interesting how many economists strongly embraced the Keynesian
doctrine; indeed, many economists whose pro-capitalist tendencies were
impeccable, the first of them being Keynes, felt that this was needed to save
capitalism. To me the identification of neoclassical economics with capitalist apologetics is certainly a little shaky. I do not deny that there are a lot
of people who are interested in neoclassical economics and find it
congenial because of their pro-capitalist tendencies. But it is also compatible in another sense. They see the world as made up of a large number of
highly selfish individuals and therefore the neoclassical system is congenial
not because capitalism is good, but because that is the way the world
actually is.

It is a little hard to deny that the empirical evidence about the Soviet
Union and its satellites has some persuasive power. People who ignore that
should not be talking quite so cattily about pro-capitalist tendencies.
During World War II Joan wrote something about a visit to Moscow in
quite glowing terms. By the 1950s she had shifted and was very critical.
What was much stronger was her pro-Chinese viewpoint which I certainly
heard her express. Current Chinese opinion does not seem to be as
persuaded of the virtues of the Cultural Revolution as she was at the time –
to put it mildly. The economic efficiency of these countries – the idea that
you get efficient allocation of resources in a socialist system – has to be
approached with some caution. Of course, these are not dead systems.
They are working. It is nonsense to say that the Soviet economy is not a
functioning system. It is not very efficient, but the capitalist system has its
problems too, as we know. In fact, it is somewhat surprising that without
the usual capitalist motives, these socialist systems seem to be working.
Perhaps it would be better to say that many of the capitalist motives simply
take different forms in the socialist system, such as power. But even income
is a motive. Currently in both China and the Soviet Union, the ideology
says that inequality is good and egalitarianism is bad. Even Stalin, at
certain phases, came out against egalitarianism. Some of us, however, feel
that the concentration of power in that system makes the concentration of
income in the US seem like a minor evil, as much as we might deplore the
latter.

Of course, one must remember that there has been a component of the
socialist movement that has stressed the importance of the market. It was a
group that I would have thought Joan should have been sympathetic to – a
group that included Lange, many other Polish economists who are either
dead or in exile, many Hungarian economists today, and many democratic
socialists like Alec Nove who has written a recent book defending market
socialism. I think that neoclassical economics as a theory of socialism has

been a significant wing of economic thought. After all in 1927, Fred Taylor, the President of the American Economic Association, devoted his Presidential Address to the economics of a socialist society. My own teacher, Harold Hotelling, was certainly of that persuasion. So, this was a very respectable group. But in all fairness, Joan has never shown any interest in how a socialist economy would operate, like Marx, but with less justification.

Feiwel: Had Joan Robinson been *au courant* of what was being done at the frontiers of theoretical economics, would her criticism still apply?

Arrow: I am sure she would have regarded her criticism as only justified had she seen what she would have regarded as the trivial niceties of the frontiers of modern economic theory. I do not think she could take, for instance, our seminars of the Institute for Mathematical Studies in the Social Sciences at Stanford – it is not her style at all, although she has written on fine theoretical points at different times in her career. *The Economics of Imperfect Competition* was certainly a difficult work for its period. In terms of logical rigor it was much more rigorous, than, say, Chamberlin. I now think that Chamberlin had more insights – as Joan herself admitted – but nothing much came of it. But she was technically very competent. I used to study her manipulation of the graphs and tried to translate them into mathematics ... Also she has an essay on the rising supply price, the papers on the golden age, the golden rule ... all these are technically very competent papers. So, when the spirit moved her she could do fancy mathematics, but clearly this was not what she was interested in.

Feiwel: If the young people working at the frontier today took Joan seriously, could they learn something from her?

Arrow: That is very hard to say. She raises profound issues and walks away from them, much as she complained about Chamberlin. That is a mixed stimulus.

Feiwel: Joan – the preacher – often criticized modern theorists for concentrating on easy questions and avoiding the real and difficult ones. Is that so? If so, why?

Arrow: Well, is there any point working on an impossible question? People do tackle difficult problems, but they try to make them easy ... and they fail. When they tackle some easy (meaning carefully circumscribed) questions – easy in the sense of being narrow, not easy in the sense of the intricacies of the thought processes involved – they can hope to solve them. You really cannot solve very complex problems. There is probably a sense in which you cannot actually describe a real-life economy in theoretical terms any more than you can describe the surface of the earth in theoretical terms.

I am fond of that analogy. Geology is a subject where in some sense the elementary laws are perfectly well known: you have water that grinds down rock; there are heat sources in the earth and you get volcanoes; there is radioactivity – the source of most heat; there is the heat of the sun; and so on. You have a system where every elementary equation is quite well known – quite different from economics. It does not mean, however, that if you asked why the mountains are in one place rather than another, you would get a good answer. The answer would refer to the plates shearing that way, but it would actually not answer the question. In other words, when one has a subject observed as a result of a lot of history, even though every step in that history can be individually explained, one cannot *really* explain it.

I read recently an amusing essay by Stephen J. Gould, a biologist who writes on scientific matters. It is a most charming essay where he was citing some recent observations of the operations of the moons of Uranus (and even before that on the moons of Saturn). He had himself written an essay where he discussed the different structure of the planets and satellites. He referred to the very simple explanation: size is everything. You have a big planet that can hold the gravitational force of the atmosphere; it is big enough to have plate tectonics, it can have earthquakes, and all that. Of course, all of these are bombarded by meteorites. On a big planet that really does not matter very much; they disappear, some of them are burned up in the atmosphere, some of the others hit the earth, but the earth is shifting around anyway ... You look at the moon, it is full of craters because it is so small; it does not have any of these properties. Radioactivity does not generate enough heat within it because of the surface–volume ratio (a bigger volume relative to the surface). Mercury is about the size of the moon and looks very much like it. However, the more you go into it, it turns out that some of the small moons around Saturn and Uranus are full of activity. Well, then what happened to the size principle? The size principle is correct, but it is only one factor among a number. What you realize is that there is a difference between a statement that explains why this particular moon is this way and a general principle.

Of course, we have a full general equilibrium theory. What it says is that this will produce such and the other often works in the opposite direction and so on. You hope that one of the forces is a lot stronger than the others. If you have that you can have a principle – a kind of historical principle. But in fact, any historical principle is likely to have offsetting forces. So, these generalizations may not really work; sometimes they do when one force is predominant. If all forces are important, you do not have a very good predictive apparatus, even though you may understand everything that happens.

And that is the way it is in the economy. It is a historical monument as a result of many, many forces. There is no hope of having a simple principle for explaining its operation. We can have a formal explanation, but ... For instance, if Walrasian theory were 100 per cent true, it would not mean that we could explain most of what we want to explain. It is not a theory that grabs a hold. It says: this happens because of this, but then this other can also happen, that may offset depending on the numerical value of the parameters, this may or may not offset, and all that. You can, of course, try to fill in every equation and just compute it. That is what people working in applied general equilibrium analysis are doing. The trouble with that is that you get into thirty, forty, or more sectors, but it is a long way from being an economy. All those people (Sherman Robinson, Shoven, Whalley, and others) do very good work. Whether it is going to yield any real insight or not I do not know. It may be useful. It certainly has been used in solving policy problems of certain kinds, but whether it is correct or not is another matter. But short of that, if you assume that no matter what you do, you cannot grab a hold of it, then you can only hope that one force is so much stronger than the others that you can neglect them. That is what monetarists think, that is what Keynesians think ... and it is probably not true.

Feiwel: Did Joan have some fundamental misconceptions about neoclassical general equilibrium, Walrasian economics? Was there a fundamental flaw in her attacks?

Arrow: Well, if you put it that way, I am not sure. Her thinking was dominated by two important considerations which, if one thinks about it, we cannot but all be influenced by. One is that there is recurrent unemployment and failure of the system to work as well as it is supposed to work according to theory. That there is conspicuous waste of resources of which the 1930s were a glaring example (and, of course, Britain had suffered considerably depressed standards in the 1920s as well, while the US and other countries did not). Therefore, the idea of the price system as a supreme coordinating mechanism did not get much support from her. The second, in later years, was the idea: how can there be this tremendous disparity among countries? In the latter case, unlike the first, she did not have much to say of a theoretical nature. In the first case she did, and extrapolated it in the long run. She saw a deficiency in the price system – an empirical deficiency. She said that prices did not serve the functions they were supposed to. Instead they serve other functions – namely, distributional functions. Then she stressed those assumptions that the real world tended to fit most conveniently, like fixed coefficients and so forth. The latter were not logically necessary; one can have a Robinsonian system with flexible coefficients, it simply cohered a lot better her way. She was obviously tremendously influenced by the poverty in the Third World. I do not know whether she had a coherent theoretical response to it. At least none that I am aware of. But surely it must have influenced the idea that you cannot claim that adopting capitalism would be very good for these countries. So, this was a negative point of view and also an argument against the neoclassical system. On the other hand, our argument that, in fact, the capitalist system has absorbed a great deal of change, has shown a flexibility in adapting to change, and that the price system has somewhat worked – all that is a point of view that did not register very much with her. To her, technological progress was something outside the system. She did not think of it as being nurtured by the system; that savings were generated by the system.

Feiwel: Did she misunderstand the theory that she attacked?

Arrow: She certainly had an idea of equilibrium that she applied in her own work, but she did not seem to perceive it in the neoclassical system. She would say: 'well, when you are out of equilibrium, you say the real wage ought to be cut, but if you do that, you will cut demand, and, in fact, you will only make matters worse'. Now, that is not an equilibrium point of view. It is true it is related to this question: how do you get into equilibrium? We would say: 'if you start out with full employment and you have the right real wage, you will stay there. And, if you do not have it, you will flounder around for a while, but presumably somehow or other you will get there. Maybe in the first instance demand will be reduced.' One of the first questions was one of timing, because, in a sense, we would say: 'if the real wage were reduced, the capitalists would hire more workers'. She would retort: 'no, because they cannot sell goods'. The thing is, however, if they *did* hire the workers, they *would* sell the goods. She would see it one way, and we another . . . and we could argue about this ad infinitum.

In some sense there is a vision of general equilibrium, with prices coordinating everything, and somehow, whether you accept it or not, you ought to at least perceive the vision. I do not think she ever did. Keynes also, even though he was trained by Marshall, does not show this perception even in his pre-*General Theory* writings. It does not actually play a role in his thinking. He understands it in a formal sense, but it is not a part of him. Not in the way it is in Marshall where it is part and parcel of his thinking. Somehow or other Marshall did not communicate his vision to the next generation.

Feiwel: What, in your opinion, are the strengths and weaknesses of Joan – the economist?

Arrow: I think that in what I have been saying so far, her strengths and weaknesses are implicit. She zeroes in on real problems. She has a tremendously expository power though it is usually done by simplifying. There is a striking contrast between her perception of real problems and the fact that she is one of the most abstract of theorists. Her virtue and her vice is that she generally picks on one problem, say, the pure theory of international trade. She just takes one point of view: it is like a very bright searchlight, she sees very quickly, and has a tremendously logical mind and sees all the implications . . . and everything else is left in the shadows. This was the case with *The Accumulation of Capital*: one way of looking at things, neglecting all sorts of other things, and then taking swipes at people for recognizing things she had neglected.

She stimulated a lot of methodological discussions: what do we mean by the stationary state? what do we mean by equilibrium? But at the end she always managed to attack even her allies on those subjects. Take for example, Harcourt's paper on Sraffa's influence on Joan. Well, there is much more to her than Sraffa's influence. In her last years she attacked disciples like Milgate and Eatwell, claiming that they did not understand the question of historical versus logical time. The point is that her position tended to such a uniqueness that there was no theory possible. And if it were, it would not have satisfied her criteria. But in the end, she forced people to think.

An interesting property of Joan's is a kind of honesty. Sometimes she would come out with statements that undercut what would seem to be her basic viewpoint. Take that marvellous statement (I think in *Economic Philosophy*) where, referring to Third World countries, she said that the one thing worse than having been exploited is never having been exploited. It is not what one would expect from her, but it has the concision and wit typical of her at her best. Like that great line in her paper on international trade that says: 'the invisible hand always works, but it sometimes works by strangulation'.

Feiwel: Would you be good enough to share with us your personal recollections of Joan?

Arrow: I do not think it would be correct to say that we were close, but there has been a great deal of mutual respect and a certain amount of warmth. Not too much of that because I did not find her personality too congenial . . . and she might not have found mine to be such either. I do not mean uncongenial, but it was not such as allowed much closeness. Our total number of encounters were not too many, certainly not more than two dozen or so. We shared a critical attitude to the existing structure; we did not agree in our perspectives on economic analysis; but we got along very well.

She was very friendly when I first came to Cambridge in 1963 – friendly in a remote sort of way, not in a personal sense, rather in an official sense. We had a number of conversations ... particularly at coffee or tea in the faculty common room. As I recall, morning coffee was the more controversial time. She would attack me about something or other (she was always very civil): 'wasn't the rate of interest a fiction?' or something like that. The trouble was that the questions she would ask were not posed the way I would pose them. Frequently it was not possible to give a straight answer without trying to give a lecture, restating the question.

She had a very strong personality. There was a certain self-created leadership element in it. She took herself as being a leader and imposed it on others, most of whom were willing to accept it one way or another. Let me tell you a story illustrative of this. When I was in Cambridge in 1963–4, in the spring of 1964 my colleague at Stanford, Paul Baran, died of a heart attack. I got a call from Mel Reder telling me about this. I thought I would share it with someone and immediately thought of Joan. I did not know her well enough to telephone, so I decided to do what I had always read in English novels ... I wrote a letter. (I then began to understand why they write letters ... they are delivered immediately!) I wrote this letter at about 5 pm, 7 am the following morning there is a phone call from Joan. We had a young child then and had a Danish au pair girl – a bright, intelligent girl. She knocked at our door: 'Mr Arrow, there is a telephone call for you.' Here it was 7 am: 'Joan Robinson here. Got your note. Baran was a very courageous man. He did not back down when others did,' and so on. She said some very nice words, much as I had expected. But, imagine not only was she up and ready to telephone, but the mail had already been delivered! After I hung up, the Danish girl said: 'I did not want to wake you up, but she sounded so severe, I did not dare tell her you were still sleeping.' This girl did not know who Joan Robinson was, and Joan probably did not even identify herself – it was all in the tone of voice.

I had another interesting encounter with her that showed another facet of her character and perspicacity. I believe it was in 1970 when I came to Cambridge for only a couple of months. On my first day, I was walking across a bridge on the Cam and she came the other way. She stopped immediately and greeted me: 'You have got to get an honorary degree or a visiting professorship for Kalecki.' I had known from previous encounters with the Soviet Union that an American commendation was the death sentence. I was very suprised by her stance. She quickly explained about Kalecki's troubles, of which I was aware. Of course, I said I would do anything I could, but would not a visiting professorship in the US only add to his troubles? 'No!' She was right, of course. The situation had changed. Now there was a responsiveness to public opinion abroad. I am telling this story to emphasize two points: one was her concern – I was not surprised at that, but it was nice to see – and two was the astuteness of her political judgment. She had assessed the changed situation much better than I did.

Now to make you known in the US was, in fact, something of a safety net, not the condemnation it certainly would have been under Stalin.

We met a few more times. I remember she gave a seminar at Harvard – the standard attack on neoclassical economics. Steve Marglin tried to make me get up and act as the defender. I was not interested and only picked on some minor issues. The difficulty of such discussion is that when you think the whole phrasing of the argument is not quite right, it is hard to unravel it. Besides, on the negative side I found a lot to agree with her. The problem is: what do you do with all this? There is unemployment, there is monopoly (though she has not stressed that so much in recent years) . . . But the question is: where do you go from there?

She was not really a Marxist – at least never thoroughly commited herself to any Marxist position of any kind. In fact, she always attacked Marxian value theory. She had a strong sympathy for certain communist regimes and a certain sarcastic view of imperialism (American or British). It seemed to me that she had a lot of focused emotion, but not a coherent philosophical viewpoint – at least not one that I could detect. It all tended to express itself best in a negative way both about economic theory and about social systems in general. I was always somewhat hard put to know what I was dealing with.

She was a social critic, but she was often off the mark. She did not seem to have a strong, concrete interest in the British economy or in the British working class. The focus of her emotion seems to have been on the Third World, at least since the early 1960s. My knowledge of her is admittedly fragmentary, but I never heard her express herself about poverty in Britain. There was a somewhat similar viewpoint among some leftist groups in the US at the time. Take, for instance, someone like Paul Sweezy, who is by no means an austere, logical person, who also at one time more or less abandoned the working class in the US. Joan seems to have fallen in that category.

4 Some Assumptions of Contemporary Neoclassical Economic Theology

Peter J. Hammond*

Economics is not only a branch of theology. (Joan Robinson, 1962, p.25)

Belief in the free market is a common form of idolatry born of an ideology which hits hardest at the worst-off in society. (The Rt Revd David Jenkins, Bishop of Durham, speaking in the House of Lords; cited in the *Manchester Guardian Weekly*, 23 June 1985)

'But then . . .' I ventured to remark, 'you are still far from the solution . . .'
'I am very close to one,' William said, 'but I don't know which.'
'Therefore you don't have a single answer to your questions?'
'Adso, if I did I would teach theology in Paris.'
'In Paris do they always have the true answer?'
'Never,' William said, 'but they are very sure of their errors.'
'And you,' I said with childish impertinence, 'never commit errors?'
'Often,' he answered. 'But instead of conceiving only one, I imagine many, so I become the slave of none.' (from Umberto Eco, *The Name of the Rose*, near the end of 'Nones' on the 'Fourth Day')

1 ASSUMPTIONS ARE NOT TO BE COMPARED WITH REALITY

'The two questions to be asked of a set of assumptions in economics are these: Are they tractable? and: Do they correspond to the real world?' (Joan Robinson, 1932 p.6)

*A respectful tribute to the late Joan Robinson. Although her teaching failed to prevent me from committing the double sin of becoming both a 'neoclassical' and a welfare economist, I hope that, even so, she might have agreed that amongst much else her classes in economic theory at least taught us some healthy skepticism, as well as how to discuss theory without using squiggles. My thanks to Mervyn King for very detailed and helpful comments, to George and Ida Feiwel for their encouragement and helpful suggestions, to Avinash Dixit for pointing out that Keynes himself devised the neoclassical synthesis, to John Taylor for his efforts to teach me some macroeconomics and to Mordecai Kurz for reducing my errors by at least one.

TABLE 4.1   List of assumptions

1. Assumptions are not to be compared with reality
2. Consumer sovereignty
3. Unbounded rationality
4. Unbounded forethought
5. Unbounded cooperation
6. Pareto efficiency is sufficient for ethical acceptability
7. The distribution of wealth is ethically acceptable
8. Consumers can survive without trade
9. Income effects are negligible
10. Pareto efficiency is necessary for ethical acceptability
11. There is a representative consumer
12. Distortionary taxes create deadweight losses
13. Domestic public expenditure programs are wasteful
14. Transfer programs confer no benefits
15. Capital markets are perfect
16. Anticipated monetary and fiscal policies are ineffective
17. Inflation is caused by an expanding money supply
18. There is a representative worker
19. The current level of unemployment is ethically acceptable
20. There is a representative capital good
21. Product markets are perfectly competitive or at least contestable
22. Neoclassical economics need not be theological.

In her classes in Advanced Economic Theory at the University of Cambridge, Joan Robinson would frequently say to us students, 'Always state your assumptions.' As a model, chapter 1 of her first major book, *The Economics of Imperfect Competition*, is indeed entitled, 'The Assumptions'. Moreover, in her later books, *Economic Philosophy* and *Economic Heresies*, she discussed the assumptions underlying standard neoclassical economics, all too many of which are all too often left implicit, and explained why she thought so many economists seem willing to accept those assumptions unquestioningly. So I propose to return to this theme and to consider the assumptions listed in Table 4.1. Too many people who discuss economic policy these days appear to take many of these assumptions for granted, despite their not being securely based either on empirical fact or on acceptable ethics.

The very first assumption to be discussed is Friedman's (1953) contention that the assumptions of economic theory should not be compared with reality. This drastic assumption appears to deny Joan Robinson the freedom to choose to speak out against the assumptions of neoclassical economics, as she did so effectively throughout her career. Friedman argues for his approach to positive economic analysis in the following words:

One confusion that has been particularly rife and has done much damage is confusion about the role of 'assumptions' in economic analysis. A meaningful scientific hypothesis or theory typically asserts that certain forces are, and other forces are not, important in understanding a particular class of phenomena. It is frequently convenient to present such a hypothesis by stating that the phenomena it is desired to predict behave in the world of observation *as if* they occurred in a hypothetical and highly simplified world containing only the forces that the hypothesis asserts to be important ...

Such a theory cannot be tested by comparing its 'assumptions' directly with 'reality'. Indeed, there is no meaningful way in which this can be done. Complete 'realism' is clearly unattainable, and the question whether a theory is realistic 'enough' can be settled only by seeing whether it yields predictions that are good enough for the purpose in hand or that are better then predictions from alternative theories. (Friedman, 1953, pp.40–1)

I have heard this interpreted to mean that one should not compare *simplifying* assumptions with reality. This makes Friedman's bland statement a little more palatable, providing that one follows his view of what economic theory should be about. Indeed, the fundamental flaw with Friedman's approach to positive economics, in my view, is its failure in practice to heed data other than a narrow selection of empirical economic data. For, especially in connection with topics like price theory and the quantity theory of money, the only economic data considered often involve only aggregate quantities or aggregate commodity demands, and pay almost no attention to the distribution of money holdings, commodities, etc. Unless one is very careful, a model of the economy that predicts just prices and aggregate quantities becomes thereby more acceptable than one which notices the possibility of inequalities of income and poverty leading to people dying of starvation, committing suicide as a result of depression brought on by a prolonged spell of unemployment, or other important human phenomena that are often not well captured by economic statistics. A positive economic theory that completely neglects social statistics is a poor and inhuman theory, too dangerous to be acceptable in policy analysis. As Joan Robinson wrote in her note on welfare economics, at the end of *The Accumulation of Capital*:

If we want to form an opinion on the economic well-being of a community, we look to such things as the food consumed, the conditions of housing and work-places, the variety of different kinds of goods being consumed (for we know that with rising wealth families purchase more kinds rather than greater quantities of goods). We look to such phenomena as the infant death rate for pointers to the effect of the level of consumption on the health of the community, and to such phenomena as the prevalence of alcoholism and neurosis to judge how great a strain the rules of the game that they are playing put upon human nature. (Robinson, 1956, p.390)

In one sense, I shall not disobey Friedman's assertion that, in positive economics, one should not discuss the (simplifying) assumptions on an *a priori* basis. This is because my primary concern will be with normative rather than positive economics. Yet, in another sense, I will be disputing his claims rather vigorously, in arguing that much of positive economics is based on assumptions that are so unrealistic as to make coherent normative analysis of economic policy at best impossible and at worst highly misleading.

The fact that so many completely unrealistic or unethical assumptions appear to underlie a great deal of contemporary economic policy analysis prompts two questions. The first is why such absurd assertions masquerading as assumptions continue to enjoy such widespread acceptance. The second is what can be done to relax the more obnoxious assumptions. Of these two questions, the first received an answer from Joan Robinson herself; indeed, in large measure this was precisely the question she addressed in *Economic Philosophy*, from which the following is taken:

It is precisely the pursuit of profit which destroys the prestige of the business man. While wealth can buy all forms of respect, it never finds them freely given.

It was the task of the economist to overcome these sentiments and justify the ways of Mammon to man. ... It is the business of the economists, not to tell us what to do, but to show why what we are doing anyway is in accord with proper principles.

In what follows this theme is illustrated. ... in an attempt to puzzle out the mysterious way that metaphysical propositions, without any logical content, can yet be a powerful influence on thought and action. (Robinson, 1962, pp.24-5)

This is as good an explanation as any other I am aware of, and it is one that we ignore at our peril. So I shall also consider how so many of the results of neoclassical economic analysis appear to support *laissez faire* policies, without necessarily wishing to suggest that neoclassical economics has worked backwards from the *laissez faire* policies to the assumptions that sustain them. And I shall in some cases discuss how one might proceed to improve the quality of economic policy analysis by replacing the more objectionable assumptions with others that are not only more acceptable on both empirical and ethical grounds, but may also not be impossibly difficult to use in practice when analyzing policy questions.

The first part of the essay will concentrate upon microeconomics, and especially the two fundamental efficiency theorems of welfare economics

which are often used to justify *laissez faire* policies. The last few assumptions
concern topics more closely associated with macroeconomics, such as money
and unemployment, although I shall discuss these from a microeconomist's
point of view.

Assumptions 2 to 6 concern the first of the two fundamental efficiency
theorems of welfare economics, which states that complete markets in
perfectly competitive or Walrasian equilibrium produce an allocation which
is Pareto efficient. Assumption 2 is the ethical value judgment of consumer
sovereignty, which is absolutely essential to give this theorem any ethical
significance. So is 'unbounded rationality', included as Assumption 3, which
denies that consumers are boundedly rational in the sense of Simon (1982).
An extension of the concept of bounded rationality to deal with a dynamic
economy is considered next; Assumption 4 calls this 'unbounded forethought', which is a concept designed to recognize the replacement of the old
perfect foresight assumption by the newer one of rational expectations.
Indeed, unbounded forethought is in some sense a generalization of rational
expectations which allows for the possibility that agents may never receive
enough information to learn the whole truth.

A crucial assumption of the first efficiency theorem is the absence of
externalities, or at least their internalization through a system of property
rights. This is considered in Assumption 5, which deals with 'unbounded
cooperation'. It is also argued that these three assumptions of unbounded
rationality, forethought, and cooperation are quite unnecessary unless one is
determined to give *laissez faire* an ethical justification. But they can only
possibly do this, in general, if it is accepted that Pareto efficiency is sufficient
for ethical acceptability, which is Assumption 6. Not surprisingly, Pareto
efficiency is found wanting because of its failure to take into account the
distribution of income or wealth.

This brings us to the second fundamental efficiency theorem of welfare
economics. This theorem characterizes all the Pareto-efficient allocations in
an economy – except those that give trouble as in Arrow's (1951) 'exceptional
case'. With enough convexity and continuity in the economy to ensure that
Walrasian equilibrium exists, the second efficiency theorem tells us that any
Pareto-efficient allocation can be achieved by setting up complete and
perfectly competitive markets, and allowing them to reach an appropriate
Walrasian equilibrium. This relies on Assumption 7, however, requiring that
the initial distribution of wealth is exactly right so that each consumer can
just afford to buy what he is supposed to in the given Pareto-efficient
allocation. So, in order to ensure that an ethically acceptable allocation really
is achieved in perfectly competitive markets, one must effectively assume that
the initial wealth distribution is, if not optimal, then at least ethically
acceptable.

I trust that it would be generally agreed that the initial distribution of
wealth is ethically unacceptable when some consumers are so poor that they

find themselves at or below the margin of subsistence. This problem in economic theory is usually circumvented by Assumption 8, that all consumers can survive without trade, in which case, of course, free trade cannot drive them down below the margin of survival. Assumption 9 then turns to the common procedure in applied economics of ignoring all income effects. Apart from simple laziness or sloppiness, this may be to avoid recognizing the importance of income distribution, which undermines the ethical appeal of *laissez faire* policies.

The physical feasibility constraints of the economy require that no agent supply more than he is able to, given the extent to which his demands are met, and also that the obvious resource balance contraints are satisfied. The second efficiency theorem characterizes (virtually all) the allocations which are Pareto efficient among this set of physically feasible allocations. Yet the appropriate schemes of lump-sum redistribution of wealth which are needed to give the second efficiency theorem its ethical significance use a great deal of information about individuals' needs, abilities, and other relevant personal characteristics. Much of this information is originally private to the individual. The 'revelation principle' of the recent literature on incentive compatibility then says that, because individuals have to be induced to reveal any private information which the mechanism uses, truly feasible allocation mechanisms have to satisfy additional 'incentive constraints' as well as the physical feasibility constraints. When trading in an 'underground economy' cannot be effectively prohibited, further incentive constraints are added which may even imply that only Walrasian allocations are truly feasible, so that markets have to be seen as constraints upon rather than the instruments of good economic policy. The ethical significance of the second efficiency theorem of welfare economics therefore relies on Assumption 10, which is that Pareto efficiency, in the usual first-best sense, is necessary for ethical acceptability. This assumption neglects the incentive constraints.

This serious lapse is often circumvented, especially in macroeconomics, by Assumption 11, that there is a representative consumer. Thereafter, Assumption 12 denies an often neglected implication of the incentive constraints which prevent optimal lump-sum redistribution, namely, that the deadweight losses created by 'distortionary' taxes are illusory, since there is really no way of eliminating them. Indeed, optimal taxes may well be distortionary, as in Diamond and Mirrlees (1971). Assumptions 13 and 14 then embody the rather extreme claims we sometimes hear that domestic public expenditure programs are wasteful, and that transfer programs confer no benefits. One of the arguments supporting such claims is that public expenditure and transfer programs, even if they are not inherently distortionary, at least rely on distortionary taxes for their finance. Once we accept that distortions are inevitable, the force of such arguments is greatly reduced.

Assumption 15 is that capital markets are perfect – one of the most common assumptions of much contemporary neoclassical analysis. Yet it will be argued that lenders always face moral hazard in capital markets because some borrowers have an incentive to borrow more than they could ever afford to repay. So perfect capital markets are impossible, and some form of non-price rationing of credit to limit each borrower's maximum permissible debt is inevitable. This lends theoretical support to the 'Clower' or 'cash in advance' constraint which has played a prominent role in some of the better recent work in macroeconomics. Then Assumption 16 considers what underlies the remarkable recent contention of some macroeconomists that no policy can be effective – or at least efficient – unless it catches people by surprise. This contention is closely linked to Assumption 17 concerning the neutrality of money, the quantity theory, and the monetarists' belief that inflation can only be caused by an expanded monetary supply.

After money, the next macroeconomic topic is unemployment, and Assumption 18, that there exists a representative worker. It is suggested that this assumption makes it virtually impossible for most of macroeconomic theory to explain unemployment. Also, while the Keynesian concept of involuntary unemployment is hard to explain unless one follows Kalecki and others in introducing imperfect competition and administered money prices and wages, there may be a useful concept of 'involuntary hardship' – a state in which many people with very limited job opportunities may well find themselves even if there is Walrasian market clearing. Assumption 19, that the level of unemployment is ethically acceptable – or that there is little that can be done about it – leads to a brief discussion of the 'neoclassical synthesis' (starting with a suggestion of Keynes himself), and of the 'bastard Keynesians' who saw fit only to consider economies in which the government had been able to find and to pursue a macroeconomic policy resulting in continuous full employment.

It seems that many young economists think of Joan Robinson primarily as a capital theorist, who happened also to write extensively on Marxian economics, development, and also wrote an early book on imperfect competition. None of these topics is touched on in the first nineteen Assumptions of this paper (except perhaps development, in connection with Assumption 8 and the possible non-survival of very poor consumers). Yet both her collected papers and her classes were full of relevance to almost every topic considered in those nineteen Assumptions. Of the four topics just mentioned, I shall leave others to write about Marx and about development. The next two assumptions, however, concern capital theory and imperfect competition.

The capital theory debate was really about Assumption 20, which postulates the existence of a 'representative capital good'. One must agree with many others – including even Joan Robinson – that the whole debate was really a waste of time, because the assumption is clearly unreasonable, and anyway nothing very important hangs upon it. Nor is steady state growth very interesting in a world of exhaustible resources.

As for imperfect competition, Assumption 21 embodies the recent attempt of Baumol (1985) and his associates to use the theory of 'contestable' markets to set a new normative standard for judging the performance of a given industry. The defects of the perfect competition defense of *laissez faire* simply reappear in a new guise. And even if the new normative standard were acceptable, it would seem *a priori* that many partly unionized labor markets are much closer to meeting it than the markets for the outputs of large corporations.

The obvious conclusion of this essay is that the future of neoclassical economics depends crucially upon the validity of Assumption 22 – that neoclassical economics need not be theological. What case there is for *laissez faire* has to be based on the cost of intervening in the economy rather than on theological arguments concerning 'efficient' or 'optimal' allocations. If I do continue to pursue neoclassical welfare economics, it is because I believe that, when it has been purged of its theological content, it has the best chance of providing useful policy advice, and of suggesting improvements to the form of public intervention in the economy.

2 CONSUMER SOVEREIGNTY

The central doctrine of orthodox economics is the defence of the freedom of anyone who has money to spend, to spend it as he likes. (Robinson, 1979a, p.92 and 1980a, p.99)

The grammar which professional economists use to discuss economic policy is, of course, welfare economics. A fundamental value judgment that is made in almost all welfare analyses is the sovereignty of consumer choice – that the preferences revealed by a consumer's demand behavior correspond exactly to an ordinal indicator of his welfare, or even to a cardinal indicator if choice under uncertainty is being discussed and if the expected utility hypothesis is satisfied.

Consumer sovereignty is popular with economists for a number of reasons, of which the most important is that the fundamental efficiency theorems of welfare economics acquire all their ethical significance from this particular value judgment. The first fundamental theorem, due to Arrow (1951), says that any allocation which results from perfect competitive markets in general equilibrium must be Pareto efficient. That is, there is no other feasible allocation which simultaneously moves each consumer to a new bundle of goods which he or she could choose in preference to the old bundle. So far, this is just a factual statement about what each consumer would choose among two hypothetical alternative commodity bundles. The consumer sovereignty ethical value judgment is then used to overcome the distinction between facts and ethical values, called 'Hume's Law' by philosophers, in order to be able to claim that the fact of moving each consumer to a preferred position is desirable as an ethical value. As Joan Robinson puts it in *Economic Philosophy*:

> We are told nowadays that since *utility* cannot be measured it is not an operational concept, and that 'revealed preference' should be put in its place. Observable market behaviour will show what an individual chooses. Preference is just what the individual under discussion prefers; there is no value judgement involved. Yet, as the argument goes on, it is clear that it is a Good Thing for the individual to have what he prefers. This, it may be held, is not a question of satisfaction, but freedom – we want him to have what he prefers so as to avoid having to restrain his behaviour.
>
> But drug-fiends should be cured; children should go to school. How do we decide what preferences should be respected and what restrained unless we judge the preferences themselves?
>
> It is quite impossible for us to do that violence to our own natures to refrain from value judgements. (Robinson, 1962, p.50)

So the first efficiency theorem is converted into an ethical proposition, because Pareto-efficient allocations like those that result from perfectly competitive markets have the property that it is infeasible to make all consumers better off than they are in the efficient allocation.

The second fundamental efficiency theorem, due to Arrow (1951) and Debreu (1951), says that, under conditions like continuity, convexity, and local non-satiation of preferences, as well as resource-relatedness of consumers, any Pareto-efficient allocation can be decentralized through a complete system of perfectly competitive markets, provided that the initial distribution of property rights is determined in exactly the right manner to produce that particular efficient allocation in equilibrium. Provided discussion is limited to what individuals actually choose, this is again just a purely factual proposition, like the first efficiency theorem. Without a value judgment like consumer sovereignty, allocations that individuals would actually prefer to choose have no normative significance whatsoever. To give such allocations the normative significance that economists usually accord to them, *some* ethical value judgment has to be introduced; consumer sovereignty just happens to be the most obvious and attractive one that works.

So one reason why consumer sovereignty has been popular with economists is that it justifies the invisible hand and *laissez faire* economic policies that business-minded economists naturally feel sympathetic toward. A better reason may simply be that, although consumer sovereignty is undoubtedly a value judgment, it is much less obnoxiously paternalistic than alternative value judgments would have to be, since they would have to specify what was good for an individual if what that individual wanted was not good. Thus, consumer sovereignty is obviously closely related to the libertarian position in ethics, which makes the rights of the individual the supreme arbiter of all ethical questions, as in Nozick (1974). And Rawls' *Theory of Justice* (1971), which puts liberty prior to any other 'primary good', is another way of advocating consumer sovereignty, in effect.

Nevertheless, making rights supreme turns out to be a much stronger statement than saying that Pareto superior allocations are ethically preferred. Libertarians regard any form of coercive taxation as unjustifiable in any circumstances. This relates closely to Assumption 7, that the distribution of wealth is ethically acceptable to the extent that no redistribution is required.

This general acceptability of the consumer sovereignty value judgment is what I believe lies behind Archibald's (1959) otherwise extraordinary claim that welfare economics should become a branch of 'positive economics' and confine itself to finding ways of satisfying those preferences of consumers that happen to dictate their behavior in the marketplace. Lerner (1972) has also made an energetic defense of consumer sovereignty. I single out these two authors only because they at least realized that there really is an issue here, and that consumer sovereignty is a value assumption. Of course, many of the more philosophically inclined economists, apart from Joan Robinson, such as Sen (1973) and Broome (1978), have also discussed and indeed heavily criticized the consumer sovereignty value judgment. Nor should one forget the work of Harsanyi (1954) and Gintis (1972a, 1972b, 1974) criticizing consumer sovereignty when tastes are endogenous.

From a more practical perspective, it is clear – indeed, even tautological – that we would prefer to be able to exercise our choices as freely in the marketplace as anywhere else. Evidently, purchasing decisions that cause externalities such as pollution and congestion are clear instances of when some control seems desirable. But wanting to control such purchasing decisions does not really violate the sovereignty of consumers as a whole, because the reason for wanting to interfere with the demand of one consumer is precisely that it affects the objects of preference of other consumers. Standard examples of desirable paternalism – such as seatbelts in cars, young children and drug-takers – may really just be other instances of externalities, rather than examples of the undesirability of consumer sovereignty, although there are some reasons to believe that the individuals in question really are not making the best decisions according to their genuine long-run preferences in these cases.

Yet consumer sovereignty is not universally desirable by any means. If it were, it would always be beneficial – externalities apart – to widen the range of opportunities available to any one consumer. Who, however, has not sometimes felt bewildered when suddenly faced with a wide range of choice over some important issue, such as the choice of a pension plan? And almost preferred to have the opportunity to choose taken away – provided, of course, that the right choice winds up being made on the individual's behalf! An even more convincing example of the undesirability of complete consumer sovereignty is when individuals are imperfectly informed, and indeed even know that they are. An ill-informed consumer knows that somebody else with better information – an 'expert', perhaps – could make a better decision on his behalf. It might be better still if that consumer could become better informed himself, but we should admit that consumers can easily become overloaded with information – 'confused', in fact. That brings us to bounded rationality which is my next subject.

3   UNBOUNDED RATIONALITY

In short, no economic theory gives us ready-made answers. Any theory that we follow blindly will lead us astray. To make good use of economic theory we must first sort out the relations of the propagandist and the scientific elements in it, then by checking with experience, see how far the scientific element appears convincing, and finally recombine it with our own political views. The purpose of studying economics is not to acquire a set of ready-made answers to economic questions, but to learn how to avoid being deceived by economists. (Robinson, 1960, p.17)

Thus does Joan Robinson conclude her lectures on 'Marx, Marshall, and Keynes', delivered at the Delhi School of Economics in 1955. If people are so easily deceived by economists, then how much more unreasonable is it to assume that they are capable of making perfectly rational decisions. In fact, Simon (1982, 1983) and others have given convincing and extensive discussions of how people who actually make decisions exhibit various forms and degrees of 'bounded rationality', in the sense that they do not appear to be maximizing a consistent preference ordering in the way that neoclassical economic theory typically presumes. Even when confronted with relatively simple decisions, in which the objectives are unambiguous and the contraints fairly obvious, people do not always behave in a manner which is consistent with neoclassical economic theory. Indeed, once decision problems become rather complex, one faces the paradox that too much rationality is irrational, because it is far too costly in time and trouble to discover what decision really maximizes one's preferences, even if it is possible at all. Similarly, in their psychological experiments, Tversky and Kahneman (1981, 1986) in particular have shown how the outcome of a decision-making process can be systematically influenced by the way in which the decision problem is 'framed', just a line segment which is in fact shorter than another can be made to appear longer simply by attaching suitable arrows to each segment in order to suggest contraction or expansion, as appropriate. Yet a fundamental tenet of rational behavior – indeed, I would even claim that it is *the* fundamental tenet – is precisely that the decision should be unaffected by the way in which the decision problem is framed. Rather, it should be determined solely as a function of the available consequences of each possible decision. I shall now argue why this casts considerable doubt on the applicability of consumer sovereignty to the market behavior of the boundedly rational consumers who certainly exist in the world, even if they do not in neoclassical economics.

Recall the role of the consumer sovereignty value judgment, which we discussed in the previous section. It is used to lend normative significance to Pareto-efficient allocations, which can then be categorized as ethically desirable. Now, I am willing to assert that any social norm should be 'consequentialist' in the sense that it should prescribe decisions based solely on the consequences of all the possible decisions – the 'fundamental tenet of rationality' was how I referred to this in the previous paragraph. This is actually a highly controversial assumption in moral philosophy, as can be inferred from the extensive critical discussion it has received, to which I refer to some extent in Hammond (1986a). No less controversial is the ethical doctrine of 'utilitarianism', which is actually rather stronger than consequentialism. Nevertheless, I am also willing to assert that most of the controversy arises because most of the critics of consequentialism in ethics have too narrow a concept of the relevant consequences in mind. Respect for individuals' rights, feelings of personal integrity, the wider acceptability of certain standards of behavior like truthfulness and honesty, even the effects of ethical education and of exemplary behavior on people's motives for behavior, are all rather subtle examples of consequences which, if they are ignored, leave consequentialism open to the kinds of troublesome examples which Williams (1973) in particular has drawn to our attention.

For consumer sovereignty to have the best possible chance of ethical acceptability, the social norm should obviously be based upon individual preferences. In particular, it must coincide exactly with individual preferences for those very special hypothetical societies in which it just so happens that all individuals are identical and one is choosing among economic allocations in which all consumers have equal amounts of every private good. But this coincidence is only possible, of course, if each individual's preferences just happen to be equal to the social norm of the 'clone' society in which everybody is identical to the given individual. So each individual's preferences must amount to a consequentialist 'individual norm', which is just a copy of the social norm for a particular clone society. Since consequentialism requires decisions always to maximize fully the individual's preference ordering over the set of all possible consequences, it is entirely inconsistent with bounded rationality. This explains formally what many will find intuitively obvious anyway – namely, that bounded rationality is inconsistent with consumer sovereignty.

Such inconsistency is troubling for those neoclassical economists who would like to claim that equilibrium allocations in complete, perfectly competitive markets can give us the best of all possible worlds. But then they deserve to have such trouble, because they are looking for unbounded rationality in the choice of an economic system and of its resultant allocations, even when individuals are boundedly rational. The invisible hand can hardly be unboundedly rational when individuals are not. Critics of the invisible hand must be wary, however. They may well be tempted to claim that, because individual's market behavior is boundedly rational, markets should be replaced by planning mechanisms. The obvious disadvantage of this is that the rationality of those administering a planning mechanism is usually no less bounded than that of the typical market participant; indeed, as Hayek has often emphasized, because such administrators inevitably face enormously complex decision problems involving the handling of much more information than is relevant for the typical participant in competitive markets, their rationality is likely to be extremely circumscribed.

It is true that various forms of bounded rationality can have a significant impact on the nature of equilibrium outcomes, as has been pointed out recently for rather different economic environments by Akerlof and Yellen (1985a, b) and by Russell and Thaler (1985). Nevertheless, to me, bounded rationality on the part of economic agents is just one more kind of constraint to be taken into account in determining what economic allocations are truly feasible, let alone optimal. Since, as I shall argue in Section 10 below, first-best allocations are almost certainly unattainable anyway, and since market allocations have no very special claim to our attention either, the fact that economic agents may not always be maximizing fully what it would be best for them to maximize is not really a fundamental problem. Individual behavior effectively operates as a constraint on the set of truly feasible allocations. And full rationality is not an essential requirement for descriptive models of economic behavior, as Becker (1962) explained long ago.

Moreover, recognizing that agents may be boundedly rational has some useful implications which cannot emerge otherwise. In positive economics, we can account for the existence of all sorts of agencies and professional services which exist to give their clients advice on how to make better decisions. In normative economics, we can advocate the provision of public services such as the Citizens' Advice Bureau in Britain which offer free advice to those who can perhaps most benefit from it.

I conclude that, even though bounded rationality is inconsistent with consumer sovereignty, this is not really troublesome unless one is looking for an economic system which functions like an unboundedly rational invisible hand. Indeed, the arguments I have just given, for regarding unbounded rationality as an unnecessary assumption in properly done welfare analyses, apply equally to consumer sovereignty. The fact that consumers may not be behaving in the way that the ethical norm would prescribe simply serves as yet one more kind of constraint to be taken into account in our discussions of economic policy and their effects on economic allocations.

4 UNBOUNDED FORETHOUGHT

> Keynes brought back *time* into economic theory. He woke the Sleeping
> Princess from the long oblivion to which 'equilibrium' and 'perfect
> foresight' had condemned her and led her out into the world here and now.
>   This release took economics a great stride forward, away from theology
> towards science; now it is no longer necessary for hypotheses to be framed
> in such a form that we know in advance that they will be disproved.
> Hypotheses relating to a world where human beings actually live, where
> they cannot know the future or undo the past, have at least in principle the
> possibility of being set out in testable form. (Robinson, 1962, pp.73–4)

The last section discussed unbounded rationality by a single agent acting in
isolation in the world, however, there are many agents whose decisions
interact with each other in an enormously complex fashion. Of course, one of
the beauties of competitive markets in Walrasian equilibrium is precisely that
the agents in the economy do not really have to know anything about each
other at all. Each agent simply interacts with the Walrasian 'auctioneer' who
learns the excess demand functions of all the agents and then adjusts prices
through some kind of *tâtonnement* process in order to clear all markets. All
the individual agent needs to know is the market clearing price vector set by
the auctioneer.

An obvious problem with this approach is that the world does not contain
any Walrasian auctioneers. The closest approximations we are ever likely to
see are government appointed price controllers told to balance supply and
demand, rather than their usual task of trying to hold back inflation, and
market makers in security markets (see Howitt, 1979, pp.621–2; Glosten and
Milgrom, 1985, and the papers cited in the latter). Even if there were a
perfectly functioning auctioneer, however, the Walrasian model of the
economy would still face enormous problems in realistic environments. The
reason is that there can never be complete contingent commodity markets
with perfect foresight, as so much of contemporary economic theory
assumes. Even in abstract theory, such complete markets can really only
function if all the agents in the economy are equally informed whenever
markets are open. Otherwise, those traders who happen to be better
informed will typically be able to exploit their superior information by
suitable market transactions. As Milgrom and Stokey (1982) and Sebenius
and Geanakoplos (1983) have recently shown formally, an agent facing an
offer of a trade contingent upon an event about which he knows that he is less
well informed than the person making the offer, will be rational to refuse that
offer, unless he has different preferences which make the trade mutually
beneficial anyway, or he believes that he has different prior as well as
posterior beliefs concerning the probabilities of the various contingencies.
But usually trading takes place sufficiently anonymously that one is never

sure whether a prospective trading partner has some privileged information, or if indeed he did start off with different prior beliefs. That is why insider trading in company shares (as discussed recently by Kyle (1985) in particular) needs to be prohibited if a stock market is to function 'perfectly', why in practice so many outsiders find it difficult to earn significant profits on stock exchanges, and why market makers on the stock exchange need to maintain bid prices below asking prices (Copeland and Galai, 1983; Glosten and Milgrom, 1985).

Private, or asymmetric, information also creates the problems of moral hazard and of adverse selection in insurance markets that have rightly received so much attention recently from economic theorists. And recent work by Mervyn King shows that share repurchases, as opposed to dividends, may suffer from similar problems – i.e., if management tries to spend the money it would have paid out as dividends in order to buy back equity, this may be misinterpreted as an indication that the firm's prospects have improved, so that the shares become too expensive to repurchase, and dividends are worthwhile after all, despite their tax disadvantages.

Indeed, once asymmetric or private information is admitted, trading must take place sequentially – it is impossible to have a single market for all contingent commodities for all time, as in Debreu (1959). One reason is that the unborn and others whose tastes are as yet not completely formed will find it very difficult to arrange or have arranged for them the pattern of taste-contingent demand they would like to have in Debreu complete contingent commodity markets. Another reason is that transaction costs are bound to limit the contingencies that can be covered in contingent commodity markets, as well as the number of periods in the future, etc. Either way, agents will try to foresee what prices will be in markets that are yet to open in the future.

In the seventies this problem of foreseeing the future was generally resolved by postulating perfect foresight concerning at least the mean, if not the entire probability distribution of market prices. Econometricians and macroeconomists tended to concentrate on linear-quadratic models with certainty equivalents in which foreseeing the mean of the distribution was good enough, in the tradition of Muth (1961). Microeconomists were more concerned about the whole probability distribution. If there are markets in Walrasian equilibrium and there is common information, this amounts to each agent foreseeing perfectly what prices will be in each exogenous state of the world, as in Radner's (1972) generalization of Arrow's (1953, 1964) work on contingent security markets. With private or asymmetric information *ex ante*, the microeconomists found serious problems in proving existence of equilibrium unless prices in equilibrium were so informative as to create common expectations *ex post*, after agents have learned what they can from the fact that the equilibrium price vector clears market demands and supplies. Thus all agents become fully informed in equilibrium. Notable exceptions are such special models as Lucas (1972, 1983); Ausubel (1984), and those surveyed in Jordan and Radner (1982).

Thus, although the assumption of perfect foresight in the strict sense has been abandoned, because agents remain uncertain about the exogenous state of the world, surprisingly often there is no additional uncertainty arising from the economic system itself. For each possible history of exogenous events, the contingent history of market-clearing price vectors is often completely known. The only exceptions occur in connection with the partially revealing equilibria of Lucas, Ausubel and Jordan and Radner, as mentioned above. Notice that the 'sunspot equilibria' of Cass and Shell (1983) also have the feature that contingent prices are perfectly foreseen. Indeed, such equilibria were considered in order to try to explain how one can have speculative bubbles even with rational expectations. The novelty of these sunspot equilibria is that states of the world – such as sunspots – which have no bearing on the exogenous variables of the economy – such as tastes and technology – may nevertheless influence equilibrium prices and produce inefficient equilibria. The point is that everybody foresees precisely how equilibrium prices do depend on extrinsic events.

A presumption of almost all this literature on general equilibrium with uncertainty and incomplete markets is that eventually the state of the world is revealed to all agents in the market. If this were not true, it would be impossible to see how agents could ever learn how prices come to depend on the state of the world. A much more plausible assumption instead is that each agent only ever sees rather a small part of the whole picture of the economy. This leads to a weaker concept of equilibrium, in which agents' beliefs about how prices depend on their own information regarding the true state of the world are correct. In an economy whose history can be summarized at any moment of time by a (possibly very long) list of state variables describing the set of agents and their tastes, information, beliefs, holdings of physical and financial capital assets, one can then look for a 'Markov' Walrasian equilibrium in which prices at each moment of time are determined as functions of all the state variables. For this to be an equilibrium, not only do prices have to clear all markets in every possible state of the economy; in addition, agents must have correct beliefs about the Markov stochastic process relating their information at the end of any period to their information at the start of the same period.

Though I believe such Markov equilibria to be interesting and conceptually important, they remain almost entirely unexplored. In the small literature that there is, they have often gone under other names, such as 'self-generating distributions' (Shefrin, 1981) and 'recursive equilibria' (Prescott and Mehra, 1980). Shefrin drew his inspiration from Hahn (1973a) and the others from Lucas (1978). Shefrin has differing agents but a non-economic environment in which the set of possible states of the game is finite: Lucas, Prescott, Mehra and others only have results for Walrasian equilibrium when there is a continuum of identical individuals, and the economy always performs optimally from the point of view of each individual. Spear (1985) has recently taken matters rather further, but we still lack a satisfactory existence theorem for Markov Walrasian equilibria, other than in very special cases. The difficulties of proving existence come about because the space of Markov price process is inherently infinite-dimensional, even in a two-class economy. To apply the usual kind of fixed-point theorem one has to be sure that demands and supplies are suitably continuous, and these are far from straightforward issues in an infinite-dimensional function space.

Such mathematical technicalities seem far removed indeed from realistic models of actual economic agents' rather incompletely formed view of the workings of the economy on which they base their expectations. They are also far removed from even the most sophisticated of the 'applied general equilibrium' models (Shoven and Whalley, 1984). The modelling problem has become so complicated that mathematical economists are only just getting around to demonstrating the possibility of the existence of an equilibrium. Yet equilibrium models of the economy presume implicitly that agents are much smarter than even the mathematical economists, because they are somehow able to learn and react to an immensely complex model of the economy, which includes as state variables everything which they might know something about – for example, the entire contents of both the *Financial Times* and the *Wall Street Journal*, all the economic statistics ever published, etc. At this stage it becomes impossible to regard such equilibrium models at all seriously. Even if they no longer involve perfect foresight, the notion of unbounded rationality considered for a single agent in Section 3 has extended itself to infinite-dimensional spaces in a form which I think should be called 'unbounded forethought'.

The above discussion has been concerned with Walrasian equilibrium, or the economics of perfect competition. Each agent needed only a model for predicting the sequence of observations he would make over time, including the prices he would be facing in any time period. Other individual agents are of no importance; it is only in the aggregate that they affect the prices faced by the single agent under consideration. That is an enormous simplification because it removes the possibilities for strategic interaction between different economic agents. Mathematically, each agent behaves as if he were in a game with a continuum of players, in which only the distribution of strategies chosen by the other players matters. When there is imperfect competition, strategic interaction does become important, of course, and has mostly been modelled in recent years using the theory of 'games', to use the terminology that has become standard since the work of von Neumann and Morgernstern. Yet even the word 'game' fails to convey the full complexity of the world in which economic agents must make their decisions. For, in real games, even enormously complex games like chess and go, each player knows a great deal about his opponent and about what that opponent must do in order to try to win the game. Whereas, in real economies, it is far from clear who are the 'players' in the 'game', let alone what the objectives of these players really are.

All might still be well if we had an adequate theory of such games, at least for simple cases. Yet right now the theory of extensive form games is in a state of great turmoil, with even the notion of rational behavior appearing self-contradictory. For example, if a game like prisoner's dilemma is played an arbitrary finite number of times, the standard notion of rationality prescribes that each player should always confess, and never cooperate with the other player in the game. Yet the recent work of Axelrod (1981, 1984) shows the apparent superiority of playing a 'tit-for-tat' strategy, in which each player cooperates if and only if the other player cooperated the previous period. The interesting paradox is that, if it looks as though the other player is likely to continue playing tit-for-tat, then a player does best by playing tit-for-tat right up to near the end of the game. But then it becomes 'rational', in a sense that is still unclear, for that other player to play the strategy that was originally irrational, because it may well convince the first player to play tit-for-tat. The analysis has already gone far beyond the work of Kreps, Milgrom, Roberts, and Wilson (1982) but has not yet reached anything like a final resting place. The very concept of rationality has become extremely unclear (see also Campbell and Sowden, eds., 1985) and so has placed the foundations of equilibrium theory upon extremely shaky ground.

5   UNBOUNDED COOPERATION

> Then consider the notorious problem of pollution. Here again the econo-
> mists should have been forewarned. The distinction that Pigou made
> between private costs and social costs was presented by him as an
> exception to the benevolent rule of *laissez faire* ... The economists were
> the last to realize what is going on and when they did recognize it they
> managed to hush it up again. *Laissez faire* and consumer's sovereignty
> were still absolute except for a few minor points discussed under the
> heading of 'externalities' that could easily be put right. (Robinson, 1972,
> p.7)

In Section 2 mention has already been made of how externalities limit the scope of consumer sovereignty. For, in the presence of externalities – be they external economies or diseconomies – consumers pursue goals which are inconsistent with Pareto efficiency, and they could be better off as a whole if their freedom to create external diseconomies, and their freedom not to create external economies, could somehow be limited. So much can be learned even from elementary economics. Externalities, in fact, undermine the conclusions of both the fundamental efficiency theorems. The first theorem becomes invalid because, in the absence of suitable markets for the creation of external effects, competitive markets do not generally bring about Pareto-efficient allocations. Private costs and benefits, which ignore external effects, differ at the margin from social costs and benefits, which do include such effects. Similarly, the second efficiency theorem also fails. Unless special markets are created to encourage the creation of external economies and to deter the nuisance of external diseconomies, no competitive market system can possibly bring about a given Pareto-efficient allocation, in general.

Such is the theory of how externalities undermine the effectiveness of a perfectly competitive market system as a good allocator of economic resources. There is also the practical experience we share of acid rain, smog, leaded fuel, noisy airports, and the other forms of pollution which industrial society inflicts upon our bodies, our minds, our personal property, and even our public monuments. Yet, despite the clear evidence around us, there remain all too many governments and their economic advisers who seem to think that externalities can be safely ignored.

To be able to ignore externalities in a way that their masters in business and even in government find most convenient, *laissez faire* conservative economists need to be able to blind themselves with a suitable theory. Demestz (1967) and Buchanan and Stubblebine (1962) were able to find one for them to use, based upon a theory of property rights. The 'Coase (1960) theorem' showed that Pigou taxes or subsidies on externalities were equivalent to an assignment of property rights, and that, in the presence of transactions costs, some assignments of property rights could be more efficient than others. Then the property rights doctrine, as it is usually called, is formulated to claim that, when several parties find themselves imposing external economies on each other, or failing to create external economies for their mutual benefit, the resulting Pareto inefficiency can be resolved by having the interacting parties come together and agree how best to create property rights governing the external effects, so that the divergence between marginal private benefits and costs and marginal social benefits and costs gets removed. Thus the fundamental efficiency theorems have their validity restored. Such mutual arrangements will indeed lead to Pareto-efficient outcomes, so that externalities can be ignored. Even if such mutual arrangements prove to be impossible, because of legal obstacles (which should anyway be done away with, according to this doctrine) or because of transactions costs or limited information, then *laissez faire* still gives rise to constrained Pareto-efficient allocations, in the sense that no truly feasible allocation which respects the legal obstacles and does not make use of information that is unavailable can possibly be Pareto superior. Really, then, the property rights doctrine is merely a special case, dealing with externalities, of what I like to call the 'efficiency tautology'. This assumes that any feasible Pareto improvement in institutional arrangements will always be found, and then claims that the economic allocation which actually results must be Pareto efficient!

In fact, for defenders of *laissez faire* who are also satisfied with Pareto efficiency as a sufficient condition for ethical acceptability, despite the faults with Assumptions 6 and 7 discussed below, the efficiency tautology is a marvellous result. It guarantees Pareto efficiency, because if there were a way to find a Pareto improvement, it would already have been found! This is unbounded rationality *par excellence*, applied not only to single individuals but also to groups of possibly arbitrarily large size. A similar objection applies, of course, to the core, when unrestricted coalition formation is postulated as it usually is. Indeed, since core allocations must be Pareto efficient, when they exist, the core has also been a useful refuge for those whose ethical sensibilities have not progressed beyond the sufficiency of Pareto efficiency.

The last three sections have discussed how the neoclassical theory of economic equilibrium presumes an absurd degree of ability among economic agents. Of course, it is very comforting to be able to believe that all agents are so rational, so full of forethought, and so ready, able, and willing to cooperate, that between them they produce the best of all possible economic worlds. It is high time that the most outrageous of these assertions started to be relaxed. Individuals are bounded in their rationality, their foresight, and their ability to cooperate. Recognizing these patently obvious facts would allow us economists to work with a picture of the world in which we are not useless, because we can surely teach people how to make decisions which display more rationality, more forethought, and more cooperation.

This is not to suggest that equilibrium models should be entirely abandoned. Indeed, our objections have almost nothing to do with the concept of equilibrium *per se*. It still makes perfect sense to look for an equilibrium of supply and demand in the economy. Rather, it is the interpretation of the demand and supply functions which changes. One no longer pretends that demands and supplies are truly those which maximize the correctly perceived objectives of each private agent in the economy. As the young Becker (1962) realized, for one, equilibrium theory does *not* require the behavioral assumption of maximization, let alone unbounded rationality, or unbounded forethought.

So, the *concept* of equilibrium does not require any kind of rationality or forethought. But when it comes to matters of *normative interpretation* it is true, of course, that equilibrium models need to heed the bounded rationality and the bounded forethought of any human being, even the smartest of the mathematical economists. It appears that one needs to describe each agent in the economy not only by his tastes and his feasible set, but also by the simplified model of the world which he will use to reach his decisions. The existing models of economic decision making are as if every agent has enough rationality and forethought to be able to play games like chess perfectly. Yet even existing computers play chess rather imperfectly by grandmaster standards. On the other hand, if one wanted to simulate how most inexpert players actually play, most existing chess programs are far too good at avoiding blunders leading to checkmate in two moves or to the early loss of a valuable piece. Many economic decisions in real life, however, have many of the characteristics of a blunder in a game of chess, and predictive models which neglect this lead to normative conclusions which are fundamentally flawed. Even if such models happen to predict the aggregate level of measured unemployment fairly well, for example, they completely miss the fact that many of the unemployed are not very good at searching systematically for a job. Indeed, if they were, that in itself would be a skill that would qualify them for a much wider range of employment opportunities. The neglect of their limited ability to find suitable jobs leads too easily to the false normative conclusion that people are unemployed because they have a preference for leisure – or, less euphemistically, because they are lazy. Kay and King (1978, p.108) make a similar point concerning the tax system when they write, 'It is worth bearing in mind that one reason the poor are poor is that they are not qualified as chartered accountants.'

At least the recent paper by Russell and Thaler (1985) is a step in the right direction. So is the earlier paper by Myerson (1983), even though it presumes an unbounded ability to formulate and solve appropriate linear programs; there is bounded forethought, however.

6   PARETO EFFICIENCY IS SUFFICIENT FOR ETHICAL ACCEPTABILITY

> In this diminished kingdom [of Keynes's *General Theory*] *laisser faire* can still flourish; from this ground it can make sallies to recapture lost territory. It is this rallying of the old ideological forces round their oriflamme – the optimum distribution of resources in long period equilibrium – that accounts for the slow progress that has been made in bringing the so-called theory of Value and Distribution into touch with historic time and the so-called theory of Welfare into touch with human life. (Robinson, 1962, p.82)

The two fundamental efficiency theorems of welfare economics characterize Pareto-efficient allocations as those which emerge from perfectly functioning complete competitive markets in general equilibrium. Assumptions 2 and 3 – consumer sovereignty and unbounded rationality – are used in order to give Pareto-efficient allocations ethical significance, and so make these two fundamental theorems into ethical justifications of free market allocations. There is still a major obstacle to such a justification, however, which also relates to the difference between the first and the second efficiency theorems.

It is the second theorem that tells us that virtually *any* Pareto-efficient allocation is a possible outcome of perfectly competitive markets in general equilibrium. But there is a most important proviso in the statement of the theorem; achieving any particular Pareto-efficient allocation generally requires redistribution of purchasing power through lump-sum taxes or subsidies, so that the distribution of wealth allows that allocation to occur in equilibrium. Whereas the first efficiency theorem says that a perfectly competitive equilibrium allocation is Pareto efficient regardless of the distribution of income.

Despite the elementary distinction between the two results, they often get confused in a way that happens to be convenient for defenders of *laissez faire* and of the *status quo*. Such defenders love to appeal to the first efficiency theorem in order to assert that we should remove all distortionary taxes and other obstacles to perfectly competitive allocations. They are much more vociferous in their advocacy of free markets than they are in recognizing that removing, for example, welfare benefits financed by distortionary taxes, is likely to hit hard the poorest members of a society who, almost by definition, are least able to prosper in a competitive economic environment. It is true that a move to perfectly competitive markets without distortions will pass the kind of compensation test originally devised by Barone, but more usually attributed to Kaldor and Hicks. But there is no Pareto improvement unless compensation is *actually paid* to those adversely affected by the winds of increased competition. In the absence of such compensation, the gains of some groups must be balanced against the losses of others. Since there are some fundamental difficulties in paying suitable compensation, as will be seen in Sections 10 and 11 below, the case for *laissez faire* remains seriously and fundamentally incomplete.

In fact, as soon as one is concerned about the ethics of income distribution, the first efficiency theorem is stripped of its ethical significance. There is no guarantee whatsoever that *laissez faire* will produce a just distribution of income, or even one that avoids very gross injustice, in which some people barely subsist in abject poverty, while others are extremely affluent. Indeed, both market and Pareto-efficient allocations can be even worse than that, because it is quite possible for both to be consistent with widespread starvation, as I shall discuss in the next section. Pareto efficiency is *not* sufficient for ethical acceptability, even though many defenders of *laissez faire* may want to claim, at least implicitly, that it is. Nor is the first efficiency theorem really of any ethical significance either. Instead, it is the *second* efficiency theorem that has some claim to ethical significance, because it characterizes *any* Pareto efficient allocation – in particular, any Pareto-efficient allocation with an ethically acceptable distribution of income.

As Joan Robinson (1949, and 1951a, p.173) wrote in her review of Harrod's *Dynamic Economics*: 'to discuss either the distribution of income or measures to increase useful investment brings politics into the economic argument. But [there] is no way to keep politics out. [The] resolution to avoid these questions is itself a political decision.'

7   THE DISTRIBUTION OF WEALTH IS ETHICALLY ACCEPTABLE

> All but a few fanatics admit that the overall amount of saving (at full-capacity operation of the economy) depends upon the distribution of wealth and income within society and upon the policy of firms in respect to withholding profits for self-finance. To represent the corresponding rate of accumulation as that 'desired by society', it is first necessary to show that the existing distribution of wealth is desirable; this is the question, of all others, that *laissez-faire* ideology is least anxious to discuss. Robinson (1965, p.142)

Assumption 6 amounts to the irrelevance of the distribution of wealth; Pareto sufficiency on its own is sufficient for ethical acceptability. Here, I consider an assumption which, while formally weaker, nevertheless rules out any further discussion of inequality or poverty in the economy. This is the assumption that, while the distribution of wealth is a matter of legitimate ethical concern, it is beyond the scope of economic policy to do anything to improve it. In particular, it is commonly assumed that wealth distribution has already been optimized by a system of suitable lump-sum taxes and subsidies. Such an assumption seems patently absurd in a world plagued by poverty, hunger, and mass unemployment. Yet the assumption of an optimal wealth distribution certainly played a prominent role in the theoretical work of Samuelson and others during the 1950s.

One's first reaction might be that, since the existing wealth distribution reflects the values of the society, it must be at least ethically acceptable, if not optimal. The allocation and distribution of resources in the economy are supposed to reflect the 'revealed preference' of government, an idea which may hark back to Pareto (1913, p.340; see Bergson, 1983, p.42). Yet I know of no government in the world that is choosing its policies very systematically, let alone anything like optimally. If I thought *that*, there would be nothing left to discuss in welfare economics, or almost any other kind of economics. Of course, it may well be true that what the welfare economist regards as 'optimal' is unattainable, although then one must question whether the true constraints on optimal policy have been properly recognized. We shall not be able to improve economic policy by throwing up our hands at the difficulties – political and otherwise – in making worthwhile changes. That is a counsel of despair which, if we are not very careful, will prevent us from trying to do anything about the pressing problems of poverty and inequality in the world economy as it stands now. Before knowing whether what we actually have is ethically acceptable, we have to consider what alternatives are feasible. Otherwise we are taking the attitude described by Joan Robinson's (1962, p.130) memorable phrase, 'our system is the best system that we have got'. Such complacency enables one simply to sit back and admire the optimally functioning economy, just as *laissez faire* economists want us to be able to sit back and observe the 'invisible' hand working its magic.

Closely related to assuming ethical acceptability of the distribution of income or wealth is the adoption of aggregate wealth maximization as an ethical criterion. (See especially the work of Posner (1981), reviewed in Hammond (1982).) Aggregate wealth maximization means adding up money-metric measures of utility over the whole population, and maximizing the sum total of everybody's dollars without any regard to the ethical desirability of weighting the dollars of the very poor more highly (or more lowly, for that matter, if one's ethical values are very inegalitarian) than those of the rich. It involves very special – and especially obnoxious – distributional value judgments. It is true that when the distribution of wealth happens to be fully optimal, all individuals' dollars have equal social value at the margin. For, if they did not, the distribution of wealth could have been improved by lump-sum transfers of wealth from those individuals whose dollars have low marginal social value to those whose dollars have high marginal social value, until the marginal values of all individuals' dollars are indeed equalized. Then aggregate wealth maximization is a first order approximation to the social welfare function in the neighborhood of the initial point at which the distribution of wealth has been optimized. Only in this case do I see any ethical justification for aggregate wealth maximization, and it is clear to me that this is not an accurate description of the world economy in which we now find ourselves.

Indeed, there are good theoretical reasons why, even if a national or world government really were maximizing society's values using the economic policy instruments it has available, the distribution of wealth might well still not be optimal, because those policy instruments are insufficiently powerful to redistribute wealth perfectly. In Section 10 below, I am going to argue that this is generally the case. Then, of course, it is somewhat harder to argue that the current unequal wealth distribution is ethically unacceptable, because the scope for redistributive policy is less. Clearly, however, the argument of the previous paragraph for equality of the marginal social value of all individuals' dollars has fallen apart completely, so that unweighted aggregate wealth maximization is no longer even an approximation to an ethically satisfactory objective of economic policy. Since most economists – let alone policy makers – appear not to understand the economic theory which is relevant to this issue, and since there is manifest poverty and injustice in the world, this leaves enlightened economists above all with the task of applying expertise toward trying to identify feasible policies which really can improve wealth distribution, rather than just looking for policies to increase total wealth. The concluding paragraphs of Joan Robinson's *Economic Philosophy* and of her *Economic Heresies* both serve to summarize where we now stand:

> The first essential for economists, arguing among themselves, is to 'try very seriously', as Professor Popper says that natural scientists do, 'to avoid talking at cross purposes' and, addressing the world, reading their own doctrines aright, to combat, not foster the ideology which pretends that values which can be measured in terms of money are the only ones that ought to count. (Robinson, 1962, p.137)

> National economic success is identified with statistical GNP. No questions are asked about the content of production . . . [M]odern capitalism . . . has not succeeded in helping (to say the least) to promote development in the Third World. Now we are told that it is in the course of making the planet uninhabitable even in peacetime.
>
> It should be the duty of economists to do their best to enlighten the public about the economic aspects of these menacing problems. They are impeded by a theoretical scheme which (with whatever reservations and exceptions) represents the capitalist world as a kibbutz operated in a perfectly enlightened manner to maximize the welfare of all its members. (Robinson, 1971, pp.143–44)

8   CONSUMERS CAN SURVIVE WITHOUT TRADE

> A good deal of present-day discussion of international trade seems to be based on the notion that there always is a position of equilibrium to be found by relying upon the operation of the pricing system, and it is necessary to recognize that the classical doctrine does not exclude starvation from the mechanism by which equilibrium tends to be established. (Robinson, 1946, and 1951a, p.189)

Most professional economists will be willing to admit, perhaps rather reluctantly, that Pareto efficiency is indeed insufficient for ethical acceptability in the absence of a just income distribution. But as Sen (1981b) has pointed out, almost all of general equilibrium theory assumes that every individual consumer has the means to survive without trade. More specifically, almost all of general equilibrium theory assumes that every consumer has a fixed endowment vector of commodities which lies within his feasible consumption set. Indeed, to guarantee the appropriate continuity of demand functions – or, more generally, of set-valued demand correspondences – as required for proving existence of a Walrasian equilibrium, it is usual to assume that the endowment vector lies in the *interior* of the consumption set, for each consumer. In more general models, where consumers are endowed not with a fixed vector of commodities but with a production possibility set, as in Rader (1964) and Coles and Hammond (1986), one assumes that the consumption and production sets of the agent intersect – or, to ensure continuity of net trade functions – that their intersection has a non-empty interior.

In all cases, then, the standard assumption of general equilibrium theory is that each consumer certainly has the means to survive without trade. Since trading opportunities enhance the consumer's feasible set, it then follows that no rational consumer can ever be pushed below the margin of survival involuntarily, except by a heavy poll tax or some other form of taxation based upon the consumer's endowment. So the possibility of the very poor starving in a world of plentiful aggregate food supplies is virtually excluded by assumption. Yet Sen (1977, 1981a,b) has provided much evidence to show that famine is in fact more often due to gross inequality of income than it is to the total food supply falling so low that it becomes impossible to feed all the population adequately.

Walrasian equilibrium without survival presents a number of technical problems, as discussed in Coles and Hammond (1986). For example, both existence of equilibrium and the second efficiency theorem of welfare economics rely on convexity of individuals' preferences and of their feasible sets. When the survival of individual consumers is at issue, the number of survivors becomes an endogenous discrete variable, leading to fundamental non-convexities. To prove results which correspond to the standard existence and efficiency theorems, we had to obtain convexity by smoothing over a continuum of individuals, using the techniques pioneered by Aumann (1964, 1966) and Hildenbrand (1974). Then the proportion of individuals who survive becomes the relevant variable, and that of course is a continuous variable in a continuum economy.

So the possibility of non-survival places no fundamental obstacle in the way of the usual efficiency, existence, and core equivalence theorems. In particular, competitive equilibria can occur with a large proportion of the population below the margin of survival. Such equilibria are even Pareto efficient, because feeding the starving would require sacrifices from some of those whose survival is not at risk. Really, that mass starvation can occur in competitive equilibrium, and still be consistent with Pareto efficiency, merely serves to dramatize the criticism of Assumptions 6 and 7 – namely, that Pareto efficiency is by no means a sufficient condition for ethical acceptability, and there is also no good reason to presume that the distribution of wealth is ethically acceptable within any one country, let alone within the whole world. Moreover, one should hardly need to add that when some individuals are at or even below the margin of survival, aggregate wealth maximization is rather obviously an unethical criterion for the choice of economic policy. Indeed, as Joan Robinson herself wrote:

that the form of investment is controlled by the principle of maximizing the welfare of society, is being discredited by the awakening of public opinion to the persistence of poverty – even hunger – in the wealthiest nations, the decay of cities, the pollution of environment, the manipulation of demand by salesmanship, the vested interests in war, not to mention the still more shocking problems of the world outside the prosperous industrial economies. The complacency of neo-*laisser faire* cuts the economists off from discussing the economic problems of today just as Say's Law cut them off from discussing unemployment in the world slump. (Robinson, 1971, pp.xiv–xv)

These problems arise in the economies that boast of their wealth. Perhaps they can afford the luxury of an economics profession that builds intricate theories in the air that have no contact with reality. But this luxury is too expensive for the so-called developing world where the doctrines of *laissez faire* and the free play of market forces are exported along with armaments to keep them from looking for any way out of their infinitely more grievous situation. (Robinson, 1972, pp.7–8)

9   INCOME EFFECTS ARE NEGLIGIBLE

With every pair of hands God sends a mouth, but a mouth without a shilling to buy bread does not constitute a market. (Robinson, 1951a, pp.115–6)

In Section 7, it was seen that aggregate maximization is a valid approximate welfare criterion in the special case when the distribution of wealth has been optimized, but is unjustified otherwise, in general. Nevertheless, the assumption remains in common use in elementary textbook treatments of welfare issues, based on partial equilibrium analysis. There it ties in closely with another dubious assumption, which is that all income – or wealth – effects can be neglected, and so welfare can be measured as the sum of total Marshallian consumer surplus together with total net expenditure on all other goods. It happens to be very convenient for these partial analyses that surplus can then be measured simply by looking at the area to the left of an aggregate demand curve, and then adding the consumer's expanditure on all other goods.

The general condition for a measure of Marshallian consumer surplus to be a well-defined line integral – to be 'path-independent' – requires homothetic preferences for the goods whose prices are changing, and income elasticities of demand for these goods all equal. The condition for Marshallian consumer surplus to give an exact measure of welfare is even more stringent and should be well known; namely, the income elasticities of demand for all goods whose prices are varying must be zero. Yet, since the time of Engel, if not earlier, economists have known a great deal about income elasticities of demand, and known that many differ substantially from zero. Indeed, the budget identity tells us that the wealth share weighted average income elasticity of demand is equal to one, and so there are bound to be some goods with income elasticities not only significantly positive, but greater than one – except, that is, in the special case of homothetic preferences for all goods, where all income elasticities are equal to one.

The elementary and intermediate textbooks no doubt ignore income effects and use Marshallian consumer surplus because many of their writers have never learned better, or because they are unwilling to face the task of explaining to students how to construct 'artificial' compensated demand curves which do allow for income effects. Even more advanced texts make similar excuses, however, claiming that compensated demand curves are 'unobservable', whereas Marshallian uncompensated demand curves are supposed somehow to be 'observable'. This despite the fact that, as far as I know, demand curves – be they uncompensated or compensated – are only observed within the pages of economics textbooks. What we actually observe in the world are prices, quantities, incomes, etc. and it is the task of the econometrician to estimate market demand functions. Any satisfactory estimation procedure has to overcome the standard identification problem of disentangling demand from supply. One possible approach is to assume that the demand curve has been fixed throughout and that all changes in prices and quantities are entirely due to shifts in supply. Generally, however, except in the special case when the income elasticity of demand is zero and so Marshallian consumer surplus is an accurate measure, one knows that the demand curve has also been shifting in response to income changes, if not to changes in the prices of complements and substitutes. Then one cannot solve the identification problem satisfactorily without including aggregate income – or, even better, the distribution of income – within the demand equation. An obvious implication is that it is virtually impossible to estimate price elasticities of demand without simultaneously estimating income elasticities of demand. Then the standard Slutsky equation can easily be used to calculate the compensated elasticity of demand. So the claim that uncompensated demand curves are somehow easier to observe than compensated demand curves becomes very difficult to substantiate outside the mythical world of economics textbooks which seem to presume that uncompensated demand curves are given to us as data.

Textbook sloppiness is one thing, but journal articles in applied economics also abound with what I am tempted to call 'surplus economics' masquerading as applied welfare economics. Some progress is being made, however, because now many writers do understand that using surplus to measure welfare is a mistake. However, they usually proceed almost immediately to excuse themselves on the grounds that surplus is a good approximation to an accurate measure of welfare. The excuse is accompanied by a ritual reference to Willig (1976), conveniently overlooking the articles by Markandya (1978) and Hausman (1981) which point to the possibility of serious inaccuracies in Marshallian consumer surplus approximations. Less forgivably, nobody I am aware of – except the above-mentioned authors – has yet cared to provide an estimate of just how inaccurate the surplus approximation is for the particular application they are considering. The easy road of ignoring income effects altogether is the one usually taken.

Many theoretical results in partial equilibrium welfare analysis are admittedly very much easier when income effects are neglected and so the partial equilibrium is known to maximize total Marshallian consumer surplus. Correcting surplus calculations for income effects brings one face to face with the inconvenient need to discuss the distribution of income in the economy. The reason is that, except in the very special Gorman (1953, 1976) case when all individuals have parallel linear Engel curves relating expenditure on the goods in question to income, total demand depends upon the distribution of income. A special case of this, of course, is when all Engel curves are horizontal straight lines, which is what is required to make Marshallian consumer surplus an exact measure of welfare. Sometimes, however, one wonders if failing to make the correction is due merely to the desire to avoid extra algebra, or whether it is rather due to the wish that the income distribution could be ignored lest its consideration should make evident the unreasonableness of aggregate wealth maximization as the ethical criterion underlying total surplus maximization.

It would be wrong to end this section without due acknowledgment that there is also much recent work which does properly account for income effects in making estimates of welfare gains and losses. Particular examples are King (1983) and many recent articles by Jorgenson and his colleagues.

10   PARETO EFFICIENCY IS NECESSARY FOR ETHICAL ACCEPTABILITY

In its own day, however, the neo-classical scheme was rather barren of results ... There was a twofold reason I think for this sterility.

First, the questions being discussed were of no practical importance. The policy recommended was *laisser faire*, and there was no need to describe in detail how to do nothing ...

The second reason why the neo-classicals were so much isolated from practice was the dominance of the concept of equilibrium in the theory itself ... The soothing harmonies of equilibrium supported *laisser faire* ideology and the elaboration of the argument kept us all too busy to have any time for dangerous thoughts. Robinson (1962, pp.68–70 *passim*)

The last four Assumptions have concerned the distribution of wealth, and how one should not presume, as far too many economists seem to do in at least some of their work, that this distribution is no matter for ethical concern, either because it has already been made acceptable, or because wealth distribution is not a legitimate concern of economists. If these extraordinary assertions were valid, they would provide a good case for *laissez faire*, which may be why they retain their popularity. Fortunately, many economists, especially those who work in public finance and related areas, now do recognize that income distribution matters and that it is imperfect. So the first efficiency theorem of welfare economics loses its force because, although complete and perfectly competitive markets will bring about a Pareto-efficient allocation, they do not guarantee an ethically acceptable distribution of wealth. Indeed, the experience of real economies suggests rather strongly that an unacceptable distribution of wealth is all that free markets can guarantee.

One last assumption is often used to defend *laissez faire*. It is based on the second efficiency theorem of welfare economics. This, remember, tells us that, under conditions discussed in Section 2 (as well as many standard textbooks, of course), any welfare optimum can be achieved through equilibrium in perfectly competitive complete markets provided that the distribution of wealth is made ethically acceptable through appropriate lump-sum redistribution.

After my arguments in the last four sections, the reader should be in no doubt that I regard the proviso concerning redistribution of wealth to be extremely important. Yet, as many economists are willing to admit, we do not see enough redistribution in the world around us. One reason may be that we cannot agree what would be an optimal redistribution. Indeed, such lack of agreement is undeniable, but there are instances of redistribution that almost everybody can agree are ethically desirable, such as the alleviation of extreme poverty by taxes levied on those most able to afford to pay them. So why do they not occur?

The problem with the lump-sum redistribution which the second efficiency theorem of welfare economics requires for its ethical significance is that it is not really feasible. Any redistribution scheme is bound to affect incentives. Hahn (1973b) did once remind us of the differential lump-sum taxes which used to be levied on different classes of the English nobility, but such taxes must have affected somewhat decisions regarding what type of noble a person wanted to become, if any. Current proposals for the reform of local taxes in Britain involve a reversion to poll taxes, in effect. But if these vary between different local authorities, they will affect taxpayers' choices of the area in which to live. Even uniform poll taxes and subsidies are clearly likely to affect incentives governing the family planning decisions of prospective parents with sufficient forethought. True lump-sum taxes must be levied on the basis of individuals' fundamental and unalterable characteristics, and not be based on decisions by those individuals. Such characteristics are usually private information to the person possessing those characteristics, even if we understand clearly what precise kind of characteristic it is that we are looking for. To the extent that a personal characteristic, like how much support an apparently very poorly endowed person might need to survive, remains private information, individuals will always be tempted to exploit that privacy by claiming to need more support than would be the truth. On the other hand, those who are truly well endowed are also likely to conceal their true endowments in order to escape paying too high a 'lump-sum' tax, based on their apparent taxable capacity. Indeed, the latter kind of manipulation by those who are really very well endowed is presumably rather more likely, because more skilled individuals are likely to understand better how to exploit the system.

Anyway, it is clear that differential 'lump-sum' taxes based upon apparent taxable capacity are not really lump-sum taxes at all, because taxpayers will tend to adjust their economic circumstances in order to reduce their tax liability. Yet it is precisely such differential lump-sum taxation that is needed in order to give ethical significance to the second efficiency theorem of welfare economics. In the jargon of the times, one says that differential lump-sum taxation is generally 'incentive incompatible'. The work of Hurwicz and Schmeidler (1978), Hurwicz (1979), Schmeidler (1982), among others, showed that among all Pareto-efficient allocations, only the Walrasian allocations without differential lump-sum taxes can be implemented by some incentive compatible mechanism. For the important special case of symmetric allocations (in which identical consumers are treated equally) in a continuum economy, one can also characterize incentive allocations as those which correspond to 'public finance mechanisms' with various kinds of commodity and income taxation, non-linear pricing, etc. This is formally stated and proved in Hammond (1979, 1987) and discussed much less formally in Hammond (1985). The conclusions of Hurwicz and Schmeidler on the incentive incompatibility of differential lump-sum taxation become reinforced, especially when free trade in an underground economy cannot be prevented. Really, all this just formalizes what Lerner (1947) and Graaff (1957) were already well on the way to understanding in their discussions of the difficulties of achieving fully optimal economic allocations.

This work changes the nature of welfare economics rather drastically, by showing that most of the Pareto-efficient allocations, considered in the second efficiency theorem of welfare economics, are not really feasible once one allows for the incentive constraints that arise because individuals' characteristics are, at least in part, private information. Indeed, the only Pareto-efficient allocations which are truly feasible in general economic environments are those which can be brought about by complete markets in perfectly competitive equilibrium without any differential lump-sum taxes which depend upon individuals' private information. In the case when nothing is known about individuals' characteristics in an exchange economy, and if there is a unique Walrasian equilibrium in this exchange economy, then this unique equilibrium allocation is the only truly feasible Pareto-efficient allocation. If, in addition, it is impossible to prevent trade on perfectly competitive underground markets, then in this case there is precisely one truly feasible allocation, which is the unique Walrasian equilibrium. Thus markets emerge as constraints upon rather than the instruments of economic policy. It relates to the only 'important advantage of the free-market pricing system' which Joan Robinson described in her paper on 'The Philosophy of Prices':

> The advantage is that each family, within the limits of the purchasing power provided by its own production, can purchase whatever it pleases and each family is led to specialize upon what it can best produce. No one has to be ordered to do anything and there is no need for any allocation or rationing. Where there are no laws there are no crimes. The system polices itself. (Robinson, 1960, p.31)

Later, in summarizing the main conclusion of this paper for the collection *Contributions to Modern Economics*, she put it even better:

> I never could understand the claim that the free play of market forces establishes an optimum pattern of prices, but discussions with Polish and Soviet economists made me realize that there are very great merits in a system of prices for consumer goods in which flows of demand for particular goods are in line with available supplies. Distribution according to queuing power is no more just and much more wasteful than distribution according to purchasing power, and it moreover invites corruption. (Robinson, 1979b, p.xx)

Ironically enough, according to Jaffé's (1977) interpretation, Walras himself may even have intended his description of a perfectly competitive economy to represent the best that was possible in the economy subject to a rather unusual form of 'justice' in the sense that all traders face identical prices. This relates to Schmeidler and Vind's (1972) notion of 'fair net trades', which are Pareto efficient subject to the constraint that nobody could be better off with another agent's net trade vector, and must coincide with Walrasian equilibrium net trades.

As Graaff (1957) for one certainly realized, this inability to redistribute wealth or to control markets in the underground economy makes the usual concept of Pareto efficiency quite redundant in general. The usual concept involves a kind of 'first best' in which the only constraints on the choice of an economic allocation are the physical feasibility and resource balance constraints. Private information imposes additional incentive constraints, and so the appropriate concept of Pareto efficiency is a kind of 'second best' which respects these extra constraints. Moreover, these constraints appear much more natural than those considered by Meade (1955) and by Lipsey and Lancaster (1956) in their work on the second best. Indeed, they are so natural that Maskin (1980) for one regards an incentive constrained optimum as really a 'first best' allocation.

This, then, finally robs the second efficiency theorem of just about all its ethical significance. The theorem characterizes only those allocations that are first best Pareto efficient, when one ignores the incentive constraints. Most of the allocations which it characterizes are not truly feasible once the force of these incentive constraints is recognized. Generally, when some degree of public intervention in the economy is possible, there is no such simple characterization of second best Pareto-efficient allocations – i.e. allocations which are Pareto efficient among those that satisfy the various kinds of incentive constraints. In particular, there is now no justification whatsoever for continuing to claim that only *laissez faire* economic policies are worthy of consideration. Nor for restricting attention to the set of allocations which happen both to satisfy the incentive constraints and also to be first best Pareto efficient, since they will typically exclude most of the allocations which are second best Pareto efficient. Hence the title of this section; first best Pareto efficiency is not a necessary condition for ethical acceptability, except in those rare cases where the second best optimal allocation happens also to be first best Pareto efficient. It is true that such cases are not impossible; one occurs for instance in Dasgupta and Hammond (1980), but I regard that as a special example which suggests the possibility of more powerful forms of redistributive taxation, rather than as a case which is likely to occur in any actual economy.

11   THERE IS A REPRESENTATIVE CONSUMER

> There is no treatment at all of the determination of the distribution of income in orthodox teaching, and precious little about its consequences. What to the general public appears one of the most interesting of all questions in economics is simply left out of the syllabus. Robinson (1985, p.160)

So concern with the distribution of income, together with incentive constraints which limit its redistribution, undermine much of the standard work in welfare economics and public finance. Even so, the issues raised in the previous sections are avoided surprisingly often. In particular, a large amount of work, both theoretical and empirical, is based upon the assumption that there exists a single representative consumer.

Obviously, this is a common assumption in macroeconomics, where I would argue that it causes much of the trouble macroeconomists seem to have both with microeconomic foundations and indeed with finding any predictive model of an economy which outperforms the vector autoregressive techniques used by Sims (1980) and others. In principle such techniques often have no theoretical economic content whatsoever beyond the choice of variables to include in the vector autoregression. Moreover, it is quite unforgivable of certain macroeconomists to claim that they are considering models of 'maximizing' economic *agents* and then to proceed to consider economies which are indistinguishable from those with one single 'representative' maximizing *agent*. After all, it is now over thirty years since Gorman (1953) first pointed out the very restrictive conditions that need to be satisfied for a representative consumer to exist – namely that, for each good, all consumers' Engel curves must be parallel straight lines. Things may be changing, however, because now authors like Stoker (1986) have taken the trouble to test the representative consumer model in macroeconomics, and not surprisingly they were able to reject it. Indeed, the model fails the kind of direct test based on the weak axiom of revealed preference, as discussed by Deaton (1986).

The popularity of single consumer models in macroeconomics has had a strange side-effect. If there were *really* a single immortal (presumably) representative consumer, economics would become pretty trivial and uninteresting. In particular, any economic fluctuations would have to be wobbles desired by this one consumer. So, in order to have interesting dynamics, macroeconomists have taken to misusing the overlapping generations model which Samuelson (1958) originally developed in order to explain the usefulness of very long-lived financial assets, and how money can have a positive value which would be illogical in any finite time horizon economy (Gale, 1982). Now each generation is represented by a single consumer, but two or three generations co-exist in any time period. This may be an interesting model of the very long-run dynamics, but can hardly be taken seriously as a suitable framework for discussing short term macroeconomic fluctuations.

Although in macroeconomics the assumption of a representative consumer is arguably rather damaging, in microeconomics, welfare economics, and public finance it is devastating. For then it is usually also presumed that the welfare of the representative consumer indeed represents the welfare of the whole society. Also, when there is only one representative consumer in an economic model, nothing whatsoever can be said about issues relating to the distribution of income in the economy, including the way that this distribution interacts with other variables of interest. Obviously, too, the representative consumer models sweep under the carpet all the important issues connected with income distribution which I have been discussing in the last five sections. Specifically, welfare optimality and Pareto efficiency coincide, and so Pareto efficiency is clearly sufficient for ethical acceptability – at least if one grants consumer sovereignty. Wealth is automatically optimally distributed. Either the single representative consumer can survive on his (her?) own or else nothing can be done. And the incentive incompatibility of lump-sum redistribution does not matter when there is no other person to redistribute to or from. It is true that the errors of neglecting income effects and measuring welfare using consumer surplus are just as possible and just as stupid in a one consumer economy, but this is not worth discussing any further.

There are two ways left to attempt to rescue the representative consumer. The first way harks back to the question of measuring national income and constructing social indifference curves, as in Samuelson (1950, 1956). Samuelson, however, postulated the unrealistic optimal lump-sum transfers which I discussed in Sections 7 and 10 above. Thereafter, Mirrlees (1969) considered the same issue in an economy where the assumption of optimal lump-sum transfers was replaced by an assumption of Diamond and Mirrlees (1971) optimal commodity taxes. Having progressed this far, it is not too difficult to take the next step and construct social indifference curves in the space of aggregate commodity vectors to represent an 'indirect' Bergson social welfare function, which measures social welfare on the presumption that the government uses whatever fiscal instruments it can to optimize the distribution of the aggregate commodity vector between all the individuals in the society. This was done in Hammond (1980) and some similar results have recently appeared in Varian (1984). However, this representative consumer is likely to be quite different from all the actual consumers in the economy. For example, even though all consumers may have strictly convex preference orderings, this artificial representative may well have preferences which are not even convex.

A second way of rescuing the representative consumer is suggested by Sen's (1976, 1979) approach to the problem of measuring national income. This treats each individual's consumption of a particular good as a 'social' commodity which is separate from the consumption of any other individual of the same good. In other words, different individuals' consumptions of the same physical good are treated as different social commodities. Moreover, in a perfectly competitive market economy in Walrasian equilibrium, there is a 'social price' of each such social commodity which is given by the product of the market price with the welfare weight of the relevant individual. This welfare weight represents the marginal value to society of allocating a marginal dollar (or other *numéraire*) to purchasing goods optimally for the individual in question – i.e. the social marginal utility of income. The society is then represented by one 'representative consumer' who buys all the social commodities at appropriate social prices, with tastes represented by a Bergson social welfare function. Inequality between different individuals' social marginal utilities of income is possible, reflecting the impossibility of arranging optimal lump-sum transfers. Like the first artificially constructed 'representative consumer' considered in the previous paragraph, this second one also may be quite unlike any of the actual flesh and blood consumers we are used to thinking about. In particular, the 'social prices' which he faces reflect social marginal utilities of income which may change in complicated ways in response to other changes in the economy. After all, these social prices are not just the usual kind of market clearing prices.

Both these artificial representative consumers are useful constructs in thinking about issues in theoretical welfare economics. They are far removed, however, from the usual kind of representative consumer, whose whole *raison d'être* seems to be the desire to avoid the distributional questions that are carefully taken into account in the two constructions I have just been discussing.

12 DISTORTIONARY TAXES CREATE DEADWEIGHT LOSSES

Ideally it would be best to assess each enterprise with an annual lump-sum tax, reflecting its special advantages, so that it is equally hard to earn a profit everywhere, and profit reflects only the efficiency of the enterprise. But in practice this assessment would involve precisely the kind of friction which it is the aim of the self-regulating price system to avoid, and a profits tax, leaving the enterprise with whatever share is considered an adequate incentive to efficiency, is probably to be preferred. (Robinson, 1960, p.44)

Once one recognizes the incentive incompatibility of lump-sum redistribution, and starts to consider second best allocations which respect the incentive constraints due to private information, much of standard public finance theory is inapplicable. In particular, it is no longer necessarily true that 'distortionary' taxes are inefficient, or that they create deadweight losses. To show that there are such deadweight losses, standard theory considers replacing any distortionary tax – such as an income or commodity tax, or an import tariff – by an alternative system of lump-sum taxation which raises the same revenue. Usually, the analysis is conducted under the representative consumer assumption of the previous section. Then it is not difficult to show that the single consumer is better off paying over a given sum as a lump-sum rather than having his demand and supply decisions distorted through a system of commodity and/or income taxes which raise the same revenue. The consumer's willingness to pay to have the distortionary taxes replaced by a lump-sum tax is then a measure of the deadweight loss created by the distortions (see Pazner and Sadka (1980), Zabalza (1982) and King (1983) for recent discussions of some pitfalls in measuring deadweight loss for a single consumer).

The problem with measuring deadweight loss come once one gets beyond the unrealistic case of the representative consumer. Then one has to argue that distortionary taxes can be replaced by alternative lump-sum taxes on all consumers (except some of the poorest who may receive lump-sum subsidies) so that all consumers are better off. If this were true, measuring the total over all consumers of the willingness to pay for having distortionary taxes replaced by lump-sum taxes is indeed a measure of the welfare loss occasioned by the distortionary taxes. Even if not all consumers are made better off, but the distortionary taxes are replaced by an optimal system of lump-sum taxes, so that a first best welfare optimum is achieved, one can still measure deadweight loss by the willingness of the society to pay to do away with distortionary taxes.

Once the argument is laid bare in this way, so are its inadequacies. For in Section 10 it was shown that lump-sum redistribution is generally infeasible because it violates incentive constraints. In particular, it is simply not possible in general to replace distortionary taxes by Pareto or welfare superior lump-sum taxes. Individuals will usually understate their true ability to pay the lump-sum taxes which are intended to replace the distortionary taxes. This involves a new kind of welfare loss which standard theory overlooks.

Indeed, the basic point can be made very simply. With incentive constraints, the kind of taxes which usual theory regards as 'distortionary' will feature in almost any second best Pareto efficient allocation. The 'optimal taxes' of Diamond and Mirrlees (1971) are not misleadingly described; they really are optimal when lump-sum taxes are incentive incompatible and when in addition non-linear pricing is impossible because consumers facing different marginal prices can do a deal on the side (Hammond, 1987). Even to call such taxes 'distortionary' is unfortunate, because they do not necessarily distort the economic allocation away from what is entirely desirable, provided that the taxes are set very carefully. The 'deadweight losses', of course, are then entirely illusory.

13   DOMESTIC PUBLIC EXPENDITURE PROGRAMS ARE WASTEFUL

When there is unemployment and low profits the government must spend on something or other – it does not matter what. As we know, for twenty-five years serious recessions were avoided by following this policy. The most convenient thing for a government to spend on is armaments. The military-industrial complex took charge. I do not think it plausible to suppose that the cold war and several hot wars were invented just to solve the unemployment problem. But certainly they have had that effect ... It was the so-called Keynesians who persuaded successive presidents that there is no harm in a budget deficit and left the military–industrial complex to take advantage of it. So it has come about that Keynes's pleasant daydream was turned into a nightmare of terror ...

Hitler had already found how to cure unemployment before Keynes had finished explaining why it occurred. (Robinson, 1972, pp.6–7 and p.8)

building weapons that become obsolete faster than they can be constructed has turned out far better than pyramids ever did to keep up profit without adding to wealth. (Robinson, 1962, p.92)

Another part of *laissez faire* economics is the hypothesis that public expenditure is usually wasteful. For some reason which no doubt has much to do with the persuasive power of what President Eisenhower, as he was retiring from office, called the 'military–industrial complex', that part of public expenditure which is allocated to what is usually euphemistically called 'defense' is exempted from this claim. But the purpose of this essay is to moralize about the state of neoclassical economic theology rather than about the arms race. So I shall concentrate upon non-military public expenditure and the claim that this is wasteful.

Of course, there is no doubt that as much, if not more, waste is created by public bureaucracies as by those in private corporations and institutions. What must be strongly contested, however, is the apparently common view that the 40 per cent or so of total national product that is spent by various public agencies is a wasteful drag upon the rest of the economy. For one thing, some of that 40 per cent represents transfer programs to the poor and elderly, which have a great deal of ethical justification, and only reduce the national product to the extent that they are financed by distortionary taxes, as will be argued in Section 14 below. Here, I want to discuss public provision of certain goods and services, from crime prevention to libraries, cultural events, publicly funded research, etc.

Extreme *laissez faire* economists argue that all such public expenditure is wasted. There seem to be two reasons for this claim, so far as I can understand them. The first reason goes so far back as to suggest that even the benefits of public goods may be misleading. The second simply focuses on the costliness of public goods, without denying that there may be benefits.

A deep objection to public expenditure may be the idea that all its benefits are illusory. It is hard for me to say, since it is not an argument that I readily understand, I must admit. What seems to be claimed is that publicly provided goods and services serve only to undermine the 'moral fibre' of the community or the nation. They devalue self-reliance. Private charity is to be preferred to public support. Such claims may be a disguised form of libertarianism, in which case they might deserve our respect in a world where institutions were indeed always set up when it was advantageous to do so. This reverts to Assumption 5, unbounded cooperation, and the 'efficiency tautology'. Alternatively, such claims may simply reflect the ideological belief that *laissez faire* is inherently the ideal economic system, in which case further discussion of the kind I have been providing throughout this paper is clearly of no interest.

It may be rare even for politicians to claim that only military public expenditure is beneficial. But a related claim which has often been heard recently in the UK is that only jobs which are created within or by the private sector have any permanent value. Of course, given the way public expenditure gets treated these days, many public sector jobs have become much less secure than they used to be. But the pretence that, for instance, workers for British Telecom were socially unproductive until they started to carry out essentially identical jobs for the privatized near-monopoly they now work for, is clearly absurd. Yet that is what passes for logic in some political speeches these days.

Let me return to the cost issue, where there is at least a coherent argument which I can discuss. It focuses on the need to finance public goods with distortionary taxes, actually recognizing for once that the old theoretical ideal of lump-sum taxes is unattainable. Nor are the Lindahl taxes for public goods which modern first best theory also prescribes. Indeed, once the level of public good provision is fixed, personalized Lindahl tax payments become equivalent to lump-sum redistribution of income, based, however, on willingness to pay for public goods at the margin. Anyway, such tax schemes typically violate incentive constraints. A uniform lump-sum or poll tax would be incentive compatible, but if it were set high enough to cover the expenses of the public goods like good education which the wealthy appear to desire, and rightly so, there is no way that the poor could afford to pay for it. So there is no truly feasible way of financing public expenditure in general without some distortionary taxes. The standard theory of public finance would then ascribe the deadweight loss from these distortionary taxes as being an additional cost of public expenditure. But, where lump-sum taxes are incentive incompatible, it was shown in Section 11 that a measure of deadweight loss has no practical significance. Just as optimal commodity taxes really are optimal in the presence of incentive constraints, etc., so having public expenditure financed by 'distortionary taxes' may well be part of a second best welfare optimum.

So far I have said little about 'privatization' in Britain or 'deregulation' in the US. These are important matters, but they have far less to do with the desirability of public expenditure on public goods than with the question of the organization of industry and the desirability of public as against private ownership and control. These are subtle questions, without simple answers. There is some evidence that private ownership and control work better on incentive grounds, and some theoretical reasons for believing that price controls may be the best way of dealing with the problems that arise with natural monopolies, but like all interesting policy questions in economics, there is no simple answer one can be dogmatic about. I shall have a little more to say about industrial organization in connection with Assumption 21.

14   TRANSFER PROGRAMS CONFER NO BENEFITS

> In its general influence on educated public opinion, orthodox teaching has been not merely feeble and confused but positively pernicious. It gives support to the view that expenditure by a government that is beneficial to the inhabitants of its territory is 'socialism' and must be prevented at all costs. This reconciles an otherwise more or less sane and benevolent public opinion to the arms race which seems to be dragging us all to destruction. But that is another story. (Robinson, 1985, p.160)

Here I want to consider the argument that transfer programs should be abolished. There are two aspects to this argument. One says that the benefits of transfer programs are illusory, because they remove people's incentives to provide for themselves. The second says that, even though it may be conceded that transfer programs do convey some benefits to their recipients, they only do so at an unacceptably large cost.

The first argument brings in incentive constraints with a vengeance, and says that they are so strong that redistributive policy is powerless because all it achieves is to replace private insurance and saving arrangements, and does so inefficiently and wastefully as a rule. This might be an argument with some validity in a world of perfect capital and insurance markets. But we do not see such perfect markets outside economics articles and textbooks, for reasons which I have already alluded to in Section 4 and will allude to again in Section 15 below. To give one very concrete example, it is only state pension schemes in both the UK and the US, and no doubt in many other countries too, which are indexed to the cost of living and so provide some reasonably safe guarantee against the adverse effects of inflation. Even with complete markets, however, some coordinated action is still needed to remedy past inequalities and injustices. The poor will always be with us and some of them will always be genuinely needy, even if some are not and choose to exploit whatever system of poverty relief is instituted. This exploitation by those who are not genuinely needy seems to be an inescapable feature of any transfer program, and one should certainly bear it in mind when designing the system. But it is no reason to abandon the truly needy.

The cost argument is also much exaggerated. To take an extreme case, if transfer payments were financed entirely by 'non-distortionary' lump-sum taxes, that part of 'public expenditure' would not really be additional expenditure at all – it is like having part of a family's income being spent by the children instead of by the parents. In fact, of course, transfer payments, like any other form of public expenditure, have to be financed by 'distortionary' income or commodity taxes. Even so, just as with the need to finance public expenditure, which was considered in Section 13, much of the 'cost' of such 'distortionary' taxes in the form of 'deadweight loss' is entirely illusory, for reasons that were explained in Section 11. Indeed, transfer payments, together with the taxes used to finance them, should really be seen as parts of an overall scheme to replace incentive-incompatible lump-sum redistribution by an incentive-compatible public finance mechanism. Distortions and even abuses are inevitable in a world of limited information, but they are no reason to abandon the idea of redistribution completely. Far better to try to avoid such abuses by measures such as replacing 'welfare' by 'workfare' in the state of California.

Libertarians may object that if the redistribution that is brought about by transfer payments is something that the society truly desires, then it would be better to leave such transfers to voluntary charitable contributions. This, however, ignores the public good aspect of charitable contributions, and the temptation for different donors to 'free-ride'. It is true that Sugden (1982, 1983) has shown pretty convincingly that charity is not just motivated by the benefits conferred upon the recipients, so that the public good argument loses some of its force. Individuals who choose to give to charity for the very sake of giving are not so likely to be free riders. It may even be true, as some have claimed, that the growth of welfare state transfer programs has promoted the decline of private charity, because it fosters the belief that all the truly needy are receiving adequate support. Nevertheless, private charity has always been a somewhat ramshackle approach to providing relief for the needy. In addition, it often turns out to be a form of exploitation of those with exceptionally strong charitable feelings, who wind up much worse off than those who remain entirely selfish. Finally, given the kind of economic theology that many people have been taught in the past, in my view it would be highly unwise, if not downright unethical, to base transfer programs exclusively upon what individuals are willing to give voluntarily to poorer fellow human beings, at least until there has been time for influential people first to learn and then to teach some better economics.

15   CAPITAL MARKETS ARE PERFECT

Among the disadvantages of various kinds of assets compared to money we may distinguish ... [l]ender's risk; that is, the fear of partial or total failure of the borrower. (Robinson, 1951b, p.94, and 1960, p.248)

I was unemployed with debts of £400,000. I know what unemployment is like – and a lot of it is getting off your backside and finding yourself a job. (Jeffrey Archer, vice-chairman of the UK Conservative Party, in a speech on the eve of the annual party conference, as reported in the *Manchester Guardian Weekly* 13 October 1985)

Gad, Jeffrey Archer is right! If only these layabouts would all go and get themselves into debt for a few hundred thousands, the unemployment problem would be solved. (Basil Mager, letter published in the *Manchester Guardian*, 20 October 1985)

So far, no mention has been made of imperfections in capital markets, particularly for financial assets. Much of neoclassical theory ignores such imperfections, with the result that the microeconomics of money has remained in an extremely unsatisfactory state, despite the recent work of Gale (1982, 1983). We know that credit rationing and bankruptcy or default are endemic features of virtually all economic systems, be they past, present, or in the conceivable future. Yet Stigler's (1967) plea for an exploration of what really underlies 'imperfections in the capital market' still goes largely unanswered, despite much recent work by Stiglitz and Weiss (1981, 1983, 1985) amongst others.

The existing literature on credit rationing has tried to integrate bankruptcy and credit rationing within a model of market equilibrium. Yet this is probably premature, since an important prior problem is to characterize what allocations of credit are truly feasible in a sequence economy. After all, in a static exchange economy, a Walrasian equilibrium allocation happens to be a particular kind of feasible allocation in which all agents are maximizing their preference subject to budget contraints, determined by their endowments and by the market-clearing price vector. In a static economy of pure exchange it is trivial to characterize the set of feasible allocations – at least in the case when all information is common. Sequence economies present new difficulties in enforcing debt repayment, however. And the only allocations that are truly feasible in a sequence economy are those in which, if a loan is ever to be repaid, there must be some mechanism for enforcing its repayment and preventing the borrower from escaping scot-free from his obligations. Indeed, as Townsend (1979) pointed out in connection with contingent contracts, the eventual outcome of an unenforceable contract is identical to the outcome of an equivalent contract which respects the constraints that arise because only enforceable repayments ever get collected.

Virtually all the theoretical work to date ignores this important issue of enforcement by assuming that a borrower will always choose to repay whenever he can afford to. Default only occurs when something unforeseen happens, and so never in a world of unbounded forethought. Yet in reality far from all borrowers are this honorable. If unlimited, unsecured loans were truly available, one would hear of far more people borrowing far more than they could ever afford to repay, and then running off to some remote desert island for a life of sun-drenched luxury. Of course, this is a form of fraud that can be punished under the criminal law, but not if the desert island in which they seek refuge makes a point of harboring immigrants of dubious reputation provided that they bring with them plenty of cash. Bank robberies would cease, since would-be robbers could simply take out loans which they have no intention of ever repaying, thus robbing the banks with the consent of the bankers.

If banks and individual savers are not both to be stripped of all their assets, credit rationing becomes unavoidable. There is simply no way to decentralize enforceable credit allocations through ordinary competitive markets as one can decentralize incentive compatible allocations in static economies (Hammond, 1979, 1985, and Section 10 above). A form of fiat money can be used to enforce credit rationing, but only provided that the amount which is issued to any one agent is itself subject to a form of non-price rationing. Agents who secure their borrowings by pledging tangible assets as collateral may be able to increase the credit they are allowed, but they will still face a credit ceiling which depends on the value of the collateral. Decentralization is lost because some central agency is required to monitor each agent's total borrowings and pledges of collateral in order to ensure that the credit ceiling is never exceeded. Otherwise, an agent may find it worthwhile to borrow a small amount from a large number of lenders before absconding to his desert island. In the event that a borrower does default, the distribution of his assets between different creditors also requires some form of central coordination, such as bankruptcy courts try to provide.

The inevitability of credit rationing in any sequence economy promises to have profound implications which are only just beginning to be explored. For a start, the 'Clower' or 'cash in advance' constraint (see Clower, 1963a, b; and Lloyd, 1964, 1968), which has been so prevalent in recent literature on the microeconomic foundations of monetary economics, may now receive a much more satisfactory theoretical foundation. At last economic theory is moving a little closer to common sense.

Much recent work in game theory has grown out of Selten's (1965, 1973) concept of perfection for extensive form games. This has forced economists to think about what happens off an equilibrium path in an extensive form game, and how that influences the appropriate kind of Nash equilibrium when players foresee that some equilibrium strategies require entirely unreasonable behavior when a player finds himself off the presumed equilibrium path. As Joan Robinson herself put it on p.25 of *Essays in the Theory of Economic Growth*, 'A world in which expectations are liable to be falsified cannot be described by the simple equations of the equilibrium path.' More recently, Kreps and Wilson (1982) have extended Selten's notion of perfection and introduced the term 'sequential equilibrium'. An implication of the work reported in this section is the amusing paradox that, in a sequence economy with financial markets, a Walrasian equilibrium is not a sequential equilibrium once one considers what is to be done to borrowers who deliberately avoid repayment. The result will come as no surprise to Shubik (1973, 1974), though the simplicity of the argument might.

16 ANTICIPATED MONETARY AND FISCAL POLICIES ARE INEFFECTIVE

> There is in some quarters a great affection for credit policy because it seems the least selective and somehow lives up to the ideal of a single overall neutral regulation of the economy. The enormous ideological attraction of the Quantity Theory of Money, that kept it going for nearly forty years after its logical content was exploded (in Keynes's *Tract on Monetary Reform*), is due to the fact that it conceals the problem of political choice under an apparently impersonal mechanism.
>
> Recent experiments have shown, however, that there is no such thing as a purely quantitative, overall financial policy ... There is no simple right policy. (Robinson, 1962, p.93)

A great deal of recent work in macroeconomics has been misdirected toward such fruitless questions as whether money is neutral (or even 'superneutral') in the sense that anticipated monetary policy affects only the value of some suitably perfect price index which is called 'the price level'. A more subtle and interesting contention is that if monetary or fiscal policies do have any real effects, they do so only by bringing about deleterious changes, or, at best, by moving the economy around the Pareto frontier. It is asserted that such policy can never generate a Pareto improvement, and so is never essential for Pareto efficiency. It has also been claimed that the national debt has no effect on the real economy, because agents foresee that they or their descendants will have to pay extra taxes in the future in order to service and eventually repay the debt. Some of the relevant writings are by Barro (1974, 1976), Sargent (1973), and Sargent and Wallace (1975). Of course, it is probably only a minority of macroeconomists who have taken such arguments at all seriously. Nevertheless, as with most of the dubious assertions which I have been discussing, it seems that those who propound them may be having undue influence. One fears this may be because they provide the message which some politically powerful proponents of *laissez faire* wish to hear.

If Robinson Crusoe is one lone consumer, transacting with nobody else at all on his desert island, then his demand prices for each good, measured in terms of money, are indeed likely to be proportional to the number of monetary units over which he has command. If we face him with not only a Walrasian budget constraint, but also with a liquidity constraint to prevent him from borrowing excessively intending never to repay (as we must in a sequential environment for reasons which I discussed in the previous section), then again demand prices will be proportional to the number of units of liquidity to which Robinson Crusoe has access. In such an economy, then, money really is neutral, and monetary policy affects only nominal prices; it cannot get in the way of Robinson Crusoe choosing an optimal plan for producing, collecting, and consuming his coconuts or whatever else is available to him upon his island. Policy is and should be completely ineffective, unless it induces Crusoe to depart from his optimum somehow.

The Robinson Crusoe example may seem rather far-fetched, yet much of contemporary macroeconomic analysis is conducted using such a model. A little more sophisticated are those models with a continuum of identical individuals, some of which I mentioned in Section 4. They allow both trade and borrowing and lending between different individuals, at least in principle, even if in equilibrium no such trade or borrowing and lending actually takes place. They also provide some scope for introducing jointly owned firms with limited liability. As soon as such firms are introduced, however, there is scope for monetary or fiscal policy. For, when firms' liability is limited, the credit limits faced by those firms matter, as well as those faced by all the identical individual consumers. Notice that *both* consumers and firms do need to be constrained in their borrowing, in general, otherwise some joint owners of firms are likely to use the unconstrained borrowing facilities of their firms in order to escape from the restrictions on their personal borrowing, which are needed to ensure existence of equilibrium. When consumers are identical and have convex preferences and when the technology is also convex, there is a symmetric Pareto-efficient allocation in the economy which one may call 'optimal' with some justice. Unless the ratio of the credit limit of each consumer to that of each firm is suitable, however, this optimum may be unattainable in any competitive equilibrium of the economy, because either all the identical individuals or at least one of the firms may find themselves prevented by liquidity constraints from choosing an optimal borrowing plan. Mind you, in this case of identical consumers, ensuring that such liquidity constraints never bind might seem rather easy. Nevertheless, the point is made that money may not always be neutral, and that monetary policy may well have real effects unless that policy takes a very special form which preserves the proportions of the total money stock held by each agent in the economy.

This conclusion is not seriously affected, moreover, by the 'classical invariance principle' discussed by Patinkin (1965), Archibald and Lipsey (1958), Clower and Burstein (1960) and Samuelson (1968) (all collected in Clower, 1969), according to which long-run equilibrium is invariant to whose liquidity constraints are alleviated; all that matters is the total nominal amount of credit. The point this analysis overlooks is the possibility of permanent harm being done by the short-run effects of credit constraints, upon the investment of business firms, or the 'human capital' of individuals, possibly including their state of health or even their very survival.

The other possibility that arises in moving from Robinson Crusoe to an economy of many identical individuals is that there are externalities and public goods. It is surely significant that much of recent macroeconomics considers models of the economy in which, if tax revenue is raised, it is spent – or rather it is dissipated – in ways that have no effect on the representative consumer's utility. Not surprisingly, then, in these models the optimal fiscal policy is to have no public expenditure and no taxes at all. Perhaps the macroeconomists were trying to take too seriously Keynes's suggestion that useful public works might include digging holes in the ground only to refill them again immediately. Or else implicitly admitting that much of the share of public expenditure devoted to armaments really does do nobody any good. However that may be, they should at least consider the possible direct benefits of public expenditure, even if many of them seem predisposed to think that those benefits are likely to be zero. A better case for neglecting public goods in macroeconomics is the assumption that preferences for private goods are independent of public goods. With such separable preferences, one can legitimately neglect the influence of public goods on the private economy, once one has reckoned with the need to finance the public goods. Once the size of the public budget is fixed, there may be neutrality in this separable case. But such separability is not very plausible, because much public expenditure is on services like education and health which clearly affect the demand for privately provided alternatives, if nothing else.

So far, I have remained within the representative consumer framework, stultifying though this is. Outside it, there is much more scope for both monetary and fiscal policy, affecting the distribution of wealth and of credit constraints within the population. Although if there is sufficient altruism between different consumers in the economy, it turns out that almost every economic policy which does not affect production directly is completely ineffective, because its direct effects would be completely offset by the transfer policies undertaken by individual altruists. These conclusions of Bernheim and Bagwell (1988) could be dismissed as laughable if it were not for the fact that they simply extend the application of those arguments used by Barro (1974) to prove his 'Ricardian equivalence theorem'.

A more interesting question is whether fiscal and monetary policy can generate Pareto improvements in the economy, so that they are likely to be required in order to achieve any Pareto-efficient allocation. In the first place, it should be pointed out yet again that, because Pareto efficiency is insufficient for ethical acceptability, this question is somewhat beside the point; if fiscal and monetary policies are suitable means for redistributing wealth, then an optimal allocation may well rely on such policies. A more appropriate but entirely artificial test, therefore, is to assume that optimal lump-sum redistribution has already occurred, and then ask whether there is any scope for such policy. In a first best world of full information, the answer is that fiscal policy may still be required in the sense that certain public goods have to be financed, and that monetary or credit policy must ensure that each agent in the economy is not prevented by liquidity constraints from achieving his part of an optimal allocation. Once we move on further, however, into an economy with private information in which the truly feasible allocations must satisfy incentive constraints, then there is even more scope for both kinds of policy, and some forms of monetary and fiscal policy will indeed be Pareto superior to others, in general. Indeed, remember that even 'distortionary' taxes may now be Pareto efficient, and some distortionary tax schemes Pareto superior to others. Moreover, the analysis of Guesnerie and Roberts (1984) shows that some quantity rationing may be preferable to having only commodity taxation even in a static economy; so, *a fortiori*, it seems very likely that appropriate forms of credit rationing will be Pareto superior to other forms once one enters a sequence economy.

17   INFLATION IS CAUSED BY AN EXPANDING MONEY SUPPLY

Inflation is always and everywhere a monetary phenomenon in the sense that it is and can be produced only by a more rapid increase in the quantity of money than in output. (Friedman, 1970, p.24)

Thus does Friedman deny that inflation can ever be due to an increase in the velocity of circulation of money, or caused by non-monetary phenomena such as an oil price shock which, while having nothing to do with the supply of money function, happen coincidentally to increase either the velocity of circulation or even the measured quantity of money. It is the old quantity theory, in its strictest form, whose inadequacies were pointed out by, among others, Joan Robinson. The *Review of Economic Studies* is a journal (published by a group of young economists) which she helped to found – see Robinson (1979b, p.xv) for her very brief account of some of the relevant history. In its very first issue, following a translation by another founder, Ursula Webb (later Hicks), of Umberto Ricci's tribute to Pareto, the second article was by Joan Robinson and related to Keynes's recently published *Treatise of Money*. Included in it we find the following piece of satire:

It was in protest against this naive view of the theory of money that Mr Kahn set out the Quantity Equation for hairpins. Let P be the proportion of women with long hair, and T the total number of women. Let $1/V$ be the daily loss of hairpins by each woman with long hair, and M the daily output of hairpins. Then $M = PT/V$, and $MV = PT$. Now suppose that the Pope, regarding bobbed hair as contrary to good morals, wishes to increase the proportion of long-haired women in the population, and asks a student of economics what he had best do. The student sets out Mr Kahn's equation, and explains it to the Pope. 'All you need to do', he says, 'is to increase M, the daily output of hairpins ... and the number of long-haired women is bound to increase.' The Pope is not quite convinced. 'Or, of course', the student adds, 'if you could persuade the long-haired women to be less careless, V would increase, and the effect would be the same as though the ouput of hairpins had increased.'

Now the experts in the Theory of Money avoided these crude errors, but when they recognized that their equations were tautologies without causal significance they were beset by an uneasy feeling that their theory only provided them with wisdom after the event. Anything that had happened could always be explained in terms of their truisms, but they were never very confident in predicting what would happen next. (Robinson, 1933, pp.22–6; and 1951a, pp.54–5)

Later, after Friedman had made his impact upon the economics profession, she was hardly less forthright:

A great part of [the] work [of the modern Chicagoans, led by Milton Friedman] consists in historical investigations of the relationship between changes in the supply of money and national income in the United States. The correlations to be explained could be set out in quantity theory terms if the equation $[MV = PT]$ were read right handed. Thus we might suggest that a marked rise in the level of activity is likely to be preceded by an increase in the supply of money (if M is widely defined) or in the velocity of circulation (if M is narrowly defined) because a rise in the wage bill and in borrowing for working capital is likely to precede an increase in the value of output appearing in the statistics. Or that a fall in activity sharp enough to cause losses deprives the banks of credit-worthy borrowers and brings a contraction in their position. But the tradition of Chicago consists in reading the equation from left to right. Then the observed relations are interpreted without any hypothesis at all except *post hoc ergo propter hoc*.

There is an unearthly, mystical element in Friedman's thought. The mere existence of a stock of money somehow promotes expenditure. But insofar as he offers an intelligible theory, it is made up of elements borrowed from Keynes. An increase in the basis of credit, say by open-market operations, permits the banks to satisfy part of the 'fringe of unsatisfied borrowers' or to offer loans on easier terms; part of additional bank lending goes to various financial intermediaries and part goes into the market for bonds. A general easing of interest rates puts up the Stock Exchange. In various ways this permits investment plans to be carried out that otherwise would have been frustrated for lack of finance, as well as encouraging purchases, especially of consumer durables, both because loans are easier to get and because, with a rise in the capital value of placements, rentiers reduce their rate of saving. Thus, *other things equal*, an increase in the quantity of money promotes an increase in activity. (Robinson, 1971, pp.86–87)

These rather obvious considerations, not to mention those concerning the effects of credit policy in Section 16, imply that the 'quantity theory' of money is an excellent example of Friedman's contention that a theory is all the better if its assumptions appear unrealistic to start with. Indeed, it is especially illuminating to keep the quantity 'theory' in mind when reading 'The Methodology of Positive Economics', particularly passages like the following:

> The difficulty in the social sciences of getting new evidence for ['the class of phenomena the hypothesis is designed to explain'] and of judging its conformity with the implications of the hypothesis makes it tempting to suppose that other, more readily available, evidence is equally relevant to the validity of the hypothesis – to suppose that hypotheses have not only 'implications' but also 'assumptions' and that the conformity of these 'assumptions' to 'reality' is a test of the validity of the hypothesis *different from* or *additional to* the test by implications. This widely held view is fundamentally wrong and productive of much mischief. Far from providing an easier means for sifting valid from invalid hypotheses, it only confuses the issue, promotes misunderstanding about the significance of empirical evidence for economic theory, produces a misdirection of much intellectual effort devoted to the development of positive economics, and impedes the attainment of consensus on tentative hypotheses in positive economics.
>
> In so far as a theory can be said to have 'assumptions' at all, and in so far as their 'realism' can be judged independently of the validity of predictions, the relation between the significance of a theory and the 'realism' of its 'assumptions' is almost the opposite of that suggested by the view under criticism. Truly important and significant hypotheses will be found to have 'assumptions' that are wildly inaccurate descriptive representations of reality, and, in general, the more significant the theory, the more unrealistic the assumptions (in this sense). The reason is simple. A hypothesis is important if it 'explains' much by little, that is, if it abstracts the common and crucial elements from the mass of complex and detailed circumstances surrounding the phenomena to be explained and permits valid predictions on the basis of them alone. To be important, therefore, a hypothesis must be descriptively false in its assumptions; it takes account of, and accounts for, none of the many other attendant circumstances, since its very success shows them to be irrelevant for the phenomena to be explained.
>
> To put this point less paradoxically, the relevant question to ask about the 'assumptions' of a theory is not whether they are descriptively 'realistic', for they never are, but whether they are sufficiently good approximations for the purpose in hand. And this question can be answered only by seeing whether the theory works, which means whether it yields sufficiently accurate predictions. (Friedman, 1953, pp. 14–15)

These views on methodology represent what Samuelson (1963) called the 'F-twist' (see also Wong, 1973). So extreme are they that not even all monetarists seem to have been in agreement with them. Yet Johnson (1971) was definitely of the opinion that Friedman's methodology is crucial for the rise of the new monetarism; as he writes of the monetarist counter-revolution:

> The demand for clarification of the mechanism by which results can be explained is contrary to the methodology of positive economics, with its reliance on the 'as if' approach. But it will have to be answered satisfactorily if the monetarist counter-revolution is to win general acceptance among the profession; and the attempt to answer it will necessarily involve the counter-revolutionaries in the opposing methodology of general-equilibrium systems and multi-equation econometric models. (Johnson, 1971, p.13)

On Friedman's terms, therefore, the quantity 'theory' is no more than a hypothesis which stands or falls according to how consistent it is with just aggregate data. When one looks for a theory in the usual sense of the word, all that one finds is that the effect of an expanded money supply cannot be predicted in general without knowing much more about whose access to credit was eased, and what distributional effects ensue. The quantity 'theory' is therefore no more than the empirical hypothesis that, in predicting the rate of inflation of price indices measured by various government statisticians, all the distributional effects of any worthwhile theory get swamped by the effects of the money stock itself, as measured by a different set of statisticians. This may have been right for a relatively closed economy like the US used to be for much of the period which Friedman and Schwartz (1963) had originally studied, despite the problems with their statistical tests pointed out by Hendry and Ericsson (1983) in connection with the later study of both the US and the UK (Friedman and Schwartz, 1982). But unless expectations are explicitly incorporated in the empirical study, there is no way of telling whether the quantity of money is to be blamed for inflation directly, or if the supply of money adjusts to the expected rate of inflation, as monetary authorities try to cap nominal interest rates through open market operations. Notice that if this were the case, increases in the money supply could well lead inflation, as the quantity theorists claim that they have, without actually being the cause of inflation.

This alternative explanation of any correlation between increases in the money supply and inflation may seem more plausible for the UK, in which for many years the Bank of England did indeed profess to follow a monetary policy of pegging simultaneously both the sterling/dollar exchange rate, and – with somewhat less success – nominal interest rates. But the UK was a much more open economy than the US, of course, even under exchange controls. So it may not be too surprising that the rate of inflation for the UK seems to be more influenced by the money supply of the US rather than that of the UK, according to Cuddington (1981). Indeed, one of the reasons for the collapse of British manufacturing industry in 1980–2 may have been the inclusion in UK money supply statistics of various foreign holdings of sterling, at a time when foreign capitalists decided to hold far more sterling assets following the 1979 oil crisis, and also because of the high interest rates caused by the restrictive monetary policy itself. The effect was to make monetary policy based on money supply targets excessively restrictive when it was being used to try to eliminate the inflation which had largely been caused by higher fuel prices and a higher rate of value added tax. In such circumstances, basing policy on the quantity 'theory' is not only unscientific, but can also bring about a catastrophic 'Friedmanic' depression.

18   THERE IS A REPRESENTATIVE WORKER

Full Employment is a Good Thing, and it is conceived to be attainable by wise policy. It is a blessed state, like equilibrium. We must be able to say what it is.

Beveridge proposed the criterion of the relation between the number of unfilled vacancies and of registered unemployed. Both figures are obviously very rough indicators of what they are intended to indicate and, even if they were quite exact, an over-all equality between them would not represent a critical point in the relation of supply and demand for labour, since the very coincidence of unfilled vacancies and unemployed workers shows that they do not fit, either because they are geographically separated or because the vacancies are for particular types of work which the unemployed cannot offer. (Robinson, 1962, pp.86 and 88)

Another problem with theoretical macroeconomics is its tendency to discuss *the* labor market, as though there were not many markets for many different kinds of labor. Then it is usual to consider the aggregate demand and the aggregate supply of labor, and ascribe all of unemployment to the discrepancy between the two. Yet it is quite obvious that a strong demand for some types of labor often co-exists with a much weaker demand and indeed unemployment of many of the suppliers of other types of labor. Moreover, in most countries one finds significant regional variations in unemployment rates among similar types of workers.

These obvious empirical facts are hard to explain in any model of Walrasian equilibrium with only one aggregate labor market. And even if labor were properly differentiated according to type, it seems at first rather hard to account for the wide diversity of employment opportunities among people who are very similar in aptitude and background, though perhaps not in employment history. To account for this diversity, any Walrasian type of model has to be greatly disaggregated. It also has to recognize the non-convexities in labor markets (Coles, 1986; and Funaki and Kaneko, 1986) which arise from the costs of travelling to and from work, the difficulties of organization, etc. Why else do people work at only one or two regular jobs at any one time, instead of spending a small fraction of their time on each of a large number of jobs?

Indeed, what most theories of labor markets neglect is the peculiar characteristics of many jobs, as discussed by Akerlof (1981), and the peculiar circumstances of each potential worker. Workers have to be matched with jobs, which leads to an assignment problem which is somewhat different from the kind of allocation problem usually considered in economics – see, for instance, Crawford and Knoer (1981), Roth (1982). This matching problem is greatly complicated by the difficulties both potential employers and employees have of discovering each other's true characteristics before agreeing, at least provisionally, to a match.

Another important feature of labor markets is the slowness of turnover (Hall, 1982). It appears that employees experience significant costs of relocation and adjustment to new jobs, while many employers find that a new employee takes a long time to train to perform a new job satisfactorily. Both sides gain from maintaining a long-term employment relationship. Firms featherbed workers during periods of low demand, and use expensive overtime rather than inexperienced new workers when demand is high. Workers who are made redundant suffer real hardship because it is difficult to find a new employer who values their work as much as their former employer did.

All of these features of realistic labor markets could be included in a Walrasian model in which the wage attached to each job and to each type of worker, with each different history of past employment, would clear all labor markets in the sense of matching mobile workers to vacant jobs at each moment of time. Such perfection in matching is unlikely to be achieved in practice, of course, but it is interesting to explore its theoretical implications. There are likely to be a lot of asymmetries, in the sense that identical workers receive very different kinds of jobs, because of the inherent non-convexities and the large costs of adjustment. Some who are particularly unfortunate may not receive any wage offer at all above subsistence, and so choose to rely on unemployment benefit, begging, or whatever other means of support they find available. While their unemployment is 'voluntary' in the sense they choose to be unemployed rather than to take up any of the extremely unattractive job offers they receive, their hardship certainty is not voluntary. Much fruitless debate might have been avoided had Keynes chosen to speak of 'involuntary hardship' rather than 'involuntary unemployment'.

It must be admitted that Walrasian models of labor markets with perfect and complete information, and unbounded rationality and forethought on the part of the workers, are unlikely to explain much of the hardship currently being experienced by many of the unemployed. Once such imperfections are added, however, it seems likely that the very limited job opportunities faced by at least a majority of the unemployed will be laid bare. And that even those who face reasonable job opportunities, if they knew better how to go about finding them, may still wind up facing severe hardship. There may even be a possibility of involuntary unemployment if employers judge the quality of applicant workers by the wage at which they are willing to work. For it can happen that the expected contribution of a worker, conditional upon the wage he is willing to accept, is less than the wage, no matter how low that wage may be. This is the possibility underlying the efficiency wage model of unemployment due to Stiglitz (1974, 1976, 1984) (see also Weiss 1980, Malcomson 1981 and Yellen 1984). Indeed, with imperfect information, it may even be optimal to face some individuals with such poor job opportunities that they will not want to take them. That does not imply, however, that such individuals should be made to face undue hardship; rather, society should be willing to pay a price to support its least productive members, if it really is impossible or too costly to find suitable jobs for all.

Thus involuntary hardship together with unemployment is a real possibility once one admits the possibility of incomplete information. Recognizing the bounds on individuals' rationality and foresight merely strengthens the above explanation, and also explains why it is so hard for the afflicted to escape their plight. Whether employment is voluntary or involuntary is largely beside the point. What is crucial, however, is avoiding excessive aggregation and the concept of a representative worker to summarize all the different workers and different types of worker. Indeed, if such aggregation is insisted upon, a more accurate approximation to reality may involve two different kinds of worker – one employed at the representative wage, and a second without any job opportunities whatsoever – rather than the fiction that all workers can be employed at the representative wage. In the first approach, the second kind of worker is effectively involuntarily unemployed. Thus, although the concept of involuntary unemployment (as opposed to grossly unequal opportunities and the possibility of involuntary hardship) is hard to justify in any microeconomic model, it may provide a better approximation to reality in a macroeconomic model.

All the above was concerned with that part of unemployment that is measured and apparent to all. One must not overlook the additional 'disguised unemployment' whose very existence was apparently first pointed out by Joan Robinson in an article published in the same year as Keynes's *General Theory*. The concluding sentence gives a clear pointer to how much is lost by assuming a representative worker holding a representative job, with no possibility of misallocating labor between different labor markets: 'The analysis of disguised unemployment makes it clear that while everybody is *occupied* for twenty-four hours a day, so that the total amount of occupation can never be increased, yet *employment* can be said to increase when part of a man's time is transferred from an occupation in which its productivity is lower to one where it is higher (Robinson, 1936, p.237).

19   THE CURRENT LEVEL OF UNEMPLOYMENT IS ETHICALLY ACCEPTABLE

> A new orthodoxy was soon established by a simple device. A substitute for Say's Law was provided by the assumption that a well-managed Keynesian policy keeps investment running at the level which absorbs the saving forthcoming at full employment. The rest of the doctrines of the neoclassics could then be revived. (Robinson, 1971, p.x)

So far I have avoided many of the issues with which Joan Robinson concerned herself repeatedly in her writings. In particular, I have not discussed Say's law and the meaningfulness of the closely associated Keynesian notion of involuntary unemployment. Nor have I mentioned capital theory or the economics of imperfect competition. All of these are undeniably important, but also unecessarily contentious; I have preferred to gnaw away at those fundamental assertions in economics which contemporary fashion finds less contentious. I shall do the same in connection with the 'neoclassical synthesis', which Joan Robinson associated with a relative of Keynesianism of dubious parentage.

The neoclassical synthesis she had in mind is usually ascribed to Samuelson (see Feiwel, 1982, 1985c), although actually it is inspired by Keynes's *General Theory* (1936, pp.378–9):

> I conceive, therefore, that a somewhat comprehensive socialisation of investment will prove the only means of securing an approximation to full employment ... But beyond this no obvious case is made out for a system of State Socialism which would embrace most of the economic life of the community ... If the State is able to demonstrate the aggregate amount of resources devoted to augmenting the instruments [of production] and the basic rate of reward to those who own them, it will have accomplished all that is necessary ...
>
> Our criticism of the accepted classical theory of economics has consisted not so much in finding logical flaws in its analysis as in pointing out that its tacit assumptions are seldom or never satisfied, with the result that it cannot solve the economic problems of the actual world. But if our central controls succeed in establishing an aggregate volume of output corresponding to full employment as nearly as is practicable, the classical theory comes into its own again from this point onwards. If we suppose the volume of output to be given, *i.e.* to be determined by forces outside the

classical scheme of thought, then there is no objection to be raised against the classical analysis of the manner in which private self-interest will determine what in particular is produced, in what proportions the factors of production will be combined to produce it, and how the value of the final product will be distributed between them ... Thus, apart from the necessity of central controls to bring about an adjustment between the propensity to consume and the inducement to invest, there is no more reason to socialise economic life than there was before.

This passage is very near the end of Keynes's *General Theory*, whereas the neoclassical synthesis *starts* with the presumption that macroeconomic policy somehow always ensures full employment – whatever that may mean – and then describes what should happen in the rest of the economy. With full employment assured by assumption, neoclassical economists could go back to their old pre-Keynesian models of Walrasian equilibrium. This assumption is therefore very like Assumption 7 above, that the government would always ensure an optimal, or at least an ethically acceptable, distribution of wealth. Yet little if any discussion is provided of the difficulties in achieving this elusive goal of full employment, just as orthodox first best welfare economics neglects the question of how to implement wealth redistribution.

I contested Assumption 10 with the observation that there is in fact no truly feasible mechanism for redistributing wealth that does not involve commodity taxes and other kinds of economic policy, which first best welfare theory regards as distortionary. Moreover, this realization comes from considering the problem of redistribution explicitly in an economy with private information. The neoclassical synthesis promises something similar. Once we understand much better what really are the causes of so much distressing unemployment, we are unlikely to feel able simply to assume unemployment away in all the rest of our economic analysis. Instead we may begin to realize how the unemployment problem interacts with many other aspects of the economy, including imperfect capital markets. The current situation seems to be that economists are in disarray over the causes of unemployment, leaving the field free for politicians to claim that nothing much should be done about it because the unemployed are too lazy to want a job, or because many of the unemployed are really participating in the underground economy while simultaneously claiming unemployment benefit, or because unions set wages and working conditions too high to allow firms to hire enough new workers to eliminate unemployment. Such claims are all the more dangerous for being at least half truths.

So, rather than pretend that unemployment is abnormal, or that there is some 'natural' rate of unemployment, it is time for economists to abandon some of the assumptions that make unemployment seem so abnormal. The sections above contain plenty of suggestions, including bounded rationality, and disaggregated labor markets which incorporate non-convexities. There is the risk that making unemployment seem less abnormal may also make us too tolerant of the imperfections in labor markets of which it is the symptom. On the other hand, recognizing that even rather well-functioning labor markets may leave some unfortunate individuals facing real hardship may lead to more acceptance of the welfare programs that are set up to alleviate such hardship, even if they are expensive, rely on fairly heavy 'distortionary' taxes, and make more payments than would be ideal to those whose hardship is self-inflicted or else more apparent than real. As we read in Robinson (1936, p.228):

> The attitude of mind, prevalent even now in certain quarters, that unemployment is the result of a vicious idleness of disposition in the unemployed individuals, pandered to by the dole, is largely an anachronism which had some plausibility in an epoch when there was open access to the land, so that any active and laborious individual could make a livelihood, when he fell out of employment, not glaringly different from what he had obtained in his former trade.

20 THERE IS A REPRESENTATIVE CAPITAL GOOD

> The latter-day neoclassicals have made the basis of the old orthodoxy much clearer than it was at the time when Keynes was trying to diagnose it. In their models it is explicitly assumed that there is and has always been correct foresight, or else 'capital' is malleable so that the past can be undone (without cost) and brought into equilibrium with the future; in short, they abolish time. (Robinson, 1971, p.89)

> In Solow [(1956a) he] had three assumptions which allowed him to ignore expectations: (i) malleable capital, (ii) constant savings ratio, (iii) instantaneous adjustment of all markets. If any one of these three is dropped, the dynamic paths are drastically changed. (Stiglitz, in Mirrlees and Stern, 1973, p.163)

> It was fun to tease Samuelson, but this debate took attention away from the main issue. (Robinson, 1979b, p.xviii)

This is the third aggregation problem considered in this essay, following the problems of aggregating the consumption side of the economy into one representative consumer, and that of aggregating all labor markets and all workers into one representative worker. I have saved the capital aggregation problem until the last of the three because, at this stage of our knowledge of economics, it seems much less important than the other two. This probably just reflects the fact that we are still struggling with important aspects of static and stationary economies; difficulties with capital aggregation will play a more prominent role in the future, I hope, when static and stationary economies become much more perfectly understood. Yet it is the capital aggregation problem that has had by far the most ink spilt over it. Just a small sample of relevant writings are: Robinson (1953, 1956); Champernowne (1953); Solow (1956a,b, 1963); Samuelson (1962); Bruno, Burmeister and Sheshinski (1966); Harcourt (1972); Stiglitz (1973); Bliss (1975); Patterson and Schott (1979); and Burmeister (1980).

The most revealing exposition of what the capital theory debate was all about may be in the pages of Mirrlees and Stern (1973) – especially in the discussions of the papers by Stiglitz and Hahn. Originally Joan Robinson (1953) had considered capital aggregation as a problem even before Solow's (1956a) fundamental paper on economic growth. Solow did away with the knife-edge instability problems of the older Harrod–Domar model by having a variable capital output ratio which could adjust in order to maintain full employment at all times. The 'warranted' rate of growth based on the demand side of the economy, including the demand for investment goods, could be brought into line with the 'natural' rate of growth based on the supply of labor, adjusted to accommodate labor-saving technical progress. The adjustment was achieved by varying both the real wage and the real rate of interest in order to clear the three markets for output, labor and capital simultaneously. The result was a stable economy tending toward a steady state, or at least toward a balanced growth path.

As was shown in particular by Hahn (1966, 1968), the achievement of long-run steady states or balanced growth becomes a great deal harder in the presence of many capital goods. Even with perfect foresight, once there is more than one capital good, a steady-state equilibrium typically becomes unstable; it will only be reached if the initial prices of the various capital goods are exactly right, reflecting precisely appropriate expectations about future prices of capital goods.

Mathematically, this reflects the stability properties of any dynamic system. In continuous time, if there is only one state variable, the asymptotic properties of solutions to a differential equation in that single state variable are relatively trivial. Either the solution converges to one of the (possibly many) stable stationary states of the system, or else it diverges off to infinity. In the Solow (1956a) growth model, the quantity of the single capital good is the one state variable of the system. The corresponding co-state variable is the price of capital or, if the price of output is normalized to one, a discounted average of future rates of return to capital. This too is stable. However, if time is discrete, or if there is more than one state variable in the system, no such simple asymptotic properties are possible. Even the asymptotic dynamics of the system may be chaotic – i.e. effectively indistinguishable from random – even though the system may be deterministic, like the procedures used to calculate 'random' numbers within a computer (see Brock 1986).

Like so many of the other assumptions I have been considering, this one too hardly appears to be worth further discussion. Any realistic model of an economy is bound to have many state variables – e.g. one state variable to represent each individual's wealth, for a start. It is entirely appropriate that the capital theory debate should have been put away into some dusty corner because it has now become irrelevant; most economists simply do not use one capital good growth models any more, except for teaching purposes. Would that the same were true of the other assumptions considered in this essay.

21 PRODUCT MARKETS ARE PERFECTLY COMPETITIVE, OR AT LEAST CONTESTABLE

The theory ... [of contestable markets] ... offers a standard for public policy that is far broader and more widely applicable than the traditional ideal of perfect competition. (Baumol, 1985, p.326)

[T]he whole notion of normal profits is beset with difficulties. Mr Shove [(1933)] has pointed out that there is not one level of normal profits, but two. The level of profits which will attract new enterprise into an industry is usually higher than the level which is just sufficient to retain existing enterprise. Entry into a trade is likely to involve considerable expense, and often involves, as Marshall was fond of pointing out, a lean period of low profits before the name of the firm becomes known. (Robinson, 1934, and 1951a, p.23)

In the previous sections of this essay, I have hardly stepped outside the bounds of Walrasian equilibrium analysis, suitably modified in all sorts of ways such as recognizing bounds on individuals' rationality and forethought, and the desirability of introducing 'distortionary' taxes both in order to achieve desirable redistribution of real purchasing power, and also to finance the provision of public goods. The only major departure from modified Walrasian analysis was in Section 15, where we were forced to recognize the impossibility of having perfect Walrasian credit markets in anything like a recognizable form, because credit rationing is inevitable. Yet obviously it would be remiss of me not to discuss at all the theme of Joan Robinson's first major book, *The Economics of Imperfect Competition*. Moreover, one can find in contemporary economic theology the assertion that monopoly power exercized by labor unions is bad, and one of the prominent causes of persistent unemployment, whereas monopoly power exercized by large corporations is largely illusory. I am unable to conclude this essay without a few remarks upon this topic, prompted especially by the recent work of Baumol and his associates on the subject of contestable markets (Baumol, 1982, 1985; Baumol, Panzar and Willig, 1982).

Baumol (1985, pp.315–16) provides this definition: 'a market is perfectly contestable if any entrant who changes his mind can exit without sacrificing any of the investment the entry decision required. For then the entrant risks nothing by taking advantage of any earning opportunity presented by the high price of an incumbent.'

Thus, perfect contestability effectively requires that 'hit and run' entry should be possible for any firm in the competitive fringe. The authors' favorite example seems to be that of airlines, with large fixed costs for each plane in the fleet, but flexibility (in the present deregulated state of the industry in the US) to adjust routes very quickly to take advantage of any overpricing by the incumbent airlines. The airline industry may be an extremely special case, however, and even within it there may be more impediments to hit and run entry than is required for anything like perfect contestability. For one thing, it takes airlines quite a while to earn a good reputation on a new route, and to build up passenger goodwill or loyalty.

The most plausible example of a perfectly contestable market, oddly enough, is a labor market. For unless a union or an association is granted special privileges under the law, which have the effect of placing a statutory restriction on entry into the trade or profession, it is surely in labor markets where hit and run entry is easiest, especially for unions of blue collar workers rather than for statutorily restricted professional associations of lawyers, doctors, etc. Yet there are many economists who claim that it is labor unions who abuse their monopoly power and cause unemployment by holding wage rates too high; many of those same economists seem too willing to suggest that the monopoly power of even the largest corporations is largely illusory, despite the obstacles to hit and run entry into the relevant industries.

The principal conclusions of this new theory of contestable markets are that all supernormal profits will be removed by the threat of hit and run entry, as will any choice of inputs which does not minimize total cost, and cross-subsidization of any of a firm's many different products which a potential entrant is capable of producing. Moreover, if an industry can sustain more than one competing firm producing a single common product, the threat of hit and run entry by new firms drives each of the two or more existing firms to charge a price equal to marginal cost, as in the usual theory of perfect competition.

This is a large body of work which does us the service of at last treating seriously the theoretical problem of how a monopolistic firm interacts with a 'competitive fringe' of potential entrants. Not that it is by any means the first work to do so. Nor is it the most coherent in its modelling of the sequence of decisions that are taken by the incumbent monopolist and the potential competitors, as should be clear from the conceptual problems faced by

Mirman, Tauman and Zang (1985) in placing contestability on more secure game-theoretic foundations. When time is continuous, the theory of perfect contestability requires easily reversible fixed costs to be clearly distinguished from sunk costs, and this distinction is by no means as clear as it might be (Weitzman, 1983). Nevertheless, I propose to ignore these objections – even quibbles, perhaps – and examine what seems to be the central thesis of the work, which is that perfect contestability, rather than perfect competition, is the appropriate standard by which to judge an industry, particularly an industry with average cost curves which are decreasing for at least some important set of outputs, so that in fact a Walrasian equilibrium may well not exist.

Now, I have already raised plenty of objections to *laissez faire* perfect competition even when all industries and all firms have convex production possibility sets. These objections apply *a fortiori* to perfect contestability in more general economic environments which may have non-convex technologies. It is rather more difficult, however, to contest a more sophisticated version of perfect contestability, which recognizes the general desirability of commodity taxation, as in Diamond and Mirrlees (1971). They and Hahn (1973b) and also Mirrlees (1972) have shown that, when optimal commodity taxes are being maintained throughout, then overall production efficiency is often desirable. Thus, when all technology sets are convex, the optimal organization of industrial production in the economy can be achieved by setting uniform producer prices for the inputs and outputs of all firms. These producer prices generally differ from consumer prices through commodity taxes and subsidies. Nevertheless, all producers should have marginal rates of transformation in production equal to producer price ratios, which implies, in the case of a firm which produces a single output commodity, that the producer price should be equal to marginal cost, when cost is also evaluated in producer prices. Thus one might think that, provided taxes are set optimally so that firms do calculate their costs and revenues in terms of suitable producer prices, perfect contestability might prove to be an appropriate generalization for non-convex environments of the Diamond and Mirrlees idea of having private producers act as if they are perfect competitors, facing producer prices.

There are a number of serious difficulties with such an argument, however. For one thing, even the original Diamond and Mirrlees argument only works when any profits made by firms are taxed either at the rate of 100 per cent or else some other optimal rate, equivalent to an optimal tax on the entrepreneurial services supplied by the owners of the firm, to which profits are the imputed reward. The attempted extension to firms with non-convex consumption sets is therefore not generally valid. Moreover, it is important that optimal commodity taxes be maintained; if they are not, the case for production efficiency becomes invalid even if all firms have constant returns to scale technology sets, as shown by Diewert (1983) and Hammond (1986b).

So the attempt of Baumol and his associates, to rescue *laissez faire* from those who object to apparently inefficient monopolies, fails because it is fundamentally misconceived. Perfect competition simply is not the right normative standard with which to judge industrial performance, even when all technology sets are convex, and so neither is perfect contestability when there are non-convexities.

There is a more subtle but much weaker defence of perfect competition available, to which I alluded back in Section 10. This is that perfect competition may well be unavoidable when the power of government agencies to monitor and to tax transactions is limited, so that an underground economy flourishes. The presence of small private corporations makes little difference to that argument. With significant economies of scale in some industries, however, there may not exist any Walrasian equilibrium in the underground economy. Then we face new problems that have scarcely been considered in the existing work on incentive constraints in general economic environments. It is very unlikely, however, that we shall see perfect contestability playing the same role in the analysis with non-convexities that perfect competition did when there were many agents with convex possibility sets. Hit and run entry, after all, is rarely possible in practice. Even if it were, government efforts to tax and monitor the transactions of economic agents are surely rather easier when at least one of the parties is a corporation that has grown large because of economies of scale. So is the administration of prices by a public body seeking to act in the public interest, as well as the taxation of price increases in an effort to check inflation, whenever prices are now administered by corporate managers acting in their own interest. The welfare economics of industrial organization is likely to be a much more complex topic than the theory of contestable markets suggests.

22   NEOCLASSICAL ECONOMICS NEED NOT BE THEOLOGICAL

Progress is slow partly from mere intellectual inertia. In a subject where there is no agreed procedure for knocking out errors, doctrines have a long life. A professor teaches what he was taught, and his pupils, with a proper respect and reverence for teachers, set up a resistance against his critics for no other reason than that it was he whose pupils they were. (Robinson, 1962, p.76)

'I require all members of the class to have a personal daily copy of *The Wall Street Journal*. I advise them that The Journal will be the textbook for the rest of their professional lives.' (A named professor at a far from unknown American university, quoted in an advertisement for a scheme whereby professors of economics get a free subscription if they sign up seven or more of their class for reduced subscriptions.)

I have discussed some of the commonly used assumptions – more properly regarded as assertions, actually – which underlie a great deal of contemporary economic policy analysis. Far too many of them have been found to be untenable. The empirical assertions have little grounding in reality, especially when consumers are treated as individuals and firms are considered one at a time, rather than being aggregated together. Some assertions amount to ethical assumptions, yet are rarely recognized as such. When they are, these ethical assertions are also highly questionable. It is high time to purge neoclassical economics of such theology. But, if we do, will there be anything left? The last assumption which I shall discuss is that there can be. Of course, there is a danger of a paradox here, because the assumption that theology is inessential to neoclassical economics is itself almost a theological assumption. But if this difficulty were fatal, it would also be the case that value-free science of any kind is impossible.

The essential content of neoclassical economic theory is that individual agents follow regular predictable behavior patterns and that their environment adjusts to their decisions in a way that produces some kind of overall equilibrium. Joan Robinson was a strident critic of such theory for at least two reasons. The first reason was the patent unreality of most of the assumptions of neoclassical economics, which this essay has already discussed at length. The second reason was the use of neoclassical economic theory to support *laissez faire* economic theology which to her, as a disciple of Keynes, was obviously perverted. She was unable to see how neoclassical theory in any form could be disentangled from *laissez faire* theology. This is entirely understandable, since it is only some of the most recent developments in economic theory and in the theory of games which are beginning to make such disentanglement possible. This essay was concerned with some of them, but by no means all, since I chose to concentrate upon how Walrasian general equilibrium theory can be modified in order to relax some of the most contentious assertions underlying *laissez faire* theology.

As the discussion of Section 21 begins to make clear, however, there are still many problems in trying to escape from Walrasian theory, and deal seriously with the monopoly power of the modern corporation. It is probably this monopoly power, moreover, which will ultimately provide the best theoretical explanation for the Keynesian phenomenon of money wages and prices being rigid in the (very) short run, especially once it is recognized that price setters are no more exempt from bounded rationality than any other kind of economic agent (see, for instance, Kalecki, 1971; Nikaido, 1975; Negishi, 1979; Hart, 1982; Akerlof and Yellen, 1985b; and Roberts 1987). The problems of imperfect competition and of Keynesian disequilibrium were ones which Joan Robinson wrestled with all her life. My failure to discuss them more than I have reflects partly the fact that this essay is already long, but much more the inherent difficulties of these problems. It is just as well that Joan Robinson devoted herself to never allowing us to forget them for long, as well as to making the theologically inclined as uncomfortable as possible whenever they tried to sweep such inconvenient problems under the carpet.

It is perhaps less fortunate that her legitimate objections to neoclassical ideology did not allow her to understand that some of us might still want to look for a residual neoclassical theory, purged of theology. In particular, she never really seemed to give due credit to Hicks' (1946) notion of temporary equilibrium, as brought up to date by Grandmont (1982, 1983) and others. This does allow history to have a role to play in determining the equilibrium outcome of the economy, and is not the usual sterile notion of a stationary state or long-period equilibrium to which she was quite right in objecting so strongly. Indeed, it seems that her justified hostility to the behavioral assumptions of standard neoclassical theory – unbounded rationality, unbounded foresight, etc. – was so strong that it completely blinded her to the possibility of having useful equilibrium models of an economy, particularly for purposes of prediction, without all the neoclassical baggage. And if this really is a failing, she would certainly have wished me to point it out – preferably long ago, when there would still have been time for her to respond – for as she wrote in the first volume of her *Collected Economic Papers*, dedicated to her pupils: 'I do not add the usual reservation to my acknowledgement to my pupils, for I think they should be held responsible for any errors that they have allowed me to maintain.'

Nor even are the recent harsh criticisms of Weintraub (1985) entirely misplaced, though they only tell a small part of the whole story. Contemporary economists cannot afford to forget what Joan Robinson stood for, unless they are content to remain as the slaves of business interests. Above all, our teaching of economics, especially of welfare economics, or of what is meant by good economic policy, clearly needs to depart from the present state, which is still far too often close to how Joan Robinson described it twenty-eight years ago in Bombay's *Economic Weekly*:

> The serious student is often attracted to economics by humanitarian feeling and patriotism – he wants to learn how to choose economic policies that will increase human welfare. Orthodox teaching deflects these feelings into the dreary desert of so-called Welfare Economics, a system of ideas based on a mechanistic psychology of a completely individualistic pursuit of pleasure and avoidance of pain, which no one believes to be a correct account of human nature, dished up in algebraic formulae which do not even pretend to be applicable to actual data. As he goes deeper into the matter, he reads some brilliant and subtle authors who debunk the whole subject and show conclusively that its methodology was inadmissible. For most, this is too bitter a pill to swallow and they desperately cling to some scraps of what they have learned because no other way has been offered of formulating the vague benevolent feelings with which they began.

The serious student was hoping, also, to learn something that would help him to make up his mind on the great question that lies open before all the developing countries. How far can private-enterprise capitalism be made to serve national ends? . . .

He soon begins to notice that, without any overt discussion of the question, he is being indoctrinated with notions soaked in a prejudice for *laissez-faire*. This is partly the result of a mere time-lag. Nineteenth-century economic teaching was built up round the conception of the merits of the free market, and in particular, of free trade (which at that time favoured British national interests, though it was damaging to India); the modern text-books are still much influenced by the masters of that period. It is partly the result of the choice of curriculum. A large proportion of his time is taken up by the theory of relative prices. The question of the distribution of *given* resources amongst alternative ends, subject to the condition that there is an equitable (and not very unequal) distribution of purchasing power among the families concerned, lends itself to exhibiting a free market in a favourable light; the student is required to work out exercises devised to show how, in these conditions, interference with the free play of the forces of supply and demand causes harm to the individuals who make up the market. All this is very complicated, and when modified by modern embellishments such as the theory of oligopoly and imperfect competition, may well occupy a year of lectures and reading. If the serious student has the hardihood to ask: But are resources given, and is income distributed equitably? he is made to feel foolish. Do you not understand that these are necessary simplifying assumptions for the analysis of prices? You cannot expect to do everything at once.

It is true that we cannot, in the time available, teach everything we would like. But why do we pick out for treatment just that selection of topics that is least likely to raise any questions of fundamental importance? (Robinson, 1965, pp.2–3)

References

Akerlof, G. A. (1981) 'Jobs as Dam Sites', *Review of Economic Studies*, 48: 37–49.
Akerlof, G. A. and J. L. Yellen (1985a) 'Can Small Deviations from Rationality Make Significant Differences to Economic Equilibria?' *American Economic Review*, 75: 708–20.
Akerlof, G. A. and J. L. Yellen (1985b) 'A Near-Rational Model of the Business Cycle, with Wage and Price Inertia', *Quarterly Journal of Economics* 100: 823–38.
Archibald, G. C. (1959) 'Welfare Economics, Ethics, and Essentialism', *Economica*, 26: 316–27.
Archibald, G. C. and R. G. Lipsey (1958) 'Value and Monetary Theory: Temporary *versus* Full Equilibrium', *Review of Economic Studies*, 26: 1–22.
Arrow, K. J. (1951) 'An Extension of the Basic Theorems of Classical Welfare Economics', pp. 507–32 of J. Neyman (ed) *Proceedings of the Second Berkeley*

Symposium on Mathematical Statistics and Probability (Berkeley: University of California Press).

Arrow, K. J. (1953, 1964) 'Le rôle des valeurs boursières pour la répartition la meilleure des risques', *Econometrie* (Colloques Internationaux du Centre National de la Recherche Scientifique) 11: 41–7, translation of 'The Rôle of Securities in the Optimal Allocation of Risk-Bearing', *Review of Economic Studies*, 31: 91–6.

Aumann, R. J. (1964) 'Markets with a Continuum of Traders', *Econometrica*, 32: 39–50.

Aumann, R. J. (1966) 'Existence of Competitive Equilibria in Markets with a Continuum of Traders,' *Econometrica*, 34: 1–17.

Ausubel, L. (1984) 'Partially Revealing Equilibria', PhD dissertation, Stanford University.

Axelrod, R. (1981) 'The Emergence of Cooperation among Egoists', *American Political Science Review*, 75: 306–18, reprinted as ch. 19, pp.320–9 of Campbell and Sowden (eds.) (1985).

Axelrod, R. (1984) *The Evolution of Cooperation* (New York: Basic Books; Cambridge: Cambridge University Press).

Barro, R. J. (1974) 'Are Government Bonds Net Wealth?' *Journal of Political Economy*, 82: 1095–1117.

Barro, R. J. (1976) 'Rational Expectations and the Role of Monetary Policy', *Journal of Monetary Economics*, 2: 1–33.

Baumol, W. J. (1982) 'Contestable Markets: An Uprising in the Theory of Industry Structure', *American Economic Review*, 72: 1–15.

Baumol, W. J. (1985) 'Industry Structure Analysis and Public Policy', ch. 8, pp.311–27 of G. R. Feiwel (ed) (1985).

Baumol, W. J., Panzar J. C. and Willig R. D. (1982) *Contestable Markets and the Theory of Industry Structure* (San Diego: Harcourt, Brace, Jovanovich).

Becker, G. S. (1962) 'Irrational Behavior and Economic Theory', *Journal of Political Economy*, 70: 1–13.

Bergson, A. (1983) 'Pareto on Social Welfare', *Journal of Economic Literature*, 21: 40–6.

Bernheim, B. D., and K. Bagwell (1988) 'Is Everything Neutral?', *Journal of Political Economy* (to appear).

Bliss, C. J. (1975) *Capital Theory and the Distribution of Income* (Amsterdam: North-Holland).

Brock, W. A. (1986) 'Distinguishing Random and Deterministic Systems: Abridged Version' *Journal of Economic Theory*, 40: 168–95.

Broome, J. (1978) 'Choice and Value in Economics,' *Oxford Economic Papers*, 30: 313–33.

Bruno, M., Burmeister E. and Sheshinski E. (1966) 'Nature and Implications of the Reswitching of Techniques', *Quarterly Journal of Economics*, 81: 526–53.

Buchanan, J. M. and W. C. Stubblebine (1962) 'Externality', *Economica*, 29: 371–84; reprinted as pp.199–212 of K. J. Arrow and T. Scitovsky (eds.) *Readings in Welfare Economics* (Homewood: Irwin; London: George Allen & Unwin Ltd).

Burmeister, E. (1980) *Capital Theory and Dynamics* (Cambridge: Cambridge University Press).

Campbell, R. and Sowden L. (eds) (1958) *Paradoxes of Rationality and Cooperation* (Vancouver: University of British Columbia Press).

Cass, D. and K. Shell (1983) 'Do Sunspots Matter?' *Journal of Political Economy*, 91: 193–227.

Champernowne, D. G. (1953) 'The Production Function and the Theory of Capital: A Comment', *Review of Economic Studies*, 21: 112–35.

Clower, R. W. (1963a) 'Classical Monetary Theory Revisited', *Economica*, 30: 165–70.

Clower, R. W. (1963b) 'Permanent Income and Transitory Balances: Hahn's Paradox', *Oxford Economic Papers*, 15: 177–90.

Clower, R. W. (ed) (1969) *Monetary Theory* (Harmondsworth: Penguin Modern Economics Readings).

Clower, R. W., and M. L. Burstein (1960) 'The Classical Invariance Principle', *Review of Economic Studies*, 28: 32–6.

Coase, R. H. (1937) 'The Nature of the Firm', *Economica*, 4: 386–405, reprinted as ch. 16, pp.331–51 of G. J. Stigler and K. E. Boulding (eds) (1952) *Readings in Price Theory* (Homewood: Irwin).

Coase, R. H. (1960) 'The Problems of Social Cost', *Journal of Law and Economics*, 3: 1–44.

Coles, J. L. (1986) 'Nonconvexity in General Equilibrium Labor Markets', *Journal of Labor Economics*, 4: 415–37.

Coles, J. L. and P. J. Hammond (1986) 'Walrasian Equilibrium without Survival: Existence, Efficiency and Remedial Policy', Stanford University Institute for Mathematical Studies in the Social Sciences, Economics Technical Report No. 483, presented at the 5th World Congress of the Econometric Society, Boston.

Copeland, T. and D. Galai (1983) 'Information Effects on the Bid Ask Spread', *Journal of Finance*, 38: 1457–69.

Crawford, V. P. and E. M. Knoer (1981) 'Job Matching with Heterogeneous Firms and Workers', *Econometrica*, 49: 437–50.

Cuddington, J. T. (1981) 'Money, Income, and Causality in the United Kingdom, *Journal of Money, Credit, and Banking*, 13: 342–51.

Dasgupta, P. S. and P. J. Hammond (1980) 'Fully Progressive Taxation', *Journal of Public Economics*, 13: 141–54.

Deaton, A. (1986) 'Life-Cycle Models of Consumption: Is the Evidence Consistent with the Theory?', National Bureau of Economic Research, Working Paper No. 1910.

Debreu, G. (1951) 'The Coefficient of Resource Utilization', *Econometrica*, 19: 273–92.

Debreu, G. (1959) *Theory of Value: An Axiomatic Analysis of General Equilibrium* (New York: John Wiley).

Demsetz, H. (1967) 'Toward a Theory of Property Rights', *American Economic Review, Papers and Proceedings*, 57: 347–59.

Diamond, P. A. and J. A. Mirrlees (1971) 'Optimum Taxation and Public Production, I and II', *American Economic Review*, 61: 8–27 and 261–78.

Diewert, W. E. (1983) 'Cost-Benefit Analysis and Project Evaluation: A Comparison of Alternative Approaches', *Journal of Public Economics*, 22: 265–302.

Feiwel, G. R. (1982) 'Samuelson and the Age after Keynes', ch. 14, pp.202–43 of G. R. Feiwel (ed) *Samuelson and Neoclassical Economics* (Boston: Kluwer-Nijhoff).

Feiwel, G. R. (ed) (1985a) *Issues in Contemporary Microeconomics and Welfare* (London: Macmillan).

Feiwel, G. R. (ed) (1985b) *Issues in Contemporary Macroeconomics and Distribution* (London: Macmillan).

Feiwel, G. R. (1985c) 'Quo Vadis Macroeconomics? Issues, Tensions and Challenges,' ch. 1, pp.1–100 of Feiwel (ed) (1985b).

Friedman, M. (1953) *Essays in Positive Economics* (Chicago: University of Chicago Press).

Friedman, M. (1970) *The Counter-Revolution in Monetary Theory* (London: Institute of Economic Affairs).

Friedman, M. and A. J. Schwartz (1963) *A Monetary History of the United States, 1867–1960* (Princeton: Princeton University Press).

Friedman, M. and A. J. Schwartz (1982) *Monetary Trends in the United States and the United Kingdom: Their Relationship to Income, Prices, and Interest Rates, 1867–1975* (Chicago: University of Chicago Press).

Funaki, Y. and M. Kaneko (1986) 'Economies with Labor Indivisibilities: I, Optimal Tax Schedules, and II, Competitive Equilibria under Tax Schedules', *Economic Studies Quarterly*, 37: 11–29 and 199–222.

Gale, D. M. (1982, 1983) *Money: In Equilibrium*, and *Money: In Disequilibrium* (Welwyn: Nisbet).

Gintis, H. (1972a) 'A Radical Analysis of Welfare Economics and Individual Development', *Quarterly Journal of Economics*, 86: 572–99.

Gintis, H. (1972b) 'Consumer Behavior and the Concept of Sovereignty: Explanations of Social Decay', *American Economic Review, Papers and Proceedings*, 62: 267–78.

Gintis, H. (1974) 'Welfare Criteria and Endogenous Preferences: The Economics of Education', *International Economic Review*, 15: 415–30.

Glosten, L. R. and P. R. Milgrom (1985) 'Bid, Ask, and Transaction Prices in a Specialist Market with Heterogeneously Informed Traders', *Journal of Financial Economics*, 14: 71–100.

Gorman, W. M. (1953) 'Community Preference Fields', *Econometrica*, 22: 63–80.

Gorman, W. M. (1976) 'Tricks with Utility Functions', in M. Artis and R. Nobay (eds) *Essays in Economic Analysis* (Cambridge: Cambridge University Press).

Graaff, J. de V. (1957) *Theoretical Welfare Economics* (Cambridge: Cambridge University Press).

Grandmont, J.-M. (1982) 'Temporary General equilibrium Theory', ch. 19, pp.879–922 of K. J. Arrow and M. D. Intriligator (eds) *Handbook of Mathematical Economics*, Vol. II (Amsterdam: North-Holland).

Grandmont, J.-M. (1983) *Money and Value: A Reconsideration of Classical and Neoclassical Monetary Economics* (Cambridge: Cambridge University Press).

Guesnerie, R. and K. W. S. Roberts (1984) 'Effective Policy Tools and Quantity Controls', *Econometrica*, 52: 59–86.

Hahn, F. H. (1966) 'Equilibrium Dynamics with Heterogeneous Capital Goods', *Quarterly Journal of Economics*, 80: 633–46.

Hahn, F. H. (1968) 'On Warranted Growth Paths', *Review of Economic Studies*, 35: 175–84.

Hahn, F. H. (1973a) *On the Notion of Equilibrium in Economics: An Inaugural Lecture* (Cambridge: Cambridge University Press).

Hahn, F. H. (1973b) 'On Optimum Taxation', *Journal of Economic Theory*, 6: 96–106.

Hall, R. E. (1982) 'The Importance of Lifetime Jobs in the US Economy', *American Economic Review*, 72: 716–24.

Hammond, P. J. (1979) 'Straightforward Individual Incentive Compatibility in Large Economies', *Review of Economic Studies*, 46: 263–82.

Hammond, P. J. (1980) 'Cost Benefit Analysis as a Planning Procedure', ch. 8, pp.221–49 of D. A. Currie and W. Peters (eds) *Contemporary Economic Analysis*, Vol. 2 (London: Croom Helm).

Hammond, P. J. (1982) '*The Economics of Justice* and the Criterion of Wealth Maximization', *Yale Law Journal*, 91: 1493–507.

Hammond, P. J. (1985) 'Welfare Economics', ch. 13, pp.405–34 of G. R. Feiwel (ed) (1985a).

Hammond, P. J. (1986a) 'Consequentialist Social Norms for Public Decisions', ch. 1, pp.3–27 of W. P. Heller, R. M. Starr, and D. A. Starrett (eds) *Social Choice and Public Decision Making: Essays in Honor of Kenneth J. Arrow*, vol. I (Cambridge: Cambridge University Press).

Hammond, P. J. (1986b) 'Project Evaluation by Potential Tax Reform', *Journal of Public Economics*, 30: 1–36.

Hammond, P. J. (1987) 'Markets as Constraints: Multilateral Incentive Compatibility in Continuum Economies', *Review of Economic Studies*, 54: 399–412.

Harcourt, G. C. (1972) *Some Cambridge Controversies in the Theory of Capital* (Cambridge: Cambridge University Press).

Harsanyi, J. C. (1954) 'Welfare Economics of Variable Tastes', *Review of Economic Studies*, 21: 204–13.

Hart, O. D. (1982) 'A Model of Imperfect Competition with Keynesian Features', *Quarterly Journal of Economics*, 97: 109–38.

Hausman, J. A. (1981) 'Exact Consumer's Surplus and Deadweight Loss', *American Economic Review*, 71: 662–76.

Hendry, D. F., and N. R. Ericsson (1983) 'Assertion without Empirical Basis: An Econometric Appraisal of Friedman and Schwartz' "Monetary Trends in the . . . United Kingdom" ', pp.45–101 of *Monetary Trends in the United Kingdom*, Bank of England Panel of Academic Consultants, Panel Paper No. 22.

Hicks, J. R. (1946) *Value and Capital* (2nd edn) (Oxford: Oxford University Press).

Hildenbrand, W. (1974) *Core and Equilibrium in Large Economies* (Princeton: Princeton University Press).

Howitt, P. (1979) 'The Role of Speculation in Competitive Price-Dynamics', *Review of Economic Studies*, 46: 613–29.

Hurwicz, L. (1979) 'On Allocations Attainable through Nash Equilibria', *Journal of Economic Theory*, 21: 140–65.

Hurwicz, L. and D. Schmeidler (1978) 'Outcome Functions which Guarantee the Existence and Pareto Optimality of Nash Equilibria', *Econometrica*, 46: 1447–74.

Jaffé, W. (1977) 'The Normative Bias of the Walrasian Model: Walras versus Gossen', *Quarterly Journal of Economics*, 91: 371–87.

Johnson, H. G. (1971) 'The Keynesian Revolution and the Monetarist Counter-Revolution', *American Economic Review, Papers and Proceedings*, 61: 1–14.

Jordan, J. and R. Radner (1982) 'Rational Expectations in Microeconomic Models: An Overview', *Journal of Economic Theory*, 26: 201–23.

Kalecki, M. (1971) *Selected Essays in the Dynamics of the Capitalist Economy, 1933–1970* (Cambridge: Cambridge University Press).

Kay, J. A. and M. A. King (1978) *The British Tax System* (Oxford: Oxford University Press).

Keynes, J. M. (1936) *The General Theory of Employment, Interest and Money* (London: Macmillan).

King, M. A. (1983) 'Welfare Analysis of Tax Reforms Using Household Data', *Journal of Public Economics*, 21: 183–214.

Kreps, D. M., P. Milgrom, J. Roberts, and R. Wilson (1982) 'Rational Cooperation in the Finitely Repeated Prisoners' Dilemma', *Journal of Economic Theory*, 27: 245–52.

Kreps, D. M. and R. Wilson (1982) 'Sequential Equilibrium', *Econometrica*, 50: 863–94.

Kyle, A. S. (1985) 'Continuous Auctions and Insider Trading', *Econometrica*, 53: 1315–35.

Lerner, A. P. (1947) *The Economics of Control* (London and New York: Macmillan).

Lerner, A. P. (1972) 'The Economics and Politics of Consumer Sovereignty', *American Economic Review, Papers and Proceedings*, 62: 258–66.

Lipsey, R. G. and K. J. Lancaster (1956) 'The General Theory of Second Best', *Review of Economic Studies*, 24: 11–32.

Lloyd, C. L. (1964) 'The Real-Balance Effect and the Slutsky Equation', *Journal of Political Economy*, 72: 295–9.

Lloyd, C. L. (1968) 'Two Classical Monetary Models', ch. 12, pp.305–17 of J. N.

Wolfe (ed) *Value, Capital and Growth: Papers in Honour of Sir John Hicks* (Edinburgh: Edinburgh University Press).

Lucas, R. E. (1972, 1983) 'Expectations and the Neutrality of Money', and 'Corrigendum', *Journal of Economic Theory*, 4: 103–24, and 31: 197–9.

Lucas, R. E. (1978) 'Asset Prices in an Exchange Economy', *Econometrica*, 46: 1429–45.

Malcomson, J. M. (1981) 'Unemployment and the Efficiency Wage Hypothesis', *Economic Journal*, 91: 848–66.

Markandya, A. (1978) 'The Quality of Current Approximations to the Measurement of Compensation Costs', *Oxford Economic Papers*, 30: 423–33.

Maskin, E. S. (1980) 'On First Best Taxation', ch. 1, pp.9–22 of D. Collard, R. Lecomber and M. Slater (eds) *Income Distribution: The Limits to Redistribution* (Bristol: Scientechnica).

Meade, J. E. (1955) *Trade and Welfare: Mathematical Supplement* (Oxford: Oxford University Press).

Milgrom, P. and N. Stokey (1982) 'Information, Trade, and Common Knowledge', *Journal of Economic Theory*, 26: 17–27.

Mirman, L. J., Y. Tauman and I. Zang (1985) 'Monopoly and Sustainable Prices as a Nash Equilibrium in Contestable Markets', ch. 9, pp.328–39 of G. R. Feiwel (ed) (1985a).

Mirrlees, J. A. (1969) 'The Evaluation of National Income in an Imperfect Economy', *Pakistan Development Review*, 9: 1–13.

Mirrlees, J. A. (1972) 'On Producer Taxation', *Review of Economic Studies*, 39: 105–11.

Mirrlees, J. A. and N. H. Stern (eds) (1973) *Models of Economic Growth* (London: Macmillan).

Muth, J. (1961) 'Rational Expectations and the Theory of Price Movements', *Econometrica*, 29: 315–35.

Myerson, R. B. (1983) 'A Dynamic Microeconomic Model with Durable Goods and Adaptive Expectations', *Journal of Economic Behaviour and Organization*, 4: 309–51.

Negishi, T. (1979) *Microeconomic Foundations of Keynesian Macroeconomics* (Amsterdam: North-Holland).

Nikaido, H. (1975) *Monopolistic Competition and Effective Demand* (Princeton: Princeton University Press).

Nozick, R. (1974) *Anarchy, State, and Utopia* (New York: Basic Books; Oxford: Blackwell).

Pareto, V. (1913) 'Il massimo di utilità per una collettività in sociologia', *Giornale degli Economisti e Rivista di Statistica*, 46: 337–41.

Patinkin, D. (1965) *Money, Interest and Prices* (2nd edn) (New York: Harper & Row).

Patterson, K. D. and K. Schott (eds) (1979) *The Measurement of Capital: Theory and Practice* (London: Macmillan).

Pazner, E. A. and E. Sadka (1980) 'Excess-Burden and Economic Surplus as Consistent Welfare Indicators', *Public Finance/Finances Publiques*, 35: 439–49.

Posner, R. A. (1981) *The Economics of Justice* (Cambridge, Mass.: Harvard University Press).

Prescott, E.C. and R. Mehra (1980) 'Recursive Competitive Equilibrium: The Case of Homogeneous Households', *Econometrica*, 48: 1365–79.

Rader, T. (1964) 'Edgeworth Exchange and General Economic Equilibrium', *Yale Economic Essays* 4: 133–80.

Radner, R. (1972) 'Existence of Equilibrium Plans, Prices and Price Expectations in a Sequence of Markets', *Econometrica*, 40: 289–303.

Rawls, J. (1971) *A Theory of Justice* (Cambridge, Mass.: Harvard University Press; Oxford: Oxford University Press).

Roberts, D. J. (1987) 'General Equilibrium Analysis of Imperfect Competition: An Illustrative Example', ch. 12, pp. 415–38 of G. R. Feiwel (ed) *Arrow and the Ascent of Modern Economic Theory* (London: Macmillan).

Robinson, J. (1932) *Economics is a Serious Subject* (Cambridge: Heffer).

Robinson, J. (1933) 'The Theory of Money and the Analysis of Output', *Review of Economic Studies* 1: 22–6, reprinted in Robinson (1951a, 1979b).

Robinson, J. (1934) 'What is Perfect Competition?', *Quarterly Journal of Economics*, 49: 104–20, reprinted in Robinson (1951a).

Robinson, J. (1936) 'Disguised Unemployment' *Economic Journal*, 46: 225–37, reprinted in Robinson (1973).

Robinson, J. (1946–7) 'The Pure Theory of International Trade', *Review of Economic Studies*, 14: 98–112, reprinted in Robinson (1951a).

Robinson, J. (1949) 'Mr Harrod's Dynamics', *Economic Journal*, 59: 68–85, reprinted in Robinson (1951a).

Robinson, J. (1951a) *Collected Economic Papers* (Oxford: Blackwell; New York: Augustus M. Kelley).

Robinson, J. (1951b) 'The Rate of Interest', *Econometrica*, 19: 92–111, reprinted in Robinson (1979b).

Robinson, J. (1953) 'The Production Function and the Theory of Capital', *Review of Economic Studies*, 21: 81–106, partly reprinted in Robinson (1979b).

Robinson, J. (1956; 2nd edn, 1965) *The Accumulation of Capital* (London: Macmillan).

Robinson, J. (1960) *Collected Economic Papers*, Vol. II (Oxford: Blackwell).

Robinson, J. (1962) *Economic Philosophy* (Watts, and Harmondsworth: Pelican, 1964).

Robinson, J. (1965) *Collected Economic Papers*, Vol. III (Oxford: Blackwell).

Robinson, J. (1971) *Economic Heresies; Some Old-Fashioned Questions in Economic Theory* (New York: Basic Books; London: Macmillan).

Robinson, J. (1972) 'The Second Crisis of Economic Theory', *American Economic Review, Papers and Proceedings*, 62: 1–10, reprinted in Robinson (1979b).

Robinson, J. (1973) *Collected Economic Papers*, Vol. IV (Oxford: Blackwell).

Robinson, J. (1979a) *Collected Economic Papers*, Vol. V (Oxford: Blackwell).

Robinson, J. (1979b) *Contributions to Modern Economics* (Oxford: Blackwell).

Robinson, J. (1980a) *What are the Questions? and Other Essays* (Armonk, NY: M. E. Sharp).

Robinson, J. (1980b) *Further Contributions to Modern Economics* (Oxford: Blackwell).

Robinson, J. (1985) 'The Theory of Normal Prices and Reconstruction of Economic Theory', ch. 4, pp.157–65 of Feiwel (ed) (1985b).

Roth, A. E. (1982) 'The Economics of Matching: Stability and Incentives', *Mathematics of Operations Research* 7: 617–28.

Russell, T. and R. Thaler (1985) 'The Relevance of Quasi Rationality in Competitive Markets', *American Economic Review*, 75: 1071–82.

Samuelson, P. A. (1950) 'Evaluation of Real National Income', *Oxford Economic Papers*, 2: 1–29.

Samuelson, P. A. (1956) 'Social Indifference Curves', *Quarterly Journal of Economics*, 70: 1–22.

Samuelson, P. A. (1958) 'An Exact Consumption-Loan Model of Interest with or without the Social Contrivance of Money', *Journal of Political Economy*, 66: 467–82.

Samuelson, P. A. (1962) 'Parable and Realism in Capital Theory: The Surrogate Production Function', *Review of Economic Studies*, 29: 193–206.

Samuelson, P. A. (1963) 'Problems of Methodology – Discussion' *American Economic Review, Papers and Proceedings*, 53: 231–6.

Samuelson, P. A. (1968) 'What Classical and Neo-Classical Monetary Theory Really Was', *Canadian Journal of Economics*, 1: 1–15.

Sargent, T. J. (1973) 'Rational Expectations, the Real Rate of Interest, and the Natural Rate of Unemployment', *Brookings Papers on Economic Activity*, 2: 429–72.

Sargent, T. J. and N. Wallace (1975) 'Rational Expectations, the Optimal Monetary Instrument and the Optimal Money Supply Rule', *Journal of Political Economy*, 83: 241–54.

Schmeidler, D. (1982) 'A Condition Guaranteeing that the Nash Allocation is Walrasian', *Journal of Economic Theory*, 28: 376–8.

Schmeidler, D. and K. Vind. (1972) 'Fair Net Trades', *Econometrica*, 40: 637–42.

Sebenius, J. K. and J. Geanokopolos (1983) 'Don't Bet on It', *Journal of the American Statistical Association*, 78: 424–26.

Selten, R. (1965) 'Spieltheoretische Behandlung eines Oligopolmodells mit Nachfrageträgheit', *Zeitschrift für die gesamte Staatswissenschaft*, 121: 301–24, and 667–89.

Selten, R. (1973) 'A Simple Model of Imperfect Competition, where 4 Are Few and 6 Are Many', *International Journal of Game Theory*, 2: 25–55.

Sen, A. K. (1973) 'Behaviour and the Concept of Preference', *Economica*, 40: 241–59.

Sen, A. K. (1976) 'Real National Income', *Review of Economic Studies*, 43: 19–39.

Sen, A. K. (1977) 'Starvation and Exchange Entitlements: A General Approach and Its Application to the Great Bengal Famine', *Cambridge Journal of Economics*, 1: 33–59.

Sen, A. K. (1979) 'The Welfare Basis of Real Income Comparisons: A Survey', *Journal of Economic Literature*, 17: 1–45.

Sen, A. K. (1981a) *Poverty and Famines: An Essay on Entitlement and Deprivation* (Oxford: Clarendon Press).

Sen, A. K. (1981b) 'Ingredients of Famine Analysis: Availability and Entitlements', *Quarterly Journal of Economics*, 95: 433–64.

Shefrin, H. (1981) 'Games with Self-Generating Distributions', *Review of Economic Studies*, 48: 511–19.

Shove, G. F. (1933) 'The Imperfection of the Market: A Further Note', *Economic Journal*, 43: 113–24.

Shoven, J. B. and J. Whalley (1984) 'Applied General-Equilibrium Models of Taxation and International Trade: An Introduction and Survey', *Journal of Economic Literature*, 22: 1007–51.

Shubik, M. (1973) 'Commodity Money, Oligopoly, Credit and Bankruptcy in a General Equilibrium Model', *Western Economic Journal*, 11: 24–38.

Shubik, M. (1974) 'Money, Trust, and Equilibrium Points in Games in Extensive Form', *Zeitschrift für Nationalökonomie*, 34: 365–85.

Simon, H. A. (1982) *Models of Bounded Rationality* (2 vols.) (Cambridge, Mass.: MIT).

Simon, H. A. (1983) *Reason in Human Affairs* (Stanford: Stanford University Press).

Sims, C. A. (1980) 'Macroeconomics and Reality', *Econometrica*, 48: 1–48.

Solow, R. M. (1956a) 'A Contribution to the Theory of Economic Growth', *Quarterly Journal of Economics*, 70: 65–94.

Solow, R. M. (1956b) 'The Production Function and the Theory of Capital', *Review of Economic Studies*, 23: 101–8.

Solow, R. M. (1963) *Capital Theory and the Rate of Return* (Amsterdam: North-Holland).

Spear, S. E. (1985) 'Rational Expectations in the Overlapping Generations Model', *Journal of Economic Theory*, 35: 251–75.

Stigler, G. (1967) 'Imperfections in the Capital Market', *Journal of Political Economy*, 85: 287–92.

Stiglitz, J. E. (1973) 'The Badly Behaved Economy with the Well-Behaved Production Function', and 'Recurrence of Techniques in a Dynamic Economy', chs. 6 and 7, pp.117–37 and 138–61 of Mirrlees and Stern (1973).

Stiglitz, J. E. (1974) 'Wage Determination and Unemployment in LDC's: The Labor Turnover Model', *Quarterly Journal of Economics*, 88: 194–227.

Stiglitz, J. E. (1976) 'The Efficiency Wage Hypothesis, Surplus Labor, and the Distribution of Income in LDC's', *Oxford Economic Papers*, 28: 185–207.

Stiglitz, J. E. (1984) 'Theories of Wage Rigidity', National Bureau of Economic Research, Working Paper No. 1442.

Stiglitz, J. E. and A. Weiss (1981) 'Credit Rationing in Markets with Imperfect Information', *American Economic Review*, 71: 393–410.

Stiglitz, J. E. and A. Weiss (1983) 'Incentive Effects of Terminations: Applications to the Credit and Labor Markets', *American Economic Review*, 73: 912–27.

Stiglitz, J. E. and A. Weiss (1985) 'Credit Rationing', mimeo.

Stoker, T. M. (1986) 'Simple Tests of Distributional Effects on Macroeconomic Equations' *Journal of Political Economy*, 94: 763–95.

Sugden, R. (1982) 'On the Economics of Philanthropy', *Economic Journal* 92: 341–50.

Sugden, R. (1983) *Who Cares? An Economic and Ethical Analysis of Private Charity and the Welfare State* (London: The Institute of Economic Affairs).

Townsend, R. (1979) 'Optimal Contracts and Competitive Markets with Costly State Verification', *Journal of Economic Theory*, 21: 1–29.

Tversky, A. and D. Kahneman (1981) 'The Framing of Decisions and the Psychology of Choice', *Science*, 211: 453–58.

Tversky, A. and D. Kahneman (1986) 'Rational Choice and the Framing of Decisions', *Journal of Business*, 59 (Supplement): 67–94.

Varian, H. (1984) 'Social Indifference Curves and Aggregate Demand', *Quarterly Journal of Economics*, 99: 403–14.

Weintraub, E. R. (1985) 'Joan Robinson's Critique of Equilibrium: An Appraisal', *American Economic Review, Papers and Proceedings*, 75: 146–169.

Weitzman, M. L. (1983) 'Contestable Markets: An Uprising in the Theory of Industry Structure: Comment', *American Economic Review*, 73: 486–87.

Weiss, A. (1980) 'Job Queues and Layoffs in Labor Markets with Flexible Wages', *Journal of Political Economy*, 88: 526–38.

Williams, B. A. O. (1973) 'A Critique of Utilitarianism', in J. J. C. Smart and B. Williams, *Utilitarianism: For and Against* (Cambridge: Cambridge University Press).

Willig, R. (1976) 'Consumer Surplus without Apology', *American Economic Review*, 66: 589–97.

Wong, S. (1973) 'The "F-twist" and the Methodology of Paul Samuelson', *American Economic Review*, 63: 312–25.

Yellen, J. T. (1984) 'Efficiency Wage Models of Unemployment', *American Economic Review, Papers and Proceedings*, 74: 200–5.

Zabalza, A. (1982) 'Compensating and Equivalent Variations, and the Deadweight Loss of Taxation', *Economica*, 49: 355–9.

5 The Economic Principles of Joan Robinson

Lawrence R. Klein

The fundamental nature of the underlying economic problem, i.e. *economics* in the abstract, has never really been fathomed because in the 200 or more years since Adam Smith's *Wealth of Nations* we have had a continuous outpouring of fresh textbooks on 'Principles' without ever finding the definitive statement. True enough, Alfred Marshall and Paul Samuelson both survived many editions, but there are always new statements forthcoming, attempting to displace the masterful renditions. Many of these new attempts succeed. There seems to be an ever ready market for a new packaging of the fundamentals of our subject.

Joan Robinson was most noted, and will be remembered, for her handling of intricate and subtle problems in economics that go far beyond 'Principles'. Her treatment of capital theory, employment theory, imperfect competition, Marxian theory, and many other advanced subjects, which justly establish her claims to fame are not for the economics beginner. They are not really for the undergraduate, but her 'Introduction' (Book I) to *The Accumulation of Capital* (1956) is a truly masterful statement of economic principles, especially principles of macroeconomics, that could serve better than almost any other 'Principles' textbook in laying bare the fundamental aspects of our subject to the beginner – if not the freshman beginner, at least to the second- or third-year student who is reconsidering the subject at a slightly more advanced (intermediate) level.

Of course, Joan Robinson could make, with apparent ease, that masterful statement because she knew her subject so well, as a truly creative person. She had a beautiful sense of the English language and a way of putting arguments in economics that would be victorious over her opponents' views simply on the basis of her flair for style of expression.

I have had my share of arguments with Joan Robinson, although I was never a close colleague and I do not feel that my own work was strongly influenced by her, except on a few specific issues. However, I was much taken by her 'Introduction' when writing a review of *Accumulation of Capital*.

Some universities have insisted that students learn basic subjects by reading 'the Great Works' as textbooks. This would never do for much of modern science and technological subjects, but it would surely be a feasible route to learning for many philosophical, humanistic, or purely intellectual subjects. 'The Great Books' would not be suitable for use in those branches of economics that rely heavily on institutional detail or on newly discovered concepts – econometrics, game theory, linear programming, portfolio analysis, foreign exchange speculation, and the like. But for an introduction to the principles of our subject, principles that should remain invariant over the decades or centuries, classic statements by masters ought to serve as well as the flashy packages in the fresh spate of modern textbooks.

Joan Robinson has not been out of this world long enough to be grouped with the statements of Smith, Marx, Ricardo, J. S. Mill, or Marshall, but she had an unusual command of the subject and is senior enough to have her statement about the underlying principles of macroeconomics serve as a definitive version of the issues.

The student will not learn much about the functioning of the Federal Reserve System, the Bank of England, the Chicago Board of Trade, the International Monetary Fund, any modern corporation, any modern trade union, or farmers' cooperative, but the student will learn a great deal about the structure of the capitalist market economy, why it differs from the socialist economy, and the way the different macroeconomic departments of a total system fit together. It is better for the new student to know these underlying patterns, as exposed by Joan, than to be able to draw a box diagram of the chain of command within the Federal Reserve System, replete with duration of appointment, responsibility to Congress, etc.

The institutional knowledge must be taught (memorized) in order that the student be knowledgeable as a good citizen who knows what is happening in the everyday world, but deeper understanding of the institutional detail and the way it fits into the system as a whole is better conveyed by Joan's presentation.

She began her overview of the economy as a whole by discussing the economic life of the robin. This is a more primitive starting point than the typical Robinson Crusoe economy often used by economic theorists (see Lange, 1936). Although Joan started out at a more primitive level than did the Crusoe analysts, by the time she completed the sixty pages of introduction she had gone more fully into the workings of a modern economic system. I believe that she provided the maximum framework that did not become institution-specific. Yet her presentation is very compact and can be consumed in just a few sittings. To me, it is far more satisfying than the Crusoe studies.

Joan Robinson, trained in the best neoclassical traditions of Cambridge economics, leaned towards Marxism after a certain spell, and the introduction is replete with insightful references and contrasts for slave, socialist, and capitalist economies.

Basically the book and its introduction are concerned with the working of the capitalist economic system. She began her analysis of capitalism by discussing finance in relation to kinds of income. She distinguished between equities and debt instruments, the latter being grouped into mortgages, bills, and bonds. This seems to me to be immensely useful for the modern undergraduate even though there is no treatment of anything like passbook savings, certificates of deposits, mutual funds, and other institutional devices. Nevertheless, she distilled the essence of the working of credit markets.

At the end of her discussion of *rentier* income she made a typical Robinsonian remark with deep meaning, beautifully put, 'A holding of Old Consols is nothing but a placement, and a soft-boiled egg is nothing but a consumption good. As always with economic categories we must rely on rough common sense distinctions, not on scholastic definitions of words more precise than the concepts to which they apply.' Here, she was illustrating the point that economic concepts are not necessarily precise but do separate clearly at the extremes, a Consol and an egg. But it is refreshing to find her impatient about being overly pedantic and willing to settle for some common-sense distinctions. What could be better advice for the young student?

In connection with her discussion of *finance* as an income-making activity she came down hard on the socio-economic usefulness of wheeler-dealers who make money by speculating. She said, 'This involves a utilisation of finance, and an expenditure of brain power and nerves, which are quite out of proportion to any contribution that they make to the productivity of the economy.' By this remark, she showed her social and philosophical biases quite clearly.

With the treatment of professional income, where she had first-hand experience and information, she showed a keen appreciation of the concepts associated with human capital. It is no surprise that she attributed a significant role to education for training and building a good stock of professional personnel.

In summing up the chapter on sources of income, Joan showed how close she was to real world events and how far she had gone from the robin's or Crusoe's economy. She pointed out that individuals have income from several sources, that people play dual roles (e.g. rentier and entrepreneur), that professional people invest their earnings in portfolios that generate income from various sources. One may have thought of Joan as having lived in an ivory tower for the greater part of her life, but she was keenly aware of the practical world of everyday economics in practice.

A difficult point to get across immediately to freshmen in economics is the distinction between income and wealth. Her second chapter starts out with a discussion of the meaning of wealth and explained the distinction in her own admirable style. She fully reflected her Marshallian training in this section of the introduction.

With respect to the discussion of the concept of wealth, Joan Robinson's biases on the possibilities of defining and measuring wealth come out clearly. She wrote, 'Economics is the scientific study of wealth, and yet we cannot measure wealth. This seems a sad state of affairs.' From the point of her research for *The Accumulation of Capital*, through her debates with economists from the other Cambridge, she stood by her arguments about the impossibility of doing more than listing a 'Who's Who of Capital'. On this point of debate, I always felt that she was excessively negative and came out on the wrong side, even to the extent of carrying misconceptions about the meaning of production function, but in the chapter on wealth in the introduction she introduced the students to two related issues of great importance. She drew, early on in the whole professional discussion of the issue, an excellent distinction between *expenditures* for consumer goods and *consumption* (see Friedman, 1957; Modigliani and Brumberg, 1955). This distinction has played an important role in the most sophisticated estimates of the consumption function for macroeconometric models.

A second excellent discussion in the chapter is her subtle treatment of the index number problem for measuring purchasing power. She recognized that there was no unique solution for a best measure and showed why we must be satisfied with bracketing the true number between upper and lower bounds. She ended the discussion of purchasing power with one of her inimitable, beautiful statements: 'If a consumer from either group is dropped into the life of the other, he feels himself (according to temperament) in a desert of privation or in a paradise of unaccustomed delights.'

The chapter on money is good. It is clear, but not particularly outstanding in comparison with some of the other chapters. Again she showed a flair for language: 'It is necessary, to keep the system running, that the plain man should act as though he thought that, as he quaintly puts it: A shilling is a shilling, even when he is vaguely aware that it is not.' Remarks like these should surely be able to drive home the point for the beginner student that the value of money depends on our confidence in the monetary system.

She also made a very shrewd observation about the nature of the capitalist system by noting that it was *necessary* to invent money in order to develop a capitalist economy. Regardless of Joan's views about the optimality or desirability of capitalism, she really knew what constituted the system.

In the chapter on capital and income, Joan Robinson showed herself to be a capable 'woman of affairs'. The public debt was no mystery. She noted that it was built up for financing military expeditions, or 'blowing things to bits'.

In discussing finance market strategies, she showed a clear grasp of fundamentals of portfolio management. She would have recommended stretching out bond portfolios when interest rates were expected to fall over a horizon of a year or two. That was precisely the kind of advice that portfolio managers were giving in the early autumn of 1982 as the Federal Reserve shifted towards an easier monetary stance. If Joan Robinson had been sitting on the various finance committees that command my attention she would have been taken in as an astute advisor.

Finally, she fully recognized and appreciated the role of profit as a driving force in our economy. She observed that the search for profits, for their own sake, led to the remarkable development of an economic system that has been shown to be both viable and capable of generating great wealth. Strange as it may seem to have that observation from a woman of the left, we can only conclude that she was a good one for calling things just as they are.

Although Joan Robinson was a member and key contributor to the inner circle of thinkers who worked with Keynes, to develop the *General Theory*, she was no 'knee-jerk' Keynesian in a crude sense. In her consumption and investment she saw clearly the double-edged nature of savings. Savings add to the sources of fund flows to make capital accumulation possible, yet consumption, not savings, is needed to maintain effective demand at a high level and also capital formation. She pointed out clearly the paradoxical nature of the capitalist system and the role of thrift in it.

Her final chapter of the introduction deals with the meaning of equilibrium. She did not operate or analyze the economy in a static framework; therefore equilibrium for her meant a smoothly moving system, one in which a 'regular rate of sales at steady prices is taking place'. She was not thinking about constant sales or prices, but steady sales and prices. The magnitudes can thus move in a steady time pattern. She coined the concept of *tranquility* for an economy

> when it develops in a smooth regular manner without internal contradictions or external shocks, so that expectations based on past experience are very confidently held, and are in fact constantly fulfilled and therefore renewed as time goes by. In a state of perfect tranquility the prices ruling today, in every market, are those which were expected to rule today when any relevant decisions were taken in the past.

This is an excellent early appreciation of the role of expectations and their relation to decision making in a dynamic setting.

She went on to develop notions of a higher state of equilibrium – *lucidity* (awareness of the situation in all markets), and *harmony* (understanding and acceptance of the rules of the game by all economic participants).

These are all highly abstract and unrealistic conditions, and she was fully aware of their remoteness from the actual state of affairs. She reasoned that if such conditions were to prevail there would have been no capitalist incentives to break out in new directions, yet she also recognized that if disturbances to these ideal conditions were too severe the economy would have collapsed. She ended the whole discussion with a typical gemlike expression, in the Robinsonian manner: 'The persistence of capitalism till today is evidence that certain principles of coherence are imbedded in its confusion.'

If an anthology of economics were to be put together with contributions from the great minds of our times – over the 200 plus years since the *Wealth of Nations* or over the twentieth century, no matter which – in order to provide comprehensive understanding of our whole scheme of thought, my choice for the 'Principles' component to provide an overview of the working of the system as a whole would be Joan Robinson's Introduction from *The Accumulation of Capital*. It would stand nicely beside Joseph Schumpeter's treatment of the circular flow in his *Theory of Economic Development* (1934). These are the thoughts of geniuses which should inspire our beginner students. They represent economics at its best.

References

Friedman, M. (1957) *A Theory of the Consumption Function* (Princeton: National Bureau of Economic Research).

Lange, O. (1936) 'The Place of Interest in the Theory of Production', *Review of Economic Studies*, 3 (June): 159–92.

Modigliani, F. and R. Brumberg, (1955) 'Utility Analysis and the Consumption Function: An Interpretation of Cross Section Data', K. Kurihara (ed), *Post Keynesian Economics* (London: George Allen & Unwin).

Robinson, J. (1956) *The Accumulation of Capital* (London: Macmillan).

Schumpeter, J. (1934) *The Theory of Economic Development* (Cambridge, Mass.: Harvard University Press).

6 Theoretic Models: Mathematical Form and Economic Content

Gerard Debreu*

I

The steady course on which mathematical economics has held for the past four decades sharply contrasts with its progress during the preceding century, which was marked by several major scientific accidents. One of them occurred in 1838, at the beginning of that period, with the publication of Augustin Cournot's *Recherches sur les Principes Mathématiques de la Théorie des Richesses*. By its mathematical form and by its economic content, his book stands in splendid isolation in time; and in explaining its date historians of economic analysis in the first half of the nineteenth century must use a wide confidence interval.

The University of Lausanne was responsible for two others of those accidents. When Léon Walras delivered his first professional lecture there on 16 December 1870, he had held no previous academic appointment; he had published a novel and a short story but he had not contributed to economic theory before 1870; and he was exactly 36. The risk that his university took was vindicated by the appearance of the *Eléments d'Economie Politique Pure* in 1874–7. For Vilfredo Pareto, who succeeded Walras in his chair in 1893, it was also a first academic appointment; he had not contributed to economic theory before 1892; and he was 45. This second gamble of the University of Lausanne paid off when Pareto's *Cours d'Economie Politique* appeared in 1896–7, followed by his *Manuel d'Economie Politique* in 1909, and by the article 'Economie Mathématique' in 1911.

In the contemporary period of development of mathematical economics, profoundly influenced by John von Neumann, his article of 1928 on games and his paper of 1937 on economic growth also stand out as major accidents, even in a career with so many facets.

*This chapter is a revised version of the Frisch Memorial Lecture delivered at the Fifth World Congress of the Econometric Society held at MIT, 17–24 August 1985, published in *Econometrica*, 54 (6): 1259–70. Permission to use is acknowledged.

I thank Irma Adelman, George and Helen Break, Jean-Michel Grandmont, Birgit Grodal, Werner Hildenbrand, Alan Manne, Andreu Mas-Colell, Herbert Scarf, John Shoven, George Stigler, Karl Vind, and Jean Waelbroeck for many helpful comments. The support of the National Science Foundation is also gratefully acknowledged.

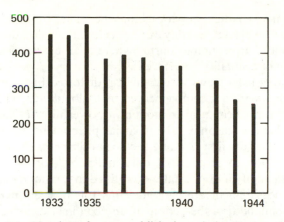

Figure 6.1   Number of pages published yearly by *Econometrica*

The date of the foundation of our society, and its very existence, do not seem to have been historically determined either. Charles Roos and Carl Christ have told about the visit made by Ragnar Frisch and Roos to Irving Fisher's home in New Haven for a weekend in April 1928. Their purpose was to discuss the possibility of founding a society that would bring together economics, mathematics and statistics. Fisher, who had attempted to organize such a society as early as 1912, was pessimistic but at length 'said that if Frisch and Roos could name one hundred people in the world who would join ... he would become an enthusiastic partner'. Delighted with Fisher's response, Frisch and Roos set to work, but 'after three days they had to give up with about seventy likely prospects. Fisher looked over their list and suggested about a dozen additional names. He was quite surprised that they had found so many and he agreed that eighty justified going ahead' (Christ, 1952, pp.5–6). Eventually the Econometric Society was born in Cleveland, Ohio, on 29 December 1930, and two years later *Econometrica* began publication with the financial backing of Alfred Cowles. The boldness of the move made in Cleveland can be read in the statistics of the number of pages published yearly by *Econometrica*. The data for the period 1933–40 suggest a downward trend, which became more distinct under the impact of World War II. The founding fathers of our society may have wondered on occasion whether its birth was premature. In one respect it was not. Roos has recounted how in 1926–7 he had unsuccessfully submitted an article in turn to an economic, to a statistical, and to a mathematical journal. Each one of the three editors offered to publish his paper if the author would eliminate the parts dealing with the other two fields, which Roos was unwilling to do. The creation of *Econometrica* was intended to break such impasses, and in his editorial for the first issue Frisch stated, 'no paper shall be rejected solely on the ground of being too mathematical. This applies no matter how highly involved the mathematical apparatus may be.' That promise was honored, and *Econometrica* played, notably during its first three decades, an irreplaceable role as a leading economic journal where the use of unusual mathematical tools did not disqualify an article.

The preceding local views would yield a distorted historical perception, however, if they were not complemented by a global view which sees in the development of mathematical economics a powerful, irresistible current of thought. Deductive reasoning about social phenomena invited the use of mathematics from the first. Among the social sciences, economics was in a privileged position to respond to that invitation, for two of its central concepts, commodity and price, are quantified in a unique manner, as soon as units of measurement are chosen. Thus for an economy with a finite number of commodities, the action of an economic agent is described by listing his input, or his output, of each commodity. Once a sign convention distinguishing inputs from outputs is made, the action of an agent is represented by a point in the commodity space, a finite-dimensional real vector space. Similarly, the prices in the economy are represented by a point in the price space, the real vector space dual of the commodity space. The rich mathematical structure of those two spaces provides an ideal basis for the development of a large part of economic theory.

Finite dimensional commodity and price spaces can be, and usually are, identified and treated as a Euclidean space. The stage is thus set for geometric intuition to take a lead role in economic analysis. That role is manifest in the figures that abound in the economics literature, and some of the great theorists have substituted virtuosity in reasoning on diagrams for the use of mathematical form. As for mathematical economists, geometric insight into the commodity-price space has often provided the key to the solution of problems in economic theory.

The differential calculus and linear algebra were applied to that space at first as a matter of course. By the time John Hicks' *Value and Capital* appeared in 1939, Maurice Allais' *A la Recherche d'une Discipline Economique* in 1943, and Paul Samuelson's *Foundations of Economic Analysis* in 1947, they had both served economic theory well. They would serve it well again, but the publication of the *Theory of Games and Economic Behavior* in 1944 signaled that action was also going to take new directions. In mathematical form, the book of von Neumann and Oskar Morgenstern set a new level of logical rigor for economic reasoning, and it introduced convex analysis in economic theory by its elementary proof of the MinMax theorem. In the next few years convexity became one of the central mathematical concepts, first in activity analysis and in linear programming, as the *Activity Analysis of Production and Allocation* edited by Tjalling Koopmans attested in 1951, and then in the mainstream of economic theory. In consumption theory as in production theory, in welfare economics as in efficiency analysis, in the theory of general economic equilibrium and in the theory of the core, the picture of a convex set supported by a hyperplane kept reappearing, and the supporting hyperplane theorem supplied a standard technique for obtaining implicit prices. The applications of that theorem to economics were a ready consequence of the real vector space structure of the commodity space; yet they were made more than thirty years after Minkowski proved it in 1911.

Algebraic topology entered economic theory in 1937, when von Neumann generalized Brouwer's fixed point theorem in a lemma devised to prove the existence of an optimal growth path in his model. The lag from Brouwer's result of 1911 to its first economic application was shorter than for Minkowski's result. It should, however, have been significantly longer, for von Neumann's lemma was far too powerful a tool for his proof of existence. Several authors later obtained more elementary demonstrations, and David Gale in particular based his in 1956 on the supporting hyperplane theorem. Thus von Neumann's lemma, reformulated in 1941 as Kakutani's fixed point theorem, was an accident within an accidental paper. But in a global historical view, the perfect fit between the mathematical concept of a fixed point and the social science concept of an equilibrium stands out. A state of a social system is described by listing an action for each one of its agents. Considering such a state, each agent reacts by selecting the action that is optimal for him given the actions of all the others. Listing those reactions yields a new state, and thereby a transformation of the set of states of the social system into itself is defined. A state of the system is an equilibrium if, and only if, it is a fixed point of that transformation. More generally, if the optimal reactions of the agents to a given state are not uniquely determined, one is led to associate a set of new states, instead of a single state, with every state of the system. A point-to-set transformation of the set of states of the social system into itself is thereby defined; and a state of the system is an equilibrium if, and only if, it is a fixed point of that transformation. In this view, fixed point theorems were slated for the prominent part they played in game theory and in the theory of general economic equilibrium after John Nash's one-page note of 1950.

A perfect fit of mathematical form to economic content was also found when the traditional concept of a set of negligible agents was formulated exactly. In 1881, in *Mathematical Psychics*, Francis Edgeworth had studied in his box the asymptotic equality of the 'contract curve' of an economy and of its set of competitive allocations. Basic to his proof of convergence is the fact that in his limiting process every agent tends to become negligible. A long period of neglect of his contribution ended in 1959, when Martin Shubik brought out the connection between the contract curve and the game-theoretic concept of the core. After the second impulse given in 1962 by Herbert Scarf's first extension of Edgeworth's result, a new phase of development of the economic theory of the core was under way; and in 1964 Robert Aumann formalized the concept of a set of negligible agents as the unit interval of the real line with its Lebesgue measure. The power of that formulation was demonstrated as Aumann proved that in an exchange economy with that set of agents, the core and the set of competitive allocations coincide. Karl Vind then gave, also in 1964, a different formulation of this remarkable result in the context of a measure space of agents without atoms, and showed that it is a direct consequence of Lyapunov's theorem of 1940 on the range of an atomless measure. The convexity of that range explains the convexing effect of large economies. In the important case of a set of negligible agents, it justifies the convexity assumption on aggregate sets to which economic theory frequently appeals. A privileged place was clearly marked for measure theory in mathematical economics.

An alternative formulation of the concept of a set of negligible agents was proposed by Donald Brown· and Abraham Robinson in 1972 in terms of Non-standard Analysis, created by Robinson in the early 1960s. Innovations in the mathematical tools of economic theory had not always been immediately and universally adopted in the past. In this case, the lag from mathematical discovery to economic application was exceptionally short, and Non-standard Analysis had not been widely accepted by mathematicians themselves. Predictably the intrusion of this strange, sophisticated new tool in economic theory was greeted mostly with indifference or with skepticism. Yet it led to the form given by Robert Anderson to inequalities on the deviation of core allocations from competitive allocations, which are central to the theory of the core. In the article published by Anderson in 1978 those inequalities are stated and proved in an elementary manner, but their expression was found by means of Non-standard Analysis.

The differential calculus, which had been used earlier on too broad a spectrum of economic problems, turned out in the 1970s to supply the proper mathematical machinery for the study of the set of competitive equilibria of an economy. A partial explanation of the observed state of an economic system had been provided by proofs of existence of equilibrium based on fixed point theorems. A more complete explanation would have followed from persuasive assumptions on a mathematical model of the economy ensuring uniqueness of equilibrium. Unfortunately, the assumptions proposed to that end were excessively stringent, and the requirement of global uniqueness had to be relaxed to that of local uniqueness. Even then an economy composed of agents on their best mathematical behavior (for instance, each having a concave utility function and a demand function both indefinitely differentiable) may be ill-behaved and fail to have locally unique equilibria. If one considers the question from the generic viewpoint, however, one sees that the set of those ill-behaved economies is negligible. This time the ideal mathematical tool for the proof of that assertion is Sard's theorem of 1942 on the set of critical values of a differentiable function. By providing appropriate techniques for the study of the set of equilibria, differential topology and global analysis came to occupy in mathematical economics a place that seemed to have been long reserved for them.

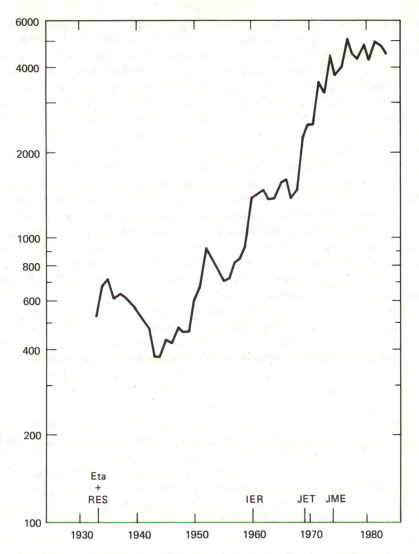

Figure 6.2   Number of pages published yearly by the leading journals in mathematical economics (Abbreviations: *Econometrica*, Eta; *Review of Economic Studies*, RES; *International Economic Review*, IER; *Journal of Economic Theory*, JET; *Journal of Mathematical Economies*, JME.)

As new fields of mathematics were introduced into economic theory and solved some of its fundamental problems, a growth-generating cycle operated. The mathematical interest of the questions raised by economic theory attracted mathematicians who in turn made the subject mathematically more interesting. The resulting expansion of mathematical economics was unexpectedly rapid. Attempting to quantify it, one can use as an index the total number of pages published yearly by the five main periodicals in the field: *Econometrica* and the *Review of Economic Studies* (which both started publishing in 1933),[1] the *International Economic Review* (1960), the *Journal of Economic Theory* (1969), and the *Journal of Mathematical Economics* (1974). The graph of that index is eloquent. It shows a first phase of decline to 1943, followed by a thirty-three-year period of exuberant, nearly exponential growth. The annual rate of increase that would carry the index exponentially from its 1944 level to its 1977 level is 8.2 per cent, a rate that implies doubling in slightly less than nine years and that cannot easily be sustained. The past eight years have indeed marked a pause that will soon resemble a stagnation phase if it persists. Among its imperfections the index gives equal weights to *Econometrica*, the *Review of Economic Studies*, and the *International Economic Review*, all of which publish articles on econometrics as well as on mathematical economics, and to the *Journal of Economic Theory* and the *Journal of Mathematical Economics*, which do not. But giving lower relative weights to the first three yields even higher annual rates of exponential growth of the index for the period 1944–77.

The sweeping movement that took place from 1944 to 1977 suggests an inevitable phase in the evolution of mathematical economies. The graph illustrating that phase hints at the deep transformation of departments of economics during those thirty-three years. It also hints at the proliferation of discussion papers and at the metamorphosis of professional journals like the *American Economic Review*, which was almost pure of mathematical symbols in 1933 but had lost its innocence by the late 1950s. The graph does not reveal, however, other changes that have altered the lives of economists. Several members of this Congress belong to the 1000-mile-a-week club, and a few may hope to emulate a high-energy physicist who travels 1000 miles a day. But jetting from colloquia to symposia, some of us will be touched by nostalgia as we evoke the memory of John von Neumann crossing the Atlantic on a liner in the 1930s and jotting down the notes for a theory of money later found in his personal papers.

II

As a formal model of an economy acquires a mathematical life of its own, it becomes the object of an inexorable process in which rigor, generality and simplicity are relentlessly pursued.

Before 1944, articles on economic theory only exceptionally met the standards of rigor common in mathematical periodicals. But several of the exceptions were outstanding, among them the two papers of von Neumann of 1928 and of 1937, and the three papers of Abraham Wald of 1935–6 on the existence of a general economic equilibrium. In 1944, the *Theory of Games and Economic Behavior* gained full rights for uncompromising rigor in economic theory and prepared the way for its axiomatization. An axiomatized theory first selects its primitive concepts and represents each one of them by a mathematical object. For instance, the consumption of a consumer, his set of possible consumptions, and his preferences are represented respectively by a point in the commodity space, a subset of the commodity space, and a binary relation in that subset. Next, assumptions on the objects representing the primitive concepts are specified, and consequences are mathematically derived from them. The economic interpretation of the theorems so obtained is the last step of the analysis. According to this schema, an axiomatized theory has a mathematical form that is completely separated from its economic content. If one removes the economic interpretation of the primitive concepts, of the assumptions and of the conclusions of the model, its bare mathematical structure must still stand. This severe test is passed only by a small minority of the papers on economic theory published by *Econometrica* and by the *Review of Economic Studies* during their first decade.

The divorce of form and content immediately yields a new theory whenever a novel interpretation of a primitive concept is discovered. A textbook illustration of this application of the axiomatic method occurred in the economic theory of uncertainty. The traditional characteristics of a commodity were its physical description, its date, and its location when in 1953 Kenneth Arrow proposed adding the state of the world in which it will be available. This reinterpretation of the concept of a commodity led, without any formal change in the model developed for the case of certainty, to a theory of uncertainty which eventually gained broad acceptance, notably among finance theorists.

The pursuit of logical rigor also contributed powerfully to the rapid expansion of mathematical economics after World War II. It made it possible for research workers to use the precisely stated and flawlessly proved results that appeared in the literature without scrutinizing their statements and their proofs in every detail. Another cumulative process could thus gather great momentum.

The exact formulation of assumptions and of conclusions turned out, moreover, to be an effective safeguard against the ever-present temptation to apply an economic theory beyond its domain of validity. And by the exactness of that formulation, economic analysis was sometimes brought closer to its ideology-free ideal. The case of the two main theorems of welfare economics is symptomatic. They respectively give conditions under which an equilibrium relative to a price system is a Pareto optimum, and under which the converse holds. Foes of state intervention read in those two theorems a mathematical demonstration of the unqualified superiority of market economies, while advocates of state intervention welcome the same theorems because the explicitness of their assumptions emphasizes discrepancies between the theoretic model and the economies that they observe.

Still another consequence of the axiomatization of economic theory has been a greater clarity of expression, one of the most significant gains that it has achieved. To that effect, axiomatization does more than making assumptions and conclusions explicit and exposing the deductions linking them. The very definition of an economic concept is usually marred by a substantial margin of ambiguity. An axiomatized theory substitutes for that ambiguous concept a mathematical object that is subjected to definite rules of reasoning. Thus an axiomatic theorist succeeds in communicating the meaning he intends to give to a primitive concept because of the completely specified formal context in which he operates. The more developed this context is, the richer it is in theorems and in other primitive concepts, the smaller will be the margin of ambiguity in the intended interpretation.

Although an axiomatic theory may flaunt the separation of its mathematical form and its economic content in print, their interaction is sometimes close in the discovery and elaboration phases. As an instance, consider the characterization of aggregate excess demand functions in an l-commodity exchange economy. Such a function maps a positive price vector into an aggregate excess demand vector, and Walras's Law says that those two vectors are orthogonal in the Euclidean commodity-price space. That function is also homogeneous of degree zero. For a mathematician, these are compelling reasons for normalizing the price vector so that it belongs to the unit sphere. Then aggregate excess demand can be represented by a vector tangent to the sphere at the price vector with which it is associated. In other words, the aggregate excess demand function is a vector field on the positive unit sphere. Hugo Sonnenschein conjectured in 1973 that any continuous function satisfying Walras's Law is the aggregate excess demand function of a finite exchange economy. A proof of the conjecture (Debreu, 1974) was suggested by the preceding geometric interpretation since any vector field on the positive unit sphere can be written as a sum of l elementary vector fields, each one obtained by projecting a positive vector on one of the l coordinate axes into the tangent hyperplane. There only remains to note that every continuous elementary vector field is the excess demand function of a mathematically well-behaved consumer. Mathematical form and economic content alternatively took the lead in the development of this proof.

The pursuit of generality in a formalized theory is no less imperative than the pursuit of rigor, and the mathematician's compulsive search for ever weaker assumptions is reinforced by the economist's awareness of the limitations of his postulates. It has, for example, expurgated superfluous differentiability assumptions from economic theory, and prompted its extension to general commodity spaces.

Akin in motivation, execution, and consequences is the pursuit of simplicity. One of its expressions is the quest for the most direct link between the assumptions and the conclusions of a theorem. Strongly motivated by aesthetic appeal, this quest is responsible for more transparent proofs in which logical flaws cannot remain hidden, and which are more easily communicated. In extreme cases the proof of an economic proposition becomes so simple that it can dispense with mathematical symbols. The first main theorem of welfare economics, according to which an equilibrium relative to a price system is a Pareto optimum, is such a case.

In the demonstration, we study an economy consisting of a set of agents who have collectively at their disposal positive amounts of a certain number of commodities and who want to allocate these total resources among themselves. By the consumption of an agent, we mean a list of the amounts of each commodity that he consumes. And by an allocation, we mean a specification of the consumption of each agent such that the sum of all those individual consumptions equals the total resources. Following Pareto, we compare two allocations according to a unanimity principle. We say that the second allocation is collectively preferred to the first allocation if every agent prefers the consumption that he receives in the second to the consumption that he receives in the first. According to this definition, an allocation is optimal if no other allocation is collectively preferred to it. Now imagine that the agents use a price system, and consider a certain allocation. We say that each agent is in equilibrium relative to the given price system if he cannot satisfy his preferences better than he does with his allotted consumption unless he spends more than he does for that consumption. We claim that an allocation in which every agent is in equilibrium relative to a price system is optimal. Suppose, by contradiction, that there is a second allocation collectively preferred to the first. Then every agent prefers his consumption in the second allocation to his consumption in the first. Therefore the consumption of every agent in the second allocation is more expensive than his consumption in the first. Consequently the total consumption of all the agents in the second allocation is more expensive than their total consumption in the first. For both allocations, however, the total consumption equals the total resources at the disposal of the economy. Thus we asserted that the value of the total resources relative to the price system is greater than itself. A contradiction has been obtained, and the claim that the first allocation is optimal has been established.

This result, which provides an essential insight into the role of prices in an economy and which requires no assumption within the model, is remarkable in another way. The two concepts that it relates might have been isolated, and its symbol-free proof might have been given early in the history of economic theory and without any help from mathematics. In fact that demonstration is a late byproduct of the development of the mathematical theory of welfare economics. But to economists who have even a casual acquaintance with mathematical symbols, the previous exercise is no more than an artificial *tour de force* that has lost the incisive conciseness of a proof imposing no bar against the use of mathematics. That conciseness is one of the most highly prized aspects of the simplicity of expression of a mathematized theory.

In close relationship with its axiomatization, economic theory became concerned with more fundamental questions and also more abstract. The problem of existence of a general economic equilibrium is representative of those trends. The model proposed by Walras in 1874–7 sought to explain the observed state of an economy as an equilibrium resulting from the interaction of a large number of small agents through markets for commodities. Over the century that followed its publication, that model came to be a common intellectual framework for many economists, theorists as well as practitioners. This eventually made it compelling for mathematical economists to specify assumptions that guarantee the existence of the central concept of Walrasian theory. Only through such a specification, in particular, could the explanatory power of the model be fully appraised. The early proofs of existence of Wald in 1935–6 were followed by a pause of nearly two decades, and then by the contemporary phase of development beginning in 1954 with the articles of Arrow and Debreu, and of Lionel McKenzie.

In the reformulation that the theory of general economic equilibrium underwent, it reached a higher level of abstraction. From that new viewpoint a deeper understanding both of the mathematical form and of the economic content of the model was gained. Its role as a benchmark was also perceived more clearly, a role which prompted extensions to incomplete markets for contingent commodities, externalities, indivisibilities, increasing returns, public goods, temporary equilibrium ...

In an unanticipated, yet not unprecedented, way greater abstraction brought Walrasian theory closer to concrete applications. When different areas of the field of computable general equilibrium were opened to research at the University of Oslo, at the Cowles Foundation, and at the World Bank, the algorithms of Scarf included in their lineage proofs of existence of a general economic equilibrium by means of fixed point theorems.

This chapter has credited the mathematical form of theoretic models with many assets. Their sum is so large as to turn occasionally into a liability, as the seductiveness of that form becomes almost irresistible. In its pursuit, researchers may be tempted to forget economic content and to shun economic problems that are not readily amenable to mathematization. I do not intend, however, to draw a balance sheet, to the debit side of which I would not do justice. Economic theory is fated for a long mathematical future, and others will have the opportunity, and possibly the inclination, to choose as a theme 'Mathematical Form v. Economic Content'.

Note

1. For its first twenty-nine years the *Review of Economic Studies* was published on an academic rather than on a calendar year basis. As a result, only one issue appeared in 1933 as against three in 1934; hence the spurious initial increase in the graph.

References

Allais, M. (1943) *A la Recherche d'une Discipline Économique* (Paris: Imprimerie Nationale).

Anderson, R. M. (1978) 'An Elementary Core Equivalence Theorem', *Econometrica*, 46, 1483–7.

Arrow, K. J. (1951) 'An Extension of the Basic Theorems of Classical Welfare Economics', in J. Neyman (ed.) *Proceedings of the Second Berkeley Symposium on Mathematical Statistics and Probability* (Berkeley: University of California Press) pp.507–32.

Arrow, K. J. (1953) 'Le Rôle des Valeurs Boursières pour la Répartition la Meilleure des Risques', *Économétrie* (Paris, Centre National de la Recherche Scientifique) 41–8.

Arrow, K. J. and G. Debreu (1954) 'Existence of an Equilibrium for a Competitive Economy', *Econometrica*, 22, 265–90.

Arrow, K. J. and F. H. Hahn (1971) *General Competitive Analysis* (San Francisco: Holden Day).

Arrow, K. J. and M. D. Intriligator (eds) (1981–5) *Handbook of Mathematical Economics*, Vols. I, II and III (Amsterdam: North-Holland).

Auman, R. J. (1964) 'Markets with a Continuum of Traders', *Econometrica*, 32, 39–50.

Balasko, Y. (1986) *Foundations of the Theory of General Equilibrium* (London: Academic Press).

Brouwer, L. E. J. (1911) 'Über Abbildung von Mannigfaltigkeiten', *Mathematische Annalen*, 71, 97–115.

Brown, D. J. and A. Robinson (1972) 'A Limit Theorem on the Cores of Large Standard Exchange Economies', *Proceedings of the National Academy of Sciences of the USA*, 69, 1258–60.

Christ, C. (1952) 'History of the Cowles Commission 1932–1952', in *Economic Theory and Measurement, A Twenty Year Research Report 1932–1952*, Cowles Commission for Research in Economics (Chicago: University of Chicago Press).

Cournot, A. (1838) *Recherches sur les Principes Mathématiques de la Théorie des Richesses* (Paris: L. Hachette).

Debreu, G. (1951) 'The Coefficient of Resource Utilization', *Econometrica*, 19, 273–92.

Debreu, G. (1952) 'A Social Equilibrium Existence Theorem', *Proceedings of the National Academy of Sciences*, 38, 886–93.

Debreu, G. (1959) *Theory of Value: An Axiomatic Analysis of Economic Equilibrium* (New York: Wiley).

Debreu, G. (1970) 'Economies with a Finite Set of Equilibria', *Econometrica*, 38, 387–92.

Debreu, G. (1974) 'Excess Demand Functions', *Journal of Mathematical Economics*, 1, 15–21.

Debreu, G. (1977) 'The Axiomatization of Economic Theory', unpublished lecture given at the University of Bonn on 22 April, 1977.

Debreu, G. (1982) 'Existence of Competitive Equilibrium', chapter 15 in: K. J. Arrow and M. D. Intriligator (eds) (1981–5).

Dierker, E. (1974) *Topological Methods in Walrasian Economics* (Berlin: Springer Verlag).

Dierker, E. (1975) 'Gains and Losses at Core Allocations', *Journal of Mathematical Economics*, 2, 119–28.

Dierker, E. (1982) 'Regulator Economies', chapter 17 in: K. J. Arrow and M. D. Intriligator (eds) (1981–5).

Edgeworth, F. Y. (1881) *Mathematical Psychics* (London: Kegan Paul).

Frisch, R. (1933) 'Editorial', *Econometrica*, 1, 1–4.

Gale, D. (1956) 'The Closed Linear Model of Production', in *Linear Inequalities and Related Systems*, H. W. Kuhn and A. W. Tucker (eds) (Princeton: Princeton University Press) pp.285–303.

Hildenbrand, W. (1974) *Core and Equilibria of a Large Economy* (Princeton: Princeton University Press).

Hildenbrand, W. (1982) 'Core of an Economy', chapter 18 in: K. J. Arrow and M. D. Intriligator (eds) (1981–5).

Hicks, J. R. (1939) *Value and Capital* (Oxford: Clarendon Press).

Kakutani, S. (1941) 'A Generalization of Brouwer's Fixed Point Theorem', *Duke Mathematical Journal*, 8, 457–59.

Koopmans, T. C. (ed) (1951) *Activity Analysis of Production and Allocation*, (New York: Wiley).

Lyapunov, A. A. (1940) 'Sur les fonctions-vecteurs complètement additives', *Izvestija Akademii Nauk SSSR*, 4, 465–78.

Mantel, R. (1974) 'On the Characterization of Aggregate Excess Demand', *Journal of Economic Theory*, 7, 348–53.

Mas-Colell, A. (1985) *The Theory of General Economic Equilibrium: A Differentiable Approach* (Cambridge: Cambridge University Press).

McKenzie, L. W. (1954) 'On Equilibrium in Graham's Model of World Trade and Other Competitive Systems', *Econometrica*, 22, 147–61.

Minkowski, H. (1911) 'Theorie der konvexen Körper', *Gesammelte Abhandlungen*, II, 131–229 (Leipzig-Berlin: Teubner).

Nash, J. F. (1950) 'Equilibrium Points in N-Person Games', *Proceedings of the National Academy of Sciences of the USA*, 36, 48–9.

Neumann, J. von (1928) 'Zur Theorie der Gesellschaftsspiele', *Mathematische Annalen*, 100, 295–320.

Neumann, J. von (1937) Über ein ökonomisches Gleichungssystem und eine Verallgemeinerung des Brouwerschen Fixpunktsatzes', *Ergebnisse eines mathematischen Kolloquiums*, 8, 73–83.

Neumann, J. von and O. Morgenstern (1944) *Theory of Games and Economic Behavior* (Princeton: Princeton University Press).

Pareto, V. (1896–7) *Cours d'Economie Politique* (Lausanne: Rouge).

Pareto, V. (1909) *Manuel d'Économie Politique* (Paris: Giard).

Pareto, V. (1911) 'Economie Mathématique', *Encylcopédie des Sciences Mathématiques* (Paris: Gauthier-Villars), tome 1, vol. 4, 591–640.

Robinson, A. (1966) *Non-standard Analysis* (Amsterdam: North-Holland).

Roos, C. F. (1948) 'A Future Role for the Econometric Society in International Statistics', *Econometrica*, 16, 127–34.

Samuelson, P. A. (1947) *Foundations of Economic Analysis* (Cambridge, Mass.: Harvard University Press).

Sard, A. (1942) 'The Measure of the Critical Points of Differentiable Maps', *Bulletin of the American Mathematical Society*, 48, 883–90.

Scarf, H. (1962) 'An Analysis of Markets with a Large Number of Participants', in *Recent Advances in Game Theory*, The Princeton University Conference.

Scarf, H. (1973) (with the collaboration of T. Hansen), *The Computation of Economic Equilibria* (New Haven: Yale University Press).

Scarf, H. (1982) 'The Computation of Equilibrium Prices: An Exposition', chapter 21 in: K. J. Arrow and M. D. Intriligator (eds) (1981–5).

Scarf, H. E. and J. B. Shoven (1984) *Applied General Equilibrium Analysis* (Cambridge: Cambridge University Press).

Shubik, M. (1959) 'Edgeworth Market Games', in *Contributions to the Theory of Games, Vol. IV, Annals of Mathematical Studies*, 40 (Princeton: Princeton University Press).

Smale, S. (1981) 'Global Analysis and Economics', chapter 8 in: K. J. Arrow and M. D. Intriligator (eds) (1981–5).

Sonnenschein, H. (1973) 'Do Walras' Identity and Continuity Characterize the Class of Community Excess Demand Functions?', *Journal of Economic Theory*, 6, 345–54.

Vind, K. (1964) 'Edgeworth-allocations in an Exchange Economy with Many Traders', *International Economic Review*, 5, 165–77.

Wald, A. (1935) Über die eindeutige positive Lösbarkeit der neuen Produktionsgleichungen', *Ergebnisse eines mathematischen Kolloquiums*, 6, 12–20.

Wald A. (1936a) Über die Productionsgleichungen der ökonomischen Wertlehre', *Ergebnisse eines mathematischen Kolloquiums*, 7, 1–6.

Wald A. (1936b) 'Über einige Gleichungssysteme der mathematischen Ökonomie', *Zeitschrift für Nationalökonomie*, 7, 637–70.

Walras, L. (1874–7) *Éléments d'Économie Politique Pure* (Lausanne: L. Corbaz).

7 An Essay in Synergetic Economics

Richard M. Goodwin*

When Roy Harrod (1948) said that, since investment raised demand and higher demand led to more investment, (a) he completed the Keynesian system; (b) he demonstrated the instability of capitalism; and (c) he contradicted a basic tenet of traditional economic analysis. When a firm or an individual makes an investment, any influence on its or his demand is negligible. This apparent contradiction between micro and macro has to be resolved and its resolution should be illuminating. The physicist faces a somewhat similar problem to that of the economist: he has a very large number of variables, the individual behavior of which he cannot hope to predict. The German physicist Haken (1983) has proposed a suggestive approach called 'synergetics'. One or a few parameters may act in such a way as to produce uniform changes in the behavior of very large numbers of independent entities; he calls this 'self-organization'.

Such a conceptualization seems appropriate to some aspects of economics. Individual industries or markets show very diverse behavior, some rising, some falling, some steady. But then, from time to time, gradually they all, or most, begin to move in the same direction, though at different rates. To explain this one can proceed as follows: a decline, following an expansion, means that, with wages high and excess capacity, profits are drastically reduced to low or negative values. The desperate search for profit leads to the implementation of new processes or new goods, which require prior investments, investments which are not inhibited by the existence of excess capacity, nor do they require increased demand. If these new productive structures are large enough, or pervasive enough in their impact, they will drive the economy increasingly into the region where more and more firms reach the threshold where they experience the need to invest in increased capacity. This excites a 'self-ordering' of the economy into a general state of expansion. Even though this threshold is a region not a point, it seems

*I offer this brief essay as a tribute to the memory of one of the more remarkable persons I have ever known. Joan Robinson was an embodiment of 'the desire and pursuit of the whole' and her passing is a great loss to her friends, and, though often unacknowledged, to the profession as a whole. She had an uncanny and rare ability to unravel the daunting complexities of economic life by the exercise of logic alone. To this austere activity she dedicated unselfishly the bulk of her adult life. For the many of us who stood in awe and admiration of the purity and power of her devotion to the understanding of our world, a light has been extinguished.

appropriate to call it a *bifurcation* from a stable state to an unstable one. Previously, the economy was tending towards the level of output determined by demand and would level off if the demand remained constant. Once enough firms have begun investing in extensions of existing facilities, the economy's growth is self-sustaining, until inhibited by some exogenous constraint.

It is easy to see this in aggregative terms. If the rate of change of output is set equal to the difference between demand and output, thus

$$\varepsilon \dot{q}^- = aq + A(t) - q ,$$

$A(t)$ being all exogenous real demand. The system is stable to its multiplier value $A/1 - a$. Calling κ the capital–output ratio and letting excess capacity go to zero, the economy, in deviations from equilibrium, becomes

$$\dot{q}/q = \frac{1-a}{\kappa - \varepsilon}, \text{ where } \kappa > 1 > \varepsilon, a > 0, \text{ so that } \frac{1-a}{\kappa - \varepsilon} > 0.$$

Consequently the system grows exponentially, having bifurcated from stability to instability. When the economy reaches the region of full employment, the rate of growth must decline, so that the accelerator cuts out; the system bifurcates back to the previous stable state.

The problem is to explain how these two self-ordered states are produced in a decentralized economy of thousands of enterprises. No single firm, or grouping of firms, has a significant, direct effect on its own demand. Therefore the familiar multiplier-accelerator mechanism is not relevant. It was a serious shortcoming of Schumpeter's original exposition of his theory of innovations, that he based it on single market analysis. Even more disastrous was the fact that he firmly and totally rejected the Keynesian doctrine of the determination of the output by effective demand. Potentially this idea provides the missing element in his own theory: however, it cannot be deployed in partial equilibrium analysis.

Consider a large number, n, of sectors producing goods, with inputs linearly variable with output, and a stock of durable capital goods similarly variable. To keep to essentials, let the flow matrix $[a]$ include labor inputs and the consumption resulting therefrom. Choose the largest indecomposable sub-set of sectors, so that all sectors are interdependent, directly or indirectly. Divide real exogenous demands into $A(t)$ and innovational investment, $B(t)$. With excess capacity

$$q_d = [a] \, q + A + B, \text{ and } [\varepsilon] \dot{q} = q_d - q ,$$

so that equilibrium outputs are

$$\{\hat{q}\} = [I - a]^{-1} \{ \{A(t)\} + \{B(t)\} \}.$$

B may consist of the investment demands of a single large sector or a constellation of sectors. Measuring in deviations from equilibrium, the dynamics of the system are

$$[\varepsilon]\dot{q} = -[I-a]q + [b]\dot{q}$$

$$[[b]-[\varepsilon]]\dot{q} = [I-a]q$$

where the *i*th column of $[b]$ remains zero until $q_i \geqslant$ desired capacity.

When and if, as a result of innovational investment, or state expenditure, or export demand, the various sectors experience rising output, first one, then several, then many, will reach the critical point of desired capacity. They then begin induced, accelerational investment, which is endogenous to the system. The conception is analogous to the familiar notion of reaching the critical temperature in starting a fire, or to the less familiar notion of critical mass in an atomic explosion. Once started it is self-sustaining until exhaustion of the conditions. For one or two equations, this constitutes a bifurcation point, beyond which the system becomes unstable. For such a large system, specification of a unique critical point cannot be done, but one can see the necessity for at least one by contrasting two pure cases. With all sectors having excess capacity, the system is definitely stable; with all sectors having output greater than desired capacity, it is clear that the system is dynamically unstable. For whatever expansion path the economy follows, there must be a threshold beyond which it becomes unstable. This point will be different for each different time shape of the output vector $\{q(t)\}$.

To see the qualitative nature of the problem, make the implausible assumption that $[b-\varepsilon]$ is non-singular and hence has an inverse. Then

$$\dot{q} = [b=\varepsilon]^{-1}[I-a]q = [Z]q.$$

The stability condition for this is given by the Trace of Z. If $TrZ < 0$, the system is asymptotically stable; if the $TrZ > 0$, it is unstable. All we know about $I-a$ is that its Trace is positive. Therefore, since all $\varepsilon_i > 0$, with universal excess capacity, and hence $b = 0$, the $TrZ < 0$, so that the system is stable. Hence as successive sectors are excited into accelerational investment, more and more positive elements are added to b. This has the consequence that the Trace of Z becomes smaller and smaller negative, passes through zero to positive values, thus bifurcating the system from a stable to an unstable dynamical state. The point of bifurcation depends on the order and magnitude with which sectors are excited into endogenous investment.

The resulting exuberant expansion tends to reach unmaintainable growth rates, since it gradually infects the whole of the economy which thus orders itself into a general expansion. Since unemployment declines, these diverse growth rates cannot be maintained. The result is a deceleration which destroys the necessary condition for the endogenous investment and so the economy reverts to the stable regime.

References

Haken, H. (1983) *Synergetics*, 3rd edn (Berlin: Springer Verlag).
Harrod, R. F. (1948) *Towards a Dynamic Economics* (London: Macmillan).

Part II

Equilibrium and Time

8 Ideology and Time: Criticisms of General Equilibrium

Harvey Gram*

1 INTRODUCTION

In her first published paper, Joan Robinson stated the following methodological position: 'a serious subject, in the academic sense, is neither more nor less than its own technique ... [gradually developed in] an austere and disinterested search, not 'for the Truth', but for a single self-consistent system of ideas' (1932, pp. 3–4).[1] She saw the intellectual activity of providing unreal answers to unreal questions as part and parcel of the laborious task of finding a set of assumptions at once *tractable* and *realistic*. This view of economic theory 'as a sequence of conceptual *models* that seek to express in simplified form different aspects of an always more complicated reality' is defended by Tjalling Koopmans, who remarks that 'most economists when pressed will agree to one formulation or another of such a view of the logical structure of economic knowledge' (Koopmans, 1957, pp. 142–43). In defense of general equilibrium theory, Frank Hahn takes a similar position, arguing that 'the Arrow–Debreu machinery gives us the best base camp for sallies into new territory' (Hahn, 1984, p. 10).[2]

Robinson did not include that first essay in any of the volumes of her *Collected Economic Papers*. She later remarked that she had 'soon ceased to believe in its main argument – that if economists could avoid certain bad habits and arrive at a consistent set of assumptions, however abstract, they could approach reality step by step merely by making more complicated models' (*CEP*, V, p. 110). It is just such an act of faith in the ultimate explanatory power of a still maturing analytical technique which motivates the search for new general equilibrium models capable of explaining real world phenomena such as bankruptcy and unemployment. The consequence of this step by step approach is to limit the range of questions which can be placed on the agenda of research to those which appear well defined from the point of view of existing theory. As a participant in the Keynesian revolution,

*Helpful comments from Vivian Walsh and Richard Roud are gratefully acknowledged. They are not responsible for remaining errors.

Robinson rejected any such limitation on theoretical argument, and with it the method she herself had pursued in *The Economics of Imperfect Competition* (1933). We are too timid if we proceed only to make minor improvements in an *a priori* set of assumptions distilled from the work of previous generations. It is necessary instead to begin, as Keynes had done, by 'making a radical critique of the relationship between the traditional assumptions and the actual economy that they pretended to describe' (*CEP*, V, p. 114).

Robinson's radical critique led her to reject standard interpretations of the works of Marx, Marshall, and even Keynes (*CEP*, II, pp. 1–17). and to insist that, 'We must throw out concepts and theorems that are logically self-contradictory, such as the general equilibrium of supply and demand, the long-run production function, the marginal productivity of capital and the equilibrium size of firms' (1980, p. 94). Concerning her own early work (in *The Economics of Imperfect Competition*), she wrote, 'In reality, evidently, an individual curve (for a particular product produced by a particular firm) is a mere smudge, to which it is vain to attribute elegant geometrical properties' (*CEP*, II, p. 229). And, as for the long period theory which is central to *The Accumulation of Capital* (1956) and to so many of her other books and articles, Robinson concluded in a posthumously published paper that because 'the argument is conducted strictly in terms of comparisons of logically possible positions ... [it] must remain in a perpetual fog' (1985, p. 161).

These negative conclusions were reached by asking questions which either cannot be posed within the framework of existing general equilibrium theory or which present themselves to modern theorists only as conundrums thrown up by their own formal models. The only arguments Robinson appeared to accept without reservation were essentially open-ended ones, often giving expression to some important aspect of Marxian, Marshallian, or Keynesian theory. The reason for this was that she saw in the resolution to every interesting economic problem an essentially unresolvable political dilemma. She came to suspect that any *complete* theory would be only 'another box of tricks' (*CEP*, V, p. 119). Robinson meant by *complete* any argument which specifies, independently of *historical* and *institutional* context, short-period reactions to unanticipated events. (She certainly rejected as a waste of intellectual effort the contemplation of equilibrium in a world of *complete* markets for all contingent commodities further distinguished by location and date of delivery.) Thus it was that Robinson summed up the two aspects of her challenge to traditional economic theory:

> The lack of a comprehensible treatment of *historical time*, and the failure to specify the *rules of the game* in the type of economy under discussion, make the theoretical apparatus offered in neo-classical text-books useless for the analysis of contemporary problems ... (*CEP*, V, p. 58, italics added)

What follows is a discussion of the basis for this two-pronged indictment as it exists *within* the structure of general equilibrium theory itself.

2 THE PURE THEORY OF EXCHANGE

The Pure Theory of Exchange provides the simplest illustration of a general equilibrium of supply and demand. Does the usual statement of this theory entail an institutional structure reflecting its ideological content?

Models of pure exchange rarely specify a relevant social context for the simple reason that there are few real world market structures for which the models are directly relevant.[3] Rather, their theoretical importance lies in illustrating a way of thinking about economic problems which may be labelled 'neoclassical' (cf. Hahn, 1984, pp. 1–2). In particular, the explanation of the reallocation of initial endowments among traders is located in the actions of *individual* agents who are assumed to behave *rationally*. The theory shows how the information embodied in a set of *equilibrium* price ratios is sufficient to establish a consistent set of trades, i.e. one characterized by zero excess demand. It is recognized, of course, that equilibrium prices need not be unique, although each of the associated equilibrium allocations is Pareto-efficient. Moreover, any Pareto-efficient allocation can be made to correspond to an equilibrium of supply and demand through an appropriate choice of initial endowments (subject to a condition of convexity on each trader's preference ordering). In this way, a distinction is drawn between the *positive* and *normative* aspects of the theory: a competitive equilibrium is not claimed to be a *just* solution to the exchange problem – it is only one set of Pareto-efficient solutions that the theory does not rank. A 'small pie, evenly divided' (an inefficient allocation at the center of the Edgeworth box, for example) might well be preferred on some normative grounds to the particular equilibrium solution(s) associated with any given initial endowments.

If Robinson's criticisms of the theory of supply and demand had turned simply on a misunderstanding of the claims that can be made on behalf of an equilibrium allocation, they would have been easily dismissed. Her contention that equilibrium theory in the Marshallian tradition and in modern microeconomics implies a defense of *laissez-faire* policy does ignore the fact that the existence of multiple equilibria completely undermines any such claim. Robinson's main point, however, was a *theoretical* criticism, and not simply a complaint about the connotations of the words *efficient* and *equilibrium*. Moreover, it is implicit in the structure of the theory itself. Equilibrium prices can include zero prices, and so the value of particular endowments can be zero. What happens to the trading agents whose incomes are zero? Is their initial endowment tacitly assumed to be a subsistence endowment, guaranteeing survival independently of trading opportunities? Will the group of traders, as a social entity, accept the allocation of goods associated with a supply and demand equilibrium, however unequal it may be? Or will they instead voluntarily accept some institutionally determined Rules of the Game for the purpose of reconciling their individual egoistic impulses with the needs for group survival and social harmony. These questions cut at the root of *reductionism*, the attempt, characteristic of neoclassical theory, to locate explanation in the behavior of individuals *as individuals*.

It is interesting to note that in the proof of the existence of a competitive equilibrium price vector in an exchange economy, a *formal* difficulty arises in connection with zero prices, a difficulty which, properly interpreted, raises precisely the issues which lie at the heart of Robinson's first complaint about traditional theory: its refusal to recognize its own ideological content. Thus, Arrow and Hahn note:

> The problem created by discontinuity of uncompensated demand functions when some prices are zero was recognized by Arrow and Debreu [1954, Section 4 and 5]; they stated a condition that the endowments of any household are desired directly or indirectly, by others, so that incomes cannot fall to zero. A general and very elegant formulation of such a condition is due to McKenzie [1959, 1961], based on an earlier suggestion of Gale [1957]. The definitions of resource relatedness and indirect resource relatedness used in Section 5.4 are variants of McKenzie's. (Arrow and Hahn, 1971, p. 127)

Discontinuity of demand functions alerted mathematical theorists to the fact that the initial distribution of endowments cannot, in fact, be arbitrary, as less formal versions of the theory had supposed. Every household must have a positive income in a competitive equilibrium. Otherwise, if bankrupt households are allowed, the formal argument requires that their utility levels be set equal to zero. This result is not innocuous. It is interpreted by Arrow and Hahn as defining 'the minimum level [of utility] that society insists on providing for every household, even those that cannot achieve this level in the marketplace' (Arrow and Hahn, 1971, p. 120).

The Pure Theory of Exchange arrives, by its own route, at precisely the *pre*-analytic point where Robinson thought the discussion should begin — with a specification of the social mechanisms or Rules of the Game used to reconcile the unavoidable conflict between the freedom of individuals to exchange and the undesirable social consequences which may follow. The failure to recognize the opposition of egoism and altruism, both necessary for survival, is the failure to recognize the ideological component of economic theory. The consequence is to leave unclear the relationship between the theory and the problems with which it is ostensibly concerned.

It has been said of formal economic theory that 'it allows us to pinpoint difficulties precisely and to be precise about the difficulties' (Hahn, 1984, p. 51). Literary argument, in less than expert hands, can be unconvincing. Still, mathematical reasoning ought to do more by enabling problems to be formulated in such a way as to shed light on the manner in which they might be resolved. When it stops short of this, obfuscating a central issue by treating it as a formal difficulty to be solved by an appropriate assumption, mathematical economics cannot be said to have advanced to the stage of Political Economy and hence to the formulation of policy. Perhaps this is intentional, its objective being to discover economic principles of such universal relevance that social and political context can be ignored. Robinson saw in this a recipe for cutting theory off from any contact with the real world.

3 GETTING INTO EQUILIBRIUM

The other element in Robinson's criticism of neoclassical theory – its lack of a 'comprehensible treatment' of *historical* time – arises in connection with the *process* by which equilibrium prices are established. The irreversible passage of time, even within a single trading period, can only be ignored by some sleight of hand. A famous example is the fictitious *auctioneer*, who calculates hypothetical excess demands at arbitrary initial prices, and then adjusts those prices to eliminate all excess demands, prior to any trade taking place. Stability of an equilibrium price vector must then be interpreted in terms of the convergence properties of the computing procedure by which the vector is found.[4] To be convincing, this solution to the problem of *getting into equilibrium* would have to be supplemented by an analysis of how markets mimic the behavior of the *auctioneer*.

Another sleight of hand consists in the statement that an Arrow–Debreu equilibrium 'makes no formal or explicit causal claims at all' (Hahn, 1984, p. 47). On this view, it is readily admitted that no theory exists as to how supply and demand are *prereconciled* – that the proof that 'orderly states (equilibria) are possible . . . provides [no] answer to the question of how order is imposed' (Hahn, 1984, p. 11). The wall thus erected around the theory may be protecting nothing at all, for 'it is a fair question whether it can ever be useful to have an equilibrium notion which does not describe the termination of actual processes' (Hahn, 1984, p. 48).

Robinson had no patience with either of these lines of reasoning, arguing instead that the potential strength of a supply and demand theory of prices lay in its ability to focus on the problems of *speculation* and the *formation of coalitions*. She saw these as the inherent political aspects of any coherent theory of markets.

The axiom that individuals act rationally must allow for the rational formation of groups. The 'canker at the heart of the theory' (Hahn, 1984, p. 79), the 'deep-seated inconsistency in the assumptions' (*CEP*, V, p. 162), is simply this:

> When every individual is pursuing his own advantage, atomistic competition cannot persist, for any group of sellers or of buyers can secure a monopolistic or monopsonistic gain by acting together and share the benefits among individual members of the group. Perfect competition, like free trade amongst nations, can persist only when there is some rule of behaviour which overrides pure self interest. (*CEP* V, p. 162)

Robinson thought that economic theory ought to concern itself with such rules, drawing hypotheses from a study of actual markets. There has been a tendency instead to look for assumptions sufficient to rule out market power.[5] One approach is to consider models in which the removal of a single trading agent leaves unchanged the allocations of goods and services among the remaining agents (Hahn, 1984, p. 79). Another is to show how the *core* – that set of allocations which no coalition can *block* by trading among themselves – reduces to a competitive equilibrium allocation as the number of traders increases without limit. Because the theory of competitive equilibrium takes the number of agents to be finite, a question arises concerning the *closeness* of the set of core allocations to the set of competitive equilibrium allocations. In this analysis it is assumed that all possible coalitions *can* and *will* form to block the actions (by bribing some members) of any group of traders who think they can do better among themselves by opting out of the competitive (or any other *core*) allocation. This assumption leaves unanswered the question as to what coalitions are both technically possible and politically viable under the Rules of the Game.

Failing to deal with the process of coalition formation in a way relevant to the social setting is failing to allow for the political constraints on the process of price formation which exist, at least implicitly, in even the purest model of exchange. Robinson's insistence on making clear the ideological content of economic theory is thus revealed as an essential aspect of the dynamic process by which prices are established.

Speculation, as an element in the process of price formation, cannot arise in a theory which assumes a complete set of markets for all commodities, the latter being distinguished not only be their physical characteristics, location, and date of delivery, but also by the state of the world in which they exist. Such a theory is descriptively bogus (as shown by the existence of sequential trading), and logically incoherent when states of the world depend on the actions of trading agents (Radner, 1968; cited by Hahn, 1984, p. 53). *Temporary* competitive general equilibrium theory is seen as a step closer to reality because market prices are assumed to exist only for current goods. Forward contracts are entered into, but the future prices at which those contracts will be settled are not known – every holder of such a contract has become a speculator. In proving the existence of a sequence of market clearing price vectors, it is found that a necessary and sufficient condition is 'the occurrence of some agreement about future spot prices' (Grandmont, 1982, p. 892). The condition is required so that no trader-speculator will entertain the possibility of unlimited profitable arbitrage – none will attempt to take an unlimited forward position in any market.[6]

Rather than being immune to Robinson's critique, temporary general equilibrium theory arrives, again by a somewhat circuitous route, at exactly the point where she thought discussion should begin. Thus, the *postulate* of sufficient agreement among traders as to the future state of markets merely sidesteps the potentially interesting inquiry into the political and institutional arrangements which might be conducive to such agreement. It is an assumption which deals with the formal difficulties presented by the mathematical argument, while leaving unanswered the central question concerning the role of speculation (and bankruptcy) in the process of price information. Robinson commented on this aspect of formal reasoning in her early paper on method:

> there is a word more to say about the logical type of argument. The account which the economist gives of the assumptions required for his technique is often very misleading. 'The formulae are wiser than the men who thought of them', and the technique knows a great deal more about the assumptions that it requires than the economist who is expounding it. (1932, p. 8).

4   HISTORICAL TIME

Independently of ideological considerations, Robinson rejected much of traditional economics because she regarded the notion of getting into equilibrium as self-contradictory. One cannot go back in time to correct errors. The analysis of economic behavior must therefore include an analysis of the consequences of making mistakes. Equilibrium, because it entails the realization of expectations (on average, at least) is therefore bound to misrepresent the outcome of decentralized decision making in a world in which unexpected events occur. This is the world of *historical time*, in which the unexpected cannot be reduced to a statistically well-behaved random event.

General equilibrium theorists have long recognized that getting into equilibrium represents an unsolved problem. They conclude that the theory is incomplete, not that it misrepresents a supply and demand equilibrium. Arrow comments that:

there exists a logical gap in the usual formulations of the perfectly competitive economy ... It is not explained whose decision it is to change prices ... Each individual participant in the economy is supposed to take prices as given and determine his choices as to purchase and sales accordingly; there is no-one left over whose job it is to make a decision on price. (Arrow, 1977, pp. 380, 382)

Hahn proposes a limited defense:

the Arrow–Debreu equilibrium ... is motivated by a very weak causal proposition. This is that no plausible sequence of economic states will terminate, if it does so at all, in a state which is not an equilibrium ...; agents will not continue in actions in states in which preferred or more profitable ones are available to them nor will mutually inconsistent actions allow given prices to persist. (Hahn, 1984, p. 47)

He goes on to argue, however, that even this proposition is false because an allocation belonging to the *core* need not be an Arrow-Debreu competitive equilibrium, and yet can still qualify as a *social* equilibrium. Moreover, to account for the existence of firms, it is necessary to allow for increasing returns, and, in that event, the *core* may be empty so that no competitive equilibrium exists. Thus, although 'the Arrow–Debreu construction ... is [not] quite useless ... it is the case that it must relinquish the claim of providing necessary descriptions of terminal states of economic processes' (Hahn, 1984, p. 53).

To regard general equilibrium theory as merely incomplete, because it lacks an explanation of how equilibrium is established, is to suggest that new theoretical work should continue to be directed toward filling this gap in the analysis. Hahn argues that 'information processes and costs, transactions and transactions costs and also expectations and uncertainty [should be] explicitly and essentially included in the equilibrium notion' (Hahn, 1984, p. 53). In such a reformulation of the theory, the manner in which agents *learn* about their economic environment should be specified and yet should not be capable of being described by a structurally stable set of equations unless the economy is already *in* a state of equilibrium.

Robinson saw the lack of an explanation of how equilibrium gets established as evidence that general equilibrium theory had asked an unanswerable question and that the entire conceptual framework should be abandoned. One should not try to solve the problem of *getting into equilibrium.*[7] The economic environment changes because of short-period inconsistencies[8] and because of unpredictable long-period changes in technology, the availability of natural resources, and the structure of institutions. There is no stable position about which to learn.

Hahn and Robinson come to similar sounding conclusions. 'When the agent is learning ... there is a change in regime so that one would require a 'higher level' theory of the learning process. Such a theory is *not available at present* ... In our present state of knowledge ... it is routine behaviour and not behaviour [sic] which we can hope to describe' (Hahn, 1984, p. 56, italics added). 'In reality, disturbing events occur on disequilibrium paths. The resulting turbulence is *beyond the skill of model builders to analyse*' (Robinson, 1962b, p. 27, italics added). When expectations about future prices are exogenous, Hahn notes that market clearing in each short period (of a temporary competitive equilibrium) 'will no longer ensure Pareto efficiency in the usual sense. On this account, then, the economy *staggers from one short period equilibrium to another*, and a good deal of this rests on unexplained expectations formation' (Hahn, 1984, p. 82, italics added). Robinson, commenting on supply and demand models, but not assuming continuous, short-period market clearing, concludes that, 'To make the argument applicable to actual situations, we have to leave equilibrium analysis behind and approach the problem in terms of a historical procss, the system continually *lurching from one out-of-equilibrium position to another*' (1962b, p. 7, italics added).

The agreement thus reached about the inadequacies of general equilibrium theory should not hide the fact that this pessimism derives from rather different arguments and leads to fundamentally different conclusions. The argument of the general equilibrium theorists derives from a consideration of the internal structure of their own models. The assumption of a complete set of markets in all commodities (which is central to the theory) is rejected not only because it is recognized that markets cannot be formed costlessly when buyers and sellers are required to 'look' for one another, but also because *moral hazard* and *asymmetric information* imply the non-existence of markets (for certain contingent commodities). The inadequacy of the supply and demand equilibrium concept and, by implication, the need for a 'Keynesian' theory of *coordination failures*, is viewed as a consequence of this inherent incompleteness. In effect, the proof that markets are incomplete is the proof that the future cannot be collapsed into the present (Hahn, 1984, p. 81). Trade necessarily occurs at every date in a 'sequence' economy instead of only once 'at the beginning'. Robinson's defense of Keynes was more direct:

On the plane of academic theory, the importance of the Keynesian revolution was to show that all the familiar dogmas are set in a world without time and cannot survive the simple observation that decisions in economic life, are necessarily taken in the light of uncertain expectations about their future consequences ... [The enormous intellectual labor which has gone into reaching the conclusion that a theory] in which the difference between the past and the future cannot arise ... could have been saved by recognizing that, at any moment in real life when a decision is taken, the past is already irrevocable and the future is still to come. (*CEP*, V, p. 112)

Their paths having crossed, the defenders and critics of general equilibrium theory might be thought ready to join forces, having reached a
common ground for discourse. The general equilibrium conception, however, appears to have a persuasive power of its own. Theorists have simply
given up the search for an explanation of how equilibrium gets established in
the short period and have resorted to *rationally formed* expectations in order
to solve the problem of establishing a sequence of equilibria. The 'invisible
hand' is thus seen to have two separate functions. With respect to short
period market clearing, 'we seem to be prepared to live on faith' (Hahn, 1984,
p. 94). With respect to the coherence of a sequence of equilibria, the rational
expectations hypothesis not only assumes than an equilibrium position
exists, but also assumes that agents are *able* to learn everything that *can* be
learned about it. It 'substitutes an internal and psychic hand for the market.
Each individual somehow has learned how the invisible hand would have
performed if it had been given markets in which to perform' (Hahn, 1984,
pp. 123–4). As a consequence, 'fully informed agents have no need for a price
mechanism to inform them about what is happening. Prices merely reflect
what they already know' (Leijonhufvud, 1983, p. 80). Thus, prices are no
longer a *source of information* any more than they would be in an Arrow–
Debreu model with a complete set of markets for all contingent commodities.
Hahn concludes that the rational expectations hypothesis is as much a matter
of faith as the market clearing hypothesis:

> Just as classical general equilibrium theory has never been able to provide
> a definitive account of how equilibrium prices come to be established, so
> rational expectation theory has not shown how starting from relative
> ignorance, everything that can be learned comes to be learned. The
> obvious route here is via Bayes' Theorem but there are formidable
> difficulties in general equilibrium application. (Hahn, 1984, p. 82).

Robinson did not participate directly in the 'rational expectations debate'.
But if one agrees that the 'spin-off from this approach ... [is that] in the
formation of expectations, in whatever manner and however imperfectly
people do form them, account will be taken of expected government policy'
(Hahn, 1984, p. 123), then one can certainly find in her writings a recognition
of this neglected proposition: 'Shock treatment that consists in an occasional
unexpected rise in interest rates loses its efficacy if it is used often; all the more
so if it is advertised as official policy' (*CEP*, III, p. 129). And if one agrees
that, in policy discussions, great weight is placed on the rational expectations
hypothesis in precisely those situations in which it is least plausible – during
periods of changing circumstances when expectations are most fluid –
Robinson's only comment on that hypothesis may seem apt:

It is strange that the concept of 'rational expectations' over the long run has come into fashion among economists just at a moment (1980) when prospects for the capitalist world are more uncertain and more threatening than they have been ever since capitalism came into existence. (1985, p. 160)

5 ROBINSON VS. SAMUELSON?

Robinson's detailed criticisms of the problem of *getting into equilibrium* arose in the context of another debate, the 'capital theory controversy', which began with her famous paper on the aggregate production function (*CEP*, II, pp. 114–31). She was concerned with long-period positions in which expectations are continuously realized. Her debate with Samuelson focused on the meaning of movements along a wage–profit frontier or pseudo-production function (1969, pp. 411–25). A change in the distribution of income between wages and profits entails a change in the physical composition of the stock of capital, not only because of a difference in the profit-maximizing technique of production, but also because of a difference in the composition of demand, and therefore output, corresponding to the new distribution of income. Such changes, in Robinson's view, could not be analyzed in terms of the equilibrium relationships of the long period. Indeed, *no change* could be analyzed without taking into account the short-period consequences of reconciling regrets about the past with those expectations about the future which guide current actions. Samuelson argued that the transition from one long-period position to another could be analyzed in terms of an intertemporal equilibrium of supply and demand. He did not claim that this would entail a movement along the curves that characterize a set of long-period positions; and he did not claim that the transition path would be unique (Samuelson, 1975).

This was an inconclusive debate. Robinson had previously analyzed 'the neo-classical problem of accumulation in an economy where the labour force and the state of knowledge are constant, with the rate of profit falling and the real-wage rising as time goes by' (*CEP*. II, p. 132). The conclusion she drew concerning this movement from one stationary state to another was simply that

there is no warrant for postulating that the expectations guiding investment plans will turn out to be correct in their turn. Indeed, there is no reason why all the various expectations being held independently should be consistent with each other. It is not possible for each firm to know what all the others have planned to do, and to deduce from this knowledge how its own position will be affected. Since the expectations being held are not self-consistent, they are not capable of being justified by the event. The investment now being done is going to create another out-of-equilibrium stock of capital goods. (*CEP*, V, p. 85)

Samuelson's conclusion was in the same spirit:

> a skeptic might legitimately doubt that ... a competitive market system will have the 'foresight' or the perfect-futures markets to approximate in real life such warranted paths that have the property that, if everyone knew in advance they would occur, each will be motivated to do just that which gives rise to them. (Samuelson, 1975, p. 45)

Robinson concluded that Samuelson simply had an opinion different from hers about a purely logical point. But, in fact, he was his own skeptic, writing elsewhere about the market in the following way:

> The image in my mind is that of a bicycle. The rider of the bicycle is the bulk of the market, a somewhat mystical concept to be sure – like its analogue, the well-informed speculator who gets his way in the end because his way is the correctly discerned way of the future; and those who think differently are bankrupted by their bets against (him and) the future. (It is easier to identify the well-informed speculator *ex post* than *ex ante*, and the image can easily dissolve into an empty tautology.) ... Even if there is something valid in this heuristic reasoning, one must admit that the system need not – and, generally, will not – move from its present position to the golden age in the most efficient way: it will hare after false goals, get detoured, and begin to be corrected only after it has erred. (Samuelson, 1967, p. 229)

Here there is no difference of opinion. Robinson's insistence that getting into equilibrium requires an act of faith finds formal expression in the analysis of an intertemporal equilibrium path. The act of faith is the belief that markets generate the discrete changes in prices and quantities required to place the economy on a new market-clearing, convergent path (following any disturbance) in a model in which long-period equilibrium is represented by a saddle point position.

Saddle points are endemic to models of intertemporal equilibrium (Shell, 1967). It might be thought that to regard such models as in any way descriptive would entail a denial that long-period equilibrium positions are 'centers of gravitation'. For, as Samuelson remarks, they could only be reached by a careful *aiming* of the system (Samuelson, 1967, pp. 228–30), and this naturally suggests some form of market intervention. Not surprisingly, however, a seeming fault has recently been turned into a virtue by the proponents of the rational expectations hypothesis. Their argument is that the ridge-like path which leads to a saddle point equilibrium, 'far from being an unlikely freak case, provides the only sensible basis for forward looking expectations when individuals are well informed about the structure of the economy' (Begg, 1982, p. 40).

Agreement that the problem of *getting into equilibrium* is a serious one for general equilibrium theory has clearly led to very different conclusions. The rational expectations hypothesis maintains that well-informed agents have expectations which are consistent with a sequence of short-period market clearing allocations converging to a long-period equilibrium. The central analytical importance of the long-period position is thus maintained. General equilibrium theorists, critical of the rational expectations hypothesis, insist that the *process* by which agents learn about an economy's changing structure be specified. Until that is done, long-period equilibrium positions have limited analytical significance. Robinson argued that it is impossible to 'learn' about a position which changes as a result of the 'learning process', and for independent reasons as well. She maintained, however, that long-period equilibrium analysis has a limited usefulness in shedding light on the causes and consequences of disequilibrium and instability.[9]

6   CONCLUSION

Obtaining a plausible answer to an interesting question within the framework of a coherent model counts as a contribution to economic theory. Insisting on the incompleteness of argument and the contradictions inherent in real reactions to real events, does not. But the indeterminacies and inconsistencies one sees need not to be arbitrary ones. Robinson's sometimes underdetermined, sometimes overdetermined models were formulated with a view to understanding contemporary problems rather than admitting only the formal difficulties generated by an existing theory. Taking the latter route appears often to lead to a point where the initial question (such as the problem of getting into equilibrium) simply reappears in a new form (as in the problem of formulating a learning theory appropriate to non-routine behavior). Perhaps this is the nature of theoretical development, but it must be asked if the claim that general equilibrium theory is safe 'from a bombardment of soap bubbles' (Hahn, 1984, p. 78) is true only because the theory is able to transmogrify itself into more complex forms without coming to grips with its essential difficulties.

Robinson's theoretical framework is purposely open-ended, for she takes as an axiom that the objective of firms is simply to grow (1962a, pp. 13–15, 47). Profit maximization in the long run is a meaningless concept because the future is unknown (cf. Hahn, 1984, p. 82), but growth for the sake of growth leaves undetermined the detailed course of future development. This, and the multifarious reactions of firms to the vicissitudes of unplanned growth (which Robinson considers in detail), help to explain why her arguments cannot be reduced to a neat and manageable form. Her point of view, however, is not without parallel.

Nicholas Georgescu-Roegen, arguing from a different perspective, decries 'the wholesale attachment of almost every economist of the last one hundred years to the mechanistic dogma . . . which [either] leaves nothing indeterminate . . . [or allows for a] freedom . . . limited only to random, not to permanent, variation . . . [It thus ignores] the *emergence of novelty by combination*' (Georgescu-Roegen, 1971, pp. 2, 13). He concludes that 'no social scientist can possibly predict through what kinds of social organizations mankind will pass in its future; [that] in the long run or even in the not too long run the economic . . . process is inevitably dominated by a qualitative change which cannot be known in advance . . . so that no system of equations can describe the development of [such] an evolutionary process' (Georgescu-Roegen, 1971, pp. 15, 17). The resulting indeterminancy 'leaves us no choice but to recognize the role of the cultural tradition in the economic process [forcing us to account for] an irreducible social conflict' (Georgescu-Roegen, 1971, pp. 11, 18–19). Mechanistic models must themselves be seen as overdetermined in so far as they reduce the unknowable consequences of the future to an equilibrium of opposing forces of supply and demand.

Georgescu-Roegen credits Marshall with keeping alive a truly dynamic conception of the economic process, but fails to mention either of his intellectual heirs, Keynes or Robinson:

> [A]mong the economists of distinction, only Alfred Marshall intuited that biology, not mechanics, is the true Mecca of the economist. And even though Marshall's antimechanistic proclivities were reflected mainly in his famous biological analogies, we must impute to them his salient discovery of the irreversibility of long-run supply schedules. Unfortunately, Marshall's teaching caused no lasting imprint and the fact that irreversibility is a general feature of all economic laws received no attention. (Georgescu-Roegen, 1971, p. 11)

For half a century, Joan Robinson insisted on the importance of the fact that time moves in only one direction from an irrevocable past to an uncertain future. And, of course, the awareness of what Georgescu-Roegen describes as an 'irreducible social conflict' was central to her concept of the Rules of the Game, that framework of social conventions and institutional arrangements within which economic development takes place. It never occurred to her to build a model in which 'the sparse information system of prices only . . . [would completely explain] a coherent economic disposition of resources' (Hahn, 1984, p. 114).

In *Economic Philosophy*, Robinson defends the need for a consideration of the Rules of the Game. Our 'uncertain, ill-disciplined subject . . . would never have developed except in the hope of throwing light upon questions of policy. But policy means nothing unless there is an authority to carry it out' (1962b, p. 117). Authority, in turn, relies on coercion and/or a sense of community reflecting the moral and institutionalized sanctions used to back up group interest. Group interest presupposes a social conscience to generate those altruistic feelings of sympathy necessary to alleviate unmitigated egoism. Where then, are the boundaries of group interest? 'Evolution will not answer the greatest of all moral questions, Who is my neighbour?' (1962b, p. 120). The answer we give, consciously or unconsciously, is our ideology.

Certainly, Robinson considered the moral dimensions of economic problems and applauded the general equilibrium theorists when they did the same thing (*CEP*, V, p. 9). She saw the spirit of Internationalism stymied by Nationalism, 'a solid unchanging lump of ideology that we take so much for granted that it is rarely noticed' (1962b, p. 117). In turn, the rational pursuit of national goals comes up against the ideology of Full Employment and a Stable Price Level; namely, the belief that the level of effective demand can be discussed independently of the content of new investment, and that the wage–price spiral can be discussed without reference to the division of income between work and property. And, at the most basic level, the rational pursuit of the accumulation of capital comes up against the ideology of the Firm: that *patriotism* which managers and employees develop for the organizations in which they work, independently of the interests of society in maintaining and enhancing the productivity of the stock of capital, broadly defined so as to include the environment and the general level of education.

Robinson's discussion of these issues includes many prescient observations. Free Trade policy is often recommended on grounds of efficiency, but the argument remains vacuous without discussion of the implications of free trade for income distribution and the pattern of economic development. Full Employment policy takes the course of least resistance, pushing industry 'further down the grooves it has worn for itself' (*CEP*, V, p. 43), and paying no attention to the resulting bias 'in favour of products and services for which it is easy to collect payment [as opposed to] investments [which] cannot be enjoyed except collectively and are not easy to make any money out of . . . When you come to think of it, what can easily be charged for and what cannot, is just a technical accident' (1962b, p. 124). On the stability of the price level, 'It seems to me that the question of whether it is possible to have full employment without a falling value of money cannot be answered until we know whether or not it is possible to have full employment without the cold war' (*CEP*, II, pp. 278–9). Regarding the Firm, and the *patriotism* which develops for it, Robinson (twenty-five years ago) offered a warning which may yet take on new meaning in the wake of recent mergers. To welcome take-overs is to concede 'to the profits of financial manipulations the halo that once belonged to the "reward of Enterprise" [and to ignore the risk that] the exaltation of the shareholder [will] make managers cynical and Trade Unions agressive' (1962b, p. 136). The personal zeal, which appears to be transformed by firms into institutional commitment, may be threatened. Whatever the outcome, a fundamental question remains. Is there a set of Rules of the Game which will transform institutional commitment into social commitment so as to satisfy communal and global needs, and to generate a feeling of obligation to the future inhabitants of the earth? On such a broad question, Robinson regarded traditional theory as systematically diverting the attention of those who take up the study of economics. She criticized neoclassical theory because she saw it as incapable of allowing the important questions any hearing at all. And indeed, one general equilibrium theorist has stated unequivocally that there is 'no way of building a bridge between this view [on an economy satisfying the conditions for a general equilibrium of supply and demand] and the workings of a capitalist economy or, for that matter, the process of planning in a controlled one' (Hahn, 1984, p. 92).

Notes

1. References to works by Robinson will be given by date only except in the case of her *Collected Economic Papers* which will be indicated by *CEP*, followed by volume and page numbers.
2. The 'base camp', in Hahn's usage, appears to be an informal idea rather than an immutable set of hard core propositions which remain unchanged as the model set expands.
3. Perhaps the most famous example is the discussion of exchange relationships in a Prisoner-of-War Camp (Radford, 1946). The theory of exchange has also been used by Sen in his essay on *Poverty and Famines* (1981).
4. Hahn points out that 'even that congenial circumstance when all goods are gross substitutes will not allow us to deduce that our artificial invisible hand is doing well [in its *computing* task], should the process be described by a set of finite difference equations. The speed of adjustment however also plays a crucial role' (Hahn, 1984, p. 89).
5. Of course, this may be seen as a prelude to the study of market power in the sense that it narrows the field of study.
6. This goes some way toward preventing bankruptcy, although the problem of initial debts remains (Grandmont, 1982, p. 892). Bankruptcy in a competitive equilibrium framework appears to be a contradiction in terms, however, 'since the risk of default obviously depends on the size of forward commitments made by a particular agents [and so] ... it is not clear why the prices of forward contracts should be independent of their size ... imperfect competition must be taken into account when analysing forward markets' (Grandmont, 1982, p. 8).
7. Robinson was as critical of long-period equilibrium models with a uniform rate of profit (even though she used such models) as she was of general equilibrium models of supply and demand. Of the former, she asked, '*When* is the long-run position with prices corresponding to a uniform rate of profit? Is it in the future or the past? Or only in a journal article?' And, concerning the latter, in their

intertemporal form, she remarked, 'for my part, I have never been able to make that theory stand up long enough to knock it down' (1980, p. 128).

8.   Disequilibrium models which allow for *false trading* might be thought to allow for short-period inconsistencies since the vector of utilities is never declining while *false trading* takes place. But this assumes barter transactions. If trade requires the use of a medium of exchange, then, during the interval of time when *money* is held, prices may change in such a way that utility falls for some traders during the process of exchange. When production decisions are allowed to take place at disequilibrium prices, the existence of durable goods implies that profits need not increase at each stage in the process of getting into equilibrium. 'The path of the system will at any time be strewn with the remnants of past mistakes' (Hahn, 1984, p. 90). In Robinson's view, the consequences of such mistakes rendered meaningless the notion of getting into equilibrium.

9.   This is to be contrasted with another point of view, inspired by the work of Straffa (1960) and set forth by Garegnani (1976) and Eatwell and Milgate (1983, pp. 1–17), which maintains that long-period positions (characterized by a uniform rate of profit) play a predictive role in the analysis of competitive capitalism. Convergence to such positions, regarded as 'center of gravitation', is based on Keynesian arguments extended to the long period.

References

Arrow, K. J. (1977) 'Toward a Theory of Price Adjustment', in K. J. Arrow and L. Hurwicz (eds) *Studies in Resource Allocation Processes* (Cambridge: Cambridge University Press).

Arrow, K. J and F. H. Hahn (1971) *General Competitive Analysis* (San Francisco: Holden-Day).

Begg, D. K. H. (1982) *The Rational Expectations Revolution in Macroeconomics* (Baltimore: Johns Hopkins University Press).

Eatwell, J. and M. Milgate (eds) (1983) *Keynes's Economics and the Theory of Value and Distribution* (London: Duckworth).

Garegani, P. (1976) 'On a Change in the Notion of Equilibrium in Recent Work on Value and Distribution', in M. Brown, K. Sato and P. Zarembka (eds) *Essays in Modern Capital Theory* (Amsterdam: North-Holland) also in Eatwell and Milgate (eds) (1983).

Georgescu-Roegen, N. (1971) *The Entropy Law and the Economic Process* (Cambridge, Mass.: Harvard University Press).

Grandmont, J. M. (1982) 'Temporary General Equilibrium Theory', in K. J. Arrow and M. D. Intriligator (eds) *Handbook of Mathematical Economics*, Vol. II (Amsterdam: North-Holland).

Hahn, F. H. (1984) *Equilibrium and Macroeconomics* (Cambridge, Mass.: MIT).

Koopmans, T. C. (1957) *Three Essays on The State of Economic Science* (New York: McGraw-Hill).

Leijonhufvud, A. (1983) 'What was the Matter with IS-LM?', in J. P. Fitoussi (ed.) *Modern Macroeconomic Theory* (Oxford: Blackwell).

Radner, R. (1968) 'Competitive Equilibrium under Uncertainty', *Econometrica*, 36 (January): 31–58.

Radford, R. A. (1946) 'The Economic Organization of a Prisoner of War Camp', *Economica* 12 (November): 189–201.

Robinson, J. V. (1932) *Economics is a Serious Subject* (Cambridge: Heffer).

Robinson, J. V. (1933) *The Economics of Imperfect Competition* (London: Macmillan).

Robinson, J. V. (1951, 1960, 1965, 1973, 1979) *Collected Economic Papers*, Vols. I–V. 'Introduction' to Vols. II and III (1975) (Oxford: Blackwell).

Robinson, J. V. (1956, 1965 and 1969) *The Accumulation of Capital* (London: Macmillan).

Robinson, J. V. (1962a) *Essays in the Theory of Economic Growth* (London: Macmillan).

Robinson, J. V. (1962b) *Economic Philosophy* (London: C. A. Watts).

Robinson, J. V. (1980) *What are the Questions? and Other Essays, Further Contributions to Modern Economics* (Armonk, NY: M. E. Sharpe).

Robinson, J. V. (1985) 'The Theory of Normal Prices, and Reconstruction of Economic Theory', in G. R. Feiwel (ed.) *Issues in Contemporary Macroeconomics and Distribution* (London: Macmillan).

Samuelson, P. A. (1967) 'Indeterminancy of Development in a Heterogeneous–Capital Model with Constant Saving Propensity', in Shell (1967)

Samuelson, P. A. (1975) 'Steady-State and Transient Relations: A Reply on Reswitching', *Quarterly Journal of Economics*, 89 (February): 40–7.

Sen, A. K. (1981) *Poverty and Famines: An Essay on Entitlement and Deprivation* (Oxford: Clarendon Press).

Shell, K. (1967) (ed.) *Essays on the Theory of Optimal Economic Growth* (Cambridge, Mass.: MIT).

Sraffa, P. (1960) *Production of Commodities by Means of Commodities: Prelude to a Critique of Economic Theory* (Cambridge: Cambridge University Press).

9 Joan Robinson and 'Getting into Equilibrium', in Short and Long Periods

Vivian Walsh

> What could have made her peaceful with a mind
> That nobleness made simple as a fire,
> With beauty like a tightened bow, a kind
> That is not natural in an age like this,
> Being high and solitary and most stern?
> Why, what could she have done, being what she is?
> Was there another Troy for her to burn?
>
> William Butler Yeats (1957)

It is not my purpose in this brief note to alter anything in that restrospective treatment of Joan Robinson's economics in which I had a share (Gram and Walsh, 1983), but rather to add some further thoughts on the specific topic of her objections to the notion of 'getting into equilibrium', in both short periods and long. In particular, I shall argue that her well-known objections to 'getting into equilibrium' have been vindicated by some of the most recent theoretical work on both short- and long-period models. What is both sad and ironic is that she was probably seldom in the minds of the (relatively) younger theorists whose herculean mathematical labors have led them at last to reach a 'Pole' (an image of hers) where her by now somewhat tattered flag has been flying for so many years.

Perhaps it is unnecessary to warn the reader that nothing in this note is to be read as implying that Robinson *herself* would have approved of the technical methods which have led these younger explorers to within sight of her Pole. It is, in any case, primarily their *negative* results which I shall argue constitute her vindication.

1 'GETTING INTO EQUILIBRIUM AND THE SHORT PERIOD

Many years ago Robinson wrote:

The prices of manufactures in the nature of the case are administered prices. With short-period fluctuations of demand, prices vary very little as long as money costs are constant . . . Even in a seller's market when output is up to the limit set by capacity, firms usually prefer to lengthen delivery dates or ration customers, rather than to choke off demand by raising prices today for fear that it might be permanently lost. Movements of demand affect profits strongly, but prices hardly at all. (Robinson 1969, p. vii–viii)

That firms in a seller's market, where they are on the short side, engage in the quantity rationing of consumers, was long known to her, and the contemporary temporary equilibrium theorist, who often turns to price fixing imperfectly competitive firms, should note that it was in her discussion of 'Imperfect Competition Revisited', which was first published as long ago as 1953, that she wrote:

In a seller's market, where demand, even at highly profitable prices, exceeds capacity output, it is often found that powerful firms prefer not to raise prices but rather to delay delivery, thus making an investment in goodwill for the future. (Robinson, Vol. II, p. 233)[1]

The point that must be stressed immediately is that when Robinson denied that a real world economy could be expected to 'get into equilibrium' in the short period, she meant get into a *market clearing* equilibrium, with demands equal to supplies on all markets. She was *not* denying that an economy could get, as it were, *stuck* in what we would nowadays call a quantity-constrained temporary equilibrium, with unsold goods and/or unemployed workers and unused capacity. Commenting on Pigou's transformation of Marshall's firms into perfect competitors, she wrote 'Under perfect competition, any plant that was working at all must be working up to capacity . . . Imperfect competition came in to explain the fact, in the world around us, that more or less all plants were working part time' (Robinson, 1969, p. vi).

Firms which perceive quantity constraints on the output they can sell can hardly regard themselves as perfect competitors. As Jean-Paul Fitoussi has remarked, 'Imperfect competition more than perfect competition, would then constitute the reference model for macroeconomics. In such a structure individual agents determine their prices on the basis of conjectured supply and demand functions' (Fitoussi, 1983, p. 15). In a well-known model of Frank Hahn, monopoly powers do not have to be *assumed*, since, as Hahn put it, 'the "price flexibility" implied by the conjectures does not ensure a competitive equilibrium' (Hahn, 1978, p. 7). Elsewhere Hahn has remarked that recent work 'seems to have been on the right track in arguing that Keynesian dynamics is ill-served by a perfect competition postulate . . . The possibility of bankruptcy is alone sufficient to make of every demand for a loan a "named" demand. That is, every debt differs by the actual borrower' (Hahn, 1977, p. 37). Now these struggling firms, each with highly individual situations, seem to me to within hailing distance of Robinson's firms, and miles apart from the perfectly competitive producing agents in those complete intertemporal neo-Walrasian models which were the favorite objects of her attack.

It is important to realize that Robinson would not have expected her *opponents* to accept as an *equilibrium* a state of affairs where demands and supplies are not equal, quantity constraints are perceived and being taken into account, firms are making conjectures as to what they can sell and are fixing prices accordingly, in situations which involve acting with seriously incomplete information and the threat of going bankrupt. Getting stuck in a state like this for a short period is not 'getting into' a very posh equilibrium!

Her arrows were simply not aimed at what we nowadays call non-Walrasian equilibria, which is, of course, not to say that she would have welcomed recent formal work of this type as giving any new insights about how a real world economy works. The point, rather, is that such work vindicates her insistence that short-period positions are messy, inconsistent, transient states of affairs.

Pierangelo Garegnani has remarked that 'Marshall's short-period equilibrium appears to be a complement to the long-period equilibrium of the system and not an alternative to it' (Garegnani, 1983, p. 139, note 25). Robinson's short-period analysis was developed from that of Marshall, of course, but some questions have recently been raised as to the role of long-period positions in her thought, particularly towards the end of her life.

2 'GETTING INTO EQUILIBRIUM' AND THE LONG PERIOD

I have heard the suggestion that in the last years of her life Robinson changed certain of her views . Perhaps she did. But one thing I am sure of: she did *not* change her view of the status of the Sraffa system, or of 'getting into' long-period equilibrium. Beginning with our meeting in the early 1970s, Harvey Gram and I developed an account of matters such as the allocations of surplus output in a modern classical model (including the special case of a Sraffa model) which Joan Robinson subjected to detailed criticism and discussion each time she came to stay with one or the other of us and we met to discuss the latest version of our work. Our view, thus influenced, early became, and remained, that:

A comparison of points along any given surplus possibilities schedule is a comparison of different economic systems, each with its own particular past investment in commodity capital. An analysis of 'movement' or 'change' from one point along the schedule to another is therefore even more problematical than an analysis of changing factor allocations along the boundary of the set of feasible outputs in a neoclassical model. (Walsh and Gram, 1980, p. 281)

But as early as 1961, Robinson had been fully aware that the word 'change' does not have its usual implications in Sraffa's description of his model:

The wage 'changes' only in the sense that the value of x changes as we run our eye up and down a curve ... we need not take the word 'change' literally. We are only to compare the effects of having differing rates of profit, with the same technical conditions and the same composition of output. (Robinson, Vol. III, p. 8)

Compare this with what she wrote much later, in an article which first appeared in 1977:

In Saffra's model ... [w]e are presented with, so to speak, a snapshot of a process of production going on in a particular industrial economy ... Now, everything in physical terms remaining the same, the share of wages in net output is run through every value from unity to zero ... These calculations must be regarded purely as an intellectual experiment. In an actual economy of which a snapshot is taken, some particular pattern of prices is ruling. The 'changes' of the share of wages in the argument are not actual historical events, only calculations by the observing economist. (Robinson, Vol. V, pp. 64–5)

Finally, and consistently with what she had always argued when Gram and I discussed these questions with her, she wrote in 'Spring Cleaning' that we can imagine a variety of techniques 'but we cannot imagine switching from one to another at an instant of time. A switch would require availability of the appropriate stocks of inputs already in existence' (Robinson, 1980, p. 10).

For Robinson the Sraffa system was always a 'snapshot' of a system with certain prices that yielded a uniform rate of profit. It was never for her (nor was it for Sraffa) the center of gravitation of a dynamic process of 'getting into' equilibrium. Now recently Marco Magnani has described Robinson as a fundamentalist Keynesian (Magnani, 1983, pp. 248–9) and remarked that 'the rejection of the long-period method is common in Fundamentalists. Joan Robinson, for example, has described long-run equilibrium (and the associated general rate of profit) as "floating above historical time as a Platonic idea" (Robinson, 1979, p. 180)' (Magnani, 1983, pp. 249–50).

Robinson's reference to Plato's Theory of Forms, which occurred in a brief note commenting on a well-known article by Pierangelo Garegnani, may have been unwise, since it is at best an analogy, and those who remember their ancient philosophy may be fastidious enough to feel that it is a rather bad analogy, but in any event this reference need not be interpreted as implying that Robinson had changed her views on the legitimate uses of the concept of the long-period. Her view in 1969 was, as it had always been from the time when she first wrote about Sraffa, that Sraffa prices represented the result of an intellectual experiment: they were those prices which one could set out here and now as being consistent with the reproduction of the imaginary economic system. Thus (in a competitive model) they *necessarily* embodied a uniform intersectorial rate of profit. They were *not* in the process of being attained in the future, as a result of some process taking place in historical time. As she wrote back in 1961 in her review of Sraffa's book: 'The commodities reproduce themselves with a physical surplus. The condition that the rate of profit is uniform throughout the economy settles their relative prices' (Robinson, Vol. III, p. 8). To put it brutally, and in a language she would not have approved, the uniform rate of profit is either the duality condition linking a set of quantity and price relations, in which case its meaning is perfectly precise and it has a clearly defined role in a wide and important class of models for the theory of general equilibrium, or it is an (as yet) unjusified speculation about real world prices in historical time.

Magnani is correct that Robinson had much to say (throughout her life, by the way) about uncertainty and expectations, when such topics were appropriate. But these issues were beside the point in discussing the Sraffa system, since the latter is in logical time, and is always in the only state defined for it by Sraffa, namely equilbrium characterized by a uniform rate of profit.

As Gram and I noted in 1983, Christopher Bliss has made a useful distinction between 'two approaches that have been adopted with regard to economic equilibrium' (Bliss, 1975, p. 27). There is first of all the modest approach, which confines itself to specifying the conditions for a model being *in* equilibrium; this, of course, is what I have been claiming was always Robinson's approach to the Sraffa system. Then there is the heroic approach, which attempts to specify a dynamic process leading to general equilibrium in a given model: 'This is what Robinson has long rejected' (Gram and Walsh, 1983, p. 520).

Now it happens that in recent years a number of modern classical theorists have attempted to provide a formal dynamic process analysis for modern commodity reproduction structures. As has been noted by Luciano Boggio, with a few exceptions, such as M. Egidi (1975), 'the problem was practically ignored until the work of Garegnani (1976), which posed such a question using an expression taken from the classics: "gravitation"' (Boggio, 1984, p. 1). In a well-known paper, first published in 1976, Garegnani had pointed out that the original classics, and also Marshall

> understood the long-period position as the 'centre' towards which the competitive economy would gravitate in the given long-period conditions.

> The basis of the argument had been laid down by Adam Smith with his distinction between the 'market price' and 'natural price' of a commodity. (1983, p. 131)

The original classics, however, clearly had in view a tendency which they believed to exist in real world economies; what is more, they did not claim that such a tendency would lead to a full-scale general equilibrium. The recent formal models, on the contrary, characteristically concern themselves with the convergence, to general equilibrium with prices of production,[2] of models in logical (or in computer) time. As Gérard Dumenil and Dominique Levy, authors of some of the most important models, '[u]ne autre différence importante avec l'analyse classique est que ce modèle reste un modèle de convergence et non de gravitation' (Dumenil and Levy, 1984, p. 21, note).

It is possible, however, to argue on the basis of this literature that Robinson overstated her case. In purely formal terms, models *can* (and have been) specified which are so simple that they can be shown to converge, if slightly displaced, to equilibrium with production prices. These results should give little aid and comfort to Robinson's opponents on the question of 'getting into equilibrium', however. This is because the positive results so far obtained, though extremely interesting, seem to be far less notable, in the eyes of their originators, than the difficulties which this work has thrown into a clear light. Indeed the leading contributors to this literature have been notably modest in their claims as to what has yet been achieved. What they repeatedly insist on is rather the extreme difficulty of obtaining general analytic results. Even the use of computer simulation has only yielded positive results in the case of very simple models, and that at the cost of abandoning the generality and force of analytical results in the conclusions thus obtained. Thus Richard Arena, Claude Froeschle and Dominique Torre conclude that '[l] a question de la gravitation est donc aujord'hui ouverte' (Arena, Froeschle and Torre, 1984, p. 4) and refer to the prudent (and agnostic) conclusion of Ian Steedman on the matter. They note what they call:

> le caractère le plus souvent local de la stabilité des modèles de gravitation. Les auteurs s'opposent en effet fréquemment que les réactions comportementales aux déséquilibres de marché ne sont pas brutales et n'impliquent que de très petites variations des grandeurs étudiées. (Arena, Froeschle and Torre, 1984, pp. 10–11)

In fact they found that the number of convergences was greater the more moderate the movements of capital:

> Lorsque les mouvements de capitaux sont brutaux, le risque s'accroit de voir l'economie se spécialiser de manière excessive dans les productions les

plus rentables, sans pouvoir assurer la fabrication de certains biens qui demeurent nécessaires en raison des interdépendences sectorielles. (Arena, Froeschle and Torre, 1984, p. 27)

When it is borne in mind that most of the existing models assume that there is no fixed capital, are confined to two sectors (or have increasing problems with more) and describe processes (often computer simulations) in logical time, it can be seen why some theorists should hesitate to use the term 'gravitation', suggestive of Adam Smith and real world processes in historical time, to refer to these modern studies of convergence to equilibrium in formal models. Dumenil and Levy, as we have seen, are careful to note that an important difference between their model and the analysis of the classics is that theirs is a model of convergence and not of gravitation.

Whatever else they have done (and obviously they have done much that is highly interesting) the authors of recent papers on the question of gravitation have made it impossible simply to *assume* that a modern commodity reproduction structure, if displaced, will 'get into equilibrium', or (even more) to assume that systems of Sraffa prices are the center of gravity of real world economies. And that, when all is said and done, was what Joan Robinson wanted admitted.

Notes

1. All references to the Collected Economic Papers will be to the MIT Press edition, 1980. For brevity, only one volume and page numbers will be included in parentheses following quotations. Where the *original* date of publication of a paper is important to the argument, this will be mentioned in the text.
2. I use the phrase 'general equilibrium with prices of production' rather than 'with a uniform inter-sectorial rate of profit' because commodity reproduction models have been constructed where intersectorial differences in profit rates exist, possibly due to monopolistic elements. See Boggio (1984, *passim*) and the literature cited there; also Willie Semmler (1984).

References

Arena, R., C. Froeschle and D. Torre (1984) 'Gravitation et Reproductibilité: un Point de Vue Classique', in Bidard (ed.) (1984).

Bidard, C. (1984) *La Gravitation*. Cahiers de la RCP, Systèmes de Prix de Production, nos. 2, 3, University of Paris, Nanterre.

Bliss, C. J. (1975) *Capital Theory and the Distribution of Income* (Amsterdam, North-Holland).

Boggio, L. (1984) 'Convergence to Production Prices under Alternative Disequilibrium Assumptions', in Bidard (ed.) (1984).

Dumenil, G. and D. Levy (1984) 'Une Restauration de l'analyse Classique de la dynamique Concurrentielle', in Bidard (ed.) (1984).

Eatwell, J. and M. Milgate (eds) (1983) *Keynes's Economics and the Theory of Value and Distribution* (New York: Oxford University Press).

Egidi, M., 'Stabilità ed instabilità negli schemi sraffiani', *Economia Internazionale*, vol. 27 (1975).

Fitoussi, J. P. (1983) 'Modern Macroeconomic Theory, an Overview', in *Modern Macroeconomic Theory*, (ed.) J. P. Fitoussi (New Jersey: Barnes & Noble, 1983).

Garegnani, P. (1983) 'On a Change in the Notion of Equilibrium in Recent Work on Value and Distribution', in J. Eatwell and M. Milgate (eds). Originally printed in M. Brown, K. Sato and P. Zarembka (1976) (eds), *Essays in Modern Capital Theory* (Amsterdam: North-Holland)

Gram, H. and V. Walsh 'Joan Robinson's Economics in Retrospect', *Journal of Economic Literature*, vol. 21 (1983).

Hahn, F. H. (1977) 'Keynesian Economics and General Equilibrium Theory: Reflections on some Current Debates', in G. C. Harcourt (ed.) *The Microeconomic Foundations of Macroeconomics* (Boulder, Col.: Westview Press).

Hahn, F. H. (1978) 'On Non-Walrasian Equilibria', *Review of Economic Studies*, vol. 45.

Magnani, M. (1983) '"Keynesian Fundamentalism": A Critique', in J. Eatwell and M. Milgate (eds).

Robinson, J. V. (1969) *The Economics of Imperfect Competition*, 2nd edn, (New York: St Martin's Press.

Robinson, J. V. (1983) 'Garegnani on Effective Demand', in J. Eatwell and M. Milgate (eds). Reprinted from *Cambridge Journal of Economics*, vol. 3, (1979).

Robinson, J. V. (1980a) *Collected Economic Papers*, vols. I–V, (Cambridge, Mass.: MIT; originally printed by Basil Blackwell, Oxford, 1951–79).

Robinson, J. V. (1980b) 'Spring Cleaning', mimeo, Cambridge.

Semmler, W. (1984) *Competition, Monopoly and Differential Profit Rates. On the Relevance of the Classical and Marxian Theory of Production Prices for Modern Industrial and Corporate Pricing* (New York: Columbia University Press).

Walsh, V. and H. Gram (1980) *Classical and Neoclassical Theories of General Equilibrium: Historical Origins and Mathematical Structure*, (New York, Oxford University Press).

Yeats, W. B. (1957) *The Variorum Edition of the Poems of W. B. Yeats*. ed. P. Allt and R. K. Alspach (New York: Macmillan).

10 Stability Analysis in Micro and Macro Theory: An Interview

Franklin M. Fisher

Feiwel: Are there any differences in the treatment of questions of stability by mathematical economists (say, since Samuelson) and the literary economists pursuing Keynesian questions?

Fisher: Aside from the question of tools employed, one could reasonably say that these two groups of economists are talking about the same topic in different ways. More precisely, stability involves the question whether in a dynamic system rest points (I often use this term to mean equilibria) are approached if one departs from them. As I understand the Keynesian question, it asks: if you have a competitive economy that for some reason departs from full employment, will it tend to return to a full-employment equilibrium or will it tend to get stuck in some underemployment equilibrium or, for that matter, will it tend to wander without reaching any equilibrium? That is a macroeconomic problem and like most macroeconomic problems it is a description in very aggregate terms of a much more complicated microeconomic problem. Let me now rephrase the same question, perhaps more generally. One could ask in general equilibrium terms: one has an economy consisting of many different agents, many different markets, many different prices, many different goods, and so on, and there are equilibria at which all markets clear. If one starts from a point at which that is not true, does the dynamic system that describes the entire economy tend to return the economy to a position where all markets clear? Does it tend to return the economy to some other stationary point? Or, does it tend to wander forever?

In the most general terms, the Keynesian problem could be described as exactly the same. The question of approaching other stationary points is the question whether the dynamic system has a tendency to approach positions where the economy gets stuck, perhaps because some people think that they cannot buy as much as they want; they cannot buy as much as they want because they are unsure that they can sell, and that sort of thing. In recent years that has become known as the Clower problem, but, in one form or another, it is the same as the Keynesian problem.

I would say that the Keynesian approach to macroeconomics (or the Keynesian problem in macroeconomics) is an attempt to deal, using rather coarse and aggregate tools, with a central problem of stability analysis more rigorously dealt with, with much finer tools, but unfortunately not with better solutions, within the context of general equilibrium theory.

Feiwel: Some scholars claim that the *General Theory* was about the instability of the capitalist economy and the tools to correct it. It is also this kind of instability with which, say, Hy Minsky is at pesent concerned. Is this sort of question of interest to modern theorists?

Fisher: That is not the question studied by stability theorists, but perhaps it ought to be. One can describe that as an instability question, with the economy embedded in a much larger dynamic system describing politics, history, and so forth, but nobody does that. I suppose it is true that one can have a dynamic model of a general equilibrium system which would show that the inevitable result is some sort of chaos or permanent underemployment and that there is no way to fix it. But that would be a rather special result. There are very few modern stability theorists, in my sense. Three of them are at present in this building [Encina Hall, Stanford University, summer of 1986] – and that is a very large fraction of the total. No, that is not what we mean when we talk about people working on stability in general equilibrium.

Feiwel: In an attempt to correct some of the critics' misperceptions, would you share with us what the notion of equilibrium means to you?

Fisher: Within the context of this discussion an equilibrium has to mean a rest point – and I shall elaborate on this presently. There is a lot of confusion in the use of the terms. A rest point refers to the action of a dynamic system. It is a point such that if the system gets to it, there is no tendency for the system to move away from it. 'Equilibrium' is often used in economics to mean a point at which markets clear. 'Equilibrium' is sometimes used, in general equilibrium theory anyway, to mean 'Walrasian equilibrium'. There certainly are dynamic systems that have the property of having rest points that are not Walrasian, for example, such as the Clower problem and the Keynesian problem. The term 'equilibrium' has no meaning unless it means a point such that when you are at it, there is no tendency to depart from it. Of course, one can speak in terms of temporary equilibria, partial equilibria, moving equilibria, and the like. Those usually mean that some things are held constant, but not all things. For example, one can think of an equilibrium for a given population size. In a dynamic system where the population would be held constant, that would mean a point from which there is no tendency to depart. In a larger system where there is a population dynamic, that would not be a rest point.

Feiwel: What does the concept of stability mean to you? What are the achievements and lacunae of stability analysis?

Fisher: I think that stability and disequilibrium dynamics is *the* principal unsolved problem of economic theory – both macro and micro economic theory. Economists are supposed to know how the price system works and how resources get allocated. We do not actually know how the price system really works in time. We have an elaborate and very elegant theory of individual agents, how they make plans and an equilibrium theory of what they do when these plans get fulfilled. But we have very little theory – and this is what stability is about – about what happens if they start from a position where the plans are not mutually compatible. We do not actually know how these things get adjusted.

Stability theory is very difficult. Modern stability theory began in the late 1930s with the introduction of serious dynamics into the study of markets. But, perhaps because equilibrium theory at the level of the individual agent is so much easier than disequilibrium theory, very little attention was paid for a very long time to the question of modelling the process that goes on out of equilibrium. That had a couple of consequences: one of them is the long-run consequence that people simply ignore the fact that it was a problem at all, and they talk about things as if one could talk about equilibrium all the time without worrying about the dynamics of a system where equilibria are embedded. The other was that the early models worked in terms of *tâtonnements* where the only things that changed out of equilibrium were prices and prices moved in the direction of excess demand. Very little attention was paid to the question of *why* they should move in the direction of excess demand, in the sense of whose behavior was it that was being described. The models resorted to a fiction – the auctioneer. Since, in fact, individual firms adjust pries, that is not very satisfactory. Very little attention was paid until well into the 1960s to the question best put as follows: in a model where everyone takes prices as given, how do prices ever change?

In any event, the study of *tâtonnements* – a study of a very unrealistic model, not only because the price change was obscured, but because it was as if nothing ever happened until equilibrium was reached – turned out to be very unsatisfactory. It did not actually get very far. It ended in a position that said: that sort of thing is stable if one is willing to make very, very strong restrictions on the nature of utility functions, production functions, and so on. About 1960 Herbert Scarf showed that, in some sense, one needed such strong restrictions; that there was not going to be a general theorem.

At about that time the subject began to advance in a more serious way because, in being forced to think about how to model trade out of equilibrium – a departure from *tâtaonnement* – people had to think about sensible trading rules. Two of them were suggested: one by Uzawa who suggested that one might make use of the proposition that people only trade when they think they are going to gain something. The other by Hahn who suggested that what we mean by markets is a system sufficiently organized that after trade there are not both people who want to sell and cannot and people who want to buy and cannot; they can meet each other (this is now sometimes called the orderly markets assumption). Fairly quickly, with both the Uzawa and the Hahn process (Uzawa named his the 'Edgeworth process', Hahn's was called the 'Hahn process' by Hahn's co-author, Negishi), it became evident that we were on to something. We now had simple models of at least exchange where one could prove stability all the time. Thinking about what was wrong with those models, the subject was on to something that turned up increasingly interesting problems. In particular, it is very hard to talk about the Hahn process very long without introducing money in a serious way. And there is a whole set of problems associated with that. That was the early 1960s, the introduction of money is perhaps 1970, the introduction of firms is perhaps the middle 1970s.

Since then not many people have worked on this. My principal work centers on the introduction of a model where the agents are not stupid. One of the problems with stability theory, at least through the mid-1970s, was that the agents involved never realized that they are in disequilibrium. They always behave stupidly as if prices will never change and as if they will complete their transactions, even though common observation reveals that is not the case. An obvious question – perhaps *the* central one – is the following: if you have an economy characterized by sensible agents (possibly rational agents) who understand that they are in disequilibrium and take advantage of arbitrage opportunities, is it or is it not true that the actions of those agents will push the economy towards an equilibrium? And, if it does, will that equilibrium be Walrasian or not? (That, as I said before, is in part the Keynesian question.)

I say that is *the* central question because all of economic theory (at least all of microeconomic theory) presumes that the answer to that question is: yes. It presumes that one really can deal with economies as if they were always in some sort of equilibrium – not necessarily Walrasian equilibrium. Indeed, all the rational expectations literature also assumes that the answer to that question is yes. Yet it is not obvious that the answer to that question is yes. There is – and here I am wandering a little – some confusion between the proposition that if one is not at an equilibrium, there is a tendency to move – which is perfectly true, in fact, that is the definition of not being at an equilibrium – and the proposition that, therefore, there must be a tendency to approach equilibrium – which is a widely different proposition. For instance, rational expectations theorists typically mistake the proposition that if there is a systematic opportunity to make money, people will take advantage of it – which is perfectly true – for the proposition that, therefore, the economy must always be in positions where there are no systematic opportunities to make money.

That may be true, but it requires proof – a proof that lies with what I mentioned before as the central question. Namely, does an economy of rational agents, acting on arbitrage opportunities, make those opportunities disappear and restore equilibrium?

My work on the subject has tried to build models where the agents actually do understand what is going on and plan in quite sophisticated ways to take advantage of it. That is an interesting thing to do, but the answer turns out to be very difficult. I do not know what the answer to that question is. I only know what the answer is under some strong general circumstances. Namely, if in some very strong sense, the agents do not keep on perceiving new opportunities for arbitrage, then it is true that the old opportunities will disappear. One can show that in quite a general way. That is more or less what one wants, but only more or less.

What one would like to have is a proposition that says: suppose there is a shock to the economy – Columbus discovers America or a Schumpeterian entrepreneur makes a new invention. What one would like to be able to show is that the actions of agents who respond to the opportunities turned up by that bring the economy back to some point of equilibrium. And one would even like to show that it happens very quickly so that one can analyze the economy by looking only at equilibrium. And one wants to show that it happens if the economy is not disturbed again. Unfortunately, that is not what I show. The problem is that what I can show is that, if the economy is not disturbed again *and* if the process of adjustment does not keep on turning up opportunities not foreseen by the agents when they started out, one does get to an equilibrium, which may not be Walrasian, by the way. The problem is that second condition: after Columbus discovered America, there were many opportunities no one ever thought of, opportunities turned up by the interaction of agents who acted on that discovery. And, that is not so simple!

What one knows at present is, I think, a very weak, very general stability theorem. It appears as if the more one moves into the direction of a realistic model where agents understand what is happening, the weaker the results tend to be. It is a hard subject. If I had to point to the weakness of stability theory, I would say that for a very long time it did not really ask the central question head on. When it does, it turns out that one gets many interesting digressions and some answer, but not a very satisfactory one. Of course, I would like to turn that around and say: 'The weakness of economic theory is that people do not work on this question.'

Feiwel: If one were to look for imperfections of competition as one of the problems explaining the prevalence of disequilibrium, how would this affect the study of stability?

Fisher: Nobody really understands much about how to deal with that kind of complication. The closest there is is Negishi's *General Equilibrium Theory* *and International Trade* where he does deal somewhat with that problem. Imperfect competition is hard enough to understand in equilibrium terms. Understanding what happens out of equilibrium in a general economy is very difficult. I am not now talking about specific partial models or particular markets. It is hard because until one understands how a competitive economy operates out of equilibrium, it is probably harder to understand in a formal way how a non-competitive economy operates.

Feiwel: Paul Samuelson once quipped: 'My theory is dynamic, every one else's is static.' To dot the i, how do you recognize that a theory is dynamic?

Fisher: It is not dotting the i, but dotting other variables because dots usually stand for time derivatives – putting dots on p, actually. Seriously, dynamic theory has to talk about the way in which things change all the time and the paths that they take. I do not know when Paul said this, but he might well have said it in the early 1940s when he was writing *Foundations of Economic Analysis*. He was probably reacting to the fact that in *Value and Capital* Hicks had introduced what is now known as Hicksian perfect stability. That has to do with whether demand curves slope down in various complicated ways. To a modern eye, the thing that stands out about that is that the discussion about whether or not demand curves slope down in such ways – however interesting it is, and we now know it is very interesting for the question as to whether there is unique general equilibrium – has nothing whatever to do with changes over time. It tells you nothing about what happens out of equilibrium. Of course, what Hicks thought he was doing was describing something which meant that, in some sense, if the economy was displaced there would be a tendency to come back. But there is no explicit modelling of time. What Paul did very early was to observe that fact and then produce the first kind of serious analysis of an explicit adjustment process in general equilibrium theory.

Feiwel: You once mentioned a distinguished economist (Friedman?) who quipped: 'It is obvious that the economy is stable and if it is not we are all wasting our time.' Would you respond in a serious way to this cavalier statement?

Fisher: Certainly. In the first place, I do not think that was a perceptive statement. In the first chapter of my book I said some specific things about this. The only reason I do not name him there is that he sort of said this to me in passing almost thiry years ago and I would not want him to get stuck with it if he does not remember it by now. I remember the occasion, but I bet he does not.

   In the first place, it is not obvious that the economy is stable. A position of stability for general equilibrium would be a point at which relative prices do not change. That is not true; relative prices do change. They change all the time! It is perfectly possible that the economy is stable in the sense that the equilibrium is moving and the economy is always rather close to the moving equilibrium and that accounts for the relative price changes. But I do not think that you can look at the economy and say, 'Yes, that is obviously true.' What he probably meant when he made that statement was: 'It is pretty obvious that most markets clear most of the time.' Probably that is true. It is not clear, however, that most markets are in long-run equilibrium much of the time. Supply and demand do change. It is a close question whether it is obvious that the economy is stable.

That, however, is not the unperceptive part of the remark. The unperceptive part of the remark was the rest of it. By the way, the full remark was: 'There is no point in studying stability because it is obvious that the economy is stable and if it is not we are all wasting our time.' The truth of the matter is that we are all wasting our time in some sense if the economy is not stable, because all of microeconomic theory rests on the proposition that one can analyze equilibria. If the economy is not stable, the properties of equilibria do not matter very much and incidentally all of welfare economics is down the tube and so is the prescription that the government ought not to intervene – something in which this particular economist is quite interested.

The real question is: does the theory lead to the proposition that the economy is stable? If it is not true that one can embed competitive equilibrium in a disequilibrium story that is stable, there is no point in discussing competitive equilibrium. So, it is a matter of considerable intellectual importance to study stability theory, in order to understand whether that is true or not. I must say that the study of stability theory does point to a couple of lessons that suggest that these considerations are very important: one proposition is that if one takes a dynamic system that describes a competitive economy, it is quite difficult to make that dynamic system have a competitive ending, even if it is stable. The second proposition – and this is quite a general proposition, one whose importance is simply not perceived – is that everything we know about stability says that one cannot get stability out of a dynamic system where only prices change. One gets stability where trade takes place out of equilibrium. And, if trade takes place out of equilibrium, it means that the place to which the economy goes, given initial conditions, is not the place to which static equilibrium theory would predict the economy would go. What that means in more general terms is that comparative statics – a major tool of static equilibrium theory – is on very, very shaky ground.

Feiwel: Does the real world offer hints to the stability analyst?

Fisher: Certainly. That is why the prominent economist we mentioned before said that obviously the economy is stable. If one looks around one typically does not see long lines of people who want to buy things the stores are not carrying. That suggests that there is no gross kind of instability all the time. The economy appears to function reasonably well. Of course, that was not true during the Great Depression. But it looks as if most of the time assuming markets are in equilibrium is a reasonable approximation. The problem is that we are not really sure why.

Feiwel: What about unemployment? Is it voluntary?

Fisher: That is an important issue. In what I just said I was overlooking unemployment. I did not mean to imply that when one looks one necessarily sees that labor markets clear all the time. On the other hand, even if labor markets do not clear, that would not tell you which of two propositions you were seeing, and I am sure there are more: one proposition is that the economy is not stable. The other proposition is that the economy is stable and it is, in fact, at a rest point, but that rest point happens to be a Keynesian one – that equilibrium involves unemployment. That is possible also. What I said in answer to your previous question was: 'If you look around and it looks as if most markets clear, then you know you are fairly close to a Walrasian equilibrium and that suggests that something good is going on.' But I take the point, we have something like 7 per cent unemployment. We have had it for a long time. I do not believe unemployment is voluntary. That suggests that either we are stuck at an underemployment equilibrium or the economy is not stable. And just from that you cannot tell which it is.

Feiwel: Some macroeconomists tend to see very little difference between the picture of an economy stuck in a very bad equilibrium, say, 10 per cent unemployment, and one where the economy moves exceedingly slowly towards full employment. Theoretically is this a correct approach?

Fisher: I almost never comment directly on macroeconomic issues, but I will comment on that one in a more general form. First of all, in some policy sense this statement is true. In order to justify the use of equilibrium tools, one has to believe the economy is close to equilibrium most of the time. Since we know that there are shocks, that requires believing two things: first, that the economy is stable, in the sense that it can absorb shocks; secondly, that it absorbs shocks quickly so that the speed of adjustment is very fast.

Feiwel: This depends on the endogenous economic mechanism?

Fisher: Yes, the endogenous mechanism that could absorb shocks quickly. The above statement is quite correct in two senses: The first is if one is going to work with theory that says all one has to worry about is full employment, and one never need think about anything else, and, in fact, it takes a very long time for unemployment to be reduced to full employment, then by the time that happens many other shocks would have occurred. Looking at the full employment equilibrium to which the system would move if one left it alone and gave it enough time is not informative as to where the actual economy is going to be. It will never be informative because what will matter is the transient behavior – what happens on the way to equilibrium – and not the equilibrium to which it gets if the system were left undisturbed. There is, of course, the second point in terms of policy, in terms of welfare economics, and in terms of the losses to the people who are unemployed. It would not have been very comforting to the people on the bread lines in the 1930s to have been told that if they just live long enough in 100 years full employment would be restored.

Feiwel: Indeed, broadly speaking, the critics of equilibrium (like Joan Robinson) say that since what characterizes an economy is change, and circumstances always alter, the concept of equilibrium as such is inapplicable. May we have your comments?

Fisher: I think that is wrong. It depends what one means by equilibrium; what dynamic system one has in view. You can imagine certain things that change slowly, let us call them parameters such as population size. That changes, of course, but it does not change very fast. Then there are things that change rapidly, such as prices, quantities, and things like that. It is perfectly possible that the following is true: at any level of the slow moving parameters (for instance, populations size), the fast moving variables adjust very quickly and the economy is stable in the sense that it is near equilibrium all the time, that is, for the fixed level of the parameters. Then the parameters change (for instance, the population grows) and the adjustment process in the fast moving variables takes place very quickly, so that, once again, one is very close to equilibrium. And that happens so fast that the economy can usefully be described as in a moving equilibrium, whose movements are controlled by the movements of the slow moving parameters. That would be a version where the economy is changing all the time. But it does make a lot of sense to talk about it in terms of equilibrium. If one wanted to redefine the problem somewhat differently, once could think of equilibrium as an equilibrium path, rather than an equilibrium state. Equilibrium does not have to be a point; it could be a time path to which the system tends to return if disturbed.

Feiwel: When a good econometrician speaks of structural change, does he in a sense mean what you were saying?

Fisher: In some sense that is quite right. Econometricians specify structural equations – equations that describe behavior and are estimated over some periods of time. Typically econometricians do not attempt to behave as though the same parameters, the same coefficients, and the same structural equations describe phenomena over very, very long periods of time. Nobody supposes that the demand for wheat in the UK is the same in the 1980s as it was in the 1780s, though it may well be characterized by some of the same variables. The reason for that is that, of course, some things do change: tastes change, populations change, new goods appear, and so forth. That does not make it any the less useful to say that over periods of time, involving twenty or thirty years, one can, in fact, describe the economy with stable equations. If one does not think that in some sense that is true – that is, that given the appropriate variables, one can describe the economy and economic behavior in equations that will stay put long enough to be worth looking at – then there is no point in talking about economic theory at all, equilibrium or not.

Feiwel: Is there anything else you would like to emphasize about the difficulties of stability theory?

Fisher: Although I have said much of this in passing, I would like to stress that too many people think that stability theory is a poor subject. In fact it is a subject with poor answers to very important questions. People tend to shy away from it sometimes by confusing the notion of what equilibrium means. One version, for some rational expectations economists, defines everything as an equilibrium, in the sense that something happens; there is an outcome. Therefore, people must have been at least temporarily satisfied to produce that outcome. That is not a sensible way of answering the question whether the economy is stable, because one has to answer why that outcome instead of another. If the notion of equilibrium is to mean anything, one has to admit the possibility of points that are not equilibria. Otherwise there is no content. So, one always has to think in terms of smaller or larger dynamic systems where the rest points are what we call equilibria and then ask: what happens if one is not at that rest point? As I said before, there is a tendency to confuse the view that if one is not at an equilibrium, one will not stay where one is, with the view that one must approach equilibrium – and that is quite a different and much harder proposition. Perhaps because equilibrium tools are so elegant and so relatively easy, economists always work in terms of those. As I guess I have indicated, there is a big gaping hole in the center of what economists know, namely, the question of what happens out of equilibrium and whether we ever get close to equilibrium, and so forth. It is an important gaping hole because most of what we do depends on assuming that it is not a problem. And we really have very little basis for that.

Feiwel: Given differences in taste, why does such a fascinating subject as stability analysis fascinate Frank Fisher and a few others only who are in a minority?

Fisher: Considering who some of the people are who are interested in stability, one might say that it is simply a peculiar perversion, able to be appreciated only by those of us with otherwise jaded palates. I am not sure of the answer; there are several possible ones, some of which are connected: one of them is that it is really hard ...

Feiwel: Is it mathematically intractable?

Fisher: No. Perhaps if we had more and better mathematical tools it might be easier, I do not know. But I do not think that is the reason. The mathematics do not appear to be particularly complex. The economics is very hard. As I said before, the problem is that we have a very elegant theory of how agents, households, and firms make plans. If those plans are fulfilled, there is no need to go any further. It then becomes a natural question to ask whether there exist situations where all these plans are fulfilled. That is what one means by positions of competitive equilibrium.

To study disequilibrium seriously, one has to study what happens when plans are not fulfilled. That means asking how agents behave when they are disappointed. Well, we do not have a good theory about that. The theory of the individual agent does not help very much. To do that really right one has to endow the agents with uncertainty and to ask how they behave under uncertainty. That adds another level of complication that is not adequately handled – at least, I do not know how to handle it – in the context of a dynamic model where part of the uncertainty is generated by the actions of the agents themselves. That kind of thing is very hard. No one has actually dealt with this in the context of a serious theory. My model deals with it by assuming that agents can be wrong but they have point expectations – which makes them 'economists', by the way; they are often wrong, but they are never uncertain.

Thus one reason why so few people work on stability is that to do so one has to depart from the usual ways of thinking. And the results do not pay off a lot. So, one possibility is that the marginal costs are very high and the marginal revenues very small. Economists can make maximizing calculations better than most people. Yet, there is more to it than that. The fact that there is a major problem is typically unnoticed and is not taught to students as a major problem. Exactly why that is, I am not sure.

Another possibility is historical. As I know somewhat more about the history of this subject than most people, I find it a little hard to understand. It is fair to say that there was a big boom in stability theory, such as it was, in the 1950s. That big boom was the study of *tâtonnement*, produced very largely by the publication of the papers by Arrow and Hurwicz, and Arrow, Hurwicz, and Block. For a short time, it looked as though there was going to be a lot of mileage in this subject. Particularly Japanese authors began to turn out papers that tried to generalize the proofs of *tâtonnement* stability from things like gross substitutes to weak gross substitutes and to various other minor extensions. There was a sort of mini-industry in this. Then about 1960 came Herb Scarf's paper which – in my present interpretation with twenty-six years' hindsight – said pretty clearly: *tâtonnement* is not always stable and, what is more, it is not even almost always stable, because we *now* know that the Scarf example is true on an open set. Without very strong assumptions it is not going to be true that one can prove stability. The assumptions under which one had been able to prove stability under *tâtonnement* were very, very strong and very, very unrealistic. The subject appeared to have come to a dead end right there.

What is peculiar is that it did not in fact come to a dead end. At about the same time the next stage of the subject was taking off, namely, the study of what happens when there is trade out of equilibrium, involving the Hahn and Edgeworth processes with which the names of Hahn, Negeshi, and Uzawa are associated. One could get a lot further with that. I have found, however, that even today, even among my own colleagues (not so much among the latter because I have been bullying them about this for ten years), when one says one is working on stability, it is tacitly assumed that one is working on *tâtonnement*. One's interlocutors immediately think: that is a silly model, it does not involve anyone's behavior, and we know it does not go anywhere, why would anyone want to be working on this? The existence of a whole subsequent literature (few people, but a lot of articles) is simply overlooked. There is then a tendency to say: 'Well, there are not enough results to teach students.' And so, one doesn't. I think that students are, in fact, steered away from the subject.

11 On Long-run Equilibrium in Class Society

Edward Nell*

The notion of equilibrium and the distinction between two kinds, long run and short, has been fundamental to almost all economic analysis of the past century. By contrast, the classics and Marx sought for the 'laws of motion' of capitalism. These latter do not define a long-run equilibrium, and it will be the claim here that a full-fledged, long-run equilibrium is not possible in a class society. This is not exactly Joan Robinson's position, but it is close, and it builds on some of her favorite themes.

We shall take it that the predominant sense of 'equilibrium' describes a position of the economy in which no agent has any incentive to change behavior; it is therefore a behavioral concept. The classics, by contrast, analyzed structure, and turned to behavioral notions only when dealing with market fluctuations around the economy's 'natural' position. (By 'behavior' we mean stimulus-response patterns, as in supply or demand functions; 'structure', on the other hand, refers to roles and institutions, which have to be maintained or reproduced. Of course, structure implies propensities to kinds of behavior, and behavior occurs in a structural setting, but the two are nevertheless significantly different.) Such 'natural' positions are inherent in the economy's structure; attempts to interpret them as positions of long-run (behavioral) equilibrium must be rejected, if the contentions of this paper are correct. To see what is involved, let's examine the notion of equilibrium.

Arrow, in concert first with Debreu (1954) and later with Hahn (1971), has greatly deepened our understanding of Hicks' (1939) notion of 'temporary equilibrium', itself a development of the older notion of short-run equilibrium, elaborated most fully by Marshall (1895). Marshall's 'short period' was defined by the fact that some or most factors of production could be varied, so that output could be adjusted, but at least one factor remained fixed. In simple models, labor was treated as variable while land and/or capital were held fixed. So, ignoring non-competing groups and other barriers to entry, the wage rate would be made uniform across different lines of work by competition. But if capital is fixed (and in modern 'temporary equilibrium' all factors are fixed in amount), then in the short period returns

*Thanks for comments and discussions on earlier versions of this paper go to G. C. Harcourt, Cigdem Kurdas, Heinz Kurz and Anwar Shaikh.

to capital invested in different lines of activity might vary, for the forces of competition would not have time to take effect. In the long run, however, capital, too, could be shifted between lines of activity, and this ebb and flow in search of the most profitable opportunities would only cease when returns to capital invested stood in the same proportion in all spheres. For if returns were non-uniform, there would exist an incentive to disinvest in low return areas and reinvest where returns are high. The analogy with the 'law of one price' is exact.

Ricardo and Marx both recognized this, and made the establishment of uniformity in the rate of profit central to their analysis of the formation of prices, though not in an equilibrium context. Likewise, the early neoclassical thinkers, Marshall, Walras, Wicksell, Clark, and others, all held both that uniformity in the rate of profit was essential to the establishment of long-run equilibrium, and that the analysis of the economy's long-period positions was a central task of economic theory, perhaps even its most important one.

But starting in the 1930s both these tenets were abandoned, as mainstream thinkers came to adopt the approach of 'temporary equilibrium'. The chief difference between this and the older notion of short-run equilibrium is that it no longer relies on the broad concept of a factor of production, such as labor in general, or capital, considered as a fund capable of adopting different forms – that is, of being invested in different sets of productive equipment. Instead, it takes each type of labor and each particular capital good as given, and it determines the appropriate shadow price or rental value. The ratio of this rental value to supply price is not considered; only the supply and demand conditions are examined, and the equilibrium prices are those that clear the markets. But such equilibria are temporary, and therefore it may be appropriate to investigate sequences of them. One of the properties of such sequences could be that rental value – supply price ratios for the various capital goods would tend to converge as the sequence lengthens to infinity. But this has not been much investigated; it is likely, however, that along the way the relations between capital values and the rates of return may be highly irregular or 'perverse'.

1 THE QUESTION OF THE RATE OF PROFIT

Serious questions can be raised about this approach, particularly when we require our models to exhibit fully the production of means of production, i.e. of capital goods. Why would owners of any capital goods accept a lower rate of return on the value of their productive equipment than was available to others, even in the short run? The short-period equilibrium is either reached by a process of *tâtonnement*, or through recontracting, either of which would provide plenty of opportunity for owners to search out and compete for the best returns. Information, foresight and mobility are all assumed to be perfect, so all owners of capital goods (and, *mutatis mutandis*, labor) not only know where the best returns will be, but could threaten to shift their activity there. Moreover, some aspects of methods of production are normally assumed to be variable, so that the temporary equilibrium will reflect a cost-minimizing choice of technique. That makes it even harder to see why owners of factors would not insist on the best rate of return on their investment.

The crucial missing element in this approach is what Marshall called 'free capital', and Hicks (1965) has referred to as the 'fund' concept of capital. Capital, as J. B. Clark knew very well, alternately takes the form of a fund of value and a set of productive goods. As the goods are used up in production, output results and is sold, returning the capital in the form of investible funds, which will at all times seek the highest returns. Thus even in the short period, there will be some capital in the form of funds – last period's depreciation, plus this period's new saving – which will potentially be shifting about in search of the highest rate of return. Even if this process is not modelled explicitly, its implication – the tendency to seek the highest rate of return – must be incorporated.

So long as the returns from using equipment in relation to its supply price are unequal, the pressure for such shifting will continue to exist. Once the rate of return is uniform, capital will no longer tend to move about, disrupting prices. But this brings us face to face with a surprising and in some quarters unwelcome implication, namely that, given a set of methods of production with certain commonly assumed characteristics (single product, 'productive', constant returns, no technical change, at least one basic good, and one primary factor – labor), the establishment of a uniform rate of profit is sufficient to determine both the choice of the method of production and the set of equilibrium prices, including the real-wage, independently of demand, and therefore of market clearing. Such prices have nothing to do with scarcity; they reflect embodied labor (Arrow and Hahn, 1971, p. 45; Pasinetti, 1975, ch. 5). Or, to put the point perhaps more revealingly, in a manner favored by Joan Robinson, they reflect a different conception of the function of the price system. Instead of indicating the most preferred choice among constrained alternatives, thus measuring scarcity as it affects behavior, prices show the exchanges that would be required to bring about the reproduction of the system with a particular distribution. This is a structural notion; it doesn't picture behavior occurring in response to stimuli, so it doesn't depend on assumptions about knowledge, rationality, veridical perceptions, mobility of factors, or the like, all of which are crucial to behavioral theories (Nell, 1967, 1984). This view of the price system, therefore, does not involve the concept of equilibrium in the sense we are using the term, although as we shall see, Hicks has given it an equilibrium interpretation, treating it as simply an alternative approach, on the same level as the method of temporary equilibrium.

2   THE 'METHOD OF GROWTH ECONOMICS'

The different way that prices work seems to be the chief reason that Hicks came to consider what he called 'Growth Economics', in which prices are determined by the rate of profit (itself inversely related to the real wage), as a separate 'method' of dynamic economics, on the same level of generality as the 'Temporary Equilibrium' method, but more useful because more suited to combination with 'Fixprice' thinking, i.e. the microeconomics of Keynes, Robinson, Harrod and the cycle theorists (Hicks, 1965, Part I). The 'Temporary Equilibrium' method is defective, in Hicks's view, because of its inadequate treatment of uncertainty, its assumption of perfect competition, but, above all, because it assumes, it *has* to assume (for otherwise prices would not be determinate), that markets clear each period. Because in 'Growth Economics' prices are determined by distribution, rather than by supply and demand, it is not necessary to assume unrealistic market clearing; hence the model is capable of providing the price-theoretic foundations for macroeconomics. But this introduces a new dimension, the growth of the economy, as a result of investment. The relationship of this to profits and distribution in long-run equilibrium must now be considered.

3   THE UNIFORM GROWTH RATE

The essential idea of a growth equilibrium is that all variables expand at the same positive rate, which must also be determined. This replaces the earlier, static idea of long-run equilibrium, in which all variables are fully adjusted, but essentially fixed, i.e. growing at the rate of zero. This requires closer examination.[1]

Growth in long-run equilibrium must be uniform; that is, all industries and sectors must be expanding at the same rate. If some industry were growing faster than its suppliers, for example, once inventories of suppliers were exhausted (and the running down of inventories itself would represent a change in capital holdings) the suppliers would have to try to change their output allocation in order to sustain the fast-growing industry. But they would not be able to do so, because (in an interdependent system with at least one basic) *their* suppliers would not be able to keep up. So the faster-growing industry would have to slow down. Similarly, if an industry were growing more slowly than its suppliers – or customers – then it would both have the incentive and the means to expand more rapidly. Of course, non-uniform growth is easily possible, at least for short periods, even when the economy is operating at or near normal full capacity. But it is not sustainable without changes in inventories and/or in average costs, so it is not a possible position of equilibrium. Only a uniform rate could be that.

A rate of growth is the ratio of output at the end of one period to output at the end of the previous period. But when the good in question is a produced means of production – a capital good, a 'basic' – then the growth rate (the potential, or full capacity growth rate) is the ratio of the output of the good to the amount of it used directly and indirectly as input. Such a ratio can be defined for every capital good. Assume either that capital goods last one period only, or that they all have the same lifetime and depreciate linearly. Then consider the set of all capital goods used directly or indirectly in each other's production – Sraffa's basics. The growth rate of this set will be constrained by the lowest ratio of output to the vertically integrated means of production; and the highest growth rate sustainable from period to period will be achieved when all such output to use-as-input ratios are uniform (Pasinetti, 1975; Brody, 1970; Mathur, 1965). But in that case the ratios of the various outputs to one another will be the same as the ratios of the various inputs to one another; the economy's output will be a 'composite commodity' consisting of the same goods in the same proportions as the aggregate of its capital goods inputs. (This conception can be extended to the case of capital goods with different lifetimes and different patterns of depreciation (Sraffa, 1960).)

4   THE RATE OF PROFIT AND THE RATE OF GROWTH

Finally, let's examine the relation between the rate of profit and the rate of growth in equilibrium. First, consider the question of uniformity. Movements of capital from low to high profit industries generate the uniform rate of profit; but it is also movements of capital, from slack to 'bottleneck' industries, which bring uniformity in growth rates. Hence, if either the growth or the profit rate is upset, causing capital to shift about, the uniformity of the other will be threatened. Since the same cause (movements of capital between sectors) establishes both uniformities, anything which incites such movements threatens both. The uniformities must therefore be considered interdependent.

Next, taking the two rates as uniform, consider the relations between them. We will begin with some quite specialized institutional assumptions, but these have been chosen to bring out certain connections, which hold more generally. Consider a set of capitalists who deal only in machinery and capital goods. They themselves do not operate the equipment; they merely lease it out to entrepreneurs. Each period they buy the entire output of the capital goods industries, which they then make available to producers in both the consumer goods industries and in the capital goods sector itself. Let us suppose that all production is organized in this way; producers are entrepreneurs who earn only salaries and 'pure profits', which are zero in long-run equilibrium. Hence the equilibrium leasing fees, or rentals, must enable the capitalists to cover their own consumption and to purchase this period's output of capital goods. Part of current output will simply replace the capital goods used up or depreciated in the course of current production; if the leasing fees cover no more than this there will be no net profit. But if the current output of the capital goods sector is greater than replacement and depreciation, the ratio of such current output to the capital goods used to produce it will be the rate of growth of the capital stock, and the leasing fees will have to be sufficient to permit the capitalists to purchase this current output. The surplus of the leasing fees over the amount required for depreciation will be the capitalists' net profit, which will have to exactly equal their consumption plus what they need to buy the additional output which represents the growth of this period's production over last period's. If we neglect capitalist consumption for the moment, this period's net leasing fees go to purchase the capital goods which will serve as next period's net investment. The rate of profit is given by the ratio of the leasing fees to last period's output (this period's invested capital), while the rate of growth is the ratio of next period's invested capital to this period's, and in equilibrium these will clearly have to be equal, since there could be arbitrage between owning the leasing industry and owning producing industries.

This argument made some very special institutional assumptions, but it brought to light the general relationship between accumulation in value terms, based on profits minus planned capitalist consumption, and real investment, which is the acquisition and installation of the equipment produced by the capital goods producers. In long-run equilibrium, growth must be balanced and growth in value and in real terms must proceed at the same rate.[2]

To put it another way: if either the rate of profit or the rate of accumulation is non-uniform, we *know* that prices and outputs must change from period to period, and, moreover, we will often have enough information to say which prices and/or which outputs will change and in which directions they will move. So if we are to define a long-period equilibrium, by contrast to temporary equilibrium, as a position in which agents are not only satisfied, but which will be maintained from period to period so long as the fundamental data remain unchanged, we must require uniformity of these two rates (automatically achieved in a zero-profit stationary state, for both rates are then uniform at zero), and the appropriate relationship between them.

5   A CLAIM OF THE CRITICS

But critics of orthodox economics have claimed that the notion of equilibrium itself was inconsistent with capitalism. (Lenin's notion of uneven development surely implies this.) To put it in contemporary terms, can capitalism proceed along a path of steady growth? Alternatively, can capitalism be studied using the 'method' of Growth Economics, that is, by comparing (hypothetical) situations of economies, similar in various respects, but growing at different rates, and/or with different rates of profit? We have now developed the concept of long-run equilibrium in a capitalist economy; let's examine the challenge of the critics.

We began from the dual nature of capital, as freely movable funds, and as produced means of production, which led to the notions of the uniform rate of profit and of accumulation, and the critique of the Temporary Equilibrium approach. But we have not yet considered the implications of the most basic fact about the capitalist system: that it is a class society.

6   CAPITALISM AND SOCIAL CLASSES

The concept of class, as it is used in sociology, is ambiguous and multidimensional, but for the purposes of developing an abstract economic theory we can adopt a simple and consistent notion, such as figured in the work of Smith and Ricardo (and to some extent, Marx, although his use of the concept goes beyond economics and raises new problems). For our purposes, class is based on the kinship system: classes are classes of families, that is, of working household units, which function both as consumers, supporting the workers and decision makers of this generation, and as producers of the next generation. Working-class families own very little wealth, not enough to provide a living income, and so must be supported by working for wages. Working-class offspring will generally marry within the working class, just as children of capitalist families will marry within their class. Capitalist families are defined by the ownership of wealth on a substantial scale, which yields profit income, and entails rights to make decisions about the uses to which means of production will be put. But working-class families will normally save, for precautionary reasons, if for no other, and so will accumulate wealth, which will yield them profit income, in addition to their wages. And capitalists will have to manage their wealth, making decisions about how and where to invest it. By normal definitions this is work, entitling them to a salary, particularly in view of the fact that managing investments requires skill and information. (Moreover, because of such specialization, capitalist managers will also handle the savings of workers.) Hence, in addition to profit income, capitalist households will normally also draw salaries. The *per capita* level of salaries, however, will be much higher than the working class wage rate, reflecting both the ability of the status and prestige conferred by wealth to command income, and returns to the investment in the acquisition of skills.

7   A SIMPLE MODEL OF GROWTH EQUILIBRIUM

If we were to write it out in full there would be at least three sectors, one producing capital goods (of various kinds), another consumer goods for workers, and one producing a higher grade of consumer goods for capitalist households. However, for simplicity we can aggregate the sectors. It is necessary to assume that all household income expenditure functions are linear; otherwise, and realistically, as the system expands the proportions of spending on different goods would change. For simplicity we shall assume that all households in each class are identical. For the system to be in Growth Equilibrium, the various sectors must all expand at the same rate, and industries must earn the same rate of profit on their invested capital. Under these circumstances prices will remain constant, making it easy to aggregate output, income and capital. Hence, using an obvious notation, we can write, using 'w' and 'c' to indicate workers and capitalists,

$$Y = C_w + C_c + I = W + P = xK \tag{1}$$

where $W = W_c + W_w$, $P = P_c + P_w$, $K = K_c + K_w$, and

$$L_w = nK, \text{ and } L_c = mK \tag{2}$$

where x, n and m are the ratios of output, factory labor and management, respectively, to capital.

Now consider the implication of long-run equilibrium for the class structure: the relative wealth and income of the two classes must remain constant (if either changed, the ratio Cw/Cc would have to change), so both classes must find their wealth expanding at the same rate, and must receive income from wealth in the same proportion, which is to say that their wealth holdings yield the same rate of profit. So we can write,

$$\frac{P_c}{K_c} = \frac{P_w}{K_w} = r \tag{3}$$

and

$$\frac{S_c}{K_c} = \frac{S_w}{K_w} = g \tag{4}$$

showing that the wealth holdings of the two classes both earn returns at the same rate and grow at the same rate. However, the wealth of the two classes is very different *per capita*, capitalists being substantially wealthier, though how much is not at issue here. So,

$$\frac{K_c}{L_c} = \frac{aK_w}{L_w} \tag{5}$$

where $a > 1$ is the coefficient indicating the extent to which capitalists are wealthier.

Next we must consider wages and salaries. The possession of wealth not only provides direct returns in the form of profits, but (notoriously) confers advantages in the earning of income, partly through the influence of position, and partly through the development of skills – so-called 'human capital'. In long-run equilibrium the effect of wealth on earning power must be the same for all forms and holdings of wealth and all types of work. Hence the ratio of salaries *per capita* to the wage-rate must be the same as the ratio of capitalist wealth to working-class wealth. So,

$$\frac{W_c}{L_c} = \frac{aW_w}{L_w} \tag{6}$$

Dividing (5) into (6) and then into (4) gives us,

$$\frac{S_c}{W_c} = \frac{S_w}{W_w} \tag{7}$$

so that, writing 's_c' and 's_w' for the respective saving propensities, which reflect the different circumstances of the classes,

$$\frac{s_c(P_c + W_c)}{W_c} = \frac{s_w(P_w + W_w)}{W_w}. \tag{8}$$

Dividing (6) into (5) and then into (3) yields,

$$\frac{P_w}{W_w} = \frac{P_c}{W_c} = \frac{P}{W} \tag{9}$$

so we can rewrite (8)

$$s_c\frac{P}{W} + s_c = s_w\frac{P}{W} + s_w \tag{10}$$

from which it follows that,

$$\frac{P}{W} = \frac{s_w - s_c}{s_c - s_w} = -1, \; s_w \neq s_c. \tag{11}$$

(When $s_w = s_c$ the result will be indeterminate.)[3]

8   CLASS WEALTH AND THE SALARY/WAGE DIFFERENTIAL

Should we assume that the salary/wage differential echoes the wealth ratio of the two classes? The argument is that in long-run equilibrium the power of capital to increase wages, or more generally earned incomes, must be the same everywhere. Otherwise, there would be attempts to create institutions to take advantage of the ability of capital to produce higher earnings in some areas. Suppose capital could augment worker earnings in some particular line; workers could then pool savings, and then boost the earnings of some select few, who would then divide the additional earnings among those who had contributed to the pool (very much as the extended family chips in to send a promising son to college). Note that the argument is not that this will tend to equalize returns; it is rather that if returns are not equalized, then these disequilibrium movements will occur.

Still, let's consider the case where, instead of (6) we have

$$W_c/L_c = bW_w/L_w \qquad (6')$$

from which we get

$$S_c/W_c = a/b(S_w/W_w). \qquad (7')$$

Manipulating further

$$P/W = [a/bs_w - s_c]/[a/b(s_c - s_w)] \qquad (11')$$

which will be > 0 if and only if $a/bs_w > s_c$, i.e. $as_w > bs_c$, or $a/b > s_c/s_w$. This is both arbitrary and implausible. For the profit–wage ratio to be positive, wealth must augment capitalist salaries very little if it affects their saving very much; the higher s_c in relation to s_w, the lower b has to be in relation to a. But if wealth promotes class differences in saving, will it not also bring about class differences in earned income?

9   GROWTH EQUILIBRIUM V. CLASS BEHAVIOR

A negative profit–wage ratio does not make sense; the system is inconsistent. Let us see what has gone wrong. From (5) and (6) we obtain,

$$\frac{W_c}{K_c} = \frac{W_w}{K_w} \qquad (12)$$

hence adding to (3),

$$\frac{P_c + W_c}{K_c} = \frac{P_w + W_w}{K_w}. \tag{13}$$

Income per unit of wealth is the same in the two classes, although, of course, income *per capita* is higher for the capitalists, so the growth rates of wealth cannot be the same unless the saving ratios are identical. But the respective saving ratios reflect the different positions of the classes; higher *per capita* wealth and income should produce a higher saving ratio. Working-class households will spend most of their income on essentials; saving will therefore be expensive in terms of forgone necessities. By contrast capitalists will only have to give up luxuries in order to save.[4]

Looking at it another way, since their current consumer needs are well provided for, capitalist households can afford to set funds aside for the future, whereas working-class households must give prime consideration to filling current needs. So it is inherent in the concept of a class society that the saving–consumption behavior of the two classes should be different, but the conditions of long-run equilibrium require their behavior to be the same.

10 DIFFERENT PROPENSITIES TO SAVE OUT OF WAGES AND PROFITS

This last point is more complicated than it might seem. Clearly if both classes have the same proportional saving function both will accumulate at the same rate. But this is not necessary; from (3) and (12), we find

$$\frac{P_c}{W_c} = \frac{P_w}{W_w}. \tag{14}$$

So if the saving propensities out of profits and out of wages are the same for both classes, even though different for the different kinds of income, then each class will have the same average propensity to save, overall, and hence will accumulate at the same rate.

Granted that there can be good reasons for saving to take place at different rates out of different kinds of income, e.g. that the payments of wages and profits were timed differently, but there is equally good reason to suppose that the respective patterns of saving behavior will be different in the two classes.[5] Suppose we add further subscripts to distinguish each class's propensity to save out of each kind of income. Then we have four distinct saving propensities, two for each class, and we write:

$$S_c = s_{cp}P_c + s_{cw}W_c \text{ and } S_w = s_{wp}P_w + s_{ww}W_w \tag{15}$$

so, following the same procedure, we find

$$s_{cp}\frac{P_c}{W_c} + s_{cw} = s_{wp}\frac{P_w}{W_w} + s_{ww}, \text{ yielding}$$

$$\frac{P}{W} = \frac{s_{ww} - s_{cw}}{s_{cp} - s_{wp}}. \tag{16}$$

The most plausible case will be $s_{cp} > s_{cw} > s_{wp} > s_{ww}$, which implies that P/W will be negative. Since $s_{cp} > s_{wp}$ is very reasonable, a positive ratio would require that workers save more from wages than capitalists from salaries, which does not make economic sense, given our assumptions on the nature of the class system.

11 MANY SOCIAL CLASSES

These results can easily be generalized. Suppose there are m classes, $i = 1, \ldots,$ m, each receiving both kinds of income. Then we rewrite (3) and (4),

$$P_i = rK_i \tag{3'}$$

$$S_i = gK_i. \tag{4'}$$

Next we suppose that earned income for any class consists of two parts, a basic socially determined subsistence wage – the same for all – and an additional portion which reflects the command of wealth. This last may be thought of as due to investment in the acquisition of skills in proportion to wealth, with the skills also being rewarded proportionally. This amounts to contending that 'human capital' must be held in proportion to non-human, as a requirement of long-run equilibrium. But this then poses the problem that the two kinds of capital, human and non-human, must either earn the same rate of return, or we must explain the differential. Alternatively, the fraction of earned income proportional to wealth could be considered as a command over income provided by privilege and social prestige, a kind of monopoly rent available to those with the inside information and contacts which follow from the ownership of property. In any case, let woi stand for the conventionally determined subsistence component of the wage; then,

$$w_i = w_{oi} + b_i K_i \tag{17}$$

where w is the total wage received by each class, basic plus wealth-determined, and b is the coefficient for each of the i social classes indicating the influence of its wealth in procuring earned income. In the 'human capital' interpretation, however, b would have to be uniform for all groups, since everyone's capital must earn the same return in equilibrium. Taking the more general case where b can vary between different classes.

$$S_i = s_i(w_i - w_{oi} + P_i) \tag{18}$$

which states that saving by the *i-th* class will take place out of profits and wealth-related earned income. Alternatively,

$$S_i = s_{wi}(w_i - w_{oi}) + s_{pi}P_i. \tag{18'}$$

Then using (17) we have

$$S_i = s_i(b_i + r)K_i, \text{ or from (18'): } S_i = (s_{wi}b_i + s_{pi}r)K_i. \tag{19}$$

It follows that,

$$s_i(b_i + r) = g = s_j(b_j + r) \tag{20}$$

or:

$$s_{wi}b_i + s_{pi}r = g = s_{wj}b_j + s_{pj}r.$$

And this in turn implies

$$r = [s_jb_j - s_ib_i]/(s_i - s_j) \tag{21}$$

which will be > 0 if and only if $b_j/b_i > s_i/s_j$. Alternatively,

$$r = [s_{wj}b_j - s_{wi}b_i]/(s_{pi} - s_{pj}) > 0 \text{ iff } b_j/b_i > s_{wi}/s_{wj}.$$

In both cases the condition is wholly arbitrary; even worse, it implies that the class whose wealth generates more income must save less out of it, as a condition for the rate of profit to be positive in long-run equilibrium, i.e. for the system to make minimal economic sense. (This is a generalization of 11'.) Now consider

$$[s_kb_k - s_ib_i]/(s_i - s_k), \ k \neq j.$$

If either s_k or b_k differ from s_j or b_j, then the calculated value of r will differ also. If there are more than two classes whose saving behavior, or the earning power of whose wealth differ, then the rate of profit cannot be uniform, even if the conditions for its being positive are met.

Finally, from (21), in the human capital case, where $b = b_j = b_i$, it follows that $r = -b$. If wealth invested in human skills contributes to earning power at a positive rate, uniform in all social classes, and if saving takes place at different rates in these classes, then non-human wealth will suffer loss at the same rate that human wealth earns returns, in order for the classes to accumulate at the same rate, i.e. for their wealth holdings to maintain a constant ratio.

12   MORE ON HUMAN CAPITAL

Suppose the return on human capital were treated as another form of the return to capital as such, so that the part of the earnings from work which are due to the holding of wealth were added to ordinary profits to determine the (augmented) rate of profit. Then we would have,

$$P_i + b_i K_i = r K_i, \text{ or } r = P_i/K_i + b_i. \tag{3''}$$

Clearly for r to be uniform all classes must have the same wealth–salary coefficient, b. Since wages are now w_{oi}, the socially determined subsistence wages, all saving will come out of wealth-related income, i.e. augmented profits. Hence,

$$S_i = g K_i = s_i(b_i + P_i/K_i)K_i = s_i r K_i \tag{4''}$$

Hence for g to be uniform,

$$s_i r = s_j r = g,$$

all classes must have identical saving behavior.

13   CORPORATE RETAINED EARNINGS

So far we have worked with a highly simplified picture of capitalism, in which its most characteristic institution, the modern corporation, has not even been mentioned. To rectify this, while keeping the argument manageable, we continue to assume that there are two classes of households, workers and capitalists, both receiving both profit and wage income, in proportion to their wealth. But now their (non-human) wealth is held explicitly in the form of shares in corporations, the number and distribution of which we take to be fixed. Income from such wealth comes in the form of dividends distributed by the corporations. Hence, in addition to distributed earnings, there will or may be undistributed earnings retained by the companies. These when invested will increase the value of the corporations' operating systems. So in anticipation of such successful investments, the shares of the companies will appreciate, and this appreciation along with savings will determine the expansion of wealth holdings.

Each class, therefore, saves and spends out of its income, which it receives as wage and dividend payments, but passively accepts the capital gains which result from the rise in the value of the shares it holds. As before, the classes can be presumed to have different consumption patterns, so that long-run equilibrium will require their wealth holdings to grow at the same rate:

$$[s_w(W_w + D_w) + N_w\Delta\$]/N_w\$ = [s_c(W_c + D_c) + N_c\Delta\$]/N_c\$ \tag{22}$$

where D_w and D_c are the dividends received by the two classes, N_w and N_c are the numbers of shares held respectively by the classes, while '$\$$' is the price of a share, and Δ is the operator 'delta'. Then, since corporations borrow and invest the savings of households, company growth will be:

$$g = [RP + s_w(W_w + D_w) + s_c(W_c + D_c)]/N\$ \tag{23}$$

where P is total profits, so that RP is retained earnings and $(1 - R)P = D_w + D_c = D$, distributed profit. In long-run equilibrium company growth must equal the expansion in household wealth; hence adding the numerators and denominators of (22) and comparing to (23), we see that the rate of increase in share values must equal the ratio of retained earning to the value of corporate invested capital.

Just as accumulation rates must be equal, so must profit rates; hence

$$[D_w + N_w\Delta\$]/N_w\$ = [D_c + N_c\Delta\$]/N_c\$ = P/N\$ = r \tag{24}$$

which implies,

$$D_w/N_w\$ = D_c/N_c\$ = D/N\$ = (1 - R)P/N\$. \tag{25}$$

As before we have,

$$W_c/L_c = aW_w/L_w, \text{ and } N_c\$/L_c = aN_w\$/L_w \tag{26}$$

from which

$$W_c/N_c\$ = W_w/N_w\$ = W/N\$. \tag{27}$$

Hence, using (24)

$$W_c/W_w = N_c\$/N_w\$ = [D_c + N_c\Delta\$]/[D_w + N_w\Delta\$] \tag{28}$$
$$= \{W_c + D_c + N_c\Delta\$\}/\{W_w + D_w + N_w\Delta\$\} = Y_c/Y_w$$

where Y stands for the total income of a class.

Similarly, we can derive

$$[D_c + N_c\Delta\$]/W_c = [D_w + N_w\Delta\$]/W_w = P/W. \tag{29}$$

Thus in long-run equilibrium both class incomes and functional shares are determined in a fixed ratio.

Now divide (22) by (27) and rearrange, obtaining

$$s_w(1 + D_w/W_w) + N_w\Delta\$/W_w = s_c(1 + D_c/W_c) + N_c\Delta\$/W_c. \tag{30}$$

But from (27) and (29) we know that $N_w/W_w = N_c/W_c$ and that $D_w/W_w = D_c/W_c = P/W$, so rewriting, we get

$$s_w + s_w P/W = s_c + s_c P/W \tag{31}$$

which yields

$$P/W = [s_c - s_w]/(s_w - s_c) = -1 \tag{32}$$

as before.

Introducing corporations does make a difference; under the assumptions here, the higher the retention rate, the higher will be the equilibrium growth rate (since there is no consumption out of capital gains). The corporation is the institutional form designed to promote capital accumulation in modern conditions (see Marglin, 1974). But it does nothing to resolve the conflict between the conditions required for long-run equilibrium and the differential behavior patterns inherent in class society, which results in the economically impossible equation (32).

14   ACCUMULATION, RELATIVE SHARES AND CLASS SIZES

The problem, of course, arises from imposing the condition of equal rates of accumulation on an economy in which saving and consuming behavior will be conditioned by social class. Let us now see what happens when we drop that requirement.

From (2) we see that the ratio of the sizes of the two classes is m/n, and we can now relate this to relative rates of growth and relative shares. From (5), then, we have,

$$K_c/K_w = aL_c/L_w = am/n. \tag{33}$$

But we know that

$$K_c/K_w = P_c/P_w = W_c/W_w \tag{34}$$

so that $P/W = am/n$.

From (1) and the definitions we can derive

$$\frac{dK}{K} = \left(\frac{K_c}{K}\right)\frac{dK_c}{K_c} + \left(\frac{K_w}{K}\right)\frac{dK_w}{K_w} \quad \text{or}$$

$$g = \theta gc + (1 - \theta)gw, \text{ where } \theta = K_c/K. \tag{35}$$

Hence from (33)

$$\theta = (am/n)/[am/n + 1], \text{ and } 1 > \theta > 0. \tag{36}$$

Next suppose that the saving behavior of the classes is such that their saving propensities are directly proportional to their *per capita* wealth. If the constants of proportionality are the same,

$$s_c = as_w, \text{ and since } Y_c/K_c = Y_w/K_w, g_c = ag_w. \tag{37}$$

Hence,

$$g = [(1 + \theta(a - 1)]g_w, \text{ and } g_c > g > g_w. \tag{38}$$

Next from (1) and (2) we find

$$dY/Y = dK/K = g = dL_w/L_w = dL_c/L_c. \tag{39}$$

Now consider (5): $K_c/L_c = aK_w/L_w$. We know that

K_c grows at rate g_c
L_c and L_w grow at rate g
K_w grows at rate g_w

so K_c/L_c tends to rise over time while K_w/L_w tends to fall. But it is an important feature of the class system, on the assumptions here, that wealth makes it possible to command additional earned income, and just as the rate of profit must be uniform in equilibrium, so must be this power to command earned income, as in (12). But this brings us to (6): $W_c/L_c = aW_w/L_w$. The salaries per head of capitalists will tend to rise, while the wage per worker will fall. In quite a literal sense, the rich get richer and the poor get poorer.

To maintain the consistency of the equations, the parameter a must rise over time, at the rate $g_c - g_w = g_w(a - 1)$. This ensures the consistency of equations (5), (6) and (12). But it also means that θ rises over time: capitalists' share of total wealth increases, and, accordingly, P/W also rises. It is common in models of growth equilibrium to assume that g is given by the requirement that capital should accumulate at the same rate that the labor force (in efficiency units) is growing. In this case, (38) implies that gw must be falling over time. In any event, if a is rising, gc/gw will also rise at the same rate. Hence, in the very long run, in the limit, all wealth must tend to concentrate in the hands of capitalists. Working-class wealth must shrink to an insignificant proportion of total wealth, and working-class earnings must tend to the socially determined subsistence level.

15　METHODS OF ECONOMIC ANALYSIS

The message is not that, under capitalism, wealth will tend to concentrate: that may or may not be true, but an argument as abstract as this cannot decide the issue. What has been shown is rather that the idea of long-run equilibrium sits uncomfortably in a model of class society. Yet this conclusion raises a considerable methodological problem. For we have previously seen that the method of Temporary Equilibrium is defective. To correct these defects it was necessary to allow for the formation of a rate of profit, which made it possible to determine prices on the basis of distribution and technology, independently of supply and demand, thereby creating a theory of value capable of providing a basis for macroeconomics. Yet the rate of profit is necessarily connected to the rate of growth; one cannot be in equilibrium without the other. But once we consider the equilibrium rate of growth, we are in trouble with the relative wealth of the classes. However, if long-run equilibrium is impossible in a class society, then the method of Growth Economics must similarly be considered defective. But can we do without the notion of equilibrium? Joan Robinson certainly thought so. But then how can the position of the economy at a moment of time, or its movement through time, be determined?[6]

The problem lies in the notion of equilibrium as a position in which no agent has an incentive to change his pattern of behavior. This is always problematical, because in a competitive, class society various groups are always struggling with one another, and so will always be on the lookout for new means or methods to improve their positions. This is one basic reason why such systems are technologically and organizationally innovative. And it means that any approach which defines equilibrium in terms of the absence of incentives to change behavior is thereby precluded from studying the incentives to innovation. But even when questions of innovation are ruled out, as in the context of the preceding discussion, the equilibrium approach demands that the social order be modelled as reaching a *settled* state. Yet it may be one of the deepest truths about capitalism that it is never settled, that it is always changing, and that this is built into the fabric of the class structure itself.

To abandon equilibrium is not to abandon economic theory. Smith, Ricardo and Marx looked for 'laws of motion' rather than positions of short-term or long-term equilibrium. To be sure, Marx's 'prices of production' and his condition for sectoral balance can be interpreted as equilibrium conditions in the modern sense. But that is not how they have to be understood. Instead, they could be seen as conditions for *reproduction*, structural conditions which have to be met if the system is to reproduce itself, that is, maintain itself in its present state (which may be a state of proportional or non-proportional expansion). Given these structural conditions, we can then ask whether the system is likely to produce behavior which will satisfy them. In other words, the problem is broken into two parts: on the one hand, there is the calculation of the conditions for the system to continue to operate successfully – and, on the other hand, the analysis of what happens when these are not met. These comprise the structural analysis. Such structural conditions need not be thought of as 'centers of gravitation'; they may function simply as regulating ideals – benchmarks to which actual behavior can be compared, not only by the observing economists, but more importantly by the agents of the system themselves. Then there follows the study of behavior, to see what behavior is required to fulfill the structural conditions, and whether the system will tend to generate it. This method, which Adolph Lowe has long advocated (Lowe, 1965, 1976; Hollis and Nell, 1975; Nell, 1984), derives from classical thinking and because it partitions the question of the economy's position into structural and behavioral components, it avoids determining variables by relying on a notion of harmonious reconcilation, in which no one will have any incentive to change their course of action.

Notes

1. The built-in static bias of neoclassical theory has tended to obscure the fact that for a capitalist economy the normal condition must be a state of growth. The problem of optimal allocation under scarcity is essentially static; it is an important subject, but it is not a good point from which to start the study of industrial capitalism. Capitalists compete, and in general size will provide advantages in competition; faster growing firms will tend to displace more slowly growing ones in the long run. Hence, even if most firms were willing to opt for the easy life, the few ambitious ones would force the rest to follow suit. So long as even one capitalist or firm proposes to improve its competitive position by investing, the rest must follow suit, or lose out in the long run – unless it can be assumed that size confers no competitive advantages whatsoever. Since this is unrealistic, in general competition will tend to lead a capitalist system to expand.
2. Garegnani (1976) and others have argued recently that the proper approach to economic theory is to determine the 'long-period position' of the economy, and then compare alternative positions for different values of key parameters. The long-period position is chiefly defined by the existence of a uniform rate of profit, and it is suggested that the development of the Temporary Equilibrium method came about because neoclassical theory had difficulty working out a 'supply and demand' treatment of capital and the rate of profit. For Garegnani the normal rate of profit and the associated prices are 'centers of gravitation', towards which the economy tends to move. Hence the idea of Temporary

Equilibrium cannot be accepted, but by the same token, the rate of profit cannot be formed without Growth Equilibrium. A theory of 'gravitation' must also be a theory of investment. And if the 'long period' is sufficient to establish the uniformity of the rate of profit, it must also establish the uniform rate of growth, for the reasons given in the text.

3.   This discussion has some affinity to a celebrated argument of Pasinetti's (1962). But in Pasinetti's system workers receive both forms of income, but capitalists only get profits. Hence, dividing (4) into (3), we get an expression for r/g, which is

$$P_c/s_cP_c = P_w/s_w(W + P_w), \text{ and simplifies to}$$
$$s_cP_w = s_w(W + P_w).$$

Substitute this into the investment–savings equation:

$$I = s_w(W + P_w) + s_cP_c$$
$$= s_c(P_w + P_c) - s_cP, \text{ and dividing by } K$$
$$g = s_cr.$$

Worker's saving can be ignored because, in equilibrium, what they save out of all forms of income must equal what the capitalists would have saved, had they received the profits which go to the workers. But the entire argument turns on the assumption that capitalists receive only profits, although they both save and consume. A similar argument can be advanced on the assumption that workers receive only wages, although they both save and consume. The justification is that their wealth – accumulated savings – must be managed by capitalists, whose (monopoly) charges for their services eat up the entire earnings. Alternatively, we can think of the bulk of worker savings as being institutional, pension funds, managed by capitalists for their own benefit. It can be objected that workers would not save if they received no profit returns, but this is wrong, for their accumulated wealth raises their wages above subsistence. ('Subsistence' here means a conventional level; if it were biological they would not be able to save.) So (3) is irrelevant, and the system consists of (4), (5) and (6), from which we derive (7), and then

$$s_c(P + W_c)/W_c = s_wW/W_w, \text{ so that}$$
$$s_c(P + W_c) = s_wW_c,$$

which states that the savings of capitalists are equal in long-run equilibrium to what the working class would have saved had they received the wages which went to capitalist managers. Substituting in the investment–saving condition;

$$I = s_wW_w + s_c(P + W_c) = s_wW_w + s_wW_c = s_wW. \text{ So we can write,}$$
$$g = s_w(1/v - r),$$

where v is the capital–output ratio and r the rate of profit. The growth rate is independent of the capitalist saving propensity.

4.   Saving propensities must be constant because of the assumption that income expenditure functions are linear. Without such an assumption long-run equilibrium would not be possible, for rising incomes would then lead to changes in the composition of output.

5.   Moreover there are good reasons to avoid such an assumption. Consider,

$$S_w = s_wW + s_pP_w = gK_w$$
$$S_p = s_pP_c = gk_c$$
$$P_c/K_c = P_w/K_w = r.$$

Following the procedure above to obtain r/g and simplifying, we find,

$s_p P_w = s_w W + s_p P_w$, which implies
$s_w W = 0$, which is absurd.

6. Disequilibrium methods are now widely used to provide microfoundations for macroeconomics (Harcourt, 1977). But such methods simply explain one mystery by another: macro quantity adjustments are explained by the assumed rigidity of some wage rate or price, but this rigidity is itself left unexamined, apart from casual references to unions and oligopoly. The purpose of the exercise is to retain the supply and demand framework, which determines prices and quantities together, yet still make room for macroeconomics. From the perspective taken here, the *ad hoc* assumptions of rigidity simply show up the defects of the Temporary Equilibrium method.

References

Arrow, K. J. and F. Hahn (1971) *General Competitive Analysis* (San Francisco: Holden-Day).

Brody, A. (1970) *Proportions, Prices and Planning* (New York: American Elsevier).

Eatwell, J. and M. Milgate (eds) (1983) *Keynes' Economics and The Theory of Value and Distribution* (New York: Oxford University Press).

Garegnani, P. (1976) 'On a Change in the Notion of Equilibrium in Recent Work on Value and Distribution', reprinted in Eatwell and Milgate (1983).

Harcourt, G. C. (ed.) (1977) *The Microeconomic Foundations of Macroeconomics* (London: Macmillan).

Hicks, J. (1965) *Capital and Growth* (Oxford: Clarendon Press).

Hollis, M. and E. Nell (1975) *Rational Economic Man* (Cambridge: Cambridge University Press).

Laibman, D. and E. Nell (1977) 'Reswitching, Wicksell Effects and the Neoclassical Production Function', *American Economic Review*, vol. 67, no. 5, December.

Lowe, A. (1965) *On Economic Knowledge* (New York: Harper & Row).

Lowe, A. (1976) *The Path of Economic Growth* (Cambridge: Cambridge University Press).

Marglin, S. A. (1974) 'What Do Bosses Do? The Origin and Functions of Hierarchy in Capitalist Production', *Review of Radical Political Economy*, vol. 6, no. 2, Summer.

Mathur, G. (1965) *Planning For Steady Growth* (Oxford: Blackwell).

Nell, E. (1967) 'Theories of Growth and Theories of Value', *Economic Development and Cultural Change*, vol. XVI, no. 1, October, reprinted in Harcourt and Laing (eds), *Capital and Growth* (Harmondsworth: Penguin).

Nell, E. (1984) 'Structure and Behavior in Classical and Neoclassical Theory', *Eastern Economic Journal*, vol. 11, no. 2, April.

Pasinetti, L. (1962) 'Rate of Profit and Income Distribution in Relation to the Rate of Economic Growth', *Review of Economic Studies*, vol. 29.

Pasinetti, L. (1974) *Growth and Income Distribution* (Cambridge: Cambridge University Press).

Pasinetti, L. (1975) *Lectures on the Theory of Production* (New York: Columbia University Press).

Robinson, J. *Collected Economic Papers*, 5 vols (Oxford: Blackwell).

Sraffa, P. (1960) *Production of Commodities by Means of Commodities* (Cambridge: Cambridge University Press).

12 Some Notes on Capital, Expectations and the Analysis of Changes

Pierangelo Garegnani*

A PREMISE

When I was asked to contribute to this volume I thought that the following work, done back in 1976 as part of a discussion with Joan Robinson, might be of some interest to a wider public. It is presented here in the spirit of the kind of commemoration she would have preferred – a discussion of her work in order to further the construction of a more satisfactory economic theory: the aim she single-mindedly pursued in her work, earning the respect and admiration of both those who did and those who did not share her critical stance.

The discussion to which I am referring, and of which the following forms but one episode, had been going on for some time (she herself was to refer to it later, see Robinson, 1980, pp.123–40). At that particular stage it had been sparked off by some remarks I made (see Garegnani, 1976, pp.42–44) about a convergence between her position and that of Paul Samuelson on the impossibility of analyzing changes in the economy by means of the traditional comparison between 'normal positions' of the system.[1] Joan Robinson reacted to those remarks by writing a short comment (Appendix I of this paper); I replied with the paper which follows; and her rejoinder is printed as Appendix II.

As I said, the discussion had been going on for some time. Differences had emerged earlier between our standpoints on 'marginal' theory. (I shall here use the expressions 'marginal' and 'marginalist' theory for what is more frequently called 'neoclassical' theory;[2] however, if readers prefer, they can safely replace 'marginal' or 'marginalist' theory with 'neoclassical' theory whenever the former expressions appear.) In particular, Joan Robinson had

*I wish to thank Sir Austin Robinson for permission to print Joan Robinson's two comments in the Appendices to this chapter. (A version of this chapter, and of Joan Robinson's comments, has appeared in Italian as an Appendix to Garegnani, 1979c.) Except for an attempt to clarify the concept of 'long-period position' by reference to the concept of 'normal' levels of the variables and for some stylistic changes, this chapter has remained the same as the paper circulated in 1976–7. Financial assistance from the Consiglio Nazionale delle Ricerche is gratefully acknowledged.

objected to Garegnani (1970), where the criticism of marginal theory centered on the difficulty entailed in deducing long-period demand functions for productive factors from the existence of alternative methods of production and of consumers' choice. My argument there, she felt, had conceded to marginal theory what should not have been granted: the possibility of analyzing changes in the economy by means of a comparison between equilibria. In some private exchanges that followed, this initial difference soon brought others to light, chiefly regarding the interpretation of the classical economists. It was because of these disagreements that I took the occasion of her comment to Garegnani (1976) for attempting to clarify and state more systematically our respective standpoints.

The discussion surfaced again in a later public exchange (Robinson, 1979; Garegnani, 1979b), following the English publication (Garegnani, 1978 and 1979a) of work I had done in the early 1960s on the relevance of the capital theory debate for Keynes's analysis of effective demand – a public exchange that may perhaps be better understood in the light of the earlier exchange presented here.

The paper which follows has, therefore, to be viewed in strict association with Garegnani (1976) to which Joan Robinson was reacting. The purpose of that paper was threefold: the first was to notice the change in the concept of equilibrium that has increasingly occurred in the theoretical writings of the last few decades; the second was to argue that this change originated in the attempt to overcome the deficiencies surrounding the notion of capital; the third and final purpose was to indicate some additional difficulties that change had brought in its train.

With respect to the first purpose, the starting point was the fact that earlier marginal theory had based its general explanation of distribution and relative prices on equilibria allowing for an adjustment of the physical composition of the capital stock to the equilibrium outputs and methods of production. This was implied in the condition of a uniform effective rate of return over the supply price of the capital goods characterizing the equilibria under conditions of free competition the qualification 'effective' applied to the rate of return, indicates here that changes over time in the relative prices of the capital goods, if at all considered in the theory, should of course be taken into account in defining the uniform rate of return[3]).

In the last few decades, however, such equilibria have been increasingly replaced by equilibria where the (initial) endowment of each kind of capital good is assumed given and, therefore, the composition of the (initial) capital stock is not allowed to adjust to the equilibrium outputs and methods of production. The result is that this equilibrium is incompatible with a uniform, effective rate of return over the supply price of the capital goods (Garegnani, 1976, p.34).

Now, when this drastic change in the concept of equilibrium has been noticed at all, it has been explained by claiming that the earlier equilibria related to *stationary economies* (or economies in steady growth) and could not be used beyond those hypotheses. The second purpose of Garegnani (1976) was to dispute that explanation of the change. Focusing on an examination of Hicks's *Value and Capital* (1946) – a book that had a decisive influence in starting these developments in the English speaking world – we argued that the motives for the change had to be sought in a different direction. The abandonment of the concept of equilibrium, characterized by an adjusted physical composition of capital, had had the advantage of avoiding the earlier reference to capital as a *single* factor of production, which could change 'form' without changing in 'quantity' (Hicks, 1932, p.20; also quoted in Garegnani, 1976, p. 35), and had accordingly to be measured in value terms – with all the difficulties that are by now well known. In fact, the new concept of equilibrium made it possible to treat the different kinds of capital goods as so many factors measurable in physical terms (as was earlier done by Walras who was, however, inconsistently retaining the condition of uniform rate of return over the supply prices of the capital goods (see Garegnani, 1960)).

However – and here we come to the third and main purpose of my 1976 article – that same change in the concept of equilibrium raises several additional difficulties. In the first place, the arbitrary physical composition of the (initial) capital stock prevents the corresponding 'short period' or 'temporary' general equilibrium from being persistent enough to be conceived as a center of gravity for the observable prices and quantities.[4] In this way economic theory appears to lose the link with observable magnitudes it had since its very inception; which consisted of conceiving the *theoretical* levels (e.g. the 'normal' prices, or the 'normal' outputs), as those the corresponding *actual magnitudes tend to and gravitate about*, thus enabling the theoretical position to be a guide to some average of the actual positions of the system (Garegnani, 1976, p.38; cf. also Section 1.4.2 below).

Secondly, the same purely temporary character of the equilibrium imposes a consideration of its dependence on the changes it will undergo in the future – changes that could safely be ignored in the case of the earlier equilibrium, endowed with sufficient persistence. The result of this was to face the general theory of prices and distribution with the unhappy choice between the hypothesis of complete markets for future commodities and the indefiniteness of results associated with introducing subjective price expectations with a determining role in the equilibrium (Garegnani, 1976, pp.38–9).

A third, connected shortcoming of the new notion of equilibrium is due to the fact that the changes of the stocks of the several capital goods over time will be governed by the tendency of the physical composition of capital to adapt to prevailing outputs and methods. This means that the supply of each capital good, unlike that of the single factor 'capital' in the earlier notion of equilibrium, cannot be treated as an *independent variable* in comparing equilibria. This, in turn, imposes an analysis of changes over time by means of a sequence of equilibria; it prevents, that is, the theory from using the most effective analysis of changes that appears to be available in economics, the *comparison* between the position of the system before and after the assumed change. As Marshall noted, in economics a 'complete dynamical solution' of economic problems is, in fact, unattainable (Marshall, 1898, p.37).

I have referred to *additional* difficulties which marginal theory faces because of the above change in the concept of equilibrium. Indeed, these difficulties – not unconnected with the present widespread disquiet at the relation between contemporary price theory and observable phenomena – do not seem to have been a price paid for overcoming the deficiencies of the former conception of a 'quantity of capital'. That conception has to re-emerge in the savings–investment market, and appears to be inseparable from demand-and-supply theory of the returns to capital.

1 CAPITAL, EXPECTATIONS AND THE ANALYSIS OF CHANGES: A REPLY

1.1 Introduction

This chapter focuses on three issues. The first pertains to the implications of the criticism of the traditional concept of capital. The second deals with Joan Robinson's criticism of traditional theory, based on the impossibility of analyzing changes by comparing equilibria, and with the methodological status of this criticism. The third issue concerns the legitimacy of Joan Robinson's apparent extension of her criticism from the comparison of marginalist equilibria to the more general method based on comparing 'normal positions' of the economic system (cf. Section 1.4.2 below), a method also used in earlier economic theory. The following three major sections deal with these three issues in the order given above.

1.2 Full Employment Equilibrium and the 'Quantity of Capital'

1.2.1

In 'History versus Equilibrium' (1974, p. 1) Joan Robinson writes, 'As soon as the uncertainty of expectations ... is admitted equilibrium drops out of the argument'. We shall consider the equilibrium Joan Robinson refers to there, and see how its validity may be questioned independently of any consideration regarding expectations. We shall use the same example of equilibrium Joan Robinson uses in her paper, namely, that from H. G. Johnson (1973), where two consumer goods x and y are produced with labor and what Joan Robinson calls 'putty-capital' (*i.e.* means of production consisting of some malleable substance) supplied in given quantities.

1.2.2

In that example the possibility of determining distribution depends on whether, as the 'putty-capital' rental falls relative to the wage, the quantity of 'putty-capital' employed with a constant labor force increases. In fact this inverse relation constitutes the decreasing 'demand function' for the service of 'putty-capital' which, in conjunction with its 'supply', will determine the unique and stable equilibrium Johnson needs and assumes (Johnson, 1973, p. 57), in order to determine the rental of 'putty-capital', the wage, the outputs and the relative price of goods x and y.

That decreasing demand function in turn results from two kinds of substitutability, between 'putty-capital' and labor:

(a) a technical substitutability for which, as the rental of 'putty-capital' falls, more of it will be employed per worker in each of the two industries (so as to equalize its marginal product with the falling rental);
(b) a consumers' substitutability for which a higher proportion of the given labor force will be employed in producing the more 'putty-intensive' commodity, say x, which consumers will generally demand in a higher proportion as it becomes cheaper relative to y with the fall of the putty-capital rental.[5]

1.2.3

This, would be the argument if capital were 'putty-capital'. But neoclassical theory was founded on the idea that though capital is not a physical 'putty', it is, so to speak, a 'value-putty'. As it wears out, 'capital' re-emerges as amortization quotas, 'free' to be reinvested in a different physical form.[6] It would thus become substitutable for labor through both route (a) and (b) above. A decreasing demand function for 'capital' in terms of the rate of interest (profits) would then tend to ensure a unique stable equilibrium determining rate of interest, real wage, prices and outputs, just as the demand for 'putty-capital' did for the respective variables.

1.2.4

It is important to note that this decreasing demand function for 'capital' (cf. Section 1.4.2 below), would only operate by means of a succession of decreasing demand functions for investment as, over time, the labor force becomes itself 'free' to be re-equipped with 'capital' of the most appropriate form (cf. Garegnani, 1976, p. 40 n. 32, and 1978, pp. 346–8, 352).[7]

1.2.5

Let us now suppose for a moment that we deny, as Joan Robinson does in her Comment (Appendix I), that different techniques co-exist in time. We would thus deny the substitutability between factors through route (a) above, and we would cause equilibrium to drop out of the argument, even for an economy with putty capital and quite independently of the uncertainty of expectations. There would, of course, remain the substitutability between factors along route (b) based on consumers choice: but if, for the sake of argument, we supposed a fixed consumption basket, no decrease in the rental for 'putty capital' would generally allow the amount of the 'capital' employed with the given labor force to increase.[8] No 'equilibrium' rates of interest and wages would generally exist at which the 'demand' and 'supply' of each of the two factors could be made equal: output, distribution and relative prices could *not* be determined by the marginalist demand and supply forces because the possibility of substitution between factors would have vanished. (In fact only zero-wage, or zero-interest-rate, or 'indifferent' equilibria would be possible, depending upon whether the proportion of labour to 'putty capital' in the initial endowment happened to exceed, fall short of or coincide with that in which the two factors have to be employed.)

1.2.6

We may now begin to see why 'reswitching' and 'reverse capital deepening' are of central importance in the criticism of marginalist theory.[9] By invalidating the traditional notion of substitutability between factors and the corresponding decreasing demand functions, these phenomena have negative implications for the notion of an 'equilibrium' between demand and supply not unlike those which, as we have just seen, would follow from the denial of the existence of alternative techniques. Moreover, reswitching and reverse capital deepening are as destructive of 'substitutability' between labor and capital through consumers' choice and route (b), as they are through route (a) and the alternative of techniques (cf. e.g. Garegnani, 1970, p. 424). And, above all, these phenomena reveal an inconsistency in the theory and do not merely consist of the denial of a long-accepted factual assumption like that of the existence of alternative techniques. The argument runs as follows: even if capital were in some sense 'malleable' through replacement, and even if the rate of interest were sufficiently flexible in the face of net saving (assumed to be consistently definable) – even then, contrary to what has long been believed, decreasing demand functions for factors could not be deduced from the existence of alternative techniques and of consumer choice. Accordingly, the explanation of distribution, prices and outputs by the marginalist demand and supply forces would lose much of its basis (Garegnani, 1985, pp. 82–3) which lay in that deduction, and not in any observed empirical regularities.

If this is true, it is hardly surprising that reswitching should play an important role in that 'Prelude to a Critique of Economic Theory', represented by Sraffa's (1960) book. Nor is it surprising that the marginalist side should have shown considerable concern in attempting to deny the phenomenon, or to limit its sphere of application.

1.3   On Joan Robinson's Methodological Criticism of Marginal Theory

1.3.1

However in Joan Robinson's view, the major criticism of marginalist theory is different: it is that the economy will not tend towards equilibrium because of the incorrect expectations of the individuals and of the uncertainty with which these expectations are held.[10]

She argues that, given the 'non-malleability' of capital (cf. Section 1.3.3 below), a tendency to equilibrium would require that a 'clear concept' of the equilibrium position exists from the beginning in the 'minds of dealers', and this cannot generally be the case because, short of perfect foresight, that concept could only come from experience; that is, from equilibrium having already been established in the past. As she wrote (1953, p. 84), 'it is impossible for a system to get into a position of equilibrium, for the very notion of equilibrium is that the system is already in it, and has been in it for a certain length of past time'. To have thought otherwise, she continues, is a 'profound methodological error, which makes the major part of neoclassical doctrine spurious'. Again, referring to the analogy of the pendulum which 'may be said to be tending towards the vertical even at those moments when it is moving away from it', Joan Robinson writes: 'this metaphor can be applied to a market in which there is a clear concept in the minds of dealers as to what the equilibrium position is. In such a case it is true to say that price is always tending towards equilibrium, even if it never settles there' (J. Robinson 1962, p. 23). (The word 'tending' in this passage should however be noted. It helps to clarify Joan Robinson's treatment of the question. At times, as in the first of the passages above, she argues as if the simple fact that equilibrium is not generally reached were sufficient to rule out its usefulness in the representation of reality (cf. e.g. J. Robinson, 1974, p. 2; 1962, p. 17). But as the sense of the word 'tending' here makes clear, she does recognize that equilibrium is supposed to provide a guide to reality, not by ever being exactly achieved, but simply by being a position towards which the economy tends and about which it gravitates: cf. Section 1.4.2 below.)

Joan Robinson's central criticism of marginalist theory outlined above explains, on the other hand, two characteristic theses she holds with regard to method.

The first thesis concerns the relevance of the equilibrium position, confined to the analysis of stationary economies, or economies in 'steady state': it is only in such economies that the above 'clear concept' of the equilibrium position can be assumed to exist in the 'minds of dealers'.[11]

The second thesis is that the changes occurring in an economy cannot be studied by means of comparisons between equilibria as was done traditionally.[12] Indeed, if no tendency to equilibrium can be assumed, because of uncertainty and incorrect expectations, the comparison between the two equilibria, corresponding, respectively, to conditions before and after the assumed change in circumstances, can provide no guidance at all to the actual effects of the change.

1.3.2

But what exactly are Joan Robinson's grounds for arguing that expectations and uncertainty prevent a tendency to equilibrium?

This is a natural question to ask because traditional theory (from the classical economists and Marx, down to Marshall and the marginalists) had a way of dealing with these phenomena that led to entirely different conclusions. It seems in fact that the 'accidental causes' (Ricardo, 1951, pp. 91–2) traditionally thought to make actual or 'market' prices deviate from their long-period levels, could mostly be described in terms of incorrect expectations. And precisely the incorrectness of these expectations (that is, their contrast with subsequent experience) was supposed to lead to their progressive revision as part of the process by which the economy tends to the 'normal position' (cf. Section 1.4.2 below) corresponding to the given conditions and gravitates about it. The tendency to the normal position was therefore supposed to be the result of objective experiences, independent of the normal levels of the variables being in the 'minds of dealers' from the beginning. This was the argument with respect to incorrect expectations. 'Uncertainty', on the other hand, could even be conceived as favoring the process of gravitation described above, in so far as it rendered expectations more responsive to present experience.

Clearly it is to Keynes that we must refer in order to answer our question and trace the origin of Joan Robinson's argument against that traditional view, for which uncertainty and lack of foresight could keep the economy out of equilibrium, but would not prevent its gravitation about the equilibrium. In the *General Theory*, Keynes had argued that uncertainty about the future, acting both through the volatility of expectations and liquidity preference, would prevent investment from *tending* to the level set by full-employment saving and would therefore prevent the economy from *tending* to an equilibrium where the quantity of labor demanded would be equal to the quantity supplied. This idea about the role of uncertainty was, of course, formulated by Keynes in the context of the short period where capital equipment is given, but he evidently thought that its consequences went further. What Joan Robinson does is to attempt to draw these consequences. She argues that through a sequence of short-period situations – where the level of investment may, or may not, allow full utilization of the productive capacity existing in each situation – there will be no tendency to reach, or preserve, a full employment equilibrium with the corresponding long-period quantities and prices. As she wrote: 'The argument of the General Theory . . . cannot be true at each moment of time and yet untrue in the long run'

(Robinson, 1962, p. 14). And elsewhere: 'Nor can we say that normal prices represent a position towards which actual prices are *tending* to move' (Robinson, 1956, p. 356; our emphasis).

1.3.3

For the sake of clarity and completeness it should also be noted that the same Keynesian basis appears to underly another strain of criticism of marginal theory raised by Joan Robinson: the strain concerning the *irreversibility* of movements in time.[13] This strain seems also to emerge in her *Comment* (Appendix I) where she writes: 'it is unacceptable methodology to draw a plane diagram, showing relations between variables, and then to introduce movements about on the page. A movement must take place in time; which can be represented by a third dimension at right angles to the page.'

Two potentially distinct questions seem to be raised here and in similar passages (e.g. Robinson, 1974, p. 5). The first (to which the immediate context of the *Comment* points)[14] is the previously considered criticism about the illegitimacy of studying changes in the economy by means of comparisons of equilibria: the 'movements about on the page', would then consist of analyzing the change by comparing the two equilibrium positions 'lying on the page'. However, no assumption about 'reversibility' of movements would seem implied in any such analysis of changes. The theorist using that method would not commit himself to arguing that the ceasing of circumstance *A*, which has brought the equilibrium of the system from position (I) to position (II), would bring the equilibrium back to position (I): he may well admit that by the time circumstance *A* has ceased to operate other determinants of the equilibrium have changed as well.

Where the assumption of 'reversibility' would come in is in a second, distinct question: the use of demand and supply functions in order to argue a tendency towards the position indicated by their intersection (the movements which 'must take place in time'). There, it is indeed implied that the process involved will not affect the demand or supply functions and therefore that one can, so to speak, move backwards on the same function on which one has moved forward. It is in fact to this second issue that Joan Robinson refers (1956 p. 58) when she says that the case of a market cannot be likened to that of a pair of scales which 'however it wobbles about will come to rest in the same position' because, unlike the case of the scales, 'the path the market follows . . . has a long persisting effect on the position that it reaches'.

However, the only example given there for this 'long-persisting effect' is the overinvestment in plant that may occur in a particular market in response to a sudden increase in demand.[15] And with this irreversibility of investment decisions we seem to be moving again on strictly Keynesian grounds, rather than on grounds like that of the irreversibility of movements along a downward sloping supply curve that troubled Alfred Marshall in his use of demand and supply functions, and to which Joan Robinson seems to refer at times.[16] Indeed through the irreversibility of investment decisions, the 'non-malleability' of capital emerges, alongside expectations and their uncertainty as the second fundamental characteristic of reality that provides the basis of Keynes's criticism: uncertainty and incorrect expectations alone could not prevent a tendency to equilibrium if the capital originating from investment could always be shifted to any destination at no cost (cf. Joan Robinson, 1975, p. vii).

(What we have just seen may also explain an aspect of Joan Robinson's criticism of the neoclassical concept of capital – the nature of which has perhaps not been sufficiently noted. She stresses the absence of a 'malleability' of capital, rather than the quite different questions of reswitching and reverse capital deepening. Indeed non-malleability, unlike reswitching, can be viewed as an integral part of the Keynesian criticism based on uncertainty and incorrect expectations.)

1.3.4

Later, in Section 1.4.5, we shall discuss Joan Robinson's arguments for her denial of the tendency of an economy towards equilibrium, or, more generally, towards a normal position. What interests us here is primarily a consequence which would seem to follow from her criticism. It appears that the significance of the concept of equilibrium for an analysis of reality essentially depends on the existence, under sufficiently general conditions, of forces capable of bringing the economy towards the equilibrium position. (Marshall, for example, would qualify an equilibrium as 'real' only if it were stable (Marshall, 1949, App. H. par. 2; cf. also Section 1.4.2 below).) Thus to deny, as Joan Robinson does, the existence of any general tendency to an equilibrium characterized by full employment of labor would seem to entail the rejection of that concept; the rejection, that is, of the conception of demand and supply forces as envisaged in marginal theory explaining distribution, prices and outputs by their equilibrium. The task facing the theoretician would then seem to be that of attempting to ascertain the true central levels about which actual prices and outputs gravitate – the task, that is, of developing an alternative theory of distribution, prices and outputs, with the corresponding concept of a normal position, alternative to the marginalist 'equilibrium'.[17]

Indeed when the problem arose for Keynes in his short-period analysis, he did follow that procedure. Thus he determined short-period centers of gravitation or 'normal positions' of the system, compatible with underutilization of productive equipment and labor unemployment, which he called 'equilibria' (1936, e.g. p.3), and by which he replaced the corresponding normal positions characterized by the full utilization of equipment and full employment of labor, to which traditional theory had implicitly referred for such short-period analysis. Indeed when long-period questions akin to those on which Joan Robinson focuses her interest did crop up in the *General Theory*, Keynes referred to what he called 'long-period positions' of the economy, that is, to normal positions characterized by a uniform rate of return on capital, allowing for labor unemployment (1936, pp. 48–9).

Joan Robinson, however, does not seem to recognize this need to refer to alternative 'centers of gravitation' of the economic system, at least when she deals with method. The question as she sees it, is: 'to leave equilibrium analysis behind and approach the problem in terms of a historical process, the system continually lurching from one out-of-equilibrium position to another' (J. Robinson, 1962, pp. 6–7).

This idea according to which what is required is fundamentally a change of method (from the 'equilibrium' analysis to the 'out-of-equilibrium' analysis of a 'historical process'), rather than the development of an alternative explanation of the normal levels of the variables, has some implications we must consider in the rest of this section and in the next.

1.3.5

The first implication is that a demand and supply equilibrium is still supposed to exist, though it is never actually reached. It would only be reached, according to Joan Robinson, if uncertainty did not exist or it were rendered innocuous by the malleability of capital. The neoclassical 'opposing sets of forces' of demand and supply (Marshall, 1949, V, i, I) founded on the substitutability between factors, are apparently not disputed in themselves (cf. however Section 1.2.5 above). What is disputed is the capacity, traditionally attributed to these forces, of impelling the system towards a position where they are in balance, thus making the system gravitate about such a position.

However, as we argued in Section 1.2.6, these demand and supply forces are those whose existence is thrown into doubt by reswitching and, more generally, by the criticism of the marginalist concept of capital. It would therefore seem that the notion itself of these demand and supply forces might be responsible for the error of asserting a tendency to an 'equilibrium' characterized by the full employment of labor. And the error would then be independent of whether, in an economy where the substitutabilities between factors existed as envisaged in marginal theory, uncertainty and expectations would, or would not, prevent a tendency towards the corresponding equilibrium.[18]

1.4 'Equilibrium Positions' and 'Normal Positions' of the Economic System

1.4.1

Joan Robinson's methodological criticism of marginal theory has a second implication, besides the uncertainty it leaves about the role of the traditional demand and supply forces. It is that her denial of a tendency to equilibrium appears to be extended into a denial of the tendency to a 'normal position' of the economic system, however determined.

1.4.2

Before discussing this point it is, however, necessary to consider more explicitly the distinction already implied in this chapter, between, on the one hand, the general theoretical concepts of a 'normal position' and a 'long period position' of the economic system, and, on the other hand, their marginalist specifications as 'equilibrium' and 'long-period equilibrium'.

By 'normal' level of a variable, we refer here to the concept traditionally used by economic theorists – whatever their school – of a theoretical central level, which the actual level of the variable will tend to and gravitate about (cf., e.g. Adam Smith's distinction between the 'natural price' and the 'actual or market price', 1950, pp. 48–9).[19] This concept of the normal level of a variable appears to provide in economics for the 'rules of correspondence' between theory and observable phenomena involved in any scientific undertaking.[20] At any given moment of time the actual or observable level of the variable can coincide with its theoretical counterpart only by a fluke: however, the above tendency or gravitation gives us reason to suppose that over a sufficient interval of time, the deviations of the actual values from their theoretical counterparts will tend to compensate each other – letting the theoretical value emerge as a sufficiently accurate guide to some average of the actual levels.[21]

Analogously by 'normal' position of the economic system we have indicated (in Section 1.3.4) the position of the economic system defined by normal values of the relevant set of variables, which the actual position of the system at any given moment of time will tend to and gravitate about, and which can therefore provide a sufficiently accurate guide to the actual positions of the system (cf. Garegnani 1976, p. 38).

These concepts of the normal value of a variable and of the normal position of the system, evidently imply a sufficient *persistence* of the forces determining them relative to those other forces that at any given time will keep the actual value or position away from them.[22] With respect to a general explanation of distribution and relative prices this persistence has been traditionally thought to impose the reference to positions of the economic system where the physical composition of the capital stock is that most suitable to the outputs and methods of production prevailing in the position itself.[23] Using the specific Marshallian meaning of 'long period', I have accordingly labelled this kind of normal position 'long period position'.[24] Under free competition, the condition of an adjusted physical composition of the capital stock is expressed by a uniform effective rate of return over the supply price of the capital goods.[25]

Now, both the concept of a normal position and that of a long-period position are, so to speak, neutral with respect to the theory by which the rate of remuneration, prices and outputs are determined. Long-period positions are, for example, those to which Smith's and Ricardo's 'natural prices', or Marx's 'prices of production' referred. There, the real wage was explained by economic or social circumstances, examined before and independently of profits and prices. Accordingly profits resulted as the residual of the social product obtained after deducting wages (and the rent of land).

When, therefore, the normal position is specified in accordance with marginal theory, we have a second concept: that of an 'equilibrium' between the 'opposing sets of forces' of demand and supply (Marshall, 1961, II, p. 593). These demand and supply forces are the ones we described schematically in Section 1.2.4. With consumers' tastes, endowment of factors, and technical knowledge given, the substitutability between goods for the consumer and the existence of alternative techniques would originate demand and supply functions in the markets for the 'factors of production'. The 'equilibrium' between these demands and supplies would determine the remuneration of factors and, simultaneously, the prices of products and the quantities produced.

In particular, we shall have the concept of a 'long-period equilibrium' when the general notion of a 'long period position' is specified in accordance with marginal theory and, therefore, is seen as the result of an equilibrium between demand and supply forces so defined as to allow for the above mentioned adjustment of the physical composition of capital.

1.4.3

This distinction between the general concept of a 'normal position' and its marginalist specification does not seem to be drawn by Joan Robinson.[26] In particular, she does not seem to recognize the nature of long-period positions such as those of the classical economists. This favors her view of the deficiency of marginal theory as being fundamentally one of method, making it almost inevitable that the rejection of the tendency to a marginalist full employment 'equilibrium' should be extended to cover a rejection of long-period 'normal positions' in general.[27] Examples of these implications of Joan Robinson's criticism of marginal theory may be found in her Comment (Appendix I), and it is to these that we turn now.

1.4.4

We may begin with the way in which the long-period position, to which

Sraffa refers his prices, appears to be there interpreted by Joan Robinson as a marginalist equilibrium. In the next section we shall proceed to consider how, as a consequence of this, she appears to extend to Sraffa's normal positions her negative conclusions concerning marginalist equilibria.

In her Comment (Appendix I) Joan Robinson writes that Samuelson's (1966) fault lay in comparing the two 'Sraffa systems' corresponding to two different rates of interest, in order to draw conclusions about the amount of saving necessary to pass from one system of production to the other.[28] However, in Samuelson the idea about accumulation lowering the interest rate, to which Joan Robinson refers, results from comparing two marginalist *equilibria*; it would not follow from comparing two of Sraffa's long-period positions. Indeed, it is only by referring to marginalist theory and its equilibria, that Samuelson can suppose:

(a) that the labor force will tend to be fully employed, both before and after the hypothetical *net* accumulation (assumed to be definable in a consistent way), so that, under constant technical conditions, such accumulation could only be taken up by a switch to more capital intensive processes;

(b) that during the transition, the propensity to save will tend to be met by a corresponding amount of investment, owing to appropriate adjustments in the rate of interest (profits), so that full employment of labor will tend to be maintained.

The comparison between two of Sraffa's long-period positions would, on the other hand, have left open the following other possibilities: (a) that accumulation (no need here to distinguish between net and gross accumulation) might have gone into equipping additional labor, or into compensating for capital destruction; (b) that the propensity to save during the period might have materialized in lower aggregate output and not in capital accumulation.

In other words, Samuelson's propositions result from the *theory* by which he determines prices, distribution and outputs, and not from the *method* by which he studies the changes that occur in these variables.[29]

1.4.5

The way in which Joan Robinson then proceeds to extend her denial of the tendency to marginalist equilibria to Sraffa's long-period positions can be found in her Comment (Appendix I) where she argues that the 'Sraffa model can only be referred to situations where techniques and prices have remained unchanged over a long stretch of historical time'. Accordingly, the model would be confined to stationary situations, and would be suitable for 'intellectual experiments' (like that of constructing a 'pseudo-production function'), but not for the 'analysis of reality'.

However, at least in the aspects Joan Robinson refers to, Sraffa's determination of the rate of profits and relative prices in no way differs from that of Ricardo or of Marx.[30] And she would surely not have argued that those authors were only concerned with stationary economies, or intellectual experiments or that they were incorrect in applying their determination of profits and prices to ascertaining the effects of changes in economies that were clearly not stationary or in steady growth. On the contrary, she often takes Ricardo and Marx as examples of the 'historical' method she herself intends to follow (cf. e.g. Robinson, 1974, p. 1)[30] thus implicity admitting, it would seem, that the positions of the economy to which Ricardo and Marx referred their 'natural prices', or 'prices of production', were different from marginalist equilibria.

In fact let us consider the two arguments Joan Robinson uses in her Comment (Appendix I) in order to exclude the applicability to reality of Sraffa's long-period positions. The first argument is that Sraffa needs the assumption that means of production are replaced in kind in order to allow for a *physical net product*. This in turn would imply that 'the same technique will continue to be used over the next period' and, therefore, that the economy is stationary. The shortcoming of this argument is that Sraffa only uses the physical net product for analyzing the *relations* between distribution and prices; and, therefore, only for the sake of the clarity of that analysis, themselves valid quite generally, independently of whether the means of production are replaced in kind, and of whether the economy is or is not stationary.

The second argument in Joan Robinson's Comment concerns the need to exclude changes in technical conditions during the lifetime of plant. However, it appears that for the prices and outputs of a long-period position to be effective – that is, for the actual prices and outputs to gravitate about them – it is sufficient that *some* of the producers should have adopted the 'dominant technique' appearing in the production equations; competition among those who have adopted the dominant technique, and between them and the producers still using the old methods would seem sufficient to enforce those prices (cf. Garegnani, 1979b, p. 185). When this is recognized it will also emerge that the existence of obsolescent fixed capital is compatible with Sraffa's long-period positions, just as it was generally thought to be compatible with the long-period positions of both the classical and marginalist authors.

The real basis of Joan Robinson's doubts about whether Sraffa's analysis is applicable to reality becomes however clear elsewhere, for example, when (1974, p. 3) she writes that when Sraffa's system is confronted with an unforeseen change 'we cannot say anything at all before we have introduced a whole fresh system specifying how the economy behaves in short-period disequilibrium'. Clearly her view here is that the tendency to the long-period positions Sraffa refers to would meet the same obstacles that are met by the tendency to the long-period equilibrium position of marginal theory.

This idea does not, however, seem to be justified. We saw in Sections 1.3.2 and 1.3.3, above, that Joan Robinson's arguments against gravitation to 'equilibrium' can be traced, fundamentally, to Keynes's critique of the tendency to full employment. But the full-employment equilibrium – the tendency to which Keynes denied – was the *marginalist* normal position, and an application of his criticism beyond the bounds of marginal theory appears to be entirely unwarranted.

Thus, Keynes's criticism cannot be used to deny gravitation to the long-period positions envisaged by the classical economists, Marx or Sraffa. Such a gravitation did *not* entail an adaptation of the level of investment to the savings out of aggregate income obtainable with full utilization of existing productive equipment. In particular it did not entail such an adaptation by means of a negative elasticity of demand for investment with respect to the rate of interest, and by means of flexibility of the latter. When the classical economists failed to realize the possibility of a deficient aggregate demand (as was the case with Ricardo), or when they failed to provide a consistent argument for that possibility (as was the case with Malthus and, to some extent with Marx) it was not because of any idea that the price mechanism would tend to bring about a full long-run utilization of existing equipment. The reason was rather a failure to separate with sufficient clarity between what today we distinguish as decisions to save and decisions to invest. As I argued elsewhere, the classical analysis of distribution and relative prices was in fact open with respect to possible deficiencies of aggregate demand: – as is not the case for marginal theory, based as the latter is on the tendency to an equality between demand and supply of factors, where the demand and supply of the factor or factors grouped under 'capital' have to take the shape of demand for investment and supply of savings (cf. Garegnani, 1978, pp. 338–41; 345–8; 352 respectively; cf. also Section 1.2.2 above).

Another basic aspect of this openness – which, I believe, Joan Robinson fails to perceive – is that, whatever their theoretical positions with respect to the tendency to a full utilization of existing equipment, the classical authors up to Ricardo did not take their long-period positions to be characterized by the full employment of labor. And this is the feature of marginal theories with which Joan Robinson appears to be chiefly struggling, since it is hardly compatible with any long-run impact of deficiencies of aggregate demand.[31]

1.4.6

In conclusion, Joan Robinson seems to underestimate the implications of the criticism of the marginalist conception of capital that she contributed so much to bringing to the center of discussion.[32] In particular she underestimates these implications when she sees the principal weakness of the orthodox theory – and of its assertion of a long-run tendency to full employment – in the obstacles uncertainty and expectations raise against that tendency. That underestimate and that thesis appear to impose on her work a methodological stance which, if strictly applied, would severely limit the possibilities of economic theory,[33] and hinder the necessary work of theoretical reconstruction. It would prevent the use and development of the firm basis for such work provided by the approach to distribution and accumulation of the classical economists.

APPENDIX I: COMMENT ON GAREGNANI'S PAPER

Joan Robinson

Garegnani and I have been on the same side in the 'capital' controversy and I agree with most of what is in this paper. In particular, I agree with what he says about uncertainty; we must bring uncertainty into a discussion of the operations of capitalism because it is a fact of life, not because it is a logical necessity. However, I do not see what it is that he is accusing me of at the end of the paper.

I understand the Sraffa model to depict a process of production going on with a single technique represented by the 'system' of equations. The definition of net output requires that all basic inputs are being replaced as they are used up. This implies that the same technique is going to continue to be used over the next period.

Formally, we could bring fixed plant into the model by taking the least common multiple of the turnover period of every ingredient in the process and treat this as the turnover period for the technique in use. This would not be a useful procedure for analysis of reality because in reality a single technique is not in use over a long stretch of historical time. But we might adopt this concept for the intellectual experiment of constructing a pseudo-production function. I regard a pseudo-production function as representing a series of Sraffa systems each with its own inputs being reproduced, that is, with its own future and its own past.

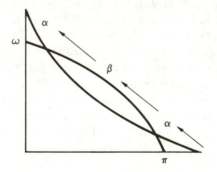

My objection to Samuelson is that he combined this concept with the notion of accumulation 'moving from higher to lower interest rates' along a speudo-production function. This was particularly absurd when he accepted reswitching. When the economy moves over the lower switch point it is 'splashed with net consumption' without extra saving (although net output per man with the Beta technique is lower than with Alpha). But it was not much less absurd when he used his own version of the pseudo-production function with labor-value prices for each technique. How is it possible to move from one techique to another?

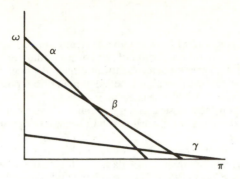

The ingredients for one Sraffa system could be changed into those for another only by a long process of investment and scrapping taking place out of steady state conditions.

Moreover, in real life, different techniques do not co-exist in time in a ready-made book of blueprints; they are evolved as accumulation goes on. In general, it is unacceptable methodology to draw a plane diagram, showing relations between variables, and then to introduce movements about on the page. A movement must take place in time, which can be represented by a third dimension at right angles to the page.

Garegnani makes a number of suggestions of what might have led me to this view and even accuses me of agreeing with Samuelson. I maintain that I hold this view because it is correct and I cannot believe that Garegnani disagrees with it.

APPENDIX II: REJOINDER

Joan Robinson

I am at a loss to understand what this controversy is about. My objection to Samuelson is simple and, I should have thought, unanswerable. He depicts a pseudo-production function as a list of the wage–profit profiles of a number of eventually non-superior techniques, arranged in ascending order of input per unit of labor. He proceeds to argue that 'society' saves, sacrificing present consumption for more consumption later, amasses 'capital' and climbs up the series of techniques from lower to higher outputs.

Apart from the general objections to this account of capitalist accumulation, it is based on a methodological error. A plane diagram, showing a punctual relation between two variables, does not allow of movements between one point and another on it. Movement takes place only in the third dimension of time. Accumulation is an historical process accompanied by the discovery and evolution of ever new techniques which cannot have been listed at some base date in a preconceived pseudo-production function.

Garegnani prefers to attack the neoclassical position from another angle. I long since welcomed his critique and I do not understand why he wants to disallow mine.

Notes

1. By 'normal position' of the economic system I am here expressing the general notion of a centre of gravitation of the corresponding observable magnitudes. With respect to a general determination of relative prices and distribution, this notion coincides with what I labelled 'long-period position' in Garegnani, 1976: cf. section 1.4.2 of this chapter.

2. The expression 'neoclassical theory' implies a basic continuity between that theory and the 'classical' theory that had been developing from William Petty and Quesnay to Adam Smith and Ricardo. This continuity between the two theories has become particularly questionable after the clarification of Ricardo's analysis (and indirectly, of Adam Smith's) that we owe to Sraffa's edition of Ricardo's *Works* (1951). On the other hand, the expression 'marginal' or 'marginalist' theory seems not inappropriate, in that through its reference to the twin concepts of marginal productivity and marginal utility, or to the corresponding 'marginal rates of substitution' (all of which can, of course, be redefined to allow for 'corners' in the relevant functions), it focuses on the fundamental role the 'substitutability' between factors of production plays in that theory, by providing the necessary basis for its characteristic explanation of distribution by demand and supply. This role of substitutability remains basic even when, as happens in recent reformulations, the main mathematical tools are less explicit about the concept of 'margin'. (On the origin of the concept of a 'neoclassical theory', and on the deficiencies of this concept cf. also Aspramourgos, 1986.)

3. Cf. note 25 below.

4. The former equilibria could in fact be characterized as 'long period' in the strict Marshallian sense of a period of time, allowing for a full adjustment of the physical capital to the prevailing outputs and methods of production. This Marshallian sense needs to be stressed today, because of a tendency in recent literature to use 'long period' in the different meaning of a stationary or steady-state situation (cf. e.g. Hahn and Matthews, 1964, p. 818, where, 'short period' or 'momentary' equilibrium are used to indicate a situation characterized by both a uniform rate of return over the supply price of the capital goods, and given endowments of capital and labor – a *long period*, and not a short period equilibrium, in the traditional Marshallian sense). These new, vaguer meanings of the expression 'long period' are perhaps what has misled some readers of Garegnani (1976) into thinking that the idea of a 'long-period position', there referred to in order to cover both marginalist long-period equilibria and the analogous positions of the classical economists, excludes by itself the existence of an 'instability' in the economic system, in the sense of wide oscillations, and rapid changes, of aggregate demand and employment, or rapid changes in technology. In fact, what appears to be at stake in the conception of a 'long-period position' is only an application of the general theoretical concept of *normal* levels of the variables to a general explanation of distribution and relative prices. Thus Marx, who, of course, always stressed the 'instability' of the present economic system, based his analysis on 'long-period positions' – as is evident from the presence in his analysis of its hallmark – a uniform rate of profits – and of the corresponding 'prices of production'. Of course, no expression like 'long period' was needed for such positions at the time (Marshall's distinction was only used for the 'particular equilibrium' of an individual industry), since it was taken as a fact that a general theory of prices and distribution could only be formulated in those terms. The expression had

to be used in Garegnani (1976) because the theoretical development outlined there had tacitly abandoned that standpoint.

5. For simplicity, we may leave aside the 'perverse' possibility of 'putty' owners having a strong preference for 'putty-intensive' goods, so that as the putty rental falls, the relative demand for the putty-intensive good would fall instead of rising.

6. Cf. e.g. the passage in Hicks (1932) commented on in Garegnani (1976) p. 33, n. 12. For the notion of free capital see, e.g., Wicksell (1935) p. 145.

7. The above notions of demand and supply 'value-putty' explain why it is difficult to agree with Joan Robinson's statement that 'the level of Marshall's normal profits and Wicksell's natural rate of interest . . . was never explained' (Robinson, 1974, p. 8). It was explained, I believe, in the way sketched in Section 1.2.2 above. (Cf. e.g. Wicksell, 1954, e.g. p.127; Marshall 1949, VI, ii, 4.)

8. See Appendix I below.

9. In fact reswitching or reverse capital deepening only constitute striking aspects of the more general difficulties connected with the notion of capital as a factor of production (another aspect pertains, for example, to the concept of net savings mentioned in Section 1.4.4 below).

10. Gram and Walsh (1983, p. 528) note a shift away from the difficulties surrounding the notion of quantity of capital in Joan Robinson's 'recent criticism of marginalist theory'.

11. 'The strict logic of the neoclassical theory of wages and profits applies to stationary states' (Robinson, 1956, p. 390). For the rationale of this statement cf., e.g., the distinction drawn between approaching an equilibrium from an arbitrary initial position and doing so after a displacement from an equilibrium that has long been established (Robinson, 1974, p. 2). It is there implied that only the second kind of movement is possible because the notion of where the equilibrium lies remains in the 'minds of dealers'.

12. Cf. e.g.: 'The major point [in the criticism of the neoclassical doctrines] is that what they pretend to offer as an alternative or rival to the post-Keynesian theory of accumulation is nothing but an error in methodology – a confusion between comparisons of imagined equilibrium positions and a process of accumulation going on through history' (J. Robinson, 1974, p. 11).

13. For this strain of argument cf. e.g. Robinson, 1973, p. 255; 1974, p. 5; 1956, p. 58.

14. It is there stated that Samuelson has used the *comparison* between two Sraffa systems in order to support the notion of accumulation 'moving [the economy] from higher to lower interest along a pseudo-production function' (cf. Section 1.4.4 below).

15. Cf. similar statements in Robinson, 1956, p. 356.

16. Cf. Marshall, 1949, appendix H. For hints at these questions in Joan Robinson, cf. e.g. Robinson, 1973, p. 258.

17. As I noted (in 1976, p. 43), Joan Robinson herself seems in fact often to rely on the comparison of normal positions in her analysis of changes.

18. It may be important to observe in this connection how what Keynes himself regarded as the essential constructive idea in the *General Theory* – namely that it is through changes in income that decisions to save are equalized with decisions to invest – is independent of his treatment of uncertainty and expectations (Cf. Garegnani, 1976, p. 39–42). The main role of that treatment was the negative one of refuting the orthodox doctrine of the rate of interest as the equilibrator between saving and investment. And today, after the criticism

of the marginalist conception of capital, this orthodox doctrine of interest – an expression of the theory of distribution in terms of demand and supply for factors (see Section 1.2.3 above) – appears to be questionable quite independently of Keynes' criticism based on uncertainty and expectations.

19. Cf. also, e.g., J. S. Mill (1909, p. 453) who expressly refers to the notion of 'natural' price of Smith and Ricardo and describes it as 'the centre value towards which ... the market value of a thing is constantly gravitating, and any deviation from which is but a temporary irregularity; which the moment it exists sets forces in motion tending to correct it'; Wicksteed (1933, p. 214): 'the actual market price at any moment ... constantly tends to approach [the ideal equilibrium value]'; Wicksell (1935, p. 53): 'the relative prices of commodities will more or less rapidly approach a certain equilibrium position or else oscillate about it'; Walras (1954, p. 380): 'Such is the continuous market, which is perpetually tending towards equilibrium without ever actually attaining it ... the market is like a lake agitated by the wind where the water is incessantly seeking its level without ever reaching it'; and Pareto (1896–7, pp. 25–6): 'Walras has shown how the competition of entrepreneurs and traders is a way to solve by groping the equations of the equilibrium of production'. Cf. also the quotations from Ricardo, J. S. Mill, Marx, J. B. Clark, Marshall given in notes 21 and 22 below, concerning the closely associated aspects of the correspondence between 'normal' and 'average' price, and of the persistence of the forces determining the normal price, respectively.

20. About the general 'rules of correspondence' between theoretical variables and observable phenomena in science cf. e.g. Nagel, 1961, p. 105.

21. Cf. 'On an average of years sufficient to enable the oscillations on one side of the central line to be compensated by those on the other, the market value agrees with the natural value, but it very seldom coincides with it at any particular time' J. S. Mill (1909, p. 453). 'These deviations [of market prices from prices of production] mutually balance one another, so that in the course of certain longer periods the average market prices equal the prices of production', Marx (1974, p. 356). 'This tendency towards costs of production ... fixes the level at which, in the long run, the market values ... tend to conform' J. B. Clark (1911, ch. VI, pp. 85–6).

   Also Marshall's statement to the effect that in a stationary state alone 'average price' and 'normal price' are convertible terms (Marshall, 1949, V, v, 4, p. 309) is in fact an indication of the *kind* of correspondence he expected to find between theoretical variables and observable magnitudes. It is indeed clear that when the normal price is changing, then the normal price such as it exactly is at some particular moment of time cannot be expected to be an average of actual prices over a *period of time*, any more than the normal price at any *other* moment over that period. There, a correspondence can only exist between the path of the changing normal price and the trend-line traced by the actual prices. In any case it seems clear that a normal price or position need not coincide with an *exact* average, or trend, of the observable prices or positions in order to provide an adequate guide to these observable prices or positions (cf., e.g., the phrase 'the market value *agrees* with the natural value' in J. S. Mill's passage above; our italics).

22. 'Having fully acknowledged the *temporary effects* which, in particular employments of capital, may be produced on the prices of commodities as well as on the wages of labour, and the profits of stock, by accidental causes, without influencing the general price of commodities, wages or profits, since these effects are equally operative in all stages of society, we will leave them entirely out of consideration, whilst we are treating of the laws which regulate natural prices, natural wages, and natural profits.' (Ricardo, 1951, ch. IV, pp. 91–2,

our italics) where the argument for 'leaving entirely out of consideration' the deviations of market from natural values of the variables rests ultimately on the 'temporary' nature of these deviations in contrast with Ricardo's concern with lasting changes.

And a similar argument is used by Marshall (1949, V, iii, 7, p. 291): 'The actual value at any time, the market value as it is often called, is often more influenced by passing events, and by causes whose action is fitful and short lived, than by those which work persistently. But in long periods these *fitful* and irregular causes in large measure efface one another's influence so that in the long run *persistent* causes dominate value completely' (our italics).

23. On the change that has occurred in this respect in the theoretical literature of the last few decades and on the role played in that change by the difficulties surrounding the conception of capital, cf. Garegnani (1976, pp. 25–36). Cf. also Section 1.1 of this chapter.

24. Cf. Garegnani, 1976, p. 26; cf. also note 3 above.

25. The need to refer to an adjusted capital stock is evidently present whatever the form of the markets for outputs and inputs. Under conditions other than free competition, the uniformity of the effective rates of return over the supply price will have to be replaced by other conditions which will entail the adjustment in the physical composition of the capital stock no less than the competitive uniformity of the rates of return.

In the text we have referred to 'effective rates of return' on the supply price of capital goods because if changes in relative prices over time are envisaged, these changes will have to be considered in estimating the rates of return. Thus, in the competitive case, equal effective rates will manifest themselves in a lower, e.g. rate of return for a capital good the relative price of which will be higher in the next period.

26. This absence of a clear distinction is partly reflected in, and partly favored by, Joan Robinson's tendency to use the word 'equilibrium' both for marginalist equilibria and for what are in fact long-period positions of a different kind (cf. e.g., 1974, pp. 1–2; also, 1975b, pp. 9–12, where the prices in Sraffa, 1960, are called 'equilibrium prices'), though many of the properties she attributes to such equilibria are then peculiar to the marginalist concept (for other instances of this cf. Joan Robinson, 1973, p. 254–5 or 1962, p. 22).

27. As mentioned in Section 1.3.4 above, Keynes's short-period equilibrium was understood to be a center of gravitation and therefore to be a 'normal position' in our sense here. Joan Robinson would therefore seem to admit *short-period* 'normal' positions like those of Keynes, and an analysis of short-period changes by means of comparisons of *these* positions.

28. According to Joan Robinson, in doing this Samuelson would ignore that it is possible to move from one system of production to the other 'only by a long process of investment and scrapping taking place out of steady state conditions'. We may however note in this connection that the mere change of system need not require the long process of investment and scrapping Joan Robinson refers to. It seems that for the new price system to become effective (that is, for actual prices to gravitate about the new, rather than the old, price system) it is sufficient that *some* of the producers should have adopted the new method: cf. Section 1.4.5 below.

29. It may be noted, however, that Samuelson's considerations about accumulation 'moving from higher to lower interest rates' could also have been derived (and in his 1966, they were in fact derived) from the analysis of a *process* consisting of a sequence of equilibria, rather than from a *comparison* of equilibria.

30. It can be said that Sraffa,(1960) provides a consistent version of what we may

call the 'core' of the surplus theories of Ricardo or Marx: the determination, that is, of the relationships linking the real wage, the rate of profits and prices. (Joan Robinson herself, e.g. in 1975b, p. iv, has referred to Sraffa's system as a 'restatement of the classical theory of profits'; cf. also Robinson, 1975a, p. 35.)

31.   In fact – as already realized by Keynes (cf. Section 1.3.4 above) – long-period positions would seem to be the necessary basis for an analysis of the implications of deficient aggregate demand, when productive equipment changes as a result of investment. The central problem which emerges, then, is to show that the position about which the economy tends to oscillate will not generally be that of full employment as argued in marginal theory. Cf. Garegnani (1983, pp. 76–8).

32.   On the origin of the critique concerning capital cf. J. Robinson 1970, pp.144–5.

33.   As Dennis Robertson wrote (1963, p. 94): 'It seems to me that anybody who rejects these two ideas, that a system can move towards equilibrium and that it may never get into it – has made it extremely difficult for himself to interpret the course of events in the real world', where Robertson's 'equilibrium' may be more generally interpreted as 'normal position'.

References

Aspramourgos, T. (1986) 'On the Origin of the term "Neoclassical"', *Cambridge Journal of Economics* 10, pp. 265–70:

Clark, J. B. (1907) *Essentials of Economic Theory* (New York); French transl., 'Principes d'économique', (Paris: Giard et Brière, 1911).

Garegnani, P. (1960) *Il capitale nelle teorie della distribuzione* (Milan: Giuffrè).

Garegnani, P. (1970) 'Heterogeneous Capital, the Production Function and the Theory of Distribution', *Review of Economic Studies*, 37 (June): reprinted in Hunt, E. K., and Schwartz, J. G. (eds) *A Critique of Economic Theory* (London: Penguin Books, 1972).

Garegnani, P. (1976) 'On a Change in the Notion of Equilibrium in Recent Work on Value and Distribution: A Comment on Samuelson', in M. Brown, K. Sato and P. Zarembka (eds) *Essays in Modern Capital Theory* (Amsterdam: North-Holland).

Garegnani, P. (1978, 1979a, 1979b) 'Notes on Consumption, Investment and Effective Demand', in *Cambridge Journal of Economics*, Part I, 3 (December): Part II, 4 (March): 'A Reply to Joan Robinson', 4 (June): in that order.

Garegnani, P. (1979c) *Capitale e domanda effettiva* (Turin: Einaudi).

Garegnani, P. (1983) 'Two Routes to Effective Demand: Comment on Kregel', in J. Kregel (ed.) *Value, Distribution and Effective Demand* (Amsterdam: North-Holland).

Garegnani, P. (1985) 'Sraffa: Classical versus Marginalist Analysis', paper delivered at the Conference 'Sraffa's *Production of Commodities* After Twenty Five Years', mimeo.

Gram, H. and V. Walsh (1983) 'Joan Robinson's Economics in Retrospect', *Journal of Economic Literature* 21 (June).

Hahn, F. H. and R. C. O. Matthews (1964) 'The theory of Economic Growth', *Economic Journal*, 74 (December).

Hicks, J. R. (1932) *The Theory of Wages* (London); 2nd edn (New York: St Martin's Press, 1964).

Hicks, J. R. (1946) *Value and Capital*, 2nd edn. (Oxford: Clarendon Press).

Johnson, H. G. (1973) *The Theory of Distribution*, (London: Gray, Mills).

Keynes, J. M. (1936) *The General Theory of Employment Interest and Money* (London: Macmillan).

Marshall, A. (1898) 'Distribution and Exchange', *Economic Journal*, 88.

Marshall, A. (1901) *Principles of Economics*, 2nd edn (London: Macmillan).

Marshall, A. (1961) *Principles of Economics*, 8th edn, 2 vols (London: Macmillan).

Marx, K. (1974) *Capital*, vol. 3 (London: Lawrence & Wishart).

Mill, J. S. (1909) *Principles of Political Economy* (London: Longmans, Green).

Nagel, E. (1961) *The Structure of Science* (New York: Harcourt Brace).

Pareto, V. (1895–6) *Cours d'économie politique*, 2 vols; Italian tr., (Turin: Boringhieri, 1961).

Ricardo, D. (1951) *'Principles of Political Economy'*, vol. 1, *Works*, Sraffa ed (Cambridge: Cambridge University Press).

Robertson, D. H. (1963) *Lectures on Economic Principles* (London: Collins).

Robinson, J. (1953) 'The Production Function and the Theory of Capital', *Review of Economic Studies*, 21(2): 81–106.

Robinson, J. (1956) *The Accumulation of Capital* (London: Macmillan).

Robinson, J. (1962) *Essays in the Theory of Economic Growth* (London: Macmillan).

Robinson, J. (1970) 'Capital Theory Up-to-Date', *Canadian Journal of Economics*, (May); repr. in *Collected Economic Papers*, vol. IV (Oxford: Blackwell, 1973) pp. 144–54.

Robinson, J. (1973) *Collected Economic Papers*, vol. IV (Oxford: Blackwell).

Robinson, J. (1974) 'History versus Equilibrium', *Thames Papers in Political Economy*, (London: Thames Polytechnic). Rpt. in *Collected Economic Papers*, vol. 5 (Oxford: Blackwell, 1979), pp. 48–58.

Robinson, J. (1975a) 'The Unimportance of Reswitching', *Quarterly Journal of Economics*, 89 (Feb).

Robinson, J. (1975b) *Collected Economic Papers*, vol. II (Oxford: Blackwell).

Robinson, J. (1980) *Further Contributions to Modern Economics* (Oxford: Blackwell).

Samuelson, P. A. (1978) 'The Canonical Classical Model of Political Economy', *Journal of Economic Literature*, 16 (December).

Smith, A. (1950) *The Wealth of Nations*, vol. 1 (London: Dent and Sons).

Sraffa, P. (1960) *Production of Commodities by Means of Commodities* (Cambridge: Cambridge University Press).

Walras, L., 1954, *Elements of Pure Economics*, Jaffé ed. (London: Allen & Unwin).

Wicksell, K., 1935, *Lectures on Political Economy*, 2 vols. (London: Routledge).

Wicksell, K., 1954, *Value, Capital and Rent* (London: Allen & Unwin).

Wicksteed, P. H., 1933, *The Common Sense of Political Economy*, 2 vols. (London: Routledge).

13 On Sraffa's Contribution to Economic Theory

Pierangelo Garegnani*

1. It is not only during the last few decades that Sraffa has acquired an important place in discussions of economic theory. An article on the laws of variable returns published as early as 1926 (Sraffa, 1926) when he was 28, in which he was already pointing towards a criticism of the demand and supply theory of value, attracted much attention as soon as it appeared. At that time however the interest focused on some remarks on the theory of the firm, which were to be developed later by Joan Robinson in her theory of imperfect competition. The work by Sraffa which is at the heart of the discussion today belongs mainly to the period since 1951. I am referring to the *Works* of Ricardo (1951–73) which Sraffa edited for the Royal Economic Society, and to his book, *Production of Commodities by Means of Commodities*, (1960). These works relate to two connected themes which are important (more important, perhaps, than is immediately apparent) for an understanding of the present situation of economic theory. The two themes are the criticism of the dominant demand-and-supply theory of distribution and relative prices, and the revival of a different approach to these problems: that of the British classical economists down to Ricardo. An attempt, however brief, at reporting Sraffa's contribution therefore requires some preliminary words about the dominant and the classical approaches to distribution, and the criticism levelled against the former.

2. I have referred to the 'modern' theory of distribution and relative prices, and to Sraffa's role in the criticism of it. By that I mean the theory based on the 'marginal' method that has held almost undisputed sway over economic thought since the last quarter of the nineteenth century. At its basis lies the idea of a substitutability between factors of production, traditionally founded upon the twin concepts of 'marginal utility' (i.e. the increment of satisfaction derived from a unit-increment of the consumption of a particular good) and 'marginal productivity' (i.e. the increment in output with a unit-increment of the 'factor of production' applied), By correlating a decrease (whether 'smooth' or 'by steps' is irrelevant here) in marginal utility and

*With some modifications regarding the arrangement and presentation of the material, this text is the same as that published in Italian, together with texts by other authors, in the weekly paper *Rinascita* of 4 August 1978, on the occasion of Sraffa's eightieth birthday. It was therefore intended for a public consisting mainly of non-economists.

marginal productivity with an increase in the use of the good and of the factor of production respectively, this theory has sought a rational foundation capable of sustaining the notion of 'demand functions' for factors of production (traditionally: labor, capital and land). These 'demand functions' are then assumed to determine the remunerations of the factors by their intersection with the corresponding 'supply' functions. This intersection or 'equilibrium' of the demand and supply of factors of production can be then shown to entail similar equilibria on the markets for the products, thereby determining the relative prices and outputs of the latter. In the words of the author who, more than anybody else among the initiators of the theory, contributed to its extraordinary success, Alfred Marshall:

> The normal value of everything, whether it be a particular kind of labour or capital or anything else, rests, like the keystone of an arch, balanced in equilibrium, between the contending pressure of its two opposite sides. The forces of demand press on one side, those of supply on the other. (*Principles*, 1st ed., Vii, i; Marshall, 1961, II, p. 593)

The practical implications of this theory for our view of the economy and of its management are, of course, far-reaching. Thus, for example, the theory underpins the generally accepted idea according to which competitive prices tend to reflect the 'scarcity' of 'factors of production' and products, and to guarantee a maximum of satisfactions for the community in some exactly definable sense.

3. Now, marginal theory, with its complex analytical structure, has been increasingly called into question as a result chiefly of two theoretical developments of the last four or five decades. The first development goes back to the late thirties and is a result of Keynes's work, and of the experience of the great economic crisis of those years. The idea was then admitted that, at least in the short period, there would be no spontaneous tendency to that equality between the quantity of labor demanded and supplied on which the theory relied for its determination of wages, profits and prices.

However, Keynes's criticism did not question the basic premises of orthodox theory and in particular the idea of a regular 'substitutability' between factors of production ensuring an inverse relation between the quantity of these employed and their relative rates of remuneration. On the contrary, Keynes explicitly accepted those premises. It was the second of the two theoretical developments referred to above that went on to question these premises. This was done, essentially, by criticizing the concept of capital as a factor or set of factors of production characteristic of the theory. This criticism has already shown the invalidity of some central propositions of the theory – such as that which postulates a direct relationship between 'capital intensity' and real-wage rates. It has also shown that a production technique which has been abandoned because of a rise in wages may profitably 'return' after wages have undergone a further rise: the phenomenon which has become known as the 'reswitching of techniques'. Of course, the latter possibility directly contradicts the proposition according to which wage rises lead to the introduction or expansion of more capital-intensive processes, thereby reducing the level of labor employment compatible with a given endowment of capital. And it was this proposition that was supposed to provide the rational basis for declining 'demand curves' of labor and the other factors of production and hence 'stable equilibria', thus supplying the foundation for an attempt to explain the distribution of the social product in terms of the marginalist supply and demand.

4. However, if we are to understand the place which Sraffa's work occupies in today's economic theory – it is not enough to refer to the criticism of marginal theory. We must also take a step back in the history of economic thought. As mentioned already, marginal theory was preceded by the theoretical approach which had been progressively worked out up to the time of the French Physiocrats and was then developed by the classical economists, particularly Ricardo. The analytical problems we shall presently mention (par. 5) were important in favoring the abandonment of this earlier approach, but no doubt important was also the theoretical support which the socialist movement was able to derive from Ricardo's work, especially in England, and already before the time of Marx.

In that earlier theoretical approach, the wage was not seen to be determined by an equilibrium between counterposed forces of demand and supply for factors of production. It was rather seen to be regulated by socioeconomic forces such as the historically determined level of subsistence (François Quesnay, Ricardo) or, more generally, the relative bargaining position of the social classes involved (Adam Smith, Marx). As a result the wage could be explained *independently* of the other forms of income: that is to say, it could be taken as a known quantity when determining the other forms of income, and especially the profits on capital.

Incomes other than wages could accordingly be calculated as what remained of the social product after deducting the known amount allotted to the workers: that is, income other than wages appeared as a 'surplus' over and above that amount – regardless of whether this surplus was determined in value form, as a 'surplus-value' or in physical terms, as a 'surplus-product'.

5. We now have the main elements for attempting to situate Sraffa's contribution. The importance of his work for today's economic theory seems to me to rest essentially on the three following elements: (i) his rediscovery of the theoretical approach characteristic of the classical economists; (ii) his solution to a number of analytical difficulties that were not resolved by Ricardo and Marx; (iii) his criticism of marginal theory.

For the first of these three elements, we should refer, apart from *Production of Commodities*, to the critical edition of Ricardo's work which absorbed the middle years of Sraffa's life. (cf Ricardo, 1951–73: for this classic among critical editions in all subjects, the Swedish Academy of Sciences awarded him the gold medal for the economic sciences, an honor which he shares only with Keynes and Myrdal.) It was in fact in his 1951 *Introduction* to the first volume of that edition, and especially in the pages of it dealing with Ricardo's need to measure the product in terms independent of its distribution, that Sraffa succeeded in bringing back to light the approach peculiar to the classical theories (Sraffa, 1951, pp. xxx–xxxvii). As he himself was later to say, this approach had been 'submerged and forgotten' (Sraffa, 1960, p.v). It had been submerged and forgotten beneath a thick layer of interpretations depicting Adam Smith and Ricardo as primitive precursors of subsequent marginal theories. There may indeed be a sense in which this first aspect of Sraffa's work is the most fundamental one since it provides the basis on which the remaining two stand.

As regards the second element, we should turn to *Production of Commodities by Means of Commodities* (1960). Here we find Sraffa's solution to the problem of determining the rate of profits and the relative prices of commodities, a solution based on more general hypotheses than those under which commodities would exchange in accordance with the labor necessary in order to produce them. These latter hypotheses were those to which the solution put forward by Ricardo and Marx had remained confined, because of the difficulties of the general case which they did not succeed in fully overcoming, and which were to play the role already mentioned in the abandonment of the classical approach.

Finally, with regard to the third main element of Sraffa's contribution, the same book rigorously sets out the propositions concerning that 'reswitching of techniques' which we already mentioned, and whose implications for a criticism of marginalism were then to be developed further by other writers.

6. These three main elements of Sraffa's contribution may help to clarify an issue which has been frequently aired in discussions both in Italy and elsewhere: the relationship between Sraffa's work and that of Marx. The question is a complex one which does not lend itself to a short answer. A first thing which may be said is that the conception which some people appear to have concerning that relationship is to my mind seriously misleading. In order to reach a correct understanding of the matter we should first try to understand the relationship between Marx and the classical economists, particularly Ricardo.

As I have argued elsewhere (Garegnani, 1984, pp. 305–9) this relationship should be seen in terms of a strict continuity at the level of economic analysis. This constitutes no contradiction of the obvious fact that unlike Ricardo and the classical economists, Marx sought to show that the capitalist mode of production is no more permanent than the modes which had preceded it – the fact, that is, that Marx aimed at a 'critique of political economy'. There is no contradiction between the two things because it is normal that one author operating within a given theoretical approach should reach conclusions which were not reached by his predecesors, and which, for that matter, may then be either confirmed or disproved by the work of his successors. This is just the way in which a theoretical approach develops, so long as it is alive. This, I believe, is exactly the kind of relationship which Marx saw, and we can see, between his 'critique of political economy' and the work of Ricardo. Thus Marx deduced the transitory character of capitalism from a kernel of analysis whose contents is what he often called the 'inner' or 'intrinsic' connections of the bourgeois system and, in particular, the antagonistic relation between wages and profits (cf. e.g. Marx, 1969, pp. 164–6; 216–22). Now, as Marx himself repeatedly stated these 'inner connections' were discovered by the classical economists, and especially by Ricardo in connection with his theory of the rate of profits. And it was precisely this theory of profits which Marx took up and developed for his 'critique'.

Once this continuity between the classical economists and Marx is correctly understood, it becomes easy, I believe, to grasp the true relation between Sraffa and Marx. A resumption of the classical approach had naturally to start from the highest points of analytical development which that approach had achieved in the past – and in many respects these points are those at which we find that approach in Marx' work.

7.   Once the relation between Marx and Sraffa is understood in these terms we are in better condition to deal with one aspect upon which the current discussion on the relation between Marx and Sraffa has sometimes insisted. A criticism of Marx has sometimes been seen to be implicit in the fact that we do not find in Sraffa the labor theory of value. It appears, however, that this point simply brings us back to the second of the three aspects of Sraffa's work we mentioned above: namely, the solution he provided for the problem of value for more general hypotheses than those under which Ricardo and Marx had solved it. Solving this problem and abandoning the labor theory of value as understood by Ricardo and by Marx are, in reality, two sides of the same coin. As should not need recalling, any living theoretical approach does develop, that is, it modifies some of its propositions.

In fact the idea according to which Sraffa would have exposed the invalidity of Marx's economic theory, since we do not find there Marx's labor theory of value, can only be understood, I believe, by recalling the ethical or sociological meanings ascribed to the labor theory of value by that Marxist tradition which had its beginnings at the end of the nineteenth century, following upon the criticism of Marx and of the labor theory of value by marginalist authors. I have argued elsewhere (cf. Garegnani, 1981, pp. 71–3; 76–88) that these meanings of the labor theory of value were not in fact present in Marx. They were developed later, largely as an answer to the marginalist criticism, and appear to have reflected the obfuscation which, by that time, had spread over the approach of the classical economists. That obfuscation appears in particular to have prevented an understanding of the analytical role which the labor theory of value played in allowing Ricardo and Marx to overcome the basic error by which Adam Smith had overlooked the constraint which binds the real wage and the rate of profits, given the technical conditions of production. It is significant that this role of the labor theory of value (which was a discovery of Ricardo, and not of Marx) should have been brought back to light by Sraffa himself, in his Introduction to Ricardo's *Principles* (Sraffa, 1951, pp.xxxii–xxxiii). In this way, far from criticizing Marx for his use of that theory, Sraffa in fact made an effective defense of it in the analytical sense in which it had been used by Ricardo and by Marx. It should be recalled in this connection how Marx himself had always been contemptous of any attempt to draw ethical or sociological conclusions from the labor theory of value (cf. e.g. Marx, 1970, p. 62 n.).

8. This having been said, it is important to remember that Sraffa only laid the premises for a resumption of the classical approach to distribution and relative prices. He did this by clarifying anew the basic elements of that approach, and by providing a solution to the problems of value theory that had been left open by Ricardo and Marx. It would therefore be a mistake to seek in *Production of Commodities* what is not actually there: to seek, that is, an explanation of capital accumulation, or even (except for some hints) an analysis of the way in which social relations determine the division of the product between wages and profits. As indicated above, so far as these problems are concerned, Sraffa appears to refer us to the places where they have received the most advanced treatment in the framework of this theoretical approach, and therefore to all the work which has to be done in order to develop the ideas of the classical economists in conformity with the present state of economic reality and of economic knowledge.

9. Another basic issue, which has been aired in current discussions in Italy and elsewhere, concerns the relation that can be established between the analysis of Sraffa and that of Keynes. I can attempt to say something on this issue here only after reformulating it in terms of the relationship which in my opinion exists between Keynes and the resumption of the classical theoretical approach which has been initiated by Sraffa. For, in his published writings, Sraffa has only marginally concerned himself with Keynes.

Looking at things in this more general light, we are immediately struck by Keynes's complex relationship to marginal theory. True, Marshall's variant of this theory constituted the entire horizon within which Keynes received his training and beyond which, in a sense, he never went. In this respect, Sraffa's work is of a profoundly different character, being directed from the very beginning to a criticism and replacement of marginal theory. Yet, at the same time, Keynes dealt a serious blow to that theory when he disputed the tendency to an equality between the supply and the demand of labor. This second element could not fail to draw Keynes close to those, like Sraffa, who criticized such a theory.

In my view, however, this negative, critical element is not the only, or even the main contribution which the contemporary resumption of classical theory can draw from Keynes's work. As I said, this resumption inevitably has in Marx's analysis one of its main starting points. Now, unlike what is true in subsequent marginal theory – indeed, unlike in Ricardo himself – the idea that aggregate demand tends to adjust to the productive capacity of the economy is quite foreign to Marx's analysis. As is well known, Marx's theory of crises clearly raises the very problems of 'effective demand' which are posed by Keynes. Keynes's 'multiplier' principle, which does a great deal to explain the mechanism by which slumps come about, may provide us with a highly valuable element for developing the analysis of the link between economic cycles and the process of accumulation. As a matter of fact, the principles of the 'multiplier' and of 'effective demand' are entirely independent of other Keynesian concepts bearing the traces of marginal theory (like the concept of a regular inverse relation betweeen investment and the interest rate), which are also those that allowed marginal theory to achieve some success over the last thirty years in its attempt to reabsorb Keynes's criticism.

References

Garegnani, P. (1981) *Marx e gli economisti classici* (Torino: Einaudi).
Garegnani, P. (1984) 'Value and Distribution in the Classical Economists and Marx', *Oxford Economic Papers*, no. 36.
Marshall, A. (1961) *Principles of Economics*, Variorum edition, 2 vols (London: Macmillan).
Marx, K. (1969) *Theories of Surplus Value*, vol. II (London: Lawrence & Wishart).
Marx, K. (1970) *Critique of Political Economy* (Moscow: Progress Publishers).
Ricardo, D. (1815) *An Essay on the Influence of a Law Price of Corn on the Profits of Stock*, in Ricardo (1951–2) Vol. IV.
Ricardo, D. (1817) *Principles of Political Economy and Taxation*, in Ricardo (1951–2) Vol. I.
Ricardo, D. (1951–73) *Works and Correspondence of David Ricardo*, Sraffa ed, 11 vols. (Cambridge: Cambridge University Press).
Sraffa, P. (1926) 'The Laws of Returns under Competitive Conditions', *Economic Journal*, 36 (December): 535–50.
Sraffa, P. (1951) Introduction to Ricardo's *Principles*, in Ricardo (1951–73) Vol. I.
Sraffa, P. (1960) *Production of Commodities by Means of Commodities* (Cambridge: Cambridge University Press).

Part III

Capital, Growth, Distribution

14 Accumulation and Capital Theory

Edward Nell

As Joan Robinson's views matured, the study of expansion through the accumulation of capital moved more and more to central stage, and she increasingly sought to group other questions around it. Yet it proved a difficult nut to crack. Accumulation has been analyzed by economists in two very different ways, between which she moved uneasily. The most common has been to see it as the expansion of the productive potential of an economy with a given technology, which may be improved in the process – this was her basic stance. But it has also been understood as the outright transformation of the technical and productive organization of the economy, an outlook of which she thoroughly approved, but which played almost no role in her analytics.

The first approach bases its thinking on the idea of steady growth, subsuming the concerns of the second under the heading of 'technical progress'. The resulting analysis rests on a conception of capital as productive goods, or, in more sophisticated versions, as a fund providing command over productive goods. This is not wrong; it is merely inadequate. Capital must also be understood, and this is the second approach, as a way of organizing production and economic activity, so that the accumulation of capital is the extension of this form of organization into areas in which production, exchange and distribution were governed by other rules. This conception of capital, in contrast to the first, more limited notion, emphasizes the importance of organization; so understood, technology and engineering are not abstract science, existing apart from capital; they are ways of organizing production, and so have an institutional dimension. Accumulation then implies the transformation of institutions as well as production, and steady growth is not applicable (except perhaps as a benchmark.)

Besides the distinction between steady state and transformational growth, there is another principal division in the way that economists have thought about accumulation, and here Joan Robinson chose sides quite unambiguously. One view sees it as 'ploughing back' part of the surplus arising from production; the other as the process of adjusting a scarce resource to its optimal uses, as determined by the market. According to the first, the classical 'surplus' approach, accumulation consists of the productive investment of part of society's net product – the surplus of output over necessary consumption and the requirements for maintaining capital intact – in order

377

to expand productive capacity to take advantage of new or developing markets. The study of accumulation, therefore, needs to explain both the availability of the surplus and the motivation for ploughing it back – and, referring to the previous distinction, this can be examined either as steady-state expansion or as part of a process of transformation.

The originators of the classical tradition saw accumulation primarily as a transformation of the economy. Smith stressed institutional changes, in particular the development of markets and the removal of state barriers, but his analytics were incomplete and partially incorrect. Ricardo offered only a rudimentary explanation of the surplus, in the 'iron law of wages'; accumulation, however, he saw as the natural activity of capitalists, although it would be limited by the rise of food prices caused by the extension of cultivation to marginal lands, shifting distribution in favor of rent. Marx located the origin of the surplus in the exploitation of labor, and found the cause of the tendency of the rate of profit to fall in the interaction of competition and technological advance, rather than in pressure on marginal land. Rosa Luxemburg accepted Marx's framework, but located the limits to accumulation in a systematic failure of domestic demand to keep pace with the expansion of capacity, requiring the conquest of overseas markets. Each offered a picture with a grand sweep, painted in large strokes. Modern 'surplus' theory, even Joan Robinson's, is more circumspect and less interesting.

The other approach, which Joan Robinson totally rejected, sees accumulation or decumulation of capital simply as the adjustment of a particular factor of production to its equilibrium level, as determined by supply and demand. In this conception (exemplified, e.g. by Hayek, 1941, ch.xx), factor equilibrium is defined in terms of the optimal allocation of scarce resources to competing tasks (in turn defined by the equilibrium final bill of goods, again determined by supply and demand). The supply of capital may either be taken as given, along with that of land and labor, or it may be seen as governed by saving behavior, and so responsive, through time preference, to the rate of interest. Demand for capital will be governed by its productivity at the margin, as with the other factors. Equilibrium in a particular sector comes when supply to that sector equals the demand for capital arising in it; equilibrium in general comes when the overall supply of capital equals the overall demand for it. So, according to this conception, accumulation occurs only when the economy is in disequilibrium – it is the movement along the path to equilibrium, or to a new equilibrium, occasioned perhaps by a shift in preferences or the effects of a technical innovation. The central economic problem is the optimal allocation of scarce resources, and accumulation of capital is simply an adjustment towards this objective – a perspective which Joan not only rejected, but held to be incoherent, since 'capital' was not a factor of production in the required sense. Nor could such an approach account for technical progress.

This last judgment may have been misguided. Allocation is a matter of given resources and given competing ends; it is clearly not suited, therefore, to the analysis of transformation. But neoclassical ingenuity should not be underestimated. Technical knowledge itself can be treated as a scarce resource, and the incentives to produce it and allocate it optimally can be studied by neoclassical methods. Thus the allocation approach can give rise to an account, albeit a little far-fetched, of the long-term transformation of the economy. But it does address the issue of the incentives to innovate, which Joan never did.

But a reallocation process has a natural ending at the equilibrium point, whereas capital accumulation appears to be limitless. A stationary equilibrium must be a point of 'bliss', in which no further capital can be usefully employed. Hence net saving must be zero, and all net income consumed. Locked into such an allocation/disequilibrium framework, the supply and demand approach would be unable even to examine adequately the (Keynesian) contention that a capitalist system must either expand or collapse into recession, the starting point for Robinson's approach. It was saved from this fate by the development of the neoclassical growth model, based on the aggregate production function, and thus combining aspects of the traditional 'surplus' approach with supply and demand, a mix to which Joan Robinson fiercely objected. The neoclassical model provides an account of 'steady growth' over the long run, that is, uniform expansion of all outputs and all inputs, taking place together with regular technical progress. Its working, in turn, is based on the traditional theory of competitive factor markets, with substitution between labor and capital in the process of production, where both factors are expressed in aggregate terms, and where 'factor prices' function analogously to commodity prices in the usual theory of markets.

1 THE KEYNESIAN PROBLEMATIC

The question of substitution initially arose because a simple Keynesian growth model with a given capital–output ratio led Harrod to the disturbing conclusion that neither steady growth nor optimal allocation could be achieved. Aggregate demand equals investment times the multiplier, or I/s, in the simplest case, where s is the average and marginal propensity to save. Aggregate supply, then, is the capital stock times its productivity, or K/v, where v is the capital–output ratio. So the growth rate, $G = I/K = s/v$. This is the rate which equates supply and demand; hence it is the one that business will find satisfactory. But nothing has been said about the labor force or employment; so the equilibrium growth rate need not be consistent with the growth of the labor force (adjusted for neutral technical progress), a condition which cannot be optimal. Nor is that the only problem. When I is too low, so that $I/K <$ full employment s/v, $I/s < K/v$, and there will be excess capacity; so businesses will be inclined to reduce I still further. Similarly when I is too large, there will appear to be capacity shortage, and businesses will be inclined to increase I still more. The system gives the wrong signals, and a deviation from steady growth will tend to worsen, rather than correct itself.

Joan Robinson's reaction was to question the use of the capital–output ratio as an accelerator in the account of deviations from the steady path. Investment decisions were more complex and the possibilities more numerous and less disastrous than this suggested. But the neoclassicals got in first.

2   THE NEOCLASSICAL RESPONSE

Substitution in response to price signals appears to 'correct' these Keynesian problems. The neoclassical model determines a path of steady and stable full employment growth. For instance, when the rate of growth of labor, in efficiency units (the 'natural' rate of growth), persistently exceeds the rate, s/v, determined by the propensity to save and the capital–output ratio (the rate that will just balance aggregate demand and aggregate supply), the real-wage will tend to fall, leading firms to substitute labor for capital. As a result, v, the capital–output ratio will decline, raising the rate of growth, s/v. So long as the production function is 'well behaved' (linear and homogeneous, positive first and negative second derivatives, marginal product of capital tends to infinity as K/L tends to zero, and tends to zero as K/L to infinity), there will exist a value of v that will equate s/v to any natural rate of growth. Technical progress which leaves the K/Y ratio unchanged (Harrod-neutral) will not affect the steady-growth path; technical progress which leaves the ratio of the marginal products of capital and labor unchanged (Hicks-neutral) will change the path, but the economy should adjust smoothly to the new equilibrium. In the Keynesian case, investment determined savings; here that causality is reversed (and so the instability disappears – by fiat): in the long run, all saving > will be invested; persistent excess capacity (resulting from planned saving) planned investment at full employment) would drive down the rate of interest by lowering the return (or raising the risk) on existing securities; the lower rate of interest will then raise investment up to the full employment level.

Of course, Joan Robinson would have none of this. It was pre-Keynesian in its approach to saving and investment, and it treated capital as a scarce factor, whose price – the rate of interest – fell as its amount relative to other factors rose. But capital is not a simple factor; it consists of miscellaneous produced means of production added together in value terms. Nor is this 'adding-up' arbitrary or insignificant; capital is shifted about from one line of industry to another precisely in response to the return obtained on the *amount* of it, as measured in value. This led to the famous controversy. But Joan Robinson objected to the neoclassical model even on its own terms.

3 OPTIMALITY AND THE GOLDEN RULE

In neoclassical theory, equilibria tend also to be optimal, but very early in the game she showed that in general the steady-growth path will not be. An optimal path ought to be one along which *per capita* consumption is at a maximum. Consumption is output minus investment, and investment must grow at a fixed rate in order to fully employ the growing labor force. Now consider different capital–output ratios: if the marginal product of capital at a certain v adds more to output than is required to equip the labor force, consumption rises; if it adds less, consumption falls. Since the marginal product falls as v rises when the marginal product of capital just equals the additional investment required for the growing labor force, consumption will be at a maximum. But there is no reason to expect this level of the marginal product to be associated with the capital–output ratio that makes s/v just equal to the rate of growth of the labor force.

The proposition that consumption per head is maximized when the rate of profit equals the rate of growth is sometimes called the 'Golden Rule of Growth'. Under constant returns, it has another disconcerting implication for neoclassical theory. In the stationary state, a positive rate of profit implies that the choice of technique (of the capital–output ratio) is suboptimal. In the stationary state (the normal assumption underlying textbook price theory), only a zero rate of profit is consistent with optimal technique. But a zero rate of profit implies that the labor theory of value governs long-run prices! Either long-run prices are determined by growth theory, or they reflect labor values, or the techniques in use are suboptimal. (Non-constant returns make this more complicated, but the heart of the problem remains: allocation theory cannot determine long-run prices and optimal techniques independently of growth theory, and therefore of the 'surplus approach'.) Joan Robinson opted for the last of these, arguing that a 'benevolent authority' would choose the optimal technique because it would set prices so that the rate of profit equalled the planned growth rate, whereas the market system, in general (and in practice), would not. But the choice of technique was only part of the conventional story; there was also the matter of the impact of a new technique, and how to analyze this.

4 TECHNICAL PROGRESS

Treating technical progress as a shift of one kind or another in the production function limits the field of study to changes in method, overlooking the introduction of new products, and indeed, whole new sectors. Treating it as autonomous or as a function of time, even, as in 'learning-by-doing', time on the job, ignores the important influence of demand pressures. Neo-Keynesians, by contrast, treat technical progress as primarily occurring in manufacturing as a response to the growth of demand, so that the rate of technical progress depends on the relative size of manufacturing and on the rate of growth of demand, a relationship known as 'Verdoorn's Law', which has been widely confirmed. But Joan herself was inconsistent on the subject. In her programmatic remarks she stressed the transformational effects of technical changes, but her analytic work was largely confined to attempts to classify innovations according to their impact on distribution, considered primarily from the supply side, but taking into account the impact of changes in distribution on effective demand. The obvious fact that new products transformed household technology, and so altered living patterns and the structure of family life, radically changing demand, nowhere figured in her analytical work. The distributional effects, however, can also lead to changes in the valuation of capital, a favorite topic of hers. For such changes in valuation invalidated the modelling of capital and distribution in terms of supply and demand.

5   CAPITAL THEORY

The standard version of neoclassical theory treats capital as a factor of production, on a par with labor and land, where factors are understood in broad terms, and are supplied by households and demanded by firms. The scarcity principle rules: prices are high when a factor is relatively scarce, low when it is plentiful. (The activity analysis version likewise rests on relative scarcity, but it treats each capital good and each form of land or labor separately, determining its marginal product as a shadow price, thereby avoiding difficulties over capital-in-general. But for that very reason activity analysis cannot easily analyze the forces that bear on capital as a whole – for instance, saving and investment and their relation to the rate of interest.) The 'surplus' approach of the classics, especially as developed by Marx, conceives capital as an institution: it is a way of organizing production by means of control over produced means of production, which permits processes of production to be valued so they can be bought and sold. These two approaches are obviously different, but are they necessarily incompatible? Joan Robinson thought so; the high priests of Cambridge, Massachusetts, did not. The capital theory controversy developed over the neoclassical attempt to show that the aggregate production function's implied ordering of techniques, according to an inverse relationship between profitability and capital intensity, could be constructed in a disaggregated classical or 'surplus' model.

Each point on a neoclassical production function (whether aggregate or not) represents the adoption of a method of production: the firm or the economy as a whole has fully adjusted its plant and equipment. Moving from one point on a production function to another thus means scrapping old plant and replacing it with new, which implies a burst of exceptionally high activity in the capital goods sector. This will normally be compatible with continuous full employment in the neoclassical framework only if the consumption goods sector is the more capital intensive, a condition for which there is no economic rationale (Uzawa, 1961), or if certain other special conditions are met (Solow, 1962; weakened by Drandakis, 1963). Moreover, even neoclassical theorists have shown that very special and strong assumptions, excluding a wide range of plausible technologies and initial conditions, are needed to bring about equilibrium growth (Hahn, 1966). And once we step outside the neoclassical framework the problem of 'traverse' (moving from one growth path to another), even with a *given* technique, can be shown to imply capacity surplus or shortages in one or more sectors, normally accompanied by temporary overall unemployment (Hicks, 1965; Lowe, 1976). All these points at least indirectly serve to validate Joan Robinson's long-standing contention that mainstream theory construes equilibrium as the end-point of a dynamic process, but has never produced a satisfactory, general account of how or why an economy out of equilibrium would ever get into it. But while Joan finally came to feel that this was her deepest line of criticism, the capital controversy revolved around the application of the scarcity principle to capital and its 'price', the rate of return.

In marginal productivity theory a technique is uniquely designated by $(K/Y, K/L)$; moreover, each K/Y is uniquely paired to its corresponding K/L, and as a direct consequence, each K/L is uniquely associated with a marginal product of capital. But suppose a technique were most profitable at one rate of profit (marginal product of capital), and then also proved the most profitable at another level of the profit rate. If this could happen, the neoclassical production function would not uniquely determine the choice of method of production. Yet the general possibility of this phenomenon ('reswitching') is easily demonstrated (see Appendix). Moreover, the inverse 'demand' relationship between capital intensity and the rate of profit need not hold; hence the principle of scarcity cannot be invoked to explain the 'use' of capital in production (see Appendix).

Not only the neoclassical approach is at risk here, however. If the technique of production which is chosen is the most profitable, and if, in general, there are no grounds for presuming that increasing capital intensity is associated with a lower rate of profit, the Marxian doctrine of the falling rate of profit is likewise rendered suspect (Okishio, 1961) (see Appendix).

Profit-maximizing businesses, operating in competitive conditions, will never choose a technique with a lower rate of profit. Joan Robinson always insisted that Marx's analytics be subjected to the same harsh criticism she inflicted on the orthodox.

6   CONCEPTUALIZING PRODUCTION

Orthodox economists have argued that the capital controversy revealed nothing more than some anomalous cases which create trouble for the theory of adjustment to equilibrium. But the problem Joan Robinson initially posed concerned the *meaning* of capital as a produced element in the process of production.

Neoclassical production theory, whether aggregate or not, postulates diminishing marginal output as the amount used of a factor is varied in relation to other factors. If factors are paid the value of their marginal products, as the theory of competitive behavior asserts, then factor reward, e.g. the rate of profit, should fall as the amount of the factor, capital, increases in relation to labor. (If reswitching occurs, it can be demonstrated that at least one of the switches will show a positive relation between capital per worker and the rate of profit.) Once we step outside the conventional approach this inverse relationship is not intuitively plausible: increasing the amount of capital employed in a production process is a more complex matter than employing more labor. Capital consists of all the various means of production; it is a *set* of inputs. In fact, it is more (and more complicated) than that: at the beginning of production the capital of an enterprise consists of its plant and equipment, its inventory of materials and its wage fund (minus various obligations). A little later it consists of somewhat depreciated plant and equipment, together with the worked-up inventory of marketable goods, while the materials and wage fund have disappeared. But (allowing for changes in indebtedness during production, etc.), although the actual goods in which its capital is embodied are different in the two situations, the business will sell for the same price – it has the same capital value. To vary the amount of capital is to change the size or the nature of the entire process, and it is not at all obvious what effect this will have on the rate of profit.

A second problem concerns influences running in the other direction, from the rate of profit to the amount of capital. When the rate of profit changes, competition requires prices to change. (Suppose, *ceteris paribus*, that the real-wage rose, requiring the general rate of profit to fall; to keep the rate uniform, so capital will not tend to migrate to the relatively high-profit industries, the prices of labor-intensive products will have to rise relative to capital-intensive ones.) But if the prices of produced means of production change, then the 'amount of capital' embodied in *unchanged* plant and equipment can vary, and this can come about because of variation in the rate of profit. Moreover, the amount of capital embodied in unchanged equipment can vary in either direction when the rate of profit changes, since the direction of relative price changes depends only on relative capital intensity, about which no general rules can be given. The neoclassical ranking of techniques according to capital intensity and the rate of return has to be considered an inadequate representation of the real complexities involved in choosing techniques and using capital in production. So the neoclassical answer to the Keynesian problem is not adequate, nor can the neoclassical theory of scarcity and substitution be applied to the problem of understanding the forces behind accumulation. Neoclassical theory *misconceives* capital.

7 NEO-KEYNESIAN THEORY

But, paradoxically, the alternative to the neoclassical theory of steady growth, developed in Cambridge by Joan Robinson and others, provides an answer that also appears to imply a stable full employment equilibrium, guaranteed by market price flexibility, although based on a different conception of the market, but still retaining the conception of accumulation as the expansion, rather than the transformation, of a given system. The overall saving ratio is considered the weighted average of saving out of wages and profits, the weights being the respective income shares. Here the propensity to save out of profits is assumed to be relatively high, and that out of wages to be low. Then, if the natural rate of growth $> s/v$, eventually the money-wage rate would tend to fall, and this, *ceteris paribus*, would raise the profitability of investment. As a result the overall saving ratio would rise, bringing s/v up to the full employment level. If s/v is greater than the natural rate, on the other hand, the resulting excess capacity would lower profitability, and tend to bring s/v down. Thus it is not necessary to assume easy and unrealistic substitution; the capital–output ratio can remain fixed, and yet market adjustments will direct the system towards the full employment growth path. (Moreover, such a 'classical' saving function could replace the proportional saving function in the neoclassical growth model, with the result that shifts in the production function would affect the K/Y ratio, but leave the rate of profit unchanged, rather than the reverse.)

Like the neoclassical, this scenario sees the natural rate of growth as the center of gravitation, towards which the system adjusts. But it has sometimes been given another, more Keynesian, interpretation. If, at the level of normal capacity utilization, investment demand were to exceed savings, multiplier pressure would drive up prices – since output could not be (easily) increased. Money wages, on the other hand, would not be driven up, since employment could not be (easily) increased, either, for when plant and equipment is operating at full capacity there are no more places on the assembly lines – the full complement of workers has already been hired. Thus the excess demand for goods will *not* translate into excess demand for labor, and prices will be driven up relative to money-wages: a profit inflation. Thus the overall saving ratio will rise, until the pressure of excess demand is eased. So, in the long run as well as in the short, savings adjusts to investment. Understood in this way, as Joan Robinson and Luigi Pasinetti insisted, the second scenario contradicts the neoclassical one, rather than complementing it.

8   INVESTMENT AND THE ACCELERATOR

But this is still not fully Keynesian, or at least not Harrodian, for the emergence of excess or shortage of capacity must be allowed to influence investment plans – the 'accelerator', or capital stock adjustment principle. Joan Robinson objected to this, on the reasonable grounds that Harrod's (and especially Samuelson's) use of the idea was too mechanical, and less plausibly, that it was not obvious to business that a change in demand would be permanent. But business success depends on being able to make that kind of judgment correctly; that is what marketing is all about. Once long-run demand has changed, either capacity or utilization has to be adjusted. But if capacity utilization is flexible, then there is no reason for prices, or, therefore, distribution, to change. Since Joan Robinson argues that prices and distribution do adjust, she must accept that capacity constrains upward movements and is expensive to carry when demand falls. Hence she must accept some form of modified 'accelerator'.

Starting from full capacity, when $s/v >$ actual or current I/K, there will be a slump; when $s/v < I/K$ prices will be bid up relative to money-wages. Money wages, in turn, will tend to rise or fall according to whether the actual rate of growth lies above or below the natural. If the actual rate lies above the natural, this will tend to raise the natural and lower the actual. There are thus three rates of growth: the actual, I/K, the warranted, s/v, and the natural, and six possible permutations of these. It can be shown (Nell, 1982) that in only two cases is there an unambiguous tendency for all three rates to converge; in these cases the actual rate lies between the warranted and the natural rates, so that money-wage inflation and price inflation move in opposite directions, causing the real wage to change. A rise in the real wage will lower the warranted rate and (less certainly) raise the natural rate; a fall will do the opposite. Hence in the two cases where the change lies in the right direction, the rates will tend to converge. In two others, the rates of inflation lie in the same direction, but plausible additional assumptions imply that they will not be equally rapid, so that the real wage will change, bringing a tendency to converge. But in two cases the real wage will tend to move in the wrong direction, and there seems to be no possibility of convergence at all; quite the opposite (Nell, 1982). So the Keynesian approach suggests that the full employment (or, indeed, any) steady-growth path should not be treated as a center of gravitation; it may or may not be what the market tends to bring about.

9   CAPACITY CONSTRAINTS?

It has been objected (Vianello, 1985, following a suggestion of Garegnani) that business routinely carries excess capacity, so that there are no binding constraints. But this is a misconception; 'normal capacity' will be a point or range of optimal usage. It can be exceeded, but at a cost, which means lowering profits below their normal range. Hence if the additional demand is permanent it will require additional capacity, either through new construction or by incurring once-for-all expenses for reorganizing present plant. In either case, we have investment expenditure, but the first means additional output from the capital goods industries, and must be underwritten by a reduction in consumption. The second, however, is a form of technical progress; no additional capital goods are required and no changes in consumption are necessary. What is required are changes in the methods and allocation of labor and in the organization of work. It may be costly to bring these about, but the costs will largely be labor and forgone output. Incurring these costs is an investment, but not one which has to be underwritten by a change in the real wage; it will normally come about through a cutback in production, while labor and managerial costs continue to run (though for different purposes). Thus the investment will be financed by the once-for-all *reduction in profits*, to be repaid by higher output and profits later. This is the mechanism which accounts for the fact that increases in the growth rate, as in the US during World War II, can be accompanied by an unchanged or even substantially increased real-wage. Contrary to the Vianello–Garegnani argument, there is no need to discard the insight that the full or normal capacity rate of growth is connected to the normal rate of profit through the propensity to save/retain earnings. But there are other difficulties.

10   CAPITAL VALUE AND PROFIT

Ironically, this neo-Keynesian approach falls foul of the same problems that plague the neoclassical standard version. For once we leave the one-sector framework, the neo-Keynesian theory implies that excess aggregate demand will bid up, not the price level in general, but the relative price of capital goods – for the excess demand is entirely concentrated in the investment goods sector, and there is no discussion of how this could be transmitted to the consumer goods sector. Moreover, if both prices did rise relative to money wages, consumer goods demand would fall. But this would not indicate a possible equilibrium, for such price increases would leave the profit rate unequal in the two sectors. Thus the neo-Keynesian claim must be that a bidding up of the relative price of capital goods will raise the rate of profit, leading to higher savings, etc., but in a two-sector model it is easily seen that this will only be the case when the capital goods sector is the more capital intensive (see Appendix). So the validity of the approach depends on an arbitrary condition (which becomes even more arbitrary as the number of sectors increases).

Even worse, suppose that the capital goods sector is the more capital intensive, and consider a small rise in the growth rate to a new equilibrium level, requiring an increased production of capital goods (alternatively, a fall in the actual rate below the equilibrium). The corresponding new overall capital–labor ratio will be higher than the initial one; but to maintain full employment there will have to be a diversion of resources to the industry with the lower capital–labor ratio. To preserve full employment the capital goods sector would have to be contracted; but to increase the growth rate it has to expand. (A similar argument holds for a decline in the equilibrium growth rate.) In the case where a rise in the price of capital goods would increase the rate of profit, permitting the neo-Keynesian mechanism to work, the system could not adjust to the new steady-growth path, since the two conditions for adjustment contradict one another (see Appendix).

In fact, adjustment from one steady-growth path to another turns out to be difficult in general, even without changes in technique. A change in the growth rate requires changes in the relative sizes of sectors, which means shifting labor and resources, but these are normally used in different proportions, or in different combinations. And some can only be used in certain sectors and not in others. The 'traverse' from one steady path to another will normally involve both unemployment and shortages, and it may be difficult to actually reach a new path before the conditions determining it change. The 'steady-growth' approach to accumulation may face insurmountable problems, if it is supposed that equilibrium paths trace out stylized history. But that profit and growth incentives may contradict one another, or that traverses may be difficult in no way undermines the theory. Indeed, these may be crucial insights, even if still oversimplified, into real problems of accumulation.

11   THE SIGNIFICANCE OF STEADY GROWTH

But, then, what is the importance of the steady-growth path? For the neoclassical approach it is an extension of the concept of equilibrium to the case of expansion over time; for some neo-Keynesians it represents a center of gravitation, a point towards which the system would move, or around which it would oscillate. For others it may simply be a point of reference –

how the system would work *if* certain contrary-to-fact assumptions held. Real processes will normally be different, and can be classified by their distance from such a point of reference.

Following Joan Robinson, steady growth with continuous full employment has been termed a 'golden age'; desired capital accumulation equals the natural rate of growth. But a low desired rate, well below the initial natural rate, might create a large reserve army of unemployed, forcing down real wages and lowering the birth rate, so that the natural rate would fall to the depressed desired rate – a 'leaden age'. A desired rate above the natural rate may bid up real wages enough to lower the rate of profit until the desired rate falls to the natural – a 'restrained golden age'. A 'bastard golden age' occurs when the desired rate cannot be achieved because the real wage cannot be driven down sufficiently, the attempt resulting in inflation. Other possibilities can be envisioned, depending on the adjustment mechanisms postulated. For example, when the initial stock of capital is not appropriate to the desired rate of accumulation, it will have first to be adjusted but the part of the capital goods sector that produces capital goods for its own use may be too large or too small for easy adjustment to the desired rate, giving rise to 'platinum age' patterns of accumulation. The catalogue is endless, but its value is limited, as Joan Robinson herself came to see.

But her disillusionment with growth theory arose from an increasing concern for the texture of history, coupled with a growing disdain for the smooth and polished surfaces of equilibrium. These latter are crystalline and timeless, collapsing the unknowable future and the unalterable past into an artificially determinate present. History, by contrast, is rough edged and open ended, filled with conflicts, accidents and mistakes. The models show us smooth sailing; the real world is awash in rough seas.

This contrast is surely overdrawn. Equilibrium cannot model history, but equilibrium models may, nevertheless, have a point. Not all concepts of equilibrium are neoclassical. Consider 'reproduction' models: what conditions must be met for the present system to reproduce itself with its present (or some other) distribution of income? Or: what conditions must be met for the present system to expand at the maximum rate permitted by its present (or some other) distribution of income and propensities to save? Or: what conditions must be met for the present system to move from its present growth path to one implied by a new distribution of income? Such questions are not only not meaningless; they must be answered if we are to analyze the actual movement of an economy – or try to plan and control such movement. Steady-growth models have a point, but they are not the whole story.

Steady growth, in fact, appears to be best analyzed as a supply-side concept. Its most elaborate development, in fact, is strictly supply side – as the von Neumann ray, or, in Sraffa's terms, the standard commodity, where the industry sizes of the system have been so adjusted that the net product of the economy as a whole consists of the same commodities in the same ratios as its aggregate means of production. The warranted rate of growth, by contrast, balances supply and demand. But it is an imperfect growth concept, for it balances aggregate supply and aggregate demand *at a moment of time*; it does not balance the growth of supply with the growth of demand. The von Neumann ray is an analysis of the growth of supply – but so far there does not exist a comparably detailed analysis of the growth of demand.

12   ACCUMULATION AND TECHNICAL CHANGE

This not only brings to light a defect in the theory of steady growth; it also raises the question of the relation of steady growth to the accumulation of capital. For the best established empirical proposition in the study of consumer behavior states that as income increases consumer demand will increase non-proportionally – it will shift in a characteristic manner. Hence there is little point in trying to complete the theory of steady growth with an account of steady growth in demand; it doesn't happen.

In actual fact, steady growth has never taken place. The history of capitalism is a history of successive booms and slumps, but perhaps even more striking, of slow but persistent long-term shifts in crucial relationships. (Joan Robinson seems to have largely overlooked this regularity in her concentration on the disorderliness of history.) For two centuries labor shifted out of agriculture and migrated to the cities to work in manufacturing industry. For over half a century now labor has shifted into services, first from agriculture and then, later, from manufacturing as well. For almost a century the relative size of the government sector has been rising, whether measured by share of GNP or by share of employment.

These points lead to a major criticism of the treatment of technical progress in accumulation: whether it is presented as shifting the production function, as learning by doing, or in a 'technical progress' function, and whether conceived as embodied or disembodied, it has been treated as leading to the extraction of greater output from given resources, in the context of steady growth. But technical progress introduces new products as well as new processes, and together these change the forms of social life. This is reflected in the changing importance of the major sectors of the economy, in the changing class structure, and in the changing patterns and nature of work. None of these points seem to have been captured by Joan Robinson's work, nor do they figure in most current analyses, in part because of the preoccupation with steady growth, based on an overly simplified concept of capital as productive goods. When capital is understood as also being a form of organization, then the link between accumulation and the transformation of institutions can be forged. Another reason, perhaps, may be that technical progress has been approached too timidly, and without understanding its dual relation to the growth of demand. For technical progress both stimulates the growth of demand and responds to it.

13   STEADY GROWTH v. TRANSFORMATIONAL GROWTH

In practice, steady growth is an impossibility, for at least three reasons. First, land and natural resources are limited, and high-grade ores and high-fertility lands are the first to be used. As they are used up over time, productivity falls unless and until technical progress offsets the decline – but such technical progress will have to involve new products. Second, as mentioned, Engel curves imply that consumption patterns will be changing. And finally, if propensities to save differ in the different social classes (and if workers receive interest on their savings, and capitalists salaries for managing capital) then the relative wealth of the classes will be changing over time, leading to changes in the composition of demand (see ch.11, this volume). The first point implies that costs will tend to rise, the second two that demand for consumer goods will tend to rise more slowly, as time passes. All three, therefore, point to long-term stagnation in the absence of major technological changes.

This does not simply mean increasing the productivity of currently employed processes; it means the development of new processes and new products – both for consumers and for industry. It means electrification, or the internal combustion engine, the airplane, or perhaps, the computer. The changes must be of sufficient importance to lead to an investment boom resulting from widespread scrapping of present plant and equipment, as well as the development, concurrently, of large-scale new markets, as consumers introduce the new products into their living patterns. And as new plants are built economies of scale can be realized, making it possible to lower prices, so as to reach new markets in lower levels of the income distribution. Capital organizes markets and marketing as well as production.

New household products have emerged because a way has been found to perform some normal daily activity better or more cheaply, by, in effect, shifting it from the household to industry, capitalizing it. New industrial processes, usually involving new products as well, have emerged as the result of mechanizing activities formerly performed by workers, enabling them to be done better, or more cheaply, or more reliably. Mass production goods have replaced home crafts; the mechanization of agriculture, in conjunction with Engel's Law, has displaced farm labor; the rise of manufacturing, to build the factories and then to supply the new goods, has provided employment for the displaced labor – but at greatly reduced hours of work per week, providing more hours to spend on consuming.

The rise of mass production and the consequent urbanization have created new problems, among others periodic mass unemployment, which in turn had to be dealt with by an expanded government. And today, traditional mass production is being transformed by the computer and the chip, with consequences we cannot yet fully foresee.

The interlocking emergence of new products and new processes, creating new markets and new industries, can be termed 'transformational growth', in contrast to steady growth. This is what is missing in Joan Robinson's work. But it is here that the true story of the accumulation of capital, and the causes of the wealth of nations, will be found, although to date this study has been left to the province of economic historians.

APPENDIX

The main points of the capital controversy can be illustrated in a simple two-sector model, of consumer goods and capital goods, sometimes interpreted as agriculture and industry.

The Model

Price:	$1 = r\alpha p + wB$		(1)
	$p = rap + wb$		(2)
Quantity:	$1 = gbT + cB$		(3)
	$T + gaT + c\alpha$		(4)

Greek letters stand for consumer goods. Roman for capital, as and αs for capital inputs, bs and Bs for labor inputs. The price and quantity of the consumer goods are taken as unity. r is the rate of profit, g the rate of accumulation; w is the wage rate and c the rate of consumption per worker. p is the price of capital goods and T the output of capital goods, both in relation to consumption goods. The unit volume of consumption goods can be taken as the basic basket of goods required to support a unit amount of labor, and the quantity equations can then be interpreted so that T is capital goods per head and c consumption per head.

This model will now be elaborated in various contexts to present significant results that were demonstrated in fuller and more sophisticated ways during the course of the controversy.

The Rate of Profit and General Equilibrium

First, convert this model to a simple activity analysis model; instead of the ratio T of capital goods (iron) to consumption goods (corn), we have the absolute outputs of each, x_c and x_1, and instead of the price ratio, p, we have p_c and p_1.

The standard version of neoclassical theory deals with factors in competitive conditions: laborers compete with one another for jobs, and capital funds flow towards the highest rate of return. The activity analysis model determines the earnings, for example, of particular machines or workers. But these earnings are rents and are subject to the requirement that

> [the] permanent fund of capital . . . is put into such forms that the rent secured by one concrete form or capital-good, is as large a fraction of its value as is that received by another . . . This equalizing force determines the number of capital-goods of each kind; and this, again, governs the rents they severally earn. (Clark, 1956, p.125)

The question confronting us is whether the modern activity analysis model is compatible with the capital theory of the standard version.

The implications of admitting that some of the goods in the initial endowments may be produced means of production are dramatic. Consider a simple model, containing two such goods:

$$\text{Max: } x_c p_c + x_1 p_1 \qquad\qquad \text{Min: } Cv_c + Iv_1$$
$$\text{Subject to: } Bx_c + Gx_1 \leqslant C \qquad \text{Subject to: } Bv_c + av_1 \geqslant p_c$$
$$\alpha x_c + ax_1 \leqslant I \qquad\qquad Gv_c + av_1 \geqslant p_1$$
$$x_c, x_1 > 0 \qquad\qquad v_c, v_1 > 0$$

Let the demand function $F(p,v)$ be such that prices satisfying it result in the production of both corn and iron, and further suppose that these quantities permit the necessary replacement to take place. No loss of generality is involved; this merely guarantees a solution compatible with replacement. Consider the diagram first of the maximizing (Fig. 14.A1a), then of the minimizing (Fig. 14.A1b) problem.

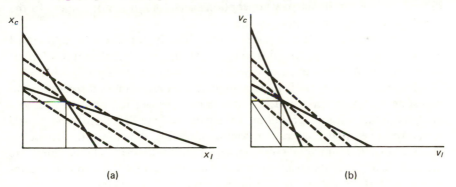

(a)   (b)

Figure 14.A1

In Figure 14.A1a, as long as the slope of the price ratio lies between the slopes of the two constraints, both goods will be produced.

In Figure 14.A1b, if both goods are produced, both resources will be assigned positive values. The minimizing problem yields these shadow values, which represent the rentals that can be obtained from the commodities. The slope of the line joining the optimal value of v_l to the optimal value of v_c gives the ratio of the rental values.

The slope of v_l/v_c need not equal p_l/p_c. If it did, p_l/p_c could not be changed without changing v_l/v_c as long as the change stays within limits prescribed by the slopes of the constraints.

Shift the intersection of the constraints in the max problem to the origin. Then construct perpendiculars to the constraint lines at the origin. These normal lines span a cone, and any line in this cone will be perpendicular to a line through the origin, *between* the constraints. The cone therefore defines the set of price vectors for which the optimal point remains unchanged.

But if $(v_l/v_c) \lessgtr (p_l/p_c)$, then $(v_l/p_l) \lessgtr (v_c/p_c)$; that is, the ratio of rental earnings to supply price for the two goods will be different. But capitalists will invest their capital in (pay the supply price of) equipment whose earning power is the highest. Hence in the Walras–Cassel equilibrium model, all capital funds will flow into the purchase of only *one* of the goods, the one whose rental value in relation to supply price is the greatest.

Clearly, this is inconsistent with the reproduction of the initial supplies of the model, which means that reproduction, in turn, is incompatible with the notion of capital as a freely moving fund, responsive to competitive pressures and opportunities. It follows that the standard version and the activity analysis approaches are *not* mutually compatible. The standard version rests on a *broad* conception of factor, allowing for a wide substitution among particular capital goods and workers in its account of the equilibrium of the firm. But this leads straight to the internal difficulties discussed earlier and, fundamentally, to the Cambridge (UK) critique (Laibman and Nell, 1977).

Activity analysis, since it has no theory of the firm, has no such internal difficulties, and on its narrow conception of factors, it is not subject to the Cambridge critique of factor pricing.

But for precisely these reasons, it stands directly opposed to the standard version and to the important idea that the cost and return on capital will both be uniform in different areas and will tend to equality with each other.

Without a theory of the firm, it is difficult to examine market structure and adjustments. But a theory of the firm cannot be grafted onto the activity analysis model without providing an account of the firm's *cost and capital structure*. The model cannot accommodate this, however, for it would require consideration of factor markets broadly defined. Hence these are mutually exclusive approaches rather than alternative tools in the economist's famous kit, and both stumble over the capital concept.

The Cambridge critics think they know what has gone amiss: net income is not, in general, a payment for a productive contribution; rather, it is the distribution of a surplus in accordance with property rights that reflect mostly class position. 'Capital' is not a factor of production, nor is it to be identified with a set of material means of production: raw materials, instruments and means of subsistence:

> What is a Negro slave? A man of the black race. The one explanation is as good as the other. A Negro is a Negro. He only becomes a slave in certain relations. A cotton spinning jenny is a machine for spinning cotton. It becomes *capital* only in certain relations. Torn from these relationships it is no more capital than gold in itself is money ... Capital ... is a social relation of production. (Marx, 1976)

The Uniform Rate of Profit and the Balanced Growth Rate

Steady growth means expansion along a balanced path, investment in which is underwritten largely by saving out of profits, which must be earned at a uniform rate. Both the balanced growth rate and the uniform profit rate are conventionally supposed to be established by movements of capital in response to competitive incentives – yet these movements are inconsistent.

Assume that agriculture is the relatively labor-intensive sector. Then let us suppose that initially, the wage – equal in both sectors – stood at its maximum level, with profit sufficient only for replacement. Assume, further, that all wages are consumed and all profit invested. Now let the wage fall from its maximum level to subsistence. Since agriculture is the relatively labor-intensive sector, it will now have the highest profit in relation to the value of its means of production. Thus, according to the implicit theory, capital should flow into agriculture, expanding supply while reducing it in industry, thus bidding down grain prices relatively to the prices of industry's products.

But a capitalist economy is an expanding one; the point of profits is that they underwrite accumulation. As the rate of profit is formed profits are invested and the capital stock expands. In order to expand in a balanced way, however, the sectors must stand in the correct proportions to one another. Moving from zero expansion – simple replacement – to expansion at the maximum rate requires an increase in the relative size of industry, which is to say a shrinkage in agriculture, just the *opposite* of the movement required to equalize the rate of profit!

Writing out the system in full, assuming circulating capital and that profit is figured in advanced wages:

Price Equations

(1a) $(1+r)(a+wb\pi)=1$

(2a) $(1+r)(\alpha+w\beta\pi)=\pi$

Quantity Equations

(3a) $(1+g)(a+ca\theta)=1$

(4a) $(1+g)(b+c\beta\theta)=\theta$

Here (a,α) are the machinery inputs in industry and agriculture, respectively, and (b,β) the consumer good requirements at subsistence level; w and c are the wage rate and the rate of consumption per head (both are *percentages* of subsistence levels); π and θ are relative prices and relative quantities, respectively (taking capital goods as the unit this time).

Eliminating w and c we obtain,

$$\pi = \frac{\beta}{b}[1 - (1+r)a] + (1+r)\alpha \tag{3}$$

$$\theta = \frac{\beta}{\alpha}[1 - (1+g)a] + (1+g)b$$

$$\frac{\delta\pi}{\delta r} = a - \left(\frac{a\beta}{b}\right) < 0 \qquad \frac{\delta\theta}{\delta g} = b - \left(\frac{a\beta}{\alpha}\right) < 0 \tag{4}$$

So the movement of capital into agriculture which will reduce π, so as to raise r, will raise θ and so reduce g, which contradicts the assumption that $r = g$, since all and only all profits are invested. More generally, when $r = g$,

$$\theta = \frac{b}{\alpha}\pi \tag{5}$$

Equilibrium θ and π must always move together. But to effect a change in π by means of supply and demand, capital must move so that the ratio of industry sizes moves inversely with π. So a movement of capital which brings prices nearer to prices of production moves outputs away from those required for balanced growth. This cannot be. The whole picture is mistaken. Capital almost never moves in response to current price differentials. Investment depends on expected market growth; and prices are set to provide the profits to finance investment. So they have little or nothing to do with current supply and demand. (See below, 'Two Concepts of Price'.)

The Marginal Productivity Theory of Wages

Neoclassical economists have held that distribution was determined in the factor market in the same way that prices and quantities were determined in the product market. The theory of marginal productivity, which has always been the foundation of this view, holds that: (1) in competition each unit of a factor will receive the value of the extra product the employment of an extra unit of the factor brings as reward, and (2) that as employment of a factor increases, with other factors constant, the amount of extra product from further employment declines. This can be shown easily in a diagram. Plot output per employed plant, Y/K, on one axis, and amounts of labor per plant, L/K, on the other. As we apply more men to the factory, output goes up, but by a smaller amount each time. For a certain ratio of labor to capital, L^*/K, there will be a corresponding Y^*/K. The tangent to the curve at that point will measure the marginal product, and the point where the tangent intersects the vertical axis will divide the output of the factory between wages and profits. The slope of the tangent is $(\text{wages}/K)/(L^*/K)=w$ (see Fig. 14.A2).

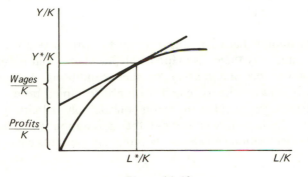

Figure 14.A2

The wage rate, and by definition:

$$\frac{Y^*}{K}=\frac{\text{wages}+\text{profits}}{K}$$

These basic ideas can be developed in a number of ways, for instance: the relationship may be conceived as one between aggregate output – the whole capital and entire labor force of the society; total wages; profits and output can be determined together with investment, savings and growth. Whatever method is used, the ultimate thought remains that factor rewards represent productive contributions at the margin and that these contributions diminish as factor employment increases.

The claim that distribution is really a form of exchange and that factor incomes are proportional to contributions has always encountered opposition. In the past, this centered on the difficulties in separating the contributions made by the various contributing factors. Cassel has commented that 'If a pit has to be dug, the addition of one more man will make little difference ... unless you give the man a spade.' A homely illustration; yet, one can translate the example to the modern factory and consider adding a man to a well-designed, properly running assembly line, where his marginal product will be zero. Subtracting a man – if the plant is well designed, without redundant workers or featherbedding – will bring the process to a halt: the marginal product will equal the total. Sir Dennis Robertson (1951), commenting on Cassel's observation, provided the neoclassical answer:

If ten men are set to dig a hole instead of nine, they will be furnished with ten cheaper spades instead of nine more expensive ones; or, perhaps, if there is no room for him to dig comfortably, the tenth man will be furnished with a bucket and sent to fetch beer for the other nine. Once we allow ourselves this liberty, we can exhibit in the sharpest form the principle of variation – the principle that you can combine varying amounts of one factor with a fixed amount of all the others; and we can draw, for labor or any other factor, a perfectly definite descending curve of marginal productivity.

Robertson admits that where the technique of production is rigidly fixed, marginal productivity theory is inapplicable; he claims that it applies where technique is variable and that under such conditions, a unique inverse relation exists between the wage and the labor to capital ratio.

In fact, Robertson qualifies the claim considerably, admitting 'that there seems to be a certain unreality about the assumption' [that the forms of capital and organization can change without the amounts changing].

Examination of Robertson's Claims

One can adopt some well-known theorems from current literature and analyze these three claims. With a little mathematics – but not much – the results will prove to be of striking simplicity, yet great generality. Start with the income identity in real terms:

$$Y = wN + rK \tag{6}$$

where Y is output; w, the wage; N, the number of workers; r, the rate of profit; and K, the total capital stock. Then, dividing by K:

$$\varphi = wn + r \tag{7}$$

where φ equals Y/K and n equals N/K. Differentiating:

$$d\varphi = ndw + wdn + dr \tag{8}$$

from which it follows that

$$w = \frac{d\varphi}{dn} \tag{9}$$

if and only if $-n$ equals dr/dw. This is to say that the wage will equal the marginal product of labor if, but only if, a certain special condition is met.

This condition is that all sectors in the economy must have the same capital to labor ratios – a most unlikely circumstance. In general, therefore, with a given technique – or, for that matter, if techniques vary – the wage will not equal the marginal product of labor.

Consider the second claim and suppose there are two techniques, competitive in the sense that for a given wage both return the same rate of profit:

$$\varphi_1 = wn_1 + r$$

and

$$\varphi_2 = wn_2 + r \tag{10}$$

This means that below the given wage technique 1 would yield a slightly higher r, than would technique 2. Combine the two equations and regroup:

$$w = \frac{\varphi_1 - \varphi_2}{n_1 - n_2} \tag{11}$$

At the so-called switching point, the wage identically, even trivially, equals the marginal product of labor. Lest anyone think this somehow profound, observe that equation (11) states no more than that when two techniques, operating at a given rate of profit and paying everything out as wages or profits, also pay the same way, then the technique using more labor per unit of capital must produce proportionately more output per unit of capital.

Modern analysis confirms the first two of Robertson's propositions. What about the third? When methods of productions can be varied – that is, when nine expensive spades can be turned into nine cheaper ones, a bucket and beer – is the result a 'perfectly definite descending curve of marginal productivity'?

The answer is devastating, unambiguous and by now well known. The law of scarcity requires that as labor becomes more plentiful with respect to capital, the real wage should decline and the marginal product diminish. However, the distribution variables (w and r), the real-wage rate and the profit rate – defined as identical with marginal products at switching points – moves in a capricious and haphazard way as the relative scarcity of labor to capital varies. In fact, the marginal product might rise, jump about discontinuously or move in any imaginable manner, without apparent rhyme or reason. There appears to be no way that a monotonic, inverse relation between the real-wage or profit rates and relative scarcity can be derived; therefore, most neoclassical writers introduce it simply as a postulate, a method which, in the words of Bertrand Russell, 'has many advantages; the same as theft over honest toil' (1919, p.71).

These are strong words, but the demonstration is simple. The two sectors –

agriculture and industry – set out above and some high school algebra will suffice. The equations showed revenues equal to cost-plus in each sector:

$$p = rap + wb$$
$$1 = r\alpha p + w\beta$$

Solving each for p, equating the results and rearranging:

$$\frac{(1/\beta - w)(1/a - r)}{rw} = \frac{\alpha/\beta}{a/b} \tag{12}$$

This can be illustrated by a simple, very instructive diagram which shows the relatedness of prices, profits and wages. Plot w against r, marking off $1/\beta$ and $1/a$ on the w and r axes, respectively: $1/\beta$ is the maximum wage rate; $1/a$, the minimum rate of profit consistent with positive prices; α/β is the machine to man ratio in agriculture; a/b, the machine to man ratio in industry. Consider the shaded portions of the diagrams; they represent the left side of equation (12). When $\alpha/\beta < a/b$, that is, whenever industry uses more machines relative to manpower than agriculture, the curve bulges outwards; when $\alpha/\beta > a/b$, that is, when agriculture uses more machinery per man than industry, the curve bends inwards. This means that, for a given real-wage, the rate of profit will be higher for both sectors whenever industry is more heavily mechanized than agriculture.

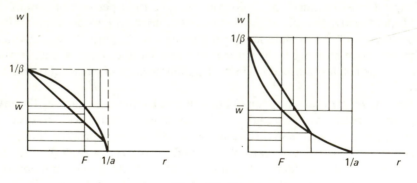

Figure 14.A3

Prices

Now for prices. Income, by definition, equals wages and profits – ignoring land and rents. In equilibrium, income also equals consumption and investment. Dividing all these magnitudes by the total labor force:

$$y = rk + w \tag{13}$$

$$y = gk + c \tag{14}$$

where y is output per man; k is capital per man; g is growth rate; gK/N = investment/labor force; and c is consumption per head. In general, it follows that:

$$k = \frac{c - w}{r - g} \tag{15}$$

In particular, however, ratios of capital value to labor for techniques producing the same good are to be compared. Let this be the consumption good, grain. Then g equals 0; so, $c = 1/\beta$ is the maximum value, the same as the maximum wage. Hence:

$$k = \frac{1/B - w}{r} = \frac{1}{n} \tag{16}$$

and k, the capital to labor ratio, will be indicated by the dotted lines in the diagrams.

Clearly, when the curve bulges out – when industry is more mechanized – as w increases, the slope measuring k gets flatter. That is, as w increases the ratio of labor to value of capital also increases. Thus, contrary to accepted opinion, the wage varies directly, rather than inversely, with the ratio of labor to capital. Honest toil is not producing results; if purity of doctrine is to be preserved, there will have to be resort to theft.

Before the dunce cap is placed on the heads of the wise men of modern economics, one had better look again at those switch points, We saw earlier that if $dr/dw = -n$, the wage would equal the marginal product of labor. A close look at equation (12) gives a clue: when $\alpha/\beta = a/b$, equation (12) will be a straight line:

$$w = \frac{1}{\beta} - \frac{ar}{\beta} \tag{17}$$

or rearranging:

$$\frac{-a}{\beta} = \frac{1/\beta - w}{r} \tag{18}$$

and

$$\frac{dw}{dr} = \frac{1}{n} = \frac{-a}{\beta} \tag{19}$$

The straight line case is a good candidate for the neoclassical conditions. Consider two such techniques which cross. As the wage falls, it becomes profitable to switch from technique *I* to *II* – that is, from a technique with less labor to capital to one with more plentiful labor in relation to capital. This confirms the neoclassical picture, although in but a very special case.

Suppose that technique *I* bends inwards and *II* outwards; for low levels of the wage, technique *I* will be most profitable. For middle-level wages, technique *II* will be best; finally, for high wages technique *I* will be best again (see Fig. 14.A5).

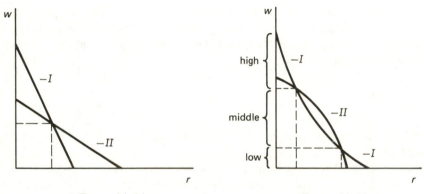

Figure 14.A4   Figure 14.A5

At the high-wage switching point, the system moves from a more labor-using technique to a less labor-using one as the wage rises. At the low-wage switching point, the movement is reversed. As the wage rises, the highest profit is obtained is more labor-intensive techniques are used. As the wage rises, it becomes profitable to adopt a method of production which uses more labor in relation to capital. This result simply cannot be reconciled with neoclassical doctrine, and there is no way to avoid a plentiful supply of such cases.

The Rate of Profit and the Marginal Product of Capital

It is easy to show that in *general* the rate of profit will not equal the marginal product of capital. Write the income distribution equation in *per capita* terms.

$$y = rk + w \qquad\qquad (13)$$

Then

$$dy = kdr + rdk + dw \tag{20}$$

and $dy/dk = r$ if and only if $dw/dr = -k = K^*/L$, i.e. $\tan \Omega = \tan \theta$ (Fig. 14.A6).

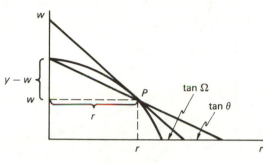

Figure 14.A6

There is no reason to suppose that this condition will normally, or indeed, ever, be met.

Consider a conventional returns-to-scale neoclassical production function, $Y = Y(K,L)$. This can be written $Y/L = Y(K/L,1)$ or $y = y(k)$. From Euler's theorem

$$w = \delta Y/\delta L = y(k) - ky^{\cdot}(k) \tag{21}$$

and

$$r = \delta Y/\delta K = y^{\cdot}(k), \; (y^{\cdot}(k) = dy/dk) \tag{22}$$

Then, $dw = y^{\cdot}dk - ky^{\cdot\cdot}dk - y^{\cdot}dk = -ky^{\cdot\cdot}dk; \; dr = y^{\cdot\cdot}dk$.
Hence,

$$\frac{dw}{dr} = \frac{-ky^{\cdot\cdot}dk}{y^{\cdot\cdot}dk} = -k = \frac{-K}{L} \tag{23}$$

This, we saw above, is the condition which must be met for the rate of profits to equal the marginal product of capital, and is met in the labor theory of value case. Hence, when the latter holds, the wage–profit trade-off frontier can be represented by a neoclassical production function.

However, in one special and implausible case, suppose all industries, whatever they produce, use capital goods and labor in the *same proportions*. Then when the wages rise and the rate of profit falls, no revaluation of capital goods will be necessary.

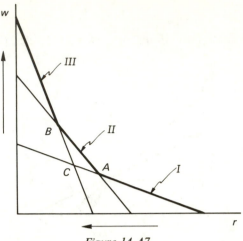

Figure 14.A7

Hence, $w/r = dw/dr = K/L$ (ignoring signs). In this special case, then, marginal productivity theory will hold. Such a wage–profit rate of trade-off can be drawn as a straight line, and three such lines will cross at switch points *A*, *B* and *C* (Fig. 14.A7). *C*, of course, will never appear, since the economy will move along the 'frontier' indicated by the heavy shading. Switch points *A* and *B* are 'neoclassical' – as *w* rises and *r* falls the system moves to more capital-intensive techniques. (Consider the switch from *I* to *II* at *A*: *II* has the higher output per man – maximum wage – so to have equal profit rates at *A*, *II* must have a higher value of capital per man.)

Capital Theory and the Golden Rule

Solving for *p* and *T*, as in Nell (1971):

$$p = \frac{b}{B + r(ab - aB)} \tag{24}$$

$$T = \frac{\alpha}{B + g(ab - aB)} \tag{25}$$

and then the value of capital per man will be:

$$pT = \frac{\alpha b}{[B + r(ab - aB)][B + g(ab - aB)]} \tag{26}$$

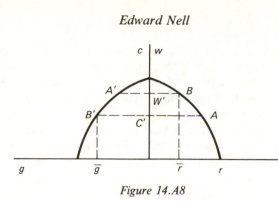

Figure 14.A8

The wage–profit trade-off can be written:

$$w = \frac{1 - ar}{B + r(ab - aB)} \tag{27}$$

so that

$$\frac{dw}{dr} = -\frac{ab}{[B + r(ab - aB)]^2} \tag{28}$$

Hence, when $r = g$, when the golden rule holds,

$$pT = \frac{-dw}{dr} \tag{29}$$

and

$$\frac{r}{w} pT = -\frac{r}{w} \frac{dw}{dr} = \frac{r}{w} k \tag{30}$$

When $r = g$, price and real Wicksell effects exactly offset one another. So even though the $w - r$ relationship is not a straight line, the value of capital per man is given by its slope, and its elasticity measures the distribution of income.

Neoclassical distribution theory will not find much comfort from this. Adopting a diagram and notation by Spaventa (4, 1970), we can first show the above case and then the more general one. Let $v = pT$, or the value of capital per man, $H = w + rv = c + gv$, or the value of net output per man. Then, from the ratio theorem, $v = c - w/r - g$ which can be seen in Figure 14.A8 as the slope either of the line AB or the line $A'B'$. Clearly as $r - g \rightarrow 0$ this line will tend to approach the tangent.

When $g=0$, on the other hand, the value of capital will equal Tan θ. Suppose, then, that $r=g$, so the tangent measures the value of capital per man, and the elasticity at a point relative shares. Then in Figure 14.A2 which illustrates the case in which the capital sector is the more capital intensive, as the rate of profit falls with a given technique the value of capital per man will also fall, just the reverse of the neoclassical postulate. Now consider a second technique which double-switches with the first. If $g=r$ then *both* switches will be forward, but the value of capital per man will still vary directly rather than inversely with the rate of profit on the section of the frontier between the two switches. For discrete techniques this can only be eliminated by postulating, implausibly enough, that the consumer goods sector is the more capital intensive of all techniques appearing on the frontier. *Two* special conditions must hold before the neoclassical relation between r and v can be justified.

As I just indicated, the second switch will not necessarily be backward, if the rate of growth is not zero. The general condition is easily seen from Figure 14.A9. If $g=g_{s1}$, then when $r=r_{s2}$ and the techniques switch, both techniques have the same value of capital per man. So, if $g>g_{s1}$, when $r=r_{s2}$, and the switch goes from II to I, the movement will be from a higher to a lower value of capital per man, a forward switch. Similarly, when $g<g_{s1}$ and $r=r_{s2}$ the switch will be backward, from a lower to a higher value of capital per man.

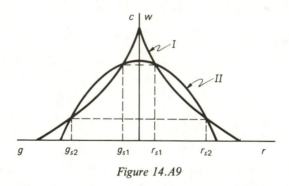

Figure 14.A9

Exactly parallel remarks hold for the first switch. If $g=g_{s2}$ and $r=r_{s1}$ then the value of capital per man in the two techniques will be the same. If $g<g_{s2}$ the switch will be forward, but if $g<g_{s2}$, then technique I will have the lower value of capital per man, so with a small rise in the rate of profit at r_{s1} the system will go from a less to a more capital-intensive technique.

Two Concepts of Price

Scarcity prices are flexible, rising in times of shortage and falling when supplies are plentiful. Scarcity prices are therefore indicators of the relative availability of goods. Production prices, by contrast, do not vary with shortages and surpluses, or with changes in output – special circumstances aside – because they are set to provide the profits needed to finance the capital required for production. Production prices are not wholly indepen-dent of demand, but what is considered in setting them is not the current market, but the possibilities of market growth.

Joan Robinson repeatedly contrasted these two, stressing that each was appropriate to certain economic conditions, and/or to certain aspects of economic problems.

The significance of the capital theory controversy in this regard is that it has shown that production prices cannot be treated as a special kind of scarcity price, with capital as the scare factor, whose marginal productivity is reflected in the rate of profit. The two conceptions of price are totally distinct: scarcity prices make sense in certain kinds of planning, and in non-industrial, pre-capitalist markets, whereas production prices are those which rule under industrial capitalism.

Since production prices do not vary with changes in output, they provide, as Hicks (1965) noted, an appropriate setting for the Keynesian theory of effective demand. So, contrary to much modern literature, it is not necessary to assume 'sticky' money-wages or prices to establish the Keynesian picture.

The Falling Rate of Profit and the Choice of Technique

Some Marxists have argued that if we discard the neoclassical conception of competition, we can see pressures at work which will explain the tendency of the rate of profit to fall as the outcome of competitive choices of methods of production. Firms will seek to increase their profit margins by reducing their variable costs through an expansion of their fixed plant and equipment. They will, in short, substitute equipment for workers. With higher margins, they can afford to cut price and intensify the competitive struggle for markets. Since anyone can gain by doing this – attracting customers from the rest – all will adopt this course, and the prevailing method of production will more or less rapidly change to one with a higher margin but lower profit rate.

Formally, this argument is the same as that advanced by Gallaway and Shukla in the capital theory controversy – that firms will maximize profits rather than the rate of profits, so from any set of possible techniques, they will always choose the method of production with the highest profits per head (Gallaway and Shukla, 1974; Laibman and Nell, 1977). This is an argument about which method of production will be chosen under the influence of competitive pressures, not about the path of movement of the economy over time. To convert this point into a story of movement, Marxists must explain why firms find themselves, in the first place, operating tech-niques with lower profits per head but higher rates of profit than the one entailed by the profit margin maximization criterion. Presumably, the more capital-intensive, lower profit rate techniques are invented later, under the pressure of competition. But this is an *ad hoc* explanation, not a theory.

A further problem arises in trying to use this choice of technique argument to explain the tendency of the *rate* of profit to fall. But the *rate of* profit in general – uniform across all industries – only exists because of the pressures of competition: according both to Marx and the classical tradition, capital flows from low *rate* of profit areas to high profit rate areas, leading to rising prices in the former and falling ones in the latter, until actual prices have come to approximate prices of production, and the rate of profit has reached an appropriate degree of uniformity. Marx was explicit: 'capital withdraws from a sphere with *a low rate* of profit and invades others, which yield a higher' (italics mine) (Marx, vol. III, ch.10).

But this means that capitalists are motivated to disinvest in one sphere of industry and invest in another by consideration of the rate of profit. Marx describes this as a process of competition between capitals. Why, then, would capitalists come, at another point, to *ignore* the rate of profit and invest on the basis of profit margins, rather than profit rates? Moreover, by so shifting capital, they would (as we have shown) create a 'disproportionality crisis', bringing about a collapse in growth. (This point is independent of objections to the 'implicit theory' of the movement of capital, for such objections argue for an even more fully specified theory of investment, which would rule out simple profit maximization.)

But the most serious problem with this argument is that it misconceives the theoretical position of the capitalist firm in two important respects. It fails to understand or analyze the firm as a unit of capital, and therefore as *constantly expanding, i.e. accumulating.* And it fails to appreciate the fact that firms undertaking large investments in fixed capital must normally raise funds to do so. Competition faces two ways – towards the market for products, but also towards the markets for labor and finance capital. Neglect of accumulation, on the one hand, and of competition in the market for funds, on the other, have allowed the story to seem plausible. Once these are properly fitted into the picture it will be clear that competitive firms must consider their profit rates, and cannot ever choose techniques on the basis of profit margins.

What follows is a study of the *logic* of choosing methods of production under capitalist institutions, on the assumption that a uniform rate of profit exists, and outputs are priced accordingly.

As a preliminary, it is useful to see that once accumulation is taken into account, the argument can run into trouble even on its own grounds. For simplicity and to avoid a long discussion over depreciation, assume a circulating capital model, with profit calculated on advanced wages (variable capital). Then in an obvious notation, in per capital terms:

$$w(1+r)+rk = c+g(w+k) \tag{31}$$

On the left we have net national income as wages plus profits, on the right, net national product as consumption plus investment. Manipulating, we find

$$w + k = \frac{c - w}{r - g};$$ (32)

that is, the value of capital per worker is given by the slope of a chord connecting the wage–profit rate point and the consumption growth rate point on the contours representing the respective trade-offs. As is well known, these contours will normally be duals and will be identical in shape (Nell, 1970; Spaventa, 1970; Laibman and Nell, 1977). They can both therefore be represented by a single curve. Let the vertical axis measure c and w, the horizontal, r and g. When $g = 0$, then c equals the maximum level of w, and the intercept of the curve measures the value of net output *per capita*. But when $g > 0$, and $g = r$ the vertical intercept of the chord measures net output *per capita* (point H). So the profit margin will be $H - w$, so the mark-up will be $(H - w)/w$, and clearly the size of this margin depends not only on w, but also on g.

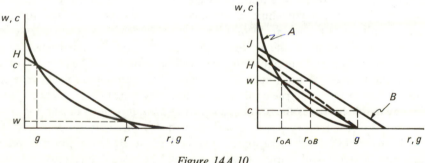

Figure 14A.10

Now consider two of these curves, A and B, which cross at one switch point. Initially the economy uses method A. Let us take the wage rate as given, at w. Assume little or no capitalist consumption and substantial savings out of wages. The growth rate will then be g, the maximum attainable with method A, and the rate of profit will be r_{oA}. Method B then becomes known and available. For simplicity, assume it is a straight line. The profit maximization criterion indicates a shift to method B, since $J - W_o > H - W_o$. However, as is evident from the diagram (Fig. A10), this shift also results in a *higher* rate of profit! Far from an explanation of the tendency of the rate of profit to fall, we now have a tendency of the rate of profit to rise. Moreover, if we have chosen W_o appropriately, the chord giving the value of capital per head in method A will be parallel to the straight line representing method B; i.e. the organic (value) composition of capital will be the same in both techniques! By choosing W_o a little higher, then, we could arrange it so that the value composition of capital was *higher* in method A. In that event, going from method A to method B would mean a falling organic composition and a rising rate of profit. Many other combinations can be worked out, as a little experimentation will show. There can be no *general* presumption here any more than in neoclassical theory, that the 'profit maximizing' criterion will uniformly lead to a succession of techniques in which the organic (value) composition of capital is higher and the rate of profit lower. (For an example of 'reswitching' according to this criterion, see Laibman and Nell, 1977.) On the contrary, it could lead to a succession of techniques with progressively lower organic compositions and higher rates of profit, or for that matter, to almost any other combination of changes. No definite rules can be laid down. (Note that this has nothing to do with the question of mechanization. There are many reasons for believing that technical progress in capitalism will take the form of displacing labor by machinery, but this is no guarantee that *value* of capital per man will rise in any regular way.)

Now let us return to the analysis of the actual process by which competitors move from the use of one method of production to another. This is supposedly the result of competitive pressure. Let us assume that the techniques, the growth rate and the wage rate are such that the preceding story will hold: the new technique will have a higher organic composition, a lower profit but a higher profit margin.

At the conclusion of the write-off period, or upon the emergence of a purchaser for the existing plant, the firm will have on hand the money value of its 'method A' plant. This will consist of its equity plus its borrowed capital. The latter it will presumably have to repay or roll-over. Hence it will have available for investment only *its equity in the initial plant* (assuming that it received a satisfactory purchase price or that it successfully recovered its initial investment before scrapping). The new plant, by assumption to have the same capacity, will employ fewer workers, but more fixed capital. Hence long-term borrowing requirements will rise, though short-term working capital needs will be less. Thus the firm contemplating a switch to 'method B' will have to increase its long-term debt–equity ratios. However, at the same time it faces a serious difficulty: method B generates a lower *rate* of profit. Hence, while it has a larger long-term debt it also has a reduced ability to pay. The competitive market interest rate will either equal the rate of profit or differ from it by a fixed margin, representing the premium for risk, etc. In any case, its movements will be governed by the rate of profit (or the rate of growth). Let us assume that the rate of interest equals the initial rate of profit. To pay the interest on the debt required to finance the method B plant, the firm will either have to *reduce its retained earnings* or *cut its dividend payments*. Either way it reduces the value of its equity. If it cuts dividends, its shares will no longer be so welcome in portfolios; if it reduces its retention ratio, s_c, it will not be able to expand as fast as its competitors, for *two* reasons: a lower rate of profit and a lower retention ratio. Thus the original growth rate of the firm was $g_o = s_{co} r_A$, whereas the later one will be $g_1 = s_{c1} r_B$, where $s_{co} > s_{c1}$ and $r_A > r_B$. Other firms which do not make the shift to method *B* will be able to maintain their retention ratios intact, so they will continue to grow at the rate g_o; hence the firm or firms that switch to method *B* will grow more slowly and their market shares will fall.

Of course, it is more likely that, foreseeing competitive disaster, banks would refuse to finance a plant constructed to operate method *B*. The argument was that firms would be *forced* to adopt method *B*, because anyone who does can cut price, having a larger margin. But the margin over variable costs has to cover fixed costs and investments, and before a firm can shift into method *B*, it must enter into fixed-cost contracts for the financing of its new plant. Even if a firm did use its higher margin to cut price temporarily (postponing its debt servicing?; postponing further investment?) it could not *supply* the new business it attracted, without expanding still further, which its reduced profit rate makes it impossible to do so.

References

Arrow, K. J. (1962) 'The Economic Implications of Learning by Doing', *Review of Economic Studies*, 29: 155–73.

Cassel, G. (1932) *The Theory of Social Economy* (London: E. Benn).

Clark, J. B. (1956) *The Distribution of Wealth* (New York: Kelley).

Domar, E. (1957) *Essays in the Theory of Economic Growth* (New York: Oxford University Press).

Drandakis, E. (1963) 'Factor Substitution in the Two Sector Growth Model', *Review of Economic Studies*, 84: 217–28.

Gallaway, L. and V. Shukla (1974) 'The Neo-Classical Production Function', *American Economic Review*, 64: 348–58.

Garegnani, P. (1970) 'Heterogeneous Capital, the Production Function and the Theory of Distribution', *Review of Economic Studies*, 37: 407–36.

Goodwin, R. (1970) *Elementary Economics from the Higher Standpoint*, (Cambridge: Cambridge University Press).

Harrod, R. (1939) 'An Essay in Dynamic Theory', *Economic Journal*, 49: 14–33.

Hahn, F. (1966) 'Equilibrium Dynamics with Heterogeneous Capital Goods', *Quarterly Journal of Economics*, 80: 633–46.

Hayek, F. (1941) *The Pure Theory of Capital* (London: Routledge).

Hicks, J. R. (1965) *Capital and Growth* (Oxford: Clarendon Press).

Kaldor, N. (1955) 'Alternative Theories of Distribution', *Review of Economic Studies*, 23: 83–100.

Laibman, D. and E. J. Nell (1977) 'Reswitching, Wicksell Effects, and the Neo-Classical Production Function', *American Economic Review*, 67: 878–88.

Lowe, A. (1976) *The Path of Economic Growth*, (Cambridge: Cambridge University Press).

Marx, K. (no date) *Capital*, Vols. I, II, III (New York: International Publishers).

Nell, E. J. (1967) 'Theories of Growth and Theories of Value', *Economic Development and Cultural Change*, 16: 15–26.

Nell, E. J. (1970) 'A Note on Cambridge Controversies in Capital Theory', *Journal of Economic Literature*, 8: 41–44.

Nell, E. J. (1982) 'Growth Distribution and Inflation', *Journal of Post-Keynesian Economics*, 5: 104–13.

Nell, E. J. (1988a) *Prosperity and Public Spending* (Boston and London: Allen & Unwin).

Nell, E. J. (1988b) 'Transformational Growth and Stagnation', in Kurdas *et al, The Imperilled Economy* (New York: Monthly Review Press).

Okishio, N. (1961) 'Technical Change and the Rate of Profit', *Kobe University Economic Review*, 7: 85–90.

Pasinetti, L. (1977) *Lectures on the Theory of Production* (New York: Columbia University Press).

Robertson, D. (1951) 'Wage Grumbles', *Readings in the Theory of Income Distribution* (eds) W. Fellner and B. Haley (Chicago: Richard Irwin) pp. 221–36.

Robinson, J. (1953) 'The Production Function and the Theory of Capital', *Review of Economic Studies*, 21: 81–106.

Robinson, J. (1956) *The Accumulation of Capital* (London: Macmillan).

Robinson, J. (1962) *Essays in the Theory of Economic Growth* (London: Macmillan).

Robinson, J. (1963) *Exercises in Economic Analysis* (London: Macmillan).

Russell, B. (1919) *Introduction to Mathematical Philosophy* (London: Allen & Unwin).

Solow, R. (1956) 'A Contribution to the Theory of Economic Growth', *Quarterly Journal of Economics*, 70: 65–94.

Solow, R. (1962) 'Substitution and Fixed Proportions in the Theory of Capital', *Review of Economic Studies*, 29: 207–18.

Spaventa, L. (1970) 'Rate of Profit, Rate of Growth and Capital Intensity in a Simple Production Model', *Oxford Economic Papers*, 22: 129–47.

Sraffa, P. (1960) *Production of Commodities by Means of Commodities*, (Cambridge: Cambridge University Press).

Uzawa, H. (1961) 'On a Two Sector Model of Economic Growth', *Review of Economic Studies*, 29: 40–8.

Vianello, F. (1985) 'The Pace of Accumulation', *Political Economy: Studies in the Surplus Approach*, 1: 33–51.

15 Trotting Platinum Ages

Gautam Mathur*

1 ROBINSONIAN GOLDEN AGE

This presentation is a token of homage to Joan Robinson, from whom I learnt the method of analysis which goes with her name. Her life was a constant effort to rationalize the manner of thinking in economics and she insisted on rigor in the formulation of ideas.

In capital theory, instead of starting with *n* goods and *m* processes, she contented herself by building simple models which contained essential elements representing notional features of reality. The golden age model can be seen to be essentially a two-commodity model intended to represent a vastly more complex reality – just as the Keynesian one was a one-commodity formulation designed for the same purpose. The models were capable of drawing the analysis nearer to reality by a series of acts of successively dropping off the simplifying assumptions. But no simplifying assumptions were encouraged to be made of a type whereby, were those particular simplifications removed, the whole edifice would crumble.

For example, we can take the assumption of capital being malleable. The heterogeneous capital school, as evidenced in the works of Piero Sraffa, Joan Robinson and Professor Lord Kahn, on this side of the Atlantic, and of John von Neumann, on the other side, looks upon capital as embodied pieces of equipment and physical stocks of work in progress and of consumption goods. No assumption of malleability of capital is necessary to be made in the model of golden age at zero rate of technical progress – even if the number of goods is expanded in the model from two to any higher finite number. However, for change in capital intensity and productivity (as a result of technical advance rather than managerial reorganization with the same equipment), the assumption of heterogeneity of capital definitely entails a change in technique and requires, therefore, no simpler methodology than a proper study of the traverse from one technique to another.

* Revised version of paper read at a seminar in May 1985 under the chairmanship of Professor Geoffrey Harcourt to the members and scholars of Cambridge University, Faculty of Economics and Politics. The author is grateful to Professor Frank Hahn and Dr John Eatwell for sponsoring this seminar, as a tribute to the late Joan Robinson. He is also grateful to Professor Nehru, Professor Sukhamoy Chakravarty, Professor Mohd Dore and Dr Jayanti Ghosh for their valuable comments.

The author acknowledges the help of I. C. Awasthi in the preparation of the script and research assistance connected therewith. He is also indebted to G. Sreedhar Reddy and G. Ramalingam for helpful comments.

For positive rates of technical progress, the assumption of malleable capital would be very helpful, and the golden age system with positive rate of technical progress also leans on some form of it (Mathur, 1962, pp.118–87). But, unfortunately, it keeps alive an illusion by which, if the malleability assumption were removed (to bring the model nearer to reality), the system and its fundamental equations would disappear. The same vanishing magic would affect a Cobb–Douglas function as much as a constant elasticity function (based on the meaningless symbol K). Heterogeneous capital goods make it necessary to break up the economy into a number of sub-economies, each with equipment of a different vintage. All that one can do in the case of technical progress is to consider different technologies, and to compare sub-economies – each adjusted to its production conditions and manpower distribution.

In those sub-economies, if the wage rate is taken to be uniform throughout the sub-economy (as in the Robinsonian model), each would then have a different rate of growth and a corresponding rate of profit. In full employment, workers of the sub-economy with near-zero profit would leapfrog to work upon equipment fabricated during operations of current investment, in the most productive sub-economy. If, instead of the uniformity of wage and a declining series of profit rates as in the Robinsonian version, different wage rates are assumed (as an alternative version taken in Mathur, 1965), a galaxy of golden ages existing simultaneously would appear (ranked according to different wage rates, but each having the same rate of profit). In the absence of any deviation from a uniform propensity of entrepreneurs to consume, the rate of growth would also be the same for each sub-economy.

The Accumulation of Capital (Robinson, 1956) spells out the main economic determinants, but gives no methodology by which the valuation of heterogeneous capital may be done in an actual or even a hypothetical economy. This was rectified by providing a von Neumann input–output base to Robinsonian measurement of capital in labor time (Mathur, 1986). Many of the restrictive assumptions of the Joan Robinson formulation of the golden age system have been dropped (as required by conditions of reality), and the model extended at various times towards greater approximation to actuality. The basic structure has survived (which has been the test of the Robinsonian model) to explain reality and to suggest actions to remove inequities and disequilibria. It is some of these attempts on which we shall focus our attention in the rest of the presentation.

2　THE SRAFFA AND THE von NEUMANN MODELS

All the time while *The Accumulation of Capital* was being written by his colleague, the late Professor Lord Kaldor had been talking of the necessity of looking more closely into the von Neumann model. Two years after the publication of *The Accumulation of Capital*, as part of his group of research students receiving preparatory grounding in advanced economic theory, this duty was allocated to me by him at the suggestion of Lal Jaywardene. It made it obligatory for me to study the basic aspects of the original von Neumann model (1945–6), and also gave me an opportunity to look at its generalizations by Kemeny, Morgenstern and Thompson (1956) and Gale (1956).

The next exercise was an act of stripping the models of mathematical embellishments. Following the hints contained in the paper of Professor Champernowne (1945), one was led in 1958 to the reinterpretation of the von Neumann model deriving all its propositions without use of even simple mathematics, not to talk of topology. The substitution of numerical economic examples for mathematical symbols made it possible to give the systems (of equations and inequalities) economic content in the light of its interpretation as a bastard golden age growth state – steady in character, but with non-employment around. This is the version contained in the Stevenson Prize Paper of 1959 (see Mathur, 1962).

The von Neumann model provides a methodology for determining the level of the constant rate of growth, of distribution of labor and of pricing (without technical progress or change of wage rate).

In 1960, the book by Piero Sraffa came out. It sent a ripple of excitement around Cambridge University circles. Here was the long-awaited product of forty years of hard labor condensed into an average of two (meticulously conceived) pages per year; though the basic propositions had been, presumably, completed before the advent of the 1930s (for they had been discussed with the young scholar Frank Ramsey before his untimely death). Not only were the economists wonderstruck by its style, but scholars of other subjects were also fascinated. Dr Luigi Spaventa of Trinity College even reported that in one of the colleges a young physics don, researching into trajectories of propulsive materials, had been inspired to prepare a manuscript entitled 'The Destruction of Commodities by Means of Commodities, being a Prelude to a Critique of the Theory of Ballistic Missiles'!

To those familiar with the von Neumann model, there were apparent similarities in the structure of the Sraffa model and that of von Neumann. One had, firstly, to rewrite the Sraffa model by sticking to his suggestion in article 9 of his book and taking wage as being paid in advance of production. One had, secondly, to substitute 'investment' for 'consumption of the entire share of entrepreneurs in the surplus' and, thirdly, to introduce constant returns to scale (avoided by Sraffa through guiding the thrust of his research into a stationary state model without investment). Fourthly, one had either to introduce inequalities instead of equations in the Sraffa model or deal with only a core sub-economy consisting merely of goods (and not things (Mathur, 1965, p.331) – with necessarily zero price) and then counting equations (Schefold, 1978) would be a meaningful procedure.

All these transformation devices would ultimately demonstrate that the two models could be shown, under certain conditions, to almost coincide in material format, though not in the objectives. The simplest meaningful form of this model can be depicted with only two types of equipment, one of lower order and the other of higher order. Both types of equipment may be displayed in a matrix with a set of figures of unity displayed in the diagonal. Only then can the Robinsonian assumption of heterogeneous capital be translated into matrix depiction, for a non-malleable machine. For instance, one cannot have in one process one-tenth part of a particular equipment tended by one man and one-ninth in another process at full capacity with same type of labor, without changing the shape of the equipment.[1] In the special system of heterogeneous capital one uses the principle of one bus–one driver per shift, whether the bus is used for carrying workmen in a biscuit factory or in a switchgear unit. The principle gives a specific form of matrix to analyze the system for a growing economy.

3   THE SRAFFA–von NEUMANN MODEL

In the simplest format of the Sraffa–von Neumann model pertaining to a first-order equipment case, we have two processes – one in the consumption sector and the other in the equipment-production sector. The system has two goods – one a consumption good C, and the other an equipment E. The equipment E (being of first order) produces C, but is capable of reproducing itself. The model was first used for analysis of technique progress prior to the publication of (or any knowledge about the contents of) Sraffa's *Production of Commodities by Means of Commodities*, but christened after the said publication. The special basic format of the model used has since September 1960 (see Rostow, 1963) been referred to as the Sraffa–von Neumann one-capital good model. In its simplest form it may be depicted as shown in Table 15.1, where the wage equal to subsistence is taken to be a unit basket of goods. Now if output in the consumption sector, z, is four baskets of corn

Table 15.1

Man	,	C	E		C	E
1	,	1	1	→	z	1
1	,	1	1	→	0	$m+1$

and in self-reproducing equipment sector, m, it is one piece of self-producing equipment, like a stone axe, the system can be seen to be in a form of golden age growth, steadily maintainable by allocating manpower in the ratio $2:3$, at the constant rate of growth, 60 per cent (Table 15.2).

Table 15.2

Man	,	Basket	Equipment		Basket	Equipment
2	,	2	2	→	8	2
3	,	3	3	→	0	6
5	,	5	5		8	8

It can be verified that the relative price vector (1 4) satisfies all the criteria of golden age measurement of capital, giving a uniform rate of profit of 60 per cent. The rate of profit equals the rate of growth; not by any mathematical property of minmax saddle point – as claimed by von Neumann – but by virtue of his original assumption that wage earners do not save and entrepreneurs do not consume whereby profits and investment are equalized and in economic terms – though not in topology – the rate of growth formulation interacts with its dual (of the rate of profit) from the very beginning.

3.1   Two Capital Goods

The model with two capital good processes (of different order) has, in addition to the consumption good process, a higher order capital good, H, as self-reproducing equipment, and lower order capital good, M, as machine for producing the consumption good, C. This can be shown as in Table 15.3.

Table 15.4 results from giving values to w, q, x and y, where $q = 51$ bags, $x = 5$, $y = 2$, the wage rate, w, is equal to 30 bags. The entrepreneurs do not consume. We have the following equilibrium solution showing balanced rate

Table 15.3

Man	,	C	M	H		C	M	H
1	,	w	1	0	→	q	1	0
1	,	w	0	1	→	0	x	1
1	,	w	0	1	→	0	0	$y+1$

Table 15.4

Man	,	w	,	C	M	H		C	M	H
1	,	30	,	30	1	0	→	51	1	0
1	,	30	,	30	0	1	→	0	5	1
1	,	30	,	30	0	1	→	0	0	$2+1$

Table 15.5

Man	w	C	M	H		C	M	H
30	30	900	30	0	→	1530	30	0
3	30	90	0	3	→	0	15	3
1	30	30	0	1	→	0	0	3
		1020	30	4		1530	45	6

of growth of 50 per cent, with process intensity, or distribution of manpower in the various sectors as (30 3 1) (Table 15.5).

The relative prices as (1:12:30) can be seen to give a uniform rate of profit equal to the rate of growth (because there is no propensity to consume of entrepreneurs):

$$30 + 12 \rightarrow 51 + 12 \qquad \text{or} \quad 42 \rightarrow 63, \; r = 50\%$$
$$30 + 30 \rightarrow 5 \times 12 + 30 \qquad \text{or} \quad 60 \rightarrow 90, \; r = 50\%$$
$$30 + 30 \rightarrow 3 \times 30 \qquad \text{or} \quad 60 \rightarrow 90, \; r = 50\%$$

The logic of the Sraffa–von Neumann format as regards the input side and the diagonal matrix (output side) has been adopted by Professor Ian Steedman (1979) also, who has used it for international trade analysis. It is possible that, in time, this format would lend itself to analysis in other branches of capital theory as a basic aid to Robinsonian golden age analysis as well as for exploring the properties of the von Neumann model and the Sraffa system.

4   THE PLATINUM AGE

In the Kemeny–Thompson generalization of the von Neumann model a number of von Neumann sub-economies can exist if they do not have trade between them. If they have trade, then with mobility of labor, we are in the fold of the original von Neumann model and there would be only one sub-economy with a uniform rate of profit. We have already considered its working as a golden age system.

In the absence of trade or absence of labor mobility (due to sociological causes or owing to lack of a frictionless economic world) there appears the possibility of a steady-growth sub-economy growing at the highest rate, and of other sub-economies outside it. With perfect mobility of factors, two different profit rates cannot exist, but as the assumption of perfect mobility of factors from one sub-economy to another has been dropped already, two or more different rates of profit may simultaneously exist. The galaxy of golden ages (referred to earlier) (Mathur, 1965, ch.15) is a manifestation of this phenomenon. The aggregate of these sub-economies would display a non-uniform rate of growth of different goods – and, hence a non-steady growth situation.

Where the technology which would have generated the fastest growing sub-economy had the wage been at golden age level is such that it can also offer a higher wage than other sub-economies, we have a special case of an advanced economy. This could, however, be analyzed to be a state of traverse (see Harcourt, 1979) in which labor is in the process of being shifted to the highest profit sub-economy in the galaxy. This is depicted in a setting of employment of a few workers in a steady-growth island with higher profit, and surrounding it a sea of poverty of the non-employed population. One is then led to identifying it, no doubt, as a model of steady growth, but in a continuing environment of misery. It is, therefore, an unapproved form of the golden age carrying, in heraldic nomenclature, a bar sinister across its coat of arms. On this account, following the nomenclature suggested by Professor Lord Kahn (1959), one may find it appropriate to categorize it as a form of bastard golden age.

The possibility of existence of a sub-economy with lower wage than is the Robinsonian golden age, but with higher rate of growth, led Professor Ian Little (1957) at Oxford to look for a growth state called the platinum age. Joan Robinson had two sub-classifications of it, with growth rates decelerating and accelerating, respectively – called creeping and galloping platinum ages.

5 GALLOPING AND CREEPING PLATINUM AGES

When we made the assumption of a transient disequilibrium compatible with steady states, then one of the following devices (based upon the extension of the concept of sub-economies) is required to be used. In the total economy referred to as the galaxy there are no longer only other sub-economies growing at a slow rate which will, in time, lose their manpower. The unsteady-state portion (comprising different bunches of goods, each bunch growing at its own rate) is composed of different islands of growth. We can now visualize at least one steady-growth sub-economy growing at a particular rate as the parent or the core, and a periphery consisting of:

(a) one or more sub-economies growing at a lower rate (this is the Kemeny–Thompson case, or a galaxy of golden ages);
(b) a dependent process (Mathur, 1966) growing at a lower pace; or
(c) unused stocks of non-bottleneck goods existing.

In each of these cases and in general as a group, there is a core which is a von Neumann sub-economy, and a periphery. The latter may consist either of another slower growing (Kemeny–Thompson) sub-economy, or, secondly, as per the present assumption, of a dependent process which could not have existed without the parent sub-economy (or grown at its existing pace, without subsidy from the fastest growing sub-economy), or, thirdly, the periphery may consist of a stock of redundant goods.

The galloping platinum age is a manifestation of two sub-economies growing at different rates (at an average not less than that pertaining to golden age growth). The sub-economy with the higher growth rate attains dominance in time, while the average growth rate shows acceleration – as the system approximates, asymptotically, to the higher growth rate. The galloping platinum age exhibits what happens to the von Neumann model when technical interlinking assumption, and assumption of adjustment before start of analysis, are both removed. Instead of the slowest growing good determining the growth rate of the economy, it is the most dynamic and fastest growing set of goods which attains dominance, and it replaces the rest in importance – and, consequently, in full employment it results in exterminating the slower growing set of sub-economies altogether.

In the creeping platinum age, the obverse of this device does not work, because if the sub-economies are both having negative rates of growth (say, on account of a declining population), the one with the lesser decline of output will gain dominance and the average rate of growth will still be rising from a bigger negative to a smaller negative value; for instance, an economy with minus 3 per cent growth rate settling down to an asymptotic value of minus 1 per cent is not a creeping, but a galloping platinum age!

If the assumption of technical interdependence of all processes (which had been removed at the beginning of and for the purposes of this section) were restored, the system will shift from the dominance of the fastest growing sub-economy to the shackles of the slowest growing set of goods – which is one of the prime propositions of the von Neumann model. This would be so, because each Kemeny–Thompson sub-economy would then be dependent on some other for at least one commodity, and that commodity would offer a bottleneck to faster growth. The sub-economy with the lowest rate of growth would then be (as in the original von Neumann model) the bottleneck sub-economy and all others would adjust to it. The faster growing sub-economies would then lose some output every year because of lack of goods of bottleneck character. Where the slowest growing economy has a growth rate above the golden age (on account of a wage rate below golden age level), the process of change and adjustment in this context would exhibit the characteristics of a creeping platinum age.

Hence, in all the cases of non-steady growth, an element of steady state is present as a core. The physical or a biological system is composed of rigidly fixed functional requirements and unused stocks – like deposits of fat, or excess of vitamins and otherwise beneficial (but redundant) salts expelled from the organic system (but existing outside the system). It may be noted that if the goods were not beneficial, we would call them 'things' (like waters of the sewers from which manuring substances and metal recycling have been extracted). They would not be counted as commodities.

6 TROTTING PLATINUM AGE

Where the growth rate is neither accelerating nor decelerating, the platinum age also is neither galloping nor creeping, but has a steady pace. This type of growth is termed the trotting platinum age (Mathur 1967, 1986). The demesne of this type of growth is not confined to absence of galloping or creeping patterns of growth. The compulsion of the non-malleable capital approach indicates that the trotting pattern of growth is an essential component of even the galloping as well as creeping ages. In a galloping age the fastest growing sub-economy forms the core part; while in a creeping age it is the slowest growing sub-economy which becomes the core. But the core is always composed of a trotting age. The periphery, also, may contain sub-economies and, hence, trotting portions. The term trotting platinum age is confined to the trotting portions where the rate of growth is higher than golden age as a result of restraint upon the current consumption level. It, therefore, forms the basis for nearly overtaking the golden age system and is, hence, at the base of attempts at progressive relative development.

In a world looking like a jumble of goods, the core is always an orderly set of processes forming a sub-economy and growing in a steady manner. What is unsteady growth to the unaided eye, may be a pattern of steady-growth islands (Mathur, 1986) – one or more trotting age sub-economies along with one or more dependent processes, as also stocks of non-bottleneck goods produced in the past (and unutilized in the current period – being redundant in each of the used processes). If the goods were bottleneck goods they, along with others lying unused as stocks, would be included in the core sub-economy, and would not be unused outside it.

The depiction of goods includes educated operatives as units of human capital fabricated by the educational manufactures, called colleges (incidentally, also very aptly called Halls which noble term was also used to be applied to work-sheds).

The realization that the trotting platinum age surrounds us universally and ubiquitously (because we are parts of a growing economy) has another significance. Trotting platinum age is not merely a form of steady-growth state. It is a vehicle of converting an underdeveloped country into an advanced country through using certain strategies. It is the instrument of effecting a traverse from a lower state of the technical arts to a higher state. It represents what in post-von Neumann literature is termed as a turnpike. The multitude of techniques generate separate sub-economies – some meaningful, some not. The development process is composed of a multiplicity of turnpikes. The choice out of these is the essence of the problem rather than an incidental aspect. The prime problem is not where to get into each turnpike, and where to drop off.[2] The trotting platinum ages represent a multiplicity of turnpikes. The selection of the optimum long-run strategy of development is the analysis of this choice but is, in a sense, the essence of the path. It is this aspect which has since 1961 been the distinguishing feature of the Sraffa–von Neumann approach to development as distinct from the post-von Neumann models (like DOSSO[3] and its extensions). The choice of techniques (depicted in sub-economies) depends upon the strategy rather than upon the relative benefit–cost ratios (as in the traditional literature).

The strategies use sub-economies in which certain socially desirable goods grow and the undesirable ones are sought to be excluded from a place in the growth process. It is possible to make a normative judgment about the criteria for considering certain goods as desirable, or for adopting certain techniques of production, but they can also follow from an exercise simulating the path which would be optimal under perfectly competitive conditions. The capitalist competitive model and the planned economy system would coincide on the depiction of an efficient program of long-term capital accumulation.

7 DEVELOPMENT DIFFERENTIATED FROM GROWTH

The proper functioning of a trotting platinum age requires the realization that the implications of the traverse are not confined to the less-developed underdeveloped countries. According to one definition (given by Professor Simon Kuznets many years ago) highly industrialized countries also would be, with respect to scientific advances and technical potentialities, considered to be underdeveloped countries. In relation to the vast reservoir of unutilized technical knowledge which applied scientific advance has created and which the explosion of fundamental research augments, for the economist dealing with long-term development, there is only a matter of degree between economically more-underdeveloped countries, and the less-underdeveloped ones. All countries are then underdeveloped – some less and some more so, howsoever economically advanced the former may appear to be in comparison with the more-underdeveloped countries.

Having noted the point that, with respect to technical level (dependent upon implementation of scientific advance already accomplished), every country is as yet underdeveloped, the more-underdeveloped type of country should be ready to imbibe in relevant spheres the benefits which technical advance (following from scientific research) gives, or can potentially give, in any less-underdeveloped country and which can be extended to more-underdeveloped countries without deflecting from the path of equity. To achieve full development, a renewal of the capital stock is periodically necessary at full employment, even in less-underdeveloped countries. When it is not merely a question of changing the type of mirrors in a car, but it is a question of whether the vehicle will run on the ground or hover in the air a few inches above the ground, the total technical base may have to be renewed. Such a change becomes due when the highest order pieces of equipment (the self-reproducing parent machines themselves) have to change their form – both as regards the source of energy and the main material of fabrication.

For instance, in the primitive economy, the type of machine tools, basic materials and the source of power were quite different from the one in the modern mechanized technology in use at present. The infrastructure which produced the giant waterwheels of Samarkand or the dams of the Singhala people were quite different from the power and fuel complex of the set of second-order capital goods of modern times.

The acts of using and expanding the existing type of highest order industry (H), and improving its productivity along with that of the lower order machinery (N) which it manufactures, ought not merely to be taken as being parts of the theory of development, but also of the theory of growth with normal technical progress. Or rather, the students of less-underdeveloped countries should be made to realize that their problems cannot be adequately solved by a study of growth economics alone, but major procedures of development economics need to be absorbed by them in their minds. The economist specializing in growth of industrialized countries usually commits an error – both of diagnosis and of remedy – by considering that their problem is one of a growing economy, whereas what this presentation purports to show is that the problems could be much better treated if they are perceived to be problems similar to those in a developing economy.

Growth economists purport to deal with a hypothetical concept called golden age (with positive rate of technical progress) after assumed adjustments of the basic machinery to current level of technical knowledge has taken place.[4] This is similar to the cavalier assumption made by Professor Pigou in *Economics of Welfare* that for measuring marginal product of labor, the amount of capital is kept constant but its shape and the organization is adjusted to requirements. The crux of the problem lies in making this adjustment and the whole of development theory (as distinct from growth theory) addresses itself to the process when it entails basic machinery changes and organizational cultures being recast.

Development economics deal with the process of adjusting the type of capital stock in the basic machinery sector to technical change in any country – more underdeveloped or less so. The former type of a country's development problem can be dealt exclusively with the help of development economics. The last phase of a development strategy (in which the basic machinery H being sufficient and of the latest type and only M is to be adjusted) could possibly also be dealt with under growth theory – though not exclusively by the latter.

When the target proportions of basic machines and of mechanized machinery (being golden age rates) have been reached, and do not further change, growth will be taking place unambiguously. It can be seen that the sway of growth theory in a real situation is very limited, and the domain of development theory much larger, since most more-developed countries have very much the problem of adjustment of the ratios of their highest order machinery to lower order machines or the reverse. In all cases where

H is adequate and M is to be adjusted,
or M is adequate and H is to be adjusted,
or alternatively H and M are both inadequate but H/M is to be adjusted as also quantum of H and of M are to be brought to equilibrium proportions with manpower at full employment,

development theory is the proper instrument of change – for a strategy of development is required for the process.

When the H/M ratio is correct for golden age requirement and both are adequate for full employment and full development, and the provision of expansion of both is only for the current assertions of manpower with no backlog of unemployment to be cleared, it is the jurisdiction of growth theory. This gives a criterion for demarcating the exclusive jurisdictions of the theory of development and theory of growth. In case of a conflict of jurisdictions, the solutions pertaining to development theory which has both long-run and short-term connotations ought to prevail. This is analytically a vast field (Mathur, 1982) but for practical applications hardly any so-called advanced country does (or is likely to) qualify as a candidate for the application of growth theory.

As technical progress takes place all the time and every decade M is to be replaced by M^+, and in every generation H by H^+, the sphere of growth theory seems to be rather limited in practical application, though it is immensely important to study the properties of hypothetical systems. Capital theorists of growth may survive, but only if they are also development theorists and know what the application of their theory is meant for – to serve as defining a target of development strategies. Development theorists would survive – but only if they fully comprehend the properties of the target state. Applied development economists have a chance of survival if they escape the charge of being superficial by understanding the capital theory of development well. In this dispensation, the applied growth economists who are only that, would, ideally, have rather a limited sphere.

Correspondingly, there is no validity of any group of planners who count themselves as applied manpower research workers or manpower experts unless they have a full understanding of development theory. Consequently, one cannot have research confined to applied aspects of manpower without basic manpower research (as a part of theory of development) being conducted; for the question remains as to what is the body of basic theoretical knowledge which applied manpower planners are supposed to apply.

By the same token, scientists dealing with development, not having mastered the theory of development as capital theory of economics views it (and by confining themselves to applied economics orientation courses) or geographers coming to the field of development with the same inadequacy as scientists, or public administrators becoming development specialists, must remove the inadequacy. It cannot be done in one-week reorientation courses (as professional trainers are led to believe by authorities who cannot arrange for longer courses due to administrative bottlenecks).

In such a situation, even in a less-underdeveloped country – the so-called advanced countries – the strategy of long-term development becomes relevant. It can be seen to deal with the pattern of trotting platinum age which may be followed for the traverse[5] in a country which is at a certain level of development and wishes to reach an appreciably higher level and style of living with the aid of a set of highest order industries (H^+) completely different from the H-industries it has got at the start of the development period. For that traverse, trotting platinum age sub-economies would be the vehicles of non-bottleneck growth – with wages restrained, and goods in balance in a standard commodity (or an equilibrium–proportions) vector for a high level of non-inflationary steady growth.

8 DEVELOPMENT WITH SOCIAL JUSTICE

The path which appears to be optimum for a large span of time, requires that during that span, the H-sector should recycle a large proportion of its output back into itself. The essential element of a strategy for development with social justice is the realization that this type of desired growth is made possible by a much lower leakage of the products of H towards the lower order machinery (M) entering in the manufacture of the consumption goods. This requires the use of H-conserving (but improved techniques) in the consumption sector. The economy, thus, is able to accumulate its basic capital goods for the future, by having highly mechanized techniques as well as lower degrees of mechanization in the H-sector, but only of the less-mechanized sort in the consumption sector.

The consumption sector, therefore, provides the consumption goods for itself and for the H-sector in an optimum manner by not depleting the resources which have alternative and essential use in the H-sector itself, but looks as far as possible for the forms of traditional lower order machinery of lesser productivity (L^-) – which requires little products from the higher order equipment H. This procedure prevents the shortage of consumption goods (and, hence, ensures non-inflationary growth), while at the same time enhancing the possibility of H products to be recycled into that sector itself.

The device of the trotting platinum age also prevents unemployment usually encountered in shifting from less-mechanized to more-mechanized techniques. The path followed for Soviet planning was

$$H^- \text{---} M^- \text{---} C^- \text{ to } H \text{---} M \text{---} C \text{ to } H^+ \text{---} M^+ \text{---} C^+$$

This shows that for consumer goods production one uses techniques M^-, M, M^+ successively. In addition to high capital intensity in the H-sector (H^-, H or H^+) if the consumption sector also uses high capital intensity (in M^-, M, M^+) the whole economy follows the path which is highly mechanized. In labor surplus countries, this would be fraught with trauma of unemployment unless the rate of investment is stepped up by contravening the principle of non-inflationary growth (and thus depressing the standard of living).

But while giving priority to H^- (and introducing H) one may use the subsystem H^-, L^-, C^- and while giving priority to H (and introducing H^+), one may use the subsystem H, L, C and when giving priority to H^+ (and introducing H^{++}), the subsystem used may be H^+, L^+, C^+. One may notice that one follows the path in the consumption sector of L^-, L, L^+ which is uniformally of low capital intensity, while H^-, H, H^+ are of either high capital intensity, or low.

The low capital intensity in the consumption sector would keep high the demand for manpower (with high as well as low degrees of skill) because L^- is a more employment-creating technique than M^-, L more than M and L^+ more employment creating than M^+. In addition, L^-, is a technique conserving H^- to a large extent in comparison to M^-, and hence it permits the base of long-term growth to be strengthened. Similarly, L is more H-conserving in relation to M, and L^+ would conserve H^+ more than M^+ would. The L^-, L, L^+ system (in contrast to M^-, M, M^+), therefore, allows growth to greater heights of technology more rapidly with priority to heavy investment throughout, along with yielding current social justice. This is manifested in the form of an abundance of consumption goods (previously thought in general to be impossible), more employment and better functional and personal income-distribution (which lesser degree of mechanization gives for a fixed subsistance wage). By this process one has built up a base of H^- to introduce H and then H expands itself through a high degree of recycling. Similarly, to introduce H^+, a sufficient base of H is required and further H^{++} for its introduction requires H^+ to make it (and L^+ to feed the people engaged in building H^{++}).

The trotting platinum age used in development planning for less-underdeveloped (and so-called advanced countries) as well as for less-advanced countries delineates a strategy of just deal for the future and for the current generation – that is, of intergenerational equity. It combines development (growth of relevant goods) with social justice, by the economic system following an efficient program of capital accumulation (Dorfmann, Samuelson and Solow, 1958) through a development strategy for less-underdeveloped (and so-called advanced) as well as more-underdeveloped countries.

9 THE ROLE OF LOWER-ORDER MACHINERY

It may be noticed that in the type of long-term growth proposed there are three phases (Table 15.6) of higher-order machinery (H in its various forms), namely its introduction, its build up through priority and its replacement when newer forms (H^+) appear, and later when they are being rapidly popularized through priority to that sector. For the consumption sector during the first phase, L^- is being used, during the second L and in the third phase L^+. During a period of very rapid growth of modern higher-order investment (H^+), it is the improved type of lower-order machinery (L^+) which has to be made to grow at a rapid pace, rather than the modern type of lower-order machinery (M^+), and when H is to be built up, it is L rather than M which is to be provided. This runs counter to the general belief that the mechanized type of lower-order machinery M^-, M, M^+ should grow fast to displace the labor-intensive type L^-, L, L^+.

In successive phases I, II, III, as higher order machinery, H, appears in different columns (2, 3, 4, successively conveying introduction, hey-day and waning), the lower-order machinery (L^-, L, L^+) is being improved as drawing some minimal input-sustenance from higher and higher forms of H-technology (H^-, H, H^+). This is the path of technical progress of the lower-order machinery (using the less-capital intensive part of the spectrum of techniques) (see Fig. 15.1).

Looking at Table 15.6 we notice that in the consumption sector there is a lag of one cycle of industrial revolution (during which time the higher-order equipment is revamped), before lower-order machinery (L) ought to be displaced by newer forms, L^+ (which are associated with newer types of higher-order machines, H^+ whose product it will use – but to a minimal extent). In this strategy there is also a lag of one phase between introduction of higher order improved machinery and extensive use of the corresponding improved less-mechanized, lower-order machinery. Thus while introducing H, H^- is given priority, L^- is used for providing consumption necessaries. While H^+ is being introduced, H is given priority and it is L which is used for providing C-goods, and when H^{++} (denoted as H^{+2}) is to be introduced and H^+ is given priority, L^+ is used for manufacture of consumption good, rather than L^{++} (denoted as L^{+2}) – which form would not yet have been invented.

Thus it may be noticed that the introduction of H is not accompanied by

Table 15.6 The progression of development

Phase	Introduction of higher-order machinery of type	Priority of higher machinery of type	Giving way to higher technology in higher-order machinery in place of	Actual use of lower-order machinery of type	Temporary avoidance of use of lower-order machinery of type	Permanent avoidance of use of lower-order machinery of type	Lag between col. 2 and corresponding lower-order machinery (col. 5)
1	2	3	4	5	6	7	8
I	H	H^-	H^{--}	L^-	L	M	One phase
II	H^+	H	H^-	L	L^+	M^+	One phase
III	H^{++}	H^+	H	L^+	L^{++}	M^{++}	One phase

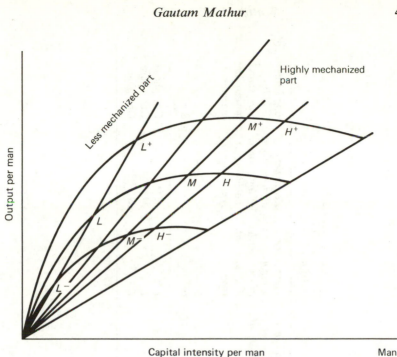

Figure 15.1 Spectrum of processes

use of L (but of L^-) while introduction of H^+ is not associated with use of L^+ (but of L). For any phase when H^{+n} is to be newly introduced, its consumption requirements are to be met. There are three possibilities – firstly, using M^{+n}; secondly, using L^{+n}; thirdly, using $L^{+(n-1)}$. The first one eats up resources of H^{+n} fast. Hence M^{+n} is to be avoided. The second one, L^{+n}, is not yet invented, or if known, not yet popularized. Hence it cannot be depended upon to be the main channel of providing the consumption requirements for H^{+n}. Hence, reliance is placed on $L^{+(n-1)}$. L^{+n} will be used when H^+ is to be given the main thrust and is to be reploughed in its own expansion rapidly, and towards the latter half of the phase (after $H^{+(n+1)}$ has ceased to be at a stage merely of introduction and has acquired importance towards being ready for priority to be allotted to it). $L^{+(n+1)}$ will be used only when $H^{+(n+1)}$ is under rapid self-regeneration, and later in the same phase when $H^{+(n+2)}$ is being introduced. The whole M series of machines, $M^{-(n-1)}$, M^{+n}, $M^{+(n+1)}$, $M^{+(n+2)}$, etc., are never used, while $L^{+(n-1)}$ with $L^{+(n+1)}$ are used with a one-phase lag.

The strategy also gives an answer to the question as to what use is H-ploughback if it does not produce M in the current phase. This question was raised by critics of Tugan-Baranovski on his suggestion that there should be a continuous ploughback of the highest order equipment (which we call H). The rapid build up of H, no doubt, prevents the use of that sector to produce

Table 15.7 The generalization of progression

Phase	Introduction of higher-order machinery of type	Priority to higher-order machinery of type	Fading out of older technology in favor of higher-order machinery	Actual use of lower-order machinery of type	Temporary avoidance of use of lower-order machinery of type	Permanent avoidance of use of lower-order machinery of type	Lag between col. 2 and corresponding lower-order machinery (col. 5)
1	2	3	4	5	6	7	8
I	H^{+n}	$H^{+(n-1)}$	$H^{+(n-2)}$	$L^{+(n-1)}$	L^{+n}	M^{+n}	One phase
II	$H^{+(n+1)}$	H^{+n}	$H^{+(n-1)}$	L^{+n}	$L^{+(n+1)}$	$M^{+(n+1)}$	One phase
III	$H^{+(n+2)}$	$H^{+(n+1)}$	H^{+n}	$L^{+(n+1)}$	$L^{+(n+2)}$	$M^{+(n+2)}$	One phase

M in the current phase of the industrial revolution; but with full development (requiring H^+ as its highest order equipment), the rapid build up of H^+ in the second phase (i.e. the next industrial revolution) would require the prevention of dissipation of its products towards M^+ (which is only *one* of the means of producing the desired consumption goods, C^+, the two others being L^+ and L). When H^+ is reproducing itself at a fast pace, the consumption requirements should come from the equipment which is H-saving (L) rather than an H-using or H^+-using technique (i.e. M or M^+). Hence, L^{+n} is not used in the first phase of introduction of H^{+n}, but is very much the instrument of supply of consumption goods in the next two phases (build up of H^{+n} and introduction of $H^{+(n+1)}$). M machines are avoided throughout (Table 15.7).

10   THE PROGRESSION OF DEVELOPMENT

The recommendations of use of techniques and their avoidance are now ready for depiction in Table 15.8. In the said table, column 2 represents a percolation strategy where there is trickling down of capital goods (in the consumption sector) and of consumption goods. Column 3 represents a percolation strategy exhibiting percolation of consumption goods. Column 4 represents the permeation strategy – saturation of the economy both with heavy equipment and with consumption necessaries of a traditional type. It requires use of less-mechanized consumption good machinery for manufacture of consumption necessaries. It stresses the use of relatively simpler equipment and production of consumption goods in common use (and hence, those satisfying the common man in his requirements). The permeation strategy represents a continuing austerity in the sense of lagged upgrading of quality of life in terms of consumption necessaries (when the economy is capable of affording the common man the goods in plentitude).

It is the aspect of austerity that captures the basic characteristic of platinum age (restraint on too quick a rise of consumption standards of the common man as regards both attributes – the quantity per head and quality of life, and restraint upon the few privileged persons improving the quality of their life when the common man is being asked to wait). In each case, the non-inflationary balance is maintained and growth is steady – the characteristics of a trotting platinum age.

In fact, it can be noticed that the proposition enunciated above was applicable to periods of rapid expansion in the industrial revolutions of the past also.

Thus, in the case of Germany, a view of the past from the statistics presented at the Konstanz Conference on the take-off (Rostow, 1963) showed that the number of handlooms expanded in the first phase of the Industrial Revolution when it was expected that their substitution by power

Table 15.8   Percolation and permeation strategies

| Phase | Combination permanently avoided
Percolation strategy for capital goods and consumer goods | Combination temporarily avoided
Percolation of consumer goods | Combination used
Percolation of capital goods and consumer goods with a lag |
|---|---|---|---|
| 1 | 2 | 3 | 4 |
| I | H^{+n}, $H^{+(n-1)}$, $M^{+(n-1)}$, $C^{+(n-1)}$ | H^{+n}, $H^{+(n-1)}$, L^{+n}, C^{+n} | H^{+n}, $H^{+(n-1)}$, $L^{+(n-1)}$, $C^{+(n-1)}$ |
| II | $H^{+(n+1)}$, $H^{+(n)}$, M^{+n}, C^{+n} | $H^{+(n+1)}$, H^{+n}, $L^{+(n+1)}$, $C^{+(n+1)}$ | $H^{+(n+1)}$, H^{+n}, $L^{+(n+1)}$, $C^{+(n+1)}$ |
| III | $H^{+(n+2)}$, $H^{+(n+1)}$, $M^{+(n+1)}$, $C^{+(n+1)}$ | $H^{+(n+2)}$, $H^{+(n+1)}$, $L^{+(n+2)}$, $C^{+(n+2)}$ | $H^{+(n+2)}$, $H^{+(n+1)}$, $L^{+(n+1)}$, $C^{+(n+1)}$ |

looms would have been taking place. The same phenomenon was witnessed in the United Kingdom also till the first phase of the Industrial Revolution was over – contrary to what was generally the impression (that the mechanized techniques immediately started throttling the less-mechanized ones out of existence).

The role of lower order equipment L^-, L, L^+ is to be the instrument of five actions during the next two industrial revolutions in which the character of H changes to H^+ (and, later on, of the latter to H^{++}).

It is, firstly, to provide plentiful consumption goods in the next industrial revolution to permit the build up of the heavy industry sector.

Secondly, it does so in a manner which conserves the products of the heavy investment sector for that sector's own expansion.

Thirdly, it provides greater employment (as L^- is more labor-using than M^-, L more than M and L^+ more than M^+).

Fourthly, it corrects the functional distribution of income, because wage–profit ratio in L^{+n} is higher than for M^{+n}.

Fifthly, it represents a lag in changeover of the quality of life too early in an industrial revolution (which can only be for a privileged few). It awaits the invention of techniques which the common man can use and whose products he can enjoy.

The less-mechanized lower-order machinery is, thus, an instrument of long-term growth and of social justice simultaneously. The highly mechanized lower order machinery, M in its various forms, negates all these – its total output per unit of investment is low; it eats into the resources for further expansion of H, it provides little employment, it generates an unfavorable functional income distribution and it is the manufacturing equipment for the goods of the privileged. Its high degree of mechanization is associated with large-scale and high profits and the unfavorable functional income distribution tends to be converted to a skewed personal income distribution. The demand for consumption goods for the privileged which this creates is again for use of machinery of type M^+ which, being even more highly mechanized, reinforces the effects noticed earlier. Lack of long-term growth and inequity are, therefore, reinforced. The economy comes under the grip of a vicious circle of affluence (see Mathur, 1983a). Thus the strategy is consistently anti-growth and anti-social justice. The characteristic of a bastard golden age is the existence of unemployment, albeit with steady growth. The trotting platinum age is a mechanism to diminish the illegitimate characteristics of high degree of non-employment. The percolation strategy with its high degree of mechanization in the consumption sector and its continuous emphasis on new type of élite consumption goods, aggravates the aspect of illegitimacy rather than diminishing it. It is, therefore, a form of progressive underdevelopment.

11 CONCLUSION

It may be seen from the foregoing discussion that planning is as relevant to the more-developed underdeveloped countries – euphemistically called advanced countries – as it is to the less-developed underdeveloped variety. In modern statecraft, a planning exercise for long-term development cannot be escaped in a development context – just as a budget and fiscal manipulation cannot be escaped (whether the economy is less underdeveloped or more underdeveloped). It is a paradox that whatever a giant corporation in private enterprise would easily do for itself (in terms of perspective planning), is not usually achieved by public authorities either in the less developed or in the more developed among the underdeveloped economies.

In both cases, the device of considering growth as a form of trotting platinum age development path allows calculation of vector of prices corresponding to a vector of distribution of manpower (to be both worked out as duals of each other with the latter being recognized as the causative factor). The shadow prices and shadow manpower distribution would be substitutes for the computation of expected prices and allocations for a perfectly competitive set of entrepreneurs had that species existed.

Equity is ensured through the type of strategy which is envisaged as the permeation strategy of intergenerational equity (Mathur, 1983b). The use of capital theory helps in framing the required strategy for progression of development. The foregoing attempt has been based on an important aspect of capital theory of development – the golden age envisaged by Joan Robinson, and the extension of her analysis to a development context through trotting platinum ages.

Notes

1. As summarized but not solved by the late Professor Sir Dennis Robertson in 1931. See Robertson (1931, 1950), p.226.
2. As, for instance, dealt with most brilliantly by Professor Lionel Mackenzie (1976).
3. Dorfmann, Samuelson and Solow (1958), referred to by Professor Sir John Hicks as DOSSO.
4. See Mathur (1962) where this assumption is described as being akin to the work of a fairy.
5. See Mathur (1965). During the period when I was working on strategies of development, Professor D. G. Champernowne was responsible for giving me the guidance as to the necessity of converting short-run models of development into long-term ones, and then warning me of many pitfalls. James Mirrlees helped exceedingly regarding looking at some mathematical problems connected therewith. A traverse using Robinsonian golden age as target and Sraffa–von Neumann system as path was thus brought into existence in 1960. Its text was deposited in March 1961 in the Cambridge University Library.

References

Champernowne, D. G. (1945) 'A Note on J. von Neumann's article on "A Model of Economic Equilibrium",' *Review of Economic Studies*, 13 (1): 10–18.

Dorfman, R., P. A. Samuelson, and R. M. Solow (1958) *Linear Programming and Economic Analysis* (New York: McGraw-Hill).

Gale, D. (1956) 'The Closed Linear Model of Production', in H. W. Kuhn and A. W. Tucker (eds), *Linear Inequalities and Related Systems* (Princeton: Princeton University Press).

Harcourt, G. C. (1979) 'Non-neoclassical Capital Theory', *World Development* 7 (October): 923–32.

Kahn, R. F. (1959) 'Exercises in the Analysis of Growth', *Oxford Economic Papers*, NS 11 (June): 145–56.

Kemeny, J. G., O. Morgenstern, and G. L. Thompson (1956) 'A Generalization of the von Neumann Model of an Expanding Economy', *Econometrica*, 24 (April): 115–35.

Little, I. M. D. (1957) 'Classical Growth', *Oxford Economic Papers*, NS 9 (June): 152–77.

McKenzie, L. (1976) 'Turnpike Theory', *Econometrica*, 44 (September).

Mathur, G. (1962) 'Technical Progress and the Production Function', in L. Spaventa (ed.) *Nuovi Problemi di Svilluppo Economico* (Turin: Einaudi).

Mathur, G. (1965) *Planning for Steady Growth* (Oxford: Blackwell).

Mathur, G. (1966) 'Von Neumann Systems and Dependent Processes', *Indian Economic Journal*, 14 (Econometrics Number): 163–90.

Mathur, G. (1967) 'Investment Criteria in a Platinum Age', *Oxford Economic Papers*, NS 19 (July): 119–214.

Mathur, G. (1982) 'Analytical Dimensions of the Problem of Poverty', in V. N. Despande *et al* (eds), *Poverty – An Interdisciplinary Approach* (Bombay: Somaiya) pp. 6–15.

Mathur, G. (1983a) 'Capital Theory of Political Economy', Presidential Address delivered to the Eighth Indian Social Science Congress, Hyderabad (July).

Mathur, G. (1983b) 'Employment and Intergenerational Equity', in E. A. G. Robinson *et al* (eds), *Employment Policy in a Developing Country* (London: Macmillan) pp. 253–75.

Mathur, G. (1986) 'Equilibrium and Disequilibrium in Development Economics', in J. Halevi and E. Nell (eds), *Revival of Growth Theory* (forthcoming).

Neumann, J. von (1945–6) 'A Model of General Economic Equilibrium', tr. by O. Morgenstern, *Review of Economic Studies* 13 (1): 1–9.

Robertson, D. H. (1931, 1950) 'Wage Grumbles', reprinted in American Economic Association, *Readings in the Theory of Income Distribution* (Homewood, Ill.: Irwin) pp. 221–36.

Robinson, Joan (1956) *The Accumulation of Capital* (London: Macmillan).

Rostow, W. W. (ed.) (1963) *Economics of Take-off into Self-Sustained Growth* (London: Macmillan).

Schefold, B. (1978) 'On Counting Equations', *Zeitschrift für Nationalokonomie*, 38: 253–85.

Steedman, I. (1979), *Trade Amongst Growing Economies* (Cambridge: Cambridge University Press).

16 Optimality and Decentralization in Infinite Horizon Economies

Robert A. Becker and Mukul Majumdar*

Analysis of current problems cannot wait until models ... have been properly worked out, the appropriate mixture selected and the interaction between them properly diagnosed. More rough-and-ready methods have to be used. All the same, simplified models can perhaps help towards an understanding of the nature of real problems, provided that their own nature is properly understood. They can certainly hinder when not properly understood. (Joan Robinson, *Essays in the Theory of Economic Growth*, 1968)

1 INTRODUCTION

The problem of economic growth was a major preoccupation of Joan Robinson. She was a major contributor to the post-Keynesian theory of economic growth that followed the publication of Harrod's seminal dynamic model. She wrote extensively and critically on the foundations of neoclassical growth theory; her concern for logically sound argument lay behind her extensive writings questioning the validity of an aggregate capital concept and the corresponding notion of an aggregate production function. Her critique of neoclassical theory placed her at the forefront of the still raging 'Cambridge controversy' in capital theory. Joan Robinson's work on capital and growth also showed a real concern that economic dynamics be studied as a process in real time. The dynamics of the stationary state might be a useful starting point, but the more serious concerns were the relationship between the short- and long-run periods in the process of accumulation and growth. She also stressed the importance of understanding the evolution of economies outside equilibrium positions.

The purpose of our paper is to discuss some issues in the development of infinite horizon capital accumulation models. We adopt the view that

* Robert Becker acknowledges the partial support of NSF Grant SES 85-20180. Mukul Majumdar acknowledges the partial support of NSF Grant SES 86-05503. Discussions with John H. Boyd III were helpful during the writing of this article. We thank Marilyn Neff for research assistance in the preparation of the paper.

aggregate capital models do have a place in economic dynamics. They do not correspond to the entire body of capital theory. The reswitching debate alerts us to the prospect that the results of the one- and two-sector models of accumulation do not extend to an arbitrary number of distinct capital goods. But there are reasons for us to pursue these models as benchmarks for testing techniques, as well as for framing the basic ideas of our theory of accumulation in the most simple fashion. These models do have at least one application in which the concept of 'capital' is unambiguous; this is the case in the economics of the fishery where the biomass plays the role of capital. From a more general viewpoint, we recall the passage quoted from Professor Robinson at the start and affirm our position that simple models have a place in the theory of capital and growth.

One of our objectives will be to formulate the major properties that are known about these 'low dimensional' models of accumulation. We shall be concerned with the welfare properties of various dynamic equilibria as well as describing the implied laws of change or comparative dynamics properties of an equilibrium path. The meaning of decentralization in dynamic economics is one of our major preoccupations. We will push to the limit of what we can say about non-steady-state equilibrium paths and how they depend on the underlying parameters of the economic model. Understanding equilibrium paths is an essential step in the process of grasping the meaning of disequilibrium growth. Applications of this theory to the economics of the fishery and capital taxation are offered as one defense for the line of inquiry which we follow in our study.

The models of accumulation which we propose can also be brought to bear on the problem of distribution. One of the major reasons for Joan Robinson's critique of aggregate capital models was her concern over the importance of understanding the relation between growth and distribution. There are three ways in which our approach is relevant to the evolution of the distribution of the national product in a dynamic economy. First, the analysis covers stationary and non-stationary equilibria. The implied pattern of factor payments may be worked out. A sharp distinction between the short run and long run may be made within this schema. The long run corresponds to the notion of an attractor for the economic system. This attractor may be a stationary state or it may take a more complex form (for example, a periodic or even 'chaotic' solution). The short run may be interpreted as the time period of the 'transient' motion observed before the economic system settles down to the attractor. We will emphasize the results of one-sector models on this front; brief comments are made on the two-sector case.

The consequences for the distribution of factor income are just one of the conclusions that may be drawn from this approach to dynamic analysis. For example, in some realizations of the heterogeneous household 'Ramsey model' there are different savings propensities out of capital and labor income in a steady state as well as along the path of evolution to the steady state. More generally, the models discussed in this review link growth theory and the Walrasian theory of value. One of Joan Robinson's observations in the preface to *The Accumulation of Capital* (1956, p.v) is the apparent divorce between value and growth theory. She laments that these two problems have not been fully reconciled; our approach offers one possible reconciliation of value and growth theory.

In Joan Robinson's (1952) essay on 'The Rate of Interest', there is a verbal discussion of the effect of thriftiness on the rate of interest (p.24). Her discussion makes a clear distinction between the very long-run results and the initial periods reaction to an increase in thriftiness. We present a dynamic equilibrium model which exhibits all the comparative dynamics properties presented in her verbal statements. In this fashion, we hope to show one way in which the construction and analysis of a mathematical model can be used to expose the assumptions lying beneath the intuitive comparisons found in the non-mathematical approach to theory and *thereby clarify the limitations of that theory*.

The paper is organized as follows: the basic issues are the subject of Section 2. One-sector optimal growth models are covered in Section 3. Decentralized one-sector models are the subject of Section 4. Concluding comments are in Section 5. Equations are numbered consecutively.

2   ISSUES

2.1   Introduction

An intertemporal optimization problem is defined by a set of possible programs, a set of attainable programs, and a welfare criterion. The interpretation of the abstract programming problem is flexible; it may represent a Ramsey-style central planner, a single household facing an intertemporal budget constraint given by market opportunities, or it may represent the planning problem faced by a single firm in a market economy. For the purposes of defining the basic framework, we adopt a central planning interpretation of the optimization problem. We will use this problem to frame an alternative market oriented interpretation in order to pose questions about the possibility of achieving a decentralized optimum. We will also discuss market equilibrium models in their own right.

The purpose of this section is to define the basic framework and questions to be addressed in the subsequent parts of the paper. We adhere to certain conventions from the start. First, we will only consider infinite horizon models with the emphasis placed on infinitely lived agent models. The overlapping generations model will be touched on in so far as it may be related to the infinitely lived agent model. Second, we abstract from the problems raised by uncertainty in order to consider only deterministic models. Many of the issues we raise in the text have analogs in the uncertainty sphere; we concentrate on the deterministic case in order to focus on the central questions in the simplest fashion. Third, we postulate an aggregate consumption good and capital good as the commodities in the model. Many of our comments apply to both one- and two-sector models (with appropriate adjustments) where the capital and consumption good are not the same physical commodity. Fourth, we treat time as a sequence of discrete periods. This allows us to carry out the discussion with a minimum of machinery and avoid certain technical problems that arise in continuous time which do not appear to have significant economic meaning.

The next section defines the basic issues. We cover the general structure of accumulation models, state the questions which we think are interesting, and comment on the potential for controversies to arise in capital theoretic model-building exercises.

2.2 Basic Issues

2.2.1 The Structure of Accumulation Models

The commodity space consists of the set of all sequences of non-negative real numbers. This set is denoted by s^+. The commodity space is a subset of the space of all sequences of real numbers which is denoted by s. An element of the commodity space is a sequence, $C = \{c_t\}$, where $t = 1,2,...$, and c_t represents the amount of the consumption good consumed within period t. Our notational convention is that boldface letters represent sets, upper-case letters represent sequences, and lower-case letters represent scalers. The commodity space represents the set of all *possible programs* (also called *profiles* or *plans*). A particular element of s^+ can be contemplated by the planner, but need not be available within the constraints which face him. The constraints facing the planner determine the set of *attainable programs*, denoted A. The set s^+ is usually endowed with a topology in order to introduce the convergence and continuity ideas required for existence theory and the analysis of the resulting optimum plans. We will endow the commodity space with the weak topology $\sigma(s,s_0)$-topology, where s_0 is the space of sequences which have finitely many non-zero terms. This topology is equivalent to the product topology on s, where s is viewed as a countable number of copies of the real line, R. It is also equivalent to the Frechet metric topology. Thus the space s is a Frechet space, i.e. it is a Hausdorff, locally convex linear topological space (see Aubin, 1977, and Robertson and Robertson, 1973, for material on Frechet spaces).

In many applications, the attainable subset of the commodity space contains only bounded sequences. This situation occurs usually as one consequence of diminishing marginal returns to capital arising from a fixed labor supply. For this reason, many authors initiate their analysis with the assumption that the commodity space is the set ℓ_∞, the space of all bounded sequences of real numbers. Unfortunately, the space ℓ_∞ is too small for many applications of the theory; the major examples occur when capital is completely durable and in equilibrium problems. We note that it is possible to give the economically relevant subset of the commodity space a topology which differs from the subspace topology induced by the $\sigma(s,s_0)$-topology. However, the choice of a topology is a delicate issue since it may imply time preference restrictions on the planner's preference order (Bewley, 1972; Koopmans, 1972; Majumdar, 1975; Brown and Lewis, 1981; Magill, 1981; Boyd, 1986a).

The preferences of the planner are described by a binary relation $\succsim$ defined on $s^+ \times s^+$, the Cartesian product of the commodity space with itself. We interpret $C \succsim C'$ to mean that C is at least as preferred to C' by the planner. In many applications of the theory, the relation $\succsim$ is described by specifying a utility function as the primitive concept in the choice problem. Given the relation $\succsim$, a *utility function* is a real valued function U defined on the commodity space such that for each C, $U(C) \succsim U(C')$ if and only if $C \succsim C'$. A utility function is an order preserving functional representation of the preference relation. The utility function is *upper semicontinuous* (u.s.c.) at C if and only if

$$\{C' \in s^+ : U(C') < U(C)\}$$

is open. *U is upper semicontinuous on A* if and only if it is u.s.c. for each $C \in A$, where A is the *attainable set* of consumption programs which satisfy the planner's constraints.

In terms of utility functions the abstract programming problem may be represented by the pair (U,A) and the problem:

$$J = \sup \{U(C') : C' \in A\}.$$

The *optimal value* of the problem is J. A program C is *U-optimal* if and only if $C \in A$ and $J = U(C)$. The basic existence theorem for utility functions is given by the Classical Weierstrass Theorem: *Every u.s.c. function defined on a non-empty compact set has a U-optimal element.*

In many models, the structure of the set A is further developed and its properties are intertwined with those of the utility function in order to demonstrate the possibility of optimal growth according to the stated criterion, as well as to uncover the qualitative properties of the given system.

We are interested in optimal growth as well as equilibrium growth. To discuss alternative equilibrium frameworks and for achieving an optimum by some decentralized mechanism, it is useful to recall the various notions of intertemporal prices. The standard treatment of commodities in general equilibrium analysis takes a commodity to be defined by its physical characteristics, the date of availability, its location, and the contingent events upon which it may depend (e.g. rain or no rain). The models addressed in this paper abstract from the latter two bases for distinguishing goods. In intertemporal analysis, the most important characteristic of a good is the date at which it is available. For this reason, we distinguish between two different views of the price system that might be used to value commodities. There are two basic forms of the valuation system: *present* and *current value* price systems. Each valuation method has its own advantages; each corresponds to a different choice of numeraire. Detailed discussions of the structure of intertemporal price system may be found in the books by Bliss (1975) and Burmeister (1980).

2.2.2 The Basic Questions

The analysis of the choice problem (U,A) forms the basic questions in the theory of optimal growth. At the most basic level, we are interested in establishing the existence of optima. A negative answer would imply the stated objective was not sensible in light of the constraints (see Koopmans, 1967, p.9). Once this problem is affirmatively answered it is possible to derive the properties of the model. First, we ask if there is a unique optimal plan. Multiple solutions signal a problem: the stated criterion is not a complete guide to optimal growth since a metacriterion would be needed for the completion of the description of what a planner *should* choose. Non-uniqueness would also create problems for deriving the laws of change implied by the model; the famous 'Cambridge controversies' are based in part on the possibility of multiple steady-state solutions.

The description of the properties enjoyed by an optimum is called the *characterization* problem. In general, we seek a *complete characterization* of an optimal program. The goal is to find necessary and sufficient conditions for an optimum in terms of shadow prices which support an optimal allocation. In the context of a centrally planned model, we are led to question the possibility of achieving the optimum by a decentralized mechanism. This usually comes down to asking if the competitive market mechanism can achieve the social optimum. We are also interested in the converse: does a decentralized market solution achieve an optimal allocation of resources in the intertemporal economy?

As Samuelson (1947, ch.2) and Hicks (1946, pp.6, 23, 27, 42–61, etc.) have taught us, we are ultimately interested in the implications of optimizing behavior whether it be that of a central planner or a household (or producer) in a market oriented economy. The characterization conditions are subjected to further analysis in order to deduce the properties exhibited by an optimal path of capital accumulation and the corresponding path of consumption. In a decentralized economy, we seek knowledge about the time paths of the various prices for goods and factors as well as the evolution and distribution of income and wealth. Finally, we are interested in the laws of change which describe the response of the optimum to shifts in the various economically important parameters or the initial data (the initial capital stock). This is called the problem of *comparative dynamics*. The optimization structure of the choice problem as well as its stability properties are combined to deduce the ways in which a parameter shift (e.g. the rate of time preference) induces a change in the dynamics of the model. In practice, these different analytical levels are often interconnected rather than taken up in sequence. We will illustrate the types of questions we find interesting in the later sections of the paper.

2.2.3 Controversies

Capital theory is one of the most controversial subjects in economic theory. Joan Robinson was one of the leading participants in the famous 'Cambridge controversies' in capital theory. That debate alone touched on such issues as the validity of an aggregate capital concept, the appropriate level of aggregation for focusing on the growth theoretic questions of interest (including the existence of a 'standard commodity'), the functional distribution of income and its relationship to the marginal productivity theory of distribution, and the possibility of deriving meaningful comparative steady-state results (much less comparative dynamics results) – indeed the very nature of the process of economic growth. There are other controversial aspects of capital theoretic models than those indicated by the Cambridge debates. For example, there is the choice of the length of the horizon, the focus on households (either finite lived or infinitely lived) versus the omniscient central planner, the optimality of market allocations, the alternative concepts of decentralization, the implications of time preference for the distribution of goods either over time or across contemporaneous agents.

We propose to look at some of the more recent issues and controversies that go beyond the celebrated Cambridge debate; we do approach elements of that controversy when we take up the subject of comparative dynamics. Indeed, Burmeister (1980, ch.4, pp.118, 154) has argued that debate can be examined by questioning the validity of steady-state comparisons either explicit or implicit in the proponents arguments. The optimizing models which we focus on have the prospect of carrying out a proper comparative dynamics program in line with Burmeister's (1980, p.165) views, as well as relating to the Hicks–Samuelson comparative statics methodology. As for directly re-examining the Cambridge controversies, we do not feel we have anything further to add to the voluminous literature under that classification; the defenders of the various positions have stated their views. A summary of the debate up to 1980 may be found in Burmeister (1980, ch.4). For an earlier (and different) account, see Harcourt (1972).

There are many theories of capital and growth. The literature on growth theory is ample testimony to the variety of opinions and arguments that the problems of economic growth and distribution raise in the economics profession. For example, in our view, neoclassical models are not solely characterized by the presence of an aggregate capital good and all the problems which this concept raises for model builders in the two Cambridges. Rather, we take the concept of aggregate capital as a useful benchmark in the modelling process, since it is the one for which our intuition is most easily developed and results may be properly worked out. Complexity may always be added at a later date.

Modelling choices arise with each of the major components of a capital theoretic model. For example, what is to be the length of an individual's horizon (finite versus infinite)? There is a controversy over whether overlapping generations or infinitely lived agent models are more useful in understanding economic dynamics. In reality, no private household agent lives forever; different generations co-exist at any time. Yet the choice of an infinitely lived agent model can still be a useful approximation for a long-lived agent exercising control and planning over the future. The overlapping generations model is not without difficulties either; bequests are a subtle issue in that framework. What is the proper length of the horizon for the economy? Capital theoretic problems are usually modelled as either finite or infinite horizon theories. Infinite horizon models will be the subject of our paper; the conception of the classical stationary state only has formal meaning in an infinite horizon framework. Recognition of the open-ended nature of the choice problem in an intertemporal setting leads inevitably to an infinite horizon – either explicitly or implicitly. The latter case arises with a predetermined finite horizon and a terminal bequest function; the bequest's meaning is derived from events occurring after the termination of the original problem.

The degree of optimizing behavior on the part of individual agents represents another choice. Optimal growth theories and dynamic equilibrium models based on optimization at the micro level may be contrasted with the 'descriptive' theories derived from fixed savings and consumption propensities as found in the neo-Keynesian and neo-Ricardian growth theories. The structure of the economic environment in which agents operate (markets versus plan), the degree of information in the possession of agents (certainty versus uncertainty), and the structure of technology including the degree of aggregation (e.g. multisector versus one sector) are other issues arising in the specification of a theoretical framework used to address an intertemporal allocation question.

The models addressed in this paper have certain common features. We postulate an aggregate capital good – see Bliss (1975) and Usher (1980) for a general discussion of the aggregation problem in growth modelling, and see Burmeister (1980, theorem 4.4, p.131) for a specific derivation of the one-sector production function from one heterogeneous capital goods model in a *steady state*. We work directly with production functions instead of with basic activities (although this distinction is blurred in the case of a linear model without choice of technique). We typically postulate either an infinitely lived planner or an infinitely lived household. The overlapping generations model is briefly discussed and related to the infinitely lived agent framework. We also discuss aspects of the 'inverse optimum' problem in order to relate our approach to the 'descriptive theories' with fixed saving propensities out of different factor shares of income. It should be stressed again that we abstract away from uncertainty and pursue perfect foresight models in order to place a manageable limit on the scope of our study.

2.3 One-Sector Technologies

The labor force is a fixed constant equal to the number of households, normalized to one in this section. Output in any period depends on the level of the variable input x (capital). Given input x, output net of depreciation is denoted by $g(x) - \mu x$, where μx allows for proportional depreciation of capital within a single period and $0 \leqslant \mu \leqslant 1$ is a given parameter. The *total output* available in the period is denoted by $f(x) = g(x) + (1 - \mu)x$. In the *classical case*, the function g is derived from a neoclassical constant return to scale production function G defined over labor and capital inputs by setting $g(x) = G(1,x)$. In the *non-classical case*, g may be derived from a quasi-concave production function in the same fashion as the classical case. The difference in the two cases is determined by the properties of g''. In both cases labor is a fixed factor; the law of diminishing returns applies to g. This law can be expressed as the requirement that the marginal product of capital, $g'(x)$, is diminishing for all input levels sufficiently large. The classical models exhibit this property at *all* positive input levels. Thus $g''(x) < 0$ for all positive x in the classical case. The non-classical case has g'' positive for input levels near 0. The non-classical case arose in the context of models of the fishery. Increasing returns to scale (at least over some output range) have also been advanced as a hypothesis in the theory of economic growth (cf. A. Young, 1928; and Romer, 1986). The case where g is linear or affine may also be subsumed in the general discussion. In this case, labor is a free factor and the law of diminishing returns does not apply to further restrict g. The *affine case* is thus defined by $f(x) = \gamma x + \xi$, where γ may be regarded as the constant marginal product of capital net of depreciation and ξ as a non-negative constant factor; the *linear case* holds whenever ξ vanishes. The linear case arises whenever the underlying economy is *closed*; this means there are no non-produced resources other than the initial capital stock.

Hypotheses restricting the technology are stated in terms of the total output function. The basic properties of f are described in the statement:

(f.1) $\quad f: \mathbb{R}_+ \to \mathbb{R}_+$, $f(0)=0$, f is continuous at 0, C^2 on $\mathbb{R}_{++}$, and $f' > 0$.

The next three assumptions are used to frame the difference between the classical and non-classical models.

(f.2) $\quad f$ is strictly concave.

The affine technologies are excluded from the class meeting (f.2). The functions satisfying (f.1) and (f.2) are called *classical* total output functions. For classical total output functions, condition (f.2) is equivalent to $f''(x) < 0$ for all x. The law of diminishing returns applies in any *open* model where there is a fixed amount of some non-produced resource that is essential for the production process.

Let $f'(a+) = \lim f'(x)$ as $x \to a$, $x > a$, be the right-hand derivative of f at a. Another axiom commonly used in the classical case is called the 'Inada condition': $f'(0+) = \infty$.

(f.3) $\quad f$ satisfies the Inada condition.

The *non-classical* total output functions are defined by the property:

(f.4) $\quad$ There exists $x\dagger$ such that $f''(x) > 0$ for $x < x\dagger$

$\quad\quad$ and $f''(x) < 0$ for $x > x\dagger$.

To simplify the exposition, any total output function found in this paper is assumed to satisfy condition (f.1) without further notice. Piece-wise linear technologies have been studied in the one-sector literature, notably by Bliss (1975) and Benveniste and Mitra (1979), but are not in the mainstream of developments of that theory. We have chosen the smoothness condition as one restriction on the scope of the paper. Given the aggregative nature of our study, this would not seem to be a major limitation.

In addition to the distinction between the classical and non-classical functions, there are two important subclasses of total output functions. They are classified according to whether $f'(x) < 1$ for x sufficiently large or $f'(x) > 1$ for all x (with equality possible only as $x \to \infty$). In the first case, f has a *maximum sustainable stock*, b, with $f(b) = b > 0$ and $f(x) < x$ whenever $x > b$. There is also a $b^* \in (0, b)$ such that $f' > 1$ on $(0, b^*)$ and $f' < 1$ *for $x > b^*$*. In this case, f is said to be *productive with maximum sustainable stock*, b. In the second case, f is *superproductive*: all positive inputs are sustainable. For example, let $g(x) = x^\rho$ for parameter ρ, $0 < \rho < 1$. This is the Cobb–Douglas function. The corresponding total output function meets the conditions in (f.1)–(f.3). If capital does not depreciate ($\mu = 0$), then f is superproductive. If capital depreciates ($\mu > 0$), then f is productive with a maximum sustainable stock b. The Cobb–Douglas function is the only member of the family of constant elasticity of substitution functions satisfying (f.1)–(f.3) and having $f(0) = 0$.

In the general one-sector model the technology may depend on time; for example, there may be exogenous technical progress. The technology is formally specified by a sequence of time varying production functions, $\mathscr{F} = \{f_t\}$.

A non-negative sequence of numbers $\{c_t, x_{t-1}\} \equiv (C,X)$ is a *possible program* if for each t

$$c_t + x_t \leqslant f_t(x_{t-1}). \tag{1}$$

where $t = 1,2,\ldots$. The assumption that goods may be disposed of without cost ('free disposal') is incorporated in (1) by use of the inequality. A possible program (C,X) is an *attainable program* of accumulation from the initial stocks k if $x_0 \leqslant k$. Let the set of attainable programs be denoted by $A(\mathscr{F},k)$. The *consumption-attainable* programs are denoted by $F(\mathscr{F},k)$ and are defined by setting

$$F(\mathscr{F},k) = \{C: (C,X)\varepsilon A(\mathscr{F},k) \text{ for some } X\}.$$

The technology is usually fixed once we initiate the analysis of optimal growth paths in a model. However, the sensitivity of an optimal path on the starting stock is a subject that is a central concern in the analysis. For this reason, we suppress the notation $\mathscr{F}$ in the representation of the possible and attainable sets when the meaning is clear.

Define f^t inductively by setting $f^1 = f_1$ and $f^t = f_t \circ f^{t-1}$ for $t = 1,2,\ldots$. The technology is said to be *stationary* if f_t is independent of time. The *path of pure accumulation* is the attainable program $(O,\{f^t(k)\})$, where $O = (0,0,\ldots)$. If the technology is stationary and f has a maximum sustainable stock b, then f has a unique fixed point at b. Moreover, $0 < f'(b) < 1$; hence for each positive k, $\lim f^t(k) = b$ as $t \to \infty$. If $k \leqslant b$, $f^t(k) \leqslant b$. In general, attainable consumption and capital at time t are always bounded by $f^t(k)$. When f has a maximum sustainable stock b and $k \leqslant b$, then b is an upper bound on attainable consumption and capital sequences. For $k > b$, $f(k)$ is the relevant bound. If f is superproductive, then the attainable set is unbounded. In applications of the theory to time varying technologies, a more precise estimate of how fast attainable consumption and capital sequences can grow is required in order to insure the existence of an optimum. For this reason, we introduce the *production correspondence* defined by

$$P(k) = \{X\varepsilon s^+ : 0 \leqslant x_t \leqslant f_t(x_{t-1}), \ x_0 = k\}.$$

The set of attainable consumption programs may be rewritten now in the notation

$$F(k) = \{C\varepsilon s^+ : 0 \leqslant c_t \leqslant f_t(x_{t-1}) - x_t \text{ for some } X\varepsilon P(k)\}.$$

Both $F(k)$ and $P(k)$ are closed in the product topology and $F(k) \subset P(k) \subset X_i^\infty[0, f'(k)]$, where X_i refers to the Cartesian product of the factor spaces. But this last set is compact by Tychonoff's Compactness Theorem, hence $F(k)$ is also compact in the product topology. The set A may now be identified with $F(k)$.

Existence and characterization theory are tied to measuring the speed at which consumption and capital may grow in their respective attainable sets. Superproductive stationary technologies exhibit an attainable set which contains unbounded sequences. To accommodate these technologies in our framework we introduce the subsets of the commodity space for which sequences do not grow faster than by a factor of β. Formally, define

$$X(\beta) = \{X \in s^+ : |X|_\beta < \infty\}$$

where $|X|_\beta = \sup |x_t / \beta^{t-1}|$ is the β-weighted ℓ_∞ norm and $\beta \geq 1$ (we identify $X(\infty)$ and s^+. These norms act as if the discount factor $1/\beta$ is built into the structure of the commodity space. The commodity space may be given a topology induced by a β-norm called the β-*topology*. The set $X(\beta)$ is called a β-*bounded* subset of the commodity space. In general, we say that a set X contained in the commodity space is β-bounded if all its elements obey the growth condition used to define $X(\beta)$. The β-topologies are used in the development of the continuity assumptions used to formulate theorems giving the existence of an optimum. They also play a role in proofs of the necessity of a transversality condition in optimal growth and perfect foresight equilibrium models. Topologies of this form were used by Chichilnisky and Kalman (1980) and Dechert and Nishimura (1980) in order to study optimal paths in classical Ramsey models. The use of weighted function spaces have also been used recently by dynamic programmers (Wessels, 1977; Waldman, 1985). Boyd (1986a) recognized their importance for the recursive utility models of optimal growth and developed the machinery we employ in our paper. The following result due to Boyd (p.15) is crucial for relating the product and β-topologies:

Lemma 1: Let $\alpha < \beta$ and let X be an α-bounded set. The β-topology and relative product topology coincide on X.

The lemma can be used to verify that the attainable consumption sets for several common technologies are actually β-compact; when combined with upper semicontinuity of the utility function, this yields existence of optimal paths. Majumdar (1975) gave an example showing that for $\alpha = \beta = 1$, the conclusion of the lemma fails. The β-topology for $\beta = 1$ is the standard sup norm topology for ℓ_∞; this topology is stronger than the relative product topology and the lemma does not go through.

Remark 1: If $\lim [f'(k)/a^t] < \infty$, then the production correspondence and the attainable consumption sets are α-bounded subsets of $X(\beta)$.

Several commonly used total output functions yield α-bounded technologies. The Cobb–Douglas total output function with depreciation parameter λ is $f(x) = Ax^\rho + (1 - \lambda)x$ where $A > 0$, $0 < \rho < 1$, and $0 \leqslant \lambda \leqslant 1$. In this case $\alpha = 1$ works if $\lambda > 0$ and any $\alpha > 1$ works when $\alpha = 0$. Any concave production function yields an α-bounded technology: just choose $\alpha > \xi$ where ξ is an arbitrary supergradient of f. This is possible since any concave function obeys the inequality $f(x) \leqslant f(a) + \xi(x - a)$ for some supergradient ξ of f at the point a. In case f is differentiable, take $f'(a) = \xi$. Let $f'(\infty)$ denote the limit of $f'(k)$ as $k \to \infty$.

Remark 2: The production correspondence of any stationary concave total output function is α-bounded for all $\alpha > f'(\infty)$.

A time-dependent technology example may be constructed by looking at a case of exogenous technical progress; set $f_t(x) = e^{\gamma t}x^\rho$. Boyd (1986a, p.16) showed that the production correspondence is α-bounded for $\alpha > \exp\{\gamma/(1 - \rho)\}$. Affine time varying technologies are also encountered in the framework of the Ramsey equilibrium problem.

2.4 Performance Criteria

We fix $A \equiv F(\mathscr{F}, k)$ for the remainder of this section. The first two criteria may be used to define preference relations which are not represented by a conventional utility function.

2.4.1 *The Efficiency Criterion*

An attainable program (C) is *inefficient* if there is another attainable program (C') offering at least as much consumption in every period and more consumption in at least one period. An attainable program is *efficient* if it is not inefficient. The *efficiency criterion* ranks programs as either efficient or inefficient. The objective is to select an efficient path. The efficiency criterion presumes that consumption may never be satiated in any period. In the standard Ramsey one-sector model an infinite number of efficient programs will exist.

2.4.2 *Extended Utilitarian Criteria*

A utilitarian criterion adds the felicities for a sequence of one-period rewards in order to evaluate a prospective program. The common element in the performance criteria proposed in this section is that the objective depends exclusively on the profile of anticipated consumption. A *felicity function, u,* maps the non-negative real numbers into the real line and $u(c_t)$ gives the single period reward from consuming c_t units of the good during period t. Properties of the felicity function are listed below.

(u.1) $U: \mathbb{R}_+ \to R$ is well defined for all $c > 0$.
(u.2) u is strictly increasing for all $c > 0$.
(u.3) u is C^2 on $\mathbb{R}_{++}$.
(u.4) u is strictly concave.
(u.5) u satisfies the Inada condition at $c = 0$, i.e. $u'(0+) = \infty$.
(u.6) Either $u(0) = 0$ and u is continuous at 0, or $u(0+) = -\infty$.

One important class of felicity functions satisfying (u.1)–(u.6) is defined by

$$u(c) = c^{1-\eta}/(1-\eta), \ \eta > 0, \ \eta \neq 1, \text{ and} \tag{2}$$

$$u(c) = \log c, \ \eta = 1. \tag{3}$$

The function $\eta(c) \equiv -cu''(c)/u'(c)$ is called the *elasticity of marginal felicity*. It is a constant function in (2) and (3). Example (2) is also a homogeneous function in c. Felicity functions such as

$$u(c) = \text{arcsec} \ (c+1) \text{ and } u(c) = \arctan (c^\alpha), \ 0 < \alpha < 1, \tag{4}$$

are not homogeneous functions.

The discussion of the extended utilitarian criteria is most easily conducted in terms of the classical Ramsey model without discounting, denoted by the pair (U^*, A), where U^* denotes the extended utilitarian pay-off given u is the felicity function over current consumption and the technology is stationary. The notation U^* is to signify that the utility function may take values in the extended real numbers. The definitions of the various objectives may be easily modified to admit a sequence of time-dependent felicities $\{u_t\}$; the most common example of this is when $u_t = \delta^{t-1}u$ for some felicity u which is independent of time; δ is called the *discount factor* and $0 < \delta \leqslant 1$. When $\delta = 1$, we say that (U^*, A) is the *undiscounted Ramsey model*; the *discounted Ramsey model* arises when $0 < \delta < 1$.

In the undiscounted Ramsey model, the utilitarian criterion with stationary felicity function would evaluate the profile C as the infinite sum of the one-period rewards $U(c_t)$. However, the resulting infinite series might not be well defined; the sums may fail to converge over some portions of the program space. An *extended utilitarian criterion* is introduced to evaluate programs for this reason. The adjective 'extended' means that the summation of felicities in the utilitarian criterion has been modified for infinite horizon planning problems. Programs are now to be compared by means of their initial segments. Different criteria arise depending on the exact ways in which programs are compared and limits of felicity sums are taken as the length of the initial segment increases. Four major criteria have been proposed for the undiscounted Ramsey model (U^*,A): optimality, weak maximality, maximality, and the long-run average criterion. We focus on the optimality criterion in this paper; see Hieber (1981) and McKenzie (1986) for an extended discussion of these alternative objectives.

An attainable program C is *optimal* if for any other attainable path C'

$$\underset{N}{\limsup} \sum_{t=1}^{N} [u(c'_t) - u(c_t)] \leqslant 0, \tag{5}$$

as $N \to \infty$. The upper (lower) limit of the sequence of partial felicity sums is denoted by limsup (liminf). The set of optimal programs is denoted by $O(U^*,A)$.

Another variant of the utilitarian criterion is based upon averaging the felicity sums over time. An attainable program C is *on average*, best, if for any other attainable program C'

$$\underset{N}{\limsup} \, (1/N) \sum_{t=1}^{N} [u(c'_t) - u(c_t)] \leqslant 0. \tag{6}$$

This objective is also known as the *long-run average* criterion. Let $L(U^*,A)$ denote the set of long-run average optimal programs. An optimal program turns out to be one of many long-run average optimal programs.

2.4.3   Intertemporal Utility

A household's preference order over alternative consumption profiles is usually described by a utility function defined on the commodity space. A utility function for time additive separable preferences may be defined whenever the felicity series converge. We are interested in other classes of utility functions which need not be defined by a series of felicity functions. The major examples are members of the recursive class of utility functions. We state the basic properties of intertemporal utility as axioms.

We assume that intertemporal preferences are defined by a utility function U which is monotonic in the sense that it is increasing in each argument. This property is to be understood as a maintained characteristic of the utility function without further comment. In an infinite dimensional commodity space context, hypotheses concerning continuity and concavity of U must be framed with some care. These properties have a simple formulation if utility is a bounded function. The axioms for this situation are stated as

(*U*1)   *U* is bounded and continuous in the $\sigma(s,s_0)$ topology.
(*U*2)   *U* is a concave function.

When (*U*1) holds, we can express *U* as the limit of finite dimensional utility functions, $U(C) = \lim_{N \to \infty} U(P_N C)$ (see Becker, Boyd and Foias, 1986). The projections P_N are defined by $P_N(C) = (c_1, c_2, ..., c_N, 0, 0, ...)$. Additional properties of utility functions are used in our theorems. Those characteristics of preferences are introduced below.

One implication of property (*U*2) is that the left- and right-hand partial derivatives of the utility function exist. These derivatives are denoted by $U_t^-(C)$ and $U_t^+(C)$, respectively. The right-hand directional derivative of *U* at *C* in the direction of $E_t = (0,0,..., 0,1,0,...)$ where 1 is in the *t*-th place, is defined as

$$U_t^+(C) = \lim_{\varepsilon \to 0^+} [U(C + \varepsilon E_t) - U(C)]/\varepsilon \tag{7}$$

The left-hand partial derivative is defined by substituting $\varepsilon \to 0^-$ in the limit. The concavity of *U* implies $U_t^+(C) \leqslant U_t^-(C)$. If equality holds, we write $U_t(C)$ for the common value and call this the partial derivative of *U* at *C* with respect to the *t*-th coordinate. Unless otherwise indicated, all directional derivatives are taken to have finite values.

In many applications, a household's preference order is described by a recursive utility function. These utility functions treat the future in the same way at each point in time. Current utility is expressed as a fixed function (aggregator) of current consumption and the utility of future consumption. Postulates governing intertemporal preference are most easily expressed in terms of the aggregator. The original work on this approach was carried out in a series of papers by Koopmans and his collaborators (Koopmans, 1960, 1972; Koopmans, Diamond and Williamson, 1964; Diamond, 1965; Beals and Koopmans, 1969). The aggregator first appeared as a primitive concept in the work of Lucas and Stokey (1984). Further development of this idea may be found in Boyd (1986a). The motivation for introducing the recursive class of functions is to encompass Irving Fisher's (1907) idea that the rate of time preference depends on the underlying consumption path – even in a steady state. The time additive separable utility functions are members of the recursive family; they are characterized by a predetermined steady-state rate of time preference.

More formally, a utility function is *recursive* if there is a function *W*, the *aggregator*, such that

$$U(C) = W(c_1, U(SC)) \tag{8}$$

where $SC = (c_2, c_3, ...)$ is the future consumption stream. The aggregator is a map from $Z \times Y$ to $\mathbb{R}$ where Z and Y are subsets of $\mathbb{R}$. We assume that the aggregator is continuous on $Z \times Y$ and increasing in each argument. Moreover, it obeys a Lipschitz condition of order one in its second argument, i.e. there is a $\delta > 0$ such that

$$|W(z,y) - W(z,y')| \leqslant |y - y'| \text{ for all } y, y' \in Y.$$

This condition represents Koopmans's notion of *uniformly bounded time perspective*. W is often concave on $Z \times Y$; however, it may be only concave in each argument and not jointly concave in some examples (see the UEH case below). At this stage, it is not necessary to assume that $\delta < 1$.

When $W(0,0) = 0$, the utility function can be computed from the aggregator as the limit of 'partial sums' by

$$U(C) = \lim_{N \to \infty} W(c_1, W(c_2, ..., W(c_N, 0))...) = \lim_{N \to \infty} U(P_N C) \tag{9}$$

(see Boyd, 1986a, for details). Note that this convergence is monotone increasing. This 'partial sum' representation is useful since there are aggregators where the utility function cannot be expressed in closed form. Further, the utility function is concave if and only if each of the 'partial sums' is concave.

The commonly used *time additive separable* (TAS) utility function $\Sigma_{t=1}^{\infty} \delta^{t-1} u(c_t)$ is recursive. This is easily verified by taking $W(z,y) = u(z) + \delta y$ where u is the felicity function. Many other types of utility functions are recursive. Koopmans, Diamond and Williamson (1964) used the KDW aggregator $W(z,y) = (1/\theta) \log(1 + \beta z^\delta + \gamma y)$ where $(z,y) \in [0,1] \times [0,1]$. $\theta = \log(1 + \beta + \gamma)$, $\beta > 0$, $1 > \delta > 0$, and $\theta > \gamma > 0$. The associated utility function does not have a closed form representation. Another example associated with an explicit utility function is the UEH aggregator $W(z,y) = (-1 + y) \exp[-u(z)]$ as used by Uzawa (1968), Epstein (1983), and Epstein and Hynes (1983). Here $y \leqslant 0$ and u is an increasing, strictly concave function with $u(z) \geqslant \varepsilon$ for some $\varepsilon > 0$. This aggregator yields the utility function

$$U(C) = -\sum_{t=1}^{\infty} \exp\left[-\sum_{s=1}^{t} u(c_s)\right] \tag{10}$$

and satisfies (U1) and (U2). The Koopmans concave quadratic aggregator (1972, p.94) is defined below by $W(z,y) = y + (z - y)(a - bz + cy)$, where $a, b, c, a - 2b, a - b - c$, and $1 - a - 2c$ are positive parameters.

The Rawls maximin utility function is another member of the recursive class. This functional ranks programs according to the lowest felicity realized over the horizon. The Rawlsian utility function is defined by setting $U(C) = \inf\{u(c_t)\}$. This is easily seen to be recursive; the aggregator is $W(z,y) = \inf\{z,y\}$, so recursivity follows. The Rawlsian utility function does not obey the strong monotonicity property assumed as an otherwise maintained assumption. An increase in consumption in finitely many periods has no impact on the utility level of a path! This criterion is very conservative; indeed it says to never sacrifice the present for the future.

One popular class of recursive utility functions are the TAS forms with a constant elasticity marginal felicity function. These examples also obey the *Inada condition at zero*, namely, $W_1 = \partial W/\partial z = u' \to \infty$ as $z \to 0^+$. However, they are not bounded and thus cannot satisfy (U1). Two useful types of bounded, concave felicity functions that enjoy the Inada property and obey $u(0) = 0$ as well as (U1) and (U2) are given by (4). The role of the Inada condition is to guarantee that households choose positive consumption at each time, income permitting.

For a general C^1 aggregator, U_t exists and is found by the formula

$$U_t(C) = W_2(c_1, U(S^1 C)) \, W_2(c_2, U(S^2 C)) \, \ldots \, W_2(c_{t-1}, U(S^{t-1} C)) \, W_1(c_t, U(S^t C))$$
(11)

where $W_2 = \partial W/\partial y$ and S^t is the t-th iterate of S. Consequently, $W_1(0+, y) = \infty$ and (11) imply the Inada condition for this class. The KDW specification meets this criterion. The UEH class can be parameterized to satisfy the Inada condition. The Koopmans quadratic aggregator and the Rawlsian aggregator do not satisfy the Inada condition.

For each consumption profile C, the *marginal rate of impatience* is defined by the number $R(C)$ given by

$$1 + R(C) = W_1(c_1, U(SC))/W_2(c_1, U(SC))W_1(c_2, U(S^2 C)).$$
(12)

By combining (11) and (12), we have $1 + R(S^{t-1}C) = U_t(C)/U_{t+1}(C)$. If C is a constant path, denoted by C_{con} with $c_t = c$, then the marginal rate of impatience reduces to the expression

$$1 + R(C_{\mathrm{con}}) = 1/W_2(c, U(C_{\mathrm{con}})).$$
(13)

For TAS utility, (13) implies $1 + R(C_{\mathrm{con}}) = \delta^{-1}$, which is independent of the underlying consumption profile. For another example, the analog of (13) in the UEH class is,

$$1 + R(C_{\mathrm{con}}) = 1/\exp(-u(c)).$$
(14)

Notice that the marginal rate of impatience in this case depends on the underlying consumption stream in contrast to the TAS case.

Unbounded utility functions must be handled with care. The TAS aggregator $W(z,y) = z^\mu + \delta y$, $0 < \mu$, $\delta < 1$, defines a utility function, U, on s^+ which is not continuous at O (see Beals and Koopmans, 1969, p.1014). Their example is manufactured with a one-sector classical stationary technology with a maximum sustainable stock b. Becker, Boyd and Foias (1986) argued this discontinuity arises because the utility function is not u.s.c., although it is lower semicontinuous (l.s.c.). There is, however, a subset of s^+ containing unbounded sequences on which this U is continuous. The choice of this subset of s^+ is designed to exclude elements that give rise to the discontinuity in the example (see Becker, Boyd and Foias, Lemma 6.1, 1986, for details). The TAS utility functions defined for felicities with constant $\eta \geqslant 1$ are also continuous on an appropriate subset of the commodity space (see Becker, Boyd and Foias, 1986).

Recall the definition of the set $X(\beta)$ for $\beta > 0$. If U is defined and continuous on $X(\beta)$, then we say that U is β-*myopic*. If U is defined and upper semicontinuous on $X(\beta)$, then we say that U is *weakly* β-*myopic*. If U is represented by the aggregator W and U is (weakly) β-myopic, then we call W *(weakly)* β-*myopic* as well. The interesting point to observe is which aggregators give rise to weakly β-myopic utility functions. (Boyd (1986a) derived several conditions that guaranteed an aggregator to be either weakly β-myopic or β-myopic. For example, if W satisfies

$$0 \leqslant W(z,0) \leqslant A(1 + z^\eta), \tag{15}$$

as would be the case if $W(z,0)$ has either asymptotic exponent or asymptotic elasticity of marginal felicity (see Brock and Gale, 1969) less than $\eta > 0$ with $\beta^\eta \delta < 1$, then U is β-myopic. Another sufficient condition for U to be β-myopic is that

$$0 \leqslant W(z,0) \leqslant A(1 + \log z), \tag{16}$$

with $\beta < \infty$ and $\delta\beta < 1$.

Existence and characterization theory are based on the assumption that utility is β-myopic. The condition $\beta^\eta\delta < 1$ illustrates the sort of joint condition on preferences and technology needed for the existence of an optimum. The inequality cannot be weakened because of Gale's (1967) cake-eating example. Let $W(z,y) = z^\mu + \delta y$ and define $f(x) = x$; note that $F(k) = \{C: \Sigma c_t \leqslant k, c_t \geqslant 0$ for $t = 1,2,...\}$. For $\delta = 1$, there is no optimal program.

Restrictions of the form (15) and (16) yield examples of utility functions which are members of the class $\mathscr{U}$ introduced below. This class of utility functions is distinguished since its members are the ones for which the transversality condition is a necessary condition for optimality in both optimal growth and perfect foresight equilibrium models. Given two sets A and B, let $C(A;B)$ denote the set of continuous maps from A to B. A function $f \in C(A;B)$ is φ-*bounded* if there exists a positive function $\varphi \in C(A;\mathbb{R})$ such that $\|f\|_\varphi \equiv \sup \{|f(x)|/\varphi(x): x \in A\} < \infty$. The φ-*norm* is $\|f\|_\varphi$; the space $C_\varphi(A;B) = \{f \in C(A;B): f$ is φ-bounded$\}$. The pair $(C_\varphi(A;B), \|f\|_\varphi)$ is a Banach space.

Notice that S is one-to-one on $X(\beta)$. Since $S \in C(X(\beta); X(\beta))$, we can compute $\|\varphi \circ S\|_\varphi$. We let $\mathcal{U}$ denote the set of all recursive utility functions U which obey the restrictions:

($\mathcal{U}$.1) $U(0) = 0$;

($\mathcal{U}$.2) U is concave;

($\mathcal{U}$.3) U is φ-bounded on $X(\beta)$ for some φ with $\delta \|\varphi \circ S\|_\varphi < 1$.

Let $\|\varphi \circ S\|_\varphi = \gamma$; taking any C_{con} in $X(\beta)$, we see that $\gamma \geqslant 1$. Thus condition ($\mathcal{U}$.3), $\delta\gamma < 1$, implies $\delta < 1$.

The following fact is implicit in Boyd (1986a) and is the consequence of membership in the family $\mathcal{U}$ needed to establish the necessity of the transversality conditions in Sections 3 and 4.

Lemma 2: If $U \in \mathcal{U}$, then $\lim\limits_{t \to \infty} \delta^t U(S^t C) = 0$.

Proof: $U \in \mathcal{U}$ implies that there is a positive number m (which may be chosen independent of t since S is one-to-one on $X(\beta)$) such that

$$0 \leqslant U(S^t C) \leqslant m\varphi(S^t C). \tag{17}$$

Use $\Phi(\tau, \tau - 1)$ to denote $\varphi(S^\tau C)/\varphi(S^{\tau-1} C)$ for $\tau = 1, 2, ..., t$ where $\Phi(1,0) = \varphi(SC)/\varphi(C)$. We have

$$\|\varphi \circ S\|_\varphi = \sup \{\Phi(t, t-1)\Phi(t-1, t-2)...\Phi(1,0)\} = \gamma^t$$

since each $\Phi(\tau, \tau - 1) \leqslant \gamma$ as $S^\tau C$ and $S^{\tau-1} C \in X(\beta)$; thus $\varphi(S^t C) \leqslant \gamma^t$. Multiply (17) through by δ^t and simplify to get

$$0 \leqslant \delta^t U(S^t C) \leqslant (\delta\gamma)^t. \tag{18}$$

Taking the limit in (18) and using $\delta\gamma < 1$ yields the result.

QED

The recursive utility functions represent stationary preference. Other utility functions have been studied in the literature. Streufert (1985) proposed a generalized recursive class. Epstein (1986) developed the implicitly additive functions. Majumdar (1975) gave a family of non-recursive utility functions.

2.4.4   Overlapping Generations Models

The major competitor of the infinitely lived household model is the overlapping generations model introduced by Samuelson (1958) in a pure exchange set-up. Diamond (1965a) extended the Samuelsonian framework to a neo-classical one-sector capital accumulation world. The major theme in their papers was the possibility that the First Fundamental Welfare Theorem could fail in an infinite horizon intertemporal model. Subsequently, Barro (1974) made the observation that the overlapping generations model with costless transfers between generations and altruism between members of different generations could be thought of as equivalent to a particular type of infinitely lived agent. Pazner and Razin (1980) argued in the exchange setting that with altruism between generations and endogeneous fertility, the efficiency of the perfect foresight equilibrium path could be established. The literature on overlapping generations models has grown substantially in recent years as theorists have found it to be of great interest in the analysis of monetary and fiscal problems in intertemporal economies (e.g. see Sargent, 1987).

We give a brief development of the overlapping generations model in this paper. We focus on two results associated with the overlapping generations model. These are Bose's (1974) characterization of efficient allocations and an important 'observational equivalence' property derived by Aiyagari (1985) relating the observed time paths of capital and consumption in a class of overlapping generations model and standard one-sector discounted Ramsey models.

The simplest overlapping generations model with capital accumulation may be described by the pair (U,A), where U now defines the utility of a member of generation born at time t. We assume that there is one member of each generation alive at any time, each agent lives for only two periods, there is no utility from bequests, and the preferences of each agent are identical. In short, there is neither population growth nor explicit intergenerational altruism in our statement of the overlapping generations model. There is a single composite capital-consumption good produced by a classical one-sector technology.

It is customary to describe the overlapping generations model in a market economy setting in which agents exercise perfect foresight over the time profiles of factor prices; a current value price system is usually used in which the price of consumption goods available in period t have unit value. An agent born at time t $(t > 1)$ lives for two periods and enjoys consumption during periods t and $t+1$ denoted by the pair $(c_t(t), c_{t+1}(t))$. That indivi-dual's pay-off is $U^t \equiv U(c_t(t), c_{t+1}(t))$. The agent works in the first period and retires in the second period. The agent is assumed to supply one unit of labor inelastically in the first period in return for a wage. The income of the young agent consists entirely of his labor income. The young agent must decide how much to consume in that period and how much to invest in order to provide capital income in the second period of retirement. In the second period, the agent consumes the income from his capital investment.

The stock of capital yielding that income is altered by the young agent alive during the 'dotage' of the older agent. The old agent is unable to convert the entire capital stock to his own consumption benefit; in this sense there is a limited bequest motive since the old agent in effect passes the ownership rights over the capital stock to the young agent. At time 1, an old agent is already on the scene; this agent is endowed with the initial capital stock of the economy. This agent consumes only his capital income. The young agent who comes into existence at the start of period 1 supplies the labor services which produce currently available goods.

A path $\{C,X\}$ represents aggregate consumption and capital; it is *attainable* if it satisfies the balance condition (1) for the one-sector model and for $t = 1,2,\dots$

$$c_t(t-1) + c_t(t) \leqslant c_t \tag{19}$$

for some non-negative numbers $c_t(t-1)$ and $c_t(t)$. The set of attainable programs (C,X) is the same for this overlapping generations model as the discounted one-sector Ramsey model. We say that $\{c_t(t-1)\}$ $(t=1,2,\dots)$ is an *attainable distribution* provided that it satisfies (19) for some attainable (C,X). The efficiency criterion for the overlapping generations model is identical to the standard concept; it applies to attainable paths (C,X). The distribution of consumption across generations alive at the same time is not a consideration when evaluating a path according to the efficiency criterion.

An attainable program (C,X) with distribution $\{c_t(t-1)\}$ is *Pareto optimal* if there is no alternative attainable path (C^*,X^*) with distribution $\{c_t(t-1)^*\}$ satisfying $c_1(0)^* \geqslant c_1(0)$, and $U^{*t} \geqslant U^t$, with strict inequality for some t. The corresponding aggregate path of consumption and capital is called a Pareto optimal path. We use $(C,X,\langle U^t \rangle)$ to denote an attainable path and corresponding pay-off sequence to the successive generations (the specific distribution in question is implicitly given by the pay-off values). Bose (1974) called this definition of optimality *long-run Pareto optimality*. An attainable path $(C,X,\langle U^t \rangle)$ is *short-run non-optimal* if there exists an attainable path $(C^*,X^*,\langle U^{*t} \rangle)$ and a positive integer T such that if t is an integer and $1 \leqslant t \leqslant T$, then

$$U^{*t} \geqslant U^t, \; U^{*T} > U^T, \; x^*_{T+1} \geqslant x_{T+1}, \; c^*_{T+1}(T) \geqslant c_{T+1}(T).$$

An attainable path $(C,X,\langle U^t \rangle)$ is *short-run Pareto optimal* if it is not short-run non-optimal. A Pareto optimal path is clearly short-run Pareto optimal and efficient. The converse is false; there may be a path which is short-run Pareto optimal over every finite collection of generations, but fails to be a long-run optimum when all generation's welfare is taken into consideration. One such example is cited in Section 3 on efficiency.

One of the issues with this model is that there may be multiple equilibria and some of those may be Pareto optimal while others may be inefficient. Aiyagari's Theorem applies to the efficient equilibria in the overlapping generations model. Bose's (1974) Characterization Theorem relates efficiency and long-run optimality. One of the most important questions with this model is whether a mechanism exists which insures that only the efficient equilibria are observable.

3   EFFICIENCY AND OPTIMALITY

3.1   Introduction

One- and two-sector models constitute the core of simple neoclassical dynamic models. The one-sector models are the simplest cases and are the focus of our presentation of optimality and decentralization results for infinite horizon economies. Many of the basic ideas can be seen in a first development based upon the efficiency criterion. This objective is the weakest of all the possible criteria discussed in our paper. The various welfare functions used to embody alternative objectives usually generate efficient programs as a by-product of achieving an optimum. Efficiency theory also takes us to the golden rule, a concept linked with the books of Joan Robinson on capital and growth. Once we have commented upon the efficiency criterion, we investigate some of the implications of alternative welfare functions. First, we recall the traditional undiscounted Ramsey model. Next, we present a generalization of the discounted Ramsey model to the case of recursive utility. The possibility of realizing the optimum by means of a decentralized resource allocation mechanism is taken up in Section 4. We also explore there the implications of alternative assumptions concerning the numbers of agents, the life-span of those agents, and the completeness of the market structure.

3.2   The Efficiency Criterion

3.2.1   Efficient Allocations

The efficiency criterion is taken to be a minimal requirement for any reasonable welfare function. As such, the efficiency criterion does not do much to single out a specific course of action for the planner. However, it can be used to eliminate some candidate optima without further reference to a specific welfare function. One example of this use of the efficiency criterion is the Phelps–Koopmans Theorem.

The interest in intertemporal efficiency stems from the seminal paper of Malinvaud (1953). He presented the first extension of Koopmans' activity analysis of efficient allocations in a static production world to an open-ended economy with a recursive technological structure. He was also the first to see that the analog of Koopmans' profit conditions for characterizing an efficient program had to be supplemented in an infinite horizon framework. The type of condition that Malinvaud formulated has since become known as the *transversality condition*. Understanding the meaning of this condition in our models will be one of our central concerns.

The existence of efficient programs is trivial to establish. For the sake of argument, we consider a stationary one-sector technology satisfying the basic assumption $(f.1)$. We do not require the function f to be classical at this stage; a non-classical total output function will work. Define a sequence of attainable programs $\{(C[T],X[T])\}$ for $T=1,2,...$, by setting (recall $f^0(k)=k$)

$$x_t[T]=f^t(k) \text{ for } t=0,1,2,...,T-1 \text{ and } x_t[T]=0 \text{ otherwise;}$$

$$c_t[T]=0 \text{ for } t \neq T, \ c_T[T]=f^T(k).$$

Given T, the path $(C[T],X[T])$ is called a T-Party program; it says that the planner follows the path of pure accumulation up to time T and has a consumption 'party' at that time leaving zero capital for the future. A T-Party program has only one period of positive consumption. The sequence of T-Party paths define the outer limit of consumption at each possible time period. Each T-Party path from k $(T=1,2,...)$ is efficient.

3.3.2 *Efficiency and the Golden Rule*

Suppose for the moment that we think of the planner as calculating a plan for an infinite sequence of generations; each generation has a felicity function u defined over its own consumption (assume u obeys the standard conditions in $(u.1)$–$(u.6)$). Here, $u(c_t)$ is interpreted as the reward received by the generation alive at time t. What is the capital-consumption pair resulting in the maximum sustainable utility? Formally, choose non-negative c and x to maximize $u(c)$ subject to $c=f(x)-x$. Since u is monotone, this is the same problem as maximizing sustainable one-period consumption, $f(x)-x$, by choice of x. The solution to this problem may be found by equating the net marginal product of capital, $f'(x)-1$, to zero. Let x^g be the root of this equation; clearly $x^g \in (0,b)$. Set $c^g=f(x^g)-x^g>0$. The pair (c^g,x^g) is termed the *golden rule*. This name is used since this combination of consumption and capital represents the savings of output (for maintainable consumption) that each generation would have past generations save for it, subject to the constraint that each generation selects the same savings rate.

The golden rule state has an important relationship to the problem of characterizing efficient programs. The specific result is called the Phelps Theorem (see Phelps, 1966, p.59). It is a sufficient condition for an attainable path to be inefficient. An attainable program (C,X) satisfies the Phelps condition if there is an $\varepsilon > 0$ and a natural number $T(\varepsilon)$ such that for all $t \geqslant T(\varepsilon)$,

$$x_t \geqslant x^g + \varepsilon.$$

The Phelps condition is equivalent to $\liminf x_t > x^g$.

Phelps Theorem: An attainable program which satisfies the Phelps condition is inefficient.

In particular, this theorem implies the path of pure accumulation is inefficient. A more interesting application of this partial efficiency characterization is to show that an inefficient intertemporal equilibrium exists.

Consider the overlapping generations model outlined in Section 2.4.4. Diamond (1965a) and Burmeister (1980, pp.53–7) have shown how this model may be used to illustrate the possibility that a dynamic equilibrium model facing an infinite horizon can generate an efficient equilibrium path. The heart of Burmeister's example is that an equilibrium program may converge to a steady-state capital stock that is greater than the golden rule stock. The limit stock yields a negative rate of return and the path is inefficient by the Phelps Theorem. Therefore, the First Fundamental Welfare Theorem *can fail* in an intertemporal setting. The inefficiency of the path is due to *capital overaccumulation* in the sense identified with the Phelps condition.

The failure of the Welfare Theorem to hold for a simple intertemporal economy is a consequence of the open-ended horizon. Indeed, the failure of the Welfare Theorem in the overlapping generations economy has been blamed on the *double infinity* of traders and time (see Shell, 1971). However, there is a complete characterization of Pareto optimal paths in the overlapping generations model (Bose, 1974). Later, we will show the welfare theorems do go through for the perfect foresight models with an infinitely lived household planner.

3.2.3 Shadow Prices and Efficient Programs

The Phelps Theorem gave a partial characterization of inefficiency. The purpose of this section is to review the criteria for the complete characterization of efficient (inefficient) programs. One of the key concepts that we introduce here is that of a competitive program. It is natural to ask if there is a duality theory for the efficiency criterion that parallels the developments found in the literature on static allocation models.

Let the technology of the economy in period t be given by the family of production functions $\mathscr{F} = \{f_t\}$. Given the initial stocks k, let $y_0 = f_0(k) > 0$. An attainable path (C,X) defines another non-negative sequence $Y = \{y_t\}$ by setting $y_t = f(x_{t-1})$ for $t \geqslant 1$. We now call X the input stock sequence and Y the output stock sequence. It will save some space to identify attainable paths as a triple (X,Y,C). Assume for the moment that each f_t satisfies:

(*f*.1)* For all $t \geqslant 1$, f_t is continuous on $\mathbb{R}_+$, $f_t(0) = 0$, and f_t is strictly increasing.

a triple (X,Y,C). Assume for the moment that each f_t satisfies: (*f*.1)*. For all $t \geqslant 1$, f_t is continuous on $\mathbb{R}_+$, $f_t(0) = 0$, and f_t is strictly increasing.

A program (X,Y,C) from y_0 is *competitive* if there exists a sequence $P = \{p_t\}$ of prices such that $p_0 \equiv 1$ and for all $t \geqslant 0$:

$$p_{t+1}y_{t+1} - p_t x_t \geqslant p_{t+1}f_t(x) - p_t x \text{ for } x \geqslant 0. \tag{20}$$

The condition (20) is often referred to as that of *intertemporal profit maximization*. We shall, for convenience, call such a sequence P satisfying (20) the *Malinvaud* prices associated with or supporting the program (X,Y,C). Observe that (*f*.1)* implies that P is a non-negative sequence. Furthermore, suppose that the input sequence X is strictly positive and we assume (*f*.1) applies to each f_t. Then, we can also show the Malinvaud prices are strictly positive and

$$p(0) \equiv 1, \ p_{t+1}f_t'(x_t) = p_t. \tag{21}$$

The *value of input* sequence $v = \{v_t\}$ associated with a competitive path is $v_t = p_t x_t$. We say that a competitive program (X,Y,C) with an associated Malinvaud price sequence P satisfies the condition of *bounded consumption value* if the sequence $\{p_t c_t\}$ is summable; and that it satisfies the *transversality condition* if

$$\lim_{t \uparrow \infty} p_t x_t = 0. \tag{22}$$

The static theory of efficiency pricing elaborated by Koopmans and Kantorovich can be readily extended to a model of intertemporal allocation with a *finite* horizon. However, the introduction of an infinite horizon poses certain mathematical difficulties, which in turn raise some conceptual problems concerning the proper definition of prices and present values. In what follows, we comment on some of the basic issues.

Suppose that (X,Y,C) is a competitive program which satisfies the bounded consumption value condition at Malinvaud prices P. It is trivial to see that given the strict positivity of $P[(f.1)]$, if

$$\sum_{t=0}^{\infty} p_t c_t \geqslant \sum_{t=0}^{\infty} p_t c_t^1 \tag{23}$$

for all attainable programs (X^1, Y^1, C^1) from y_0, then (X,Y,C) is indeed efficient. In other words, maximization of present value of consumption at Malinvaud prices (when the bounded consumption value condition is

satisfied) is sufficient to guarantee efficiency. This again, is a partial characterization of efficient competitive programs. Note that for any finite T, and
any attainable program (X^1, Y^1, C^1) from y_0 one has:

$$\sum_{t=0}^{T} p_t(c_t - c_t^1) \geq p_T x_T^1 - p_T x_T \geq -p_T x_T, \text{ or} \tag{24}$$

$$\sum_{t=0}^{T} p_t c_t \geq \sum_{t=0}^{T} p_t c_t^1 - p_T x_T. \tag{25}$$

Since (X, Y, C) is assumed to satisfy the condition of bounded consumption
value, for all $T \geq 1$

$$\sum_{t=0}^{\infty} p_t c_t \geq \sum_{t=0}^{T} p_t c_t \geq \sum_{t=0}^{T} p_t c_t^1 - p_T x_T. \tag{26}$$

If the transversality condition (22) holds, (26) implies (23) and guarantees
efficiency of (X, Y, C).

Consider, now, the case when a competitive program (X, Y, C) from y_0
satisfies the bounded consumption value condition at Malinvaud prices P
and, in addition, satisfies (23) for *any* feasible program (X^1, Y^1, C^1) from y_0.
We can show that it must necessarily satisfy the transversality condition (22).
The argument is intuitive. If the transversality condition does *not* hold there
must be some $m > 0$ and a subsequence of time periods such that

$$p_t x_t \geq m \tag{27}$$

for all t along this subsequence. But by the condition of bounded consumption value, there must exist some finite time T such that

$$\sum_{t=T}^{\infty} p_t c_t \leq m/2. \tag{28}$$

Choose some period $\tau \geq T$ such that $p_\tau x_\tau \geq m$, and define a program
(X^1, Y^1, C^1) as follows:

$(x_t^1, y_t^1, c_t^1) = (x_t, y_t, c_t)$ for $1 \leq t \leq \tau - 1$;

$(x_\tau^1, y_\tau^1, c_\tau^1) = (0, y_\tau, y_\tau)$ for $t = \tau$;

$(x_t^1, y_t^1, c_t^1) = (0, 0, 0)$ for $t > \tau$.

It is easy to verify that

$$\sum_{t=0}^{\infty} p_t c_t^1 \geq \sum_{t=0}^{\infty} p_t c_t + m/2.$$

which contradicts (23).

Thus, there is an intimate link among efficiency, the present value maximization condition (23) and the transversality condition when the competitive program satisfies the bounded consumption value condition. However, we know (from the golden rule example) that there are efficient competitive programs that *violate* the bounded consumption value condition and the transversality condition at the associated Malinvaud prices. We also know that there are competitive programs that are inefficient (violating the transversality condition) – look at the path of pure accumulation. One important direction of research has been to characterize programs that are efficient.

The non-linear total output functions cannot be used to define the class of models for which intertemporal profit maximization and the transversality conditions completely characterize an efficient allocation. This is implied by the golden rule example. There is a 'direct' characterization of the support prices; this is the Cass criterion. In its simplest form the Cass criterion for strictly concave C^2 total output functions states that an attainable program (C,X) is *inefficient* if and only if the infinite series

$$\sum_{t=0}^{\infty} \pi_t < \infty, \text{ where } \pi_t = X_{i=0}^{t-1} f'(x_i). \tag{29}$$

The interpretation of (29) is that inefficiency is linked with the speed with which the π_t (the future value of a unit of capital at period 0) converges to zero. Note that π_t is just the reciprocal of the present prices iterated according to (21).

Mitra (1979a) developed the most general form of the Cass criterion for a direct test of a program's efficiency. All the Cass-type measures of inefficiency use curvature conditions on the technology. The curvature ideas arise in part because of the attempt to measure how fast the terms of trade between the present and future deteriorate along a candidate for an inefficient path. We quote Mitra's first theorem to illustrate the generality of his results. The maintained assumption is a stationary technology meeting conditions $(f.1)$–$(f.3)$. The additional property of the technology is:

Condition S: For some $0 < m \leq M < \infty$, $N < \infty$, and $0 < \lambda \leq 1$, there exists a function $\mu(x)$ for $x \geq 0$, such that

   (a) $0 \leq \mu(x_t) \leq N$ for $x_t > 0$, $t \geq 0$, and

(b) $m\varepsilon\mu(x_t)/x_t \leqslant L(x_t,\varepsilon) \leqslant M\varepsilon\mu(x_t)/x_t$ for $0 < \varepsilon < \lambda x_t$, where
$L(x_t,\varepsilon) = \{[f(x_t) - f(x_t - \varepsilon)]/\varepsilon f'(x_t)\} - 1$.

Mitra Characterization Theorem: An attainable program satisfying Condition S is inefficient if and only if $\inf\{v_t: t = 1,2,...\} > 0$ and

$$\sum_{t=0}^{\infty} [\mu(x_t)/v_t] < \infty.$$

The original Cass criterion is a special case of this theorem. This would result if Condition S was valid for $\mu(x_t) = x_t$. However, it should be noted that the Cass type of criterion is not useful in linear models (see Majumdar, 1974, p.365).

One important application of the Cass-type efficiency criterion is Bose's proof (1974, theorem 3) of a complete characterization theorem for the long-run Pareto optimal paths in the overlapping generations model (U,A) with stationary technology f. He assumes that U is *separable*, i.e. there exists a felicity function u such that $U(c_t(t),c_{t+1}(t)) = u(c_t(t)) + u(c_{t+1}(t))$. An attainable path $(C,X,\langle U^t\rangle)$ is *interior* if aggregate consumption and capital at each time are uniformly bounded away from zero.

Bose's Characterization Theorem: Let U be separable with felicity u in the overlapping generations model (U,A). Assume a stationary technology f. Under $(f.1)-(f.3)$ and $(u.1)-(u.4)$, an interior path $(C,X,\langle U^t\rangle)$ is long-run Pareto optimal if and only if it is short-run Pareto optimal and efficient.

A second direction has been to characterize technologies in which competitive programs necessarily satisfy the conditions of bounded consumption value and maximization of present value (23). Mitra (1979b) gives sufficient conditions in terms of the technology such that *every* efficient program from a fixed starting stock has bounded consumption value.

Suppose that in addition to $(f.1)$ we assume $(f.2)$. The decisive result of Malinvaud asserts that if (X,Y,C) is an efficient program from y_0, it is competitive; i.e. a sequence P of Malinvaud prices satisfying (20) necessarily exists. It should, however, be stressed that the convexity assumption $(f.2)$ does *not* enable us to relax the monotonicity assumption in $(f.1)$. Examples of non-existence of Malinvaud prices in the presence of $(f.2)$ and $(f.1)^*$ are known from Peleg and Yaari (1970, pp.58–9) and McFadden (1975). Without going into the cumbersome algebraic manipulations that these examples entail, we can note that if the input sequence X of an efficient program (X,Y,C) is *strictly positive*, and (assuming $(f.1)$), $f'(x_t) = 0$ for at least a subsequence of time periods, the condition (2) clearly cannot hold, and Malinvaud prices supporting (X,Y,C) cannot exist.

Given such non-pathological examples of non-existence of Malinvaud prices and unbounded consumption values, one can define a *value function* as a continuous linear functional on an appropriate sub-class of programs and characterize efficiency in terms of consumption value maximization relative to such a value function. Results in this direction were reported by Radner (1967). However, a continuous linear functional need not 'generate' a price sequence P that can be used to calculate profits, or to measure intertemporal 'trade-offs' or more generally, used as convenient 'messages' in a theory of decentralization. The constant price sequence supporting the golden rule serves as an example of such a P. Given this difficulty, subsequent efforts were concentrated on two directions. First, a large class of models were identified in which (by exploiting the (ℓ_1, ℓ_∞) duality) continuous linear functionals with sequential representation could be used to derive the equivalence between efficiency and present value maximization [see the review paper by Cass and Majumdar (1979) and the references cited there]. Typically, these are models in which non-producible primary factors of production do not impose a bound on the rate of growth. A second direction explored systematically by Radner (1967) and Majumdar (1970, 1972) [see the synthesis of Kurz–Majumdar (1972)] was to show that efficient programs that are not supported by 'well-behaved' continuous linear functionals can still be approximated by 'regular' efficient programs that satisfy the criterion of present value maximization relative to continuous linear functionals that generate Malinvaud prices and define bounded consumption values. Of course, any notion of approximation involves the choice of a suitable topology on at least a subset of the program space.

3.3 Extended Utilitarianism and Optimality Theory

The purpose of this section is to illustrate the dynamics associated with the extended utilitarian criteria. We choose the classical undiscounted Ramsey model to discuss this approach since it is the fundamental example in this realm of the theory. The model (U^*,A) is understood to be fixed in the following development. The one-period felicity function is u and f is the classical total output function in this economy. The following blanket assumption is taken to be in effect throughout this section unless otherwise noted:

The model (U^*,A) satisfies $(u.1)–(u.6)$, $(f.1)–(f.3)$, and f has a maximum sustainable stock b. The initial capital k is positive.

One program plays a distinguished role in the demonstration that an optimal program exists. That program is the golden rule; it is the stationary path which is optimal given the starting stocks defining the program. Duality theory enters the theory at this stage by way of the 'value loss' concept. In turn, this leads to a new optimization problem defined for arbitrary initial data that is 'dual' to the original programming problem. This new problem is shown to have a solution. It is then shown to solve the original problem.

The golden rule has the following *support property*: by concavity of u and f, there exist non-negative functions α and β such that for every $c,x \geq 0$,

$$u(c^g) - pc^g = u(c) - pc + \alpha(c),$$

$$f(x^g) - x^g = f(x) - x + \beta(x),$$

where $p \equiv u'(c^g)$, $f'(x^g) = 1$. We say that $\delta(c,x)$ is the *value loss function*. It is defined by the formula

$$\delta(c,x) = \alpha(c) + p\beta(x).$$

If $(C,X)\varepsilon A$, set $\delta_t = \delta(c_t, x_{t-1})$; δ_t is called the *value loss of* (C,X) at time t. Let

$$D_T(C,X) = \sum_{t=0}^{T} \delta_t.$$

When the meaning is clear, we write D_T for $D_T(C,X)$. Since $\delta_t \geq 0$, it is clear that $\{D_T\}$ is a non-decreasing sequence. Therefore, either $D_T \uparrow \infty$ or $D_T \uparrow D < \infty$ as $T \uparrow \infty$. The path (C,X) is *good* if $D < \infty$, and *bad* otherwise. It can be shown that every good path converges to the golden rule.

Let $v(c) = u(c) - u(c^g)$ denote the renormalized felicity (this is the analog of Ramsey's trick with bliss). Use v as the new felicity function; the ranking of paths according to the optimality criterion will not change as a result of this alteration of u. Given attainable paths (C,X) and (C',X'), an elementary computation yields for any T:

$$\sum_{t=1}^{T} [v(c'_t) - v(c_t)] = \sum_{t=1}^{T} [u(c'_t) - u(c_t)] = p(x_T - x'_T) + (D_T - D'_T).$$

where $D'_T \equiv D_T(C^*,X')$. If both paths are good, then x_t and x'_t converge to x^g and

$$\sum_{t=1}^{\infty} [u(c'_t) - u(c_t)] = D - D'.$$

Therefore, (C,X) is optimal if and only if $D \leq D'$ for any other attainable path (C',X').

There is a good path in the attainable set for any $k \in (0,b)$ (see Majumdar and Mitra, 1982). Existence of an optimum follows once we show the set of attainable paths is compact and the value loss functional $D: A \rightarrow \mathbb{R}_+$ is a l.s.c. function. Compactness of A in the $\sigma(s,s_0)$-topology was shown in Section 2.3. Thus the remaining task is to prove D has the desired continuity property.

Lemma 3: The accumulated value loss functional D is lower semicontinuous with respect to the $\sigma(s,s_0)$-topology on the set of attainable programs.

Proof: Fix (C,X) in A. Since $D_T(C,X)$ is non-negative and continuous on G for each T, it follows that $D_T(C,X)$ increases to $D(C,X)$ as $T\to\infty$. Therefore,

$$D(C,X) = \sup_T D_T(C,X).$$

Hence D is the point-wise supremum of continuous functions and must then be lower semicontinuous.

QED

Define a set of numbers $\mathscr{D}$ by

$$\mathscr{D} = \{D(C,X): (C,X)\in A)\}.$$

The value loss minimization problem is the program defined by

$$D_* = \inf\{D: D = D(C,X)\in\mathscr{D}\}.$$

Clearly D_* is a non-negative number. It is also finite since good programs exist. A good program (C^*,X^*) has *minimal value loss* if $D(C^*,X^*) \equiv D^* = D_*$.

Brock's Lemma: A good program exists having minimal value loss.

Proof: Apply the classical Weierstrass Theorem to $-D$.

QED

The set of good paths is *not* a $\sigma(s,s_0)$-compact set since it is not a closed subset of the attainable programs. Given a good path (C,X), consider the sequence of attainable paths $(C^n,X^n)\in A(k)$ satisfying $c_t^n = 0$ for $t\leqslant n$ and $c_t^n = c_t$ for $t > n$. The point-wise limit of the consumption sequences as $n\to\infty$ is 0 for each t; the limit path is clearly bad. The set of good paths does, however, enjoy a type of 'closure' property.

A more detailed proof of Brock's Lemma would show that a sequence of good paths whose value losses are uniformly bounded above converges to a good path; this is the type of closure property alluded to above. As the good paths are the economically relevant ones in this model, it would be nice to weaken Brock's Lemma to include a result covering this sort of closure property that is weaker than compactness in the σ-topology.

This proof of Brock's Lemma was designed to emphasize the unity of the value loss method and the classical approach based on the Weierstrass Existence Theorem. By taking the negative of the value loss function, it is easy to see that Lemma 3 is another way of saying that the utility function is upper semicontinuous on the class of good paths once the origin of the felicity function has been shifted in the manner suggested by Ramsey. Brock's Lemma, therefore, is the same as saying there is an optimum. Finally, strict convexity of the value loss function at each t implies that there is at most one such program. Therefore, the value loss minimizer will be the optimal program.

Existence Theorem: There is a unique optimal program.

The golden rule state is globally asymptotically stable. This means that for each starting stock, the optimal path converges to that consumption-capital pair. This convergence property of the optimum arises because it is a good program.

Convergence Theorem: The optimal path converges asymptotically to the golden rule.

The Convergence Theorem is another example of a qualitative feature of the optimum. The mode of convergence is not described by this result. It turns out that the optimal program is monotonic. The general proof of the monotonicity property is characteristic of a large number of one-sector optimal growth models and will be given a general treatment in the section on characterization.

The uniqueness of the optimum with respect to the optimality criterion in the undiscounted model does not carry over to the long-run average optimality criterion. Indeed, *any* good program is a long-run average optimal program. Just observe that for any two good paths

$$T^{-1}\{\Sigma_1^T [u(c_t') - u(c_t)]\} \to 0 \text{ as } T \to \infty.$$

Long-run Average Existence Theorem: Any good program is a long-run average optimal program.

The long-run average optimality criterion is an example of a welfare function where the class of optima is so large as to be of little interest to a planner. The multiplicity of optima does not call for a specific plan to be chosen in order to achieve a 'best' allocation of resources. A *metacriterion* would need to be invoked in order to determine a course of action. The only real recommendation from this objective is to not choose a bad path. The uniqueness of the optimum for the optimality criterion does tell the planner to choose one particular program. There is no ambiguity about the optimal course of action.

3.4   Recursive Utility and the Ramsey Problem

The objective function of the one-sector optimal growth problem with recursive utility is usually specified in terms of an aggregator function. The main concern in our review of existence theory for recursive objectives is to stress the nature of joint conditions on preferences and technology that support the existence argument. The recursive optimal growth problem is formally defined by the programming problem:

$$J(k) = \sup W(c_1, U(SC)) = U(C) \text{ subject to } C \in F(k), \tag{$\mathscr{G}$}$$

where J is the optimal return or value function, W is the aggregator, U is the utility function, and $F(k)$ defines the set of consumption attainable programs.

The common aggregators discussed earlier are all consistent with the existence of optimal programs when the technology exhibits a positive maximum sustainable stock b. More generally, an optimum exists for any β-myopic or weakly β-myopic aggregator defined on a β-bounded set $X(\beta)$; the details are in Boyd (1986a) and are another application of the classical Weierstrass Theorem. Finally, given strict concavity of the utility and total output functions, we may conclude that there is a unique optimal program.

Given the existence of optimal paths for a large class of programs, we are interested in writing down a characterization of the optimum. Boyd's complete characterization results for recursive utility apply when $U \in \mathcal{U}$ and the technology is given by a sequence of one-period classical total output functions satisfying $f_t(0) = 0$. He also assumes that the attainable consumption set is generated by an α-bounded technology for some $\alpha < \beta$. These conditions are taken to be maintained assumptions in the next two theorems.

Envelope Theorem: The value function is increasing and concave. If U is differentiable with respect to consumption in period 1, then J is differentiable and obeys $J'(y) = U_1(C)$ where C is any optimal path from the initial income $y = f_1(k)$. If U is recursive, then $J'(y) = W_1(c_1, U(SC))$.

Proof: See Boyd (1986a), p.20.

QED

The Kuhn–Tucker conditions for an optimal path (C, X) are known as the *Euler* or *no-arbitrage equations* and are necessary conditions for optimality. These conditions are (30) where the utility function is assumed to be differentiable in each period's consumption separately and satisfying the Inada condition.

$$U_{t+1}(C)f'(x_t) \leqslant U_t(C), \text{ with equality if } x_t > 0. \tag{30}$$

(If U fails to satisfy the Inada condition, then the inequality (30) can also hold in the opposite sense if $x_t = f_t(x_{t-1})$. The Inada condition rules this out since it would now allow $c_t = 0$ in an optimal plan.) The interpretation of the Euler condition is that a one-period reversed arbitrage is not profitable on an optimal path. This means that the cost at $t = 1$ from acquiring an extra unit of capital at time t, $U_t(C)$, is at least as great as the benefit realized at time $t + 1$, discounted back to $t = 1$, from selling that additional unit of capital at $t + 1$ for consumption. The extra unit of capital yields $f'(x_t)$ units of the consumption good at time $t + 1$; each unit of that good is worth $U_{t+1}(C)$ utils in period one. For the discounted Ramsey model with TAS utility and discount factor δ, the Euler equation takes the form

$$\delta f'(x_t)u'(c_{t+1}) \leqslant u'(c_t), \text{ with equality if } x_t > 0. \tag{31}$$

The necessary condition for a stationary optimal path in the TAS case becomes $c = f(x) - x$ and $\delta f'(x) = 1$; the unique solution to the Euler equation is called the *modified golden rule*, denoted by $(c[\delta], x[\delta])$. The golden rule case results when $\delta = 1$.

The *transversality condition* holds along the attainable path (C,X) if

$$(TVC_\infty) \quad \lim_{t \to} x_t U_t(C) = 0.$$

The necessity of the transversality condition can be interpreted as a type of no-arbitrage condition for *unreversed arbitrages*. This interpretation of the transversality conditions was originally suggested by Gray and Salant (1983). We develop the intuition behind the transversality condition for the recursive utility model by use of their no-arbitrage concept. Assume that (C,X) is optimal. Suppose that the planner decides to increase the first period's consumption; this is possible if the planner forgoes one unit of capital (to be used for next period's production). The marginal gain to the planner is $U_1(C)$ in units of utility at time one. Let T be a natural number. A T-*period reversed arbitrage* occurs if at time $T + 1$ the planner reacquires the unit of capital forgone at time one. There are two costs incurred by the acquisition at time $T + 1$. First, there is the *direct cost* or *repurchase cost* of *forgone* consumption which arises from converting a unit of consumption at time $T + 1$ to a unit of capital to be saved for the next period's production. This direct cost equals $U_{T+1}(C)$ in utils of time period one. The *indirect cost* arises because the *net marginal product* of that unit of capital is lost to the planner in every period between $t = 2$ and $t = T + 1$; this is a forgone shadow interest loss. The indirect cost at time t in utils of time one is

$$U_t(C)[f'(x_{t-1}) - 1].$$

Adding those lost utils yields the present value (focal date 1) of the indirect costs of the arbitrage as the figure

$$\sum_{t=2}^{T+1} U_t(C)[f'(x_{t-1})-1].$$

Therefore, the total cost of this arbitrage equals the sum of the direct and indirect costs:

$$\sum_{t=2}^{T+1} U_t(C)[f'(x_{t-1})-1]+U_{T+1}(C).$$

A necessary condition for optimality of the program (C,X) is that for any T the marginal benefit of a T-period reversed arbitrage is equal to its marginal (discounted) cost. Thus

$$U_1(C)=\sum_{t=2}^{T+1} U_t(C)[f'(x_{t-1})-1]+U_{T+1}(C). \tag{32}$$

For $T=1$, the equation above reduces to the Euler equation. The infinite horizon means the planner could also contemplate the profitability of an *unreversed arbitrage* in which the unit of capital is permanently sacrificed at $t=1$. There are no repurchase costs associated with an unreversed arbitrage, hence the zero marginal profit condition for an unreversed arbitrage must be

$$U_1(C)=\sum_{t=2}^{\infty} U_t(C)[f'(x_{t-1})-1]. \tag{33}$$

But (32) and (33) can hold as $T\to\infty$ only if

$$\lim_{T\to\infty} U_T=0, \tag{34}$$

which implies the transversality condition. Thus, the transversality condition expresses the zero marginal profit condition for the open-ended arbitrages which are only admissible in the infinite horizon context.

Complete Characterization Theorem: An attainable path (C,X) with initial stocks k is optimal if and only if the Euler equations and the transversality conditions hold.

Proof: See Boyd (1986a), pp.20–2.

QED

Notice that the (maintained assumptions) hypotheses of the Complete Characterization Theorem are themselves only sufficient conditions for the result. The aggregator $W(z,w)=\log z+\delta w$, $0<\delta<1$, and Cobb–Douglas technology $f(x)=x^{\rho}$, $0<\rho<1$, has the optimal value function given by $J(y_1)=J(1)+[1/(1-\rho\delta)]\log y_1$ (see Boyd, 1986b). The Euler and transversality conditions are necessary and sufficient for this specification of the model.

The dynamics of the classical Ramsey model can be worked out with further restrictions on preferences and technology. For the logarithmic utility example just given, the optimal capital path can be found by iterating the difference equation $x_{t+1} = \rho\delta[x_t]^\rho$ for $t = 0, 1, \ldots$, with $x_0 = k$; notice that the optimal path is monotinic and converges to the modified golden rule capital stock $x^* = [1/\rho\delta]^{(1/\rho - 1)}$. The optimal consumption plan in this example is found by setting $c_t = [1 - \rho\delta]y_t$, where $y_t = f(x_{t-1})$. If the initial capital lies below (above) the modified golden rule, then the optimal path of capital and consumption increases (decreases) with time; the modified golden rule is the unique globally asymptotically stable steady state of the model. The dynamics of the model are such that the very long-run dynamics of the economy following the optimal path are described by approximate steady-state behavior. Furthermore, the rate of return to capital is falling (rising) and the wage rate is increasing (decreasing) over time; these pricing concepts will be clarified in the discussion of perfect foresight equilibrium.

A one-sector optimal accumulation program has the *monotonicity property* if the capital and consumption sequences are monotone functions of time. We claim that the monotonicity property of the optimal plan is one of the most important results in the one-sector model. Of course, the monotonicity property is not a general characteristic of these models when the technology is time varying. For example, introduce exogeneous technical progress into the previously given example by letting the total output function be $f_t(x) = \exp(\gamma t)x^\rho$ for some given $\gamma > 0$. By using a *symmetry argument* due to Boyd (1986b, pp.16–17, p.23), the optimal consumption plan is given by $c_t = [1 - \rho\delta]y_t$, where y_t is the planner's income at time t. The optimal consumption can be written out as

$$c_t = [1 - \rho\delta]g \exp\{\gamma(\rho^t - \rho t + t - 1)(1 - \rho^{-2} + \rho^{t-1}\log(y/g)\},$$

where $g = [\rho\delta]^{(1/(1-\rho))}$ and $y = f_1(k)$ for $k > 0$ the given initial stock of capital. Although the technology grows at a constant rate, the growth rate of consumption varies. Asymptotically, the optimal path grows at rate $\delta/(1 - \rho)$; for finite times, its behavior may vary. For example, if $\rho\gamma = 1/2$, δ is between 0 and 1, $y = g^2 = \delta^2/4$, then the first three periods' consumption turn out to be

$$c_1 = [1 - g^2]e^4, \ c_2 = [1 - g^2]e^{3.5}, \ c_1 = [1 - g^2]e^{3.75}.$$

The optimal consumption path is U-shaped over time, which is not monotonic. On the other hand, it is interesting to note that the monotonicity property is observed in some non-classical technologies with time additive separable utility. Thus, there is some interest in classifying the possible formulations of the Ramsey model on the basis of this qualitative characteristic.

Which recursive utility Ramsey models exhibit the monotonicity property?

There are two sufficient conditions for the monotonicity of the optimal path when the objective function is recursive. The first condition is due to Beals and Koopmans (1969). The second was given by Benhabib, Majumdar, and Nishimura (1986). Both sets of authors rely on a concept of 'normality'. We will argue that there is a distinction between the two concepts of normality proposed so far. We will give a simplified proof of the monotonicity property using the normality idea of Benhabib, Majumdar, and Nishimura under an additional set of restrictions which may be justified on expositional grounds. The monotonicity of the optimal program has been investigated by Leviatan (1970), Iwai (1972), and Boyer (1975) along the lines we will follow. Magill and Nishimura (1984) weaken the assumptions in Beals and Koopmans and derive the monotonicity property. Epstein (1986) introduced implicitly additive utility functions in order to study a general class of objectives yielding the monotonicity of the optimal capital path.

The proof of the monotonicity property depends on establishing the Non-crossing property; this is combined with Bellman's Principle of Optimality and the time consistency of an optimal policy to demonstrate that the optimal path of capital is a monotonic sequence.

Let $J(y)$ denote the optimal return function where $y = f(k)$ denotes the initial starting stock. The recursive structure of utility as represented by the aggregator W allows us to state that an optimal program for the model ($\mathscr{G}$) must satisfy

$$J(y) = \sup \{W(c, J(f(y-c))): 0 \leqslant c \leqslant y\}. \tag{$\mathscr{B}$}$$

Equation ($\mathscr{B}$) represents *Bellman's Principle of Optimality* and is called the *optimality equation*. This equation plays a fundamental role in the analysis of optimal programs.

Let $C(y) = \{c_t[y]\}$ and $X(y) = \{x_t[y]\}$ denote the optimal sequences of consumption and capital, respectively, given the value of the starting stock y. We say that the model ($\mathscr{G}$) has the *strong non-crossing property* if for each pair of initial stocks y and y', $y > y'$ implies $x_t[y] > x_t[y']$ for all t. The *non-crossing property* holds if for each pair of initial stocks y and y', $y > y'$ implies $x_1[y] > x_1[y']$. The solution $X(y)$ exhibits the *monotonicity property* if $\{x_t[y]\}$ is a monotonic sequence. The *(strong) consumption non-crossing and monotonicity properties* hold if the analogous conditions are met by the optimal consumption sequences $C(y)$ and $C(y')$.

Assume for the remainder of this section that the aggregator W is C^2 and concave. The aggregator W is *normal* if $D(z,y)$ is a strictly decreasing function of z for each given y, where

$$D(z,y) = W_1(z,y)/W_2(z,y);$$

we refer to this property of D as condition ($\mathscr{N}$). This normality hypothesis was first stated in Beals and Koopmans (1969). They argue (pp.1004–5) the condition ($\mathcal{N}$) is essentially a statement that consumption in neither of any two adjacent periods is inferior to that in the other period in the usual sense of demand theory. The aggregator W is *supermodular* if

$$W_{12}(z,y) \geqslant 0. \qquad (\mathcal{SM})$$

This implies their normality concept. The converse is false; use the UEH case. In the application of condition ($\mathcal{SM}$), the normality hypothesis is placed on the analog of the income consumption curve for the *induced utility function* $\omega(c,y) = W(c,J(f(y-c)))$ that is used in ($\mathcal{B}$). The normality condition for ω in the (c,y)-space originates in the papers of Leviatan, Iwai, and Boyer. Benhabib, Majumdar, and Nishimura (1986) introduced a more explicit form of ($\mathcal{SM}$) for recursive models. The term supermodularity is due to Ross (1983); the statement ($\mathcal{SM}$) is the differentiable version of his hypothesis.

The key result for paths of capital accumulation is the

Non-crossing Theorem: If either condition ($\mathcal{N}$) or ($\mathcal{SM}$) apply to ($\mathcal{G}$), then ($\mathcal{G}$) has the non-crossing property.

Proofs of this theorem may be found in Beals and Koopmans (1969) when condition ($\mathcal{N}$) holds and in Benhabib, Majumdar, and Nishimura (1986) in the other case. We give a simple proof of the theorem below for strictly concave aggregators satisfying ($\mathcal{SM}$) under the additional assumption that J is C^2. It is clear that J is also concave. The idea of the proof is to use a dynamic programming style of argument to reduce an infinite number of choices to a sequence of decisions.

We introduce the *optimal consumption function* or *policy function* $c = g(y)$ which from ($\mathcal{B}$) (and the uniqueness of the optimum given y) satisfies

$$J(y) = W(g(y), J(f(y - g(y)))).$$

The function g may be found by using the implicit function theorem on the first-order necessary conditions for the maximization problem on the right-hand side of ($\mathcal{B}$). Assuming an interior solution, that first-order necessary condition is (omitting arguments of the partial derivatives)

$$W_1 - W_2 J'f' = 0.$$

Use $N(c,y)$ to denote the function $W_1 - W_2 J'f'$. The second-order sufficient condition for this maximization exercise holds; it is recorded as $N_1 < 0$ where

$$N_1 = W_{11} - 2W_{12}J'f' + W_{22}(J'f')^2 + W_2[J''f' + J'f''].$$

The role of W strictly concave and condition ($\mathscr{SM}$) is to yield the negative sign for N_2 (below). The implicit function theorem may now be invoked to produce the optimal consumption function; note that this function is C^1 on $(0,b)$.

Lemma 4: For each $y \in (0,b)$, $0 < g'(y) < 1$.

Proof: Computing $g'(y)$ from the implicit function theorem yields $g'(y) = -N_2/N_1$ where

$$-N_2 = -W_{12}J'f' + W_{22}J'f' + W_2[J''f' + J'f''] < 0.$$

This implies $0 < g'$; by rewriting g', we have

$$g' = -N_2/\{W_{11} - W_{12}J'f' - N_2\}.$$

Comparing the numerator and denominator, it is clear that $g' < 1$ must hold.

QED

Define the *optimal investment function*, $i(y) = y - g(y)$.

Corollary. $i'(y) > 0$.

The Non-crossing Theorem is a consequence of the fact that the investment function is increasing in the starting stocks. Given the additional hypotheses on W and J stated above, we record the proof of the Non-crossing Theorem below when W satisfies the supermodular condition.

Proof (Non-crossing Theorem): Let $f(k) = y$ and $f(k') = y'$. We assume $k > k'$; thus $y > y'$ and the corollary implies

$$x_1[y] = i(y) > x_1[y'] = i(y').$$

QED

The proof of this theorem also demonstrates the weaker condition: $y' \leqslant y$ implies $x_1[y'] \leqslant x_1[y]$. If the initial stock is raised from y' to y, then the stocks go up in every period. To see this, continue the argument of the theorem inductively. This is recorded as the

Strong Non-crossing Theorem: If either condition ($\mathscr{N}$) or ($\mathscr{SM}$) apply to ($\mathscr{G}$), then ($\mathscr{G}$) has the strong non-crossing property.

The Non-crossing Theorems also imply that optimal consumption increases in every period when there is an increase in the starting stocks; this occurs because the optimal policy function g is increasing in y.

Consumption Non-crossing Theorem: If either condition $(\mathcal{N})$ or $(\mathcal{S}\mathcal{M})$ apply to $(\mathcal{G})$, then $(\mathcal{G})$ has the strong consumption non-crossing property.

Given the Non-crossing Theorems, the next result is easy to demonstrate as a consequence of the recursivity and stationarity of the objective and constraints. The Monotonicity Theorem is then a consequence of the time consistency of any solution to this model as embodied in Bellman's Principle.

Monotonicity Theorem: If either condition $(\mathcal{N})$ or $(\mathcal{S}\mathcal{M})$ apply to $(\mathcal{G})$, then an optimal capital sequence $X(y)$ for $(\mathcal{G})$ has the monotonicity property.

Proof: Let $X(y)$ be optimal for the problem $(\mathcal{G})$ with initial stocks $y = f(k)$ available at time zero. At $t = 1$, define $k' = x_1[y]$ and $y' = f(k')$. Then $\{x_t[y']\}$ $(t = 2,3,...)$ is optimal for $(\mathcal{G})$ with initial stocks y' starting at time one. Bellman's Principle yields the time consistency of the optimum; thus $x_t[y'] = x_t[y]$ for $t = 2,3,...$. But, $\{x_{t-1}[y']\}$ $(t = 2,3,...)$ is also optimal for the starting stocks y' at time zero. Therefore, if $y \leqslant y'$, the Non-crossing Theorem implies $x_1[y'] \geqslant x_1[y]$; but $x_1[y'] = x_2[y]$. Therefore, $x_2[y] \geqslant x_1[y]$. The rest follows by induction on t. If $k_1 > k$, then the weak inequality is strict. Similarly, if the optimal sequence begins by decreasing, then the inequalities are reversed.

QED

Consumption Monotonicity Theorem: If either condition $(\mathcal{N})$ or $(\mathcal{S}\mathcal{M})$ apply to $(\mathcal{G})$, then an optimal consumption sequence $C(y)$ for $(\mathcal{G})$ has the monotonicity property.

We note in passing that the monotonicity property may hold in a trivial way for a large set of values of the initial data: consider the Rawlsian aggregator $W(z,y) = \min\{z,y\}$. If the initial capital is below the golden rule capital, then the optimal path is to stay put, i.e. set $c = f(k) - k$. In the TAS case, the Monotonicity Theorem implies the modified golden rule is globally asymptotically stable (see the other works referred to for stability in the general aggregator case); uniqueness of a non-trivial steady state plus either of the conditions $(\mathcal{N})$ or $(\mathcal{S}\mathcal{M})$ imply the asymptotic stability of the steady state. It is important to note that in the general aggregator case, a steady-state capital and consumption program is determined as a stationary solution to the Euler equations. In the general aggregator case, this means that the steady-state rate of impatience is endogenously determined, in contrast to the case of the TAS aggregator with a predetermined rate of impatience $\delta^{-1} - 1$ (see Beals and Koopmans, 1969; and Lucas and Stokey, 1984, for a discussion of hypotheses on the rate of marginal impatience related to the uniqueness and stability of steady states in the non-TAS aggregator case).

Examples of aggregators satisfying one or both of the conditions $(\mathcal{N})$ or $(\mathcal{SM})$ may be given. It is straightforward to show that the TAS, UEH, and KDW aggregators satisfy condition $(\mathcal{N})$. Of these three, the TAS aggregator is the only one to satisfy $(\mathcal{SM})$; in both the UEH and KDW cases, $W_{12} < 0$. The Koopmans concave quadratic aggregator satisfies $(\mathcal{N})$ and $(\mathcal{SM})$.

The Non-crossing Theorem is a comparative dynamics result. It applies to both classical and non-classical technologies with a TAS utility function having a fixed discount factor (Majumdar and Mitra, 1982; Dechert and Nishimura, 1983). Majumdar (1984) shows it also extends to some non-stationary felicity functions. Other comparative dynamics properties of an optimal path for the Ramsey model with TAS utility have also been worked out for some experiments.

Consider the TAS model with classical technology. The analysis of the impact of a change in δ is given in the next theorem. This result addresses one of the questions raised by Joan Robinson in her essay 'The Rate of Interest', as noted in the introduction. An increase in δ corresponds to an increase in the 'level of thriftiness' in our model. In this framework we are able to give a precise meaning to the concept of thriftiness and work out the implications of a change in thriftiness on the optimal path of accumulation.

Increasing Time Preference Theorem: Fix a Ramsey model with TAS utility and classical total output function satisfying $(f.1)$–$(f.3)$ and $f(0) = 0$. Assume J is a C^2 function. Let $0 < \delta < \delta' < 1$; keep k fixed and denote by $(C[\delta], X[\delta])$ and $(C[\delta'], X[\delta'])$ the corresponding optimal paths. Let $(c[\delta], x[\delta]$ and $(c(\delta'], x[\delta'])$ denote the modified golden rule pairs for these two discount rates. Then

(1) $(c[\delta], x[\delta]) < (c[\delta'], x[\delta'])$;

(2) $x_t[\delta] < x_t[\delta']$ for all $t \geqslant 1$;

(3) There exists T such that $c_t[\delta] > c_t[\delta']$ for $t < T$ and $c_t[\delta] < c_t[\delta']$ for all $t \geqslant T$.

Proof: (1) is well known, see Burmeister and Turnovsky (1972). Results (2) and (3) may be found in Becker (1983a, 1985b).

$$\text{QED}$$

The conclusion of the previous theorem tells us that an increase in the discount factor results in a greater capital stock at each time (past zero); but this increase in the capital stock has a short-run price to be paid in terms of an initial segment of reduced consumption. Eventually, the increased capital stock provides a higher consumption stream. These results are the dynamic analog of steady-state regularity as introduced by Burmeister and Turnovsky (1972).

The comparative dynamics theorems stated above may be linked to the monotonicity property of the optimum. These results represent the *Laws of Change* for the classical Ramsey model. One of the most important questions in the one-sector theory is to prove extensions of the increasing time preference comparative dynamics results for a general recursive utility specification of the model.

The comparative dynamics properties found for the classical one-sector TAS model illustrate the importance of true dynamic comparisons instead of just comparing steady states. When a parameter shifts, the planner contemplates *all* the attainable paths that are open with the new data; the entire optimal path with the new data is compared with the old optimum on a period by period basis. Since the new steady state may not even be feasible with the new data in one step, the dynamic opportunities open to the planner form the proper frame of reference for stating a comparative dynamics result. Put differently, the comparison of steady states without a full analysis of the transition path is not a legitimate stopping point for a comparative dynamics study. Our views on comparative dynamics and the Cambridge controversy are thus in line with those voiced by Burmeister (1980). He argues (ch.4) that the failure to do a complete comparative dynamic analysis is one of the reasons for the 'misunderstanding' fuelling the debate over 'paradoxical' steady states. We shall have more to say on the subject of comparative dynamics once the market equilibrium framework is developed in the next section.

4   ONE-SECTOR MODELS: DECENTRALIZATION

4.1   The Equivalence Principle

Perfect planning and perfect markets form a dual pair. Put differently, a market equilibrium is a social optimum and a social optimum is a market equilibrium. This idea is the basis for the First and Second Fundamental Welfare Theorems in the Walrasian competitive equilibrium framework. Are there analogs of the Fundamental Theorems in infinite horizon models of capital accumulation? We have seen that a competitive equilibrium in an intertemporal economy can be inefficient due to the overaccumulation of capital. Samuelson's consumption loan model provides the example where the First Fundamental Welfare Theorem fails in an intertemporal set-up. Yet other studies find the market rates a poor second in relation to the social optimum found by the planner (see Spulber and Becker, 1986). In short, the possibility of a market equilibrium to realize a social optimum is open to question in intertemporal allocation models.

In this section we investigate the welfare theorems in the context of the one-sector Ramsey model. An infinitely lived omniscient planner is used to define the social optimum as a problem of optimal growth. The concept of a perfect foresight competitive equilibrium is introduced in order to formulate a market equilibrium model with an infinitely lived household; we concentrate on the representative household case in our initial discussion of the models. The *Equivalence Principle* states that an optimum allocation in the Ramsey optimal growth model is also a perfect foresight competitive equilibrium allocation in the market model and that the converse is also valid; the welfare theorems carry over to the Ramsey model.

The development of the Equivalence Principle for Ramsey models is discussed in Becker (1981, 1982, 1983, 1985a) and Burmeister (1980). A related idea in a partial equilibrium adjustment cost model of an industry may be found in Lucas and Prescott (1971) and Scheinkman (1978). The idea that a solution to a Ramsey model of optimal growth is an equilibrium and vice versa has been implicit in the optimal growth theoretic literature since the seminal contribution of Ramsey.

In general, the analysis of dynamic market equilibrium problems is difficult owing to the non-stationary nature of the agent's optimization problems. The prices used to define the household's budget constraint may be fluctuating over time. The validity of the Equivalence Principle for a class of optimal growth–market equilibrium models greatly simplifies the analysis of the market equilibrium problem; the properties enjoyed by an equilibrium may be read off from those of the optimal growth model. In particular, the existence, uniqueness, stability, and comparative dynamics properties of a market equilibrium solution follow from the analogous properties of the optimal growth model.

A more significant role for the Equivalence Principle is that it provides a *mechanism* by which a decentralized economy can achieve a social optimum. This aspect of the Equivalence Principle (as well as its proof) is closely tied to the necessity of a *transversality condition* in the market equilibrium model. As we saw in Section 3.4, the transversality condition is a type of no-arbitrage condition across *infinitely* many dates; the passage from an Euler necessary condition representing a no-arbitrage property for any finite number of dates to a condition stretching over the indefinite future has always been bothersome to capital theorists. Consequently, the necessity of the transversality condition has been an important issue in the debates over both the meaning and possibility of decentralization in infinite horizon capital accumulation models. This is particularly true in the discussion of the so-called *Hahn problem* first encountered in descriptive growth models (see Hahn, 1966; Burmeister, 1980, ch.6; Becker, 1981).

We postulate the optimal growth problem described by ($\mathscr{G}$) with a recursive utility objective in order to bring out the crucial assumptions needed to provide a proof of the Equivalence Principle. The utility function is assumed without further comment to be strictly concave throughout the discussion of the Equivalence Principle. We call a solution to this program a *Ramsey optimum* or a *Ramsey optimal path of accumulation*. The set of Ramsey optima is denoted by $\mathscr{R}(k)$; the dependence on the aggregator (or utility) function and technology f are suppressed in this notation since these are fixed in the discussion of the Equivalence Principle.

The market equilibrium model is based on the postulate of a representative household with perfect foresight about the time paths of output and factor prices. The representative household axiom is a proxy for the assumption of a 'large' number of identical households; in equilibrium no household will have an incentive to deviate from the behavior of the average or representative agent.

There are two alternative ways to define the household's intertemporal budget constraint. The first form is sequential; current prices are used to value goods in any period and a one-period rental-interest rate for capital goods is the price which links adjacent periods. This approach is symmetric to the recursive structure of the constraints in the optimal growth model. It is also useful for representing models where the agent cannot borrow against future labor income and therefore must face a budget constraint at each date. The alternative model is found by using present value prices and permitting the agent to borrow and lend subject to repayment of all debts as time stretches to infinity. In this view of the budget constraint, anticipated labor income may be capitalized to the present. In the representative household world, these two views of the budget constraint are essentially the same; the representative agent cannot find any agent willing to act as either a lender or borrower since all agents are identical. Therefore, it makes no difference whether we model the budget constraint in present value form or in sequential form. We will discuss the sequential form of the constraint in this paper because it is the format of the 'Ramsey Equilibrium' model with many agents and incomplete market which we take up in Section 4.5.

The representative household perfectly anticipates a profile of factor returns $R = \{r_t + 1\}$ and $\mathscr{W} = \{w_t\}$, where $r_t + 1$ is the one-period rental rate for capital goods supplied at the beginning of time t and used to produce goods of period t and w_t is the wage in period t. Notice that the factor returns at t are measured in units of the composite consumption-capital good found at time t. The rental of capital is compensated with a one-period lag in the sense that the input of capital at the start of period t equals the stock of capital at the end of period $t - 1$. The current price of the composite consumption-capital good is normalized at one in every period – this is the current value price system's numeraire.

The household's income at time t consists of capital income $(1 + r_t)x_{t-1}$, and labor income w_t. The amount of capital at time which earns interest, r_t, plus principle is x_{t-1}. The household supplies one unit of labor inelastically at each moment of time. At each time t, the household must divide its income between consumption and savings of physical capital which will provide the next period's capital income. The consumption decision is denoted by c_t and the savings decision may be represented by the terminal stock of the period, x_t. The preference relation of the household is taken to be the recursive utility function of the planner. The optimization problem of the household is stated for specific R and $\mathcal{W}$ sequences as the program:

$$\sup W(c_1, U(SC)) = U(C) \text{ subject to } C \in B(R, \mathcal{W}, k), \qquad (\mathcal{H})$$

where

$C \in B(R, \mathcal{W}, k)$ if and only if there is an X such that

$$c_t + x_t \leqslant w_t + (1+r_t)x_{t-1} \ (t=1,2,...);$$

$$c_t, x_{t-1} \geqslant 0 \ (t=1,2,...) \text{ and } x_0 \leqslant k.$$

A solution to $(\mathcal{H})$ for given R and $\mathcal{W}$ yields the planned sequence of household consumption demands, $C(R, \mathcal{W})$, and planned capital supply sequence $X(R, \mathcal{W})$. The dependence of these demand and supply sequences on the initial stock is implicit in this notation.

The production sector has the myopic profit maximization problem at each time given the anticipated sequence R:

$$\sup \{f(x_{t-1}) - (1+r_t)x_{t-1}: x_{t-1} \geqslant 0\}. \qquad (\mathcal{P})$$

The wage bill is treated as a residual payment in this model. The solution to this problem defines the production sector's demand for capital and supply of output at each time. The production sector's problem is myopic because there are no internal costs of adjusting the capital stock input; the market for capital input rentals is perfect as is the output market at each date. Therefore, there is no intertemporal decision for the production sector. Put differently, discounted profit maximization (using the interest factors $1+r_t$) is equivalent to the myopic problem $(\mathcal{P})$ at each time (see Arrow, 1964). The economically relevant intertemporal allocation decisions are concentrated in the hands of the household sector.

Definition: Sequences $\{R, \mathcal{W}, C, X\}$ constitute a Perfect Foresight Competitive Equilibrium, abbreviated PFCE, if

(a) $(C, X) = (C(R, \mathcal{W}), X(R, \mathcal{W}));$

(b) $x_{t-1} = \text{argmax} [f(x) - (1 + r_t)x]$ at each t;

(c) $w_t = f(x_{t-1}) - (1 + r_t)x_{t-1}$ at each t;

(d) $c_t + x_t \leqslant f(x_{t-1})$ at each t.

Notice that the definition of PFCE implies $x_0 \leqslant k$. The first condition says that the consumption and capital sequences are optimal for the household given the anticipated factor profiles R and $\mathscr{W}$. The second condition expresses profit maximization at each time and the third condition says that profits are distributed to the workers as a residual payment (think of labor as the entrepreneurial factor). The last condition is the goods markets balance at each time. We also refer to this condition as the *flow market equilibrium* condition. It states that the planned consumption demand and saving equals output at time t. There is also a form of *Walras Law* at each time which yields a *stock market equilibrium* condition: properties (a), (c), and (d) may be combined to show that property (b) necessarily follows in a PFCE. The equality of planned capital demand by the production sector and planned capital supply by the household sector constitutes a stock market equilibrium condition which is implicit if the remaining equilibrium conditions hold.

Let $\mathscr{E}(k)$ denote the set of PFCE allocations of consumption and capital. The *Equivalence Principle* asserts that under suitable conditions on the data (U,A), $\mathscr{R}(k) = \mathscr{E}(k)$. This means that each Ramsey optimum allocation is a PFCE allocation and vice versa. Therefore, the Equivalence Principle described a form of the First and Second Fundamental Welfare Theorems for the Ramsey model of capital accumulation. The verification of the Equivalence Principle is based on matching the no-arbitrage (Euler) and transversality conditions which characterize the solutions of the optimal growth model and the market equilibrium model. It is easy to prove the no-arbitrage conditions hold for an optimal solution of the household's problem in a PFCE; just follow the same line of reasoning given for the optimal growth model in Section 3.4. The difficult problem is to determine whether or not the transversality condition is necessary. We say that the transversality condition is valid for the PFCE (C,X,R,W) if the (TVC_∞) is a necessary condition for a PFCE.

Lemma 5: If $U \in \mathscr{U}$, then the transversality condition is valid for a PFCE path.

Proof: The proof combines the arguments in Becker (1985a) and Boyd (1986a). Let $X(\beta)$ be the β-bounded subset of s^+ for which U is represented by the aggregator W in the model $(\mathscr{G})$. Then, in a PFCE, the equilibrium consumption and capital paths are elements of $X(\beta)$; moreover, the sequence of equilibrium wages is also an element of that set. Since $U \in \mathscr{U}$, Lemma 2 implies that for any $C \in X(\beta)$,

$$\lim_{t \to \infty} \delta^{t-1} U(S^t C) = 0. \tag{35}$$

In particular, (35) applies to the equilibrium sequence of wages. We note that for the PFCE consumption and equilibrium wages $\{w_t\}$

$$\lim_{t \to \infty} \delta^{t-1}[U(S^t C) - U(S^t\{w_t\})] = 0. \tag{36}$$

Given the equilibrium sequences of rental and wage rates r_t and w_t, respectively, define a sequence of optimal return functions $J_t: (0,b) \to \mathbb{R}_+$ by setting

$$J_t(y_t'') = \sup W(c_t'', U(S^t C''))$$

by choice of non-negative sequences C'' and X'' subject to

$$c_t'' + x_t'' = y_t''$$

$$c_s'' + x_s'' = w_s + (1 + r_s) x_{s-1}'' \text{ for } s \geq t.$$

Note that at time t the wage and rental as well as the previous period's capital are fixed, so y_t'' is determined from those data. Note that the previous period's capital may differ from that period's stock realized in the given PFCE. Clearly, $J_t(0) \geq 0$ and J_t is non-decreasing in y_t''; thus $J_t \geq 0$. By mimicking the arguments in Becker (1985a, Lemma 2) and Boyd (1986a), we claim without further proof that J_t is a concave function on $[0,b]$, has a finite value at y_t corresponding to the PFCE output level at time t, and J_t is C^1 on $(0,b)$. The derivative of J_t at the PFCE y_t has the envelope property

$$J_t'(y_t) = W_1(c_t, U(S^t C)).$$

Since J_t is concave, we have the inequality

$$J_t(y_t) - J_t(0) \geq J_t'(y_t) y_t \geq W_1(c_t, U(S^t C)) f(x_{t-1}) \geq W_1(c_t, U(S^t C)) x_t \tag{37}$$

by $y_t = f(x_{t-1}) \geq x_t$ in PFCE. But

$$U_t(C) = W_2(c_1, U(SC)) \ldots W_2(c_{t-1}, U(S^{t-1}C)) W_1(c_t, U(S^t C)).$$

Let $\delta = \max\{W_2(c_i, U(S^i C)): 1 \leq i \leq t-1\}$; the properties of W imply that $0 < \delta < 1$. Thus $U_t(C) \leq \delta^{t-1} W_1(c_t, U(S^t C))$; multiplying (37) through by δ^{t-1} and simplifying implies

$$\delta^{t-1}[J_t(y_t) - J_t(0)] \geq U_t(C)) x_t \geq 0. \tag{38}$$

But $J_t(y_t) = U(S^tC)$ and $J_t(0) \geqslant U(S^t\mathscr{W})$, hence

$$\delta^{t-1}[U(S^tC) - U(S^t\mathscr{W})] \geqslant U_t(C))x_t \geqslant 0. \tag{39}$$

Letting $t \to \infty$, (36) and (39) imply that $U_t(C)x_t \to 0$, which is the transversality condition.

QED

The Inada condition implies that the household will never desire zero consumption, hence the Euler conditions will be equalities in both the household and central planner's problem. The proof of the Equivalence Principle proceeds by matching the Euler or no-arbitrage and transversality conditions of the optimality and equilibrium models. In the equilibrium model the transversality condition need only be a valid necessary condition in a perfect foresight equilibrium. Put differently, the household sector's transversality condition may not be valid for an *arbitrary* profile of wages and rentals. The matching of the first-order conditions in the two frameworks proves the Equivalence Principle because those conditions are *complete characterizations* of the agents' problems in the respective frameworks. The necessity of the transversality condition in the PFCE setting is also an extreme form of the efficient market's hypothesis since it may be interpreted as saying that the present value price of a unit of capital is equal to the discounted sum of the stream of future rental rates – just mimic the heuristic argument for the (TVC_∞) given in Section 3.4 in the PFCE set-up.

Equivalence Theorem: The Equivalence Principle holds whenever $U \in \mathscr{U}$ satisfies the Inada condition at $0, f$ is classical and satisfies the Inada condition at 0, and k is positive.

Proof: The proof is to match the Euler and transversality conditions in the PFCE and optimal growth models. The sufficiency of these conditions follows from Boyd's (1986a) arguments; their necessity follows from his arguments and our Lemma 5.

QED

The conditions of the theorem are only *sufficient* for the Equivalence Principle to obtain for the model (U,f,k). For example, let the aggregator be defined as $W(z,y) = \log z + \delta y$, $0 < \delta < 1$ given, and set $f(x) = x^a$, with $0 < a < 1$ a fixed parameter. Using Boyd's (1986b) symmetry argument we may show that the Equivalence Principle holds for this model. In fact, we can show that the transversality condition holds in the PFCE model as well.

Lemma 6: A PFCE for the Ramsey model with TAS utility, felicity function given by the logarithm of consumption, and Cobb–Douglas total output function satisfies the transversality condition.

The properties of a PFCE may now be inferred from the analogous properties exhibited by the corresponding Ramsey optimum. Since the general analysis of the recursive utility Ramsey problem remains an open question, we simply observe that the key monotonicity property of the optimum is inherited by the equilibrium path under appropriate conditions on the optimal growth model. If capital is increasing along the optimum, then the rental rate is falling and the wage is rising. Capital income is increasing along the optimum–equilibrium path whenever the neoclassical production function F underlying f has an elasticity of substitution greater than or equal to unity. Through the Equivalence Principle, the Ramsey optimization model leads to a general theory of the functional distribution of income. The distribution of factor incomes in a growth model was a central concern of Joan Robinson. Our theory gives a portrait of the model's dynamics that goes beyond a steady-state analysis.

The comparative dynamics of properties of the equilibrium model arising from time preference changes in the household sector may also be inferred as a consequence of the Equivalence Principle. As an example, for TAS utility models, an increase in the household's discount factor can be analyzed just as in the optimal growth setting. The Increasing Time Preference Theorem has an analog in the PFCE set-up. This is one result made possible as an application of the Equivalence Principle.

The Equivalence Principle provides a solution to the Hahn problem. The question raised by Hahn was formulated in a multisector model, but the basic issue arises in the one-sector model. Put briefly, the Hahn question is what determines the 'correct choice' of the initial price of capital (in present value terms) or equivalently the initial consumption in a *decentralized* market economy? Originally, Hahn's problem was bound up with whether or not the equilibrium path was stable. His contention was that the saddle point character of the long-run, steady-state equilibrium opened the possibility (and probability) that a decentralized economy would choose the 'wrong' initial prices or equivalent consumption level and fail to converge to the long-run equilibrium. This potential instability was supposed to be a fundamental flaw in dynamic market economies. There was no obvious choice of mechanism to place the economy on the stable manifold belonging to the steady state. However, stability is in fact not the real economic issue (Becker, 1981); a cyclic path may be an equilibrium in some models. There are two-sector models exhibiting cyclic equilibria (see Section 4.3 for references). This is a consequence of the Equivalence Principle for the two-sector model (see Boldrin, 1986). The stability issue is intertwined with the choice of the initial consumption (price) consistent with the perfect foresight solution in the one-sector case because of the monotonicity property.

Therefore, the Equivalence Principle tells us that whenever there is a *unique* Pareto optimal path, then there is a unique initial consumption choice or initial present price of capital which places the economy on the perfect foresight path. The decentralized perfect foresight market economy imposes a transversality condition on itself in equilibrium which gives an efficient market's connection between the initial price and the anticipated rental stream. This result applies to one-sector models that do not exhibit the monotonicity property (the existence of non-monotonic optima in the one-sector model was conjectured by Iwai (1972) using a recursive, but non-additive utility function; see Benhabib, Majumdar, and Nishimura (1986) for a recent discussion). Interestingly, Hahn (1966) conjectured that shadow prices associated with a social optimum problem might be used to place the market economy on the correct initial path (which in his case meant a stable path). The Equivalence Principle gives a rigorous formulation of this idea and shows that it can be used to resolve the problem at a *theoretical* level. Of course, it would seem that one has to accept the infinitely lived agent and long-run perfect foresight assumptions for this to be an acceptable solution. Hahn (1985, pp.5–6) states that he does not and makes his view of the matter quite clear:

> I took my result to show that warranted paths of the economy as defined by Harrod did not in general seek the steady state. It never occurred to me that anyone would wish to posit perfect foresight over the infinite future. But I was wrong: such a postulate is now commonplace. It still strikes me as dotty.

The story of the Hahn problem does not end with the Equivalence Principle. There are three additional strands of research that can be viewed as reinforcing it as the appropriate *theoretical* resolution of the Hahn problem. The first of these strands is the work on the 'inverse optimum problem'. The second line of research concerns the very conception of decentralization in the representative infinitely lived agent model. The third approach is based on Aiyagiri's Observational Equivalence Theorem for the efficient overlapping generations equilibria and the discounted Ramsey optimum. It is important to note that all three of these lines of inquiry involve additive separable forms of the recursive utility hypothesis.

4.2   Decentralizability Conditions

One of the earliest informal (but characteristically clear) discussions of the problem of decentralization of decisions in an infinite horizon model is due to Koopmans (1958). In what follows, we provide an outline of some of the recent developments that drew on the theory of economic mechanisms (developed by Hurwicz and others) and attempt to treat some aspects in a formal manner.

A concept of an informationally decentralized resource allocation mechanism has to take into account the *initial dispersal of information* with each

economic agent possessing only *partial* knowledge of all the 'given parameters' (environment) in the economy; also it has to recognize *limited
communication and information processing* capabilities of the agents.

Consider an aggregate infinite horizon economy in which an *environment E*
is defined by $E=(F,U,y)$ where $F=\{f_t\}$ is a sequence of production functions,
$U=\{u_t\}$ is a sequence of utility functions, and y is the initial stock (set
$y=f_0(k)$). The designer of the resource allocation mechanism typically does
not know the exact E, but only that E belongs to a set $\mathscr{E}$ of possible
environments (e.g. that each f_t [resp. u_t] belongs to the set of functions
satisfying $(f.1)$, $(f.2)$, and $(f.3)^*$ (defined below) [resp. $(u.1)$–$(u.6)$]). Thus, the
designer cannot calculate the resource allocation programs that meet the
evaluation criterion given the actual E (the sequence evolving over time). The
role of the designer is to set forth the response or behavior rules of the agents
in all the future periods (e.g. producers must verify the intertemporal profit
maximization condition specified in (36)).

To begin with a simple case, suppose that the set $\mathscr{E}$ is restricted as follows:
the technology sequence F is a stationary sequence $F=\{f,f,...\}\equiv F^{(\infty)}$ where
$f:\mathbb{R}_+\to\mathbb{R}_+$ must satisfy $(f.1)$, $(f.2)$, and

$(f.3)^*$ $\lim_{x\downarrow 0} f'(x)=1+\theta_1$ for some $\theta_1>0$;

$\qquad \lim_{x\uparrow\infty} f'(x)=1-\theta_2$ for some θ_2, $1>\theta_2>0$.

Next, the sequence U is of the form $u_t\equiv\delta^t u$, where $0<\delta\leqslant 1$ and u is defined
either on $\mathbb{R}_+$ or $\mathbb{R}_{++}$ with values in $\mathbb{R}$ and must satisfy felicity conditions
$(u.1)$–$(u.6)$.

A feasible program (X,Y,C) from y_0 is *optimal* if for any alternative
program (X',Y',C') starting from y_0,

$$\limsup_{T\uparrow\infty} \sum_{t=0}^{T} \delta^t[u(c_t')-u(c_t)]\leqslant 0.$$

Competitive programs provide the point of departure for formalizing the
notion of informational decentralization. A program (X,Y,C) from y_0 is
competitive if there exists a sequence $P=\{p_t\}$ of prices such that for all $t\geqslant 0$:

$$\delta^t u(c_t)-p_t c_t\geqslant\delta^t u(c)-p_t c \text{ for all } c\geqslant 0; \tag{40}$$

$$p_{t+1}f(x_t)-p_t x_t\geqslant p_{t+1}f(x)-p_t x \text{ for all } x\geqslant 0. \tag{41}$$

Observe that if (X,Y,C) is a competitive program with its associated price
sequence P, it follows that $x_t>0$, $c_t>0$, $y_t>0$, and $p_t>0$ for all $t\geqslant 0$. Next,
whether a program (X,Y,C) is competitive at a price sequence P can be
determined by a period by period verification: the 'consumer' in period t has

to verify whether $c_t > 0$ and whether the equation '$\delta^t u'(c_t) = p_t$' is satisfied [and the producer has to verify whether $x_t > 0$ and whether '$p_{t+1} f'(x_t) = p_t$' is satisfied]. The verification in period t can be carried out with only a finite number of messages (prices and quantities) and with the sole knowledge of the utility and production functions in that period. The consumer [resp. the producer] does *not* know f [resp. u] and if the agents in different periods do not communicate, then they cannot determine whether the stationarity condition holds or not! This *verification scenario* (see Hurwicz, 1986) captures an important aspect of the informal notion of informational decentralization.

With an infinite horizon, a competitive program is not necessarily optimal. Recall the 'standard' result on optimality of competitive programs in terms of the appropriate transversality condition:

Shadow Price Characterization Theorem: A program (X, Y, C) from $y_0 > 0$ is optimal if and only if it is competitive at prices P and

$$p_t x_t \text{ is bounded when } \delta = 1; \tag{42}$$

$$p_t x_t \text{ converges to 0 when } 0 < \delta < 1. \tag{43}$$

It should be stressed that neither (42) nor (43) can be verified by any agent in any period t on the basis of observing a finite number of prices and quantities. Thus, rephrasing Koopmans, we may wonder how 'even at this level of abstraction the task of meeting condition' (42) or (43) 'could be pinned down on any particular decision maker. This is a new condition to which there is no counterpart' in the finite horizon models.

The recent results attempt to replace (42) or (43) by appropriate period by period conditions in a variety of models. The following is a typical example (Majumdar, 1986):

Decentralizability Theorem: Let (X, Y, C) be a competitive program with the price system P starting from $y_0 > 0$ such that

$$(x_t - x[\delta])(p_t - p_t[\delta]) \leq 0 \text{ for all } t > 0, \tag{44}$$

where $x[\delta]$ is the unique golden rule input satisfying $\delta f'(x) = 1$ and $p_t = \delta^t u'(c[\delta])$ for $c[\delta] = f(x[\delta]) - x[\delta]$. Then (X, Y, C) is optimal from y_0. Conversely, if (X, Y, C) is the optimal program from y_0, then there is a price sequence P such that (X, Y, C) is competitive and (44) is satisfied.

The point to be stressed is that the task of verifying (44) can be assigned to the producer in period t and this verification is achievable by supplementing the 'competitive messages' by two other parameters.

The restriction to stationary sequences means, of course, that the producer in period t has the same characteristics as that in any other period; however, if the producer in any period does *not* know that the *sequence* is stationary (a fact known to the designer) then, again by observing a finite number of periods (or communicating with a finite number of producers), he *cannot* derive the stationary property. In any case, his response depends only on his *own* characteristics and a finite number of parameters (prices/quantities).

Attempts to handle non-stationary environments have so far produced mostly impossibility results (see Hurwicz and Majumdar, 1985). Suppose the class of admissible technologies in any given period contains a pair of functions that satisfy the regularity conditions like $(f.1)$, $(f.2)$, and $(f.3)^*$ whose graphs 'cross' (i.e. there is an input–output pair consistent with both functions). If the verification rule is restricted to be based on a partial knowledge of the environment, then optimal programs cannot be attained through such a sequence of verification rules. It should be emphasized that the literature is very much in its infancy. The spirit so far has been to capture equilibria based on *tâtonnement*-type adjustment processes. However, once 'real' time is introduced, it is perhaps more meaningful to look for welfare properties of the mechanisms in which decisions are made (and actions carried out) on the basis of limited information and bounded communication. Also, even in the stationary case, one can question whether the verification rule (44) is compatible with any 'natural' incentives of the producer, and how it can be achieved if there is more than one producer within a given period. However, interesting generalizations to models with many commodities have been made by Brock and Majumdar (1985), Dasgupta and Mitra (1986), and Nyarko (1986).

4.3 The Inverse Optimum Problem and the Reduced Form Model

Many growth models postulate fixed saving and consumption propensities out of the different functional income categories as primitive concepts in the model. Examples include the Keynesian consumption ·function $c = (1-s)f(x)$, where s is the constant savings ratio $(0 < s < 1)$ and the Cambridge consumption function $c = f(x) - f'(x)x$, i.e. consume all wage income. Two class savings functions are also possible in which the workers save their income and the capitalists consume their income. Which, if any, of these savings functions may be reconciled with individual optimization behavior? If we can show that one of these functions could be the optimal solution to a Ramsey model of optimal growth (in so-called *closed loop* format), then we could exploit the Equivalence Principle to conclude that savings function is consistent with a utility maximizing household exercising perfect foresight over the indefinite future. The problem of constructing an optimal growth model whose closed loop solution is the stated savings function is called the *inverse optimum problem*. The first studies of this question were made by Kurz (1968) and Goldman (1968); Kurz (1969) should also be cited here. Those studies as well as the recent extension to stochastic models by Chang (1986) were conducted in continuous time. A discrete time treatment of the problem can be found in the paper of Boldrin and Montrucchio (1987), whose result on this problem we state below.

Boldrin and Montrucchio derive their result in the context of a *reduced form model* of capital accumulation. Consider the Ramsey model with felicity $u(c)$; let x represent the stocks held at the start of the period and let y represent the period's terminal stocks. Substitute $f(x) - y = c$ into u and define $v(x,y) = u[f(x) - y]$; v is the *reduced form utility function*. It is defined on the set of pairs (x,y) which give a c value in the domain of u. For example, if $u(c) = \log c$, then D, the domain of v, is a subset of the positive orthant of $\mathbb{R}^2$, and given by

$$D = \{(x,y): f(x) - y > 0,\ x > 0,\ y > 0\}.$$

For classical technologies, D is a convex set and $v(x,y) = \log [f(x) - y]$. This v is clearly increasing in x, decreasing in y, and strictly concave on D. For $u(c) = c^{\sigma}$, $0 < \sigma < 1$, the set D takes the form

$$D = \{(x,y): f(x) - y \geqslant 0,\ x \geqslant 0,\ y \geqslant 0\}.$$

In this case $(0,0) \in D$ and D is closed in contrast to the log case. The v function shares the same monotonicity and concavity properties of the log case.

Reduced form models study problems with period-wise felicities defined over the stocks of capital at the beginning and end of a period as in the examples. The constraints are represented by a technology set D and the initial capital stock k. We write the *reduced form optimization problem* as

$$J_{\delta}(k) = \sup \{\textstyle\sum_{t=1}^{\infty} \delta^{t-1} v(x_{t-1}, x_t)\colon (x_{t-1}, x_t) \in D,\ \text{all } t,\ \text{and } x_0 \leqslant k\}. \qquad (\mathscr{RG})$$

The function $J_{\delta}(k)$ denotes the optimal return function. The optimal return function satisfies the *Bellman optimality equation* below:

$$J_{\delta}(k) = \max \{v(k,k') + \delta J_{\delta}(k')\colon (k,k') \in D\}. \qquad (\mathscr{B})$$

This allows us to formally define the *policy function* as

$$\tau_{\delta}(k) = \operatorname{argmax} \{v(k,k') + \delta J_{\delta}(k')\colon (k,k') \in D\}. \qquad (\mathscr{PF})$$

The main result of Boldrin and Montrucchio (1987) is a set of sufficient conditions for a map $\theta\colon D_1 \to D_1$ to be the policy function for some optimization problems $(\mathscr{RG})$, where D_1 is the projection of D onto the first factor space and D is assumed to have the form of a Cartesian product $D_1 \times D_1$. The restrictions which they impose on τ_δ are quite mild. They solve the inverse optimum problem for a wide class of technologies besides the one-sector model. Indeed, the major application of their result is to deduce the possibility of a *chaotic* solution to a standard two-sector optimal growth model. By coupling this result with an Equivalence Theorem for the two-sector model, we may conclude there are chaotic perfect foresight equilibria (also see Benhabib and Nishimura, 1985; Boldrin, 1986, Boldrin and Montrucchio, 1987; Deneckere and Pelikan, 1987, for more concrete results in the two-sector case).

The reduced form model is a subject of intense investigation in both aggregate and multisector models. McKenzie (1986) gives an extensive development of the general multisector version of the reduced form model. For aggregate models, Benhabib and Nishimura (1985) present sufficient conditions on v and D for the monotonicity property to hold; they also give sufficient conditions for the optimum to oscillate over time. Their sufficient condition for a monotonic (oscillatory) optimum applies to a $v \in C^2$; the sufficient condition is $v_{12} > 0$ ($v_{12} < 0$) for all points in D where v_{12} is the second-order cross partial of v. We note the similarity of this condition and $(\mathcal{SM})$. The Ramsey one-sector model with classical technology and TAS utility satisfies the monotonicity condition. Comparative dynamics results along the lines of the Increasing Time Preference Theorem were found by Becker (1985b) in the aggregate reduced form model whenever $v_{12} > 0$ held. Finally, we note that Benhabib, Majumdar, and Nishimura (1986) as well as Benhabib, Jafaray, and Nishimura (1986) have found some similar monotonicity conditions for the one- and two-sector models with recursive preferences; hypotheses on the rate of impatience are needed to rule out cyclic solutions.

4.4 Aiyagari's Observational Equivalence Theorem

Aiyagari (1985) has provided a set of conditions for the perfect foresight competitive equilibrium of an overlapping generations (OLG) model to yield a unique time path of capital which is also optimal for a classical discounted one-sector TAS Ramsey model. The preferences and technology of the OLG model are used to construct the preferences and technology for the Ramsey problem. He also proves a converse: given the optimal path of accumulation of a classical discounted one-sector TAS Ramsey model, there is a corresponding OLG model whose PFCE is the same as the given solution of the Ramsey problem. The data of the Ramsey model are used to construct the relevant OLG model. This is a striking result, since it opens an identification question in our theory: we cannot distinguish between two competing theories from a given set of observations on the time path of consumption and capital. Aiyagari's Observational Equivalence Theorem may not be a true Equivalence Theorem since it is not clear that starting from a given OLG model, passing to the Ramsey problem and then constructing an OLG model from that Ramsey problem necessarily takes us back to the original OLG model. Observational Equivalence just says that the observed paths can be reconciled with both alternative theories; it does not say that the OLG model and the Ramsey optimal growth model are in the same duality relation as the infinitely lived agent PFCE model is with the Ramsey optimal growth model. One of the interesting aspects of Aiyagari's proof is that it is essentially a clever exercise in the use of inverse optimum problems. His result only applies to the aggregate consumption path in the OLG case. Aiyagari's Observational Equivalence Theorem and Bose's Characterization Theorem tell us that in an OLG model, a long-run Pareto optimal program is observationally equivalent to the Pareto optimal program that solves an appropriate discounted Ramsey model.

4.5   Ramsey Equilibrium

4.5.1   *Borrowing Constraints and Heterogeneous Households*

The purpose of this section is to develop the concept of a Ramsey equilibrium. This is a perfect foresight equilibrium model with a single capital good and many infinitely lived households. This framework differs from the standard neoclassical one-sector model in two crucial aspects. Households are heterogeneous – they may have different intertemporal preferences over alternative consumption profiles. Markets are incomplete – there is a borrowing constraint that prevents using discounted future income to increase current consumption.

The Ramsey equilibrium is designed to focus on the interplay between the households' impatience for future consumption, the limitations on their choices due to the borrowing constraint, and the technological possibilities for capital accumulation. Borrowing constraint models in a perfect foresight set-up clarify the relation between impatience and long-run income distribution and illustrate the significant implications of capital market imperfections for macrodynamics.

When borrowing and lending are permitted, Ramsey (1928) conjectured the most patient household would emerge as the dominant consumer provided each household's utility function is time additive separable with a fixed utility discount factor (Rader, 1971; Bewley, 1982; Coles, 1985). The consumption of the relatively impatient households approaches zero as their incomes are completely devoted to debt service. Several authors (Epstein and Hynes, 1983; Lucas and Stokey, 1984; Epstein, 1987a,b) have suggested that this is an unappealing outcome. Flexible time preference alone is not sufficient to overturn this result. A borrowing constraint, changing the consumer's choice sets, would prevent this solution. Households for which the constraint is binding would always have a wage income available for consumption. Indeed, their consumption remains positive in the fixed discount factor model studied in Becker (1980) and Becker and Foias (1987), presented below.

Borrowing constraints are a type of capital market imperfection. These constraints and heterogeneity of households have been proposed as a foundation for equilibrium business cycle theories (Bewley, 1986; Scheinkman and Weiss, 1986). The latter argue there are richer dynamic possibilities for equilibrium trajectories in the constrained heterogeneous household model than in the conventional representative household business cycle theory. The Bewley paper offers a deterministic model whereas Scheinkman and Weiss present a stochastic study. In both models, the borrowing constraint arises when a household becomes unemployed; in the stochastic case, this is due to the realization of an uninsurable shock. The *certainty* model we use also exhibits a richer dynamic structure than the representative consumer case. In this model, equilibrium cycles with two heterogeneous households arise in the fixed discount factor context. The Equivalence Principle implies this would not happen in the analogous model with a representative household since the equilibrium capital sequence would be monotonic. We discuss Becker and Foias's (1987) sufficient conditions on the technology to insure monotonicity in the heterogeneous household's case.

In keeping with our focus on the intertemporal relationship between impatience, limitations on consumer choice, and technology, we will simplify the household's labor–leisure choice. We assume that each household inelastically supplies one unit of identical labor services. This assumption has three consequences. First, the evaluation of lifetime utility depends only on the household's consumption profile. Second, cross-sectional differences in income are due entirely to differences in capital holdings. Last, the technology is constant and can be represented by a total output function that depends on variable capital input with labor treated as a fixed factor.

In our model a single agent faces a sequence of budget constraints, one for each time. The household's income at each date depends on wage and capital income derived from renting the previous period's terminal capital stock to the production sector. If factor markets are competitive at each time, the household faces a sequence of time-dependent affine 'production functions'. In each period, the household divides its income into consumption and capital savings. In the framework of single-agent theories, a number of authors have examined the decision problem of an infinitely lived consumer facing a borrowing constraint under an affine technology (Schechtman, 1976; Bewley, 1977; Schechtman and Escudero, 1977; Levhari, Mirman, and Zilcha, 1980; Sotomayer, 1984; Clarida, 1985; Boyd, 1986a).

4.5.2   The Ramsey Economy

We assume discrete time t, and a single commodity serving both as capital and as consumption good. A *Ramsey economy* is a $(2H+1)$-tuple $(U^1,...,U^H,$ $k^1,...,k^H, f)$. Households are labelled by the index $h=1,...,H$. The utility function of h is U^h and it is defined over alternative consumption profiles consisting of sequences $C=\{c_t\}$ of non-negative real numbers. Consumption at date t is denoted by c_t. Household h is endowed with an amount of capital, k^h, at time zero. The labor force consists of the H households, each inelastically supplying one unit of identical labor at each date. Technology is constant and is represented by a total output function f. Capital is the only variable input and production of goods available at time t depends on the capital input made at the start of the period. We assume that capital available at the beginning of period t is equal to the capital stock at the end of period $t-1$. The total output function includes replacement of capital in case there is depreciation of capital within the period. In the remainder of the section, we present the formal structure of the household and production sectors as well as the relations between them. We also define the Ramsey equilibrium concept.

At each date, households receive capital and labor income. The initial endowment of capital is a given non-negative number. There is a sequence of constraints, one for each time. Each budget constraint has the same form as in the PFCE section. Superscripts are used to label agents. The distinguishing characteristic of the Ramsey economy is that h is subject to a borrowing constraint. This limit is expressed in the requirement that capital holdings are *non-negative at each time*. Capital markets are *incomplete*: households may not borrow against anticipated wage income. Consequently, physical capital is the only fungible asset and it must therefore remain non-negative at all times.

Households are competitive agents and perfectly anticipate the profile of factor returns $\{1+r_t,w_t\}$. The rental and wage sequences are always non-negative. Given an expected sequence of factor returns, household h solves the problem $(\mathcal{H})$ defined in Section 4.1. The usual Euler or no-arbitrage and transversality conditions are necessary for each household's optimization problem. These conditions take the same form as the ones derived in the section on the Equivalence Principle.

The labor force is a fixed constant equal to the number of households, H. Output in any period depends on the level of the variable input x. Given input x, output net of depreciation is denoted $g(x)-\gamma x$, where γx allows for proportional depreciation of capital in a single period and $0\leqslant\gamma\leqslant 1$ is a given parameter. The total output available in the period is denoted by $f(x)=g(x)+(1-\gamma)x$. We assume that g is derived from a neoclassical constant returns to scale production function G with labor input fixed at H: we write $g(x)=G(x,H)$. The maintained assumptions on f are $(f.1)$–$(f.3)$; the technology is productive. We also assume f has a positive maximum sustainable stock b.

The production sector is modelled by a sequence of profit maximization problems, one for each period. At each date, given the competitive rental price, $1 + r_t$, the production sector chooses a non-negative input x_{t-1} in order to solve problem ($\mathscr{P}$) in Section 4.1.

Let $k = \Sigma_h k^h$ denote the aggregate initial endowment of capital. We make the blanket assumption that k is positive. A sequence $\{1 + \bar{r}_t, \bar{w}_t, \bar{k}_{t-1}, \bar{c}_t^h, \bar{x}_{t-1}^h\}$ constitutes a *Ramsey equilibrium* for the economy $(U^1, ..., U^H, k^1, ..., k^H, f)$ provided $\{\bar{c}_t^h, \bar{x}_{t-1}^h\}$ solves each households' decision problem given $\{1 + \bar{r}_t, \bar{w}_t\}$, $\bar{k}_{t-1}$ solves the production sector's problem at each date given $1 + \bar{r}_t$, for each t

$$H\bar{w}_t = \bar{f}(k_{t-1}) - (1 + \bar{r}_t)\bar{k}_{t-1}, \text{ and} \tag{45}$$

$$\Sigma_h \bar{x}_{t-1}^h = \bar{k}_{t-1}, \bar{k}_0 = k. \tag{46}$$

Condition (45) says that the residual payments for labor services exhaust the 'profits' of the production sector on each date. Capital market equilibrium is expressed in (46). Output markets are necessarily in balance at each t as a consequence of the other Ramsey equilibrium conditions. This is a form of Walras Law at each date. The output market clearing condition is

$$\Sigma_h (\bar{c}_t^h + \bar{x}_t^h) = f(\bar{k}_{t-1}). \tag{47}$$

The balance (47) states that $\bar{c}_t = \Sigma_h \bar{c}_t^h$ and $\bar{x}_t = \Sigma_h \bar{x}_t^h$ constitute a feasible path of *aggregate consumption and capital* in the usual one-sector model, i.e. $\bar{c}_t + \bar{x}_t = f(\bar{x}_{t-1})$, $\bar{x}_0 = k$. If we ignore the distribution of capital and consumption, an arbitrary $\{c_t, x_{t-1}\}$ is *feasible* given (f, k) if $c_t + x_t \leqslant f(x_{t-1})$ for all t and $x_0 \leqslant k$. One special feasible program is the *path of pure accumulation*. It is found by putting $c_t = 0$ and $x_t = f^t(k)$, where f^t is the tth iterate of f. If f is productive and has maximum sustainable stock b, then $k \leqslant b$ implies $f^t(k) \leqslant b$. In this case, an equilibrium aggregate capital stock is bounded from above by b. In the remaining discussion, the overbars denoting a Ramsey equilibrium are dropped to simplify the notation when the meaning is clear.

4.5.3 Properties of Ramsey Equilibrium

The existence of a Ramsey equilibrium was demonstrated in Becker, Boyd, and Foias (1986) for a broad class of utility and total output functions. In particular, their results cover the recursive utility functions discussed earlier. Concave total output functions with or without a maximum sustainable stock are also admissible technologies provided an Inada condition is met for a zero capital input. Since the technical details of their existence proof would lead us away from the main thrust of our paper, we will concentrate on the characterization of Ramsey equilibrium. In particular, we are interested in whether or not the aggregate capital path is monotonic in an equilibrium configuration. The bulk of the qualitative results obtained for Ramsey equilibrium to date have been found in the case of a time additive separable utility function for each household; heterogeneity of households is specified by postulating that households have different discount rates. We state this as a blanket assumption for this section unless otherwise noted:

Maintained Assumption: Household h has a TAS utility function with a C^2 strictly concave and increasing felicity function u_h obeying the Inada condition at 0 and with discount factor $\delta_h \in (0,1)$. Moreover,

$$1 > \delta_1 > \delta_2 > ... > \delta_H > 0.$$

The households have been indexed from the most patient to least patient according to the magnitude of their discount factors. Recall that $\delta_h^{-1} = 1 + \rho_h$ where ρ_h is h's *pure rate of time preference.*

The usual no-arbitrage condition is necessary for each household in a Ramsey equilibrium configuration. This is recorded as

$$\delta(1 + r_{t+1})u'(c_{t+1}) \leqslant u'(c_t), \text{ with equality if } x_t > 0, \tag{48}$$

where the h labels are omitted since the meaning is clear. This inequality may also be interpreted as stating that the *marginal rate of impatience between two adjacent periods* is always greater than or equal to the market rate of interest (which equals the rental rate for capital in this one-sector model). Recall, for constant consumption profiles, the marginal rate of impatience reduces to the pure rate of time preference.

The first example of a Ramsey equilibrium is the *stationary Ramsey equilibrium* which is defined as a time invariant Ramsey equilibrium. The no-arbitrage necessary condition for each household in this equilibrium configuration reduces to

$$\delta_h f'(K) \leqslant 1, \text{ with equality if } x^h > 0, \tag{49}$$

where K denotes the total capital stock and x^h denotes h's stationary capital stock in this equilibrium. Clearly there can be an equality in (49) for at most one household (namely $h = 1$). The marginal rate of impatience for the first household determines the long-run interest rate; the marginal rates of impatience for the relatively more impatient households are above the long-run interest rate. Since f' is decreasing, there is a unique K such that (49) holds with an equality for $h = 1$. Denote this capital stock by $K(\delta_1)$. It turns out that this is the stationary Ramsey equilibrium total capital stock. The initial data must be in a particular arrangement for this stock to be realized in a Ramsey equilibrium. This is spelled out as the

Steady State Distribution Theorem: $K(\delta_1)$ is the unique stationary Ramsey equilibrium total capital stock where the Ramsey economy has the initial data $k^1 = K(\delta_1)$, $k^h = 0$ for $h \geqslant 2$. The stationary Ramsey equilibrium rental rate is $r(\delta_1) = (\delta_1)^{-1} - 1$ and the wage rate is $w(\delta_1) = f(K(\delta_1)) - f'(K(\delta_1))K(\delta_1)$. The consumption of the agents is $c^1(\delta_1) = w(\delta_1) + r(\delta_1)K(\delta_1)$ and $c^h(\delta_1) = w(\delta_1)$ for $h \geqslant 2$.

Proof: See Becker (1980).

A Ramsey equilibrium exhibits the *recurrence property* whenever the zero capital state is achieved infinitely often by households $h \geqslant 2$. If every household $h \geqslant 2$ also eventually reaches a no-capital state and maintains it thereafter, then we say that the Ramsey equilibrium has the *turnpike property*.

The main results of the non-steady-state Ramsey equilibrium theory are stated in the following theorems.

Recurrence Theorem: A Ramsey equilibrium has the recurrence property.

Proof: See Becker and Foias (1987, p.178).

The recurrence property is suggested by observing that whenever the Ramsey equilibrium converges to *anything*, then the no-arbitrage condition reduces to (49) as $t \to \infty$; it is then obvious that at most one h can hold capital for all t sufficiently large under this hypothesis. The general result applies to an arbitrary Ramsey equilibrium.

A Ramsey equilibrium has a cycle of period 2 (a 2-cycle) if for $K_1 < K_2$ the sequence $\{K_2, K_1, K_2, K_1, \ldots\}$, $K_0 = K_2$, may arise in equilibrium. Becker and Foias (1987) constructed an example of a 2-cycle equilibrium with two agents. The example was based on a situation where only the first agent held capital in equilibrium; hence the turnpike property was already in force. The details of their example may be found in the paper (pp.180–2); we concentrate on the basic intuition of the example in our discussion.

In the familiar one household perfect foresight equilibrium, total income, $f(K)$, is a monotonically increasing function of capital; this income is the sum of the wage bill $f(K) - f'(K)K$, and capital income, $f'(K)K$. In contrast, with many households and the situation of their example, the total income of the first household differs from the national income of the economy by an amount equal to the wage payments made to the non-capital holding agents. Assumptions $(f.1)–(f.3)$ alone are not sufficient to guarantee that the capital income of the first household (which is the total capital income) is increasing in capital. Thus, the most patient household's total income may not be increasing in capital; if the first household increases its capital holding from one period to the next, then its capital income may fall by more than the wage income it receives. The negative slope of the factor-price frontier implies that the wage income always increases when capital increases. In the next period, the first household naturally saves less than before thereby inducing a subsequent increase in its income. The fluctuations in income and factor prices are perfectly foreseen. Provided the first household is sufficiently impatient, the motive for that household to profit from a one-period reversed arbitrage (all other things equal) is diminished; thus, the incentive for that agent to smooth the fluctuations in consumption does not exist. Therefore, a decline in capital income as capital increases combines with the relative impatience of the first agent to provide a cyclic equilibrium capital sequence.

Cyclic Equilibrium Existence Theorem: A Ramsey equilibrium with a 2-cycle exists.

The oscillatory behavior of capital income may be eliminated by strengthening $(f.1)$–$(f.3)$. If *total* capital income, $f'(K)K$, is always increasing in the aggregate capital stocks, then the technological basis for the example is ruled out. A well-known sufficient condition for this property is that the elasticity of substitution is greater than or equal to one for the neoclassical production function giving rise to f with a fixed labor factor. This holds, for example, in the Cobb–Douglas total output function case.

Ramsey Convergence Theorem: If $f'(K)K$ is a strictly increasing function of K, then any Ramsey equilibrium converges (eventually monotonically) to the stationary Ramsey equilibrium and the turnpike property obtains.

The development of further qualitative properties of Ramsey equilibrium is an important item for future research. The development of the theory with flexible time preference is one of the main priorities. Boyd (1986c, ch.5) gave some steady-state results. For example, he showed that there was a stationary Ramsey equilibrium in which the most patient household was in the zero capital position and one of the more impatient households held positive capital.

5   CONCLUDING COMMENTS

The one-sector models we have discussed provide a framework for the analysis of capital accumulation problems consistent with optimizing individual behavior. The well-known neoclassical parable of growth and an increasing stock of capital over time is a consequence of the monotonicity property of the optimal, PFCE, or Ramsey equilibrium (when applicable) trajectory provided the initial stock of capital is smaller than the modified golden rule state. This path registers in the market economy as a rising wage and decreasing rental rate for capital. In the one-sector model, this also implies a falling rate of interest. These properties of non-steady-state growth are fairly robust to the specification of individual behavioral assumptions. For example, we can accommodate this set of results in the infinitely lived representative agent framework with a very general recursive preference structure. This pattern may also be possible in an overlapping generations model. We are also able to work out various comparative dynamic results which account for the full range of options open to the planner-household after a parameter shift 'shocks' the economy. In this fashion we have argued that it is possible to take equilibrium dynamics beyond steady-state comparisons and open the road to analysis of growth problems in real time.

Much remains to be done. The two-sector model is under active investigation now because it provides a concrete specification that is both tractable and offers a richer dynamics than the one-sector model. The agenda set out for the analysis of the one-sector model is also being followed in the case of the two-sector model. We can only hope that these simple models will provide us with the basis for developing and understanding more complex models to follow. For the time being, they can be used to develop applications to monetary theory, public finance, resource economics, and financial economics which form some of the fields with outstanding dynamic issues in need of study.

References

Aiyagari, S. R. (1985) 'Observational Equivalence of the Overlapping Generations and the Discounted Dynamic Programming Frameworks for One-Sector Growth'. *Journal of Economic Theory*, 35 (April): 201–221.

Arrow, K. J. (1964) 'Optimal Capital Policy, the Cost of Capital, and Myopic Decision Rules'. *Annals of the Institute of Mathematical Statistics*, 16: 21–30.

Aubin, J. P. (1977) *Applied Abstract Analysis* (New York: Wiley).

Barro, R. J. (1974) 'Are Government Bonds Net Wealth?', *Journal of Political Economy*, 82 (November–December): 1095–1117.

Beals, R. and T. C. Koopmans (1969) 'Maximizing Stationary Utility in a Constant Technology', *SIAM Journal of Applied Mathematics*, 17: 1001–15.

Becker, R. A. (1980) 'On the Long-Run Steady State in a Simple Dynamic Model of Equilibrium with Heterogeneous Households', *Quarterly Journal of Economics*, 47 (September): 375–82.

Becker, R. A. (1981) 'The Duality of a Dynamic Model of Equilibrium and an Optimal Growth Model: The Heterogeneous Capital Goods Case', *Quarterly Journal of Economics*, 48 (May): 271–300.

Becker, R. A. (1982) 'The Equivalence of a Fisher Competitive Equilibrium and a Perfect Foresight Competitive Equilibrium in a Multi-Sectoral Model of Capital Accumulation'. *International Economic Review*, 23 (February): 19–34.

Becker, R. A. (1983a) 'Comparative Dynamics in the One-Sector Optimal Growth Model', *Journal of Economic Dynamics and Control*, 6: 99–107.

Becker, R. A. (1983b) 'A Simple Dynamic Equilibrium Model With Adjustment Costs', *Journal of Economic Dynamics and Control*, 6: 79–98.

Becker, R. A. (1985a) 'Capital Income Taxation and Perfect Foresight', *Journal of Public Economics*, 26: 147–67.

Becker, R. A. (1985b) 'Comparative Dynamics in Aggregate Models of Optimal Capital Accumulation', *Quaterley Journal of Economics*, 47 (September): 375–82.

Becker, R. A. and C. Foias (1987) 'A Characterization of Ramsey Equilibrium', *Journal of Economic Theory*, 41 (February): 173–84.

Becker, R. A., J. H. Boyd III and C. Foias (1986) 'The Existence of Ramsey Equilibrium', Discussion Paper, Indiana University.

Benhabib, J. and K. Nishimura (1985) 'Competitive Business Cycles', *Journal of Economic Theory*, 35: 284–306.

Benhabib, J., S. Jafarey and K. Nishimura (1985) 'The Dynamics of Efficient Intertemporal Allocations with Many Agents, Recursive Preferences and Production', Working Paper, New York University.

Benhabib, J., M. Majumdar and K. Nishimura (1986) 'Global Equilibrium Dynamics with Stationary Preferences', Working Paper, New York University.

Benveniste, L. M. and T. Mitra (1979) 'Characterizing Inefficiency of Infinite-Horizon Programs in Nonsmooth Technologies', in *General Equilibrium, Growth, and Trade: Essays in Honor of Lionel McKenzie* (eds) J. R. Green and J. A. Scheinkman (New York: Academic Press) pp. 199–216.

Bewley, T. (1972) 'Existence of Equilbria in Economies with Infinitely Many Commodities', *Journal of Economic Theory*, 27: 514–40.

Bewley, T. (1977) 'The Permanent Income Hypothesis: A Theoretical Formulation', *Journal of Economic Theory*, 16: 252–92.

Bewley, T. (1980) 'The Optimum Quantity of Money', in *Models of Monetary Economics*. (eds) J. H. Kareken and N. Wallace (Minneapolis: Federal Reserve Bank of Minneapolis).

Bewley, T. (1982) 'An Integration of Equilibrium Theory and Turnpike Theory', *Journal of Mathematical Economics*, 10: 233–67.

Bewley, T. (1986) 'Dynamic Implications of the Budget Constraint', in *Models of Economic Dynamics* (ed.) H. Sonnenschein (Berlin: Springer-Verlag) pp. 117–23.

Bliss, C. J. (1975) *Capital Theory and the Distribution of Income* (Amsterdam: North-Holland).

Boldrin, M. (1986) 'Paths of Optimal Accumulation in Two-Sector Models', Working Paper, University of Rochester.

Boldrin, M. and L. Montrucchio (1987) 'On the Inderterminancy of Capital Accumulation Paths', in *Nonlinear Economic Dynamics* (ed.) J. M. Grandmont (New York: Academic Press) pp. 26–39.

Bose, A. (1974) 'Pareto-Optimality and Efficient Capital Accumulation', Discussion Paper, University of Rochester.

Boyd, J. H., III (1986a) 'Recursive Utility and the Ramsey Problem', Working Paper, University of Rochester.

Boyd, J. H., III (1986b) 'Symmetries, Equilibria and the Value Function', Working Paper, University of Rochester.

Boyd, J. H., III (1986c) *Preferences, Technology and Dynamic Equilibria*, Ph.D. Dissertation, Indiana University.

Boyer, M. (1975) 'An Optimal Growth Model With Stationary Non-Additive Utilities', *Canadian Journal of Economics*, 8 (May): 216–37.

Brock, W. A. and D. Gale (1969) 'Optimal Growth Under Factor Augmenting Progress', *Journal of Economic Theory*, 1: 229–43.

Brock, W. A. and M. Majumdar (1985) 'On Characterizing Optimality of Competitive Programs in Terms of Decentralizable Conditions', Cornell University Working Paper No. 335 (to appear in *Journal of Economic Theory*).

Brown, D. J. and L. M. Lewis (1981) 'Myopic Economic Agents', *Econometrica*, 49: 359–68.

Burmeister, E. (1980) *Capital Theory and Dynamics* (New York: Cambridge University Press).

Burmeister, E. and S. Turnovsky (1972) 'Capital Deepening Response in an Economy with Heterogeneous Capital Goods', *American Economic Review*, 62: 842–53.

Cass, D. (1972) 'On Capital Overaccumulation in the Aggregative Neo-classical Model of Economic Growth: A Complete Characterization', *Journal of Economic Theory*, 4: 200–23.

Cass, D. and M. Majumdar (1979) 'Efficient Intertemporal Allocation, Consumption-Value Maximization, and Capital-Value Transversality: A Unified View', in *General Equilibrium, Growth, and Trade: Essays in Honor of Lionel McKenzie* (eds) J. R. Green and J. A. Scheinkman (New York: Academic Press).

Chang, F. R. (1986) 'Inverse Optimal Problems: A Dynamic Approach', Working Paper, Indiana University (to appear in *Econometrica*).

Chichilnisky, G. and P. J. Kalman (1980) 'Application of Functional Analysis to Models of Efficient Allocation of Economic Resources', *Journal of Optimization Theory and Applications*, 30: 19–32.

Clarida, R. H. (1985) 'Consumption, Liquidity Constraints, and Asset Accumulation in the Presence of Random Income Fluctuations', Cowles Foundation Discussion Paper #705R, Yale University.

Coles, J. L. (1985) 'Equilibrium Turnpike Theory with Constant Returns to Scale and Possibly Heterogeneous Discount Factors', *International Economic Review*, 26: 671–9.

Dasgupta, S. and T. Mitra (1986a) 'Intertemporal Optimality in a Closed Linear Model of Production', (to appear in *Journal of Economic Theory*).

Dasgupta, S. and T. Mitra (1986b) 'Intertemporal Optimality in a Multi Sector Model when Future Utilities are Discounted', (to appear in *Journal of Economic Theory*).

Dechert, W. D. and K. Nishimura (1980) 'Existence of Optimal Paths and the Turnpike Property: The Non-convex Case with Unbounded Stocks', Working Paper, SUNY-Buffalo.

Dechert, W. D. and K. Nishimura (1983) 'A Complete Characterization of Optimal Growth Paths in an Aggregrated Model with a Non-Concave Production Function', *Journal of Economic Theory*, 31: 332–54.

Deneckere, R. and S. Pelikan (1987) 'Competitive Chaos', in *Nonlinear Economic Dynamics* (ed.) J. M. Grandmont (New York: Academic Press), pp. 26–39.

Diamond, P. A. (1965a) 'National Debt in a Neoclassical Growth Model', *American Economic Review*, 55: 1126–50.

Diamond, P. A. (1965b) 'The Evaluation of Infinite Utility Streams', *Econometrica*, 33: 170–7.

Epstein, L. G. (1983) 'Stationary Cardinal Utility and Optimal Growth Under Uncertainty', *Journal of Economic Theory*, 31: 133–52.

Epstein, L. G. (1986) 'Implicitly Additive Utility and the Nature of Optimal Economic Growth', *Journal of Mathematical Economics*, 15: 111–28.

Epstein, L. G. (1987a) 'A Simple Dynamic General Equilibrium Model', *Journal of Economic Theory*, 41 (February): 68–95.

Epstein, L. G. (1987b) 'The Global Stability of Efficient Intertemporal Allocations', *Econometrica*, 55 (March): 329–57.

Epstein, L. G. and J. A. Hynes (1983) 'The Rate of Time Preference and Dynamic Economic Analysis', *Journal of Political Economy*, 91: 611–35.

Fisher, I. (1907) *The Rate of Interest* (New York: Macmillan).

Gale, D. (1967) 'On Optimal Development in a Multi-Sector Economy', *Review of Economic Studies*, 34: 1–18.

Goldman, S. (1968) 'Optimal Growth and Continual Planning Revision', *Review of Economic Studies*, 35 (April): 145–54.

Gray, J. A. and S. Salant (1983) 'Transversality Conditions in Infinite-Horizon Models', Working Paper, Washington State University.

Hahn, F. (1966) 'Equilibrium Dynamics with Heterogeneous Capital Goods', *Quarterly Journal of Economics*, 80: 633–46.

Hahn, F. (1987) *Money, Growth and Stability* (Cambridge, Mass.: MIT Press).

Harcourt, G. (1972) *Some Cambridge Controversies in the Theory of Capital* (Cambridge: Cambridge University Press).

Hicks, J. (1946) *Value and Capital* (Oxford: Oxford University Press).

Hieber, G. (1981) *On Optimal Paths with Variable Technology* (Cambridge, Mass: Oelgeschlager, Gunn and Hain).

Hurwicz, L. (1986) 'On Informational Decentralization and Efficiency in Resource Allocation Mechanisms', in *Studies in Mathematical Economics* (ed.) S. Reiter. (The Mathematical Association of America), pp. 238–350.

Hurwicz, L. (1986) 'On Informational Decentralization and Efficiency in Resource Allocation Mechanisms', in *Studies in Mathematical Economics* (ed.) S. Reiter. The Mathematical Association of America, pp. 238–350.

Iwai, K. (1972) 'Optimal Economic Growth and Stationary Ordinal Utility – A Fisherian Approach', *Journal of Economic Theory*, 5: 121–51.

Koopmans, T. C. (1958) *Three Essays on the State of Economic Science* (New York: McGraw-Hill).

Koopmans, T. C. (1960) 'Stationary Ordinal Utility and Impatience', *Econometrica*, 28: 287–309.

Koopmans, T. C. (1967) 'Objectives, Constraints, and Outcomes in Optimal Growth Models', *Econometrica*, 35: 1–15.

Koopmans T. C. (1972) 'Representation of Preference Orderings Over Time', in *Decision and Organization* (eds) C. B. McGuire and R. Radner (Amsterdam: North-Holland).

Koopmans, T. C., P. A. Diamond and R. E. Williamson (1964) 'Stationary Utility and Time Perspective', *Econometrica*, 32: 82–100.

Kurz, M. L. (1968) 'The General Instability of a Class of Competitive Growth Processes', *Review of Economic Studies*, 35: 155–74.

Kurz, M. L. (1969) 'On the Inverse Optimum Problem', in *Mathematical Systems Theory and Economics* (eds) H. W. Kuhn and G. P. Szego (Berlin: Springer-Verlag).

Levhari, D., L. J. Mirman and I. Zilcha (1980) 'Capital Accumulation Under Uncertainty', *International Economic Review*, 21: 661–71.

Leviatan, N. (1970) 'A Diagrammatic Exposition of Optimal Growth', *American Economic Review*, 60: 302–9.

Lucas, R. E., Jr. and E. Prescott (1971) 'Investment Under Uncertainty', *Econometrica*, 39: 658–82.

Lucas, R. E., Jr. and N. L. Stokey (1984) 'Optimal Growth with Many Consumers', *Journal of Economic Theory*, 32: 139–71.

Magill, M. (1981) 'Infinite Horizon Programs', *Econometrica*, 49: 679–711.

Magill, M. and K. Nishimura (1984) 'Impatience and Accumulation', *Journal of Mathematical Analysis and Applications*, 98: 270–81.

Majumdar, M. (1970) 'Some Approximation Theorems on Efficiency Prices for Infinite Programs', *Journal of Economic Theory*, 2: 399–410.

Majumdar, M. (1972) 'Some General Theorems on Efficiency Prices with an Infinite Dimensional Commodity Space', *Journal of Economic Theory*, 5: 1–13.

Majumdar, M. (1974) 'Efficient Programs in Infinite Dimensional Spaces: A Complete Characterization', *Journal of Economic Theory*, 7 (April): 335–69.

Majumdar, M. (1975) 'Some Remarks on Optimal Growth with Intertemporally Dependent Preferences in the Neoclassical Model', *Review of Economic Studies*, 42: 147–53.

Majumdar, M. (1984) 'Some Recent Developments in the Theory of Intertemporal Allocation', Discussion Paper, Cornell University.

Majumdar, M. (1986) 'Decentralization in Dynamic Economic Models', (mimeo) Cornell University.

Majumdar, M. and M. Kurz (1972) 'Efficiency Prices in an Infinite Dimensional Space: A Synthesis', *Review of Economic Studies*, 39: 147–58.

Majumdar, M. and T. Mitra (1982) 'Intertemporal Allocation with a Non-Convex Technology: The Aggregative Framework', *Journal of Economic Theory*, 27: 101–36.

Malinvaud, E. (1953) 'Capital Accumulation and Efficient Allocation of Resources', *Econometrica*, 21: 233–68.

McFadden, D. (1975) 'An Example of the Non-Existence of Malinvaud Prices in a Tight Economy', *Journal of Mathematical Economics*, 2 (March): 17–19.

McKenzie, L. W. (1986) 'Optimal Economic Growth, Turnpike Theorems and Comparative Dynamics', in *Handbook of Mathematical Economics*, Vol. 3, (eds) K. J. Arrow and M. Intriligator (Amsterdam: North-Holland) pp. 1281–355.

Mitra, T. (1979a) 'Identifying Inefficiency in Smooth Aggregative Models of Economic Growth', *Journal of Mathematical Economics*, 6: 85–111.

Mitra, T. (1979b) 'On the Value Maximizing Property of Infinite Horizon Efficient Programs', *International Economic Review*, 20 (October): 635–42.

Nyarko, Y. (1986) 'On Characterization Optimality of Stochastic Competition Processes', (to appear in *Journal of Economic Theory*).

Pazner, E. A. and A. Razin (1980) 'Competitive Efficiency in an Overlapping-Generation Model with Endogenous Population', *Journal of Public Economics*, 13: 249–58.

Peleg, B. and M. E. Yaari (1970) 'Efficiency Prices in an Infinite-Dimensional Space', *Journal of Economic Theory*, 2: 41–85.

Phelps, E. S. (1966) *Golden Rules of Economic Growth* (New York: Norton).

Rader, T. (1971) *The Economics of Feudalism* (New York: Gordon & Breach).

Radner, R. (1967) 'Efficiency Prices for Infinite Horizon Production Programs', *Review of Economic Studies*, 34: 51–66.

Ramsey, F. P. (1928) 'A Mathematical Theory of Saving', *Economic Journal*, 38: 543–59.

Robertson, A. P. and W. Robertson (1973) *Topological Vector Spaces* (Cambridge: Cambridge University Press).

Robinson, J. (1952) *The Rate of Interest and Other Essays* (London: Macmillan).

Robinson, J. (1956) *The Accumulation of Capital* (London: Macmillan)

Robinson, J. (1960) *Collected Economic Papers: Volume Three* (Oxford: Blackwell).

Robinson, J. (1968) *Essays in the Theory of Economic Growth* (London: Macmillan).

Robinson, J. (1973) *Collected Economic Papers: Volume Four* (Oxford: Blackwell).

Romer, P. (1986) 'Increasing Returns and Long-Run Growth', *Journal of Political Economy*, 94 (October): 1002–37.

Ross, S. M. (1983) *Introduction to Stochastic Dynamic Programming* (New York: Academic Press).

Samuelson, P. A. (1947) *Foundations of Economic Analysis* (Cambridge, Mass.: Harvard University Press).

Sargent, T. J. (1987) *Dynamic Macroeconomic Theory* (Cambridge, Mass.: Harvard University Press).

Schechtman, J. (1976) 'An Income Fluctuation Problem', *Journal of Economic Theory*, 12: 218–41.

Schechtman, J. and V. L. S. Escudero (1977) 'Some Results on "An Income Fluctuation Problem",' *Journal of Economic Theory*, 16: 151–66.

Scheinkman, J. A. (1978) 'Stability of Separable Hamiltonians and Investment Theory', *Review of Economic Studies*, 45: 559–70.

Scheinkman, J. A. and L. Weiss (1986) 'Borrowing Constraints and Aggregate Economic Activity', *Econometrica*, 54: 23–45.

Shell, K. (1971) 'Notes on the Economics of Infinity', *Journal of Political Economy*, 79: 1002–11.

Sotomayer, M. D. (1984) 'On Income Fluctuations and Capital Gains', *Journal of Economic Theory*, 32: 14–35.

Spulber, N. and R. A. Becker (1986) 'Theoretical Issues in Optimal Planning', *International Journal of Development Planning Literature*, 1: 237–53.

Streufert, P. (1985) 'Dynamic Allocation with Consistent Intergenerational Benevolence', IMSSS Technical Report #471, Stanford.

Usher, D. (ed.) (1980) *The Measurement of Capital* (Chicago: University of Chicago Press).

Uzawa, H. (1968) 'Time Preference, the Consumption Function, and Optimum Asset Holdings', in *Value, Capital and Growth: Papers in Honour of Sir John Hicks* (ed.) James N. Wolfe (Edinburgh: Edinburgh University Press).

Waldman, K. H. (1985) 'On Bounds for Dynamic Programs', *Mathematics of Operations Research*, 10: 220–32.

Wessels, J. (1977) 'Markov Programming by Successive Approximations with Respect to Weighted Supremum Norms', *Journal of Mathematical Analysis and Applications*, 58: 326–35.

Young, A. A. (1928) 'Increasing Returns and Economic Progress', *Economic Journal*, 38: 527–42.

17 Capital Theory Paradoxes: Anything Goes

Andreu Mas-Colell*

1 INTRODUCTION

A first approximation to the study of the intertemporal aspects of resource allocation (capital theory from now on), consists of concentrating on the steady states (the rest points) of associated dynamical systems. Provided one does not lose sight from the fact that this is not an end in itself, there is much useful information to be gleaned from steady-state analysis – indeed, one of the prime tools of economics. No doubt, the pervasiveness of the notion of the stationary state in classical economics and the fact that there is so much one can do without invoking powerful mathematics, have also added to its popularity.

An excellent, but advanced, introduction to steady-state capital theory in the multigood case (the focus of this paper) is von Weizsäcker (1971). The books by Bliss (1975) and Burmeister (1980), which are general surveys of capital theory, also have good accounts of steady-state aspects.

In the early 1950s, Joan Robinson started the systematic comparative static analysis of the steady states of economies with several capital goods (see Robinson, 1953). Although the fundamental, and slow to sink in, contributions of von Neumann (1945–6) and Malinvaud (1953) come earlier, the emphasis on comparative statics was distinctive from the tradition she helped to launch.

The line of research initiated by Robinson culminated in the 1960s with the realization that many of the comparative statics theorems valid for the one capital good case do not generalize to the multigood case. To a sensibility educated on the former, the heterogeneous capital good case admitted models with behavior that appeared 'bizarre', 'exotic', 'paradoxical' ... I should be quick to add that this was no disappointment to J. Robinson and her followers. It was rather their point and in this they were perceptive. Many controversies and much noise accompanied the process of intellectual discussion. The story has been told many times (see the Bliss or Burmeister references; or, for a militant Robinsonian point of view, Harcourt, 1972) and I will not repeat it here.

Consider the central example with which I will concern myself in this

* The research for this paper has been helped by the support of a Guggenheim Fellowship.

paper: the dependence of steady-state consumption (say, that there is only one consumption good) on the rate of interest. For simplicity I restrict myself to a world without technological change or population growth. A basic and quite general theorem, the golden rule, asserts that the maximum consumption level is associated with a rate of interest equal to the rate of population growth, that is, zero. In addition, the standard one capital good case displays a monotonically decreasing relationship between consumption levels and the rate of interest (as in Fig. 17.1a). This does not generalize and it is now well understood that even with only two capital goods, a non-monotone association such as in Figure 17.1b is possible (see, for example, Burmeister, 1980, ch.4).

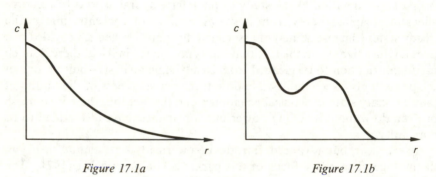

Figure 17.1a   *Figure 17.1b*

   The purpose of this chapter is to bring the above point to its logical conclusion (to out-Cambridge Cambridge, so to speak) by showing that in general (i.e. two capital goods but no specific restriction on the technology beyond convexity) there is no other theorem on the association across steady states of consumption levels and rates of interest than a slightly strengthened version of the golden rule. The result of this chapter says, roughly, that given any set of consumption and rate of interest pairs, say the one in Figure 17.2, a well-behaved technology can be found having precisely this set as the steady-state comparative static locus. The uncovering of a slight strengthening of the golden rule is a minor positive pay-off of this research strategy.

   The informed reader will notice that the project carried out in this chapter follows a parallel development in general equilibrium theory. As in capital theory, intensive research by general equilibrium theorists on comparative statics, and the closely related topic of stability, did not yield many general results and few that measured up to early hopes (the story is well told in Arrow and Hahn, 1971). The research culminated in the results by, among others, Sonnenschein, Mantel and Debreu (see Shafer and Sonnenschein, 1982, for a good survey) showing that but for the obvious restrictions (e.g. Walras Law) literally anything can be the excess demand of a well-behaved exchange economy. My intention in this paper is thus to make Joan

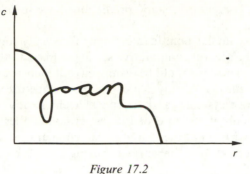

Figure 17.2

Robinson's point in the manner of the Sonnenschein–Mantel–Debreu theorem.

It is interesting to ponder why two analytically similar developments gave rise to such different styles of scientific debate: placid and consensual in general equilibrium theory; tumultuous and passionate in capital theory. I will make a couple of comments on this although I do not think that they constitute much of an explanation for the difference. More likely the reasons are to be found in the sociology of knowledge and in the fact that, perhaps because of the Marxian tradition, capital theory has tended to be more ideologically charged than other areas of economics. There has been a distressing propensity, on all sides, to draft analytical results for service at the trenches.

My first comment touches on a superficial aspect, but it may be psychologically significant. It has to do with pictures. The Edgeworth box can be made to display quite a lot of complex behavior in front of our very eyes (e.g. multiplicity of equilibria, transfer paradoxes, . . .). The ground may therefore be prepared for bad news in the *n*-good case. On the contrary, in capital theory only the one capital good case is amenable to self-evident graphical analysis. The interesting complexities arise, however, only with more than one capital good.

My second comment goes deeper and reveals, probably, my bias to view capital theory as subsumed in general equilibrium analysis. While undoubtedly general equilibrium theorists would wish to have general comparative static theorems, the news that they are not available is not looked at as the deathknell of the theory. The reason is that general foundational theorems abound (e.g. the welfare theorems) and the strength of the theory rests assured on them. The interpretation of the negative results is rather that comparative statics is not an area for armchair thinking but for empirical assessment of parameters. The 'real world' may or may not be simple. If it is, so much the better. If, as is more likely, it is not, then we still need, and have, sophisticated analytical tools to study it. But the values of the parameters determining the comparative static predictions have to be calibrated by an empirical appeal.

I believe that a similar point can be made for steady-state capital theory. There may not be general comparative static theorems (although the golden rule is general and not a result to be dismissed) but there are general theorems (e.g. short-run efficient steady state can be competitively supported by proportional price systems, a short-run efficient steady state is long-run efficient if and only if the rate of interest is not smaller than the rate of population growth). What the 'paradoxical' comparative statics has taught us is simply that modelling the world as having a single capital good is not *a priori* justified. So be it.

2   THE GOLDEN RULE THEOREM

To focus on essentials I will only consider a stationary economic situation with no technical change or population growth.

There are n capital goods. Vectors of stocks of capital goods are denoted $x, y, z \in R^n$.

There is a single consumption good, denoted c.

The intertemporal technological possibilities are described in a familiar but highly reduced form. Namely, there is a function $v(x,y)$ which gives the largest amount of consumption possible today if the capital stock vector today is x and the capital stock available tomorrow is constrained to be y.

The following standard hypotheses are made on the technology. Let $P = \{\Delta \in R^n : z \gg 0\}$. Then *v is defined on $P \times P$, it is strictly concave, continuously differentiable and satisfies*

$$v(0,y) \leqslant 0, \ \frac{\partial v}{\partial x_i}(x,y) > 0, \ \frac{\partial v}{\partial y_i}(x,y) < 0$$

for any $(x,y) \in P \times P$.

The assumption that the concavity is strict and partial derivatives exist are just a matter of simplicity. Nothing of economic substance depends on it. The same is true for the permitted possibility of negative consumption. The neglect of stock vectors with some zero component is more important. Allowing for them would require some minor qualification to our conclusion.

A *steady state* is a configuration where $x = y$. Typically we denote by z this common value.

We are not interested in any state but only in those for which their corresponding stationary trajectories are dynamically efficient. (See the references in the introduction for the relevant concepts and results on the characterization of efficiency. An excellent treatment is Gale (1973).)

A steady state (z,z) is efficient if and only if it satisfies two conditions having, respectively, a short-run and a long-run character.

The short-run condition is that the steady state be supportable by a proportional price system. More precisely, there should be an interest rate factor r_z such that

$$\nabla_y v(z,z) = -(1-r)\nabla_x v(z,z).$$

The long-run condition is that the interest factor r associated with (z,z) be at least as large as the rate of population growth. In our case, $r \geqslant 0$.

The purpose of this paper is to investigate the properties of the locus $L \subset R_+ \times R$ formed by the pairs $(r_z, v(z,z))$ of rates of interest and consumption levels as (z,z) runs over all possible efficient state states.

A first restriction on L follows from the well known, and very general,

Golden Rule Theorem: The steady states that maximize consumption among all steady states are characterized by being efficient and having an associated rate of interest equal to the rate of population growth, in our case zero.

Thus, *a fortiori* (maximization over all steady states implies maximization over the efficient subset), we have that $c > c'$ whenever $(0,c) \in L$, $(r,c') \in L$ for some $r \neq 0$, and $(0,c) \neq (r,c')$. The locus represented in Figure 17.3a is inadmissible.

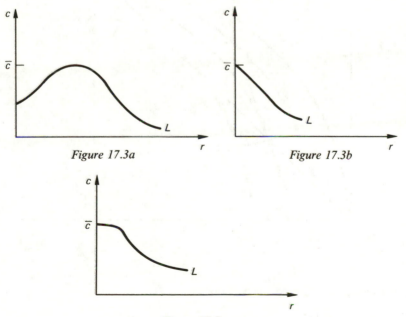

Figure 17.3a

Figure 17.3b

Figure 17.3c

The Golden Rule Theorem is very easy to prove. We should maximize $v(z,z)$ over $z > 0$. The first-order condition for this problem is:

$$\nabla_x v(\bar{z},\bar{z}) = -\nabla_y v(\bar{z},\bar{z}).$$

Hence, $(\bar{z},\bar{z})$ has an associated rate of interest which equals zero. Figure 17.4 provides a graphical illustration in the case $n = 1$.

Note that the Golden Rule Theorem would remain valid if the technology function v is merely quasiconcave (thus allowing for some degree of increasing returns in the production of the consumption good). Indeed, only the convexity of the sets $\{(x',y'): v(x',y') \geqslant v(x,y)\}$ matter to the proof. However, I shall now show that if the technology is in fact concave then the Golden Rule Theorem can be slightly strengthened. Not only is the maximum consumption reached at $r = 0$ but the consumption loss from a first-order increase in r (from $r = 0$) is of the second order. Geometrically, the top of the locus L as it intersects the vertical axis must be flat. Thus, the locus of Figure 17.3c is admissible but the one in Figure 17.3b is inadmissible. An examination of Figure 17.4 will convince the reader that Figure 17.3b could be generated from a quasiconcave v. This is because we are free to assign consumption values to the isoquants in the figure as we please.

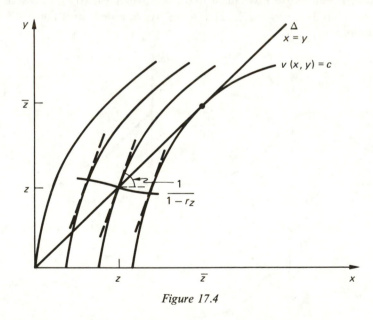

Figure 17.4

Formally the claimed property is:

Fact: Suppose that $\bar{c}$ is a golden rule consumption. If $r_m > 0$, $r_m \to 0$ and $(r_m, c_m) \in L$ then $(\bar{c} - c_m)/(r_m) \to 0$.

Proof: Let $\bar{z}, z_m$ be the capital stock associated, respectively, with the golden rule and (r_m, c_m). Denote $w(z) = v(z, z)$. Then

$$\nabla_z w(z_m) = \nabla_x v(z_m, z_m) + \nabla_y v(z_m, z_m) = r_m \nabla_x v(z_m, z_m).$$

By concavity,

$$\bar{c} = c_m = w(\bar{z}) - w(z_m) \leqslant \nabla_z w(z_m) \cdot (\bar{z} - z_m) = r_m \nabla_x w(z_m) \cdot (\bar{z} - z_m).$$

By the strictly concavity of $w(\cdot)$ we have have $z_m \to \bar{z}$. Therefore,

$$\nabla_x w(z_m) \cdot (\bar{z} - z_m) \to 0$$

and so

$$\frac{\bar{c} - c_m}{r_m} \to 0.$$

Technical Remark: I suspect, although I have only proved it for the case $n = 1$, that the above property can be strengthened to:
  There is a continuous function $\alpha: (-\infty, c] \to R$ such that

   (i) $\alpha(c) \leqslant r$ whenever $(r, c) \in L$ and

  (ii) $\displaystyle\int_{-\infty}^{\bar{c}} \frac{1}{\alpha(c)} \, dc < \infty.$

3   A CONVERSE TO THE GOLDEN RULE THEOREM

The central issue to be discussed in this section is: given a set $L \subset [0, \infty) \times R$, when can L be generated as the interest rate consumption locus of a technology v?

We will always take L to be closed and bounded above. We postulate also that for some $\bar{r} > 0$ we cannot have $(r, c) \in L$, $r \geqslant \bar{r}$ and $c \geqslant 0$. Further, we shall only care about non-negative consumption. Summarizing: we can assume without further loss of generality, that L is a closed subset of a rectangle $[0, \bar{r}] \times [0, \bar{c}]$.

Let $(0, \bar{c}) \in L$ be the golden rule point. We know from Section 2 that L should intersect the vertical axis perpendicularly and only at this point. Essentially, this will turn out to be the only restriction on L and thus the (strengthened) golden rule the only general comparative statics theorem.

The term 'essentially' in the previous paragraph is required because I will impose an extra, weak technical condition controlling the local behavior of L at $(0, \bar{c})$. The technical condition (or, for that matter, the strengthened golden rule itself) *places no restriction whatsoever on the shape of* L *over* $[\epsilon, \bar{r}] \times [0, \bar{c}]$.

Golden Rule Restriction: There is a continuous function $\alpha: (-\infty, \bar{c}] \to R$ with $\alpha(\bar{c}) = 0$ and $\alpha(c) > 0$ for $c < \bar{c}$ such that:

(i)   for a constant $k > 0$, $\alpha(c) \leqslant r \leqslant k\alpha(c)$ whenever $(r,c) \in L$, and

(ii) $\int_{-\infty}^{\bar{c}} \dfrac{1}{\alpha(c)} dc < \infty$. See Figure 17.5.

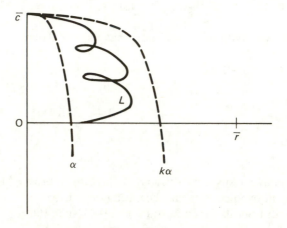

Figure 17.5

I wish to emphasize that, granted the golden rule, the technical golden rule restriction is purely local, i.e. depends only on the form of L near $(0,\bar{c})$. The condition has two parts. The first asserts the existence of a continuous function $\alpha: (-\infty, \bar{c}] \to R$ with $[1]/[\alpha(c)]$ integrable and such that its graph leaves L to its right. As indicated in the remark at the end of the previous section, this implies the perpendicularity of L at $(0,\bar{c})$ and it is only slightly stronger than this property. It may also be a necessary implication of the concavity of v (this is unsettled). The second part is that L be captured between the graphs of α and $k\alpha$. This is necessitated by our method of proof and it could be violated by the locus generated by an admissible technology. Nevertheless, this part of the condition is extremely weak. Its violation appears quite pathological. Indeed, we must be able to find $c_m \to \bar{c}$, $(r_m, c_m), (r'_m, c_m) \in L$ but with r_m, r'_m approaching zero at different rates. In particular, if for c close to $\bar{c}$ we can solve uniquely for the rate of interest $r(c)$ such that $(r(c), c) \in L$, then this second part is automatically satisfied.

After this technical digression, we are able to state the main result.

Proposition: Suppose that $L \subset [0,\bar{r}] \times [0,\bar{c}]$ is a closed set satisfying the golden rule restriction. Then L can be generated by an admissible technology function $v(x,y)$.

The proof of the proposition will be given in the next section. Only two capital goods are needed for the technology.

One could ask if the construction underlying a given L is robust in the sense that a small perturbation of the (production, and productivities) of the generating technology will change L only slightly. Informally, the answer is that, in general, the construction cannot be robust because if it is then the set L itself must belong to the 'generic class' formed by the sets which are one-dimensional smooth manifolds. In less technical terms, if the construction is robust then L should look around any of its points as a little (curved) segment, i.e. as in Figure 17.6a but not as in Figure 17.6b where the manifold condition fails at the three indicated crossing points. On the other hand, we shall observe in the next section, while carrying out the key construction of the proof, that if the set L we start with is a one-dimensional smooth manifold, then the construction is in fact robust.

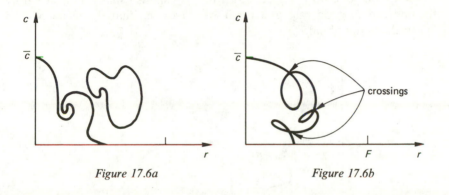

Figure 17.6a   Figure 17.6b

What can we accomplish if we are constrained to a single capital good? Actually, the proposition remains valid provided we add to the restrictions on L that for every $c \leqslant \bar{c}$ there be a unique r_c with $(r_c, c) \in L$. That this restriction is necessary is obvious from Figure 17.4. We see there that fixing c and requiring a steady state determines z uniquely and so there can be at most one rate of interest. On the other hand, in the one-dimensional case, prices across two periods are always proportional. Hence, every steady-state z has associated with it a rate of interest which equals one minus the inverse of the slope to the isoquant through z. Still referring to Figure 17.4, the basic intuition of our proof, reduced to the case $n = 1$, consists in observing that in the segment $[0, (\bar{z}, \bar{z})]$ we can assign the slopes in essentially any manner we wish. There is a slightly delicate point (which accounts for the term 'essentially'): the assignment of isoquants to slopes should be compatible with the isoquant map being generated from a concave function. It is for this that the more refined golden rule restriction (i.e. the existence of the function α) is required.

We have just argued that a set L such as the one in Figure 17.7 can be generated from a one capital good model. This seems to be in conflict with the conventional claim that the one capital good case is well behaved and yields a monotone consumption–interest rate locus. But there is no contradiction. Suppose we impose on the isoquant maps of $v(x,y)$ the following 'normality' condition: if the marginal rates of transformation of x for y are fixed at any arbitrary value, then the resulting one-dimensional curve is increasing with consumption; a higher consumption level is possible only if there is at least as much current capital and less capital requirement for the next period. With this condition, the assignment of slopes to steady state is monotone (see Fig. 17.4 again) and so will be the set L. A sufficient condition for the normality property is that $v(x,y)$ have the 'quasilinear' form $v(x,y)=f(x)-y$. In this case, the isoquants of v are generated from each other by vertical displacement. The form $v(x,y)=f(x)-y$, i.e. the capital and consumption goods are perfect substitutes, is what is usually understood by the one capital good case and for it we have seen that the claim of well behavedness does hold.

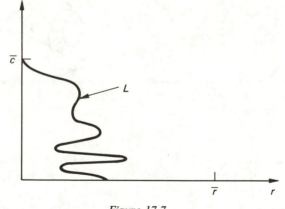

Figure 17.7

4   PROOF OF THE PROPOSITION

The proof consists of six steps. Also, we shall rest content with having $v(x,y)$ continuous and concave. The function can be made continuously differentiable and strictly concave at the cost of two extra steps. Because they are rather messy and not very interesting we skip them.

The technology function $v(x,y)$ is constructed in step 4 after preliminary work in steps 1 to 3. Steps 5 and 6 verify that v has the desired properties. Step 1 constructs v on the steady-state set $\Delta = \{(x,y) \in P \times P: x=y\}$. Steps 2 and 3 associate to every steady state an affine function on R^4 which supports v

over Δ. Step 4 then extends v to the entire $P \times P$ by taking the infimum of all the affine functions.

Without loss of generality we take $\bar{c} = 1$, $\bar{r} = 1$.

Step 1

Take $n = 2$.

There is a considerable freedom in choosing the technology function over the steady-state set $\Delta = \{(x,y) \in P \times P : x = y\}$. We shall choose one which is particularly convenient for latter constructions.

Let $\beta: (-\infty, 1]$ be an arbitrary, continuously differentiable, strictly increasing, strictly convex function with

   (i) $\beta(0) = 0$,

   (ii) $\beta(1) = 1$ and

   (iii)   there is a constant $a > 0$ such that $\beta'(c) = \dfrac{a}{\alpha(c)}$.

Such a function exists because by the golden rule restriction

$$\int_{-\infty}^{\bar{c}} \frac{1}{\alpha(c)} \, dc < \infty.$$

By putting $\beta^{-1}(t) = 1$ for $t > 1$ we can view β^{-1} as defined on $[0, \infty)$. (See Figure 17.8.)

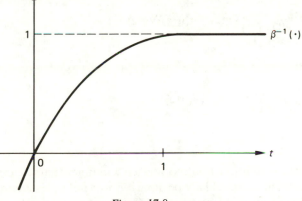

Figure 17.8

Let $e = (1,1)$ and $g: R_+^2 \to R_+$ be an increasing concave function with non-vanishing gradient and Hessian determinant. Suppose also that:

(i) $g(e) = 1$,

(ii) $g((2,0)) < 0$, $g((0,2)) < 0$ and

(iii)   there is a constant $h > 0$ such that $\frac{1}{h}\|\nabla \partial g(z)\| \leq h$ for all $z \geq 0$.

Finally, define $w: \Delta \to (-\infty, 1]$ by the order preserving transformation $w(z) = \beta^{-1}(g(z))$. (See Figure 17.9.)

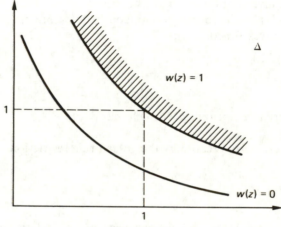

Figure 17.9

Note that for $w(z) < 1$ we have

$$\nabla w(z) = \frac{a}{\beta'(w(z))} \nabla g(z) = \alpha(w(z)) \nabla g(z).$$

Hence,

$$\frac{a}{h} \alpha(w(z)) \leq \|\nabla w(z)\| \leq ah\alpha(w(z)).$$

Step 2

The task here is to inject L into Δ in such a manner that the injection is one-to-one (note that this could *not* be done if Δ was not at least two dimensional) and the isoconsumption sections of L get mapped into the corresponding isoconsumption curves of w. See Figure 17.10.

Parameterize the region $Q = \{z \in \Delta: z \leq e, w(z) \geq 0\}$ by identifying every $z \in Q$ with $(w(z), \theta(z))$ where $\theta(z)$ is the angle in grades of the vector $z - e$. Obviously $180 \leq \theta(z) \leq 270$.

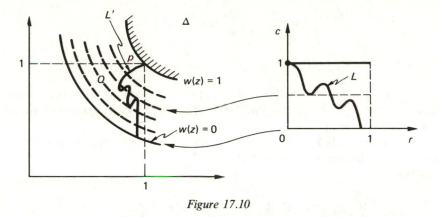

Figure 17.10

To any $(r,c) \in [0,1]^2$ associate the point $z(r,c) \in Q$ given by $(c, 200 + 50r)$. Note that, indeed, $w(z(c,r)) = c$ and that the function $z(\cdot)$ is one-to-one on L. Denote the L' the image of L.

Step 3

We now proceed to associate with every $z \in \Delta$, $0 \leqslant w(z) < 1$, a certain affine function q_z on R^4 majorizing w on Δ. But first we need to pick two auxiliary functions whose existence is a consequence of the closedness of L'.

Let $r: \Delta \to [0,1]$ be a continuous function such that:

   (i) $\alpha(w(z)) \leqslant r(z) \leqslant k\alpha(w(z))$ for any $z \in \Delta$ and

   (ii) if $z \in L'$, then $r(z)$ is the correct rate of interest associated with z, i.e. $z(r(z), w(z)) = z$.

Let $\gamma: \Delta \to (-\tfrac{1}{2}, \tfrac{1}{2})$ be an arbitrary continuously differentiable function such that, whenever $0 \leqslant w(x) \leqslant 1$, we have $\gamma(z) = 0$ if and only if $z \in L'$. In addition, if L (and therefore L') happens to be a smooth one-dimensional, then γ can be chosen so that $\nabla_z \gamma(z) \neq 0$ whenever $\gamma(z) = 0$. It is this requirement which guarantees the robustness of our construction in the case that L is a smooth manifold.

Finally, for every z with $0 \leqslant w(z) < 1$, define $q_z: R^4 \to R$ by

$$q_z(x,y) = b_z^x \cdot x + b_z^y \cdot y + d_z$$

where:

$$b_z^x = \frac{1}{r(z)} \left([1 + \gamma(z)] \frac{\partial w}{\partial z_1}(z), \frac{\partial w}{\partial z_2}(z) \right) \gg 0$$

$$b_z^y = -\frac{1-r(z)}{r(z)}\left(\left[1+\frac{\gamma(z)}{1-r(z)}\right]\frac{\partial w}{\partial z_1}(z),\ \frac{\partial w}{\partial z_2}(z)\right) \ll 0$$

$$d_z = w(z) - (b_z^x + b_z^y)\cdot z.$$

Observe that $b_z^x + b_z^y = \nabla w(z)$ and $q_z(z,z) = w(z)$. Therefore, if $x = y = v$, we have $q_z(v,v) = (b_z^x + b_z^y)\cdot v + d_z = \nabla w(z)\cdot(v-z) + w(z)$, i.e. on Δ q_z coincides with the gradient of w at z.

The vectors b_z^x, b_z^y have been designed so that they are proportional if and only if $z \in L'$, in which case $b_z^y = -(1-r(z))b_z^x$.

Finally

$$\|q_z\| = \|(b_z^x, b_z^y)\| \leqslant \frac{ah\alpha(w(z))}{r(z)} + (1+\gamma(z))\frac{ah\alpha(w(z))}{r(z)} \leqslant 3ah$$

and

$$\|q_z\| \geqslant \|b_x^z\| \geqslant \frac{1}{r(z)}\|\nabla w(z)\| \geqslant \frac{a}{h}\frac{\alpha(w(z))}{r(z)} \geqslant \frac{a}{hk}.$$

Therefore, the collection $\{\|q_z\|:\ 0\leqslant w(z)<1\}$ is uniformly bounded above and below.

Step 4

Define the technology function $v: P\times P\to R$ by:

$$v(x,y) = \mathrm{Inf}\,\{q_z(x,y):\ z\in\Delta,\ 0\leqslant w(z)<1\}.$$

By construction, v is concave. Because of the boundedness property claimed at the end of the previous section, $v(x,y) > -\infty$ for all (x,y) and, also, every subgradient vector is non-trivial and has components of the right (weak) sign. We have in addition that $c(z,z) = w(z)$ on Δ.

To conclude the proof we should show, therefore, that a steady state (z,z) admits a supporting rate of interest $r \geqslant 0$ and consumption $c \geqslant 0$ if and only if $(r,c)\in L$. Step 5 (resp., step 6) establishes the if (resp., only if) part.

Step 5

The if part is trivial. Let $(r,c)\in L$. Take $z = z(r,c)\in L'$. Then $c = v(z(r,c))$ and by construction q_z, which supports $v(x,y)$ at (z,z), has

$$b_z^y = -(1-r(z))b_z^x = -(1-r)b_z^x.$$

Step 6

The only if part is slightly more delicate.

The key fact is that for any $0 \leqslant w(z) < 1$, the function $v(x,y)$ has q_z as the *unique* gradient at (z,z). This implies that if a (z,z) with $1 > v(z,z) \geqslant 0$ admits a rate of interest r, then this r can only come from q_z, i.e. we must have $b_z^y = -(1-r)b_z^x$. Hence, $z \in L'$ (otherwise b_z^x, b_z^y are not proportional) and therefore $r = r(z)$, which yields $(r, v(z,z)) \in L$, the desired conclusion. As for $c = 1$, since $w(\ )$ has a maximum value equal to one it follows from the Golden Rule Theorem that $c = 1$ can only be associated with the rate of interest $r = 0$.

We should therefore prove that if $0 \leqslant w(z) < 1$ then q_z is the unique supporting affine function to $v(x,y)$ at (z,z). We argue by contradiction and suppose that there was another one, denoted p.

Take $au \neq 0$ such that

$$p((z,z) + u) < q_z((z,z) + u).$$

Since $p(z,z) = q_z(z,z)$, this implies $p(u) < q_z(u)$.

By definition of v there is a sequence z_m such that

$$q_{z_m}\left((z,z) + \frac{1}{m}u \right) < v\left((z,z) + \frac{1}{m}u \right) + \frac{1}{2^m} \leqslant p\left((z,z) + \frac{1}{m}u \right)$$

$$+ \frac{1}{2^m} < q_z\left((z,z) + \frac{1}{m}u \right) + \frac{1}{2^m}.$$

By the strict convexity of w on a neighborhood of z and the boundedness of $\{q_z: 0 \leqslant w(x) < 1\}$, we can find $\delta_n \to 0$ such that if $\|z' - z\| > 1/n$, then $q_{z'}((z,z) + \varepsilon v) > q_z((z,z) + \varepsilon v) + \delta_n$ for $\varepsilon < \delta_n$.

Combining the last two paragraphs, we conclude $z_m \to z$.

Rearranging terms and multiplying by m, we get:

$$m(q_{z_m}(z,z) - p(z,z)) + q_{z_m}(u) - p(u) \leqslant \frac{m}{2^m}.$$

The left-hand side goes to zero. The first term of the right-hand side is non-negative because $q_{z_m}(z,z) \geqslant q_z(z,z) = w(z) - p(z,z)$. Therefore, $q_{z_m}(u) \to p(u)$. But $z_m \to z$ implies $q_{z_m} \to q_z$. Therefore, $q_z(u) = p(u)$, which constitutes the desired contradiction.

QED

References

Arrow, K. and F. Hahn (1971) *General Competitive Analysis* (San Francisco: Holden-Day).

Bliss, C. (1975) *Capital Theory and the Distribution of Income* (Amsterdam: North-Holland).

Burmeister, E. (1980) *Capital Theory and Dynamics* (Cambridge: Cambridge University Press).

Gale, D. (1973) 'On the Theory of Interest', *American Mathematical Monthly*, 80: 8.

Harcourt, G. C. (1972) *Some Cambridge Controversies in the Theory of Capital* (Cambridge: Cambridge University Press).

Malinvaud, E. (1953) 'Capital Accumulation and Efficient Allocation of Resources', *Econometrica*, 21.

Neumann, J. von (1945–6) 'A Model of General Economic Equilibrium', *Review of Economic Studies*, 13.

Robinson, J. (1953–4) 'The Production Functions and the Theory of Capital', *Review of Economic Studies*, 21.

Shafer, W. and H. Sonnenschein (1982) 'Market Demand and Excess Demand Functions', ch. 14 in *Handbook of Mathematical Economics*, Vol. II, K. Arrow and M. Intriligator (eds) (Amsterdam: North-Holland).

Weizsäcker, C. C. von (1971) *Steady State Capital Theory* (New York: Springer-Verlag).

18 Steady States and Determinacy of Equilibria in Economies With Infinitely Lived Agents

Timothy J. Kehoe, David K. Levine and
Paul M. Romer*

1 INTRODUCTION

Joan Robinson frequently argued that neoclassical general equilibrium theory could not determine the rate of interest in intertemporal models (see, for example, Robinson, 1973). There were two aspects to this critique: First, neoclassical marginal productivity theory depended on the notion of an aggregate capital stock. Because of aggregation problems, notably reswitching, this concept could not be defined without resorting to circular reasoning except in the most unrealistic of models. Second, for any rate of interest there is a different short-period equilibrium in a neoclassical model. There are not enough equilibrium conditions to determine what this rate of interest is.

This paper focuses on the latter issue: whether the rate of interest is determinate in the neoclassical model. It is well known that this need not be true with overlapping generations: Kehoe and Levine (1985c) give a simple example of an overlapping generations model that has no cycles, is not chaotic, and has a robust continuum of Pareto-efficient equilibria that converge to the same Pareto-efficient stationary state. If we focus on the neoclassical case of the behavior of a production economy with a finite number of heterogeneous, infinitely lived consumers and equilibria that converge to a non-degenerate stationary state or cycle, however, we find that the set of equilibria are determinate, that is, locally unique for almost all endowments.

Our result shows that the determinacy of the rate of interest depends critically on whether or not there are finitely or infinitely many agents. The example in Kehoe and Levine (1985c), clearly shows that indeterminacy has nothing to do with whether or not equilibrium prices lie in the dual of the

* We are grateful to NSF grants SES 85-09484 and SES 83-20007, and to the ULCA Academic Senate for financial support.

commodity space. More strongly, Kehoe, Levine, Mas-Colell, and Zame (1986) show that robust indeterminacy can arise when both the commodity and price spaces are the same Hilbert space, provided there are infinitely many consumers. Consequently, it is the assumption of finitely many consumers that drives our results in this paper.

Our results extend those of Muller and Woodford (1986), who consider production economies with both finitely and infinitely lived agents. They show that there can be no indeterminacy if the infinitely lived agents are sufficiently large. Their results are local, however, and concern only equilibria that converge to a particular stationary state. We prove a global theorem: for a given starting capital stock, there are only finitely many equilibria that converge to any non-degenerate stationary state. One particular implication is that when the discount factor is sufficiently close to one, which implies that there is a global turnpike, then equilibria are determinate.

We assume that markets are complete and that the technology and preferences are convex. Consequently, the behavior of equilibria in our model can be characterized by the properties of a value function. This is because the second theorem of welfare economics holds; that is, any Pareto-efficient allocation can be decentralized as a competitive equilibrium with transfer payments. If the preferences of consumers can be represented by concave utility functions, then an equilibrium with transfers can be calculated by maximizing a weighted sum of the individual utility functions subject to the feasibility constraints implied by the aggregate technology and the initial endowments. Showing that an equilibrium exists is equivalent to showing that there exists a vector of welfare weights such that the transfer payments needed to decentralize the resulting Pareto-efficient allocation are zero. This approach has been pioneered by Negishi (1960) and applied to dynamic models in a series of papers by Bewley (1980, 1982). Using this approach, Kehoe and Levine (1985a) have considered the regularity properties of an infinite horizon economy without production.

In general, calculating the transfers associated with a given set of weights requires the complete calculation of equilibrium quantities and prices. In a dynamic model with an infinite number of commodities, this can be awkward. To simplify the calculation, we adopt an alternative strategy based on the simple geometric observation that any convex set in R^n can be interpreted as the cross-section of a cone in R^{n+1}. To exploit this fact, we add a set of artificial fixed factors to the economy and include them as arguments of the weighted social value function. These factors are chosen so that the augmented utility and production functions are homogeneous of degree one. Thus, the usual problem of choosing a point on the frontier of a convex utility possibility set is converted into a problem of choosing a point from a cone of feasible values for utility. This extension has theoretical advantages analogous to those that arise when a strictly concave production function is converted into a homogeneous of degree one function by the addition of a fixed factor. When the technology for the firm is a cone, profits and revenues are completely accounted for by factor payments. Analogously, making the social value function homogeneous of degree one simplifies the accounting necessary to keep track of the transfers associated with any given Pareto-efficient allocation. The present value of income and expenditure for each individual can be calculated directly from an augmented list of endowments and from the derivatives of the augmented social value function, without explicitly calculating the dynamic paths for prices or quantities. This is the framework for studying multi-agent intertemporal equilibrium models developed by Kehoe and Levine (1985b).

In such a setting equilibria are equivalent to zeros of a simple finite dimensional system of equations involving the derivatives of the social value function and the endowments. Intuition says that since the number of equations and the number of unknowns in this system are both equal to the number of agents, equilibria ought to be determinate. To do the usual kind of regularity analysis, however, we require that the system of equations that determines the equilibria be continuously differentiable. Because these equations involve derivatives of the social value function, they are C^1 if the value function is C^2.

Unfortunately, the question of when the value function is C^2 has not been entirely answered. Consequently, we are led to augment the system of equations with vectors of capital sequences, and focus on equilibria that converge to non-degenerate steady states. Using methods pioneered by Araujo and Scheinkman (1977), we can then prove determinacy using infinite dimensional transversality theory.

If the dimension of the stable or unstable manifold of a stationary state changes as the welfare weights change, or if the total number of stationary states changes, then the system bifurcates. In this case, the dynamical system at stationary states must have unit roots, and our theorem does not apply. Alternatively, the system may have cycles of unbounded length, in which case we loosely refer to it as chaotic. Consequently, our results may be summarized by saying that, in the class of economies that have no bifurcations and no chaos, determinacy is generic.

These results complement those of Kehoe, Levine, and Romer (1987), who make use directly of the differentiability of the value function. There it is shown that if the discount factor is large, there is a global turnpike and the value function is C^2. This overlaps with the results here. On the other hand, if the discount factor is small, the value function is also C^2. This covers most known examples of chaotic systems, as well as systems that satisfy the non-bifurcation condition outlined above. This paper shows that with the non-bifurcation condition, we do not need for the value function to be globally C^2, nor do we need discount factor conditions.

In the next section we present a highly aggregated neoclassical general equilibrium model. We use this model to motivate the approach that we follow and to provide an overview of our results. In Section 3 we establish some preliminary mathematical details about concave functions. Section 4 describes the economy. Section 5 defines and analyzes the savings function of the economy. In the Appendix we prove our major results on the genericity of regularity.

2   AN EXAMPLE

Consider a simple two-person neoclassical growth model. The preferences of each consumer take the usual additively separable form, discounted by the common factor β, $0 < \beta < 1$. The utility function for consumer i, $i = 1,2$, is $\sum_{t=0}^{\infty} \beta^t u_i(c_{it})$ where the momentary utility function u_i is strictly concave and monotonically increasing. The initial endowment of the single productive factor is $\bar{k}^0$, and θ_i is the share of consumer i. Obviously, $\theta_1 + \theta_2 = 1$, and $\theta_i \bar{k}_0$ is the endowment of consumer i. The technology is described by a strictly concave, monotonically increasing aggregate production function $g: R_+ \to R$. Any profits are distributed to consumers in shares φ_i where $\varphi_1 + \varphi_2 = 1$.

A competitive equilibrium for this model consists of a sequence $p_0, p_1, \ldots$ of prices for the consumption good, a price r for the initial capital stock, a consumption allocation $c_{i0}, c_{i1}, \ldots$ for each consumer i, a sequence of capital stocks $k_0, k_1, \ldots$, a sequence of outputs of the consumption good $q_0, q_1, \ldots$, and a level of total of profits π. Given the prices p_t and r_t and the profits π, the consumption allocation c_{it} must solve the utility maximization problem for consumer i:

$$\max \sum_{t=0}^{\infty} \beta^t u_i(c_{it})$$

$$\text{s.t.} \sum_{t=0}^{\infty} p_t c_{it} \leq \theta_i r \bar{k}_0 + \varphi_i \pi.$$

Furthermore, given the prices p_t, the production plans k_t, q_t must maximize profits:

$$\max \sum_{t=0}^{\infty} p_t q_t - r k_0$$

$$\text{s.t.} \quad q_t + k_{t+1} \leq g(k_t), \quad t = 0,1,\ldots$$

In addition, the profits π that enters into the consumers' budget constraints must be those actually generated by the production plans k_t, q_t:

$$\pi = \sum_{t=0}^{\infty} p_t q_t - r k_0.$$

Finally, demand must equal supply for the consumption good in every period and for the initial capital stock:

$$c_{1t} + c_{2t} = q_t, \quad t = 0, 1, \dots$$

$$k_0 = \bar{k}_0.$$

Let us assume that the functions u_i and f are such that at any equilibrium the utility maximization problems of the consumers and the profit maximization problem of the production sector have interior solutions. Assuming that these functions are also continuously differentiable, we can characterize these solutions using first-order conditions. For the utility maximization problem of consumer i, these are

$$\beta^t u_i'(c_{it}) - \lambda_i p_t = 0, \quad t = 0, 1, \dots$$

$$\sum_{t=0}^{\infty} p_t c_{it} = \theta_i r \bar{k}_0 + \varphi_i \pi.$$

Here $\lambda_i > 0$ is the marginal utility of income of consumer i. The first-order conditions for profit maximization are

$$p_t - \mu_t = 0, \quad t = 0, 1, \dots$$

$$-r + \mu_0 g'(k_0) = 0$$

$$-\mu_{t-1} + \mu_t g'(k_t) = 0, \quad t = 1, 2, \dots$$

Here $\mu_t > 0$ is the Lagrange multiplier associated with the constraint in period t. These conditions can be simplified to

$$g'(k_0) = \frac{r}{p_0}$$

$$g'(k_t) = \frac{p_{t-1}}{p_t}, \quad t = 1, 2, \dots$$

Let us now consider the social planning problem of determining a Pareto-efficient consumption allocation and production sequence. Given non-negative welfare weights (α_1, α_2), we maximize a weighted sum of the individual consumers' utilities subject to feasibility constraints:

$$\max \sum_{i=1}^{2} \alpha_i \sum_{t=0}^{\infty} \beta^t u_i(c_{it})$$

$$\text{s.t.} \sum_{i=1}^{2} c_{it} + k_{t+1} \leqslant g(k_t) \quad t=0,1,...$$

A solution to this problem can be characterized using the first-order conditions

$$\alpha_i \beta^t u_i'(c_{it}) - p_t = 0, \quad i=1,2; \ t=0,1,...$$

$$-p_{t-1} + p_t q'(k_t) = 0, \quad t=0,1,...$$

$$p_0 g'(k_0) - r = 0.$$

Here $p_t > 0$ is the Lagrange multiplier associated with the constraint on output in every period and r is the Lagrange multiplier associated with the constraint on the initial capital stock. (In addition to these conditions there is a transversality condition of the form $p_t k_t \to 0$ as $t \to \infty$.)

Notice that, if we set $\alpha_i = 1/\lambda_i$, $i=1,2$, then a competitive equilibrium satisfies all of the conditions for a Pareto-efficient consumption allocation and production sequence. (It is trivial to show that the transversality condition must be satisfied if the profit maximization problem has a finite solution.) This is the first theorem of welfare economics, that every competitive equilibrium is Pareto efficient. Notice too that, if we set $\lambda_i = 1/\alpha_i$, $i=1,2$, then a solution to the social planning problem satisfies all of the conditions for a competitive equilibrium except, possibly, the individual budget constraints. This is the second theorem of welfare economics, that every Pareto-efficient consumption allocation and production plan can be implemented as a competitive equilibrium with transfer payments. In this case, the transfer payments necessary to implement the consumption allocation and production plan associated with the welfare weights (α_1, α_2) are

$$\sum_{t=0}^{\infty} p_t(\alpha) c_{it}(\alpha) - \theta_i r(\alpha) \bar{k}_0 - \varphi_i \pi(\alpha), \quad i=1,2,...$$

where

$$\pi(\alpha) = \sum_{t=0}^{\infty} p_t(\alpha) \sum_{i=1}^{2} c_{it}(\alpha) - r(\alpha) \bar{k}_0.$$

A competitive equilibrium corresponds to a vector of welfare weights α for which these transfer payments are equal to zero.

Let us develop a characterization of solutions to the social planning problem, and of competitive equilibria, in dynamic programming terms. Given an aggregate endowment of capital k_0 and a vector of non-negative welfare weights (α_1, α_2), define a value function $V(k_0, \alpha_1, \alpha_2)$ as the maximum of

$$\sum_{i=1}^{2} \alpha_i \sum_{t=0}^{\infty} \beta^t u_i(c_{it})$$

subject to the constraint

$$\sum_{i=1}^{2} c_{it} + k_{t+1} \leqslant g(k_t).$$

The envelope theorem allows us to treat the derivative $D_1 V(k_0, \alpha_1, \alpha_2)$ as the price for capital r and use it to calculate the value of the endowment $\theta \bar{k}_0$ for each individual. To calculate the transfers associated with these weights, we must also calculate the profits of the firm, if any, and the expenditure of each individual. For profits this is straightforward: If f is not homogeneous of degree one, introduce a fixed factor $x \in \mathbb{R}$ and define $G(k,x) = g(k/x)$. Specify endowments φ_i of this fixed factor equal to the ownership shares of the individuals in the aggregate firm. Then define $V(k_0, x, \alpha_1, \alpha_2)$ as the maximum of the weighted objective function subject to the constraint $\Sigma_{i=1}^{2} c_{it} + k_{t+1} \leqslant G(k_t, x)$. In equilibrium the aggregate endowment of the factor x is equal to 1, but it is useful to allow for the hypothetical possibility that it takes on other values so that we can calculate derivatives. Formally, we can treat x as a factor of production analogous to k and conclude that the share of the profits for agent i is φ_i multiplied by the price $D_2 V(k_0, x, \alpha_1, \alpha_2)$. Since $G(k,x)$ is homogeneous of degree one, profits net of the new factor payments are zero. McKenzie (1959) has observed that any convex production possibility set could be interpreted as a cross-section of a cone in precisely this fashion and suggested that x be interpreted as an entrepreneurial factor.

Alternatively, x could denote the input of inelastic labor. In this interpretation each consumer is endowed with a constant amount φ_i of labor in every period, and units are normalized so that the total supply of labor in every period is one. What we have called profits is actually labor income. Here $g(k_t) = G(k_t, 1)$ and our construction helps us recover the 'lost' factor.

The next step is to show that strictly concave utility functions can also be made homogeneous of degree one. If we interpret the fixed factor x as an accounting device used to keep track of producer surplus – the difference between revenue and expenditure – it is clear that a similar factor can be used to account for consumer surplus – the difference between utility and expenditure. Introduce an additional, person-specific fixed utility factor w_i

for each agent, and endow agent i with the entire aggregate supply of one unit of factor i. (For simplicity, we make no distinction in the notation between the individual's holdings of factor w_i and the aggregate endowment.) Just as we do for production, define an augmented utility function $U_i(c,w_i) = w_i u_i(c/w_i)$. In the next section, we show that this augmented utility function can always be defined and is well behaved even when u_i is unbounded from below. Now define a value function $V(k_0, x, w_1, w_2, \alpha_1, \alpha_2)$ as the maximum of the weighted sum of the augmented utility functions subject to the augmented technology.

If we let c_{it} denote the optimal consumption of agent i at time t, the first-order conditions from the maximization imply the equality

$$\beta^t \alpha_i D_1 U_i(c_{it}, w_i) = \beta^t \alpha_j D_1 U_j(c_{jt}, w_j).$$

As a result, discounted marginal utility for either consumer can be used as a present value price for consumption at time t. The only difference from the usual representative consumer framework is that the weights α convert the individual marginal utility prices into a social marginal value price. We can then evaluate the expenditure of consumer i in period t as c_{it} multiplied by this price. Using the properties of homogeneous functions, we can decompose period t utility for consumer i into the sum of a term of this form and an analogous term involving the added utility factor:

$$U_i(c_{it}, w_i) = c_{it} D_1 U_i(c_{it}, w_i) + w_i D_2 U_i(c_{it}, w_i).$$

If the term involving the utility factor is interpreted as a measure of consumer surplus, expenditure on goods in period t is simply utility minus consumer surplus. Using the envelope theorem, we can calculate the present value of consumer surplus for agent 1 as the derivative of the social value function $V(k_0, x, w_1, w_2, \alpha)$ with respect to w_1 multiplied by the endowment w_1:

$$w_1 D_3 V(k_0, x, w_1, w_2, \alpha_1, \alpha_2) = \sum_{t=0}^{\infty} \beta^t \alpha_1 w_1 D_2 U_1(c_{1t}, w_1).$$

Similarly, we can calculate the discounted sum of utility for consumer 1, measured in social value units, as the derivative of the social value function with respect to α_1 multiplied by α_1:

$$\alpha_1 D_5 V(k_0, x, w_1, w_2, \alpha_1, \alpha_2) = \sum_{t=0}^{\infty} \beta^t \alpha_1 U_1(c_{1t}, w_1).$$

Then the present value of expenditure by agent 1 is simply the difference

$$\alpha_1 D_5 V(k_0, x, w_1, w_2, \alpha_1, \alpha_2) - w_1 D_3 V(k_0, x, w_1, w_2, \alpha_1, \alpha_2).$$

The transfer to agent 1 necessary to support this equilibrium is zero if and only if this expenditure is equal to the time zero value of the agent's endowment

$$\theta_1 k_0 D_1 V(k_0,x,w_1,w_2,\alpha_1,\alpha_2) + \varphi_1 D_2 V(k_0,x,w_1,w_2,\alpha_1,\alpha_2).$$

Formally, this equality can be interpreted in terms of an augmented economy where trade in the production factor x and the utility factors w_i actually takes place. In this case, this equality can be interpreted as a requirement that the value of the augmented endowment for agent 1, $\theta_1 k_0 D_1 V + \varphi_1 D_2 V + w_1 D_3 V$, equals the amount of social utility purchased, $\alpha_1 D_5 V = \alpha_1 \sum_{t=0}^{\infty} \beta^t U_1$.

It is useful to define a net savings function s_1 for consumer 1 as

$$s_1(k_0,\theta,\varphi,\alpha) = \theta_1 k_0 D_1 V(k_0,1,1,1,\alpha_1,\alpha_2) + \varphi_1 D_2 V(k_0,1,1,1,\alpha_1,\alpha_2)$$

$$+ D_3 V(k_0,1,1,1,\alpha_1,\alpha_2) - \alpha_1 D_5 V(k_0,1,1,1,\alpha_1,\alpha_2).$$

The savings function for consumer 2 is defined symmetrically. For a given set of welfare weights α the transfer for each individual needed to support the social optimum as a competitive equilibrium is the negative of the net savings for that individual. A competitive equilibrium is therefore a vector of weights α such that $s(k_0,\theta,\varphi,\alpha) = 0$. In general, if m is the number of individuals, $s(k_0,\theta,\varphi,\cdot)$ is a map from $\mathbb{R}^m$ into $\mathbb{R}^m$, and the existence of an equilibrium can be established using a standard fixed point argument in a finite dimensional space.

This characterization of equilibria as zeros of an equation involving endowments and the derivatives of an augmented value function is quite general. All that is required is that the second welfare theorem hold and that the preferences of the consumers can be represented using concave utility functions.

3 HOMOGENEOUS EXTENSION OF CONCAVE FUNCTIONS

In describing equilibria, we shall need the fact that it is possible to convert any concave utility function into a homogeneous function by adding a fixed factor. This does not follow immediately from results for production functions because utility functions need not be bounded from below. The analysis that follows would be considerably simpler if we restricted attention to utility functions that are bounded, but functions like logarithmic utility and isoelastic utility, $u(c) = -c^{-\sigma}$ where $\sigma > 0$ are widely used in applications of this kind of model. In the formal analysis we accommodate these functions using the concepts and terminology from convex analysis for dealing with extended real valued functions; see Rockafellar (1970) for a complete treatment.

If n_c denotes the number of consumption goods in this economy, a utility function u is a function that is defined on the non-negative orthant $R_+^{n_c}$ in commodity space, and that takes on values in $R \cup \{-\infty\}$. On the strictly positive orthant $R_{++}^{n_c}$, u is finite, but to accommodate functions like logarithmic utility, we want to allow for the possibility that $u(c)$ is equal to $-\infty$ if one of the components of c is equal to zero. We can define a topology on $R \cup \{-\infty\}$ by adding the open intervals $[-\infty, a)$ to the base for the usual topology of R. Note that $(-\infty, \infty)$ is not a closed set in this topology and that convergence to $-\infty$ has the usual interpretation: a sequence $\{b^n\}$ in R converges to $-\infty$ if, for all $M \in R$, there exists an N such that $n \geq N$ implies $b^n \in [-\infty, M)$. With this topology, the natural assumption on preferences is that $u : R_+^{n_c} \to R \cup \{-\infty\}$ be continuous. For example, the utility functions $u(c) = -c^{-1/2}$ and $u(c) = ln(c)$ can both be represented as continuous functions from R_+ to $R \cup \{-\infty\}$.

The extension of $u(c)$ to the homogeneous function $U(c,w) = wu(c/w)$ does not preserve continuity on the non-negative orthant in R^{n_c+1}. A discontinuity can arise at the point $(c,w) = (0,0)$. This extension does, however, preserve a weaker notion of continuity. Recall that for a function $g : R \to R$, g is *upper-semi-continuous* (u.s.c.) if the inverse image $g^{-1}([a,\infty))$ is always a closed set. If we allow the function g to take values in $R \cup \{-\infty\}$ instead of R, we can make an identical definition. Equivalently, g is u.s.c. if, for any sequence $\{y^n\}$ in R converging to y, $\lim_{n \to \infty} \sup g(y^n) \leq g(y)$. Since an u.s.c. function has a maximum over a compact set, upper-semi-continuity is strong enough for our purposes. If the function g is concave, define the *recession function* of g, $r_g : R_+ \to R \cup \{-\infty\}$, as

$$r_g(y) = \lim_{t \to \infty} \frac{g(z + ty) - g(z)}{t}$$

where z is any point such that $g(z)$ is finite. Since g is concave, it can be shown that r_g is homogeneous of degree one and does not depend on the choice of z in the definition. Roughly speaking, $r_g(y)$ describes the asymptotic average slope of g along a ray from the origin passing through the point y.

Given these definitions, we can now state the key lemma for our construction. See Rockafellar (1970, p.67) for a proof.

Lemma 1: Let $g : R_+ \to R \cup \{-\infty\}$ be concave and continuous. Let

$$G : R \times R \to R \cup \{-\infty\}$$

be defined by

$$
G(y,\rho)=
\begin{cases}
\rho g(y/\rho) & \text{if } \rho>0 \text{ and } y\in\mathbb{R}_+, \\
r_g(y) & \text{if } \rho=0 \text{ and } y\in\mathbb{R}_+ \\
-\infty & \text{otherwise}
\end{cases}
$$

Then G is concave, u.s.c., and homogeneous of degree one.

If g is a production function, hence non-negative, $G(y,\rho)$ is increasing in ρ. If g represents a utility function that takes on negative values, $G(y,\rho)$ is decreasing in ρ for some values of y. In the artificial equilibrium where we allow for trade in the utility factors, this may imply that the price associated with the utility factor is negative. Implicitly, the strategy here is to consider first an equilibrium with explicit markets in all goods, including the fixed factors in the utility functions. Prices are such that each individual consumes his endowment (equal to one) of the utility factor. Then prices and quantities for all other goods do not depend on whether or not trade in the utility factors is possible. The possibility of negative prices for utility factors in the complete markets equilibrium poses no problem for proving existence because it is not necessary to assume free disposal of the utility factors. As long as each individual is endowed at time zero with a positive amount of capital or some other factor with positive value, strictly positive consumption of all true consumption goods is feasible. The total value of any individual's endowment may be negative, but it is always possible to use up the utility factor, that is, consume it, leaving strictly positive income to be spent on the true consumption goods.

4 FORMAL EQUILIBRIUM MODEL

Assume that there are m consumers in the economy. Let n_k denote the number of reproducible capital stocks, n_c the number of consumption goods. Let k_0 denote the n_k vector of initial aggregate capital stocks. Let φ denote the m vector of ownership shares for the single aggregate firm. Each agent has a utility function $u_i\colon \mathbb{R}^{n_c}\to\mathbb{R}\cup\{-\infty\}$; let $U_i\colon \mathbb{R}^{n_c}\times\mathbb{R}\to\cup\mathbb{R}\times\{-\infty\}$ denote the homogeneous extension of u_i as defined in Lemma 1. Naturally $U_i(c_{it},1)=u_i(c_{it})$.

We assume that all consumers have the same discount factor $\beta>1$. Conceptually, there is no difficulty with different consumers having different discount factors. Kehoe and Levine (1985b) show how to integrate this into the formal model. Moreover, the proof of the existence of an equilibrium remains straightforward. For simplicity, assume that the technology that relates period t to period $t+1$ can be described in terms of an aggregate production function. Let c_t, k_t, and k_{t+1} denote the aggregate consumption at time t, and capital at time t and $t+1$. Then the technology is described by the constraint $f(k_t, k_{t+1}, c_t) \geqslant 0$, where $f: R_+^{lk} \times R^{lk} \times R_+^{lc} \to R$. In our simple example,

$$f(k_t, k_{t+1}, c_t) = g(k_t) - k_{t+1} - c_t.$$

Formally, it is convenient to allow f to be defined when the terminal stock k_{t+1} lies outside the non-negative orthant. Hypothetically, if it were possible to leave negative capital for next period, f describes the additional current consumption that would be possible. In the intertemporal optimization problems we explicitly impose the constraint that k_{t+1} be non-negative.

In this specification of the aggregate technology, we have not made explicit the dependence of output on factors of production that are in fixed supply. Formally, it is as if we have given ownership of all such factors to the aggregate firm. Individuals sell any endowments of land and labor for an increased ownership share in the firm. To consume a specified amount of leisure or of consumption services from land, an individual must purchase these like any other consumption good. This is merely a notational convenience. To make these factors explicit, we would simply need to augment the argument list for the production function and specify individual endowments in these additional factors.

By Lemma 1, there exists a homogeneous function $F(k_t, k_{t+1}, c_t, x)$ such that $F(k_t, k_{t+1}, c_t, 1) = f(k_t, k_{t+1}, c_t)$. Given the additional fixed factor x, the aggregate technology set is a cone. Its representation in terms of an aggregate production function is convenient because it allows a simple specification of the smoothness properties of the technology. If F is smooth, the boundary of the cone is smooth. A more general treatment along the lines of Bewley (1982) would start from assumptions about the separate technologies available to individual firms, but our interest here lies not so much with the specification of the technology, but rather with the specification of preferences and endowments.

We can now specify the properties assumed for the preferences and technology. The assumptions concerning continuity and smoothness are standard. For convenience, the usual monotonicity assumptions are strengthened, but this is not essential. A more important restriction is that the utility function be strictly concave and that the production possibility set for output capital stocks be strictly convex when the input capital stocks and aggregate consumption are held constant.

Assumption 1: For all i, the utility function $u_i: R_+^{lc} \to R \cup \{-\infty\}$ is concave, strictly increasing, and continuous. On the strictly positive orthant R_{++}^{nc}, u is C^2 and has a negative definition Hessian.

Assumption 2: The production function f: $\mathbb{R}_+^{n_k} \times \mathbb{R}^{n_k} \times \mathbb{R}_1^{n_c} \to \mathbb{R}$ is concave and continuous, with $f(0,0,0)=0$. On the interior of its domain, f is C^2, strictly increasing in its first argument, and strictly decreasing in the second and third arguments. Also the matrix of second derivatives with respect to the vector of terminal stocks, $D_{22}f(k_t,k_{t+1},c_t)$, is negative definite.

In his discussion of the von Neumann facet, McKenzie (1983) has emphasized that it is restrictive to assume that f is strictly concave. If fixed factors in production can be allocated between different constant returns to scale industries (for example, labor in the multisector neoclassical growth model), there can exist an affine set of initial and terminal capital stocks that produce the same consumption goods vector. In the usual case where consumption and next period capital can be exchanged one for one, the weaker assumption that $D_{22}f(k_t,k_{t+1},c_t)$ is negative definite requires that, given k_t, the set of possible output combinations have a production possibility frontier with positive curvature.

If we define $f(k_t,k_{t+1},c_t)$ as $g(k_t)-k_{t+1}-c_t$ in our simple example, then $D_{22}f(k_t,k_{t+1},c_t)=0$. Suppose instead we set

$$f(k_t,k_{t+1},c_t)=h(g(k_t))-h(k_{t+1}+c_2)$$

where h is a function that satisfies $h'>0$ $h''>0$. If $g''<0$, then we can choose h so that the composition $h(g(k_t))$ is still concave. Consequently, f now satisfies Assumption 2. We should stress that we have made our assumptions very strong to keep our exposition as simple as possible. Most of our results could be derived under weaker assumptions.

Because some of the factors of production are in fixed supply, output exhibits diminishing returns as a function of the initial capital stock. The next assumption strengthens the diminishing returns so that feasible output stocks are bounded.

Assumption 3: (Boundedness) There exists $k_{max} \in \mathbb{R}_+^{n_k}$ and a bound $b<1$ such that $k_t \geqslant k_{max}$ and $k_{t+1} \geqslant bk_t$ implies that k_{t+1} is not feasible.

This assumption states that capital stocks larger than k_{max} cannot be sustained. By the definition of F, this bound also holds when $f(k_t,k_{t+1},c)$ is replaced by its homogeneous extension $F(k_t,k_{t+1},c,x)$ for any value of x less than or equal to one. This boundedness assumption is stronger than is needed for existence of a social optimum or an equilibrium, but it is required to rule out unbounded growth paths in the proof of the existence of an optimal stationary value for the capital stock.

Proving the existence of an optimal stationary state also requires the other half of a set of Inada-type conditions on production. Assumption 4 ensures that there exist strictly positive feasible paths for capital and consumption, and that at least one such path does not converge asymptotically to zero consumption and capital. Recall that R^k_{++} denotes the strictly positive orthant in R^k and that $\beta < 1$ is the discount factor.

Assumption 4: (Feasibility) For all $k_t \in R^k_{++}$ there exists $k_{t+1} \in R^k_{++}$ and $c \in R^c_{++}$ such that (k_t, k_{t+1}, c) is feasible, that is, $f(k_t, k_{t+1}, c) \geq 0$. Furthermore, for some point $k_t \in R^k_{++}$, k_{t+1} and c can be chosen so that $c \in R^c_{++}$ and $\beta k_{t+1} > k_t$.

The smoothness arguments that follow require that the optimal values of the capital stock and consumption lie in the interior of the domain of the production function and the consumption function respectively. This is guaranteed here by infinite steepness conditions on the boundary of the domains. For a concave function $g: R^r \to R \cup \{-\infty\}$, the generalization of a derivative is a subgradient. The set of *subgradients* of g at y, denoted $\partial g(y)$, is defined by

$$\partial g(y) = \{p \in R^r : g(z) - g(y) \leq p(z - y) \text{ for all } z \in R^r\}.$$

Note that we follow the unfortunate, but well-established, convention of letting a term like subgradient have a different meaning for concave and convex functions. For a convex function $h(z)$, the definition of $\partial h(z)$ is given by reversing the direction in the inequality in the definition given here. Let $\{y^n\}$ be a sequence in R_{++}. Suppose g is a differentiable function with the property that one of the components of the gradient $\partial g(y^n)$ has a limit equal to ∞ as y^n approaches a point y. Then $\partial g(y)$ is empty. By the assumption of concavity, a point like y can arise only on the boundary of the domain of g. For a function like $g(y_1, y_2) = y_1^{0.3} y_2^{0.3}$, the limit of the gradient as (y_1^n, y_2^n) goes to $(0,0)$ cannot be defined, but it is still the case that $\partial g(0,0)$ is empty.

Assumption 5: (Infinite steepness on the boundary)
(a)   If c is an element of the boundary of the domain of u_i, the set of subgradients $\partial u_i(c)$ is empty.
(b)   If any component of k_t is 0, the set of subgradients of f with respect to its first argument, $\partial_1 f(k_t, k_{t+1}, c)$, is empty.

Part (a) implies that the marginal utility of any good is infinite starting from zero consumption of that good. As stated, it allows u to be finite or to equal $-\infty$ on the boundary. It implies that every individual consumes some amount of every good in equilibrium, but weaker conditions could be used. All that is necessary is that a strictly positive amount of each good be produced in equilibrium. Part (b) is the usual assumption of infinite marginal productivity of each capital good starting from zero usage.

5 SOCIAL RETURN AND SAVINGS FUNCTIONS

We now define the return and savings functions derived from the social planning problem. These are then used to define an equilibrium. Given the underlying preferences and technology, we define a weighted momentary social return function $v: R_+^{lk} \times R^{lk} \times R_+ \times R_+^m \times R_+^m \to R \cup \{-\infty\}$ as follows: If $F(k_t, k_{t+1}, 0, x) \geq 0$, that is, if non-negative aggregate consumption is feasible,

$$v(k_t, k_{t+1}, x, w, \alpha) = \max \sum_{i=1}^{\infty} \alpha_i U_i(c_i, w_i)$$

$$\text{s.t. } F\left(k_t, k_{t+1}, \sum_{i=1}^{\infty} c_{it}, x\right) \geq 0$$

$$c_i \geq 0.$$

If $F(k_t, k_{t+1}, 0, x) < 0$,

$$v(k_t, k_{t+1}, x, w, \alpha) = -\infty.$$

If we were to work only with utility functions that are bounded from below on a suitably chosen domain, v would be a familiar, real valued saddle function. It is concave and homogeneous of degree one in (k_t, k_{t+1}, x, w), convex and homogeneous of degree one in α. It would also be continuous in the usual sense, instead of u.s.c. as established below. The following proposition, characterizing v, is proven in Kehoe, Levine, and Romer (1987).

Proposition 1: Under Assumptions 1–5, the following results hold:

(a) v is well defined.
(b) For $\alpha \in R_{++}^m$, $v(\cdot, \cdot, \cdot, \cdot, \alpha)$ is concave, u.s.c., and homogeneous of degree one, with the same monotonicity properties as F.
(c) For any $(k_t, k_{t+1}, x, w) \in R_+^{lk} \times R^{lk} \times R_+ \times R_+^m$, the function $v(k_t, k_{t+1}, x, w, \cdot)$: $R_{++}^m \to R \cup \{-\infty\}$ is convex and homogeneous of degree one.
(d) For any $(x, w, \alpha) \in R_+ \times R_+^m \times R_+^m$, the set of subgradients of the concave function $v(\cdot, \cdot, x, w, \alpha)$ is empty at every point on the boundary of its domain.
(e) On the interior of its domain, v is C^2.
(f) Evaluated at any point in the interior of the domain of v, $D_{22}v(k_t, k_{t+1}, x, \alpha)$ is negative definite.

Next, we consider the optimization problem

$$\max \sum_{t=0}^{\infty} \beta^t v(k_t, k_{t+1}, x, w, \alpha). \tag{1}$$

Here, the maximization is over all non-negative sequences $\{k_t\}$ having an initial value equal to k_0. The constraint that the sequence be feasible is implicit in the maximization problem since v must take on the value $-\infty$ at some point along an infeasible sequence. Let $\ell_\infty^{n_k}$ denote the Banach space of bounded sequences in R^{i_k} under the sup norm, $|k| = \sup_t |k_t|$, where $|k_t|$ denotes any norm equivalent to the usual norm on R^{n_k}; let $(\ell_\infty^{n_k})_+$ denote the positive orthant in $\ell_\infty^{n_k}$. For convenience, assume that the first component of any sequence in $\ell_\infty^{n_k}$ has an index $t = 1$. Define the mapping associated with the Euler equation, $\xi: (\ell_\infty^{n_k})_{++} \times R^{i_k}_{++} \times R^n_{++} \to \ell_\infty^{n_k}$, by the rule

$$\xi(k,k_0,\alpha)_t = D_2 v(k_{t-1},k_t,1,1,\alpha) + \beta D_1 v(k_t,k_{t+1},1,1,\alpha), \quad t \geq 1.$$

By the usual sufficient conditions for concave maximization problems, any path k_t that remains bounded and satisfies the Euler equation $\xi(k,k_0,\alpha)=0$ is an optimal path. Conversely, any optimal path k starting at an interior point $k_0 \in R^{i_k}_{++}$ satisfies this equation and remains bounded. Consequently, $k \in (\ell_\infty^{n_k})_+$ is optimal if and only if $\xi(k,k_0,\alpha)=0$.

To define the savings functions we need to specify the matrices of individual endowments. Let θ denote the $n_k \times m$ matrix of non-negative capital shares. Naturally $\Sigma_{j=1}^m \theta_{ij} = 1$. Let k_0 denote the $n_k \times n_k$ diagonal matrix of capital stock corresponding to an n_k vector k_0, and let A denote the $m \times m$ diagonal matrix of welfare weights corresponding to an m vector α. Also let φ denote the m vector of endowment shares of the fixed factor of production. We say that the endowment shares θ and φ and initial stock k_0 are *admissible* if all of the components are non-negative, if the aggregate supplies k_0, are strictly positive, if every individual is endowed with a positive amount of some capital good, and if the shares sum to one. If we let θ^T denote the transpose of θ and interpret all the following products as matrix products, we can define the savings function for any admissible k_0,θ,φ and $\alpha \in R^m_+$ as follows:

$$\sigma(k,k_0,\alpha,\theta,\varphi) = \theta^T k_0 D_1 v(k_0,k_1,1,1,\alpha) + \varphi \sum_{t=0}^\infty \beta^t D_3 v(k_t,k_{t+1},1,1,\alpha)$$

$$+ \sum_{t=0}^\infty \beta^t D_4 v(k_t,k_{t+1},1,1,\alpha) - A \sum_{t=0}^\infty \beta^t D_5 v(k_t,k_{t+1},1,1,\alpha).$$

Notice that, in defining the savings function, we have set $x = 1$ and $w_i = 1$ for $i = 1,...,m$. At these values the augmented functions $U_i(c_{it},w_i)$ and $F(k_t,k_{t+1},c_t,x)$ reduce to the original specifications u_i and f. The next proposition establishes the basic properties of σ, and of the optimal stationary capital stock k^{ss}.

Proposition 2: Let $k_0 \in R^{i_k}_+$, let $x \in R_+$, and let $\alpha \in R^m_+$. Under Assumptions 1–5 the following results hold:

(a)   The maximization problem (1) has a unique solution.
(b)   There exists an optimal stationary value $k^{ss} = k^{ss}(\alpha)$; that is, the sequence defined by $k_t = k^{ss}$ solves the problem (1) beginning at k^{ss}; every optimal stationary value lies strictly in the interior.
(c)   The pair (ξ, σ) is C^1.
(d)   The pair (ξ, σ) is homogeneous of degree one in α.
(e) $\Sigma_{i=1}^n \sigma_i(k, k_0, \alpha, \theta, \varphi) \equiv 0$.

See the Appendix for the proof. Kehoe, Levine, and Romer (1987) prove the following result.

Proposition 3: For given k_0, θ, and φ, k and α are an equilibrium if and only if

$$\xi(k, k_0, \alpha) = 0$$

$$\sigma(k, k_0, \alpha, \theta, \varphi) = 0.$$

Moreover, an equilibrium exists for any k_0, θ, and φ that are admissible.

Because (ξ, σ) is homogeneous and $\Sigma_{i=1}^m \sigma_i = 0$, we should delete one variable and one equation from our equilibrium system. Fix $\alpha_m = 1$. For notational simplicity we assume hereafter that $\alpha = (\alpha_1, \alpha_2, ..., \alpha_{m-1})$. We shall also assume hereafter that σ consists of σ_1 to σ_{m-1} only. Our procedure is analogous to that used with systems of excess demand functions where homogeneity of degree zero is used to impose a numeraire and Walras's Law is used to drop an equation.

We now define a non-degenerate steady state and prove that, for generic initial conditions, there are only finitely many equilibria converging to non-degenerate steady states. Define $D_h\xi = [D_1\xi \, D_2\xi]$. Let $D_{ij}v_t$ denote $D_{ij}v(k_t, k_{t+1}, \alpha)$. Then we can write the component t of $D_h\xi(k, k_0, \alpha)h$ as

$$\beta D_{12}v_t h_{t+1} + (\beta D_{11}v_t + D_{22}v_{t-1})h_t + D_{21}v_{t-1}h_{t-1}.$$

In other words, $D_h\xi h = 0$ gives rise to a linear dynamical system. At a stationary state, the coefficients are time independent, so we omit the time subscript. For emphasis we write $D_h\xi^{ss}$ to emphasize we are considering a stationary state. By the roots of $D_h\xi^{ss}$ we mean the eigenvalues of the associated linear dynamical system. We call a stationary state *non-degenerate* if $D_h\xi^{ss}$ has no roots on the unit circle and if $D_{12}v$ is non-singular.

That $D_{12}v$ is non-singular ensures that the dynamical system can be solved both forwards and backwards since $D_{21}v$ is the transpose of $D_{12}v$. In economic terms, this means that the model must be stated using a minimal set of capital goods. To see what this rules out, consider a Cobb–Douglas neoclassical growth model stated in terms of two capital goods, two consumption goods, and a fixed endowment of labor that must be allocated between identical production functions for the two consumption goods. Let two individuals have identical preferences $ln(c_1) + ln(c_2)$. The economy satisfies Assumptions 1–5. It is straightforward to show by direct algebraic manipulation that independent of the initial stocks of capitals, the subsequent aggregate stocks of the capital goods in the social planning problem for and set of weights α are always chosen in fixed proportions. (The consumption goods are also consumed in fixed proportions.) The model is not in any relevant sense two dimensional: the two capital goods and the two consumption goods can be combined into single composite capital and consumption goods. The dynamical system associated with the social planning problem for this economy always maps k_{t+1} onto a line in R^2. One can also show directly that $D_{12}v(k_t, k_{t+1}, \alpha)$ is everywhere singular in this case. This kind of collapse in the dimensionality of the model is prevented, even locally, by assuming that $D_{12}v$ is non-singular.

At a non-degenerate steady state, it is well known that R^{2n_k} can be written as the direct sum of a stable and unstable manifold. We refer to n_k minus the dimension of the stable manifold as the *index* of $D_1\xi^{ss}$. In Lemma 3 below we show that $D_1\xi^{ss}$ is one to one. It follows directly that the index is non-negative. We call a path k non-degenerate for α and k_0 if k_t converges to a non-degenerate stationary state $k^{ss}(\alpha)$ and if, whenever index $k^{ss}(\alpha) \geqslant 1$, $D_{12}v(k_t, k_{t+1}, \alpha)$ is non-singular for $t = 0, 1, \dots$.

Note that these definitions may easily be extended to allow cycles in place of stationary states. Consider a cycle with period p. We redefine periods with $n_c p$ commodities and $n_k p$ types of capital per period so that all cycles appear as stationary states. This kind of trick is frequently used with overlapping generations models. Consequently, the subsequent propositions apply equally to paths converging to cycles.

Let $\bar{E}(k_0)$ denote the set of pairs $(k, \alpha) \in (\ell^{n_k}_\infty)_+ \times R^{m-1}$ such that k is non-degenerate for α and k_0. In other words, we restrict attention to paths that converge to a non-degenerate stationary state. Our goal in this section is to prove the following result:

Proposition 4: For fixed φ and a full measure subset of k_0 and θ there are finitely many equilibria in $\bar{E}(k_0)$.

Notice incidentally, that by Fubini's Theorem, the fact that Proposition 4 holds for fixed φ and a full measure subset of k_0 and θ implies that it holds for a full measure subset of k_0, θ, and φ.

We can now define an equilibrium to be regular if the operator

$$\Sigma = \begin{bmatrix} D_1\xi & D_3\xi \\ D_1\sigma & D_3\sigma \end{bmatrix}$$

is non-singular. Since the inverse function theorem and implicit function theorem work as well in infinite dimensions as in finite, it follows that the equilibria of a regular economy are locally unique. Unfortunately, since $(l^\pi k) \times R^{n-1}$ is infinite dimensional, the set of possible equilibrium values of (k, α) is not compact. We do not know, therefore, that the number of equilibria is necessarily finite.

Our preliminary goal is to study the circumstances under which Σ is non-singular.

Lemma 2: $D_1\xi$ is one to one.

Proof: Araujo and Scheinkman (1977) provide a proof under the assumption that $v(\cdot,\cdot,\alpha)$ is strictly concave, but this is stronger than is necessary. Proposition 2 demonstrates the uniqueness of solutions for this model and this is all that is required for their argument.

QED

With this preliminary we can now give a sufficient condition for Σ to be non-singular.

Lemma 3: If Σ is onto, then it is non-singular.

Proof: We must show Σ is one to one. Let

$$\kappa = \{h_a \in R^{n-1} |\text{ there exists } h_k \in \ell^{n_k}_\infty \text{ such that } D_1\xi h_k + D_3\xi h_a = 0\}.$$

Since $D_1\xi$ is one to one by Lemma 2, there is a unique linear operator B: $\kappa \to \ell^{n_k}_\infty$ such that $D_1\xi Bh_a + D_3\xi h_a = 0$. Notice that, since B has finite dimensional domain, it is a continuous operator.

Suppose $h \in \ker \Sigma$. Then $h_a \in \kappa$ and $h_k = Bh_a$, which implies that $(D_1\sigma B + D_3\sigma)h_a =)$. On the other hand, $D_1\sigma B + D_3\sigma$ is onto. Let $y_a \in |R^{n-1}$ and let $0 \in \ell^{n_k}_\infty$ with $y = (0, y_a)$. Since Σ is onto, let $\bar{h}$ be a solution of $\Sigma \bar{h} = y$. Then $\bar{h}_a \in \kappa$ and $\bar{h}_k = B\bar{h}_a$. This implies that $(D_1\sigma B + D_3\sigma)\bar{h}_a = y_a$, which implies that $D_1\sigma B + D_3\sigma$ is onto. Finally, since $D_1\sigma B + D_3\sigma$ is a finite dimensional square matrix, it is also one to one. We conclude that if $h \in \ker \Sigma$, since $(D_1\sigma B + D_3\sigma)h_a = 0$, then $h_a = 0$. Since $h_k = Bh_a$, we find that $h = 0$.

QED

We should emphasize that the picture is already very different from that with infinitely many agents. If we follow standard practice in infinite dimensional transversality theory, we would call an equilibrium regular if Σ is onto and its kernal has closed complement. We have just shown that this definition of regularity implies that Σ is non-singular. This should be contrasted with the robust indeterminacy that occurs with infinitely many agents. In that case the fact that Σ is regular, that is, onto, does not imply that it is one to one. The kernal of Σ is simply the tangent space to the manifold of equilibria. Since the manifold deforms smoothly with respect to small perturbations, they change neither the fact that Σ is regular, nor the dimension of the kernal. The indeterminacy is robust. For a more detailed discussion of this point, the reader is referred to Kehoe, Levine, Mas-Colell, and Zame (1986).

Lemma 4: At a non-degenerate steady state $D_h\xi^{ss}$ is onto and dim ker $D_h\xi^{ss} = n_k -$ index $D_h\xi^{ss}$.

Proof: That dim ker $D_h\xi^{ss} = n_k -$ index $D_h\xi^{ss}$ means that dim ker $D_h\xi^{ss}$ has the same dimension as the stable manifold; since multiple solutions to $D_h\xi^{ss}h = 0$ are indexed by pairs (h_0, h_1) on the stable manifold, this follows. That $D_h\xi^{ss}$ is onto follows from the fact that the stable manifold is robust at a non-degenerate stationary state with respect to small non-stationary perturbations; see the proof of the local stable manifold theorem in Irwin (1980). Consequently, $D_h\xi^{ss}h = b$ has non-empty stable manifold for small enough b, and since it is linear, for all b. In particular, $D_h\xi^{ss}h = b$ has at least one solution.

QED

The next task is to show that, if k converges to a non-degenerate stationary state, then $D_h\xi(k,k_0,a)$ is onto.

Proposition 5: If k is a non-degenerate path for α and k_0, then $D_h\xi(k,k_0,\alpha)$ is onto and has index equal to that at $k^{ss}(\alpha)$.

Proof: First we show that $D_h\xi$ is onto. Araujo and Scheinkman (1977) give a proof for the case where index $D\xi^{ss} = 0$. We examine only the case where index $D\xi^{ss} \geqslant 1$. Let $F: \ell_\infty^{n_k} \to \ell_\infty^{n_k}$ be defined by the rule $Fk = (k_2, k_3, ...)$. Since $k_t \to k^{ss}(\alpha)$ and small perturbations of $D_h\xi^{ss}$ are also onto, for some finite T, $D_h\xi(F^Tk, k_T, \alpha)F^Th = F^Tb$. Then, since $D_{12}v_t$ is by assumption non-singular, we simply solve recursively backwards to find

$$h_{t-1} = -D_{21}^{-1}v_{t-1}[(\beta D_{11}v_t + D_{22}v_{t-1})h_t + \beta D_{12}v_th_{t+1} - b_t].$$

Since only a finite number of steps are involved, $h \in \ell_\infty^{n_k}$.

The fact that $D_h\xi$ and $D_h\xi^{ss}$ have the same index follows from the fact [shown, for example, in Araujo and Scheinkman (1977)] that they differ by a compact operator, and the fact that the index of a Fredholm operation is invariant under the addition of a compact operator.

QED

Let $\bar{E}_i(k_0)$ denote the set of pairs $(k,\alpha) \in (\ell_\infty^{n_k})_+ \times \mathbb{R}^{n-1}$ such that k is non-degenerate for α and k_0 and is of index i. Recall now that $0 \leqslant i \leqslant n_k$. We are interested in $\bar{E}(k_0) = \cup_{i=0}^{n_k} \bar{E}_i(k_0)$.

Proposition 6: For any fixed φ and a full measure subset of k_0 and θ every equilibrium in $\bar{E}(k_0)$ is regular.

Proof: In steps 1–4 we consider a fixed index i and $\bar{E}_i(k_0)$.

Step 1

We must find an open domain for ξ in order to do calculus. If $(k,\alpha)\in\bar{E}_i(k_0)$, then there is an open neighborhood $E_i(k_0)$ of (k,k_0,α) such that if $(k',k_0',\alpha')\in E_i(k_0)$ and $\xi(k',k_0',\alpha')=0$, then $(k',\alpha')\in\bar{E}_i(k_0')$; in other words, locally paths either converge to a non-degenerate stationary state, or leave; they do not remain bounded nearby without converging. This is shown in the proof of the robustness of the stable manifold; see, for example, Irwin (1980). We may also assume that, in $E_i(k_0)$, $D_h\xi(k',k_0',\alpha')$ is onto and has kernal of dimension $n_k - i$. This follows from the facts that the set of operators of this type is an open set (see Abraham and Robbin, 1967) and that $D_h\xi$ is a continuous function of its arguments by Proposition 2. Finally, let $E_i - \cup_{k_0} E_i(k_0)$. This open set we take to be the domain of ξ.

Step 2

Consider the matrix function on $E_\ell \times \mathbb{R}^{n_k(m-1)}$

$$\mu = \begin{array}{cccc} \underline{k} & \underline{k_0} & \underline{\alpha} & \underline{\theta} \\ \begin{bmatrix} D_1\xi & D_2\xi & D_3\xi & 0 \\ D_1\sigma & D_2\sigma & D_3\sigma & D_4\sigma \end{bmatrix} \end{array}$$

In Kehoe, Levine, and Romer (1987) it is shown that $D_2\sigma$ is onto; and by construction $[D_1\xi\,D_4\xi]=D_h\xi$ is into. It follows that μ is onto. Moreover, since $D_4\sigma$ is non-singular, and $[D_1\xi\,D_2\xi]$ is onto with an n_k-i dimensional kernal, it is clear that dim ker $\mu=n_k-i+m-1$. The implicit function then implies that the set of (k,k_0,α,θ) such that (α,k) is an equilibrium is an $n_k-\ell+m-1$ dimensional C^1 manifold.

Step 3

To apply the parametric transversality theorem in step 4 below, we must show that the equilibrium manifold is second countable; that is, that every open covering has a countable subcovering. Since $\ell_\infty^{n_k}$ is not separable, it is not itself second countable. It is clearly sufficient, however, that the set of (k,k_0,α) in E_i with $\xi(k,k_0,\alpha)=0$ is second countable. By construction such k converge to a non-degenerate stationary state, and such convergence must be exponential, so it suffices to show that the space of convergent sequences converging at the rate $1/t$ is second countable. This is the product of the second countable space $\mathbb{R}^{n_k}$, containing the limits, and the space of sequences converging to zero at the rate $1/t$. The latter space of sequences is second countable because it is the union of sequences dominated by N/t as $N \to \infty$, and each of these spaces is compact. Finally, we observe that the product of second countable spaces is second countable.

Step 4

This step is identical to the finite dimensional proof of the parametric transversality theorem. See, for example, Abraham and Robbin (1967). Consider the projection $\Pi(k,k_0,\alpha,\theta) = (k_0,\theta)$ restricted to the equilibrium manifold. This is a C^1 map between second countable $n_k - i + (m-1)$ and $n_k + (m-1)$ dimensional C^1 manifolds; moreover, the point (k,k_0,α,θ) is a regular equilibrium if and only if it is a regular value of Π. By Sard's Theorem, however, the set of regular values (k_0,θ) are of full measure. This shows regular equilibria are full measure for each i.

Step 5

Since the countable union of measure zero sets has measure zero, the intersection of the full measure sets for each i has full measure.

QED

Observe that in step 4 the map to which Sard's Theorem applies is from an $n_k - i + m - 1$ dimensional manifold to an $n_k + m - 1$ dimensional one. It follows directly that if $i \geq 1$ then the equilibria in $E_i(k_0)$ are regular by virtue of not existing at all. Moreover, as we have remarked above, Araujo and Scheinkman show that $D_1\xi$ is onto at a steady state with index 0. Consequently, under the hypothesis of Proposition 4, we may assume that there are finitely many equilibria, and that every equilibrium has $D_1\xi$ non-singular.

APPENDIX

Proof of Proposition 2: See Kehoe, Levine, and Romer (1987) for the proof of parts (a), (b), (d), and (e).

To show part (c) consider any function $\psi_t = w(k_t,k_{t+1},\alpha)$ where w is C^1. Since (k_t,k_{t+1},α) may be restricted to a compact domain, the operator defined by

$$(D\psi(k,\alpha)h)_t = D_1 w(k_t,k_{t+1}),\alpha)h_t + D_2 w(k_t,k_{t+1},\alpha)h_{t+1} + D_3 w(k_t,k_{t+1},\alpha)h_\alpha$$

is bounded and therefore continuous. Moreover, if $|k-k'|, |a-a'| \leqslant \varepsilon$ and $|h| \leqslant |$, then

$$\sup |[D\psi(k,a) - D\psi(k',a')]h|$$

$$\leqslant 3 \sup |D_j w(k_t, k_{t+1}, a) - D_j w(k'_t, k'_{t+1}, a')|.$$

The compactness of the domain implies that $D_j w$ is uniformly continuous: as $\varepsilon \to 0$, $|D\psi(k,a) - D\psi(k',a')| \to 0$, in other words $D\psi$ varies continuously.

Finally, we can show that $D\psi$ is actually the derivative of ψ by again using the uniform continuity of $D_j w$ to show that the integral form of the remainder in period t, which is made of terms of the form

$$\int_0^1 (1-s)[D_j w(k_{t-1} + sh_{t-1}, k_t + sh_t, a + sh_a) - D_j w(k_{t-1}, k_t, a)]ds$$

vanishes uniformly across periods as $h \to 0$.

This shows that ξ is C^1. Moreover, the mapping $B: \ell_\infty^{nk} \to \mathbb{R}$ defined by $B(k) = \sum_{t=0}^\infty \beta^t k_t$ is continuous and linear, and thus C^∞. Since σ is then a composition of the form $B(\psi)$, it too is C^1.

QED

References

Abraham, R. and J. Robbin (1967) *Transversal Mappings and Flows* (New York: Benjamin).

Araujo, A. and J. A. Scheinkman (1977) 'Smoothness, Comparative Dynamics and the Turnpike Property', *Econometrica*, 45: 601–20.

Benveniste, L. M. and J. A. Scheinkman (1975) 'On the Differentiability of the Value Function in Dynamic Models of Economics', *Econometrica*, 43: 727–32.

Bewley, T. (1980) 'The Permanent Income Hypothesis and Long Run Economic Stability', *Journal of Economic Theory*, 22: 252–92.

Bewley, T. (1982) 'An Integration of Equilibrium Theory and Turnpike Theory', *Journal of Mathematical Economics*, 28: 221–34.

Blume, L., D. Easley and M. O'Hara (1982) 'Characterization of Optimal Plans for Stochastic Dynamic Programs', *Journal of Economic Theory*, 28: 221–34.

Boldrin, M. and L. Montrucchio (1985) 'The Emergence of Dynamic Complexities in Models of Optimal Growth', Rochester Center for Economic Research Working Paper No. 7.

Boldrin, M. and L. Montrucchio (1986) 'On the Indeterminacy of Capital Accumulation Paths', *Journal of Economic Theory*, 40: 26–39.

Brown, D. J. and Geanakopoulos (1985) 'Comparative Statics and Local Indeterminacy in OLG Economies: An Application of the Multiplicative Ergodic Theorem', Cowles Foundation Discussion Paper No. 773.

Debreu, G. (1959) *Theory of Value* (New York: Wiley).

Deneckere, R. and S. Pelikan (1986) 'Competitive Chaos', *Journal of Economic Theory*, 40: 13–25.

Hildenbrand, W. (1974) *Core and Equilibria of a Large Economy* (Princeton: Princeton University Press).

Irwin, M. C. (1980) *Smooth Dynamical Systems* (New York: Academic Press).

Kehoe, T. J. and D. K. Levine (1985a) 'Comparative Statics and Perfect Foresight in Infinite Horizon Economies', *Econometrica*, 53: 433–53.

Kehoe, T. J. and D. K. Levine (1985b) 'Empirical Implications of Complete Contingent Claims', UCLA Department of Economics.

Kehoe, T. J. and D. K. Levine (1985c) 'Indeterminacy of Relative Prices in an Overlapping Generations Model', UCLA Department of Economics.

Kehoe, T. J., D. K. Levine, A. Mas-Colell, and W. R. Zame (1986) 'Determinacy of Equilibrium in Large Square Economies', *Journal of Mathematical Economics*, forthcoming.

Kehoe, T. J., D. K. Levine, and P. M. Romer (1987) 'Determinacy of Equilibria in Economics with Production and Finitely Many Infinitely Lived Consumers', University of Minnesota.

Kydland, F. E. and E. C. Prescott (1982) 'Time to Build and Aggregate Fluctuations', *Econometrica*, 50: 1345–70.

McKenzie, L. W. (1959) 'On the Existence of General Equilibrium for a Competitive Market', *Econometrica*, 27: 54–71.

McKenzie, L. W. (1983) 'Turnpike Theory, Discounted Utility and the von Neumann Facet', *Journal of Economic Theory*, 30: 330–52.

McKenzie, L. W. (1986) 'Optimal Economic Growth, Turnpike Theorems and Comparative Dynamics', in *Handbook of Mathematical Economics*, Vol. 3, K. J. Arrow and M. D. Intriligator (eds) (Amsterdam: North-Holland) pp. 1281–355.

Mas-Colell, A. (1985) *The Theory of General Economic Equilibrium: A Differentiable Approach* (Cambridge: Cambridge University Press).

Muller, W. J. and M. Woodford (1986) 'Stationary Overlapping Generations Economies with Production and Infinitely Lived Consumers', *Journal of Economic Theory*, forthcoming.

Negishi, T. (1960) 'Welfare Economics and Existence of Equilibrium for a Competitive Economy', *Metroeconomica*, 23: 92–7.

Robinson, J. (1973) 'Marginal Productivity', *Collected Economic Papers*, Vol. 4 (Oxford: Blackwell) pp. 127–38.

Rockafellar, R. T. (1970) *Convex Analysis* (Princeton: Princeton University Press).

Varian, H. (1984) *Microeconomic Analysis* (New York: W. W. Norton).

19 Dynamic Optimization Under Uncertainty: Non-convex Feasible Set

Mukul Majumdar, Tapan Mitra and Yaw Nyarko*

[The] object [of the book] is refinement, not reconstruction; it is a study in 'pure theory'. The motive back of its presentation is twofold. In the first place, the writer cherishes, in the face of the pragmatic, philistine tendencies of the present age, especially characteristic of the thought of our own country, the hope that careful, rigorous thinking in the field of social problems does after all have some significance for human weal and woe. In the second place, he has a feeling that the 'practicalism' of the times is a passing phase, even to some extent, a pose; that there is a strong undercurrent of discontent with loose and superficial thinking and a real desire, out of sheer intellectual self-respect, to reach a clearer understanding of the meaning of terms and dogmas which pass current as representing ideas. (Frank H. Knight, in *Risk Uncertainty and Profit*)

1 INTRODUCTION

An editorial note in the *Economic Journal* (May 1930) reported the death of Frank Ramsey, and his 1928 paper was described as 'one of the most remarkable contributions to mathematical economics ever made'. In the same issue the editor organized a symposium on increasing returns and the representative firm. This symposium seems to be a natural follow-up of a number of papers published by the Journal during 1926–8, including the well-known article of Allyn Young (1928) that is still available, and duly remembered. The problems of equilibrium of a firm under increasing returns, or more generally, of designing price-guided resource allocation processes to cope with increasing returns, has since been a topic of continuing interest. Ramsey's contribution was enshrined as a durable piece with a resurgence of

* Research support from the National Science Foundation is gratefully acknowledged. The research of the first author was also supported by the Warshow endowment at Cornell and that of the second author by an Alfred P. Sloan Research fellowship. We would also like to thank Professors R. N. Bhattacharya, C. Clark, J. Chipman and L. Hurwicz for helpful suggestions.

interest in intertemporal economics in the fifties. But neither John Keynes, the editor of the *Economic Journal* who was most appreciative of Ramsey's talents, neither the subsequent writers on 'growth theory' in Cambridge, England (nor, for that matter, those in Cambridge, Massachusetts), have made any precise suggestion towards incorporating increasing returns in a Ramsey-type exercise.

A concise discussion about a phase of increasing returns in a production process appeared in Frank Knight's Ph.D. thesis at Cornell (subsequently published as *Risk, Uncertainty and Profit* (1921), see pp.100–1), and casual references to increasing returns in the context of capital accumulation were, of course, made from time to time. Joan Robinson (1956, chapter 33) and John Hicks (1960) alluded to the importance of Young's ideas, but somehow, increasing returns had to be discussed by crossing 'the boundary of topics that can usefully be discussed in the framework of ... simplifying assumptions' (Robinson (1956), p.336). Systematic and formal expositions of increasing returns in a Ramsey-type model of dynamic optimization emerged much later, and, mostly in the context of relatively recent 'pragmatic' concern in the economics of exhaustible and natural resources. The paper by Clark (1971) in *Mathematical Biosciences* is indeed a landmark in this area, and our primary objective is to bring together a collection of subsequent results in a fairly simple framework of dynamic optimization under uncertainty. To be sure, a *deterministic* exercise can be viewed as a very special case of our formal stochastic model, and our development of ideas and exposition owe much to the insights gained from such deterministic exercises following up Clark's paper. As with Frank Knight, our object is refinement (not reconstruction), rigor – not realism.

1.1   Recent Literature: An Overview

Discrete time deterministic models of dynamic optimization with an 'S-shaped production function' have been explored by Majumdar and Mitra in (1982) and (1983). These papers dealt with three different evaluation criteria: intertemporal efficiency, maximization of a discounted sum of one-period felicities (linear felicities in (1983)), and the case of undiscounted optimality in the sense of 'overtaking'. The linear case had been studied earlier by Clark (1971). Dechert and Nishimura (1983) made significant improvements of results obtainable in the discounted case, and further extensions in different directions were made by Majumdar and Nermuth (1982), and Mitra and Ray (1984).

One-good models of dynamic optimization under uncertainty in the classical 'convex' environments were studied by Brock and Mirman (1972) (strictly concave felicities), Jaquette (1972) and Reed (1974) (linear felicities, multiplicative shocks). A useful source of related references is Mirman and Spulber (1982).

1.2   A Reader's Guide

We develop the formal model of sequential decision making under uncertainty as a special case of the stochastic discounted dynamic programming model explored by Blackwell (1965) and others. The set of technologically feasible 'plans' or policies is non-convex, but the evaluation criterion is a discounted sum of expected (concave) felicities. In Section 2, we summarize some basic theorems on the existence of optimal stationary policies. These are obtained for both linear and strictly concave felicities. The value function is shown to be continuous and to satisfy the functional equation of dynamic programming (see (8) and (9)). In Section 3, the main result (Theorem 2) is that any optimal investment policy function $h(y)$ is monotonically non-decreasing in the stock y. Such a policy function is a selection from a correspondence, and is, in general, not unique. Without the assumption of convexity of the feasible set, the optimal consumption policy function $c(y)$ is not necessarily monotone non-decreasing in y. In fact, under some additional assumptions, we prove that $c(y)$ is non-decreasing if and only if the value function V is concave. In Section 4, we identify conditions under which optimal policies are interior and can be characterized (in the case of strictly concave felicities) by a stochastic version of the Ramsey–Euler condition (see (13)). We should emphasize that we could prove the interiority property only under the assumption that utility of zero consumption is minus infinity. In the context of convex models, an 'Inada condition' on the boundary (namely, that marginal utility goes to infinity as consumption drops to zero) is sufficient to guarantee that optimal input, consumption and stock processes are interior (see Theorem 19). Without convexity, however, we were able to assert only that input and stock (but not necessarily consumption) processes are interior. Theorem 18 and Example 3 clarify this issue. Section 5 deals with the problem of non-uniqueness of optimal processes in non-convex models. The value function is differentiable at an initial stock if and only if there is a unique optimal process from the same stock, and non-differentiability can only arise on a set that is at most countable. In Section 6, some results on the convergence of optimal inputs are obtained (see Theorems 11–13), and the behavior of optimal inputs in non-convex models is contrasted with that in convex models.

In convex stochastic models, the 'turnpike' property obtains: regardless of the initial stock, the optimal input process converges in distribution to a unique invariant distribution. With non-convexity, there are potentially many invariant distributions and, furthermore, the one to which an optimal input process converges depends on the initial stock (the turnpike one takes depends on the point of departure!). The analysis of the optimal process that leads to Theorems 11 and 12 depends, however, on the assumptions that there are finitely many random events at any date, and (more importantly) that the technology satisfies an Inada condition at the origin (see (T.8)). A different 'splitting' condition ensuring that there is sufficient variability in production yields a strong turnpike result (Theorem 13). Section 7 contains additional incidental results and provides a technical overview of the related literature. All the proofs are relegated to Section 8.

1.3   The Role of Non-convexity

What are the most striking differences in the qualitative properties of optimal decisions when non-convexities are introduced? Ignoring uncertainty for the moment, let us stress a couple of important aspects (see Majumdar and Mitra (1982) for details). In a deterministic model with an S-shaped production function, it turns out that *average productivity* along a feasible program has a crucial role in signalling intertemporal inefficiency in contrast with the classical model where the remarkable Cass condition can be precisely expressed solely in terms of marginal productivities. Secondly, when future utilities are discounted, the qualitative properties of optimal programs depend critically on the magnitude of the discount factor. Roughly speaking, when discounting is 'mild', optimal programs behave as in the undiscounted case (converging to a unique optimal stationary program), when discounting is 'heavy', optimal programs approach extinction. Also, in the 'intermediate' range of discounting, the long-run behavior depends critically on the initial stock. Contrast this with the 'classical' turnpike literature where the long-run behavior of optimal programs is invariant with respect to the initial stock.

The fact that solutions to dynamic optimization problems in one-good models display striking monotonicity properties has been an important by-product of research efforts in the area reviewed in the present paper. As noted above, a version of monotonicity continues to hold even when uncertainty is introduced, and such properties have been exploited to study the dynamic behavior of optimal decisions. The main shortcoming of the present paper, however, is an inadequate analysis of the nature of optimal processes under uncertainty with an S-shaped production function introduced by Frank Knight. (The Inada condition (T.8) in Section 6.1 is *not* consistent with an S-shape.) A deeper understanding of this case is certainly desirable, and – to us – is the most important gap in the literature on stochastic dynamic optimization with non-convexities.

2   THE MODEL

2.1   Sequential Decisions

The standard framework of stochastic dynamic programming (see, e.g., Blackwell, 1965; Maitra, 1968) is used to describe a problem of intertemporal resource allocation under uncertainty. In each period t, the planner observes the current stock y_t of a particular good, and chooses 'an action': some point a in $A \equiv [0,1]$. One interprets a as the fraction of y_t to be used as input in period t, and refers to $x_t \equiv ay_t$ as the *input* in period t. As a result of the decision on a, the stock in the next period $t+1$ is determined according to the following relationship:

$$y_{t+1} = f(x_t, r_{t+1}) \equiv f(ay_t, r_{t+1}) \tag{1}$$

where f is the gross output function (satisfying the assumptions introduced below), and (r_t) is a sequence of independent, identically distributed random variables ('shocks' to the production process). Choice of a also determines the consumption $c_t \equiv (1-a)y_t$. Consumption generates an immediate return or utility according to a function u (satisfying the assumptions listed below). In other words, choice of a generates utility defined as

$$u(c_t) \equiv u((1-a)y_t)$$

Note that the decision on a is made *before* the realization of r_{t+1}; in the next period, y_{t+1} is observed after the realization of r_{t+1} and the same choice problem is repeated.

A *policy* π is a sequence $\pi = (\pi_t)$ where π_t specifies the action in the t-th period as a function of the previous history $\eta_t = (y_0, a_1, ..., a_{t-1}, y_t)$ of the system, by associating with each η_t (Borel measurably) an element a of A (hence, the input $x_t^{(\pi)} \equiv ay_t \equiv \pi_t(\eta_t)y_t$ and the consumption $c_t^{(\pi)} \equiv (1-a)y_t \equiv [1 - \pi_t(\eta_t)]y_t$). Any Borel function $g: R_+ \to A$ defines a policy: whenever $y \geq 0$ is observed, choose $a = g(y)$ irrespective of when and how the stock y is attained. The corresponding policy $\pi = (g^{(\infty)})$ is a stationary policy and g is the policy function generating the stationary policy.

A policy π associates with each initial stock y a corresponding t-th period expected utility $Eu(c_t(\pi))$ and an expected discounted total utility defined as

$$V_{\underline{\pi}}(y) = \sum_{t=0}^{\infty} \delta^t Eu(c_t(\underline{\pi})), \tag{2}$$

where δ is the discount factor, $0 < \delta < 1$. The measure theoretic foundation underlying the expectation operation in (2) is fully spelled out in Blackwell (1965).

A policy $\pi^* = (\pi_t^*)$ is optimal if $V_{\pi^*}(y) \geq V_{\pi}(y)$ for all $y > 0$ and all policies π. We call V_{π^*} the optimal) value function defined by π^*. Note that if π^* and $\bar{\pi}$ are both optimal policies, $V_{\pi^*} = V_{\bar{\pi}}$. Hence, we shall often drop the subscript in referring to the value function V.

2.2   Environment, Technology and Utility

Let $\mathcal{E}$ be a compact set of positive real numbers. Two examples of $\mathcal{E}$ are of particular interest: (a) $\mathcal{E}$ is a finite set; (b) $\mathcal{E}$ is a closed interval $[b_1, b_2]$ in positive reals. The elements of $\mathcal{E}$ are alternative states of the environment in any period. Let (r_t) be a sequence of independent, identically distributed random variables with values in $\mathcal{E}$ and a common distribution γ.

The technology is described by a gross output function $f: R_+ \times \mathcal{E} \to R_+$ satisfying the following:

(T.1)   There is $\beta > 0$ such that for all $x \ge \beta$, $x > f(x,r)$ for all $r \in \mathcal{E}$.

(T.2)   For each $r \in \mathcal{E}$, $f(\cdot, r)$ is continuous on R_+.

(T.3′) For each $r \in \mathcal{E}$, $f(\cdot, r)$ is non-decreasing on R_+.

A stronger version of (T.3′) is

(T.3)   For each $r \in \mathcal{E}$, $f(\cdot, r)$ is strictly increasing on R_+.

The immediate return or utility function $u: R_+ \to R$ is assumed to satisfy

(U.1) u is continuous on R_+.

(U.2) u is strictly increasing on R_+.

(U.3) u is strictly concave on R_+.

We shall point out that most of the important results can also be proved if instead of (U.1) we have

(U.1′) u is continuous on R_{++} and $\lim_{c \downarrow 0} u(c) = -\infty$.

Under (U.1′), to ensure that the value function is finite, i.e. $V(y) > -\infty$, we impose the following assumption:

(T.4)   There is a $k > 0$ such that for all $0 < x < k$, $f(x,r) > x$ for each r.

When we want to accommodate a linear utility function we replace (U.3) by:

(U.3′) u is concave on R_+.

Given an initial stock $y > 0$, a policy $\underset{\sim}{\pi} = (\pi_t)$ generates an *input* process

$x^\pi = (x_t^{(\pi_t)})$, a consumption process $c^\pi = (c_t^{(\pi_t)})$ and a *stock* process $y^\pi = (y_t^{(\pi_t)})$ according to the description in Section 2.1. Formally,

$$x_0 \equiv \pi_0(y)y, \; c_0 \equiv [1 - \pi_0(y)]y, \; y_0 = y \tag{3}$$

and, for each $t \geq 1$, and for each partial history $\eta_t \equiv (y_0, a_0, \ldots, y_{t-1}, a_{t-1}, y_t)$ one has:

$$x_t(\eta_t) \equiv \pi_t(\eta_t)y_t, \; c_t \equiv [1 - \pi_t(\eta_t)]y_t, \; y_t \equiv f(x_{t-1}, r_t) \tag{4}$$

Clearly,

$$c_0 + x_0 = y_0;$$

$$c_t + x_t = f(x_{t-1}, r_t) \text{ for all } t \geq 1; \tag{5}$$

$$c_t \geq 0, \; x_t \geq 0 \text{ for all } t \geq 0.$$

For brevity, we call $(x^{\pi*}, c^{\pi*}, y^{\pi*})$ an optimal (resp. input, consumption, stock) process generated by an optimal policy π^* (when it exists).

We first note a useful boundedness property in our model.

Lemma 1: Assume (T.1), (T.2) and (T.3'), and let $y > 0$ be any initial stock. If π is any policy generating the stock process y^π, then for all $t \geq 0$

$$0 \leq y_t \leq \max(\beta, y) \tag{6}$$

Proof: An induction argument on t is easy to construct.

QED

It follows from (5) and (6) that the processes x^π and c^π generated by π also satisfy for all $t \geq 0$

$$x_t \leq \max(\beta, y), \; c_t \leq \max(\beta, y) \tag{7}$$

In what follows we restrict the initial stock $y \leq \beta$. Define $S \equiv [0, \beta]$ and denote by $q(\cdot|y, a)$ the conditional distribution of y_{t+1} given the stock y and action a in period t [as determined by f and the common distribution γ of r_{t+1}]. One can verify:

Lemma 2: Under (T.2), if a sequence $(y^n, a^n) \in S \times A$ converges to $(y, a) \in S \times A$, the sequence $q(\cdot|y^n, a^n)$ converges weakly to $q(\cdot|y, a)$.

2.3   Existence of an Optimal Stationary Policy

The basic existence theorem of Maitra (1968) when applied to our case leads to the following:

Theorem 1: Assume (T.1), (T.2), (T.3') and (U.1). There exists an optimal stationary policy $\underset{\sim}{\pi}{}^* = (\hat{h}^{(\infty)})$ where $\hat{h}$: $S \to A$ is a Borel measurable function. The value function $V_{\underset{\sim}{\pi}{}^*}$ defined by $\underset{\sim}{\pi}{}^*$ on S is continuous and satisfies

$$V_{\underset{\sim}{\pi}{}^*}(y) = \max_{a \in A} \left[u((1-a)y) + \delta \int V_{\underset{\sim}{\pi}{}^*}[f(ay,r)]d\gamma \right] \tag{8}$$

$$= u[y - \hat{h}(y)\cdot y] + \delta \int V_{\underset{\sim}{\pi}{}^*}[f(\hat{h}(y)y,r)]d\gamma \tag{9}$$

Remarks

(1)   The existence of $\underset{\sim}{\pi}{}^*$ requires assumptions weaker than those listed above. The stronger continuity conditions are used to establish the continuity of $V_{\underset{\sim}{\pi}{}^*}$ by readily adapting the proof in Maitra (1968).

(2)   If (U.1) is replaced by (U.1') one appeals to Schäl (1975) to establish Theorem 1.

(3)   We refer to the function $h(y) \equiv \hat{h}(y)\cdot y$ as an optimal investment policy function and the function $c(y) \equiv [1 - \hat{h}(y)]y$ as an optimal consumption policy function.

To simplify notation, we write (x^*, c^*, y^*) to denote the optimal input, consumption and stock processes generated by $\underset{\sim}{\pi}{}^*$ (see (4) and (5)).

3   MONOTONICITY OF OPTIMAL INVESTMENT POLICY FUNCTION

3.1   Strictly Concave Utility Function

We first establish a (weak) monotonicity property of optimal investment policy functions. In all of this section, (U.1) can be replaced with (U.1') and (T.4).

Theorem 2: Assume (T.1)–(T.3) and (U.1)–(U.3). Then if h is an optimal investment policy function, h is non-decreasing, i.e. '$y > y'$' implies '$h(y) \geqq h(y')$'.

Remarks

(1) Strong monotonicity ['$y > y''$ implies '$h(y) > h(y')$'] of h is proved later when the optimal process is characterized by the stochastic Ramsey–Euler conditions.

(2) The proof of Theorem 2 relies critically on *strict* concavity of the utility function u.

(3) It should be emphasized that Theorem 2 is concerned with the monotonicity of the optimal investment policy function $h(y) \equiv \hat{h}(y) \cdot y$ where the existence of $\hat{h}$ is proved in Theorem 1. However, $\hat{h}$ is a selection from a correspondence and is, in general, not unique. (Uniqueness of $\hat{h}$ leads to the continuity of $\hat{h}$ (hence h) and is obtainable in the classical 'convex' model studied by Brock–Mirman–Zilcha.)

(4) The strategy of proof that we follow in Theorem 2 is due to Dechert and Nishimura (1983), who established a parallel result in their deterministic model with a non-convex technology.

(5) In Theorem 2 above we may replace (T.3) with (T.3').

The functional equation characterizing the value function V can be recast as (see (8)):

$$V(y) = \max_{0 \leqslant x \leqslant y} \, [u(y-x) + \delta \int V[f(x,r)]d\gamma] \tag{10}$$

$$= u(c(y)) + \delta \int V[f(h(y),r)]d\gamma \tag{11}$$

Given $y > 0$, define $\varphi(y)$ to be the set of all values x where the right side of (10) attains its maximum. The continuity properties in our model imply that $\varphi(y)$ is non-empty, and that $h(y)$ is a selection from the correspondence φ.

It is important to note that a stronger version of Theorem 2 is true. If $\{x_t\}_0^\infty$, $\{x_t'\}_0^\infty$ are optimal input processes from y, y' then $y > y'$ implies $x_0 \geqslant x_0'$. This implies the following ordering relation on φ. If A and B are two subsets of R_+, then we say $A \geqslant B$ if $a \in A$ and $b \in B$ implies $a \geqslant b$. φ then has the property that $y > y'$ implies $\varphi(y) \geqslant \varphi(y')$.

Define

$$\underline{h}(y) = \min \, [x : x \in \varphi(y)]$$

$$\bar{h}(y) = \max \, [x : x \in \varphi(y)]. \tag{12}$$

3.2   Concave Utility Function

In this subsection, we assume (T.1)–(T.3), (U.1), (U.2) and (U.3'). It should be stressed that the strict concavity assumption (U.3) on u is replaced by the less restrictive concavity assumption (U.3'). Our first result provides a characterization of the correspondence φ and its selections $\underline{h}$ and $\bar{h}$.

Theorem 3: Under (T.1), (T.2), (T.3'), (U.1), (U.2) and (U.3'):

(a) φ is an upper semicontinuous correspondence;

(b) $\underline{h}$ is well defined, left continuous and non-decreasing;

(c) $\bar{h}$ is well defined, right continuous and non-decreasing.

Corollary 3: There is a Borel selection $\hat{h}$: $S \rightarrow A$ such that the corresponding optimal investment policy function $h(y) \equiv \hat{h}(y) \cdot y$ is non-decreasing and right continuous.

Remark

There is also a selection such that h can be made to satisfy left continuity (and weak monotonicity).

4   INTERIOR OPTIMAL PROCESSES AND THE STOCHASTIC RAMSEY–EULER CONDITION

We now impose (U.1') and (T.4) and derive the property that the optimal processes are interior (a.s.). In addition to (T.1)–(T.4) and (U.1')–(U.3), we make the following assumptions in this section:

(T.5) $f(x,r)=0$ if and only if $x=0$.

(T.6) $f(x,r)$ is continuous on $R_+ \times \mathcal{E}$.

Theorem 4: (Interiority) Under (T.1)–(T.6) and (U.1')–(U.3), if (x^*,c^*,y^*) is an optimal process from some initial stock $y>0$, then for all $t \geq 0$, $x_t^*(\eta_t)>0$, $c_t^*(\eta_t)>0$ and $y_t^*(\eta_t)>0$ for all η_t.

In studying the dynamic behavior of optimal processes, it is useful to exploit the stochastic Ramsey–Euler conditions characterizing an optimal process. We now introduce additional assumptions:

(T.7)   For each r in $\mathcal{E}$, the derivative of $f(x,r)$ with respect to x exists, and is continuous at each (x,r) for which $x>0$.

(U.4) $u(c)$ is continuously differentiable at $c > 0$.

Theorem 5: (Stochastic Ramsey–Euler Condition) Under (T.1)–(T.7) and (U.1')–(U.4) if h is an optimal investment policy function and $c(y) = y - h(y)$,

$$u'(c(y)) = \delta \int u'(c(f(h(y),r)))f'(h(y),r)dy \qquad (13)$$

Corollary 5: If (13) holds, $h: R_+ \to R_+$ is strictly increasing.

So far we have discussed monotonicity of the optimal investment policy function. The following result throws light on monotonicity of the optimal consumption policy function.

Theorem 6: If the value function V is concave, then it is differentiable at each $y > 0$. Furthermore, $c(y)$ is non-decreasing if and only if V is concave.

5   SOME PROPERTIES OF THE VALUE FUNCTION AND UNIQUENESS OF OPTIMAL PROCESSES

We now establish some differentiability properties of the value function and relate these to the question of uniqueness of optimal processes. Recall that in the classical 'convex' model, with the assumption (U.3), there is a unique optimal process. With a non-convex technology, uniqueness cannot be asserted even in deterministic models. However, the nature of non-uniqueness can be clarified by examining the value function V. In this section we assume that (U.1'), (U.2)–(U.4) and (T.1)–(T.7) all hold.

Going back to (10), recall that the correspondence $\varphi(y)$ is not in general single valued, and an optimal investment policy function is a selection from $\varphi(y)$.

Lemma 3: There is a countable set D in S, such that if y is not in D, $\varphi(y)$ is single valued.

Remark: Recall that φ is upper semicontinuous as a correspondence, hence if $\varphi(y)$ is single valued, continuity of $h(y)$ and $c(y)$ follows.

Lemma 4: The left- and right-hand derivative (denoted by V^-, V^+, respectively) of V exist at all $y > 0$; $V^-(y) \leq V^+(y)$. Furthermore, $\{y: V^-(y) < V^+(y)\}$ is at most countable.

The following theorem throws light on non-uniqueness of optimal processes:

Theorem 7: Suppose (x,c,y) and (x',c',y') are optimal from $y > 0$. If $x_0 = x'_0$, then $x_t = x'_t$ and $c_t = c'_t$ for all $t \geq 1$. Furthermore, V is differentiable at some $y > 0$ if, and only if there is a unique optimal process from y.

Remark: The results reported above are stochastic versions of the parallel deterministic results in Dechert and Nishimura (1983).

Finally, we come to the useful 'envelope theorem':

Theorem 8: Suppose that V is differentiable at some $y > 0$. Then

$$V'(y) = u'(c(y)) = \delta \int V'[f(h(y),r)]f'(h(y),r)d\gamma \tag{14}$$

6   DYNAMIC BEHAVIOR OF AN OPTIMAL INPUT PROCESS

We now focus on the stochastic process

$$x_{t+1} = h[f(x_t, r_{t+1})] \tag{15}$$

where h is an optimal investment policy function. Two cases are considered. First, we assume that $\mathcal{E}$ is finite and that the production function satisfies the Inada condition at the origin ('infinite derivative at zero'). One can allow for a phase of increasing returns once a specific positive level of input has been committed. The dynamic behavior of the process (15) turns out to be quite different from that in the 'classical' case of a strictly concave f. Next, we impose a condition that requires that there be sufficient variability in the production function. We then conclude that the distribution function of x_t converges uniformly to the distribution function of a unique invariant distribution, regardless of the level of initial stock.

In both cases we shall use a result of Dubins and Freedman (1966); to state this result we require the following notation.

Recall that γ is the probability distribution of r on $\mathcal{E}$. Let $\gamma^n = \gamma x ... x \gamma$ (n-times) be the product measure induced by γ on $\mathcal{E}^n$. Let $r^n = (r_1,...,r_n)$ be a generic element of $\mathcal{E}^n$ and define for any x in S

$$H(x,r) = h[f(x,r)]$$

$$H^n(x,r^n) = H(H(...(H(x,r_1),r_2),...,r_n) \tag{16}$$

If μ is any probability on S, define the probability $\gamma^n\mu$ on S by the relation

$$\gamma^n\mu(A) = \int_S \gamma^n(\{r^n \in \mathcal{E}^n | H^n(x,r^n) \in A\})\mu(dx) \tag{17}$$

where A is any Borel subset of S.

Let S' be a closed interval in S. S' is said to be γ-invariant if $\gamma(\{r \text{ in } \mathcal{E} | H(x,r) \in S' \text{ for all } x \text{ in } S'\}) = 1$. $\bar{x}$ in S is a γ-fixed point if the singleton set $\{\bar{x}\}$ is γ-invariant.

Let S' be γ-invariant. For any $n = 1,2,\dots$, the probability γ^n is said to split on S' if there is a z in S' such that

$$\gamma^n(\{r^n \text{ in } \mathcal{E}^n | H^n(x,r^n) \leq z \text{ for each } x \text{ in } S'\}) > 0 \tag{18}$$

$$\gamma^n(\{r^n \text{ in } \mathcal{E}^n | H^n(x,r^n) \geq z \text{ for each } x \text{ in } S'\}) > 0$$

A probability μ on S is said to be an invariant probability on S' if the support of μ is a subset of S', and for any Borel set A in S,

$$\gamma\mu(A) = \mu(A) \tag{19}$$

An invariant distribution is the distribution function of an invariant probability. We may now state a modification of Dubins and Freedman (1966, Corollary 5.5, p.842):

Theorem 9: Suppose for some γ-invariant closed interval S', and for some integer n, γ^n splits on S'. Suppose further that there are no γ-fixed points $\bar{x}$ in S', and also that the function $H(\cdot,r)$ is monotone non-decreasing on S', for γ a.e. r in $\mathcal{E}$. Then there is one and only one invariant probability μ on S'; and for each probability v whose support is a subset of S', the distribution function of $\gamma^n v$ converges uniformly to the distribution function of μ.

6.1 Optimal Input Process When $\mathcal{E}$ Is Finite and the Inada Condition Holds

In this subsection, in addition to (T.1)–(T.7) and (U.1')–(U.4), we assume that the following conditions hold:

(E.1) $\mathcal{E}$ is finite.

(T.8)   For each $r \in \mathcal{E}$, $\lim_{x \downarrow 0} f'(x,r) = \infty$ (Inada condition at the origin).

(T.9)   For any fixed $x > 0$, there does not exist any $\bar{y}$ in S such that

$$\gamma(\{r \in \mathcal{E} | f(x,r) = \bar{y}\}) = 1.$$

Since, from Corollary 5, h is strictly increasing, (T.9) implies there are no positive γ-fixed points in S. Roughly speaking, we show that the optimal process (14) enters one of a number of disjoint sets and stays in it. Unlike the

Brock–Mirman–Zilcha case of strictly concave production functions (in which x_t converges in distribution to an invariant distribution irrespective of the initial stock), the set into which x_t eventually enters depends very much on the starting point.

Some new notations are (alas!) needed. Let

$$f_m(x) \equiv \min_r f(x,r) \text{ and } f_M(x) \equiv \max_r f(x,r).$$

Clearly, f_m and f_M are well-defined continuous functions on R_+. Recall $H(x,r) \equiv h[f(x,r)]$. Define

$$\bar{H}(x,r) \equiv \bar{h}[f(x,r)] \tag{20}$$

$$\underline{H}(x,r) \equiv \underline{h}[f(x,r)]$$

where the functions $\bar{h}$ and $\underline{h}$ are defined in (12). Finally, let

$$H_m(x) = \min_r H(x,r) \text{ and } H_M(x) = \max_r H(x,r).$$

$\bar{H}_m, \bar{H}_M$ and $\underline{H}_m, \underline{H}_M$ may be similarly defined by replacing H by $\bar{H}$ and $\underline{H}$. From the monotonicity of f and h, one can show that (we prove this in Section 8):

$$H_m(x) = h(f_m(x)), \; H_M(x) = h(f_M(x)) \tag{21}$$

The main results on the long-run behavior of x_t rely on an analysis of fixed points of the maps just introduced. Fortunately, these fixed points are independent of the choice of optimal policy function. This is stated formally below.

Lemma 5

(a) $H, \bar{H}, \underline{H}$ all have the same fixed points;

(b) $H_M, \bar{H}_M, \underline{H}_M$ all have the same fixed points;

(c) $H_m, \bar{H}_m, \underline{H}_m$ all have the same fixed points.

The following lemma is important for the results that follow.

Lemma 6: There exists $\varepsilon > 0$ such that $H(x,r) > x$ for all x in $(0,\varepsilon)$ and all r in $\mathcal{E}$.

Next, let us define

$$y_m = \min \{x > 0: H_m(x) = x\}, \; y_M = \max x > 0: H_M(x) = x\} \tag{22}$$

$$x_m = \max \{x > 0: H_m(x) = x\}, \; x_M = \min \{x > 0: H_M(x) = x\}$$

It should be stressed that Lemma 5 implies that the numbers x_m, y_m, x_M, y_M in (22) are independent of the selection of h. The following facts are gathered in the form of a lemma:

Lemma 7

(a)   The points x_m, y_m, x_M, y_M are well defined;

(b) $y_m > 0$;

(c) $H_m(x) > x$ for all x in $(0, y_m)$, $H_m(x) < x$ for all x in (x_m, ∞);

(d) $H_M(x) > x$ for all x in $(0, x_M)$ and $H_M(x) < x$ for all x in (y_M, ∞);

(e) $y_m \leq x_M$ and $x_m \leq y_M$.

From Lemma 7, there are two possible configurations:

(A) $x_m \leq x_M$ and (B) $x_m > x_M$ (see Fig. 19.1 below).

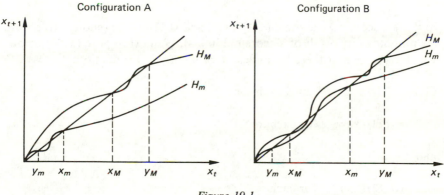

Figure 19.1

Configuration A holds when for each r, $f(\cdot, r)$ is strictly concave. (See Theorem 17 in Section 7.1.) One can, however, give examples of non-convex technologies where configuration A still holds.

The dynamic behavior of the optimal input process under configurations A and B is stated in Theorems 11 and 12 below. In both cases we exploit Theorem 9 via another theorem of Dubins and Freedman (1966), which we state below:

Theorem 10: Let S' be a γ-invariant closed interval in S. Suppose that for γ a.e. r in $\mathcal{E}$, $H(\cdot, r)$ is continuous and monotone non-decreasing on S', and there are no γ-fixed points in S'. If there is a unique minimal γ-invariant closed interval in S' then for some integer n, γ^n splits and the conclusions of

Theorem 9 hold. The hypothesis that $H(\cdot,r)$ be continuous on S' for γ a.e. r in $\mathcal{E}$, may be dropped if instead we assume that $\mathcal{E}$ is finite and Lemma 5(a) holds.

We now state two main results characterizing the asymptotic properties of the optimal input process, $\{x_t\}$. Let $F_t(x)$ be the distribution function of x_t, i.e. $F_t(x) = \mathrm{Prob}\,(\{x_t \leqslant x\})$.

Theorem 11: If configuration A holds, $F_t(x)$ converges as $t \to \infty$ uniformly in x to a unique invariant distribution $F(x)$, independently of initial stock y_0. The support of F is $[x_m, x_M]$.

Theorem 12: Suppose configuration B holds. If $x_0 \in (0, x_M]$ (resp. $x_0 \in [x_m, \infty)$) then $F_t(x)$ converges as $t \to \infty$ uniformly in x to the invariant distribution $\bar{F}(x)$ (resp. $\underline{F}(x)$) whose support is a subset of $[y_m, x_M]$ (resp. $[x_m, y_M]$). $\bar{F}(x)$ (resp. $\underline{F}(x)$) is the unique invariant distribution with support a subset of $(0, x_M]$ (resp. $[x_m, \infty)$).

6.2   Case When Production Is 'Very Stochastic'

In this subsection we assume (T.1)–(T.3) and (U.1)–(U.3) (enough to ensure the monotonicity result of Theorem 2 holds). We next impose (T.10) below, which requires that there be sufficient variability in production:

(T.10)   There is $z > 0$ in S such that

$$\gamma(\{r \in \mathcal{E}\,|\,f(x,r) \leq z \text{ for each } x \in S\}) > 0$$

and

$$\gamma(\{r \in \mathcal{E}\,|\,f(x,r) \geq z \text{ for each } x \in S\}) > 0$$

Recall that $F_t(x)$ is the distribution function of x_t.

Theorem 13: $F_t(x)$ converges as $t \to \infty$ uniformly in x to a unique invariant distribution $F(x)$, independently of the initial stock.

Example: Suppose $f(x,r) = 1/\{1 + me^{-kx}\} + r$, with $k > 0$ and $m > 0$. This is the logistic growth function with additive shocks. If $\mathcal{E} = [a,b]$ is the support of γ, then $b - a > m/1 + m$ will ensure that (T.10) holds and we obtain the conclusions of Theorem 13.

7 SOME ADDITIONAL RESULTS

7.1 The Convex Environment: An Overview

We now indicate how the standard results that hold in the 'convex environment' (i.e. with a strictly concave production function) can be obtained as special cases of our earlier results. Suppose that we impose the following concavity assumption:

(T.11)   For each fixed $r \in \mathcal{E}$, $f(\cdot, r)$ is strictly concave on S.

The following results summarize some uniqueness and concavity properties when (T.11) is added to our model:

Theorem 14: Under (T.1)–(T.3), (T.11), (U.1), (U.2) and (U.3):

(a)   If (x, c, y) and (x', c', y') are optimal (resp. input, consumption and stock) processes from the initial stock $y > 0$, then for each $t \geq 0$, $x_t = x'_t$, $c_t = c'_t$ and $y_t = y'_t$ a.s.

(b) $\varphi(y)$ is single valued at each $y > 0$.

(c)   The value function $V(y)$ is concave in y.

(d)   If, in addition, (U.3) holds, the value function, $V(y)$, is strictly concave in y.

Remarks

(1)   In Theorem 14 above, (U.1) may be replaced with (U.1′) and (T.4).

(2)   Without (U.3), the strict concavity of u, Theorem 14(d) may not hold.

From Theorem 2 we obtained the monotonicity of the optimal investment policy function, $h(y)$. In general, the monotonicity of the optimal consumption policy function, $c(y)$, cannot be asserted for non-convex technologies. Further, the functions $h(y)$ and $c(y)$ are not necessarily continuous.

We indicate below, however, that in the special case where (T.11) holds, such monotonicity and continuity results may be obtained.

Theorem 15: Under (T.1)–(T.3), (T.11), (U.1), (U.2) and (U.3′):

(a) $h(y)$ is continuous and non-decreasing in y;

(b) $c(y)$ is continuous and non-decreasing in y.

Remarks

(1)   Again we note that in Theorem 15, (U.1) may be replaced with (U.1′) and (T.4).

(2)   Theorem 15 uses the weaker assumption (U.3′), hence allows for linear utility functions.

Next, we obtain the differentiability of the value function and the 'envelope theorem'.

Theorem 16: Under (T.1)–(T.7), (T.11) and (U.1′), (U.2)–(U.4):

(a)   The value function, $V(y)$, is differentiable at each $y > 0$;

(b)   The following 'envelope theorem' holds at each $y > 0$;

$$V'(y) = u'(c(y)) = \delta \int V'(f(h(y),r))f'(h(y),r)d\gamma \tag{23}$$

The following corollary strengthens Theorem 15.2

Corollary 16: Under the hypotheses of Theorem 16.3:

(a) $h(y)$ is continuous and strictly increasing in y;

(b) $c(y)$ is continuous and strictly increasing in y.

Next, recall that in Section 6.1 we obtained the dynamic behavior of optimal input processes. We indicated that this behavior depends upon whether configuration A or B holds. We now show that under (T.11), configuration A holds and we obtain the convergence of the optimal input process to a unique invariant distribution irrespective of where the process begins.

Theorem 17: Assume (T.1)–(T.9), (T.11), (U.1′), (U.2)–(U.4) and (E.1). Then configuration A, hence, the conclusions of Theorem 11 hold.

Remarks

(1)   The proof of the result above that configuration A holds under (T.11) is due to Mirman and Zilcha (1975, lemma 2).

(2)   In Theorems 16 and 17 the assumptions (U.1′) and (T.4) are used. This is because (U.1′) and (T.4) are required to show that optimal processes are interior (Theorem 4); this is then used to prove the stochastic Ramsey–Euler condition (Theorem 5), which is crucial to the proofs of Theorems 16 and 17. Consider the following Inada condition at the origin:

(U.5) $\lim_{c \downarrow 0} u'(c) = \infty$

In Theorem 19 of Section 7.2 below, we indicate that Theorem 4 (Interior Optimal Processes), continues to hold if (U.1') and (T.4) are replaced with (U.1), (U.5) and (T.11). Hence, in Theorems 16 and 17, we may replace (U.1') and (T.4) with (U.1) and (U.5).

7.2 Interior Optimal Processes

In this subsection we discuss Theorem 4 (Interior Optimal Processes) when the assumptions (U.1') and (T.4) are replaced with (U.1) and (U.5) (the 'Inada condition' at the origin), which we repeat here:

(U.5) $\lim_{c \downarrow 0} u'(c) = \infty$.

We will also require,

(T.12) $\liminf_{x \downarrow 0} f'(x,r) > 0$ for each r.

First we indicate that if (U.1') and (T.4) are replaced with (U.1), (U.5) and (T.12) in Theorem 4, we can show that the optimal input and stock processes are interior.

Theorem 18: Under (T.1)–(T.3), (T.5)–(T.7), (T.12), (U.1) and (U.2)–(U.5), if (x^*, c^*, y') is an optimal process from some initial stock $y > 0$, then for all $t \geq 0$, $x_t^*(\eta_t) > 0$ and $y_t^*(\eta_t) > 0$ for all histories η_t.

Remarks

(1) Under the hypotheses of Theorem 18, we are unable to show that optimal consumption processes are interior.

(2) Theorem 18 may fail if (T.12) does not hold (see Section 7.3, Example 3).

(3) Notice that (T.11) is not required in Theorem 18.

We now indicate that under (T.11), Theorem 18 may be strengthened to show that optimal consumption processes (as well as input and stock processes) are interior.

Theorem 19: Under (T.1)–(T.3), (T.5)–(T.7), (T.11), (U.1) and (U.2)–(U.5), if (x^*, c^*, y) is an optimal process from some initial stock $y > 0$, then for all $t \geq 0$, $x_t^*(\eta_t) > 0$, $c_t^*(\eta_t) > 0$ and $y_t^*(\eta_t) > 0$ for all histories η_t.

7.3 Some Examples

We shall now present a collection of examples where one or more of the assumptions in our model do not hold, and as a result, some conclusions that we have derived fail to remain valid.

Example 1: We relax the assumption (U.3) in Theorem 2 and show that with a linear utility function, an optimal investment policy function need not be monotone non-decreasing.

Let $u(c) = 1/\delta c$ for $c \geqslant 0$ and $f(x,r) = 1/\delta x$ if $0 \leqslant x \leqslant M$, $M > 0$ and for all r in $\mathcal{E}$ and $f(x,r) = M/\delta$ for $x > M$. (We bound $f(x,r)$ from above so that it satisfies the assumptions we placed earlier on our production function, $f(x,r)$).

Let $\bar{y} \in (0,M)$, and let $\{x_t\}_{t=0}^{\infty}$ be an optimal input process from y. Suppose $x_1 < 1/\delta x_0$ and $x_0 < \bar{y}$.
Let $0 \leqslant \varepsilon \leqslant \bar{y} - x_0$. Construct a process $\{c_t', x_t'\}_0^{\infty}$ as follows:

$$x_0' = x_0 + \varepsilon, \ c_0' = c_0 - \varepsilon$$

$$c_1' = \frac{1}{\delta}(x_0 + \varepsilon) - x_1, \ x_1' = x_1$$

$$\{c_t', x_t'\} = \{c_t, x_t\} \text{ for all } t \geqslant 2$$

Then clearly $\{c_t', x_t'\}$ is feasible from $\bar{y}$. Furthermore,

$$\sum_{t=0}^{\infty} \delta^t u(c_t) - \sum_{t=0}^{\infty} \delta^t u(c_t') = u(c_0) + \delta u(c_1) - u(c_0') - \delta u(c_1')$$

$$= \frac{1}{\delta}(c_0) + \delta \left(\frac{1}{\delta}\right)\left(\frac{1}{\delta}x_0 - x_1\right) - \frac{1}{\delta}(c_0 - \varepsilon) - \delta\left(\frac{1}{\delta}\right)\left(\frac{1}{\delta}(x_0 + \varepsilon) - x_1\right) = 0$$

Hence, the process $\{x_t'\}_0^{\infty}$ is optimal. In particular if x_0 is optimal from y, and $x_0 \leqq x_0' \leqq y$ then x_0' is also optimal from y. Thus $h(y) = y$ for y in $[0,M]$ is an optimal policy function.
Under the assumption that $x_0 < \bar{y}$ we obtain the following as an optimal policy function, on $[0,M]$.

$$h(y) = y \text{ for all } y \neq \bar{y}$$

$$h(\bar{y}) = x_0 < \bar{y}.$$

Clearly this optimal investment policy function is *not* monotone non-decreasing.

If $x_0 = \bar{y}$ and $x_1 < 1/\delta x_0$ we can use the above method and define

$$\varepsilon = \frac{x_0 - \delta x_1}{2}, \; x_0' = \bar{y} - \varepsilon < \bar{y}, \; h(y) = y \text{ for all } y \neq \bar{y} \text{ and } h(\bar{y}) = x_0' < \bar{y}$$

and obtain the result that $h(y)$ is *not* monotone non-decreasing.

Finally, we note that $x_1 = 1/\delta x_0$ *and* $x_0 = \bar{y}$ cannot hold for any $\bar{y} \in (\bar{M}, M)$ where $\bar{M} = \delta M$ (see Fig. 19.2)

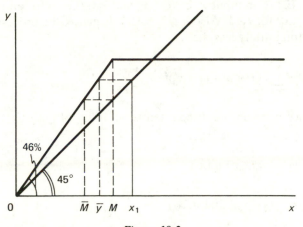

Figure 19.2

For in the case notice that x_1 lies in the horizontal flat portion of the production function. Thus we may put $x_1' = x_1 - \varepsilon$ with $\varepsilon > 0$ small enough so that x_1' also lies in the horizontal flat portion. Then output in the next period, period two, is unchanged; hence, defining $c_1' = \varepsilon$ and $\{x_t', c_t'\} = \{x_t, c_t\}$ for $t > 1$ we obtain a process with higher expected discounted total utility.

Example 2: Now we present an example where the production function is not uniformly bounded away from zero for each positive input level, and as a result, Theorem 5 (Stochastic Ramsey–Euler Condition) ceases to remain valid. Suppose $u(c) = -1/c$, $f(x,r) = rx^{1/2}$ and r is uniformly distributed on $[0,1]$. Then, since $c(f(h(y),r)) \leq f(h(y),r)$, if the stochastic Ramsey–Euler condition holds,

$$u'(c(y)) \geq \delta \int u'(f(h(y),r)) f'(h(y),r) dy = \frac{\delta}{2}[h(y)]^{3/2} \int_0^1 \frac{1}{r} dr = \infty$$

This is a contradiction as, from Theorem 4, $c(y) > 0$, hence $u'(c(y))$ is finite.

Example 3: Here we show that without (T.12), Theorem 18 may fail. Let $u(c) = c^{1/2}$, $f(x,r) = f(x) = x^4$ for $0 \le x \le 1$, $y = \frac{1}{2}$, $\delta = \frac{1}{2}$. If (x,c,y) is any process from y, since $y < 1$ and $f(x,r) \le x$ for $0 \le x \le 1$, then $0 \le x_t \le 1$ for each t, hence the definition of $f(x,r)$ for $x > 1$ is unimportant in the discussion below. Notice that (T.12) does not hold. Define the process (x^*,c^*,y^*) from initial stock y, by $y_0^* = c_0^* = y$, $x_0^* = 0$ and for all $t \ge 1$, $x_t^* = c_t^* = y_t^* = 0$. We will show that (x^*,c^*,y^*) is optimal from initial stock y, hence Theorem 18 does not hold.

The discounted total utility of (x^*,c^*,y^*) is $(\frac{1}{2})^{1/2}$. Let (x,c,y) be any process from initial stock y with some fixed input level $x_0 > 0$. We shall show that the discounted total utility of (x,c,y) is less than $(\frac{1}{2})^{1/2}$. Define the total accumulation process $\{\bar{x}_t\}$ from input x_0 by $\bar{x}_0 = x_0$ and $\bar{x}_t = f(\bar{x}_{t-1})$ for all $t \ge 1$. Notice that $\bar{x}_t = x_0^{4^t} \le x_0^{4t}$ for $t \ge 1$. Also $c_t \le \bar{x}_t$ for $t \ge 1$, hence, the process (x,c,y) has discounted total utility less than

$$(\tfrac{1}{2} - x_0)^{\frac{1}{2}} + \sum_{t=1}^{\infty} (\tfrac{1}{2})^t (x_0^{4t})^{\frac{1}{2}} = (\tfrac{1}{2} - x_0)^{\frac{1}{2}} + \frac{\frac{1}{2}x_0^2}{1 - \frac{1}{2}x_0^2} \tag{24}$$

The difference between the discounted total utility of (x^*,c^*,y^*) and (x,c,y) exceeds

$$D(x_0) \equiv (\tfrac{1}{2})^{\frac{1}{2}} + q_1(x_0) + q_2(x_0) \tag{25}$$

where $q_1(x_0) = -(\tfrac{1}{2} - x_0)^{\frac{1}{2}}$ and $q_2(x_0) = -\dfrac{\frac{1}{2}x_0^2}{1 - \frac{1}{2}x_0^2}$

To show that (x^*,c^*,y^*) is optimal, it suffices to show that $D(x_0) > 0$ for $x_0 > 0$. Notice that $D(0) = 0$, so we only have to show that $D'(x) > 0$ for $0 < x \le \frac{1}{2}$. However, one can check that $q_1(x)$ is convex so $q_1'(x) \ge q_1'(0) = (\tfrac{1}{2})^{\frac{1}{2}} > 1/1.5$ and also that $q_2(x)$ is concave so $q_2'(x) \ge q_2'(\tfrac{1}{2}) > -1/1.5$ for $0 < x \le \frac{1}{2}$. Addition then yields $D'(x) > 0$ for $0 < x \le \frac{1}{2}$. So (x^*,c^*,y^*) is optimal and hence Theorem 18 fails to hold.

8 PROOFS

Proof of Theorem 1: One may readily adapt the basic existence theorem of Maitra (1968) to obtain Theorem 1. We now indicate how to obtain Theorem 1 using (U.1′) in place of (U.1) [see Remark 2 following the statement of Theorem 1]. Since S is compact, (U.1′) implies u is bounded above on S, hence, using Lemma 2, one may check that all the conditions of Schäl (1975, theorem 16.1) hold, so we conclude there exists an optimal stationary policy $\pi^* = (\hat{h}^{(\infty)})$ where $\hat{h}: S \to A$ is a Borel measurable function. The functional equation (eqs (8) and (9)), follow from the same theorem. From Schäl (1975,

Corollary 6.3) we obtain that the value function, V, is upper semicontinuous (u.s.c.). Since, clearly, V is monotone non-decreasing, this implies that V is right continuous. To show that V is left continuous, fix any $y > 0$, and suppose x^* is an optimal input from y, and $c^* = y - x^*$. Assume $c^* > 0$, for otherwise $V(y) = -\infty$ and left continuity of V at y is trivial. Next, let $y_n \uparrow y$, so that for large enough n, $y_n - x^* \geq 0$. Then, from the functional equation,

$$V(y) = u(c^*) + \delta \int V(f(x^*,r))\gamma(dr)$$

$$V(y_n) \geq u(y_n - x^*) + \delta \int V(f(x^*,r))\gamma(dr)$$

hence, $V(y_n) - V(y) \geq u(y_n - x^*) - u(c^*)$, and taking limits gives

$$\lim_{n \to \infty} V(y_n) \geq V(y),$$

so combining with the fact that V is u.s.c. yields the left continuity of V.

QED

Proof of Theorem 2: We will now prove a stronger version of Theorem 2. Theorem 2(S): Suppose $y > y'$, and $\{x_t\}_0^\infty$, $\{x'_t\}_0^\infty$ are optimal input processes from y, y', respectively. Then $x_0 \geq x'_0$.

Proof: Theorem 2 follows from Theorem 2(S) by defining $x_0 = h(y)$ and $x'_0 = h(y')$.

Suppose, on the contrary, that $x_0 < x'_0$. Define new input processes from y, y' as follows. Let $\bar{x}_t = x'_t$ for all $t \geq 0$. Then $\bar{x}_0 = x'_0 \leq y' < y$, and for $t \geq 1$, $\bar{x}_t = x'_t \leq f(x'_{t-1},r_t) = f(\bar{x}_{t-1},r_t)$, hence $\{\bar{x}_t\}$ is feasible from y. Next, define $\bar{x}'_t = x_t$ for $t \geq 0$. Then $\bar{x}'_0 = x_0 < x'_0 \leq y'$ and for $t \geq 1$, $\bar{x}'_t = x_t \leq f(x_{t-1},r_t) = f(\bar{x}'_{t-1},r_t)$, hence $\{\bar{x}'_t\}$ is feasible from y'. Let $\{\bar{c}_t\}, \{\bar{c}'_t\}$ be the consumption processes corresponding to $\{\bar{x}_t\}, \{\bar{x}'_t\}$, respectively.

Using the functional equation (see eqs (10) and (11)) we obtain

$$u(c_0) + \delta \int V(f(x_0,r))\gamma(dr) = V(y) \geq u(\bar{c}_0) + \delta \int V(f(\bar{x}_0,r))\gamma(dr)$$

$$u(c'_0) + \delta \int V(f(x'_0,r))\gamma(dr) = V(y') \geq u(\bar{c}'_0) + \delta \int V(f(\bar{x}'_0,r))\gamma(dr) \qquad (26)$$

Adding these two inequalities and noting that $x_0 = \bar{x}'_0$, $x'_0 = \bar{x}_0$ we obtain

$$u(c_0) + u(c'_0) \geq u(\bar{c}_0) + u(\bar{c}'_0) \qquad (27)$$

Now, $\bar{c}_0 = y - x'_0 > y' - x'_0 = c'_0$ and $\bar{c}_0 = y - x'_0 < y - x_0 = c_0$, so there is a $0 < \theta < 1$ such that $\bar{c}_0 = \theta c_0 + (1 - \theta)c'_0$. Then $\bar{c}'_0 = y' - x_0 = (y - x_0) + (y' - x'_0) - (y - x'_0) = c_0 + c'_0 - \bar{c}_0 = (1 - \theta)c_0 + \theta c'_0$. This gives, using the strict concavity of u,

$$u(\bar{c}_0) > \theta u(c_0) + (1-\theta)u(c'_0) \tag{28}$$

and

$$u(\bar{c}'_0) > (1-\theta)u(c_0) + \theta u(c'_0) \tag{29}$$

so by addition

$$u(\bar{c}_0) + u(\bar{c}'_0) > u(c_0) + u(c'_0) \tag{30}$$

(30) contradicts (27), and proves that $x_0 \geq x'_0$ for $y > y'$.

QED

Remark: The proof of Theorem 2 above is a modification of the proof of Dechert and Nishimura (1983, theorem 1).

Proof of Theorem 3

(a) $\varphi(y)$ is the set

$$\{x: x \text{ solves } \max_{0 \leq x \leq y} \ u(y-x) + \delta \int V(f(x,r))\gamma(dr)\}$$

Since both u, and V are continuous, (a) follows from the Maximum Theorem (see, e.g., Berge (1963), p.116). (b) $\varphi(y)$ is a subset of S, hence is bounded. For fixed y in S, since φ is upper semicontinuous, $\varphi(y)$ is closed. $\underline{h}(y)$ is therefore the minimum of the compact set $\varphi(y)$, and hence is well defined.

Next, we show that $\underline{h}(y)$ is monotone non-decreasing. Notice that if u were strictly concave then the result would follow from Theorem 2(S).

If u is concave (not necessarily strictly) we modify the proof in Theorem 2(S) as follows. Suppose $y > y'$ and let $\{x_t\}$, $\{x'_t\}$ be the optimal input processes from y,y', respectively, using $\underline{h}$. Without strict concavity of u, eqs (28), (29) and hence (30) hold only with weak inequalities, in the proof of Theorem 2. However, we may still derive a contradiction to (27) by noting that (27) in this case holds with strict inequality, since $\bar{x}'_0 = x_0 < x'_0 = \underline{h}(y') = \min \varphi(y')$. Hence, $\bar{x}'_0$ is not optimal from y', so (26), and therefore (27), hold with strict inequality. Hence, $\underline{h}$ is monotone non-decreasing.

Next, we show that $\underline{h}(y)$ is left continuous. Let $y_n \uparrow y_0$. Since $\underline{h}(y_n)$ is monotone non-decreasing and bounded above we obtain that

$$x'' \equiv \lim_{n \to \infty} \underline{h}(y_n)$$

exists. But for all n, $\underline{h}(y_n) \leq \underline{h}(y_0)$, so

$$x'' \leq \underline{h}(y_0) \tag{31}$$

Next, let $x_n = \underline{h}(y_n) \in \varphi(y_n)$, and notice that $x_n \to x''$, $y_n \to y_0$ and $x_n \in \varphi(y_n)$. Since φ is upper semicontinuous, $x'' \in \varphi(y_0)$. Hence,

$$x'' \geq \min \varphi(y_0) = \underline{h}(y_0) \tag{32}$$

From (31) and (32),

$$\lim_{y_n \uparrow y_0} \underline{h}(y_n) = \underline{h}(y_0);$$

so $\underline{h}$ is left continuous.

(c)   Proof is similar to that of (b) with obvious changes.

QED

Proof of Corollary 3: Choose $h(y) = \bar{h}(y)$ (or $\underline{h}(y)$ if left continuity is required), and apply Theorem 3.

QED

Proof of Theorem 4: First we show that under (T.4), $V(y) > -\infty$ for $y > 0$. Fix any $y > 0$. Given the $k > 0$ in (T.4), choose any $0 < x_0 < \min \{y, k\}$. Then the following input and consumption process is feasible: For each t, and history $\eta_t, x_t(\eta_t) = x_0$, $c_0 = y - x_0 > 0$ and for $t \geq 1$, $c_t = f(x_{t-1}, r_t) - x_t = f(x_0, r_t) - x_0 > 0$. Using (T.6) and compactness of $\mathcal{E}$, there exists a $c' > 0$ such that $c_t \geq c'$ for all $t \geq 1$. Then

$$V(y) \geq u(y - x_0) + \sum_{t=0}^{\infty} \delta^t u(c') = u(c_0) + \frac{\delta}{1-\delta} u(c') > -\infty \tag{33}$$

If from any $y > 0$, $c(y) = 0$, then (U.1') implies $V(y) = -\infty$, contradicting (33). Hence, $c(y) > 0$ for $y > 0$. Finally, if $h(y) = 0$, then by (T.5), next period stock, and hence consumption, is zero, which by (U.1') implies $V(y) = -\infty$, again contradicting (33). Hence, $h(y) > 0$, from which the theorem follows.

QED

Proof of Theorem 5: First we prove the following lemma.

Lemma 2A: If $A = [a_1, a_2]$ with $0 < a_1 < a_2 < \infty$, then

$$\inf_{y \in A} c(y) > 0.$$

Proof: Suppose, on the contrary, that

$$\inf_{y \in A} c(y) = 0 \text{ and suppose } y^n \in A \text{ and } \lim_{n \to \infty} c(y^n) = 0.$$

Since A is compact we may assume without loss of generality that $y^n \to y^* \in A$. Define $\underline{c}(y) = y - \underline{h}(y)$ and $\bar{c}(y) = y - \bar{h}(y)$. If y^n contains a subsequence (retain the same index n) converging to y^* from below such that $y^n < y^{n+1}$ for all n, then by Theorem 2(S), $h(y^{n-1}) \leq \underline{h}(y^n) \leq h(y^{n+1})$ so taking limits as $n \to \infty$,

$$\lim_{n \to \infty} \underline{h}(y^n) = \lim_{n \to \infty} h(y^n) \text{ or } \lim_{n \to \infty} \underline{c}(y^n) = \lim_{n \to \infty} c(y^n) = 0.$$

Then using the left continuity of $\underline{c}(y)$ yields $\underline{c}(y^*) = 0$, which contradicts Theorem 4. A similar contradiction may be obtained if there is a subsequence $y^n \downarrow y^*$. This concludes the proof of the lemma.

We now proceed to prove Theorem 5. Fix $y^* > 0$, and define $c^* = c(y^*)$, $x^* = h(y^*)$ and $\bar{x}(r) = h(f(x^*, r))$. Define

$$H(c) \equiv u(c) + \delta \int u[f(y^* - c, r) - \bar{x}(r)] \gamma(dr) \tag{34}$$

for all c such that the expression is well defined. We begin with:

Claim 1: The following maximization problem (P) is solved by c^*:

$$\text{'max } H(c) \text{ subject to } 0 \leq c \leq y^* \text{ and } f(y^* - c, r) \geq \bar{x}(r)\text{'} \tag{P}$$

To verify claim 1, note that if c^* did not solve (P), there is some $\hat{c}$ such that $0 \leq \hat{c} \leq y^*$, $f(y^* - \hat{c}, r) \geq \bar{x}(r)$ and $H(\hat{c}) > H(c^*)$. Define a new process $(\hat{c}, \hat{x})$ as follows: $\hat{c}_0 = \hat{c}$, $\hat{x}_0 = y^* - \hat{c}$, $\hat{c}_1 = f(\hat{x}_0, r) - \bar{x}_1(r)$, $\hat{x}_1 = \bar{x}_1(r)$, $\hat{c}_t = c_t$, $\hat{x}_t = x_t$ for all $t \geq 2$, where $(\underline{c}, \underline{x})$ is an optimal process from y^*. The difference between the expected total discounted utility of $(\underline{c}, \underline{x})$ and $(\hat{c}, \hat{x})$ is $H(c^*) - H(\hat{c}) < 0$, a contradiction to optimality of $(\underline{c}, \underline{x})$. This establishes claim 1.

Claim 2: There exists a $\xi > 0$ such that for all c in $U \equiv (c^* - \xi, c^* + \xi)$, the contraints '$0 \leq c \leq y^*$' and '$f(y^* - c, r) - \bar{x}(r) \geq 0$' are satisfied.

To prove claim 2, note that from Theorem 4, $0 < c^* < y^*$, so let $\xi_1 > 0$ be such that $0 < c^* - \xi_1 < c^* + \xi_1 < y^*$. Then for c in $U_1 \equiv (c^* - \xi_1, c^* + \xi_1)$ the first constraint in claim 2 is satisfied.

Since $\mathcal{E}$ is compact, (T.6) implies that the following are well defined and positive for $x > 0$;

$$f_m(x) \equiv \min_{r \in \mathcal{E}} f(x, r) \text{ and } f_M(x) \equiv \max_{r \in \mathcal{E}} f(x, r).$$

Then $f(x^*, r) \in [f_m(x^*), f_M(x^*)]$, so Lemma 2A implies there is a $k > 0$ such that

$$f(x^*, r) - h(f(x^*, r)) \geq k \quad \gamma - \text{a.e.} \tag{35}$$

f is continuous on the compact set $S \times \mathcal{E}$ and so is uniformly continuous in (x, r), hence there exists some $\xi \, \varepsilon (0, \xi_1)$ such that

$$\sup_r |f(x^* + \varepsilon, r) - f(x^*, r)| < \frac{k}{2}$$

for all ε in $(-\xi, \xi)$. Define $U \equiv (c^* - \xi, c^* + \xi)$. Then for any c in U, putting $\varepsilon = c^* - c$, we obtain

$$f(y^* - c, r) - \bar{x}(r) = f(x^* + \varepsilon, r) - \bar{x}(r) = f(x^* + \varepsilon, r) - h(f(x^*, r))$$
$$= [f(x^*, r) - h(f(x^*, r))] + [f(x^* + \varepsilon, r) - f(x^*, r)] > k - \frac{k}{2} = \frac{k}{2};$$

i.e. for c in U

$$f(y^* - c, r) - \bar{x}(r) > \frac{k}{2} \quad \gamma \text{ a·e} \tag{36}$$

In particular the second constraint is satisfied for each c in U. Since $U \subset U_1$, the first constraint is also satisfied for each c in U. This completes proof of claim 2.

For c in U and any ε such that $c + \varepsilon$ is also in U, $[H(c+\varepsilon) - H(c)]/\varepsilon = A(c, \varepsilon) + \delta \int D(c, \varepsilon, r) \gamma(dr)$ where $A(c, \varepsilon) = [u(c+\varepsilon) - u(c)]/\varepsilon$ and $D(c, \varepsilon, r) = [u(f(y^* - c - \varepsilon, r) - \bar{x}(r)) - u(f(y^* - c, r) - \bar{x}(r))]/\varepsilon$.

Claim 3: There is an $M < \infty$ such that for each c in U and for any ε such that $c + \varepsilon$ is in U, $|D(c, \varepsilon, r)| \leq M$ γ – a.e.

To prove claim 3, suppose c is in U, and ε is such that $c + \varepsilon$ is in U. Then (36) implies for some $k > 0$, $f(y^* - c - \varepsilon, r) - \bar{x}(r) \geq k/2$ and $f(y^* - c, r) - \bar{x}(r) \geq k/2$ γ a.e. Since $y^* - c - \varepsilon \leq y^* - c^* + \xi$ we obtain $f(y^* - c - \varepsilon, r) - \bar{x}(r)$ and $f(y^* - c, r) - \bar{x}(r)$ both lie in the interval $[k/2, f_M(y^* - c^* + \xi)]$ where

$$f_M(x) \equiv \max_{r \in \mathcal{E}} f(x, r).$$

Hence, (U.4) implies there is an $M_1 > 0$ such that for each c and $c + \varepsilon$ in U,

$$\left| \frac{u(f(y^* - c - \varepsilon, r) - \bar{x}(r)) - u(f(y^* - c, r) - \bar{x}(r))}{f(y^* - c - \varepsilon, r) - f(y^* - c, r)} \right| \leq M_1 \quad \gamma - \text{a.e.} \tag{37}$$

Also, since $y^* - c - \varepsilon$ and $y^* - c$ both lie in $[x^* - \xi, x^* + \xi]$, (T.7) implies there is an $M_2 < \infty$ such that for all c and $c + \varepsilon$ in U,

$$\left| \frac{f(y^* - c - \varepsilon, r) - f(y^* - c, r)}{\varepsilon} \right| \leq M_2 \quad \gamma - \text{a.e.} \tag{38}$$

But (37) and (38) imply $|D(c, \varepsilon, r)| \leq M_1 M_2$, so putting $M = M_1 M_2$ then proves claim 3.

Now

$$\lim_{\varepsilon \to 0} A(c,\varepsilon) = u'(c).$$

Also

$$\lim_{\varepsilon \to 0} D(c,\varepsilon,r) = -u'(f(y^* - c,r) - \bar{x}(r))f'(y^* - c,r),$$

so using claim 3 above and the Dominated Convergence Theorem yields

$$\lim_{\varepsilon \to 0} \frac{H(c+\varepsilon) - H(c)}{\varepsilon} = u'(c) - \delta \int u'(f(y^* - c,r) - x(\bar{r}))f'(y^* - c,r)\gamma(dr) \quad (39)$$

Hence, $H(c)$ is differentiable at each c in U, and $H'(c)$ equals the expression on the right of (39).

Finally, since c^* solves the problem 'maximize $H(c)$ subject to $c^* - \xi < c < c^* + \xi$', and H is differentiable on the open constraint set, we obtain by the classical first-order conditions of calculus that $H'(c^*) = 0$ and the stochastic Ramsey–Euler condition follows immediately.

QED

Proof of Corollary 5: $h(y)$ from Theorem 2 is monotone non-decreasing. Suppose there exists $\underline{y}$, $\bar{y}$ with $\bar{y} > \underline{y} > 0$ such that $h(\underline{y}) = h(\bar{y}) \equiv h^*$ (say). Then for all $y \in [\underline{y},\bar{y}]$, $H(y) = h^*$. From the stochastic Ramsey–Euler conditions, this implies

$$u'(c(y)) = \delta \int u'(c(f(h(y),r)))f'(h(y),r)\gamma(dr)$$

$$= \delta \int u'(c(f(h^*,r)))f'(h^*,r)\gamma(dr) = m^*, \text{ say, for all } y \in [\underline{y},\bar{y}].$$

Hence, since u is strictly concave, $c(y) = c^*$ (say) for all y in $[\underline{y},\bar{y}]$, so $y = h(y) + c(y) = h^* + c^* = y^*$ (say) for all y in $[\bar{y},\underline{y}]$ which is a contradiction, proving that $h(y)$ must be strictly increasing.

QED

We shall prove Theorem 6 after we have proved all the results of Section 5.

Proof of Lemma 3: Let $E = \{y \in S | \bar{h}(y) - \underline{h}(y) > 0\}$. Given any integer n, let $E_n = \{y \in S | \bar{h}(y) - \underline{h}(y) > 1/n\}$. Then $E_n \uparrow E$ as $n \uparrow \infty$. Let $C = \{y \in S | \underline{h}(y)$ is continuous at $y\}$. Since $\underline{h}(y)$ is monotone non-decreasing, $C' = S - C$ is at most countable (see, e.g., K. L. Chung (1974), p.4). Fix an n and let $y_0 \in C \cap E_n$, and $y_k \downarrow y_0$. Then

$$\lim_{k\to\infty} \underline{h}(y_k) = \underline{h}(y_0)$$

since $y_0 \in C$; so there is a $k^* = k^*(n)$ such that for all $k > k^*$,

$$\underline{h}(y_k) \leq \underline{h}(y_0) + \frac{1}{2n} < \underline{h}(y_0) + \frac{1}{n} \leq \bar{h}(y_0). \tag{40}$$

The last inequality is from the hypothesis that $y_0 \in E_n$. Pick any $k > k^*$ and let $y' = y_k$, $x' = \underline{h}(y_k)$ and $x_0 = \bar{h}(y_0)$. Then (40) tells us that even though $y' > y$ we have $x' < x$. This contradicts Theorem 2(S); so for all n, $C \cap E_n$ is empty. Thus $E_n \subset S - C = C'$, so E_n is at most countable.

Finally, since

$$E = \bigcup_{n=1}^{\infty} E_n, \ E \text{ is a countable union of countable sets and hence is}$$
countable.

Proof of Lemma 4: Fix $y > 0$ and let $\underline{y}^n \uparrow y$. Let $\{x_i^n\}_0^\infty$ be the optimal input process from $\underline{y}^n$ obtained using the optimal investment policy function $\underline{h}$. We proceed to show

$$u'(y - x_0) \leq \lim_{n\to\infty} \inf \frac{V(y) - V(\underline{y}^n)}{y - \underline{y}^n} \leq \lim_{n\to\infty} \sup \frac{V(y) - V(\underline{y}^n)}{y - \underline{y}^n} \leq u'(y - x_0)$$

which implies $V^-(y) = u'(y - x_0)$. By the left continuity of $\underline{h}(y)$, $x_0^n = \underline{h}(\underline{y}^n)$ $\uparrow \underline{h}(y) = x_0$ where $\{x_i\}_0^\infty$ is the optimal input process from y (using $\underline{h}$ again). By Theorem 4, $x_0 < y$. Thus $\underline{y}^n \uparrow y$ implies that there is an n^* such that $x_0 \leq \underline{y}^n$ for all $n > n^*$. So by the functional equation

$$V(y) = u(y - x_0) + \delta \int V(f(x_0, r)) \gamma(dr).$$

$$V(\underline{y}^n) \geq u(\underline{y}^n - x_0) + \delta \int V(f(x_0, r)) \gamma(dr) \text{ for } n > n^*.$$

This leads to

$$V(y) - V(\underline{y}^n) \leq u(y - x_0) - u(\underline{y}^n - x_0)$$

$$\leq u'(\underline{y}^n - x_0)[y - \underline{y}^n] \text{ from concavity of } u.$$

So
$$\lim_{n\to\infty} \sup \frac{V(y) - V(\underline{y}^n)}{y - \underline{y}^n} \leq u'(y - x_0) \tag{41}$$

Since $\underline{h}$ is monotone non-decreasing,

$$x_0^n = \underline{h}(\underline{y}^n) \leq \underline{h}(y) \leq y.$$

Hence, by the functional equation

$$V(y) \geq u(y - \underline{x}_0^n) + \delta \int V(f(\underline{x}_0^n, r)) \gamma(dr).$$

$$V(\underline{y}^n) = u(\underline{y}^n - \underline{x}_0^n) + \delta \int V(f(\underline{x}_0^n, r)) \gamma(dr).$$

We then obtain $V(y) - V(\underline{y}^n) \geq u(y - \underline{x}_0^n) - u(\underline{y}^n - \underline{x}_0^n) \geq u'(y - \underline{x}_0^n)[y - \underline{y}^n]$ from concavity of u, so

$$\liminf_{n \to \infty} \frac{V(y) - V(\underline{y}^n)}{y - \underline{y}^n} \geq u'(y - x_0). \tag{42}$$

Combining (41), (42) yields $V^-(y) = u'(y - x_0)$. Similarly, by letting $\bar{y}^n \downarrow y$ and using the optimal investment policy function $\bar{h}$ one obtains $V^+(y) = u'(y - \bar{x}_0)$ where $\bar{x}_0 = \bar{h}(y)$. Hence, the right and left derivatives exist. Further using $\bar{h} \geq \underline{h}$ and concavity of u,

$$V^-(y) = u'(y - \underline{h}(y)) \leq u'(y - \bar{h}(y)) = V^+(y) \tag{43}$$

To prove the last part of the theorem, we obtain from Lemma 3 that $\underline{h}(y) = \bar{h}(y)$ except for countably many values of y. Hence, except for those countable values of y, $x_0 = \underline{h}(y) = \bar{h}(y) = \bar{x}_0$, so $V^-(y) = u'(y - x_0) = u'(y - \bar{x}_0) = V^+(y)$, and $V'(y)$ exists outside this countable set.

QED

Proof of Theorem 7: Suppose from $y > 0$, $\{x_0, x_1, x_2, ...\}$ and $\{x_0, x_1', x_2', ...\}$ are optimal input processes. By induction, it suffices to prove that $x_1 = x_1'$ a.s. Suppose, *ad absurdum*, that $\bar{h}(f(x_0, r)) > \underline{h}(f(x_0, r))$ with strictly positive γ probability. Define $\bar{c}(y) = y - \bar{h}(y)$ and $\underline{c}(y) = y - \underline{h}(y)$. Then, under the hypotheses of the stochastic Ramsey–Euler condition, since $\bar{c}(f(x_0, r))$, $\underline{c}(f(x_0, r))$ are *both* optimal consumptions from $f(x_0, r)$, we obtain

$$u'(y - x_0) = \delta \int u'(\bar{c})f(x_0, r)))f'(x_0, r)\gamma(dr)$$

and

$$u'(y - x_0) = \delta \int u'(\underline{c}(f(x_0, r)))f'(x_0, r)\gamma(dr)$$

so

$$\int [u'(\bar{c}(f(x_0, r))) - u'(\underline{c}(f(x_0, r)))]f'(x_0, r)\gamma(dr) = 0. \tag{44}$$

But $\bar{c}(f(x_0, r)) \leq \underline{c}(f(x_0, r))$ for each r, with strict inequality holding with γ positive probability. Since u is strictly concave (U.2), and f is assumed increasing (T.3), the left-hand side of (44) is strictly positive. This is a contradiction, and proves that $\underline{h}(f(x_0,r)) = \overline{h}(f(x_0,r))$ so $x_1 = x'_1$ a.s.

We now prove the second part of the theorem. If the optimal path is uniquely determined then $\bar{x}_0 = \overline{h}(y) = \underline{h}(y) = x_0$, hence from equation (43) above we see that $V^-(y) = V^+(y)$ so V is differentiable.

If V is differentiable, since u is strictly concave we obtain from eq. (43) that $\bar{x}_0 = \overline{h}(y) = \underline{h}(y) = x_0$. Then the first part of this theorem implies that the entire input process is uniquely determined.

QED

Proof of Theorem 8: From eq. (43), for $y > 0$, since $y - \overline{h}(y) \leq c(y) \leq y - \underline{h}(y)$, we obtain $V^-(y) = u'(y - \underline{h}(y)) \leq u'(c(y)) \leq u'(y - \overline{h}(y)) = V^+(y)$. If V is differentiable at y, then $V'(y) = u'(c(y))$, which is the first equality in eq. (14).

Since V is differentiable at $y > 0$, Theorem 7 implies that there is a unique optimal process from y; so for γ a.e. r, there is a unique optimal process from $y_1 = f(h(y),r)$; hence, using Theorem 7 again, V is differentiable at $y_1 = f(h(y),r)$. The second equality in (7) then follows immediately from the stochastic Ramsey–Euler condition, and the first equality (replacing y with $y_1 = f(h(y),r)$).

QED

Proof of Theorem 6: Concavity of V implies that for all $y > 0$, $V^-(y) \geq V^+(y)$. Combining this with equation (43) proves the first assertion. Next, suppose that V is concave. Then V is differentiable, so from Theorem 8, $V'(y) = u'(c(y))$. Monotonicity of $c(y)$ then follows from concavity of V and u. Finally, if $c(y)$ is monotone non-decreasing, to prove that V is concave, it suffices to show that $u'(c(y)) = V'(y)$ for all $y > 0$. Let C be the set of points $y > 0$ where the equality does not hold. From Lemma 4 and Theorem 8, C is the set of points where V is not differentiable, and C is at most countable. To complete the proof we will show that C is empty. Suppose, instead, that $y \in C$. Since C is countable, we may choose sequences $\{\underline{y}_n\}, \{\bar{y}_n\}$ such that $\underline{y}_n \uparrow y, \bar{y}_n \downarrow y$ with $\underline{y}_n, \bar{y}_n$ outside C for all n. Using eq. (43) and the right continuity of $\overline{h}$, gives

$$V^+(y) = u'(y - \overline{h}(y)) = \lim_{n \to \infty} u'(\bar{y}_n - \overline{h}(\bar{y}_n)) = \lim_{n \to \infty} V'(\bar{y}_n).$$

Similarly, we may show

$$V^-(y) = \lim_{n \to \infty} V'(\underline{y}_n).$$

Monotonicity of $c(y)$ implies $V'(\bar{y}_n) = u'(c(\bar{y}_n)) \leq u'(c(\underline{y}_n)) = V'(\underline{y}_n)$, so taking limits $V^+(y) \leq V^-(y)$, which from eq. (43) means V is differentiable at $y \in C$, contradicting the definition of C. Hence, C is empty.

QED

Proof of eq. (21):

$$H_m(x) = h(f_m(x)), \; H_M(x) = h(f_M(x)) \tag{21}$$

We prove only the first equation, the second following similarly. By definition, $f_m(x) \leq f(x,r)$ for all r, hence from monotonicity of h, $h(f_m(x)) \leq h(f(x,r))$ for all r, so

$$h(f_m(x)) \leq \min_{r \in \mathcal{E}} h(f(x,r)) \equiv h_m(x) \tag{45}$$

Next, since $\mathcal{E}$ is finite,

$$\min_{r \in \mathcal{E}} f(x,r)$$

is attained at some r'; i.e. $f_m(x) = f(x,r')$. Hence,

$$h(f_m(x)) = h(f(x,r')) \geq \min_{r \in \mathcal{E}} h(f(x,r)) \equiv h_m(x) \tag{46}$$

From (45) and (46) we obtain the first equation in (21).

QED

Proof of Theorem 9: One checks that if $H(\cdot,r)$ is monotone non-decreasing (but not necessarily continuous) γ a.e., one may still apply Dubins and Freedman (1966, corollary 5.5) [see, e.g., Bhattacharya, 1985].

Proof of Lemma 5

(a)   Suppose for some fixed r, x^* is a fixed point of $H(\cdot,r)$ but is not a fixed point of one of $\bar{H}(\cdot,r)$, $\underline{H}(\cdot,r)$. Then $H(x^*,r) = x^*$ and $\bar{H}(x^*,r) > \underline{H}(x^*,r)$. Let $y = f(x^*,r)$. Define two processes (x,c,y) and (x',c',y') from y as follows: the process (x,c,y) is obtained by using h in the initial period, and $\underline{h}$ in each subsequent period. The process (x',c',y') is obtained using the policy h in the initial period, and the policy function $\bar{h}$ in each subsequent period.

Then (x,c,y) and (x',c',y') are both optimal processes from the initial stock $y > 0$, and $x_0 = x'_0 = h(y) = h(f(x^*,r)) \equiv H(x^*,r) = x^*$. Let $x_1(r)$, $x'_1(r)$ denote the inputs in period one corresponding to the processes (x,c,y), (x',c',y'), respectively, when the shock occurring in period one is r. Then

$$x_1(r) = \underline{h}(f(x_0,r)) = \underline{h}(f(x^*,r)) \equiv \underline{H}(x^*,r) < \bar{H}(x^*,r) \equiv \bar{h}(f(x^*,r))$$

$$= \bar{h}(f(x'_0,r)) = x'_1(r).$$

Under (E.1), the shock r occurs with positive probability, so we obtain a contradiction to the uniqueness result of Theorem 7.

(b) Suppose that $x_0 = H_M(x_0)$, and that the maximum defining $f_M(x_0)$ is attained at r_M (see eq. (21)), i.e. $f(x_0, r_M) = f_M(x_0)$. Then $x_0 = H_M(x_0) = h(f(x_0, r_M))$; hence, by (a) above, $\bar{H}(x_0, r_M) = \underline{H}(x_0, r_M) = x_0$ which gives, using eq. (21), $\bar{H}_M(x_0) = \underline{H}_M(x_0) = x_0$. Therefore, H_M, $\bar{H}_M$, $\underline{H}_M$ all have the same fixed points. Proof of (c) is similar to (b).

$$\text{QED}$$

Proof of Lemma 6: We require the following:

Claim 1: Suppose $G: S \rightarrow S$ is monotone non-decreasing and there exists $x_1 < x_2$ in S such that $G(x_1) > x_1$ and $G(x_2) < x_2$. Then there exists an x_3 in (x_1, x_2) with $G(x_3) = x_3$.

The claim can be proved using a simple sequential argument.

Claim 2: Fix an r in $\mathcal{E}$. Then $H(\cdot, r)$ cannot have a sequence of positive fixed points $\{x_n\}$ such that $x_n \rightarrow 0$ as $n \rightarrow \infty$.

Proof: Fix an r in $\mathcal{E}$. Suppose, contrary to the claim, that $H(x_n, r) = x_n$ for each n, and $x_n \rightarrow 0$ as $n \rightarrow \infty$. From the stochastic Ramsey–Euler condition,

$$u'(c(f(x_n, r))) = \delta \int u'(c(f(H(x_n, r), \sigma)))f'(H(x_n, r), \sigma)\gamma(d\sigma)$$

$$= \int u'(c(f(x_n, \sigma)))f'(x_n, \sigma)\gamma(d\sigma)$$

$$\geq \delta\gamma(\{r\})u'(c(f(x_n, r)))f'(x_n, r)$$

Hence, $\qquad 1 \geq \delta\gamma(\{r\})f'(x_n, r)$.

Under (T.8), the Inada condition at the origin, the right-hand side of the above inequality tends to infinity as n tends to infinity, which is a contradiction, which completes proof of claim 2.

Now we prove Lemma 6. Since $\mathcal{E}$ is finite it suffices to show that for fixed r, there exists an $\varepsilon_r > 0$ with $H(x, r) > x$ for all x in $(0, \varepsilon_r)$. Fix an r in $\mathcal{E}$. Define $M' = \inf\{x > 0 | H(x, r) = x\}$, then by claim 2, $M' > 0$. Suppose, *ad absurdum*, that there is no $\varepsilon_r < M'$ such that $H(x, r) > x$ for each x in $(0, \varepsilon_r)$. Pick any M in $(0, M')$ such that $H(M, r) < M$. If there is a $z < M$ with $H(z, r) > Z$, then claim 1 implies there is a $z' > 0$ with $z < z' < M < M'$ such that $H(z', r) = z'$. This contradicts the definition of M'.

Therefore,

$$H(x, r) < x \text{ for each } x \text{ in } (0, M) \tag{47}$$

Next, we show there is a K in $(0, M)$ such that

$$c(f(h(y), r)) > c(y) \text{ for each } y \text{ in } (0, K) \tag{48}$$

To prove (48) pick any y in $(0,M)$. Then from the stochastic Ramsey–Euler condition

$$u'(c(y)) = \delta \int f'(h(y),\sigma) u'(c(f(h(y),\sigma))) \gamma(d\sigma)$$

$$\geq \delta \gamma(\{r\}) f'(h(y),r) u'(c(f(h(y),r)))$$

Hence,

$$\frac{1}{\delta \gamma(\{r\}) f'(h(y),r)} \geq \frac{u'(c(f(h(y),r)))}{u'(c(y))}.$$

Since $f'(h(y),r) \to \infty$ as $y \to 0$, the left-hand side of the above inequality tends to zero as $y \to 0$. Choose K in $(0,M)$ such that for all y in $(0,K)$,

$$\frac{u'(c(f(h(y),r)))}{u'(c(y))} < 1,$$

so by strict concavity of u, $c(f(h(y),r)) > c(y)$ and (48) follows.

Next, pick any $y_0 \in (0,K)$ and define $x_0 = h(y_0)$, $c_0 = y_0 - h(y_0)$ and for $n \geq 1$, $x_n = H(x_{n-1},r)$, $y_n = f(x_{n-1},r)$ and $c_n = y_n - x_n$.

Claim 3: $H(x,r) < x$ for all x in $(0,M)$ [i.e. (47)], implies $x_n \to 0$, $y_n \to 0$ and $c_n \to 0$ as $n \to \infty$.

To prove claim 3 it suffices to show $x_n \to 0$ as $n \to \infty$. $x_0 \leq y_0$ and $y_0 \in (0,M)$ implies $x_0 \in (0,M)$. If $x_{n-1} \in (0,M)$ then since $x_n = H(x_{n-1},r) < x_{n-1}$, we have $x_n \in (0,M)$. So by induction $x_n \in (0,M)$ for each n, hence $x_{n+1} = H(x_n,r) < x_n$ for each n, and $x_n \downarrow x^*$ (say). We will show $x^* = 0$. Using the monotonicity result of Theorem 2(S), since $x_{n+1} < x_n < x_{n-1}$, $\bar{H}(x_{n+1},r) \leq H(x_n,r) \leq \bar{H}(x_{n-1},r)$. Taking limits and using the right continuity of $\bar{H}$,

$$\bar{H}(x^*,r) = \lim_{n \to \infty} \bar{H}(x_n,r) = \lim_{n \to \infty} H(x_n,r) \equiv \lim_{n \to \infty} x_{n+1} = x^*. \tag{49}$$

Hence, x^* is a fixed point of $\bar{H}$. From Lemma 5(a), x^* is a fixed point of H. Clearly $x^* < M$. If $x^* > 0$, we obtain a contradiction to the definition of M; so $x^* = 0$, and this completes proof of claim 3.

However, by putting $y = y_n$ in (48) we obtain $c_{n+1} > c_n$ for each n, so $c_n > c_0$ for each n. By Theorem 4, $c_0 > 0$, hence c_n cannot converge to zero, contradicting claim 3. So for fixed r, there is an $\varepsilon_r > 0$ with $H(x,r) > x$ for all x in $(0,\varepsilon_r)$, and r is in $\mathcal{E}$, a finite set.

QED

Proof of Lemma 7

(a) We shall show only that y_m is well defined, the others following similarly. Suppose $x^k \downarrow y_m$ with $H_m(x^k) = x^k$ for all k. Then Lemma 5(c) and eq. (21) imply $x^k = \bar{H}_m(x^k) = x^k$)). Taking limits, and using the continuity of $f_m(x)$ and right continuity of $\bar{h}$, $y_m = \bar{h}(f_m(y_m)) = \bar{H}_m(y_m)$. Applying Lemma 5(c) again, we get $y_m = H_m(y_m)$, hence y_m is well defined.

(b) Follows from Lemma 6.

(c) If $H_m(x) < x$ for some x in $(0, y_m)$ then claim 1 in proof of Lemma 6, and Lemma 6 itself, would imply there is some $x' \in (x, y_m)$ such that $H_m(x') = x'$ and this contradicts definition of y_m. Hence, $H_m(x) > x$ for $x \in (0, y_m)$. Similarly, using (T.1) which implies $H_m(\beta) < \beta$, we can show that $H_m(x) < x$ for x in (x_m, ∞).

The proof of (d) is similar to that of (c). (e) follows immediately from (c), (d) and the fact that $H_m(x) \leq H_M(x)$ for all x.

QED

Proof of Theorem 10: Let $S' = [c, d]$ and let $[a, b]$ be the unique minimal γ-invariant subset of S'. We proceed to show that for some integer m, γ^m splits, and in particular,

$$\gamma^m(\{r^m \varepsilon \mathcal{E}^m | H^m(x, r^m) \leq \frac{a+b}{2} \text{ for all } x \text{ in } S'\}) > 0$$

and

$$\gamma^m(\{r^m \in \mathcal{E}^m | H^m(x, r^m) \geq \frac{a+b}{2} \text{ for all } x \text{ in } S'\}) > 0 \tag{50}$$

Define $a_n = \sup \{z | H^n(d, r^n) \geq z, \text{ for all } r^n \in \mathcal{E}^n\}$ and $a^* = \inf_n a_n$. We will show $a^* = a$. First, since $[a, b]$ is γ-invariant, $H^n(d, r^n) \geq H^n(b, r^n) \geq a$ for all $r^n \in \mathcal{E}^n$. Hence, $a_n \geq a$ for each n, and $a^* \geq a$. Next, to show $a^* \leq a$, we will prove that $[a^*, d]$ is γ-invariant, which implies, since $[a, b]$ is minimal, that $[a, b] \subset [a^*, d]$ so $a^* \leq a$. To show $[a^*, d]$ is γ-invariant, it suffices to show

$$H(a^*, r) \geq a^* \text{ for all } r \tag{51}$$

First we prove the following general lemma. Recall $\bar{H}(x, r) = \bar{h}(f(x, r))$ where $\bar{h}$ is defined in (12). From Theorem 3(c), $\bar{H}$ is right continuous.

Lemma 8

$$\bar{H}(a^*,r) \geq a^* \text{ for each } r. \tag{52}$$

To prove Lemma 8, we will first prove the following claim:

Claim: Fix an n. Then for all r in some subset B_n of $\mathcal{E}$ with $\gamma(B_n) = 1$

$$\bar{H}\left(a_n + \frac{1}{n}, r\right) \geq a_{n+1} \tag{53}$$

Proof: Suppose the claim is false. Then on some subset D of $\mathcal{E}$ with $\gamma(D) > 0$,

$$a_{n+1} > \bar{H}\left(a_n + \frac{1}{n}, r\right) \geq H\left(a_n + \frac{1}{n}, r\right).$$

By definition of a_n, for r^n in some subset A_n of $\mathcal{E}^n$ with $\gamma^n(A_n) > 0$, $H^n(d, r^n) \leq a_n + 1/n$. Hence, for $r^{n+1} = (r^n, r) \in A_n \times D$,

$$H^{n+1}(d, r^{n+1}) \equiv H(H^n(d, r^n), r) \leq H\left(a_n + \frac{1}{n}, r\right) < a_{n+1},$$

which, since $\gamma^{n+1}(A_n \times D) = \gamma^n(A_n) \cdot \gamma(D) > 0$, contradicts the definition of a_{n+1}. This completes the proof of the claim.

To prove Lemma 8, define

$$B = \bigcap_{n=1}^{\infty} B_n,$$

then $\gamma(B) = 1$. Since $H(d,r) \leq d\gamma$ a.e., by induction $H^{n+1}(d, r^{n+1}) \leq H^n(d, r^n)$ so $a_{n+1} \leq a_n$ for each n, hence $a_n \downarrow a^*$. Taking limits in (53), and using the right continuity of $\bar{H}$ gives (52), for $r \in B$. This completes the proof of Lemma 8.

If H were continuous, then a simple modification of the proof of Lemma 8 results in (51). We now show

Lemma 9: The inequality (51) holds if we assume that $\mathcal{E}$ is finite and Lemma 5(a) holds.

Proof: Define $B_0 = \{r \in \mathcal{E} \mid \underline{H}(a^*,r) < a^*\}$ and suppose *ad absurdum* that $\gamma(B_0) > 0$. Since $\mathcal{E}$ is finite, for some r' in B_0,

$$M \equiv \max_{r \in B_0} f(a^*, r) = f(a^*, r'),$$

so

$$\underline{h}(M) = \underline{h}(f(a^*,r')) \equiv \underline{H}(a^*,r') < a^* \tag{54}$$

If $\bar{H}(a^*,r) = a^*$ for some r in B_0, we obtain an immediate contradiction to Lemma 5(a), so from (52),

$$\bar{H}(a^*,r) > a^* \text{ for each } r \text{ in } B_0 \tag{55}$$

and, in particular,

$$\bar{h}(M) = \bar{h}(f(a^*,r')) \equiv \bar{H}(a^*,r') > a^* \tag{56}$$

For r *not* in B_0, $\underline{h}(f(a^*,r)) \equiv \underline{H}(a^*,r) \geq a^* > \underline{h}(M)$; so from monotonicity of $\underline{h}$, $f(a^*,r) > M$, and hence by monotonicity of $\bar{h}$ and (56),

$$\bar{H}(a^*,r) \equiv \bar{h}(f(a^*,r)) \geq \bar{h}(M) > a^* \text{ for each } r \text{ not in } B_0 \tag{57}$$

From (55) and (57), $\bar{H}(a^*,r) > a^*$ for all r in $\mathcal{E}$. Since $\mathcal{E}$ is finite, there is some $\xi > 0$ such that

$$\bar{H}(a^*,r) > a^* + \xi \text{ for all } r \in \mathcal{E} \tag{58}$$

and $a^* + \xi \leq d$ (the latter inequality is possible since $a^* < d$; this follows from the fact that $H(d,r) \leq d$ for all r, hence by (T.9), $H(d,r'') < d$ for some r'', hence $a^* \leq a_1 \leq H(d,r'') < d$).

We will show that (58) leads to a contradiction. Define $\bar{a} = a^* + \xi$. Then for each r, $H(\bar{a},r) \equiv H(a^*+\xi,r) \geq \bar{H}(a^*,r) > a^* + \xi = \bar{a}$ (where the first inequality follows from Theorem 2(S), and the second follows from (58)). Then $H(d,r) \geq H(\bar{a},r) > \bar{a}$, so by induction, $H^n(d,r^n) \geq \bar{a}$ for each r^n. Hence, $a_n \geq \bar{a}$ for each n, so $a^* \geq \bar{a} = a^* + \xi$, a contradiction. This shows that $H(a^*,r) \geq \underline{H}(a^*,r) > a^*$, and concludes proof of Lemma 9.

Hence, we have shown that $a^* = a$. The proof of Theorem 10 then proceeds just as in Dubins and Freedman (1966, theorem, 5.15). We provide the rest of the proof here for the sake of completeness.

Since there are no γ-fixed points, $a < b$, so $a^* = a < a + b/2$. Hence, for some n_1, there is an $\bar{r}^{n_1} \in \mathcal{E}^{n_1}$ in the support of γ^{n_1} such that $H^{n_1}(d,\bar{r}^{n_1}) < a + b/2$. Repeating a similar argument, there is an integer n_2 and an $\underline{r}^{n_2} \in \mathcal{E}^{n_2}$ in the support of γ^{n_2} such that $H^{n_2}(c,\underline{r}^{n_2}) > a + b/2$.

Define $\bar{r}^{n_1+n_2} = (\underline{r}^{n_2}, \bar{r}^{n_1}) \in \mathcal{E}^{n_1+n_2}$, i.e. the first n_2 coordinates are $\underline{r}^{n_2}$, and the last n_1 are $\bar{r}^{n_1}$. Then for each x in $S' = [c,d]$,

$$H^{n_1+n_2}(x,\bar{r}^{n_1+n_2}) \leq H^{n_1+n_2}(d,\bar{r}^{n_1+n_2})$$

$$\equiv H^{n_1}(H^{n_2}(d,\underline{r}^{n_2}),\bar{r}^{n_1})$$

$$\leq H^{n_1}(d,\bar{r}^{n_1})$$

$$< \frac{a+b}{2}.$$

Similarly, if we define $\underline{r}^{n_1+n_2} = (\bar{r}^{n_1},\underline{r}^{n_2}) \in \mathcal{E}^{n_1+n_2}$ then $H^{n_1+n_2}(x,\underline{r}^{n_1+n_2}) > a+b/2$ for each $x \in S'$. Putting $m = n_1 + n_2$ proves (50) and concludes proof of Theorem 10.

QED

Proof of Theorem 11: From Lemma 6 there is an $\varepsilon > 0$ such that for all r, $H(x,r) > x$ for all x in $(0,\varepsilon)$, so we may redefine our state space to be $S' = S - [0,\varepsilon)$. We proceed to show that $[x_m,x_M]$ is the unique minimal γ-invariant closed interval in S', so that by applying Theorem 10 we may conclude the proof of this theorem. First, $[x_m,x_M]$ is a closed γ-invariant set, since for $x \in [x_m,x_M]$, $x_m = H_m(x_m) \leq H_m(x) \leq H(x,r) \leq H_M(x) \leq H_M(x_M) = x_M$, so γ a.e., $H(x,r) \in [x_m,x_M]$. Next, we show that $[x_m,x_M]$ is a minimal closed γ-invariant set. Suppose $[a,b] \subset [x_m,x_M]$ is γ-invariant. If we assume $x_m < a$, then $[a,b]$ γ-invariant implies $H(a,r) \geq a$, so $H_m(a) \geq a$, which contradicts Lemma 7(c). Hence, $x_m = a$. Similarly, we may show $b = x_M$, so $[x_m,x_M]$ is a minimal closed γ-invariant set.

Finally, we show that $[x_m,x_M]$ is the only minimal closed γ-invariant subset of S'. Suppose $[a,b]$ with $b \leq x_m$ is γ-invariant. Then $H(b,r) \leq b$ so $H_M(b) \leq b$, which, since $b \leq x_m < x_M$, contradicts Lemma 7(d). Similarly, we may show that $[a,b]$ with $a \geq x_M$ cannot be γ-invariant. Hence, $[x_n,x_M]$ is the unique minimal closed γ-invariant subset of S', hence applying Theorem 10 concludes proof.

QED

Proof of Theorem 12: Define $x_{m-} = \max\{x \in [y_m,x_M] | H_m(x) = x\}$, and proceed as in Lemma 7(a) to show that x_{m-} is well defined. From Lemma 6, there is an $\varepsilon > 0$ such that $H(x,r) > x$ for any x in $(0,\varepsilon)$ and for all r. Define $S'' = [\varepsilon,x_M]$, then one can check that S'' is γ-invariant. We may then follow the steps in the proof of Theorem 11 to show that $[x_{m-},x_M]$ is the only minimal γ-invariant closed interval in S''. An application of Theorem 10 then proves that if $x_0 \in (0,x_M]$, then $F_t(x)$ converges as $t \to \infty$ uniformly in x to an invariant distribution $\underline{F}(x)$ with support $[x_{m-},x_M]$.

Similarly, if we define $x_{M+} = \min\{x \in [x_m,y_M] | H_M(x) = x\}$, we may show that if $x_0 \in [x_m,\infty)$ then $F_t(x)$ converges as $t \to \infty$ uniformly in x to an invariant distribution $\bar{F}(x)$ with support $[x_m,x_{M+}]$.

QED

Proof of Theorem 13: From (T.10), with $z' = h(z)$, we obtain

$$\gamma(\{r \in \mathcal{E} \mid H(x,r) \leq z' \text{ for each } x \text{ in } S\}) > 0$$

and

$$\gamma(\{r \in \mathcal{E} \mid H(x,r) \geq z' \text{ for each } x \text{ in } S\}) > 0$$

So γ splits, and we may apply Theorem 9 to complete the proof of the theorem.

QED

Proof of Theorem 14

(a) Suppose (x,c,y) and (x',c',y') are optimal processes from some initial stock $y > 0$. Define a new process $(\bar{x},\bar{c},\bar{y})$ as follows: Fix any α in $(0,1)$. Let $\bar{x}_t \equiv \alpha x_t + (1-\alpha)x'_t$ for $t \geq 0$; $\bar{y}_0 \equiv y$ and for $t \geq 1$, $\bar{y}_t \equiv f(\bar{x}_{t-1},r_t)$; and for $t \geq 0$, $\bar{c}_t \equiv \bar{y}_t - \bar{x}_t$. Clearly, $\bar{x}_t \geq 0$ and $\bar{y}_t \geq 0$ for each $t \geq 0$. Further, using (T.11),

$$\bar{c}_t = f(\bar{x}_{t-1},r_t) - \bar{x}_t = f(\alpha x_{t-1} + (1-\alpha)x'_{t-1},r_t) - \alpha x_t - (1-\alpha)x'_t$$

$$\geq \alpha f(x_{t-1},r_t) + (1-\alpha)f(x'_{t-1},r_t) - \alpha x_t - (1-\alpha)x'_t \tag{59}$$

$$= \alpha c_t + (1-\alpha)c'_t \tag{60}$$

$$\geq 0$$

Hence, $(\bar{x},\bar{c},\bar{y})$ is a well-defined (resp. input, consumption and stock) process from initial stock y. Under (U.2), the monotonicity of u, we obtain from (60),

$$Eu(\bar{c}_t) \geq Eu(\alpha c_t + (1-\alpha)c'_t) \text{ for each } t \geq 0 \tag{61}$$

If for some $\tau \geq 1$, $x_{\tau-1}$ is different from $x'_{\tau-1}$ on a set with strictly positive probability, then under (T.11) (the *strict* concavity of f), (59) above holds with strict inequality; hence, (60) holds with strict inequality for $t = \tau$, so under (U.2), the strict monotonicity of u,

$$Eu(\bar{c}_\tau) > Eu(\alpha c_\tau + (1-\alpha)c'_\tau) \tag{62}$$

Then, using (61) and (62),

$$\sum_{t=0}^{\infty} \delta^t Eu(\bar{c}_t) > \sum_{t=0}^{\infty} \delta^t Eu(\alpha c_t + (1-\alpha)c'_t)$$

$$\geq \alpha \sum_{t=0}^{\infty} \delta^t Eu(c_t) + (1-\alpha) \sum_{t=0}^{\infty} \delta^t Eu(c_t') \text{ [from U.3')]} \tag{63}$$

$$= \alpha V(y) + (1-\alpha)V(y) \text{ [Since } (x,c,y), (x',c',y') \text{ are optimal]}$$

$$= V(y)$$

This is a contradiction, hence proves $x_t = x_t'$ a.e. for each $t \to \geq 0$. From this one obtains immediately that $y_t = y_t'$ and $c_t = c_t'$ a.e. for each $t \geq 0$.

(b) This follows immediately from (a) above.

(c) Fix any y, y' and suppose $y > y' \geq 0$. Let (x,c,y) and (x',c',y') be optimal processes from initial stocks y and y', respectively. Fix any α in $(0,1)$. Define a new process $(\bar{x}, \bar{c}, \bar{y})$ as follows: For all $t \geq 0$, $\bar{x}_t \equiv \alpha x_t + (1-\alpha)x_t'$; $\bar{y}_0 \equiv \alpha y + (1-\alpha)y'$ and for $t \geq 1$, $\bar{y}_t \equiv f(\bar{x}_{t-1}, r_t)$; and for all $t \geq 0$, $\bar{c}_t \equiv \bar{y}_t - \bar{x}_t$. One employs an argument used in (a) above to show that $(\bar{x}, \bar{c}, \bar{y})$ is a well-defined (resp. input, consumption and stock) process from $\bar{y}_0 \equiv \alpha y + (1-\alpha)y'$; and,

$$Eu(\bar{c}_t) \geq Eu(\alpha c_t + (1-\alpha)c_t') \text{ for each } t \geq 0. \tag{64}$$

Then, $V(\alpha y + (1-\alpha)y') = V(\bar{y}_0) \geq \sum_{t=0}^{\infty} \delta^t Eu(\bar{c}_t)$

$$\geq \sum_{t=0}^{\infty} \delta^t Eu(\alpha c_t + (1-\alpha)c_t') \text{ [from (64)]}$$

$$\geq \alpha \sum_{t=0}^{\infty} \delta^t Eu(c_t) + (1-\alpha) \sum_{t=0}^{\infty} \delta^t Eu(c_t') \text{ [from (U.3')]}$$

$$= \alpha V(y) + (1-\alpha)V(y') \tag{65}$$

Hence, V is concave.

(d) To show that V is strictly concave under (U.3), we modify the proof in (c) above as follows: Let y, y', α, (x,c,y), (x',c',y') and $(\bar{x}, \bar{c}, \bar{y})$ be as in (c) above.

If at some date $\tau \geq 0$, c^τ is different from c_τ' on a set with strictly positive probability, then (64) and (U.3) imply,

$$Eu(\bar{c}_\tau) \geq Eu(\alpha c_\tau + (1-\alpha)c_\tau') > \alpha Eu(c_\tau) + (1-\alpha)Eu(c_\tau') \tag{66}$$

If, alternatively, $c_t = c_t'$ for each $t \geq 0$, then since $y > y'$, we have $x_0 > x_0'$. So one may mimic the argument used to obtain (62) above, to show that

$$Eu(\bar{c}_1) > Eu(\alpha c_1 + (1-\alpha)c_1') \tag{67}$$

Finally, repeating the arguments used to obtain (65), with the aid of (66) and (67), we obtain,

$$V(\alpha y + (1-\alpha)y') > \alpha V(y) + (1-\alpha)V(y') \tag{68}$$

Hence, V is strictly concave.

QED

Proof of Theorem 15

(a)   From Theorem 14(b), $\varphi(y)$ is single valued, hence $h(y) = \bar{h}(y) = \underline{h}(y)$ for each $y > 0$ (where $\bar{h}$, $\underline{h}$ are defined in (12)). The monotonicity and continuity of h then follows from Theorem 3(b) and (c).

(b)   Since $c(y) = y - h(y)$, the continuity of $c(y)$ follows from the continuity of $h(y)$, which has been established in (a) above.

To prove the monotonicity of $c(y)$ we use a method similar to that used in Theorem 2. Let $y > y' > 0$ and suppose on the contrary that $c_0 \equiv c(y) < c(y') \equiv c_0'$. Define $x_0 \equiv h(y)$ and $x_0' \equiv h(y')$.

Let $\bar{x}_0 \equiv y - c_0'$. Then $y \geq y - c_0' \equiv \bar{x}_0$ and $\bar{x}_0 \equiv y - c_0' > y' - c_0' = x_0' \geq 0$. Hence, $\bar{x}_0 \in [0, y]$. From Theorem 14(a), the optimal process from y is unique. However, $\bar{x}_0 \equiv y - c_0' < y - c_0 = x_0$, and x_0 is the unique optimal input from y, hence $\bar{x}_0$ is not an optimal input from y. Then, using functional equation (see (10) and (11) above),

$$u(c_0) + M(x_0) = V(y) > u(y - \bar{x}_0) + M(\bar{x}_0) \tag{69}$$

where

$$M(x) \equiv \delta \int V(f(x,r))\gamma(dr) \tag{70}$$

Next, let $\bar{x}_0' \equiv y' - c_0$. Then $y' \geq y' - c_0 \equiv \bar{x}_0'$ and $\bar{x}_0' \equiv y' - c_0 > y' - c_0' = x_0' \geq 0$. Hence, $\bar{x}_0' \in [0, y']$. So using the functional equation again we obtain

$$u(c_0') + M(x_0') = V(y') \geq u(y' - \bar{x}_0') + M(\bar{x}_0') \tag{71}$$

Adding (69) and (71), and noting that $y - \bar{x}_0 = c_0'$ and $y' - \bar{x}_0' = c_0$, we obtain

$$M(x_0) + M(x_0') > M(\bar{x}_0) + M(\bar{x}_0') \tag{72}$$

Notice that $\bar{x}_0 \equiv y - c_0' < y - c_0 = x_0$ and $\bar{x}_0' \equiv y - c_0' > y' - c_0' = x_0'$.

Hence, there is a θ in $(0,1)$ such that $\bar{x}_0 = \theta x_0 + (1-\theta)x_0'$. Then $\bar{x}_0' \equiv y' - c_0 = (y - c_0') + (y' - c_0') - (y - c_0') = x_0 + x_0' - \bar{x}_0 = (1-\theta)x_0 + \theta x_0'$. Under (T.11) and the concavity of V (Theorem 14(c)), $M(x)$ is concave. Hence,

$$M(\bar{x}_0) \geq \theta M(x_0) + (1 - \theta) M(x_0') \tag{73}$$

$$M(\bar{x}_0') \geq (1 - \theta) M(x_0) + \theta M(x_0') \tag{74}$$

so by addition,

$$M(\bar{x}_0) + M(\bar{x}_0') \geq M(x_0) + M(x_0') \tag{75}$$

This contradicts (72) and concludes proof of the theorem.

QED

Proof of Theorem 16

(a)   This follows immediately from Theorem 14(c) and Theorem 6.

(b)   This follows immediately from (a) above and Theorem 8.

Proof of Corollary 16

(a)   This is Corollary 5!

(b)   Let $y > y' > 0$. From Theorem 14(d), $V(\cdot)$ is strictly concave, hence $V'(\cdot)$ is strictly decreasing. Then, using Theorem 16(b), $u'(c(y)) = V'(y) < V'(y') = u'(c(y'))$; so under (U.3), the strict concavity of u, $c(y) > c(y')$ for $y > y' > 0$. Finally, if $y > y' = 0$, then $c(y') = 0$ and, from Theorem 4, $c(y) > 0$, so $c(y) > c(y')$. Hence, $c(y) > c(y')$ for all $y > y' \geq 0$.

QED

Proof of Theorem 17: Let x_1, x_2 be any fixed points of H_m, h_M, respectively. We will show that $x_1 \leq x_2$, from which the conclusion follows.

Since $\mathcal{E}$ is finite, there exists r_m, r_M in $\mathcal{E}$ such that

$$x_1 = H_m(x_1) = H(x_1, r_m) \text{ and } x_2 = H_M(x_2) = H(x_2, r_M) \tag{76}$$

From the stochastic Ramsey–Euler condition (Theorem 5),

$$u'(c(f(x_1, r_m))) = \delta \int u'(c(f(H(x_1, r_m), \sigma))) f'(H(x_1, r_m), \sigma) \gamma(d\sigma)$$

$$= \delta \int u'(c(f(x_1, \sigma))) f'(x_1, \sigma) \gamma(d\sigma) \tag{77}$$

But, $f(x_1, r_m) = f_m(x_1) \leq f(x_1, \sigma)$ for each σ in $\mathcal{E}$, so since $c(y)$ is monotone non-decreasing (Theorem 6), and u is concave, we obtain $u'(c(f(x_1, r_m))) \geq u'(c(f(x_1, \sigma)))$ for each σ in $\mathcal{E}$. Putting this in (77) gives

$$1 \leq \delta \int f'(x_1, \sigma) \gamma(d\sigma) \tag{78}$$

Similarly, we may show that $1 \geq \delta \int f'(x_2, \sigma) \gamma(d\sigma)$; so combining with (78)

$$\int f'(x_1,\sigma)\gamma(d\sigma) \geq \int f'(x_2,\sigma)\gamma(d\sigma) \tag{79}$$

Strict concavity of $f(\cdot,\sigma)$ for each σ implies that the function $\int f'(x,\sigma)\gamma(d\sigma)$ is decreasing in x, so from (79) we obtain $x_1 \leq x_2$.

$$\text{QED}$$

Proof of Theorem 18: We shall show that for each $y>0$, $\underline{h}(y)>0$ (where $\underline{h}$ is defined in (12)). This will conclude the proof of the theorem; for, suppose $(x,\underline{c},y)$ is any optimal process from a given initial stock $y>0$. Then by definition of $\underline{h}$, $x_0 \geq \underline{h}(y)$; then using (T.5), $y_1 = f(x_0,r)>0$ for each r; hence $x_1 \geq \underline{h}(y_1) = \underline{h}(f(x_0,r))>0$ for each r. Repeating such an argument, we obtain that for each date $t \geq 0$, $x_t>0$ and $y_t>0$ a.s.

To prove $\underline{h}(y)>0$, for all $y>0$, fix $y>0$ and let $(x,\underline{c},y)$ be the optimal process from initial stock y, generated by the optimal investment policy function $\underline{h}$, and suppose on the contrary that $x_0=0$ and $c_0=y$. Then under (T.5), $x_t=0$, $y_t=0$ and $c_t=0$ a.s. for all $t \geq 1$. Fix any ε in $(0,y)$. Then define a new process $(x',\underline{c}',y')$ as follows: $y_0' \equiv y$, $x_0' \equiv \varepsilon$, $c_0' \equiv y - \varepsilon$, $y_1' \equiv f(x_0',r) = f(\varepsilon,r)$, $x_1' \equiv 0$, $c_1' \equiv y_1' = f(\varepsilon,r)$ and for all $t \geq 2$, $c_t' = x_t' = y_t' = 0$ a.s. Clearly, $(x',\underline{c}',y')$ is a well-defined (resp. input, consumption and stock) process from y.

Let $\tilde{V}(y)$ be the expected discounted total utility of the process $(x',\underline{c}',y')$. Then since $(x,\underline{c},y)$ is an optimal process from y,

$$0 \leq V(y) - \tilde{V}(y) = \sum_{t=0}^{\infty} \delta^t E[u(c_t) - u(c_t')]$$

$$= u(y) - u(y-\varepsilon) + \delta \int [u(0) - u(f(\varepsilon,r))]\gamma(dr)$$

Hence,

$$\int [u(f(\varepsilon,r)) - u(0)]\gamma(dr) \leq \frac{1}{\delta}[u(y) - u(y-\varepsilon)] \tag{80}$$

Define

$$A(\varepsilon,r) = \frac{u(f(\varepsilon,r)) - u(f(0,r))}{f(\varepsilon,r) - f(0,r)}$$

and $B(\varepsilon,r) = [f(\varepsilon,r) - f(0,r)]/\varepsilon$.

Then using Fatou's lemma (see, e.g., Chung (1974), p.42),

$$\int \liminf_{\varepsilon \to 0} A(\varepsilon,r) \cdot \liminf_{\varepsilon \to 0} B(\varepsilon,r)\gamma(dr) \leq \int \liminf_{\varepsilon \to 0} A(\varepsilon,r)B(\varepsilon,r)\gamma(dr)$$

$$\leq \liminf_{\varepsilon \to 0} \int A(\varepsilon,r)B(\varepsilon,r)\gamma(dr)$$

$$= \liminf_{\varepsilon \to 0} \int \frac{u(f(\varepsilon,r)) - u(f(0,r))}{\varepsilon} \gamma(dr)$$

$$\leq \liminf_{\varepsilon \to 0} \frac{1}{\delta} \left[\frac{u(y) - u(y - \varepsilon)}{\varepsilon} \right] [\text{from (80)}]$$

$$= \frac{1}{\delta} u'(y) < \infty \ [\text{from (U.4)}] \tag{81}$$

This is a contradiction since the left-hand side of (81) is infinite under (U.5) and (T.12).

QED

Proof of Theorem 19: From Theorem 18 above, we obtain that optimal input and stock processes are interior (notice that (T.11) and (T.3) imply (T.12)). It remains to show that optimal consumption processes are interior. It suffices to show that $c(y) > 0$ for each $y > 0$, where $c(\cdot)$ is the optimal consumption policy function; for suppose $c(y) > 0$ for each $y > 0$. Then if (x,c,y) is an optimal process from some fixed initial stock $y > 0$, we obtain from Theorem 18 that $y_t > 0$ a.s., hence $c_t = c(y_t) > 0$ a.s. for each $t \geq 0$.

To show $c(y) > 0$ for each $y > 0$, fix $y > 0$; let (x,c,y) be the optimal process from initial stock y, and suppose on the contrary that $c_0 = 0$ and $x_0 = y$. From the functional equation (see (10) and (11)), for all $0 < \varepsilon < \frac{1}{2}y$,

$$u(0) + \delta \int V(f(y,r))\gamma(dr) = V(y) \geq u(\varepsilon) + \delta \int V(f(y - \varepsilon,r))\gamma(dr)$$

hence

$$\frac{u(\varepsilon) - u(0)}{\varepsilon} \leq \delta \int \frac{V(f(y,r)) - V(f(y - \varepsilon,r))}{f(y,r) - f(y - \varepsilon,r)} \cdot \frac{f(y,r) - f(y - \varepsilon,r)}{\varepsilon} \gamma(dr) \tag{82}$$

Recall $f_m(x) \equiv \min_r f(x,r)$ and $f_M(x) \equiv \max_r f(x,r)$. Since the value function, V, is concave (Theorem 14(c)), and $f(y,r) \geq f(y - \varepsilon,r) \geq f_m(\frac{1}{2}y)$,

$$\frac{V(f(y,r)) - V(f(y - \varepsilon,r))}{f(y,r) - f(y - \varepsilon,r)} \leq \frac{V(f_m(y/2)) - V(0)}{f_m(y/2)} \tag{83}$$

Next, since the production function is concave (T.11),

$$\frac{f(y,r) - f(y - \varepsilon,r)}{\varepsilon} \leq \frac{f(y/2,r)}{y/2}$$

for each r in $\mathcal{E}$; also,

$$\frac{f(y/2,r)}{y/2} \leq \frac{f_M(y/2)}{y/2}.$$

Putting this and (83) into (82) gives,

$$\frac{u(\varepsilon) - u(0)}{\varepsilon} \le \delta \frac{V(f_m(y/2)) - V(0)}{f_m(y/2)} \cdot \frac{f_M(y/2)}{(y/2)} < \infty \tag{84}$$

Taking limits as $\varepsilon \to 0$ in (84) yields a contradiction since the left-hand side tends to infinity under (U.5), while the right-hand side is finite.

QED

References

Berge, C. (1963) *Topological Spaces* (Edinburgh: Oliver & Boyd).

Bhattacharya, R. (1985) 'Notes on Convergence of Probability Measures', mimeo.

Bhattacharya, R. and M. Majumdar (1981) 'Stochastic Models in Mathematical Economics: A Review', in 'Statistics: Applications and New Directions', *Proceedings of the Indian Statistical Institute*, Golden Jubilee International Conference, 1981; pp. 55–99.

Blackwell, D. (1965) 'Discounted Dynamic Programming', *Annals of Mathematical Statistics*, 36: 226–35.

Brock, W. and L. Mirman (1972) 'Optimal Growth and Uncertainty: The Discounted Case', *Journal of Economic Theory*, 4: 479–513.

Chung, K. L. (1974) *A Course in Probability Theory* (New York: Academic Press).

Clark, C. (1971) 'Economically Optimal Policies for the Utilization of Biologically Renewable Resources', *Mathematical Biosciences*, 12: 245–60.

Clark, C. (1976) *Mathematical Bioeconomics* (New York: John Wiley).

Dechert, W. and K. Nishimura (1983) 'A Complete Characterization of Optimal Growth Paths in an Aggregated Model with Nonconcave Production Function', *Journal of Economic Theory*, 31: 332–54.

Dubins, L. and D. Freedman (1966) 'Invariant Probabilities for Certain Markov Processes', *Annals of Mathematical Statistics*, 37: 837–48.

Hicks, J. (1960) 'Thoughts on the Theory of Capital – The Corfu Conference', *Oxford Economic Papers*, 12.

Jacquette, D. (1972) 'A Discrete–Time Population–Control Model with Set-up Cost', *Operations Research*, 22: 298–303.

Knight, F. (1921) *Risk, Uncertainty and Profit* (Boston and New York: Houghton Mifflin).

Maitra, A. (1968) 'Discounted Dynamic Programming on Compact Metric Spaces', *Sankhya*, Ser. A, 30: 211–21.

Majumdar, M. and T. Mitra (1982) 'Intertemporal Allocation with a Nonconvex Technology', *Journal of Economic Theory*, 27: 101–36.

Majumdar, M. and T. Mitra (1983) 'Dynamic Optimization with Nonconvex Technology: The Case of a Linear Objective Function', *Review of Economic Studies*, pp. 143–51.

Majumdar, M. and M. Nermuth (1982) 'Dynamic Optimization in Nonconvex Models with Irreversible Investment', *Zeitschrift für Nationalokonomie*, 42: 339–62.

Mirman, L. and D. Spulber (eds) (1982) *Essays in the Economics of Renewable Resources* (Amsterdam: North-Holland).

Mirman, L. and I. Zilcha (1975) 'Optimal Growth Under Uncertainty', *Journal of Economic Theory*, 11: 329–39.

Mitra, T. and D. Ray (1984) 'Dynamic Optimization on a Nonconvex Feasible Set', *Zeitschrift für Nationalokonomie*, 44: 151–71.

Ramsey, F. (1928) 'A Mathematical Theory of Savings', *Economic Journal*, 38: 543–49.

Reed, W. (1974) 'A Stochastic Model of the Economic Management of a Renewable Animal Resource, *Mathematical Biosciences*, 22: 313–34.

Robinson, J. (1956) *The Accumulation of Capital* (London: Macmillan).

Schäl, M. (1975) 'Conditions for Optimality in Dynamic Programming and for the Limit of n-Stage Optimal Policies to be Optimal', *Z. Wahrschein-lichkeitstheorie und Verw. gebiete*, 32: 179–96.

Sotomayor, M. (1984) 'On Income Fluctuations and Capital Gains with a Non-concave Production Function', mimeo.

Young, A. (1928) 'Increasing Returns and Economic Progress', *Economic Journal*, 38: 527–42.

20 Stochastic Capital Theory

William A. Brock, Michael Rothschild and Joseph E. Stiglitz*

1 INTRODUCTION

Many problems in capital theory – particularly 'Austrian' capital theory – take the following form: an asset has an *intrinsic value* $X(t)$ at time t. If he takes a particular action at time T, then the asset's owner gets $X(T)$ at T. In anticipation of future usage we shall call the action taken at T *stopping* and refer to T as a *stopping time*. This set-up raises two natural, and related, questions. When should the intrinsic process be stopped? What is the present value of the asset? The standard examples are when to drink the wine whose quality at t is given by $X(t)$ or when to cut down the tree which contains lumber with a value of $X(t)$. If the discount rate is r then these questions may be simply answered. The optimal stopping time T^* maximizes $e^{-rT}X(T)$ and the present value of the tree is its discounted value

$$V(t) = e^{-r(T^*-t)}X(T^*). \tag{1}$$

To distinguish from intrinsic value, call this latter quantity the *market value* of the asset.

An implication of (1) is that as long as $t < T^*$ the market value of an asset grows at a constant exponential rate. Note that this is true even though intrinsic value $X(t)$ cannot in general grow at a constant rate. Suppose, to the contrary, that $x(t) = x_0 e^{gt}$. Then if $g < r$, the asset will be stopped immediately; if $g > r$, its present value is infinite and it will never be stopped; only if $g = r$ is it possible that the asset will have a finite value and not be stopped immediately. While g could equal r for some (Fisherian) general equilibrium reasons, it does not seem a likely occurrence if the asset is a small part of a large economy. In this chapter we examine how these problems of timing and evaluation change when the asset's intrinsic value evolves stochastically rather than deterministically.

Suppose an asset will be worth $X(t,\omega)$ if stopped at time t when $X(t,\omega)$ is a

*This is a revision of NBER technical paper 23 (May 1982). The research reported here is part of the NBER's research program in Financial Markets and Monetary Economics. We are grateful to the National Science Foundation and the University of Wisconsin Graduate School for Research support. Rothschild and Stiglitz held the Oskar Morgenstern Distinguished Fellowship, Mathematica and Brock was Sherman Fairchild Distinguished Scholar, California Institute of Technology while some of the work on this paper was done.

stochastic process. We want to know when it should be stopped and what its market value is. We ask these questions because we believe that, as in the deterministic case, such an analysis leads to the solution of other interesting questions of valuation and timing. In the next section we discuss some examples where $X(t,\omega)$ is a discrete time stochastic process; however, our main concern is with the case where intrinsic value is a diffusion.

Some examples of the general optimal stopping problem analyzed in this chapter are: First, is the problem of finding the optimum time to erect a plant whose construction cost is F and whose net profits are generated by a stochastic process. In this case we seek the market value of the *rights* to contruct such a plant as a function of the current state of profit potential. The optimal stopping time is just the time at which the plant is built. Brock, Miller, and Scheinkman (1982) analyze this and other entry and exit problems in industrial organization which can be formulated as optimal stopping problems. Formally identical is the problem of deciding when to stop accumulating human capital and start working. Here human capital is measured by the discounted value of expected future earnings.

Second, is the problem of valuing an American option which gives its owner the right to purchase the present discounted value of future net cash flows from an asset by paying the exercise price.

Third, McDonald and Siegel (1982) show that an important class of questions in cost–benefit analysis can be posed as the problem of deciding when (or whether) to take an irreversible decision. An example is the decision to build a canal through the Everglades National Park or dam up the Grand Canyon. McDonald and Siegel show how such problems can be formulated as optimal stopping problems which are formally identical to those considered here.

Fourth, Dothan (1981) has considered the problem of finding the optimal time, from the point of view of the stock-holders, to default on bond-holders as an optimal stopping problem. Fifth, Ye (1983) has shown how the techniques developed here can be applied to the problem of optimally replacing a machine whose maintenance costs increase stochastically. Sixth, Miller and Voltaire (1980, 1983) have applied the techniques developed in previous versions of this paper to repeated stopping problems.

We hope we have said enough to justify the interest of economists in general problems of optimal stopping. What distinguishes our paper from existing literature on this problem is that we show how to derive comparative statics propositions for optimal stopping problems where the instantaneous mean and variance functions are arbitrary functions of the state variables. Most work in economics which has used diffusion processes has been restricted to processes which are either linear or geometric Brownian motion with constant coefficients. Each specification is unsatisfactory. In many cases, linear Brownian motion is unappealing or implausible as we show in Section 3.1 below. In all cases the optimal stopping problem is uninteresting or ill posed if the asset's intrinsic growth process is geometric Brownian motion. This should not surprise. The optimal stopping problem for an asset whose intrinsic value grows at a constant exponential rate is ill posed in the certainty case.

The analytic method we use, adapted from Krylov's (1980) work on optimal stopping of controlled diffusion processes, is simple and powerful. We believe it is new to the economics literature.

The rest of the introduction summarizes our results.

In Section 2 we analyze an asset whose growth follows a discrete time stochastic process. We obtain three main results. First, for processes which are strictly increasing, as uncertainty increases so does the value of the asset: however, the size at which it is cut down is not affected by uncertainty. Second, for processes which can decrease, the reverse may be the case. Third, the results for discrete time processes, particularly those which can decrease, are not as sharp as we would like them to be because they are confounded by round-off problems. Assets which follow a discrete time process necessarily grow by leaps and bounds. They cannot be cut down and harvested at an exact size. These problems of overshooting and undershooting make it difficult to obtain the kind of strong qualitative results we are looking for. Thus the remainder of the paper analyzes assets whose growth paths are continuous, i.e., they are governed by diffusion processes.

In Section 3 we pose and solve the optimal stopping problem for assets whose intrinsic value follows a diffusion process with instantaneous mean $b(x)$ and instantaneous variance $\sigma^2(x)$. The other parameters of the problem are r, the discount rate and a lower boundary condition. Because diffusion processes can decrease as well as increase, it is necessary to specify what happens to the asset when it reaches some lower boundary. The probability theory literature is replete with different boundary conditions; we consider the three most natural boundary conditions – a boundary at infinity, an absorbing boundary, and a reflecting boundary. Our methods work for all these boundary conditions.

We may summarize our results as follows: suppose the asset's value is defined over an interval $J=[Q,Z]$ where Q and Z are, possibly infinite, upper and lower boundaries. Then we may break up the interval J into two sets, a continuation set $\mathscr{C}$ and a stopping set $\mathscr{S}$. The market value of the asset is a function of its intrinsic value $V(x)$. On the stopping set $\mathscr{S}$, $V(x)=x$ while on the continuation set $\mathscr{C}$, $V(x)>x$. Also, on the continuation set, $V(x)$ satisfies a simple second order linear differential equation whose coefficients are the parameters of the growth process, $\sigma^2(x)$, $b(x)$ and the interest rate r. In the deterministic case the optimal stopping rule is to stop the asset when its growth rate is equal to the interest rate. The expected growth rate of the asset's value is just $b(x)/x$; thus the expected growth rate is greater than the interest rate if $b(x)>rx$. If $b(x)\geqslant rx$ then x belongs to the continuation region. In many instances (including the important case when the expected growth rate, $b(x)/x$, is declining) the optimal stopping rule is easily described. Don't stop the asset until its value hits a critical point y^* on the upper boundary of $\mathscr{C}$ where both $V(y^*) = y$ and $V'(y^*) = 1$. At y^*, $b(y^*)/y^* < r$. On the continuation region market value $V(x)$ follows a diffusion process such that $dV/V = rdt + A(x)dW(s)$ where $A(\cdot)$ is some function. Thus, $\log(EV(t)) - \log V(t_0) = r(t - t_0)$. This is an exact analogue of the result that under certainty the market value of an asset grows at the interest rate as long as it is held. Both the stopping value y^* and the market value function $V(x)$ are determined by the parameters of the problem – $\sigma^2(x)$, $b(x)$, and r. Our comparative statics results show how changes in the parameters affect y^* and V. Any parametric change which increases $V(x)$ at a point x increases $V(y)$ for all y in a neighborhood of x. Such a change also increases y^*. Thus all changes are either good, in which case they increase value uniformly over a neighborhood and they increase the optimal stopping size when x is near y^*, or bad, in which case they decrease value uniformly over a neighborhood and cause the asset to be stopped when smaller. Increases in the growth rate $b(x)$ are good. Increases in the discount rate are bad. Whether increases in variance, $\sigma^2(x)$, are good or bad depend on where they take place. If the market value function $V(x)$ is convex near x, a local increase in variance at x is good; it increases value and it will increase cutting size if x is near y^*. If the value function is concave near x, then a local increase in variance is bad. Near y^*, $V(x)$ is convex but there may be a region where $V(x)$ is concave. If there is an absorbing barrier, there will always be such a region. The ambiguous effects of variance on increases in value stand in sharp contrast to the option pricing literature. Increases in the variance of an asset increase the value of most financial options (like calls) written on that asset.

In Section 4 we show how the same techniques can be applied to optimal stopping problems in which the asset is described by a d dimensional diffusion process. An example would be a tree whose value is a function of its size and the price of lumber.

2   DISCRETE TIME-STOCHASTIC PROCESSES

This section contains observations about assets whose intrinsic value follows a discrete time stochastic process. We believe these observations provide considerable intuition about the way in which uncertainty affects market value and stopping times. They also indicate why we have chosen to analyze continuous processes at greater length in succeeding sections of this paper. In the examples that follow we suppose that at a time t the lumber in a tree is worth x_t where x_t is a discrete Markov process. The tree's owner seeks a stopping time τ, which will maximize $EX_\tau e^{-r\tau}$.

Example 1

Let

$$X_{t+1} = X_t + \varepsilon_t. \tag{2}$$

The ε_t are independent, identically distributed (i.i.d.) random variables with

$$Pr\{\varepsilon_t = 2\} = Pr\{\varepsilon_t = 0\} = 1/2.$$

Let $r = .1$ so $e^{-r} = .905$. Consider a tree of size 8 which will be cut down the first time it is size 10. Then $V_{10}(8)$, its present value, must satisfy the equation

$$V_{10}(8) = .905[(1/2)V_{10}(8) + (1/2)10]$$

or

$$V_{10}(8) = 8.26. \tag{3}$$

If the tree is now size 10 and will be cut down at size 12, its present value, $V_{12}(10)$, satisfies

$$V_{12}(10) = .905[(1/2)V_{12}(10) + (1/2)12]$$

so that

$$V_{12}(10) = 9.92 < 10. \tag{4}$$

A comparison of (3) and (4) suggests that an optimal policy is to cut down the tree when it first reaches size 10. (That this is so is a consequence of Proposition 1 below.) Note that this is the rule which would be followed if the tree grew constantly at a rate equal to its mean rate of growth. In this case we would have in the notation of the previous section $X'(t) = 1$, so the optimal cutting size X^* satisfies $X^{*'}/X^* = r = .1$ or $X^* = 10$; a tree of size $X < 10$ would be worth $W(X) = 10e^{-.1(10-X)}$. Thus

$$W(8) = 8.19. \tag{5}$$

Comparing (5) and (3) we see that uncertainty increases the value of the tree. Given the form of the optimal stopping rule – harvest the tree when it first reaches the optimal cutting size X^* – this is quite reasonable. The tree's expected present discounted value is then just $EX^*e^{-r\tau_{X^*}}$ where τ_{X^*} is the first time the tree reaches the size X^*. The only uncertain quantity in this expression is τ_{x^*} and our valuation function is the expected value of a *convex* function of this random variable. Since uncertainty increases the expected value of convex functions it is not surprising that uncertainty should increase the value of the tree. The next example shows that this intuition is not always correct.

Example 2

Consider a tree which grows according to the same rules as the tree in Example 1. Its present size is 9.5. Its owner can either sell it now or let it grow. Since the tree grows two units at a time, if he elects to let it grow, he must wait until it is at least 11.5 units tall. It is easy to calculate that

$$V_{11.5}(9.5) = 9.504$$

so that it is worthwhile to keep the tree. Since $V_{13.5}(11.5) = 11.15 < 11.5$ it seems the best policy is to keep the tree until it reaches 11.5. On the other hand, if growth of the tree is certain, then

$$W(9.5) = 10e^{-.05} = 9.512 > V_{11.5}(9.5). \tag{6}$$

In this case uncertainty decreases the value of the tree. The explanation for this anomaly is straightforward. As we will prove shortly, if the tree grows according to

$$X_{t+1} = X_t + \varepsilon_t$$

where the ε_t are non-negative independent, identically distributed (i.i.d.) random variables with $E\varepsilon_t = \mu$, an optimal policy is to cut down the tree the first time it reaches or exceeds $\bar{X}$ where $\bar{X}$ is the solution to

$$\bar{X} = \beta(\bar{X} + \mu) \tag{7}$$

or

$$\bar{X} = \frac{\beta}{(1-\beta)} \mu \tag{8}$$

and $\beta = e^{-r}$. In our case $\mu = 1$ and $\beta = e^{-1} = .905$, so

$$\bar{X} = 9.508.$$

The tree's owner would like to cut down the tree the first time it exceeds 9.508. Ideally, he would cut it down when its size reached $\bar{X} = 9.508$. Since the tree grows in steps of 2, he cannot cut it down exactly at $\bar{X}$. If it is currently of a size 9.5 he can only plan to cut it down at size $9.5 < \bar{X}$ or at 11.5 which overshoots the optimal harvesting size. It is not so much uncertainty *per se* which is responsible for the inequality (6) as the fact that the uncertain process is discrete and the tree cannot be cut down at its optimal size.

To see that this is correct, consider a tree now worth X. Next period it will be $Y = X + \Delta$ with probability $(1 - p)$. The discounted value of expected returns from realizing Y the first time the tree reaches Y is

$$V = YEe^{-rN_Y}$$

where the random variable N_Y is the number of periods to wait until the tree reaches Y. Since $EN_Y = 1/p$, Jensen's inequality implies $Ee^{-rN_Y} > e^{-r/p}$. But if the tree grew at the rate $\mu = p\Delta$ per period for certain, it would reach Y in exactly $1/p$ periods; its value would be $Ye^{-r/p}$. The uncertain tree is worth more – if it can be cut down precisely at Y.

In the simple examples we have given so far, we have suggested that uncertainty does not change the form of the optimal stopping rule. In Proposition 1, we use a simple heuristic argument (for which we are grateful to Herbert Scarf) to show that this is so if ε_t is non-negative (and thus the tree's size is a non-decreasing process). Let X be the optimal cutting time for the tree.

Proposition 1: If (2) holds and if

$$P\{X_{t+1} \geqslant X_t\} = 1 \tag{9}$$

then it is optimal to cut down the tree the first time $X_t \geqslant \bar{X}$ *where $\bar{X}$ is given* by (7).

Proof: Let $V(X)$ be the value of having a tree of size X assuming it will be cut down when it reaches the optimal size. Then if $\hat{X}$ is the cutting size it must be that

$$V(X) = X, \text{ for } X \geqslant \hat{X} \tag{10}$$

and

$$V(X) > X, \text{ for } X < \hat{X} \tag{11}$$

Also at $\hat{X}$, the tree owner must be indifferent between cutting the tree down now and letting it grow for a period. That is, $\hat{X}$ must satisfy

$$V(\hat{X}) = \beta E \max[(\hat{X} + \varepsilon), \ V(\hat{X} + \varepsilon)]. \tag{12}$$

However, since ε is non-negative, $V(\hat{X} + \varepsilon) = \hat{X} + \varepsilon$ and (12) becomes

$$\hat{X} = \beta E[\hat{X} + \varepsilon] = \beta(\hat{X} + \mu)$$

which is the same as (7). Since the solution to (7) is unique, $\hat{X} = \bar{X}$.

The proof of Proposition 1 makes clear that the assumption that X_t is increasing is crucial. If the tree can shrink as well as grow, the conclusion does not hold. Suppose that (2) holds but ε_t may be negative. If, for example, ε has a density function $f(.)$ with support on $[-1, +1]$, then the optimal cutting size $\hat{X}$ exceeds $\bar{X}$. For in this case (12) becomes

$$\hat{X} = \beta \left[\int_{-1}^{0} V(\hat{X} + \varepsilon) f(\varepsilon) d\varepsilon + \int_{0}^{1} (\hat{X} + \varepsilon) f(\varepsilon) d\varepsilon \right]$$

$$> \beta \left[\int_{-1}^{0} (\hat{X} + \varepsilon) f(\varepsilon) d\varepsilon + \int_{0}^{1} (\hat{X} + \varepsilon) f(\varepsilon) d\varepsilon \right] = \beta(\hat{X} + \mu).$$

Thus, $\hat{X} > \dfrac{\mu\beta}{1 - \beta} = \dfrac{\mu}{r} = \bar{X}$.

The mere fact that decreasing processes can go down leads to another reason why processes which can decrease are different from processes which grow certainly or processes which are uncertain but increasing. A process which can decrease can get stuck. Uncertainty makes this unhappy prospect possible and thus can decrease the value of the tree even when there is no overshooting problem. The reader will have no difficulty constructing examples which illustrate this point.

These observations give rise to something of a dilemma for the researcher who wants to build simple but general models to analyze the effect of uncertain growth on such Austrian assets as trees and wine. Examples 1 and 2 suggest that continuous models yield the most easily interpretable results. If the asset's value evolves continuously it can be stopped at any point. Problems of overshooting – which are responsible for the anomalous results of Example 2 – will be avoided. On the other hand, we have seen that strictly increasing processes behave very differently from processes which can decrease. Unfortunately, processes with continuous sample paths cannot be both genuinely stochastic and increasing. The only non-deterministic processes with continuous sample paths are diffusions and such processes behave locally like Brownian motion. Sample paths of Brownian motion are not monotonic. They increase and decrease. See Karlin and Taylor (1981, pp.162–9) and Krylov (1980, chapter 11). We have resolved this problem by focusing in the sequel on continuous (and thus possibly decreasing) processes.

3 ONE-DIMENSIONAL DIFFUSION PROCESSES

In this section we analyze the value of an asset whose intrinsic value, $x(t)$, evolves according to

$$x(t) = x_0 + \int_0^t \sigma(x(s))dW(s) + \int_0^t b(x(s))ds \qquad (13)$$

where W is a Weiner process. A common shorthand notation for (13) is

$$dx = \sigma(x)dW + b(x)dt \qquad (14)$$

The meaning of equations (13) and (14) is roughly that $x(t)$ behaves locally like Brownian motion with instantaneous drift $b(x)$ and instantaneous variance $\sigma^2(x)$. Thus, if $\Delta x = x(t + \Delta t) - x(t)$

$$E\Delta x \approx b(x)\Delta t \qquad (15)$$

$$E(\Delta x)^2 \approx \sigma^2(x)\Delta t \qquad (16)$$

Many texts have explained in detail the meaning of equations like (13) and (14). Two excellent examples are Arnold (1974) and Karlin and Taylor (1981).

The most general continuous time stochastic processes, which have sample paths continuous with probability one, can be written in the form (13) or (14) with the requirement that the coefficients $\sigma(.)$ and $b(.)$ satisfy some regularity conditions, see Karlin and Taylor (1981, section 15.1) and Krylov (1980, chapter 11). We make two significant restrictions by assuming that $a(.)$ and $b(.)$ are functions of the asset's current value alone. First, we assume that the process which affects the asset's growth is stationary; growth is not a function of time. Second, we assume that the only factor which determines the asset's growth is its current value. This is quite a severe restriction. One might naturally suppose that the value of a tree was a function of its monetary value $V(t) = p(t)x(t)$ where $p(t)$, the price of lumber in board feet, also follows a diffusion process. In the next section we show that our techniques can be applied to assets whose growth is determined by more general diffusion processes.

We will impose the mild regularity conditions that $\sigma(x)$ and $b(x)$ are bounded and satisfy a Lipschitz condition. We will also insist that the process be genuinely stochastic so that $\sigma(x)$ is bounded away from 0 for all x.

3.1 Heuristics and Boundary Conditions

To begin our analysis we *assume* that the optimal stopping rule is of the form: For some number y stop when intrinsic value first reaches y. Then the asset's market value is

$$H(x_0, y) = E[ye^{-rT_y}|x_0 = x] \tag{17}$$

where

$$T_y = inf\{t|x(t) = y\}.$$

Suppress y for a minute and consider the market value of the asset as a function of its current intrinsic value alone. The market value $V(x)$ must satisfy the linear second-order differential equation

$$L[V] = 0$$

where

$$L[u](x) = ru(x) - b(x)u'(x) - a(x)u''(x) \tag{18}$$

and

$$a(x) = \tfrac{1}{2}\sigma^2(x) \tag{19}$$

That this is so follows from general results stated in Krylov (1980) or Shiryayev (1978). We give a heuristic argument on which the more rigorous proofs are based. Suppose $x(t) < y$. Since $x(t)$ is continuous, if Δt is sufficiently small we may be sure that $x(t + \Delta t) < y$ and the asset will not be stopped before $t + \Delta t$. Thus

$$V(x) = e^{-r\Delta t}E[V(x(t + \Delta t))|x(t)] \tag{20}$$

Use (15), (16) and (17) to expand the right-hand side of (19) in a Taylor series so that

$$V(x) = e^{-rt}E[V(x) + V'(x)(\Delta x) + \tfrac{1}{2}V''(x)(\Delta x)^2 + \ldots]$$

$$= (1 - r\Delta t + \ldots)(V(x) + V'(x)b(x)\Delta t + V''(x)a(x)\Delta t + \ldots).$$

Rearrange and discard all terms of order $(\Delta t)^2$ and higher to get (18).

An immediate implication of equation (18) is that whatever process (as described by the coefficients $a(x)$ and $b(x)$ which governs the asset's intrinsic value), the asset's expected market *value* grows approximately exponentially.

Proposition 2:   Let the initial size x_0 at date 0 be in the continuation region, then for $t > 0$, t small, we have

$$\log(EV(x(t))) - \log(V(x_0)) = rt. \tag{21}$$

Here E denotes expectation conditioned at date 0.

Proposition 2 is a generalization of the result in the deterministic case that the present value of an asset that will be stopped at t^* is $V(x(t)) = x(t)e^{-r(t^*-t)}$; thus if $t < t^*$, $\log V(x(t)) - \log V(x(t_0)) = r(t - t_0)$.

Proof: Applying Ito's lemma to the process $V(x)$ we obtain

$$dV = [V'(x)b(x) + \tfrac{1}{2}V''(x)\sigma^2(x)]dt + V'(x)\sigma(x)dW.$$

Using (18) we see that

$$dV = rVdt + V'\sigma dW. \tag{22}$$

Taking expectations, using the fact that the stochastic integral is a martingale, so that

$$E\left[\int_0^t V'(x(s))\sigma(x(s))dW(s)\right] = 0, \tag{23}$$

we obtain (21), for t small enough so that (22) remains valid.

Proposition 2 emphasizes the distinction between the market value process and the intrinsic value process. The stochastic process which the tree's value follows is a generalization of geometric Brownian motion. Equation (22) would be exactly geometric Brownian motion if the term $V'(x)/V(x)\sigma(x)$ were a constant. In general this term will not be a constant, but we shall discuss a special case on page 604 below where it is.

As in the certainty case, processes of growth cannot in general satisfy an equation like (22). If $dx = b(x)dt + A(x)dW$ with b constant then b must be equal to r. For if $b > r$, then the asset would never be stopped and would have an infinite value. If on the other hand $b < r$, the asset's value is maximized if it is stopped and sold immediately. This is an immediate consequence of Proposition 3 (a rephrasing of general results due to Miroshnichenko (1975) below). However, the explanation of this result is familiar. By the definition of market value, if the owner of an asset of intrinsic value x were offered $V(x)$ he would be indifferent between selling the asset or holding on to it. Thus if a man had an asset whose intrinsic value followed the same process (22) as the market value of another asset, he would at any moment be indifferent between stopping it and letting it grow.[1] If the asset's growth rate were not r, he would no longer be indifferent. If such processes were freely available to the economy (constant returns) then, this requirement would determine the equilibrium interest rate. However, this seems as unlikely in the stochastic case as it is in the deterministic case. Thus if an asset's intrinsic value grows according to geometric Brownian motion (or to a process like (22)), it must be that the growth rate is exactly equal to r. Because this is such an implausible specification for physical processes we have sought, in this paper, results which hold for general diffusion processes.

We return to the problem of analyzing the market value and optimal stopping rule for an asset. We have shown so far that V must satisfy (18). A second order differential equation like (18) is completely determined by two boundary conditions. One boundary condition which V must satisfy is

$$V(y) = y \tag{24}$$

which is an immediate consequence of (17). Another consequence of (17) is that *if y is chosen optimally*

$$V'(y) = 1. \tag{25}$$

• Rigorous proofs of the necessity of (25) – known as the smooth pasting condition – can be found in Krylov (1980) and Shiryayev (1978). We give a heuristic argument which holds only for the special case where the function $H(x, y)$ of (17) can be written in the form

$$H(x, y) = f(x)g(y). \tag{26}$$

(We will observe shortly that (26) holds for some interesting special cases.) In this case it follows from the definition of H in (17) that $H(y, y) = y$, so $f(y)g(y) = y$ or $g(y) = y/f(y)$.

We have

$$V(x) = \sup_y \left(f(x) \cdot \frac{y}{f(y)} \right) = f(x) \sup_y \frac{y}{f(y)} \tag{27}$$

and

$$V'(x) = f'(x) \frac{y}{f(y)}. \tag{28}$$

When y is chosen optimally, y must maximize $y/f(y)$; thus

$$f(y) - f'(y)y = 0. \tag{29}$$

Using (29) to evaluate (28) at y we obtain (25).

We have argued that the market value V must satisfy a second-order differential equation $L[v] = 0$ and the two boundary conditions (24) and (25). This might at first sight seem to determine V completely as the two boundary conditions determine a unique solution to a second-order differential equation.

However, this reasoning is incorrect since (24) and (25) are meant to determine the optimal stopping boundary y while, as Hartman shows (1973, chapter XI, section 6), for *every* y there is a solution to the differential equation $L[u] = 0$ satisfying $u(y) = y$, $u'(y) = 1$. Obviously all y cannot be optimal so the problem must be rethought. The most straightforward approach is to look for another boundary condition. We stated that a distinctive aspect of diffusion processes was that they could go down as well as up. A natural question to ask is whether there is some obvious lower bound to the intrinsic value of the asset and if there is, what the value of the asset should be if it ever reaches that value.

This leads us to a discussion of lower boundary conditions. We ask the reader's patience as we proceed. The literature suggests many different boundary conditions. Some boundary conditions are plausible for some applications, others for others. We freely admit that the stories we use to motivate a particular boundary condition are not compelling. However, our techniques will work for all the boundary conditions we analyze and can, we suspect, be adapted to others. This does not mean boundary conditions are unimportant. We will see that the effect of changes in variance on market value and stopping rules depends on boundary conditions.

One possible solution to the lower boundary problem is to suppose that there is no lower boundary. Then we must be prepared to evaluate assets of any intrinsic value; in other words $V(x)$ must make sense for arbitrarily large negative x. This requirement provides the needed missing boundary condition. To see this most easily, consider the constant coefficients case where $a(x) = a$ and $b(x) = b$. Then the requirement that $L[V] = 0$ implies that

$$rV - bV' - aV'' = 0 \tag{30}$$

or

$$V(x) = A_1 e^{\lambda x} + A_2 e^{\mu x} \tag{31}$$

where λ and μ are roots of the characteristic equation of (30). Let

$$\lambda = \frac{-b + (b^2 + 4ar)^{1/2}}{2a} > 0 \tag{32a}$$

and

$$\mu = \frac{-b - (b^2 + 4ar)^{1/2}}{2a} < 0. \tag{32b}$$

Since for all x, $V(x) \geqslant x$ it follows from (31) and (32) that if

$$\lim_{x \to -\infty} |V(x)| < 0$$

then $A_2 = 0$ and

$$V(x) = A_1 e^{\lambda x}. \tag{33}$$

This is the example we promised on p.601 above; (33) implies $V'(x)/V(x) = \lambda$, a constant for all x. Equation (22) now states that market value follows geometric Brownian motion. For other boundary conditions, A_1 and A_2 are non-zero; V'/V is not constant.

Note that (33) is of the separable form (26) with the constant A_1 playing the role of $g(y)$. If the asset is stopped at y, we must have $A_1 = ye^{-\lambda y}$, so that $V(x) = ye^{-\lambda(y-x)}$. If y is chosen optimally it maximizes $ye^{-\lambda y}$, thus $y = \lambda^{-1}$ and

$$V(x) = \lambda^{-1} e^{\lambda x - 1}. \tag{34}$$

If the coefficients $a(x)$ and $b(x)$ are not constant, an analogous technique applies. It follows from general results of Hartman (1973, chapter XI, section 6) that if $a(x)$ and $b(x)$ satisfy the conditions set forth in Section 3.1 above, then there is a solution $V(x)$ to $L[w] = 0$ which satisfies

$$\lim_{x \to -\infty} |V(x)| < \infty. \tag{35}$$

Furthermore, if $V(x)$ is a solution to $L[v] = 0$ satisfying (35), so is $AV(x)$ for any constant A. Once again these solutions satisfy (26). The optimal upper boundary y is determined in the same way as in the constant coefficient case.

For some applications, it makes sense to postulate a lower bound to the intrinsic value of the asset; there is some value Q below which the asset's value cannot sink. We must ask what determines this boundary and what the market value of the asset is if it ever hits this boundary. One straightforward procedure would be to assume that when an asset hits an absorbing barrier at Q it dies and is worth nothing. In this case we add to the conditions (24) and (25) the condition

$$V(Q)=0. \tag{36}$$

Unfortunately this condition is suspect on economic grounds. If Q is positive it is not clear that the optimal policy is simply to let the asset die if it reaches Q. It would seem better to stop at size $Q+\varepsilon$ where $\varepsilon>0$. Since ε can be arbitrarily small, we can approximate this boundary condition arbitrarily closely by

$$V(Q)=Q. \tag{37a}$$

To avoid troublesome technicalities of little economic interest, we restrict attention to absorbing barriers which are non-negative so that

$$Q\geqslant 0. \tag{37b}$$

Consider stocks bought on margin to see that the condition (37) has appeal. Suppose I buy one share of stock on margin. When I buy it, its price is x_0 and I pay $P<x_0$, borrowing x_0-P from my broker. If the price gets so low that the amount I have borrowed is greater than or equal to γ times the current value of the stock, my broker will sell me out at the current market price. Thus I will get sold out at price $Q=(x_0-P)/\gamma$. When a sale is made at price S at time T (either voluntarily by me or involuntarily by my broker) I receive S and pay off my loan. If I can borrow at my discount rate r, then I must pay back a sum of $(x_0-P)e^{rt}$ which has a present value of (x_0-P). Thus the value of the transaction to me will be

$$\hat{R}(y,\tau)=ye^{-r\tau}-(x_0-P)$$

if I sell voluntarily and

$$\hat{R}(Q,\tau)=Qe^{-r\tau}-(x_0-P)$$

if I am sold out at Q. Since the term (x_0-P) is a constant independent of anything I do, I may as well analyze $R(y,\tau)=\hat{R}(y,\tau)+x_0-P$.

$$V(x_0)\equiv\sup_{\tau}E[R(y(\tau),\tau)|x(0)=x_0]$$

satisfies (18) as well as the boundary condition (37).

As we observed, while (37) is appealing on economic grounds, it does not have the homogeneity property of (22) which the other previous boundary conditions we have discussed had.

We mention one other boundary condition which is homogeneous. Probabilists who analyze diffusion processes often consider reflecting barriers. This corresponds to an asset, which when it reaches a size Q simply bounces off and starts again. As can be proved by a Taylor series argument (Cox and Miller, 1968) if there is a reflecting barrier at Q, then

$$V'(Q) = 0. \tag{38}$$

It is difficult to imagine cases where (38) makes sense when (13) represents the value of an asset. However, it is not hard to imagine processes which could be modelled by diffusion processes for which the boundary condition (38) is appropriate. In models of invention (38) corresponds to 'Oh, well, back to the drawing board.' (This case might also be modelled by a process which stuck on the boundary for a random period of time before it bounced back.) See Karlin and Taylor (1981, chapter 15) for a discussion of a variety of boundary conditions.

3.2   Comparative Statics – An Example

To illustrate the kind of results we seek it will be well to begin with the constant coefficient case with the boundary condition that V be bounded below at $-\infty$. As we saw the optimal cutting size is $y = \lambda^{-1}$ and the value of a tree of size x is $V(x) = \lambda^{-1} e^{\lambda x - 1}$ is given by (32a). Since $V(x)$ is a decreasing function of λ, the parameters of the problem (a, b, and r) change value and stopping size through their effect on λ. It is straightforward to calculate $d\lambda/dr > 0$; $d\lambda/db < 0$ so that increases in the discount rate decrease value and stopping size, while increases in the growth rate b have the opposite effect. Similarly, $d\lambda/da > 0$ so that increased variance increases both cutting time and value. This result is consistent with the observations we made in the preceding section that barring overshooting problems and the possibility of falling into a disaster, uncertainty should increase value and cutting time because e^{-rt} is a convex function of t.

3.3   Comparative Statics – General Principles

Here we show how to obtain similar results when $a(.)$ and $b(.)$ are functions rather than constants and the process satisfies any of the four boundary conditions (35), (36), (37) or (38).

Before we begin our analysis it will be well to restate somewhat more formally the characterization of the optimal stopping problems we are studying. Let $x(t)$ be a diffusion process which grows according to (13) on $I = [Q, Z]$ where $-\infty \leqslant Q < Z \leqslant +\infty$ and which satisfies the boundary conditions (35) or (37) where $Q\varepsilon[-\infty, +\infty)$ and $Z\varepsilon(-\infty, +\infty]$. (For boundary conditions (36) and (38), the statement of the results must be changed slightly in obvious ways.)

We seek a stopping time τ which maximizes $Ee^{-r}x(\tau)$. Krylov (1980, p.39), Shiryayev (1978, p.161), and Miroshnichenko (1975) have shown that the solution to this problem is characterized as follows. If $a(x)$, $a(x)^{-1}$ and $b(x)$ are bounded and satisfy a Lipschitz condition on I, then we may divide I into two disjoint regions:

(a) A closed set $\mathcal{S}$ called the stopping region on which $V(x) = x$.
(b) An open set $\mathcal{C}$ called the continuation region on which $V(x) > x$.

Furthermore if $\Gamma(E)$ is the boundary of the set E

(c) $L[V] = 0$ for $x \, \varepsilon \, \mathcal{C}$
(d) $V'(x) = 1$ for $x \, \varepsilon \, \Gamma(\mathcal{C})$
(e) The optimal stopping rule is to stop on the first entry into $\mathcal{C}$.
    (If $x_0 \, \varepsilon \, \mathcal{S}$ the asset should be stopped immediately.)

These conditions are sufficient as well as necessary. If there is a function $\hat{V}$ and regions $\mathcal{C}$ and $\mathcal{S}$ satisfying (a), (b), (c), and (d) and if $\hat{V}$ is absolutely continuous on I, then $\hat{V} = V$ and (e) describes the optimal stopping rule.

These conditions are best understood graphically. In Figure 20.1 we have

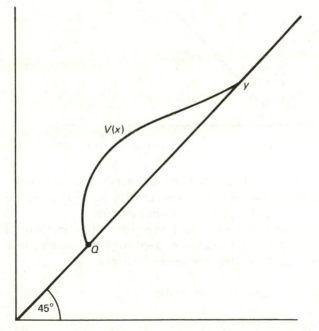

Figure 20.1   Coerced boundary at Q, free boundary at y

drawn the function $V(x)$. The continuation region $\mathscr{C}$ corresponds to the areas where $V(x)$ is above the 45° line. On the stopping region $\mathscr{S}$, $V(x)=x$ and thus coincides with the 45° line. There are two boundaries of $\mathscr{C}$ in Figure 20.1. The first is at Q and there it is not true that $V'(x)=1$ at $x=Q$. We will call such a situation a *coerced* boundary. There is a *free* boundary at y and at that point $V'(y)=1$ (in accordance with condition (d)). Other examples of possible boundaries and continuation regions are shown in Figures 20.2 and 20.5. Figure 20.2 corresponds to a continuation region which is unbounded below.

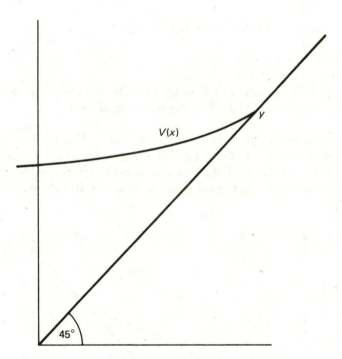

Figure 20.2   No lower boundary, free boundary at y

Figure 20.3 corresponds to two free boundaries (the boundary at Q is not coerced), Figure 20.4 to a disconnected continuation region, Figure 20.5 to an asset which is always stopped immediately.

We begin our analysis of the optimal stopping time with a result which implies that in general assets are kept until they are at least as valuable under uncertainty as they are under certainty.

Proposition 3:   Consider the region

$$A = \{x \in I; \ b(x)/x > r\}$$

then

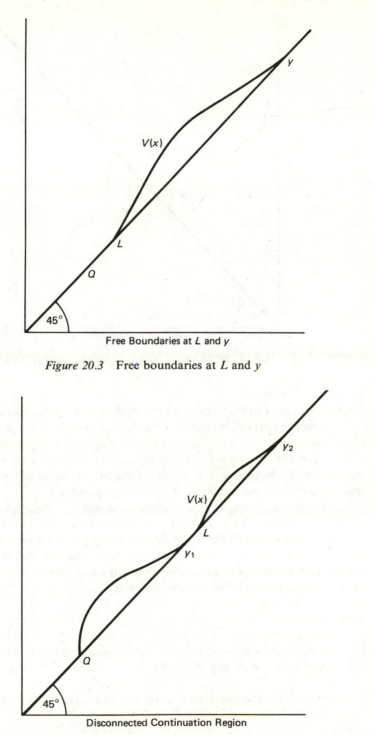

Free Boundaries at *L* and *y*

Figure 20.3   Free boundaries at *L* and *y*

Disconnected Continuation Region

Figure 20.4   Disconnected continuation region

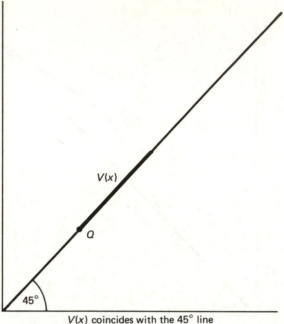

V(x) coincides with the 45° line

Figure 20.5   V(x) coincides with the 45° line

(a) $\mathscr{C} \subset A$

(b) Each interval of $\mathscr{C}$ contains an interval of A. In particuler if A consists of a single interval, $\mathscr{C}$ consists of a single interval, if A is empty so is $\mathscr{C}$.

Proof: This result is due to Miroshnichenko (1975) who established it for finite horizon problems; it is straightforward to adapt his proof to our special case if we assume away the existence problems.

   Since $b(x)$ is the average rate of physical growth of the asset, $b(x)/x$ is its (expected) growth rate; if $b(x)/x > r$, the expected growth rate of the tree is greater than the interest rate. The rule for selling an asset under certainty is to let it grow as long as the growth rate exceeds the interest rate. Proposition 3 generalizes and strengthens this rule. We note without proof some obvious consequences of Proposition 3.

Corollary 1

(a) If $b(x)/x > r$ for all $x \in I$, then $\mathscr{C} = (Q,Z)$, and $\Gamma(\mathscr{C}) = \{Q,Z\}$.

(b) If $b(x)/x \leqslant r$ for all $x \in I$, then $\mathscr{S} = I$.

   Note that (a) corresponds to Figure 20.3 and (b) to Figure 20.5. The next result gives necessary conditions for Figure 20.1 to describe the stopping region.

Corollary 2

If $Q > 0$ and

$$b(x)/x \text{ is decreasing and } b(Q)/Q > r \tag{39}$$

then the continuation region consists of a single interval. Furthermore, there is a coerced boundary at Q.

We have shown that the value function $V(x)$ and the optimal cutting size y satisfy the differential equation

$$rV(x) = a(x)V''(x) + b(x)V'(x) \tag{40}$$

the boundary conditions

$$V(y) = y, \quad V'(y) = 1 \tag{41}$$

and one of the boundary conditions (35), (36), (37) or (38). We now analyze how $V(x)$ and y change when the functions $a(x)$ or $b(x)$ are changed. We continue to use the symbol Q to stand for the lower boundary condition. That is, if the analysis refers to boundary condition (36), (37) or (38) Q is a number, while if it refers to (39) $Q = -\infty$. This convention will allow us to handle all three boundary conditions together.

Our approach to comparative statics will consist of changing the parameters $a(x)$ and $b(x)$ in a small interval $J \subset (Q, y)$ and leaving them unchanged outside of J. Specifically, we increase both instantaneous mean $b(x)$ and instantaneous variance $a(x)$ and ask whether this will increase the value of the asset. Krylov's (1980, p.39) analysis of the optimal control of diffusion processes motivates our results. Krylov shows that if a diffusion evolves according to

$$x(t) = x_0 + \int_0^t \sigma(x(s), \alpha(s)) dW(s) + \int_0^t b(x(s), \alpha(s)) ds$$

where $\alpha(s)$ is a control variable, whose values are restricted to lie in some control set A, then on the continuation region the value function $V(x)$ satisfies

$$a(x, \alpha^*(x)) V''(x) + b(x, \alpha^*(x)) V'(x) - rV(x) = 0 \tag{42}$$

where $\alpha^*(x)$ in A is chosen to maximize the left-hand side of (42). Suppose that increases in α correspond to increases in variance, that is $a(x,\alpha)$, is increasing in α, while $b(x,\alpha)$ is independent of α. Then α will be set as high as possible if $V''(x) > 0$ or if the value function is convex near x; if $V''(x) < 0$, then α will be set as low as possible. Since choosing to set α high means voluntarily accepting more variance, whether or not local increases in variance increase or decrease value depends on whether the value function is convex or concave. Similarly, increases in mean will increase value if the valuation function is increasing.

We now show that this heuristic argument is correct. Consider an optimal stopping problem with parameters $a(x)$ and $b(x)$ and continuation region $= (u, y_0)$. Let $V_0(x)$ and y_0 be the market value function and the optimal stopping boundary for this problem. Let $J = (c,d)$ be an interval such that $u < c < d < y_0$.

Let

$$a(x,\alpha) = a(x) + \alpha \eta(x) \tag{43}$$

and

$$b(x,\alpha) = b(x) + \alpha \eta(x) \tag{44}$$

where η is a smooth function which is zero off J and positive on J. Then we say $a(x,d)$ is a *local increase* in a on J; $b(x,d)$ is a local increase in b on J. Let $V_\alpha^*(x)$ be the value functions for the process with parameters $a(x,\alpha)$ and $b(x,\alpha)$.

Theorem 1

Suppose that for $x \in J$ it is the case that $V_0'(x) > 0$ *and* $V_0''(x) > 0$. Then there is an $\epsilon > 0$ such that if $0 < \alpha < \epsilon$, then for all of the boundary conditions (35–38),

$$V_\alpha^*(x) > V_0(x) \quad \text{for } x \in J$$

$$V_\alpha^*(x) \geqslant V_0(x) \quad \text{for } x \in [Q, y_0] \backslash J$$

Proof: In general the optimal upper boundary for the α process, y_α, will not equal y_0. Let $V_\alpha(x)$ be the unique solution to the differential equation

$$rV_\alpha(x) = a(x,\alpha)V_\alpha''(x) + b(x,\alpha)V_\alpha(x) \tag{45}$$

with boundaries

$$V_a(y_0) = y_0 \tag{46}$$

and

$$V_a(u) = u, \ u \geqslant 0 \tag{47a}$$

$$V_a'(u) = 0, \tag{47b}$$

or

$$\lim_{x \to \infty} |V_a(x)| < \infty. \tag{47c}$$

Clearly $V_a^*(x)$ is the value of a process with parameters $a(x,a)$ and $b(x,a)$ which will be stopped at size y_0. Since a person owning the process with these parameters could have stopped it at size y_0 rather than the optimal y_a, it must be that $V_a^*(x) \geqslant V_a(x)$. We prove the proposition by showing that $V_a(x) > V_0(x)$ for $x \in J$ and $V_a(x) \geqslant V_0(x)$ for $x \in (u,y_0) \backslash J$.

It is straightforward to adopt standard arguments showing that solutions of ordinary differential equations are continuous in parameters to show that the solution $V_a(x)$ and its first two derivatives $V_a'(x)$ and $V_a''(x)$ are continuous in a. Thus there is an ϵ such that $0 < a < \epsilon$ implies that for $x \in J$, $V_a''(x) > 0$ and $V_a'(x) > 0$. Now for $x \in (u,y_0)$ we have,

$$(a(x) + a\eta(x))V_a''(x) + (b(x) + a\eta(x))V_a'(x) = rV_a(x) \tag{48}$$

$$a(x)V_0''(x) + b(x)V_0'(x) = rV_0(x) \tag{49}$$

Subtract (48) from (49) and let $Z(x) = V_a(x) - V_0(x)$. Thus

$$a(x)Z''(x) + b(x)Z'(x) - rZ(x) = f(x)$$

or

$$Z(x) = (a(x)Z''(x) + b(x)Z'(x) - f(x))/r \tag{50}$$

where

$$f(x) = -a\eta(x)(V_a''(x) + V_a'(x)) \tag{51}$$

so that

$$f(x) < 0 \text{ for } x \in J \text{ and } f(x) = 0 \text{ for } x \in (u,y_0) \backslash J. \tag{52}$$

Furthermore (46) and (47) imply that Z satisfies the boundary conditions

$$Z(y_0) = 0 \tag{53}$$

and

$$Z(Q) = 0,$$

$$Z'(Q) = 0 \tag{54b}$$

or

$$\lim_{x \to -\infty} |Z(x)| < \infty. \tag{54c}$$

We now show that Z is non-negative everywhere. Suppose to the contrary that there were an $\hat{x}$ such that $Z(\hat{x}) < 0$. Then since $Z(y_0) = 0$, it must be that there is an $x \in (\hat{x}, y_0)$ such that $Z(x) \leqslant 0$ and $Z'(x) > 0$. But this implies either (i) $Z'(x) > 0$ for all $\hat{x} < x$, or (ii) there is a largest $\hat{x} < x$ such that $Z'(\hat{x}) = 0$. Clearly (i) cannot hold, for if it does $\hat{x} < x$ implies that

$$Z''(x) = \frac{f(x) + rZ(x) - b(x)Z'(x)}{a(x)} < 0$$

which is incompatible with any of the boundary conditions (54). However, if (ii) holds, then

$$Z''(\hat{x}) = \frac{f(\hat{x}) + rZ(\hat{x})}{a(\hat{x})} < 0$$

which implies that Z attains a local maximum at $\hat{x}$ which is also impossible. Thus we see that $Z(x) \geqslant 0$ for all $x \in (Q, y_0)$.

A similar argument shows that $Z(x) > 0$ for $x \in J$. If there were an $x \in J$ such that $Z(\hat{x}) = 0$ it would have to be a local minimum for Z. Thus $Z'(\hat{x}) = 0$. But this implies

$$Z''(\hat{x}) = f(\hat{x})a(\hat{x}) < 0$$

so that Z attains a local maximum at $\hat{x}$. This contradiction completes the proof.

3.4 Comparative Statics – Results

We make three points in this section. The first is that Theorem 1 is easy to use. The second is that some quite general comparative statics results are to be had. The third is that boundary conditions do matter. The effects of increases in variance are quite different for absorbing barriers than for reflecting barriers or barriers at $-\infty$. Throughout this section Q will denote a lower barrier and y^* a free upper boundary of the continuation region. We analyze the effect of local changes in b, mean, and σ^2, variance on V and y^*. We also analyze the effects of changes in the discount rate, r, and the level of the absorbing barrier, Q.

1. Changes in mean. The result here is, as is to be expected, simple and straightforward.

Corollary 3

Suppose that $V(x)>0$ for $x\in\mathscr{C}$. Then local increases in $b(x)$ increase both $V(x)$ and y^*.

Proof: In view of Theorem 1 it is only necessary to prove that $V'(x)>0$ for all $x\in\mathscr{C}$. By the smooth pasting condition, $V'(y^*)=1$. Suppose by way of contradiction that there is an $\hat{x}\in\mathscr{C}$ such that $V'(\hat{x})\leqslant0$. Then there is a largest $\hat{x}<y^*$ such that $V'(\hat{x})=0$. By definition of $\hat{x}$ (18), and positivity of V it follows that $V''(\hat{x})>0$. If there is a closest $\hat{x}<x$ that is a local maximum or inflection point of V then (18) yields an immediate contradiction to $V(\hat{x})>V(\hat{x})>0$. Hence $V'(x)<0$ for all $x<\hat{x}$. We claim that $V''(x)>0$ for all $x<\hat{x}$. Suppose not. Then there is a largest $x^*<\hat{x}$ such that $V''(x^*)=0$. But (18) and $V'(x^*)=0$ contradict $V(\hat{x}^*)>V(x)>0$. Hence $V''(x)>0$ for all $x<\hat{y}$. But then it is impossible for V to meet any of the boundary conditions (35–38). The reader will see this immediately if he/she draws a graph. This contradiction aids the proof.

One comment is necessary before we continue. The assumption that $V(x)>0$ for $x\in\mathscr{C}$ is modest. It will hold if the drift $b(x)$ is bounded away from zero for all x and there is no absorbing barrier. This is so because all the asset holder has to do at any initial x_0 is to hold the asset long enough until its intrinsic value x becomes positive. Thus $V(x_0)$ must be positive. Alternatively if there is an absorbing barrier $Q\geqslant0$, it is the case that $V(x_0)>0$ for $x_0\geqq Q$ provided that $b(x)>0$ for all x. However, if $Q<0$ then for x_0 close enough to Q we would have $V(x_0)<0$ even if $b(x)>0$ for all x. This is so because there is high probability of being absorbed at Q for x_0 close to Q.

2. Changes in the discount rate. The same type of argument used to establish Theorem 1 shows that value and stopping size are decreasing functions of the discount rate. The details of the proof are omitted.

Corollary 4

Suppose that $V(x) > 0$ for $x \in \mathscr{C}$, then $V(x)$ and y^* are decreasing functions of r.

3. **Changes in variance.** It follows from Theorem 1, that if V is convex in a neighbourhood of x_0, then local increases in variance at x_0 increase both value and the optimal stopping size y^*. If V is concave near x_0 a local increase in variance has the opposite effect. Thus to determine the effect of an increase in variance it is necessary to find out in which parts of the continuation region, V is convex. This is easy to do in some cases.

Corollary 5

A local increase in variance near a free boundary increases V and y^*.

Proof: We must show that near a free boundary at y, $V'' > 0$.

Consider $h(x) = V(x) - x$. Then $h(x)$ satisfies

$$a(x)h''(x) + bh'(x) - rh(x) = rx - b(x)$$

If y is a free boundary, $h(y) = 0$ and $h'(y) = 0$. Thus

$$a(y)h''(y) = ry - b(y),$$

which is positive by Proposition 3. Since $a(y) > 0$ and $h''(y) = V''(y)$, we conclude that $V''(y) > 0$.

Local increases in variance near coerced boundaries may have the opposite effect.

Corollary 6

If Q is an absorbing barrier and if $b(Q)/Q > r$, then in a neighborhood of Q, local increases in variance decrease V and y^*.

Proof: We must show that $V'''(Q) < 0$. From (18),

$$\begin{aligned} a(Q)V''(Q) &= rV(Q) - b(Q)V'(Q) \\ &= rQ - b(Q) - b(Q)(V'(Q) - 1) \\ &= rQ - b(Q) - b(Q)h'(Q) < 0. \end{aligned}$$

Thus if $b(x)/x$ is decreasing, increasing variance near a lower absorbing boundary decreases value while increasing variance near the free boundary value has the opposite effect. If one is edging gingerly away from a precipice, one is not pleased if required to make the trip on roller skates.

The effects of increased variance are quite different for other boundary conditions. Let us first deal with a reflecting boundary at Q. Suppose that $C=[Q,y^*]$ for some y^*. If there is a reflecting boundary at Q then (18), and (38), imply that $V(Q)>0$ provided that $V(Q)>0$ which we assume as a maintained hypothesis. In this case V must be convex in the lower parts of the continuation region. Since V'' is non-negative at the free upper boundary y^*, a condition which guarantees that there cannot be a point $\hat{x}$ at which V switches from being convex to concave as x increases will imply that V must be convex everywhere. If there were such a point, it would have to satisfy $V''(\hat{x})=0$ and $V'''(\hat{x})\leqslant0$. However, (18) implies that if $V''(\hat{x})=0$,

$$V'''(\hat{x})=(V'(\hat{x})/a(\hat{x}))(r-b'(\hat{x})).$$

Since $V'(\hat{x})/a(\hat{x})>0$, this proves

Corollary 7

If $r>b'(x)$ for all x and there is a reflecting boundary at Q then all local increases in variance increase V and y^*.

Using a somewhat similar argument we may prove

Corollary 8

Suppose that (i) $r>b'(x)$ for all x, (ii) $V(x)>0$ for all x, (iii) $\mathscr{C}=(-\infty,y^*)$ for some y^*, (iv) the boundary condition at $-\infty$ is given by (35). Then $V''(x)>0$ for all $x\in\mathscr{C}$, and, hence, all local increases in variance increase V and y^*.

Proof: At all zeroes of V'' on $\mathscr{C}$ we must have $V'''>0$ by (18) and (i). Hence there can be at most one zero of V'' on $\mathscr{C}$. Suppose by way of contradiction that there is one zero of V'', call it $\hat{x}$, on $\mathscr{C}$. Since $V'''(\hat{x})>0$ it must be the case that $V''(x)<0$ for $x<\hat{x}$. But

$$V(y)-V(\hat{x})=-\int_y^{\hat{x}}V'(\zeta)d\zeta<-V'(\hat{x})(\hat{x}-y)=V'(\hat{x})(y-\hat{x}) \tag{55}$$

for $y<\hat{x}$. This is so because $V'(\zeta)>V'(\hat{x})$ for $\zeta<\hat{x}$. Now let y go to $-\infty$ in (55). We have $V'(x)>0$ by Corollary 3. Hence $V(y)\to-\infty$, $y\to-\infty$. But this contradicts (35). The proof is complete.

Before moving on it is useful to remind the reader that Proposition 3 gives sufficient conditions for $\mathscr{C}$ to be of the form $[Q,Y^*]$ or $(-\infty,y^*)$.

The different implications of the condition $r>b'(x)$ for absorbing barriers emphasizes the importance of boundary conditions. With an absorbing barrier, $r>b'(x)$ implies the continuation region is broken up into two parts. In the upper portion V is convex, and more variance is welcome. In the lower portion V is concave and more variance is shunned.

4.   Changes in the absorbing barrier. Our last exercise in comparative statics is to analyze the effect of changes in the level of a coerced absorbing barrier at Q. Common sense suggests that since a coerced absorbing barrier is a constraint, making the constraint more stringent will make things worse. That is, if Q increases we expect both $V(x)$ and y^* to increase. This is correct. Suppose $\mathscr{C} = (Q, y^*)$ and let $V_1(x)$ and y_1^* be the value and optimal stopping barrier if there is an absorbing boundary at $Q_1 > Q$.

Corollary 9

For $x \in \mathscr{C}$, $V(x) > V_1(x)$; furthermore $y^* > y_1^*$.

Proof: Let $\mathscr{C}_1 = (Q_1, y_1^*)$, the continuation region when the absorbing barrier is Q_1. We consider only the case where $Q_1 \in \mathscr{C}$ for if $Q_1 > y^*$, then by Proposition 3, $\mathscr{C}_1$ is empty and the Corollary is obviously true. Since any policy which could be followed when the absorbing barrier is Q_1 could have been followed when the absorbing barrier is Q, $V(x) \geqslant V_1(x)$ all $x \in [Q_1, Z]$. Thus $\mathscr{C}_1 \subset \mathscr{C}$ and $y_1^* \leqslant y^*$. Let

$$g(x) = V(x) - V_1(x).$$

It will suffice to prove that

$$g(x) > 0 \text{ for } x \in \mathscr{C}_1.$$

On $\mathscr{C}_1$, $g(x)$ satisfies (18). Also $g(x) \geqslant 0$. Thus if there were an $\hat{x} \in \mathscr{C}$ such that $g(\hat{x}) = 0$ it would be a relative minimum of $g(.)$. But this implies that $g'(\hat{x}) = 0$; thus $g''(\hat{x}) = 0$ and g is the trivial solution of (18) and is identically equal to 0 on $\mathscr{C}_1$. However, $V(Q) > V_1(Q_1) = Q_1$ so $g(Q_1) > 0$. Thus g is not identically equal to zero on $\mathscr{C}_1$. This contradiction completes the proof.

4   GENERAL DIFFUSION PROCESSES

In this section we present versions of Proposition 2 and Theorem 1 for the case where the current state of an asset is characterized by a d-dimensional vector X which evolves according to the stochastic differential equation

$$dX = f(X)dt + G(X)dW \tag{56}$$

where W is an m dimensional Weiner process, $f(.)$ is a d-dimensional vector and $G(.)$ is a d by m matrix. Let $R(X)$ be a function which gives the reward which the owner of an asset reaps if he stops the asset's growth and sells it when the state variable is X. For example, suppose the asset is a tree, the two components of X are the price of lumber and the number of board feet of lumber in the tree; then $R(x_1,x_2)=x_1 x_2$. For simplicity we will suppose that the process must stop if X ever exits from a compact set D contained in R^d. Thus we define the market value of an asset in state X as

$$V(X)=\sup_{\hat{\tau}} Ee^{-r\hat{\tau}}R(X(\hat{\tau}))$$

where τ is a stopping time, $\tau(D)$ is the first time $X(t)$ leaves D, and $\hat{\tau}\equiv\min(\tau,\tau(D))$. We assume V exists.

Simple generalizations of Proposition 2 and Theorem 1 hold for this more general problem. Again standard results contained in Krylov (1980, p.160) imply that if certain regularity conditions are satisfied, then there is a continuation region $\mathscr{C}$ in D such that if $x\in\mathscr{C}$, the market value function satisfies

$$rV= V_x f+\tfrac{1}{2}tr[GG'V_{xx}]. \tag{57}$$

The process is stopped on the boundary of $\mathscr{C}$, $\Gamma(\mathscr{C})$. If $\hat{X}\in\Gamma(\mathscr{C})\backslash\Gamma(D)$ then $\hat{X}$ is a free boundary. At a free boundary, the smooth pasting condition,

$$R_x(\hat{X})= V_x(\hat{X}),R(\hat{X})= V(\hat{X}),$$

must hold.

The proof of Proposition 2 applies almost without change so that on

$$\frac{dV}{V}=rdt+ H(X)dW \tag{58}$$

and value grows approximately like geometric Brownian motion.

We now show that a generalization of Theorem 1 provides the basis for analysis of the effects of changes in diffusion coefficients on the value of the asset. That theorem stated roughly, that if V is increasing and convex at X_0, then a local increase of mean and variance at X_0 will increase V. The instantaneous mean of the diffusion process X is the vector $f(X)$; an increase in mean is an increase in all of the components of $f(x)$. The analogue of the instantaneous variance of X is the matrix $G(X)G'(X)$. We define an increase in variance as a change to a matrix $H(X)$ such that

$$H(X)H'(X) - G(X)G'(X)$$

is positive definite.

Let J be an open set in the continuation region and suppose $\eta(X)$ is a function from R^d to R^d such that $\eta(X) \geqslant 0$ for $x \in J$ and $\eta(X) = 0$ for $X \in J$. Let $\delta(X)$ be a function from R^d to R^{dm} such that $\delta(X) = 0$ for $X \notin J$ while if $X \in J$,

$$\delta(X)G'(X) + G'(X)\delta(X) \text{ is non-negative definite,} \tag{59a}$$

and

$$\delta(X)\delta'(X) \text{ is positive definite.} \tag{59b}$$

Now consider the asset which evolves according to

$$dX = (f(X) + \alpha\eta(X))dt + (G(X) + \alpha\delta(X))dW \tag{60}$$

If $\alpha > 0$, this asset has a greater mean and a larger variance on J than does the asset which evolves according to (56). As above let $\hat{V}^\alpha$ be the value of the asset which evolves according to (60) and is stopped optimally.

Theorem 2

Suppose that for $X \in J$, V is strictly increasing and strictly convex. Then there is an $\epsilon > 0$ such that

$$\hat{V}^\alpha(X) > V(X) \text{ for } X \in J;$$

$$\hat{V}^\alpha(X) \geqslant V(X) \text{ for } X \notin J.$$

Proof: The proof of Theorem 2 is essentially the same as that of Theorem 1. To apply these arguments, we need a simple result in matrix algebra.

Lemma: If U is a symmetric matrix then $tr(AU) > 0$ for all non-trivial, non-negative definite A if and only if U is positive definite.

Proof: Let $U = C'\Lambda C$ where Λ is a diagonal matrix of the eigen values of U. Since A is non-negative definite there is a matrix B such that $A = BB'$. Then

$$tr(AU) = trBB'C'\Lambda C = trB'C'\Lambda CB = trG\Lambda G' = tr\Lambda G'G = \sum_i \lambda_i g'_i g_i,$$

where g_i is the ith column of the matrix $G' = CB$ and λ_i is the ith eigen value of U.

Proof of Theorem 2: Let V^α be the value of the asset which evolves according to (60) but which is stopped whenever it leaves $\mathscr{C}$. Since this is not the optimal stopping rule for an asset which evolves according to (60),

$$\hat{V}^{\alpha}(X) \geqslant V^{\alpha}(X).$$

Let $Z(X) = V^{\alpha}(X) - V(X)$. Proceeding as in the proof of Theorem 1, we see that

$$rZ(X) - Z_x f(X) - \tfrac{1}{2} tr(G(X) G'(X) Z_{xx}(x)) = Q(X) \tag{61}$$

where

$$Q(X) = \alpha[f(X) V_x^{\alpha}(X) + tr H(X) V_{xx}^{\alpha}(x)]$$

and

$$H(X) = G(X) \delta(X)' + \delta'(X) G(X) + \alpha \delta(X) \delta'(X).$$

Now $Q(X) = 0$ for $X \notin J$. We will prove that

$$Q(X) > 0 \text{ for } X \in J. \tag{62}$$

Since $V_x^{\alpha}(x)$ and $V_{xx}^{\alpha}(x)$ are continuous functions of α, there is an $\epsilon > 0$ such that $V_x^{\alpha}(X) \gg 0$ and $V_{xx}^{\alpha}(X)$ is positive definite for $\alpha < \epsilon$ and $x \in J$. Thus the Lemma and (59) imply (62).

To prove Theorem 2 it will suffice to prove that

$$Z(X) \geqslant 0 \text{ for } X \in \mathscr{C}.$$

For $X \in \Gamma(\mathscr{C})$, $Z(X) = 0$. Suppose there is an $\hat{X}$ on the interior of $\mathscr{C}$ such that $Z(\hat{X}) < 0$. Then there is an $X \in \mathscr{C}$ such that Z has a local minimum at $\hat{X}$ and $Z(\hat{X}) < 0$. At $\hat{X}$, $Z_x(\hat{X}) = 0$ and therefore (61) implies

$$Z(\hat{X}) = r^{-1}[Q(\hat{X}) + \tfrac{1}{2} tr(G(\hat{X}) G'(\hat{X}) Z_{xx}(\hat{X}))]$$

However, at a local min, Z_{xx} is positive semidefinite so that the Lemma implies $Z(\hat{X}) \geqslant 0$. This contradiction completes the proof.

Notes

1. Those familiar with the optimal stopping literature will recognize this as a consequence of (or another way of stating) a basic result of optimal stopping theory: on the continuation region the value of a process that will be optimally stopped is a martingale.
2. See Brock and Rothschild (1986) for further discussion of material in this section.

References

Arnold, L. (1974) *Stochastic Differential Equations: Theory and Applications* (New York: Wiley).

Brock, W. A., R. Miller and J. Scheinkman (1982) 'Natural Monopoly and Regulation', Department of Economics, University of Wisconsin, Madison and Chicago.

Brock, W. A. and M. Rothschild (1986) 'Comparative Statics for Multidimensional Optimal Stopping Problems', pp.124–138 in *Models of Economic Dynamics* (ed.) Hugo F. Sonnenshchein, Springer-Verlag *Lecture Notes in Economics and Mathematical Systems*, vol. 214.

Brock, W. A., M. Rothschild and J. E. Stiglitz (1982) 'Stochastic Capital Theory', NBER Technical Report No. 23.

Chow, Y. S., H. Robbins and D. Siegmund (1971) *Great Expectations: The Theory of Optimal Stopping* (Boston: Houghton Mifflin).

Cox, D. R. and H. D. Miller (1968) *The Theory of Stochastic Processes* (New York: John Wiley).

Dothan, U. (1981) 'Debt, Investment Opportunities, and Agency'. Kellogg School of Management, Northwestern University.

Hartman, P. (1973) *Ordinary Differential Equations*, 2nd edn (Baltimore: privately published).

Karlin, S. and H. M. Taylor (1981) *A Second Course in Stochastic Processes* (New York: Academic Press).

Krylov, N. V. (1980) *Controlled Diffusion Processes* (New York: Springer-Verlag).

McDonald, R. L. and D. Siegel (1986) 'The Value of Waiting to Invest', *Quarterly Journal of Economics*, 101: 707–28.

Miller, R. and K. Voltaire (1980) 'A Sequential Stochastic Tree Problem', *Economic Letters*, 5: 135–40.

Miller, R. and K. Voltaire (1983) 'A Stochastic Analysis of the Tree Paradigm', Carnegie Mellon University, Graduate School of Industrial Administration, Working Paper 35–82–83, January.

Miroshnichenko, T. P. (1975) 'Optimal Stopping of the Integral of a Weiner Process', *Theory of Probability and Its Applications*, 20: 387–91.

Shiryayev, A. N. (1978) *Optimal Stopping Rules* (New York: Springer-Verlag).

Wentzell, A. D. (1981) *A Course in the Theory of Stochastic Processes* (New York: McGraw-Hill).

Ye, M. H., PhD Thesis, Department of Economics, University of Wisconsin, Madison, 1983.

21 Demand Composition, Income Distribution, and Growth

Lance Taylor*

An enduring theme in Cambridge economics – and Joan Robinson's work in particular – is that the overall macroeconomic situation is intimately linked with income distribution. Following in Robinson's footsteps, Rowthorn (1982), Taylor (1983), and Dutt (1984) have recently presented models of how growth and distribution interact in a one-sector setting, under two alternative modes of macroeconomic adjustment. The first is based on changes in output or capacity utilization, along lines stressed by Keynes in the *General Theory*, and Kalecki (1971) and his followers. One striking Kaleckian result is that income redistribution favoring workers may lead to higher capacity utilization and faster growth. The second, 'neo-Keynesian' adjustment mechanism functions via income redistribution to create forced saving in response to higher investment demand. In such models (as proposed by Keynes in his *Treatise on Money*; Kaldor, 1960; and Robinson, 1962, for example) faster growth is necessarily associated with an endogenous distributional shift away from labor. The tenor of these results carries over when inflationary mechanisms and financial markets are brought into the models – see Marglin (1984) and Taylor (1985) for neo-Keynesian and Kaleckian variants, respectively.

Not much work has been done extending these models to a multisectoral context, though radical economists have long argued that the sectoral composition of demand, affecting and affected by the income distribution, strongly influences capacity utilization and growth. An early example is in the work of the Swiss reformist Sismondi (1819), who taught that industrial stagnation results from an unequal distribution. He argued that the poor can afford no more than essential foodstuffs and clothing, while the rich purchase luxurious handicrafts and foreign goods. Capitalism cannot flourish when there is income inequality, since there is no demand for products from the capitalist industrial sector. This same sort of market insufficiency shows up in the writings of the Russian *narodniki* or Populists in the late nineteenth century and in Baran's (1957) well-known book on economic development and growth. The theme is hotly debated in India

* Research support from the Ford Foundation is gratefully acknowledged.

today – see Chakravarty (1979) for the political economy which stimulated Dutt's (1984) formalization.

This argument was turned on its head by Latin American structuralist authors in the 1950s and 1960s – Lustig (1984) gives a useful survey. The hypothesis is that growth after an early phase of 'easy' import substitution requires rapid expansion of 'key' or 'dynamic' sectors such as consumer durables and capital goods. The key sectors have economies of scale or investment demand functions that respond readily to increases in output. Since the poor do not consume the products of the dynamic sectors in large quantity, raising the purchasing power of the majority of the population is costly in terms of growth stimulus from the side of demand. From that, it is a small step to assert that income concentration proceeds *pari passu* with expansion of the leading sectors. Taylor and Bacha (1976) provide a formalization along neo-Keynesian lines. On the empirical side, these theories stimulated dozens of input–output studies on the possible effects of redistribution on capacity utilization, employment, and growth. Clark (1975) gives a partial survey. The results of these investigations were inconclusive, for reasons that will appear below.

In this paper, a simple two-sector model is presented in which demand composition can have long-term effects – the idea is to see under what circumstances Sismondi and successors might be right. Most authors in this tradition assume that both capacity utilization and the rate of growth can be changed by shifts in demand composition or income distribution – they are a long way from neo-Keynesian models in which full utilization of capacity is the order of the day. Hence, we have to set up a Kalecki-style of stagnationist model in which sectoral outputs are determined by demand. Saving rates and consumption functions of recipients of wage and non-wage incomes (workers and capitalists) differ, to allow room for changes in demand composition. Once installed in a sector, capital stock is assumed immovable. There are separate sectoral investment functions which differ in their responsiveness to rates of profit or capacity utilization – highly elastic demand can be assumed typical of a key sector. The main questions we want to ask are whether policies aimed at redistribution can bear fruit either in the form of reduced income concentration or faster growth. The answers are ambiguous, and it is interesting to explore the reasons why. Intersectoral differences in technology, demand preferences, and (especially) investment responsiveness make the potential outcomes from distributional experiments far from clear-cut.

1   THE SHORT RUN

Each sector has a fixed capital stock in the short run. This hypothesis is realistic, and also allows sectoral rates of profit and capacity utilization to differ, stimulating differential levels of investment demand. A sector's production function implicitly is of the Leontief fixed-coefficients form, though available capital (or capacity) is never fully utilized. Under such circumstances, it is natural to postulate mark-up pricing, along lines long urged by Kalecki (1971), Sylos Labini (1984), and other authors. The price P_i in sector i is given by:

$$P_i = (1 + \tau_i)wb_i, \quad i = w \text{ or } p. \tag{1}$$

Here, τ_i is the sector i mark-up rate, b_i is its labor–output ratio, and w is the wage. We will not be greatly concerned with inflation or relative price changes, so that it is simplest to normalize wages and prices at unity,

$$P_p = P_w = w = 1, \tag{2}$$

though price terms will be carried in the equations to clarify the analysis. Under this normalization, the mark-up rate is high when the labor–output ratio is low – the non-wage income share will be large in high productivity sectors.

The sector indexed by w is assumed to produce wage-goods, e.g. food, clothing, simple services, etc. The sector indexed by p produces goods consumed by high income profit recipients as well as capital goods – consumer durables, high-tech services, machinery and equipment, etc. The price of capital-in-place is P_p, and one can define sectoral profit rates as:

$$r_i = \frac{P_i X_i - wb_i X_i}{P_p K_i}, \quad i = w \text{ or } p, \tag{3}$$

where X_i is sector i's output level and K_i is its available capital stock. The profit rate r_i represents the sector's cash flow relative to capital stock. It will obviously rise when output goes up. Simple algebra – details in Taylor (1983) – gives the profit rate as:

$$r_p = \frac{\tau_p}{1 + \tau_p} \frac{X_p}{K_p} \tag{4}$$

and

$$r_w = \frac{\tau_w}{1 + \tau_w} \frac{P_w}{P_p} \frac{X_w}{K_w}. \tag{5}$$

A more neoclassical production specification based on, say, CES cost functions would give expressions like (4) and (5) but with the X_i/K_i ratios taken to an exponent. The extra complexity would be a frill in the present context.

Suppose that only recipients of mark-up or profit incomes (or the companies that they own) save. Then the investment–saving balance in short-run macro equilibrium takes the form:

$$P_p(I_w + I_p) = sw[\tau_w b_w X_w + \tau_p b_p X_p], \tag{6}$$

where I_w and I_p are levels of investment in the two sectors, and s is the saving rate of recipients of profit income from either sector. Let $g_i = (dK_i/dt)/K_i$ be growth rate of capital stock (*not* output) in sector i and $\lambda = K_w/K_p$ be the ratio of capital in the two sectors. With these definitions, (6) can be transformed to the intensive form:

$$\lambda g_w + g_p - s(\lambda r_w + r_p) = 0. \tag{7}$$

Equation (7) is a generalization of the Cambridge equation – a weighted average of growth rates in the two sectors must be financed by saving from the same weighted average of profit rates. The weighting factor λ reflects the relative sizes of the sectors, as measured by their capital stocks.

Consumption demand by sector depends on non-saved income. Workers' income Y_w is given by the equation:

$$Y_w = w(b_w X_w + b_p X_p), \tag{8}$$

while capitalists' income Y_p depends on mark-up rates in the form:

$$Y_p = w(\tau_w b_w X_w + \tau_b b_p X_p). \tag{9}$$

The simplest assumption is that only workers consume the wage-good. In real terms, they purchase C_w^w of w-goods and C_p^w of p-goods only. With these specifications (implications of relaxing them are discussed below) consumer demand functions can be written as:

$$P_w C_w^w = \theta P_p(K_w + K_p) + \alpha Y_w, \tag{10}$$

$$P_p C_p^w = -\theta P_p(K_w + K_p) + (1 - \alpha) Y_w, \tag{11}$$

and

$$P_p C_p^p = (1 - s) Y_p. \tag{12}$$

Workers' marginal propensity to consume wage-goods from current income is α. The terms involving θ are meant to reflect secular trends towards consumption of wage-goods (when θ is positive). Examples include the following:

(1)   There can be Engel effects in consumption. These are not easily handled in steady-state growth models, such as the present one. However, as Pasinetti (1981) points out, the more fundamental tendency under capitalism is that demand for specific commodities for a time grows more rapidly than the rest of the economy, then saturates and declines. Pasinetti formalizes these changes with time trends in consumption; equations (10) and (11) relate demand shifts to real wealth or 'size' of the economy $P_p(K_w + K_p)$. With θ positive, overall growth in the system shifts workers' consumer demand towards w-goods. The stylized fact in this formalization is, of course, the opposite – demand for simple commodities declines as the economy expands and $\theta < 0$.

(2)   In practice, these broad trends are affected by actions of an interventionist government and the private sector. The government may stimulate or try to inhibit production of p-type or w-type commodities. Typical policies include production controls and licensing, advertising, etc. Commodity examples are very common – big cars and small cars or scooters, color and black and white TV, foreign and domestically produced cigarettes. Private companies attempt to influence the mix of available commodities in similar ways.

(3)   Beyond the manipulation of both the state and the corporations are broader shifts in demand patterns. If environmental protection were a high-tech commodity, for example, then there would be non-market forces in the system making θ negative in (10) and (11). Growth in regulatory activity and 'intermediate' inputs of government services to the production process (Kuznets, 1971) could be formalized in similar fashion.

(4)   Policies aimed explicitly at income redistribution affect demand patterns. For example, a lump-sum tax T on capitalists' *consumption* which is transferred to wage earners would increase demand for the wage-good by the amount αT. If the tax is scaled to overall wealth, $T = \mu P_p(K_w + K_p)$, then we arrive at (10) with $\theta = \alpha\mu$. An interesting extension is the case in which capitalists' marginal propensity to consume the wage-good is α_p and the workers' propensity is $\alpha_w > \alpha_p$. Then the demand shift term θ becomes $(\alpha_w - \alpha_p)\mu$. The tax/transfer policy will affect resource allocation only in so far as consumption propensities differ between the classes – a theorem perhaps first stated for saving behavior by Lubell (1947). Empirical evidence suggests that the differential may be small – transfers on the order of 5 per cent of GDP might be required to raise wage-goods demand by 1 per cent or so.

(5)   Finally, other implicit taxes could be modelled. For example, Rowthorn (1982) argues that accelerated technical progress could accelerate scrapping of old equipment, in effect reducing firms' cash flows. If firm-owners consume wage-goods, then θ in (10) would become negative. The

saving–investment balance (7) would be unaffected, if replacement of scrapped capital goods automatically occurs. (Equal terms for 'deprecia-tion' and 'replacement' would be added to each side of (6).)

In any of these versions, θ enters as a parameter in the condition that excess demand for wage-goods should equal zero in equilibrium,

$$\theta P_p(K_p + K_w) + aw(b_w X_w + b_p X_p) - P_w X_w = 0.$$

After a bit of manipulation, this formula can be restated as:

$$-\frac{\beta\lambda}{\tau_w}r_w + \frac{\alpha}{\tau_p}r_p + \theta(\lambda + 1) = 0, \tag{13}$$

where $\beta = (1 + \tau_w - \alpha) > 0$.

The saving–investment balance (7) and the commodity material balance equation (13) form a convenient system for determining the profit rates r_w and r_p (and implicitly sectoral output levels, the income distribution, etc.). Note that the two profit rates trade off inversely at given level of saving. A rise in one rate would generate excess saving that would have to be offset in equilibrium through a fall in the other rate. This relationship is shown by the negatively sloped 'Saving' line in Figure 21.1.

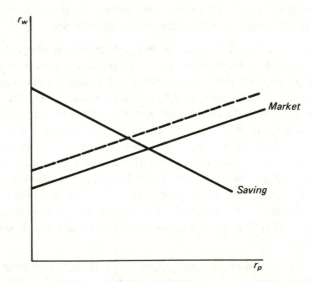

Figure 21.1   Determination of the sectoral profit rates r_w and r_p in the short run. The shift in the market locus results from an increase in the trend term θ towards consumption of wage-goods.

In the market for w-goods, an increase in r_w is associated with excess supply – the marginal propensity to consume wage-goods from the income generated by an increase in output X_w is less than one. An increase in r_p raises demand. Hence, to hold excess demand to zero, r_w and r_p trade off along the positively sloped 'Market' line in Figure 21.1 – a rise in r_p calls forth an increase in supply (associated with a higher r_w) to restore equilibrium.

Various comparative static exercises can be carried out in this framework – we mention just two. An increase in autonomous demand for wage-goods (a higher θ) shifts the market locus upward, leading to a higher r_w (and X_w) and lower r_p (and X_p). Faster scrapping shifts the market locus downward, and r_p rises while r_w falls. These shifts do *not* unambiguously affect growth rates and income distribution. To see why, we have to bring more analytical apparatus to play.

2   DYNAMICS IN THE SHORT RUN

For the record, it is useful to write the saving–investment and commodity market equilibrium conditions together in matrix form:

$$
\begin{bmatrix} s\lambda & s \\[2mm] -\dfrac{\beta\lambda}{\tau_w} & \dfrac{\alpha}{\tau_p} \end{bmatrix}
\begin{bmatrix} r_w \\[2mm] r^p \end{bmatrix}
=
\begin{bmatrix} \lambda g_w + g_p \\[2mm] -\theta(\lambda+1) \end{bmatrix}
\tag{14}
$$

From (14), the short-run determinant is:

$$
\text{Determinant} = s\lambda\left[\frac{\alpha}{\tau_p} + \frac{\beta}{\tau_w}\right] = \frac{s\lambda\alpha}{\tau_p}(1+\Delta),
$$

where

$$
\Delta = \frac{\tau_p}{\alpha}\frac{\beta}{\tau_w} = \frac{\tau_p}{\alpha}\frac{(1+\tau_w-\alpha)}{\tau_w}.
\tag{15}
$$

The explicit solutions for the profit rates are:

$$
r_w = \frac{1}{(1+\Delta)\lambda}\left[\frac{\lambda g_w + g_p}{s} + \frac{\tau_p(1+\lambda)}{\alpha}\theta\right]
\tag{16}
$$

and

$$r_p = \frac{1}{(1+\Delta)} \left[\frac{\Delta(\lambda g_w + g_p)}{s} - \frac{\tau_p(1+\lambda)}{\alpha} \theta \right]. \tag{17}$$

If demand effects as represented by the terms involving θ are 'small', then an increase in λ or the relative abundance of capital in the w-goods sector will lower r_w and raise r_p, as might be expected. However, this result can reverse for a large negative θ, or a demand trend away from w-goods. As is typical in models with differential saving rates between classes, a rise in either sector's growth rate will increase the profit rates to generate more saving.

In a system with excess capacity, growth itself depends on investment demand. In each sector, entrepreneurs' desired growth g_i can be assumed to be a function of the profit rate r_i and capacity utilization (X_i/K_i) as a proxy for an accelerator term. But from (4) and (5) rates of capacity utilization can be uniquely related to profit rates, so the investment demand functions become:

$$g_i = g_0 + \varphi_i r_i, \quad i = w \text{ or } p. \tag{18}$$

The term g_0 here is autonomous demand for investment, assumed for simplicity to be the same in the two sectors. Its level may depend on institutional factors, population growth, and (as argued below) technological change. The response terms φ_w and φ_p can differ – a more 'dynamic' or 'entrepreneurial' sector might be expected to have a higher coefficient.

Since r_w and r_p are given by (16) and (17), one can use (18) to solve for the growth rates as:

$$g_w = \frac{1}{\Gamma} \left\{ g_0 \left[1 + \frac{1}{(1+\Delta)s} \left(\frac{\varphi_w}{\lambda} - \varphi_p \Delta \right) \right] \right.$$
$$\left. + \frac{\varphi_w}{\lambda(1+\Delta)} \left(1 - \frac{\varphi_p}{s} \right)(1+\lambda)\tilde{\theta} \right\} \tag{19}$$

and

$$g_p = \frac{1}{\Gamma} \left\{ g_0 \left[1 - \frac{\lambda}{(1+\Delta s} \left(\frac{\varphi_w}{\lambda} - \varphi_p \Delta \right) \right] \right.$$
$$\left. - \frac{\varphi_p}{1+\Delta} \left(1 - \frac{\varphi_w}{s} \right)(1+\lambda)\tilde{\theta} \right\} \tag{20}$$

where $\tilde{\theta} = (\tau_p/\alpha)\theta$.

In these expressions, Γ is another determinant:

$$\Gamma = 1 - \left[\frac{\Delta\varphi_p}{(1+\Delta)s} + \frac{\varphi_w}{(1+\Delta)s} \right]. \tag{21}$$

The usual expectation is that Γ should be positive, for reasons given below.

We can now ask what happens to the income distribution in the short run when the demand trend parameter θ changes, for any of the reasons mentioned in Section 1. Let asterisks denote wage and non-wage income flows divided by the p-sector capital stock.

$$Y_w^* = \frac{Y_w}{P_p K_p} = \frac{r_w}{\tau_w}\lambda + \frac{r_p}{\tau_p} \tag{22}$$

and

$$Y_p^* = \frac{Y_p}{P_p K_p} = r_w\lambda + r_p. \tag{23}$$

A natural measure of inequality is ω, the ratio of wage to non-wage income:

$$\omega = \frac{Y_w}{Y_p} = \frac{Y_w^*}{Y_p^*} = \frac{(r_w/\tau_w)\lambda + (r_p/\tau_p)}{r_w\lambda + r_p}. \tag{24}$$

The economics of distributional shifts is straightforward. On the assumptions of the model Y_w and Y_p represent labor and non-labor content of total output. Assume for a moment that there is no effect of profit rates on investment or growth rates. In two-factor/two-commodity models of international trade, the well-known Rybczynski (1955) theorem states that an increase in one factor will raise the production of the commodity intensive in its use, and lower production of the other commodity. The converse is also true, that if demand for one good rises and the other one falls, then if the good with rising demand is more labor intensive, the total labor content of output will go up.

An increase in θ shifts the composition of demand in the present model towards wage-goods. The labor–output ratios in the two sectors are b_w and b_p, and from the price equations (1) and (2) if wage-goods are labor intensive with $b_w > b_p$, then $\tau_p > \tau_w$. This criterion enters into the formal expression for $d\omega/d\theta$, which also takes account of the feedback of the profit rates r_i into growth rates g_i. The ratio of wage to non-wage income will rise with θ when the following condition is satisfied:

$$(\tau_p - \tau_w)\left[r_p\left(1 - \frac{\varphi_p}{s}\right) + \lambda r_w\left(1 - \frac{\varphi_w}{s}\right) \right] > 0. \tag{25}$$

The following observations are immediate:

(1)   If the bracketed term on the right of (25) is positive, a demand shift towards wage-goods will shift the distribution towards wages when $\tau_p > \tau_w$ or wage-goods are a low productivity sector. If this intensity condition is reversed, an income transfer towards wage earners will shift the distribution towards profits, presumably not the desired result.

(2)   At the level of aggregation used here, it is by no means obvious empirically that $b_w > b_p$. The message of many of the input–output demand composition studies mentioned in the introduction was that the consumption basket of the well-to-do may be quite labor intensive – in high-tech services like medical care in rich countries and in domestic servants in poor ones. A serious empirical question arises about the likely impact of redistributive policies.

(3)   The effect of a shift in θ is attenuated in so far as the investment response coefficients φ_p and φ_w approach the saving rate. Suppose that in the dynamic p-goods sector φ_p even exceeds s – a rise in the profit rate stimulates more investment demand than it raises saving. If φ_p is big enough to make the bracketed expression in (25) negative, then a shift in demand *away* from p-goods as θ rises would depress the economy but release labor for wage-goods production if the p-sector were labor intensive. The income distribution would shift towards wages but stagnation would result. This outcome resembles the Latin American structuralist story mentioned in the introduction.

The next step is to extend this analysis to the long run, conventionally represented by a steady state. A modest amount of additional work is required in the following section.

3   THE STEADY STATE

The system will be in steady state when g_w and g_p – the sectoral capital stock growth rates – are equal. Since $\lambda = K_w/K_p$, it (and other variables such as profit rates, the ratio of wage to non-wage income, etc.) will be constant at steady state. The growth rate of λ is $(d\lambda/dt)/\lambda = g_w - g_p$. Using (19) and (20), one can show that λ evolves over time according to the equation

$$\frac{d\lambda}{dt} = \frac{\lambda(1+\lambda)}{\Gamma(1+\Delta)} \left\{ \frac{g_0}{s} \left(\frac{\varphi_w}{\lambda} - \varphi_p \Delta \right) \right.$$

$$\left. + \left[\frac{\varphi_w}{\lambda} \left(1 - \frac{\varphi_p}{s} \right) + \varphi_p \left(1 - \frac{\varphi_w}{s} \right) \right] \tilde{\theta} \right\} . \tag{26}$$

The interesting steady state occurs when the term in curly brackets is zero. So long as θ is not excessively negative (for $\varphi_p < s$) or positive (for $\varphi_p > s$) the derivative of the bracketed term with respect to λ is negative. Hence, for $\Gamma > 0$, the economy will approach steady state.

From (21) the condition that $\Gamma > 0$ is equivalent to:

$$s > \frac{\Delta\varphi_p}{1+\Delta} + \frac{\varphi_w}{1+\Delta}, \tag{27}$$

or the saving rate from profits must exceed a weighted average of sectoral investment demand responses to a higher profit rate. If the inequality is violated because of overly sensitive investment demand, then the economy will be unstable around its 'warranted' steady-growth path, along the lines suggested by Harrod (1939).

Note from (19) and (20) that when $\Gamma > 0$, g_w decreases as a function of λ, while g_p goes up. Relatively more capital in place in the w-sector reduces the profit rate there, and thus the sector's investment demand. At the same time, the p-sector's profit and investment rates rise. Figure 21.2 gives a graphical representation, with the steady state determined at a point A

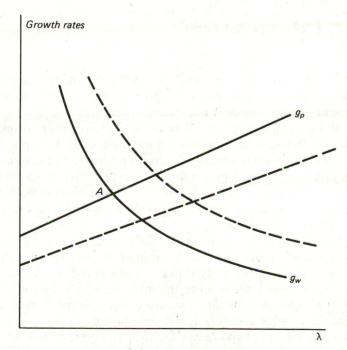

Figure 21.2 Determination of steady-state values of the growth rate g and sectoral capital stock ratio λ. An initial equilibrium is A, and the dashed lines represent the effect of an increase in trend consumption towards wage-goods.

where the loci for g_w and g_p intersect. An increase in θ raises g_w for a given λ, again by shifting the profit rate. By a similar mechanism, g_p declines. The outcome (dashed lines) is a rise in the steady-state capital stock ratio λ, but an ambiguous shift in the rate of growth.

In one extreme case, if investment in wage-goods is lethargic and φ_w close to zero, then the dominant shift will be in the g_p schedule, and the steady-growth rate will fall. Redistribution towards wages in this case would slow growth in the long run. If φ_p is near zero while φ_w is relatively large, the opposite result of faster growth would occur. The sign of the effect of an increase in θ depends only on the investment parameters, as the algebraic solutions for steady-state values of g and λ (derived by setting the right side of (26) to zero) reveal:

$$g = \frac{1}{\Gamma} \left\{ g_0 - \left[\frac{\varphi_p - \varphi_w}{1 + \Delta} \right] \tilde{\theta} \right\} \tag{28}$$

and

$$\lambda = \frac{\varphi_w \left[\dfrac{g_0}{s} + \left(1 - \dfrac{\varphi_p}{s} \right) \tilde{\theta} \right]}{\varphi_p \left[\dfrac{g_0 \Delta}{s} - \left(1 - \dfrac{\varphi_w}{s} \right) \tilde{\theta} \right]}. \tag{29}$$

If θ (or $\tilde{\theta}$) is less than zero, so that there is a secular shift in spending away from wage-goods by workers, then growth will be fast when $\varphi_p > \varphi_w$. Dynamic investment response and consumption trends interact synergistically in this case. The result would be stronger if investment demand itself responds to technical change. As argued above, more rapid technical advance could foster scrapping and make θ negative. At the same time, g_0 (or separate sectoral analogs) might rise. In that case, from (28) growth would be doubly accelerated. A further cumulative effect could come from stimulation of technical progress by growth, as in the 'Verdoorn's Law' of Kaldor (1966).

Two last questions have to do with possible equalization of profit rates in the long run and steady-state redistributional effects. Even though sectoral growth rates are equal in steady states, the same need not be true of profit rates, as can be seen directly from the investment demand functions (18). Only if the response parameters φ_i are equal will profit rates equalize. Uniformly responsive investors across the whole economy may or may not be a plausible long-run hypothesis. As Pasinetti (1981) points out, negative values of trend demand for most 'old' sectors and positive values for a few 'new' ones are likely in a multisectoral system. The natural offset would be

differential investment parameters by sector, even though the whole economy might be tending towards steady state.

The final issue is the effect of changes in θ on the steady-state income
distribution. When $g_w = g_p = g$, the ratio ω of wage to non-wage income
becomes:

$$\omega = \frac{\tau_p + \tau_w \Delta}{\tau_w \tau_p (1 + \Delta)} + (\tau_p - \tau_p) s(\tilde{\theta}/g). \tag{30}$$

As in the short run, a change in θ affects distribution directly through the
factor-intensity term $\tau_p - \tau_w$. However, θ also influences the steady-state
growth rate g from (28), and a change in g should alter the income
distribution by shifting the saving supply required to meet investment
demand.

Remarkably, differentiation of (30) and substitution from (28) show that
this latter effect washes out around a stable steady state. The algebraic
reason is that g in (28) is a linear function of $\tilde{\theta}$, so that in the ratio $\tilde{\theta}/g$ in
(30), the growth-rate derivative cancels out. More generally, factor-inten-
sity considerations will determine distributional response so long as growth
is not dramatically affected by changes in θ. In (30), with long-run stability
($\Gamma > 0$), the long-run wage-share rises with θ when $\tau_p > \tau_w$, or wage-goods
are the low productivity sector. But from (28) the distributional improve-
ment comes at the cost of slower growth, if the p-sector has the more
dynamic investment response. A demand trend away from wage-goods
helps both distribution and growth when p-goods are labor intensive. Does
the future well-being of post-industrial countries require that their dynamic
service sectors maintain low labor productivity? If so, attempts to improve
distribution by tax/transfer policies will go awry. A better tack could be to
stimulate investment dynamism in wage-goods sectors – or so Sismondi
might say.

4 SUMMARY

Our main conclusion is that in a demand-driven model, shifts in trend
consumption towards wage-goods can affect income distribution in both
the short run and steady state, as well as the long-run growth rate. The
income distribution change between wages and profits depends on differences in sectoral labor productivity levels, while the growth rate response
depends on the sectoral sensitivity of investment demands to profit rates.
With plausible values of the parameters there may be relationships of either
sign between the growth rate and the wage share in the long run.

The consumption demand trend is partly a result of taste shifts and Engel effects, but could also result from redistributive policy. In the latter case, its magnitude will depend on differing marginal propensities to consume wage-goods between classes, and may not be large.

These results all depend on the demand-driven causality in the model which is consistent with the long literature in economics on interactions between demand composition and relative stagnation. Details would be different if more neoclassical production and demand formulations were employed, but the main thrust of the results would carry through. It would even reach to discussion of capital-deepening in a multisectoral neoclassical growth model, with growth determined as the natural rate from the supply side. The details are tedious, and not interesting to work through when one realizes that the key to the economics comes from the Robinson/Cambridge emphasis on the interaction of investment demand and income distribution in the long run.

References

Baran, P. (1957) *The Political Economy of Growth* (New York: Monthly Review Press).

Chakravarty, S. (1979) 'On the Question of the Home Market and Prospects for Indian Growth', *Economic and Political Weekly*, Special Number, 1229–42.

Clark, P. B. (1975) 'Closing the Leontief Model: Consistency and Macroeconomic Planning', in C. R. Blitzer, P. B. Clark and L. Taylor (eds) *Economy-Wide Models and Development Planning* (New York: Oxford University Press).

Dutt, A. (1984) 'Stagnation, Income Distribution and Monopoly Power', *Cambridge Journal of Economics*, 8: 25–40.

Harrod, R. F. (1939) 'An Essay in Dynamic Theory', *Economic Journal*, 49: 14–33.

Kaldor, N. (1966) *Causes of the Slow Rate of Growth of the United Kingdom* (New York: Cambridge University Press).

Kaldor, N. (1960) *Essays on Economic Stability and Growth* (London: Duckworth).

Kalecki, M. (1971) *Selected Essays on the Dynamics of the Capitalist Economy* (New York: Cambridge University Press).

Kuznets, S. S. (1971) *Economic Growth of Nations: Total Output and Production Structure* (Cambridge, Mass.: Harvard University Press).

Lubell, H. (1947) 'Effects of Redistribution of Income on Consumers' Expenditure', *American Economic Review*, 37: 157–70.

Lustig, N. (1984) 'Underconsumption in Latin American Economic Thought: Some Considerations', *Review of Radical Political Economics*, 12: 35–43.

Marglin, S. (1984) 'Growth, Distribution, and Inflation: A Centennial Synthesis', *Cambridge Journal of Economics*, 8: 115–44.

Pasinetti, L. L. (1981) *Structural Change and Economic Growth* (Cambridge: Cambridge Univeristy Press).

Robinson, J. (1962) *Essays in the Theory of Economic Growth* (London: Macmillan).

Rowthorn, B. (1982) 'Demand, Real Wages, and Economic Growth', *Studi Economici*, (no. 18): 3–53.

Rybczynski, T. M. (1955) 'Factor Endowments and Relative Commodity Prices', *Economica*, 22: 336–41.

Sismondi, J. C. L. S. (1819) 'Political Economy', *Edinburgh Encyclopedia* (Sir D. Brewster), 17: 37–8.

Sylos Labini, P. (1984) *The Forces of Economic Growth and Decline* (Cambridge, Mass.: MIT).

Taylor, L. (1983) *Structuralist Macroeconomics* (New York: Basic Books).

Taylor, L. (1985) 'A Stagnationist Model of Economic Growth', *Cambridge Journal of Economics*, to appear.

Taylor, L. and E. L. Bacha (1976) 'The Unequalizing Spiral: A First Growth Model for Belindia', *Quarterly Journal of Economics*, 90: 197–218.

22 Three Fundamental Productivity Concepts: Principles and Measurement

William J. Baumol
Edward N. Wolff*

The literature on productivity devotes considerable and deserved attention to a variety of measurement problems and to distinctions such as that between labor productivity and total factor productivity. However, some of the basic definitional issues that arise implicitly in many of the discussions do not seem to have been examined to the degree they merit. In this paper, we contrast three different basic concepts of productivity, discuss the differences in their interpretation and significance, and then demonstrate empirically that use of different notions of productivity can give rise to great differences in measurements of productivity growth.

1 THREE PRODUCTIVITY GROWTH CONCEPTS

In writings on productivity growth at least three different connotations are implicitly assigned to the term. Most often, it is interpreted as a measure of the increase in productive 'capacity' *attributable to technical change* – the shift in the production frontier. Sometimes it is interpreted as a measure of the increase in consumer and producer welfare produced per unit of input, regardless of the source of the improvement, whether technical change, better allocation of resources given the state of technology, or some other influence. Finally, usually with some embarrassment, statistical studies sometimes deal with changes in what we will call crude productivity – number of units of output produced per unit of input, and with little or no attempt to take account of changes in output quality. In this paper we will refer to these, respectively, as growth in productive capacity, welfare productivity, and crude productivity.

* We would like to express our gratitude to the Division of Information Science and Technology of the National Science Foundation, the Fishman-Davidson Center for the Study of the Service Sector, and the C. V. Starr Center for Applied Economics at New York University for their support of the research reported here.

We will show that the (monotonically descending) pecking order that seems at least implicitly to be assigned to these three concepts in the literature is misleading. For, as will be demonstrated, each of them has its legitimate and significant use both in analysis and in application. In particular, the crude productivity measure will be shown to be extremely important in explaining the behavior over time of the relative prices of different goods and services, in budgetary planning for various public sector activities, and in planning to meet future manpower requirements. It will be seen that in some cases the productive capacity measure may deviate systematically from the welfare productivity measure, and in those circum- stances the former will be inappropriate for an analysis of standards of living.

Some observations will be offered about the nature of the measurement issues raised by each of these concepts. It will be shown why only in very special cases is an unambiguous scalar index of growth in productive capacity possible. On the other hand, welfare productivity, at least in principle, turns out to be easier to measure than may be expected, despite the important role of changes in the quality of the products in question which are, of course, difficult to identify and describe and sometimes all but impossible to quantify.

2   ON PRODUCTIVE CAPACITY MEASURES

One frequently encounters the view that a pure measure of productivity growth should confine itself to the consequences of technical change and changes in the quality of the available inputs, e.g., in the skills of the labor force, leaving out of consideration changes in output per unit of input that result, e.g., from elimination of inefficiencies.[1]

Specifically, indices of growth in productive capacity seek to measure the rate of outward shift of the production frontier hypersurface in product quantity space, holding constant the quantities of inputs utilized. That is, of course, straightforward when the shift is equiproportionate, as that from frontier *AA* to *BB* in Figure 22.1. One need only take the ratio of *RS*, the increment in length of any ray, *OS*, between the two frontiers and the length of ray *OR* to the inner frontier. But matters are not so straightforward when the outward shift is uneven, as that from *AA* to *DD*. Then there simply exists no one number which can adequately measure the enhanced productive capacity. The problem is exacerbated when a new production technique expands the ability to produce one good at the expense of another, so that what may be described (somewhat barbarically) as the new technique-specific frontier (*EE'* in Fig. 22.2) crosses the old frontier, *AA'*. One may then assume that the new production frontier for the economy will be the envelope, *EHA'*, of *EE'* and *AA'*, and in these circumstances, while

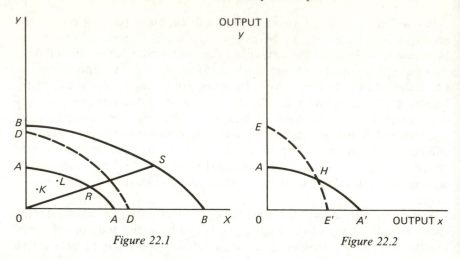

Figure 22.1   Figure 22.2

no part of the economy's frontier will have shifted inward, only some portion of it will have shifted outward.[2]

This indicates why those who seek to estimate some measure of growth of productive capacity usually adopt assumptions of some degree of severity about the nature of the production set and the character of technical change. Their premises are designed to offer them an expansion path for the production frontier which can be described uniquely by a scalar measure, as in the shift from *AA* to *BB* in Figure 22.1. Unfortunately, reality need not follow such a simple course and then *any* scalar measure of productivity growth as an index of expansion of productive capacity per unit of input becomes at best a rough indicator of a development which can be described fully only by a multivariable function.

3 IMPERFECT ASSOCIATION OF PRODUCTIVE CAPACITY AND WELFARE

However one may choose to define standard of living or level of welfare (more will be said about that presently), it is clear that there are ways other than an increase in productive capacity to enhance welfare or living standards. For one thing, allocative or *X* inefficiency may be reduced without any technological change. This moves the economy from a point inside the production frontier to another point closer to the frontier, but involves no shift in the frontier itself. Moreover, the product mix that constitutes output can be adapted better to consumer preferences, thereby clearly contributing to consumer welfare. Consequently, it should not be surprising that the association between growth of productive capacity and growth in welfare productivity is imperfect. In addition, disparities between the measures need not occur only haphazardly. An illustration will show how systematic differences between the two may arise.

Consider the use of a patent system to stimulate economic growth. To permit the use of a two-dimensional diagram, we employ a model with a single commodity and a two-period horizon, though our conclusions will be perfectly general. In period 1 the community has a choice between adoption or rejection of a patent law. The patent system will yield innovations which enhance productive capacity but it will employ as its incentive the provision of monopoly power to the innovator. The innovator will use that power to influence prices, thereby distorting the allocation of resources. Let us also assume that without patents the economy will be perfectly competitive.

Figure 22.3 describes the consequences of society's choice between adoption and rejection of the patent policy. The axes represent y_t and y_{t+1}, outputs in the initial and the subsequent periods. In the absence of the patent arrangement, the production frontier is AA. With a patent system, the frontier shifts outward to BA. Clearly, with the economy's resources given, patents increase productive capacity.

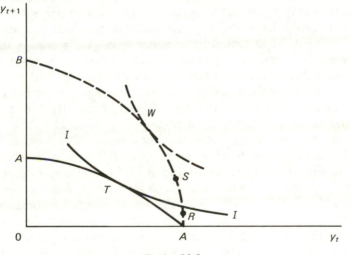

Figure 22.3

Welfare productivity, however, is another matter. Without patents, the economy's (competitive) equilibrium point is T, the point of tangency between production frontier, AA, and an indifference curve, II, of the social welfare function.

However, under a second period monopoly instituted via the patent system, output is distorted. Second period output, y_{t+1}, is restricted below its optimal level so that instead of the optimal point, W, the equilibrium lies to its right at a point such as R or S. If it happens to fall at R, which lies below II, the indifference curve through the patentless equilibrium, welfare productivity will clearly have fallen even though productive capacity has grown. This is no fortuitous relationship. The divergent behavior of the two productivity measures in this case may, rather, be taken as striking evidence that the patent arrangement in question is not well designed.

4   ON WELFARE PRODUCTIVITY AND ITS MEASUREMENT

The preceding discussion may suggest, with good reason, that welfare productivity, however it may be defined, is the appropriate measure of the effectiveness with which the economy is pursuing the goals of the people who compose it. After all, we are not concerned ultimately with the size of the collection of physical objects (and services) the economy turns out, but with the degree of satisfaction they yield. That concern, for example, underlies attempts to take account of changes in product quality in the measurement of productivity growth.

Growth in welfare productivity is in some ways a more amorphous concept than that in productive capacity. Yet in one important attribute it is far more easily definable. It is more difficult to get at because welfare productivity can be increased in so many ways – via a change in output composition or a change in product quality as well as by elimination of inefficiencies. However, it is a simpler concept because, unlike productive capacity growth, it corresponds to a move from one given point to another point in output space, not to the shift of an entire frontier. We ask by how much the move from point K to point L in Figure 22.1 had increased welfare, not how much of an increase in the distance of the frontier from the origin is constituted by the move from AA to DD. In mathematical terms, growth in welfare productivity is a function of the vector of outputs while that in productive capacity is a functional, i.e. a function of a non-denumerable infinity of variables: the set of points on the production frontier.

Since welfare productivity depends on product quality, this feature alone would appear to be a source of intractable difficulties. After all, it is a formidable task just to enumerate the quality changes that must be taken into account in determining what has happened, say, to the productivity of the phonograph industry or the medical profession since 1930, and all but impossible to quantify and aggregate the changes in quality of their products. This has been the bane of economists engaged in measurement of productivity in practice.

What seems at least sometimes to have been overlooked, however, is that by taking welfare productivity as a phenomenon in which we are interested, we do *not* thereby enmesh ourselves more deeply in the intractable complexities of measurement of quality changes. On the contrary, the welfare productivity approach, at least in principle, automatically solves those problems at a single stroke.

Here, as in so many other issues, the price mechanism once more demonstrates its amazing efficacy as a conveyor of information. In an economic sense, an improvement in product quality, after all, is not a mere concatenation of modified technological specifications – higher quality transistors, reduced lubrication requirements, and the like. Rather, it is a matter of the utility that these changes offer consumers. And on our usual premises, that contribution to utility is unambiguously measured by the behavior of a product's relative price. If a product has become better, consumers will be willing to pay more *for a given quantity* of the item. There is no need to go behind the change in this component to seek to determine what part of it is attributable to which element in the complex set of quality changes that the product may have undergone. One may even suspect that further inquiry into quality measurement can only be misleading and counterproductive.

Thus, price analysis is the proper way of dealing with the measurement of changes in product quality and disposes of the problem with one blow. Yet, there is a complication. We cannot for the purpose simply use the behavior of actual market prices, even in theory. True, market prices do tell us what happens to relative *marginal* utilities as a result of improvements in product quality. But marginal utility is not the pertinent criterion. It is easy to see that it can even be totally misleading if not interpreted with care. Thus, suppose an improvement in the quality of some product increases quantity that is sold which, in turn, elicits scale economies and a consequent reduction in price. Are we to conclude that because the product's relative price and marginal utility have fallen, its quality has deteriorated? The answer, of course, is that the fall in price has added to (and certainly not reduced) the consumers' surplus contribution of the change in product quality, which is, ultimately (together with its producers' surplus effect), the most reasonable measure of the change. That is, in measuring the welfare productivity of the particular industry, it would appear that the proper measure is the behavior of the sum of producers' and consumers' surplus per unit of input.

The need to measure changes in consumers' and producers' surpluses complicates empirical evaluation of quality changes considerably, but it certainly does not amount to total retreat to the impossible task of identification and evaluation of all the changes in the attributes of a product that occur with the passage of time. Measurement of changes in surpluses is a far more manageable task than that. This is definitely true in principle, and to a considerable degree it is so in practice. To calculate true productivity growth in automobile production, for example, one need not undertake the (perhaps even undefinable) task of evaluating the degree of improvement in quality of a 1982 model over, say, its 1972 counterpart, including the modifications in comfort, safety, reliability, appearance, etc. In theory, for the purpose one need only estimate the relevant demand and cost relationships and use them to calculate the change in consumers' and producers' surpluses, armed with Professor Willig's (1976) assurance that the procedure is (almost perfectly) legitimate. That is, one can use the definable and conceptually observable cost and demand functions to evaluate indefinable and unmeasurable quality changes. Moreover, in practice, as a good deal of work on hedonic indices has shown, it is actually possible to obtain reasonable econometric estimates of the required magnitudes. Thus, the procedures just described transform measurement of quality changes from a mysterious and ill-defined exercise into one whose outlines, at least, are clear.

5   CRUDE PRODUCTIVITY AND THE SERVICES

Anyone who has thought about the subject is apt to be uncomfortable about discussions of productivity in the services because the very concept is so elusive. Just what is the 'product' of education or medical care, and how does one measure it? Is one really forced, as is often done in the services, to measure output quantities via the quantity of input used in their production so that calculated productivity remains stagnant, just because of the way it is measured?

Fortunately, for many purposes we do not have to face up to these difficulties. To explain why, we must turn to the concept of crude productivity. Crude productivity, in the calculation of which absolutely no effort is made to adjust for quality changes, is often easy to measure and is, fortunately, the correct information required for some significant types of analysis.

Crude productivity is simply a measure of number of units of observable 'output' per unit of input. For example, in musical performance we can define crude productivity of labor as number of audience members (or number of concert performances) per labor hour. Similarly, in the case of higher education, the crude measure of labor productivity can be taken simply as the number of students attending colleges and universities divided by the number of faculty hours devoted to teaching, that is, the student–teacher time ratio. These are obviously easy to measure and the figures readily available. Analogous measures of multifactor productivity in musical performance and education, taking into account other inputs besides musician or teacher time, are also easily constructed.

Why should we ever be interested in crude productivity rather than in a measure that is adjusted for quality changes? The answer is that it is the former, not the latter, that is the primary determinant of the budgets, costs, and prices of the products in question. For example, ignoring other inputs, the cost of education per student is simply the wage per faculty hour multiplied by the number of faculty hours used, all divided by the number of students. But crude productivity equals number of students divided by the number of faculty hours. Therefore, the cost per student is simply the reciprocal of the index of crude productivity multiplied by the average hourly faculty salary. Immobility of labor often permits faculty salaries to lag behind wages and salaries elsewhere in the economy. But, in the long run, trends in faculty salaries seem to be determined preponderantly outside the university because of the long-run mobility of labor and tend, over long periods, to be similar everywhere. This means that the only way that university administrations can affect the ratio between education cost per student and cost per unit of output in the remainder of the economy is by changing the rate of growth of crude productivity in colleges and universities. If crude productivity in education lags behind that in the rest of the economy, the cost per student *must* rise faster than cost per unit of output in the rest of the economy, and university fees and total budgets must follow along commensurately.

An oversimplified example will explain most clearly some important applications of productivity measurement for which it is simply wrong to take quality changes into account. In particular, we will see why this is true of certain types of budgeting decisions affected by differentials in productivity growth and for associated resource allocation decisions.

Consider an economy which produces only two outputs, call them performance of string quartets and electronic (video) game machines. Suppose the quartets are all written for a half-hour performance, so that they always require just four musical instruments and two person hours of labor input per performance. Consequently, whatever the changes in quality of the product, crude productivity must remain absolutely fixed and immutable. Suppose also that electronic games improve in quality, in some sense, with the passage of time, and that crude total factor productivity in their manufacture grows at a rate of 7 per cent per year, hence doubling every decade. Let this economy be perfectly competitive and its overall price level, P_t, stationary so that

$$P_t = P(P_{ct}, c_t, P_{gt}, g_t) = k \qquad (1)$$

(where P_{ct} is the price of admission to a concert, c_t is the number of concerts performed, etc.). Suppose, finally, that both industries use similar inputs with identical input prices and that income and price elasticities of demand are such that the output proportion (i.e. the machine–concert ratio) remains absolutely constant.

Several conclusions follow. First, the price of electronic games, P_g, must fall and the price of concerts, P_c, must rise at constant percentage rates satisfying (1) and

$$\left(\frac{\dot{P}_c}{P_c}\right) \Big/ \left(\frac{\dot{P}_g}{P_g}\right) = 1.07. \tag{2}$$

Second, with output proportions constant, the share of the economy's *inputs* devoted to concerts must increase steadily, at a rate given by the production functions and input prices for the two outputs. It should be emphasized that to calculate this change in allocation of inputs there is no need to measure the change in quality of either concert performance or electronic games.

Next, let us consider the following two applications:

(1)   Schools in our imaginary economy plan how many classrooms to build for the training of musicians *vis-à-vis* the number they need for the training of electronic game assemblers. A moment's consideration confirms that *crude* productivity growth is the only required productivity datum. For example, if labor were the only input, and in 1970 the labor force had been divided equally between the two outputs, by 1980, since crude productivity in games doubles each decade while crude productivity in music remains constant, the fixity of output proportions requires that

$$\frac{L_{c80}}{2L_{g80}} = \frac{L_{c70}}{L_{g70}} = 1, \tag{3}$$

where L_{g80} is the size of the 1980 labor force in game production, etc. Hence, we know from our calculation of crude productivity growth alone that two-thirds of the economy's 1980 labor force must be trained as musicians *regardless of developments in quality*.

(2)   As a second application, suppose that half the cost of each concert is obtained by public subsidy. Then budget planning by the arts support agency of the government can be carried out completely with the aid of (1), (2), and (3) which determine *exactly* the growth in real cost of each concert and the number of concerts on the basis of crude productivity growth data alone.

It is true, of course, that developments in quality enter the matter implicitly by determining the course of the relative demands for the two outputs, which were here subsumed in the premise that output proportions remain fixed. However, the point is that nowhere do we have to *measure* or even define or describe quality change to determine input training proportions or the arts subvention budget. For this we need only know *crude* productivity growth and changes in output proportions – both directly observable magnitudes.

6 SOME EMPIRICAL COMPARISONS

We shall now show, using actual data, that these concepts can yield very different measurements of both annual and average annual productivity growth. Moreover, we will show that because of ambiguities in the concept of growth in productive capacity, legitimate measures of this may yield values that vary widely.

We use data for the railroad industry, which have been compiled with care by Caves, Christensen and Swanson (1980) and have already been used extensively in estimation work. We will only offer estimates of growth in crude productivity and in productive capacity, since welfare productivity is more difficult to measure.[3] We will show, in particular, that the estimated value of growth in productive capacity is quite sensitive to the assumptions used to impose equiproportionate movements upon the production function over time. It should be noted that although the analysis is carried out for just a single industry, the conclusions apply with equal (if not greater) force to the aggregate production function – that is, the measurement of aggregate productivity growth must also be very sensitive to the assumptions used to impose equiproportionate growth.

We begin with what would seem to be the productivity concept whose measurement is most straightforward: crude productivity. Crude productivity growth measures the increase of output that can be produced with various combinations of inputs. In general, measurement of crude productivity growth is complicated by the fact that input quantities do not all grow in the same proportion with time, and more than one output is produced by any industry. This is certainly so in the railroad industry. As a result, to measure crude productivity growth it is necessary to define it as the difference in the rate of growth of an output *index* and a rate of growth of an input *index*. We can define an output index, $Y(t)$, and an input index, $X(t)$, at time t, respectively, as

$$Y(t) = v_1 y_1(t) + v_2 y_2(t) + \ldots + v_m y_m(t), \text{ all } v_i \geqslant 0, \Sigma v_i = 1$$

$$X(t) = w_1 x_1(t) + w_2 x_2(t) + \ldots + w_n x_n(t), \text{ all } w_j \geqslant 0, \Sigma w_j = 1.$$

Crude productivity at time t is, then, given by

$$CP(t) = Y(t)/X(t)$$

and crude productivity growth by

$$CP(t)/CP(t-1)=\{Y(t)/Y(t-1)\}/\{X(t)/X(t-1)\}.$$

There is, unfortunately, no uniquely preferable set of weights either for the input index or the output index. We have used three sets of weights in measuring crude productivity growth in the railroad industry: (i) first period cost share weights, (ii) last period cost share weights, and (iii) an average of first period and last period cost shares. Five inputs are used in constructing the input index: (i) labor, (ii) way and structure, (iii) equipment, (iv) fuel, and (v) materials. Two outputs enter the output index: (i) freight ton miles and (ii) passenger miles; revenue shares are used as weights.

Table 22.1   Estimates of annual rates of crude productivity growth in the railroad industry, 1951–74

	First year wts	Last year wts	Average wts
1951–2	2.405%	2.021%	2.214%
1952–3	1.079	0.995	1.038
1953–4	2.000	1.762	1.882
1954–5	7.813	8.080	7.946
1955–6	3.844	3.830	3.837
1956–7	0.026	−0.153	−0.063
1957–8	−0.653	−1.177	−0.914
1958–9	3.884	3.929	3.907
1959–60	1.932	1.840	1.886
1960–1	3.187	2.911	3.050
1961–2	5.435	5.466	5.451
1962–3	4.361	4.403	4.382
1963–4	4.481	4.433	4.457
1964–5	6.544	6.576	6.560
1965–6	4.734	4.685	4.709
1966–7	−1.325	−1.449	−1.387
1967–8	2.462	2.502	2.482
1968–9	2.352	2.315	2.334
1969–70	−2.055	−2.012	−2.034
1970–1	−2.014	−1.917	−1.966
1971–2	7.608	7.906	7.756
1973–4	5.045	4.999	5.022

Average annual productivity growth, 1951–74

	2.927%	3.014%	2.940%

Estimates of both annual and annual average crude productivity growth are shown in Table 22.1 for each of the three indices. Estimates of annual rates of crude productivity growth turn out to be relatively insensitive to the choice of weights. The maximum difference in estimates resulting from the substitution of first year for last year weights is 0.53 percentage points (1957–8), and in only one other case (1951–2) does the difference exceed 0.3 percentage points. There is only one case in which the sign is different (1956–7). Except for 1956–7, where the signs differ, there are only two cases where the percentage difference between estimates of *CP* growth resulting from the use of the two sets of weights differs by more than 10 per cent: 1951–2 and 1957–8. The two estimates of average annual *CP* growth over the entire period 1951–74 differ by only 0.09 percentage points, or 3 per cent.

7 MEASUREMENT OF GROWTH IN PRODUCTIVE CAPACITY[4]

The measurement of productive capacity growth differs from that of crude productivity in that we need to know at what rate the amount of output that can be produced with *each* combination of inputs increases over time. The basic problem, as has been noted, is that, in general, this will be *different* for different combinations of inputs. Indeed, the only practical way of measuring growth in productive capacity is the adoption of fairly restrictive assumptions about the nature of the techniques available to an industry and the way they change over time. In particular, it is necessary to assume that productivity grows at the same rate for each combination of inputs. But even this assumption does not yield a unique productivity growth figure, since there are various ways of imposing equiproportionate productivity growth on a production function.

We shall compare three such measurements of growth in productive capacity. The first uses a standard Divisia index and the other two are measures constructed by Caves, Christensen and Swanson explicitly for use in the railroad industry. The reader may be quite surprised at how different the estimates are from each other and from the crude productivity measurements.

In this section we describe the three measures of growth in productive capacity that we used. Then, in the next section, the results of the statistical analysis will be reported.

7.1 The Divisia Measure

We will, in general, follow the derivation of the Divisia index in Hulten (1978).[5]

The assumptions are the following:

Assumption 1 The technology of a sector can be represented as a production function of the form:

$$Y = F(x_1, x_2, \ldots, x_n, t)$$

where Y is the output, F is an algebraic function, x_1 through x_n are the input quantities, and t represents time. This rather general premise already rules out discrete and abrupt changes in technology, which are common to most industries. The presence of the time parameter, t, in the production function also implies that technological change is 'disembodied' (and, in particular, is Hicks-neutral).

Assumption 2   The technology represented by this production function is strictly quasi-concave and continuously differentiable.

Assumption 3   All input prices are determined in competitive markets.

Assumption 4   Producers minimize cost.

The next and critically important premise is

Assumption 5   The production function exhibits constant returns to scale (CRTS).

This assumption serves two purposes. First, it ensures that productivity growth is the same for each combination of inputs. Second, it ensures that the full value of the output is exhausted by the inputs. This last relationship is needed to derive the Divisia index.

We now define the Divisia rate of growth of productive capacity, DP^*, as:

$$DP^* = \partial(\ln Y / \Sigma\, w_i \ln x_i) / \partial t.$$

Define the rate of growth of each input X_i as

$$x_i^* = d(\ln x_i)/dt$$

and the rate of growth of output as

$$Y^* = d(\ln Y)/dt.$$

Then, the Divisia rate of productive capacity growth is given by:

$$DP^* = Y^* - (w_1 x_1^* + w_2 x_2^* + \ldots + w_n x_n^*)$$

where q is the price of output Y, p_i is the price of input x_i, and

$$w_i = \frac{p_i x_i}{qY}.$$

In the case of multiple outputs, $y_1,...,y_m$, the Divisia output index is

$$Y^* = v_1 y_1^* + ... + v_m y_m^*$$

where

$$q_i = 1_i y_1 / \Sigma \, q_i y_i$$

and q_i is the price of output i.

7.2 Adjustment for Returns to Scale

To measure productive capacity growth in the railroad industry, Caves, Christensen and Swanson (1980) propose a measure alternative to the Divisia index which allows explicitly for non-constant returns to scale. Their approach uses a general transformation function and its corresponding multiproduct cost function. Differentiation of the cost function leads to a productivity index which is a weighted sum of output growth less a weighted sum of input growth. The weights for output are the elasticities of total cost with respect to the output levels, and the input weights are the elasticities of total cost with respect to the corresponding input prices.

Formally, following the work of McFadden (1978) they adopt the following premises:

Assumption 1'   The technology of the railroad industry can be represented as an implicit production function of the form

$$f(y_1, y_2, ..., y_m; \ x_1, x_2, ..., x_n; \ t) = 0 \tag{4}$$

where f is an algebraic function, y_1 through y_m are various outputs, and x_1 through x_n are the inputs. This function is used because it is not, in general, possible to assign unique input quantities to each of the several outputs. As a result, the production structure must be defined implicitly as a general algebraic transformation function. As in Assumption 1, discrete and abrupt changes in techniques are ruled out in this formulation and it is again assumed that technological change is disembodied.

Assumption 2'   The transformation function has a strictly convex structure.

Assumption 3'   Producers are cost minimizers.

Assumption 4'   While economies of scale may be present, their effects can be separated out.

Economies of scale mean that as the output level increases, *measured productivity may increase* – without any change in technology. Roughly speaking, crude productivity – that is, the measured ratio of outputs to inputs – will increase either because of economies of scale or changes in technology. It is crucial to separate out these two influences when measuring productive capacity growth in an industry, since by the latter we refer only to the portion of the change in the measured ratio of outputs to inputs strictly ascribable to *changes in technology*. The Caves–Christensen–Swanson formulation here thus differs from the Divisia index by netting out the economies of scale factor (compare Assumption 5).

Assumption 5′   Prices need not be determined in competitive markets. In particular, as noted above, cost elasticities rather than relative prices are used to weight both outputs and inputs in the Caves–Christensen–Swanson productivity growth measure.

Technically, for this purpose, the transformation function represented by equation (4) must first be reformulated as a cost function of the form

$$C = g(y_1, y_2, \ldots, y_m; p_1, p_2, \ldots, p_n; t) \tag{5}$$

where g is an algebraic function; p_1 through p_n are the prices of inputs x_1 through x_n, respectively; and C is total cost given by

$$C = \sum_{i=1}^{n} p_i x_i.$$

Next, let the elasticity of the cost function with respect to input price i, η_i, be given by

$$\eta_i = \frac{\partial \ln g}{\partial \ln p_i}$$

and the elasticity of the cost function with respect to output y_i, e_i, be given by

$$e_i = \frac{\partial \ln g}{\partial \ln y_i}.$$

Then it can be shown that Assumption 4′ yields the following properties: First, the elasticity of the cost function with respect to input price is equal to the share of the input in the cost of the product:

$$\eta_i = \frac{\partial \ln g}{\partial \ln p_i} = \frac{p_i x_i}{C} = s_i$$

where s_i is the share of input i in total cost. Second, it can be shown that the rate of productive capacity growth, EP^*, is now given by:

$$EP^* = \sum_{i=1}^{m} e_i y_i^* - \sum_{i=1}^{n} s_i x_i^*.$$

7.3 Adjustments for Returns to Scale and Capacity Utilization

In a follow-up article, Caves, Christensen and Swanson (1981) provide two advances over their earlier paper (1980). These are explicit measurement of economies of scale in the railroad industry and allowance for the possibility that inputs are not optimally employed.

The measurement of returns to scale uses an analytical procedure similar to the one the authors employed in the earlier article. They begin with a general transformation function describing the structure of production, which is given by

$$H(\ln y_1, ..., \ln y_m; \ln x_1, ..., \ln x_n; t) = 1 \qquad (6)$$

where H is an algebraic function and all other symbols are defined as before.

They argue that in the case where an industry produces only one output, productive capacity growth is defined as the rate at which output can grow over time with inputs held constant (i.e. $\partial \ln Y / \partial t$). In the case of multiple outputs, a 'natural' definition of productive capacity growth is the common rate at which all outputs can grow with inputs held fixed:

$$\pi_y^* = \frac{d\ln y_i}{dt} = \frac{d\ln y_j}{dt} \quad \text{subject to } d\ln X = 0,$$

where π_y^* is the rate of productive capacity growth from the output side. it can be shown that

$$\pi_y^* = \frac{\partial F / \partial t}{\sum_{i=1}^{m} \partial F / \partial \ln y_i}. \qquad (7)$$

It is equally 'natural' to define productive capacity growth as the common rate at which all inputs can be decreased over time, with outputs held fixed:

$$\pi_x^* = \frac{d\ln x_i}{dt} = -\frac{d\ln x_j}{dt} \quad \text{subject to } d\ln Y = 0$$

where π_x^* is the rate of productive capacity growth from the input side. It can be shown that:

$$\pi_x^* = \frac{\partial F/\partial t}{\sum_{i=1}^n \partial F/\partial \ln x_i}. \tag{8}$$

Next, it can be shown that π_y^* and π_x^* are related by the degree of returns to scale (*RTS*) in the transformation function. *RTS* is defined as the proportional increase in all outputs that result from a given proportional increase in all inputs, holding the production structure and hence time fixed. That is to say,

$$RTS = -\sum_{i=1}^n \partial F/\partial \ln x_i / \sum_{i=1}^m \partial F/\partial \ln y_i.$$

As a result,

$$\pi_y^* = RTS \, \pi_x^*. \tag{9}$$

The returns to scale factor *RTS* can be estimated directly from the cost side. If there is a convex input structure and the firm minimizes cost with respect to all inputs, then the transformation function (6) associated with it has a unique cost function:

$$\ln C = G(\ln y_1, \ldots, \ln y_m; \ \ln p_1, \ldots, \ln p_n; \ t) \tag{10}$$

where all symbols are as before and G is the cost function. *RTS* is then given by

$$RTS = \left[\sum_{i=1}^n \partial \ln C/\partial \ln y_i \right]^{-1}. \tag{11}$$

The second major advance of the Caves, Christensen and Swanson follow-up article (1981) is allowance for the possibility that not all inputs are employed optimally. As the authors argue, productivity growth estimates typically assume that the firm is in a position of static equilibrium – in particular, that the firm is at a position of minimum cost with respect to *all inputs*. That is to say, it is normally assumed that the firm is operating at an efficient point in its production set. In reality, of course, firms often are not perfectly efficient. As the authors note, if the assumption of minimum cost is violated, 'then estimates of [crude] productivity growth include the effects of . . . movements toward or away from equilibrium, in addition to shifts in the structure of production' (p. 994).

Their way of measuring productive capacity growth when some inputs are not in equilibrium is ingenious. Because the total cost function given by equation (10) will not be satisfied, they do not attempt to use it. Instead, they assume that the firm minimizes cost with respect to a subset of inputs (the so-called 'variable' factors of production whose quantities can be changed in the short run) subject to the other input quantities remaining fixed. (These are referred to as 'fixed' or 'quasi-fixed' inputs.) In this way they can derive a variable cost function

$$\ln CV = G^*(\ln y_1,\ldots,\ln y_m;\ \ln p_1,\ldots,\ln p_{n-q};\ \ln z_1,\ldots,\ln z_q;\ t) \tag{10'}$$

where CV, the variable cost, is given by

$$CV = \sum_{i=1}^{n-q} p_i x_i.$$

G^* is the new cost function, and the z_i are the fixed inputs. The formulae for output productivity growth π_y^*, input productivity growth π_x^*, and returns to scale RTS must now be modified. It is shown (Caves, Christensen and Swanson (1981)) that the new equations are

$$\pi_y^* = -(\partial \ln CV/\partial t)/\sum_{i=1}^{m} (\partial \ln CV/\partial \ln y_i) \tag{7'}$$

$$\pi_x^* = -(\partial \ln CV/\partial t)/\left[1 - \sum_{i=1}^{q} (\partial \ln CV/\partial \ln z_i)\right] \tag{8'}$$

and

$$RTS = \left[1 - \sum_{i=1}^{q} (\partial \ln CV/\partial \ln z_i)\right]/\sum_{i=1}^{m} (\partial \ln CV/\partial \ln y_i).$$

It still remains true that

$$\pi_y^* = RTS\ \pi_x^*.$$

This formulation of productivity growth is particularly useful when the railroad industry is not operating at full capacity.

8 EMPIRICAL RESULTS

We shall now see that estimates of productive capacity growth are very sensitive to the choice of measure. We use the data provided in Caves, Christensen and Swanson (1980, pp.171, 172, and 175). Three measures will be employed as estimates of annual productivity growth. The first, which we have called the 'full Divisia index', measures productivity growth as the difference between a Divisia index of output and a Divisia index based on five inputs. The Divisia output index is a weighted sum of freight ton-miles and passenger miles, with revenue shares as weights. The Divisia input index is a weighted sum of the following inputs – (i) labor, (ii) way and structures, (iii) equipment, (iv) fuel, and (v) materials – with cost shares as weights. The second measure is also a Divisia index. It differs from the first in that only two inputs are used in the index – labor and capital – and the inputs are weighted by the share of labor and capital in the national income generated in the railroad industry. The third measure is the Caves–Christensen–Swanson index *EP**, based on five inputs and two outputs.

The estimates are shown in Table 22.2. First, it is instructive to look at the estimates of annual average productivity growth over the period 1951–74. These estimates range from the 1.5 per cent value of *EP** to the 3.6 per cent value of the two-input Divisia index, a 240 per cent difference.

Table 22.2 Estimates of annual rates of productivity growth in the railroad industry using three different capacity productivity indices

Year	Full Divisia index (DP*)	Divisia index using national income weights (DP*)	Caves–Christensen–Swanson measure EP* (Bell Journal)
1951–2	−0.3%	0.5%	0.1%
1952–3	0.0	0.7	−0.6
1953–4	−0.2	2.3	0.1
1954–5	9.1	9.0	6.7
1955–6	3.8	4.3	3.1
1956–7	−0.5	0.6	−1.0
1957–8	−2.2	1.4	−2.0
1958–9	4.2	4.6	2.6
1959–60	1.7	2.7	1.3
1960–1	2.8	4.1	2.3
1961–2	5.7	5.9	4.6
1962–3	4.6	5.0	2.9
1963–4	4.4	4.3	3.4
1964–5	6.4	8.5	4.4
1965–6	4.6	5.5	3.4
1966–7	−1.5	1.2	−2.3
1967–8	2.5	3.6	0.1
1968–9	2.3	2.9	0.9
1969–70	−2.0	−1.4	−3.5
1970–1	−1.9	1.0	−4.4
1971–2	7.9	10.9	7.0
1972–3	5.5	5.2	4.6
1973–4	−0.2	−0.6	1.3

Average annual productivity growth rate, 1951–74

2.5%	3.6%	1.5%

Moreover, the two Divisia indices differ by 0.9 percentage points, or by 40 per cent. The estimate of crude productivity growth over this period is about 3 per cent per year, which also differs significantly from each of the three productive capacity growth measures.

Estimates of annual productivity growth are even more sensitive to the choice of measure. For 1952–3, estimates vary from *negative* 0.6 per cent per year to positive 0.7 per cent. In 1953–4, they range from −0.2 per cent to 2.3 per cent. In 1956–7, they range from −1.0 to 0.6; in 1957–8, from −2.6 to 1.4; in 1958–9, from 2.6 to 4.6; in 1959–60, from 1.3 to 2.7; in 1964–5, from 4.4 to 8.5; in 1966–7, from −2.3 to 1.2; in 1967–8, from 0.1 to 3.6; in 1968–9, from 0.9 to 2.9; in 1970–1, from −4.4 to 1.0; and in 1973–4, from −0.6 to 1.3 per cent per year. There is almost no consistency between any two of these measures.

Table 22.3   Estimates of annual average productivity growth in the railroad industry, 1955–74, using different capacity productivity indices

Measure	*Productivity growth*
1. Full Divisia index (DP*)	2.5%
2. Divisia index using national income weights (DP*)	3.7%
3. Caves–Christensen–Swanson (1980) measure EP*	1.5%
4. Caves–Christensen–Swanson (1981) measure π^*	
a. π_y^* (Equation (7): Total cost function)	0.9–1.0%
b. π_x^* (Equation (8): Total cost function)	0.8%
c. π_y^* (Equation (7'): Variable cost function)	1.8–2.0%
d. π_x^* (Equation (8'): Variable cost function)	1.8%

Estimates of π_y^* and π_x^* are available only for average annual productivity growth for the period from 1955 to 1974. Comparisons of these with the three measures in Table 22.2 are provided in Table 22.3. The estimates of π_y^* and π_x^* based on the total cost function (equations (7) and (8)) range from 0.8 to 1.0 per cent per year,[6] which are considerably lower than the Divisia estimate and lower than the *EP** index. The estimates of π_y^* and π_x^* based on the variable cost function (equations (7') and (8')) fall in the range 1.8 to 2.0 per cent per year, about twice the total cost function figures but still lower than the Divisia-based estimates of productive capacity growth.

9   CONCLUSION

In this paper we have shown that three basic concepts of productivity growth – welfare productivity, productive capacity, and crude productivity – have very different meanings and uses and can behave very differently. All three of them are shown to be significant, even the crude productivity growth measure which makes no adjustments for quality changes and which may seem basically indefensible on first consideration. We have seen also why it may be impossible to devise any robust scalar representation of growth in productive capacity. We saw why explicit adjustments for changes in product quality may be unnecessary. That is, at least in principle, one can hope to deal with the quality change problem through reasonably accurate measurement of growth in welfare productivity. This, moreover, may in some ultimate sense, have the best claim as the true measure of productivity growth for purposes of economic analysis.

The empirical results demonstrate that estimates of both annual and annual average productivity growth over fairly long periods are highly sensitive to choice of productivity concept. Measures of crude productivity differ greatly from those of productive capacity. Moreover, estimates of productive capacity growth are very sensitive to the assumptions used to impose an equiproportionate shift on the production function over time.

Notes

1. Where we deal with multifactor productivity, the concept of a unit of input clearly involves serious aggregation problems. For the discussion here, however, that is an irrelevant complication and it will therefore be ignored. We will, in effect, proceed on the assumption that all input is homogeneous or that we are concerned with labor productivity. We will return to the aggregation issues later.
2. It is even arguable that a new technique sometimes literally reduces the economy's ability to produce some outputs. For example, the use of concrete in the construction of buildings has probably reduced the opportunities for on the job training of stonemasons, whose quality of work on churches and gothic college buildings may thereby have been impeded.
3. The calculation of the consumers' surplus clearly requires estimates of the demand schedules for railroad output. We will also make no attempt to measure levels of or change in X-inefficiency over time.
4. This section describes the assumptions and the mathematical expressions used in the three measures of growth in productive capacity. The reader who is interested only in the results can proceed directly to Section 8 which is comprehensible without knowledge of the formulas.
5. A similar derivation can be found in Gollop and Jorgensen (1980).
6. Two measures of π^*_y were provided, based on alternative methods of estimation of the returns to scale (*RTS*).

References

Caves, D., L. R. Christensen and J. A. Swanson (1980) 'Productivity in US Railroads, 1951–1974', *Bell Journal of Economics*, 11: 166–81.

Caves, D., L. R. Christensen and J. A. Swanson (1981) 'Productivity Growth, Scale Economies, and Capacity Utilization in US Railroads, 1955–74', *American Economic Review*, 71, 5: 994–1002.

Gollop, F. M. and D. W. Jorgensen (1980) 'US Productivity Growth by Industry, 1947–73', in J. W. Kendrick and B. N. Vaccara (eds), *New Developments in Productivity Measurement and Analysis*, (Chicago: University of Chicago Press).

Hulten, C. R. (1978) 'Growth Accounting with Intermediate Inputs', *Review of Economic Studies*, 45 (3), 141: 511–18.

McFadden, D. (1978) 'Cost, Revenue, and Profit Functions', in M. A. Fuss and D. McFadden (eds) *Production Economics: A Dual Approach to Theory and Applications*, (Amsterdam: North-Holland).

Willig, R. (1976) 'Consumer Surplus Without Apology', *American Economic Review*, 66: 589–97.

23 Technical Progress, Research and Development

Thomas K. Rymes*

> The real dispute is not about the *measurement* of capital but about the *meaning* of capital. (Joan Robinson, 1975, vi)

1 INTRODUCTION

Measures of the rate of technical advance, sometimes called sources of growth, total factor productivity, residuals, or measures of our ignorance are now commonplace. It is, however, not a commonplace to find recognition that there are basically two such measures: (i) the traditional measure, based on the early work of Hicks, and (ii) newer ones, based on the theoretical work of the late Sir Roy Harrod and Joan Robinson.

The traditional measures do not take account of the reproducibility of capital inputs, in all their forms, while the newer measures do (Rymes, 1986; Rymes and Cas, 1985). The traditional measures attempt to separate reproducible capital accumulation and technical progress, the newer measures take into account that some of observed reproducible capital accumulation is really the result of technical progress and cannot meaningfully be distinguished from such technical progress. Indeed, it is increasingly being recognized that traditional measures seriously *understate* measured rates of technical advance. (See Rymes 1971, 1972, 1983; Hulten, 1979; Peterson, 1979; Usher, 1980; Postner and Wesa, 1983; and Steedman, 1983 and 1985.)

Joan Robinson, in her work on capital accumulation and technical progress, stressed the unsatisfactory nature of considering capital accumulation in a *given* state of technical knowledge. It was impossible, she argued, to distinguish in the traditional way between capital accumulation and technical progress, particularly when account is taken of the fact that some capital expenditures are designed to bring about advances in technical knowledge (Robinson 1962, 1965).

* I am grateful for comments on an earlier draft by Geoff Harcourt, Jeffrey Bernstein, and Marc Lavoie.

Her deep theoretical insights into such problems are now being reflected in current empirical work. Professor Griliches (1984, p.18) has recently admitted, dealing with the relationship between research and development expenditures and traditional measures of total factor productivity, that

> we are more aware of both the conceptual and the measurement difficulties involved in productivity measurement and less sure about the relevance of the existing measures to the issues at hand.

This paper first sets out a Robinsonian theory of the relationship between capital accumulation and induced technical progress. It then shows that traditional measures of total factor productivity will be of no use in detecting what relationship might exist between capital-type research and development expenditures and measures of technological progress, and that newer measures based on the theoretical work of the late Sir Roy Harrod and Joan Robinson will be of potentially greater use in detecting such relationships. Joan Robinson's theoretical work is demonstrated, then, to have immediate relevance to some very important contemporary empirical and policy questions in the economics of capital accumulation and technical progress.

2   THE ROBINSONIAN THEORY OF ACCUMULATION AND TECHNICAL PROGRESS

Joan Robinson's growth theory was essentially concerned with the relationship between the rate of technical progress and capital accumulation. She argued (Robinson, 1962) that the desired rate of accumulation undertaken 'today' by entrepreneurs, given their 'animal spirits', will be a positive function of the expected net rate of return to capital, but that it is not possible to be more precise about the non-linearity of the relationship. Thus, one can write

$$g = g(\hat{R}) \quad g' > 0 \quad \text{and} \quad g'' = 0, \tag{1}$$

where g is the desired rate of accumulation and $\hat{R}$ is the expected net rate of return. The expected net rate of return to capital is a positive function of 'today's' rate of return, but at a diminishing rate because entrepreneurs are rationally cognizant of the limits of current experience in forming expectations about the future,[1] i.e.

$$\hat{R} = \hat{R}(R) \quad \hat{R}' > 0 \quad \text{and} \quad \hat{R}'' < 0, \tag{2}$$

where $\hat{R}$ is the expected rate of return to investment and R is the current rate of return. Therefore, 'today's' desired rate of accumulation is a positive but diminishing function of 'today's' net rate of return, i.e.

$$g = g(\hat{R}(R)) \quad g'\hat{R}' > 0 \quad \text{and} \quad g'\hat{R}'' + \hat{R}'g'' < 0. \tag{3}$$

The steady state net rate of return is said to be the actual rate of accumulation as modified by the rate of saving out of net returns to capital (or, following Pasinetti (1974) rather than Robinson, the rate of saving carried out by the individuals of the economy who derive all their income as returns to capital), i.e.

$$g = S_c(R)R \quad S'_c(R) > 0. \tag{4}$$

Relations (3) and (4) together determine equilibrium net rates of accumulation and net rates of return, as illustrated in Figure 23.1.

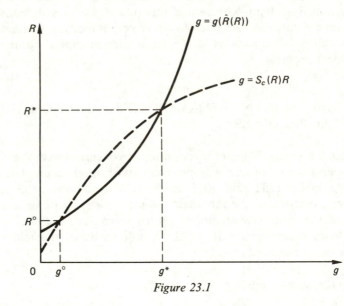

Figure 23.1

In Figure 23.1, the desired rate of accumulation function $g = g(\hat{R}(R))$ illustrates the proposition that the higher the rate of return, the higher the desired rate of accumulation, but in a diminishing way reflecting the manner in which expectations are formed. As the curve is drawn, entrepreneurs must anticipate some positive rate of return before they undertake any accumulation at all. The Cambridge saving relation illustrates the proposition that the higher the rate of accumulation, the higher the net rate of return, but at a diminishing rate reflecting the argument that a higher rate of return will be associated with an even greater rate of saving out of returns to capital. As the latter curve is drawn, even if the rate of accumulation were zero, there would be some minimum positive rate of return, at which point the fraction of net returns to capital saved would have fallen to nil, even if growth were zero.

Mrs Robinson suggested that multiple equilibria could result with (g_0, R_0) being an unstable low-level equilibrium and (g_1, R_1) being a stable high-level equilibrium. Only at the stable steady-state equilibrium is it possible and meaningful to talk about the desired and actual net rate of accumulation being the same. As well, only in stable steady-state equilibrium will the expected net rate of return to capital equal the actual net rate of return.

We now introduce induced technical progress into Joan Robinson's determination of the rate of accumulation and the net rate of return to capital.

The rate of growth of the economy in steady-state equilibrium is $g = n + n'$, i.e. it is equal to the rate of growth of primary inputs such as labor and waiting[2] and the improvement in their efficiency or the rate of Harrod-neutral technical progress. The rate of technical progress may be divided into two parts: $n_1 + n_2(g)$ where n_1 is the rate which is independent of accumulation yet favorably affects accumulation and n_2 is a positive but diminishing function of the desired rate of accumulation. We may reconstruct Mrs Robinson's argument by rewriting relation (3) as

$$g_d = g_d(n + n_1, \hat{R}(R)). \tag{5}$$

The desired rate of accumulation is positively related to the exogenous rate of growth of primary inputs in Harrod-efficient terms, and, as before, the expected net rate of return to capital. The actual rate of accumulation is given in relation (6).

$$g_a = n + n_1 + n_2(g_d). \tag{6}$$

The actual rate of accumulation will be equal to the *overall* rate of growth of Harrod-efficient primary inputs, with part of such increases in efficiency being brought about by the new techniques accompanying the rate of accumulation entrepreneurs desire.

The desired rate of accumulation will equal the actual rate when relation (7) holds.

$$n + n_1 + n_2(g_d(n + n_1, \hat{R}(R))) = g_d(n + n_1, \hat{R}(R)). \tag{7}$$

For different exogenous rates of growth of Harrod-efficient primary inputs, the desired and actual rates will be equal for different current net rates of return to capital, exhibited by the $g_d = g_a$ locus in Figure 23.2.[3]

Relation (4) must be rewritten to stress that it arises from the connection

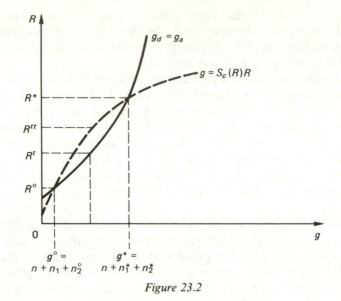

Figure 23.2

between the actual rate of accumulation and the current net rate of return, as in relation (8).

$$n + n_1 + n_2(g_d(n + n_1, \hat{R}(R))) = S_c(R)R. \tag{8}$$

The relationship between exogenous rates of growth of Harrod-efficient primary inputs and the net rates of return to capital from (8) is exhibited also in Figure 23.2.

Figure 23.2 reveals that again the possibility of multiple equilibria arises when we recognize that (i) higher rates of technical progress may be the result of higher desired rates of accumulation, and (ii) higher given rates of technical progress may result in higher desired rates of accumulation. In particular, it must be noted that, as in Mrs Robinson's case, a more robust analysis is required when situations other than the steady states (such as $[n + n_1^0 + n_2^0, R^0]$ and $[n + n_1^* + n_2^*, R^*]$) are contemplated (Gram and Walsh, 1983; Asimakopulos, 1984). If there were a different rate of growth of Harrod-efficient primary inputs, while there may exist a net rate of return, R^t, such that equal desired and actual rates of accumulation could be associated with such a rate of return, as is shown in Figure 23.2, when preferences are introduced, the actual rate of accumulation would be associated with a net rate of return to capital, R'', which would not equilibrate desired and actual rates of accumulation.

What the analysis does suggest, however, is that overall rates of technical progress and that kind of capital accumulation said to be productive of technical progress would be positively associated. Since

$n_2 = n_2(g_d(n + n_1, \hat{R}(R)))$, higher rates of exogenous technical progress would be associated with higher rates of capital accumulation. Such higher rates of accumulation would themselves induce additional technical progress. Both the higher rates of exogenous and endogenous technical progress, by bringing about higher net rates of return to capital, would again reinforce even higher rates of accumulation and induce further endogenous technical progress. While it is clear that the empirical separation of the relationships between technical progress and accumulation will be difficult, the Robinsonian theory would predict a positive relationship between the capital accumulation said to produce technical progress and measures of technical progress or total factor productivity. Let us call such capital accumulation 'research and development'. How would measures of such capital accumulation and total factor productivity be related? We turn now to contemporary measures of technical progress or productivity and see how the traditional and newer Harrod–Robinson constructs would shed light on the relationship.

3 MEASURES OF TECHNICAL PROGRESS AND THE ECONOMIC ACCOUNTING SYSTEM

Consider a simple case first. Suppose the economy in question has primary inputs which are used to produce homogeneous intermediate output which as intermediate input together with the primary inputs produce homogeneous final output. The simple accounts for such an economy are

$$WL + PM \equiv PC + PM \equiv PQ, \tag{9}$$

where WL is a row vector of primary input prices times a column vector of primary input quantities, P is the price of the homogeneous product, M is the scalar quantity of intermediate input or output, C is the scalar quantity of the final (consumption) output, and Q is the scalar quantity of gross output.

Where starred variables represent instantaneous proportionate rates of change, consider now two Divisia index measures of technical progress. The traditional one would be

$$Q^* - \left[\frac{WL}{PQ}(L^*) + \frac{PM}{PQ}(M^*) \right] \equiv T^* \equiv$$
$$\left[\frac{WL}{PQ}(W^*) + \frac{PM}{PQ}(P^*) \right] - P^*, \tag{10}$$

where the proportionate rate of technical progress, T^*, is, with respect to quantities, equal to the proportionate rate of growth of gross output, less the weighted sum of the proportionate rates of growth of the primary inputs and the producible intermediate inputs[4] and, with respect to prices, equals the weighted sum of the proportionate rates of growth of the prices of the primary and intermediate inputs less the growth rate of the price of gross output.

The newer measures of technical progress take into account the obvious fact that there is a fundamental difference between the non-reproducible primary inputs and the producible intermediate inputs. The new Harrod–Robinson measures would be

$$Q^* - \left[\frac{WL}{PQ}(L^*) + \frac{PM}{PQ}(M^* - H^*) \right] \equiv H^* \equiv$$

$$\equiv \left[\frac{WL}{PQ}(W^*) + \frac{PM}{PQ}P^* + H^*) \right] - P^*. \tag{11}$$

It is immediately clear, in a comparison of relations (10) and (11), that H^* will exceed T^*; that $M^* - H^*$ is a measure of the proportionate rate of growth of the primary inputs necessary to produce the intermediate outputs and inputs and that $P^* + H^*$ is a measure of the proportionate rate of growth of the prices of the primary inputs involved in the production of the intermediate outputs and inputs. Of course, if the traditional measures were constructed for the accounts, exhibited by relation (12),

$$WL \equiv PC \tag{12}$$

the *revised* traditional measures of technical progress would equal the newer ones.

If the economy is composed of a number of heterogeneous activities, then the accounts for any activity, j, would be

$$WL_j + P_i M_{ij} \equiv P_j C_j + P_j M_{ji} \equiv P_j Q_j, \tag{13}$$

where M_{ij} is the (vector) flow of intermediate inputs from activity i into activity j while M_{ji} is the (vector) flow of intermediate outputs from activity j into activity i. Traditional measures of technical progress[5] for activity j would be

$$Q_j^* - \left[\frac{WL_j}{P_j Q_j}(L_j^*) + \frac{P_i M_{ij}}{P_j Q_j}(M_{ij}^*) \right] \equiv T_j^* \equiv$$

$$\equiv \left[\frac{WL_j}{P_j Q_j}(W^*) + \frac{P_i M_{ij}}{P_j Q_j}(P_i^*) \right] - P_j^* \tag{14}$$

where not only is the producibility of the intermediate inputs and outputs ignored but, as a consequence, so is the interactivity interdependence of the technology. The new measures would be

$$Q_j^* - \left[\frac{WL_j}{PQ_j}(L_j^*) + \frac{P_iM_{ij}}{P_jQ_j}(M_{ij}^* - H_i^*) \right] \equiv H_j^* \equiv$$

$$\equiv \left[\frac{WL_j}{P_jQ_j}(W^*) + \frac{P_iM_{ij}}{P_jQ_j}(P_i^* + H_i^*) \right] - P_j^*. \qquad (15)$$

A remarkable characteristic of the new measures can now be seen. The vector $M_{ij}^* - H_i^*$ refers to the 'deflation' of the quantities of intermediate inputs from activity i used in activity j to represent the primary inputs, in activity i, indirectly used in activity j. One cannot assess the rate of technical progress in activity j without knowing the rate of such progress in activity i; i.e. the advances in the activities directly and indirectly involved in the production of the gross output of activity j. Furthermore, when it is recalled from relation (13) that activity j produces intermediate outputs which appear as intermediate inputs in other activities, one cannot solve for the measure of the rate of technical progress in activity i, without knowing the rate of progress in activity j. However, it is precisely the knowledge of the interdependence of technology exhibited in modern input–output accounts that permit the *simultaneous* solution for the measures of technical progress in the technologically interdependent activities (see Rymes and Cas, 1985). The argument immediately generalizes to more complex cases involving the treatment of capital inputs. The accounts for any activity j would be

$$WL_j + P_iM_{ij} + R_jP_kK_{kj} \equiv P_jC_j + P_jM_{ji} + P_j\Delta K_{jk} \equiv P_iQ_j, \qquad (16)$$

where capital consumption allowances on durable reproducible capital goods are treated as intermediate inputs, $P_j\Delta K_{jk}$ is the net capital formation in activity k produced in activity j, and $R_jP_kK_{kj}$ is the (vector) flow of the net returns to capital goods in activity j producible in activity k.

The traditional measure of technical progress for activity j would be

$$Q_j^* - \left[\frac{WL_j}{P_jQ_j}(L_i^*) + \frac{P_iM_{ij}}{P_jQ_j}(M_{ij}^*) + \frac{R_jP_kK_{kj}}{P_jQ_j}(K_{kj}^*) \right] \equiv T_j^* \equiv$$

$$\equiv \left[\frac{WL_j}{P_jQ_j}(W^*) - \frac{P_iM_{ij}}{P_jQ_j}(p_i^*) + \frac{R_jP_kK_{kj}}{P_jQ_j}(R_j^*P_k^*) \right] - P_j^* \qquad (17)$$

while the new Harrod–Robinson measures would be

$$Q_j^* - \left[\frac{WL_j}{P_jQ_j}(L_j^*) + \frac{P_iM_{ij}}{P_jQ_j}(M_{ij}^* - H_i^*) + \frac{R_jP_kK_{kj}}{P_jQ_j}(K_{kj}^* - H_k^*) \right] \equiv H_j^* \equiv$$

$$(18)$$

$$\equiv \left[\frac{WL_j}{P_jQ_j}(W^*) + \frac{P_iM_{ij}}{P_jQ_j}(P_i^* + H_i^*) + \frac{R_jP_kK_{jk}}{P_jQ_j}(R_j^* + P_k^* + H_k^*) \right] - P_j^*.$$

4   CAPITAL ACCUMULATION, CAPITALIZED EXPENDITURES, AND RECORDED TECHNICAL PROGRESS

The essence of the problem to be discussed now can be seen by considering relation (17) for any economy where strict Harrod–Robinson *neutral* technical progress was being exhibited, not only at the aggregate economy level but, more restrictively, at the individual activity levels as well. In that case we would have

$$Q_j^* = M_{ij}^* = K_{kj}^* \ \forall_{i,j,k}$$

and

$$P_i^* = P_j^* = P_k^* \ \forall_{i,j,k} \quad \text{and} \quad R_j^* = 0, \ \forall_j$$

so that relation (17) would be

$$\frac{WL_j}{P_jQ_j}(Q_j^* - L_j^*) \equiv T_j^* \equiv \frac{WL_j}{P_jQ_j}(W^* - P^*)$$

$$(19)$$

and relation (18) would be

$$Q_j^* - L_j^* \equiv H_j^* \equiv W^* - P_j^* \equiv R_j^* + P_k^* - P_j^* + H_k^* \equiv R_j^* + H_k^*.$$

$$(20)$$

Relation (17) would have it that the less important were primary non-reproducible inputs (the smaller is WL_j/P_jQ_j), the lower would be the rate of technical progress. Relation (18) would correctly report that the rate of technical progress would be equal to the proportionate rate of growth of the productivity of all *primary* (not necessarily just labor) inputs.

Relation (18) would show that the rate of improvement in Harrod-efficiency of the non-reproducible inputs would be equal to the rate of increase in the own-product price of labor, $W^* - P_j^*$, and for the non-reproducible input associated with reproducible capital, $R_j^* + P_k^* + H_k^* - P_j^* = R_j^* + H_k^*$. There is, of course, not the slightest reason to imagine such comprehensively ubiquitous Harrod neutrality in technological progress to hold in reality. The assumption is used merely to demonstrate how susceptible are the traditional measures to reclassification of capital accumulation and the capitalization of expenditures. To that matter, we now turn.

Activity j will be incurring a variety of expenditures which might be called 'R & D'. The activity can be purchasing 'research and development' from other activities (extramural) or can be producing 'R & D' within its own activity (intramural). In the case of 'research and development' expenditures provided by other activities, they could be treated as either current intermediate inputs or as capital expenditures. In the case of 'research and development' expenditures within the activity, they will be expenditures on intermediate inputs, expenditures on (say) scientific equipment which will be already treated as capital expenditures by activity j, and the wages and salaries of 'scientists' employed within the activity. All of these expenditures by activity j (not just those associated with the purchase of scientific equipment) could be capitalized.

Clearly, whether or not the 'research and development' expenditures are capitalized by the activities themselves or by the economist studying the problem will be a function of tax laws, government policies, and the accompanying accounting and economic theories. Given strict Harrod-neutrality, differences in capitalization should not affect measures of technical progress.

If the extramural expenditures were treated as a current intermediate input from another 'research and development'-producing activity, traditional measures of technical progress treat the increase in the physical quantities of such inputs as an explanatory factor in accounting for the growth of the gross output of the purchasing activity. *Ceteris paribus*, the larger the share of such expenditures in the purchasing activity's gross output, the *lower* will be the recorded rates of technical progress in the purchasing activity. That is, the lower is WL_j/P_jQ_j because the higher is P_iM_{ij}/P_jQ_j, the lower will be T_j^*.

Capitalization of such extramural expenditures would have a similar effect. The flow expenditures would no longer be treated as intermediate inputs but as part of the capital consumption experienced by the capital stock of the purchasing activity. The share coefficients would be revised such that, for the component under review,

$$\frac{R_jP_iK_{ij} + \delta P_iK_{ij}}{P_jQ_j} > \frac{P_iM_{ij}}{P_jQ_j},$$

i.e. the gross rentals on the capitalized extramural 'research and development' expenditures as a fraction of the purchasing activity's gross output will be greater than the fraction with respect to the expenditure when classed as intermediate inputs. The strong assumption of Harrod-neutrality implies all produced outputs and inputs are expanding at the same rate, and the implication once again that the mere capitalization of certain inputs produced elsewhere accounts for a lower measured rate of technical progress in the purchasing activity. It is clear that if the capitalization of extramural 'research and development' were the result of government policy, then it would appear that 'research and development' would be accounting for technical progress. The traditional measures would show that a greater share in the growth rate of the purchasing activity's gross output would be accounted for by 'research and development' – i.e. by the activity producing the 'research and development'. It is equally immediately clear that, when Harrod-neutrality prevails, the rate of technical progress in the purchasing activity, which takes into account the advances in technology in all activities directly and indirectly supplying the purchasing activity with reproducible inputs, whatever their form, will be unaffected by such accounting and capitalization procedures. Traditional measures of technical progress at the activity level will be brittle with respect to such classifications.[6]

With respect to intramural 'research and development' expenditures, the effect of the capitalization of such expenditures is even more clear. Consider *just* the expenditures on the wages and salaries of 'scientists'.[7] What are the effects of capitalization of such expenditures, of treating them as part of technical progress inducing capital accumulation? In a technically progressing economy the real wage and salary rates of scientists (the output price of all non-reproducible inputs) will be rising at the overall rate of Harrod-neutral technical progress. The capitalization of such expenditures will result in the human component of the stock of 'research and development' growing more rapidly than the number of 'scientists'. That is, of course, the same thing as a reduction in the shares of non-reproducible inputs in activity j's gross output – i.e. a reduction in WL_{ij}/P_jQ_j. As we have seen, this reduces the traditional measure of the rate of technical progress in the activity capitalizing its intramural 'research and development' expenditures.

Again, the newer measures of activity technical progress would be invariant to these mere conventional accounting relations. The traditional measures would again say that increases in capital accumulation such as 'research and development' expenditures would account for ('explain') a part of the residual, would reduce our ignorance of the sources of economic growth. In the case of intramural 'research and development' expenditures, one cannot claim that the accounting for technical progress comes from outside the activity in question – it comes merely from the capitalization.

Traditional measures of technical progress are always reduced by decreases in the shares (i.e. under competitive conditions, the partial elasticities of output with respect to inputs) of the non-reproducible inputs. The reclassification of in-house or intramural non-reproducible inputs by capitalization to reproducible inputs, in a technically progressive world, results in a higher observed rate of growth of such inputs and a corresponding reduction in the observed rate of technical progress. The new measures of technical progress are always expressed in terms of the changing efficiency of non-reproducible inputs, never mix up the roles of non-reproducible and reproducible inputs, and they are thus not susceptible to the reclassification of inputs from non-reproducible to reproducible by the capitalization of certain expenditures considered to be productive of technical progress.

'Research and development' expenditures are said by theory to be positively correlated with technical progress. If one uses traditional measures of technical progress, since the activity ranking of such measured rates of technical progress is suspect, being dependent solely on the shares or partial elasticities of non-reproducible inputs, the idea that such measured rates of technical progress will be positively correlated with 'research and development' expenditures – even if such correlation were observed – would in no way support the theory. If there were observed negative correlations, then such observations could *not* be said to fail to support the theory. Since the traditional measured rates of technical progress are faulty there is no point in seeing how 'research and development' expenditures contribute to such measured technical progress.

If such 'research and development' expenditures are capitalized to provide measures of the *stock* of 'research and development', then it follows that, when such expenditures are capitalized, it will be said that the growth of such stocks will account for (some) measured traditional rates of technical progress. We have seen, in the context of strict Harrod-neutrality, how such an accounting of the sources of growth is merely an artifact of statistical and accounting conventions, and the fact that traditional measured rates of technical progress at the activity level fail to distinguish between reproducible and non-reproducible inputs.

If the new measures of technical progress were employed, then studies relating such measures to 'research and development' expenditures might shed light on that component of the rate of technical progress which is endogenous and related to capital accumulation, for, in general, the mere capitalization of 'research and development' expenditures will not affect the Harrod–Robinson measures of technical progress.

With Harrod-neutrality, the new measures of technical progress will reveal the various interdependent rates of increase in technical efficiency. Such measured rates will not be susceptible to the mere capitalization of those expenditures, such as R & D, which are said to be productive of technical advance. The traditional measures, susceptible to such taxonomic exercises, will show that capitalized R & D expenditures will 'explain' a greater share in the rate of growth of output and the share of 'residuals' in the growth rate being reduced by accounting artifact.

The foregoing discussion has assumed, for analytical clarity, that measured technical progress, at the activity and aggregate level, would exhibit strict Harrod-neutrality. What of the argument when Harrod non-neutral technical progress is observed?

Harrod-neutrality is observed when all real rates of return to capital are constant (i.e. $R_j^* =$ zero, $\forall_j$) and *either* all produced input–output ratios are constant (e.g. $Q_j^* = M_{ij}^* = K_{ij}^*$, $\forall_{i,j}$), and all reproducible input own-product prices are constant (i.e. $P_i^* - P_j^* =$ zero, $\forall i,j$), i.e. one has strict neutrality, *or* all value shares are constant (e.g. $P_i^* + M_{ij}^* - [P_j^* + Q_j^*] =$ zero, $\forall_{i,j}$). Therefore, non-neutrality in Harrod's sense will be that state when the value shares are changing (i.e. $P_i^* + M_{ij}^* - [P_j^* + Q_j^*]/$zero, $\forall_{i,j}$). In the second case of neutrality, if activity i supplies 'research and development' intermediate inputs into activity j, if $P_i^* < P_j^*$, then $M_{ij}^* > Q_j^*$ so that the rate of Harrod-neutral progress in activity i exceeds that in activity j. The traditional measures would have none of this greater technical progress in activity i showing up in activity j, the newer measures would show this precisely. The newer measures would indeed predict that for those activities experiencing the lowest rates of Harrod-neutral progress, the produced input–output relations, when the output of the most rapidly technically advancing activities would be appearing as the inputs in such input–output relations, would all be rising at the highest rate, whereas the non-produced input–output relations would all be falling at the lowest rates.

In the case, then, of different but neutral rates of technical progress, if an activity were producing 'research and development' output and that activity were experiencing high rates of technical progress, all other activities using such 'research and development' outputs as inputs would be sharing in such technical progress and would therefore themselves be showing high Harrod-measured rates of technical progress.

It follows that if Harrod non-neutrality were observed so that $P_i^* + M_{ij}^* - [P_j^* + Q_j^*] > 0$ then the argument would be that the non-neutrality of the measured technical progress would entail increased integration of the ith into the jth activity. Hence higher Harrod-measured rates of technical progress in the ith sector, supplying the jth sector with intermediate inputs, would result in even higher Harrod-measured rates of technical progress in the jth activity than would be the case if strict neutrality were observed.

If the intermediate inputs were, in fact, extramural research and development expenditures in the ith activity purchased by the jth activity, then even higher rates of technical progress in the provision of research and development would 'explain' even more of the growth recorded in the jth activity, would reduce even further the traditionally measured total factor productivity advance in the jth activity. If such extramural expenditures were capitalized, then the traditionally measured rate of technical progress in the jth activity would be even further reduced.

The Harrod-measures, with non-neutrality appearing as closer integration of the two activities, would show higher rates of productivity advance in the ith activity being exhibited as correspondingly higher rates of productivity advance in the jth activity. The traditional measures would show just the opposite result and would not only be unable to explain the differences amongst measured productivity advances across activities, but also would not offer any meaningful account of the changing degrees of integration among activities exhibited by non-neutral interactivity dependent Harrod–Robinson technical progress.

Two important points may now be summarized. (i) In the purchasing activities, if the extramural 'research and development' intermediate input expenditures were capitalized then the shares of such expenditures would be increased and the Harrod-measured rates of technical progress in the purchasing activities correspondingly *increased*, not decreased. The interdependence of the industries would be increased by the capitalization and capital accumulation would thus be shown to be correlated with induced technical progress. (ii) If the progress were non-neutral, and shares of 'research and development' expenditures in the purchasing industries were increasing – technical progress would be described as Harrod-biased 'research and development' using – then the integration between the activities would be increased. Again, capital accumulation in such 'research and development' expenditures would be seen to be contributing to technical progress. However, if the technical progress were Harrod-biased 'research and development' saving – the shares of such expenditures in the purchasing activities would be falling – then the contribution of 'research and development' to measured technical progress in the purchasing activities would be reduced *because* the bias in the technical progress would be reducing the degree of integration between the producing and using activities.

Thus, the contribution of desired rates of accumulation to endogenous rates of technical progress is correctly observed if and only if the measured rates of technical progress are of the new or Harrod–Robinson type. This satisfactory conclusion must, of course, be modified by the recognition that exogenous rates of Harrod–Robinson technical progress may, as argued above, encourage capital accumulation. Observed positive correlation between capital accumulation and technical progress may result as much from the fact that high rates of technical progress may encourage high rates of capital accumulation, such as capitalized 'research and development' expenditures, as from the fact that capital accumulation in the form of 'research and development' expenditures may contribute (unless the progress were 'research and development' saving) to technical progress.[8]

5 CONCLUSION

Joan Robinson argued that it was not helpful to study capital accumulation in the context of a given state of technical knowledge. In this paper, I have attempted to show that if and only if Harrod–Robinson or new measures of technical progress at the activity level are constructed, will it be possible to have predictable and well-behaved relationships between capital expenditures such as 'research and development' outlays and technical progress. Mrs Robinson supported Harrod's concept of technical progress which obviates confusion between non-reproducible and reproducible inputs because Harrod–Robinson measures of technical progress permit a better understanding of the role of capital accumulation in a *changing* state of technical knowledge.

Notes

1. The problem of the rational formation of expectations about future events, based on current empirical support for competing theories, when faced with the problem of induction, was dealt with by Sir Roy Harrod (1956). Harrod's basic thinking was foreshadowed by Keynes (1921) and was implicitly adopted by Joan Robinson.
2. See Harrod, 1961.
3. Figure 23.2 is derived from Figure 23.1a.

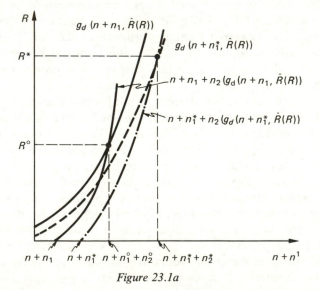

Figure 23.1a

An exogenous rate of growth of Harrod-efficient primary inputs, $n + n_1$, will be associated with a desired rate of accumulation function, $g_d(n + n_1, \hat{R}(R))$ and an induced rate of technical progress function $n_2(g_d(n + n_1, \hat{R}(R)))$ so that the actual rate of accumulation will be $n_1 + n_2(g_d(n + n_1, \hat{R}(R)))$. The desired and actual rates of accumulation will be equal at the intersection of the two functions, indicated by the pair $[n + n_1^0 + n_2^0, R^0]$. A higher exogenous rate of growth of Harrod-efficient primary inputs, $n + n_1^*$, will be associated with higher desired and actual rates of accumulation, illustrated by the dashed lines, which will again be equal at the intersection of the shifted functions, indicated by the pair $[n + n_1^* + n_2^*, R^*]$. The locus $g_d = g_a$ in Figure 23.2 is the set of all such intersection points and will have the shape indicated because the actual accumulation function, for which $0 < \delta n_2/\delta g_d < 1$, shifts more than does the desired accumulation function.

4. The weights will be equal to the shares in gross output and, under competitive conditions, can be interpreted as the partial input-output elasticities, e.g. $WL/PQ = \frac{\delta Q}{\delta L} \frac{L}{Q}$.

5. When certain aggregation procedures are carried out in these cases, the traditional aggregate measures will correspond to the newer measures with the possibility that the aggregate traditional measures, subject to an aggregation problem, would show higher rates of technical progress than any of the individual activity traditional measures (see Hulten, 1978; Domar, 1961). For an illustration of the confusions which result when intermediate inputs are considered in traditional measures of total factor productivity, see Sato and Suzawa (1983).

6. For a discussion of a closely related phenomenon, see L. L. Pasinetti's defense of his concept of vertically integrated sectors in Pasinetti, 1980 and 1981, chap. 6, 'The Empirical Significance of Vertically Integrated Analysis'.

7. One gets the same results, of course, if one capitalizes the services of 'salesman', the wages and salaries of whom could be said to be a lasting contribution to the activity's production and profitability.

8. The new measures of total factor productivity may also help in understanding externalities some authors (e.g. Nelson, 1982) argue are associated with interactivity R & D expenditures.

References

Asimakopulos, A. (1984) 'Joan Robinson and Economic Theory', *Banca Nazionale del Lavoro Quarterly Review*, 151: 381–409.

Domar, E. (1961) 'On the Measurement of Technological Change', *Economic Journal*, 71: 709–29.

Gram, H. and Walsh, V. (1983) 'Joan Robinson's Economics in Retrospect', *Journal of Economic Literature*, 21: 518–50.

Griliches, Z. (ed.) (1984) *R & D, Patents and Productivity* (Chicago: University of Chicago Press for the National Bureau of Economic Research).

Harrod, R. F. (1956) *Foundations of Inductive Logic* (London: Macmillan).

Harrod, R. F. (1961) 'The "Neutrality" of Improvements', *Economic Journal*, 71: 300–4.

Hulten, C. (1978) 'Growth Accounting With Intermediate Inputs', *Review of Economic Studies*, 34: 511–18.

Hulten, C. (1979) 'On the "Importance" of Productivity Change', *American Economic Review*, 69: 126–36.

Keynes, J. M. (1921) *A Treatise on Probability*, reprinted as vol. VIII, *The Collected writings of John Maynard Keynes* (London: Macmillan, 1973).

Nelson, R. (1982) 'The Role of Knowledge in R & D Efficiency', *Quarterly Journal of Economics*, 97: 453–70.

Pasinetti, L. L. (1974) 'The Rate of Profit in an Expanding Economy', *Growth and Income Distribution: Essays in Economic Theory* (Cambridge: Cambridge University Press).

Pasinetti, L. L. (1980) 'The Notion of Vertical Integration in Economic Analysis' (ed.) L. L. Pasinetti, *Essays on the Theory of Joint Production* (New York: Columbia University Press).

Pasinetti, L. L. (1981) *Structural Change and Economic Growth* (Cambridge: Cambridge University Press).

Peterson, W. (1979) 'Total Factor Productivity in the UK: A Disaggregated Analysis' (eds) K. D. Patterson and Kerry Schott, *The Measurement of Capital: Theory and Practice* (London: Macmillan).

Postner, H. and L. Wesa (1983) *Canadian Productivity Growth: An Alternative (Input–Output) Analysis* (Ottawa: Economic Council of Canada).

Robinson, J. (1962) *Essays in the Theory of Economic Growth* (London: Macmillan).

Robinson, J. (1965) *The Accumulation of Capital*, 3rd edn (London: Macmillan).

Robinson, J. (1975) 'Introduction 1974', in *Collected Economic Papers*, vol. 3 (Oxford: Blackwell).

Rymes, T. K. (1971) *On Concepts of Capital and Technical Change* (Cambridge: Cambridge University Press).

Rymes, T. K. (1972) 'The Measurement of Capital and Total Factor Productivity in the Context of the Cambridge Theory of Capital', *Review of Income and Wealth*, 18: 70–108.

Rymes, T. K. (1983) 'More on the Measurement of Total Factor Productivity', *Review of Income and Wealth*, 39: 297–316.

Rymes, T. K. (1986) 'The Measurement of Multifactoral Productivity in an Input–Output Framework: New Canadian Estimates', *Problems of Compilation of Input–Output Tables* (Baden, Austria: Austrian Statistical Society).

Rymes, T. K. and A. Cas (1986) 'On the Feasibility of Measuring Multifactor Productivity in Canada' (Ottawa: Statistics Canada (Input–Output Division)), Cambridge University Press, forthcoming.

Sato, R. and G. S. Suzawa (1983) *Research and Productivity: Endogenous Technical Change* (Boston, Mass.: Auburn House.)

Steedman, I. (1983) 'On the Measurement and Aggregation of Productivity Increase', *Metroeconomica*, 35: 223–33.

Steedman, I. (1985) 'On the "Impossibility" of Hicks-Neutral Technical Change', *Economic Journal*: 95: 746–58.

Usher, D. (1980) *The Measurement of Economic Growth* (New York: Columbia University Press).

24 The Wage-share and the Rate of Exchange of Labor Time

Robert Dixon

Joan Robinson subscribed to an elegant model of the real wage in which the wage is related to the average product of labor in the wage-goods sector and the proportion of the total workforce which is engaged in the production of wage-goods. Clearly, this model also suffices to account for the distribution of income (between wages and profits) within the wage-goods sector. Elsewhere (Dixon, 1981), I have set out a model of the wage-share in the economy as a whole, using Robinson's model of the wage-goods sector as a starting point. In that paper it was shown that the proximate determinants of the economy-wide wage-share are: the proportion of the total workforce which is engaged in producing wage-goods, the price level of wage-goods relative to the general price level, and the level of the average product of labor in the wage-goods sector relative to the average product of labor in the economy taken as a whole. In this contribution I wish to demonstrate that these last two items (i.e. relative prices and relative labor productivities), taken together, are a measure of the rate of exchange of the labor time expended in the production of the various outputs produced in the economy. We are thus able to derive an expression for the economy-wide wage-share in terms of the sectoral composition of employment and the (implicit) rate of exchange of labor time.

I begin with a (re)statement of a model of distribution in which the wage-share is related to the proportion of the workforce which is employed in the wage-goods sector, relative labor productivities and relative prices. It is then shown that the terms involving aggregate prices and productivities may be disaggregated into weighted averages of sectoral phenomena and thereby arrive at an expression for the (economy-wide) wage-share in terms of the division of labor between the sectors and (a ratio of) the prices and labor productivities prevailing in the two sectors. In the final sections, the notion of the rate of exchange of labor time is introduced and it is demonstrated that it is this rate of exchange which is measured by the ratio of prices times productivities in the two sectors. For simplicity, we will restrict ourselves to a classical model in which we have two (vertically integrated) sectors, one producing wage-goods and the other capital goods and where (it is assumed that) all profits are saved and that all wages are spent on consumer goods and services in the current period.

1   A MODEL OF LABOR'S SHARE

We may define the wage-share for the economy as a whole to be the ratio between the total wages bill in all sectors of the economy (W) and the value of aggregate output in current prices (Y). The total wages bill will equal the total number of workers employed (L) multiplied by the (assumed uniform) money wage per worker (w_m). Aggregate output in current prices will equal the product of the (implicit) price deflator (p) of aggregate output times the level of real output in all sectors of the economy over the relevant period (Q). So that the economy-wide wage-share (ω) may be measured as:

$$\omega = \frac{W}{Y} = \frac{w_m L}{pQ} = \frac{w_m}{p(Q/L)} \tag{1}$$

The ratio of aggregate real output (i.e. output measured at constant prices (Q)) to total employment (L), is simply a measure of the average product per worker in the economy as a whole (A), so that our expression for the economy-wide wage-share may be written as:

$$\omega = \frac{w_m}{pA} \tag{2}$$

which is to say that the wage-share in the economy as a whole will equal the ratio between the average money wage per worker (w_m) and the (average) value of output per worker in current prices (pA).

We turn now to an examination of Joan Robinson's model of the relationship between the wage-share in the wage-goods sector (assumed to be fully integrated) and the proportion of the total workforce which is engaged in the production of wage-goods (see Robinson, 1960, p. 23ff).

Given that workers do not save, the total amount of money spent on wage-goods in any period will equal the value of the total wages-bill (in the economy as a whole) over that period. The quantity of wage-goods which will be purchased (Qd_{wg}) will depend upon the total value of expenditure on wage-goods in money terms ($w_m L$) and the (average) price of wage-goods (p_{wg}). The real value of demand for wage-goods will therefore equal:

$$Qd_{wg} = \frac{w_m L}{p_{wg}}$$

The output of wage-goods (Q_{wg}) will equal the number of workers in the wage-goods sector (L_{wg}) multiplied by the average amount of wage-goods produced per worker (A_{wg}), so that:

$$Q_{wg} = A_{wg}L_{wg}$$

Let us assume that real output in any period is just equal to the real value of demand (= sales). This equality could come about because the price of wage-goods varies (relative to the money wage-rate) so as to quickly 'clear' the market for wage-goods, or it could be that, with prices inflexible (in Hicks's sense) the level of output adjusts quite rapidly to the level of demand. Given that current output equals current demand, we have:

$$\frac{w_m L}{p_{wg}} = A_{wg}L_{wg} \tag{3}$$

We may rearrange (3) to yield an expression for the share of wages in the value of output of the wage-goods sector; as

$$\frac{w_m}{p_{wg}A_{wg}} = \frac{L_{wg}}{L} \tag{4}$$

Given that the real-wage is equal to the money wage deflated by the price of (a basket of) wage-goods (w_m/p_{wg}), we see from (4) that 'the real wage bears the same proportion to the average output per man employed in producing [wage-goods] that employment in that sector bears to total employment' (Robinson, 1964, p. 411). Alternatively, we may say that, the larger the proportion of the workforce which is engaged in the production of wage-goods, the nearer will the money wage approximate the average revenue per worker in the wage-goods sector, and the larger will be the wage-share in the wage-goods sector.

Notice that we may now establish a relationship between the economy-wide wage-share and the ratio (L_{wg}/L). From (2), it must be the case that:

$$\omega = \frac{w_m}{pA} = \frac{w_m}{p_{wg}A_{wg}} \frac{p_{wg}A_{wg}}{pA} \tag{5}$$

Substitution of (4) into (5) yields an expression for the economy-wide wage-share:

$$\omega = (L_{wg}/L)((p_{wg}A_{wg})/(pA)) \tag{6}$$

which is to say that the share of wages in income in the economy as a whole will depend upon the proportion of the workforce which is engaged in the production of wage-goods and also upon relative prices and relative labor productivities.

In the following section of this paper I will show that the ratio $[(p_{wg}A_{wg})/(pA)]$ in equation (6) may be expressed in terms of the particular prices and labor productivities prevailing in the two sectors of the economy. This yields an alternative expression for the economy-wide wage-share.

2   AN ALTERNATIVE EXPRESSION FOR THE WAGE-SHARE

In the classical two-sector model, all activity may be classified as taking place in either the wage-goods sector (denoted, as before, by the subscript *wg*) or the capital-goods sector (denoted by the subscript *cg*). (We will assume that each sector is fully integrated.)

Our expression for the wage-share (equation (6)) refers *inter alia* to the ratio between the price level and labor productivity in the wage-goods sector and the price level and labor productivity in the economy as a whole. In this section of the paper, we shall investigate the relationship between that ratio (i.e. $(p_{wg}A_{wg}/pA)$) and the particular prices and labor productivities prevailing within the wage-goods sector and the capital-goods sector.

If we multiply the economy-wide price level by (p) the economy-wide level of labor productivity (A), the result is simply equal to the value of aggregate output measured in current prices per worker (i.e. (Y/L)). Thus:

$$[(p_{wg}A_{wg})/(pA)] = [(p_{wg}A_{wg})/(Y/L)] \tag{7}$$

The value of total output measured in current prices (Y) will equal the sum of the values of price times output in each sector. So that:

$$Y = p_{wg}Q_{wg} + p_{cg}Q_{cg}$$

It follows that the value of output per worker in current prices will equal:

$$pA = Y/L = p_{wg}(Q_{wg}/L) + p_{cg}(Q_{cg}/L)$$

The above may be rewritten as:

$$pA = p_{wg}(Q_{wg}/L_{wg})(L_{wg}/L) + p_{cg}(Q_{cg}/L_{cg})(L_{cg}/L)$$

which becomes:

$$pA = p_{wg}A_{wg}(L_{wg}/L) + p_{cg}A_{cg}(1 - (L_{wg}/L)) \tag{8}$$

We may therefore say that the ratio of the value of output per worker in the wage-goods sector to the value of output per worker in the economy as a whole (both measured in current prices) will equal:

$$\frac{p_{wg}A_{wg}}{pA} = \frac{p_{wg}A_{wg}}{p_{wg}A_{wg}(L_{wg}/L) + p_{cg}A_{cg}(1 - (L_{wg}/L))}$$

which may be rewritten as:

$$\frac{p_{wg}A_{wg}}{pA} = \frac{1}{(L_{wg}/L) + (1 - (L_{wg}/L))((p_{cg}A_{cg})/(p_{wg}A_{wg}))} \tag{9}$$

Substitution of (9) into (6) yields an expression for the economy-wide wage-share in terms of sectoral prices and labor productivities:

$$\omega = \frac{1}{1 + \frac{(1 - (L_{wg}/L))}{(L_{wg}/L)}((p_{cg}A_{cg})/(p_{wg}A_{wg}))}$$

Since $(1 - (L_{wg}/L))$ is equal to (L_{cg}/L) the above expression becomes:

$$\omega = \frac{1}{1 + L_{cg}/L_{wg}((p_{cg}A_{cg})/(p_{wg}A_{wg}))} \tag{10}$$

which is to say that the economy-wide wage-share depends upon the sectoral division of labor and also upn the relative prices and relative labor productivities prevailing in the two sectors.

In the next section we shall see that the terms in equation (10) which involve relative prices and labor productivities may be interpreted as the implicit rate of exchange of the labor time expended in the two sectors.

3 THE RATE OF EXCHANGE OF LABOR TIME

Our model of the distribution of income (10) contains an expression representing not (just) relative prices, but rather the relative (money) values of output per worker in the two sectors.[1] I will now proceed to demonstrate that the ratio which the value of output per worker in one sector (or industry) bears to the value of output per worker in another, is in fact a measure of the amount of labor time in one sector which 'exchanges' for one unit of labor time in another.[2] Using the symbol A to stand for, say, daily output per worker, the amount of money represented by the multiplication of price and the average product of labor for the capital-goods sector (i.e. $(p_{cg}A_{cg})$), is a measure of the amount of money the product of one day's labor in the capital-goods sector will fetch in the market. If we divide this by the price of wage-goods (p_{wg}) we will have an expression for the amount of wage-goods which 'exchange' for the results of one day's labor in the capital-goods sector (i.e. $[(p_{cg}A_{cg})/(p_{wg})]$). If we now divide this expression by the average (daily) product of labor in the wage-goods sector, we will have an expression for the amount of labor time in the wage-goods sector which (implicitly) 'exchanges', in the market for commodities, for one unit of labor in the capital-goods sector $[(p_{cg}A_{cg})/)p_{wg}A_{wg}]$.[3]

Notice, in passing, that if $(p_{cg}/p_{wg}) = (A_{wg}/A_{cg})$ (this is the 'labor values' case; see Dixon (1981, p. 400ff) for details), the rate of exchange of labor time will equal unity, i.e. one hour in the capital-goods sector will (implicitly) exchange for one hour's labor in the wage-goods sector. In addition it will be observed that if, in some 'early and rude state of society' (Smith, 1950, p. 53), prices are simply equal to unit labor cost (and given that the money wage is uniform across sectors), the relative price ratio will equal $(p_{cg}/p_{wg}) = ((w_m/A_{cg})/(w_m/A_{wg})) = (A_{wg}/A_{cg})$, that is, prices will be exactly proportional to embodied labor time, and the implicit rate of exchange of labor time $((p_{cg}A_{cg})/(p_{wg}A_{wg}))$ will equal $((A_{wg}/A_{cg})(A_{cg}/A_{wg}))$, which (again) equals unity.

4 THE RATE OF EXCHANGE OF LABOR TIME FURTHER CONSIDERED

We have seen that the economy-wide wage-share has as its proximate determinants, the social division of labor (that is, the proportion of the total workforce which is engaged in the production of wage-goods) and the (implicit) rate at which labor-time is exchanged between the two sectors. This stress upon the rate of exchange of labor time is appropriate because in a system of capitalist commodity production 'the exchange of commodities is an exchange of the products of the labor of individual producers' (Sweezy, 1942, p. 27).[4] It follows that the labor is alienated labor.[5] This is because 'labor does not only create goods; it also produces itself and the worker as a *commodity*, and indeed, in the same proportion as it produces goods. This fact simply implies that the objects produced by labor, its product, now stands opposed to it as an *alien* being, as power independent of the producer' (Marx, in Fromm, 1966, p. 95). Furthermore, our approach illustrates the doctrine of commodity fetishism[6] because, in revealing that the rate of exchange of labor time is implicit in the model of the wage-share, we have presented '... an example of a peculiar fact which pervades the whole economy and has produced serious confusion in the minds of the bourgeois economist – economics is not concerned with things but with relations between persons, and in the final analysis between classes; these relations, however, are always bound to things and appear as things' (Engels, in Marx, 1970, p. 226).

Seen in the light of the preceding paragraph, it is clear that our model of the wage-share (based as it is upon Robinson's model of the wage-goods sector), is rich in classical and Marxian insights.

Notes

1. By definition (and using the notation introduced earlier):

$$[(p_{cg}A_{cg})/(p_{wg}A_{wg})] = [((p_{cg}Q_{cg})/L_{cg})/((p_{wg}Q_{wg})/L_{wg})]$$

    All of which is to say that amongst the terms on the RHS of (10) is a term which measures the relative (nominal) values of output per worker in the two sectors.
2. I am mindful of Marx's statement that 'we should not say that one man's hour is worth another man's hour, but rather that one man during an hour is worth just as much as another man during an hour. Time is everything, man is nothing; he is at the most time's carcass' (Marx, 1963, p. 54).
3. I am tempted to define this ratio to be 'mediated value' or 'value in exchange', that is, labor acquiring a comparative worth through the mediation of the market. However, the adoption of this language may confuse the reader familiar with Marx.
4. 'The notion that the exchange of commodities is in essence the exchange of the labor of the men who produce them, became something of a common place as the [eighteenth] century progressed' (Meek, 1973, p. 41).
5. For an excellent exposition of this point, see Colletti (1972, pp. 82–92).
6. Heilbroner describes this doctrine as asserting that 'a commodity is not just a thing, but also a container of invisible social relationships' (Heilbroner, 1980, p. 102).

References

Colletti, L. (1972) *From Rousseau to Lenin* (London: New Left Books).

Dixon, R. (1981) 'A Model of Distribution', *Journal of Post Keynesian Economics* 3: 383–402.

Fromm, E. (1961; new edn 1966) *Marx's Concept of Man* (New York: Frederick Ungar).

Heilbroner, R. L. (1980) *Marxism: For and Against* (New Year: Norton).

Marx, K. (1963) *Poverty of Philosophy* (New York: International Publishers).

Marx, K. (1970) *Contribution to the Critique of Political Economy* (Moscow: Progress Publishers).

Meek, R. (1956; 2nd edn 1973) *Studies in the Labour Theory of Value* (London: Lawrence & Wishart).

Robinson, J. (1960) *Exercises in Economic Analysis* (London: Macmillan).

Robinson, J. (1964) 'Solow on the Rate of Return', *Economic Journal* 74: 410–17.

Smith, A. (Cannan edn 1950) *The Wealth of Nations* (London: Methuen).

Sweezy, P. (1942) *The Theory of Capitalist Development* (New York: Modern Reader Paperbacks).

Part IV

Development and Trade

25 The Theory of International Trade, Steady-state Analysis and Economics of Development

T. N. Srinivasan*

1 INTRODUCTION

In one of her many lucid critiques of mainstream economics, Joan Robinson wrote:

> Micro questions – concerning the relative prices of commodities and the behaviour of individuals, firms and households – cannot be discussed in the air without any reference to the structure of the economy in which they exist and to the process of cyclical and secular change. Equally, macro theories of accumulation and effective demand are generalizations about micro behaviour: the relation of income to expenditure for consumption, of investment to the pursuit of profit, of the management of placements, in which financial wealth is held, to rates of interest and of wages to the level of prices results from the reactions of individuals and social groups to the situation in which they find themselves. *Even the artificial conception of a stationary state has to be specified in terms of the behaviour of its inhabitants.* [Emphasis added.]

She went on to add that 'if there is no micro theory, there cannot be any

*I first met Mrs Robinson (in 1959 or thereabouts) when I was a graduate student at Yale. She gave a talk based on her book *The Accumulation of Capital*, in which she excoriated neoclassical capital theory and the notion of marginal productivity of capital. My classmate, Mordecai Kurz, and I, met with her after her talk. We pointed out that for defining marginal productivity of capital one does not require a neoclassical malleable aggregate of capital, and that in a model with time phasing and a disaggregated set of capital goods, Malinvaud (1953) was able to articulate a perfectly well-defined marginal productivity of capital. She graciously listened to us but we did not succeed in convincing her! For that matter, many writers in the Sraffian tradition to this day continue to assert mistakenly that there is no meaningful marginal productivity of capital once the heterogeneity of capital goods is recognized. I saw Mrs Robinson subsequently on one or two occasions during her many visits to India, but we never discussed capital theory again!

macro theory either' (Robinson, 1977, p.1320). She approvingly quoted Hicks in the same article to the effect that models of steady growth (i.e. growing economy counterparts of the classical stationary state) are futile and the whole point of a steady state is to study disturbances (including policy shifts) that take the economy away from it.

It will be argued below (Section 2) that some of the radical critiques[1] of the neoclassical presumption that free trade is the optimal policy for a small open economy, are based on irrelevant comparisons of steady-state equilibria associated with autarky (or more generally restricted trade) and with free trade, thus committing the very mistake against which Joan Robinson warned us. Also, a class of models meant to address issues of trade between developing and developed countries that goes under the generic name North–South Models will be discussed in Section 3. These models often arrive at their conclusions that are at variance with mainstream analysis, mainly because of their economy-wide or macro assumptions that have no basis in rational micro behavior, thus underscoring the importance of Mrs Robinson's insistence on a satisfactory micro theory as a foundation for any macro theory.

It is well known that Mrs Robinson, along with E. Chamberlain, was a pioneer in the attempts to break away from the confines of perfect competition, a centerpiece of neoclassical analysis. She, along with Kaldor, was also critical of the assumption of non-increasing returns to scale in production, which is one of the sufficient conditions on which much of neoclassical competitive equilibrium theory is based. Interestingly, recent developments in the theory of international trade, unlike the pure competition-based traditional models of Ricardo and Heckscher–Ohlin–Samuelson (H–O–S), incorporate increasing returns to scale and non-competitive behavior in the analysis. The relevance of some of these models and their rehabilitation of policy intervention in international trade for the development strategies and policies of developing countries will be assessed in the fourth and final section of the paper.

2   PROBLEMS WITH STEADY-STATE ANALYSIS[2]

Ian Steedman's (1979) book inspired by Joan Robinson was intended to provide an alternative approach to what he viewed as the static H–O–S theory for analyzing trade among growing economies. By adopting a neo-Ricardian framework in which production is time-phased and all of the capital used is in the form of working capital, he showed that some of the H–O–S propositions about patterns of trade and the effects of trade policy do not hold. Ethier (1979) argued that this assertion has to be qualified, once appropriate modifications are made to the standard H–O–S analysis to account for time-phasing. This was disputed by Metcalfe and Steedman

(1981) but reaffirmed by Ethier (1981). This debate need not concern us here. What concerns us is Steedman's deliberate choice to consider only steady growth paths and thereby restrict his analysis to comparative dynamics of such paths. As he put it: 'Thus processes of transition from one steady growth path to another will not be discussed: it may be noted in particular that the states of autarky and free trade (or restricted trade) will only ever be compared and *no attempt will be made to analyse the process of adjustment from one such state to another*' (Steedman, 1979, p.11) (emphasis added).

In his insightful review of Steedman's book, Avinash Dixit (1981) pointed out the limitations of steady-state models. He concentrated on three things, namely, the alternatives to steady-state analysis, the questions that can or cannot be answered in that framework, and how the same questions could be answered by using more general modes of analysis. There is no need to go over the ground covered so well by Dixit. It is enough here to concentrate on the free trade/autarky comparison emphasized by Steedman. In particular, we will argue that once the appropriate behavioral assumptions are incorporated and proper account is taken of the adjustment process from one steady state to another, it will *always* be in the interest of a small open economy to follow the policy of free trade, even though in the steady state welfare under autarky may be higher (and *if* higher in the specific example of the Appendix to this paper) than the welfare under free trade. Thus, a steady-state analysis can in this instance lead to wrong policy conclusions.

The time-phased Ricardian character of Steedman's analysis is not essential for establishing the above assertions. We will therefore use the traditional two-commodity, two-factor H–O–S model.[3] The only non-produced primary factor of production is labor which is assumed to grow exponentially at a given rate n. One of the two commodities is a pure consumption good and the other a pure investment good. All consumers in this economy are identical and each derives an instantaneous utility $U(C)$ from his or her consumption C and her intertemporal welfare is represented by the discounted sum (at a non-negative rate ρ) of instantaneous utilities. Leisure does not enter the utility function so that each consumer inelastically supplies labor up to her endowment. Under autarky the investment needs of the economy have to be met from domestic output of investment goods. For simplicity let us assume that capital depreciates exponentially at a specified rate δ. Then the optimal growth path of the economy solves the following problem (Problem I):

$$\text{Maximize} \int_0^\infty e^{-\rho t} U(C(t)) dt \text{ subject to} \tag{0}$$

$$\dot{k}(t) = 1_i(t) f(k_i(t)) - (n+\delta)k(t) \tag{1}$$

$$C(t) = (1 - 1_I(t))g(k_C(t)) \tag{2}$$

$$k(t) = 1_I(t)k_I(t) + (1 - 1_I(t))k_C(t) \tag{3}$$

$$1_I(t), k_I(t), k(t), c(t), k_C(t) \geqslant 0 \text{ for all } t \tag{4}$$

and $k(0)$ given, where $\tag{5}$

$k(t)$ is the aggregate capital–labor ratio at time t

$\dot{k}(t)$ rate of change of aggregate capital–labor ratio at time t
$1_I(t)$ proportion of labor force employed in producing investment goods
$k_I(t), k_C(t)$ capital–labor ratios in the production of investment and consumption goods, respectively, at time t
$C(t)$ per worker consumption at time t
$f(k_I(t)), g(k_C(t))$ average product of labor at time t in the production of investment and consumption goods, respectively.

The assumption of constant returns to scale in production of both goods has been utilized in setting up the problem in terms of variables that are normalized by the size of the labor force. Also, for simplicity, it is assumed that the labor force is a constant proportion of total population implying that *per capita* consumption is a constant proportion of consumption per worker. This constant proportionality is subsumed in the function $U(C)$. Also, it is assumed that the production functions are such that it will not be optimal to depart from employing available labor and capital stock fully at each t.

It is well known that given $\rho > 0$ a solution to the above problem exists and it converges to a unique steady state (that is, independent of the given initial capital–labor ratio $k(0)$) characterized by:

$$f'(k_I^A) = n + \rho + \delta \tag{6}$$

$$\frac{f(k_I^A) - k_I^A f'(k_I^A)}{f'(k_I^A)} = \frac{g(k_C^A) - k_C^A g'(k_C^A)}{g'(k_C^A)} \tag{7}$$

$$(n + \delta)k^A = 1_I^A f(k_I^A) \tag{8}$$

$$1_I^A = \frac{k_C^A - k_C^A}{k_I^A - k_C^A} \tag{9}$$

$$C^A = (1 - 1_I^A)g(k_C^A) \tag{10}$$

The interpretation of (6)–(10) is straightforward. The rate of growth of labor force (n), the pure rate of time preference (ρ), and the depreciation rate (δ) of capital stock together determine the own rate of interest on capital, i.e. the marginal product of capital in the production of investment goods. This is shown in (6). Equation (7) represents the condition that the factor allocation between the two sectors is efficient, i.e. the marginal rate of substitution between capital and labor (that is, the ratio of marginal product of labor to that of capital) is the same in the two sectors. Equation (8) says that the investment needed to maintain the aggregate capital–labor ratio constant (as it has to be along a steady state) equals the output of investment goods per unit of labor. Equations (8) and (9) together determine the aggregate capital labor ratio k^A and the proportion of labor 1_I force employed in the production of investment goods. Equation (10) gives *per capita* consumption along the steady state.

It can be shown that C^A, the *per capita* consumption (and hence $U(C^A)$ the instantaneous utility of *per capita* consumption) is a decreasing function of ρ, the rate of pure time preference. As $\rho \to 0$, $C^A \to$ its maximum value. Let us denote by p_C^A the autarky steady-state relative price of consumer goods in terms of investment goods. By definition $p_C^A = f'(k_I^A)/g'(k_C^A)$.

Suppose now the economy has an opportunity to trade with the rest of the world at a *constant relative price* p_C^T of consumption goods in terms of capital goods (that is, the economy is assumed to be too small to influence p_C^T). With the maximand the same as in Problem I, and denoting by $q_C(t)$ the *per capita* outputs of consumption goods and by $C(t)$ *per capita* consumption, the constraints of the problem of the trading economy (Problem II) become (assuming that there is no foreign lending or borrowing so that trade is balanced):

$$\dot{k}(t) = 1_I(t)f_I(k_I(t)) + p_C^T\{q_C(t) - C(t)\} - (n+\delta)k(t) \tag{1'}$$

$$q_C(t) = (1 - 1_I(t))g(k_C(t)) \tag{2'}$$

Constraints (3) and (5) remain the same as in Problem I with $q_C(t)$ added to the list of variables required to be non-negative. Equation (1') is nothing but the statement that trade is balanced or equivalently that gross domestic expenditure $p_C^T C(t) + \dot{k} + (n+\delta)k(t)$ (i.e. the sum of consumption expenditure $p_C C(t)$ and gross investment expenditure $\dot{k} + (n+\delta)k(t)$ equals gross income or value of output $p_C^T q_C(t) + 1_I(t)f_I(k_I(t))$.

From a comparison (1)–(5) and (1'), (2'), (3)–(5) it is easily seen that *any feasible* solution to Problem I yields a *feasible* solution to Problem II if we set $q_C(t) = C(t)$. This is just another way of saying that autarky is a *feasible* policy option even when trading opportunity is available. But it is not necessarily an optimal policy. As such the maximized value of the objective function (i.e. intertemporal welfare) of Problem II cannot be lower than that achieved in Problem I. Thus, having the option to trade cannot lower welfare.

One can go further. Assuming that there are no factor intensity reversals in the usual sense, it can be shown that the optimal solution to Problem II exists and converges to a unique steady state in which the economy is specialized in the production of consumer goods (investment goods) if the relative price p_C^A of consumer goods in the autarky steady state is less than (greater than) the world market price p_C^T, i.e. the economy specializes in the good in which it has a comparative advantage. If $p_C^T = p_C^A$, there are a continuum of steady states consistent with trade to one of which the optimal solution to Problem II will converge depending upon the initial capital labor ratio $k(0)$. Although the steady state to which the optimal solution converges is one of complete specialization in one of the goods when $p_C^T \neq p_C^A$, along the optimal path the economy can start from an initial specialization in the other good, then pass through a phase of incomplete specialization, and then in the final phase specialize in the good associated with the steady state. Thus, confining one's attention to the steady state can be misleading in that it conceals the trade pattern reversal that can take place as the economy matures. *But for all t along the optimal path trade will be free, i.e. for a small open dynamic economy free trade is the optimal policy.*

More specifically, if $p_C^A \neq p_C^T$ the trading economy's optimal path will converge to the steady state characterized by:

Specialization in Consumer Goods	Specialization in Investment Goods	
$(p_C^A < p_C^T)$	$(p_C^A < p_C^T)$	
$q_C^T = g(k_C^T)$	$q_C^T = 0$	(11)
$p_C^T g_C'(k_C^T) = n + \rho + \delta$	$f_I'(k_I^T) = (n + \rho + \delta)$	(12)
$p_C^T C^T = p_C g(k_C^T) - (n + \delta)k_C^T$	$p_C^T C^T = f_I(k_I^T) - (n + \delta)k_I^T$	(13)

It can be shown that regardless of specialization (i.e. whether $p_C^A < p_C^T$ or $p_C^A > p_C^T$) the steady-state consumption C^T is a decreasing function of ρ approaching its maximum as ρ approaches zero. Although the difference $C^T - C^A$ between trading and autarky steady-state consumptions is *positive* for $\rho = 0$, there is nothing to preclude $C^T - C^A$ becoming *negative* as ρ increases. In other words, for sufficiently large positive values of ρ, C^A could exceed C^T, i.e. the autarky steady-state consumption (and hence welfare) can exceed the free trade steady-state consumption and welfare. An example in which this happens is provided in the Appendix. Given such a value of ρ, an analyst looking only at steady states may conclude that autarky is the superior policy. But as we argued earlier, the maximized value of the objective function, i.e. intertemporal welfare in Problem II, can never be lower than that in Problem I. Thus, a comparison of steady-state welfares leads to an inappropriate ranking of policies.

There is nothing paradoxical about the above conclusion. It arises simply from the fact of neglecting the gains and losses in welfare in moving from one steady state to another through a non-steady-state adjustment process. Thus, in the situation where C^A exceeds C^T, even if the economy is initially on the autarky steady state and has the option to continue on it and reap the welfare $U(C^A)$ every instant, it is optimal to utilize the trading opportunity freely by changing resource allocation even though the economy eventually will converge to a lower level steady-state welfare. What happens is that along the optimal path (see Figure 25.1), initially welfare will exceed $U(C^A)$, equal it at some point t^*, and eventually fall below it to reach $U(C^T)$. However, the *discounted* sum of the difference in utilities compared to $U(C^A)$ is positive.

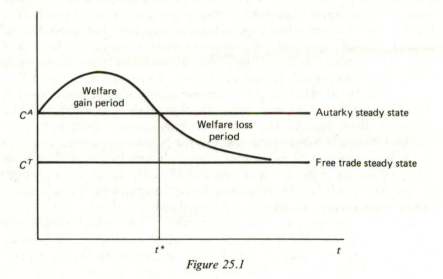

Figure 25.1

3 NORTH–SOUTH MODELS[4]

There is a growing literature (see, for example, Findlay, 1980; Vines, 1985; Vines and Kanbur, 1985; Galor, 1986) devoted to formal models of trade, aid, and factor movements between the developing countries and the developed or industrialized countries. These models called variously as North–South, Centre–Periphery or Dependency models, are all based on some *assumed* structural difference between the two groups of countries. Many, though not all, of the models concentrate their attention only on the steady-state properties of the models. The fundamental problem with these models is that, first, they rarely link the structural rigidities to some underlying exogenous features of technology, tastes, or institution. Second, and more important, they assume that the rigidities and inflexibilities will remain forever and not, more plausibly, just in the short or medium run. It is enough here to consider one such model for illustrative purposes.

Findlay (1980) considers a two-region model in which each region is *specialized* in producing its export good. The North produces a single homogeneous manufacture under a constant returns to scale neoclassical technology with capital and labor as inputs, saves a fixed proportion of its output, fully employs its exponentially growing labor force in a competitive market for goods as factors. The part of the output that is not saved (and invested) is spent either on domestic manufactures or on imports of primary products from the South. The South's technology for the production of exports is again neoclassical with capital and labor as inputs, except that labor supply to the export sector is infinitely elastic at a fixed product wage. Southern workers consume all their wages and capitalists save part of their profits. Consumption expenditures of workers and capitalists is divided between spending on home-produced primary products and imported manufactures depending upon relative prices.

A unique steady-state equilibrium in which North and South grow at a rate equal to the growth rate of the effective supply of labor in the North is shown to exist. Also, convergence to this steady state from arbitrary initial conditions is established. The comparative dynamics (i.e. impact on the steady-state equilibrium) of increases in the Northern propensity to save and improvements in its technology are simply that its *per capita* income increases and its terms of trade improve while the South *loses* on both counts. As discussed earlier in Section 2, such comparisons of steady states can be misleading, if not wrong in their policy implications.

As Findlay himself admits, the assumptions of the model, such as the absence of capital mobility in response to differing profit rates between North and South, production specialization and, above all, the assumption of unlimited labor supply at a fixed real wage in the South, are very restrictive. It is unlikely that the savings behavior of households remains unaffected by the evolution of their incomes and the opportunities for investment. Nor is it likely that capitalists will not compare the returns from alternative uses to which their capital can be put, at home and abroad. Even less likely is the evolution of terms of trade over time that will ensure that both regions continue to be specialized in the production of their products. To paraphrase Joan Robinson's admonition, even the artificial conception of trade in a steady state between regions has to be specified in terms of rational behavior of all its inhabitants, in the North as well as the

South, workers as well as capitalists! Findlay's and most other North–South models can be criticized for ignoring this requirement.

4 IMPERFECT COMPETITION, INCREASING RETURNS, INTERNATIONAL TRADE AND DEVELOPMENT[5]

In the last decade some perceptive theorists saw an opportunity to engage in intellectual arbitrage by the application of developments in the field of industrial organization to the theory of international trade and policy. From a positive perspective, one class of applications appeared to explain better some stylized facts (such as intra-industry trade in differentiated products between countries with similar factor endowments) by taking into account a distinguishing feature of modern industrial technology, namely, increasing returns to scale and the associated non-competitive market structure, modelled as the large group Chamberlinian monopolistic competition with free entry. From a normative perspective, another class of applications based on partial equilibrium oligopoly models generated an active role for government intervention under certain circumstances. And some analysts in Western developed countries, particularly in the USA, saw in the latter both an explanation of the success of the Japanese in capturing a large share of the world markets in many products including, in particular, the so-called high-technology industries and an argument for an industrial policy in their own countries. Some development economists, particularly those predisposed to government intervention, also saw the latter as refuting what they viewed as the neoclassical prescription of free trade (Stewart, 1984; Helleiner, 1985).

The arguments that emerge from the new theories in favor of an interventionist trade policy can be grouped into three categories: profit-shifting arguments, neo-infant industry arguments, and Research and Development (R & D) expenditure arguments. The profit-shifting argument is simply that appropriate government policy intervention can shift part of the oligopoly rents earned by foreigners to the home economy. In traditional trade theory, intervention in trade is appropriate only for a country that has market power in international trade that is not perceived by its price-taking domestic producers and consumers. As long as its trading partners do not retaliate, such a country, by levying an appropriate tariff, can optimally exploit its market power at the expense of its partner countries.

In contrast, the oligopoly model of rent extraction or profit shifting through trade policy instruments may be appropriate even if a country has no market power in the traditional sense. In other words, it can be argued that tariffs are appropriate policy instruments even for an open economy that is 'small' in the traditional sense as long as there are some foreign firms earning rents in the home market through oligopolistic behavior. Since most developing countries are 'small' and in many of them oligopolistic multinational firms allegedly operate, some (e.g. Helleiner, 1985) see in this an activist role for governments in foreign trade.

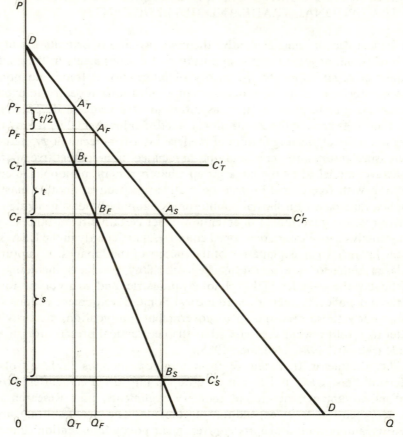

Figure 25.2

The argument is illustrated in Figure 25.2 where, for simplicity, it is assumed that there is no home production of the importable, and the foreign firm's marginal cost curve $C_F C_F'$ is horizontal. With a downward-sloping home demand curve DD (assumed to be linear for simplicity), in free trade the foreign firm will sell $0Q_F$ (at a price $0P_F$) where marginal revenue equals marginal cost, thereby earning a monopoly rent equal to the area $P_F A_F B_F C_F$. Now, imposition of a specific tariff at the rate t shifts the cost curve up to $C_T C_T'$, reduces sales to $0Q_T$, and raises prices to $0P_T$. Given linearity of the demand curve, the rise in price is only $t/2$, i.e. only half the amount of the tariff, and the monopoly rent falls to $P_T A_T B_T C_T$. Thus, the tariff diverts rents to the home economy. However, the rise in price induced by the tariff cuts into the consumer surplus by increasing the wedge between marginal cost and consumer price. The home government can, however, achieve rent diversion as well as eliminate the wedge between marginal cost and consumer price by *subsidizing* imports by the amount s equalling $C_F C_S$, and charging the monopolist a lump-sum fee (for the right to sell in the home market) equalling the total subsidy cost. It can thereby ensure that the price in the home market equals the marginal cost $0C_F$, an outcome that occurs in a competitive market and that the entire monopoly rent is shifted to the home economy! Thus, two instruments, a lump-sum tax and an import subsidy both optimally set, eliminate the wedge between marginal cost and consumer price due to monopoly as well as succeed in making the monopolist finance the subsidy he receives! While the logic of this argument is impeccable, whether many developing country governments are capable of designing and credibly implementing such a two-part tariff is open to doubt.

There are a number of other issues that arise in assessing profit-shifting arguments for trade policy (Krugman, 1986). First, a country that accounts only for a small share of the global market of an oligopolistic firm may obtain concessions even without intervention that the firm may not offer to larger countries. In any case, a small country may be unable to formulate and commit itself to a set of policies specific to the market structure in different commodities. Second, few small economies (in terms of GNP) are home bases of multinational firms so that diversion of rent in third markets from competitors to home firms through strategic trade policy is irrelevant. Third, although Krugman is correct in suggesting that the new theory justifies marketing boards for centralizing purchases of *imports* so that the boards bargain with the oligopolies supplying imports to obtain price discounts that individual importers would be unable to obtain, the available evidence on the performance of such boards is not particularly encouraging. Even without the benefit of the analytical support offered by theory, some developing countries such as India have canalized the imports of some commodities through state trading corporations. There is no strong evidence, however, that such canalization resulted in the realization of deep price discounts. Besides, as Krugman himself recognizes, the operation of such boards in the social interest presumes the existence of highly competent and honest bureaucrats at their helm. But in the real world, political patronage considerations often influence the appointment of top officials of state enterprises. Instances of corruption and division of oligopolistic rents between import suppliers and the executives of the public sector trading companies are not rare either.

The neo-infant industry argument for protection, that is, import protection-as-export promotion, is based on the existence of a *sizeable domestic market* for the product under consideration so that closing the domestic market to foreigners can speed up the learning process. Except perhaps for a few large developing economies that are at the same time sufficiently advanced technologically, developing countries by and large are unlikely to have domestic markets for high-technology products that are large enough for this argument for protection to be of any significance.

Krugman (1986) suggests that while the substantial differences in the factor endowments between the developed and developing countries will continue to influence the pattern of trade between the two groups along traditional lines of comparative advantage, to the extent investment in *non-traded* infrastructure is necessary for engaging in *trade*, increasing returns in the provision of infrastructure bring an element of arbitrariness in which countries succeed in making the investment in infrastructure. It will also open the door for the strategic use of policies to encourage such investment. A small investment subsidy by one country can tilt comparative advantage in its favor in the absence of an activist policy by other countries.

Dixit (1985) also finds an analogous 'knife-edge' result in R & D expenditures: even a small policy-created advantage to firms in one country can eliminate R & D expenditures altogether by its competitors. Krugman points out that in his model countries are likely to engage in a non-cooperative subsidy war that will end up in their duplicating infrastructural facilities and dissipating any profits that they could have shifted from their rivals. Dixit also cautions against the social desirability of policy-created advantage to home firms, pointing out that the promotion of one country's dominance through R & D will turn out to be economically costly. In any case, the R & D-based argument is unlikely to be relevant for many developing countries. Even if there are any for which it is conceivably relevant, unless the government can pick the winning industries and firms *ex ante* with certainty and exclude others, such countries will gain little from intervention.

APPENDIX

Let $f(k_I) = k_I^\alpha$ and $g(k_C) = k_C^\beta$. The autarky steady state is given by:

$$\alpha(k_I^A)^{\alpha-1} = (n+\rho+\delta) \Rightarrow k_I^A = \left(\frac{\alpha}{n+\rho+\delta}\right)^{1/1-\alpha} \tag{A.1}$$

$$\left(\frac{1-\alpha}{\alpha}\right) k_I^A = \left(\frac{1-\beta}{\beta}\right) k_C^A \Rightarrow k_C^A = \lambda k_C^I \quad \text{where } \lambda = \left[\frac{\beta(1-\alpha)}{\alpha(1-\beta)}\right] \tag{A.2}$$

$$(n+\delta)k^A = \left(\frac{k^A - k_C^A}{k_I^A - k_C^A}\right) (k_I^A)^\alpha = \frac{(k^A - \lambda k_C^A)}{(1-\lambda)} \tag{A.3}$$

$$(k_I^A)^{\alpha-1} = \left(\frac{k^A - \lambda k_I^A}{1-\lambda}\right) \cdot \left(\frac{n+\pi+\delta}{\alpha}\right)$$

or

$$k^A = \theta k_I^A \quad \text{where } \theta = \frac{\lambda(n+\rho+\delta)k_I^A}{[(n+\rho+\delta)-\alpha(1-\lambda)(n+\delta)]}$$

$$C^A = \left(\frac{k_I^A - k^A}{k_I^A - k_C^A}\right)(k_C^A)^\beta \tag{A.4}$$

$$= \left(\frac{1-\theta}{1-\lambda}\right)\lambda^\beta(k_I^A)^\beta$$

$$p_C^A = \frac{\alpha(k_I^A)^{\alpha-1}}{\beta(k_C^A)^{\beta-1}} = \frac{(n+\rho+\delta)}{\beta} \cdot (\lambda k_C^A)^{1-\beta} \tag{A.5}$$

Let $p_C^T < p_C^A$ so that the economy specializes in investment goods in the free trade steady state. The latter is given by:

$$\alpha(k_I^T)^{\alpha-1} = (n+\rho+\delta) \Rightarrow k_I^T = \left(\frac{\alpha}{n+\rho+\delta}\right)^{1/1-\alpha} = k_C^A \tag{A.6}$$

$$p_C^T C^T = (k_I^T)^\alpha - (n+\delta)k_I^T = \left[\frac{n+\rho+\delta}{\alpha} - (n+\delta)\right]k_I^T \tag{A.7}$$

or

$$C^T = \left[\frac{(n+\rho+\delta)-\alpha(n+\delta)}{\alpha p_C^T}\right]k_I^T$$

Now

$$\frac{C^T}{C^A} = \frac{(1-\lambda)[(n+\rho+\delta)-\alpha(n+\delta)]}{(1-\theta)\alpha\lambda^\beta(k_I^A)^\beta p_C^T}k_I^T$$

Noting $k_I^T = k_I^A$ and using (A.5) we get:

$$\frac{C^T}{C^A} = \frac{(1-\lambda)[(n+\rho+\delta)-(n+\delta)]}{(1-\theta)\alpha\lambda^\beta p_C^T} \cdot \frac{\beta p_C^A}{(n+\rho+\delta)\lambda^{1-\beta}}$$

$$= \left(\frac{1-\lambda}{1-\theta}\right)\left(\frac{\beta}{\alpha}\right)\left(\frac{(n+\rho+\delta)-(n+\delta)}{(n+\rho+\delta)}\right)\frac{1}{\lambda}\frac{p_C^A}{p_C^T}$$

Can we choose parameters including p_C^T such that $P_C^T < p_C^A$ and $C^T < C^A$? Now $C^T < C^A \Rightarrow p_C^T > \mu p_C^A$ where

$$\mu = \left(\frac{1-\lambda}{1-\theta}\right) \frac{(n+\rho+\delta) - \alpha(n+\delta)}{n+\rho+\delta} \cdot \frac{\beta}{\alpha\lambda}$$

If μ can be made sufficiently small by appropriate choice of parameters, then by setting p_C^T sufficiently close to but below p_C^A one can ensure that $C^T < C^A$.

It can be verified by substitution for λ and θ that

$$\mu = \frac{(1-\beta)\rho + (1-\beta)(n+\delta)}{(1-\alpha)(n+\rho+\delta)} \tag{A.8}$$

If $\rho = 0$ then $\mu = 1$ so that with $p_C^T < p_C^A$ we *cannot have* $C^T < C^A$. That is, if the pure rate of time preference is zero, welfare will always be higher in the free trade steady state compared to autarky as asserted in the text. However, as $\rho \to \infty$, $\mu \to 1 - \beta/1 - \alpha$. Thus, by choosing ρ sufficiently large and β sufficiently close to 1 one can make μ as small as one likes, thus ensuring $C^T < C^A$.

Notes

1. Not all radical critiques will be discussed. In particular, the literature on *Unequal Exchange* following Emmanuel (1972), from which Mrs Robinson often quoted approvingly, will not be covered.
2. This section draws on Bhagwati and Srinivasan (1980).
3. Mrs Robinson strongly disapproved calling one of these factors malleable 'capital'. Although our results could be established without using neoclassical production functions with a malleable capital stock as one of the inputs, it would have involved messier algebra.
4. This section draws on my paper (Srinivasan, 1986a).
5. This section draws on my paper (Srinivasan, 1986b).

References

Bhagwati, J. N. and T. N. Srinivasan (1980) 'Trade and Welfare in a Steady State', in J. S. Chipman and C. P. Kindleburger (eds) *Flexible Exchange Rates and Balance of Payments* (Amsterdam: North-Holland) pp. 209–22.

Dixit, A. (1981) 'The Export of Capital Theory', *Journal of International Economics* 11(2): 279–94.

Dixit, A. (1985) 'The Cutting Edge of International Technological Competition', mimeo, Department of Economics, Princeton University.

Emmanuel, A. (1972) *Unequal Exchange: A Study of the Imperialism of Trade* (New York, Monthly Review Press).

Ethier, W. (1979) 'The Theorems of International Trade in Time-Phased Economies', *Journal of International Economics* 9: 225–38.

Ethier, W. (1981) 'Reply to Metcalfe and Steedman', *Journal of International Economics* 11(2): 273–7.

Findlay, R. (1980) 'The Terms of Trade and Equilibrium Growth in the World Economy', *American Economic Review* 70: 291–9.

Galor, O. (1986) 'Global Dynamic Inefficiency in the Absence of International Policy Coordination: A North–South Case', *Journal of International Economics* 21(1/2): 137–50.

Helleiner, G. (1985) 'Industrial Organization, Trade and Investment: A Selective Literature Review for Developing Countries', paper presented at a conference on *Industrial Organization, Trade and Investment in North America: Mexico, Canada and the USA*. Merida, Mexico.

Krugman, P. (1986) 'New Trade Theory and the Less Developed Countries', paper presented at the Carlos Diaz-Alejandro Memorial Conference, World Institute for Development Economics Research, Helsinki.

Malinvaud, E. (1953) 'Capital Accumulation and Efficient Allocation of Resources', *Econometrica* 21: 233–68, and 'Efficient Capital Accumulation: A Corrigendum', *Econometrica* (July 1962), 570.

Metcalfe, J. S. and I. Steedman (1981) 'On the Transformation of Theorems', *Journal of International Economics* 11(2): 267–71.

Robinson, J. (1977) 'What are the Questions?', *Journal of Economic Literature* XV, 4: 1318–39.

Srinivasan, T. N. (1986a) 'International Trade and Factor Movements in Development Theory, Policy and Experience', in G. Ranis and T. Paul Schultz (eds) *The State of Development Economics: Progress and Perspectives* (Oxford: Blackwell).

Srinivasan, T. N. (1986b) 'Recent Theories of Imperfect Competition and International Trade: Any Implications for Development Strategy?', mimeo, Yale University, Department of Economics, Economic Growth Center.

Steedman, I. (1979) *Trade Among Growing Economies* (Cambridge: Cambridge University Press).

Stewart, F. (1984) 'Recent Theories of International Trade: Some Implications for the South', in H. Kierzkowski (ed.) *Monopolistic Competition and International Trade* (London: Oxford University Press) pp. 84–107.

Vines, D. (1985) 'North–South Growth Model Along Kaldorian Lines', Discussion Paper No. 26, London: Centre for Economic Policy Research.

Vines, D. and R. Kanbur (1985) 'North–South Interaction and Commodity Control', *Journal of Development Economics*.

26 Joan Robinson as a Development Economist

Irma Adelman and David Sunding*

Economic development was not a major focus for Joan Robinson's research. Nevertheless, she considered the subject important and returned to it throughout her life.

Joan Robinson's development economics did not evolve in a vacuum. It began from a common intellectual framework with mainstream development economics, reacted to it, developed in idiosyncratic ways, and was based on a particular ideological and historical perspective. At times, it interweaved with the mainstream; at times, it was more extreme than the mainstream but in the same direction; at other times, it diverged from the mainstream in direction as well as in extent; and, toward the end, it again touched base with some of the strands in mainstream development economics which it influenced.

1 DEVELOPMENT ECONOMICS IN THE 1950s AND 1960s

To understand the evolution of Joan Robinson's development writings, one must place them in the perspective of mainstream development economics to which they were a counterpoint.

Mainstream development economics sprang from the classical economists – particularly Ricardo.[1] The classical economists focused on accumulation processes combined with technical change and institutional evolution as the primary determinants of steady-state growth. The economy was decomposed into two sectors – one dominated by increasing returns called 'industry' and the other by decreasing returns called 'agriculture'. The process of raising income *per capita* required the transfer of labor from the decreasing returns sector into the increasing returns sector. It depended upon the speed of capital accumulation relative to the rate of growth of the labor force since the increasing returns sector was also the capital-intensive sector. In a steady state, the rate of growth of income *per capita* depended upon the rate of growth of the capital–labor ratio, the rate of technical change, and upon the relative contribution of institutional change to economic growth.

*We are indebted to Sherman Robinson for his excellent comments with, of course, the usual disclaimer of responsibility.

Lewis's adaptation of the Ricardian model to developing economies (Lewis, 1954) focused attention on industrialization as the mainspring of development. The main role of agriculture was to provide a surplus for the accumulation of industrial capital and to release labor.

Subsequent development economists added an emphasis upon the role of externalities and economies of scale in generating the initial impetus to economic development (Scitovsky, 1954 and Nurkse, 1963). Big push theories (Rosenstein-Rodan, 1943), based on the need to generate externalities, emphasized the necessity for rapid capital accumulation and for an active role for the state in initiating the development process.

The role of institutional change was stressed by 'stage theories' of economic growth (Rostow, 1960) and by historical theories of economic development (Kuznets, 1966). A theory of institutional 'prerequisites' and of substitution for these missing prerequisites (Gershenkron, 1962) supplemented the view that identified accumulation processes as the main determinants of economic development.

Both the accumulation-externality view of development and the stage theories of development emphasized the role of government and of economic planning as active initiators of the development process. A technical apparatus for planning evolved[2] starting from single-equation partial equilibrium models (Chenery, 1960); proceeding to two-sector open economy generalizations of the Harrod–Domar model (Chenery and Strout, 1966); and to multisector linear (Leontief, 1953) and non-linear (Chenery and Raduchel, 1971; Adelman and Robinson, 1978), optimizing models. Work with these models, in turn, led to a recognition that international trade and foreign capital inflows are important determinants of the efficiency of domestic resource use. Trade strategies and foreign aid could contribute significantly to domestic resource accumulation and technical and institutional change in accelerating the rate of economic development.

Most of mainstream development economics was dominated by the historical experience of four sets of countries: the firstcomers to the Industrial Revolution (England and Belgium), where spontaneous economic development led to widespread industrialization combined with the growth of a highly productive agricultural sector; the latecomers to the industrial revolution (Germany, Russia, and Japan), where government-led economic growth was used to substitute for missing 'prerequisites' in a narrower industrialization process combined with a more backward agriculture than in the firstcomers to the industrial revolution; the Marshall Plan countries, where foreign aid led to rapid industrialization; and the class of large, overpopulated, low productivity, largely agricultural economies of which India is a prime example.

2   JOAN ROBINSON'S DEVELOPMENT ECONOMICS

The lines of thought sketched above form a backdrop for Joan Robinson's development economics. She began with an intellectual heritage shared with mainstream development economics – the classical economists. However, other elements were mixed in – Marx, Keynes, Kalecki, and Fel'dman; and, while other development economists learned their lessons from the experiences of England, Germany, and India, Joan Robinson focused primarily on socialist economies.

Joan Robinson's development economics was firmly rooted in her *Accumulation of Capital* (1956). She shared with the early development economists the stress on capital accumulation and, particularly, on investment in physical capital as the major determinant of economic development; but, in her stress on the rate of capital accumulation, she was rather more extreme than mainstream development economists. Unlike mainstream development economists, she placed less emphasis on externalities, technical change, institutional change, and the accumulation of human capital as important contributors to economic development.

Roughly, three periods can be discerned in Joan Robinson's writings on economic development. The first coincides more or less and is inspired by her vision and conception explicated in *The Accumulation of Capital*. The second is steeped in her disenchantment with the post-war changes in capitalist countries, the post-war experience and revelations of failures in East European countries, and her fascination with Maoist China. The third, just before her death, is still conditioned by the first two factors of the second, but also modified by a more critical view and some disenchantment with China. There are few formal writings from this last period, and we shall not consider it explicitly. Moreover, one must distinguish between her analytical writings in economics where, as a good model builder, she focused on technical issues, abstracting from others, or taking them for granted, and her more general writings (or lectures) where her human concerns – about equality of income distribution, improvement of standard of living, health care, and the like – are underlined. (An example of the latter is her 'Teaching Economics' (1960).)

During the 1950s and 1960s, Joan Robinson's development economics stressed rapid economic growth to the virtual exclusion of other objectives. She favored rapid economic development in the Third World primarily because it would alter the balance of power among nations and improve collective welfare rather than because it would be a route to reducing individual poverty and improving the individual welfare of the world's impoverished masses. She preferred socialism as a form of organization of production and distribution for developing countries not simply because of the better income distribution achieved by socialist economies, but also because she viewed the socialist mode of production as a more efficient method of extracting an investable surplus from productive enterprises (Robinson, 1957b, pp. 74–5 and Robinson, 1957b, p. 98). In her writings of this period, she was aware of the trade-off between consumption and investment inherent in socialist growth schemes, and was willing to limit consumption in the interests of sustained accumulation (Robinson, 1957b, pp. 98–9).

In her later writings, Joan Robinson seemed to broaden and soften her views. Exposure to Chinese economic development sensitized her to the importance of agriculture. She more readily admitted that East European socialist economies had overdone the repression of worker consumption, and she modified her view that the repression of all consumption was desirable arguing instead that primarily non-wage-goods and luxury consumption be curbed. Her later writings thus assumed a more humanitarian stance.

3   GROWTH AND ACCUMULATION

The central problem of economic development, as Joan Robinson saw it, was the problem of rapid accumulation. Thus, she wrote:

> The underdeveloped economies are those which are dissatisfied with their present economic condition and want to develop. To do so, it is necessary for them to increase their present rate of accumulation, and this is what, in one way or another, they are struggling to do, or at least talking about planning to do. (Robinson, 1957b, pp. 96–7)

For her, the process of economic development was synonymous with the process of industrialization. She and Eatwell put this proposition bluntly:

> To rise out of this situation [of underdevelopment], industralization is necessary, for industrialization means the application of power to produc-tion and transport, to supplement human and animal muscle. The Chinese have shown how much can be done by mobilizing the population to work 'with their bare hands', but output (and therefore consumption) per head cannot begin to rise towards modern levels without mechanical aids. 'Development' is, therefore, rightly identified with industrialization, in the general sense in which it applies as much to agriculture as to manufactures. (Robinson and Eatwell, 1973, p. 232)

Her views on the relations between accumulation and development had both Keynesian and neoclassical elements. In her view, Keynes, unlike his neoclassical predecessors, understood rightly the relation between savings and investment. Whereas the neoclassicals pointed to a willingness to forgo consumption as the source of accelerated accumulation, Keynes 'shifted the emphasis from the rentier aspect of capital as the product of thrift to the entrepreneur aspect of capital as the product of enterprise' (Robinson, 1957b, p. 89). In this view, 'the development of wealth depends not upon prudence but upon energy' (Robinson, 1957b, p. 89); and the enemy of accumulation is flagging 'animal spirits'.

On the other hand, she claimed that, unlike in Keynesian economics where there is no trade-off between consumption and investment, there is such a dilemma in socialist and in developing countries. When writing on socialist planning in 1973, she pointed out that, 'if near-full employment is going to be maintained in any case, then a faster rate of accumulation must be associated, in a given technical situation, with a lower level of consumption' (Robinson and Eatwell, 1973, p. 274). For this reason, she called Keynes a Cassandra for, as soon as his teaching becomes widely accepted, it ceases to be true. That is, once full employment is the accepted goal of government policy, the ends of investment become more important than the process of investment – 'investment becomes a present sacrifice instead of being the vehicle for a present benefit' (Robinson, 1957b, p. 91); and, given the level of wages, the rate of accumulation is higher the more thrifty are the capitalists. Even in this case, however, she did not return to the pre-Keynesian notion that savings governs investment. Rather, she held to the view that decisions about how much real investment to undertake determine the rate of accumulation.

In light of the fact that Joan Robinson clearly distinguished between situations of full and underemployment, recognized that one of the most widely emphasized characteristics of developing countries is the prevalence of underemployment, and was concerned about this issue, it seems odd that her early analysis of underdeveloped economies was worked out in the context of an expanding economy with continuous full employment. For example, in her 1957 article, 'Notes on the Theory of Economic Development', she assumes the existence of a full employment economy producing wage and investment goods and populated by two classes – workers (who receive a wage) and capitalists (who receive all profits). If capitalists save the whole of their profits, then, given the technique of production, the average level of real-wages is determined by the rate of accumulation (or, equivalently, by the allocation of labor between the two departments). The larger the investment sector, the lower the real-wage rate since

the total selling value of a year's output of consumption goods is equal to a year's wages bill. The excess of the receipts for the sale of consumption goods over their wages cost is the wages bill of the investment sector. The profit margin on the sale of consumption goods prevents the workers in the consumption sector from consuming the whole of their own output, and makes it possible for the workers in the investment sector to share in consumption. The larger the investment sector, the higher the profits margins and the lower the real wage rate. (Robinson, 1957b, pp. 93–4)

She extended her analysis at this point to include the more realistic case in which capitalists consume a part of what they receive as profits. In this model, she echoed Kalecki's familiar doctrine when she held that, 'for the capitalists considered as a class, it is spending that is meritorious, for it is spending that generates profits' (Robinson, 1957b, p. 95). Their expenditure out of profits drives up the selling value of the consumption good and, in turn, generates additional profits. However, she was quick to point out that what is a virtue for capitalists (spending) may be a vice from a larger point of view. While capitalists would prefer the public to spend and then finance investment from their own undistributed profits, a 'fundamental proposition' derived from Robinson's analysis is that, 'given the level of real wages, the less thrifty is the community, the lower the rate of accumulation that it can undertake' (Robinson, 1957b, p. 95). A successful development strategy must then force the capitalist class to reduce consumption out of profits.

Joan Robinson's analysis of investment criteria for developing countries (Robinson, 1977) differed from her analysis of investment criteria in full employment economies (Robinson and Eatwell, 1973, pp. 277–8). For developing countries, she followed Kalecki (Feiwel, 1975, ch. 15) in rejecting the Sen–Dobb criterion that the appropriate guide for the choice of technique should be the maximization of the surplus over the wage bill. She did so because she believed that in developing countries this criterion would lead to a greater amount of luxury consumption, a lower share of wages in the national product, and ultimately to less rapid capital accumulation. Indeed, she felt that prices (which are, of course, implicit in the evaluation of the surplus) cannot be used as guides for project evaluation and investment planning at all. Instead, she suggested that 'the way to generate the maximum possible surplus is to organise employment of all available workers, provide them with an acceptable minimum standard of life and to direct all who are not required to provide the ingredients of the minimum into investment industries' (Robinson, 1977, p. 235). This approach would transform a situation of underemployment into a situation of full employment and avoid divorcing the savings decision from the investment decision at the cost, however, of both decisions being made by the state rather than by the aggregation of individual choices. She felt that the question of the level at which the minimum living standard is to be set, and when to let it rise, is a political (Robinson, 1977, p. 235) rather than a welfare economics problem.

The mainstream development economists also saw a problem with using market prices for project evaluation. They solved it somewhat differently, however. Instead of using market prices, they advocated using shadow prices based on a Bergson–Samuelson welfare function which, for example, would maximize the stream of consumption over time. They also suggested (in a somewhat unconvincing sleight of hand) that the shadow prices might be approximated by world prices (see, for example, United Nations Industrial Development Organization, 1972 and Little and Mirrlees, 1968).

4   JOAN ROBINSON AND SOCIALISM

In the light of her stress on the mobilization of savings by repressing consumption and on the need for a prime mover to implement an investment program, it is not surprising that, throughout her life, Joan Robinson was an unfailing supporter of socialism in the Third World. Because socialist governments have complete control over the surplus from production, there is no income from property and the savings problem which plagues capitalist economies is automatically solved. She correctly saw this fact as the primary reason socialist economies can grow faster than their capitalist counterparts. Also, 'in the socialist economies, power is in the hands of those who are determined to carry through the process of development at the fastest possible pace. There is no question of hestitation or ambivalence or flagging "animal spirits"' (Robinson, 1957b, p. 97).

Robinson's early conception of socialist economic development rested theoretically on the model of the two-sector economy wherein all surplus (profits in the market economy formulation) is reinvested. In a socialist version of this model, the Soviet-style 'turnover tax' serves precisely the same role as the profit margin in allowing investment sector workers to consume. While, in her later writing, she acknowledged the undesirability or even the impossibility of repressing worker consumption in underdeveloped nations, her early development economics, nevertheless, had in common with pre-Keynesian theory the notion that saving is a public virtue and that the rate of development is determined by the willingness to forgo present consumption.

Joan Robinson advocated market socialism in the sense that prices in socialist economies should be set by equating supply and demand. She observed that in socialist economies the favorable effects of market clearing prices would be the same as in market economies (Robinson, 1958, pp. 35–6), while some of the negative effects would disappear. This would be particularly true of equity reasons for overriding market prices. Since the distribution of wealth is considerably more equal in socialist economies, the prices established by equating supply and demand would come closer to having desirable ethical properties (Robinson, 1958, p. 40; Robinson, 1964b, p. 70). She even hoped that, with appropriate institutional reforms designed to create a class of functionaries whose role it is to see that consumer demand is satisfied, socialist countries would become the true systems with consumer sovereignty.

She worried about the extended functional distribution of income in socialist economies, especially between farmers and urban workers (Robinson, 1958, pp. 33–6), and recognized that in both socialist and market economies the agricultural terms of trade must be politically determined. For purposes of accumulation, at least initially agricultural terms of trade should be kept below market clearing prices. But this cannot be overdone since the marketable surplus would be siphoned off into the second economy.

In her later writings, particularly *Aspects of Development and Underdevelopment*, Joan Robinson emphasized the ability of socialist governments to repress luxury consumption rather than consumption in general. Theoretically, this shift in attention was mirrored by her use of a three-sector model with the consumption goods sector divided into a wage good and a luxury good sector. This kind of model became popular with the Latin American structuralist school of development economics in the 1970s (Taylor, 1979; Deere and de Janvry, 1979). Joan Robinson used this model to attack the 'orthodox' view that 'accumulation is due to saving and it is necessary for society to have a wealthy class because only the rich save' (Robinson, 1981, p. 32). When rentier consumption is allowed to go unchecked, she saw that

profits are easier and quicker to make in the markets fed by rentier consumption than in supplying wage goods or in building up the capacity of basic industry to produce means of production. Moreover, a large part of the investment that caters for the consumption of the rich is not really adding to productive capacity at all; it is merely taking over the market for precapitalist handicraft production or from small-scale family businesses, so reducing employment and increasing the inequality of income which keeps its own market expanding. (Robinson, 1981, pp. 33–4)

For Joan Robinson, then, capitalist development not only results in a lower rate of accumulation than socialist governments can attain but the benefits of growth are distributed more unequally; and some groups may even expect their economic welfare to deteriorate.

Although Joan Robinson remained an advocate of socialism in the Third World, in her later writings, she expressed disillusionment with East European socialism, disillusionment that sprang from what she perceived as major blunders of socialist planners (especially Soviet planners). Joan Robinson came to believe that agriculture was treated badly in the Soviet drive to industrial accumulation. She claimed that the policies of Preobrazhensky and others, that expropriated a surplus from cultivators and made little investment in agricultural technology, acted as a 'drag on the development of countries in the Soviet sphere' (Robinson and Eatwell, 1973, p. 318). With respect to industry, it is clear that she regarded alienation to be at least as prevalent in East European societies as in their Western counterparts. Consequently, 'the greatest problem for all countries in the Soviet sphere is to find some way to get the workers to work; it is made all the more difficult by the cynicisn which has been generated by years of sanctimonious official propaganda' (Robinson and Eatwell, 1973, p. 316). Low worker morale is reinforced, in her view, by the repression of consumption typical of Stalinist growth – a tendency of which she was aware since her earliest writings (Robinson, 1957b, p. 98). Finally, Joan Robinson grew pessimistic about the prospects for economic reform in the Soviet Union in particular. Whereas Yugoslavia was able to (somewhat) effectively implement a system of worker control and of planning based on profit considerations, she saw no indications that the Soviets were willing to follow Yugoslavia's lead. Moreover, she held that the reforms necessary to rejuvenate Soviet industry were of a fundamental nature: 'When the original ideals of socialism have been worn down by years of cynicism and discouragement, they cannot be restored merely by making some alterations in the directives given to industry' (Robinson and Eatwell, 1973, p. 321).

5 JOAN ROBINSON AND THE MAINSTREAM IN THE 1970S

Oddly enough, Joan Robinson's later writings on economic development were more out of tune with the mainstream than her early writings even though the mainstream became more radical and her influence on a subset of development economists (the Latin American structuralist school) increased.

In the 1970s, the dominant view of mainstream development economics shifted drastically. It was realized that, even though the period from 1950 to 1970 had been one of greatly accelerated economic growth in *per capita* income, this growth had been accompanied by a decline in the share of income accruing to the poor and an increase in the number of poor and malnourished (Adelman and Morris, 1973). A reformulation of development goals toward establishing the satisfaction of basic needs for all (within a relatively short time) as a major objective of national development policy ensued (International Labor Organization (ILO), 1972; Chenery *et al.*, 1974; and Adelman, 1975). Growth *per se* was de-emphasized; the quality of growth and how the fruits of growth were distributed became an important focus for mainstream development economics. In contrast to earlier strategies based on the two-sector labor–surplus model that advocated an indirect approach to development based on capital accumulation in the modern sector, alternative development models were proposed that focused more directly on poverty reduction (for a summary, see Emmerij, 1986; Streeten, 1986). These alternative models advocate supporting the modern formal sector while at the same time attempting to raise productivity and incomes in the informal urban sector and in the rural traditional sector. They also stress labor-intensive, employment-generating growth and focus on the design of investment and trade strategies that will lead to such growth. The new focus of mainstream development economics, which became known as the basic needs approach, involves a more complex view of the development process, a reformulation of development objectives with a stress on employment creation, equality of income distribution, and statisfaction of basic needs.

Joan Robinson never joined the basic needs camp although some of the themes she pursued in the last decade of her life were consonant with it. She continued to focus on economic growth albeit with a greater awareness of the costs of that policy in East European socialist countries. At the same time, some of the three-factor models she used to analyze development permeated into the Latin American structuralist literature. She also shared with the mainstream of the 1970s an increasing recognition of the importance of agriculture, and her advocacy of the Chinese strategy of 'walking on two legs' is reminiscent of some of the basic needs strategies advocated by the ILO (see, for example, ILO, 1972).

6 DEVELOPMENT STRATEGY

As in conventional development economics, trade policy was important in Joan Robinson's development economics. She was against foreign trade as the engine of growth especially when primary commodities are the principal export. The greatest drawback to trade in primary commodities, Joan Robinson observed, is the instability of prices in these markets. She objected to export-led growth in manufactures as well because of her mistaken[3] view that 'the very essence of the process involves a low share of wages in the value of output, that is, a high rate of exploitation of labour' (Robinson and Eatwell, 1973, p. 331). She did acknowledge that, 'all the same, workers who are being exploited by capitalists are better off than those who are existing at near starvation in disguised unemployment in the cities and as landless labour in the countryside' (Robinson and Eatwell, 1973, p. 331).

Joan Robinson favored import substitution as a development strategy without, however, distinguishing between the stages of import substitution. In 1973, she wrote that

> since foreign exchange is always in short supply, the first rule for development should be to economize on imports, that is, to aim for the greatest possible home production per unit cost of imports. This involves eliminating, by prohibitions or tariffs, the import of goods that can be done without or substituted by home production, and allowing in only those that contribute to the programme of development. (Robinson and Eatwell, 1973, p. 331)

She conceded that, in reality, industries set up in this manner typically operate at low capacity implying that the cost of investment has been extravagant relative to output and employment. Furthermore, she observed that protection is often not designed in a manner which promotes employment growth; production processes often utilize a great deal of machinery. But she argued that these ills flow 'not from industrialisation as such, but, first, from the planners' choice of investment projects on the basis of "willingness to pay", say, for passenger cars, and secondly from imitating Western industry and allowing or inviting Western businesses to organise industry for them' (Robinson, 1981, p. 107).

Joan Robinson predicted that import substitution in industry has the greatest chance of success in countries where accumulation of the means of production has already reached a modest level and where planners are sympathetic to the process of equitable development. When a nation has the capacity to produce intermediate inputs, real saving of foreign exchange can take place; and, if investment in import-substituting industries follows the Chinese principle of walking on two legs, employment can grow well.

In her advocacy of import substitution, Joan Robinson diverged from the mainstream – especially the mainstream of the 1970s and beyond. While during the 1950s and 1960s, most development economists either extolled the advantages of import-substitution-based development (Prebish, 1959) or emphasized the advantages of export-led growth (Chenery, 1961), a consensus favoring export-led growth began evolving in the 1970s. Thinking in this area was strongly influenced by the experience of a group of Far Eastern countries, the 'Gang of Four', whose growth rates shot up and basic needs performance became very good once they shifted from an early phase of import substitution toward export-led growth. Studies of their growth patterns indicated that countries having more open, outward-looking policies enjoyed higher growth rates and responded more quickly and effectively to disturbances originating in international markets than did more closed economies (Balassa, 1986).

Under the influence of her exposure to China, in her last writing on the subject, Joan Robinson advocated import substitution in agriculture for countries at lower levels of development. Indeed, she claimed that, 'from every point of view – political, economic, and humane – the first necessity for the Third World is to increase production of basic foodstuffs' (Robinson, 1981, p. 132). Because many underdeveloped nations are dependent on imports of food, Joan Robinson saw that 'production of food is the most effective form of import-saving investment' (Robinson, 1981, p. 132). In elaborating this point, she emphasized that

> a frontal attack on mass poverty and unemployment requires an increase in the output of food but also an equalisation of consumption. The only way to combine both results is to go back to small-scale, labor-using agriculture and then to advance gradually from that base. But there seems to be little chance of such a drastic reversal taking place. (Robinson, 1981, p. 134)

To achieve the increase in agricultural productivity, she recommended that 'technical research should be directed to land-saving improvements – those which merely reduce labour per unit of product should wait until industry is ready to draw workers from the land into employment' (Robinson, 1981, p. 134). To this end, she advocated increasing productivity in agriculture within the framework of rural collectives. She favored this form because she doubted that the most obvious alternatives – individual ownership and cooperatives – can generate a marketable surplus.

> To produce an agricultural surplus without having to rely on the extreme misery of the cultivators, it is necessary to increase productivity, and at the same time, to provide the cultivators with the means and the motive to part with a considerable portion of their products. One way of extracting a surplus from independent peasants is by instituting a tax. The other is by organizing marketing and providing some commodities or services that the rural population want to acquire. (Robinson and Eatwell, 1973, p. 324)

There is a growing number of mainstream development economists who would agree with her on the desirability of an import substitution strategy in agriculture as preferable for industrialization and for egalitarian growth in the international climate of the 1980s (Mellor, 1976; Singer, 1979; Adelman, 1984). These economists argue that, after an initial phase of industrialization, policy toward agriculture should change its emphasis from surplus extraction to surplus creation and to the generation of demand linkages with the rest of the economy. Such a policy can best be implemented by improving the productivity of land as Joan Robinson recommended. But the mainstream development economists would part way with Joan Robinson in her advocacy of collectives as the best form of rural organization. Looking at the performance of post land-reform agricultural sectors in Japan, Taiwan, and South Korea, they would advocate small- to medium-sized freehold agriculture as a superior institutional structure for the farm sector. The farm sectors in these countries yielded good distributions of income while superior incentives were generated for improving agricultural productivity. The rates of growth of agricultural productivity in these countries substantially exceeded the Chinese rates (Perkins and Yusuf, 1984).

7 JOAN ROBINSON AND CHINA

The bulk of Joan Robinson's writings on China concerns the agricultural collectives which she greatly admired. Indeed, she regarded Chinese institutions as a model for the Third World in general and Asia in particular. In her review of Gunnar Myrdal's *Asian Drama* she wrote

The Chinese have shown what institutions the modernisation of Asian agriculture requires. First of all, a drastic land reform in each village put almost every family into the position of a 'middle peasant', that is, brought about a land to labour ratio that permitted everyone to work his own holding with his own family labor. (Robinson, 1968, p. 109)

In her last writings on the subject, she praised the Chinese commune system (in contrast with other types of agricultural organizations) as an example of an agricultural system that does not proceed from inequality or have an inherent tendency toward it. Communalization and the equation of individual and social welfare – 'it is in China that the people seriously try to put into practice the ideal: combat egoism and reject privilege' (Robinson, 1968, p. 113) – succeed both in increasing agricultural output and improving the welfare of all producers (Robinson, 1981, pp. 58–9).

Joan Robinson regarded active state participation as the primary reason for the success of the Chinese case. Reiterating themes that appear throughout her writings, she held that

it is not easy for cooperative agriculture to be established except in the framework of a government policy genuinely directed to the interests of the peasantry. (Robinson and Eatwell, 1973, p. 325)

In China the state is anything but soft. By gradual stages the socialist sector absorbed the whole of industry and commerce, so that the conflict of interest and jockeying for advantage between private and public enterprises are inhibited. At the same time, devolution and local initiative mitigate the rigidity of a monolothic plan. The question of personal taxation does not arise. Unearned income is a mere remnant of the manner in which the 'patriotic bourgeoisie' was let down lightly by the revolution. (Robinson, 1968, p. 107)

It is significant that she spoke favorably of both the ability of the Chinese government to acquire productive surplus and the uses to which this surplus was put. Specifically, she seemed to admire the principle of walking on two legs as a strategy for rapid, but equitable, development. Under this rule, investment is carried out so as to maximize increases in productive capacity and employment. In industry, a dualistic strategy is employed: a small proportion of output in each sector is produced with modern, capital-intensive technology and the rest with labor-intensive traditional methods.

These views stand in marked contrast to her early claims that socialism is suitable for the task of economic growth simply because of the powerful control that socialist governments exert over profits and consumption. In short, Joan Robinson's exposure to the Chinese case, and her disillusionment with Fel'dmanite development in East European socialist countries, seem to have had a humanizing influence on her development theory as she became more aware of the need to increase employment and worker consumption throughout the course of economic development.

8   JOAN ROBINSON AND THE STYLIZED FACTS OF ECONOMIC DEVELOPMENT

The review of Joan Robinson's approach to economic development presented above has indicated some points of convergence and some points of divergence with the mainstream. One way of assessing the respective claims of competing theories is to compare their assumptions or predictions with the stylized facts. This is what we shall do in the present section. The comparison will draw upon several major studies of the development experience of less-developed countries during the period 1955 to 1975 (Chenery, Robinson, and Syrquin, forthcoming; Nishimizu and Robinson, 1984; Feder, 1983).

Joan Robinson emphasized the role of capital accumulation almost to the exclusion of other factors as a determinant of the rate of economic growth of national income. A review of studies performed by various authors who decomposed the sources of growth in national value added from 1950 to 1973 in thirty-nine countries is summarized in Chenery *et al.* (chapter 2, table 2.2). The decomposition used Dennison-type growth accounting to attribute the sources of growth to the growth in factor use, on the one hand, and to total factor productivity improvement, on the other. For the Organization for Economic Cooperation and Development (OECD) countries, about half of the growth came from productivity change, 30 per cent from the growth of the labor force, and only 20 per cent from the growth of capital. In the less-developed, semi-industrial countries, the picture is reversed: about 70 per cent of the growth in total GNP came from the growth of factor supplies and only 30 per cent from growth in total factor productivity. Of the growth in factors, the growth in employment accounted for 40 per cent of the contribution of factor growth to the growth in GNP and the growth of capital to 60 per cent. In centrally planned economies, about 35 per cent of the growth came from the growth in total factor productivity, 56 per cent from capital accumulation, and 44 per cent from the growth in employment. Centrally planned economies indeed grew significantly faster (8.2 per cent) than the other less-developed countries (6.3 per cent) or the OECD countries (5.4 per cent). Most of the difference in performance (60 per cent) between less-developed countries and socialist countries was due to the significantly more rapid rate of capital accumulation in the socialist nations. (The rate of accumulation in socialist countries was 1.5 times that in semi-industrial and OECD economies.) But the productivity of capital in the socialist countries was only 88 per cent that of the less-developed countries, and the growth in total factor productivity was only 70 per cent that of the OECD countries.

Thus, Joan Robinson's emphasis on accumulation as the major source of growth and on socialism as a more efficient engine for accumulation is borne out by the stylized facts.

But what are the policy prescriptions that follow from these observations? Mainstream economists would emphasize the need to raise the rate of growth of total factor productivity in less-developed countries so that a higher rate of growth can be combined with an increase in both total and *per capita* consumption by farmers and workers. Joan Robinson stressed primarily the need to speed up accumulation.

With respect to development strategies, Joan Robinson emphasized import substitution over export-led growth. Regressions of total factor productivity by sector and in the aggregate upon, *inter alia*, the growth of exports and the growth in import substitution reported in Nishimizu and Robinson (1984) and Feder (1983) indicate that import substitution contributed negatively to the growth of total factor productivity in Korea, Turkey, Yugoslavia, and Japan, while export growth contributed positively to factor productivity growth. In most industries, an early period of import substitution, with a negative contribution to total factor productivity, preceded a period of export expansion, with a positive contribution to total factor productivity growth. The suggestion from these and other studies (Balassa, 1982; Bhagwati, 1978; and Krueger, 1978) is that continuation of inward-looking policies beyond the infant industry phase is a costly policy that makes economic growth more difficult to achieve. There is also some evidence from socialist countries that have switched from closed to open strategies (Hungary and post-reform China); it indicates that this switch, when combined with institutional changes, led to an improvement in their growth rates.

What of import substitution in agriculture? Here the verdict is not in yet. There are suggestive experiences of a few countries (notably China and India) and suggestive modelling results (Adelman, 1984) supporting the proposition that investment in land-augmenting innovations, coupled with a trade strategy that discriminates neither in favor nor against international trade in agricultural commodities, would improve the rate of economic growth, the distribution of income, and reduce poverty and malnutrition.

Finally, what of China as a model for developing countries? As Joan Robinson herself admitted in a postscript to the preface of *Aspects of Development and Underdevelopment* (Robinson, 1981), the evidence now coming out of Chinese statistics indicates that her conceptions of China, formed largely during the Cultural Revolution, were idealized. The average grain yield per hectare in China in 1979 was substantially above the world and Asia average; but it was also below that in South Korea, Taiwan, and Japan (Perkins and Yusuf, 1984, p. 38). The average rate of growth of grain yields from 1955 to 1979 in China (2.7 per cent per year (Perkins and Yusuf, 1984, p. 40)) was above that of two-thirds of developing countries but below that of the upper third (Food and Agriculture Organization of the United Nations, 1981, p. 39). However, the sources-of-growth accounting performed by Perkins and Yusuf (1984, chapter 4, especially pp. 68–9) indicates a negative growth of total factor productivity in Chinese agriculture between 1959 and 1979. Perkins and Yusuf (1984) interpret this result as signifying that

> production increases were achieved at the cost of increasing mismanagement, declining personal incentives, and other sources of reduced efficiency in the raising of crops . . . Mao's methods did greatly increase the inputs available to Chinese agriculture, but the organization required for this achievement (such as communes, mass campaigns, and so forth) played such havoc with management and incentives that many of the benefits of increased inputs, both modern and traditional, were lost. (Perkins and Yusuf, 1984, p. 69)

Even if one abstracts from the staggering human costs involved in the Cultural Revolution, the performance of Chinese agriculture has thus been mixed. The evidence now coming out of China suggests that the very feature of China that Joan Robinson extolled (collectivized agriculture) may well have been more of a liability than an asset in productivity terms.

China's development efforts since 1952 may be divided into six periods. First, the years from 1952 to 1958 saw the socialist transformation of agriculture through land reform initially, and then through the establishment of producer and consumer cooperatives. This period was also characterized by sectoral imbalances as nearly 90 per cent of all state investment went into capital goods. Second, the Great Leap Forward, which began in 1958 and ended in 1961, successfully collectivized Chinese agriculture. The concurrent withdrawal of Soviet aid led to a temporary collapse of many sectors of the economy. Third, the period 1961–6 was characterized by the adjustments and reforms designed by Liu ShaoQi. The state's role in planning was increasingly decentralized in hopes of achieving a more widespread use of production incentives. For example, in agriculture, peasants were permitted to own private plots. The relative economic normalcy of this reform period was followed by the massive social unrest of the fourth period, the Cultural Revolution, which ran from 1966 to 1968. The aftermath of the Cultural Revolution lasted from 1968 to 1979. During this period agricultural expansion, largely untouched by the Cultural Revolution, continued at a moderate rate, and was accompanied by accelerated industrialization. Finally, Deng ShaoPing and his 'rehabilitated' colleagues ushered in the latest economic policy regime – the Second Spring. This plan is based on balanced growth via retrenchment in heavy industry's capital formation, adjustment of industrial wages, improving commodity circulation, and decollectivization in agriculture (Shen, 1985, p. 12; Adelman, 1977).

These changes in Chinese economic policy have been associated with changes in the size distribution of income, the sectoral distribution of income, and the rate of economic growth. Table 26.1 presents Gini coefficients estimated for the years 1952 to 1983 on the basis of recently released income, employment and population data. The table indicates that China was and remains one of the developing countries with the most equal distribution of income.

Table 26.1   Chinese income inequality: 1952–83

Year	Policy regime	Gini coefficient	Urban/ rural income ratio	Year	Real net material product (average annual growth %)
1983	Second Spring	.237	1.681	1983	
1979	Aftermath	.317	2.603	1980	5.9
1968	Cultural Revolution	.310	2.563	1970	8.3
1966	Adjustment and Reform	.324	2.742	1966	14.7
1961	Great Leap Forward	.315	2.570	1962	− 3.1
1958	Capital Accumulation	.378	3.723	1958	8.9
1952		.226	1.800	1952	

Source: Columns 1 to 4: Adelman and Sunding (forthcoming); columns 5 and 6: The World Bank (1983), p. 76.

During the 1952–8 period of collectivization and massive capital accumulation, the distribution of income worsened dramatically due to stagnating agricultural production and rapidly rising urban incomes. During the Great Leap Forward, administrative inefficiency and the loss of Soviet aid combined to depress urban wages by nearly 10 per cent, while average peasant income rose by 10 per cent in this same period. As a result the distribution of income improved greatly. The reform period of 1961–6 was associated with little systematic movement in the size distribution of income since rural and urban incomes moved closely together. The slight decline in worker income precipitated by the Cultural Revolution, coupled with the steady increase in peasant income from 1966 to 1968, resulted in low levels of inequality. From its bottom at the end of the Cultural Revolution, inequality in China increased steadily during the 1968–79 aftermath. Average urban income increased by 51 per cent while average rural income increased by 48 per cent.

More dramatic movements in the distribution of income were associated with the introduction of the most recent reforms in agriculture and industry, initiated in 1979. Although decollectivization has resulted in a more inequitable distribution of rural income, as evidenced by Table 26.2, the rapidly

Table 26.2   Chinese rural income inequality

Year	Gini
1983	.240
1978	.227
1952	.226

Source: Adelman and Sunding (forthcoming).

declining gap between rural and urban incomes has equalized the overall distribution. Thus, the Gini coefficient for the 1983 distribution of income is nearly identical to that for 1952!

As a result, the level of poverty decreased dramatically as well. In the five years since 1978, the percentage of population in poverty has fallen to less than a third of its 1978 level. By contrast, in the twenty-five years from 1952 to 1978, the rural distribution remained more or less unchanged, and the overall distribution deteriorated because urban incomes increased more rapidly than rural incomes. The percentage of population in poverty declined but much more slowly than in the post-reform period. The ratio of people in poverty fell to about a third of its 1952 value in twenty-five years. Thus, the rate of decline of the poverty ratio more than quintupled since the decollectivization of the rural sector and the introduction of the other reforms associated with the 'system of responsibility'.[4]

Where one comes out in one's evaluation of the Chinese performance thus depends on value judgments pitting production versus productivity, social justice versus basic needs, and the human costs of the Cultural Revolution and of the Great Leap Forward versus the human costs associated with the periodic mass famines so prevalent in pre-revolutionary China.

9   POSTSCRIPT

Joan Robinson spent a lifetime fighting neoclassical economics. Economic development, as a field, has been mainly structuralist though, at times, it employed neoclassical techniques for structuralist analysis. Most development economists find that the neoclassical assumptions require major qualification for less-developed countries, and that the neoclassical concern with short-period equilibrium is of limited value in the analysis of long-run structural change and medium-run structural adjustment. There should, therefore, have been a close relationship between Joan Robinson and mainstream development economics with communality of interests, cross-fertilization, and interaction. Sadly, this did not happen. The mainstream of the development field found her extreme; and she, in turn, ignored it.

Notes

1. For a summary of classical growth economics, see Adelman (1961).
2. For a review of this literature, see Blitzer *et al.*, 1975.
3. In South Korea, for example, the share of wage payments in Gross National Product is about 66 per cent; the average share of wages in socialist countries is 60 per cent (Chenery *et al.*, table 2.2).
4. The sources and methodology on which these statements are based are described in Adelman and Sunding, forthcoming.

References

Adelman, I. (1961) *Theories of Economic Growth and Development* (Palo Alto: Stanford University Press).

Adelman, I. (1975) 'Development Economics – A Reassessment of Goals', *American Economic Review*, 64: 302–9.

Adelman, I. (1977) 'Redistribution Before Growth: A Strategy for Developing Countries', Inaugural Address for the Cleveringa Chair, University of Leiden.

Adelman, J. (1984) 'Beyond Export Led Growth', *World Development*, 12: 937–49.

Adelman, I. and C. T. Morris (1973) *Economic Growth and Social Equity in Developing Countries* (Palo Alto: Stanford University Press).

Adelman, I. and S. Robinson (1978) *Income Distribution Policy in Developing Countries* (Palto Alto: Stanford University Press).

Adelman, I. and D. Sunding (forthcoming) 'Income Distribution in China'.

Balassa, B. and Associates (1982) *Development Strategies in Semi-industrial Economies* (Baltimore: Johns Hopkins Press).

Bhagwati, J. (1978) *Foreign Trade Regimes and Economic Development: Anatomy and Consequences* (Cambridge, Mass.: Ballinger Press).

Blitzer, C. R., P. B. Clark and L. Taylor (1975) *Economy-wide Models and Development Planning* (Oxford: Oxford University Press).

Chenery, H. B. (1961) 'Comparative Advantages and Development Policy', *American Economic Review*, 51: 18–51.

Chenery, H. B. (1960) 'Patterns of Industrial Growth', *American Economic Review*, 50: 639–54.

Chenery, H. B. *et al.* (1974) *Redistribution with Growth* (New York: Oxford University Press).

Chenery, H. B. and W. Raduchel (1971) 'Substitution in Planning Model', in H. B. Chenery (ed.) *Studies in Development Planning* (Cambridge, Mass.: Harvard University Press) pp. 379–98.

Chenery, H. B. and A. M. Strout (1966) 'Foreign Assistance and Economic Development', *American Economic Review*, 56: 679–733.

Chenery, H. B., S. Robinson and M. Syrquin (forthcoming) *Industrialization and Growth: A Comparative Perspective* (New York: Cambridge University Press).

Deere, C. D. and A. de Janvry (1979) 'A Conceptual Framework for the Empirical Analysis of Peasants', *American Journal of Agricultural Economics*, 61: 601–11.

Emmerij, L. (1986) 'Alternative Development Strategies Based on the Experience of the World Development Program', in I. Adelman and J. E. Taylor (eds) *The Design of Alternative Development Strategies* (Rothak India: Jan Tinbergen Development Institute) pp. 8–26.

Feder, G. (1983) 'On Exports and Economic Growth', *Journal of Development Economics*, 15: 59–74.

Feiwel, G. (1975) *The Intellectual Capital of Michal Kalecki* (Knoxville: University of Tennessee Press).

Food and Agriculture Organization of the United Nations (1981) 'Agriculture: Toward 2000' (Rome: Food and Agricultural Organization).

Gershenkron, A. (1962) *Economic Backwardness in Historical Perspective* (Cambridge, Mass.: Harvard University Press).

International Labor Organization (1972) 'Employment, Incomes, and Equality: A Strategy for Increasing Productive Employment in Kenya' (Geneva: International Labor Organization).

Krueger, A. (1978) *Foreign Trade Regimes and Economic Development: Liberalization* (Cambridge, Mass.: Ballinger Press).

Kuznets, S. (1966) *Modern Economic Growth* (New Haven: Yale University Press).

Leontief, W. (1953) *Studies in the Structure of the American Economy* (New York: Oxford University Press).

Lewis, W. A. (1954) 'Economic Development with Unlimited Supplies of Labor', *The Manchester School*, 33: 139–91.

Little, I. M. D. and J. A. Mirrlees (1968) *Manual of Industrial Project Analysis* (Paris: Organization for Economic Cooperation and Development).

Mellor, J. (1976) *The New Economics of Growth: A Strategy for India and the Developing World* (New York: Twentieth Century Fund).

Nishimizu, M. and S. Robinson (1984) 'Trade Policies and Productivity Change in Semi-industrial Countries', *Journal of Development Economics*, 16: 177–206.

Nurkse, R. (1963) *Problems of Capital Formation in Underdeveloped Countries* (Oxford: Oxford University Press).

Perkins, D. and S. Yusuf (1984) *Rural Development in China* (Baltimore: Johns Hopkins Press).

Prebish, R. (1959) 'Commercial Policy in the Underdeveloped Countries', *American Economic Review*, Papers and Proceedings, 49: 251–73.

Robinson, J. (1952) 'The Model of an Expanding Economy', *Economic Journal*; repr. in Robinson (1960) pp. 74–87.

Robinson, J. (1956) *The Accumulation of Capital* (London: Macmillan).

Robinson, J. (1957a) 'India, 1955: Unemployment and Planning', *Capital: Annual Supplement*; repr. in Robinson (1965b) pp. 182–91.

Robinson, J. (1957b) 'Notes on the Theory of Economic Development', *Annales de la Faculté de Droit de Liège*; repr. in Robinson (1960) pp. 88–106.

Robinson, J. (1958) 'The Philosophy of Prices', *The Manchester School*; repr. in Robinson (1960) pp. 27–48.

Robinson, J. (1960) *Collected Economic Papers*, Vol. II (Oxford: Blackwell).

Robinson, J. (1964a) 'China, 1963: The Communes', *The Political Quarterly*; repr. in Robinson (1965b) pp. 192–206.

Robinson, J. (1964b) 'Consumer's Sovereignty in a Planned Economy', *Essays in Honor of Oskar Lange*; repr. in Robinson (1965) pp. 70–81.

Robinson, J. (1965a) 'Korea, 1964: Economic Miracle', *Monthly Review*; repr. in Robinson (1965b) pp. 207–15.

Robinson, J. (1965b) *Collected Economic Papers*, Vol. III (Oxford: Blackwell).

Robinson, J. (1967a) 'Growth and the Theory of Distribution', *Annals of Public and Cooperative Economy*; repr. in Robinson (1979) pp. 71–5.

Robinson, J. (1967b) 'Marginal Productivity', *Indian Economic Review*; repr. Robinson (1973b) pp. 129–38.

Robinson, J. (1968) 'The Poverty of Nations', *Cambridge Quarterly*; repr. in Robinson (1973b) pp. 106–13.

Robinson, J. (1973a) 'Formalistic Marxism and Ecology Without Classes', *The Journal of Contemporary Asia*; repr. in Robinson (1979) pp. 241–7.

Robinson, J. (1973b) *Collected Economic Papers*, Vol. IV (Oxford, Blackwell).

Robinson, J. (1974) 'Reflections on the Theory of International Trade', Lectures given at the University of Manchester; repr. in Robinson (1979) pp. 130–45.

Robinson, J. (1976) *Economic Management in China* (London: Anglo-Chinese Educational Institute).

Robinson, J. (1977) 'Employment and the Choice of Technique', *Society and Change*; repr. in Robinson (1979) pp. 228–40.

Robinson, J. (1979) *Collected Economic Papers*, Vol. V (Oxford: Blackwell).

Robinson, J. (1981) *Aspects of Development and Underdevelopment* (New York: Cambridge University Press).

Robinson, J. and J. Eatwell (1973) *An Introduction to Modern Economics* (Maidenhead, Berkshire: McGraw-Hill).

Rosenstein-Rodan, P. N. (1943) 'Industrialization of Eastern and Southeastern Europe', *Economic Journal*, 53: 202–11.

Rosenstein-Rodan, P. N. (1957) 'Notes on the Theory of the Big Push', mimeo, International Economic Association.

Rostow, W. W. (1960) *The Stages of Economic Growth* (Cambridge: Cambridge University Press).

Scitovsky, T. (1954) 'Two Concepts of External Economies', *Journal of Political Economy*, 62: 143–51.

Shen, R. (1985) 'A Perspective of Economic Development in PRC', *Review of Business*, 7: 10–13.

Singer, H. (1979) 'Policy Implications of the Lima Target', *Industry and Development*: 17–32.

Streeten, P. P. (1986) 'Basic Needs: The Lessons', in I. Adelman and J. E. Taylor (eds) *The Design of Alternative Development Strategies* (Rothak, India: Jan Tinbergen Development Institute) pp. 27–38.

Taylor, L. (1979) *Macro Models for Developing Countries* (Cambridge, Mass.: MIT Press).

United Nations Industrial Development Organization (1972) *Guidelines for Project Evaluation* (New York: United Nations).

World Bank (1983) *China: Socialist Economic Development*, Vol. I (Washington, DC: The World Bank).

27 Disguised Unemployment and Underemployment

Paul Streeten

In her well-known essay 'Disguised Unemployment' Joan Robinson coined this term for a situation widely observed in the Great Depression in which men, thrown out of regular employment, crowded into occupations like carrying bags, rendering small services or selling matches in the Strand. The reasoning underlying her argument can be brought out by a simple two-sector model: in one sector money wages are rigid downwards; in the other, where self-employment is common, incomes are flexible. In competitive full employment equilibrium, the marginal productivity of labor is the same in both sectors. If then a fall in aggregate demand below the full employment level occurs, men will be thrown out of work in the rigid wage sector, but, rather than become unemployed, will move into the flexible income sector. Money income per man in this sector will fall as more men are accommodated to spread a smaller work load. Productivity differentials (measured in terms of man-years, man-weeks, or man-days, but not in terms of man-hours, for productivity of hours *not* worked is not meaningful, though it is not clear how hours spent waiting for work, or in search of work, should be counted) will increase, but no visible unemployment will appear. The difference between a situation of general low labor productivity (say due to absence of skills) and a situation of disguised unemployment in this sense is that a rise in the level of effective demand will shift workers back into the high-productivity, rigid-wage sector and remove the disguised unemployment. The workers are adapted to the requirements in this sector and, if the time spent in the flexible sector has not been too long, so that they have not forgotten their skills, have remained well fed and healthy and have not been demoralized, a rise in effective demand is a sufficient remedy.

Although the same term has been used, it is immediately obvious that the situation in the rural sector of developing countries is quite different from that described by Joan Robinson. It is true that the rural subsistence sector, in which smallholdings are cultivated by families, resembles the flexible income sector in that it is capable of spreading a constant or slowly growing work load and product over a rapidly growing number of people. But it is not true that an increase of effective demand would, by itself, absorb the excess population in industry. Clearly a series of additional measures would be necessary. Machinery and equipment would have to be provided, infrastructure would have to be constructed, a workforce would have to be trained, disciplined and educated in cooperation, nutrition and health may have to be improved, public services would have to be provided, objections to factory work would have to be removed, etc.

But, looking at the problem simply from the point of view of rural surplus population, it may make sense to ask the question: how many people can be removed from agriculture without reducing output? Rosenstein-Rodan, in a subtle analysis, distinguishes between two basic concepts: the static and the dynamic, according to whether methods of cultivation are assumed not to change or whether they are assumed to change, when the surplus population is removed, while output remains constant.

Rosenstein-Rodan (1956–7) claims that the static concept is clear, whereas the dynamic concept requires a detailed specification of what changes in methods of cultivation are envisaged. These changes might vary from minor changes 'obtained merely through a rearrangement of work with but small additions of circulating capital' to thoroughgoing and even revolutionary changes 'including additional use of both fixed and variable capital'. The dynamic concept, carried to the extreme, becomes irrelevant for policy, because it raises questions such as what would surplus population be if the agricultural sector of an underdeveloped country were cultivated under Dutch conditions.

Rosenstein-Rodan (1956–7) discusses two methods of measuring disguised unemployment in agriculture. The first and *direct method* is based on empirical sample enquiry with questionnaires distinguishing between different types of cultivation, different sizes and forms of property, the composition of the labor force and the 'labor diagram' (number of labor hours required and supplied). Such an enquiry would distinguish between permanent disguised unemployment and frictional or seasonal unemployment.

The *indirect method* may be used in three variants:

(a)   The number of labor hours required to produce a given output is subtracted from the number of labor hours available from the active agrarian population. The difference represents the agrarian surplus population.

(b)   The density of population deemed adequate for a given type of cultivation is subtracted from the actual density of population. In order to take into account different grades of fertility of the soil, conversion coefficients of arable equivalents are used, for example: 1 hectare of garden = 3 hectares of cultivated area; 1 hectare of meadow = 0.4 hectares of cultivated area, etc. (J. Poniatowski, quoted in 'Population in Agriculture', League of Nations, 1939.)

(c)   The number of hectares required under a given type of cultivation to provide one person with a 'standard income' is contrasted with the number of hectares and the agrarian population available. The difference represents people for whom there is no land available and who are therefore 'surplus'. For income calculation, 'crop units' are used by H. E. Moore, instead of the arable equivalents (area conversion coefficients) of J. Poniatowski.

But even on the most stringent static assumptions, amounts of labor required, adequate density and adequate income are vague concepts and involve value judgments.

Rosenstein-Rodan (1956–7) employs the *direct method* to calculate disguised unemployment in southern Italy and spells out very lucidly the assumptions which have to be made in such an enquiry:

(a)   Only agricultural small holdings of 'direct cultivators' (peasant owners and tenants) are considered. Employed workers, even though they may spend time in idleness, are assumed not to be underemployed.

(b)   The agricultural area is divided into representative types of cultivation and each of these types is grouped into holdings by size.

(c)   As labor force in each holding, he assumes active population to comprise persons from 14 to 65 years of age. Fractions can be attached to children below 14 and adults over 65.

Those who work outside their own holdings are excluded. Problems arise if outside work is part-time and if certain jobs are traditionally done by women and others by men and they object to changing this.

(d)   It is assumed that one woman in a household of four is occupied in household activities and not available for cultivation. For larger-sized families greater numbers are assumed.

(e)   It is assumed that those who are in surplus are involuntarily unemployed. Where, owing to custom or religion, women do not accept work outside the home, they should not be counted as disguised unemployed. But it is not entirely clear how men are to be treated who would not wish to do more work than they are doing now, or who would object to different kinds of work from the one they carry out now.

(f)   Labor hours required for each type of cultivation over the whole year, month by month, are counted and compared with available labor hours. In the resulting seasonal underemployment, two kinds are distinguished: (i) 'seasonal underemployment of the productive capacity', which depends on biological and technical factors in growing crops; and (ii) 'seasonal underemployment proper', which takes into account labor not available for climatic reasons, such as snow, and institutional reasons, such as holidays. These reduce the number of working days available during the year.

(g)   Next, allowance is made for the fact that the number of labor hours available in different months varies: fewer in the winter and more in the summer.

(h)   After labor hours have been calculated in terms of labor units (men and women), allowance must be made for the fact that not all underemployed thus calculated could be removed without causing output to decline. Only entire labor units (men and women) whose removal would not cause such a decline can be considered as surplus. Rosenstein-Rodan therefore distinguishes between (i) removable disguised underemployment; (b) disguised fractional underemployment, i.e. labor hours not used through the year which do not add up to an entire labor unit. These cannot be removed without a decline in output but they can be provided with part-time work in rural industries, rural public works, etc.; and (c) seasonal underemployment due to climatic factors. Even a brief seasonal peak, together with a serious adherence to *ceteris paribus*, greatly reduces the amount of disguised unemployment.

(i)   A slight relaxation of the strict *ceteris paribus* rule can be permitted; to allow for reorganization of peak loads of up to two months, and in this way the size of the surplus population can be considerably increased – doubled in southern Italy.

Reference

Rosenstein-Rodan, P. N. (1956–7) 'Disguised Unemployment and Underemployment in Agriculture', *Monthly Bulletin of Agricultural Economics and Statistics*, 6(7–8): 1–7.

28 International Economics in Embryo

Martin Bronfenbrenner

When we buy foreign goods, we get the goods and the foreigner gets the money. When we buy our own goods, we get the goods and the money both. *Abraham Lincoln* (?)

Two circumstances inspire this venture into ancient history, or prehistory if you will. The first circumstance is the current (1985–6) relapse of the international monetary system into an oligarchy of Central Bank and Finance Ministry discretion (and indiscretion) for however long the oligarchs can agree among themselves and leave the rest of us bedazzled by their perspicacity. The second circumstances is only the fortieth anniversary of my own initial attempt to teach International Economics to undergraduates (at Roosevelt University in Chicago, in the spring of 1947). Before my ageing memory fails completely, I shall try to reconstruct what was being taught to American college students of that day about the macroeconomic side of international economics in that epoch of intractable – some even said, of *permanent* – dollar shortage.

I base this effort on two models which differ drastically from each other. One of these is Lord Keynes's essay on 'My Early Beliefs', and we might recall that he had passed away only one year before I began international-economics teaching, although I was already a chalky veteran in some other branches of the economics curriculum. My second model (or anti-model) has been the prolonged squabble among Milton Friedman, Don Patinkin, Paul Samuelson, and others about 'what neoclassical monetary theory really was', especially at Chicago, before the Keynesian revelation and/or revolution of 1936.

An autobiographical paragraph or two may be in point to conclude this introduction.

My teacher of international economics had been Jacob Viner at Chicago, but when I attended his lectures in 1935, they had stressed doctrinal history and we had read in manuscript the first half, more or less, of his classic *Studies in the Theory of International Trade*. It is all very well to consider in some detail the genesis of received doctrine when one knows in elementary fashion what this doctrine is, and Professor Viner may have justifiably expected his graduate students to have absorbed the conventional wisdom as undergraduates. But I, for one, lacked any such background.[1] If I recall

727

correctly, the main substantive controversy to engage much class time was that sparked by Keynes and Bertil Ohlin on the transfer problem of German reparations after World War I – whether or not one could prove the existence of a 'secondary burden' on Germany owing to deterioration in the German terms of trade. (The class concluded, though I disagreed, that such a proof was impossible within the rules of the trade theory 'game', making Ohlin right and Keynes wrong in the real world!) And since 1935 anteceded the great micro-macro bifurcation in theoretical economics, Viner took pains to defend the classical and neoclassical trade theorists (including himself and his teacher, F. W. Taussig of Harvard) from charges of neglecting 'income effects' in the mechanism of trade-balance adjustment. (A later fashion has been to assume income and employment constant in trade theory, leaving to 'open-economy macroeconomics' the exploration of their variations as related to international factors, and decrying the muddying of distinctions between the two.)

My performance in Viner's trade theory and policy classes having been mediocre, I had finished graduate school with no desire for further work in international economics. It was Japan which reversed this decision – wartime background under US Navy auspices in the country's language and history, followed by direct personal exposure in Northern Kyushu to its overriding economic question of the immediate post-war period. The question: could the new Japan, after the loss of the entire overseas Empire, the war damage at home, and some 6 million extra repatriates and demobilized troops to be fed, ever recover to the point of economic self-support? And if so when, how, and at what approximate percentage of its pre-war living standard? The Occupation view, as expressed by the geographer Edward Ackerman's *Japan's Prospect*, was highly pessimistic, the shell-shocked Japanese seemed equally so, although I later learned that some of their economic statesmen were not.[2]

Such questions were by no means peculiar to Japan, but they were perhaps more acute there than in some other countries, the more so because Japan's status as defeated enemy and 'War Criminal, Inc.' brought no special claim on the victors' largesse. And need I say, graduate school international economics had provided no 'handle' for dealing with these questions.

In the bloodless and unemotional terms of professional economic discourse, the problem of feeding the hungry was soon translated into the problem of 'dollar shortage'. I believe the translation was accepted quite early in 1946. For countries toward which dollar countries' aid policy was expected to be niggardly or worse, could dollars be earned for the materials of reconstruction and recovery without imposing mass starvation on the populace? And for the remainder of the non-dollar world, what were the prospects of shortening and minimizing dependence on fickle or conditional American generosity?

The pessimistic thesis of 'structural dollar shortage' argued the necessity of discrimination against dollar exports wherever possible, and rationing them as a second-best substitute. Discrimination and rationing might last into the indefinite future. For American 'productivity' advantages, achieved or enhanced during the war, would surely grow with time as America continued to learn by doing and devoted resources to research and development (R&D), while potential rivals were limited to reconstruction of basically pre-war facilities wihtout funding for adequate R&D. ('Structural' means in this case that a problem has no free-market equilibrium solution, that any equilibrium solution is unstable, or that a stable solution is precluded by political or social constraints impossible to override within the conventional parameters of market economics, principally exchange-rate and wage adjustments.) The Keynesians of the Left, following Thomas Balogh and Michal Kalecki and including Mrs Robinson, were decidedly of this persuasion.

But I was myself a dollar-shortage optimist, like most of my colleagues at the several 'Chicagoland' universities and research institutions.[3] I believed the dollar-shortage problem basically the over-evaluation of foreign currencies against both dollar and gold. It was therefore amenable to devaluation of these currencies against dollars and gold,[4] by the wise men of the International Monetary Fund (IMF) under the 'fundamental disequilibrium' clause of that agency's charter. The processes of devaluation might require repetition from time to time, but there was no need to float exchange rates and risk revival of the competitive devaluations of the pre-war decade. Neither was there need to invoke the 'scarce currency' clause of the same IMF charter outside of brief and pathological situations. (This clause authorized IMF sanction for discrimination against the exports of countries which were in persistent excess demand at official rates, but where the disequilibrium was less than 'fundamental!'[5] It believed, in other words, that the foreign-exchange markets were stable, and the Marshall–Lerner stability conditions accordingly satisfied nearly all the time, the sum of a country's long-term demand for its own imports and the world's long-term demand for the country's exports adding to at least unity.

At that time I considered myself a Keynesian, albeit perhaps a right-wing deviationist as indicated by an essay on 'The Dilemma of Liberal Economics' which I had published in the *Journal of Political Economy* in the previous summer (August 1946). But I was among the minority of Keynesians as impressed with 'Keynes's last article' as with anything in the *General Theory* itself. That article, which appeared in the *Economic Journal* in the spring of 1946, dealt with 'The Balance of Payments of the United States'. In this essay Keynes had spoken of America as 'a high-living, high-cost country' from which little need be feared in the long run as regards international competitiveness. With this view I agreed most thoroughly, for 1946 was the year of the '54-for-40' strikes. In this wave of strikes, the American organized-labor movement strove, and largely succeeded, in combining the money (and real) incomes of the wartime fifty-four-hour work week with the easier life of the peacetime forty hour one. But to the true-blue Keynesian with Kaleckian overtones, 'Keynes's last article' was a sick man's relapse into childish conventionality, to be passed over in embarrassed silence, (Of such schism in the Keynesian church, I became aware only much later.)

But however lapsing might be my Keynesian faith, I was less of a 'free market' man than I think I am today. To secure the right exchange rates and appropriate devaluations of pounds and francs and guilders and such, I was placing my trust in the impartial expertise of the IMF's wise men, not in the world's financial markets. (Milton Friedman's call for 'clean' floating of exchange rates was not written until 1950 and not published until his *Positive Economics* of 1953; I make no claim to anticipating him.)

Sidney Alexander's 'absorption approach', an alternative to depreciation in dealing with the dollar shortage, was equally far over the horizon; it appeared in 1952. But I was among many – 'policy activists' we might now be called – thinking along similar lines in 1947 and even before. My private variant, in fact, involved greater scope for administration discretion than Alexander's, being less aggregative. Rather than cutting back generalized or overall domestic absorption (the textbook $C + I + G$) to permit a rise in the foreign balance (textbook $X - M$ or $X - Im$) with given resources and continuing high unemployment, I thought deficit countries like Britain should balance their international accounts in part by disarmament and in part by limitations or outright bans on luxury housing and the construction of entertainment facilities.[6] Such limitations might not eliminate the need for currency depreciation – here I may have been less sanguine than Alexander – but they would lessen the size, shock, and strain of the necessary devaluations. I was still puritanical enough to think that 'luxury' investments (and imports) could be defined and restricted with neither incentive effects nor diversion of domestic production into black markets.

So far I have been able to proceed with some degree of overall complacency and self-satisfaction overall. So far but no further, for I had no inkling whatever that the same forces which I trusted to mitigate the dollar shortage might lead on to dollar glut, or that the United States might, within little more than a generation, join the sick men's club of the international economy, or that Japanese recovery would assume 'miraculous' proportions. So I propose to spend the remainder of these pages pinpointing a few causes for my poor foresight in the specific contexts of America, of Japan, and of Japanese–American economic relations. I naturally hope that some part of my explanations will have broader applications – to other pairs of countries and other situations as well as to the shortcomings of other economists.

It turns out, I now believe, that my errors transcended conventional economics. They cannot be blamed on my professional ground or on any of my teachers. They may even add up to a case for a more interdisciplinary or multidisciplinary approach in international studies than I have been willing to advocate. At any rate, I associate my failures with the following six factors, some rather technical and some expressed in terms more abstract than meaningful:

1. A 'back to normalcy' syndrome.
2. An underestimate of the difficulties of shifts or 'transitions' between equilibrium positions.
3. An overestimate of the advantages of exchnage-rate stability, even at 'wrong' rates.
4. An underestimate of the international-economic consequences for America of its political commitment to high employment 'at whatever cost'.
6. And possibly, some elements of possible racism in my underestimate of the economic potential of Japanese labor.

I beg your indulgence in considering these six considerations in order, some of them at considerable length.

1 'BACK TO NORMALCY'

This ungrammatical term we owe to one of America's least-admired Presidents, Warren G. Harding (1921–3). The underlying idea, however, was shared by many European contemporaries of greater repute, especially in Britain and France. It surfaced again in 1945–6 with respect to Japan.

I, for example, considered as 'normal' – meaning 'workable' but by no means 'Utopian' – a Japan in the economic situation of the mid-1930s. This was *after* the country's rapid recovery from the Great Depression, a recovery I ascribed to 'Takahashi finance' rather than to the Manchurian expansion of 1931. The period was also *before* Japan's large-scale invasion of China in 1937, before the Tripartite Pact with the European Axis Powers, and before the war-industry build-up which accompanied these events. For all its brevity, its eventual futility, and its undercurrent of military terrorism, this interlude seemed in retrospect a taste of 'belle epoque', like the pre-1914 decade in Western Europe and North America. It was a period of high employment and considerable prosperity in low-wage, labor-intensive economy, churning out light industrial goods like textiles and garments along with economy or budget or utility models of medium industrial goods like cameras and bicycles, aimed at the world's poor. (By 'the world's poor' I mean not only the less-developed countries but also those in the richer countries who made do with 'cheap junk' from 'bargain basements'.)

This was the role I anticipated Japan might and should play again, this time on a larger scale in a more prosperous world. I accordingly viewed with some doubt and a little suspicion both American Occupation and Japanese

Government policies to maintain or raise real-wages, to keep young people in school longer and reduce the size of the labor force, to raise the skilled-labor intensity of the country's industrial output, and increasingly to move 'up-market' in the world economy.[7] To me, such policies seemed reckless and perhaps even suicidal, moving Japan suddenly from positions of comparative advantage (competitive with less-developed countries) to positions of comparative disadvantage (losing out to Europe and America). It was like forcing a successful 5-and-10-cent store chain like Woolworth's into competition with Macy's and Bloomingdale's if not with Saks Fifth Avenue. I feared that its motivation might include the safeguarding of American firms from the most dangerous sorts of Japanese price competition; I was surprised to see such Japanese agencies as MITI carry the program further and faster after the Occupation packed its carpet-bags and went home.

In terms of Japan's international competitiveness in various industries, I could easily anticipate trouble for American exporters in Third World countries, and indeed for labor-intensive American industries in the home market – the 'dollar blouses' of 1954–5 are examples I remember. I could even anticipate problems with Japanese cameras and bicycles within the home market, or some Japanese 'econo-box' competing with the Volkswagen 'beetle' and with second-hand American cars – or for that matter (at the other end of the scale) a Japanese competitor with Cadillac, Mercedes-Benz, and Rolls-Royce for the carriage trade. But anything more was beyond the realm of possibility. Automobiles and tractors and electrical goods were *ours* by divine right, just as our balance of trade had always been positive ever since the 1890s! Such were the parameters of 'normalcy' – and I need not add that I was completely wrong.

2   ECONOMIC ADJUSTMENT PROCESSES

Like many another economic pedagogue before and since, I was in the classroom habit of comparing the overall effectiveness of economic 'laws' and 'forces' in the real world to that of gravity in a world of feathers with a high wind blowing. But at the same time, my 'policy' thinking for particular markets tended along conventional lines. Equilibrium positions were statistically stable while evolving at the pace of 'molasses going uphill in winter'. Overshooting adjustments were strongly damped when they existed at all. Quantities of inputs and outputs were supplied or demanded entirely on present or anticipated near-future prices, not on rates of price change or the relation of prices to some other prices regarded rightly or wrongly as normal, fair, or just.

Exchange, money, and other markets impinging directly upon international trade and capital movements have come to violate these implicit assumptions. (Perhaps, indeed, they always did – a strong case for such institutions as metallic standards and exchange controls and even quotas.) In the short term, exchange markets may be unstable; the Marshall–Lerner conditions may not hold, and the course of trade balances for devaluating countries may follow 'J-curve' patterns.[8] Movements of equilibrium may be both sudden and substantial; the world 'oil shock' makes this point even more sharply than the outbreaks of two World Wars. A strong speculative element may win or lose fortunes on the basis of right or wrong extrapolations of price-change series, based themselves on 'new information' – which may be deceptive 'disinformation' circulated and contradicted with a view to rocking markets and increasing speculative gains. And at another extreme, considerations of 'fairness' retard adjustments to prices which violate them, even when these prices result from such impersonal forces as technical progress, exchange fluctuations, and interest-rate changes. If excessive price volatility is the economic equivalent of chorea, price rigidity corresponds to arthritis and arteriosclerosis. In a world beset by both sets of ailments, long-term decision-making becomes additionally difficult. And in such a world, 'getting the prices right' is both a more arduous and a less effective task than I presumed in my early ventures into international-economics teaching. For, even when we have got the prices right, what are the probabilities of their remaining so?

3 STABILITY FOR ITS OWN SAKE

At the same time, and inconsistently into the bargain, I was overly impressed with the convenience and associated advantages of exchange-rate stability as an end in itself, and without sufficient attention for the realization of the level being stabilized. My prime example is, naturally enough the Y360 to the dollar exchange rate of 1949–71. Hindsight suggests that it should have been brought down in easy stages by the IMF to perhaps Y300 by 1970, to recognize the 'fundamental disequilibrium' brought on by Japanese recovery and its 'miraculous' *kōdō-seichō* (high growth) period (1955–73). But I was 'too little and too late' in realizing what was going on, bemused undoubtedly by three circumstances. Obviously the Y360 rate made Japan, even Tokyo, a relatively cheap place for my family and myself to live on our fairly frequent visits there. And although that rate was originally regarded by the Occupation authorities as a special favor to Japanese export and self-sufficiency in 1949, when a Y320 rate would have been closer to purchasing-power parity, I myself thought that rate too low in view of black-market rates of Y400, Y450, and even Y500 I had known as late as the outbreak of the Korean War. (I am not sure how these (probably disequilibrium) rates are to be explained.[9]) And finally, I had a vested interest in rate fixity, having been the monetary-fiscal policy member of the Occupation team which fixed the exchnage rate for the *Ryūkyūan* (Okinawan) yen at 120 to the dollar and 3

Japanese yen. (I was proud that this rate stuck until 1958, when the Ryukyus temporarily adopted the United States dollar – a political error which smacked of 'economic imperialism' but lasted until the reversion of the islands to Japan.)

4   PROCESSING ECONOMIES

One reason for my spellbound fixation on things as they were, or on pre-war conceptions of 'normalcy', was my emphasis on the role of natural resources in limiting a country's industrial export potential. I took quite seriously the rationale of various LDCs for import-substitution policies on the grounds of having 'nothing to export'. In the Japanese case, I knew the facts of cotton textile exports based since the middle of the Meiji Era on the processing of imported raw cotton, but without thinking that similar arrangements might occur in the newer heavy industries – at a level more important for value-added than the final assembly stage. I had seen in late 1945 the big steel complex at Yawata on the north coast of Kyushu, but again, without reflecting upon its meaning. In fact I thought the sea coast combination of imported ore, imported coke, and domestic limestone to be an uneconomic wasteful expedient undertaken for exclusively military reasons. But what was that complex in actuality, underneath the rust and grime of minor war damage and major wartime neglect of upkeep? The shape of things to come! Not only in steel, but in oil refining and petrochemicals and chemicals in general and many another branch of manufacture. And not only in Japan, but in Korea and Taiwan and Singapore and virtually anywhere else with harbor facilities and skilled labor. Harbor facilities and skilled labor: given these, a country's need for specialized resources was minimal. The processing economies could rival the resource economies to a steadily increasing degree, Japan being an early case in point.

5   HIGH EMPLOYMENT 'AT WHATEVER COST'

We may well dispute the strength, sincerity, and limits of the American commitment to either 'high' or 'full' employment, as embodied in the Employment Act of 1946. But on one point we can agree: it is impossibly bad politics for even the most conservative or reactionary American Administration, or its economic spokesmen, to tell a major union or labor federation under any circumstances that: 'Your last set of gains was uneconomically high, and will lower employment in your industry. That loss in employment will be your own fault, and you may stew in your own juice.' Instead key increases tend to be quietly – and in some Administrations incompletely – validated or accompanied by expansionary (inflationary) monetary and fiscal policies.

(the monetary ones have been, in my opinion, the more effective.) And there has been insufficient concern with international repercussions. That is to say, wage increases in domestic or 'sheltered' industries like the building and service trades have been treated much like those in export or import-competing industries like steel and autos. Wage increases were passed through to consumers; collective bargaining became in large measure collusive, across the board. Which was all very well for America in the heyday of 'dollar shortage'.

But with the recovery and expansion of Western Europe, and the onset of *kōdō-seichō* in Japan, the situation changed in some degree. Sheltered industries could engage in collective or collusive bargaining as before, but the international ones – whether exporting, import-competing, or in rapid transit from the first to the second status – were in different positions entirely. I for one anticipated a novel brand of dualism in the American wage structure, with international competitive pressure moderating union demands and strengthening employer resistance in one international industry after another, while the sheltered industries continued ever onward and upward. But I had either reckoned without the American labor movement's 'instinct of equity' or mistaken the direction in which it would operate. Given the American political climate, the international industries too felt compelled to continue their now-outmoded but still-convenient strategies: wage-push, collusive-bargain, pass-through. And then, when unemployment and profits both declined as anticipated, with the shrinkage of export markets and import competition gaining ground at home, management and labor – particularly labor – have 'bayed at the moon' with complaints – often justified in special cases.[10] These complaints were (1985–6) reflected in protectionist rumblings and dollar devaluations *de facto*, where I in my ignorance had anticipated moderation or demise of cost-, sellers'-, administered-, or similar inflationary pressures from the supply side.

6 RACISM?

I wish that racist elements on the American side of the festering Japanese–American trade 'frictions' – a certain alternation of unjustified condescension with unreasoning hostility – were less obvious. (And also, that the Japanese side did not respond in kind.) My question is only whether, despite the special advantages of a semi-professional Japanologist, I have avoided sharing in my countrymen's racism, at least in its condescending phases.

For I recall being asked by an industrial consultant, in 1950 or 1951, whether I thought Japanese workers might someday be taught to manufacture zippers. And also being asked some years later (1958) by an industrial engineer whether Japanese workers might someday be taught to manufacture computers, or at least computer parts. In each case I said, factually enough, that I did not know. In each case, my answer should have been a strong affirmation, since Japanese workers are now second to none in both these branches of industrial endeavor. At the very least, I should have said something like this: 'If the employer does an adequate job of worker selection – weeding out incompetents, problem children, and potential trouble-makers in advance,[11] of course Japanese workers are as good as Westerners!' How could I have made such mistakes? What explanation is there, other than racist condescension?

Two explanations, both flawed, present themselves. One candidate is a misinterpretation of Japanese wartime performance, and the other, an overly pessimistic assessment of Occupation educational reforms.

I knew something about Japan's unanticipated advances in military technology, ranging from the Zero fighter plane to the light tank to nocturnal binoculars, and not forgetting the Yawata steel complex already mentioned. But since 'defence is of much more importance than opulence' (Adam Smith, *Wealth of Nations*), especially in wartime, perhaps such advances were impractical in peacetime. Many things, we know, are technically possible but not worth doing, Adam Smith's famous example being viticulture in the inhospitable climate of his native land: 'By means of glasses, hotbeds, very good grapes can be raised in Scotland, and very good wine can be made from them at about thirty times the expense for which at least equally good can be bought from foreign countries.' As I have admitted, I had written off Yawata in my own mind as another 'Scottish winery'.

It likewise seemed to me, as early as 1949–50, that the Japanese skilled-labor potential (like the American!) was threatened with diversion from cheap, short, private, cook-bookish, but eminently practical institutes or *semmon gakkō*, often with apprenticeship features, in the holy name of educational democracy for working-class children. It was being diverted, after nine years of public education, into conventional, standardized, three-year senior high school (*kōtō-gakkō*) programs in mathematics, science, literature, social studies, and the English language. 'Better a first-class electrician or mechanic than another marginal engineering trainee,' I thought, and criticized my Civil Information and Education (CIE) colleagues in the SCAP bureaucracy especially sharply because neither the kids nor their parents, aside from an academically talented minority, showed great enthusiasm for longer education disguised as higher.[12] What I was here ignoring was primarily the effectiveness of Japanese OJT (on-the-job training – and retraining!) programs which companies already had for the screened and selected high-school graduates they had hired for long-term, blue-collar employment. And neither was I making adequate allowance for the absence, in Japan, of Western-style craft unionism with its built-in job classifications, jurisdictional disputations, and resistances to retraining.

And so, in conclusion, I admit to having been wrong, but deny that my rationalizations for error are to any significant extent racist.

I entitled this paper 'International Economics in Embryo' before starting to write it. As the writing proceeded, I felt more than once that I should change the title to 'An International Economist in Embryo'. But, of course, the two topics are interrelated at least by the accident of time, and perhaps the title I retained has the greater generality of coverage and possibly even appeal.

But at the same time, the paper's purpose is in fact to a large extent subjective. It would be pleasing to inspire other international economists – American, Japanese, European, socialist, or underdeveloped – to similar exercises in intellectual and personal history and autobiography covering the same approximate period. In particular, I should like to learn, from sources closer to the seats of power, why American policy drifted as it did, and also why the IMF role was reduced to that of passive bystander.

The comparative study of such accounts, however subjective and even biased, would benefit both standard doctrinal history and the contemporary fad of 'economic rhetoric'. Would that the 'first Keynesian generation', before passing completely from the scene, might have left us more of such memorials than we seem likely to obtain!

Notes

1. As a concession to underprepared students like me, Viner permitted for term-paper purposes the soft option of writing a comparative review of the 'trade theory' chapters of elementary textbooks, with special attention to the mechanism of trade-balance adjustment. Of the half-dozen texts I chose to consider for this assignment, the first edition of the 'Minnesota' one (by F. B. Garver and Alvin Hansen) impressed me as best by a wide margin.
2. See, for example, Dr Okita Saburo's autobiography, entitled in English *Japan's Challenging Years*. The relevant chapters are 4–5.
3. In addition to Roosevelt University and the University of Chicago, these included, listing only places where I had friends and acquaintances, Northwestern University, the Chicago campus of the University of Illinois, the Federal Reserve Bank of Chicago, and the Economic Club of Chicago.
4. 'Dollars and gold' were used almost synonymously, in view of the fixed dollar price of gold ($35 an ounce). I cannot recall hearing any proposals to alleviate the dollar shortage by up-valuing the dollar (lowering the price of gold).
5. The clause was probably intended as a threat against countries with trade and payments supluses who might be tempted to deflationary macroeconomic policies.
6. Night clubs, movie theatres, and questionable 'hotels' were my especial targets in 1947, as I had seen the large-scale construction of such facilities (for Occupation Forces) take precedence over housing construction in immediate post-war Fukuoya, Japan. Sports arenas, stadiums, and race tracks came next, soon to be followed by soft-drink bottling plants. (On moving to the University of Wisconsin in the autumn of 1947, I was disappointed to find promised housing delayed for a large Coca-Cola bottling plant.)
7. At the very top of the market, where artisanship and craftsmanship merge with fine art, Japan had also competed pre-war and could compete again. By

moving 'up-market' I mean only moving into the great 'middle mass' segments.

8. The free-market, floating-rate reaction to payments imbalances tends to up-value currencies in excess demand (those of surplus countries) and to devaluate currencies in excess supply (those of deficit countries). The Marshall-Lerner condition – that the reciprocal demands of each pair of countries for each other's goods should add to at least unity – provides that in a pure-trade world without capital movements these exchange-rate changes will in fact shift international balances in an equilibrating direction ... The J-curve phenomenon trades the course of the trade balance of a deficit country when the Marshall-Lerner condition is satisfied in the long run but not immediately.

9. Two theories: (1) Japan banned capital exports, and the Occupation was rumored to be keeping records of military and civilian personnel converting 'too much' military currency into greenbacks when leaving the country. Tax evaders, black-marketeers, and others anxious to move funds out of the country in a hurry were raising the value of the greenback; (2) Japanese, unusually eager for luxuries obtainable only at Occupation Post Exchanges (PXs) for dollars, would bid up the dollar when such items were available – often only at rare intervals.

10. Readers familiar with the 'Scandinavian' theory of inflation and its international transmission will note that I have stood on its head, in a sense, the doctrine associated with the Norwegian economist Odd Aukrust. In Aukrust's analysis, 'Korean' and 'Vietnamese' war inflations came to neutral Norway through rising freight rates and windfall profits for marine industries, shared with workers in the seafaring and shipbuilding trades. Considerations of equity then extended these wage gains to the sheltered industries and macroeconomic policy accommodation followed to maintain employment in these sheltered industries ... In both the Norwegian and American cases, 'equity' worked in only one direction – upward.

11. On these 'screening' problems, see my (much later) 'Essays on Negative Screening', in T. Shishido and R. Sato (eds) (1986) *Economic Policy and Development: New Perspectives*, ch. 14.

12. A perceptive Japanese-born critic (Mrs Bronfenbrenner) inquires skeptically whether I am accusing either the Occupation or CIE of trying to sabotage Japanese productivity for fear of future commercial competition. Such an accusation would be nonsense, and I do not make it. These people were sincere disciples of 'educational democracy' as an end in itself, whatever its side effects on productivity and economic growth.

29 The Classical Transfer Problem and the Theory of Foreign Exchanges

John S. Chipman*

The theory of the exchanges may be regarded as the analysis of the manner in which movements of the balance of trade and the balance of lending are equated to each other. (Joan Robinson)

1 INTRODUCTION

This essay analyzes a model that, for over a hundred years, has lurked behind discussions of the transfer mechanism and the theory of foreign exchanges, yet has never been made explicit. The model originates with John Stuart Mill (1848, vol. II, book III, ch. XXI) and was developed by Taussig (1917, 1927), Keynes (1930), and Robinson (1937a) among others. It underlies what Samuelson (1952) called the 'orthodox presumption' in the theory of the transfer problem; and it also lies at the basis of the simplest expositions of the so-called 'elasticity approach' to the balance of payments. Of course, one cannot say definitely that the model presented here faithfully represents the notions adhered to only subconsciously by all these writers; but it does reproduce (and make plausible) some of the most prominent propositions associated with these doctrines, as well as expose (and explain) some of the fallacies involved in their misapplication and misinterpretation.

The essential features of the model may be depicted diagrammatically in Figure 29.1. There are two countries and three commodities; commodities 1 and 2 are tradable (with no transport costs) and commodity 3 in each country is non-tradable. There is a single factor of production (labor) which, in each country, is allocated freely between the export good and the non-tradable under conditions of constant returns to scale. Neither country produces any amount of the import good. Assuming (by convention) that country k exports commodity k, and denoting by y_j^k country k's output of commodity j ($=k,3$), each country has a linear (Ricardian) production-

*I wish to thank the Stiftung Volkswagenwerk, Hannover, and the Riksbankens Jubileums-fond, Stockholm, for research support.

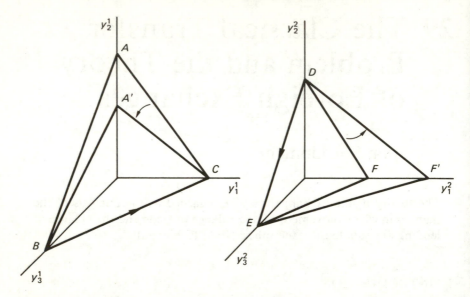

Figure 29.1 Country 1 (depicted on the left) makes a transfer to country 2 (depicted on the right). There results a movement along country 1's production-possibility frontier *BC* in the direction of more output of its export good (commodity 1) and less of its non-tradable (commodity 3). There is a similar movement along country 2's production-possibility frontier *DE* in the direction of more output of its non-tradable (commodity 3) and less of its export good (commodity 2). With higher world output of commodity 1 and lower world output of commodity 2, country 1's terms of trade may be expected to deteriorate; this is shown by country 1's budget triangle swinging inward from *BCA* to *BCA'*, and country 2's swinging outward from *DEF* to *DEF'*.

possibility frontier as between its export good and its non-tradable. Assuming that all goods are required in consumption, each country must produce a positive amount of both its export good and its non-tradable; in equilibrium, the relative prices of these goods are therefore fixed. This is the only logical meaning, in a general equilibrium model, that one can attach to the assumption of an 'infinite elasticity of supply of exports'.

Now consider the transfer problem. In an initial equilibrium, the prices faced by consumers in each country are depicted by budget triangles whose bases are the production-possibility segments. If country 1 now makes a transfer to country 2, consumers in the receiving country will (if all goods are superior) wish to consume more of their non-tradable (commodity 3), which they can do only if resources are transferred out of the export industry (as indicated by the arrow); the reverse reallocation must take place in the paying country. As a result of these reallocations, the world supply of commodity 1 is increased and that of commodity 2 is diminished. Under some fairly plausible conditions (e.g. equal marginal propensities to consume tradables as between countries, independently of expenditure levels and prices of non-tradables) this will result in a fall in the price of commodity 1 relative to commodity 2, i.e. in a deterioration of country 1's terms of trade. This is the so-called 'orthodox presumption'.

Mill (1848, II, p.158; 1895, II, p.183) analyzed the workings of this process under a gold standard. Referring to the paying country (England) he stated:

> The currency is accordingly contracted: prices fall, and among the rest, the prices of exportable articles; for which accordingly, there arises, in foreign countries, a greater demand: while imported commodities have possibly risen in price, from the influx of money into foreign countries, and at all events have not participated in the general fall.

He went on to explain how the change in the terms of trade would lead to adjustments in supply and demand restoring equilibrium in payments.[1]

Taussig (1917; 1927, ch.26) analyzed the same process under conditions of flexible exchange rates, assuming each country to have a fixed money supply (1917, p.397; 1927, p.341), and concluded that the currency of the receiving country would appreciate while nominal prices of non-tradables would remain unchanged. The nominal prices of imports would fall in the receiving country and rise in the paying country.[2] The analyses of Keynes (1930) and Robinson (1937a) followed in this tradition, Keynes specifically acknowledging his indebteness to Taussig (Keynes, 1930, I; p.334n.) and Robinson likewise to Keynes of the *Treatise* (Robinson, 1937a, p.183n.; 1947a, p.134n.). But Taussig's explicit assumptions concerning the role of the money supply and of non-tradables were lost in the process. These explicit assumptions were restored by Meade (1951a,b).

In the model developed in Section 2, in which preferences in each country are assumed to be aggregable, it is shown that each country has a 'trade-demand function' (cf. Chipman, 1979) expressing net imports of the two tradables as a function of the two prices and the balance of payments on current account, and that this function is generated by maximizing a 'trade-utility function', which has the two trades (net imports) as arguments, subject to a balance-of-payments constraint. This generalizes Meade's (1953) construction to the case of non-tradables, and allows one to draw strictly-convex-to-the-origin trade-indifference curves in the space of imports and exports, and to use the entire Marshallian offer-curve apparatus.[3] Since, in this model, the real exchange rate (defined as the price of country 2's non-tradable – in units of country 1's currency – relative to the price of country 1's non-tradable – in units of its own currency) is a constant proportion of country 2's terms of trade, Marshallian analysis can be validly used whenever monetary conditions are such that the nominal exchange rate (the price of country 2's currency in units of country 1's currency) is proportional to the real exchange rate, i.e. the ratio of own-currency prices of non-tradables is constant. The latter condition can be guaranteed by assuming that each country stabilizes the nominal price (in its own currency) of its non-tradable.[4] This is assumed in Section 3 below. If the demand for money is proportional to income (as opposed to expenditure or 'absorption'), this condition can be ensured by assuming a constant money supply in each country – as was done by Taussig. If the demand for money is proportional to expenditure, then a varying money supply would be required; if each country's money supply were constant, then the Marshallian analysis would no longer be valid.

In Section 3 it is shown that Samuelson's (1952) criterion for a transfer to worsen the paying country's terms of trade can be applied without change to the trade-demand functions; in place of the countries' marginal propensities to consume are the 'marginal trade-propensities to import', i.e. the partial derivatives of the trade-demand functions with respect to the current-account deficit. In the receiving country (country 2), the marginal trade-propensity to import its import good (commodity 1) is equal to its marginal propensity to consume this good – since it is not produced in the country. However, the marginal trade-propensity to import its export good (commodity 2) is the sum of the marginal propensity to consume this good and a term equal to the product of the marginal propensity to consume the non-tradable and the cost ratio between the non-tradable and the export good (formula (32) below). Intuitively (assuming all three goods to be superior), when country 2 receives a transfer, it will expend a certain proportion of it on imports in accordance with the marginal propensity to consume the import good; but it will have to divert resources from the export industry to the non-tradables industry to produce its extra requirements of the non-tradable, hence its increased demand for exportables will consist of the direct demand plus the indirect demand needed to make up for the diversion of resources. A similar analysis holds for country 1. Hence, if it is assumed that preferences as between the countries are such that the marginal propensities to consume the tradables are the same, independently of the price of the non-tradable and the level of expenditure, then the two countries' marginal propensities to consume each commodity will be the same. The indirect effect then insures that country 2 will have a larger marginal trade-propensity to import its own export good than country 1. There is no need to make artificial assumptions concerning countries' relative preferences for their own export goods; production conditions fully account for the 'orthodox presumption', in accordance with Mill's original explanation.

In a general model of flexible exchange rates, one would want to allow for variations in countries' money supplies as an additional source of variations in exchange rates. Some models go to the other extreme and rule out capital movements by assumption, and thus allow no other than monetary explanations for the exchange rate.[5] These, of course, lead essentially to some form of 'purchasing-power–parity' doctrine. The 'elasticity approach', requiring one to be able to interpret nominal exchange rates as proportional to real exchange rates, and thus requiring the above stabilization assumptions, leaves capital movements as essentially the only exogenous variable of interest. It is, therefore, essentially the theory of the transfer problem. This theory has tended to be narrowly identified with the theory of the effect of a transfer on the terms of trade; it does reduce to that under the special assumptions of this paper.[6] More broadly, it is the theory of how a change in the capital account brings about an equal and opposite change in the current account.

The main use to which the 'elasticity approach' was put during the Bretton Woods era was in the analysis of the effect of a devaluation. But here there has been a fundamental confusion. I can do no better than quote from Kemp (1962, p.314):

> If one country devalues its currency in terms of other currencies, what will happen to its terms of trade, its price level, and its balance of payments? ... The problem of determining the impact of a once-over devaluation on the balance of payments has often been identified with *the question of dynamic exchange stability*. In fact the questions are quite dissimilar ... The question of exchange stability calls for a model in which the rate of exchange appears as a *variable*, the value of which is to be determined by the system itself. The questions posed in the preceding paragraph, however, call for a model in which the rate of exchange appears as a *parameter*.

The confusion arises out of the fact that if the dynamic-adjustment process posits the rate of change of a country's exchange rate as a sign-preserving function of the world excess demand for its exports,[7] then it is a sign-preserving function of the *value* of the world excess demand for its exports – which is equal to the surplus in its current account associated with this disequilibrium excess demand, less the existing (exogenous) rate of lending to foreign countries (see formula (42) below). Dynamic stability requires that this disequilibrium surplus be a decreasing function of the exchange rate. This condition is often misinterpreted as meaning that a devaluation will improve the country's *equilibrium* current-account balance.[8]

The conventional argument to the effect that a devaluation will improve the balance of payments proceeds as follows:[9] with higher value of foreign currency, the demand schedule for imports and the supply schedule for exports (both in terms of foreign currency) will shift downward, hence (if the stability condition holds) the value of imports less the value of exports (in foreign currency) will fall. The problem with this argument, however, is that a country can devalue its currency only by purchasing more foreign currency with domestic currency, and this it can do only by creating more domestic currency. Unless it cuts down on its borrowing (in terms of foreign currency), the increased money supply will (eventually, at least) erase the effects of the devaluation: the demand and supply schedules will not shift at all, and there will be no change in the balance of payments (in foreign currency). If the government directly cuts down on its borrowing, the exchange rate (if left to itself) will fall without the need of any intervention (assuming stability).

The proviso just mentioned provides the key to the analysis in Section 4 of this paper. Currency depreciation is a policy instrument used by countries which are experiencing unsustainable current-account deficits. By 'unsustainable' it is meant that the country cannot count on these capital inflows continuing in the future.[10] If it could count on their continuation, there would be no need for the currency depreciation. If a capital inflow is unsustainable, most likely it represents a demand for funds expressed in domestic currency. There is a ubiquitous source of such borrowing, namely government budget deficits. When a country with a substantial budget deficit, resulting from expenditures representing commitments denominated in domestic currency, devalues its currency, it automatically lowers the foreign-currency value of this debit item in the balance of payments. Thus, the devaluation creates an instantaneous transfer to the foreign country, or if one prefers, an instantaneous reduction in the pre-existing rate of transfer from the foreign country.

This simple point was made by Corden (1977, p.12). A similar point, but with respect to the effect of a devaluation on real balances, was made by Dornbusch (1973a, pp.899, 905).

In Section 4 a model of pegged, adjustable exchange rates is developed in which it is shown that if either (i) the current-account balance of the devaluing country is exogenously determined in terms of the foreign currency, or (ii) this balance is exogenously determined in terms of the domestic currency, but equal to zero, then a devaluation has no real effect. That is, it has no effect (in equilibrium) on resource allocation and relative prices. If the country's current account is exogenously given in terms of the domestic currency, and if both the 'orthodox presumption' and the dynamic stability conditions hold, then a devaluation will improve the balance of payments (in foreign currency) if the current account is initially in deficit, and worsen it if the current account is initially in surplus. These results are fully in accord with Mill's doctrine (1848, vol. II, book III, ch.XXII, §3, p.175; 1895, II, p.200) that 'a depreciation of the currency does not affect the foreign trade of the country', given his assumption (ch.XX, §2) of balanced trade. But Mill's doctrine needs the obvious modification indicated above in the case (also considered by Mill) of unbalanced trade.

2 THE BASIC CLASSICAL MODEL

The assumption of an 'infinite elasticity of supply of exports' can presumably mean only one thing: infinite elasticity of transformation between a country's export good and its non-tradable. This leads to the specification that each country specializes in its export and non-tradable goods, which it produces under constant returns to scale with a single factor of production.

It will be assumed that there are two countries, indicated by the superscript $k = 1,2$, each of which consumes three commodities in amounts x_1^k, x_2^k, x_3^k, the third of which is non-tradable. Denoting the output of commodity j in country k by y_j^k, it is assumed that country k produces commodity k and its non-tradable commodity 3, and imports commodity $j \neq k$. (Analytically, the respective countries' non-tradables must be treated as different commodities.) The endowment of the unique factor in country k will be denoted ℓ_1^k, the subscript being included to allow for subsequent generalization to two or more factors.

Let p_j^k denote the price of commodity j in country k, denominated in country k's currency. The exchange rate will be introduced in the next section.

2.1 Production Relations

Letting v_{1j}^k denote the allocation of the unique factor 1 to industry j in country k, the production function for commodity j in country k is assumed to satisfy the constant-returns-to-scale property

$$y_j^k = f_j^k(v_{1j}^h) = \lambda^{-1} f_j^k(\lambda v_{1j}) \quad \text{for } \lambda > 0$$

whence the factor–output ratio in each industry is fixed and given by

$$b_{1j}^k = v_{1j}^k / y_j^k = 1/f_j^k(1). \tag{1}$$

The full-employment condition $v_{1k}^k + v_{13}^k = \ell_1^k$ then yields the production-possibility frontier

$$b_{1k}^k y_k^k + b_{13}^k y_3^k = \ell_1^k \quad (k = 1,2). \tag{2}$$

Now it is assumed that the production is carried out efficiently, and that commodities k and 3 are produced in positive amounts, i.e. that the value of national product

$$Y^k = p_k^k y_k^k + p_3^k y_3^k \tag{3}$$

is maximized subject to (1), and that the solution of the maximum problem satisfies $y_k^k > 0$, $y_3^k > 0$. Obviously this entails

$$p_3^k = p_k^k b_{13}^k / b_{1k}^k \quad (k = 1,2). \tag{4}$$

2.2   Demand and Supply Relations

Preferences in each country k are assumed to be aggregable, yielding demand functions

$$x_j^k = h_j^k(p_1^k, p_2^k, p_3^k, E^k) \quad (j = 1,2,3; \ k = 1,2) \tag{5}$$

which maximize a utility function $U^k(x_1^k, x_2^k, x_3^k)$ subject to the budget constraint

$$\sum_{j=1}^{3} p_j^k x_j^k \leqq E^k = Y^k + D^k, \tag{6}$$

where E^k is expenditure ('absorption'), Y^k is the value of the national product, and D^k is the deficit in the balance of payments on goods and services, all denominated in country k's currency. It is assumed that preferences are non-satiating, so that equality holds in (6).

Net imports are denoted

$$z_j^k = x_j^k - y_j^k \quad (j,k = 1,2). \tag{7}$$

For the import good – commodity $j \neq k$ – by assumption, $z_j^k = x_j^k$, so (5) gives the demand for imports. However, since p_3^k and E^k themselves depend on p_1^k, p_2^k, and D^k from (3), (4), and (6), we shall want to express the demand for imports as a function of these three variables.

For the export good – commodity k – the demand relation (5) must be combined with a supply relation. From (2) we have $y_k^k = (\ell_1^k - b_{13}^k y_3^k)/b_{1k}^k$, and since by definition of a non-tradable we must have

$$x_3^k = y_3^k \quad (k = 1,2) \tag{8}$$

in equilibrium, our supply relation may be expressed as

$$y_k^k = \ell_1^k / b_{1k}^k - (b_{13}^k / b_{1k}^k) h_3^k(p_1^k, p_2^k, p_3^k, E^k). \tag{9}$$

Again, we wish to express this as a function of p_1^k, p_2^k, and D^k.

The variable p_3^k is eliminated from (5) and (9) by substituting (4). Combining (3), (4), and (2) we obtain

$$Y^k = p_k^k \ell_1^k / b_{1k}^k, \tag{10}$$

expressing national income as the product of the factor endowment ℓ_1^k and its rental $w_{1k}^k = p_k^k / b_{1k}^k$. We thus obtain for our import demand and export supply functions the *trade-demand functions*[11]

$$z_j^k = \hat{h}_j^k(p_1^k, p_2^k, D^k) \equiv \tag{11}$$

$$\equiv h_j^k(p_1^k, p_2^k, p_k^k b_{13}^k / b_{1k}^k, p_k^k \ell_1^k / b_{1k}^k + D^k) \quad j \neq k$$

$$z_k^k = \hat{h}_k^k(p_1^k, p_2^k, D^k) \equiv h_k^k(p_1^k, p_2^k, p_k^k b_{13}^k / b_{1k}^k, p_k^k \ell_1^k / b_{1k}^k + D^k) -$$

$$- \ell_1^k / b_{1k}^k + (b_{13}^k / b_{1k}^k) h_3^k(p_1^k, p_2^k, p_k^k b_{13}^k / b_{1k}^k, p_k^k \ell_1^k / b_{1k}^k + D^k).$$

We verify from the budget constraint (6) (with equality holding) that these trade-demand functions satisfy

$$\sum_{i=1}^{2} p_i^k \hat{h}_i^k(p_1^k, p_1^k, D^k) = D^k \quad (k = 1, 2). \tag{12}$$

For future reference we note that

$$\frac{\partial \hat{h}_j^k}{\partial p_j^k} = \frac{\partial h_j^k}{\partial p_j^k} \quad (j \neq k); \qquad \frac{\partial \hat{h}_j^k}{\partial D^k} = \frac{\partial h_j^k}{\partial E^k} \quad (j \neq k); \tag{13}$$

$$\frac{\partial \hat{h}_j^k}{\partial p_k^k} = \frac{\partial h_j^k}{\partial p_k^k} + \frac{b_{13}^k}{b_{1k}^k} \frac{\partial h_j^k}{\partial p_3^k} + \frac{\ell_1^k}{b_{1k}^k} \frac{\partial h_j^k}{\partial E^k} \quad (j \neq k);$$

and

$$\frac{\partial \hat{h}_k^k}{\partial p_j^k} = \frac{\partial h_k^k}{\partial p_j^k} + \frac{b_{13}^k}{b_{1k}^k} \frac{\partial h_3^k}{\partial p_j^k} \quad (j \neq k); \qquad \frac{\partial \hat{h}_k^k}{\partial D^k} = \frac{\partial h_k^k}{\partial E^k} + \frac{b_{13}^k}{b_{1k}^k} \frac{\partial h_3^k}{\partial E^k}; \tag{14}$$

$$\frac{\partial \hat{h}_k^k}{\partial p_k^k} = \frac{\partial h_k^k}{\partial p_k^k} + \frac{b_{13}^k}{b_{1k}^k} \frac{\partial h_k^k}{\partial p_3^k} + \frac{\ell_1^k}{b_{1k}^k} \frac{\partial h_k^k}{\partial E^k} + \frac{b_{13}^k}{b_{1k}^k} \left[\frac{\partial h_3^k}{\partial p_k^k} + \frac{b_{13}^k}{b_{1k}^k} \frac{\partial h_3^k}{\partial p_3^k} + \frac{\ell_1^k}{b_{1k}^k} \frac{\partial h_3^k}{\partial E^k} \right].$$

2.3 Integrability of the Trade-demand Functions

The Slutsky terms of the demand functions (5) and the trade-demand functions (11) are defined respectively by

$$s_{ij}^k = \frac{\partial h_i^k}{\partial p_j^k} + \frac{\partial h_i^k}{\partial E^k} h_i^k \quad (i, j = 1, 2, 3); \quad \hat{s}_{ij}^k = \frac{\partial \hat{h}_i^k}{\partial p_j^k} + \frac{\partial \hat{h}_i^k}{\partial D^k} \hat{h}_j^k \quad (i, j = 1, 2). \tag{15}$$

Routine computations show that the 2×2 and 3×3 Slutsky matrices $\hat{S}^k = [\hat{s}^k_{ij}]$ and $S^k = [s^k_{ij}]$ are related by

$$
\begin{bmatrix} \hat{s}_{jj} & \hat{s}_{jk} \\ \hat{s}_{kj} & \hat{s}_{kk} \end{bmatrix} = \begin{bmatrix} 1 & 0 & 0 \\ 0 & 1 & b^k_{13}/b^k_{1k} \end{bmatrix} \begin{bmatrix} s^k_{jj} & s^k_{jk} & s^k_{j3} \\ s^k_{kj} & s^k_{kk} & s^k_{k3} \\ s^k_{3j} & s^k_{3k} & s^k_{33} \end{bmatrix} \begin{bmatrix} 1 & 0 \\ 0 & 1 \\ 0 & b^k_{13}/b^k_{1k} \end{bmatrix} \quad (j \neq k \tag{16}
$$

(cf. Chipman, 1981, p.54, formula (63)). Since S^k is symmetric and non-positive definite (because h^k is, by assumption, derived from utility maximization), the same is necessarily true of $\hat{S}^k$. Further, denoting $\hat{p}^k = (p^k_j, p^k_k)'$ and $p^k = (p^k_j, p^k_k, p^k_3)'$ for $j \neq k$, it follows from (16) and (4) that

$$
\hat{p}^{k\prime} \hat{S}^k \hat{p}^k = p^{k\prime} S^k p^k = 0. \tag{17}
$$

By the results of Hurwicz and Uzawa (1971) it follows that there exists a trade-utility function $\hat{U}^k(z^k_j, z^k_k)$ $(j \neq k)$ which, when maximized subject to the balance-of-payments constraint

$$
p^k_j z^k_j + p^k_k z^k_k \leqslant D^k \quad (j \neq k) \tag{18}
$$

yields the trade-demand functions (11).[12]

Since the trade-demand functions (11) are single-valued, the indifference curves of the trade-utility function $\hat{U}^k$ are strictly convex – this, despite the fact that the country operates on a flat production-possibility frontier. For $D^k = 0$ the functions (11) trace out a Marshallian offer curve as p^k_1/p^k_2 varies. The elasticity of country k's demand for imports is defined as

$$
\eta^k = -\frac{p^k_j}{\hat{h}^k_j} \frac{\partial \hat{h}^k_j}{\partial p^k_j} \quad \text{for } j \neq k. \tag{19}
$$

Differentiating (12) with respect to p^k_j and multiplying the result through by $p^k_j/p^k_k \hat{h}^k_k$, we obtain the formula

$$
-\frac{p^k_j}{\hat{h}^k_k} \frac{\partial \hat{h}^k_k}{\partial p^k_j} = \frac{p^k_k \hat{h}^k_j}{-p^k_k \hat{h}^k_k} (\eta^k - 1) \quad (j \neq k) \tag{20}
$$

which will prove useful in the next section. Note that the factor on the right in (20) is the ratio of imports to exports in country k (denominated in country k's currency); when $D^k = 0$ this ratio is equal to 1.

3 A MODEL OF FLEXIBLE EXCHANGE RATES

The exchange rate will be defined as the price of country 2's currency expressed in units of country 1's currency. Arbitrage in commercial and foreign-exchange markets then entails

$$p_j^1 = e p_j^2 \quad \text{for } j = 1, 2. \tag{21}$$

It will be further assumed in this section that each country pursues a monetary policy that stabilizes the price of its non-tradable, denominated in its own currency. Then $p_3^k = \bar{p}_3^k$, and from relation (4), $p_k^k = \bar{p}_3^k b_{1k}^k / b_{13}^k \equiv \bar{p}_k^k$, so both producer prices are fixed in nominal terms in each country. From (10), so are the nominal national products $Y^k = \ell_1^k \bar{p}_k^k / b_{1k}^k = \ell_1^k \bar{w}_1^k \equiv \bar{Y}^k$.

3.1 The Dynamical System

It will be supposed that country 1 makes a loan to country 2 of L^1 units of its currency. The following dynamical system will be postulated:

$$\dot{e} \propto h_2^1(\bar{p}_1^1, e\bar{p}_2^2, \bar{p}_3^1, \bar{Y}^1 - L^1) + h_2^2(\bar{p}_1^1/e, \bar{p}_2^2,$$

$$\bar{p}_2^3, \bar{Y}^2 + L^1/e) - \ell_1^2/b_{12}^2 + y_3^2 b_{13}^2/b_{12}^2$$

$$\dot{y}_3^1 \propto h_3^1(\bar{p}_1^1, e\bar{p}_2^2, \bar{p}_3^1, \bar{Y}^1 - L^1) - y_3^1 \tag{22}$$

$$\dot{y}_3^2 \propto h_3^2(\bar{p}_1^1/e, \bar{p}_2^2, \bar{p}_3^2, \bar{Y}^2 + L^1/e) - y_3^2.$$

The first relation of (22) states that the rate of change of the exchange rate is proportional to the world excess demand for commodity 2 (country 2's export good), this excess demand being a function of the exchange rate and the output of the non-tradable in country 2 (see (2)). The second and third relations state that, in each country, the rate of change in the output of the non-tradable is proportional to the excess demand for it. By Walras' Law, the supply and demand for commodity 1 are determined by the above.

Equilibrium is defined as a state in which $\dot{e} = \dot{y}_3^1 = \dot{y}_3^2 = 0$. It will be assumed that an isolated equilibrium of the system (22) exists, i.e. that there are locally unique values of the variables e, y_3^1, y_3^2 for each predetermined value of L^1. Denoting these functions by $\bar{e}(L^1)$, $\bar{y}_3^1(L^1)$, $\bar{y}_3^2(L^1)$, their derivatives are given by the solution of

$$
\begin{bmatrix}
\dfrac{\partial h_2^1}{\partial p_2^1}\bar{p}_2^2 - \dfrac{\partial h_2^2}{\partial p_1^1}\dfrac{\bar{p}_1^1}{e^2} - \dfrac{\partial h_2^2}{\partial E^2}\dfrac{L_1}{e^2} & 0 & \dfrac{b_{13}^2}{b_{12}^2} \\[3mm]
\dfrac{\partial h_3^1}{\partial p_2^1}\bar{p}_2^2 & -1 & 0 \\[3mm]
-\dfrac{\partial h_3^2}{\partial p_1^1}\dfrac{\bar{p}_1^1}{e^2} - \dfrac{\partial h_3^2}{\partial E^2}\dfrac{L^1}{e^2} & 0 & -1
\end{bmatrix}
\begin{bmatrix}
\dfrac{d\bar{e}}{dL^1} \\[3mm]
\dfrac{d\bar{y}_3^1}{dL^1} \\[3mm]
\dfrac{d\bar{y}_3^2}{dL^1}
\end{bmatrix}
\begin{bmatrix}
\dfrac{\partial h_2^1}{\partial E^1} - \dfrac{\partial h_2^2}{\partial E^2}\dfrac{1}{e} \\[3mm]
\dfrac{\partial h_3^1}{\partial E^1} \\[3mm]
-\dfrac{\partial h_3^2}{\partial E^2}\dfrac{1}{e}
\end{bmatrix}.
\tag{23}
$$

As is well known, dynamic stability requires that the principal minors of the above Jacobian matrix be alternatively non-positive and non-negative.[13] Since an isolated solution of (23) is assumed to exist, the determinant of this matrix, to be denoted Δ, must be negative. This determinant is readily computed to be

$$
\Delta = \frac{1}{e}\left\{ p_2^1 \frac{\partial h_2^1}{\partial p_2^1} - p_1^2 \left[\frac{\partial h_2^2}{\partial p_1^1} + \frac{b_{13}^2}{b_{12}^2}\frac{\partial h_3^2}{\partial p_1^1} \right] \right\} - \frac{L^1}{e^2}\left[\frac{\partial h_2^2}{\partial E^2} + \frac{b_{13}^2}{b_{12}^2}\frac{\partial h_3^2}{\partial E^2} \right]
\tag{24}
$$

where use is made of (21). From (13) and (14) and the fact that $L^1 = eD^2$, this may be written as

$$
e\Delta = p_2^1 \frac{\partial \hat{h}_2^1}{\partial p_2^1} - p_1^2 \frac{\partial \hat{h}_2^2}{\partial p_1^2} - D^2 \frac{\partial \hat{h}_2^2}{\partial D^2}.
\tag{25}
$$

3.2 Derivation of the 'Marshall–Lerner Condition'

The stability condition $\Delta < 0$ may be expressed in elasticity form as follows. Let

$$
\delta^k = -\frac{D^k}{\hat{h}_k^k}\frac{\partial \hat{h}_k^k}{\partial D^k}
\tag{26}
$$

denote the elasticity of country k's excess demand for its exportable with respect to its balance-of-payments deficit (keeping in mind that $\hat{h}_k^k < 0$). Then, using formulae (19) and (20) of the preceding section we obtain as our stability condition

$$
-(e/\hat{h}_2^1)\Delta = \eta^1 + \frac{p_1^2 \hat{h}_1^2}{-p_2^2 \hat{h}_2^2}(\eta^2 - 1) + \delta^2 > 0.
\tag{27}
$$

The term $p_1^2 \hat{h}_1^2 / (-p_2^2 \hat{h}_2^2)$ is country 2's import–export ratio. When $D^2 = 0$ this ratio is 1 and $\delta^2 = 0$, hence (27) reduces to the notorious 'Marshall–Lerner condition'[14]

$$\eta^1 + \eta^2 > 1. \tag{28}$$

The more general necessary condition (27) corresponds to that of Hirschman (1949), except that Hirschman omitted the term δ^2.

3.3 Effect of a Transfer on the Exchange Rate and Terms of Trade

Returning to the solution of (23), by Cramer's rule and (14) we have

$$\frac{de}{dL^1} = \frac{1}{\Delta} \left\{ \frac{\partial h_2^1}{\partial E^1} - \frac{1}{e} \left[\frac{\partial h_2^2}{\partial E^2} + \frac{b_{13}^2}{b_{12}^2} \frac{\partial h_3^2}{\partial E^2} \right] \right\} = \frac{1}{\Delta} \left(\frac{\partial \hat{h}_2^1}{\partial D^1} - \frac{1}{e} \frac{\partial \hat{h}_2^2}{\partial D^2} \right). \tag{29}$$

Multiplying the above expressions through by p_2^1 and making use of (21) we see that, assuming the stability condition $\Delta < 0$ to hold, a loan from country 1 to country 2 will strengthen country 2's exchange rate if and only if

$$p_2^1 \frac{\partial \hat{h}_2^1}{\partial D^1} - p_2^2 \frac{\partial \hat{h}_2^2}{\partial D^2} = p_2^1 \frac{\partial h_2^1}{\partial E^1} - p_2^2 \frac{\partial h_2^2}{\partial E^2} - p_3^2 \frac{\partial h_3^2}{\partial E^2} < 0. \tag{30}$$

Condition (30) may be analyzed from two points of view. Consider first the condition $p_2^1 \partial \hat{h}_2^1/\partial D^1 < p_2^2 \partial \hat{h}_2^2/\partial D^2$. This is equivalent to the conditions derived by Pigou (1932) and Samuelson (1952) for a transfer to improve the receiving country's terms of trade. In the present model, this is $p_2^2/p_1^2 = (\bar{p}_2^2/\bar{p}_1^2)e$, that is, we are dealing with the very special situation in which the terms of trade vary directly with the exchange rate. As long as

$$0 < p_i^k \partial \hat{h}_i^k/\partial D^k < 1$$

for $i = 1,2$ and $k = 1,2$, the first inequality of (30) can be written in Samuelson's form (1952, p.286):

$$\frac{p_2^2 \partial \hat{h}_2^2/\partial D^2}{p_1^2 \partial \hat{h}_1^2/\partial D^2} > \frac{p_2^1 \partial \hat{h}_2^1/\partial D^1}{p_1^1 \partial \hat{h}_1^1/\partial D^1}. \tag{31}$$

The reason why (31) is a plausible condition in the present model is that the trade-preferences in the respective countries satisfy the asymmetric conditions

$$\frac{\partial \hat{h}_j^k}{\partial D^k} = \frac{\partial h_j^k}{\partial E^k}; \quad \frac{\partial \hat{h}_k^k}{\partial D^k} = \frac{\partial h_k^k}{\partial E^k} + \frac{b_{13}^k}{b_{1k}^k} \frac{\partial h_3^k}{\partial E^k} \quad (j \neq k). \tag{32}$$

Thus, the loan in country 2 is partially absorbed in increased consumption – and therefore production – of its non-tradable, leading to an increase in the net demand for exportables caused by the withdrawal of resources from the production of exportables.

The other approach to the analysis of (30) follows directly from the above considerations. Suppose that preferences as between the two countries are similar in the sense that both have the same marginal propensity to spend on tradables.[15] Then the second inequality of (30) reduces simply to the condition $\partial h_3^2/\partial E^2 > 0$, i.e. that the non-tradable in country 2 be a superior good. If the reverse is true, i.e. if country 2's non-tradable is an inferior good, then the exchange rate and the balance of payments will be *inversely* related, even though the stability condition (29) holds.

The condition $\Delta < 0$ is only a necessary condition for stability; it is not sufficient. However, it is immediately apparent that the remaining stability conditions will hold if the first diagonal element in (23) is non-positive. Thus, we need to supplement (27) by

$$p_2^1 \frac{\partial h_2^1}{\partial p_2^1} - p_1^2 \frac{\partial h_2^2}{\partial p_1^2} - D^2 \frac{\partial h_2^2}{\partial E^2} \leqq 0. \tag{33}$$

It is not hard to see that this condition follows from $\Delta < 0$ if the non-tradable in country 2 is a superior good and $D^2 \leqq 0$ or D^2 is positive and sufficiently small. Otherwise the condition is stronger; but it does not appear worthwhile to provide further details.

3.4 A Simpler but Less Plausible Dynamic Formulation

A limiting case of the model (21) is that in which the speeds of adjustment in the second and third relations become infinite. The equilibrium conditions can then be substituted in the first relation to yield the very simple dynamical system

$$\dot{e} \propto \hat{h}_2^1(\bar{p}_2^1, e\bar{p}_2^2, -L^1) + \hat{h}_2^2(\bar{p}_1^1/e, \bar{p}_2^2, L^1/e). \tag{34}$$

The total derivative of the expression on the right with respect to e is then precisely Δ, as given directly by (25), and the condition (27) becomes necessary and sufficient. This corresponds to the method for deriving the stability condition given by Kemp (1964, pp.61–3). However, it should be noted that in the real world, prices and exchange rates adjust rapidly and production adjusts slowly, which is the reverse of the specification leading to (34).

A pair of specifications very similar to (34) are worth examining closely, owing to their prominent role in the literature. Multiplying the expression on the right in (34) by $e\bar{p}_2^2$, we may express the first of these specifications as

$$\dot{e} \propto F^1(e,D^1) = e\bar{p}_2^2 \hat{h}_2^1(\bar{p}_1^1, e\bar{p}_2^2 D^1) + e\bar{p}_2^2 \hat{h}_2^2(\bar{p}_1^1/e, \bar{p}_2^2, -D^1/e). \tag{35}$$

F^1 furnishes the value of the world excess demand for commodity 2 denominated in country 1's currency. Using the budget identity (12) this function may be expressed in the form

$$F^1(e,D^1) = e\bar{p}_2^2 \hat{h}_2^1(\bar{p}_1^1, e\bar{p}_2^2, D^1) - \bar{p}_1^1 \hat{h}_1^2(\bar{p}_1^1/e, \bar{p}_2^2, -D^1/e) - D^1. \tag{36}$$

Defining $L^1 = -D^1$ as in the previous subsection, and defining the function

$$T^1(e,L^1) = \bar{p}_1^1 \hat{h}_1^2(\bar{p}_1^1/e, \bar{p}_2^2, L^1/e) - e\bar{p}_2^2 \hat{h}_2^1(\bar{p}_1^1, e\bar{p}_2^2, -L^1), \tag{37}$$

we have from (35) and (36) the relation

$$\dot{e} \propto L^1 - T^1(e,L^1). \tag{38}$$

The function T^1 consists of the excess of the demand (by country 2) for country 1's exports over the demand (by country 1) for country 1's imports, denominated in country 1's currency. It is therefore the implied or scheduled balance of payments on current account of country 1 that would result from the exchange rate, e, and country 1's lending, L^1. Recalling that the exchange rate is here defined as the price of country 2's currency in terms of country 1's, the relation (38) makes precise the dynamic-adjustment postulate set forth by Robinson (1937a, p.195; 1947a, p.144): 'If, at a given exchange rate, the balance of trade falls short of the balance of lending the exchange depreciates.'

The second specification replaces the right side of (35) by the value of the excess demand for commodity 2 denominated in country 2's currency:

$$\dot{e} \propto F^2(e,D^2) = \bar{p}_2^2 \hat{h}_2^1(\bar{p}_1^1, e\bar{p}_2^2, -eD^2) + \bar{p}_2^2 \hat{h}_2^2(\bar{p}_1^1/e, \bar{p}_2^2, D^2), \tag{39}$$

and similarly one may express the function F^2 in the form

$$F^2(e,D^2) = \bar{p}_2^2 \hat{h}_2^1(\bar{p}_2^1, e\bar{p}_2^2, -eD^2) - (\bar{p}_1^1/e)\hat{h}_1^2(\bar{p}_1^1/e, \bar{p}_2^2, D^2) + D^2. \tag{40}$$

Defining $L^2 = -D^2$ and

$$T^2(e,L^2) = \bar{p}_2^2 \hat{h}_2^1(\bar{p}_1^1, e\bar{p}_2^2, eL^2) -$$

$$- (\bar{p}_1^1/e)\hat{h}_1^2(\bar{p}_1^1/e, \bar{p}_2^2, -L^2), \tag{41}$$

we may express (39) and (40) in the form

$$\dot{e} \propto T^2(e, L^2) - L^2. \tag{42}$$

Since T^2 represents the excess of country 1's demand for country 2's exports over country 2's demand for its own imports, denominated in country 2's currency, (42) is a literal formalization of Robinson's postulate quoted above. For the case $L^2 = 0$ (41) corresponds (but with opposite sign) to the expression given in Sohmen (1958, p.611).

Necessary and sufficient conditions for the asymptotic stability of (35) and (39) are respectively that $\partial F^1/\partial e < 0$ and $\partial F^2/\partial e < 0$. In terms of (38) and (42) these reduce to $\partial T^1/\partial e > 0$ (a devaluation of 1's currency should improve its balance of trade) and $\partial T^2/\partial e < 0$ (a devaluation of 2's currency should improve its balance of trade).

Using (19), (21), and the fact that $D^1 = -eD^2$, we find that

$$\frac{\partial F^1}{\partial e} = \bar{p}_2^2 \hat{h}_2^2 \left[\eta^1 - 1 + \frac{(\bar{p}_1^1/e)\hat{h}_1^2}{-\bar{p}_2^2 \hat{h}_2^2} \left(\eta^2 - \frac{D^2}{\hat{h}_1^2} \frac{\partial \hat{h}_1^2}{\partial D^2} \right) \right]. \tag{43}$$

Differentiating the budget constraint (12) with respect to D^k we obtain the formula

$$p_j^k \hat{h}_j^k \left[1 - \frac{D^k}{\hat{h}_j^k} \frac{\partial \hat{h}_j^k}{\partial D^k} \right] + p_k^k \hat{h}_k^k \left[1 - \frac{D^k}{\hat{h}_k^k} \frac{\partial \hat{h}_k^k}{\partial D^k} \right] = 0. \tag{44}$$

From (44) and (26) (with $k = 2$), (43) reduces to

$$\frac{\partial F^1}{\partial e} = \bar{p}_2^2 \hat{h}_2^2 \left[\frac{(\bar{p}_1^1/e)\hat{h}_1^2}{-\bar{p}_2^2 \hat{h}_2^2} (\eta^2 - 1) + \eta^1 + \delta^2 \right]. \tag{45}$$

Since $\hat{h}_2^2 < 0$, the condition $\partial F^1/\partial e < 0$ leads precisely to (27).

In similar fashion we find that

$$\frac{\partial F^2}{\partial e} = \frac{\bar{p}_1^1 \hat{h}_1^1}{e^2} \left[\eta^2 - 1 + \frac{(\bar{p}_2^2/e)\hat{h}_2^1}{-\bar{p}_1^1 \hat{h}_1^1} \left(\eta^1 - \frac{D^1}{\hat{h}_2^1} \frac{\partial \hat{h}_2^1}{\partial D^1} \right) \right]. \tag{46}$$

Using (44) and (26) (with $k = 1$) this becomes

$$\frac{\partial F^2}{\partial e} = \frac{\bar{p}_1^1 \hat{h}_1^1}{e^2} \left[\frac{(\bar{p}_2^2/e)\hat{h}_2^1}{-\bar{p}_1^1 \hat{h}_1^1} (\eta^1 - 1) + \eta^2 + \delta^1 \right]. \tag{47}$$

Since $\hat{h}_1^1 < 0$, the condition $\partial F^2/\partial e < 0$ leads to the condition that the bracketed term in (47) be positive.

It should be noted that the traditional formulae derived in the literature (Robinson, 1937a, p.194n.; 1947a, pp.142–3; Hirschman, 1949; Sohmen, 1958; Chacholiades, 1968) are faulty since they omit the terms δ^2 and δ^1 in (45) and (47), that is, they overlook the dependence of the balance-of-trade functions (37) and (41) on the 'balance of lending' (L^1 and L^2, respectively). It should also be noted – and this is much more serious – that the formulae are often misinterpreted as showing the effect of a change in a pegged exchange rate on the equilibrium balance of trade. On the contrary, formulae (45) and (47) are *disequilibrium relationships* in a model of *freely flexible exchange rates*.[16] The contrast between the two models will be displayed in the next section.

3.5 Monetary Implications of the Model

It has been assumed that in each country the monetary authority acts to stabilize the price of the non-tradable, $p_3^k = \bar{p}_3^k$, and that from this it follows that the price of the export good, $p_k^k = \bar{p}_3^k b_{1k}^k / b_{13}^k = \bar{p}_k^k$, and the nominal national product $Y^k = \ell_1^k \bar{p}_k^k / b_{1k}^k = \bar{Y}^k$, are stabilized also. If the demand for money in each country is proportionate to the national product, by $M^k = \kappa^k Y^k$, then this result is easily taken care of by assuming that each country stabilizes its money supply. However, a more reasonable assumption to make would be that the demand for money is proportionate to expenditure (absorption), according to $M^k = \kappa^k (Y^k + D^k)$; in that case, it must follow the rule $M^k = \kappa^k \bar{p}_3^k \ell_1^k / b_{13}^k + \kappa^k D^k$, rising with capital inflows and falling with capital outflows.

4 A MODEL OF PEGGED, ADJUSTABLE EXCHANGE RATES

The model developed in the previous section assumed a flexible exchange rate, and was used to analyze the effect on the exchange rate of an exogenous change in the balance of payments on current account. For some purposes, such a model may be adequate to represent the situation a country finds itself in when it is experiencing 'balance-of-payments difficulties'. For example, if a country's exchange rate is being artificially propped up by borrowing to enable it to 'live beyond its means', there may come a time when creditors are no longer willing to supply the funds; a currency devaluation in such circumstances may appear to be a tool which successfully reduces the country's balance-of-payments deficit, when in reality it may be no more than an official recognition of the inevitable market pressure leading to a lower exchange rate once the flow of foreign funds is cut off. This would be analogous to the actions of a Central Planning Board in a planned economy adjusting prices to more realistic market-clearing levels.

There is no doubt, however, that there are circumstances in which a currency devaluation is conceived to have a strong effect of its own in reducing a country's balance-of-payments deficit. To investigate this possibility, it is necessary to modify the model of Section 3 to allow for an exogenously controlled exchange rate.

4.1 Formulation of the Model

Let M^k denote the supply of money in country k, denominated in its own currency, and let M denote the world stock of money denominated in country 1's currency; then

$$M^1 + eM^2 = M. \tag{48}$$

Country 1 will be regarded as the 'reserve-currency country', and the exchange rate will be assumed to be determined by the activities of the monetary authorities in country 2. In each country the demand for money will be represented by a simple Cambridge equation, but making it proportional not to income but to expenditure ('absorption'):

$$M^k = \kappa^k E^k = \kappa^k (Y^k + D^k) \quad (k = 1, 2). \tag{49}$$

Equilibrium in world payments requires, by 'Cournot's Law' (cf. Mundell, 1960a, p.102),

$$D^1 + eD^2 = 0. \tag{50}$$

From (48)–(50) and (10) we then have as a condition for world equilibrium

$$\kappa^1 \frac{\ell_1^1}{b_{11}^1} p_1^1 + \kappa^2 \frac{\ell_1^2}{b_{12}^2} e p_2^2 + (\kappa^1 - \kappa^2) D^1 = M. \tag{51}$$

To formulate an appropriate dynamic-adjustment process I shall assume that the relation (51) holds out of as well as in equilibrium, for given values of the variables e, M, D^1, D^2 satisfying (50), (51), and (10). Differentiating (51) with respect to time, t, and denoting $\dot{p}_j^k = dp_j^k/dt$, we have

$$\kappa^1 (\ell_1^1/b_{11}^1) \dot{p}_1^1 + \kappa^2 (\ell_1^2/b_{12}^2) e \dot{p}_2^2 = 0. \tag{52}$$

From (12,), (21), and (50) we have

$$p_1^1 [\hat{h}_1^1 (p_1^1, e p_2^2, D^1) + \hat{h}_1^2 (p_1^1/e, p_2^2, D^2)] + \tag{53}$$

$$+ e p_2^2 [\hat{h}_2^1 (p_1^1, e p_2^2, D^1) + \hat{h}_2^2 (p_1^1/e, p_2^2, D^2)] = 0.$$

The simplest way to assure compatibility of (52) and (53) is to posit the equality of the two expressions term by term:

$$\kappa^j(\ell^j_1/b^j_{1j})\dot{p}_j = p^j_j[\hat{h}^1_j(p^1_1,ep^2_2,D^1) + \hat{h}^2_j(p^1_1/e,p^2_2,D^2)] \quad (j=1,2). \tag{54}$$

This leads at once to our dynamical system

$$\frac{\dot{p}^j_j}{p_j} = P_j(p^1_1,p^2_2; D^1,D^2) \equiv \frac{\hat{h}^1_j(p^1_1,ep^2_2,D^1) + \hat{h}^2_j(p^1_1/e,p^2_2,D^2)}{\kappa^j\ell^j_1/b^j_{1j}} \quad (j=1,2), \tag{55}$$

where (50) holds.

From (55) and (53) we obtain (52) back again; and integrating (52) we obtain a linear relation in p^1_1 and p^2_2 of which (51) is a particular integral. When $\kappa^1 = \kappa^2$ (equal velocities of circulation of money in the two countries), (51) is an international version of Fisher's equation.

4.2 Stability Conditions

Stability of the system (55) may be analyzed by considering the Taylor approximation around an equilibrium set of prices (p^1_2,p^2_2), defined as a set of prices for which $P_j=0$ for $j=1,2$, after transforming the prices to their logarithms. The Jacobian of this system, to be denoted $A = [\partial P_i/\partial \log p^j_j]$, is given by

$$\begin{bmatrix} \dfrac{1}{\kappa^1\ell^1_1/b^1_{11}} & 0 \\[2ex] 0 & \dfrac{1}{\kappa^2\ell^2_1b^2_{12}} \end{bmatrix} \begin{bmatrix} \dfrac{\partial\hat{h}^1_1}{\partial p^1_1}p^1_1 + \dfrac{\partial\hat{h}^2_1}{\partial p^1_1}\dfrac{p^1_1}{e} & \dfrac{\partial\hat{h}^1_1}{\partial p^2_2}ep^2_2 + \dfrac{\partial\hat{h}^2_1}{\partial p^2_2}p^2_2 \\[3ex] \dfrac{\partial\hat{h}^1_2}{\partial p^1_1}p^1_1 + \dfrac{\partial\hat{h}^2_2}{\partial p^1_1}\dfrac{p^1_1}{e} & \dfrac{\partial\hat{h}^1_2}{\partial p^2_2}ep^2_2 + \dfrac{\partial\hat{h}^2_2}{\partial p^2_2}P^2_2 \end{bmatrix}. \tag{56}$$

From the homogeneity of degree 0 of the trade-demand functions $\hat{h}^k_j$ we have, using Euler's Theorem,

$$\frac{p^k_j}{\hat{h}^k_j}\frac{\partial\hat{h}^k_j}{\partial p_j} + \frac{p^k_k}{\hat{h}^k_j}\frac{\partial\hat{h}^k_j}{\partial p_k} + \frac{D^k}{\hat{h}^k_j}\frac{\partial\hat{h}^k_j}{\partial D^k} = 0. \tag{57}$$

Combining (57) with (20) and (12) we obtain

$$\frac{p^k_k}{\hat{h}^k_k}\frac{\partial\hat{h}^k_k}{\partial p_k} = \frac{p^k\hat{h}^k_j}{-p^k_k h^k_k}(\eta^k - 1) + \delta^k \quad (j \neq k) \tag{59}$$

and

$$\frac{p_k^k}{\hat{h}_j^k}\frac{\partial \hat{h}_j^k}{\partial p_k^k} = \eta^k - 1 + \frac{-p_k^k \hat{h}_k^k}{p_j^k \hat{h}_j^k}(\delta^k + 1) \quad (j \neq k), \tag{59}$$

where δ^k is defined by (26). Using these formulae, and defining the generalized Marshallian stability expression

$$\mu^k = \frac{p_j^k \hat{h}_j^k}{-p_k^k \hat{h}_k^k}(\eta^k - 1) + \eta^j + \delta^k \quad (j \neq k = 1,2), \tag{60}$$

(compare (47) and (45)), we find that

$$A = \begin{bmatrix} \dfrac{1}{\kappa^1 \ell_1^1/b_{11}^1} & 0 \\[2ex] 0 & \dfrac{1}{\kappa^2 \ell_2^2/b_{12}^2} \end{bmatrix} \begin{bmatrix} -\hat{h}_1^2 & -\dfrac{p_2^2 \hat{h}_2^2}{p_1^2} \\[2ex] -\dfrac{p_1^1 \hat{h}_1^1}{p_2^1} & -\hat{h}_2^1 \end{bmatrix} \begin{bmatrix} \mu^1 & 0 \\[2ex] 0 & \mu^2 \end{bmatrix}. \tag{61}$$

The middle matrix in this product has rank 1, on account of (21) and the material-balance conditions $\hat{h}_j^1 + \hat{h}_j^2 = 0$; hence, the characteristic equation is

$$|I\lambda - A| = \lambda(\lambda - \text{trace } A) = 0.$$

A necessary and sufficient condition for stability is then that trace $A < 0$, or

$$\bar{\mu} \equiv \frac{\hat{h}_1^2}{\kappa^1 \ell_1^1/b_{11}^1}\mu^1 + \frac{\hat{h}_2^1}{\kappa^2 \ell_1^2/b_{12}^2}\mu^2 > 0. \tag{62}$$

That is, a weighted sum of the generalized Marshallian stability expressions is positive. A sufficient condition for stability is

$$\mu^k > 0 \quad \text{for } k = 1,2. \tag{63}$$

In the special case of balanced payments, (60) reduces to $\mu^k = \eta^1 + \eta^2 - 1$ and (62) reduces to

$$\left[\frac{\hat{h}_1^2}{\kappa^1 \ell_1^1/b_{11}^1} + \frac{\hat{h}_2^1}{\kappa^2 \ell_1^2/b_{12}^2}\right](\eta^1 + \eta^2 - 1) > 0. \tag{64}$$

In this case the 'Marshall–Lerner condition' (28) is necessary and sufficient for dynamic stability.[17]

4.3 Case 1: The Transfer Denominated in Country 1's Currency

Expressing the capital movement between country 1 and country 2 in terms of country 1's currency, we have from (21), (50), (51), and the material-balance condition $z_2^1 + z_2^2 = 0$ for commodity 2 the system of two equations

$$\hat{h}_2^1(p_1^1, ep_2^2, D^1) + \hat{h}_2^2(p_1^1/3, p_2^2, -D^1/e) = 0$$

$$\kappa^1 \frac{\ell_1^1}{b_{11}^1} p_1^1 + \kappa^2 \frac{\ell_1^2}{b_{12}^2} ep_2^2 + (\kappa^1 \kappa^2) D^1 - M = 0 \tag{65}$$

in the two unknowns p_1^1 and p_2^2, the variables D^1 and e (as well as ℓ_1^1, ℓ_1^2, and M) being exogenous. The second equation of (65) is (51). (The material-balance condition for commodity 1 follows from (65), (12), and (50).) Equations (65) define implicitly the functions

$$p_1^1 = \bar{p}_1^1(D^1, e), \quad p_2^2 = \bar{p}_2^2(D^1, e), \tag{66}$$

where ℓ_1^1, ℓ_1^2, and M are held constant.

Differentiating each of the two expressions of (65) with respect to p_1^1 and p_2^2 we obtain the Jacobian matrix

$$J = \begin{bmatrix} \dfrac{\partial \hat{h}_2^1}{\partial p_1^1} + \dfrac{1}{e}\dfrac{\partial \hat{h}^2}{\partial p_1^2} & e\dfrac{\partial \hat{h}_2^1}{\partial p_2^2} + \dfrac{\partial \hat{h}_2^2}{\partial p_2^2} \\[2mm] \kappa^1 \dfrac{\ell_1^1}{b_{11}^1} \cdot & e\kappa^2 \dfrac{\ell_1^2}{b_{12}^2} \end{bmatrix} = \begin{bmatrix} -\dfrac{\hat{h}_1^1}{p_2^1}\mu^1 & -\dfrac{\hat{h}_2^1}{p_2^1}\mu^2 \\[2mm] \kappa^1 \dfrac{\ell_1^1}{b_{11}^1} & e\kappa^2 \dfrac{\ell_1^2}{b_{12}^2} \end{bmatrix}. \tag{67}$$

the second expression following from (60) and the relation derived above between (56) and (61). Its determinant is

$$|J| = \kappa^1 \frac{\ell_1^1}{b_{11}^1} \kappa^2 \frac{\ell_1^2}{b_{12}^2} \frac{1}{p_2^2} \bar{\mu}. \tag{68}$$

From (62), $|J| > 0$ in stable equilibrium.

Making use of (19), (20), and (58)–(60), the matrix of the negatives of the partial derivatives of the two expressions of (65) with respect to D^1 and e is found to be

$$- \begin{bmatrix} \dfrac{1}{p_2^1}\left[p_2^1 \dfrac{\partial \hat{h}_2^1}{\partial D^1} - p_2^2 \dfrac{\partial \hat{h}_2^2}{\partial D^2} \right] & \dfrac{\hat{h}_2^2 \mu^2}{e} \\[3mm] \kappa^1 - \kappa^2 & p_2^2 \kappa^2 \ell_1^2 / b_{12}^2 \end{bmatrix}. \tag{69}$$

4.3.1 The Effect of an Increase in the Nominal Rate of Transfer

Replacing the respective columns of J in (67) by the first column of (69) we obtain by Cramer's rule

$$\frac{\partial p_1^1}{\partial D^1} = \frac{-1}{p_2^2 |J|} \left\{ \frac{\kappa^2 \ell_1^2}{b_{12}^1} \left[p_2^1 \frac{\partial h_2^1}{\partial D^1} - p_2^2 \frac{\partial h_2^2}{\partial D^2} \right] + (\kappa^1 - \kappa^2) \hat{h}_2^1 \mu^2 \right\}$$

$$\frac{\partial \bar{p}_2^2}{\partial D^1} = \frac{1}{p_2^1 |J|} \left\{ \frac{\kappa^1 \ell_1^1}{b_{11}^1} \left[p_2^1 \frac{\partial h_2^1}{\partial D^1} - p_2^2 \frac{\partial h_2^2}{\partial D^2} \right] + (\kappa^1 - \kappa^2) \hat{h}_1^1 \mu^1 \right\}.$$

(70)

Thus, the effect of a transfer on the absolute prices decomposes into what may be called a *terms-of-trade effect* and a *velocity effect*. The effect of a transfer to country 1 on its terms of trade is

$$\frac{\partial}{\partial D^1} \left(\frac{\bar{p}_1^1}{e\bar{p}_2^2} \right) = \frac{-1}{(p_2^1)^2 p_2^2 |J|} \left\{ \left[\frac{\kappa^1 \ell_1^1}{b_{11}^1} p_1^1 + \frac{\kappa^2 \ell_1^2}{b_{12}^2} p_2^1 \right] \left[p_2^1 \frac{\partial h_2^1}{\partial D^1} - p_2^2 \frac{\partial h_2^2}{\partial D^2} \right] \right.$$

$$\left. - (\kappa^1 - \kappa^2) [p_1^1 \hat{h}_1^1 \mu^1 + p_2^1 \hat{h}_2^1 p^2] \right\}.$$

(71)

We find from (60), (12), and (26) that

$$p_1^1 \hat{h}_1^1 \mu^1 + p_2^1 \hat{h}_2^1 \mu^2 = D^1 \left[p_2^1 \frac{\partial h_2^1}{\mu D^1} - p_2^2 \frac{\partial h_2^2}{\partial D^2} \right],$$

(72)

hence, taking account of (51), (71) reduces to

$$\frac{\partial}{\partial D^1} \left(\frac{\bar{p}_1^1}{e\bar{p}_2^2} \right) = \frac{-M}{(p_2^1)^2 p_2^2 |J|} \left[p_2^1 \frac{\partial h_2^1}{\partial D^1} - p \frac{\partial h_2^2}{\partial D^2} \right],$$

(73)

in conformity with (29) and (30). Since stability implies $|J| > 0$, this yields the Samuelson criterion for a transfer to improve the receiving country's terms of trade, but expressed in terms of the trade-demand functions.

4.3.2 The Effect of a Currency Devaluation

Replacing the respective columns of J in (67) by the second column of (69) we obtain by Cramer's rule and use of (67) and (62),

$$\frac{e}{\bar{p}_1^1} \frac{\partial \bar{p}_1^1}{\partial e} = 0; \quad \frac{e}{\bar{p}_2^2} \frac{\partial \bar{p}_2^2}{\partial e} = -1.$$

(74)

Thus, a devaluation by country 2 of its currency has no effect on the nominal price (in country 1's currency) of country 1's export good, and increases the normal nominal price (in country 2's currency) of country 2's export good by the same percentage as the devaluation. Denominated in country 1's currency, the prices of the traded goods are unchanged, hence the terms of trade are unchanged:

$$\frac{\partial}{\partial e}\left(\frac{\bar{p}_2^2}{\bar{p}_1^1/e}\right) = \frac{\partial}{\partial e}\left(\frac{e\bar{p}_2^2}{\bar{p}_1^1}\right) = 0. \tag{75}$$

Thus, in accordance with classical doctrine, a devaluation has no real effect.

4.4   Case 2: The Transfer Denominated in Country 2's Currency

Expressing the capital movement from country 1 to country 2 in terms of country 2's currency, we have from (50) the following system of equations in place of (69):

$$\hat{h}_2^1(p_1^1, ep_2^2, -eD^2) - \hat{h}_2^2(p_1^1/e, p_2^2, D^2) = 0$$

$$\kappa^1 \frac{\ell_1^1}{b_{11}^1} p_1^1 + \kappa^2 \frac{\ell_1^2}{b_{12}^2} ep_2^2 - (\kappa^1 - \kappa^2)eD^2 - M = 0. \tag{76}$$

This system defines implicitly the functions

$$p_1^1 = \bar{\bar{p}}_1^1(D^2, e), \quad p_2^2 = \bar{\bar{p}}_2^2(D^2, e), \tag{77}$$

where ℓ_1^1, ℓ_1^2, and M are held constant.

The Jacobian matrix of partial derivatives of (76) with respect to p_1^1, p_2^2 is exactly the same as (67). The matrix of the negatives of the partial derivatives of the two expressions of (76) with respect to D^2 and e is found to be

$$- \begin{bmatrix} -\dfrac{1}{p_2^2}\left[p_2^1 \dfrac{\partial \hat{h}_2^1}{\partial D^1} - p_2^2 \dfrac{\partial \hat{h}_2^2}{\partial D^2} \right] & \dfrac{p_1^1 \hat{h}_1^1}{e p_2^2} \mu^1 \\ \\ (\kappa^1 - \kappa^2)e & \dfrac{\kappa^2 \ell_1^2}{b_{12}^2} p_2^2 - (\kappa^1 - \kappa^2)D^2 \end{bmatrix} \tag{78}$$

4.4.1   *The Effect of an Increase in the Nominal Rate of Transfer*

Replacing the respective columns of J in (67) by the first column of (78) we obtain

$$\frac{\partial \bar{p}_1^1}{\partial D^2} = \frac{1}{p_1^1 |J|} \left\{ \frac{\kappa^2 \ell_1^2}{b_{12}^1} \left[p_2^1 \frac{\partial h_2^1}{\partial D^1} - p_2^2 \frac{\partial h_2^2}{\partial D^2} \right] + (\kappa^1 - \kappa^2) \hat{h}_2^1 \mu^2 \right\}$$

(79)

$$\frac{\partial \bar{p}_2^2}{\partial D^2} = \frac{1}{p_2^2 |J|} \left\{ \frac{\kappa^1 \ell_1^1}{b_{11}^1} \left[p_2^1 \frac{\partial h_2^1}{\partial D^1} - p_2^2 \frac{\partial h_2^2}{\partial D^2} \right] + (\kappa^1 - \kappa^2) \hat{h}_1^1 \mu^1 \right\}.$$

The effect of an increase in the rate of transfer from country 2 to country 1 on country 1's terms of trade is

$$-\frac{\partial}{\partial D^2} \left(\frac{\bar{p}_1^1}{e\bar{p}_2^2} \right) = \frac{-1}{p_2^1 (p_2^2)^2 |J|} \left\{ \left[\frac{\kappa^1 \ell_1^1}{b_{11}^1} p_1^1 + \frac{\kappa^2 \ell_1^2}{b_{12}^2} p_2^1 \right] \left[p_2^1 \frac{\partial h_2^1}{\partial D^1} - \frac{\partial h_2^2}{\partial D^2} \right] \right.$$

(80)

$$\left. - (\kappa^1 - \kappa^2) [p_1^1 \hat{h}_1^1 \mu^1 + p_2^1 \hat{h}_2^1 \mu^2] \right\}.$$

From (72) and (50) this reduces to

$$-\frac{\partial}{\partial D^2} \left(\frac{\bar{p}_1^1}{e\bar{p}_2^2} \right) = \frac{-M}{p_2^1 (p_2^2)^2 |J|} \left[p_2^1 \frac{\partial h_2^1}{\partial D^1} - p_2^2 \frac{\partial h_2^2}{\partial D^2} \right].$$

(81)

Note that this is just a multiple, e, of the expression (73). Thus, the currency in which the transfer is denominated makes no difference to the effect of the transfer.

4.4.2   *The Effect of a Currency Devaluation*

Replacing the first column of J in (67) by the second column of (78) we obtain

$$\frac{\partial \bar{p}_1^1}{\partial e} = \frac{-1}{p_2^1 |J|} \left\{ \frac{\kappa^2 \ell_1^2}{b_{12}^2} [p_1^1 \hat{h}_1^1 \mu^1 + p_2^1 \hat{h}_2^1 \mu^2] - (\kappa^1 - \kappa^2) D^2 \frac{(p_2^1 \hat{h}_2^1 \mu^2)}{p_2^2} \right\}.$$

(82)

Using (72), (51), and (50) this becomes, after a few manipulations,

$$\frac{\partial \bar{p}_1^1}{\partial e} = \frac{eD^2}{p_2^1 |J|} \left\{ \frac{\kappa^2 \ell_1^2}{b_{12}^1} \left[p_2^1 \frac{\partial h_2^1}{\partial D^1} - p_2^2 \frac{\partial h_2^2}{\partial D^2} \right] + (\kappa^1 - \kappa^2) \hat{h}_2^1 \mu^2 \right\}.$$

(83)

Note that this is equal to the expression in the first equation of (79), times the factor $D^2 p_2^1 / p_2^2$. Thus, a devaluation of country 2's currency (a fall in e) has the same effect (times this constant) on the price of country 1's export good as an exogenous decrease in D^2. If country 2 starts out with a balance-of-payments deficit (i.e. $D^2 > 0$), then a currency devaluation accomplishes the same thing as an exogenous transfer from country 2 to country 1. If country 2 starts out with a balance-of-payments surplus (i.e. $D^2 < 0$), then a currency devaluation on the part of country 2 accomplishes the same thing as an exogenous transfer from country 1 to country 2.

Replacing the second column of J in (67) by the second column of (78) and making use of (50) and (51), we obtain

$$\frac{\partial \bar{p}_2^2}{\partial e} = \frac{\hat{h}_1^1 \mu^1 M}{e p_2^1 |J|} < 0, \tag{84}$$

the inequality following from the sufficient stability condition (63) (given (68) and (62)). Thus, a devaluation necessarily increases the prices of country 2's imports.

To determine the effect of a devaluation on country 2's terms of trade, we compute

$$\frac{\partial}{\partial e}\left(\frac{\bar{p}_1^1}{e \bar{p}_2^2}\right) - \frac{\bar{p}_1^1}{e^2 \bar{p}_2^2}\left[\frac{e}{\bar{p}_1^1}\frac{\partial \bar{p}_1^1}{\partial e} - \frac{e}{\bar{p}_2^2}\frac{\partial \bar{p}10_2^2}{\partial e} - 1\right]. \tag{85}$$

After some manipulations we find from (83) that

$$\frac{e}{\bar{p}_1^1}\frac{\partial \bar{p}_1^1}{\partial e} - 1 = \frac{eM}{p_1^1(e p_2^2)^2 |J|}\left\{eD^2\left[p_1^2 \frac{\partial \hat{h}_2^1}{\partial D^1} - p_2^2 \frac{\partial \hat{h}_2^2}{\partial D^2}\right] + p_1^1 \hat{h}_1^1 \mu^1\right\}, \tag{86}$$

and from (84) we have

$$\frac{e}{\bar{p}_2^2}\frac{\partial \bar{p}_2^2}{\partial e} = \frac{M}{p_2^1 p_2^2 |J|}\hat{h}_1^1 \mu^1. \tag{87}$$

Consequently, (85) becomes

$$\frac{\partial}{\partial e}\left(\frac{\bar{p}_1^1}{e \bar{p}_2^2}\right) = \frac{D^2 M}{p_1^1 (p_2^2)^2 |J|}\left[p_1^1 \frac{\partial \hat{h}_2^1}{\partial D^1} - p_2^2 \frac{\partial \hat{h}_2^2}{\partial D^2}\right]. \tag{88}$$

If the 'orthodox presumption' holds, the bracketed term is negative; hence, a devaluation will worsen country 2's terms of trade if its balance of payments is initially in deficit, but improve its terms of trade if its balance of payments is initially in surplus. If country 2 starts from a position of balanced payments on current account, *then* the classical proposition holds that a devaluation will have no real effect.

Note that (88) is related to (81) simply by

$$\frac{\partial}{\partial e}\left(\frac{\bar{\bar{p}}_1^1}{e\bar{p}_2^2}\right) = D^2\frac{\partial}{\partial D^2}\left(\frac{\bar{\bar{p}}_1^1}{e\bar{p}_2^2}\right). \tag{89}$$

Thus, a devaluation by country 2 simply accomplishes a transfer to country 1, if $D^2 > 0$, or a reverse transfer from country 1, if $D^2 < 0$. This is quite obvious when one gives the matter a little thought, since a devaluation by country 2 simply lowers the real value of its pre-existing current-account deficit; if this is positive, the effect is equivalent to a transfer to country 1, and if it is negative, the effect is the opposite. If country 2's current account is initially balanced, then in agreement with (75) the devaluation has no real effect.

The question usually posed concerning a current devaluation is: will it improve the country's balance of payments? The way the model (76) has been set up, it is obvious that a devaluation can have no effect on country 2's balance of payments denominated in its own currency; it can only have an effect on the balance of payments denominated in country 1's currency. The effect is given simply by

$$-\frac{\partial D^1}{\partial e} = -\frac{\partial(-eD^2)}{\partial e} = D^2. \tag{90}$$

If country 2's balance of payments is initially in deficit ($D^2 = -D^1/e > 0$), a devaluation will reduce this deficit when denominated in country 1's currency (i.e. raise D^1 towards 0). However, it will have the opposite effect if its balance of payments is initially in surplus ($D^2 < 0$). It will have no effect if the current account is already balanced.

4.5 Devaluation and the 'Neutrality of Money'

The results of Sections 4.3 and 4.4 pertaining to the 'neutrality of money' can be easily understood directly from the basic equations (65) and (76), without going through any detailed, mechanical evaluations of derivatives.

If in (65) we set $ep_2^2 = p_2^1$ (i.e. we replace the endogenous variable p_2^2 by the endogenous variable p_2^1), we see by the homogeneity of degree 0 of $\hat{h}_2^2$ that the equations reduce to

$$\hat{h}_2^1(p_2^1,p_2^1,D^1) - \hat{h}_2^2(p_1^1,p_2^1,-D^1) = 0$$

$$\kappa^1\frac{\ell_1^1}{b_{11}^1}p_1^1 + \kappa^2\frac{\ell_1^2}{b_{12}^2}p_2^1 + (\kappa^1-\kappa^2)D^1 - M = 0. \tag{91}$$

The exchange rate, e, has disappeared from the equations. A devaluation by country 2 thus has no real effect.

On the other hand, if we make the same substitution of p_2^1 for p_2^2 in (76) then, again making use of the homogeneity of degree 0 of $\hat{h}_2^2$, these become

$$\hat{h}_2^1(p_1^1,p_2^1,-eD^2)+\hat{h}_2^2(p_1^1,p_2^1,eD^2)=0$$

(92)

$$\kappa^1\frac{\ell_1^1}{b_{11}^1}p_1^1+\kappa^2\frac{\ell_1^2}{b_{12}^2}p_2^1-(\kappa^1-\kappa^2)eD^2-M=0.$$

These differ from (91) only by the substitution $D^1=-eD^2$. In (92), the variables, e and D^2 appear only in the combination eD^2. Thus, a devaluation by country 2 (a fall in e) is a way of accomplishing the same thing as would be achieved by a nominal transfer to country 1 (a fall in D^2) – if $D^2>0$, or by a nominal transfer from country 1 (a rise in D^2) – if $D^2<0$. If $D^2=0$ a devaluation accomplishes nothing at all.

In the model (91), since a devaluation leaves country 1's prices unaffected, and country 1's current account (denominated in its own currency) is by hypothesis unchanged, the variables p_1^2, p_2^2, D^2 all rise (in absolute value) proportionately to the devaluation; in particular, therefore, if $D^2>0$ the devaluation, of course, 'worsens' country 2's balance of payments (denominated in its own currency) by the percentage devaluation. Country 2's money supply, satisfying

$$eM^2=\kappa^2\left(\frac{\ell_1^2}{b_{12}^2}p_2^1-D^1\right),$$

(93)

also rises by the percentage of the devaluation.

In the model (92), a devaluation leaves country 2's balance of payments unaffected in terms of its own currency (by hypothesis), and automatically 'improves' it in terms of country 1's currency, if it was initially in deficit (and 'worsens' it if it was initially in surplus). The effect on the money supply is somewhat more complex than the previous case, since the devaluation causes a real transfer out of country 2 (if $D^2>0$ initially), contributing to a lessening of the transactions demand for money. However, to devalue its currency country 2 must purchase country 1's currency with its own, and to provide the wherewithal it must create more money. Since from (49) and (10) its money supply is determined by

$$M^2=\overline{M}^2(D^2,e)=\kappa^2\left[\frac{\ell_1^2}{b_{12}^2}\bar{p}_2^2(D^2,e)-D^2\right],$$

(94)

we find from (84) and assuming the sufficient stability condition (63) to hold that

$$\frac{\partial \overline{M}^2}{\partial e} = \frac{\kappa^2 \ell_1^2 \hat{h}_1^1 \mu^1 M}{e p_2^1 b_{12}^2 |J|} < 0.$$

Thus, a devaluation results in an increased money supply in country 2.

4.6   Concluding Observations

The model developed in this section necessarily contains a basic asymmetry. If country 2 has a current-account deficit, its ability to alter the value of this deficit in terms of country 1's currency, whether directly or by a realignment of the currency, implies a completely passive mode of behavior on the part of lenders in country 1.[18] In effect, this assumes an infinite elasticity of supply of loanable funds (at zero interest rate) from country 1 to country 2. This obviously cannot be regarded as a very satisfactory theory. An adequate general equilibrium treatment of credit markets would require an intertemporal model allowing for responsiveness of lending to real interest rates.

The aim of this essay has not been to provide a complete or even the best explanation of the market for foreign exchange, but to provide a general equilibrium formulation of the most prominent model that has been used to this end, and to exhaust its implications. A specialized version of this model – involving the assumption of infinite elasticities of supply of exports – has been studied; but it should be clear that the basic logical problems inherent in the static approach would not disappear, and might even be obscured, by a study of a more general version of the model.

The basic problem in analyzing the phenomenon of a 'successful devaluation' is that, as Alexander (1952) showed, one must explain how or why a currency depreciation should be capable of altering the difference between total expenditure (absorption) and total income. In a static framework, any discrepancy between expenditure and income on the part of an individual economic agent is a violation of its budget constraint.[19] One may therefore ask: why should a change in the value of the currency affect agents' budget constraints? Within the context of a static, flow-oriented model, there appears to be only one way: to alter the foreign-currency value of existing rates of borrowing.

Can such a simple subterfuge be the real explanation for a 'successful devaluation'? It may be objected, as was done in a related context by Mundell (1960b), that this presupposes 'money illusion': workers are willing to accept cuts in their real wages resulting from the inflationary effects of a devaluation, but not in their money wages. In the case of the present model, recipients of government welfare payments are willing to accept cuts in their real benefits but not their pecuniary ones. However, in both cases it appears that the issue is one of power rather than money illusion. Unions are no more fond of cuts in real than in money wages, but they have power to affect the nominal wage rate but not the exchange rate; union leaders would take the blame for the former but could pass the blame to others for the latter. Likewise, in the case of pressure groups and lobbyists for recipients of government transfer payments.

It is not pretended that the effect of devaluation on the foreign-currency value of the existing rate of borrowing is the only, or even the most important, explanation for the effect of a devaluation on the balance of payments – although it is not easy to think of examples of countries that pursued such policies successfully that did not start out with large public-sector deficits. But the most common alternative explanation – that a devaluation lowers the real value of cash balances (or other forms of wealth) and causes agents to cut down on their expenditures in order to accumulate cash (or wealth) (cf. Kemp, 1969; Dornbusch, 1973b) – amounts to showing another way in which a devaluation will bring about a real reverse transfer (albeit a temporary one) from the devaluing country to the rest of the world (cf. Dornbusch, 1973a). The chain of causation is not from devaluation to changes in relative prices to a change in the balance of payments; rather, it is from devaluation to a change in the balance of payments to changes in relative prices.

The Bickerdike–Robinson–Machlup–Metzler theory of the foreign exchanges, especially as formulated by Robinson, is essentially a theory of how the real exchange rate adapts to bring the current and capital account into equilibrium. This is also the Mill–Marshall theory, since the comparative statics and the stability conditions are the same under flexible exchange rates as under a gold standard with flexible prices. The confusions and controversies that have arisen with regard to the 'elasticity approach' result largely from two interrelated misconceptions: (i) failure to distinguish sharply between models in which the exchange rate is an endogenous variable from models in which it is an exogenous variable; (ii) failure to recognize that proportionality between the nominal and real exchange rate requires special monetary assumptions, and that these assumptions can (but need not) be fulfilled in a model of freely flexible exchange rates, but are incapable of being fulfilled in a model of pegged, adjustable exchange rates.

Notes

1. Mill explicitly (1848, II, p. 157; 1895, II, p. 182) stated that he was concerned with dynamic stability, in the words: 'The trade is in a state like that which is called in mechanics a condition of stable equilibrium.' The passage quoted in the text was followed by the following sentences, of which the first will be recognized as coming very close to a statement of the so-called 'Marshall–Lerner condition':

> But until the increased cheapness of English goods induces foreign countries to take a greater pecuniary value, or until the increased dearness (positive or comparative) of foreign goods makes England take a less pecuniary value, the exports of England will be no nearer to paying for the imports than before, and the stream of the precious metals which had begun to flow out of England, will still flow on. This efflux will continue, until the fall of prices in England brings within reach of the foreign market some commodity which England did not previously send thither; or until the reduced price of the things which she did send, has forced a demand abroad for a sufficient quantity to pay for the imports, aided, perhaps, by a reduction of English demand for foreign goods, through their enhanced price, either positive or comparative.

Mill's explicit discussion of the effect of a transfer (as opposed to stability conditions) came later (1848), vol.II, book III, ch.XXI, §4, pp.166–7; 1895, II, pp.191–2).

2.   There was some variation in Taussig's theory between 1917 and 1927. In 1917 he followed Mill in (tacitly) assuming that the countries did not produce import-competing goods; he also assumed that the paying country (Britain) was on the gold standard (hence would lose gold) and that the receiving country (the US) had flexible exchanges (with a constant money supply). He held (1917, pp.378, 397) that nominal prices of exportables and non-tradables ('domestic commodities') would also fall in the receiving country while nominal income remained constant. In 1927, he allowed for the production of import-competing goods and held (1927, pp.348–9) that nominal income and nominal prices of both exportables and importables would fall. He stressed that a general price index in the receiving country would fall under flexible exchanges but rise under a gold standard.

3.   The possibility of such a construction exists under very general conditions, and is not limited to the particular model under consideration here. See Chipman (1981).

4.   In the present model, since exportables and non-tradables are produced at constant cost, this implies that each country stabilizes the price of its export good (as well as its wage rate). This is the assumption made by Meade (1949; 1953, ch.VII). Meade's entire geometrical apparatus can be used without change, but reinterpreted to allow for non-tradables in the background.

5.   Cf., e.g. Johnson (1976, p. 263). Johnson justified this assumption on the ground that 'international capital movements would make no difference to the results'. There are cases (see Chipman, 1974, 1980) where capital movements would have no effect on relative prices (and therefore no effect on exchange rates if nominal prices of non-tradables are held constant) but this is certainly not true in general, and is not true in the case of the model under consideration here.

6.   See Chipman (1978) for a more general treatment of the relative-prices approach. As pointed out there, the Bickerdike–Robinson–Metzler formulae require the totally artificial assumption of additively separable trade-utility functions. Even with additively separable (consumer) utility functions, there are no reasonable conditions on production that will lead to this result other than a totally specific-factors technology which, in the case of fixed factor supplies, reduces to a model of pure exchange. For alternative interpretations of the 'elasticity approach' see Bronfenbrenner (1950), Jones (1961, 1974), Kemp (1964, pp. 235–6), Negishi (1968), and Dornbusch (1975).

7.   I.e. a function which is positive if the excess demand is positive, negative if the

excess demand is negative, and zero if the excess demand is zero. For stability theory in terms of sign-preserving functions, see McFadden (1968).

8. This is partially a semantic trap, since both propositions can be stated in the form: 'a decline in the exchange rate will lead to an increase in the balance of payments'. But even as careful a writer as Meade (1953, pp.93–4) appears to have fallen into it. It is true that, since a transfer from country 2 to country 1 (or a reduction in the rate of transfer from country 1 to country 2) will lower country 2's real exchange rate, a reduction in country 2's real exchange rate requires (logically) an improvement in country 2's current-account balance. The trouble is that a country normally has no power to control its real exchange rate, except by increasing its foreign lending or reducing its foreign borrowing. And in a model in which a country can control its nominal exchange rate, it will no longer be the case that the real exchange rate is proportional to the nominal exchange rate.

   A reading of the classic writings by Bickerdike (1920), Robinson (1937a, 1947a), Machlup (1939–40, 1950), Lerner (1944, pp.347, 376–9), and Metzler (1948) confirms that their concern in analyzing elasticities was with dynamic stability of a system of fluctuating exchange rates. (Marshall (1923, pp.353–4) was concerned, of course, with stability of the price mechanism, as was Mill before him.) Robinson (1937a) distinguished between the 'balance of trade' and the 'balance of lending', which were equal only in equilibrium (1937a, pp. 185–8; 1947a, pp. 136–8). She set out to explain how a 'change in the desire to lend abroad will tend to alter the exchange rate' (1937a, p.188; 1947a, p.138); subsequent references to the effect of the exchange rate on the balance of trade are all consistent with the disequilibrium interpretation. But in Robinson (1937b, 1947b) one can detect a switch to the equilibrium interpretation.

9. Cf. Haberler (1949) for the most detailed and comprehensive analysis using the 'elasticity approach'. Haberler himself (p.213) anticipated the argument presented in the remainder of this paragraph concerning the possible inappropriateness of the 'elasticity approach' for the analysis of the effect of an exogenous currency depreciation.

10. It is immaterial for this argument whether such capital inflows take the form of short-term loans or a loss of reserves.

11. Cf. Chipman (1979). These trade-demand functions are similar to Kemp's (1970) '"reduced" excess demand functions'.

12. This is a special case of a more general result derived in Chipman (1981).

13. Cf. Arrow (1974, p.185). Since (22) specifies that the rates of change be proportional (in some unspecified way) to the expressions on the right, by stability of this system I mean stability independently of the proportionality factors, i.e. independently of (positive) speeds of adjustment. Arrow's conditions correct those of Metzler (1945) whose condition was that the principal minors be alternately negative and positive.

14. Marshall's condition, derived for a model in which the variable of adjustment was the terms of trade, was stated as a condition for instability, namely that 'the total elasticity of demand of each country be less than unity, and on the average less than one half' (Marshall, 1923, p.354). This is only slightly more explicit than Mill's statement quoted in note 1 above. The first statement in the explicit form (28) was that of Bickerdike (1920, p. 121), and the next statement in words only that of Lerner (1944, p. 378). This was derived for a model of varying exchange rates. The condition was interpreted by Robinson (1947a, p.143a) (as it had been explicitly by Bickerdike), as corresponding to the special case of an infinitely elastic supply of exports in each country. Haberler

(1949, pp.204–6) suggested that Lerner may have had in mind elasticities in Marshall's sense. In the present model the two concepts coincide (see also Chipman, 1978, p. 67). The terminology 'Marshall–Lerner condition' is due to Hirschman (1949).

15. That is, the functions $\partial h_i^k(p_1^k, p_2^k p_3^k, E^*)/\partial E^*$ are independent of p_3^k and E^* and identical with one another for $i,k = 1,2$, hence the demand functions are given by

$$h_i^k(p_1^k, p_2^k, p_3^k, E^*) = \varphi_i(p_1^k, p_2^k, p_3^k) + \psi_i(p_1^k, p_2^k, p_3^k)E^* \quad (i = 1,2,3)$$

where φ_i^k and ψ_i^k are positively homogeneous of degree 0 and -1 respectively, and satisfy

$$\sum_{i=1}^{3} p_i^k \varphi_i^k(p_1^k, p_2^k, p_3^k) = 0,$$

$$\sum_{i=1}^{3} p_i^k \psi_i^k(p_1^k, p_2^k, p_3^k) = 1$$

and the special condition

$$\psi_i^k(p_1^k, p_2^k, p_3^k) = \psi_i(p_1^k, p_2^k) \text{ for } i = 1,2.$$

These functions are generated by indirect utility functions of the Gorman (1961) 'polar form'

$$V^*(p_1^k, p_2^k, p_3^k, E^*) = \frac{E^* - \Phi^k(p_1^k, p_2^k, p_3^k)}{\psi^k(p_1^k, p_2^k, p_3^k)}$$

where Φ^k and ψ^k are positively homogeneous of degree 1 and ψ^k satisfies the special separability property

$$(p_1^k, p_2^k, p_3^k) = F(p_1^k, p_2^k)^{1-\gamma}(p_3^k)^{\gamma} \quad (0 < \gamma < 1),$$

where F is positively homogeneous of degree 1. Thus,

$$\varphi_i^k(p^k) = \frac{\partial \Phi^k(p)}{\partial p_i^k} \Phi^k(p^k) \frac{\delta \log \psi^k(p^k)}{\partial p_i^k}$$

and

$$\psi_i^k(p^k) = \frac{\partial \log \psi^k(p^k)}{\partial p_i^k} = \begin{cases} (1-\gamma)\dfrac{\partial \log F(p_1^k, p_2^k)}{\partial p_i^k} & \text{for } i = 1, 2 \\[2mm] \gamma\dfrac{1}{p_i^k} & \text{for } i = 3 \end{cases}.$$

For a related result see Primont (1983).

16. Dornbusch (1973a, p.898) appears to be the first to have drawn attention to this misinterpretation. It forms the basis for the well-justified doubts expressed by Takayama (1972, pp.234–6).

17. Some authors (e.g. Negishi, 1968; Johnson, 1976, p.281) insist that (28) is not a correct stability condition for a monetary economy, but only for a 'barter economy'. The present model is certainly not one of a barter economy. This point appears to be a red herring, distracting attention from the more serious confusion discussed at the end of Section 3.4 above.

18. This is an example of what Mundell (1969, pp.29, 36–7) has called the 'redundancy problem'. Actually, country 1 will not be entirely passive since if country 2's borrowing becomes excessive, it (or the IMF) will put pressure on country 2 to devalue and/or reduce its public-sector deficit as a condition for continued lending. But this is not part of the formal model.

19. It was noted by Harberger (1950) that if all agents adhere to a budget constraint equating expenditure to income (an assumption he called 'Say's Law' following Oscar Lange's unusual terminology), a devaluation would have no effect. Both he and Laursen and Metzler (1950) emphasized the importance of the effect of the terms of trade on the propensity to save. Actually, there is no reason to focus on the terms of trade: if a devaluation lowers a country's real exchange rate (by raising domestic prices of both exportables and importables relative to non-tradables), this could be expected to have an even greater effect on intertemporal substitution than a fall in the terms of trade (a rise in import prices alone). But this does not help explain how a devaluation improves (or worsens) the balance of payments; for one still needs to explain how a fall in the nominal exchange rate will bring about a fall in the real exchange rate. For this one needs to show how a devaluation will cause a real transfer.

References

Alexander, S. S. (1952) 'Effects of a Devaluation on a Trade Balance', International Monetary Fund *Staff Papers* 2: 263–78.

Arrow, K. J. (1974) 'Stability Independent of Adjustment Speed', in G. Horwich and P. A. Samuelson (eds) *Trade, Stability, and Macroeconomics* (New York: Academic Press) pp.181–202.

Bickerdike, C. F. (1920) 'The Instability of Foreign Exchange', *Economic Journal* 30: 118–22.

Bronfenbrenner, M. (1950) 'Exchange Rates and Exchange Stability: Mathematical Supplement', *Review of Economics and Statistics* 32: 12–16.

Chacholiades, M. (1968) 'The Marshall–Lerner Condition', in C. P. Kindleberger, *International Economics*, 4th edn (Homewood, Ill.: Richard D. Irwin) pp. 569–77.

Chipman, J. S. (1974) 'The Transfer Problem Once Again', in G. Horwich and P. A. Samuelson (eds) *Trade, Stability, and Macroeconomics* (New York: Academic Press) pp.19–78.

Chipman, J. S. (1978) 'A Reconsideration of the "Elasticity Approach" to Balance-of-Payments Adjustment Problems', in J. S. Dreyer (ed.) *Breadth and Depth in Economics* (Lexington, Mass.: D. C. Heath) pp.49–85.

Chipman, J. S. (1979) 'The Theory and Application of Trade Utility Functions', in J. Green and J. A. Scheinkman (eds) *General Equilibrium, Growth, and Trade* (New York: Academic Press) pp.277–96.

Chipman, J. S. (1980) 'Exchange-Rate Flexibility and Resource Allocation', in J. S. Chipman and C. P. Kindleberger (eds) *Flexible Exchange Rates and the Balance of Payments* (Amsterdam: North-Holland) pp.159–209.

Chipman, J. S. (1981) 'A General-Equilibrium Framework for Analyzing the Responses of Imports and Exports to External Price Changes: An Aggregation Theorem', in G. Bamberg and O. Opitz (eds) *Methods of Operations Research*, vol.44: *6th Symposium on Operations Research*, vol.2 (Königstein: Verlag Anton Hein) pp.43–56.

Corden, W. M. (1977) *Inflation, Exchange Rates, and the World Economy* (Oxford: Clarendon Press).

Dornbusch, R. (1973a) 'Currency Depreciation, Hoarding, and Relative Prices', *Journal of Political Economy* 81: 893–915.

Dornbusch, R. (1973b) 'Devaluation, Money and Nontraded Goods', *American Economic Review* 63: 871–80.

Dornbusch, R. (1975) 'Exchange Rates and Fiscal Policy in a Popular Model of International Trade', *American Economic Review* 65: 859–71.

Gorman, W. M. (1961) 'On a Class of Preference Fields', *Metroeconomica* 13: 53–6.

Haberler, G. (1949) 'The Market for Foreign Exchange and the Stability of the Balance of Payments', *Kyklos* 3: 193–218.

Harberger, A. C. (1950) 'Currency Depreciation, Income, and the Balance of Trade', *Journal of Political Economy* 58: 47–60.

Hirschman, A. O. (1949) 'Devaluation and the Trade Balance: A Note', *Review of Economics and Statistics* 31: 50–3.

Hurwicz, L. and H. Uzawa (1971) 'On the Integrability of Demand Functions', in J. S. Chipman, L. Hurwicz, M. K. Richter, and H. F. Sonnenschein (eds) *Preferences, Utility, and Demand* (New York: Harcourt Brace Jovanovich) pp.114–48.

Johnson, H. G. (1976) 'The Monetary Theory of Balance-of-Payments Policies', in J. A. Frenkel and H. G. Johnson (eds) *The Monetary Approach to the Balance of Payments* (London: Allen & Unwin) pp.262–84.

Jones, R. W. (1961) 'Stability Conditions in International Trade: A General Equilibrium Analysis', *International Economic Review* 2: 199–209.

Jones, R. W. (1974) 'Trade with Non-traded Goods: The Anatomy of Interconnected Markets', *Economica* NS: 121–38.

Kemp, M. C. (1962) 'The Rate of Exchange, the Terms of Trade and the Balance of Payments in Fully Employed Economies', *International Economic Review* 3: 314–27.

Kemp, M. C. (1964) *The Pure Theory of International Trade* (Englewood Cliffs, NJ: Prentice-Hall).

Kemp, Murray C. (1970) 'The Balance of Payments and the Terms of Trade in Relation to Financial Controls', *Review of Economic Studies* 37: 25–31.

Keynes, J. M. (1930) *A Treatise on Money*, 2 vols (London: Macmillan).

Laursen, S. and L. A. Metzler (1950) 'Flexible Exchange Rates and the Theory of Employment', *Review of Economics and Statistics* 32: 281–99.

Lerner, A. P. (1944) *The Economics of Control* (New York: Macmillan).

McFadden, D. (1968) 'On Hicksian Stability', in J. N. Wolfe (ed.) *Value, Capital, and Growth* (Edinburgh: Edinburgh University Press) pp.329–51.

Machlup, F. (1939–40) 'The Theory of Foreign Exchanges', *Economica*, NS, 6: 375–97; 7: 23–49.

Machlup, F. (1950) 'Elasticity Pessimism in International Trade', *Economia Internazionale* 3: 118–37.

Marshall, A. (1923) *Money Credit and Commerce* (London: Macmillan).

Meade, J. E. (1949) 'A Geometrical Representation of Balance of Payments Policy', *Economica*, NS, 16: 305–20.

Meade, J. E. (1951a) *The Balance of Payments* (London: Oxford University Press).

Meade, J. E. (1951b) *The Balance of Payments: Mathematical Supplement* (London: Oxford University Press).

Meade, J. E. (1953) *A Geometry of International Trade* (London: Allen & Unwin).

Metzler, L. A. (1945) 'Stability of Multiple Markets: The Hicks Conditions', *Econometrica* 13: 277–92.

Metzler, L. A. (1948) 'The Theory of International Trade', in H. S. Ellis (ed) *A Survey of Contemporary Economics* (Philadelphia: Blakiston) pp.210–54.

Mill, J. S. (1848; 5th edn 1895) *Principles of Political Economy* 2 vols (London: John W. Parker; 5th edn, New York: D. Appleton).

Mundell, R. A. (1960a) 'The Pure Theory of International Trade', *American Economic Review* 50: 67–110.

Mundell, R. A. (1960b) 'The Monetary Dynamics of International Adjustment Under Fixed and Flexible Exchange Rates', *Quarterly Journal of Economics*, 74: 227–57.

Mundell, R. A. (1969) 'Problems of the International Monetary System', in R. A. Mundell and A. K. Swoboda (eds) *Monetary Problems of the International Economy* (Chicago: University of Chicago Press) pp.21–38.

Negishi, T. (1968) 'Approaches to the Analysis of Devaluation', *International Economic Review* 9: 21–227.

Pigou, A. C. (1932) 'The Effect of Reparations on the Real Ratio of International Interchange', *Economic Journal* 42: 532–43.

Primont, D. (1983) 'Aggregation of Input Price Indexes', in W. Eichhorn, R. Henn, K. Neumann, and R. W. Shephard (eds) *Quantitative Studies on Production and Prices* (Würzburg: Physica-Verlag) pp.181–91.

Robinson, J. (1937a; 2nd edn 1947a) 'The Foreign Exchanges', in J. Robinson, *Essays in the Theory of Employment* (New York: Macmillan) pp.183–209; 2nd edn (Oxford: Blackwell) pp.134–55.

Robinson, J. (1937b; 2nd edn 1947b) 'Beggar-My-Neighbour Remedies for Unemployment', in J. Robinson, *Essays in the Theory of Employment* (Oxford: Basil Blackwell) pp.210–28; 2nd edn pp.156–70.

Samuelson, P. A. (1952) 'The Transfer Problem and Transport Costs: The Terms of Trade when Impediments are Absent', *Economic Journal* 62: 278–304.

Sohmen, E. (1958) 'The Marshall–Lerner Condition', in C. P. Kindleberger, *International Economics*, revised edn (Homewood, Ill.: Richard D. Irwin) pp.610–12.

Takayama, A. (1972) *International Trade* (New York: Holt, Rinehart & Winston).

Taussig, F. W. (1917) 'International Trade under Depreciated Paper. A Contribution to Theory', *Quarterly Journal of Economics* 31: 380–403.

Taussig, F. W. (1927) *International Trade* (New York: Macmillan).

30 A Neglected Corner: Labor Unions and the Pattern of International Trade

Murray C. Kemp and Koji Shimomura

1 INTRODUCTION

It is a striking fact (and, in view of her strong social sympathies, a puzzling one) that during no phase of her long professional career did Joan Robinson seriously interest herself in the economics of labor unions. Thus in *The Economics of Imperfect Competition* there are chapters on the monopolistic and monopsonistic exploitation *of* labor but there is almost nothing about the monopolistic exploitation *by* labor. In her middle years, Keynesian preconceptions prevented her from attaching much significance to the practices of unions; see, for example, her 1945 essay 'Obstacles to Full Employment' (*Collected Essays*, vol. 1, pp.105–14). And in the final capital-theoretic phase of her career she worked almost exclusively with Ricardian models which impose blinkers of another kind.

Also noteworthy is Joan Robinson's apparent lack of interest and relative lack of achievement in the economics of open economies. What little she attempted in this field was either essentially unoriginal (her celebrated 1937 treatment of the foreign exchanges came seventeen years after Bickerdike's paper on the same topic) or routine Keynesian analysis.

In the present essay, we pay tribute to Joan Robinson not by elaborating on one of her favorite themes but by plunging into territory she has conspicuously neglected. Our purpose is to outline a theory of international trade which incorporates a maximizing labor union. As a more specific but subsidiary objective, we seek to discover whether there are circumstances in which a maximizing union, by imposing a minimum wage, may so change the effective factor–endowment ratio of a country as to reverse the direction of its trade. That an arbitrary minimum wage can achieve a reversal is well known and easy to understand. The outstanding question is whether a rationally chosen minimum wage can do so.

In Section 2 we set out some general orienting ideas. In the technical third section we deduce some of the properties of union-distorted commodity excess-demand functions. Then in Section 4 we establish general sufficient conditions for the existence of a union-ridden world equilibrium and for the reversal of trade. (In an appendix to Section 4, sharper conditions are obtained by requiring that production functions and the union's objective function be of special types.) As a welcome by-product of our analysis we obtain necessary and sufficient conditions for the existence of a labor union; that is, the union is treated not as an institutional datum but as an endogenous variable. A brief final section contains some remarks concerning the possibility of extending the analysis to other standard problems of trade theory.

A more complete treatment of our topic may be found in the authors' forthcoming *Labour Unions and the Theory of International Trade*.

2 GENERAL IDEAS

We consider a trading world of two countries, the home and the foreign. Each country is endowed with given stocks of non-tradable labor and some other non-tradable primary factor, say land; and it is capable of producing two tradable goods, one a pure consumption good, the other a pure intermediate good or raw material. (Here we follow Joan Robinson who, on many occasions, manifested her aversion to the Heckscher–Ohlin tradition of modelling trade in consumption goods only.) Production is by means of a no-joint-products technology described by concave, constant-returns production functions in which each factor is indispensable.

In the home country there is a single labor union to which all workers, employed and unemployed, belong. (The alternative assumption of fragmented unionism would be more realistic; but such an assumption would muddle the effects of unionism *per se* with those of inter-union rivalry.) The objective function of the union is written, quite generally, as $U(w,x)$, where w is the real-wage, in terms of the consumption good, x is the ratio of employed labor to land, and U is an increasing function. The union sets the minimum real-wage, say w_m, leaving competitive firms to determine the real-wage and the volume of employment. However, it is assumed that the union is rational in the sense that it knows both the employment and the wage implications of each minimum wage. The task of the union, then, is to find that w_m which maximizes $U(w,x)$, full allowance made for the dependence of w and x on w_m.

In Figure 30.1 the wage–employment curve $zd'y'$ contains the set of feasible (w,x), that is, the set of (w,x) each member of which is associated with some value of w_m; point d' is the pre-union equilibrium; and point m' is a possible post-union equilibrium. At this preliminary stage of our analysis we cannot rule out any of the three possibilities: (i) that d' and m' coincide; (ii) that m' lies to the right of d', but not so far to the right that the direction

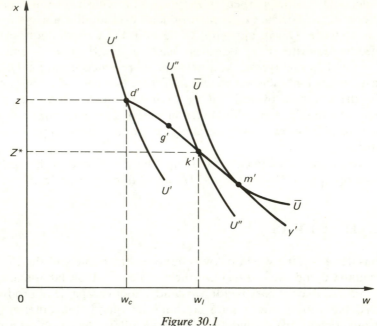

Figure 30.1

of trade is reversed; (iii) that m' lies so far to the right of d' that the direction of trade is reversed. Later, however, sufficient conditions for each outcome will be found. Those conditions will be in terms of factor endowments at home and abroad, union preferences, and social security and tax arrangements at home.

3   UNION-DISTORTED EXCESS-DEMAND FUNCTIONS

The more detailed analysis of our problem falls into two parts. In the present section we derive some of the properties of the excess-demand function for the intermediate good in the home country, given the minimum wage set by the union. The possibility and characteristics of a union-ridden world equilibrium will be derived in Section 4.

3.1   Before the Union

We begin by considering an initial, union-free situation; the material is, of course, quite familiar. Let $c^1(w,r,p)$ and $c^2(w,r)$ be the unit-cost functions of the consumption good and the intermediate good, respectively, where w, r, and p are the wage rate, the rental of land, and the price of the intermediate good, all in terms of the consumption good. Given the restrictions placed on the production functions, the system of equations

$$1 = c^1(w,r,p)$$

$$p = c^2(w,r)$$

has a unique solution $[w(p),r(p)]$ for each $p > 0$. Then, denoting the labor–land ratio of the ith industry by x_i, we have

$$x_1(p) = \frac{c_w^1[w(p),r(p),p]}{c_r^1[w(p),r(p),p]}$$

$$x_2(p) = \frac{c_w^2[w(p),r(p)]}{c_r^2[w(p),r(p)]}$$

where $c_w^i \equiv \partial c^i / \partial w$, etc. Figures 30.2a and 30.2b provide the familiar illustration. In these figures z represents the labor–land endowment ratio of the home country and $\underline{p}$ and $\bar{p}$ mark off the regions of specialization: both goods are produced if $p \in (\underline{p}, \bar{p})$, only the intermediate good is produced if $p \geq \bar{p}$ and only the consumption good is produced if $p \leq \underline{p}$.

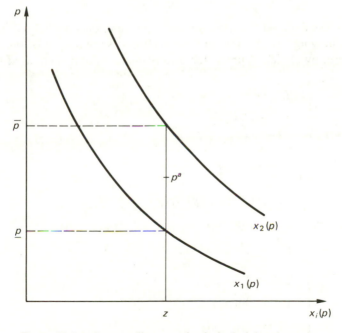

Figure 30.2a   Intermediate good relatively labor-intensive

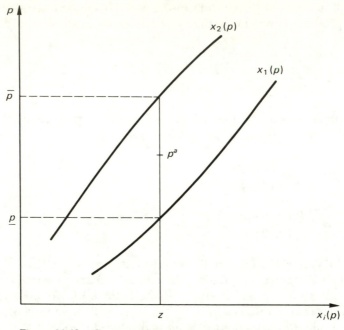

Figure 30.2b   Consumption good relatively labor-intensive

The excess-demand function for the intermediate good $ED_2(p)$ is defined by the following system of equations, where y_i is the output of the ith good and where, by choice of units, the endowment of land is equated to one.

$$\text{if } p \geq \bar{p} \quad \left\{ \begin{array}{ll} ED_2 = -y_2 \\[4pt] 1 \quad = c_r^2[w,r]y_2 \\[4pt] z \quad = c_w^2[w,r]y_2 \\[4pt] p \quad = c^2[w,r] \end{array} \right.$$

$$\text{if } p \in (\underline{p},\bar{p}) \quad \left\{ \begin{array}{ll} ED_2 = c_p^1[w(p),r(p),p]y_1 - y_2 \\[4pt] 1 \quad = c_r^1[w(p),r(p),p]y_1 + c_r^2[w(p),r(p),p]y_2 \\[4pt] z \quad = c_w^1[w(p),r(p),p]y_1 \end{array} \right.$$

$$\text{if } p \leq \underline{p} \quad \left\{ \begin{array}{ll} ED_2 = c_p^1[w,r,p]y_1 \\[4pt] 1 \quad = c_r^1[w,r,p]y_1 \\[4pt] z \quad = c_w^1[w,r,p]y_1 \\[4pt] 1 \quad = c^1[w,r,p] \end{array} \right.$$

It can be verified that $ED_2(p)$ is a declining function. Since all factors are indispensable to the production of each good, the pre-union autarkic equilibrium price ratio p^a must lie strictly between $\underline{p}$ and $\bar{p}$, as in Figure 30.3.

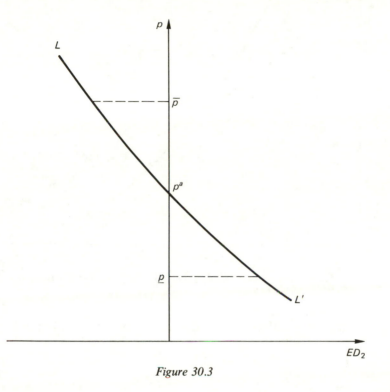

Figure 30.3

3.2 After the Union

Suppose now that a labor union is formed and that the union sets the minimum wage w_m at the level $w(p^a)$.

Imagine for the time being that the intermediate good is relatively labor-intensive, so that the wage–rental curves are as in Figure 30.4. If p is slightly less than p^a then, from the Stolper–Samuelson Theorem, $w(p) < w_m = w(p^a)$. As Figure 30.4 makes clear, only the consumption good is produced. But $x_1 < z$ near p^a. Hence unemployment emerges and the excess-demand function for the intermediate good is defined by the system

$$ED_2 = c_p^1[w_m, r, p] y_1$$

$$1 = c_r^1[w_m, r, p] y_1 \tag{1}$$

$$1 = c^1[w_m, r, p]$$

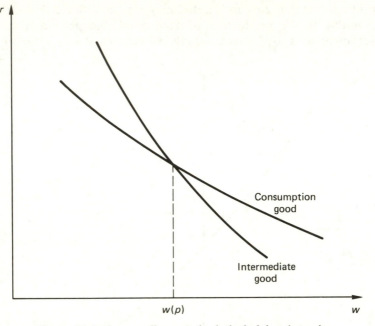

Figure 30.4   Intermediate good relatively labor-intensive

Differentiating (1) with respect to ED_2, y_1, r, and p, we find that

$$\frac{dED_2}{dp} = \frac{-1}{(c_r^1)^2} \begin{vmatrix} c_{pp}^1 y_1 & c_{pr}^1 y_1 & c_p^1 \\ c_{rp}^1 y_1 & c_{rr}^1 y_1 & c_r^1 \\ c_p^1 & c_r^1 & 0 \end{vmatrix} < 0 \tag{2}$$

since the determinant is positive. If, on the other hand, p is slightly greater than p^a then $w(p) > w_m = w(p^a)$. At w_m there will be an excess demand for labor, implying that the wage rate will rise to $w(p)$, where the union-free equilibrium will be established.

Suppose alternatively that the intermediate good is relatively land-intensive, so that the wage–rental curves are as in Figure 30.5. If p is slightly greater than p^a then, again from the Stolper–Samuelson Theorem, $w(p) < w_m = w(p^a)$; only the intermediate good is produced; hence there is some unemployment and the excess-demand function for the intermediate good is defined by the system

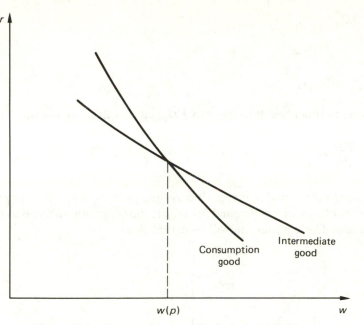

Figure 30.5   Consumption good relatively labor-intensive

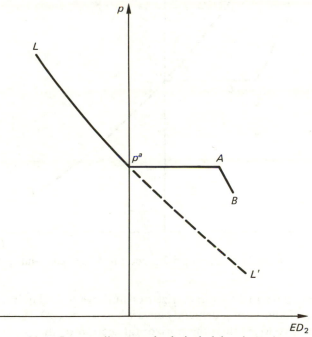

Figure 30.6   Intermediate good relatively labor-intensive

$$ED_2 = -y_2$$

$$1 = c_2^2[w_m, r]y_2 \tag{3}$$

$$p = c^2[w_m, r]$$

Differentiating (3) with respect to ED_2, y_2, r, and p, we obtain

$$\frac{dED_2}{dp} = \frac{y_2 c_{rr}^2}{(c_r^2)^2} < 0 \tag{4}$$

If, on the other hand, p is slightly less than p^a then $w(p) > w_m = w(p^a)$. At w_m there will be an excess demand for labor, the wage rate will rise to $w(p)$ and the union-free equilibrium will be established.

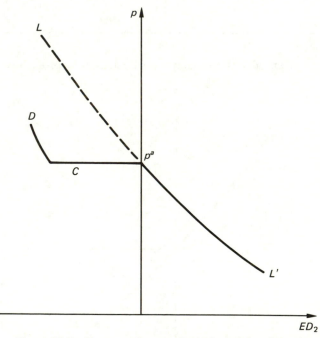

Figure 30.7   Consumption good relatively labor-intensive

Figures 30.6 and 30.7 summarize our findings to this point. They display the union-ridden excess-demand curve when $w_m = w(p^a)$. If the union sets w_m slightly above $w(p^a)$ then the horizontal section of the curve moves up or down according as the intermediate good is relatively labor-intensive or relatively land-intensive, respectively; the value of p, say p_m, through which the horizontal section passes being defined by $w_m = w(p_m)$.

4 UNION-RIDDEN WORLD EQUILIBRIUM

Let us now introduce the possibility of trade between the home and foreign countries. Given our limited objective of demonstrating the possibility of union-induced trade reversal, we find it useful to specify quite closely the technology and factor endowments of the two countries. Specifically, it is assumed that the two countries have a common technology, the same land endowment and labor endowments which slightly favor the home country. These assumptions allow us to concentrate on situations in which both countries are incompletely specialized. For brevity, we confine our attention to the case in which the consumption good is relatively labor-intensive, so that the home country is the natural importer of the intermediate good.

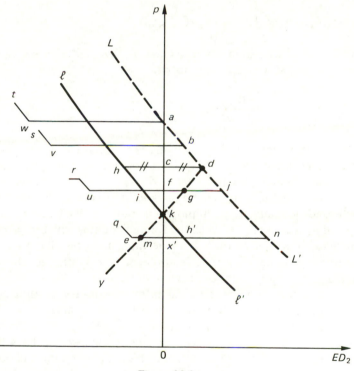

Figure 30.8

Figure 30.8 displays the pre-union home and foreign excess-demand curves (LL' and $\ell\ell'$, respectively) for the intermediate good. In the absence of a union, the equilibrium world price of the intermediate good is p^{nu}, represented by the segment Oc in Figure 30.8. The equilibrium is disturbed by the emergence of a labor union at home. As w_m is pushed above its initial value of $w(p^a)$, the home excess demand shifts in the manner described in

Section 3, taking in turn the positions *twaL'*, *svbL'*, *rujL'*, and *qenL'*. Provided p_m lies in the interval *ac*, however, the world equilibrium price remains at *Oc* and the minimum wage has no effect. Proceeding, suppose that w_m is large enough to place p_m in the interval *ck*. Then the union does play a role; p_m itself is the world equilibrium price. For example, if p_m is equal to *Of*, so that the home excess-demand curve is *rujL'*, the equilibrium price is *Of* and the foreign country exports *fi* (=*fg*) of the intermediate good. At *g* the home country suffers some unemployment. For, on the horizontal segment *uj*,

$$ED_2 = c_p^1[w_m, r(p_m), p_m]y_1 - y_2$$

$$1 = c_r^1[w_m, r(p_m), p_m]y_1 + c_r^2[w_m, r(p_m), p_m]y_2 \qquad (5)$$

$$x = c_w^1[w_m, r(p_m), p_m]y_1 + c_w^2[w_m, r(p_m), p_m]y_2$$

The shift from *j* to *g* involves a decline in ED_2. Differentiating (5) with respect to y_1, y_2, x, and ED_2, we obtain

$$\frac{dx}{dED_2} = \frac{-1}{c_r^2 c_p^1 + c_r^1}[c_r^1 c_w^2 - c_w^1 c_r^2]$$

Since the intermediate good is relatively land-intensive, the square-bracketed term is negative. Hence dx/dED_2 is positive, implying that at point *g* there is some unemployment.

   If w_m is large enough to place p_m in the interval *kO*, the equilibrium is characterized not only by unemployment but also by trade reversal. For example, if p_m is equal to *Ox'* then the foreign country will *import x'h'* of the intermediate good. Of course, it is one thing to show that there exists a trade-reversing value of w_m; it is quite another thing to show that a maximizing union might choose such a value.

   The dashed line *dgkmy* is the locus of home-country equilibrium excess demands for the intermediate good, one for each value of w_m. We now examine the behavior of employment *x* as w_m changes and the economy moves along *dgkmy*. At the end of our calculations we will have the set of feasible (wage, employment) pairs from which the union must choose. Now along the locus *dgkmy* the relationship between *x* and w_m is defined by the system

$$c_p^1[w_m, r_m, p_m]y_1 - y_2 + ED_2^*(p_m) = 0$$

$$c_r^1[w_m, r_m, p_m]y_1 + c_r^2[w_m, r_m, p_m]y_2 = 1$$

$$c_w^1[w_m, r_m, p_m]y_1 + c_w^2[w_m, r_m, p_m]y_2 = x \qquad (6)$$

$$c^1[w_m, r_m, p_m] = 1$$

$$c^2[w_m, r_m] = p_m$$

where $ED_2^*(p_m)$ is the foreign excess-demand function for the intermediate good. Differentiating (6) totally,

$$
\begin{bmatrix}
c_{pp}^1 y_1 + ED_2^{*'} & c_p^1 & -1 & 0 & c_{pr}^1 y_1 \\
c_{rp}^1 y_1 & c_r^1 & c_r^2 & 0 & c_{rr}^1 y_1 + c_{rr}^2 y_2 \\
c_{wp}^1 y_1 & c_w^1 & c_w^2 & -1 & c_{wr}^1 y_1 + c_{wr}^2 y_2 \\
c_p^1 & 0 & 0 & 0 & c_r^1 \\
-1 & 0 & 0 & 0 & c_r^2
\end{bmatrix}
\begin{bmatrix}
dp_m \\
dy_1 \\
dy_2 \\
dx \\
dr_m
\end{bmatrix}
$$

$$
= -
\begin{bmatrix}
c_{pw}^1 y_1 \\
c_{rw}^1 y_1 + c_{rw}^2 y_2 \\
c_{ww}^1 y_1 + c_{ww}^2 y_2 \\
c_w^1 \\
c_w^2
\end{bmatrix}
dw_m
$$

where $ED_2^{*'} \equiv dED_2^*/dp_m$. Solving for dx/dw_m and simplifying,

$$\frac{dx}{dw_m} = \frac{p_m ED_2^{*'}(c_r^1 c_w^2 - c_w^1 c_r^2)^2 - \psi}{p_m(c_r^1 + c_p^1 c_r^2)^2}$$

where

$$\psi \equiv -y_1[c_{rr}^1(c_w^2)^2 - 2c_r^2 c_w^2 c_{rw}^1 + c_{ww}^1(c_r^2)^2]$$

$$- y_2[c_{rr}^2(c_w^2)^2 - 2c_r^2 c_w^2 c_{rw}^2 + c_{ww}^2(c_w^2)^2]$$

Since c^i is a strictly concave function, $i=1,2$, ψ is positive. Hence dx/dw_m is negative if (as we shall assume) $ED_2^{*\prime}$ is negative. Thus we have the negative relationship between x and w_m illustrated by Figure 30.1, with d', g', k', m', and y' corresponding respectively to d, g, k, m, and y of Figure 30.8.

So far, we have confined ourselves to values of w_m consistent with the incomplete specialization of home production. However, the negativity of the wage–employment relationship is global. When w_m is sufficiently large only the relatively labor-intensive consumption good is produced at home and the relationship between w_m and x is defined by the system

$$c_p^1[w_m,r_m,p_m]y_1 - ED_2^*(p_m) = 0$$

$$1 = c_r^1[w_m,r_m,p_m]y_1$$

$$x = c_w^1[w_m,r_m,p_m]y_1 \tag{7}$$

$$1 = c^1[w_m,r_m,p_m]$$

Differentiating (7) totally one finds that $dx/dw_m < 0$ if $ED_2^{*\prime} < 0$.

It follows from the argument to this point that as w_m rises either x reaches zero at some finite value of w_m or x converges to a non-negative constant $\bar{x}$. In fact the constant must be zero; for, if it were positive, $w_m\bar{x}$, and therefore w_mx, would be unbounded, a physical impossibility. Hence we can state the following proposition concerning the existence of a union-ridden world equilibrium.

Proposition 1:   There exists a union-ridden world equilibrium if (i) x is indispensable in the sense that $U(w,0) = -\infty$ and the wage–employment curve is such that $x=0$ for some finite w or if (ii) the union's objective function U has an elasticity of substitution between w and x which is smaller than one.

The union-ridden world equilibrium may or may not involve unemployment. However, the following proposition is easy to verify.

Proposition 2:   A union-ridden world equilibrium will be attended by unemployment if and only if

$$\left|\frac{\partial U/\partial w}{\partial U/\partial x}\right| > \left|\frac{dx}{dw}\right| \tag{8}$$

at the pre-union world trading equilibrium (point d' in Fig. 30.1). In fact, condition (8) is necessary and sufficient for the existence of a labor union.

Going a step further we arrive at the following proposition concerning the possibility of union-induced trade reversal.

Proposition 3: A union-ridden world equilibrium will be attended by unemployment and trade reversal if and only if (8) holds at the no-trade point k' of Figure 30.1.

5 FINAL REMARKS

It has been shown that labor unions help to determine not only a country's employment level but also the extent and direction of its foreign trade. In particular, it has been shown that the Heckscher–Ohlin Theorem survives the recognition of labor unions only in a heavily qualified form. However, the methods of the present paper provide access to many other interesting questions. Having mastered the technical problem of accommodating a rational labor union, one can proceed to rewrite the whole of conventional barter trade theory. Thus, building on the analysis of the present paper, we have studied elsewhere the implications of unions for the Stolper–Samuelson and Rybczynski Theorems (Kemp and Shimomura, 1984), for the pattern of international indebtedness (Kemp and Shimomura, 1985a), and for the relationship between protective tariffs and unemployment (Kemp and Shimomura, 1985b,c).

APPENDIX TO SECTION 4

In this appendix we briefly consider the special case where, in each country, the unit-cost functions take the constant-elasticity-of-substitution (CES) form

$$c^1(w,r,p) = (aw^{-\rho} + br^{-\rho} + cp^{-\rho})^{-1/\rho}$$

$$\rho > -1$$

$$c^2(w,r) = (\alpha w^{-\rho} + \beta r^{-\rho})^{-1/\rho}$$

where $\sigma \equiv 1 + \rho$ is the elasticity of substitution and in which the union objective function is $U = wx$.

Making use of the equilibrium conditions

$$1 = aw^{-\rho} + br^{-\rho} + cp^{-\rho}$$

$$p^{-\rho} = \alpha w^{-\rho} + \beta r^{-\rho}$$

one may verify that

$$c_w^1 = aw^{-(1+\rho)}, \quad c_w^2 = \alpha w^{-(1+\rho)} p^{1+\rho}$$

$$c_r^1 = br^{-(1+\rho)}, \quad c_r^2 = \beta r^{-(1+\rho)} p^{1+\rho}$$

$$c_p^1 = cp^{-(1+\rho)}$$

Then, letting

$$\gamma \equiv \frac{1+\rho}{\rho}, \quad W \equiv w^{-\rho}, \ R \equiv r^{-\rho}, \ P \equiv p^{-\rho}$$

we have the equations

$$(cP^\gamma y_1 - y_2) + (cP^\gamma y_1^* - y_2^*) = 0 \tag{A.1a}$$

$$aW^\gamma y_1 + \alpha W^\gamma P^{-\gamma} y_2 = x \tag{A.1b}$$

$$bR^\gamma y_1 + \beta R^\gamma P^{-\gamma} y_2 = 1 \tag{A.1c}$$

$$aW^\gamma y_1^* + \alpha W^\gamma P^{-\gamma} y_2^* = z^* \tag{A.1d}$$

$$bR^\gamma y_1^* + \beta R^\gamma P^{-\gamma} y_2^* = 1 \tag{A.1e}$$

$$aW + bR + cP = 1 \tag{A.1f}$$

$$\alpha W + \beta R = P \tag{A.1g}$$

where asterisks indicate variables relating to the foreign country. From (A.1b) and (A.1c),

$$y_1 = \frac{\beta x W^{-\gamma} - \alpha R^{-\gamma}}{a\beta - \alpha b}$$

$$\tag{A.2}$$

$$y_2 = \frac{aR^{-\gamma} - bx W^{-\gamma}}{p^{-\gamma}(a\beta - \alpha b)}$$

and, from (A.1d) and (A.1e),

$$y_1^* = \frac{\beta z^* W^{-\gamma} - \alpha R^{-\alpha}}{a\beta - \alpha b}$$

$$\tag{A.3}$$

$$y_2^* = \frac{aR^\gamma - bz^* W^{-\gamma}}{p^{-\gamma}(a\beta - \alpha b)}$$

Hence, substituting from (A.2) and (A.3) into (A.1a),

$$\frac{x+z^*}{2} = \frac{ac+a}{\beta c+b} \left(\frac{R}{W}\right)^{-\gamma} \tag{A.4}$$

On the other hand, from (A.1f) and (A.1g),

$$\frac{R}{W} = \frac{1}{\beta c+b} \left[\frac{1}{W} - (ac+a)\right] \tag{A.5}$$

Hence, substituting from (A.5) into (A.4) and recalling that $W = w^{-\rho}$,

$$\frac{x+z^*}{2} = \frac{ac+a}{\beta c+b} \frac{(\beta c+b)^{(1+\rho)/\rho}}{[w^\rho - (ac+a)]^{(1+\rho)/\rho}}$$

$$= AB^{-1/(1-\sigma)}[w^{-(1-\sigma)} - A]^{\sigma/(1-\sigma)} \tag{A.6}$$

where $A \equiv ac+a > 0$ and $B = \beta c+b > 0$. Differentiating (A.6) and evaluating at $x = z$,

$$\frac{w}{x} \frac{dx}{dw} = -\frac{z+z^*}{z} \frac{\sigma}{1-Aw_c^{1-\sigma}}$$

where w_c is the union-free equilibrium wage rate determined by (A.6) with $x = z$.

Finally, given the union's objective function $U = wx$,

$$\frac{w}{x} \frac{dx}{dw}\bigg|_0 = -1$$

From Proposition 2, therefore, for the existence of a union-ridden world equilibrium with unemployment in the home country it is necessary and sufficient that

$$\sigma < \frac{z}{z+z^*}(1 - Aw_c^{1-\sigma})$$

Similarly, from Proposition 3, for the existence of a union-ridden world equilibrium with trade reversal it is necessary and sufficient that

$$\sigma < \tfrac{1}{2}(1 - Aw_\ell^{1-\sigma})$$

where w_ℓ is defined by Figure 30.1.

References

Kemp, M. C. and K. Shimomura (1984) 'Labor Unions and the Theory of International Trade', paper read to the Sydney meeting of the Econometric Society, August.

Kemp, M. C. and K. Shimomura (1985a) 'Do Labor Unions Drive Out Capital?' *Economic Journal*, 86, forthcoming.

Kemp, M. C. and K. Shimomura (1985b) 'Tariffs and Employment in Union-ridden Economies', University of New South Wales.

Kemp, M. C. and K. Shimomura (1985c) 'Tariffs and Employment in Union-ridden Economies: A Further Note', University of New South Wales.

31 Economic Growth Without Accumulation or Technical Change: Agriculture Before Mechanization

Gregory Clark

Economic analysis, serving for two centuries to win an understanding of the Nature and Causes of the Wealth of Nations, has been fobbed off with another bride – a Theory of Value. (Joan Robinson, 1956, p. v)

1 INTRODUCTION

Underlying much of Joan Robinson's work, particularly in the later years of her life, was the aim of explaining the process of economic growth. She considered that the theory of allocation of resources with given endowments and technology was largely vacuous and that 'a dynamic long-run analysis of how resources can be increased is now what we require' (Robinson, 1962, p. 100). In formulating such a theory of growth both she and her opponents in the neoclassical camp agreed that the major sources of growth of output per head had to be accumulation and technical progress. Their disagreement was about the effects and the determinants of accumulation, and the causes and character of technical progress. Very little progress, however, has been made in explaining economic development by either the Cambridge or the neoclassical schools. The causes of the poverty of nations remain as obscure as they were when Joan Robinson called for a rediscovery of the problem of economic growth in the 1950s, despite the enormous intellectual energy devoted to the problem since then. In the 1980s most intellectual effort in economics is once again being devoted to static allocation problems of an even more obscure variety than Robinson decried.

Joan Robinson gave pride of place in explaining economic growth to the rate of accumulation, which also accounts for much technical progress. Thus Robinson noted that 'to speed up the rate of development ... involves increasing the ratio of investment to consumption' (Robinson, 1960, p. 99). And the chief driving force behind technical progress is the scarcity of labor in relation to capital which is produced by a rate of accumulation in excess of the rate of growth of population. The chief reason for the superior performance of capitalism in the United States is that the American economy grew up in conditions of scarcity of labor. (Robinson, 1960, p.105)

This chapter, in the spirit of the later Joan Robinson, tackles the problem of economic growth and development. But it argues that she and almost all other economists, by their almost exclusive concentration on capital accumulation and technical progress, have missed another major source of growth of incomes *per capita* which is perhaps the most important element in raising incomes in preindustrial societies. It is shown below that up until the Industrial Revolution increases in the intensity of labor were perhaps the major cause of rising output per worker in British agriculture. The differences in work intensity over time in Britain are echoed by differences across countries in the nineteenth century. American workers, for example, performed simple agricultural tasks three or four times more quickly than did workers in Eastern Europe, and this fact is not explained by differences in yields or relative prices (Clark, 1987b).

Though this chapter concentrates on European agriculture prior to mechanization in the late nineteenth century, there is every reason to believe that the great differences in work intensity discussed below are found also in industrial and commercial activities. Since the inception of modern economic theory, a tension has existed between the demand of the theory that the returns to factors of production which are mobile should tend to equalize across regions, and the all too evident fact that industry and capital remained remarkably concentrated in a few developed regions, where the return to labor was high. Any number of rationalizations of this startling failure of economic reasoning to mirror reality have been offered: the workers' lack of education or industrial experience in poor countries, the lack of management skills or of an entrepreneurial tradition, the lack of appropriate institutions, economies of scale in industrial technologies, the failure of capital markets. But a study of twenty countries in the international cotton textile industry around 1910 finds that all these putative obstacles to economic development, while they certainly existed, were rather minor compared to the extraordinary cost advantages the low-wage countries had from cheap labor. Wage rates in China were only about one-sixteenth of those in New England. Economies of scale in textiles were very limited, the least developed countries had access to machinery as modern as that in the advanced countries, and they imported managers and skilled mechanics to run the factories, and often coal to power them. All this increased costs, but their cost advantages from lower wages remained overwhelming, on paper at least (Clark, 1987a, pp.142–9). Further, most of the cotton workers performed simple machine tending requiring neither literacy, nor strength, nor even much training.

What maintained a rough equality in costs in the international industry was that the intensity of work varied by as much as six to one. Workers in New England, the highest paid in the industry, did nearly six times as much work per hour as the workers in the lowest paying countries such as China, India, Japan, and Greece (Clark, 1987a, p.150). While weekly wage rates varied by as much as 16 to 1 across the different countries, the real cost of labor varied by a maximum of 3 to 1. While the south of the United States, for example, had the third highest wage rate of any area of cotton textile production in the world, its real labor costs correcting for the high efficiency of its workers were lower than in many underdeveloped economics such as Italy (Clark, 1987a, p.150). The British textile industry was the largest in the world in 1910, and was able to undersell most other countries in free markets even though its wage rates were among the highest in the world. The average wage of British textile workers was about $5.0 per week. Had work intensity been at the same level in the underdeveloped economies as in Britain, the wage in China could have been raised from $0.48 per week to $4.35 without raising Chinese manufacturing costs above the British, and the wage in India raised similarly from $0.50 to $3.93. Thus if other industries in these countries were like cotton textiles, the major source of the underdevelopment of these countries in 1910 would be the low intensity of work rather than any of the more exotic failures of the market that were listed above (Clark, 1987a, p.170).

2 WORK INTENSITY IN BRITISH AGRICULTURE, 1300–1860

There are two ways of measuring the intensity of work in agriculture. We can look at how long it took workers to perform individual tasks in agriculture, or we can look at the total output of grains per worker. I use both ways to check that we really are measuring differences in labor intensity.

Table 31.1 shows the estimated grain output per agricultural worker from 1300 to 1841. It is calculated by estimating the percentage of the population in agriculture in each year, the percentage of grain consumption which was imported, and the yields per seed. I also assume that grain consumption *per capita* was as high in 1300 as in 1841, despite the lower incomes in 1300, which will bias upwards the estimated outputs per worker for 1300 and 1661.

Examining the total output of grains per man may seem a rather odd measure of labor intensity, since it would seem to be subject to a lot of other influences such as the amount of land per worker, the relative prices of labor and grains, and the yield of land per acre. Grain output per worker is a very good measure of the efficiency, however, for the following reasons. First

Table 31.1   Grain output per male agricultural worker

Year	Percentage of population agricultural	Imports as a percentage of consumption	Yield per seed	Output per worker
c.1300	75	0	4	83
				104*
1661	60	0	6	108
	54	0	6	120
1841	26	15	10	216

Sources   See the text and the technical appendix.

Note   The output per worker denoted by * is calculated by an alternative method which does not involve assumptions about the percentage of the population in agriculture or the percentage of food requirements imported or exported. See the text for details.

labor demands in agriculture were highly peaked, with the harvest month absorbing twice as much labor as the average month in the rest of the year. Figure 31.1 below shows the payments per week to workers on a Norfolk farm employing convertible husbandry in 1733–4. The payments peak very sharply in August so that even considering the higher wages per hour at the harvest probably 2.5 times as many man-hours were worked then as in the mid winter. Thus the constraint on output per worker was the amount of grain that could be harvested per worker in the harvest period.

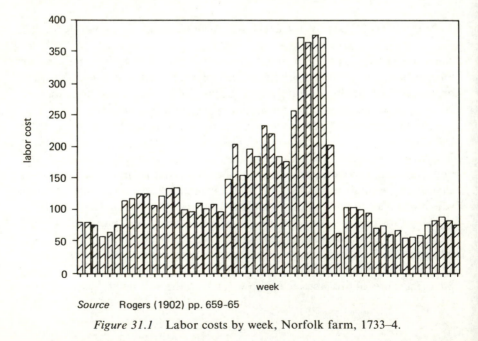

Source   Rogers (1902) pp. 659-65

Figure 31.1   Labor costs by week, Norfolk farm, 1733–4.

Second, the labor inputs per bushel of grain harvested were largely independent of the yield per acre. In the early nineteenth century, in areas of advanced agriculture the higher yields of grain crops stemming from new rotations, manure applications, and more careful cultivation seem to have resulted largely from more of the same plants being grown per acre. Wheat and barley were grown on unmanured plots and on plots with farmyard manure at the Rothamsted experimental station from 1841 onwards. The manured wheat yielded three times the 12.6 bushels of the unmanured, while the manured barley yielded about twice that of the unmanured. But the ratio of the weight of grain to that of straw varied little with the yield, and was in fact 10 to 20 per cent higher with the low-yielding unmanured crops (Hall, 1919, pp. 35, 55, 63, 72, 84, 93). Also, the number of grains per bushel of wheat was the same for a yield of 39.2 bushels per acre as it was for a yield of 12.3 bushels per acre, so the individual grains were not getting bigger (Hall, 1919, p.55). Albert Thaer gives a ratio of 1:2 for the weight of wheat grain to that of straw for the low yields of Prussia, which is about the same as the Rothamsted ratio and as the ratio given for the high yields of Britain in 1840 reported by J. R. McCulloch (Thaer, 1844, vol. 2, p.407; McCulloch, 1839, p.466).

If with denser crops all that was happening was that the plants were closer together, the labor savings in harvesting from higher yields would be very limited, since most of the labor involved cutting the stems, binding and stacking the cut grain, and carting the sheaves to the barn. With higher yields a reaper had to cover less ground per bushel, but in reaping wheat for example, at yields of 26 bushels per acre a British reaper in the nineteenth century would walk less than one mile in cutting the wheat (assuming the reaper cuts a three-foot-wide swath through the grain). Consequently, the famous German economist Johann von Thunen, who maintained an estate in Mecklenburg, noted that,

> the space of land which can be mown in a day by one labourer, depends very much on the strength of the Corn itself, and the expense of mowing ought on this ground, to be calculated rather in proportion to the quantity of produce, than to the extent of the surface . . . the expense of binding and shocking depends, like that of mowing, rather on the quantity of the produce than on that of the land. (Jacob, 1828, Second Report, p.89)

Judge Peters, in the eighteenth century, remarked that American reapers could reap a much larger area each day than English reapers because of the lighter American yields (Washington, 1803, p.75). Gervase Markham in his treatise on husbandry, written in the seventeenth century, stated that while a man and a binder should reap 1 acre per day of a standard wheat crop, they could reap 1.25 acres of thin wheat. Also a mower cut 2 to 2.5 acres of a standard crop of barley or oats per day, but 3 to 4 acres of a thin or short crop (Markham, 1683, p.113).

A nice illustration of the near constancy of reaping labor per bushel when yields varied is found in Bolton Priory during the great famine of 1315–17, when yields fell drastically. The average gross output of corn at Bolton during these years was 40 per cent less than the average in the years 1310–14, principally because yields per acre fell. Payments to reapers fell by 42 per cent between the two periods, or about proportionately to output. On the home farm the actual man-days expended in reaping was recorded, and these fell by 40 per cent in the famine (Kershaw, 1973, pp.38, 50).

An early study of the effects of manures upon wheat crops contains data showing that as the yield increased, the number of sheaves of straw increased proportionately (Morton, 1855, vol. 2, p.1144). In Scotland and the north of England reapers were often paid by the sheaf of corn reaped, not by the acre, so that the price paid per acre could vary by a factor of two, depending on the bulk of the crop (Stephens, 1952, vol. 2, pp.335–7; Morton, 1855, vol. 2, p.1145). Similarly, in both Prussia and Hungary in the early nineteenth century reapers were often paid by a share of the sheaves, not be the number of acres reaped (Thaer, 1844, vol. 1, p. 102; Blum, 1948, p.190). In a village in the north of India, in 1984, the method of payment for reaping wheat and barley was one sheaf in twenty cut, though yields per acre varied by a factor of 3 to 1 across different fields.

Third, the other important characteristic of reaping grain (and also of threshing it by hand) is that the labor input seems to have been independent of the relative cost of labor and grain. It was possible to extract a little more grain per acre by applying more labor, but the possibilities here seem to have been limited. Grain prices in Britain would vary greatly from year to year but nominal wages were fairly stable, so that real wages were low in years of bad harvests. On average in the ten-year intervals from 1701 to 1841 the highest corn price was double the lowest, yet the payment for reaping did not change with the price fluctuations, implying that in years of high prices the reapers did not reap more carefully to avoid dropping a few more ears of corn. Reaping payments show similar stability when grain prices changed from year to year in medieval England.

Further evidence that the labor input in harvesting was not sensitive to the relative price of grains and labor comes from an explanation of day wage rates and piecework payments for reaping grains in England in the period of the Black Death. When the plague struck in England in 1349 it killed between one-third and one-half of the population (Hatcher, 1977, pp.21–6). Repeated visitations of the plague from then till the mid-fifteenth century kept the population considerably below the levels reached by 1300. The reduction in populations raised real-wage levels since the supply of land relative to labor was thus increased greatly. It is hard to estimate the rise in real-wages precisely, but figures for the day wages of artisans suggest a rise in real-wages of greater than 50 per cent after 1350 (Rogers, 1866, vol. I, pp. 321–2). Nominal wages rose by more than 50 per cent but the price of grains remained constant or dropped. If it was possible to economize on labor in reaping with higher labor costs we would expect that after 1350 the cost of reaping an acre of grain should fall relative to the day wage of labor. But as Table 31.2 shows, the price paid for piecework operations such as harvesting and threshing rose proportionately to the day wage, suggesting that as many days were being devoted to these tasks as before.

Table 31.2   Wages and piece rates before and after the Black Death

Years	Average wage rates of artisans (pence)	Payment for reaping per acre (pence)	Payment for threshing per bushel (pence)
1261–1350	3.23	5.46	1.78
1351–1400	4.94	8.54	2.62
rise (%)	53%	56%	48%

Source   Rogers (1866) vol.I, pp.320–2.

Notes   The artisans for which the average wages are calculated are thatchers, carpenters, masons, tilers, slaters, and sawyers. The reaping rate is the average for reaping an acre of wheat, barley or oats. The threshing rate is the average for threshing wheat, barley or oats.

I can estimate grain output per agricultural worker in Britain, in 1841, in Table 31.1 with reasonable accuracy. In 1841, 26 per cent of the population of Great Britain was in the agricultural sector. If we assume that all males between 15 and 60 were active in the labor force this implies a male agricultural work force of 1.36 million males, or 7.2 per cent of the population in 1841.

I have assumed that women and children do not work. This assumption is close to the truth for 1841, when few women were employed and then only for the peak labor demand periods in the summer. There have been suggestions, however, that prior to 1750 women had a much greater participation in the agricultural labor force (see Snell, 1985, pp. 51–7). Without considering this suggestion in detail I can say that if true it will only strengthen the case being made here since it implies I underestimate the labor force of earlier years, which will increase its apparent productivity.

Corn outputs in British agriculture in 1841 can be estimated with some precision, as can consumption *per capita* of grains, since we have a fairly good idea of grain yields, grain acreages and of imports of grain from outside the United Kingdom and from Ireland. The details of these calculations are given in the Appendix. They show that consumption *per capita* was about 8.04 bu. of wheat-equivalent in 1841 (a bushel of barley cost 0.45 of a bushel of wheat, and a bushel of oats 0.33). This estimate is pretty close to standard assumptions on grain consumption in the eighteenth and nineteenth centuries. It implies that gross corn production, including seed and corn for farm horses, in 1841, was 216 bu. of grain per adult male agricultural worker, or 123 bu. of wheat-equivalent.

I can calculate the grain output per worker for c.1300 and for 1661 by assuming that the consumption of grains per head of the population was the same as in 1841, and estimating the percentage of the population employed in agriculture. This again will tend to overestimate output per worker in these earlier years, since income levels were lower than in 1841.

There is great uncertainty about the percentage of adult males in agriculture in 1661, but a very detailed muster roll for Gloucester in 1608 shows about 50 per cent of the population outside of Bristol in agriculture (Tawney and Tawney, 1935). At this date woollen cloth making was Britain's chief industry, and Gloucester was the most important cloth manufacturing county in England. So I take 50 per cent of the population of England and Wales in 1661 to be in agriculture, and 75 per cent of the population of Scotland, or 54 per cent for Britain overall. This gives a lower estimate than the 56 per cent in agriculture in England and Wales in 1688 suggested by Crafts on the basis of the work of Lindert (Crafts, 1985; Lindert, 1980). Correcting for the age distribution of the population in 1661 and 1841 gives the estimate that in 1661 males aged 15–60 employed in agriculture were 16.4 per cent population, more than twice the 7.2 per cent of 1841.

Gross output per agricultural worker would then be only 120 bu. of grains *per capita* in 1661, if 54 per cent of the population was in agriculture, assuming that gross yields per seed in 1661 were only three-fifths of those in 1841. We know that there were small net imports and exports of grain in this period. This is only slightly over 55 per cent of the 1841 level. I also show in Table 31.1 the output per male worker under the assumption that 60 per cent of the population were in the agricultural sector in 1661. In this case, output per male worker in 1661 would be only 108 bushels.

For 1300 I assume in Table 31.1 that 75 per cent of the population was in the agricultural sector. We have no way of estimating this figure directly but it fits with our knowledge of the occupational structure in the more agricultural countries of Europe when data becomes available in the eighteenth century. Gross grain yields per seed we know with reasonable accuracy for the medieval period, and averaged about 4 to 1 on the Winchester estates (Titow, 1972). This implies a gross output of grains per male agriculture in 1300 of 83 bushels, which is only 38 per cent of the 1841 level.

Table 31.1 shows an alternative estimate of the gross output per worker around 1300. This is derived from statistics we have on the average area of arable land cultivated by medieval peasants in England. The average peasant family in the late thirteenth century in England can be taken, from Kominsky, to have tilled 21 acres of land: 14 acres of their own and 7 acres of demesne (Kominsky, 1956, pp. 100, 216, 223). The size of the family in the

Middle Ages is disputed, but a survey of Lincolnshire in 1267–8 showed 4.7 persons per household (Hallam, 1961). Assuming the same age distribution and sex composition as in 1661 implies that there were 1.42 male workers aged between 15 and 60 years of age in each peasant household. If yields on peasant land equalled the yields of the demesnes of the Winchester Estates before 1350, this in turn implies that the output of grains was 104 bushels per male worker (Titow, 1972). This is still only about 87 per cent of the 1661 output per male worker, and a mere 48 per cent of the 1841 output.

Why were workers in 1841 able to harvest so many more bushels of grain than in 1661, or in the Middle Ages? We must consider whether the adoption of more efficient harvesting techniques, or the use of workers from outside agriculture for the harvest explains the increase if yields and prices do not.

Harvesting techniques do not seem to have changed much in the period 1661 to 1841, though techniques may have advanced somewhat between 1300 and 1661. Collins gives great importance to the replacement of reaping by mowing, which required less harvest labor, in European agriculture in the nineteenth century. But he dates the major period of transition in England as 1835–70, which implies that by 1841 there had been little change (Collins, 1969, pp. 457–8). Wheat, beans and peas were mostly reaped in 1841 as they had been since medieval times, and these crops absorbed about 55 per cent of the grain harvest labor in 1841. In the seventeenth century, in the southern two-thirds of Britain, the barley and oats were already being mown extensively, and this changed little by 1841 (Collins, 1969, pp. 456–9).

The harvest period always saw the recruitment of extra workers for the harvest tasks. These were both the wives and children of the regular laborers, and workers from the non-agricultural sector. There is no evidence that these flows were any greater in 1841 than earlier. The decline of rural domestic industry in favor of urban factories reduced the numbers who had both agricultural experience and the liberty to leave their occupations for harvest. Irish migrants were available in 1841 to help in the harvest, but these were estimated to be only 58 000, which represents an addition of only 4.3 per cent to the regular male agricultural labor force (Collins, 1969, p. 472). Labor supplied by the wives of the resident laborers would be much more important. The evidence is that this was becoming less important in the nineteenth century than it had been earlier (Snell, 1985, pp. 52–3).

The increase of output per worker from 1300 to 1661, and from 1661 to 1841 thus seems to have resulted mainly from labor input per worker, through longer hours or more intense work.

Consideration of a number of farming manuals from the mid nineteeth century suggests that in a twelve-hour harvest day a worker could harvest 11.1 bu. of corn, averaging over wheat, barley, oats, beans and peas. This figure assumes that wheat and beans were reaped, and the barley and oats mown. Total labor requirements to harvest the corn in 1841 thus were 19.4 days of twelve hours per male farm worker. The harvest period was typically four to six weeks. On one farm in Gloucestershire from 1830 to 1865 the average length of the harvest was five weeks (Jones, 1964, p. 63). Since there were other labor requirements in this period, 19.4 days of actual labor for the corn in 1841 is a reasonable figure.

These labor requirements applied to 1661 suggest that at the 1841 work rates there was only 10.8 days of harvest work per harvest worker. In the Middle Ages at these work rates there would be only 7.5 days of harvest work per male agricultural worker.

For 1841 and 1661 we can consider in more detail the other tasks of the harvest month to see whether it was changes in these which account for the impression of great underemployment in 1661 at the labor peak periods. The other major operations of the harvest period included giving the fallow the seed ploughing for wheat, cutting the grass aftermath, and hoeing the turnip crops. But as Table 31.3 shows these were relatively more important in 1841 because hoeing root crops had been added to harvest labor as a consequence of the diffusion of the turnip since 1661. Thus the total labor requirement in the harvest period per male worker in 1841 was, in 12 hour harvest days, 29.0 days per worker. In 1661, only 15.1 days were required per worker, which is only about half the 1841 requirement.

Table 31.3 Harvest labor requirements, 1661 and 1841

Activity	Man-days (12 hours) per acre	Acres (m.)	Total man-days (m.)
1661			
corn harvest	1.7	6.9	11.8
plough for wheat	0.9	2.6	2.4
cut grass aftermath	0.7	3.4	2.3
total			16.5
1841			
corn harvest	2.8	9.3	26.4
plough for wheat	0.9	3.4	3.2
hoe roots	1.7	3.2	5.5
cut clover aftermath	0.9	2.1	2.0
cut grass aftermath	0.8	2.8	2.3
total			39.4

Sources   See the Appendix and Clark (1987c).

The other way to compare labor intensity *c.*1300 with that in 1841 is to look at the man-days required to reap a bushel of wheat, or to thresh a bushel of wheat, barley or oats. Comparing the time taken to reap a bushel of wheat controls for possible changes of technique in harvesting from 1300 to 1841, such as mowing crops instead of reaping them. Mowing used less labor per bushel. The labor inputs on specific tasks confirm the overall pattern found above by looking at total harvest labor requirements.

Reaping was an old technique which varied little over time and between countries. The reaper would stoop to cut handfuls of stalks that he or she had gathered, using a short, smooth or serrated, crescent-shaped knife. Other workers would follow the reapers to bind and stack the cut stalks. No animals and very little machinery were involved. The number of bushels reaped by a worker in one day can be estimated in two ways. The first is to divide the day-wage in harvest by the payment per bushel to reapers, who received a piece rate. The second is to estimate a normal day's reaping in each area using agricultural handbooks and the observations of visitors. Table 31.4 shows the number of bushels of wheat reaped per worker per day *c.*1300 and in 1850 in Britain, calculated in both ways.

Table 31.4 Bushels of wheat reaped per worker per day

Year	Assumed yield per acre (bushels)	Reaping rate (day wage/ payment per bushel)	Reaping rate (direct estimate)
1261–1349	9	2.8	
*c.*1300	9		3.6
1389	8		2.5*
1850	26	9.1	
1846	26	10.7	8.7

Sources Rogers, 1866, vol.II, pp.273–310; Oschinsky, 1971, p.445; Curtler, 1909, pp.62, 67; *Gardener's Chronicle and Agricultural Gazette*, 27 April 1850, pp.266–7; Raynbird, 1846, pp.125, 139.

Note The reaping rate is in Winchester bushels per worker per day. The harvest work-day is assumed to be 12 hours long where the number of hours is not specified. The * denotes that this estimate, for the manor of Hawsted, is for all the grains harvested, not just wheat.

So far we have discussed exclusively the task of harvesting grains. Another major task in agriculture was the threshing of the harvesting grains over the winter. Threshing grain was the most important winter occupation in arable agriculture, and represented about 17 per cent of the arable labor input in the three-field system. Hand threshing, an ancient technique, was carried on in essentially the same fashion in all of Northern Europe and the northern United States in 1800 as in 1300. Until the threshing machine, the only advances in technique were in methods for separating the grain from the chaff. But winnowing was always a minor part of threshing labor. As Thaer notes of flails, the jointed wooden stick used to beat the corn on the barn floor, none of the modifications, either in their make or of the manner of using them, are of sufficient importance to render it worth while to take the trouble of endeavouring to teach the labourers to perform the operation in any way to which they are unaccustomed. (Thaer, 1844, vol. 2, p. 386)

Since threshing was indoor work, it was independent of local topography or climate. The labor required per unit of grain output did depend in part on the ratio of grain to straw; with more straw, more labor was required. But, as is noted above, as yields increased the proportion of straw to grain stayed constant or even increased. Grain mown with a scythe required more labor than that reaped with a sickle, since with mowing there was more straw, and it was not so tightly bound. But the differences appear to have been small, about 10 per cent according to one author. And in any case, mowing was more common in high-wage areas so that threshing rates in high-wage areas are if anything understated.

I calculate the threshing rates for Britain prior to 1349 and in 1850, in terms of the number of bushels of 'wheat-equivalent' which would be threshed per day (in the time taken to thresh a bushel of wheat roughly 1.75 bushels of barley could be threshed, and 2.25 bushels of oats), calculated by dividing the day-wage by the payment per bushel to threshers. This calculation shows that in 1850 the thresher would thresh about 4.5 bushels of wheat-equivalent per day (*Gardener's Chronicle and Agricultural Gazette*, 27 April 1850, pp. 266–7). Medieval English threshers before 1349 threshed only from 2.4 to 2.8 bushels per day. For manors whose labor accounts are recorded by Thorold Rogers the rate is 2.8 bushels a day, while Ramsey Abbey and Crowland Abbey show threshing rates of 2.4 bushels, and 2.7 bushels per day prior to 1349 (Rogers, 1866, vol. I, pp. 245, 288–9; vol. II, pp. 273–310, 329–34; Raftis, 1957; Page, 1934). So the efficiency of workers in threshing rose by between 60 and 80 per cent.

As with reaping, the labor input in threshing seems to have been invariant to the yields per acre and the relative prices of grain and labor. As Table 31.2 shows, when the Black Death increased wages by about 50 per cent relative to the price of grain it did not increase the rate at which grain was threshed to economize on labor. Thus John Howlett noted that in abundant harvests the wheat crop could be double the size of bad years, and that the amount of labor expended in threshing the crop would vary correspondingly (Howlett, 1792, p. 570). Since there was little else to do for most of the winter but thresh the grain crop, if extracting more grain was possible by careful threshing, it would be expected that the amount of labor expended in threshing would vary little with the size of the crop. The many farming handbooks do not contain any advice to vary threshing and reaping rates with the relative prices of grain and labor.

3 PRODUCTIVITY GROWTH AND TECHNICAL CHANGE, 1661–1841

I further estimate, though this calculation is extremely tentative, the overall growth of productivity in agriculture from 1661 to 1841. Then I decompose it into the part on more intense labor inputs per worker, and the part which is consequent purely on technical change. The details of the calculations of the inputs and outputs in each year are discussed in the Appendix, and in Clark (1987c).

From 1661 to 1841 the increase in output per unit of input in British agriculture was probably 50 per cent or more. We conventionally view these changes as consequent on the technical changes of the Agricultural Revolution: the enclosure of the open fields, the introduction of turnips and clover into crop rotations, the selective breeding of animals, the introduction of new machinery such as better ploughs and threshing machines. Since output per worker nearly doubled in this period, and labor was about one-third of costs, much of the overall increase in productivity is consequent on the higher output per worker. But the rise in output per worker does not seem to be explained by the technical changes of the period. Timmer, for example, shows that the major agricultural innovations of the period saved land and not labor. In fact Timmer's own initial calculation revealed that output per worker on a Norfolk farm would drop by 15 per cent with the introduction of convertible husbandry. Even when he allows for a 50 per cent increase in output per acre with the new techniques, his calculations imply only a 3 per cent increase in output per worker. The increases in productivity Timmer's calculations imply are correspondingly modest: 1.7 per cent if the yield increase under convertible husbandry was 10 per cent, 17.5 per cent if the yield increase was as high as 50 per cent (Timmer, 1968).

The calculations below show that technical change accounts for only about one-third of the productivity rise in the period of the Agricultural Revolution. Most of the productivity increase came from increased work intensity per worker.

Table 31.5 shows the actual inputs of labor, capital and land in 1841 and 1661, measured in terms of their cost at 1841 prices. The labor input is simply the number of man-years of agriculture labor available in each year multiplied by the yearly wage for 1841.

Land inputs grew fairly rapidly since, though little new land was brought into cultivation, most of the value of farmland by 1841 consisted of improvements to the land, rather than the pure site value. The improvements consisted of the clearing of the land, the removal of stones, the building of roads and fences and farm buildings, and the manuring and draining of the land, or the watering of it in the case of some meadows. For the 1850s it was estimated that improvements constituted 75 per cent of the value of farmland (Thompson, 1907). Investigations of the cost of enclosures of waste in

Table 31.5   Inputs in production (million 1841 shillings)

Input	Value 1661	Value 1841
Labor	654	815
Profits on capital	242	443
Depreciation	36	132
Land rents, taxes	416	722
Total cost	1348	2114
Output/cost	1.00	1.54

Sources   See the text and Appendix, and Clark (1987c).

Scotland in the early nineteenth century confirm this. With the Agricultural Revolution the stock of improvements per acre was increasing. Merely assuming that greater outputs per acre in 1841 required proportionately more farm buildings, and that half the land was treated with mineral manures between 1661 and 1841, while one-quarter was underdrained in some fashion, gives the increase in land inputs of the table. The increase could easily have been much greater.

Capital inputs also grew fairly rapidly since much of the capital stock was proportionate to output, and new machines were introduced. The main elements of the farmers' capital in 1841 were the animal stock (45 per cent), wages (18 per cent), horses and horse fodder (12 per cent), implements (10 per cent), rent advances (8 per cent), and seeds (5 per cent). The stock of 1661 is calculated by considering how much each of the constituents would be reduced under the techniques and outputs of 1661. The calculated stock for 1841, 4430 million shillings, accords well with McCulloch's estimate of a stock of 4220–4940m.s. for Great Britain in 1839 (McCulloch, 1839, p. 539). The stock of farm capital rises by 86–117 per cent depending on what assumption we make about the size of labor inputs in 1661, so that capital per unit of output is dropping. Physical depreciation costs are included, calculating the overall growth of capital inputs. Depreciation includes wear and tear on horses (10 per cent), implements (15 per cent), and mineral manures, drainage, and irrigation systems (for the details see the Appendix).

The overall growth of productivity can be approximated by the familiar expression,

$$\dot{A}/A = \dot{Q}/Q - a.\dot{L}/L - b.\dot{K}/K - c.\dot{T}/T$$

As is shown in the Appendix,

$$\dot{Q}/Q = \text{growth rate of output} \quad = 0.491 \text{ per cent}$$

Table 31.5 shows that from 1661 to 1841,

$\dot{L}/L$ = growth rate of labor force = 0.124 per cent

$\dot{K}/K$ = growth rate of capital (inc. depreciation) = 0.410 per cent

$\dot{T}/T$ = growth rate of land = 0.314 per cent.

In 1841, the estimated shares of labor, land and capital are 38.5 per cent, 34.2 per cent and 27.3 per cent. In 1661, the shares are 43.7 per cent, 37.1 per cent and 19.2 per cent (using the prices of 1661). These figures show labor and rent, in 1841, having a rather high share of costs, and farmer's capital a low share in comparison with contemporary estimates of their share in costs (see, for example, Bacon, 1844). But the reason may be in part that contemporary estimates include the labor of the farmer in the returns to farmer's capital.

$a = 0.39$, $b = 0.27$, and $c = 0.34$, are thus the estimated shares in total costs of labor, capital and land. Given these estimates $\dot{A}/A$ is calculated to be 0.225 per cent, and productivity increased by 50 per cent from 1661 to 1841. As can be seen, most of the rise of productivity stems from the slow growth of labor inputs compared to output.

Table 31.6 shows inputs in production in each year when labor inputs for 1661 are calculated based on the amount of labor which should have been required in the harvest peak at the work rates of 1841, as shown in Table 31.3 above, rather than being taken as the number of available workers.

Table 31.6 Counterfactual inputs in production (million 1841 shillings)

Input	Value 1661	Value 1841
Labor	330	815
Profit on capital	210	443
Depreciation	36	132
Land rents, taxes	416	722
Total cost	992	2114
Output/cost	1.00	1.14

Sources See the text and Appendix, and Clark (1987c).

The value of labor inputs in 1661 would be 326 million shillings rather than 654, and capital inputs would shrink, because of a lower wages bill to 210 million shillings. Given only the changes in technique of the Agricultural Revolution labor inputs ought to have grown at the much more rapid rate of 0.502 per cent per annum. In this case, with output per worker falling, the growth of productivity from 1661 to 1841 would be 14 per cent only, or 0.073 per cent per annum. Thus only about one-third of the growth of productivity in the Agricultural Revolution came from technological changes.

A reflection of the unimportance of new techniques in explaining the rise of productivity can be found in rent increases upon enclosure in the eighteenth century. Enclosure was often the prelude to land improvement, convertible husbandry and selective breeding. From the rent increases upon enclosure we can calculate that the productivity gain from enclosure was less than 7 per cent (Clark, 1988).

4   THE DETERMINANTS OF LABOR INTENSITY

Why should there have been such an increase in the work rate of agricultural workers from 1300 to 1841 of between 60 per cent and 150 per cent? I can conceive of four types of explanation for low labor intensity in England in 1661 and earlier: the methods of labor recruitment and supervision were inefficient; the workers did not know how to improve their performance; the preferences of the workers were different; or the workers were trapped in an equilibrium where poor nutrition made the workers inefficient, which kept wages low, and consequently nutrition poor. I cannot explore these possibilities in detail here, but I can show that some of the above explanations appear inconsistent with the evidence.

Medieval England was a servile society, where the peasants were bound to deliver labor services to the lord and were constrained by many other restricting and demanding exactions. By 1841 most agricultural workers in Britain were wage laborers who were employed on terms similar to modern industrial workers. I am sceptical, however, of these organizational features as the basis of the labor intensity differences. For a start, almost all the direct work rate estimates in the sections above are for wage workers, not for bound labor. In medieval England large amounts of labor were hired and paid piece rates for harvesting and threshing so workers had every incentive to work quickly. Second, the agricultural workers of northern Britain were more efficient than those of southern England and Ireland, and of Western Europe in the early nineteenth century, though their social situation was essentially similar as were the hiring and supervision practices (see Clark, 1987b).

Surveys of wages and the piece rates for various manual tasks in British and Irish agriculture in 1850 and 1860 by the *Gardener's Chronicle and Agricultural Gazette* (27 April 1850, pp.266–7, and 30 April 1860, pp.392–3) indicate these differences clearly. An index of work rates for reaping wheat, mowing grass and mowing clover in 1860 shows the work rate of the south of Britain to be only 69 per cent of that in the north, and the rate in Ireland to be a mere 53 per cent of the north British rate.

Interestingly, the north of Britain seems to have become a region of high worker efficiency only in the period of the Industrial Revolution. In 1700, the North was regarded as a backward region agriculturally, the advanced areas being in the South East near London. The persistent refrain of nineteenth-century writers on farming that the northern agricultural worker was far superior to the southern finds no echo in earlier days. The appearance of the northern worker as an example and a reproach to his nogood southern counterpart is contemporaneous with the rise of the North as an industrial center. In 1793, East Anglia was still regarded as an area with very efficient workers. The writer of the report on Norfolk mentions that rents would be dear in the rest of the country, but ' . . . the industry of the inhabitants render it easy', and. ' . . . there is no county where labour does a fairer day's work' (Kent, 1794). This suggests that whatever determined work rates was not some deep cultural norm, but a fairly rapidly mutable characteristic of a region.

Were low-productivity areas locked into an equilibrium where poor nutrition, because of low wages, created low productivity and consequently low wages? Traditional agriculture did involve large expenditures of energy; could workers in areas of low wages not afford the food required for effective labor? Notice that such an explanation implies that farmers in poor areas were systematically ignoring cheap ways of increasing the productivity of their workers. Since feeding workers on the farm was common, farmers could easily ensure that workers were fed adequately for high work rates. In 1862, farm workers in northern Britain were paid $0.57 per day, those in the south $0.47 (Great Britain, Parliamentary Papers, 1864, pp.216–329). But as noted above, and as was well known to agricultural commentators of the nineteenth century, northern workers performed more per day than those of the south. If southern workers had done as much as those in the north the employers would have saved $0.21 per worker per day. Edward Smith's dietary survey of 1862 suggests that northern workers were consuming about 1000 more calories per day than those in the south. If the constraint in the south was a lack of calories, it could have been lifted very profitably, since the cost of 1000 calories in the southern diet was only about $0.04. It seems unlikely, therefore, that low productivity areas were constrained by poor nutrition, at least for the methods of labor organization used in nineteenth-century Europe.

The same sources show that Irish workers in 1862 were paid only $0.25 per day, and their work rate was about half that of northern Britain. Yet they consumed nearly as many calories per day more than the southern workers who did about 31 per cent more work per day than the Irish. The Irish diet was monotonous and unattractive, consisting mainly of potatoes, maize when potatoes were not available, and yoghurt, but it was both cheap and well supplied with calories and protein.

Some might argue that the increase in work rates over time was caused by very low-level learning, but by knowledge differences none the less. Workers in 1841 knew better techniques or organized the work better. The problem here is that the manual tasks examined above had been performed over a very long period of time in Northern Europe. Reaping and threshing, for example, were done in essentially the same way in 1850 as in 1250. Threshing was not a task requiring a large team of workers, or careful coordination of the elements of the process. For 600 years most of the British labor force spent many days at reaping or threshing, both strenuous and repetitive tasks. Yet despite the millions of independent and potentially innovating reapers and threshers, methods to increase work rates happened to be discovered only in the eighteenth century, at just the same time that important industrial innovations began to proliferate.

It appears more plausible that the workers in pre-industrial British agriculture were different from the people we are familiar with. Either they worked little or they exerted themselves little when at work (that is, they had different tastes) or their mental life is otherwise alien to us. They were not merely people like us who happened to be lacking certain pieces of knowledge.

5 IMPLICATIONS

Agricultural workers in Britain in 1850 earned about 140 per cent more than those of 1300 (see Clark, 1987b, table 1). At the same time, they produced between 108 per cent and 160 per cent more grain output per worker. If we directly measure their productivity on particular tasks, they were about 200 per cent faster at reaping, and between 60 per cent and 80 per cent faster at threshing. Thus most of the higher wages of agricultural workers in 1850 can be explained by the greater intensity of work.

While the importance of technical change in economic growth is not disputed, this finding does imply that in writing the history of agriculture before the mechanization of the late nineteenth century we have tended to overplay the role of technological change as a source of growth. Labor was the major input in agriculture, either direct or embodied in land improvements. If the time taken to perform simple tasks could vary by 3 to 1 or more, then there was ample room for productivity growth before 1850 without any technical change. And until the machine age much of the rise in the productivity of British agriculture seems to have come from some such source.

TECHNICAL APPENDIX

In this Appendix I give the derivation of the technical data underlying much of the discussion of the paper. To keep it to a reasonable length the detail is reported rather sparsely, and more complete descriptions of the data can be found in Clark (1987c).

A.1 Growth of Agricultural Output

Grain outputs in 1841 and 1661 can be estimated with reasonable accuracy. The facts I need to approximate for 1841 are the net yields per acre of each crop, the acreage, the net imports of each grain, and the consumption of oats by farm horses. It is shown below that the net yields of wheat, barley and oats were 24, 30 and 32 bushels respectively. I take the acreages of each crop to be those of the first agricultural census in 1866, which implies a net output of 82.8 million bushels of wheat, 67.5 million bushels of barley, and 119.1 million bushels of oats, beans and peas. There were about 1m. horses in agriculture at this time, who were said in the farming manuals to consume 80 bushels of oats per year. This figure is for full grown working horses, so I assume an average consumption which is slightly lower at 72 million bushels per farm horse. With this deduction the net production of grains in British agriculture in 1841 is 129.4 million bushels of wheat-equivalent, where barley and oats are valued at their relative prices compared to wheat in 1836–40 of 0.46 and 0.33 per bushel.

Consumption *per capita* in wheat equivalents is found by adding to this net domestic production imports from Ireland and from outside the United Kingdom. Imports were about 14.7 per cent of British grain consumption from 1836 to 1840. Consumption *per capita* in 1841 was thus 8.04 bushels of wheat-equivalent, and 151.7 million bushels in total.

In 1661, there was little net import or export of grain from Britain. I estimate output by assuming the same consumption *per capita* by the 6.64 million population of 1661 as there was in 1841. This entails that net output rose by 142 per cent from 1661 to 1841. I take gross yields per acre in 1661 to be 60 per cent of those in 1841. I also assume that the quantity of seed per acre was the same in 1661 and 1841, which entails that gross output rose by the lower amount of 125 per cent.

The growth in production of meat, leather or wool is harder to estimate. For simplicity I assume that these outputs grew at the same rate as the output of grains. My assumption of a growth of output of 141 per cent from 1661 to 1841 is conservative compared to the Deane and Cole (1969) estimate that agricultural output grew by 139 per cent from 1701 to 1831 and Crafts' (1983) revised estimate of a growth of 144 per cent.

A.2 Crop Acreages 1841 and 1661

For want of better information I assume the acreage of corns, fallow, roots and clover in 1841 was the same as in 1866, 9.3 million acres of corn crops,

1.0 million acres of bare fallow, 3.2 million acres for roots and 4.2 million acres for artificial grasses, and 11.2 million acres of pasture. McCulloch (1839) gives estimates of acreages under different crops, but these are largely based on information from 1812 or earlier, and he seems to greatly overestimate the area of pasture in England and Wales in 1839.

Given that corn yields increased by 67 per cent the corn acreage of 1661 would be 0.76 that of 1841, once we take into account the deductions of seed from gross yield (see Clark, 1987c). I assume for 1661 one acre in fallow to every two in corn, along with no land planted in roots, clover or other rotation grasses. This implies 10.6 million acres in arable cultivation in 1661. Since the labor input per acre of arable was much greater than for pasture these assumptions are the crucial ones for determining labor requirements in agriculture in 1661. Thus though there is tremendous uncertainty in determining the total cultivated area in 1661 and hence the area of permanent pasture, the errors are relatively unimportant in determining labor requirements.

What was the total area of cultivated land in 1661, excluding hill pasture? We know that in England alone Parliamentary Enclosure brought into permanent cultivation 1.9 million acres of waste and commons by 1840 (Turner, 1980, pp. 62, 180). In the North of England the enclosed waste was 12.0 per cent of the total surface area. Applying this figure to Wales and Scotland suggests that prior to 1840 at least 4.82 million acres were added to the cultivated area. This is 17 per cent of the improved land in 1866. Applying this figure implies that there were 13.5 million acres of permanent pasture in 1661 compared to 11.2 million acres in 1841.

The 1851 population census gives farms by size class from which I can estimate the total cultivated acreage in 1851 at around 32.5 million acres. The difference between 32.5 million acres and 28.9 million acres I take to be rough grazing. For 1661 I assume that the rough grazing was this 3.6 million acres together with the 4.8 million acres which were improved.

Table 31.7 below shows the assumed acreages in 1661 and 1841 for each type of crop. The labor requirements on pasture depended importantly on the proportion of fodder crops which were fed off directly by animals and the proportion harvested for indoor consumption. The 1870 crop returns in the Parliametary Papers show that about half of rotation grasses and one-quarter of permanent pasture were cut for hay. I apply these ratios to 1841 and 1661 since they are consistent with other descriptions. For roots, in the absence of better information, I assume that half of the turnips were harvested and all of the potatoes giving the numbers shown.

Table 31.7 Assumed crop acreages in 1661 and 1841 (in millions of acres)

Crop	Area 1661	Area 1841
Corns	6.9	9.3
Fallow	3.5	1.0
Roots, harvested	0.0	2.0
fed off	0.0	1.2
Rotation grass, harvested	0.0	2.1
fed off	0.0	2.1
Total arable	10.6	17.7
Pasture, harvested	3.4	2.8
fed off	10.3	8.4
Total permanent pasture	13.7	11.2
Total improved area	24.3	28.9
Rough grazing, waste	8.4	3.6

Source See the text.

A.3 Capital Inputs

For 1841 I derive estimates shown in Table 31.8 of the various elements of the capital owned by the tenants (as opposed to land improvements and buildings) per acre of arable and permanent pasture in shillings from Morton (1855, pp.377–88), Stephens (1852, pp.516–18), Anonymous (1831), and Murrey (1840). The total agriculture capital stock belonging to farmers in each year is given in Table 31.9, in millions of 1841 shillings. The farmer's capital per acre for 1661 is derived by adjusting the figures for 1841 to reflect the smaller stock of animals per acre, the smaller stock of implements in the absence of threshing machines, horse drills etc., and the smaller labor inputs

Table 31.8 Tenants' capital stock per acre in 1661 and 1841

Type of capital	Arable (shillings)	Permanent pasture (shillings)
Horses, harnesses	17.5	3.5
Implements:		
Traditional (carts, ploughs, etc.)	14.0	2.8
New (drills, hoes, threshers)	8.5	0.0
Seeds	12.0	0.0
Horse fodder	9.0	1.8

Source See the text.

Table 31.9   Total farmers' capital stock in 1661 and 1841 (in millions)

Type of Capital	Value of capital, 1661 (shillings)	Value of capital, 1841 (shillings)
Livestock	1046	2016
Horses, harnessses: arable	148	310
permanent pasture	59	49
fodder	97	174
Implements: old	116	279
new	0	150
Seeds	96	212
Mineral manure	0	64
Wages: actual labor input	654	815
Half of rent and taxes (assuming these paid 6 months in advance)	208	361
Total capital	2422	4430
Capital per acre (shillings)	101	153

Source   See the text.

per acre and stock of mineral manures, as are described in the notes to the table below.

The livestock value in 1841 is derived from the estimate of the number and value of animals in McCulloch (1839). Following McCulloch I assume that the rate of turnover of the stock had increased by 25 per cent since 1688. Thus the value of the stock in 1661 relative to 1841 is assumed to be the relative volume of fodder output, times 25 per cent to account for the slower turnover.

I assume the stock of horses (and oxen) for traction was 25 per cent greater per arable acre in 1841 and the same per acre of pasture. I assume the stock is greater on the arable because of increased ploughings per acre, the increased volume per acre of harvested materials to be carted in, the even greater increase in the volume of manure to be carted back to the fields, and the requirements of horses for threshing, and for laying mineral manures. Counterbalancing this were improvements in carts and ploughs. A 25 per cent increase per acre thus seems reasonable. The amount of fodder is assumed proportionate to the amount of horse power required.

The stock of traditional implements in 1841 compared to 1661 is assumed proportional to output in each year, since many implements, such as carts would be needed in proportion to output. The stock of seeds is calculated based on the acreages sown to each crop in 1661 and 1841, assuming 25 per cent more seed was sown per acre in 1661, and on the cost of seed per acre for each type of crop in 1841. The stock of manure payments is assumed to be one year's expenditure by the farmer to maintain mineral manure levels. It is assumed that in 1661 there was no application of chalk, limestone, marl or clay.

The calculated capital of 4430 million shillings (or of 153 s per cultivated acre) in 1841 is close to other estimates. McCulloch estimated the total capital stock in farming in 1839 at 4220–4940 million shillings (McCulloch, 1839, p.539). Bacon (1844) estimates that a Norfolk farm in 1843 had a capital per acre of 160 s.

For 1661 the farmer's capital is derived based on the actual labor inputs in agriculture. For purposes of decomposing the productivity growth between 1661 and 1841 I also calculate the farmer's capital based on the amount of labor which should have been necessary in 1661. Instead of 654 million shillings tied up in wage payments in 1661 there would then be only 313 million shillings, reducing the 1661 capital total to 2081 million shillings from 2422 million shillings.

A.4 Land Inputs

Thompson gives estimates of the value of land improvements which are derived from the costs of clearing and preparing crown forests for cultivation in 1850–60 (Thompson, 1907). The cost of clearing and preparing the land was 144 shillings per acre, but part of this cost included cutting and removing the timber which would have been incurred anyway if the land had been kept as forest. A number of reports in the *Transactions of the Highland Agricultural Society* give the cost of clearing and grubbing land for cultivation. These costs per acre were on average of 17 instances 99 shillings. These were costs for nineteenth-century clearing and grubbing where the stones were removed to a depth of 16 inches or more. I use these as the costs of clearing land for cultivation.

The same reports give the cost of lime applied which averaged in twelve instances of reclaiming uncultivated land 57 shillings per acre. In one case where farm buildings were constructed the cost was 171 shillings per acre. In nine cases where drainage was needed the cost was 110 shillings per acre.

The value of improvements per acre in shillings and the rent attributed to each per year are shown in Table 31.10 by the class of improvement. I assume an interest rate on land improvements of 4 per cent, and that farm buildings are maintained by the landlord and depreciate at 2 per cent per annum (on the interest rate implicit in the ratio of rents to land values see Clay, 1974, Holderness, 1974). Buildings per acre are assumed proportionate to output per acre, since they are used for storing output, sheltering livestock, and processing output.

I assume that in 1841 half of the 28.9 million cultivated acres had been

Table 31.10   Value of land improvements per acre in 1661 and 1841

Improvement	1661		1841	
	Value/ acre	*Rent/ acre*	*Value/ acre*	*Rent/ acre*
Cleaning, grubbing	99	4.0	99	4.0
Roads, fencing	26	1.0	26	1.0
Buildings	70	4.2	140	8.4
Draining, manuring	0	0.0	65	2.6
All improvements	195	9.2	330	16.0

Source   See the text.

Note   The values and rents are given in shillings per acre.

treated with mineral manures such as clay, chalk, limestone and marl, at a cost of 105 shillings per acre treated. Stephens (1852, p.500) estimates that it would cost from 100 to 200 shillings per acre to put soil in bad condition into good heart. I assume that a quarter of the cultivated area had been drained or irrigated in some way at a cost of 49 shilings per acre so treated. The life of manuring treatments and pre-1840s drainage systems was about twenty-five years, so that there is 4 per cent depreciation to be charged under this heading also. However, the maintenance of soil condition and drainage was generally the responsibility of the farmer so these costs are included under the labor and depreciation bills.

Thompson argues that by the 1850s the site rent is less than 25 per cent of the total rent in the late nineteenth century, but somewhat more than this in 1815–30 when there was less drainage, and fewer farm buildings (Thompson 1907, pp.75–81). Since the average rental of land in 1841 was around 20 s. per acre these figures certainly confirm Thompson's calculations. I take the site rent in 1841 to be exactly 25 per cent of the gross rent, which I thus assume to be 21.3 shillings per acre.

From 1661 to 1841 the cultivated area is assumed to rise by 20 per cent. I assume that this land was marginal land yielding no rent, because extra capital was needed to bring it into cultivation through drainage or mineral manures to increase the fertility of the soil. In this case, the pure site rent in 1661 is assumed equal to that of 1841 for agriculture as a whole. The value of the land input into production in 1661 is thus,

$$5.33 \times 28.9 + 9.2 \times 24.1 = 350 \text{ million shillings}$$
(site rent)   (improvements)

The land input in 1841 is

$$5.33 \times 28.9 + 16.0 \times 28.9 = 616 \text{ million shillings}$$
(site rent)   (improvements)

The increase in the land inputs from 1661 to 1841 is thus 76 per cent, even though the cultivated acreage grows by only 20 per cent, and site rents are assumed to be the same (i.e. no land productive in another use such as forest was brought into agriculture).

A.5 Capital Depreciation

Inputs have to be purchased to replace depreciating machinery, horses or manures. I assume that the rate of depreciation of horses was 10 per cent and on machinery 15 per cent (following Morton, 1855, p.387), and on mineral manures 4 per cent (of which 2 per cent has already been included in the labor account). This gives, in million shillings,

	1661	*1841*
Horses	18.3	34.9
Implements	17.4	64.5
Manures	0.0	32.1
Total	35.7	131.5

References

Anonymous (1831) 'On the Capital Required in Farming', *Quarterly Journal of Agriculture*, 3; 450–76.

Bacon, R. N. (1844) *Report on the Agriculture of Norfolk*. London.

Blum, J. (1948) *Noble Landowners and Agriculture in Austria, 1815–1848* (Baltimore: Johns Hopkins Press).

Clark, G. (1987a) 'Why Isn't the Whole World Developed? Lessons from the Cotton Mills', *Journal of Economic History*, 67 (1): 141–74.

Clark, G. (1987b) 'Productivity Growth Without Technical Change: European Agriculture Before 1850', *Journal of Economic History*, 67 (2): 419–32.

Clark, G. (1987c) 'The Agricultural Revolution in Britain, 1661–1841: Changes in Technique Versus Changes in People', manuscript.

Clark, G. (1988) 'The Cost of Capital and Medieval Agricultural Technique', *Explorations in Economic History*, forthcoming.

Clay, C. (1974) 'The Price of Freehold Land in the Later Seventeenth and Eighteenth Centuries', *Economic History Review*, 27(2): 173–89.

Collins, E. J. T. (1969) 'Harvest Technology and Labor Supply in Britain', *Economic History Review,* 2nd ser., 22: 453–73.

Crafts, N. F. R. (1983) 'British Economic Growth. 1700–1831: A Review of the Evidence', *Economic History Review*, 36: 177–99.

Crafts, N. F. R. (1985) *British Economic Growth During the Industrial Revolution* (Oxford: Clarendon Press)

Curtler, W. H. R. (1909) *A Short History of English Agriculture* (Oxford: Clarendon Press).

Deane, P. and W. A. Cole (1969) *British Economic Growth, 1688–1959* (Cambridge: Cambridge University Press).

Great Britain, Parliamentary Papers (1864) *Sixth Report of the Medical Officer of the Privy Council. Appendix 6: Food of the Lowest Fed Classes*, Vol. XXVII.

Hall, A. D. (1919) *The Book of the Rothamsted Experiments* (London: John Murray).

Hallam, H. E. (1961) 'Population Densities in Medieval Fenland', *Economic History Review*, 2nd ser., 14.

Hatcher, J. (1977) *Plague, Population and the English Economy, 1348–1530* (London: Macmillan).

Howlett, J. (1792) 'On the Different Quantity and Expense of Agricultural Labour in Different Years', *Annals of Agriculture*, 18.

Holderness, B. A. (1974) 'The English Land Market in the Eighteenth Century: The Case of Lincolnshire', *Economic History Review*, 27(4): 557–76.

Jacob, W. (1828) *Tracts Relating to the Corn Trade and Corn Laws*. London.

Jones, E. L. (1964) *Seasons and Prices* (London: Allen & Unwin).

Kent, N. (1794) *A General View of the Agriculture of the County of Norfolk*. London.

Kershaw, I. (1973) *Bolton Priory: The Economy of a Northern Monastery, 1286–1325* (Oxford: Oxford University Press).

Kosminsky, E. A. (1956) *Studies in the Agrarian History of England in the 13th Century* (New York: Kelley & Millman).

Lindert, P. H. (1980) 'English Occupations, 1670–1811', *Journal of Economic History*, 60: 685–712.

Markham, G. (1683) *Markham's Farewell to Husbandry*, 14th edn. London.

McCulloch, J. R. (1839) *A Statistical Account of the British Empire*, 2nd edn.

Morton, J. C. (1855) *A Cyclopedia of Agriculture*, Vol.II (Glasgow: Blackie).

Murrey, W. (1840) 'On the Cost of Stocking a Small Farm', *Quarterly Journal of Agriculture*, 11: 76–81.

Oschinsky, D. (1971) *Walter of Henley and Other Treatises on Estate Management and Accounting* (Oxford: Clarendon Press).

Page, F. M. (1934) *The Estates of Crowland Abbey* (Cambridge: Cambridge University Press).

Pell, A. (1887) 'The Making of the Land of England: A Retrospect', *Journal of the Royal Agriculture Society of England*, New Series, 23: 355–75.

Raftis, J. A. (1957) *The Estates of Ramsey Abbey* (Toronto: Pontifical Institute of Medieval Studies).

Raynbird, H. (1846) 'On Measure Work', *Journal of the Royal Agricultural Society of England*, 7: 119–40.

Robinson, J. (1956) *The Accumulation of Capital* (London: Macmillan).

Robinson, J. (1960) *Collected Economics Papers*, Vol.II (Oxford: Blackwell).

Robinson, J. (1962) *Economic Philosophy* (New York: Anchor Books).

Rogers, J. E. T. (1866) *A History of Agriculture and Prices in England*, Vols.I and II (Oxford : Clarendon Press).

Rogers, J. E. T. (1902) A History of Agriculture and Prices in England, Vol. VII, Part 2 (Oxford : Clarendon Press).

Snell, K. D. M. (1985) *Annals of the Labouring Poor* (Cambridge: Cambridge University Press).

Stephens, H. (1852) *The Book of the Farm*, Vols.I and II, 2nd edn (Edinburgh: Blackwood).

Tawney, A. J. and R. H. (1935) 'An Occupational Census of the Seventeenth Century', *Economic History Review*, 5: 98–103.

Thaer, A. (1844) *The Principles of Agriculture*, trans. W. Shaw and C. W. Johnson. London.

Thompson, R. J. (1907) 'An Enquiry into the Rent of Agricultural Land in England and Wales During the Nineteenth Century', *Journal of the Royal Statistical Society*, 70: 587–625.

Timmer, C. P. (1968) 'The Turnip, the New Husbandry, and the English Agricultural Revolution', *Quarterly Journal of Economics*, 83: 375–95.

Titow, J. Z. (1972) *Winchester Yields: A Study in Medieval Agriculture Productivity* (Cambridge: Cambridge University Press).

Turner, M. (1980) *English Parliamentary Enclosure* (Folkestone: Dawson).

Washington, G. (1803) *Letters to Arthur Young and John Sinclair*. Alexandria, Virginia.

PART V

Economics and Philosophy

32 On Justifying the Ways of Mammon to Man

Daniel M. Hausman*

In *Economic Philosophy* Joan Robinson argues that economic theorists have been perennially concerned with whether economic behavior and its outcomes can be morally justified and that this concern has had a major impact on economics.

> It was the task of economics to overcome these [moral] sentiments and justify the ways of Mammon to man. No one likes to have a bad conscience. Pure cyncism is rather rare ... It is the business of economists, not to tell us what to do, but to show why what we are doing anyway is in accord with proper principles. (1962, p.21)

Furthermore, it is her view that this concern arises out of an insoluble problem: we can neither mend our economic ways (except in details), nor can we (or should we?) adjust our morals to fit our behavior.

> The moral problem is a conflict that can never be settled. Social life will always present man with a choice of evils. No metaphysical solution that can ever be formulated will seem satisfactory for long. The solutions offered by economists were no less delusory than those of the theologians that they displaced. (1962, p.147)

When Robinson speaks of 'the moral problem', she has in mind the conflict between individual and collectivist interest; and she is thinking of one particular purported solution to the moral problem – the doctrine of *laissez-faire*. Indeed comments elsewhere suggest that when she speaks of 'economic philosophy', what she has in mind primarily is the view that social benefits come from pursuit of individual interest:

> I want to speak about the philosophy of economics. It is an extremely important element in the view of life and the conceptions which prevail in this country. Freedom is the great ideal. Along with the concept of freedom goes freedom of the market, and the philosophy of orthodox economics is that the pursuit of self-interest will lead to the benefit of

*Michael McPherson provided useful criticism of an earlier draft of this essay.

821

society. By this means the moral problem is abolished. The moral problem is concerned with the conflict between individual interest and the interest of society. And since this doctrine tells us that there is no conflict, we can all pursue our self-interest with a good conscience. (1980b, p.43)

For Robinson the really critical events in this century in economics are the collapse of *laissez-faire* in the Keynesian revolution and the subsequent attempts at resuscitation. Ideological motivations are basic (1971, p.162).

Despite the power and brilliance of Robinson's writing, neither the moral concern nor the argument for its insolubility are presented clearly, for they are encased within a positivist view of science, metaphysics and morality that must be superseded before one can confront the serious issues. It would surely be unfair to take Robinson to task for espousing the philosophical orthodoxy of her day, but it is nevertheless informative to highlight how destructive are the constraints early logical positivism places on attempts to understand the relations between morality and economics. Only then can we turn serious attention to Robinson's important substantive claims.

1   THE PARADOX OF ROBINSON'S LOGICAL POSITIVISM

Although Robinson refers in *Economic Philosophy* to the views of Karl Popper, rather than to the views of the logical positivists, her views on metaphysics and morality and their relationship to science are much closer to the positivists than to Popper. For, unlike Popper and like the positivists, Robinson maintains that unscientific propositions are *meaningless*. Thus she asserts, for example, 'if an ideological proposition is treated in a logical manner, it either dissolves into a completely meaningless noise or turns out to be a circular argument' (1962, p. 2). Here she is talking about ideology, not metaphysics or morality, but with a rather breathtaking ease, ideology, metaphysics and morality are lumped together, the differences apparently not worth remarking! (See also her 1970, p.120). It is not only the case that metaphysical *propositions* are meaningless or empty, but metaphysical 'concepts' such as value (1962, p.26) and utility (1962, p.48) are also mere words' or 'circular' and without 'scientific content' (1962, p.52).

Thus when Robinson turns to morality, she thinks of it as matter of feelings only. Moral feelings 'are a separate part of our equipment, like our ability to learn to talk' (1962, p.11). There is no role for reason: 'Reason will not help. The ethical system implanted in each of us by our upbringing ... was not derived from any reasonable principles; those who conveyed it to us were rarely able to give any rational account of it, or indeed to formulate it explicitly at all' (1962, p.12). The result is not only an emotivism like that endorsed by the logical positivists (see, for example, Ayer, 1936, ch. 6), but in Robinson's work a quasi-relativistic view as well:

> Sophisticated people recognize the great variety of ethical systems and take a relativistic view of moral questions. But all the same, under relativism we believe in certain absolutes. There are certain basic ethical feelings that we all share. We prefer kindness to cruelty and harmony to strife; we admire courage and respect justice. Those born without these feelings we treat as psychopaths; a society which trains its members to crush them we regard as a morbid growth. (1962, p.13)

Here it seems that Robinson contradicts herself twice, first asserting the correctness of a moral relativism which is refuted by the universality of certain feelings, which turn out not to be universal at all. What is important here are not the gaffes, but Robinson's struggle to express a reasonable point of view within a philosophy that will not permit it. (Philosophers can certainly make life difficult!)[1] A thorough-going ethical relativism makes nonsense of Robinson's concern with the inevitable conflict between economics and ethics; all there can be are conflicts between economic life and some ethical codes and consistency between economics and other codes. The first problem that Robinson's positivism poses for her is this problem of relativism: how can she defend the ethical views she favors as something more than merely her prejudices?[2]

A second problem concerns the *force* and *role* of metaphysical–ideological–moral propositions. If they are but meaningless noises, how can they be so important and influential? Robinson answers: 'Yet, metaphysical statements are not without content. They express a point of view and formulate feelings which are a guide to conduct' (1962, p. 3; see also p. 52). Although they are not subject to rational scrutiny or appraisal, they can influence behavior and can lead people to do particular sorts of scientific work and to defend specific scientific propositions, even when the evidence is inadequate or unfavorable. We can thus study their influence in the same way that one studies other non-rational influences, such as diet, drugs or psychoses.

But this account of the force of ethical statements leads to a further difficulty. As presented by Robinson, this emotivist view rules out any theory of the rational formulation, use or defense of supposedly metaphysical propositions that employ concepts such as value or utility. How then can people argue about them with the appearance of coherence and rationality? Rational assesment of the limitations of the labor theory of value surely has had *some* role in that theory's decline. Indeed, if nothing rationally bears on the acceptance of ideologies, then it is unclear why ideology should have had so much influence on social theorizing. Why not just let the facts and scientific theories be as they may?

Sensibly to discuss the possible conflicts between economic behavior and outcomes and the demands of morality, requires that one take the demands of morality seriously not as the arbitrary heavings of someone's heart, but as imperatives and claims with cognitively significant content subject to rational appraisal and capable of rational influence.

Although this is not the occasion for an extended essay on the rationality and objectivity of ethics, I should say a few words about how a positivistically motivated ethical nihilism may be avoided. First, even if it is conceded that 'basic' ethical judgments – judgments that are supposed to apply[3] under all conceivable circumstances (Sen 1970, pp. 59–61), cannot be rationally defended, it does not follow that there is no role for reason in ethics. Given that so many of our ethical judgments are non-basic, there is ample role for rational deliberation concerning their applicability. Notice also that, even if rationally unarguable, basic ethical judgments might still be universal. For it might be that we are so constituted by nature that given similar experiences and agreement on the 'facts', we would also reach broad ethical agreement. 'We prefer kindness to cruelty and harmony to strife; we admire courage and respect justice' (1962, p.13). Relativism is only a possibility. Furthermore, there is no reason to believe that ethical judgments that are supposed to apply under all conceivable circumstances cannot be rationally disputed. For logic and imagination may demonstrate conflicts between basic judgments (in this sense) and strongly held non-basic ones, and there is ample role for reason in revising one's system of ethical beliefs to make it consistent and more coherent. Finally, quite apart from the ethical convictions that one attempts rationally to bring into harmony with one another, there are also non-vacuous constraints on acceptable ethical systems. For example, moralities serve social functions, and some do their tasks better than others. These differences make possible further rational assessment. Rawls, for instances, rejects egoism as an acceptable moral system because it fails to perform one of the central tasks of any morality, which is to adjudicate competing claims (1970, pp. 134–36).

Only the unacceptably narrow vision of scientific rationality defended by the logical positivists rules out a non-arbitrary and cognitivist view of morality. But that positivist vision was, unfortunately, the dominant one during Robinson's formative years, and she was unable fully to break with it. Released from such blinders by the further course of intellectual history, let us turn to the serious issues.

2   ON THE INFLUENCE OF IDEOLOGY

Robinson argues only half-heartedly for the historical thesis that the business of economics has been 'to show why what we are doing anyway is in accord with proper principles'. Indeed she cites counter-examples to the general claim, such as Keynes (1962, pp. 76–7). It seems to me that the most one can say in general about the influence of ideology in economics is that there has obviously been some. It is surely not the case that *every* economist is guided by some grand political ideology. Nor does ideology tightly constrain theory development in economics. After all, in Robinson's view Keynes and Kalecki enunciated essentially the same theories, despite drastic ideological disagreement (1973c, p. 258). Indeed she says of the case, 'In this connection we have a striking illustration of the independence of analysis from ideology (when logic is not deliberately fudged or evidence cooked)' (1973c, pp. 257–8). It is true that plausible theoretical work that paints capitalism in rosy moral colors is praised and supported by more capitalists than is more potentially subversive theorizing. But it would be surprising if the incentives of honor, wealth, and position could so effectively compromise economists' scientific integrity as to make ideology dominate theory development and appraisal in economics. Both in Robinson's view and as matter of fact, many influential economic theories have been ideologically inconvenient.

Moral and ideological factors have no doubt had their role in economics. One can discern their influence most clearly in the otherwise inexplicably bad arguments competent economists occasionally make. But apart from noting the moral and ideological motivations and implications of particular theories or applications of theories and apart from noting particular failures of scientific acumen or rationality that may have an ideological explanation, there is in my view nothing more to be said.

An interesting specific instance where Robinson finds ideology at work – the need to justify profits in particular – is the Cambridge controversy.[4] Robinson clearly thinks that there are bigger stakes at issue than some technical points in capital theory. And, in my view the gaffes, fallacious 'proofs' and exaggerations on both sides provide evidence of powerful motivations.

According to Robinson, criticisms of aggregate production functions and of capital as an input into production shake the whole edifice of neoclassical theory and the ideological justification for interest or profits and for *laissez-faire* policy. Apart from mythical stationary states, there are only capital goods, not capital. Apart from historic costs, which should be irrelevant, and current prices, which cannot be cited in explaining interest or distribution, the only sense that could be attached to a quantity of capital depends on the discounted value of the income streams different capital goods yield, which depends in turn on the estimated rate of interest (1953–4, pp. 80ff). Capital has no marginal product or productivity and talk of the quantity of capital, even when coherent, does nothing to explain the rate of interest. These conclusions are supposed to undermine neoclassical functional distribution theory (1969; 1973b, 31, 33; 1977).[5]

As I have argued elsewhere, Robinson's view of the logical or rational significance of the problems in neoclassical capital theory is somewhat exaggerated (1981, ch. 3, 10). For, on the one hand, neoclassical economic theory does little to justify the paying of profits or interest to capitalists (as Robinson concedes (1967, p. 129)) and, on the other hand, nothing in Sraffa's work undermines the justification of paying profits and interest to capitalists.

In aggregative neoclassical theory, interest equals the marginal product of capital. This equality is of no causal significance (Bliss, 1975, pp. 33–77, ch. 5). Interest and the marginal product of capital jointly depend on all the independent variables or givens of any particular neoclassical model, not on each other.

Second, quite apart from the Cambridge criticisms, within the terms of neoclassical theory itself, it is at best misleading to regard the marginal productivity of capital as one of the *determinants* of interest.[6] Except as a construal of certain misconceptions of neoclassical theory, one cannot accept Robinson's claim that. 'Its [marginal productivity theory's] main point, I think, is to find an explanation of factor prices in purely physical, technical conditions, independent of the manner in which an economy is organised' (1967, p.130). Marginal productivity is at best a theory of the demand for inputs, and this demand is not a purely technical matter, but depends on other prices and demands, or, ultimately, on all the givens to the general equilibrium system (which is how the neoclassical theorist conceives of a market economy).

Third, even if it were acceptable to regard the marginal productivity of capital as *one* of the causal determinants of interest (a) marginal *productivity* would still be only *one* of the determinants, not the sole cause and (b) marginal productivity would still be a function of tastes, technology and quantity and distribution of endowments, not some intrinsic property of capital.

And, finally, even if capital could claim its marginal productivity as its own and could lay claim to the interest which may be regarded as due, in part, to its marginal productivity, it would, as Robinson notes (1967, p. 129) still not follow that the *owners* of the capital had any morally sanctioned claim to that interest. To begin to make a case for the claims of the owners of capital, one must invoke the sacrifices of 'waiting' or 'abstinence'. But the sacrifice or marginal disutility of waiting (or the extent of one's time preference), like all marginal quantities, cannot be regarded as causally prior to prices, the rate of interest, or the value of capital.[7] Neoclassical theory does maintain that one cannot have allocative efficiency without including interest among the costs of production, but neoclassical theory does not imply that capital ought to be privately owned or that interest ought not to be heavily taxed. Fundamental neoclassical theory is non-committal on what Robinson sees as the central ideological issue.

On the other side of the controversy, Sraffa's theory is just as non-committal. Sraffa takes a snapshot of an economy with a given set of production techniques in place and a given level of output. He then shows that the 'basics' sector of each economy has a hypothetical twin in which doses of a single aggregate commodity as input are combined with labor to produce just that aggregate commodity as output. Net output over input gives the maximum rate of profit, and there is a linear trade-off between wages and profits. In the real economy, for every rate of profit between zero and some maximum, there is a wage and a price vector such that if that wage is paid and all output is sold at the calculated prices, each industry will earn that rate of profit and all markets can clear (Sraffa 1960, Part I). This result, although of formal interest, is of little economic interest, because it says nothing about what *determines* (in the relevant causal sense) wages, profits and prices.

Robinson disagrees. In her view Sraffa's work has weighty implications. Sraffa shows

> that, when we are provided with a set of technical equations for production and a real wage rate which is uniform through the economy, there is no room for demand equations in the determination of equilibrium prices. (When we take down our productive fense, and allow that changes in distribution affect the comparison of output, we shall need a fresh set of equations relating them, but that is quite another matter). (1961, p. 12)

I am not sure how to interpret this passage. Robinson seems to mean that determinant prices can be derived mathematically from Sraffa's givens and some distribution of income. This claim is surely correct; but Robinson has not said why the result is of interest. One should, I think, resist interpreting her words as a suggestion that Sraffa shows that demand does not affect prices (although some – Medio 1972, p. 325 and Eatwell 1974, p. 288 – have defended such a view). For Robinson explicitly notes that higher wages will shift demand toward generally lower priced consumption goods, while higher profits will shift demand toward investment and luxury goods (1977, p. 286). With possibly gross disequilibrium, market prices will thus diverge from calculated equilibrium prices, real-wages and profits from calculated amounts.[8]

But it is clear that Robinson believes that Sraffa's work does have some important implications, for she maintains that it shows that 'the marginal productivity theory of distribution is all bosh' (1961, p. 13).[9] It does this by demonstrating that the technical relations among inputs and outputs do not themselves imply any particular compensation for the factors of production (1961, p. 13; 1967, p. 130; 1977, p. 287).

But this claim seems unsupportable. Given a particular technique only some wage-profit pairs and their corresponding price vectors are equilibrium values. Other wage-profits pairs and corresponding price vectors appear to be irrelevant. In any equilibrium, with sufficient continuity, all the marginal equalities will hold. Nothing in Sraffa's work contests these claims. Marginal productivity theory may also be used as an account of the demand for inputs into production, and since Sraffa's system says nothing at all about how the size and composition of output, distribution, prices, or the techniques of production are determined, it also fails to contest this account.

The important point to notice about Sraffa's work is that all interesting economic action has been frozen into the given output and its given technique of production. To suppose that one then has an alternative to neoclassical theories of that economic action is unjustified. Ideological conclusions are as unfounded. Sraffa's system says nothing about why profits are as large or as small as they are (apart from the limit imposed by the ratio of net output to input) or about whom they should be paid to. To Sraffa's system itself (as opposed to misinterpretations of it) the staunchest defender of *laissez-faire* capitalism need have no ideological objection.

The only ideological danger that a defender of the status quo might find in Sraffa's work is the possibility that it might be combined with *other* more ideologically suspect views. Political ideology was afoot in the Cambridge controversy much more because of commitments to such other views and because of the hope or fear that somehow a death-blow might be dealt to neoclassical theory. None was. In assesing the episode, one should also not underestimate the passions that can arise directly from general intellectual or theoretical commitments.

3   ON THE IRREMEDIABLE IMMORALITY OF ECONOMICS

It remains clear and, indeed, obvious (although not if moral views are without content) that there are some moral standards and ideas to which contemporary economic behavior does not conform. These standards have prevailed to varying degrees, and Robinson is concerned that they are being displaced by other standards, which are more hospitable to capitalism. Indeed, she ends *Economic Philosophy* with a call 'to combat, not foster, the ideology which pretends that values which can be measured in terms of money are the only ones that ought to count' (1962, p. 148).

But then, in Robinson's view, it appears to follow that there are 'moral' standards with which market economies do accord. So even if people on the whole cannot behave in advanced societies as certain traditional moralities would oblige them to, why must there always be a conflict? Why can we not settle for something like Ayn Rand's objectivism and let dog eat dog with our highest hosannas? The answer is simple: such purported moralities are unacceptable, and not a matter of Joan Robinson's feelings but as a claim that can be rationally defended. Without the possibility of some objectivity in ethics, there is nothing but personal or collective taste here and nothing at all, apart from some claims about the emotional peculiarities of people, in the purportedly unresolvable conflict between morality and economic behavior and outcomes.

Is there indeed such an unresolvable conflict? Are social harmony and individual interest forever irreconcilable? Since human behavior depends so greatly on institutions, might not institutional change provide a means of resolution? Why in Robinson's view must such resolutions fail? The answer, I think, is that in her view institutions within which it is possible for people to shed their greed and egoism (if there are any) do not support the sort of economic productivity that people demand. In Keynes' view, which Robinson cites:[10]

> The time for all this [virtue] is not yet. For at least another hundred years we must pretend to ourselves and to every one that fair is foul and foul is fair; for foul is useful and fair is not. Avarice and usury and precaution must be our gods for a little longer still. For only they can lead us out of the tunnel of economic necessity into daylight. (Keynes 1930, p. 372)

Robinson sees no end to the tunnel. She does not believe in a utopia in which acquisitiveness can be overcome: 'the change in our sense of values that Keynes was pleading for is not in evidence. On the contrary, commercial considerations swallow up more and more of social life' (1970, p. 118). To acquiesce in a social system that perverts human values is thus not an investment with immense moral dividends. Capitalism delivers the goods and will perhaps keep delivering more and more of them; but we will never not want more still. We are thus disinclined to do without capitalism. But then we cannot be moral. We can be rich or good or neither; but we cannot be both. Economic behavior and outcomes cannot be reconciled with morality.

Even if the conflicts between morality and economics cannot be made to disappear, they can be made less serious. Just how Mammon might be tamed is, however, unclear. Robinson evidently looks to an enriched and unblinded political life (1964, p. 145) for the source of the amelioration, and she seems to have in mind standard welfare state remedies (although more effectively applied). But such remedies will only be sought if the political realm is at least in large part ruled by a morality of decency and altruism[11] (or if the plight of the poor becomes a threat to the functioning of the economy). Against the corrosive influence of economic behavior, such a morality cannot retain its force as a mere matter of habit. Without the possibility of rational defense, Robinson's call for non-monetary values can have no rational force and the mediation of the conflict between economy and morality will come through the progressive degradation of the latter.

Notes

1. Not surprisingly, philosophers have found ways to 'defuse' the non-cognitive emotivism defended by the logical positivists and to make it almost a reasonable doctrine. See Stevenson (1944) and Urmson (1969). For a brief introduction Williams (1972) is helpful, and MacIntyre (1981) provides illuminating background and useful criticism.
2. For a later and more successful formulation, see her 1971, p. 122.
3. Although this is Sen's language, it seems clear from the discussion that follows on pp. 61–4 that what Sen really means is that a basic judgment is one that an individual *in fact* sticks to, regardless of what the facts are and what other ethical commitments he or she may have. So that truly basic ethical judgments are not disputable, but it is also impossible to show that a given judgment is a basic one. With respect to any judgment, whether we judge it to be basic or not, rational argument may always be relevant. Sen would thus phrase the matter differently than I do in this paragraph.
4. Given Robinson's view that 'The unconscious preoccupation behind the neoclassical system was chiefly to raise profits to the same level of moral respectability as wages' (1962, p.59) and her claim that 'Under it [the Cambridge controversy] a deep cleavage runs down to the basis of economic theory' (1973b, p. vii), one would naturally infer that the Cambridge controversy would, in Robinson's view, be a classic instance of ideological conflict. Yet Robinson also maintains, 'The object [of the revival of pre-Keynesian neoclassical marginal productivity theory] is not overtly ideological. Fairly radical conclusions can be drawn from the analysis, such as that the distribution of dividends is harmful to society' (1965b, p. 101).
5. I am only concerned with Robinson's views on capital theory with respect to the purported role of ideology in the Cambridge controversy. This paper will thus not be concerned with her major substantive contributions to economic analysis.
6. The problem lies with the *ceteris paribus* clause involved in regarding the demand for capital as a function of its price, which is taken to be the rate of interest. The other determinants of the demand for capital that are impounded in the *ceteris paribus* clause are not sufficiently independent of the rate of interest. For a more extensive treatment of the general causal issue here, see Hausman (forthcoming).
7. Robinson also maintains that, 'The whole elaborate structure of the metaphysical justification for profit was blown up when he [Keynes] pointed out that capital yields a return not because it is *productive* but because it is *scarce*' (Robinson's emphasis) (1962, p. 77). Robinson's (and Keynes's) claim that the explanation for why capital yields a return is that capital is scarce rather than that it is productive puzzles me. From the perspective of fundamental neoclassical theory, both scarcity and productivity are consequences of tastes, technology and the size and distribution of endowments. With respect to inputs into production, they are inseparable sides of the same coin. Indeed Walras's word for marginal productivity was *rareté*.
8. In the paragraph immediately following the quotation Robinson writes, 'But to my mind it [the fact that there is no room for demanding equations in the determination of equilibrium prices] emphasizes a point which, both in its scholastic and in its political aspect, is of great importance; in a market economy, either there may be a tendency towards uniformity of wages and the rate of profit in different lines of production, or prices may be governed by

supply and demand, but not both. Where supply and demand rule, there is no room for uniform levels of wages and the rate of profit' (1961, p. 12). For an extended treatment of this claim and of related views defended by Bliss (1975, p. 294) and Hahn (1975, p. 360), see my 1981, pp. 80–93.

9. Harcourt attributes to Robinson and Sraffa the view that profits are just a surplus (1986, p. 92). But it is hard to see how Sraffa's system could support this conclusion. In Robinson's view, it does not support the related claim that the extent of profits is determined by struggle between capitalists and workers. 'Some readers have interpreted the calculation of the movement up and down of the rate of profit and the share of wages as a story about the class war. But that is a complete misunderstanding. With a single technique and a given net output, there is little scope for fighting over wages and, anyway, the movement is only the movement of the eye running up and down a curve on the blackboard' (1977, p. 287).

10. 1970, p. 117; Robinson quotes the paragraph before the one I quote.

11. The following comments of Marx's are worth recalling here: 'The political state has just as spiritual an attitude to civil society [market behavior] as heaven has to earth. It stands in the same opposition to civil society and overcomes it in the same manner as religion overcomes the limitations of the profane world, that is, it must likewise recognize it, reinstate it, and let itself once more be dominated by it' (1843, p. 46). Without Marx's revolutionary optimism, this is an awfully gloomy thought.

References

Ayer, A. (1936) *Language, Truth and Logic* (repr., New York, 1952).

Bliss, C. (1975) *Capital Theory and the Distribution of Income* (Amsterdam: North-Holland).

Eatwell, J. (1974) 'Controversies in the Theory of Surplus Value: Old and New', *Science and Society* 38: 281–303.

Hahn, F. (1975) 'Revival of Political Economy: The Wrong Issues and the Wrong Argument', *Economic Record* 51: 360–64.

Harcourt, G. (1986) 'On the Contributions of Joan Robinson and Piero Saffra to Economic Theory', in O. F. Hamouda (ed.) *Controversies in Political Economy: Selected Essays of G. C. Harcourt* (New York: New York University Press).

Hausman, D. (1981) *Capital, Profits and Prices: An Essay in the Philosophy of Economics* (New York: Columbia University Press).

Hausman, D. (forthcoming) 'Supply and Demand Explanations and Their *Ceteris Paribus* Clauses'.

Keynes, J. (1930) 'Economic Possibilities for Our Grandchildren', in *Essays in Persuasion* (London: Macmillan, 1933).

MacIntyre, A. (1981) *After Virtue* (Notre Dame: Ind. University of Notre Dame Press).

Marx, K. (1843) 'On the Jewish Question', tr. D. McClellan; repr. in D. McClellan, *Karl Marx: Selected Writings* (Oxford: Oxford University Press, 1977).

Medio, A. (1972) 'Profits and Surplus Value', in E. Hunt and J. Schwartz, (eds) *A Critique of Economic Theory* (Baltimore: Penguin) pp. 312–46.

Rawls, J. (1970) *A Theory of Justice* (Cambridge, Mass.: Harvard University Press).

Robinson, J. (1953–4) 'The Production Function and the Theory of Capital', repr. in her 1978, pp. 76–90.

Robinson, J. (1961) 'Prelude to a Critique of Economic Theory', repr. in her 1965a, pp. 7–14.

Robinson, J. (1962) *Economic Philosophy: An Essay on the Progress of Economic Thought* (New York: Doubleday).

Robinson, J. (1964) 'The Final End of *Laissez-Faire*', repr. in her 1965a, pp. 139–47.

Robinson, J. (1965a) *Collected Economic Papers*, Vol. 3 (Oxford: Blackwell).

Robinson, J. (1965b) 'Pre-Keynesian Theory After Keynes', repr in her 1978, pp. 91–102.

Robinson, J. (1967) 'Marginal Productivity', repr. in her 1973a, pp. 129–38.

Robinson, J. (1970) *Freedom and Necessity* (London: Allen & Unwin).

Robinson, J. (1971) 'A Reply [to Ferguson]', repr. in her 1973a, pp. 160–3.

Robinson, J. (1973a) *Collected Economic Papers*, vol. 4 (Oxford: Blackwell).

Robinson, J. (1973b) *Economic Heresies: Some Old Fashioned Questions in Economic Theory* (New York: Basic Books).

Robinson, J. (1973c) 'Ideology and Analysis', repr. in her 1980a, pp. 254–61.

Robinson, J. (1977) 'The Labour Theory of Value', repr. in her 1980a, pp. 280–8.

Robinson, J. (1978) *Contributions to Modern Economics* (New York: Academic Press).

Robinson, J. (1980a) *Collected Economic Papers*, Vol. 5 (Cambridge, Mass.: MIT).

Robinson, J. (1980b) 'Morality and Economics', in her 1980a, pp. 43–7.

Sen, A. (1970) *Collective Choice and Social Welfare* (San Fransisco: Holden-Day).

Sraffa, P. (1960) *The Production of Commodities by Means of Commodities: Prelude to a Critique of Economic Theory* (Cambridge: Cambridge University Press).

Stevenson, C. (1944) *Ethics and Language* (New Haven: Yale University Press).

Urmson, J. O. (1969) *The Emotive Theory of Ethics* (Oxford: Oxford University Press).

Williams, B. (1972) *Morality: An Introduction to Ethics* (New York: Harper & Row).

33 An Axiomatic Approach to Marxian Political Philosophy

John E. Roemer*

1 EXPLOITATION THEORY

Over forty years ago, Joan Robinson (1942, p. 22) wrote:

> no point of substance in Marx's argument depends upon the labor theory of value. Voltaire remarked that it is possible to kill a flock of sheep by witchcraft if you give them plenty of arsenic at the same time. The sheep, in this figure, may well stand for the complacent apologists of capitalism; Marx's penetrating insight and bitter hatred of oppression supply the arsenic, while the labour theory of value supplies the incantations.

In particular, Robinson's point applies to the theory of exploitation, which was the centerpiece of Marx's analysis of capitalism. He developed the theory of exploitation in Volume I of *Capital*, with a model postulating the labor theory of value. (It was there assumed that prices of commodities are proportional to their embodied labor contents, their 'values'.) But exploitation of workers by capitalists, in the Marxian sense, remains true even in more intricate models where prices are of the usual market clearing sort, and are not proportional to embodied labor values. While Robinson understood this in 1942, the point has now been accepted by all but the most dogmatic writers, due to its elaboration in a series of mathematical models developed in the last fifteen years.[1]

While the exploitation of workers by capitalists, and the linking of exploitation to profits, remain true despite the demise of the labor theory of value, one must nevertheless ask: why be interested in exploitation? I do not speak here of exploitation in its colloquial sense (which is obviously of interest) but in its technical, Marxian sense. A worker, more generally any agent, is exploited if he expends more labor in the process of production than is embodied in the bundle of commodities purchasable with the wages,

*I thank my co-author H. Moulin for permission to report results from our joint work.

interests, rents, and profits which he has earned (or appropriated). This is a slightly more general definition than Marx's, but the spirit is the same. The net product Y of an economy is produced by the employment of an amount of labor L. The product Y has embodied labor value L, since by hypothesis the investment goods used up in producing it have been replaced. Y is distributed to the agents in the economy in some way: say $Y = \Sigma Y^i$, where Y^i is the share which is the property of agent i. On the other hand, total labor expended can be written as $L = \Sigma L^i$, where L^i is the share performed by i^{th} agent. Let $l.v.(X)$ denote the embodied labor in a commodity vector X, which can be calculated in a variety of ways, depending on how complicated the model is. Agent i is said to be exploited if $l.v.(Y^i) < L^i$ and he is an exploiter is $l.v.(Y^i) > L^i$. Since $l.v.(Y) = \Sigma L^i$, it is generally the case that the population is partitioned into a class of exploited and a class of exploiters, with perhaps some agents who, on a knife-edge, are in neither group (because for them $l.v.(Y^i) = L^i$).

Notice this definition is quite general. It makes no reference to prices, profit rates, or sources of income. So long as there is a sensible way of defining 'labor embodied in a bundle of commodities', it makes sense. But why should one be interested in this statistic? Is it of normative or positive interest to calculate who is exploited, and if so, how much? I will argue that exploitation (always, the technical concept) is of no fundamental interest, for either positive or normative reasons. It is of interest only in so far as it is a proxy for something more fundamental; and I will describe how it fails to be a good proxy for the various fundamental things it might be taken to indicate. Thus, although exploitation can be revived independently of the labor theory of value, there is little point in the resuscitation.

What exploitation seeks to represent, but fails to do in a rigorous way, is the degree to which a class of agents is separated from the means of production. More generally, that a class of agents is exploited purports to be an injustice which is the consequence of the private and unequal ownership of alienable productive assets, a fact which characterizes capitalism. I think it is an injustice that alienable productive assets are so unequally distributed under capitalism, and that aspect of capitalist property relations constitutes the fundamental criticism that critics of capitalism must make.

Exploitation, however, is not a rigorously accurate barometer of that inequality. After demonstrating this in Section 2, I outline in Section 3 the different positions concerning property rights which characterize different schools of contemporary political philosophy. In Section 4, a model is presented which illustrates how a political philosophy with respect to property rights can be represented as the study of allocation mechanisms on a space of economic environments. In particular, it is proposed that concepts such as 'public ownership of assets' can be represented in an axiomatic way in this framework. I present a model of this type for studying the question: What distributions of society's product will respect both the private ownership by persons of their own skills, and the public ownership by society of external productive factors, such as land? This question, in Section 3, is shown to be a cogent one in contemporary political philosophy. The theorem proved in Section 5 shows that public ownership of only some assets (such as land) constrains the distribution of the product to be much more welfare-equalizing than one might have thought. This, I propose, is a way of studying the normative implications of alternatives to private property in alienable assets in a more direct and fruitful way than exploitation theory allows.

2   WHY EXPLOITATION THEORY DOESN'T WORK

To exhibit the fundamentals of exploitation theory, imagine a corn economy with two techniques for producing corn, a Factory and a Farm. The Farm is a marginal, subsistence technique, where corn can be produced from labor alone, using no capital (which in this economy is seed corn). The techniques are:

Farm: 3 days labor produces (in 1 week) 1 corn
Factory: 1 day labor plus 1 seed corn produces (in 1 week) 2 corn

There are $N = 1000$ agents, and their preferences are of a 'subsistence' nature: each wishes to consume 1 corn per week and to replace whatever seed corn he may have started with. Having done so, leisure is preferred to more labor, but preferences are strictly monotonic in corn. Suppose the total capital stock is $K = 500$ corn, and it is equally distributed, so that each agent owns .5 corn. The outcome is clear. Each agent will invest his .5 seed corn plus .5 days of his labor in the Factory technique, which will yield (at the end of the week) .5 corn for consumption, net of the capital stock which he replaces. To produce the other .5 corn he requires, he operates the Farm technology for 1.5 days. Thus each agent works 2 days, and that is all; the situation at the beginning of next week is the same as it was at the beginning of this week. Given the technology, capital stock, and preferences in this economy, the labor embodied in 1 corn is 2 days. No one is exploited.

Imagine, now, that the initial capital stock is distributed very unequally: each of 10 agents owns 50 seed corn; the other 990 own none. The 10 rich ones will now become capitalists. We suppose it is possible for a labor market to emerge. Suppose the 10 emerging 'capitalists', who own the seed stock, offered to hire labor at a wage rate of .5 corn per day. Then all 990 peasants would flock to the Factory doors, since on the Farm, they earn only .33 corn per day. There is not sufficient capital stock fully to employ all the peasants and to meet the demand for corn. So the wage offered by the capitalists, in equilibrium, must fall to .33 corn per day, in which case the peasants are indifferent to working on the Farm or in the Factory. At any higher real-wage, there is an excess supply of labor. At the equilibrium wage, the capitalists purchase 500 days of wage labor – say, provided by 500/3 workers, each of whom works for 3 days in the Factory. From this labor, 1000 corn are produced, 500 of which replace the capital stock, and 500/3 of which are paid as wages. The remaining 333.3 of the product comprise profits. The other 823.3 peasants stay on the Farm and each works 3 days for 1 corn. Thus, in equilibrium each of the 990 propertyless agents works 3 days for 1 corn, either in the Factory or on the Farm, and each of the capitalists works zero days and accumulates 33.3 corn in the week. Exploitation has emerged with the unequal distribution of the means of production, for each of the peasants and workers works 3 days for a share of the total product which embodies 2 days of labor, by the previous calculation.

Along with inequality in the distribution of the capital stock, three phenomena have emerged: exploitation, a class structure (capitalists, workers and peasants, defined according to their work relations to each other and the process of production), and accumulation. I do not think exploitation is in itself of rock-bottom interest: it may be interesting if it is intimately related to either (α) the inequality in the distribution of the means of production, or to (β) the emergence of classes, or to (γ) accumulation. For we may have independent reason to judge (α) unjust, in which case our interest in exploitation is as a barometer of that injustice; or we may judge (β) to be of importance, if we think that classes are important sociologically in forming preferences of individuals, or in episodes of collective action; and clearly (γ) is of utmost importance. But exploitation, in its technical sense, is a concept quite distant from any proximate ethical or positive concern. (Who, after all, would be interested in this abstract kind of social labor accounting for its own sake? Such an interest must be deduced from the relationship of those accounts to something palpable.) It is interesting only to the extent that it is diagnostic of one of three phenomena in question.[2] I argue, next, that it is an imperfect indicator of these phenomena.

With respect to accumulation, the 'Fundamental Marxian Theorem' of Morishima (1973), which has now generated a small literature, purports to show that exploitation is the secret of accumulation; it says that exploitation of workers exists if and only if profits are positive. This theorem carries out the legacy of Marx, who thought he had located in labor power the one commodity capable of producing more value than was embodied in it; therein lay the secret of accumulation in a system where each commodity exchanged for its competitive price, yet a surplus emerged. The Fundamental Marxian Theorem is true, but the inference is false that it is labor's exploitation which *explains* profits. For it can be shown that in a productive system, each commodity, when taken as the value numeraire, is exploited.[3] Thus, one would have to say profits are explained by the exploitation of steel, of oil, of land ... on grounds of exploitation alone, there is no reason to single out labor. If labor exploitation is important, it must be for some other reason.

Classes, indeed, are associated with exploitation in a robust way. This is the claim of the Class–Exploitation Correspondence Theorem (Roemer, 1982) which demonstrates that, very generally, agents who optimize by hiring labor are exploiters and agents who optimize by selling labor are exploited, in a general equilibrium model in which agents have general preferences and begin with some initial endowments of goods. But if one's fundamental interest is in class formation, why ask about exploitation, which is a circuitous route to the diagnosis of class? After all, class membership can be easily observed (who hires whom), but exploitation is a complicated statistic to calculate. And if classes are important historical actors, it is surely not because some exploit others, in the technical sense, but because of their relations to each other in the process of production (i.e. their class relationship), and the conflicts and consciousness those relations induce. The class relationship may involve practices which we consider informally 'exploitative', but that should not be confused with the technical statistic of exploitation, something quite different.[4]

Perhaps the strongest case for an interest in exploitation comes from its apparent link to inequality in ownership of productive assets. It is the rich, after all, who exploit the poor, and our interest in exploitation is perhaps parasitic on our views about the justice of the initial distribution of endowments. But consider the following example. There are two techniques, the Farm and the Factory as above, and two agents, Karl and Adam, whose preferences for corn and labor include the following orderings:

Karl: (2/3 corn, 0 days labor) $>_K$ (1 corn, 1 day labor)
Adam: (3.3 corn, 4 days labor) $>_A$ (3 corn, 3 days labor)

Each of these preference orderings is reasonable. Moreover, it is easy to see that these two orderings can be embedded in one well-behaved, convex ordering of bundles of corn and leisure. Thus, what has been observed about Karl and Adam is consistent with their having the *same preferences*. Now suppose Karl has an endowment of 1 seed corn and Adam of 3 seed corn. Each must, as before, reproduce his initial stock. Karl can achieve the bundle (1 corn, 1 day labor) by working up his capital stock in the Factory; likewise, Adam can achieve the bundle (3, 3) by himself. This is not Pareto optimal. Suppose instead Karl offers to hire Adam for 1 day at a wage of 1/3 corn, to work up Karl's capital stock. Karl ends up with 2/3 corn net of reproducing his capital stock, for zero days labor, an outcome he prefers to (1,1). Adam, who still works up his own 3 corn in the Factory in 3 days, ends up with the bundle (3.3, 4) which he prefers to (3,3). The new arrangement is a Pareto improvement over autarky. Moreover, the wage rate at which Karl hires Adam is the competitive one, it is the real-wage Adam could earn if he turned to the Farm to increase his corn consumption.

What's wrong? In the new arrangement, Karl is exploiting Adam. This situation could continue for many weeks, during which Karl never works, and lives off Adam's labor. But Adam is the rich one and Karl the poor one. Against whom is the injustice being perpetrated? If against the poor one, certainly not on grounds of exploitation. And if the original distribution of capital is unjust against Karl, does his exploitation of Adam nullify that? Hardly. One should, in such a case, still consider Karl to be the one who suffers an injustice as a consequence of the initial (unjust) distribution of capital.

The general proposition, which this example illustrates, is that although exploitation is well correlated with class (that is a theorem, referred to above) it is not well correlated with wealth, with the distribution of initial endowments (valued at their equilibrium prices, in more complicated models). The exploitation of the poor by the rich is contingent upon preferences displaying certain features, which I have outlined elsewhere (Roemer, 1985a). When preferences are misbehaved, as in the example, then the poor may exploit the rich. If our true concern is to champion those who own little of society's productive assets against those who own much, perhaps due to the unjust circumstances in which that distribution originated, that cannot be properly represented by an accounting of exploitation. We must turn directly to an investigation of property relations, unobscured by the veil of exploitation theory.

3   PUBLIC OWNERSHIP OF THE EXTERNAL WORLD

I have concluded that the Marxian concern with exploitation can be interpreted as a concern with the consequences of private and unequal ownership of the alienable means of production. The measure of exploitation, however, does not properly represent the concern with the distributive inequalities which are a consequence of unequal ownership of capital, as I have shown; from now on, I discuss property relations directly and avoid the circuitous detour to those concerns through exploitation theory.

Further evidence for this conclusion (that Marxism's ethical concern is with the unequal distribution of alienable productive assets) lies in Marxism's advocacy of socialization of the means of production, as the solution to the problem of exploitation. Instead of taking the radical step of abolishing private ownership of alienable productive assets as a remedy, why not recommend equal and private ownership of them? A kind of people's capitalism known as 'equal division competitive equilibrium (ED-CE)', which initially distributes property rights in all assets in the external world equally to all, and then allows markets to operate, is a system which appears to combine an appealing kind of 'starting gate equality' with the privacy and efficiency which are associated with the market mechanism. The ED-CE mechanism has been a popular one in contemporary discussions of distributive justice, among both economists and political philosophers (see the work on envy-freeness, for example, Varian (1974), and the work on resource egalitarianism of Dworkin (1981)). It is oblique to this paper's topic to discuss why equal and private ownership is eschewed by Marxism in favor of public ownership of the productive assets of society; for further discussion of that issue see Roemer (1986a).

In contemporary political philosophy it is useful to distinguish among three positions with regard to the admissible jurisdiction of private property. The liberal[5] position is that of Nozick (1974), representative of the neo-Lockean school, which argues that all assets, both those in the external world and those that are intimately associated with people (call these assets, generically, 'talents') can be held as private property. Nozick maintains that the inequalities of contemporary capitalist society could have evolved from an initial pristine state in which each person owned his own talents, the external world was unowned, and people were allowed to appropriate objects in the external world as their own under certain 'Lockean' conditions (briefly, that no one is rendered worse by such an appropriation than he would have been were the appropriated object to have been left unowned). According to this story, objects in the external world which are initially unowned become private property as a result of being associated, under certain conditions, with the talents of people, which are initially owned by those in whom the talents reside. It is arguable that, under the Lockean proviso, a world characterized by highly unequal and private ownership of the alienable means of production can result; such inequality is justified by the liberal argument.

The second position, a radical alternative to neo-Lockeanism, maintains that no person should necessarily have property rights either in the external world or in his own talents. A justification for this position is that the distribution of personal talents is morally arbitrary; if luck is not an ethically privileged means for acquiring, then there is arguably no more reason to benefit by virtue of being born with a talent than by virtue of being born with a property right in a fertile piece of land. While neo-Lockeanism derives a justified private partition of the external world from a postulated self-ownership, the radical alternative denies self-ownership, viewing personal talents as unowned property which in principle everyone should benefit from. Such a radical egalitarianism is associated with Rawls (1971) and Dworkin (1981). The maximin principle of Rawlsian justice can be viewed as a method of distributing the returns from all assets, whether land, capital, or talents, to achieve as egalitarian an outcome as is possible, constrained only by incentive considerations. Dworkin calls for equality of resources, and he specifically includes among resources personal talents. I have discussed the economics behind his proposals in detail elsewhere (Roemer, 1985b, 1986b), and will not do so here.

The third position is politically intermediate between the first two; it has been proposed by G. A. Cohen (1985, 1986). Begin with Nozick's or Locke's pristine state of nature, in which the external world is not privately owned. There is an alternative, unacknowledged by neo-Lockeans, to its being unowned: it could be jointly owned, or publicly owned by all. Suppose self-ownership is granted in regard to talents, but the external world is publicly owned. What distributions of income are compatible with these property rights? The appeal of Cohen's proposal is that it distinguishes between personal talents and external assets in a way which neither the liberal nor the radical egalitarian alternatives do. It grants to the liberal position its more appealing clause of self-ownership, and to the radical position its more appealing clause of non-appropriability of the external world. Whatever public ownership of the external world means, it probably constrains the final distribution to be more equal than the neo-Lockean property rights do.

I will summarize and make the link with classical Marxian concerns. Liberal political philosophy postulates self-ownership (of talents) and derives from that private and unequal ownership of alienable assets in the external world. Among talents are included not only skills and entrepreneurial ability, but preferences, including preferences for risk and for consumption or saving over time, which play an important role in liberal justifications of unequal ownership of alienable assets. The obvious reply to the liberal position is to deny self-ownership, on grounds of the moral arbitrariness of the distribution of talents; perhaps, alternatively, self-ownership is deduced as unjustified by a veil of ignorance argument, as in Rawls. If one pushes this position sufficiently far, one must advocate a distribution which equalizes outcomes, or welfares of individuals, as much as possible, subject only to efficiency considerations. (Such is the stated position of Rawls, and I have shown in Roemer (1986b) that this consequence holds generally for resource egalitarian theories which include among resources personal talents.) But that reply is hard to swallow, with its denial of self-ownership. The middle alternative is to grant ownership of talents by the people in whom they reside, but to constrain the degree to which people can appropriate objects in the external world by postulating it to be publicly owned. I think an investigation of the Cohen alternative is the next step towards which Marxian concerns with exploitation point. For exploitation, as I have characterized it, is an indictment of unequal ownership of alienable productive assets, and Marxism's call has been for public ownership of such assets. It has not been so radical, however, as to call for public ownership of all assets, including talents.

Perhaps that more radical alternative is appealing, but I think it is prudent as a research program, and probably historically more realistic, to proceed piecemeal, narrowing the jurisdiction of private property as slowly as possible. Capitalist revolutionaries in feudal society called for abolishing one kind of private property, that held as rights over the labor of other people, serfs. Socialist revolutionaries in capitalist society call for abolishing only capitalist property, not property in talents, as well. One could say it will be for communists (in socialist society?) to call for the abolition of private property in talents. It is perhaps ironic that, as I have outlined the three positions, the one which I have identified with the extension of Marxism is less radical in its intentions than contemporary egalitarian political philosophy, as I have reported it. (I do not hold these authors accountable to my depiction; indeed Rawls (1985) explicitly claims his theory is much less egalitarian than the Rawlsian theory I have described. I am not concerned here with the proper paternity of the theories, but with the three clear alternative theories outlined.) The question becomes: how much is inequality in the distribution of output constrained by postulating public ownership of assets in the external world in conjunction with private ownership of the self and its talents?

4 HOW SHOULD ABLE AND INFIRM SPLIT THE PRODUCT OF THEIR LABOR?

The substantial problem in answering the question posed at the end of the last section is in understanding what public ownership of the external world means. Broadly, one can take either a procedural or an outcome-oriented approach to this question. The procedural approach maintains that some procedure, such as majority vote with regard to the disposition of the asset, implements its public ownership. Or one might justify a procedure which empowers a small committee to make decisions for the public, chosen by some suitably universal franchise. On the contrary, an outcome-oriented approach does not name a procedure but claims that public ownership of an asset implies certain outcomes with respect to the welfares of those who own it, in consequence of its use. Instead of naming a procedure one requires certain properties of the final distribution of income or welfare, to wit, that everyone must benefit by virtue of the disposition of a publicly owned asset. One can ask whether the justification of a procedure which putatively implements public ownership depends, ultimately, on the outcome one expects the procedure to generate. If that were so, then the rock-bottom notion of public ownership would in either case be outcome-oriented. Without pursuing this important question, I adopt here an outcome-oriented approach to public ownership.

More specifically, an axiomatic approach will be taken to the problem of how to implement public ownership of the external world and private ownership of self. In this section I present a model which illustrates this approach. Suppose there are two people in the world, Able and Infirm. One possesses more skill than the other, and skill is used to till the land which produces corn, which they both wish to consume. They have a common utility function for corn and leisure, $u(C,l)$. Each is endowed, initially, with 1 unit of leisure. There is an amount W of land in the world and a production function $f(W,L)$ which describes the conversion of land–labor combinations into corn. The skill levels of the people measure the efficiencies of their labor; thus if person i has skill level s^i and he converts L^i units of his leisure into labor, he supplies $s^i L^i$ units of labor. I wish to model these property rights: that each person owns his own skill and labor, but the land and technology are jointly owned between them. Question: What allocations of labor and corn to the agents respect these apparently competing property rights? Suppose, for example, Infirm's skill level were zero. If he receives some corn from Able's production, does that not violate Able's self-ownership? Or perhaps not, for he jointly owns the world with Able, and does that not give him the right to reach an agreement with Able concerning the distribution of the product before permitting Able to till their jointly owned land?

To model this problem, describe an *economic environment* as a vector $\varepsilon = \langle \bar{W}, f, s^1, s^2, u \rangle$, where $\bar{W}$ is the amount of land, $f(W,L)$ is the production function, s^i the skill level of agent i, and $u(C,l)$ the utility function for corn and leisure which both agents share. Let the set of all such environments be Σ, where W, s^1 and s^2 can be any non-negative numbers, f any production function which is non-decreasing in its two components and exhibits non-increasing returns to scale, and u any utility function which is increasing in both its arguments. This defines a reasonable class of economic environments. Let F be an *allocation mechanism*, which associates to any environment ε a feasible allocation of corn and labor to the two agents:

$$F(\varepsilon) = ((C^1, l^1),(C^2, l^2)) = (F^1(\varepsilon), F^2(\varepsilon))$$

where the bundles of corn and leisure assigned to the two agents are feasible for ε. F is a function defined on Σ.

An attempt is made to capture the two kinds of property rights we wish to impose by placing axioms on the behavior of the allocation mechanism. Consider these axioms:

(A1) (Pareto-optimality), F assigns a Pareto optimal allocation in ε.
(A2) (Self-ownership). In any environment, Able should end up at least as well off as Infirm. That is, $u(F^1(\varepsilon)) \geqslant u(F^2(\varepsilon))$. (I adopt the convention that the first agent is always the one who is at least as skilled as the other.)
(A3a) (Public Ownership of the Land). If land becomes more abundant,

then both agents should become (weakly) better off under F's action. Formally, let $\varepsilon = <\bar{W},f,s^1,s^2,u>$ and $\varepsilon^* = <W^*,f,s^1,s^2,u>$ and $\bar{W}^* > \bar{W}$. Then for $i = 1,2$: $u(F^i(\varepsilon^*)) \geqslant u(F^i(\varepsilon))$.

(A3b) (Public Ownership of the Technology). If the technology becomes more productive, then both agents should (weakly) benefit under F's action. Formally, let ε be as above and $\varepsilon^* = <\bar{W},f^*, s^1,s^2,u>$ and $f^* \geqslant f$, for all (W,L).

Then for $i = 1,2$: $u(F^i(\varepsilon^*)) \geqslant u(F^i(\varepsilon))$.

(A4) (Protection of Infirm). Infirm should not suffer by virtue of Able's ability. Formally, let ε be as above, and define $\varepsilon^* = <\bar{W},f,s^2,s^2,u>$. Then $u(F^2(\varepsilon)) \geqslant u(F^2(\varepsilon^*))$.

Axiom (A1) needs no comment, and (A2) seems to be a minimal requirement for respecting the self-ownership of Able. Whatever such self-ownership means, it should at least imply that, since he and Infirm have the same preferences, that Able should end up at least as well off as Infirm. Note this comparison assumes that utility is interpersonally comparable, for axiom (A2) would have little ethical appeal as a representation of self-ownership if that were not the case.

The axioms (A3a,b) are, plausibly, necessary conditions for what public ownership of the land and technology requires. Whatever such public ownership means, at least it should imply that neither agent's welfare suffers as the publicly owned asset becomes more abundant and nothing else changes. These are the axioms which most clearly embody the outcome-oriented approach to public ownership. It should be noted, however, that these monotonicity axioms are very powerful, for they commit the allocation mechanism to performing a continuum of comparisons. The allocation assigned by the mechanism F in a given economic environment must welfare-dominate the allocation assigned in any other environment whose technology, for example, is inferior to the given technology, *ceteris paribus*. Although this sounds plausible as a representation of what public ownership of the technology requires, it may not be. For our intuitions about the welfare consequences of public ownership – if we have any – come from making discrete comparisons of possible worlds, but the axioms in question commit us to much more than that.

I am not sure how to justify axiom (A4) from the two fundamental kinds of property right which are postulated, but I find it attractive, perhaps independently of its representation of the property rights under discussion. It says that the weak agent should not end up worse off in this world than he would in a world where the other agent were just as weak as he. (A4) protects Infirm from a perverse externality he might otherwise suffer from being in a world with Able. Note that axiom (A2) implies symmetry – namely, that in the environment ε^* of (A4), both agents will receive the same utility under F. So (A4), in conjunction with (A2), requires that in the world ε where Able is more skilled than Infirm, Infirm should at least do as well as he would in the symmetric Pareto optimal allocation in ε*. Even the neo-Lockean 'enough and as good for others' proviso might be interpreted to justify (A4).

Finally, a remark on the choice of domain: it is parsimonious to assume that the two people have the same preferences for corn and leisure, since our aim is to focus upon differential talents, not tastes. The family of economic environments described is perhaps the simplest one upon which one can study the conflict of public and private property rights. The domain can be altered in various ways, and the main result is preserved.

A proof is presented in the next section that there exists a unique mechanism which satisfies axioms (A1) through (A4) on the domain Σ described: F assigns always the Pareto-optimal allocation which equalizes the utilities of the two agents. (Formally, the mechanism F itself is not unique, as there may be several allocations which equalize utility, but the utility mapping which F induces from economic environments to allocations of *utility* is unique.) Thus if we believe that public ownership of the external world (land and technology) necessitates at least what these axioms require, and even if self-ownership of Able is protected to the extent that (A2) assures, then public ownership of the external world trumps self-ownership, in the sense that Able can never strictly benefit from his superior skill. The outcome inequality which neo-Lockeans deduce from self-ownership is here completely nullified by what public ownership of the external world requires.

One may present various arguments against this conclusion. First, these axioms only represent necessary conditions for self-ownership and public ownership of the external world. A liberal could say self-ownership requires much more: for instance, that there should be at least one economic environment in which Able ends up strictly better off than Infirm. If one postulated that, then there is an impossibility theorem – no allocation mechanism would exist respecting both public and private property rights. Neo-Lockeans can use the above theorem to attack the acceptability of public ownership of the external world, since it is now shown to be inconsistent with their postulate of self-ownership, which, more strongly than (A2), requires Able to do strictly better than Infirm in some worlds. But the radical response is: one can derive complete outcome equality without socializing skills. These axioms only explicitly socialize the external world, and they even make some effort to respect self-ownership of skill. Nevertheless, no outcome inequality can be sustained under their purview. One need not take the radical position of denying people *a priori* ownership of their talents to end up with the same welfare egalitarian conclusion which that radical starting point generates.

Secondly, one might maintain that the monotonicity axioms are not necessary conditions for public ownership. Could not the owners of a publicly owned resource decide to divide it equally, let us say, and hold it as private property, trading to Walrasian equilibrium from that initial equal division? (Suppose they decided upon this disposition of the publicly owned resource by unanimous vote.) 'Equal division Walrasian equilibrium' violates technological monotonicity, but it would seem (according to the argument just proposed) to be a possible implementation of public ownership. The answer to this challenge is that it takes a procedural rather than an outcome-oriented approach to public ownership. If one advocates the procedural approach, then one could just as well justify giving all the land to one person, if the public unanimously voted that alternative. Would this be so clearly an implementation of public ownership? I think the answer to this general criticism is the one briefly alluded to earlier. If a procedural approach to implementing public ownership is adopted, it is reasonable to require that the procedure pass certain tests with respect to the outcomes it will generate. The proposed tests, now under scrutiny, are the monotonicity requirements of Axioms (3a,b). Showing that a procedure for implementing public ownership violates one of these axioms can either be taken to imply that the axioms do not capture necessary conditions for public ownership, or that the procedure does not implement public ownership. Which stance one adopts depends on an intuition for which there is no further formal justification, lacking a definition of public ownership.

Thirdly, one can criticize other axioms of the model. I doubt that the axioms of Pareto optimality (A1) and Self-ownership (A2) are questionable. One might criticize (A4) as *ad hoc*, although it seems to be a requirement in defense of Infirm that even a neo-Lockean would endorse. It is more effective to attack the domain axiom, which requires the allocation mechanism to be defined on the entire class of possible environments Σ. If the domain is sufficiently restricted, or modified, then other mechanisms might exist which would satisfy the axioms. This is always a solution to impossibility theorems or surprising characterization theorems in social choice theory. I think, in this case, the domain of economic environments is a reasonable one. Furthermore, the domain can be changed in a number of ways without modifying the result. As the reader of the proof will see, the theorem is in fact a 'single profile' result, which is true for every class of environments which are gotten by fixing W, u, s^1 and s^2, and varying only the production function f. With respect to domain considerations, therefore, the most tenable criticism is that the class of technologies which are admitted is unreasonably large.

5 PROOF OF THEOREM[6]

Theorem   Let F be an allocation mechanism defined on the domain of economic environments $\Sigma = \{< \bar{W}, f, s^1, s^2, u >\}$ where f can be any production function $f(W,L)$ of land and labor which is non-decreasing in inputs and which exhibits, for any W, constant or decreasing average returns in labor (i.e. for fixed $\bar{W}, f(\bar{W},L)/L$ is non-increasing in L), and u can be any utility function in corn and leisure which is strictly increasing in both arguments, normalized so that $u(0,0) = 0$. A unique mechanism F satisfies axioms (A1), (A2), (A3a), (A3b) and (A4). F assigns the Pareto optimal utility equalizing allocation.

First, observe that technological monotonicity (A3b) implies land monotonicity (A3a) because an increase in the amount of land can be viewed, alternatively, as a land-augmenting technical change. That is, at a Pareto-optimal allocation of an environment $\varepsilon \varepsilon \Sigma$, all the land will be used, and so we can restrict ourselves to examining environments with production functions $g(L)$ where land does not appear explicitly and the production function has only labor as an input. Think of such a function g being related to $f(W,L)$ by

$$g(L) \equiv f(\bar{W},L) \tag{1}$$

It suffices to prove the theorem for the class of environments $\hat{\Sigma} = \{< g, s^1, s^2, u >\}$ where $g(L)$ is a production function such that $g(L)/L$ is non-increasing in L and axioms (A1), (A2), (A3b) and (A4) hold. Environments in Σ are associated with environments in $\hat{\Sigma}$ through equation (1), and an allocation mechanism satisfying (A3b) on $\hat{\Sigma}$ satisfies (A3a) as well on Σ. I therefore restrict attention to the domain $\hat{\Sigma}$ where land no longer appears explicitly.

Before proceeding it is useful to define the *induced utility map* associated with an allocation mechanism F.

Definition: For an allocation mechanism F, define

$$u_F(\varepsilon) = (u(F^1(\varepsilon)), u(F^2(\varepsilon)))$$

where $F^i(\varepsilon)$ is the corn-leisure allocation assigned to person i. u_F is the induced utility map associated with F.

Lemma 1: Consider the class of environments

$$\hat{\Sigma}_{s1,s2,u} = \{< g, s^1, s^2, u > \varepsilon \; \hat{\Sigma} \,|\, (s^1, s^2, u) \text{ is fixed}\}.$$

If F satisfies (A3b) and (A1) on $\hat{\Sigma}_s 1,_s 2,_u$ then F is a monotone utility path mechanism. That is, for any two environments ε, $\varepsilon' \in \sum_s 1,_s 2,_u$, either $u_F(\varepsilon) \geq u_F(\varepsilon')$ or $u_F(\varepsilon') \geq u_F(\varepsilon)$; and so u_F traces out a monotone utility path from the origin in utility space as ε ranges over $\hat{\Sigma}_{s1,s2,u}$.

Proof

1. Given $\varepsilon = \; < g,s^1,s^2,u >$, $\varepsilon' = \; < g',s^1,s^2,u >$ two environments. Define

    $$g^*(L) = \max(g(L),g'(L)).$$

    Note g^* is a (continuous) admissible production function since it inherits the non-increasing returns to scale in labor from g and g'. Therefore the environment $\varepsilon^* = \; < g^*,s^1,s^2,u >$ is in $\hat{\Sigma}_{s1,s2,u}$.

2. By (A3b), $u_F(\varepsilon^*) \geq u_F(\varepsilon)$ (2)

    and $u_F(\varepsilon^*) \geq u_F(\varepsilon')$ (3)

    since $g^* \geq g$ and $g^* \geq g'$. But note, from the definition of g^*, that $F(\varepsilon^*)$ is a feasible allocation for either ε or ε'; say for ε. Then by (A1) and (2), $u_F(\varepsilon^*) = u_F(\varepsilon)$. From (3), $u_F(\varepsilon) \geq u_F(\varepsilon')$ which proves the lemma.

Lemma 2: Consider an environment $\varepsilon = \; < g_a,s^1,s^2,u >$ where g_a is the constant production function

$$g_a(L) \equiv \alpha, \; \geq \text{ some } \alpha > 0.$$

(A1), (A2) and (A4) imply F equalizes utilities on ε.

Proof

1. By (A1) no labor is expended since utility is strictly decreasing in labor and labor does no good in production in ε.
2. By convention, $s^1 \geq s^2$. Axiom (A2) implies symmetry: that is, in an environment where both agents have the same skill, they receive the same utility. In particular,

    $$u_F(< g_a,s^2,s^2,u >) = (u(\alpha/2,1),u(\alpha/2,1))$$

    where each consumes 1 unit of leisure (which means neither performs any labor), and they split the corn.

3. By (A4), $u(F^2(\varepsilon)) \geq u(\alpha/2,1)$.
    By (A2), $u(F^1(\varepsilon)) \geq u(F^2(\varepsilon)) \geq u(\alpha/2,1)$.

$\therefore u_F(\varepsilon) \geqq (u(\alpha/2,1), u(\alpha/2,1))$.

But $(u(\alpha/2,1), u(\alpha/2,1))$ is on the Pareto frontier in ε, and so
$$u_F(\varepsilon) = (u(\alpha/2,1), u(\alpha/2,1)).$$

Proof of Theorem

By Lemma 1, an allocation mechanism satisfying (A1) and (A3b) traces out some monotone utility path in utility space on the sub-domain $\hat{\Sigma}_{s1,s2,u}$ for any fixed vector $(_{s1,s2,u})$. By Lemma 2, an allocation mechanism satisfying the axioms must therefore trace out the equal utility ray on $\hat{\Sigma}_{s1,s2,u}$ since any point on that ray can be generated as $F(\varepsilon_\alpha)$ for $\varepsilon_\alpha = <g_\alpha,s1,s2,u>$, some α. (This uses the assumption that u is strictly increasing in corn.) Hence on every sub-domain $\hat{\Sigma}_{s1,s2,u}$, F is the equal utility mechanism.

There are some small technical points I have glossed over in the interest of presenting an uncluttered proof.[7] Furthermore, there are various domain refinements which can be made (see Moulin and Roemer, 1986).

6   CONCLUSION

The fundamental debate between advocates of socialism and capitalism reduces either to one over the moral legitimacy of self-ownership or over the rules for appropriating assets in the external world, what Marxists are fond of calling the means of production. I have argued that the theory of exploitation is a rather blunt weapon for this debate. In some peculiar cases, it gives the wrong verdict (the poor may exploit the rich). But more generally, exploitation theory does not confront the liberal challenge which maintains that the appropriation of assets in the external world by the exercize of a person's rightly owned personal traits is morally all right. Marxists have advocated public ownership of the external means of production, whatever that means. In this paper I have proposed a way to study what allocations of the fruits of labor and land can be said to satisfy two kinds of property rights: public ownership of the land and private ownership of labor. The conclusion is that public ownership of the land trumps self-ownership, in the sense that welfare egalitarianism is achieved without the radical socialization of skills. This can either be viewed as a strong case for welfare egalitarianism, as that conclusion is derived without explicit interference with self-ownership; or, by liberals, it can be taken as a strong case against public ownership of the external world, since that postulate (as modelled by the axioms here) nullifies any differential gain a person might win by virtue of his talent.

In any case, the model presented here is not intended to be the last word on this question of political philosophy, but an example of how one can use an axiomatic approach for modelling property rights and studying normative questions of distribution. I suggest that by explicitly modelling the property rights which are recommended by ethical considerations, progress can be made in welfare economics beyond what has been accomplished by traditional approaches in social choice theory and bargaining theory. These latter approaches have not provided a sufficiently concrete language for studying questions of political philosophy, a point which is elaborated upon in Roemer (1986c).

Notes

1. See, for example, Morishima (1973), Vegara (1979), Steedman (1977), and Roemer (1981).
2. Exploitation can also be proposed as a statistic for domination and alienation. I do not refute the usefulness of exploitation as a statistic for these phenomena here, but do in Roemer (1985a).
3. This 'Generalized Commodity Exploitation Theorem' has now been observed by many writers, for instance Vegara (1979, chapter 3), Bowles and Gintis (1981), and Roemer (1982, chapter 6).
4. For a treatment of class consciousness and its relationship to exploitation, see Wright (1985).
5. I use 'liberal' in its classical sense throughout this paper, to indicate the libertarian or individualist position in political philosophy. American readers may substitute 'conservative'.
6. This theorem and refinements of it are treated in Moulin and Roemer (1986).
7. For instance, I have assumed in the proof that the utility possibility frontier for an economic environment does not have any horizontal or vertical level segments. Such an environment is called 'strictly comprehensive'.

References

Bowles, S. and Gintis, H. (1981) 'Structure and Practice in the Labor Theory of Value', *Review of Radical Political Economics*, 12: 1–26.

Cohen, G. A. (1985) 'Nozick on Appropriation', *New Left Review*, 150: 89–107.

Cohen, G. A. (1986) 'Self-Ownership, World Ownership and Equality', *Social Philosophy and Policy*, 3(2).

Dworkin, R. (1981) 'What is Equality? Part 1: Equality of Welfare', *Philosophy and Public Affairs*, 10: 185–246; and 'What is Equality? Part 2: Equality of Resources', 283–345.

Morishima, M. (1973) *Marx's Economics*, (Cambridge: Cambridge University Press).

Moulin, H. and Roemer, J. (1986) 'Public Ownership of the External World and Private Ownership of Self', Department of Economics Working Paper, University of California.

Nozick, R. (1974) *Anarchy, State, and Utopia* (New York: Basic Books).

Rawls, J. (1971) *A Theory of Justice* (Cambridge: Belknap).

Rawls, J. (1985) 'Justice as Fairness: Political not Metaphysical', *Philosophy and Public Affairs*, 14: 223–51.

Robinson, J. (1942; 2nd edn 1966) *An Essay on Marxian Economics*. (New York: St Martin's Press).

Roemer, J. E. (1981) *Analytical Foundations of Marxian Economic Theory* (Cambridge: Cambridge University Press).

Roemer, J. E. (1982) *A General Theory of Exploitation and Class* (Cambridge, Mass.: Harvard University Press).

Roemer, J. E. (1985a) 'Should Marxists be Interested in Exploitation?' *Philosophy and Public Affairs*, 14: 30–65.

Roemer, J. E. (1985b) 'Equality of Talent', *Economics and Philosophy*, 1: 151–88.

Roemer, J. E. (1986a) 'Public Ownership and Private Property Externalities', in Elster, J. and Moene, K. (eds) *Comparative Market Systems* (Oxford: Oxford University Press).

Roemer, J. E. (1986b) 'Equality of Resources Implies Equality of Welfare', *Quarterly Journal of Economics*, 101: 751–84.

Roemer, J. E. (1986c) 'The Mismarriage of Bargaining Theory and Distributive Justice', *Ethics*, 97: 88–110.

Steedman, I. (1977) *Marx After Sraffa* (London: New Left Books).

Varian, H. (1974) 'Equity, Envy, and Efficiency', *Journal of Economic Theory*, 9: 63–91.

Vegara, J. M. (1979) *Economia Politica y Modelos Multisectoriales* (Madrid: Biblioteca Tecnos).

Wright, E. O. (1985) *Classes* (London: New Left Books).

PART VI

Veteris Vestigia Flammae

34 A Personal Note on Joan Robinson

Kenneth E. Boulding

It is almost impossible to separate Joan Robinson the economist, Joan Robinson the person, and Joan Robinson the Cantabrigian, that is, a participant in the extraordinary group of economists who flourished at Cambridge University in the decades following World War I. I find it also difficult to separate my own reactions as an economist, as a person, and as a non-Cantabrigian. So this note perhaps must be discounted in academic terms for its strong personal flavor.

I only saw Joan Robinson twice. The first occasion was when she gave the Ely Lecture to the American Economic Association in New Orleans, in 1971. We had a long discussion, mainly with members of the Union for Radical Political Economics (URPE), a group with which I must confess I have somewhat marginal sympathy, though I was glad to see it formed. The other occasion was when I was in Cambridge, England, at a seminar of the International Economic Association on The Grants Economy and Collective Consumption, in 1979. It was organized by Austin Robinson and Joan Robinson sat in on one or two sessions, though she was clearly not well and did not really participate.

Her first great book, *The Economics of Imperfect Competition* (1933), made a great impact on me as a budding young economist in the mid-1930s. Herbert Stein (1969, p.162) in *The Fiscal Revolution in America* notes that both Paul Samuelson and I refer to this period in terms of Wordsworth's famous statement, 'Bliss was it in that dawn to be alive, but to be young was very heaven!' although he points out also that this may have had much more to do with being 21 than with anything that actually happened. There were two aspects to that sense of a new dawn in the 1930s. One, of course, was Keynes, in the sense that at least someone was wrestling with the real causes of what looked like a catastrophic failure of the market economy in the Great Depression. The other element in that dawn was the theory of imperfect competition or monopolistic competition as developed almost simultaneously by Joan Robinson, who lived in Cambridge, England, and Edward Chamberlin, in Cambridge, Massachusetts. This seemed to liberate economics from its absurd commitment to pure competition, which everybody knew didn't exist, and opened up another possibility of a much more realistic image of market economies.

Looking back on that dawn after fifty years, it certainly looks as if it turned into a pretty cloudy day. The theory of imperfect and monopolistic competition, elegant as it was, was embalmed in the textbooks and then seemed to dry on the vine. It did not set off the process of new research, new ideas, new insights which one would have expected from something that at the time seemed almost what today would be called a 'Kuhnian Revolution' in economic thought. As far as I can see it had very little impact on economic policy or legislation. The great revival of free-market ideology and monetarism, following Milton Friedman in the 1950s, paid very little attention to imperfect competition and dismissed it in effect as a minor aberration of the free-market system.

The Keynesian Revolution, of course, had much more impact. One sometimes has an uneasy feeling that Keynes's book on *The Economic Consequences of the Peace* (1920) had much more impact than any of his later masterpieces. It could be argued that the greatest thing that emerged out of Keynesianism was the fact that the peace after World War II was so much more successful, certainly in economic terms, than after World War I. We had learned something from the utter folly of Versailles, so that we had a non-punitive, essentially creative peace settlement as far as the Western world and Japan were concerned, though, of course, it did land us in the disaster of the Cold War with the Soviet Union.

The impact of Keynes on actual economic policy remains much greater than an official ideology. Mr Reagan, after all, is one of the most Keynesian presidents the United States has ever had, in spite of the idiocies of supply-side economics, which contains maybe 5 per cent of truth. I suspect Keynes would have been horrified by the grotesque rise in interest rates and the appalling future costs of the budget deficit, even though it is about the only thing that is keeping us going in the short run. Monetarism has had a very high social cost, in terms of bringing down the rate of inflation, by what to my mind is a totally unacceptable level of unemployment and a distortion of the debt and equity structure on a world scale as well as on the national scale, which bodes much ill for the future.

If these were false dawns (and I am inclined to think they were cloudy rather than false), Joan Robinson had a good deal to do with both of them. *The Economics of Imperfect Competition* was a brilliant work, not perhaps quite so satisfactory in detail as Edward Chamberlin's version, but broader in scope and in some ways more insightful. Joan Robinson, however, also participated in the Keynesian Revolution at its very fountainhead. She was a close associate of J. M. Keynes, a constant and helpful critic of his work, and played a considerable part in the actual formulation of the *General Theory*. It is all the more striking, therefore, that she herself perceived the cloudiness of both these dawns, almost before anybody else did, especially after World War II, when she came almost to repudiate the theory of imperfect competition as almost trivial elegance, and she became acutely conscious of the gaps in the Keynesian system.

The greatest of these gaps was the failure to deal adequately with the extremely important problem of macro distribution, that is, what really determines the distribution of the national income or some suitable aggregate as between wages, profit, interest, and other shares. These gaps so haunted her thinking from the 1950s on that she was led into what some might think a rather unfortunate flirtation with Karl Marx, although she certainly never became a Marxist, and her 'Open Letter From a Keynesian to a Marxist' is as penetrating in its perception of the weakness of Marxist orthodoxy as any anti-Marxist could wish (see Robinson, 1973, p.264). Nevertheless, I think she felt that Marx had asked at least one question which neither he nor anybody else had really answered, which in its simplest form is what really determined the division of the national income between labor income and non-labor income? Beyond that, of course, is the question, what determined the distribution of non-labor income into its various components?

The sense that Marx had asked a very important question did, I think, blind her to the political as well as some of the economic defects of communist societies, of which she took what today seems far too rosy a view in light of their subsequent history. I suspect she never thought very much about political freedom and the relation of this to the institution of private property and the checks which private property places on political tyranny. For all her life, she remained very much an economist, with a certain narrowness of vision that this specialization implies. Nevertheless, her concern for world poverty and for what she felt were the pathologies of the market system, was very deep and it is hard not to be moved by it. Moreover, one cannot help feeling that sensitivity to the defects of the market system sometimes prevents people from recognizing that the cures are frequently worse than the disease.

An interesting episode in Joan Robinson's intellectual life was her contribution to the so-called 'Cambridge capital controversy' of the late 1950s and early 1960s, so called because Cambridge, England and Cambridge, Massachusetts provided some important contributors. I must confess I have always thought this was one of the most trivial controversies in the history of economic thought, parallel I am sure to some of the controversies that must have taken place among the alchemists regarding the nature of fire as an element. Joan Robinson perceived clearly, I think, that this was controversy revolving around a meaningless taxonomy of the factors of production, although she herself plunged with great skill into the diagrammatic absurdities of the controversy (witness her article on 'The Badly Behaved Production Function' with K. A. Naqvi, 1967). She saw very clearly that what economists call 'capital' is a hopelessly heterogeneous aggregate and an enormous variety of populations of different goods which it is impossible to reduce in real terms either to 'putty' or to 'steel', which she reversed delightfully as 'leets'. In this she had a somewhat unexpected ally in my old Oxford tutor, E. H. Phelps Brown, whose article on 'The Meaning of the Fitted Cobb–Douglas Function' (1957) demolished the statistical illusion that the quantity of labor and capital can be measured by a single number.

Joan Robinson had a wonderful intuitive feeling of the appalling complexity of the economic system and of the enormous amount of information that was lost in trying to reduce complexity to a single number. It was this feeling perhaps that chased her away from econometrics and ritual mathematization, the trap into which most of the economics profession fell. It may be, however, the fact that she refused to fall into this trap that made her ideas inaccessible to those who did fall into it and refused to take her seriously.

A concept which was basic to her thinking about macro distribution I have called myself the 'K-Theory', because it is to be found in some form in the writings of Keynes, Kalecki, Kaldor, and, if I may say so, Kenneth Boulding. This is the view that the amount of national income going to profits (it is not quite clear whether this includes interest) depends on the amount of private investment, plus what capitalists spend on household purchases. There are considerable variations on this theme, but this is perhaps the simplest exposition of it. Joan Robinson quotes Kalecki's famous saying that 'the workers spend what they get and the capitalists get what they spend'. She admits the phrase is not found in print in English and it seems to me one of the curious oral traditions for which Cambridge is famous. Perhaps the first recognition of this principle stems from Keynes's famous 'widow's cruse' doctrine in *A Treatise on Money* (1930). The reference, of course, is to the story of Elisha and the widow who had the cruse of oil that he blessed so that it never ran dry.

Perhaps the simplest way to perceive this principle is to imagine a stationary state with the net production or net national income (Y), divided into non-labor income (P) and labor income (W), so that in any one year $Y = P + W$. If we have a stationary state in which there is no saving or investment, everybody spends their whole income, so this is a stable equilibrium where the total volume of expenditure by households is $P + W$, this must equal Y. This is true, however, no matter what the actual values of P and W. Of a net national product of 100, P could be 20 and W 80, or P could be 30 and W 70, and the equilibrium would go on just the same. The historical process that led to the stationary state would determine the actual proportions.

In a non-stationary society in which there is positive investment and the capital stock is growing, investment represents a gross addition to the net worth of businesses taken as a whole, if cost accountants are to be believed. Then the payment of wages does not increase net worth, but simply shifts assets out from a liquid form into the product of the work with the same value. Profit can only arise if the product is revalued above cost at the moment of sale, which, of course, gives you good old 'surplus value'.

The value of the total product is more than is paid in wages if investment takes place. There are all sorts of amendments that have to be made to this principle, but it has always seemed to me that it was essentially sound. I would have thought that if anyone could have presented it in a way that would be convincing, Joan Robinson would have done so with her extraordinary facility for convincing argument. The economics profession, however, still remains almost totally oblivious to this essential addition to standard economics and continues to believe in the nonsense of distribution according to marginal productivity, which has some microeconomic meaning for the individual employer, but very little at the level of the total economy, except perhaps in the very long run. Joan Robinson was, I think, at the end of her life profoundly disappointed by the failure of the economics profession to respond to what she felt was a fundamental flaw in conventional economics.

I might add a footnote on this point myself. I came somewhat independently to the same view of the macroeconomics of distribution in my *Reconstruction of Economics* (1950) through trying to reconstruct economics by way of the balance sheet rather than the income statement. Economics, however, obstinately refused to be reconstructed and even Jan Pen, the Dutch economist who is perhaps the best historian of economic thought of the twentieth century, dismisses my *Reconstruction of Economics* in a curt footnote as a 'dead horse' (see Pen, 1971, p.24n). I doubt very much if anybody at Cambridge ever read *The Reconstruction of Economics*. Why, indeed, should anybody at the center of the world read anything that came out of Iowa? Certainly, Joan Robinson never mentions it, although it would have given substantial support to her point of view. I can sympathize personally, therefore, with the feeling which I am sure she had, of being a voice crying in the wilderness of having something very important to say that nobody would listen to. Even Martin Bronfenbrenner (1971, chapter 16) in his book on *Income Distribution*, which has the most sympathetic account of the macroeconomic theory of distribution, in the end with seeming reluctance shakes it off and goes back to what he calls the 'good old theory' of marginal productivity.

The difficulty here goes back a long way in economics to the failure to recognize that the rate of profit and the rate of interest is not a price, but a rate of growth, which does not have the dimensions of price. Economists have been singularly insensitive to the problem of the dimensions of their variables. The confusion between stocks and flows goes right back to Adam Smith. In fact the very first sentence of *The Wealth of Nations* (1776) really says the annual labor of every nation is the 'fund' which annually provides you with all the necessaries and conveniences of life. Annual labor is a flow.

By the necessaries and conveniences of life he means real income, also a flow, while the 'fund' is a stock.

Rates of profit and of interest are rates of growth with dimensions of one over time, whereas price is a ratio of the quantities of the exchangeables exchanged. This means that the rate of profit or the rate of interest cannot be determined in the market as such. What is determined in the market is the prices of securities, whether stocks or bonds, and the prices of capital goods. A bond, a certificate of indebtedness, is a promise to pay specific sums at specific dates in the future. If there is no uncertainty, the price of the bond then determines the rate of interest when the bond is held to maturity. The higher the rate of the bond, the less the rate of interest, according to a familiar formula. If the bond is not held to maturity but is sold earlier, the rate of return depends on the price at which the bond is sold as well as the price at which it was bought, for the price received for the bond when it is sold now becomes part of the payments received. Profit is a more complex phenomenon. It is the gross rate of growth of the 'bottom line', that is, of the net worth as a result of the exchange and production transactions that are taking place. The question of what exactly is gross and net in this regard is a tricky one, particularly in the case of private businesses or households. In the case of the corporation, however, it is fairly clear that gross increase in net worth is divided into the net increase plus the amount which has been distributed to owners (in the case of the corporation, the shareholders).

Profit arises entirely from the revaluation of assets. Exchange and production involve costs that is, the lessening of some assets, such as money when wages are paid, raw materials as they are destroyed in producing the finished product, and so on. The results of these activities are valued at cost according to cost accountants. They are revalued at the moment of sale at what they bring in and there is profit if what they bring in is above the cost. This again points up the fact that if profits are to persist, the total value of output must be greater than what is paid out in cost. This can only happen if either output is not sold at all, that is, it just appears as an increase in the capital goods in the goods and valuable items possessed by the business in assets, or if what is distributed to the household or the capitalists is used by them to purchase goods from businesses. Perhaps Joan Robinson was right that the resistance to this idea arises from the fear that it provides a critique of capitalism and suggests that the reward of the capitalist, on good Marxian lines, is a form of exploitation.

There is, however, an answer to this charge, which Joan Robinson never really developed. It is the recognition that production is a process which originates in what might be called 'human know-how', that is, a genetic factor, and that this is limited in its capacity to be realized by limiting factors, of which the most obvious ones are space, time, energy of many different kinds, and materials of many different kinds. The limiting factors may also include institutions, that is, in Marxist terminology, the relations of production may themselves be factors of production, especially in the limiting sense. This view of production cuts across biology and the social sciences. The fertilized egg of a human knows how to produce a human being. It does not know how to produce a rhinoceros, although it has some ideas about this. If the genetic structure cannot command energy to identify, transport, and transform materials into the shapes and structures of the product, the potential in the genetic structure will not be realized. This is as true of a horse as it is of an automobile. Indeed, I have argued that the automobile or any other human artifact is a species just like a horse in the general ecosystem of the world. The only difference is that it has a much more complicated sex life. The genetic structures which produce human artifacts are not contained in the artifacts themselves, as is the case with biological artifacts, but are contained in many other kinds of artifacts and, of course, in human minds and records. This seems to me a much more satisfactory theory of production than what I have called the 'cookbook theory' of the economics textbooks, which suppose that land, labor, and capital are simply stirred together and out pops potatoes or automobiles.

This genetic theory of production, however, throws a very different light on the comparisons between market societies and centrally planned economies than does the cookbook theory. The political power and information structure of centrally planned economies operates as a sharply limiting factor on the realization of the potential of human know-how. Market economies, of course, can also exhibit pathologies, but on the whole when they are operating well, the chance of realizing the potentials of human know-how in a product in terms of commodities seem to me much larger than in a centrally planned economy. In this sense the institutions themselves are productive because they pull back, as it were, the limiting factors, which otherwise would limit the realization of the potential of the know-how involved, especially in complex systems. The market is essentially an ecological system. In the woods and the prairie we have free private enterprise beyond the dreams of Milton Friedman and not even a mayor. Ecosystems have no political processes whatever. They are wholly governed by invisible hands. An organism, on the other hand, is a centrally planned economy from the plan in the original fertilized egg or genetic structure. Ecosystems are certainly comprised of organisms of great variety. It is this variety that has created evolution, development, and persistence. If evolution had culminated in the production of a single organism wrapped around the earth it would have died. All organisms have been programmed for death. A centrally planned economy is much more like an organism than it is an ecosystem, although it certainly has elements of an ecosystem in it, which perhaps is the thing that keeps it alive.

While I think, therefore, that Joan Robinson's criticism of market-type economics was very largely valid, her political conclusions I think were not, simply because she was never able to transcend the cookbook theory of production, although she is acutely aware of its weakness. One hopes that when the history of economic thought is written a hundred years from now she will be seen perhaps a little bit like Karl Marx as the asker of very important questions, to which the times did not permit an answer. She was indeed a remarkable mind and a great lady, someone of whom the human race can legitimately be very proud.

References

Boulding, K. E. (1950) *A Reconstruction of Economics* (New York: John Wiley).

Bronfenbrenner, M. (1971) *Income Distribution Theory* (Chicago: Aldine/Atherton).

Brown, E. H. Phelps (1975) 'The Meaning of the Fitted Cobb–Douglas Function', *The Quarterly Journal of Economics*, 71: 546–60.

Keynes, J. M. (1920) *The Economic Consequences of the Peace* (London: Macmillan).

Keynes, J. M. (1930) *A Treatise on Money* (London: Macmillan).

Pen, J. (1971) *Income Distribution*, trans. By T. S. Preston (Harmondsworth: Penguin Books).

Robinson, J. (1933; 2nd edn 1969) *The Economics of Imperfect Competition* (London: Macmillan).

Robinson, J. (1973) *Collected Economic Papers*, Vol. IV (New York: Humanities Press).

Robinson, J. and K. A. Naqvi (1967) 'The Badly Behaved Production Function', *The Quarterly Journal of Economics*, 81: 579–91.

Smith, A. (1776; repr. 1937) *The Wealth of Nations* (New York: Random House/ Modern Library).

Stein, H. (1969) *The Fiscal Revolution in America* (Chicago: University of Chicago Press).

35 Joan Robinson: Utter Fearlessness

Paul Streeten

The quality that stands out in my memory of Joan Robinson is something very rare in England and the United States, so rare indeed that there is not even a word for it. The Austrians call it *Zivilcourage*. The translation of 'moral courage' is somewhat too pompous, and 'civilian courage' does not catch the flavor. Courage and fearlessness are certainly involved, and it is a form of courage that has little to do with the courage displayed by wartime heroes in battle. Men and women of great physical courage can turn out to be utter cowards when it comes to displaying *Zivilcourage*. A test for it is the following setting: you attend a meeting of important people, whose judgment and power you respect. A topic is discussed and views are voiced round the table. A consensus emerges. Finally, it is your turn to give your views. You utterly disagree with the emerging consensus. Do you have the guts to say what you think, at the risk of being regarded a fool or a knave by all the other distinguished people, or do you modify your views or suppress them? In my experience, people with no physical courage can display great *Zivilcourage* on such an occasion, and vice versa.

Joan Robinson had to a superb degree that quality of *Zivilcourage*. On one occasion, I witnessed a combination of physical submission and moral assertion. A group of us, including David Worswick, Richard Kahn and myself, were participating in a symposium at François Perroux' institute in Paris. The subject was growth theory. François Perroux had decided that Joan should be in the chair at the meeting, but Joan had refused. Whether Perroux was making opportune use of his deafness, or whether he had not taken in her refusal, I don't know. As we entered the lecture room, Perroux physically pushed Joan into the chair to be occupied by the chairman, and Joan submitted silently and stayed there. But when it came to the discussion of the role of capital, its definition, meaning and measurement, she espoused a view that went entirely against the accepted orthodoxy. As we were walking away from that meeting up the Boulevard Sebastopol, I remember her shouting at David Worswick who maintained a doctrine of incentives to invest that Joan disagreed with, 'It's animal spirits, animal spirits.'

There are some people who derive pleasure and excitement from contradicting the established view. Such contrari-mindedness is, of course, itself a form of conformity. I remember a cartoon of Penny, the comic strip character, who said to her boyfriend, 'Can't you be different . . . like all the others?' In Joan's fearlessness there was nothing at all of this kind of contrari-mindedness, of opposition for the sake of opposition, of *épater le bourgeois*. Her views derived entirely from the way she saw reality and how things connected.

Next to this admirable and rare quality, Joan had an enormous store of human warmth, particularly for people who had no pretensions, no reputations. This contrasted nicely with her sometimes militant and abrasive manner in lectures, when she was challenged by pompous or pretentious people. When my wife studied anthropology she took an enormous interest in her work and was very encouraging. I often noticed her maternal feelings of protectiveness to friends. When we corresponded on aspects of the theory of the firm and I thought Richard Kahn's judgement on a small point would be useful, she wrote that she did not wish to trouble him, because he was tired and overworked. And it was this protectiveness and warmth that also inspired her concern for the underdog, the oppressed, the poor. She did not always find it easy to express this warmth and one felt that she was reaching out to communicate it, but sometimes failed.

A third quality I greatly admired in Joan was her simplicity. It expressed itself in the way she lived, in a little cottage at the bottom of her garden, the way she wrote, and the way she talked. She had a wonderful way of cutting through the skeins of complicated problems, and putting them in straightforward terms.

Joan was not perfect. She had faults and she could be wrong. She would favor and promote for jobs people of whose political views she approved, against better qualified people of whose views she disapproved. She could be very partial in her perception and blind to things most others saw clearly. She was wrong about Mao and, earlier, about the Soviet Union. Perhaps these were the defects of her merit, the merit of a fighter. For she was, above all, a fighter.

36 Images of Joan

I. G. Patel

I came to King's College, Cambridge, in November 1944 lured mainly by two names, Keynes and Mrs Robinson. My University of Bombay Prize consisted of three books which I had tried to read carefully soon after graduation: Keynes's *General Theory*, Mrs Robinson's *Imperfect Competition*, and James Meade's *Economic Analysis and Policy*. The first aroused my curiosity about a number of things which were not clear enough to me then. The second was crystal clear and intellectually exciting. The third convinced me that Economics was a useful subject. Someone told me that if I liked these books, I should go to King's because both Keynes and Mrs Robinson were there – little did we know of Cambridge then! I was, therefore, delighted when I learnt on arriving at Cambridge that Mrs Robinson at least was not drafted into the war effort – whether because of her radicalism or simply because of her sex, I had wondered.

The first impressions of Mrs Robinson were rather off-putting. It did not come easily to a shy Indian student to approach anyone, let alone a female teacher with a gruff voice and a sort of grunt which I did not recognize then as a characteristic of British shyness. I was afraid of approaching her, the more so because of her lectures – on monetary policy, employment, etc. – were rather different from her book on *Imperfect Competition*: not just clear and concise exposition step by step of an argument, but a commentary on views held by different persons which made little sense to someone who had read so little. It was through her books that Mrs Robinson came alive to us; and we read them avidly, particularly as they provided an intellectual rationale for our socialist inclinations. But it was only after a year or so of being at King's when I was invited to seminars where Mrs Robinson used to be present that I began to appreciate what a warm heart lay behind that stern exterior.

I would not have thought that her sense of fairness – of taking the side of those pilloried or just misunderstood – would make her defend on occasion views not her own or persons not particularly to her liking. I remember an occasion soon after the war when Samuelson came to Cambridge and gave a lecture where he annoyed everyone by the arrogant and messianic tone in which he tried to tell us what exciting advances in economic theory were being made in the other Cambridge, when British economists were merely going round and round in meaningless controversies. It was decided to invite him to address a small gathering next day in the Marshall Library where several academics, notably Sraffa were to be ready to take him on and to bring his ego down a few notches. But when the fun began and everyone was almost shouting at Samuelson, Mrs Robinson said in a loud voice drowning everyone else's, that surely what Samuelson meant was something else and went on to outline it as if she had known it all along and agreed with it, which was certainly not the case. But the point was made, Samuelson grabbed at the lifeline offered and everyone was well behaved thereafter.

But I came to know Mrs Robinson well only after I had left Cambridge in 1949. I used to return to Cambridge quite frequently in the 1950s and called on the Robinsons without fail at their Grange Road home. As a former student of both Joan and Austin, the welcome mat was always there, with a lunch certainly and a bed at night if needed. We met often in India also where she sometimes stayed with me in my Delhi bachelor flat. In 1958, soon after I was married, I was on my way to Washington to take up a semi-diplomatic assignment. India was in the midst of her first serious foreign-exchange crisis and I was to be a member of a new establishment we were setting up then in Washington to cultivate support for Western aid to India. Joan knew my wife's father (Professor A. K. Dasgupta) well and we had casually informed her that we would be in London en route for a few days. When I received a letter from Joan that she would come to London and meet us on the steps of the National Gallery, I was a bit nervous. I felt somehow that with her attitude towards America and her dislike of diplomatic flummery, she would not quite approve of my decision to accept the Washington assignment. When she came, apart from a good lunch and a tour of her favorite paintings in the Gallery and the offer of the use of her flat in London, she gave us a beautiful present which we still have – a set of beautiful china bowls on a superbly designed iron stand. What I had not expected were the shy words with which it was given: 'I thought I should find something which could be useful when you entertain people – you know, you will have to do that in your new job.'

We met often in India in the sixties and seventies. We learned how fond she was of her own family and of the grandchildren. Contrary to what many people think, she did not love or admire China more than India. I am sure she loved India and Indians; and as is often the case with love, it made her more impatient with India at times. I also have the feeling that if she admired the Cultural Revolution and stuck to Mao, it was not so much on ideological grounds as out of loyalty to a great leader. She certainly would have found it difficult to be warm towards Deng's China as she did towards Indira's India. There is something tragic as well as heroic about loyalty and love which struggle to survive despite frequent disappointments; and I am afraid both India and China have betrayed to some extent the love and trust she so generously bestowed upon both of them.

The last time Joan stayed with us in India was in 1979–80 when I was with the Reserve Bank in Bombay. She was coming from Cairo and was to spend some time with K. N. Raj in Kerala and stayed a few days with us both ways in Bombay. By then she was seriously ill, not really in control of herself and it was sad to see how that most penetrating pair of eyes was beginning to lose its focus. Age and illness and even disillusion had not dimmed her desire to discover not so much truth as a way of ending the inequity and ugliness of much of life. She lamented how it was difficult even in England to retire from time to time to some quiet corner in the Lake District. She was like a grandmother to our young daughter with whom she spent many long hours talking of things of interest to a 13-year-old; but suddenly she would forget whom she was talking to and ask her views on matters which she could hardly be aware of at that age. The spirit was still shining, but it was sad to see that body and mind were failing. With that memory, the news of the end came almost as a relief.

37 My First Encounter With Joan Robinson

Tibor Scitovsky

I am no student of Joan Robinson's: my interests lie elsewhere. But I was one of her supervisees when I got my first taste of economics at Cambridge in 1930, at age 19. I went to Cambridge only for a short time to learn English and international law; but, getting tired of law, switched to economics for my last two terms. I took Dennis Robertson's and Maurice Dobb's lectures and was assigned Joan Robinson as my supervisor, for whom I had to write fortnightly essays.

From this great distance in time, I remember only two things about Joan: her looks and her reaction to my first paper. She had a 'just married' look and was quite beautiful, in the gentle, dreamy fashion of German romanticism. Her dress and hairdo made me think of Goethe's Gretchen: she wore a Dirndl-like dress and had her long golden hair plaited into two pigtails, each rolled into what the Germans call Schnecken, large spirals plastered flat against the two sides of the head. [See the frontispiece in the companion volume.] The sweet innocence of her appearance, however, was belied by her chain-smoking out of a ten-inch cigarette holder and always sitting on a pouffe with her legs crossed.

Of the fortnightly essays I was supposed to write for her, I only remember the first one she assigned, which was on money. At that time, I had perhaps a four-weeks' acquaintance with economics and did not even know that there was something called monetary theory. But I did a prodigious amount of reading to prepare myself for what was to be my first English composition; and even dug up a non-Cambridge source (Knapp's *Staatliche Theorie des Geldes*), little suspecting the proud insularity of Cambridge economists. I finished the paper on time, Joan read it, correctly identified the various sources from which I had drawn my newly acquired knowledge and then delivered her verdict. She supposed that it was quite all right for me to read all those other writers on money but she could not find anywhere *my* theory of money. So she suggested that I go home and write the paper again, this time presenting my own ideas on the subject.

I went home devastated. Until then, my academic studies in law had not made me aware of the scope, let alone the need for independent thinking and contributions of my own. I remember spending an agonizing miserable two weeks until my next meeting with Joan, trying not to read, just to think, walking up and down or sitting with a blank sheet of paper in front of me and sweating blood and tears in my desperate effort to say something new about money. That was my first lesson in the hard labor of thinking for oneself; and I have been grateful to Joan for giving me that lesson ever since.

38 Reminiscences of Joan Robinson

John S. Chipman

As an undergraduate at McGill University I was privileged to be guided by my professors B. S. Keirstead and Benjamin Higgins through a rich fare of classics such as Böhm-Bawerk's *Positive Theory of Capital*, Hayek's *Pure Theory of Capital*, Hicks' *Value and Capital*, Lerner's *Economics of Control*, Marshall's *Principles of Economics*, Chamberlin's *Monopolistic Competition*, Robinson's *Imperfect Competition* and *Introduction to the Theory of Employment*, Keynes's *General Theory*, Haberler's *Prosperity and Depression*, and Hansen's *Fiscal Policy and Business Cycles*. To me it was all a wonderful discovery that gave me a lifelong love of economic analysis. The two works by Joan Robinson, particularly the *The Economics of Imperfect Competition,* made a deep impression on me. I was fascinated by the tools of marginal analysis, and awed by the brilliance and depth of the work – most especially the 'Digression on Rent'.

I met Joan Robinson for the first time in 1954, when I was spending a one-semester sabbatical leave from my position as Assistant Professor of Economics at Harvard University. I was staying at Oxford, but towards the end of the Easter term I was invited by Harry Johnson to visit Cambridge for a few days. I arrived at his rooms in King's College just in time for a party, and waited in excitement for the arrival of Joan Robinson, who had just returned from a trip to the People's Republic of China. Harry Johnson introduced me to her as soon as she arrived, and the conversation was all about her trip. She had nothing but unreserved praise for Mao Tse-Tung and his regime; I was astonished by how completely uncritical she was, but then I thought that perhaps she deliberately intended to shock me (which she did). The climax came when she explained the marvels of Chinese wash basins. She said, 'Do you know, they have invented the most marvellous kind of wash basins. Instead of having the hot and cold water coming out of separate taps, requiring one to insert a plug in the drain and wash one's hands in one's own dirt, they blend the hot and cold water through a single tap and dispense with the plug. So simple and so hygienic!' I could not help retorting, 'In the United States we have these types of taps too in our wash basins, as well as plugs, so you can exercise your freedom of choice.' She was so furious at the apparent rudeness of my response that she turned around right away, cut me dead, and started a conversation with somebody

868

else. I was quite shattered. I realized later, as I had learned in Oxford, what a strong current of anti-Americanism there was in Britain at the time, since this was the peak of the McCarthyist era. I must have struck her as an impertinent smart aleck. Harry Johnson told me not to worry, however, since she had invited me to join her and R. F. Kahn for lunch the following day.

The lunch could not have been pleasanter. She was absolutely charming, and introduced me to the delights of English cider. It was, nevertheless, a somewhat terrifying experience – rather like an oral examination. My knowledge of international trade was limited to what I had learned during a brief one-semester one-evening-per-week seminar conducted by Jacques J. Polak at Johns Hopkins (an excellent seminar, by the way), so when she contradicted my assertion that a devaluation would necessarily lead to a deterioration in the terms of trade, I realized that I was quite out of my depth (I had obviously not studied 'Beggar-My-Neighbour Remedies for Unemployment' with sufficient care). At this lunch I saw her wonderfully human side. This was indeed the Joan Robinson I had so learned to admire.

It was years later that I met her for the second and last time. She had been visiting a daughter in Toronto, I believe, and came to the Twin Cities (if I am not mistaken) to visit her other daughter at McAlister College in St Paul. It was in the early 1970s, when the radical movement among students was at its height. She gave a talk to our department, and there was a huge turnout. It was largely a negative talk concerning what was wrong with static and equilibrium economics. During the question period there were many questions from students but none from faculty. In a fury, she pointed her finger at the front rows where many of the faculty were sitting, and said, 'I know, as soon as I leave this place you're going to explain to the students what was wrong and mistaken about my talk. Why don't you have the courage to tell them while I'm here?' This did not evoke the hoped-for response. When some of us said after her talk that we saw the merit in her critique, and indeed that many of us were concerned precisely with problems of uncertainty, expectations, and disequilibrium, I think she thought we were just trying to be polite; she would have much preferred an argument. I felt very sorry that she should have become so embittered and disillusioned, much like that other great Cambridge figure, Bertrand Russell.

I will also remember Joan Robinson as a person of great intellect and great passion. She was a commanding figure in twentieth-century economics. Like Abba Lerner, she never received the honor from her peers that she deserved, and history will always wonder why.

39 Recollections of Joan

Paolo Sylos Labini

I made Joan Robinson's personal acquaintance in September 1950, soon after my arrival in Cambridge, where I spent an academic year on an Italian research scholarship. At that time I was studying the business cycle both from a theoretical and from an empirical point of view. (During the 1949–50 academic year I had been in the United States, first in Chicago, then at Harvard, where my supervisor was Joseph Schumpeter, the great theorist of the cyclical development of capitalism.) In Cambridge – the old Cambridge – I asked for and obtained, as my supervisor, Dennis Robertson, author of one of the best books ever written on industrial fluctuations. From the United States – at that time under the strong theory and policy influence of Keynesian ideas (*quantum mutatum ab illo!*) – I had written a long letter to an economist friend of mine in Rome, where I was criticizing rather sharply certain theses worked out by Keynes in his *General Theory*; that letter was then published (Sylos Labini, 1949).

There are several reasons why I was then so critical of Keynes. First, is the common propensity of young men to be non-conformists and even arrogant, and I was no exception. Second, the year before I had helped Alberto Breglia (I was assistant to him) work out a book on monetary theory (see Breglia, 1948) and Keynes's assumption concerning the exogenous character of the quantity of money appeared to me untenable, if not absurd; only for money issued by the central bank can that assumption be to some extent justified. Finally, I considered Keynes's praise of unproductive public expenditure to be not only analytically wrong but also very dangerous for economic policy.

True, that praise was presented as a paradox; to shock people and induce them to abandon the traditional theory. (To bury bottles filled with bank notes and then hire people to recover them, thus reducing unemployment and pushing up effective demand; pyramid-building; and so on.) Also true, even before the war Keynes wrote a long letter to *The Times* to dispel the impression created by those paradoxes and to point out the dangers of increasing unproductive expenditure. But most economists learned about this letter only recently, after the publication of volume XXVII of *The Collected Writings* edited by R. Moggridge (see Keynes, 1980). At the time, and for most economists since then, it was the paradoxical praise of 'pyramid-building' that prevailed. Considering the strong propensity of politicians of all times to spend public money, my criticism was not so out

870

of place. (I think that the present-day anti-Keynesian reaction is to some extent a reaction against the rapid expansion of public expenditure that, in spite of all provisos, is directly or indirectly related to the prescriptions derived from the Keynesian theory.)

When I arrived in Cambridge I discovered that many economists had read that letter; it was in English and had a provocative title 'The Keynesians' – provocative especially in Cambridge! Of course, Joan Robinson (at that time a passionate follower of Keynes) had read it. She invited me to luncheon. As soon as we sat down at the table, she started to ask question about my letter. Our conversation was by no means easy since Joan was passionately arguing her case and my chances of defending my views were rather limited. The conversation, however, did not degenerate; at the end Joan invited me to follow her course (on the theory of employment) and I accepted with pleasure.

In Cambridge I was in touch not only with Joan Robinson and with Dennis Robertson, but also Piero Sraffa and Nicky Kaldor; but my most systematic relations were with the first two. This was a rather strange affair, since the relations between Joan Robinson and Dennis Robertson were ice-cold, to say the least; the Keynesians wrongly regarded Robertson as a 'baleful Bourbon' and he considered them, Joan Robinson in particular, as terribly sectarian. Yet, my good relations with both of them were not disturbed at all by this state of affairs. More than that: my arrogant letter did not create problems with 'the Keynesians', who, fully consistent with proverbial English fair play, were very kind to me; more than once did they invite me to luncheon and, on one occasion, to the Arts Theater, founded by Keynes.

At the end of one of her lectures Joan handed me a short note where she tried to demonstrate why my criticisms of Keynes were wrong. At the end of the following lecture I handed her a written answer. This peculiar correspondence went on for at least a month and a half, covering not only the original issues, but also problems she was discussing in her lectures. She conceded very little (some things, however, she did concede); I conceded more – although I was and still am convinced that those two criticisms of mine, as well as others, were correct.

As should be clear by now, this was the beginning of long lasting relations between Joan and me, in spite of a non-negligible difference in age; relations that were both 'dialectical' and friendly – increasingly friendly. A few years after my stay in Cambridge, that is, at the beginning of 1956, when I was writing *Oligopoly and Technical Progress*, Joan sent me the proofs of *The Accumulation of Capital*, where, in chapter 19, she discusses the full cost principle, thus showing an unprejudiced attitude towards the theory of price formation. In fact, at that time the economists of repute who were taking seriously the full cost principle were a tiny minority; at present, they are still a minority, though less so. Interestingly Kalecki's theory of price formation in manufacturing industry is perfectly consistent with the full cost principle (see Kalecki, 1943). As I wrote in the aforementioned book, my debt to Joan is considerable (Sylos Labini, 1969, p.24, n.18); in that book I also published parts of letters exchanged with Joan concerning 'biased' technical progress (p.146, n.16).

Our relations remained relatively intense up to the end of her life. I used to send her my publications in English and she often sent me reprints or manuscripts. Several times, after some of her numerous tours around the world on her way back to England, she would stop in Rome, where she was a guest of a mutual friend, Gerda Blau, who was living in a delightful top-floor apartment with a small roof-garden in the center of Rome and extended hospitality to a number of the most distinguished economists of our time, like Nicky Kaldor, Tibor Scitovsky, Robert Triffin, to mention only three. On those occasions I used to invite Joan and a few Italian economists for supper; more than once, after dining, she gave seminars describing her impressions of certain countries that she had visited before coming to Rome – thus, she gave a seminar on India and another on China, after extensive travels in those two great countries.

Since I have, too, a rather high propensity to travel, sometimes we met somewhere in the world. Thus, in 1979 we met in Brazil, in a period in which I was giving a cycle of seminars in the department of economics of the Universidad Federal de Rio de Janeiro. She decided to attend one of my seminars and I did my best to provoke her – I meant to say things that, to my mind, should have aroused her critical reactions; but I was only moderately successful.

Before concluding this short note, two more memories concerning our intellectual relations.

First memory. In 1976, after participating in the Glasgow conference for the bicentenary of the *Wealth of Nations*, I sent a copy of my report to Joan for her comments. Among other things, I maintained the thesis that the criticism commonly raised against Smith – that he confused, after having distinguished them, labor commanded and labor embodied – is not justified; and I was giving my own interpretation of the different purposes of the two standards of value. Joan expressed her full agreement (see Sylos Labini, 1976).

Second memory. When I was visiting professor at the University of Sydney, I gave a lecture, in October 1980, on 'Technological Change under Contemporary Conditions: An Economist's View'; again, I sent Joan a copy of that paper (that subsequently was published in the August 1981 issue of *Economic Papers* edited by Peter Groenewegen and reprinted in Sylos Labini, 1984). As an answer to my paper, at the beginning of 1981 Joan sent me a mimeographed copy of her paper 'The Theory of Normal Prices: Spring Cleaning', that George Feiwel has published after Joan's death (see Robinson, 1985). On the front page Joan had written: 'Dear

Sylos (like many Anglo-Saxon friends she thought that Sylos was my second name, whereas it is the first part of my surname) 'I liked your piece on technological change very much. This is what we should be thinking about now – Joan.'

This was the last note I received from her.

References

Breglia, A. (1948; 3rd edn 1955) *L'economia dal punto di vista monetario* (Rome: Ateneo).

Kalecki, M. (1943) 'Costs and Prices', reprinted in *Selected Essays on the Dynamics of the Capitalist Economy 1933–1970* (1971) (Cambridge: Cambridge University Press).

Keynes, J. M. (1936) *The General Theory of Employment, Interest and Money* (London: Macmillan).

Keynes, J. M. (1980) *Activities, 1941–1946: Shaping the Post-War World: Bretton Woods and Reparations, The Collected Writings of J. M. Keynes*, Vol. XXVI (London: Macmillan).

Robertson, D. H. (1915) *A Study of Industrial Fluctuations* (London: King).

Robinson, J. (1956; new edn 1966) *The Accumulation of Capital* (London: Macmillan).

Robinson, J. (1985) 'The Theory of Normal Prices and Reconstruction of Economic Theory', in G. R. Feiwel (ed.) *Issues in Contemporary Macroeconomics and Distribution* (London: Macmillan), chapter 4.

Schumpeter, J. (1911); Americ. edn., 1934) *Theorie der wirtschaftlichen Entwicklung* (Berlin: Duncker und Humblot).

Schumpeter, J. (1939) *Business Cycles – A Theoretical, Historical and Statistical Analysis of the Capitalist Process* (New York and London: McGraw-Hill).

Sylos Labini, P. (1949) 'The Keynesians – A Letter from America to a Friend', *Banca Nazionale Quarterly Review* (November).

Sylos Labini, P. (orig. It. edn. 1956; Americ. edns 1962 and 1969) *Oligopoly and Technical Progress* (Cambridge Mass.: Harvard University Press).

Sylos Labini, P. (1976) 'Competition and Economic Growth in Adam Smith' and (1981) 'Technological Change under Contemporary Conditions: An Economist's View'; both essays have been reprinted in *The Forces of Economic Growth and Decline* (1984) (Cambridge Mass.: MIT).

40 Joan Robinson: An Informal Memoir

Duncan K. Foley

My first encounter with Joan Robinson was when I was a graduate student and read her *Review of Economic Studies* article on the concept of capital and the production function. This left me (and apparently many other people) bewildered; in my case not only because I had difficulty in following her argument, but also because due to defects in my education in economics, I was not very familiar with the concept of capital she was attacking. What I had studied of economic theory, general equilibrium theory, made me doubt that it was possible to summarize general production sets in a two-dimensional space, but I was in enough awe of those very successful theorists who asserted that it was possible, that I decided to avoid thinking about the problem too hard.

I began teaching at MIT in 1966, where there was, curiously enough, almost no discussion of the fundamental problem of capital theory. People were working on it, as the appearance of later articles and books testify, but no one was encouraging junior theorists to work on it. I suspect this silence reflected a belief at MIT that the only worthwhile goal of research in capital theory was to justify the aggregate production function, and a dawning suspicion in the wake of the reswitching controversy that no such results were forthcoming.

Robinson visited MIT in the late 1960s, and her personality made a considerable impact on me. She adopted what appeared to me then an extremely aggressive intellectual stance, probing directly at her interlocutors, both in personal conversation and in public meetings. She would begin with the strongest statement of the most controversial position she could formulate, and challenge her listeners either to assent or criticize. Her personal style made no allowances for differences in age, experience, rank, nationality, research interest, and certainly none for differences in intelligence and insight. She was in that sense very democratic and very intellectual. On the other hand, she was intimidating and sometimes discouraged the intellectual interchange she was trying to elicit, because many people find themselves able to explore controversial and complex questions only in a tentative, speculative tone. The sight of Robinson directly confronting the massive self-confidence of the American economic theoretical establishment left me with an indelible impression of her courage and passion.

The reaction of the American economic establishment at this time seemed to me to be that they could safely ignore Joan Robinson and her critique, on the grounds that everyone had agreed over the reswitching controversy, that general equilibrium capital theory with arbitrary *n*-dimensional commodity space was not subject to the critique, and that the aggregate production function was still a legitimate device for simplifying pedagogical expositions and models that were not directly concerned with the details of capital theory problems. It also seemed to me that there was something rude and ungenerous in this response to Robinson's intellectual challenge. I recall that one of my colleagues returned from a visit of several months to Cambridge, England complaining that he had received from Joan Robinson a stream of notes asking 'What is the marginal productivity of capital?' He was exasperated and bored by this.

My most direct interactions with Joan Robinson occurred several years later, when I had become interested in the labor theory of value, and convinced that it was possible to reconstruct a rational and consistent interpretation of Marx's discussion of that theory. Here I again encountered Joan Robinson in the periodical literature, but this time as the ally of precisely those benighted neoclassical theorists she had clashed with over capital theory, for Robinson agreed with Samuelson that the labor theory of value was a piece of mystical rubbish, without scientific value or explanatory significance. On the occasion of a visit by Robinson to Stanford University I had some conversations with her on this subject. Although I had by this time reached a state of ambiguous seniority that compelled me to engage Robinson's challenges, I cannot say that these conversations seemed very successful. Certainly she failed to persuade me of her position, and I doubt very much whether I was able to formulate my own sharply enough to convey its force to her.

It is particularly striking to me that Robinson maintained her opposition to the labor theory of value so tenaciously, because she also put forward very clearly what I regard as the key to the problem when she argued that the rate of surplus value, the ratio of profit income to wage income, plays the key role in determining potential accumulation in a capitalist economy. This is precisely the conclusion I arrived at in trying to reconstruct Marx's development of the labor theory of value by studying the conditions for the conservation of surplus value between labor value and money price accounting schemes. It seems to me that Robinson had two great difficulties in understanding Marx on the labor theory of value. First, she seems to have regarded it as a theory of relative prices, the claim that commodities will exchange at ratios proportional to their labor content. This prevented her from seeing the role of labor value concepts as conservation laws at the level of the system of commodity production as a whole, and thus from recognizing in Marx's language his attempt to formulate many of the same ideas about capital accumulation that Robinson herself put forward and developed as analytical tools. Second, I think that Robinson had difficulty in reading Marx, because of her discomfort with the concept of emergent properties of complex systems. Value, like the meaning of words in human language, emerges from the systematic interactions of people, and cannot be reduced to an account of individual behavior. Robinson could come to terms with the concept of value only by viewing it as essentially mystical, which was a pity, because it was Marx's path towards a precise formulation of the relation of money and price to commodity production and capital accumulation, and Robinson's own theories fall short of achieving a convincing synthesis of money with other aspects of production.

My last encounter with Joan Robinson was at a conference at Williams College only a few months before her death. What struck me most about this event was the image of Joan Robinson surrounded by much younger people (although, given her age, some of those younger people were not particularly young). I had mixed feelings about this sight. She was somehow isolated from the group of mature scientists and scholars who usually gather to celebrate each others' past successes and present power. But there was life and joy in the comfort Joan Robinson was taking at the end of her career from the affection of men and women far behind her on the path, and the pleasure she so abundantly had in their willingness to talk economics.

41 Memories of Joan Robinson

Harvey Gram

The effects of the capital theory controversy were first felt in the teaching of economics when I was a graduate student in the late 1960s. At the University of Wisconsin there were both defenders and critics of neoclassical theory. The critics did not appear to me to have any political axe to grind. They simply had an argument to present. I suffered a certain loss of faith in the logical coherence of the neoclassical theory I had learned, but the excitement generated by the debate was a great compensation.

Joan Robinson's contributions to the capital theory controversy were provocative, but they were hard to follow. Her opening salvo, 'The Production Function and the Theory of Capital' (1953) was on the reading list for an otherwise orthodox course in macroeconomic theory. What I had previously read of Joan's work, especially in trade theory, had always been a model of clarity. This was different. When I read, 'Capital is not what capital is called, it is what its name is called', I asked my professor for help. He candidly admitted that he did not understand what Joan was saying, and referred me to an article by Ed Nell which he thought had disproved her point, suggesting that the whole matter was likely to be settled shortly in favor of neoclassical theory.

Don Harris was giving lectures at Wisconsin in what was called *advanced* macroeconomic theory, but the issues were basic. Can capital be treated as a factor of production without arguing in a circle? It was then I discovered the meaning of that remarkable sentence in 'The Production Function and the Theory of Capital'. Don had spent time in Cambridge and so his students had access to mimeographed papers which were privately circulated. Among these was Joan's essay on 'Interest and Profit' which appeared in *Economic Heresies* (1971), a book she preferred to call by its subtitle, *Some Old-Fashioned Questions in Economic Theory*.

I first met Joan in 1971. Sidney Weintraub had hired me as a lecturer at the University of Waterloo where Joan was visiting for a term. The lectures she gave were meant to provoke discussion of the essays in *Economic Heresies*, but few of the students had read them and none seemed to realize they were controversial. I was trying to discover just what her disagreements with the neoclassics were. It was a difficult task because she did not play by the usual rules. Criticism of neoclassical theory by neoclassical

877

economists can often be traced to a minor change in the assumptions of a familiar argument. The implications of the change are then worked out within the framework of supply and demand equilibrium. Joan had long given up on this approach which characterized her early work in *The Economics of Imperfect Competition* (1933). In 'Thinking About Thinking' (1979), she also pointed out that she had given up looking for *complete* theories, which I took to mean consistent theories of equilibrium. Her interest lay in finding the causes and consequences of inconsistency and conflict. This made her arguments difficult to follow for anyone who was looking for an equilibrium solution. Moreover, by 1971 Joan's verbal and written arguments had become very terse. One need only compare *The Rate of Interest and Other Essays* (1952) with later treatments of the same topics to see a process of distillation taking place.

Joan's office was next to mine at Waterloo, and I often drove her to the next town where she was staying with her daughter's family. Most of our conversations were about economists rather than economics. I did not know how to argue outside the framework of an equilibrium model. It was pointless to sail off into formalities which didn't interest her – and presumptuous, too, in the presence of one who had discovered the reswitching phenomenon without the aid of algebra (1956, pp.109–10). We did, however, discuss the manuscript of *An Introduction to Modern Economics* (1973) she was writing with John Eatwell. I discovered then how she chose her assumptions. When they were familiar and convenient, but didn't explain the facts as she saw them, she threw the assumptions out and asked me to help her find new ones. She also showed me the drafts of her Ely lecture which was given that year at the Christmas meetings of the American Economic Association in New Orleans. The sweep of her rhetoric left me with little to say.

Joan was continuing her correspondence with Paul Samuelson on capital theory issues, trying to resolve her disagreement with him concerning the effects of changes in the rate of profit as opposed to the results of differences. She showed me a letter in which Samuelson referred to chapter 12 of his *Linear Programming and Economic Analysis* (1958), written with Dorfman and Solow, for a discussion of efficient capital accumulation. I found myself defending the theory of intertemporal equilibrium, about which Joan later wrote, 'I have never been able to make that theory stand up long enough to knock it down' (1980, p.128). My difficulties were only partly mathematical. The real problem was trying to justify the crucial assumption of perfect foresight: what Samuelson later described as the 'reaiming behavior of speculators' (Samuelson, 1967, p.228). Joan would have none of it. And when I said without perfect foresight there could be no equilibrium, she answered, 'Exactly!' At the time, I had not read her own essay on growth equilibrium with perfect foresight, 'Accumulation and the

Production Function' (1959). For her, it had been an exercise in futility, the purpose of which was to expose a neoclassical error.

In later years, Joan and I met in Cambridge and in New York. The only satisfactory response to the arguments she would make was to attempt to think through the problem under discussion in some new and interesting way. She knew the equilibrium answers. Joan was a sharp debater, and perhaps I charted too safe a course. Once, she told me she had mellowed a great deal, a reference to past confrontations about which I knew little. Those who had experienced them sometimes felt resentment towards her in spite of their agreement with her views.

At the end of her life, Joan was distressed by the course of developments in economic theory, including those in the classical tradition she had helped to revive. She regarded equilibrium as a deadening influence seeping back into every revolutionary break with neoclassical theory. The last time I saw her she was asking what had gone wrong. She thought that Keynes's theory of effective demand, enriched by Kalecki, and generalized to the long period in her own work could provide the basis for an approach to economics in which the force of history could supersede the lullaby of equilibrium. I had nothing very encouraging to offer, but she took comfort in the fact that a few 'heretics' were carrying on the debates she had begun. She was especially pleased to meet people who, independently of their political beliefs, had discovered sound theoretical reasons for abandoning the all-embracing equilibrium framework of neoclassical analysis in favor of a more rough and ready historical approach to the study of economic systems.

References

Dorfman, R., P. A. Samuelson and R. M. Solow (1958) *Linear Programming and Economic Analysis* (New York: McGraw-Hill).

Robinson, J. V. (1933) *The Economics of Imperfect Competition* (London: Macmillan).

Robinson, J. V. (1952) *The Rate of Interest and Other Essays*. Republished as *The Generalisation of the General Theory and Other Essays* (London: Macmillan, 1979).

Robinson, J. V. (1953) 'The Production Function and the Theory of Capital', in *Collected Economic Papers*, Vol. II (Oxford: Blackwell, 1960) pp.114–31.

Robinson, J. V. (1956) *The Accumulation of Capital* (London: Macmillan).

Robinson, J. V. (1959) 'Accumulation and the Production Function', in *Collected Economic Papers*, Vol. II (Oxford: Blackwell, 1960) pp.132–44.

Robinson, J. V. (1971) *Economic Heresies: Some Old-Fashioned Questions in Economic Theory* (New York: Basic Books).

Robinson, J. V. (1979) 'Thinking About Thinking', in *Collected Economics Papers*, Vol. V (Oxford: Blackwell) pp.110–19.

Robinson, J. V. (1980) 'Debate: 1970s', in *What are the Questions? and Other Essays: Further Contributions to Modern Economics* (Armonk, NY: Sharpe) pp.123–30.

Robinson, J. V. and L. Eatwell, (1973) *An Introduction to Modern Economics* (London: McGraw-Hill).

Samuelson, P. A. (1967) 'Indeterminacy of Development in a Heterogeneous-Capital Model with Constant Saving Propensity', in K. Shell (ed.) *Essays on the Theory of Optimal Economic Growth* (Cambridge, Mass.: MIT) pp.219–31.

42 A View of Joan Robinson's Last Decade

Vivian Walsh

I first met Joan in 1971, and in an important sense I met her at just the right time to be open to her influence. One of the odder characteristics of the United States in the late sixties and early seventies was the existence of younger economists (and graduate students) who, although they had become deeply distrustful of establishment *policies*, notably the war in Vietnam, still accepted more or less without question orthodox economic *theory*. Although not nearly as young as most of the people whom I have in mind, in other respects I was a case in point. I had just published what can certainly be described as a neoclassical book.

Then I met Joan in the early Fall. I would love to be able to say that as soon as I heard her speak I instantly saw the light. But the fact is that I attended a whole term of her faculty and student seminar at the University of Waterloo that Fall and, though increasingly fascinated, remained somewhat confused. Certain things, of course, struck me forcibly from the beginning. The foremost was her utter seriousness – her implicit belief that economics, properly understood, mattered – and not just to a few specialists, but to the future of the world. I do not in the least mean that she was solemn or pompous (occupational diseases of the academic profession). No one was ever less so. Her wit was lightning fast and cut like a razor, as those who have felt its edge may be left to attest. No, I mean that she had a quality which calls for an old fashioned phrase like moral seriousness – a phrase which will sound odd to those economists who still cling to the particular fact/value distinction which they long ago borrowed from logical empiricism, and which within philosophy fell with the discredited epistemology upon which it rested (see Walsh, 1987a).

Moral seriousness was the last of the graces which I had come to expect from economic theory. I expected a good deal of formal elegance, obtained at the cost of an heroic degree of abstraction from the human condition. Now suddenly I was confronted with a woman who had the stark and deadly simplicity of Antigone. She was defying the laws of the orthodoxy, simply because she must. No adornment was needed, nor could be draped over such a figure of indomitable purpose. Yet in this very simplicity there was something incomprehensible to me for, although she spoke directly and precisely, she spoke out of a whole complex intellectual tradition utterly different from that of current neoclassical economics, which I had become used to.

Then, after she had returned to England, I attended a seminar given by Harvey Gram on March 14, 1973. Later I learned that he had come back to Canada in 1971 to be with Joan. He presented and compared two models, one neo-Walrasian and the other a model of commodity reproduction which he referred to as a Cambridge model, and which was of a type which we were later to call modern classical.

Suddenly I saw clearly in what I can only call (forgive me, Joan!) a *general equilibrium* setting what I had not seen when it was presented informally: that there were at issue here two strikingly different classes of models. The next morning I was in Harvey's office, asking if he would contribute some chapters on this quite different kind of model to a book which I was then writing. He agreed, and we began to meet in the evenings to look at what I had already written and see if he could live with it. But one evening some months later I told him that I wanted to scrap everything I had written on the project, and work in equal partnership with him on a completely different book, whose whole structure would turn on the distinctions between these two different sorts of models. Our work was published some years later (1980).

In May of 1974 Joan came back to Canada and stayed with Harvey and during the following years she stayed with me several times. When she was not in North America we saw her in Cambridge, sometimes staying with her, sometimes dropping by for shorter visits when one of us was in London or Paris. She read several versions of our book during this time, and I remember one version which had her marvelous terse comments scattered over the pages. And through those long years my understanding of her, beginning absolutely from nothing, began (as I fondly and perhaps wrongly believe!) growing and changing, and has continued to do so ever since.

Yet even then, during the years up to 1980, I approached Joan from a direction which might seem very odd to anyone who knew the Cambridge of her youth. For I completely ignored Marshall and even Keynes, and approached her through Sraffa and his classical antecedents. I believed this to be dictated by the nature of the book which Harvey and I were writing. We had two main objectives. The first was historical: to show that in the primary sources of the history of economic analysis one could distinguish the developing formulations of a certain pair of significantly different classes of models. The second was analytic: to show that the crucial concepts of each of these two classes of models could be distinguished from those of the other, even in their simplest versions. We chose to end the historical part of our work with Walras, and not to treat Marshall. We could argue that Walras, and not Marshall, was the thinker whom modern neoclassics regard as their founding father. But the truth is that we chiefly avoided Marshall from self preservation – sensing that to treat him *properly* would open up immense complications! We have been justly criticized, by otherwise admiring reviewers, for this sin of omission. Keynes and Keynesian problems, on the other hand, we ruled out explicitly, on the ground that their treatment, however important, was not necessary to the formulation and comparison of the *simplest* models of either class. (On models and theory, see Walsh, 1987b.) As a result of this, my experience of Joan for a number of years was primarily of her reactions to a pair of different kinds of general equilibrium models.

At first, of course, we had great difficulty in getting her to agree to our speaking of *classical* models of general equilibrium. Nevertheless the fact of the matter is that she eventually accepted our use of this idea as a central part of our analysis. Whereas, with regard to other things which she would *not* accept, she resisted year after year until she wore us down. I think it is important to note here that the general equilibrium models (classical *and* neoclassical) which we presented her with in successive drafts always depicted each model *in* equilibrium, and made no claim that a satisfactory formal dynamic process had been specified which would bring that model *into* equilibrium, were it not already in that state. She really objected to any such claim, as indeed I have noted in Chapter 9 of this volume. But, she was always willing to *use* the Sraffa system, interpreted as a snapshot of a model economy in equilibrium.

As I read the classics, including Marx, over the years from 1973 to 1980, I came to understand much more about Joan. I began to see her as one of the surviving defenders of an ancient tradition. Of course, this was just one *aspect* of her thought – remember, I was not then looking at her work with Keynes, to mention just one of her other major contributions. Nor, on the other hand, did I at first realize that she had learned of classical ideas initially from the work of Marshall, and only later from Marx and from Ricardo (under the influence of Sraffa). Indeed, on some points I differed from her interpretation of the great original classics. The most noteworthy case, I think, was that of Adam Smith. She seemed at times to be almost willing to make the neoclassical tradition a direct descendant of Smith. Certainly it is true that he was a founder of allocation theory, but his was a theory of the allocation of surplus output (as was Cantillon's – see Walsh, 1987b). His interest lay, not in the timeless allocation of a set of parametric factor services, but in the repeated allocation of surplus to the reproduction of those inputs needed to bring about the greatest possible accumulation of capital.

Turning to the neoclassical tradition, Harvey and I also found ourselves sometimes differing from her interpretation. I will never forget her reaction to her first reading of our chapter on Walras: 'You make him out to be quite a hero!' she said. 'Yes, we do,' I replied, 'but I think he was.' He was no mere technician, I told her. An important part of the motivation for his general equilibrium model was an idea of social justice (think what you will of it) in which he believed deeply, as had his father. I told her that I had come to like Léon Walras after many happy hours spent listening to Bill Jaffé talk of the young Walras and the Paris in which he lived. He must have been a charming, romantic youth, not at all unlike the Marx of the Economic and Philosophical Manuscripts. As I spoke, I was thinking of the irony of the whole thing: Walras must have been just the sort of brilliant, idealistic young person whom (from my experience of watching her with people) Joan could not resist. But Walras for her had never come to life. I wanted to say that production by means of the services of a set of given resources was a much more strictly limited, carefully confined idea for Walras than it became in the hands of his followers – that he was very aware of the need to reach a treatment of *reproduction*, and of the fact that this would entail something fundamentally different from the model which he had been able to set up. But I sensed that she would not be sympathetic. After all, she was only just prepared to tolerate even *modern classical* general equilibrium models.

As for the revival of the classical tradition, as everyone knows now, it did not begin with Joan or Sraffa (or even with John von Neumann in the thirties). It was already very much alive in the early twentieth century work of the School of Kiel, two of whose one-time members are of course well known in America today: Wassily Leontief and Adloph Lowe (see J. Halevi, D. Laibman and E. J. Nell, eds. 1988).

I came to know Oskar Morgenstern in the early 1970s after he wrote me a charming letter praising my book (1970) and inviting me to visit him in Princeton. Indeed, some years later he read and offered helpful comments on an early draft of the work which Harvey and I were writing. The last time we ever saw him, which was in New York at a luncheon, in April 1976, he talked sadly of meeting Joan and trying to talk to her. It had not been a success. 'Joan was never fair to Johnny,' he told us. I think it must be said that Joan did not reach out to modern classical work that did not, directly or indirectly, emanate from Cambridge. It was not as if no strictly modern classical work was being done in America: Oskar Morgenstern and the younger people he influenced were keeping alive the tradition of Neumann, and the grand old man of the School of Kiel, Adolphe Lowe, was publishing and influencing younger people at the graduate faculty of the New School. Still, even if one were to list *everyone* doing work of this kind in America in the 1970s, it would have amounted to only a tiny fraction of the profession. Even the most elementary understanding of Sraffa was uncommon. Joan's view of American economics was a generalization that was unfair to a few individuals. But it was not all that inaccurate as generalizations go.

Having listened to Joan at length on these matters on many occasions from 1971 until shortly before the end of her life, my view is that she retained her bitterness towards the American economists, making few (though important) exceptions. But it must be remembered that she had seen her American opponents in the capital theory controversy fight a long drawn out rear guard action against Cambridge, England. She had seen the final admissions and concession of victory to herself and Sraffa made – only to be followed by the same old theory, as if the whole controversy had never taken place. She had seen the textbooks, those busy money changers in the temple of learning, happily conducting business as usual, selling the illegitimately drawn ideological conclusions of the marginal productivity 'theory' of distribution for the edification of the young and the ignorant.

What perhaps she did not see (or simply *would not* see!) was that her true enemies were not her intellectual opponents in the Cambridge controversy, who in the end granted her a discreet and quiet victory. Like her, they cared about serious theory, and, in their very different way, about the good of society. Her true enemies were surely those who, ignoring both sides in the capital controversy, were busily cobbling together an economic argument for the new Right. As America swung massively to the Right, during her last years, her only possible alliance there would have had to be with her former opponents, who were by then in the furthest 'left' position which had any substantial constituency. But I for one saw no trace of willingness to accept any compromise – it was simply not in her nature. And then I think she never forgave the American liberal democratic economists for what she saw as their tacit acceptance of military spending as a tool of full employment policy and their failure to condemn the Vietnam war until it became safe (and indeed fashionable) to do so.

The Bastard Keynesians fell from favor, and I heard her amusement at this, the beginnings of which she lived to see. But they were not succeeded by the Cambridge post-Keynesians: they were succeeded by people whose views would have been anathema to her. And there would surely have been bitter irony for her in the fact that whatever weakened the Bastard Keynesians had as one of its consequences the strengthening of reaction. But she did live to see all these things come to pass, and I never heard her judgment on them.

It may cause some surprise that, despite our sinful tendencies towards general equilibrium, and my flagrantly neoclassical background, Harvey and I were never given the rough edge of her tongue. That is, as far as I can recall – and it is not the sort of thing one would be likely to forget. In those years she went through successive versions of our book like an avenging wind, and was ruthless in argument. But although we argued all day (and sometimes well into the night), we were always content with our lot, because we felt that she was spotting genuine flaws in our work which needed correction, and never arguing just for victory. We never felt that the discipline was undeserved. We have heard from others that she was a tyrant, but we just did not find this to be true – and we gave her plenty of opportunity to show tyrannical qualities if she possessed them. Joan understood very deeply what a struggle it can be to escape from conventional ideas. She often quoted Keynes's famous remarks about this, and spoke of her own struggle (to escape from the pseudo production function). This made her tireless in explanation, once she was convinced that one was seriously trying to understand. But I think that her consciousness of the layers of prejudice that can come with age gave her a special love for young people, whose minds might hopefully be fresher and less closed. I know that she specifically asked to be allowed to teach beginning undergraduates – not a request that would be typical of her intellectual peers in America. As it happened, I had a vivid demonstration of Joan's love of young people shortly after we met. As I have already mentioned, I was attending her seminar but not yet understanding much of what she said, and I was certainly not finding it easy to talk to her alone. Then something totally unexpected happened. I had at that time a young friend who was there on a visit. I had taken her to hear Joan, though she knew nothing of economics, simply because I thought Joan a very remarkable human being whom it would be worthwhile for her to encounter. Then one day shortly after this, my young friend and I were walking down a university corridor past Joan's office. It was a lovely day in early Fall.

Suddenly my friend turned and shot into the office, where Joan could be seen at her desk through the open door, and announced in a crisp young English voice: 'Oh, I say, Professor Robinson – we're going for a drive in the country to an English tea shop – you probably don't think they exist in Canada – won't you come with us; we can all squeeze into the MG – it's such a lovely day!'

Joan straightened up and turned to face us and her face lit up with a positively beaming smile, and she said, 'You dear child; I'd love to!' We drove off with the top down (we had offered to put it up, but Joan said no) into the golden afternoon. We had the kind of tea I used to love when on holiday from my boarding school, with hot scones and lots of rich homemade cake, and everyone happily overate. The ladies who ran the tearoom made a great fuss over Joan. One of them was the widow of a British officer. All the while I quietly observed Joan and the young girl. Joan, her eyes shining, was drawing the girl out, asking her about her acting, her stage experience, her ambitions. They were happily chatting away as if they had known one another for years, utterly at ease. From that day forth I never felt strange with Joan again.

It occurs to me that in stressing that she was old when I met her, I may have given the impression that Joan was a frail old woman. Nothing could be further from the truth. Her step was firm and vigorous, her head with its fine bones held high. Her great mane of white hair, in public always coiled up, fell nearly to her waist when free. She was old as Yeats makes one imagine Lady Gregory to have been, firm in her undaunted pride before the vulgarity of her detractors, but with a pride that was established in humility before the inexorable demands of truth. She was the undefeated human spirit, defying age. And in her openness to the young and to the new, and in her sense of wonder, she had a freshness that could stand comparison with youth. She seemed as old as Troy but as new as morning.

Joan wanted everyone to call her by her Christian name, and at first blush this sometimes embarrassed the very young. But in no time they were doing it quite naturally. I remember with fond amusement how she insisted on one occasion that she was not to be introduced to an audience as 'Lady Robinson'. She achieved a fine blend of left wing propriety and upper class disdain for the parvenu. I was reminded vividly of certain formidable county ladies of my childhood, one of them an M.F.H. to boot. And of course county families (in the Ireland I grew up in at any rate!) were not too thrilled about new titles. I remember Joan commenting on a somewhat modestly distinguished British Worthy who had just been given a life peerage: 'Oh I'm glad he's got it, poor old thing – he needed it, you know.'

It would never do to ignore the fact that she could have a quite wicked sense of humor on occasion. I shall not forget what happened to a young Irish lad who wanted to have a full dress discussion of the labor theory of value with her. I had been warned by a young friend who saw much of Joan in Cambridge (and this was someone who was still an active rugger player) that she was likely to take one on a walk of twelve miles or so. Heedless of this warning, the Irish boy and I drove off in my M.G. for his discussion of labor values. It was early summer, but already quite hot, and Joan was under canvas in Ontario, camping with her daughter and her grandchildren, to whom she was devoted. She emerged from her tent dressed in fatigues and combat boots, and marched us off over hill and dale. After what felt like several hours, she finally sat down, in the sun, and produced refreshment. It consisted of a fifth of John Jameson. Three glasses completed her provisions, and she proceeded to pour drinks. The lad who, let it be recalled, was Irish, could not bring himself to admit that he was not really quite up to drinking drink for drink with her. She then turned on him the full force of her charm and her analytic power. He was bright, and rather well read on the transformation problem, but he was not equal to the total demands that had been made of him. As we drove home, after a picnic dinner with Joan and her family, he said, 'Ah God, I wouldn't want to be on a long march with herself. I don't remember the half of what she said, but she had great arguments. Doesn't she get tired at all?'

This, by the way, was the representative view of Joan's stamina on the part of my young friends, usually students who volunteered to help entertain her when she came to stay. She was up by seven, or eight at the latest, and did not retire before twelve or one. When Harvey and I were working with her, that occupied the day, but there were evenings, and days after our work was done. She liked good conversation with young people, as by then I knew. They came willingly, and enjoyed her, but they were usually exhausted after about four hours. So I arranged them in four-hour watches as if we were on an ocean race.

And, just as in ocean racing, the cook's role was important. Joan did not like the taste of meat (she stressed that she was not a vegetarian on moral grounds), but she would eat eggs, cheese and fish. And she loved good food and wine. Usually whoever was acting as her hostess cooked some of the meals. I cooked some, my specialty being cold poached salmon mayonnaise (a great favorite in Irish country houses during my childhood) which she clearly liked, as she also liked my trout. But the few things I do well (there are only about eight!) are unfortunately mostly made up of red meats. So volunteers were encouraged, and showed great bravery (I remember one young woman chasing lobsters all over the kitchen floor), and many of their soufflés did not fall. Despite the intensity of our work, luncheon was a serious meal (it was at one of these that the lobsters made a futile bid for freedom), and every dinner was a carefully planned occasion. Sometimes we dined out. In the village where the teashop was, there was also a little bistro run by a Basque of considerable charm and strong character (he was reputed to have chased away someone who infuriated him with a kitchen knife). He *always* called Joan 'M'Lady' and got away with it. When at the beginning she tried to stop him, his English did one of its quick disappearing acts. He would tease her in an amazing mixture of languages, in which there was just enough that was familiar to guess at his meaning. In some fashion of his own he revered her because he saw her as both a grande dame and a revolutionary. I have known simple Irish country people who would have understood his point of view.

But there was a dramatic change in her the last time she came to stay with me, early in May 1980. That Spring I was dividing my time between the graduate faculty of the New School in Manhattan, and the State University of New York at Plattsburg, and I had a cottage near the College in Plattsburg, where Joan came to stay. She gave a talk at the College, and was very well entertained by them, and clearly liked the people there. But she was very tired – the fire was dying down in her. Geoff Harcourt was also staying with me, and he gave off an Aussie cheerfulness that warmed her and got her going again on some of the old favorite themes. But anyone who had known her in her *vigorous* old age could see that now she had indeed become very frail. Her mind was as clear as ever, but long conversations tired her now, and she walked even short distances with difficulty.

Now it has been suggested that by this time she had changed her mind on certain great issues of theory. I have commented on this claim in Chapter 9 so here I will remark only that, while I have found her terribly changed as to physical stamina, I recall no change in her theoretical position. I do remember her asking me why Sraffa's ideas had taken so long simply to be known about in the United States. It was obvious from what she said that the understanding of the Sraffa system *mattered* to her – she had not stopped caring about the fate of this piece of abstract theory. So she really was not willing to abandon all theory. Nor was she questioning the *validity* of Sraffa's system: she simply wanted to hear my thoughts on why it had been so slowly known about. I mentioned some obvious reasons why Sraffa might not appeal to American tastes and then thought of something else which I think is worth repeating simply because of her reaction to it.

I laughed and said that since America was the land of salesmen, perhaps one should consider the question in terms of selling! Sraffa's book was perfectly designed for only *one* purpose: to win a logical victory on the ground of high theory. It was for all the world like a formula racing car – one could not sell it as a sportscar to be driven on the highway. And where, after all, could one get it serviced? Joan's eyes had their wicked sparkle – the one I knew so well.

But now, I argued, 'People are writing books that embody certain Sraffian ideas in models constructed using modern American (algebraic) parts, which any graduate student here will know how to take apart and put back together. There's a high powered Italian production model by Pasinetti, and others will follow!'

She was laughing now: 'Do you really think this will happen?'

I said that it might be slow, but that in time I thought it would. She had another glass of wine. This was not a woman who had come to reject all theory.

When Joan's *Collected Economic Papers* (1980) came out in their American edition, at MIT Press, Harvey and I were asked by Moses Abramovitz to write a retrospective article on her economics and specifically on her *Collected Economic Papers*. We produced a first draft fairly quickly, and Harvey went to stay with her in Cambridge, to discuss it. She told him that she was 'highly gratified,' saying much the same thing in a brief letter to me. She never saw the final published version. Everyone who has seen both versions has said that the final one is stronger, and in a way they are right. But by then we had been forced to make hard choices, and to take positions on subtle questions on which, probably, the final word will never now be said. During this period I began to ask myself whether we were becoming Bastard Robinsonians! I wondered what she would have said if she could have seen what we were writing, in our effort to make her intelligible to people trained in an utterly different tradition.

It was equally necessary to go back to *her* tradition and immerse oneself in it. I had rather dodged this, as I have already noted, while working on the book with Harvey: we had the original classics and Sraffa between us and much of Joan's intellectual background. Now there was nothing to protect us from Keynes – and even more to the point, from Marshall. As I immersed myself in Joan's writings, and especially her *Collected Papers*, it became more and more obvious that one could get nowhere without a serious study of Marshall. She was always telling us (and wrote somewhere) that 'The more I read Marshall the less I like him and the more I like his economics.'

It seemed to me that her dislike of his character needed to be simply disregarded in judging her intellectual debt to his work. She belonged to a generation who regarded everything Victorian as unspeakably despicable. The literary critics of the period dismissed Dickens as simply a vulgar best seller, who by accident had written one or two great novels like *David Copperfield*. Victorian artistic and intellectual tastes, Victorian furniture and Victorian moral attitudes were equally out of style – how could Marshall hope to survive? One wonders how Marx, who was among other things a great Victorian, got read at all! I had always loved Dickens and this now made it easy for me to read and like Marshall. And for me Marshall's occasional condescension and moral superiority were redeemed by his genuine humanity, and by a feeling for the sufferings of the poor wholly lacking in 'supply siders' and other such recent trendies.

So I was willing to dismiss Joan's dislike for the man. What was it then that was so important for her about his economics? Harvey and I took the view in our article (1983) that what was important was closely connected with the differences between Marshall's short period (from which Keynes took his start) and an elementary time interval of an Arrow-Debreu-McKenzie model. Since then I have come to feel (as I have said in Chapter 9) that *some* of the characteristics of Marshall's (and Joan's) short period are beginning to appear in the strange setting of certain current models of temporary equilibrium – despite these models' possessing a structure (Walrasian) that would have made her very cross. She hated and rejected *complete* Walrasian general equilibrium; but perhaps so-called non-Walrasian equilibrium is a horse of a different color.

As for the long period, I could not see what Marshall was up to there as long as I accepted uncritically what she said about it. She overplayed the role of demand and supply in his long-period theory. In his 'theoretically perfect long period' (Marshall, 1961, p.379) we find that 'cost of production governs value . . . there would be no reflex influence of demand' (Marshall, p.367). He is quite aware that without surplus there would be no profit and no accumulation of capital (Marshall, 1961, p.224). Joan stressed his tendency to moralize about profits, and indeed he was prone to this. But he was not analytically confused: he knew that profits reflected the existence of surplus. What initially misled me was that I did not see that Marshall had a *second* concept of the long period. He knew, as Adam Smith had known before him, that in the real world one would never see his theoretically perfect long period. But an economy would be always gravitating towards it (Marshall, 1961, p.346). And so, of course, the forces of demand *would* play a role, as is natural in a gravitation process. And this would be true even over rather long periods of *historical* time.

For all Joan's avowed liking for Marshall's economics, I never got from her the idea that he had preserved a good deal of the long-period point of view of the classics: she presented him in a way that made him appear the quintessential neoclassic. But now as I read them both, it seems to me clear that she had an essentially classical long-period point of view in work done *before* she began to re-examine Ricardo through Sraffian eyes. As I have already said, I think she got it from Marshall. But now that I know what questions I really want to ask her about Marshall, I can never have her answer.

References

Gram, H. and V. Walsh (1983) 'Joan Robinson's Economics in Retrospect,' *Journal of Economic Literature*, 21.

Halevi, J., D. Laibman and E. J. Nell (1989) (eds) *Beyond the Steady State: Essays in the Revival of Growth Theory* (forthcoming).

Marshall, A. (1961) *Principles of Economics: An Introductory Volume*, 9th (Variorum) (ed.) C. W. Guillebaud, Vol. I (London: Macmillan for the Royal Economic Society).

Robinson, J. (1980) *Collected Economic Papers*, 5 vols (Cambridge, Mass.: MIT).

Walsh, V. (1970) *An Introduction to Contemporary Microeconomics* (New York: McGraw-Hill).

Walsh, V. (1987a) 'Philosophy and Economics', in J. Eatwell, M. Milgate and P. Newman (eds) *The New Palgrave: A Dictionary of Economic Theory and Doctrine* (London: Macmillan).

Walsh, V. (1987b) 'Cantillon, Richard', in *The New Palgrave*.

Walsh, V. and H. Gram (1980) *Classical and Neoclassical Theories of General Equilibrium: Historical Origins and Mathematical Structure* (New York: Oxford University Press).

43 Joan Robinson: A Memoir

Edward Nell

When I first met her in the fifties, I liked to think of Joan playing opposite Humphrey Bogart in a John Huston film about the Resistance. She'd have been perfect – black clothes and red stockings, a commanding presence, cool, tough, single-mindedly loyal, fiercely partisan. Strong progressive opinions, but no nonsense about accepting dogmas, Marxist or otherwise. Critical of bourgeois society and its hypocrisy. A fighter, fearless and tough as they come.

Perhaps not a film, though. Joan was always part of real life, not of art. Later I thought, more like the Sandanistas – an English Nora Astorga! But again, perhaps not. Nora Astorga seems comfortable as a woman; I don't think Joan was. Which may partly account for what many found disproportionately harsh in her criticism.

Yet it was really not the harshness which was the problem; her opponents complained, but perhaps they deserved what they got. There was a lack of balance in her work between the positive or constructive and the negative and critical. Her emphasis, and the conclusions she highlighted, in her principal contributions have mostly been critical: in capital theory, of course. But consider her essay on Marx; it was her criticism of the labor theory of value that caught attention. As for Keynes, it is her critique of 'bastard Keynesianism' that is remembered. Even ingenious theorems like the 'Golden Rule' were developed during the course of a critique of marginal productivity theory. *The Accumulation of Capital* ends up in a set of disconnected scenarios designed to show what was wrong with Harrod's approach, on the one hand, and neo-classical thinking on the other. Even *The Economics of Imperfect Competition* had a primarily critical objective – to undermine the marginal productivity theory of wages, and the associated ideas of perfect competition. (Of course, it also had the positive aim of explaining the existence of excess capacity in conditions that were clearly in some sense competitive.) And finally, after initially welcoming Sraffa's great contribution, she turned critical of the efforts of some of her closest friends and associates to develop a constructive account of capitalism on the foundations Sraffa laid. It was an equilibrium theory, she argued, and equilibrium can tell us nothing about history. At a stage in her life where she might have been expected to sum up her life's work in a way that might have provided guidance for her students and followers, she offered a critique of the whole project: instead of answers, she gave us *What Are the Questions?*

Well, why not? The profession certainly needs critics, and harsh ones. Look at virtually any mainstream journal these days and you will find pre-Keynesian thinking, standard and marginal productivity theory, perfect competition, and all the rest, parading through the pages as if there were nothing wrong.

But this is exactly the point. You can't beat something with nothing. No matter how fierce the criticism, no matter how well delivered the blows, neoclassical theory never dies. Like a vampire it rises from the grave the next night, to prey on the unwary. Only those protected by the amulet of another theory will be safe from its ravages. And that is the protection that many of Joan's students and followers sought, but which she never provided.

Yet she might have. The materials were certainly there, particularly in *The Accumulation of Capital*, and the later *Essays*. The presentation may be deficient, but the conception is clear: here, for the first time in academic economics is a two-sector 'classical' growth model, turning on an inverse relationship between wages (=consumption) and growth (financed by saving out of profits). Neither prices nor choice of technique are governed by scarcity relationships; by contrast, investment, depending chiefly on 'animal spirits', governs both output and profits, (given the saving rate) and thus, indirectly, the choice of technique. Prices depend on technical coefficients and on profits, and so, ultimately on investment. Her objective was to extend Keynes's vision to the long run, showing that investment governs savings, the active dominates the passive, there also, exactly reversing the neoclassical growth models developed by Solow, Swan, Meade, Uzawa *et al*. She tried to provide both the vision and some of the technical foundations.

My favorite among her later works has always been *Exercises in Economic Analysis*, a relatively good-tempered and constructive work, full of common sense and shrewd insight. (Also excellent diagrams that students have to draw for themselves.) But it was rudimentary, from a technical point of view. It contained the basis for a theory of accumulation of the rate of profit and the rate of interest. It set forth a theory of the mark-up, and, by way of contrast, an account of scarcity prices. It contrasted socialism and capitalism, with many perceptive insights; and it dealt with effective demand, and provided important hints about the working of the monetary system. It contained criticism, of course, but the positive side was much more in evidence. These were the topics that provided a basis for an alternative account of the working of the economy. The material was there, but it needed more work, not only by Joan, but by a school of supporters. It could have been developed, but so far it has been neglected. (A later attempt, jointly with John Eatwell, fell between two stools: it did not dig deep enough to build new theory, but it was too abstract for a textbook.) Her later work became overwhelmingly critical. In her last years, she was acutely aware of what she called the failure to found an alternative school, and she lamented the drift back to neoclassicism, occurring even at Cambridge.

Yet the simplest explanation for the failure of the alternative vision is that it has never been fully developed. Where is the constructive non-neoclassical work to compare with James Meade's multivolume magnum opus? Where is the alternative to Samuelson's *Foundations*, Hicks's *Value and Capital?* To the constructions of Arrow and Debreu, or Arrow and Hahn? An alternative vision is one thing, an alternative construction quite another. *The General Theory* makes too many concessions, *Production of Commodities* is a prelude, a foundation, but the edifice is still to be built. *The Accumulation of Capital,* or the later *Exercises,* reworked and developed fully, as a positive theory, could and should have been part of such a construction, but it has yet to be erected.

44 Robinson–Hahn Love–Hate Relationship: An Interview

Frank Hahn

Feiwel: Did Joan misperceive the neoclassical economics she was criticizing? Where was she right? If so, did she go the wrong way about it?

Hahn: One ought rather to start at *The Accumulation of Capital* – a neoclassical book through and through. It is linear programming that she invented for herself. You will find that Lawrence Klein, in his review of the book, pointed this out. Linear programming, as we all know, is neoclassical economics. Joan's problem was that she took neoclassical economics as represented in the textbooks as saying that output is a function of capital and labor, rather than as a description of a general equilibrium system. She certainly completely misperceived what neoclassical economics was about. There were two reasons for this. One was that she found it difficult to understand what one means by simultaneous equations. She always held that she needed to have causality in the story somewhere. Secondly, because she did not really understand what *marginal* meant, she could not understand that someone could calculate in his head what it was worth his while to do if he had a little bit more of this or that. She always felt that the moment one thought one had a little more capital, one would have to take into account that the rest of the system would change. There was no way one could have a little bit more capital without all the prices changing straight away. She did not know the envelope theorem ... I think that a great deal of her objection was simply misperception.

However, curiously enough, she also hit on something very interesting, but she never made anything of it. The whole problem of having an aggregate measure of capital, or the Wicksell effect, or double switching has nothing whatsoever to do with the marginal productivity theory of distribution – whatever that may be – but has everything possible to do with dynamics. In other words, if the capital aggregate is ill-behaved, then it is quite possible that the dynamic system can behave very badly as well. That is to say, if you were looking out of golden age or out of steady state, and you wanted to see whether the system approached it or not, then the fact that capital goods are heterogeneous makes a great deal of difference.

Let me tell you an anecdote about this. When I wrote my piece on heterogeneity of capital goods and showed that Solow's famous paper simply did not work when there is more than one capital good, Harcourt came back from somewhere or other where I had given the first version of this and said to Joan that I had recanted. When I got back to Cambridge, I had an invitation to stop at Grange Road for a glass of sherry and she drank to my recantation. And then, after we talked for about twenty minutes, she said: 'Get out! You are hopeless, you are hopeless!'

Anyway, Joan had a number of very important things to say. If she had been trained in mathematics and had been technically more competent she could really have done more to clinch them. The things she had to say were: (1) That the future is very important to the present. That was all lost in the malleable neoclassical models with one capital good: one could always undo the capital and consume it. That was a very strong point she made. (2) She was very good in trying to distinguish between equilibrium comparisons and causal stories (for example, a comparison of two islands, one with more capital than the other – that sort of thing, and the statement 'if we increase the stock of capital, this or that will happen' or comparative statics, or comparative dynamics, compared to a genuine causal story). The contributions she made there were good, but if you look at the body of her writings in this area, they are badly flawed. A large number of Italians and Indians spent fifteen years or more in the wilderness because of following her while lacking her intelligence. By now, I think, the whole of that story is nearly dead. But at the time it was a disaster.

Moreover, Joan was very much influenced by another *non sequitur* which I have never understood. That is, she had an objection to the marginal theory of distribution, as she conceived it. She felt that if she agreed to it, she would have to agree to the further proposition that the existing income distribution was just: that everybody got his marginal product. To anyone of moral sensitivity, it is obvious that must be false, because the old statement of fairness is that someone who is very strong should be handicapped. There is no reason why people should consume their genetic rents. There is no reason at all that a society where people receive their marginal product is a just society. She, however, did not think that far.

Secondly, she had difficulties with the theory itself. That must be a very old thing. It goes back, I think, to Dennis Robertson who wrote a paper called 'Wage Grumbles' in which he pointed out that the marginal theory of distribution does not say that the marginal product *determines* people's income. It says: 'in equilibrium it measures their income'. If you write down 'the wage equals marginal product', that is not an equation from which you can determine anything because the marginal product depends on the ratio of inputs, so you need many more things to determine it. Now, take the situation where the stock of capital and labor is given. Then you might say, 'Well, now the distribution of income is given, because if l and k are given, then the marginal product of labour is determined already.' That is, of course, false because people still have the choice always of, for instance, not maintaining capital, of not using it fully ... So, there is no way one can say that there is a one-way causal arrow of marginal productivity determining the distribution of income. It is simply one of the equations.

The thing I spent the flower of my youth and middle age trying to convince Joan of (without success, because she just could not understand) is that her equations were marginal productivity equations. She would say, 'you have an Alaph technique and a Beth technique, and so on and so forth, and the switch point came when they were equally profitable'. In fact, what she was doing was choosing techniques that minimized the cost of production. Every first-year undergraduate student in England (and every first-year graduate student in the US) knows that to say that is exactly equivalent to saying that you pay the marginal product. That was the sort of thing that used to drive me mad. She had this idea that she was doing something new – and what she was doing was neoclassical economics! Double switching, as Terence Gorman always said, is one of the totally neoclassical theorems that, had anyone else produced it, Joan would have thought of as all nonsense. In fact she later wrote an article explaining why double switching does not matter, because eventually it was borne in on her that the whole of this story was purely neoclassical.

So, yes, she never understood what neoclassical economics was about. It was just very difficult for her. She had learned it from Marshall. She never had the Walrasian stuff at all. What she had was a very, very high intelligence and, in her later years, a desire to emulate Keynes in challenging what she conceived of as orthodoxy. On the whole, all the good things she had to say, like the importance of the future for the present and the sloppiness of capital aggregation, had enormous implications on the way models are constructed and were very important for dynamics –how the system evolves, whether it approaches steady state or not. But she never could do it herself ...

Most of her criticism was directed against the textbooks. I believe that American economists have done almost as much harm as Joan did in certain cases, with their ghastly little textbooks. The textbooks are the worst thing that happened to modern economics. When I came to economics, there were no textbooks: I was doing mathematics and I had joined the Air Force. My parents were worried that I would become intellectually stunted. Kalecki, who was a friend of my parents, said: 'Let him read economics, it is easy.' He lent me *Value and Capital* of which I could not understand much. The fact is, however, that the textbooks in America are mainly written as 'science' and stop recognition of the ambiguities of the subject. The macro is worse, but even the micro theory is pretty awful. If one takes what Joan said just to stop all this nonsense, she would deserve our applause.

To go back to our previous subject, *The Accumulation of Capital* is not a book in economic dynamics. It is about golden ages. The dynamics these people had, from Harrod onwards, are pseudo stationary states. As far as I know, Joan never attempted what Hicks called the 'traverse', that is, going from one steady state to another. She never did that. She would go into golden ages, leaden ages, pseudo ages . . . all that sort of thing. I think that capital theory was actually too difficult for her technically. The best book written on that since is the one by Christopher Bliss. I think he has said everything that needs to be said about the subject. He has given a very fine account of what the problems are. He was exposed to Joan just as I was.

I had no preconceptions against Joan. From my very early years, Joan was very kind to me. I had no reason to disagree with her other than that she was wrong. Now, the business about distribution of income being derived from people's propensity to save – I had that in my thesis, but I do not think it was any good. She also (and Nicky) got clobbered over this. To say that capitalists have different propensities to consume from workers (supposing workers do not save at all) in itself has nothing to say about marginal productivity theory. That is just a demand equals supply equation and is consistent with any marginal productivity theory you could ever think of. Now Nicky (Kaldor) was much better than Joan because he realized early on that the idea actually required imperfect competition. That if you have imperfect competition, so that the profit mark-up is somehow variable, you might get another kind of story out of this.

I published my article on the subject in *Oxford Economic Papers* in 1949 or 1950. I had a postcard from Joan. She felt that what I was saying was getting close to Marx. Very early on I had decided, however, that it was not very interesting. What I had got out of it was a kind of wage fund theory; that at any moment of time output is already predetermined by what happened in the previous period, and that the market clearing conditions would simply have distributional implications because of the differences on the propensities to consume. But the whole thing never worked . . .

The reason why Piero Sraffa (the only person Joan was afraid of) was so important to all those people had actually much more to do with the idea that they were going to find their way back to Marx than it had to do with a critique of neoclassical economics. And it was just a failure.

Feiwel: How do you interpret her attitude to the concept of equilibrium?

Hahn: She said some very good things about equilibrium which I like very much. For instance, she said in an article in the *Economic Journal* that to be in a golden age today you must have been in a golden age yesterday or the day before. In other words, she understood that the whole notion of steady state is very, very suspect. Because she could never work out asymptotic theory, that is, how a path might approach steady state asymptotically, she was very unhappy with it. She was also very hostile to equilibrium, but that was in a different phase. Referring to *The Accumulation of Capital*, she always said to me: 'You know, in that book I gave you all the neoclassical stuff you wanted.' But she was very hostile to equilibrium because in her (just as in Nicky) common sense kept breaking through. They saw the economy in a much more Schumpeterian way, perhaps in a Marxian way, much more historically based ... But like everybody else, Joan did not have the tools to analyze it properly. So, when she started her analysis, it turned out to be just what everybody else did. You know, we all realize there is more to economics than general equilibrium, but the question is: what to do about it? She tried her best, but she never managed ... she never got there.

Feiwel: When she spoke about equilibrium, Joan usually meant the Marshallian problem of a tendency to a long-run full-employment equilibrium. Isn't this a different question from the one of stability on which you shed so much light?

Hahn: In a sense it is different. But it is different only in so far as we try to prove some results about it. Joan, however, talked rather loosely about it. The Sraffians (of whom I suppose she was one) regard Sraffa prices as being *normal* prices – long-run prices. I published recently a long article about the neo-Ricardians and two French Marxists wrote a rebuttal in which they say, actually, that the capitalist system always tends to the golden rule – this is Marshallian thinking, though Marshall, of course, did not think in those terms. It is news to me that Marx always thought that the capitalist system tended to long-run equilibrium. Their demonstration was actually not a demonstration, because they had to assume away an essential point. To come back to Joan, she was interested in equilibrium in general terms. She probably believed that if the system were left to itself some day it would tend to that, but she never took it very seriously.

Feiwel: Do you think that for Joan (and her generation) the question of instability was somewhat different from what it is for the general equilibrium theorist?

Hahn: Oh, yes, I think so, although she herself did not speak very much about it. As far as I know, Joan never wrote on the business cycle. She never wrote on fluctuations at all. What she wrote was Keynesian unemployment equilibria. I never heard her, actually, talk very much about the instability of the capitalist system. If she did, I think she must have had something quite different in mind, like long-run secular social forces at work, classes, that sort of thing. I think she probably believed what Keynes said. That is, if your model of the capitalist economy turns out to be very unstable, throw it away. The system we observe does not fluctuate violently. And Keynes wrote that in the 1930s, remember! I do not think that they actually believed that the economy was unstable in the technical sense.

Feiwel: What do you think of the Walsh and Gram distinction (inspired by Joan) between equilibrium interpreted by the neoclassical modern Walrasians as pertaining to allocation of given resources among alternative uses and that of the classical economists, concerned with allocation of a surplus in a growing economy?

Hahn: This again is a mistake. If you take *the* most abstract of neoclassical constructions, that is, an Arrow–Debreu economy, an Arrow–Debreu equilibrium can behave through time in any way you like. As the economy unfolds through time, it can fluctuate in any way you like. All that happens – and this is Joan's expression, very well put – in the Arrow–Debreu economy is that the whole future is collapsed into the present. All transactions and all decisions are made now, but none the less the unfolding of the economy can be anything, it can even be steady state, or anything of that sort. It just is not true that it is in any way static in the sense that everything repeats itself. The easiest way to understand it is to say, 'Let us suppose we now allow for real time.' Then you can get an 'inessential sequence economy', which goes with the Arrow–Debreu economy, provided you put in rational expectations. Look at Grandmont cycles, for instance, they occur in a pure general equilibrium model.

What Walsh and Gram have in mind deep down, I think, is class problems. Now, that is something quite different – that Ricardo, or Adam Smith for that matter, was concerned with the really important questions. It is absolutely true that no general equilibrium theory has any answer to the questions: Why is Japan doing so well? Why did China not develop the industrial revolution and why did Britain? . . . It is absolutely true – one of the great criticisms of modern economic theory is that it is absolutely non-historical . . .

Feiwel: Is it possible to make it historical?

Hahn: That is what we are coming to now. In the last few years it has become obvious to us – to people who work in this area – that we have far too little information to say anything in particular because most economies seem to have a huge number of equilibria. Not only that, but they have a continuum of equilibria. Now, suppose for a moment that you have two equilibria – or three, to be more precise – and you start in some arbitrary place. The question where you will finish up will depend on your starting point; that is, the equation will depend on the initial conditions. So, history comes into it. The same is probably true of the theory of games as it is coming along now. Again, in the theory of games we find that we get a fantastic number of equilibria, for instance, the Folk Theorem. So, we do need to put some history into it. But we have not done it yet . . .

You see, the difference between people like Joan and people like us (by which I mean those she called the 'orthodox') is that we only say what we *can* say, while she said a great deal more than could be said. You know Wittgenstein's famous saying: 'Whereof you cannot speak, thereof you shall be silent.' It would be lovely if we could have the Great Theory of Society that made some kind of sense – we haven't! That is my objection to all this Marxist stuff *et sub specie acternitatis*. It is not that I have any political preconceptions of any sort – I don't really feel strongly one way or the other – but it is pseudo science; it is imprecise. At best, it is a sort of insightful poetry, but it is not the careful pursuit of things that hang together in some specific way. And my guess is that it can't be done! If the physicists cannot find a unified field theory, infinitely simpler than a unified theory of society, I do not think we have much chance. So, we have to continue to think in terms of these little partial theories.

Feiwel: Granted that (as you have often pointed out) advances in mathematical economics are responses to criticisms from within (rather than those of Joan and others), can you share with us what these advances have really been? What have we learned from modern (mathematical) economic theory? What is its fundamental message?

Hahn: I will probably repeat myself here. I usually start my lectures on principles in the following manner: If you were a man from Mars and came to earth and asked, 'how do you guys organize your economy?' and suppose you were told that 'everyone does what he wants to, everyone does the best he can for himself'. I am absolutely certain that as a Martian you would guess that that economy would be chaotic – absolutely chaotic with no one to organize it, no one to supervise it . . . And to many people it seems that way. Now, Adam Smith made a contribution of astounding value: one of these *great* intellectual contributions. He said that it need not be chaotic!

The thing that has happened in economic theory since the last war, and for a long period, until quite recently, has been for the *first time* to codify nineteenth-century economics. But that was a very important thing to do. In other words, we made absolutely clear the proposition that says under what circumstances an economy that is *entirely* decentralized can none the less be coherent. I personally believe that that is an intellectual achievement that stands alongside anything in the natural sciences. It is a purely intellectual question; as yet is says nothing about the world. Once the question has been asked, it surely deserves an answer. I do think it is a beautiful question. Adam Smith produced an answer which had to be further clarified. It is not just beauty ... it is really a fundamental intellectual insight.

Now comes the second part – usefulness. With regard to that, I have just written a long article in *The Times Literary Supplement* about Kenneth Arrow's contributions. The best thing I can do is to refer you, for instance, to Ken's article on medical care. What does he do? His approach is immensely fruitful. He says, 'suppose medical care is entirely private'. In order for it to be satisfactory, it would have to meet the conditions that we know from the theory would have to hold. And then he goes step by step through to say where these conditions are not satisfied. This produces a beautiful argument – and the same on racial discrimination. Because in the latter case, the obvious question is: why is it not profitable to have blacks on the workforce?

Now, my third claim is the following: I am quite aware that one can spend a lifetime polishing forever some general equilibrium proposition, adding more mathematics, differential topology, and what not ... it is not all that interesting. But what it does – at least for those of us who started our academic lives in this way – it keeps us honest and modest. You might think that it is peculiar for me to say so, but the mathematical economists are the only modest economists. This is a *really* serious point. When one reads a piece of mathematical economics, the critic can right away say, 'Look at your crazy assumptions!' Such a piece will have the assumptions carefully spelled out and will be at the core of what you want to prove. If you read a piece of literary economics, you don't even know what the assumptions are!

Feiwel: But that is what Joan attempted to do in *The Economics of Imperfect Competition*, didn't she?

Hahn: That book is another matter altogether. It is an exercise in the axiomatic method, well executed. But she repudiated it later. She was very hostile to her own work on this and wrongly so.

Feiwel: Why?

Hahn: I think she went through a genuine conversion. Let me explain this to you by tracing the differences between Nicky and myself. I can see as much as Nicky can that there are huge gaps or flaws in the models we have. Nicky is willing to make one of these big leaps; he is very keen on his intuition and writes things that are suggestive. There is a role for people like that. But I don't like to leap anywhere I have not explored. Actually, I think it is a genetic difference between that group (Joan, Nicky, and others) and us, for instance, at IMSSS. They are willing to say much more than they can give reasons for saying.

Feiwel: May we get back to your thinking about the axiomatic method that I interrupted?

Hahn: The point about the axiomatic method is one of those funny things. I do not really know what one is supposed to make of it, because, as far as I can see, everything we do in any branch of knowledge is axiomatic, of sorts. What does an axiom mean? I do not know what it says in the *Oxford English Dictionary*, but my guess is that it is a proposition so obvious that you take it for granted. Many axioms turn out to be not so obvious; take, for instance, Euclidean axioms. The axioms we take for example, that people have an ordering are a good illustration.

Now, Joan – who was an incredibly intelligent woman, intellectually serious and all of that – occasionally made serious mistakes. Let me give you a good example: she said, 'Preference theory simply says a man will do what he prefers to do.' And, she continued, 'When we observe him doing something funny, we simply say that his preferences have changed.' What she did not understand is that the axiom does not say that people just have preferences; what it does say is that preferences are sufficiently stable relatively to what people are doing. What this actually means is that we are more or less integrated persons. It is not that we are born with our preferences; no one can deny that they are constructed in a historical way. A piece of evidence for that is that when one goes abroad, one keeps translating back into one's own currency. Why does one do that? Obviously, the axiom of complete preferences is a huge idealization. Indeed, most of us think it is an idealization in excess of what is required by theory. For much of our purposes, we could simply have a set of local preferences. But she misunderstood that completely.

Similarly, Joan's favorite American economist, Galbraith, somehow or other believes that one can talk about a society and an economy, yet the individuals in that society are completely malleable. For example, the firm can decide what to produce and through advertising persuade people to buy the product. That is a very contradictory position to take. Again, as I tell my students, at the end of the eighteenth century, people wanted to go from London to Brighton; and they wanted to go fast, prestigiously, comfortably. All these characteristics are embodied in different goods now: automobiles, railways, helicopters, what have you, in different ratios. You might make just as good a case by saying that people's tastes have been extremely steady. We can read ancient history and, at least, it appears that many of the motives are comprehensible to us. It is not like the reading of some science fiction. So, you can make the exact opposite case. Now, I am not making that opposite case; I do think that people change. What I mean to say is that it is the kind of drastic, colorful statement that falls to pieces when you look at it closely.

Feiwel: Could the participants of the summer IMSSS seminars learn something useful from Joan?

Hahn: Absolutely. In Cambridge I am one of the strongest advocates of having, for instance, two principles courses taught by people of different persuasions. The main thing I want to avoid is textbook-style economics. That makes people believe that they are doing 'science'. I think of economic theory as a way of organizing our minds, so that we do not speak of things that are incoherent. I do not mean that we are stating the 'truth'.

Undoubtedly, Joan would be very salutary in an American setting simply because while it has its own virtues, it rarely has Joan's. Take, for instance, 'smoothing by aggregation'. Joan would say, 'Why does an intelligent person like you waste your time on this?' And she would give good reasons why there are many more important questions to be investigated. In other words, she would undervalue purely technical work, but technicians often forget what they are about. Joan had a large vision, but she would never have had an influence. One of the things that we all remark on is that Joan and Nicky have left no descendants.

Feiwel: Is it partly due to their own infighting?

Hahn: No. Look, when I was brought to Cambridge as a young man, I was to become Joan's disciple. It was just impossible! I was very friendly with her. Richard (Kahn) and she were extremely kind to me But it was often impossible to follow her; she was incoherent, that is all I can say. The fact is that she often spoiled even the good things she had to say. For instance, increasing returns are important, and one should not stick exclusively to equilibrium economics . . .

Feiwel: Forgive me for interrupting, what do you think she means exactly when she talks about equilibrium economics? Is it the Marshallian tendency to long-run full employment over time? The orthodoxy that Keynes fought?

Hahn: Let me give you a favorite sentence of hers. When she was not doing golden ages and the like, she would say: 'The way to view a capitalist economy is that it staggers from one short period to the next'. In other words, there is no intertemporal coherence in the economy, because people's expectations are wrong, they make mistakes, they do not coordinate intertemporal decisions, and so on. She could have learned a fantastic amount from the Arrow–Debreu model which I tried to explain to her on countless occasions.

Feiwel: A technical question: Is there a fundamental difference between the Marshallian (textbook) short run and the general equilibrium short run?

Hahn: As far as I know, Marshall never had a general equilibrium system at all. He talked about markets. The only people who actually had general equilibrium short-run periods, before anyone else, are Lundberg (in his book on macroeconomics), Hicks (had the 'week') and Robertson (his 'day'). But Joan and the other Cambridge people were very hostile to Hicks. He was neoclassical, you see!

But I do want to make an important point that relates to your previous question. If one understands Arrow–Debreu and that one has to have contingent futures markets in order to have the system intertemporally organized, one immediately understands Keynes. If one agrees with those who claim that the market works, one has to claim that there is a way of coordinating through contingent markets or substitutes. But once one has understood *that*, one knows where to look for evidence in favor of the claim. Let me be fair. I think that deep down in some way Joan understood all this – that is what she meant by the phrase that the future is important for the present. There is no way of taming the future in the present through futures markets because there are not enough of these markets – that is what we would say. So that the future affects the present through expectations; people make mistakes and so on. But she was so out of kilter with what was going on and so prone to misunderstanding.

... For example, Roy Radner spent a year in Cambridge and spent weeks talking to her. One day I came into coffee and Joan said: 'I have convinced Radner that general equilibrium is no good.' In the evening, Roy came to dinner in college and I said: 'Joan tells me that you recanted.' Of course it was nothing of the kind ... she simply misunderstood.

Feiwel: When Joan speaks of expectations, is her meaning the same as yours?

Hahn: Yes, I think so. I think what she said about the bastard Keynesians is quite right (for instance, the real cash balance effect). Her argument was that Keynes should never have accepted IS-LM. That the bastard Keynesians really act as if there were an auctioneer. She stressed that the equilibrating process takes place in *real* time. She never made any contribution to that theory, but her criticisms were perfectly well taken. Her emphasis on real time, staggering from period to period, was very much to the point. She said that what Keynes was really about – and she was quite right – was essentially the difficulty of equilibrating rather than bad equilibrium.

Keynes said: 'Let us imagine that money wages were actually very flexible.' He then said: 'Well, that would lead to falling prices and bankruptcies, and all the rest of it.' And somewhere in that chapter he also said: 'If wages were really flexible, the prices would fluctuate between zero and infinity.' Of course, that is Keynes being sloppy, but what he really meant is that they would be very unstable, because the price level would no longer be tied down to something. Joan had a feeling for that – for her what Keynes was about was that there were no automatic equilibrating mechanisms. An earlier remark I made that is connected with that is that she understood that it is quite different to say that there exists a money wage low enough so that all markets clear, from saying that wages should fall. These are completely different statements.

Solow and I have just shown the effects of perfectly flexible money wages in one of these models. The computer is turning out the most frightful things. So, Keynes was right! In fact, we hope to have some effect here. You see, many economists, because they could not reconcile it with their textbooks, kept on and on about Keynes assuming rigid money wages. Not a bit of it! What Keynes said – and you can document that endlessly – was that if money wages are not rigid, things are worse than if they are! Larry Summers has been doing some empirical work that seems to support some of this.

Feiwel: Joan considered the 'new classical macroeconomics' as nonsense and retrogressive. Where was she right and where wrong?

Hahn: That whole subject is dead now. It died about two or three years ago. There are many reasons why it died. One has to distinguish between Lucas and the Lucasians. The Lucas followers with their macroeconomics were not exactly admirable. Lucas's paper 'Expectations and the Neutrality of Money' is an outstanding one, because he made clear how monetary events can affect the information structure of an economy and have real effects. However, what he said there – the fundamental thing about rational expectations – turned out to be wrong. Guesnerie has shown recently, as one of the nails in the coffin, that even in that model of Lucas there are a huge number of rational expectation equilibria. It has now come increasingly to light and we now know that rational expectations and rationality are not enough to tie down anything; anything could happen. Moreover, it is not true that once you have all these equilibria, monetary policy is ineffective. Monetary policy may well eliminate some of these equilibria. There are many other things wrong. For instance, the claim about monetary policy not mattering is crucially dependent on abstracting from distribution. When you have, for instance, overlapping generations, you always have distributional effects, from the old to the young. Once you have distributional effects of changes in monetary policy, that policy could be very effective. So, I think Lucas, like Joan, served his purpose, but this whole approach is now an episode on the way to real understanding. People still play around with rational expectations, but what they do with them is to find billions of equilibria and some that cycle. Take for example, the lovely paper we heard this morning [by M. Boldrin and L. Montruccio, 'New Results on Stability and Chaos in General Equilibrium Optimal Growth Models']. What happens? Chaos! All right, you can have a chaotic, rational expectations economy. That is not going to satisfy the Lucasians either.

Feiwel: Would you care to share with us some of your personal recollections of Joan?

Hahn: I have millions of them. A lot of them have to do with my love–hate relationship. She would never leave me alone. I have some pleasant memories of her too. When she was getting old, she would send me messages and wanted me to come and see her. I did. We talked about China about which she was totally unreliable – again. None the less ...

What I liked about Joan – something that most people do not realize – was that she was cast in the tradition of the upper-class Englishwoman. In another age she would have been on a camel, riding through the desert. She was that sort of person. Her father, as you know, got into deep hot waters in World War I. A part of her personality was simply upper-class refusal to go with the herd; a need to distinguish herself from the herd. One of the most amusing things about Joan was her thinking of herself as a proletarian, when, in point of fact, she was totally a heterodox upper-class Englishwoman – a type that has been thoroughly described through history. I rather like that about her! I enjoyed it!

Another thing about Joan is, in my opinion, that she was very beautiful. I thought she had a most splendid face – a face from which intelligence shone. I met her when I was 22 (and she was in her early forties); I thought she was absolutely stunning.

Feiwel: You mentioned she was afraid of Sraffa. Why?

Hahn: I do not know. On occasion, he was quite rude to her. He would say things like, 'Shut up Joan, you don't understand.' Sraffa altogether had a curious position, I think. He was separate . . . he kept his distance. For instance, although he was obviously invited to the secret seminars, he never came. For some time I used to have dinner with Sraffa at Trinity once a month, by arrangement. I cannot claim that I was afraid of him, but sometimes I dreaded these dinner meetings. He would go into a kind of Italian screaming in a way I found unnerving. He undoubtedly had a position; he was touched by Keynes in a way others had not been. He also had *real* militant connections (Gramsci, and all that) which Joan may not have had. Joan obviously knew some leftist leaders, but I do not think she ever was part of that milieu as Sraffa was.

Feiwel: Did Kahn supply most of Joan's analytical ammunition?

Hahn: I would not go so far as to say that. I am sure Richard Kahn was very important in the development of her ideas. Richard knew a great deal more mathematics than any of the others, including Keynes (who had forgotten it all, I think). Richard was technically skilled. I suspect that Joan could not have done any of her diagrams on her own.

Feiwel: Do you think she was very much influenced by Kalecki?

Hahn: Yes, she was deeply influenced by Kalecki. She went into directions Kalecki had charted. She not only claimed that Kalecki had anticipated Keynes, but she also felt very strongly that politically he was on the right side. I imagine that she read a good deal of Kalecki into Keynes. Kalecki–whom I myself admired very much–when he had a theory about profits, for instance, finished it up with a mixed differential equation that was very hard to follow. Joan could not have possibly followed that. She simply took it for granted. Kalecki was certainly a hero of hers–there is no doubt about it.

Feiwel: How would you compare Joan with Kaldor?

Hahn: Oh, Kaldor is a greater economist by far. Nicky has made really fundamental contributions to economics, for instance, his model of the trade cycle, speculation in the trade cycle, and on and on. Nicky is one of the outliers. He is a man who *really* has ideas, lots of them absolutely nonsensical, but every so often they are gems. He cannot work them out; he needs assistance (from Champernowne, Mirrlees, or Nield). But we are there to do the plumbing for him. He is exceptionally innovative. I think it is scandalous that they have not given him the Nobel Prize.

Feiwel: What do you consider Joan's real contributions to have been?

Hahn: I think it is in monetary economics. Her work on interest rates and money was excellent – outstanding in many ways. Obviously *The Economics of Imperfect Competition* was an important book at the time. But looking back at it, Cournot had it, and almost any student at Stanford could summarize it in two pages; it is essentially marginal revenue equals marginal cost. She did get the tangency solution which is interesting. But the general consensus is, I think, that Chamberlin's book is a good deal better. On the other hand, I think that Dick Goodwin maintains that Chamberlin got all his ideas from Allyn Young. I must confess that when I met Chamberlin, I did not get the impression of a great mind. Though that book was very important to many people, it is not her lasting achievement. Her lasting achievement is, I believe, her work in monetary economics. Quite honestly, I do not think that she is going to be remembered all that much . . .

Feiwel: Could you enlarge on her contributions in monetary economics?

Hahn: She wrote some splendid papers on the structure of interest rates, on liquidity preference, on the connection between monetary economics and the exchange rate . . . all these essays she collected in *The Rate of Interest and Other Essays*. She also did a great deal to popularize Keynes. Her *Essays in the Theory of Employment* was an important book in its time. She also wrote one rather splendid, uncharacteristic article – 'Euler's Theorem and the Problem of Distribution'.

My memory of her is, however, clouded by this wretched capital theory stuff. At the very best, one can say that she irritated people out of complacency; stopped them from doing sloppy things. Let me share with you an anecdote (that you might already know): Bob Solow was in Cambridge in the 1960s and gave a talk about capital. Joan cried out immediately: 'What is capital?' Bob replied: 'This reminds me of someone standing in the street – a fellow comes up to him and asks the time. The man replies: "Ah, time . . .".' That is another thing Joan did not understand. When Keynes was talking about investment and saving, that was all right. And, she was quite willing to aggregate labor, but somehow capital was different. Now this is pure conjecture, but it seems to me that she started off by saying that she did not like the idea that profits are the marginal product of something called capital. Profits are supposed to be a surplus. So, she was hostile to that more than to the other aggregates. She never saw the point that we all the time think in terms of aggregates; she did, we all did. And all the aggregates are, of course, wrong – whether it is investment, savings, labor, or capital.

Feiwel: Samuelson commented that behind the esoteric dispute over 're-switching' or heterogeneity of capital can be found contrasting views about fruitful ways of understanding distributional analysis and affecting its content by alternative policy measures. May we have your comment on that?

Hahn: I am very surprised that he said that. There are no doubt profound questions of income distribution, but I cannot see them in the capital controversy. I cannot understand that comment. The sort of thing that is behind the controversy is that you cannot say, 'The capital per man in India seems to be less than in the UK, US, or Japan, and, therefore, you would expect the rate of profit to be higher.' I do not know where Samuelson gets that statement from. There are profound implications about income distribution in the assumption of perfect competition and in not taking game theory (bargaining) seriously – all that I can see.

45 Joan Robinson and Cambridge – A Theorist and Her Milieu: An Interview

R. C. O. Matthews

Feiwel: What in your opinion are the strengths and weaknesses of Joan as an economist?

Matthews: Joan was a zealot and a crusader and it is impossible to judge her as an economist in a technical sense in divorce from the motivation that underlay her work. The driving force was the desire to establish the truth and to refute self-interested or lazy fallacies. Her interest was not primarily intellectual – she had no interest in 'beautiful theorems' as such. Nor was she ambitious in a career sense, a fact she attributed herself to being a woman, although she did mind very much about whether her *ideas* were accepted ('I feel so lonely', she said on one occasion in the 1970s.) She held that, as Marx and Popper taught, intellectual thinking had usually an ideological basis and there is no reason to suppose she would have wished to be excluded from this herself. Even *The Economics of Imperfect Competition* is really a tract. The ideological emphasis amounts essentially to a desire to refute arguments which in her opinion economists had been too willing to put forward to justify the manifest injustices of capitalism.

With regard to intellectual originality, what Joan had achieved already by World War II was sufficient to mark her out, and so she continued. Yet in some ways her originality was more as a synthesizer than as an originator. The collection of elements on which the brew was concocted was an unusual one: Marshall (in a very large helping), Marx, Keynes, Shove, Sraffa, and Kalecki, to say nothing of Richard Kahn's contributions. Therein lay much of the originality.

In the matter of style, she did not resemble any of these authors. The hallmarks were clarity carried to the point of homeliness – the style of one anxious to convince. Her lack of mathematical background may sometimes have led her to misunderstand opponents, but it did not matter as far as her own contributions were concerned. Her indefatigable

911

worrying away at problems, with occasional help from friends, was usually enough to get her to the answer.

Joan was a theorist, and like many theorists, she was not particularly interested in empirical research. Certainly she didn't carry out empirical research herself. If challenged she would no doubt have said that the important facts were obvious enough. It was precisely for the neglect of those obvious and important facts that she upbraided her traditional opponents, and still more their 'new classical' successors.

It would be a gross exaggeration to say that all Joan's work was of a negative kind. But it is true she was better at pointing to the Emperor's nakedness than in supplying him with clothing. She was most at home in the role of critic, both in economic analysis and, especially, in drawing policy implications. I would guess this to have been a matter of temperament as much as a consequence of her ideology. The stance of opposition was as congenial to her as it had been to her father, Lieut-Gen Sir F. Maurice, whose public allegation, as a serving officer in World War I, that Prime Minister Lloyd George was a liar earned him a page in the history books as the part-source of the later split in the Liberal Party (the incident of the 'Maurice letter'). Even her role as a propagandist for the Keynesian revolution was ambivalent. She was one of the first to emphasize the potential conflict between low unemployment and price stability. The reformist aspects of Keynesianism, as expressed by James Meade, for example, were not to her liking. The logical consequence of her radical posture on policy would have required her to look at the role and the potential role of governments in the same hard-headed way as she looked at the role of the market – something she never attempted.

Joan's ideology went through a number of phases. Her best-known contributions of the 1930s (on imperfect competition, on disguised unemployment, on foreign trade elasticities) can be regarded as reformist in inspiration, even if reluctantly so. In the 1940s she became acquainted with Marx, to whom she was introduced by Erwin Rothbarth and Kalecki, and the more radical note enters. A further turn came in her old age, with her love affair with Communist China, so reminiscent of the Webbs' late love affair with the Soviet Union. Underlying that late turn came the faith she had always felt in some degree in the perfectibility of man – a doctrine with familiar antecedents in political theory, and one by no means absent in Marshall, but alien to mainstream economics as it has developed.

I have touched on the intellectual and personal origins of Joan's thinking and its shifts over time. It would be entirely in accordance with her own prescriptions to speculate on the social-class origins as well. I have little doubt that Joan's upbringing as a member of the British non-commercial upper middle class played its part. You may be right in suggesting that she did not have much *personal* fellow feeling for members of the British working class. Still less did she with the business class. Her extreme antipathy to everything American – she never visited the United States until she went quite late in life to be lionized by the American left-wingers – surely reflected a disdain, traditional to one of her upbringing for the commercial *nouveaux riches*, as well as an identification of the United States as the metropolis of capitalism. It was surely her background, as well as her gender, that accounted for her lack of academic competitiveness and her repugnance at the academic rat-race and its consequences. Her implicit reliance on governments as being at least potentially philosopher kings was of a piece with all this.

Feiwel: What is the essential originality and contribution to economic analysis of *The Accumulation of Capital?* Joan identified her work on accumulation and growth as post-Keynesian generalization of the *General Theory*. Can you comment on this?

Matthews: *The Accumulation of Capital* is a generalization of *The General Theory*, in the sense that it considers the *long-run* behavior of an economy in which ex-ante saving and investment are independently determined and are brought into equality otherwise than through the capital market. By contrast, the focus of *The General Theory* itself on a short-run in which growth and accumulation are disregarded. Harrod's work had the same purpose, as Joan generously acknowledged.

The Accumulation of Capital is a model of economic growth. It traces out the consequences of a particular set of assumptions, chiefly: (i) consumption is a function of wage income; (ii) the level of investment is a function of the attitudes and energies of entrepreneurs (subject to some constraint about reasonable profitability); (iii) the form taken by a particular amount of investment is that which is most profitable; (iv) a discontinuous set of alternative techniques exists at any time, more or less mechanized than one another; (v) capital is not malleable; (vi) the rate of technical progress is a function of labor scarcity. Some of these functions are Keynesian, others owe more to Marx (especially (vi)). This is a coherent and interesting set of assumptions. It was a valuable contribution to work out their consequences. The Keynesian aspect of the model makes it unusually well adapted for the simultaneous treatment of growth and fluctuations. The verbal rather than mathematical exposition facilitates the treatment of special cases that are deemed to be particularly important in certain contexts. Whether the assumptions are better than the neoclassical ones, where the two differ, is ultimately an empirical question (not a matter of intellectual rightness or wrongness, as both Joan and her critics too often suggested).

One characteristic of the book is the sharply different roles and motivations attributed to different types of economic agent (wage earners, entrepreneurs, rentiers). Joan was hostile to the now more fashionable notion of an undifferentiated utility maximizing economic agent. She held that economic conduct was culturally conditioned. This may seem more Marxian than Keynesian; yet she regarded it as Marshallian (*Collected Economic Papers*, Vol 3, p.101). This was a fruitful area for exploration, though, as Joan admitted, her own treatment was rudimentary. 'Economic analysis requires to be supplemented by a kind of comparative historical anthropology which is still in its infancy as a scientific study' (*Accumulation of Capital*, p.56).

The *Accumulation of Capital* reads better than her later, more polemical writings on the same theme. For all its merits, however, I don't rate it highest among Joan's writings. For originality and technical versatility, her earlier writings are more striking; and for breadth of vision, the brilliant opening and concluding chapters of *Economic Philosophy*.

Feiwel: Would you share with us your personal recollections of Joan as well as Cambridge in the 1950s and 1960s?

Matthews: I can speak only of the years up to 1965, when I left to go to Oxford. It was an exciting time, especially at the beginning. At the now famous 'secret seminar' topics connected with growth and accumulation were at the core of the agenda, though altogether different topics were included too. The seminar was 'secret', i.e. exclusive, because Joan and Richard Kahn thought that discussion between economists of totally uncongenial views was unprofitable. (Wassily Leontief, on a visit to Cambridge around 1950, opened a paper to the secret seminar by some such words as, 'I shall assume there is full employment, brought about by wage-flexibility.' He got no further – the rest of the evening was spent challenging that.) The topics were central, they were discussed in a real world context, and they were sufficiently non-technical to avoid scholastic segmentation. It would not be true to say that Joan did all the talking, but she and Richard largely determined the agenda. Nicky Kaldor's arrival in the early 1950s added another star with similar interests. The other participants of my own generation included (not all at the same time) Harry Johnson (Harry's later virulence against Cambridge economics was *never* manifested as long as he was there. Was this tact, or did his attitudes change?), Frank Hahn, Robin Marris, Amartya Sen, Aubrey Silbertson, Kenneth Berrill, Jan Graaff, and Luigi Pasinetti – quite a list and, while never a school, sufficiently like-minded to form a coherent group. Among the seniors, Dobb never attended, nor did Austin Robinson or Dick Stone, whose influence in Cambridge was exercised through a different channel, the Department of Applied Economics (DAE). Dennis Robertson, of course, was not invited. Sraffa came hardly ever. Nor did he ever lecture. It is a myth of later creation that Sraffa was an intellectually influential figure in Cambridge at this time. Any influence he may have had, except perhaps within Trinity, was mediated mainly through private conversations with Joan and Richard.

One of the reasons why the secret seminar was important to some of us was that there was throughout the 1950s no Faculty building where staff had rooms (apart from the members of the DAE). People worked in their colleges and had to make special arrangements to foregather. With the construction of the Sidgwick Avenue building in the early 1960s, contacts became easier. At the same time the secret seminar had begun to deteriorate. The disputes became more disputacious and more repetitive. Bob Solow's participation, when on a visit, though vastly enlightening to most of us, was an irritant to Joan; and there were other personality clashes. At the end the management were right to call it a day.

The endeavor by Joan and Richard to build up a Cambridge school goes back to the 1930s. It has some strongly positive effects. Great trouble was taken to make first-class appointments. Young lecturers like myself were treated very kindly, and our development was helped. At the same time there were ill-effects on those excluded from the charmed circle – not only Robertson and, earlier, Hicks, but also, for example, Michael Farrell and Malcolm Fisher. I did not sufficiently appreciate that at the time – a fact for which I now reproach myself, especially in relation to Dennis. Austin held the balance between the two sides in a way for which he can never be given too much credit. But two sides there were, and one was dominant. The dominant side in its turn began to suffer in the 1960s an erosion of its own intellectual coherence. We had reckoned ourselves to be among Joan's admirers, but we became bored by the increasingly theological disputes about the measurement of capital, about the fallacy of the marginal productivity theory, and so on. So one chapter ended. the later chapters evolved out of it – but they fall outside the scope of your question.

46 Joan Robinson – Passionate Seeker After Truth

Richard M. Goodwin

Joan was a great lady. This impression, once received, never dimmed with closer acquaintance. As a student in Oxford, when I first saw her she appeared wearing a bright green pajama suit; she was young, vigorous and beautiful; she addressed us in abstruse terms about the long-period theory of employment. I understood little but sat spellbound, and, in a sense, have remained so ever since. She had already published a great, influential book – a work which subsequently should have ensured her a Nobel prize, had she not had the two stigmas of being both a woman and a radical. The contrast between her and Edward Chamberlin is striking and highly significant. He spent the remainder of his life in self-hagiography, collecting all reviews, references and comments on his one work. Once she had published her first book, Joan more or less never mentioned it again: she charged into fresh fields, attempting to complete the Keynesian rectification of the shortcomings of Marshallian partial equilibrium.

Such totally self-abnegating dedication was awe inspiring: she was a Seeker after Truth, unrelenting, almost obsessive, and she had had considerable success in her pursuit of it. She was never personally unpleasant or aggressive, except where she felt Truth was at stake. However, she was merciless with Unbelievers and managed to make life difficult for some of her colleagues. I remember Paul Samuelson giving a talk to a small group in which he made some sort of allusion to the role of profit. Joan interrupted to demand what determined the rate of profit. He began a rather conventional explanation, at which she interrupted again with the same statement, and she continued to do so through the remainder of his presentation.

Schumpeter once said to me that Böhm-Bawerk was remarkable for the fact that he could see the resolution of complex logical and even mathematical problems without any knowledge of mathematics. This was also true to some extent for Joan (as also for Piero Sraffa). Though I was a card-carrying supporter of her, that was no protection. Once I was giving a paper on a two-sector, dynamical model, in the course of which I said that both sectors would exhibit both motions. She interrupted to say that I was wrong: there was only one motion. I denied this, and presumably carried on. But I was bothered and later, reworking the problem, discovered that she was right since the system was degenerate!

Joan was a great teacher and the fact is testified by the number of her admirers in all parts of the world. This came in spite of the fact, or perhaps partly because of the fact, that she was an outsider, never a member of the establishment. Much more it was due to her many impressive qualities: her clarity, her unswerving devotion to unpopular, progressive causes, her total sincerity and integrity, her high seriousness and her unwillingness to suffer fools gladly. In the face of increasing age and illness, she continued to go to the far corners of the world to spread the truth as she understood it. Towards the end her faith in her mission did suffer somewhat. To my wife she said, during one of her last illnesses, that in the thirties we felt we knew the answers and could make it work, and now that vision is being dissipated. Though this may seem unduly pessimistic, it may have come from a sense of the impending end of her lifelong contributions to the struggle for a better world.

47 Remembering Joan Robinson

Lorie Tarshis

The role of Joan Robinson in the writing of Keynes's *General Theory* is amply displayed in the publication of his *Collected Works*, and most particularly in volumes XIII, XIV and XXIX. Even in 1931, she was a prominent figure in that small group – the Circus – which was so influential in the debates that moved Keynes from the *Treatise on Money* to take that revolutionary step – the development of macroeconomics as set out in the *General Theory*.

In the same few years she completed the first (in a tie) treatise on imperfect competition. And for the rest of her long – but really far too short – life, she was in the forefront of most of the other significant advances in economics: economic growth, development and capital theory. Her professional achievements are well known to anyone interested in the development of economics between 1930 and 1980. I can add a few personal touches which show that she was a person with a heart – an absolutely admirable person – and a person so committed to pursuing her own ideals, that she sometimes created ill-will in place of the good-will (towards others) that she intended.

In the spring of 1933, I first encountered her in her lectures. It was at the end of a cold, dark and drizzly winter. Her lectures were unique, because she spoke directly and to the point. Most of our lectures that year, except for hers, Richard Kahn's and Keynes's, were dreary. One lecturer addressed, if that is not too strong a word, his mumbles to the blackboard on which he wrote, rubbed out and rewrote, whatever it was – invariably obscured by his own figure. Keynes was exciting because he was Keynes – brilliant and frighteningly quick. Most of the rest seemed to be saying nothing and saying it ponderously. After a few weeks, I attended only her lectures and those of Keynes and Kahn.

Her lectures were not only clear and crisp; they were delivered by a very attractive young lady – a feature which, to anyone brought up as I had been in a school and a university program that was almost totally bereft of female fellow students and teachers, was most noticeable. A strong, handsome face, a lovely smile, white teeth and bright blue eyes and a liveliness that sparkled.

I spent the following summer in Germany – Hitler everywhere – where Bob Bryce (the man who really *did* introduce Keynes to Harvard, two years later) and I had gone to learn German. We took Joan's book with us and, disappointed (I write for myself) at my inability to find a beautiful fraulein who would discover me to be irresistible, we spent a lot of time reading and fighting over it. By the time we returned to Cambridge, we had a fat stack of pages bearing comments, criticisms and deletions (of expletives).

Someone told Joan of our contribution to learning. Shortly after term began, we received an invitation to join her for tea. I, for one, was a bit scared; some of our written remarks were intended for our eyes only and it took courage to face anyone so obviously intelligent and direct. I cannot remember any of our discussion; all that remains is a memory of her grace and of her obvious pleasure in encountering students who were ready (?) to think for themselves. I know that by the end of our meeting I felt like a hero. As I saw her later in Cambridge, Stanford, India and Toronto, I have repeatedly been struck by her sincere interest in students and the encouragement she offered to any who showed a capacity for independent thought.

Her concern – commitment really – for the right was as much a part of her as her intelligence and directness. She had evidently been as a schoolgirl – so I heard from one who had been at school with her – a person of great courage and strong ideals. I saw this when on a trip with her, the Kaldors and my wife, she led a 'strike' in support of 'the dispossessed'.

The role of this Cambridge contingent was to conduct seminars for young instructors in India, Pakistan, Ceylon and Malaysia who had not studied in the US or Britain. Joan, my wife and I were put up at a somewhat shabby and very Victorian hotel in Poona; the more junior attendees were housed in barracks at the institution at which the seminars met; and the Kaldors – I say this in admiration – had, through contacts, been invited to stay with a Maharajah. Our meals were tolerable. But Joan heard that the meals served to our young colleagues were inedible, so she persuaded us to join them for lunch from then on. We did and there was a very sudden improvement. And when we were invited to end our visit with a sightseeing trip to the Taj Mahal and Joan learned that this trip was reserved for 'distinguished seniors', she again moved to force a change. She stated clearly that we would not participate unless the trip were opened to the whole group. It was.

She *acted* to support her ideals. They were not simply expressions of what she desired. In doing so and of course in her technical discussions, where again she took stands that were her own, no matter how strong was the opposition, she set a wonderful example. Unfortunately, humans, being no better than human, often resented it and she accumulated far more enmity than she deserved.

Economists, everywhere, owe her a heavy debt. At times it is difficult to feel much pride in being one of the profession. But it becomes much easier when one remembers that she too was an economist – a great economist and a great person.

Like my fellow authors in these volumes, I dedicate my essay [Chapter 26 of the companion volume] to her memory, and (for myself anyway) to the hope that her example will be followed by many: her determination to discover how things work, her insistence on writing out her findings directly and clearly, her fierce will to hold her ground, once she was persuaded of its rightness, even if she had to stand alone; and all this combined with an unclouded conscience that recognized the claims of others, the worth of friendship and the beauties that men, women and children can create.

Index*

*See also the index to *The Economics of Imperfect Competition and Employment: Joan Robinson and Beyond.*

921